The Authors

David Jary, BSc (Econ.) is Visiting Professor, Department of Cultural Studies and Sociology, University of Birmingham. Before moving to Birmingham, he was Professor of Sociology and Dean of the School of Social Sciences at Staffordshire University. Previously he was Senior Lecturer in Sociology at the University of Salford, and before that he was subject leader in Sociology at Manchester Polytechnic. His previously edited works include *The Middle Class in Politics* (with J. Garrard, M. Goldsmith and A. Oldfield), *Sport, Leisure and Social Relations* (with J. Horne and A. Tomlinson), *Giddens' Theory of Structuration* (with C. Bryant), and most recently *Anthony Giddens: Critical Assessments* (4 vols) with C. Bryant.

Julia Jary, BSc (Soc.), BA, Ma, PhD has been Senior Lecturer in Psychology at Staffordshire University and also taught general psychology and cognitive psychology for the Open University. Previously she has worked as a lecturer at the Universities of Manchester and Salford. Her current writing and research are concerned with social psychological issues in cancer care.

William Collins' dream of knowledge for all began with the publication of his first book in 1819. A self-educated mill worker, he not only enriched millions of lives, but also founded a flourishing publishing house. Today, staying true to this spirit, Collins books are packed with inspiration, innovation, and practical expertise. They place you at the centre of a world of possibility and give you exactly what you need to explore it.

Collins. Do more.

Collins dictionary of Sociology

edited by

David Jary and Julia Jary

Collins

HarperCollins Publishers
Westerhill Road, Bishopbriggs,
Glasgow G64 2QT

www.collins.co.uk

First published by HarperCollins in 1991
Second edition 1995
Third edition 2000
Reset 2005

Reprint 10 9 8 7 6 5 4 3 2 1

A catalogue record for this book is available from the British Library

ISBN 13 978-0-00-718399-9
ISBN 10 0-00-718399-2

Typeset by Davidson Pre-Press Graphics Ltd, Glasgow
Printed and bound in Italy by Legoprint.

To our parents
Phoebe and Oswald,
Rose and John,
and our children, Stephen, Jane and Daniel

Introduction

Sociology is not a tidy subject. As the 'science of society and social relations' its boundaries are wide and difficult to draw. It overlaps with all other social science disciplines, which, as the general science of society, it must take into account or can even be said to include. Since, in addition, its discourses are also continuous with those of 'lay' society, its subject matter is often controversial and charged by 'values' as well as by disciplinary disputes.

These features and other complexities of the subject are not a weakness of the subject, but are in many ways its strength: the fact that sociology reflects and interacts with real world issues and has no arbitrarily constructed disciplinary closure. However, they do present the compiler of a dictionary of sociology with considerable problems, not least the need to arrive at working criteria of inclusion and exclusion when no one set of criteria is likely to reflect all possible conceptions of the subject. It is important, therefore, to make clear what the criteria have been for this volume. Included are:

(a) major sociological terms and topic areas which have been central in the development of the subject or which are currently important, together with many more minor sociological terms;

(b) entries on other social science disciplines, including key terms from these disciplines where the terms have achieved a wide usage within sociology;

(c) entries on the most influential sociologists, and entries on major social theorists and philosophers whose influence on the subject has often been on a par with those whose disciplinary links are more explicitly with sociology;

(d) entries on the main research methods used in sociology, including basic statistical terms, together with entries on epistemological and ontological terms and issues which sociology shares with philosophy;

(e) a selection of frequently used 'common language' terms in sociology where these are likely to present problems for students.

The breadth of coverage attempted means that the volume includes a greater number of headwords than most previous dictionaries of the subject. A further general feature is that, whereas other dictionaries have mostly adopted a discursive approach in communicating the meanings of terms, in this volume a brief definition (or definitions) immediately follows every headword. This is intended to be useful to the person who wishes to use a dictionary to establish a meaning without having to sort through many paragraphs to arrive at it. This is not to say that the reader will find only short entries in the Dictionary. On the contrary, it contains many longer more encyclopedic entries, but these always begin with initial briefer definitions. It should finally be noted that this Dictionary does not set out to be a comprehensive or a definitive work of scholarship, e.g. it is relatively little concerned with the complex etymologies of terms, or to convey all usages. Rather its main aim is to function as a study aid.

Using the Dictionary

Entries are arranged in alphabetical order which treats all words appearing in the headword as a continuous word – thus **civilizing process** precedes **civil society**.

Where headwords indicate only a cross-reference in SMALL CAPITALS, the location of a definition is usually indicated by the appearance of this headword in *italics* within the cross-referenced entry.

It should not be assumed that the length of an entry reflects the importance of a term within the subject. This is true of person entries as well as those dealing with individual terms. Material of relevance on a particular entry will often be found in related entries, indicated by SMALL CAPITALS, also used more generally to indicate cross-references to key terms defined elsewhere.

Works cited in the text are listed in a general Bibliography which appears at the rear of the Dictionary, although where the title of the work is given in full in the text, these texts are not always included in the Bibliography.

The Contributors

The Dictionary is mainly the work of a team of sociologists and social psychologists based at the Division of Sociology, in the School of Social Sciences at Staffordshire University, a large Department with extensive undergraduate and postgraduate experience in teaching sociology as a single honours, joint honours and an ancilliary subject. Outside contributors have also been used where it was felt that this would improve on internal resources.

The general editors, David and Julia Jary, have been assisted by an editorial team of associate editors consisting of Tony Charles, Phil Nicholls and Alan Sillitoe.

Entries have not been individually signed, since the work is a collective one. The full list of contributors, together with their areas of main contribution, is:

Michael Ball – Anthropology, Interpretative Sociology
Christopher Bryant (University of Salford) – Intellectuals and Intelligentsia
Tony Charles – Industrial Sociology, Sociology of Organizations, New Technology
Rosemary Charles – Strategic Theory
Mike Dent – Industrial Sociology, Sociology of Organizations
Ursula Dobraszczyz – Sociology of Health and Medicine, Mass Media and Mass Culture, Urbanism
David Gatley – Research Methods
Ruth Green – Social Psychology
John Horne – Sociology of Leisure, Sociological Theory
Susie Jacobs – Class, Gender, Marxism
David Jary – General Sociology, Sociological Theory, Philosophy of Science, Methodology, Historical and Comparative Sociology, Religion, Marxism, Class, Political Sociology, Economic Sociology
Julia Jary – Psychology and Social Psychology, Research Methods, Environmental issues
Paul Keating (University of Exeter) – Sociological Theory, Historical Sociology, Religion
Derek Longhurst (Dept of Humanities, Staffordshire Polytechnic) – Poststructuralism

Adrian Oldfield (University of Salford) – Political Philosophy
Dianne Phillips (Manchester Polytechnic) – Statistics and Research Methods
John Phillips (Manchester Polytechnic) – Sociological Theory, Philosophy, Language
Jim McAuley (Huddersfield University) – Political Sociology
David Newton – Sociology of Education
Phil Nicholls – General and Comparative Sociology, Sociology of Health and Medicine
Steve Outram – Social Policy and Social Welfare, Sociology of the Family, Demography
Martin Parker – Anthropology, Sociological Theory, Philosophy
Alan Roulstone – New Technology
John Shiels – Crime and Deviance, Class and Social Stratification
Alan Sillitoe – Historical and Comparative Sociology, Sociology of Development, Marxism, Socialism and Communism
Gregory Smith (University of Salford) Interpretative Sociology
Joan Smith – Research Methods
Geof Stanley – Industrial Sociology
Martin Thomas – Social Work, Social Welfare, Family and Marriage
Colin Tipton (University of Surrey) – Marxism, Political Sociology
Lorna Warren (University of Salford) – Anthropology
Ruth Waterhouse – Sexuality and Gender, Women's Studies, Feminism, Ethnicity, Urbanism, Culture
Jim Zacune – Sociology of Higher Education

Changes in the Second Edition

Many entries have been updated or otherwise revised, a number have been removed, and more than 250 entirely new entries have been added. As a result, the new edition is considerably longer than the previous one.

Associate Editors

With his departure from Staffordshire University, Tony Charles is no longer an Associate Editor. The Associate Editors for this edition have been Phil Nicholls and Alan Sillitoe.

Contributors to the Second Edition

The following have contributed to the revision of entries or have prepared new entries in the general areas indicated:

Dr. Mike Ball – social anthropology
Prof. Christopher Bryant (University of Salford) – eastern Europe, intellectuals, nationalism
Judith Cavet – social policy
Prof. Ellis Cashmore – race and ethnicity, mass communications, social theory
Dr. Pam Cotterill – sexuality and gender, social theory
Dr. Mike Dent – sociology of organizations

Dr. Charles Fernyhough – general psychology, social theory
Ursula Dobraszczyz – sexuality and gender
John Horne (Heriot-Watt University) – sociology of sport and leisure
Dr. Ruth Green – intelligence, social psychology
Prof. David Jary – comparative and historical sociology, general sociology, higher education, social theory and methodology
Dr. Julia Jary – general, social, developmental and abnormal psychology, research methods
Prof. Christine King – sociology of religion
Dr. Elizabeth Meins – developmental and abnormal psychology
Dr. Phil Nicholls – comparative sociology, general sociology, social theory, sociology of health and medicine
Dr. Martin Parker (University of Keele) – social theory
John Pierson – social policy
Prof. Chris Rojek – cultural studies, post-modernity, social theory, sociology of sport and leisure
Maggie O'Neill – sexuality and gender, social theory
Alan Sillitoe – comparative and historical sociology, communism and socialism, eastern Europe, general sociology
Dr. Greg Smith (University of Salford) – social theory
Dr. Joan Smith – class, housing and homelessness, research methods
Geof Stanley – industrial sociology, sociology of organizations
Dr. Karen Stevenson – sexuality and gender, social theory
Colin Tipton (University of Surrey) – Marxism
Martin Thomas – social policy and social theory
Ruth Waterhouse – feminism, sexuality and gender

Changes to the Third Edition

As in the second edition, many entries have been updated and revised. A small number of entries have been removed but more than 100 new entries have been added, especially in the area of contemporary social theory and to acknowledge the new importance of what has been termed 'cyberculture'. Other areas where there are new or amended entries are the rapidly shifting terrain of social and educational policy, and the new politics of the 'Third Way'. Once again, the new edition is longer than its predecessor.

Contributors to the Third Edition

The following have contributed to the revision of entries or prepared new entries in the areas indicated:

Prof. Christopher Bryant (University of Salford) – civil religion, nationalism, intellectuals
Dr. Angie Burns – social and critical psychology
Prof. Ellis Cashmore – cultural theory and sports sociology
Dr. David Clark-Carter – statistics, research methods

Jude Courtney (Staffordshire Probation Service) – social policy
Prof. Mike Dent – sociology of work and organisation, information technology
Ursula Dobraszczyz – health, social policy, social theory
Dr. Mark Featherstone – contemporary social theory
Simon Gardner – social theory
Richard Gorton – the new politics
Dr. Siobhan Holohan – contemporary social theory, feminist theory
Prof. David Jary (University of Birmingham and Staffordshire University) – social theory, contemporary society, general sociology
Dr. Julia Jary – psychology
Rob Jones – contemporary social theory, higher and further education
Dr. Phil Nicholls – general sociology
Dr. Martin Parker (University of Keele) – social theory
Prof. Chris Rojek – cultural and leisure theory
Alan Sillitoe – comparative historical sociology
Dr. Karen Stevenson – post-feminism, the body
Dr. Greg Smith (University of Salford) – social theory, Goffman
Prof. Tony Spybey – globalization
Dr. Liz Thomas – higher education and lifelong learning, research methods, social policy
Colin Tipton – Marxism
Prof. Frank Webster (University of Birmingham) – information society
Jim Zacume – social psychology

Acknowledgements

We continue to be encouraged in our endeavours by the very positive feedback from users of the Dictionary, for which many thanks.

Additional help in the assembly and typing of entries has been received from Jill Scott and Jean Wrench at Staffordshire University Graduate School, from Sheelagh Rowbottom and Geoff Walton at Staffordshire University Library, and, last but not least, from Edwin Moore and his team at HarperCollins.

David and Julia Jary

a

abnormal deviating from the usual pattern of behaviour (or social structure), especially where this is viewed as maladjustment or DYSFUNCTION.

Any sociological use of the term faces the problem of determining 'normality'. For example, DURKHEIM made the assumption that the average social form at a particular level of social development was also the functional form. However, whilst conceptions of functional normality and abnormality may be relatively clear in relation to biological organisms, the utility of these concepts in sociology has been widely questioned. With the exception of Durkheim and functionalist sociology, sociologists have usually conceptualized individual and social variability and deviation from established patterns of behaviour in other terms than 'normality' and 'abnormality'. See also DISABILITY.

abnormal division of labour see DIVISION OF LABOUR.

abortion miscarriage of birth; the artificially induced termination of pregnancy leading to the destruction of the foetus. While abortion is officially prohibited in some societies, in many societies, including most modern societies, it is recognized as a legitimate way of terminating unwanted pregnancies. In some modern societies the incidence of recorded abortions approaches that for live births. In recent years, debates about abortion have centred on the rights of mothers as well as the rights of the unborn child. In this way the debate about abortion is also bound up with wider political struggles in modern societies, e.g. ideologies of the NEW RIGHT, as well as the WOMEN'S LIBERATION MOVEMENT. See also REPRODUCTIVE TECHNOLOGIES.

absentee landowner an owner of agricultural land who lives away from the property and is not directly involved in day-to-day production. Within a PEASANT SOCIETY this form of land ownership can be conducive to the appearance of social and political conflicts between landlords and peasants, as in prerevolutionary France and prerevolutionary China.

absolute and relative surplus value see SURPLUS VALUE.

absolute poverty that level of POVERTY defined in terms of the minimum requirements for basic subsistence.

absolute surplus value see SURPLUS VALUE.

absolutism (and **absolutist state**)

1 any political regime in which rulers are unrestrained by custom or the rule of law, and where the exercise of power can be arbitrary.

2 the doctrines justifying such a regime.

3 the specific state form and related doctrines (e.g. divine right of kings) associated with centralizing European monarchies in the 17th and 18th centuries.

4 (MARXISM) the form of Western European state which precedes the CAPITALIST STATE.

In reality no ruler possesses absolute power. The conventional view has been that absolute government was a feature of premodern, non-Western states, e.g. the Turkish sultanate or Fijian monarchy.

However, although arbitrary power and the social mobilization of subject populations (e.g. in the building of the pyramids) were a feature of such regimes, the lack of modern technologies of communication and SURVEILLANCE meant that effective power was often severely limited. Historically, Western sociologists and political scientists tended to exaggerate differences between non-European and European constitutional regimes – an aspect of the general ethnocentrism of Western social science, especially in the 19th century (see ORIENTAL DESPOTISM, ORIENTALISM).

Western European absolutism was absolutist only in comparison with the feudal monarchies that preceded it and the constitutional monarchies which followed. The Marxist view is that Western European absolutism arose from a balance of power between a traditional landowning aristocracy and a rising bourgeoisie. This enabled monarchs to establish more effective central control, including codified laws, new and more effective standing armies and more efficient systems of taxation. In practice, restraints on the centralization of political power remained, associated with the continued existence of independently powerful groups and the introduction of new constitutional rights. Debates exist in sociology as to how far absolutism in Europe was an integral element in the rise of Western capitalism, and whether it should be viewed as involving the recasting of feudal aristocratic power (as for ANDERSON, 1974b) or as the onset of modern bourgeois domination (the more conventional Marxist view).

abstracted empiricism a term used by C. Wright MILLS (1959) to refer to those forms of social survey research that involve QUANTITATIVE RESEARCH TECHNIQUES but draw little on the theoretical tradition in sociology and contribute little to sociological understanding. Somewhat unfairly, Mills singled out the work of Paul LAZARSFELD as an exemplar, which he saw as elevating research techniques and the quest for 'reliability' of data at the expense of 'relevance'. See also EMPIRICAL SOCIOLOGY. Compare EMPIRICISM.

abstract labour the basis of the measure of VALUE in Marx's economic theory. See SOCIALLY NECESSARY LABOUR. See also LABOUR THEORY OF VALUE.

access (to post-compulsory education) the process of facilitating entry to formal learning for 'non-traditional' students (e.g. CLASS, ETHNIC GROUP, AGE GROUP and disability). Theoretically, entry may be hindered in various ways including economically, culturally and institutionally. In practice, however, potential entrants may be confronted by a combination of these obstacles. Access researchers are particularly concerned with resisting and criticizing the application of 'deficit' models to potential entrants. In attempting to explain instances of under- or non-participation such models sometimes ignore wider socio-economic and cultural factors and will look to the individual, claiming, for example, that 'low aspirations' are decisive and can be acted on directly. See also ACCESS COURSES.

access courses certificated courses (in England, level 3, A-level equivalent) designed to prepare 'mature students' (usually over 21 years) for entry to HIGHER EDUCATION by providing academic preparation, study skills and an alternative entry qualification. Currently 8% of students in the UK enter HE via Access courses (UCAS, 1998).

accidental generalization see HISTORICAL GENERALIZATION.

accommodation 1 (in race relations) a process in which ethnic groups adjust to each other's existence and coexist without necessarily resolving underlying differences and conflicts (compare ASSIMILATION).
2 (more generally, e.g. in politics or in domestic life) any individual or group behaviour of the above kind.
3 (as used by the CHICAGO SCHOOL, e.g. PARK and Burgess, 1921) a fundamental social process, analogous to biological adaptation, by which societies achieve adjustment to

their environments. The vagueness and conservatism of this usage is criticized by Myrdal et al. (1944).
4 (in PIAGET's theory of CHILD DEVELOPMENT) one of the mechanisms by which development from one stage to the next is achieved. See ASSIMILATION AND ACCOMMODATION.

accounts the 'descriptions' and justifications offered by social actors for their own conduct, e.g. 'members' rational accounts' (see ETHNOMETHODOLOGY) or DEVIANCE DISAVOWALS. While it is a point of principle in forms of sociology such as ethnomethodology or symbolic interactionism to pay close attention to actors' accounts, in other forms of sociology this is not always the case.

acculturation 1 (especially in CULTURAL ANTHROPOLOGY) a process in which contacts between different cultural groups lead to the acquisition of new cultural patterns by one, or perhaps both groups, with the adoption of all or parts of the other's culture.
2 any transmission of culture between groups, including transfer between generations (although in this instance the terms ENCULTURATION and SOCIALIZATION are more usual).

accumulation (*or* **expanded** *or* **extended reproduction**) **of capital** (MARXISM) the process by which capitalism expands by employing labour to create SURPLUS VALUE in order to create new CAPITAL, which in turn is used to create further surplus value and further new capital, leading, in the long run, to a continuous increase in the overall volume of capital.

For Marx, accumulation is the most central imperative and motor of change within a capitalist economy. Unlike Weber, Marx does not see accumulation primarily as a motivational predisposition of capitalists (compare PROTESTANT ETHIC). Rather, it is the essence of capitalism that accumulation must occur, and this is essential for capitalism as a system to survive. Thus any long-term threat to this accumulation is also a threat to capitalism. See also CAPITALISM AND CAPITALIST MODE OF PRODUCTION, CIRCUITS OF CAPITAL, PRIMITIVE ACCUMULATION, CONTRADICTION, CRISES OF CAPITALISM.

acephalous (in SOCIAL ANTHROPOLOGY) (of a society) without formal leadership, e.g. with no provision for a chief or permanent political authority. See SEGMENTARY SOCIETIES, STATELESS SOCIETIES.

achieved status any social position gained through personal effort or open competition. As such, achieved status contrasts with ASCRIBED STATUS. See also ACHIEVEMENT, CONTEST AND SPONSORED MOBILITY, PATTERN VARIABLES.

achievement the gaining of social position or social status as the outcome of personal effort in open competition with others, e.g. in formal examinations or competition in a market. As such, achievement is contrasted with ascription and ASCRIBED STATUS. See also PATTERN VARIABLES.

While achievement in its widest sense can be seen as a particular feature of modern, 'open-class' society (see SOCIAL MOBILITY) (e.g. 'careers open to talents'), its opposite, *ascription* (e.g. inheriting one's father's job), is a feature especially of traditional class-divided societies. However, both modes of allocation of social position and social status will usually exist in any society. One reason for this is that some positions (e.g. historically, especially GENDER ROLES) are mainly ascribed, while other positions, e.g. where skills or talents required by the society are in short supply, tend to be subject to open competition. Another reason is that there are likely to be ascriptive elements underlying achieved status (e.g. the effects of advantages of family background underlying educational achievement). See also FUNCTIONALIST THEORY OF SOCIAL STRATIFICATION, MERITOCRACY.

achievement motivation a concept (with associated projective tests) introduced by the psychologist D.C. McClelland (1961) which purports to measure individual and cultural differences in the striving for achievement.

The concept rests on the hypothesis that the *need for achievement* (*NAch*) is stimulated by a caring parental relationship (particularly with the mother) which sets high standards of behaviour. Achievement motivation is presented as a significant determinant of individual entrepreneurial endeavour and also of different levels of economic development (e.g. between developed and undeveloped societies). This latter assumption is challenged by many sociologists who regard McClelland as failing to take into account major differences in the social and economic structures of societies apart from achievement motivation.

act 1 to carry out or perform any unit or sequence of social behaviour. See ACTION.
2 to play or act out social roles as if on a stage. See DRAMATURGY.
3 any unit of ACTION or behaviour.
4 the 'accomplished act' rather than the process of social action (Schutz, 1972). See also ACTION.

action 1 any unit or sequence of social activity or behaviour, e.g. the action of a trade union or state, as well as the action of an individual.
2 (in contrast with BEHAVIOUR; see also BEHAVIOURISM) any unit or sequence of individual social activity which is intentional or purposive and involves conscious deliberation rather than merely being the result of a biological reflex.

For Weber, *meaningful social action* consists of any course of action in which subjective meaning guides the action and where this action is oriented towards others. For a symbolic interactionist, such as BLUMER (1969), that actors act, rather than merely react, is a decisive feature of human action (see ACTION THEORY, SYMBOLIC INTERACTIONISM, MEAD). See also TYPES OF SOCIAL ACTION.

Sociologists are divided as to whether social reality is better explained with reference to individual purposive action (see ACTION THEORY, AGENCY, METHODOLOGICAL INDIVIDUALISM, MEANINGFUL UNDERSTANDING AND EXPLANATION) or as the outcome of SOCIAL STRUCTURE (see also STRUCTURALISM). There are also those sociologists (see SOCIAL PHENOMENOLOGY, ETHNOMETHODOLOGY, SCHUTZ, GARFINKEL) who argue that action theorists as well as structuralists have failed to show how actors' meanings are actually constituted.

The debate about social action in these terms is one of the most central in modern sociological theory. Various attempts have been made to reconcile action theory and structuralist perspectives (see PARSONS, STRUCTURATION THEORY, STRUCTURE AND AGENCY, GIDDENS). While no consensus exists that these attempts are entirely successful, there is an increasing recognition that sociological explanations must include reference to both action and structure (see DUALITY OF STRUCTURE).

action approach an approach within INDUSTRIAL SOCIOLOGY which stresses the influence of actors' overall orientations to work, including those emanating from beyond the workplace. The approach presents itself as a reaction against those that are more deterministic, including the SOCIOTECHNICAL SYSTEMS APPROACH. See also ORGANIZATION, ORGANIZATION THEORY.

action frame of reference see PARSONS.

action research a form of research carried out with the aim of inducing changes in social activities (e.g. increased participation in cultural events), but with the aim of also studying these changes. See PARTICIPATORY ACTION RESEARCH.

action theory a general orientation to sociological analysis particularly associated with the work of WEBER and the SYMBOLIC INTERACTIONISTS (see also ETHNOMETHODOLOGY). The aim of the approach is the MEANINGFUL UNDERSTANDING AND EXPLANATION of social reality, which is seen as the outcome of purposive social action. See ACT, ACTION, VERSTEHEN, INTERPRETATIVE SOCIOLOGY.

While all action theorists regard explanation with reference to actors' meanings (purposes, values, etc.) as an essential first step in sociological explanations, this is seen by some (notably P. WINCH, 1958) as removing all possibility of more general explanations. For most sociologists, including Weber, meaningful explanation and other types of EXPLANATION are complementary forms. See also STRUCTURATION THEORY.

Although it is sometimes suggested that action theory is 'irredeemably individualistic', this is only so in some cases (e.g. METHODOLOGICAL INDIVIDUALISM). That the contrary can be true is illustrated by the work of Weber (especially his comparative studies of European and Asiatic religions). Nevertheless, there remain significant differences between 'action theory' and other more avowedly STRUCTURALIST approaches in sociological theory, for example in the degree of VOLUNTARISM or independent AGENCY seen for social actors.

activism active involvement as a member of a POLITICAL PARTY, PRESSURE GROUP, or related political organization, e.g. a 'trades union activist'. Theories and research concerned with *political activism* suggest that the tendency is for activists generally to be of higher social status, more socially confident and often better informed than most nonactivists. Levels of political activism also vary according to political circumstances. For example, in times of political crisis many people may be drawn into politics who would not normally be politically active. Some theorists, especially in POLITICAL SCIENCE (e.g. LIPSET, 1959), have suggested that in Western societies, in such circumstances, high levels of political activity and less informed participants may pose a threat to the 'stability of democracy'. More generally, however, increased participation in politics by members of lower status minority groups (e.g. new URBAN SOCIAL MOVEMENTS) is regarded as a favourable development. See also POLITICAL PARTICIPATION, OPINION LEADERS, TWO-STEP FLOW IN MASS COMMUNICATIONS, STABLE DEMOCRACY, SOCIAL MOVEMENTS.

actor see SOCIAL ACTOR.

actor-network theory (ANT) a recently influential approach to social theory, which combines post-structuralist insights with detailed empirical study of science/technologies, organizations and social processes. Its method is to 'sum up' interactions as 'local' and 'practical'. Building especially on the work of Bruno Latour (see Latour, 'On Recalling ANT' in J. Law and J. Hassard (eds) *Actor Network Theory and After, 1999*), the focus of ANT is on the 'reality'/'transformability' of 'networks', as against such notions as 'institution' or 'society'. Its conception of the social is as a circulatory 'field of forces' beyond the agency-structure debate.

adaptation the way in which social systems of any kind (e.g. a family group, a business firm, a nation state) 'manage' or respond to their environment. According to Talcott PARSONS, 'adaptation' is one of four FUNCTIONAL PREREQUISITES which all social systems must satisfy if they are to survive. He argues that in industrial societies the need for adaptation is satisfied through the development of a specialized subsystem, the economy. See also NEOEVOLUTIONISM.

addiction see DRUG ADDICTION.

ad hoc hypothesis any hypothesis added to an explanatory theory merely to save that theory from potentially refuting evidence. In Popper's FALSIFICATIONISM, ad hoc hypotheses are regarded as illegitimate. He cites Marx and Freud as examples of social thinkers using hypotheses in this way to protect their theories from refutation.

admass see ADVERTISING.

administrative theory see MANAGEMENT SCIENCE AND ADMINISTRATIVE THEORY.

adolescence the stage in the LIFE COURSE between childhood and adulthood marked by the beginnings of adult sexuality but coming before full adult status or final detachment from the FAMILY OF ORIGIN OR ORIENTATION.

In simple societies the passage from childhood to adulthood is often marked by *rites de passage* (see RITUAL), or by the provision of young men's (and less often young women's) AGE SETS. However, it is within modern societies, with their distinctive emphasis on YOUTH CULTURE, fostered by the MASS MEDIA OF COMMUNICATION, that adolescence has achieved a particular importance. In these societies, in contrast to more TRADITIONAL SOCIETIES, adolescents must choose their CAREERS and sexual partners as well as their general LIFESTYLE. Thus adolescence, the time of educational examinations and entry into work, is also a stage in the life cycle which is associated with individual experimentation in sexual and leisure behaviour. It may also be a time for questioning received values, and of rebellion against parental patterns of behaviour (see also GENERATION). The search for independence, and the heightened sense of self-awareness and uncertainty about SELF, can also lead to psychological crisis and psychological disturbance. See also YOUTH UNEMPLOYMENT, DELINQUENCY.

Adorno, Theodor (1903-69) German social philosopher, sociologist and musicologist, and a leading member of the FRANKFURT SCHOOL OF CRITICAL THEORY. His epistemological writings and his critique of modern society and MASS CULTURE have been especially influential. Expelled from Germany by the Nazis in 1934, he went first to England and then to the US, where he remained until 1949 when he returned to Germany. In America, Adorno participated in a famous empirical research project, *The Authoritarian Personality* (Adorno et al., 1950), which involved studies of racial prejudice, nationalism and authoritarianism. In 1959 he became director of the Institute of Social Research, which had returned to Frankfurt from the US.

Adorno wrote more than 20 books on philosophy, music, literature, AESTHETICS, social psychology and sociology. His critique of capitalism particularly focused on the commodification and perversion of culture by the 'culture industry'. Popular music, for example, produced solely to sell in the economy of the market place, was standardized and mechanical and served as a 'social cement' for the existing system. Adorno's concern with repressive systems of thought and organization in what he called the 'administered world' led him to articulate opposition to traditional epistemological ideas as well as to advocate radical change in society. In his epistemological writings, e.g. *Negative Dialectics* (1973), Adorno proposed the dissolution of any theoretical frameworks and conceptual distinctions that threaten to become dogmas, including MARXISM. Both EMPIRICISM and POSITIVISM were rejected by Adorno, who regarded them as betraying Reason and as no longer leading to 'enlightenment'. In his *Aesthetic Theory* (1984) art and critical theory were invested with the 'power' to disclose 'truths' about society. Here Adorno speaks of an administered society constituted by the myth of total reason. His methodology, 'negative dialectics', was a tool for the critical analysis of society. Commentators on Adorno's life and work have regarded his stance as increasingly pessimistic and élitist, issues taken up by later representatives of the Frankfurt school, notably HABERMAS. Other important works by Adorno are: *Dialectic of Enlightenment* (with Horkheimer) (1972), *Philosophy of Modern Music* (1973), and *The Jargon of Authenticity* (1973). See also BENJAMIN, METHODENSTREIT.

advanced capitalism (MARXISM) the hypothetical final stage in the development of CAPITALISM, which is characterized by concentration of ownership and by increased state intervention in the economy. The latter arises from the need to control the effects of increasing economic and social CONTRADICTIONS and increasing tendency to ECONOMIC CRISES. The stage is seen as culminating in a final crisis of capitalism and a transition to socialism. See also CAPITALISM AND CAPITALIST MODE OF PRODUCTION, IMPERIALISM.

advertising the process and the means (press, film, TV, etc.) by which the availability and the qualities of commodities and services are notified to a wider public. Drawing on SEMIOLOGY, Jean BAUDRILLARD (1970) has argued that in modern Societies CONSUMPTION entails the 'active manipulation of the SIGN', so that the sign and the commodity have come together in the production of the 'commodity-sign'.

It is in such a context that the power of advertising has been a central issue in modern sociology. In a popular sociological exposé, *The Hidden Persuaders* (1957), Vance Packard painted a picture of an armoury of psychological and sociological advertising techniques which made these techniques appear all-powerful. In the 1950s, the novelist J. B. Priestley coined the term *admass* to describe the drive to consumption which was fuelled by mass advertising in modern societies. Packard also argued that advertising promotes consumption as a solution to personal and political problems. Advertising creates 'false needs' which are met in a fundamentally unsatisfying way by conspicuous consumption, in the belief that wellbeing and peace of mind are provided by the purchase of commodities.

Against such views, more conventional paradigms in media research have often argued that barriers to mass communications (e.g. group opinion) exist which act as a 'protective screen' against any too easy manipulation (see TWO-STEP FLOW IN MASS COMMUNICATIONS). Feminist theories of advertising have taken another line, stressing its frequent sexism, an aspect of its more general recourse to gender, ageist, and racist STEREOTYPES.

A further aspect of advertising is that in the UK and elsewhere advertising influences the general content of broadcasting. In the UK, Curran et al., commenting upon the discussion in the 1977 *Royal Commission on the Press* on press finances, argued that advertising organizes both media content and structure, and effectively operates as a system of patronage supporting capitalist production values rather than democratic political values. Markets and sections of populations which are not attractive to advertisers and manufacturers, such as older people and people with low incomes, are not serviced by the mass media because of this dependence on advertising. One final point of interest is that some advertising agencies now employ operational categories which have much in common with ideas currently being developed by academic writers using the concept 'postmodern' to describe contemporary Western societies. Postmodernism proposes that the concept of CLASS has less relevance to contemporary experience than LIFESTYLE and CONSUMPTION. In this frame of reference advertising is depicted as seductive rather than manipulative and advertising agencies are increasingly abandoning socioeconomic classification systems and replacing them with the concepts of consumption class and 'lifestyle group'. See also CONSUMER CULTURE, MASS CULTURE.

advocacy research a form of social policy research (e.g. on rape) undertaken by researchers with a strong concern about the importance of a social problem. The aim is both to collect information about the level of a social problem and to raise public consciousness.

aesthetics (PHILOSOPHY) the study of art and artistic appreciation. Among the topics considered by aesthetics is the extent to which our experience and appreciation of art is similar to or different from our experience and understanding of nature. A further question is whether the inherent qualities of the thing perceived or the contemplative experience itself is decisive in the experience.

In the work of the FRANKFURT SCHOOL OF CRITICAL THEORY (e.g. ADORNO, BENJAMIN) or postmodernists (see POSTMODERNITY AND POSTMODERNISM), the focus of aesthetics has been relocated and radically expanded to include, as Lash (1990) puts it, 'aesthetic signifiers in the flotsam and jetsam of everyday life'. In this, the 'political nature of the aesthetic' is increasingly affirmed and there is a refusal to see art as a separate order of life. This has the effect of making aesthetics central to the sociology of MASS CULTURE. See also SOCIOLOGY OF ART.

aetiology see ETIOLOGY.

affect feeling or emotion. A term used to denote the emotional or feeling side of mental experience, as opposed to the cognitive or thinking aspect. See also AFFECTIVE DISORDERS.

affective disorders disorders of mood or of the emotions. Disorders of the emotions, such as depression or anxiety, are termed 'affective disorders'.

affective involvement see PATTERN VARIABLES.

affective neutrality see PATTERN VARIABLES.

affectual action see TYPES OF SOCIAL ACTION.

affinal (of a kin relationship) arising from a link by marriage, e.g. father-in-law/son-in-law is an affinal relationship whereas the father-son relationship is a relationship of DESCENT. See also KINSHIP.

affirmative action see POSITIVE DISCRIMINATION.

affluent society 1 a description of British society, especially in the mid-1950s and early 1960s, in which it was assumed that rising living standards were leading to profound changes in social attitudes, including a decline in traditional working-class support for the Labour Party. See also AFFLUENT WORKER, EMBOURGEOISEMENT THESIS, CLASS IMAGERY.

2 (GALBRAITH, *The Affluent Society* 1958) an account of US society in the late 1950s as a society in which basic economic scarcity and insecurity had been substantially conquered, but where private affluence was accompanied by 'public squalor' (e.g. producing cars in abundance, but disregarding road improvement and pollution control), and where poor provision was made for the casualties of capitalism. If increasing state expenditure in the 1960s and 1970s led to a departure from this pattern, monetarism and the changing political climate of the late 1970s and the 1980s has again tipped the balance against state provision. Echoes of Galbraith's concerns exist, however, in the importance of environmental issues in modern politics (see GREEN MOVEMENT).

affluent worker the new type of affluent manual worker (see AFFLUENT SOCIETY), said to be distinguished by new patterns of voting behaviour and detachment from 'traditional' working-class loyalties and movement from 'traditional' working-class locations. This EMBOURGEOISEMENT THESIS, however, was challenged in a major study of the CLASS LOCATIONS and CLASS IMAGERY of industrial workers by GOLDTHORPE, LOCKWOOD, et al. (1968a & b, 1969).

African socialism see SOCIALISM.

Afro-Caribbean a person of African descent who has migrated from, or is living in, the Caribbean. In the context of the UK, the term is used to describe people who were part of the post-World War II labour migration of inhabitants of the Caribbean Islands, and their descendants in Britain.

age group any social grouping based on age. In some simple societies age groupings (see AGE SETS) have formed a crucial basis of social organization, but age groupings of varying kinds have significance within societies of all types (e.g. in modern Britain, the under-5s or the over-65s).

ageing the chronological process of growing physically older. However, there is also a social dimension in which chronology is less important than the meanings attached to the process. Different cultural values and social expectations apply according to gender and age group, and therefore there are socially-structured variations in the personal experience of ageing.

EISENSTADT (*Generation to Generation*, 1964) studied the political role of age groups and argued that age stratification is an important stabilizing influence in societies where:

(a) two sets of values coexist within the social structure – the particularism of family ties and the universalism of the public division of labour (here age groups act as buffers between the public and the private domain and give members solidarity and support as well as orienting them to the adult world of work); and
(b) the opportunity for the young to have full participation in adult society is blocked by systems of KINSHIP and DESCENT (here the age group becomes the basis for status and also power struggles between the generations).

In DEMOGRAPHY the terms *ageing society* and *youthful society* are used to indicate the age composition of the population. A youthful society is one in which there is a preponderance of people in young age groups (under 15 years) because of a high BIRTH RATE and low LIFE EXPECTANCY. An ageing society is one in which reductions in the birth rate and greater longevity have resulted in a rising proportion of the population belonging to the older age groups. For example, CENSUS data for the UK shows that in 1911 men over 65 years and women over 60 years comprised 6.8% of the population, whereas in 1981 they comprised 17.1%.

The growing proportion of older people in the population, and the spread of early retirement, has led to age being perceived as a social problem. Older people are subject to negative stereotyping and diminished SOCIAL STATUS. Even academic discourse promotes negative imagery through such terms as 'burden of dependency' and 'dependency ratio', which refer to the number of economically inactive older people in relation to the number of economically active younger people whose labour provides the services consumed by the older generation. In the US, AGEISM has become a political issue through the emergence of movements, such as the Grey Panthers, determined to safeguard the citizen rights of older people and counter the negative imagery of old age promoted by the commercialization of youth. See also MIDLIFE CRISIS, YOUTH CULTURE.

ageism any process or expression of ideas in which stereotyping of and/or DISCRIMINATION against people occurs by virtue of age. Ageism applies especially to such actions directed against older people, but the term may also be employed to refer to unreasonable stereotyping or discrimination against anyone where this occurs simply by virtue of age.

agency 1 the power of ACTORS to operate independently of the determining constraints of SOCIAL STRUCTURE. The term is intended to convey the volitional, purposive nature of human activity as opposed to its constrained, determined aspects. Although utilized in widely different ways, it is especially central in METHODOLOGICAL INDIVIDUALISM, ETHNOMETHODOLOGY, PHENOMENOLOGY, SYMBOLIC INTERACTIONISM. The importance of human intention (and possibly also FREE WILL) thus emphasized, places the individual at the centre of any analysis and raises issues of moral choice and political capacity. The political problematic is expressed by GOULDNER counterposing 'man on his back' with 'man fighting back' (1973), but the classic essay is Dawe's (1971) 'The Two Sociologies'.
2 any human action, collective or structural *as well as* individual, which 'makes a difference' to a social outcome; thus, for GIDDENS (1984), agency is equivalent to POWER. In this way Giddens opposes any simple polarization of 'structure' and 'agency'. This is related to his view that STRUCTURE must be seen as 'enabling' as well as 'constraining' (see also STRUCTURE AND AGENCY, DUALITY OF STRUCTURE).

agency and structure see STRUCTURE AND AGENCY.

Age of Enlightenment the period of intellectual ferment leading up to the French Revolution, which was distinguished by a fundamental questioning of traditional modes of thought and social organization, and sought to replace these with an exclusive reliance on human reason in determining social practices. Many thinkers and philosophers were associated with these developments, amongst them Voltaire (1694–1778), MONTESQUIEU, Holbach (1723–89), Helvétius (1715–71), Diderot (1713–84) and ROUSSEAU. Nor was the movement merely confined to France; it also embraced numerous other thinkers elsewhere, including members of the so-called SCOTTISH ENLIGHTENMENT, such as Adam FERGUSON and John MILLAR, whose work was especially sociological. Despite a common accord on the importance of reason in human affairs, major differences of view existed between thinkers: Voltaire popularized English liberal doctrines of NATURAL RIGHTS; Holbach and Helvétius took these doctrines further and argued for UTILITARIANISM and representative government; while Rousseau's concept of the SOCIAL CONTRACT led to holistic conceptions of state and society realized in the French Revolution. In retrospect, much Enlightenment thought is seen as superficial, lacking an adequate empirical research base, and above all overconfident about human PROGRESS and the ultimate triumph of Reason. However, the Enlightenment era signalled a final decisive break between traditional and modern thought, and between traditional and modern forms of social organization. See also COMTE, RATIONALISM, GRAND NARRATIVES.

age sets age-related corporate social groupings, more usually of men, which form an important basis of social organization, especially within SEGMENTARY SOCIETIES. Such age sets create a pattern of social relationships, crosscutting KINSHIP or DESCENT, performing ceremonial sociopolitical and economic functions which may include the ownership of property.

age specific birth rate see BIRTH RATE.

aggregate any collection of units or parts, however temporary or fortuitous; thus the contrast may sometimes be drawn between mere aggregates, with no internal structure or basis for persistence, and GROUPS, COMMUNITIES, etc., which will usually possess clear internal structure, coherence, cohesion and relative persistence.

aggregate data analysis any form of analysis which employs available bodies of published or other data (e.g. demographic data, suicide statistics as used by DURKHEIM) describing the characteristics of an entire population or similar aggregate of individuals. The attraction of this mode of research is that large quantities of data, including cross-cultural data, are available at little cost. The main disadvantage is that the researcher may have little awareness of how the original data were collected. See also ECOLOGICAL FALLACY OR WRONG LEVEL FALLACY, OFFICIAL STATISTICS, SECONDARY ANALYSIS, CICOUREL.

aggregate level fallacy see ECOLOGICAL FALLACY OR WRONG LEVEL FALLACY.

aggregation the process of combining diverse political interests to form a more or less coherent set of policies which can form a political programme. In representative democracies, according to Almond (1953), this function is especially undertaken by POLITICAL PARTIES, whereas the related function of *interest articulation* is carried out particularly by interest groups and PRESSURE GROUPS.

aggression a hostile attitude or action. In humans, aggressive behaviour is generally underlain by emotions such as anger or fear.

This is an area in which ETHOLOGY and PSYCHOANALYSIS as well as sociology have shown great interest, with the result that aggressive behaviour can be seen to have three possible situation determinants:

(a) (*Ethology*) in the animal kingdom certain environmental stimuli (releasing mechanisms) may evoke aggression, for example the presence of another male robin in a robin's territory;

(b) (*Psychoanalysis*) frustration in obtaining one's goals may lead to aggression, not necessarily directed at the source of the frustration. The frustration-aggression

theory of prejudice (Adorno et al., 1950) is related to this theory (see FRUSTRATION-AGGRESSION HYPOTHESIS, AUTHORITARIAN PERSONALITY);
(c) aggression may be a learnt response, i.e. behaviour that has been conditioned because it has led to positive results for the individual when displayed in certain situations in the past (see BEHAVIOURISM).

agnatic see PATRILINEAL DESCENT.

agrarian society any form of society, especially traditional societies, primarily based on agricultural and craft production rather than industrial production.
The major preindustrial civilizations, e.g. preindustrial Christendom, China, India, were predominantly agrarian societies. Sometimes simpler societies, e.g. HUNTER-GATHERERS, which are not based on settled agriculture are referred to as *preagrarian* (see Hall, 1985).

agribusiness 1 AGRICULTURE conducted as a large-scale capitalist business enterprise.
2 economic activities closely related to or directly dependent on agriculture, including the production of producer goods for agriculture (e.g. farm machinery, fertilizers) as well as the sale of agricultural produce as food and raw materials.

agricultural revolution 1 the transition from HUNTER-GATHERER to settled agricultural societies which occurred in the Middle East around 10,000 years ago, bringing about the domestication of animals and the cultivation of crops. Whether, as some theorists suggest, this agricultural revolution was the result of necessity born out of a depletion of naturally occurring supplies of food, the likelihood is that the transition occurred more than once, since patterns of transition that are apparent in the New World show marked differences from those in the Old World.
2 innovations in agricultural production and organization leading to increased food and other crop production associated with the transition from AGRARIAN SOCIETY to INDUSTRIAL SOCIETY. The example of Europe, and England in particular, is often used as the model. Transformations in agricultural production in the 17th and 18th centuries were associated with increased population, improvements in diet and growing urbanization. This is seen as one of the factors making possible the INDUSTRIAL REVOLUTION in Europe. Important changes continued throughout the 19th and 20th centuries with increases in agricultural productivity and a long-term decline in the proportion of the working population engaged in agriculture.

agriculture the cultivation of plants for food and raw materials (see also AGRICULTURAL REVOLUTION). In a more restricted sense, however, agriculture is distinguished from HORTICULTURE.

alcoholism the consumption of alcohol to excess, leading to psychological and physical dependency and addiction (see DRUG ADDICTION OR DRUG DEPENDENCY). Among other diseases associated with excessive consumption of alcohol over a long period are cirrhosis of the liver and heart disease.

algorithm any method, procedure, or set of instructions for carrying out a task by means of a precisely specified series of steps or sequence of actions, e.g. as in long division, the hierarchical sequence of steps in a typical computer program, or the steps in a manufacturing process.

allocative power see POWER.

Allport, Gordon (1897–1967) Influential US social psychologist (e.g. Allport, *Social Psychology*, 1924) who made important contributions to the development of TRAIT THEORY and the study of ATTITUDES and PREJUDICE. He regarded the SELF as a central aspect of the psychology of the individual, with the self and PERSONALITY seen as always tending to seek internal coherence. In its concern to establish the dimensions of personality and attitudes, he argued, psychology must be careful not to lose sight of the individual. He suggested that motives possess a 'functional autonomy', defying a reduction to behaviouristic accounts.

alienation

1 an individual's feelings of estrangement from a situation, group or culture, etc.

2 a concept used by MARX, in his early work, in reference to the core relationships of capitalist production and their human and psychological effects.

3 (following from **2**) a central term in different interpretations of Marx (see below).

4 as operationalized in empirical research, the term has its best known use in R. Blauner's (1964) comparison of work conditions and work satisfaction.

In religious and philosophical usage, the term dates back to medieval times and can even be found in the classical philosophy of ancient Greece. Modern sociological usage mainly derives from Marx's critique of Hegel's use of the term in Marx's *Economic and Philosophic Manuscripts* (EPM), written in 1844 but not published until 1932, and not widely known until the 1950s. In the EPM Marx gives several meanings and nuances to the term, but with three central elements: philosophical, psychological and sociological. Unlike Hegel, who uses alienation to contrast the 'objectivity' of nature with human consciousness, Marx emphasizes the importance of the relationship between human beings (in their social relations of production) and nature for social development, and therefore individual development. The psychological, or social psychological, usage is the one which is most commonly found in popular, and in many sociological, accounts. At its simplest, this refers to feelings of unhappiness, lack of involvement or only instrumental involvement with work and with others. In Marx's explanation these individual manifestations of alienation are a product of social relations. The important aspect of the concept is the sociological one. Within capitalism, workers do not work to express themselves, to develop their interests or for intrinsic satisfaction: work is essentially forced and, in work, people are subjected to the demands and discipline of others, the owners of capital. In addition to this emphasis on the relation of the worker to the act of production, Marx also stresses the importance of the relation of workers to the products which they produce. The objects which workers produce, commodities, do not belong to them, but to their employers. In effect, in work, people produce wealth and power for a class which oppresses them. Products do not belong to their producers, they are alien objects.

The philosophical element concerns a particular conception of human nature. Marx portrays human nature not as something which is 'fixed' or eternal, but as a social product. He writes about alienation, or estrangement from 'species being', by which he means those characteristics which are specifically human and distinguish human beings from other animals. These human attributes develop socially, through relations of production, and, for Marx, they have the potential for unlimited development in a favourable system of social relationships. Simply, Marx sees the process of production as central to human development. It follows that a system based upon EXPLOITATION, one in which workers are estranged from the act of production and from the products which they produce, stultifies and dehumanizes. It alienates human beings from 'species being' in the sense that it denies any possibility of the development of human potential or creativity, except for a privileged few. Alienation is thus analysed in terms of the social structure of CAPITALISM, i.e. private property, commodity production and class relations.

The 'discovery' of the EPM by Western scholars transformed sociological approaches to, and interpretations of, Marx's work. Some accounts have emphasized either a continuity between the humanist preoccupations of the EPM and later more scientific and less overtly philosophical work, or have argued that the earlier work contains a more satisfactory explanation of the human condition than the later. Others point out that Marx deliberately dropped the term 'alienation' in his later work, in part so as to distance himself from other German scholars of the time – the 'Young Hegelians' – but also, some argue, because of a rejection of humanist philosophical values. This interpretation is associated in particular with the work of ALTHUSSER who argues that a fundamental shift in Marx's approach, an 'epistemological break', occurs after 1844. This radical change involves the development of scientific concepts rather than philosophical, humanist or ideological ones. Opponents of this view argue that Marx's notebooks, published as the *Grundrisse*, show a continuing preoccupation with the concept, and also argue that the concept of 'commodity fetishism', which is used in *Das Kapital* Vol. 1, is in a direct line of descent from 'alienation'.

In addition to interpretative disputes, some Marxist or Marx-influenced writers have attempted to use the concept in concert with some themes from Freud's work, in writings on FALSE CONSCIOUSNESS and on the ways in which modern consumer capitalism creates 'false needs' which have important consequences for working-class politics (e.g. FROMM, 1941; MARCUSE, 1964).

Some sociologists and social psychologists have attempted to use the concept empirically. This operationalization has involved the attempt to divest the concept of its political and evaluative dimensions – in effect to translate it from a distinctively Marxist to a sociological framework. The best-known example of this empirical use is R. Blauner's book *Alienation and Freedom*, in which he uses a redefinition of the concept proposed by a social psychologist, M. Seeman. Seeman argued that 'alienation' could be operationalized in five aspects: powerlessness, meaninglessness, normlessness, isolation and self-estrangement. Blauner attempted to apply this typology, excluding normlessness, to an analysis of historical changes in the organization of work. He argued that in the shift from traditional craft production (e.g. the print industry) to factory production (e.g. cotton mills) and then to mass-production techniques (e.g. the car industry), alienation intensified and the number of alienating jobs increased. However, for Blauner, the further refinement of technology in process production (e.g. chemical works) had the effect of reducing alienation by giving workers enhanced feelings of autonomy, control, understanding and, generally, work satisfaction. Blauner's thesis has been criticized, especially by Marxist sociologists, on a number of grounds. It has been argued that his evidence is inadequate and his interpretation of data partial and one-sided. His work has also been depicted as psychologistic, focusing solely on inferred *feelings* of workers and ignoring the structural analysis of relations of production which is central to Marx's conception. As a related criticism, his technological determinism is seen as problematic, as is the attempt to strip the concept of its political, critical connotations.

The debates about the importance of the concept in Marx's work, and its usefulness or otherwise in sociology, have produced many fruitful arguments, but the adequacy of operationalizations of 'alienation' in empirical sociological research has not been demonstrated.

alphabet any set of letters or similar signs used in WRITING in which each letter represents one or more phonemes. Alphabets were not the earliest basis of writing, having evolved from hieroglyphs, or picture writing, as used in ancient Egypt, and syllabaries, writing whose units were syllables, as in Mycenae and also later in Egypt. The 'convergence' of writing with speech, as Quine (1987) puts it, reached its full extent, however, only with the alphabet.

alternative culture see COUNTER CULTURE OR ALTERNATIVE CULTURE.

alternative medicine therapeutic practices based on understandings of the human organism, the disease process and its treatment, which are different to those held by Western scientific medicine. Conceptualizing alternative medicine thus always implies some under standing of the principle features of orthodox 'scientific' treatment. These are usually held to be:
(a) a mechanical/materialistic understanding of the body and of disease;
(b) a doctrine of 'specific etiology', i.e. that all disease is caused by specific material pathogens such as bacteria, viruses, defective genes, etc.;
(c) a vigorous interventionist therapeutic stance using surgery or chemical drugs to correct, oppose or reverse the disease process;
(d) patient passivity and compliance with the regimen dictated by an expert profession.

Proceeding in this way towards a 'negative' definition of alternative medicine, however, has its dangers as it suggests a unity within both fields which is in fact absent. If regular medicine is materialistic, therapeutically aggressive, etc. (and it sometimes, but not always, is), then it is too easy to assume that all alternative approaches subscribe to opposite principles: viz: a holistic understanding of the body and disease, involving an indissoluble unity of mind and body; a 'sympathetic' therapeutic stance, aimed at enhancing the body's own healing processes; a cooperative relationship between therapist and patient; and an active role for the patient in regaining health. While some systems of alternative medicine do exhibit these features (for example, homeopathy), others (such as chiropractic) do not.

Sociological work on alternative medicine is a recent development, and has tended to focus on four main areas:
(a) rather than accepting therapeutic principles at 'face value', interest has been shown in the social processes underlying the negotiation of the *legitimacy* of therapeutic principles, and of medical knowledge in general (thus the regular/alternative boundary is not fixed only by epistemological criteria, but is also historically fluid, and contingent on issues of professional power);
(b) issues of organization and professionalization;
(c) the resurgence of popular (and regular medical) interest in alternative medicine (involving a complex of reasons, all related in some way to a recognition of the damaging effects of science and technology – it is no accident that interest in green politics and green medicine have emerged more or less together);
(d) the increasing interaction between regular and alternative practitioners, and the incorporation of alternative therapy into regular practice (processes which have led to the use of the term 'complementary therapy' rather than 'alternative therapy').

alternative technology forms of technology (sometimes also referred to as APPROPRIATE TECHNOLOGY or INTERMEDIATE TECHNOLOGY) which are not heavily dependent on access to the advanced technology of Western countries, and may therefore by seen as more 'sustainable' and as making better use of the available resources, including labour.

Althusser, Louis (1918–90), French Marxist social philosopher, and theorist within the French Communist Party, whose theories were especially influential in the aftermath of the student activism of 1968 and in the period of the greatest vogue of structuralist thinking in the 1970s. In particular, Althusser opposed 'humanist' and Hegelian movements within Marxism, proposing instead that Marx's mature work – especially *Das Kapital* with its emphasis on 'labour power' and class contradictions, etc. – should be seen as a 'scientific' theory on a par with that of Galileo or Darwin (*Lenin and Philosophy* (1971)). Thus, in *For Marx* (1966) and (with E. Balibar) *Reading Capital* (1970), he rejects all suggestions that the Hegelian concept of ALIENATION can have any place in Marx's mature theory. Drawing on the epistemological ideas of the French philosopher of science Gaston BACHELARD – especially his concept of the PROBLEMATIQUE – Althusser's argument was that an EPISTEMOLOGICAL BREAK exists between Marx's early philosophical (and ideological) work and his later scientific theory. Further key concepts in Althusser's account of Marx's theory are the concepts of OVERDETERMINATION – the idea that major changes in society are complex and multiply determined – and his distinction between the ideological and repressive state apparatuses (see INTERPOLATION, IDEOLOGICAL STATE APPARATUS). Together these concepts are Althusser's way of avoiding a vulgar determinism or 'economism', in that they allow, first, that the ideological superstructure is *not* merely a reflection of the economy but also in part conditions the existence of it, and, second, that IDEOLOGY must be seen *not* merely as 'false consciousness' but as an important part of real social relations. Similarly, the Marxian concept of MODE OF PRODUCTION is seen as requiring an interpretation so that it is accepted as involving in each concrete case a complex 'articulation' of economic, political and ideological practices. It is difficult now to convey the extent of the interest that Althusser's somewhat tortuous conceptions for a time aroused. However, the degree of dogmatism in his Marxism, and the fact that his theory solved few concrete issues and soon ran into self-contradiction, have meant that his star has waned – an eclipse compounded, tragically, by his murder of his wife and his own incarceration. See ALTHUSSERIAN MARXISM, CULTURAL STUDIES.

Althusserian Marxism a structuralist version of Marxism fashionable especially in the 1970s, based on the ideas of Louis ALTHUSSER. Promoted in England by the Marxist journal the *New Left Review*, Althusser's work influenced many theorists, including Stuart HALL, and Hindess and Hirst (1975). A notable criticism of the approach is E. P. THOMPSON's *The Poverty of Theory* (1978). In opposing Althusser's dogmatism with 'humanism', however, Thompson exhibits his own kind of dogmatism in resisting arguments for structural analysis. Previous supporters of Althusserian Marxism now look to sociological theory to provide a recognition of the importance of *both* STRUCTURE AND AGENCY, having failed to find this in Althusser's work (for a general discussion see T. Benton, 1984, *The Rise and Fall of Structural Marxism*). See also STRUCTURALISM.

altruism concern for the welfare of others rather than oneself. Altruistic behaviour is therefore the opposite of egoistic behaviour. It involves intention to help others when used of human behaviour, but the fact that some animal behaviour is judged to be altruistic indicates that there are two possible bases to a definition: intentionality, and behavioural effects.

The term was coined by COMTE who saw society evolving towards humanistic values through the influence of POSITIVISM. Rushton and Sorrentino (1981) suggest four possible explanations for altruism:

(a) *genetic inheritance:* this is supported by the animal evidence and by the sociobiologist R. Dawkin's (1976) 'selfish gene' theory. It proposes that altruistic behaviour towards one's kin (e.g. maternal behaviour) has the effect of preserving ones genes in common;
(b) *cognitive development:* moral reasoning and the ability to 'take the role of the other' (see G. H. MEAD) increase with age;
(c) *social learning:* SOCIALIZATION involves learning from others by observation and modelling;
(d) *prudential behaviour* helping others is likely to encourage reciprocal action from them (see EXCHANGE THEORY).

This last can be seen as dubiously altruistic, since it is likely to involve the strategic calculation of personal benefit, or mutual benefit, rather than 'purely' altruistic action. In these terms all human action could be interpreted as egoistic, but this would be to lose any distinction between altruistic and egoistic behaviour.

Psychologists have proposed a personality trait of altruism, i.e. helping behaviour is more evident in some people than in others. Altruism towards strangers is particularly influential in the philosophy behind the WELFARE STATE, and is illustrated more specifically in Titmuss's analysis of the Blood Transfusion Service, in which it is seen as a GIFT EXCHANGE OR GIFT RELATIONSHIP. See also COOPERATIVE ORGANIZATION AND COOPERATIVE MOVEMENT. Compare COMPETITION.

altruistic suicide the form of SUICIDE identified by DURKHEIM (1897) as occurring in highly integrated societies and in certain types of social organization where social integration is similarly strong. Examples of altruistic suicide are the euthanasia of the old and infirm as practised in some simple societies, or suicides of honour (e.g. among the military). See also EGOISTIC SUICIDE, ANOMIC SUICIDE.

amplification of deviance see DEVIANCE AMPLIFICATION.

analogy a comparison made to show a degree of similarity, but not an exact identity, between phenomena. In sociology, analogies are often made between social phenomena and mechanical or organic phenomena. This can be seen in classical forms of sociological functionalism in which societies are often seen as 'machine-like' or, more usually, 'organism-like' entities whose parts interrelate and reinforce each other. Although sometimes useful, and perhaps even indispensable in any science, recourse to analogies is often suspect. Assumptions made or relationships imputed (e.g. 'social needs' analogous with 'animal needs') require separate justification. The use of analogies therefore always involves risks. See MODEL.

analysis of variance (ANOVA) (STATISTICS) a procedure used to test whether differences between the MEANS of several groups are likely to be found in the population from which those groups were drawn. An example might be three groups of people with different educational backgrounds for whom the mean wage level has been calculated. ANOVA provides a way of testing whether the differences between the means are statistically significant by dividing the variability of the observations into two types. One type, called 'within group' variability, is the VARIANCE within each group in the SAMPLE. The second type is the variability between the group means ('between groups' variability). If this is large compared to the 'within group' variability it is likely that the population's means are not equal.

The assumptions underlying the use of analysis of variance are:

(a) each group must be a RANDOM SAMPLE from a normal population (see NORMAL DISTRIBUTION);

(b) the variance of the groups in the population are equal.

However, the technique is robust and can be used even if the normality and equal variance assumptions do not hold. The random sample condition is nevertheless essential. See also SIGNIFICANCE TEST.

analytical induction a method of analysis (originally formulated by Lindesmith, 1947), used especially in SYMBOLIC INTERACTIONISM and other forms of 'qualitative sociology', which involves the application of a general hypothesis to successive cases, with progressive modification of the generalization to fit all cases (see Robinson, 1951). The researcher formulates an hypothesis to explain a particular phenomenon and then attempts to search for a 'decisive negative case'. If one is found, the hypothesis is reformulated to include or disallow it, the process being followed until a degree of certainty can be claimed. The method is seen at work in BECKER's study of marijuana usage (Becker, 1953; see also DRUG TAKING FOR PLEASURE). As with any inductive method, the attempt must always be made to seek out contrary cases, but there is never any clear end point when a generalization can be regarded as final (see INDUCTION). See also GROUNDED THEORY.

analytical philosophy a general term for a type of philosophy based on analytic logic which is hostile to metaphysical speculation. It derives from the English empiricism of LOCKE, HUME and MILL, through the LOGICAL POSITIVISM of the Vienna Circle and the 'logical atomism' of the early WITTGENSTEIN and Russell. The subsequent development of ORDINARY LANGUAGE PHILOSOPHY is usually also included, but it differs in important ways by focusing on language in use. These later variants of analytic philosophy are often referred to as linguistic philosophy. See also SPEECH ACT.

analytic and synthetic (PHILOSOPHY) the distinction drawn between two types of statement or propositions:

(a) those which are true by virtue of the meanings of the terms they contain (e.g. 'all clergymen are male') – *analytic*, or logically *necessary* truths;

(b) those which are true or false only by virtue of their empirical content, and not logically implied by the meanings of the terms the statement contains (e.g. the statement which may or may not be true: that '50% of clergymen like ice-cream') – *synthetic, contingent,* or purely 'empirical' statements.

Often the distinction between the two kinds of statement has been regarded as one that admits of no exceptions. Some philosophers, however, notably Quine, have challenged this assumption, suggesting among other things that the distinction rests on unwarranted assumptions about consistency in the meanings of terms (see also DUHEM-QUINE THESIS).

In practice, in sociology, as in physical science, the production of knowledge involves both the formal definition of concepts, and statements of the logical relation between these, as well as the empirical testing of these relations. Theory and research in sociology moves between one and the other, with concepts being restated as the result of 'empirical' evidence, and the framing and interpretation of empirical evidence being altered as the outcome of changes in conceptualizations. It remains important to try to be clear when any additions to knowledge proposed depend mainly on the logical extension of an established conceptual scheme, or when these arise more from new empirical evidence. But that both of these processes can be important in the development of knowledge must be recognized, and a hard-and-fast distinction between the two realms is not one that can be sustained.

Compare A PRIORI AND A POSTERIORI, KANT.

anarchism any doctrine that advocates the virtues of social existence without governmental institutions. See also ANARCHO-SYNDICALISM.

anarchistic method see EPISTEMOLOGICAL ANARCHISM and METHODOLOGICAL PLURALISM.

anarcho-syndicalism a revolutionary movement derived, in part, from the teachings of Proudhon and MARX, and most usually associated with the doctrines of Guillaume and SOREL. The movement emerged in France in the 1890s and thereafter spread to Italy, Spain and Latin America. Anarcho-syndicalists were committed to the overthrow of capitalism by means of a workers' revolution. Their doctrines were based on a radical rejection of all political roads to socialism, and indeed of all POLITICAL PARTIES, power and planning both before and after the revolution. Such 'politics' was associated with compromise which weakened the revolutionary will of the workers. It was also associated with hierarchical party and state organization, and thus with inequalities of power and domination, which would – unless politics was repudiated – persist after the revolution and convert the DICTATORSHIP OF THE PROLETARIAT into a dictatorship over the proletariat by party hierarchs and state functionaries. Accordingly, the anarcho-syndicalist ideal lay in a producer-centred revolution: a revolution carried out at the point of production by a loose federation of decentralized, free, autonomous workers' organizations which is based on a rejection of hierarchy and domination and achieved through the medium of the general strike. This would sweep away capitalist society and the state and replace them with free, autonomous, self-governing workers' associations which would administer production and society without recourse to hierarchical organization and domination. Although anarcho-syndicalism made some impact in France, Italy and Spain, its influence was short-lived and never widespread, especially since mainstream MARXISM regarded it as a PETTY BOURGEOIS deviation which distracted the working class from its principal task of building a revolutionary party.

ancestor worship varying forms of religious rites and cult activity centred on respect for actual or mythical ancestors. Such rites (found in many types of society and in several parts of the world, e.g. West Africa, China) are usually based on membership of a LINEAGE GROUP, CLAN or

SIB, and are associated with a belief that the ancestral dead can intervene in human social life, and that religious activity can promote the wellbeing of both the living members of society and the ancestral dead. One suggestion is that ancestor worship reflects the importance of family or communal property within the societies in which it occurs. Another is that it legitimates AUTHORITY, e.g. 'eldership', while also unifying these groups against outsiders. In SEGMENTARY SOCIETIES ancestor worship can be an important aspect of the identification of the segments that make up the lineage system. In China, according to WEBER (1951), 'the cohesion of the sib undoubtedly rested wholly on the ancestor cult'. Since these cults were the only folk-cults not managed by the central state, in Weber's view they were an important aspect of the way in which in China – compared, say, with ancient Egypt – the sib was able to resist the encroachments of patrimonial central power. It is within the context of ancestor worship that a Chinese man without male descendants would often resort to adoption, or his relatives invent fictitious descendants on his behalf after his death.

ancien régime the prerevolutionary social order in France which was overthrown by the Revolution of 1789.

ancient society the Graeco-Roman epoch in the Marxist periodization of historical development (see HISTORICAL MATERIALISM, MODE OF PRODUCTION). Within classical Marxism, ancient society is seen as based on a 'slave' mode of production. More recently, however, the heterogeneity of historically existing modes of production has been emphasized by Marxist sociologists. Nevertheless, the significance of SLAVERY, together with military conquest, remains important in explaining both the expansion and the ultimate decline of Graeco-Roman society.

Anderson, Perry (1938–) British social theorist and historian. Anderson's earliest writings arose from his association with the left-wing journal *The New Left Review.* Examples of articles from this period are reprinted in *Towards Socialism* (ed. with R. Blackburn, 1965). Wide-ranging theoretical works on developments in Western Marxist theory followed – *Considerations on Western Marxism* (1976) and *In the Tracks of Historical Materialism* (1983); and in *Arguments within English Marxism* (1980) Anderson reviews the work of the socialist historian Edward THOMPSON. However, it is Anderson's two major historical works, *Passages from Antiquity* and *Lineages of the Absolutist State,* both published in 1974, which have had by far the most impact. The two works were conceived on the grand scale as a dialogue between the historical theories of MARX and WEBER. The argument advanced by Anderson is that 'what rendered the unique passage to capitalism possible in Europe was the concatenation of antiquity and feudalism', a thesis he supports by extended comparative analysis of both European and non-European societies. His suggestion is that ABSOLUTISM acts as a filter to modern CAPITALISM only where it is associated with the uniquely Western European lineage. The distinctive feature of Anderson's Marxist historical sociology, besides its impressive range and depth, is the way that it combines Marxism with Weberian perspectives while maintaining a view of social development in which the conception of a transition to socialism in Western societies is retained.

Anderson has continued as a prolific writer on historical themes, on European integration and on contemporary social theory (including *The Question of Europe,* 1997 – with P. Gowan). In 2000 he returned to edit the *New Left Review,* where he has set out his stall to provide a forum for critical leftist analysis against any apologism for the new politics of the centre left.

androcentrism the tendency to neglect the female perspective or the female contribution, i.e. male bias in cultural ideas and embodied in institutions.

animism the belief that natural phenomena, e.g. mountains or plants, are endowed with spirits or life-forces and that events in the world are the outcome of the activities of these. Compare TOTEMISM.

***Annales* school** the group of sociologically inclined French historians associated with the journal *Annales d'histoire économique et sociale,* founded in 1929 by Lucien Febvre and Marc BLOCH. Its links with Marxism have been particularly strong, as have its links with sociology. Distinguished by their opposition to traditional, national, political, chronological and narrative history, members of the school have in particular emphasized the importance of social and economic history and long-term historical trends. As well as breaking with conventional units and methods of analysis in historical studies, the approaches employed included extensive consideration of geophysical and demographic factors as well as cultural and social structural factors. An example of the work of members of the school is Bloch's *Feudal Society,* which combines comparative analysis and great novelty with scrupulous attention to detail. More recently the work of Fernand BRAUDEL, with its emphasis on writing all-embracing 'global history', has been especially influential within the social sciences, e.g. on the work of Immanuel WALLERSTEIN on the WORLD SYSTEM. See also HISTORY OF MENTALITIES.

Année sociologique the journal founded and edited by Emile DURKHEIM and contributed to by the many talented sociologists, anthropologists and historians who formed the Durkheim school, which exerted a dominating influence on French sociology.

anomic division of labour see ANOMIE, DIVISION OF LABOUR.

anomic suicide the form of SUICIDE associated with ANOMIE, i.e. with serious disruptions of the social order, such as an unexpected catastrophe or rapid economic growth, or with any similar disturbances in social expectations. Anomic suicide is the third of the three main types of SUICIDE identified by DURKHEIM (*Suicide,* 1897).

anomie *or* anomy

1 (literally 'without norms' – a concept introduced into sociology by DURKHEIM) a condition of society or of personal relation to society in which there exists little consensus, a lack of certainty on values or goals, and a loss of effectiveness in the normative and moral framework which regulates collective and individual life.

2 (a specification by Robert MERTON (1949) of Durkheim's concept) social situations and individual orientations in which a mismatch exists between culturally defined goals and the availability of institutionalized means of achieving these goals (e.g. the social conditions in which organized crime flourished in the US during the Depression).

The view of human nature held by Durkheim stands in the tradition of Thomas HOBBES, namely that there is no 'natural' or inbuilt limit to the desires, ambitions or needs of individuals. For Durkheim, the required limits must be socially produced. Anomie exists, and unhappiness and social disorders result, when society fails to provide a limiting framework of social norms. As Durkheim sees it, anomie is an 'abnormal' social form, resulting from the failure of modern societies to move fully from the MECHANICAL SOLIDARITY characteristic of premodern societies to the ORGANIC SOLIDARITY which would come to typify modern societies. Durkheim saw anomie as pervasive in modern societies. For example, an *anomic division of labour* existed because occupations were not allocated according to talents. In more general terms, economic activity in these societies remained essentially unregulated.

In *Suicide* (1897), Durkheim claims to demonstrate a correlation between rates of suicide and anomic social situations, for instance, a correlation between suicide rates and divorce rates. It should be noted that anomie can arise from an upward spiralling of social expectations (e.g. from new wealth or opportunities) as well as from more obviously adverse conditions.

As reformulated by Merton, anomie becomes a concept used in the analysis of DEVIANCE. What Merton suggests is that whenever there exists any disjuncture between culturally defined goals and the socially approved means available to individuals or groups, four logically possible responses are available (see Fig. 1):
(a) 'innovation', i.e. crime or other socially disapproved means to achieve approved goals;
(b) 'ritualism', i.e. going through the motions of pursuing approved means with no prospect or expectation of success;
(c) 'retreatism', i.e. simply opting out;
(d) 'rebellion', i.e. seeking to change the system.

If Durkheim's focus on anomie can be seen as arising from a moral conservatism mixed with a social radicalism. Merton's approach reveals how anomie may be a source of social innovation as well as a locus of social problems.

		Adoption of culturally approved means	*Acceptance of culturally approved goals*
(a)	innovation	+	–
(b)	ritualism	–	+
(c)	retreatism	–	–
(d)	rebellion	+ or –	+ or –

Fig. 1 **Anomie.** Merton's typology.

anorexia nervosa a disorder of eating behaviour. This is a psychological disturbance found predominantly in young women which leads them to perceive themselves as obese and to attempt to become slim. Their disordered eating behaviour is most usually expressed as a refusal to eat sufficiently, so that weight is lost, and in conjunction there may be episodes of *bulimia,* or bingeing, followed by the use of purgatives and self-induced vomiting. As weight loss continues menstruation ceases, and, though at first energy appears to increase, eventually the physical condition may become life-threatening.

There has been much interest in and research into this condition since the early 1970s. Among sociologists, anorexia is considered a 'pathology of self-identity', arising from the idealization of slimness (especially for women) in contemporary societies. Disordered family relationships have been suggested as a precipitating factor, the effort of the patient to return to being a child (immature figure, non-menstruating) suggesting an unwillingness to become an adult. It is also proposed that a genetic predisposition may underlie the problem. Current treatment is becoming more oriented to medical intervention to correct the biochemical imbalance, but social and psychiatric treatments are still widely used. When a patient is severely ill, needing hospitalization, the usual treatment has been behavioural, which can be effective in inducing weight gain. See BEHAVIOUR THERAPY. Psychotherapy is used to assist the patient achieve a realistic perception of her/his situation, and SELF-HELP GROUPS are found useful by many sufferers who may need long-term support. See also BODY.

anthropocentric viewing humankind as of central importance within the universe.

anthropocentric production systems see HUMAN-CENTRED TECHNOLOGY.

anthropology broadly, 'the study of humanity', but more narrowly consisting of:
(a) physical anthropology;
(b) SOCIAL ANTHROPOLOGY (in Britain) and CULTURAL ANTHROPOLOGY (in the USA).

Physical anthropology concerns itself with the genesis and variation of hominoid species and draws on evolutionary biology, DEMOGRAPHY and archaeology. Social and cultural anthropology investigates the structures and cultures that are produced by HOMO SAPIENS.

In Europe and elsewhere the term ETHNOLOGY is also employed to refer to these areas of study.

The distinction between sociology and social or cultural anthropology is primarily one of convention – sociologists have tended to study complex societies whilst anthropologists have concentrated on numerically small, non-industrialized cultures outside Western Europe and modern North America. In addition, methodological differences between the two subjects are critical; anthropologists having usually involved themselves in detailed ETHNOGRAPHY, accounts produced after long periods of PARTICIPANT OBSERVATION.

This methodological difference grew out of two considerations:
(a) many of the societies studied were pre-literate, and thus with no written records anthropologists had no alternative but to observe societies directly and to record the oral memory of the members of the societies;
(b) a reaction against speculative accounts of pre-literate societies, e.g. in early forms of social EVOLUTIONARY THEORY. See also COGNITIVE ANTHROPOLOGY, GENERATIVE ANTHROPOLOGY, STRUCTURAL ANTHROPOLOGY.

anthropomorphism the attribution of human form or characteristics to natural phenomena, animals, deities, spirits, etc. Anthropomorphism is a central feature of many systems of religion and cosmology which frequently assert a relationship between human affairs and the natural and supernatural realms.

anticipatory socialization any process in which an individual endeavours to remodel his or her social behaviour in the expectation of gaining entry to and acceptability in a higher social status or class than that currently occupied.

anticlericalism opposition, especially political opposition, to the power and influence of the church.

anti-humanism (post-structuralism) the displacement of the human subject from centre stage, e.g. as the seat of reason, history or truth. See also HUMANISM.

antinaturalism any approach to sociological analysis which opposes the adoption of a natural-science model (e.g. the formulation of natural laws), regarding this as inappropriate to the study of human social action. Reference to 'naturalism' in this sense must be distinguished from a different usage of the term 'naturalism' in sociology to refer to NATURALISTIC RESEARCH METHODS. Here the emphasis is on the study of social action in 'naturally' occurring social settings. In this case, a preference for 'natural' research methods is often associated with opposition to the slavish following of any model drawn from the physical sciences. Thus, naturalism in this second sense is often taken as implying 'antinaturalism', using naturalism in the first sense.

antinomianism the beliefs held, e.g. by the members of some Protestant sects in the 16th and 17th centuries, that, as members of 'God's elect', they could no longer be guilty of sin. As WEBER (1922) put it, such persons felt themselves 'certain of salvation', and 'no longer bound by any conventional rule of conduct'. This belief was interpreted by some believers as permitting them to engage in unorthodox marital practices, including plural marriages, as well as in sexual activity outside marriage, which they justified as bringing others to salvation. Weber's view was that antinomianism is a generally occurring phenomenon, and that the more systematically the 'practical psychological character' of a religious faith develops, the greater is the tendency for antinomianism to be the outcome.

antipsychiatry a movement of opposition against both the practice and theory of conventional psychiatry, influential especially in the 1960s and early 1970s. Associated with the work of R. D. LAING (1959) in Britain and Thomas SZASZ in the US, antipsychiatry attacks the general concept of MENTAL ILLNESS as well as the therapeutic techniques employed in treating this. Both Laing and Szasz were themselves psychotherapists. In Laing's view, 'mental illness' is a concept with little or no scientific foundation; the causation of 'mental illness' is not biological. His suggestion was that the mental and behavioural states so described would be better seen as a meaningful response to the stresses and strains and disrupted communications of family life. Such mental states 'make sense' once the social situation of the person concerned is fully considered. Doctors and the patient's family often collude, Laing proposes, in labelling a person 'mad'. The argument of Szasz was similar in key respects, though different in detail. In *The Myth of Mental Illness* (1961), he pointed out that psychiatrists rarely agreed in diagnosing SCHIZOPHRENIA. It was on this basis that he concluded that schizophrenia is not an illness. The implication of this, according to Szasz, is that patients are people who must be held responsible for their actions and treated accordingly. Both Laing and Szasz regarded the involuntary incarceration of patients in mental hospitals and the use of techniques of treatment such as electroconvulsive therapy, leucotomy, and even tranquilizing drugs, as of uncertain value and repressive, a denial of individual autonomy without good reason. Sociologists who have also exerted an influence on the antipsychiatry movement (although the overall influence of their work is much wider) are FOUCAULT and GOFFMAN – see also MADNESS, TOTAL INSTITUTION, LABELLING THEORY.

The late 1970s and 1980s have seen a great reduction in the numbers of people in mental hospitals, partly as the result of movements such as antipsychiatry. Ironically, however, the dismantling of the old apparatus of mental institutions and custodial care has given way to COMMUNITY CARE partly because mental illness has proved controllable by drugs. There are many who claim that this demonstrates that mental illness is at least in part a medical condition.

anti-Semitism hostility towards the Jewish people, ranging in form from the varying degrees of institutionalized PREJUDICE widely found in European societies historically, to the highly explicit ideology of Hitler's NATIONAL SOCIALISM.

apartheid a system of racial separation that existed in the Republic of South Africa. A separation of the population into 'whites', 'blacks', and 'coloured' or 'mixed racial' groups was defined by law, and this separation was reflected in restrictions on residence, intermarriage, areas of employment and the use of public facilities such as schools, hospitals, parks and beaches. A refusal to replace or significantly reform apartheid resulted in the Republic of South Africa becoming a pariah nation-state in the world community, and the imposition of economic and political sanctions against her, particularly the severing of sporting connections.

apocalypticism discourse that refers to theological and secular theories of the end of the world. Beyond its origins in biblical scripture, apocalyptic thought is often related to significant dates or moments of great historical change. The years 999 and 1999 both saw an increase in theories surrounding the prophesied end of the world. At times of profound historical change groups like the Diggers, Levellers, and Luddites have all informed and reflected apocalyptic belief systems. Often this form of knowledge can be equated with an anxious fear about the nature of OTHERNESS. As later examples show, contemporary apocalypticism frequently mixes with conspiratorial thought to produce events such as the Waco massacre and the Heaven's Gate suicides. In these instances apocalypticism tends to overlap millenarian thought. In the latter, the idea of the absolute end of the world is replaced by the notion of a relative apocalyptic that will result in the rebirth of a better social order. Thus the tension between UTOPIA/DYSTOPIA is implicit in apocalyptic discourse. Some examples, such as the image of the nuclear apocalypse, tend to stress the idea of absolute dystopic destruction, while others, such as the Calvinist world-view discussed by Max Weber, reflect the concept of the relative apocalypse, i.e., the dystopic death of a rotten social order and re-birth of a new 'just' utopian world.

a posteriori see A PRIORI AND A POSTERIORI.

appearance and reality (especially in MARXISM) the distinction drawn between 'surface' social relations – the *appearance* – and the underlying determinants of social *reality*, hidden from view by IDEOLOGY, etc. For example, for Marx, the LABOUR THEORY OF VALUE provides the key to a 'scientific' understanding of the true character of CAPITALISM, i.e. its 'exploitative' and 'contradictory' character, rather than the apparent 'fairness' of the CAPITALIST LABOUR CONTRACT. In drawing a general distinction between appearance and reality, Marx did not wish to suggest that surface appearances were in any sense wholly unreal, but simply that they disguised more fundamental, ultimately determining relations. The distinction also drawn between *epiphenomena* (surface) and *phenomena* (underlying reality) is another way of saying the same thing. See also COMMODITY FETISHISM, REIFICATION.

apperception (PHILOSOPHY) the mind's perception of itself. In various ways, apperception has been one important method in which philosophy has sought to ground knowledge.

applied sociology the application of sociological theories, concepts, methods and findings to problems identified in wider society. For example, sociological ideas have been applied to the practices of SOCIAL WORK, EDUCATION, INDUSTRIAL RELATIONS and planning. While sociological ideas and sociological research often lead to a redefinition of social problems (e.g. the identification of UNANTICIPATED CONSEQUENCES OF SOCIAL ACTION), the extent of the influence of sociological thinking and research is difficult to measure. There has been debate recently (e.g. Scott and Shore, 1979) as to why sociological research sometimes fails to gain applications, even though this is intended, and application seems appropriate. The explanation given by Scott and Shore is that applied research is often cast first in terms of 'disciplinary concerns' and only second in terms of the realities of the political context of much actual decision-making, where political interests often triumph over rational persuasion. See also INDUSTRIAL SOCIOLOGY, SOCIAL POLICY, SOCIAL ADMINISTRATION.

apprenticeship see CRAFT APPRENTICESHIP.

appropriate technology forms of technology which best utilize the resources and human skills available in a given society. The term has been applied particularly to poorer countries where the transfer of high technology may act to the disadvantage of the receiving country. Instead, less capital intensive and more 'environmentally friendly' technologies may be better utilized for production. Use of such technologies rejects the widespread assumption that technological advance determines general societal 'progress'. See also INTERMEDIATE TECHNOLOGY.

appropriation see EXPLOITATION.

a priori and a posteriori (literally 'what comes before' and 'what comes after') a distinction made between kinds of statements or propositions according to the manner in which we acquire knowledge of their truth; thus, whereas an *a priori* statement is one that can be known to be true or false without reference to experience or empirical evidence (e.g. the definition of a square as having four equal sides), the truth of an *a posteriori* statement can be established only by an examination of what is empirically the case. While many 'rationalist' philosophers, most notably in modern times KANT, have argued that some things can, and indeed must, be known a priori, merely from first principles, the opposing view – philosophical EMPIRICISM – holds that our ideas are derived only from 'experience' (see also HUME). More recently the view has been expressed that neither of these positions are satisfactory, that there is no fixed starting point or ultimate grounding in philosophy or knowledge. Compare ANALYTIC AND SYNTHETIC.

arbitration 1 (ANTHROPOLOGY) an arrangement, especially in stateless societies, for settling conflicts and disputes between two parties by reference to a third party who acts as arbiter. Whilst the arbiter generally has little or no ability to enforce a judgement, it is frequently the case that the disputants agree in advance to abide by the arbiter's ruling. For example, among the Nuer, the Leopard Skin Chief acts as an arbiter in this way – see EVANS-PRITCHARD (1940), GELLNER (1969).

2 (industrial relations) see ARBITRATION AND CONCILIATION.

arbitration and conciliation (INDUSTRIAL RELATIONS) one of the institutions of industrial relations which is designed to resolve stalemates in collective bargaining by means of third-party intervention (see also COLLECTIVE BARGAINING). At the request of one or more of the parties involved in an intractable dispute, independent, third-party intervention can offer:

(a) 'conciliation', the object of which is to help the parties to develop their own solutions by bringing them together and encouraging the use of agreed procedures;

(b) 'mediation', where recommendations are made by a mediator, but the parties do not

commit themselves in advance to accept an arbitration award;
(c) 'arbitration', where, compulsorily or based on the consent of both parties, and within strict terms of reference, an award can be made.

The origins of conciliation and arbitration in the UK are to be found in the establishment and voluntary use of permanent boards of conciliation and arbitration in industries where employers and unions sought to avoid lockouts and strikes. The development of state provision has preserved the voluntary principle, though there have been periods when it has been eroded. Currently, the Advisory, Conciliation and Arbitration Service, which comprises representatives of employers, trade unions and industrial relations specialists, seeks to provide these services independently of government influence. In some other societies mandatory third-party intervention precedes strikes or lockouts.

archaeology 1 the scientific or systematic analysis of the material remains, especially the artifacts, but also the physical remains of human and animal bodies, crops, etc., left by past SOCIETIES and CULTURES, where the aim is to produce an account or reconstruction of these societies or cultures. Especially important in situations where the societies and cultures in question have left no written records or where these records are few, archaeology may also be practised in any context in which the study of such remains may complement the written historical record, as recently exemplified by *industrial archaeology,* which studies the relatively recent past as evident in the physical remains left by industrial and extractive processes, modes of transportation, etc. When its focus is on societies and cultures that have left no written record, archaeology is coextensive with the discipline of *prehistory.*

Traditionally distinguished by its use of the method of excavation and careful recording of remains, nowadays archaeology employs many scientific techniques, including aerial photography, computer modelling, radiocarbon dating, and even more precise forms of dating based on the climatic record left in the fossil remains of trees. Since the remains studied are physical remains, modern archaeology often smacks more of science than does sociology itself. However, since its subject matter continues to be cultural and social phenomena, the scientific character of archaeology is not necessarily a sign of its superiority, for archaeology must work hard simply to piece together sufficient data for sociological analysis to begin. Once such sociological analysis is undertaken, the concerns and the problems of archaeology are the same as those of sociology, with the extra difficulty for archaeology that it is usually denied any very direct access to the intended meaning of the social actors involved. Thus archaeology and sociology must be seen as complementary disciplines. There are affinities and continuities, for example, especially between the archaeological study of pre-urban prehistorical societies and modern anthropological study of simple societies. The same kind of division as exists in sociology between comparative and generalizing approaches on the one hand, and the historical or meaningful understanding of unique cultures on the other hand, also exists in archaeology. In fact, a comparable range of competing theoretical perspectives to those found in sociology and anthropology also occur in archaeology, including, for example, FUNCTIONALIST and EVOLUTIONARY THEORIES, and Marxian approaches.
2 (FOUCAULT, *The Order of Things*, 1966, tr. 1973, *The Archaeology of Knowledge,* 1969, tr. 1974) a view of historical documents as 'one way in which a society recognizes and develops a mass of documentation with which it is inextricably linked' in which. Foucault particularly sought to specify the historical a priori on which certain forms of knowledge become possible. Later Foucault preferred the term GENEALOGY to describe

his method, seeing positivist elements in the notion of 'archaeology'.

archetypes see JUNG.

arena (POLITICAL SOCIOLOGY) any domain of discourse and competition, or of conflict or struggle for political power.

Arendt, Hannah (1906–1975) born in Konigsberg, and studying under HEIDEGGER, Hannah Arendt moved to the USA in 1941 after working in the Zionist movement. Her main works of political philosophy and social analysis are *The Origins of Totalitarianism* (1951), *The Human Condition* (1958) and *On Revolution* (1965). In the first of these, she identified modern totalitarianism as distinguished by IDEOLOGY as well as by violence, employed to create a regime of *terror*. In the second, she argued that philosophy and politics are not opposed and stressed the importance of political participation. In the third, she advanced a controversial account of the French and American revolutions.

aristocracy 1 (in classical Greece) 'the rule of the best'.

2 a hereditary élite or noble class, e.g. the noble class in FEUDALISM. In most large-scale, premodern societies a tendency existed for the ruling or dominant classes to transform themselves into a hereditary noble class, but counter tendencies also existed in which such claims could be resisted. See also PATRIMONIALISM.

While sense **2** is more usual, the term may be used in something like its earlier Greek sense, e.g. as in LABOUR ARISTOCRACY.

aristocracy of labour see LABOUR ARISTOCRACY.

Aristotle (384–322 BC) major Greek philosopher and tutor of Alexander the Great, whose influence on European thinking has been extensive. This influence is seen in the development of natural science, of political science, within early anthropology, and above all in PHILOSOPHY (including LOGIC and ETHICS). Aristotle studied at PLATO's academy in Athens, but, though influenced by Plato's IDEALISM, he is usually regarded as a representative of the EMPIRICIST wing of philosophy. Where relevant, his method of inquiry involved careful observation and reporting. On the other hand, he also initiated the systematic study of logic. In practice, therefore, reason and empiricism were combined in his work.

arms race the competition between NATION STATES to attain a position of military superiority over adversaries. In its contemporary usage the concept has been applied especially to the competition between the US and the USSR. This has taken the form of a dramatic increase in the size of nuclear arsenals and an intensification of weapons development. Each technological advance by one side has produced an attempt by the other side to build superior weapons, which the initial mover has then to attempt to further improve upon. The pattern can be characterized as one of action-reaction. An early statistical study of arms races in these terms was made by L. F. Richardson, *The Statistics of Deadly Quarrels* (1960).

Although arms races between major powers have attracted most attention, they also occur between minor powers (e.g. between the Arab states and Israel), where their outcome may more often lead to war than those between major powers. A major consequence of the arms race between the US and the USSR has been economic 'waste'. Although it was once suggested that its economic effect may have been to sustain a post-World War economic boom (see MILITARY INDUSTRIAL COMPLEX), more recently it has been proposed that it has acted as a brake on the economic prosperity of nation-states with the largest military commitments (e.g. the slower growth and relative economic weakness of Britain and the US compared with Germany or Japan). Undoubtedly, excessive military commitments have had this effect in the USSR, leading some commentators to suggest that the COLD WAR has been won by the Western powers as a consequence of this burden. See also NUCLEAR DETERRENCE, BALANCE OF POWER.

Aron, Raymond (1905–83) French sociologist and influential political commentator with wide interests in sociological theory, strategic studies, and the sociology of industrial societies. His contributions to the discussion of sociological theory include *German Sociology* (1935) and *Main Currents in Sociological Theory* (1965). In *The Opium of the Intellectuals* (1957) he criticized the tendency of intellectuals to suspend their critical judgements and to be too readily seduced by Marxism. On strategic studies he wrote voluminously, producing important works such as *The Century of Total War* (1951), *Peace and War* (1961) and *Clausewitz, Philosopher of War* (1976). He wrote several books on modern industrial societies, among them *Eighteen Lectures on Industrial Society* (1963) and *Democracy and Totalitarianism* (1965). Closer to TOCQUEVILLE or WEBER than to DURKHEIM or MARX in his approach, in general his work stresses the importance of the political dimension in social life, and the virtues of PLURALISM. The unpredictability he saw for political and cultural dimensions also meant that he was unimpressed by suggestions that a CONVERGENCE would occur between East and West.

art see SOCIOLOGY OF ART.

artefact *or* **artifact** any individual material object produced by a culture. The study of such objects is important in anthropology (see MATERIAL CULTURE). In ARCHAEOLOGY, the artefacts left behind by a society are the main means of reconstructing an account of that society.

articulation of modes of production (MARXISM) a concept in which separate MODES OF PRODUCTION are seen as coexisting within one society or social formation. The concept was developed particularly within a Marxist critique of DEPENDENCY THEORY to demonstrate links between so-called UNDERDEVELOPMENT and development. Especially influential was Wolpe's (1972) analysis of the reserve system in South Africa as a subordinate, precapitalist mode of production based on kinship relations, which provided cheap labour power for the industrialized capitalist economy of South Africa.

There is considerable debate within Marxism. For example, Banji (1977) offered a powerful critique of Wolpe in which he argued that the overall laws of motion of the economy define the social formation, and it is not always necessary that all elements of the capitalist mode be present to define a system as 'capitalist'. The 'subordinate modes of production' referred to by articulation theory are not, for Banji, modes of production at all, since they are devoid of their own 'laws of motion and serve to reproduce the capitalist mode of production. Such forms lack the essential ingredient of the ability to reproduce themselves'. See also NONCAPITALIST AND PRECAPITALIST MODES OF PRODUCTION.

artificial intelligence and **artificial consciousness** the human-like 'intellectual' capacity claimed to be possessed by some machines, especially computers that set out to mimic the behaviour of neurons. As Francis Crick argues in *The Astonishing Hypothesis* (1994): if the behaviour of real neurons is the basis of consciousness, then it is reasonable to begin to search for artificial consciousness among artificial neurons. Claims for artificial intelligence are controversial, however, given the complexities of the human brain and the interrelation of human consciousness and emotions, including human will.

asceticism the doctrine and practice of self-denial in which practitioners abstain from worldly comforts and pleasures. Asceticism has been a feature of many world religions, and for some practitioners (e.g. the members of some monastic orders) it may involve a fatalistic retreat from most worldly endeavours. Despite this association with fatalism and escape from the world, its challenge to mundane values has also meant that it has often been associated with resistance to political authority and been instrumental in social change. For example, according to WEBER (1922), Protestant asceticism played a decisive role in the rise of modern western capitalism (see PROTESTANT ETHIC).

ascribed status any social position to which a person is allocated by birth or directly as the outcome of family background, and which cannot readily be altered by their own ACHIEVEMENT. As such, ascribed status contrasts with ACHIEVED STATUS. See also PATTERN VARIABLES.

ascription see ASCRIBED STATUS, PATTERN VARIABLES.

Asiatic mode of production and Asiatic society (MARXISM) a mode of production and a type of society in which MARX assumed land was owned either by the state and/or self-sufficient village communities, and in which the historical development evident in European society was absent.

This is the sense in which, according to Marx, Asia 'has no history'. In making these assumptions Marx simply accepted much of the then conventional Western view of Asiatic society as state-dominated, lacking private property in land (see ORIENTAL DESPOTISM), and therefore failing to manifest the economic and political development (e.g. CIVIL SOCIETY) characteristic of European society. Marx also accepted the prevailing, but now largely discredited, view that the distinctive form of Asiatic society could be accounted for by geographical conditions which required widespread public works to build and maintain irrigation systems and flood controls (see also HYDRAULIC SOCIETY).

Today the entire concept of a single basic form of Asiatic mode of production and corresponding form of society is in doubt. This conception has been undermined, firstly, by empirical research which fails to support such a picture of Asian society, and, secondly, by the awareness that European thinking has been dominated by a Euro-centric myth of 'Oriental Society' (see Said, 1985). For Marxist theory, the concept of Asiatic society has the added disadvantage of an apparent incompatibility with the general assumption of inherent social progress involved in HISTORICAL MATERIALISM. As Brendan O'Leary (1989) remarks 'the Asiatic mode of production is the Loch Ness Monster of historical materialism, rarely sighted and much believed'. It should be noted that Marx referred to the term only once by name. See also MODE OF PRODUCTION, ORIENTALISM.

Asiatic society see ASIATIC MODE OF PRODUCTION.

assimilation (especially in race relations) the process in which a minority group adopts the values and patterns of behaviour of a majority group or host culture, ultimately becoming absorbed by the majority group (compare ACCOMMODATION). The process can involve changes for both the majority and the minority groups. It may prove more difficult to accomplish where visible signs (e.g. clear-cut distinctions of 'colour') form the basis of the original division (e.g. in the US 'melting pot', the assimilation of black minority groups).

assimilation and accommodation (in PIAGET's theory of CHILD DEVELOPMENT) the means by which changes in conceptual schemata come about.

Fundamental to Piaget's stage theory of cognitive development is the idea that each stage has a typical mode of thinking, called a *conceptual schema.* For development to take place these schemata change, the next type of schema emerging out of the current schema. This change takes place either by new experiences being *assimilated* by the current schema, which becomes fuller and more elaborated as a result, or by *accommodation,* which is necessary if the current schema cannot fully deal with new experiences and needs to make a fundamental change in order to do so.

association 1 any group sharing a common purpose or interest. See also GEMEINSCHAFT AND GESELLSCHAFT.

2 (STATISTICS) the degree to which two VARIABLES are related. See CORRELATION.

attachment 1 the emotional bond between infant and mother.

2 the types of behaviour displayed by the infant to indicate an attachment, e.g. following parents, crying, smiling.

3 the more abstract psychological tie felt towards a nurturing figure involving a mutual dependency for emotional satisfaction.

A theory of attachment was first proposed by BOWLBY (1958, 1969) who was primarily concerned with the first two interpretations, citing ethological evidence to support his claims about how human infants use certain types of behaviour to elicit psychological as well as physical care from their mothers. Attachment merely refers to whether the child has formed a tie to a caregiver, but more recently the notion of security of attachment (Ainsworth et al., *Strange Situation Behaviour of One-year Olds,* 1978) was established to assess the quality of the attachment relationship once it has been formed.

attempted suicide and **parasuicide** either a genuine attempt at self-destruction which fails, or an 'attempted SUICIDE' which is, in fact, feigned, i.e. a *parasuicide.*

The pattern of incidence of attempted suicide is different from 'true' suicide, underlining that these are different phenomena. Usually parasuicide is regarded as a 'cry for help', with little or no intention to cause self-injury. Nonetheless, the incidence of suicide among those who have previously attempted suicide remains markedly higher than for those with no previously recorded attempt.

attitude a learnt and enduring tendency to perceive or act towards persons or situations in a particular way.

The concept of attitude has provoked much consideration and investigation, both by psychologists and sociologists, as it incorporates individual and social aspects. Psychologists emphasize the conditions under which an individual develops attitudes and integrates them as part of the personality. Social psychologists are particularly interested in the way attitudes function within a social Setting. Sociologists associate social behaviours with particular social structures and situations, e.g. class relations.

There is a variety of definitions of attitude (e.g. Allport, 1935; Haber and Fried, 1975; Rokeach, 1960), some imply that holding an attitude leads to behaving in a certain way, others encompass the idea that an attitude may only exist mentally, since overt behaviour can be constrained situationally. It is therefore useful to see attitudes as involving three elements:

(a) a cognitive component – beliefs and ideas;

(b) an affective component – values and emotions;

(c) a behavioural component – predisposition to act and actions (Secord and Backman, 1964).

attitude scale the most common way of measuring attitudes, which relies on assumed consistency between attitudes and behavioural responses. Verbal statements about the attitude object, e.g. the monarchy or uncontrolled immigration, are rated according to the (degree of) agreement or disagreement felt by the respondent. Semantic differential scales allow subjects to rate the attitude object on a number of different bipolar dimensions, e.g. good-bad. There are different methods of constructing these scales, depending on whether they are based on the subjective judgement of many subjects (LIKERT SCALE), on the ratings of 'judges' (Thurstone and Chave, 1929), or on response pattern analysis (GUTTMAN SCALE). See also SCALING, POLITICAL ATTITUDES.

attribute see VARIABLE.

attribution theory a collection of theories, originating in the work of F. Heider (*The Psychology of Interpersonal Relations,* 1958), which seek to explain how people attribute causes to others' and their own behaviour.

A distinction is made between internal or dispositional causes, located within the individual, e.g. 'she failed the exam because she is lazy', and external or situational causes, e.g. 'he was late for work because of the traffic jam'. Attributional errors are made when we favour dispositional over situational explanations (the fundamental attribution error). We are also more likely, with regard to our own behaviour, to make a dispositional attribution for success and a situational attribution for failure (the self-serving bias). Attribution theory provides a useful framework for the analysis of everyday explanations of social issues such as unemployment, criminality, and health and illness-related behaviours.

audience segregation see DRAMATURGY.

audit a process in which the performance of organizations is monitored by independent agencies. Compared with direct observation and control of behaviour (see SURVEILLANCE), audit usually does its work by an examination of the records of the processes and/or outcomes of organizational activity. Audits are a prominent part of what has been termed the 'new governance' in contemporary advanced societies. As well as the more familiar financial audits of business organizations, there are today organizational audits of hospitals, schools and universities as well as environmental audits. See also AUDIT SOCIETY.

audit society (M. Power, *The Audit Explosion*, 1994, *The Audit Society*, 1997) a society 'which has come to understand the solution to many of its problems in terms of AUDIT'. (Power, 1997:5). Power's contention is that audits 'do not passively monitor ... performance 'but shape the form of the performance in crucial ways (Power, 1994:8). Partly because they become formulaic and 'ritualistic' they may have side-effects and pathologies that frustrate the original intention to produce transparency and improvement of performance. The origins of an increase in audit are bound up with the phenomenon of RISK SOCIETY, with the new economic and ecological uncertainties – 'new environments of trust and risk' – associated with REFLEXIVE MODERNIZATION and GLOBALIZATION.

autotelic self (GIDDENS, 1994) a self-directing 'self', possessing 'inner confidence and self-respect', grounded in a sense of 'ontological security' originating in 'basic trust', and also capable of a positive appreciation of social difference'. This kind of self is that which Giddens sees as conducive to levels of personal 'responsibility' and 'pluralism' increasingly demanded by contemporary societies.

aura the distinctive quality of a thing, e.g. a particular work of art, and (as defined by BENJAMIN, *Charles Baudelaire*, 1983) also 'a unique manifestation of distance'. Benjamin's reading is dependent on a quasi-religious understanding of society. Thus social order requires certain objects in society to be popularly regarded as sacred. For example, objects like the Emerald Buddha in Thailand or Stonehenge possess an aura. They are socially distant from us in the sense of occupying the symbolic apex of culture; and they also require us to make an inner journey away from the surface preoccupations of everyday life to a posited deeper, immemorial reality. In his troubled paper on the effects of mechanical reproduction, Benjamin (*Illuminations*, 1955) argued that the duplication of these objects as artefacts and symbols within mass culture weakens their auratic power. They become clichéd and hackneyed. Authenticity and the sacred are lost, and the social integration of society falters. See also SIMULATION, POSTMODERNISM.

Austro-Marxism an influential group of Neo-Marxist theorists, prominent in Austria from the late 19th century until the mid-1930s, whose members included Max Adler, Rudolf Hilferding, Otto Bauer and Karl Renner. Influenced by NEO-KANTIANISM, one distinctive perspective of the school, articulated especially by Adler, involved an emphasis on 'socialized humanity', a concept seen as transcendentally given (see also KANT). Perhaps the most famous work by a member of the school is Hilferding's *Finance Capitalism* (1910), in which he described the growth of cartels and monopolies as a new phase of capitalism (*organized capitalism*), ideas which influenced LENIN's thinking on IMPERIALISM. Renner's main contribution was to the Marxist SOCIOLOGY OF LAW. Austro-Marxists were also among the earliest Marxist theorists to point to the need for fundamental revisions of Marxist theory to take account of an increasing differentiation of the working class and overall changes in the class structure of advanced societies – e.g. Renner's conception of the SERVICE CLASS.

autarchy 1 absolute sovereignty or despotic rule.
2 see AUTARKY.

autarky *or* **autarchy** the practice or policy of economic self-sufficiency.

authenticity see DASEIN.

authoritarianism see AUTHORITARIAN PERSONALITY.

authoritarian personality a person who prefers or believes in a system in which some individuals control while others are controlled. This, therefore, involves dominance and submission, and may be regarded as the obverse of a democratic preference.

The term *authoritarian personality* was introduced by ADORNO et al. (1950). After studying ANTI-SEMITISM, Adorno extended his interest to the negative attitudes to 'outgroups' displayed by 'ingroup' members. He found that these negative attitudes were only part of a cluster of related attitudes which could be seen in political, religious and social behaviour, and also within the family setting. Thus, the whole PERSONALITY is authoritarian: *authoritarianism* is not only expressed under certain eliciting conditions, it is a way of behaving which is a persistent personality characteristic.

Various theories exist as to the conditions which encourage the formation of an authoritarian personality, these being closely associated with the formation of PREJUDICE. In particular, having experienced authoritarian treatment, or the frustration of self-expression, seem to be conditioning factors. See also FRUSTRATION-AGGRESSION HYPOTHESIS, ETHNOCENTRISM.

authoritarian right see NEW RIGHT.

authority the established political rule within a community or STATE when this rule also possesses a grounding in one or more possible forms of political legitimacy. See LEGITIMATE AUTHORITY.

autocracy rule by one person, especially arbitrary or absolute rule. Compare ABSOLUTISM.

automation any form of industrial production in which the productive process is carried out substantially or entirely by machines, with a consequent reduction in the requirement for routine manual labour. As the undertaking and control of productive processes in this manner has become more commonplace (especially with the development of computer technology), the term has tended to fall out of use, being replaced by other general terms such as INFORMATION TECHNOLOGY or simply NEW TECHNOLOGY.

Both popular and sociological debate about automation have been concerned with its consequences for levels of employment: whether it will lead to an overall decline in the requirement for labour, increases in unemployment, the onset of a new age of LEISURE, and so on. What seems clear, however, is that while it may involve a decrease in the demand for unskilled or routine forms of manual labour, the demand for educated labour – necessary in the design and maintenance of the new machines and in the management of the new processes – is likely to increase. However, how far these new jobs will themselves tend to become routinized (e.g. involve routine keyboard work) remains an unresolved issue (see DESKILLING). The implications of automation and new technology for overall control of the LABOUR PROCESS is a further topic of general importance. See also INTELLECTUAL LABOUR.

autonomous man and plastic man a distinction made by Hollis (1977, 1987) between the choosing, rational, self-determining SOCIAL ACTOR, capable of fulfilling goals and expressing his own interests, i.e. *autonomous man*, and *plastic man*, who is determined by social structures and biology. Hollis's aim in drawing the distinction is to argue that a model which includes elements of both is required for a satisfactory sociological explanation. As such, his is a more poetic rendering of a widespread modern emphasis in sociology on STRUCTURE AND AGENCY. According to Hollis, while acknowledging that some social outcomes are the direct result of the intended actions of individual actors, an adequate model must also take account of social outcomes that 'go on behind our backs', including 'unintended consequences'. For Hollis, *homo sociologicus* should be framed as a role player, guided by norms and influenced by structures, but capable of genuine choice and of trust and morality. See also FREE WILL, RULES AND RULE-FOLLOWING, RATIONAL CHOICE THEORY.

autonomy 1 the capacity possessed by the individual SELF for choice. The case for DEMOCRACY, as David Held (*Models of Democracy*, 1987) has shown, is linked crucially to the principle that individuals possess autonomous capacity. Compare DECENTRED SELF.

2 The capacity for self determination (see SOVEREIGNTY) possessed by an independent STATE.

autonomy of sociology the viewpoint, as expressed by DURKHEIM in particular, that sociology must be formulated as a distinctive science, dealing with a level of reality that cannot be explained by reduction to other disciplines such as psychology or biology. Durkheim's view was that 'society' has a reality 'sui generis' – i.e. of its own kind. See also SOCIAL FACTS AS THINGS, SUICIDE.

average see MEASURES OF CENTRAL TENDENCY.

aversion therapy a type of BEHAVIOUR THERAPY which relies on negative reinforcement. Negative reinforcement occurs when the individual learns that by acting in a certain way, an unpleasant consequence can be avoided. The reinforcer of that behaviour therefore lies in the avoidance of pain or unpleasantness. An example of the clinical application of aversion therapy is in the treatment of alcoholism by use of an emetic. Thus the avoidance of alcohol leads to avoidance of sickness. The same principle can be seen at work in changing smoking behaviour through strong social disapproval.

avoidance relationship a mode of behaviour that involves one person continually avoiding another, usually on the grounds of respect or deference. The most common case is when a man has the duty to avoid meeting his wife's mother. Structural-functionalist anthropologists have explained this pattern as a mechanism that expresses and prevents latent conflict. More latterly, symbolic anthropologists have classed it as a form of TABOO which reflects native classification systems.

axiom (as in geometry, but also in social theory) the taken-for-granted assumption or postulate of a model or theory from which other propositions can be derived. See also FORMAL THEORY AND FORMALIZATION OF THEORY.

b

Bachelard, Gaston (1894–1962) widely influential French social philosopher and philosopher of science who, among other things, introduced the term EPISTEMOLOGICAL BREAK and influenced ALTHUSSER and FOUCAULT. Parallels exist between Bachelard's thinking and that of Thomas KUHN on revolutionary science.

back region any area of social context, in contrast with the FRONT REGION, in which a person is able to relax from the ROLE playing and 'performance' required by the front region. See also DRAMATURGY, GOFFMAN.

backward supply curve for labour (ECONOMICS) a situation in which an increase in the rate of pay reduces, rather than increases, the willingness to work extra hours. For example, peasants in a traditional economy or students working part-time during a degree course, may have 'target incomes', required to supplement income from land or from a grant or loan, and thus choose to work fewer hours as the rate of pay increases.

Bakhtin, Mikhail (1895–1975) Russian thinker, whose ideas on the nature of dialogue have proved highly influential in a number of fields, including literary theory, social theory, anthropology, linguistics and psychology. Central to Bakhtin's theory (e.g. Bakhtin, *Speech Genres and Other Late Essays,* 1986) is the notion of *voice* as a manner of speaking unique to a particular location in the physical and social worlds. The word in living contexts is therefore socioculturally situated, betraying the belief and value systems of the speaker. Bakhtin claimed that SAUSSURE ignored genres and thus missed much of the essential working of language. The directed nature of speech also means that any utterance involves a *dialogic interplay* between the voice of the speaker and that of the addressee for whom the utterance is intended. The importance of Bakhtin's ideas in this area for sociology consists mainly in his claims for the sociocultural situatedness of the utterance in everyday language, with its implications for the question of whether anyone can be said to 'own' the utterances to which he or she gives voice. His emphasis is on the 'polyphonic' and dynamic character of language. These ideas are seen applied in his writings on POPULAR CULTURE, especially the CARNIVAL (*Rabelais and his World,* 1969), which have attracted recent interest in sociology. He shows how, historically, the carnival operated as a site of 'ambivalence' (e.g. regarding death and the 'debasements' of the body, such as defecation and copulation) as well as a source of a COUNTER CULTURE to more hierarchical forms of culture.

Bataille, Georges (1897–1962) French poststructuralist thinker who mixed fictional and scientific discourse in order to explore the nature of horror, baseness, and obscenity. During the 1930s Bataille attended Alexandre Kojeve's lecture course on Hegel's phenomenology. Taking his reading of Hegel from Kojeve, Bataille argued that the quest for absolute knowledge overlooked the importance of horizontal thinking and the horror of basic existence. Following Kojeve, this position suggested that Hegel's system threatened to produce too much knowledge. In his key work, *The Accursed Share* (1991), Bataille elaborates on this idea by showing how 'verticality' creates horror and obscenity by virtue of its excessive determinism, the structural imperative that masks the essential nature of horizontal being. Throughout Bataille's thought, the return of this axis (horror, baseness, and obscenity) is referred to as that which corrupts the restricted economy. It short-circuits the structure of vertical knowledge because it exists within the aneconomic domain, the world beyond exchange value. By concentrating on the eternal return of this excessive remainder, Bataille's work on sacrifice argues for Marcel MAUSS' system as an economy of loss rather than a system of balanced exchange. This theory, which looks at how GIFT EXCHANGE is broken by pure-consumption, followed the position adopted by Bataille on HEGEL's phenomenology. See DELEUZE, ORDER/DIS-ORDER.

balance of power (INTERNATIONAL RELATIONS) a situation (actually achieved or the objective of policy) in which a rough balance is sought in the military capacity of major powers. In an era of nuclear weaponry, the term *balance of terror* has also been used. See also NUCLEAR DETERRENCE, ARMS RACE.

band a small group with a simple social structure. This form of social organization is regarded by US evolutionary anthropologists as existing prior to the TRIBE, CHIEFDOM or the STATE, and is usually associated with hunting and gathering societies. For definitional purposes it is regarded as having no differentiated political institutions and no complex social institutions.

banditry see SOCIAL BANDITRY.

barbarism the stage of development typified by pastoralism identified in early theories of social evolution (see EVOLUTIONARY THEORY). MONTESQUIEU was the first to use the term in this way, arguing that the three main stages in social development were: (a) hunting or SAVAGERY; (b) herding or barbarism; and (c) CIVILIZATION. Later 19th-century evolutionary thinkers, such as E. B. TYLOR and L. H. MORGAN, also adopted the concept.

bar chart a diagrammatic method for displaying FREQUENCY DISTRIBUTIONS, in which bars of equal width are drawn to represent each category, with the length of each bar being proportional to the number, or frequency of occurrence, of each category (see Fig. 2). Bar charts are used not because they present different information than can be displayed in tables, but because they can display it in a way that is easier to understand. See also HISTOGRAM.

barter and barter economy a form of economic exchange and a related form of economy in which goods are exchanged for goods rather than for money. In some subsistence societies, MONEY as a medium of exchange is entirely absent.

Barthes, Roland (1915–80) French social theorist and leading exponent of SEMIOLOGY. Usually associated with the structuralist approach, his work was also

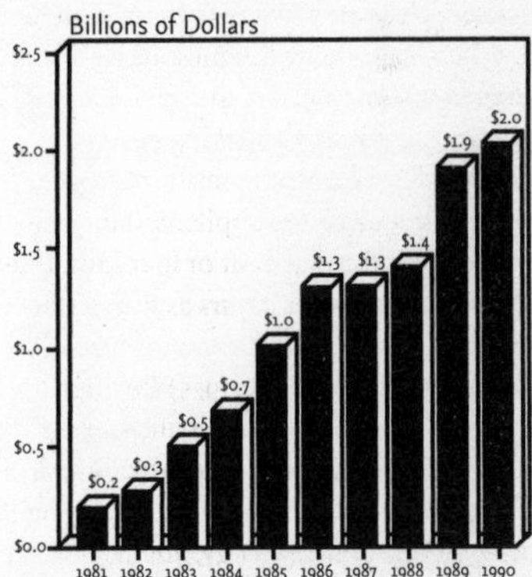

Fig. 2 **Bar Chart.** A diagrammatic display of a frequency distribution in which bars of equal width represent each category, with the length of each bar being proportional to the number or frequency of occurrence for each category. In the above example, the annual student loan default in $US is represented for the years 1981–1990.

influenced by social anthropology and Marxism. His most notable contributions include works on myth, IDEOLOGY and popular culture. He was an influential figure in cultural studies because of his contribution to semiology and his concentration upon the TEXT, rather than its author, as the object of study. He wrote about commonplace events, images and activities in order to show the prevalence of ideology in areas sometimes considered free of any political significance (e.g. posters advertising wine or margarine). He enlarged on the anthropological definition of myth by describing it as one of the ways in which the norms of a society are endowed with a taken-for-granted status as facts of nature. He regarded myth as a prevalent aspect of culture; composed of the SIGN systems through which we understand and express ourselves. FASHION, for example, can be regarded as a system of meanings, one which differentiates between clothes by stressing the significance of detail, and locating the wearer within a constantly changing symbolic order. Barthes argued that cultural forms are essentially ambiguous and permit varied interpretations or readings. Among the key works by Barthes are *Mythologies* (1957) and *Elements of Semiology* (1964).

base and superstructure MARX's metaphor to express the relationship between the economy, as the foundation and determining influence of society (the *base*), and other parts of society (the *superstructure*). Thus the assumption is that at each level of economic development the form of the economy (more particularly the sum total of productive relations) broadly determines the existence of the particular forms of the state, legal system, etc. If this is a general assumption of Marxism, however (see also HISTORICAL MATERIALISM, ECONOMIC INTERPRETATION OF HISTORY), Marx was aware that the actual historical determination of economic and social systems is more complex than suggested by any vulgar notion of base and superstructure. Rather, the historical, specific determinants of social arrangements must be analysed separately within the general framework provided by the concept of base and superstructure. This must include recognition that the relation between base and superstructure is, in part, a two-way relationship in which superstructural forms can feedback to exert a 'relatively autonomous' influence on the base, without necessarily undermining the idea of determination by the economy 'in the last instance' (see also RELATIVE AUTONOMY).

basic human needs the conception that all human beings share fundamental needs (including health and AUTONOMY) by virtue of their humanity (see L. Doyal and I. Gough, *A Theory of Human Need*, 1991). The fulfilment of these basic needs is seen as an 'essential precondition for full participation in social life'. The alternative view is that human needs are relative, a matter of individual or cultural preference. See also JUSTICE, RAWLS, NEEDS, CITIZENSHIP.

basic trust see TRUST, ONTOLOGICAL SECURITY AND INSECURITY.

Bateson, Gregory (1904–80) widely influential US cultural anthropologist with academic interests ranging from zoology, social anthropology, philosophy, psychology and communication studies to mysticism. He was part of the first generation to follow in the ethnographic footsteps of MALINOWSKI. Bateson's first, and now classical, ethnographic contribution, was his study *Naven* (1936), a fascinating addition to the developing anthropological mosaic with its analytical framework for the study of symbolism. He introduced the concept of *schizmogenesis* (to describe the process of social fission and conflict), and he employed the more familiar concepts *ethos* and EIDOS to capture the inherent principles of belief systems. He also argued that explanatory and descriptive categories employed in data analysis could be reshuffled and changed, that data were not beholden to a single framework.

Bateson's second anthropological classic,

Balinese Character (1942), of which Margaret MEAD was co-author, contributed to the vogue in the study of *culture and personality* in US cultural anthropology especially in the 1940s. A further aspect of his work is that he made pioneering use of still photographs and moving film as constituents of both ethnographic fieldwork and report writing. In his later work he ranged from 'humanistic psychology' and cybernetics to communication studies, investigating aquatic mammals and dolphins. His work influenced GOFFMAN and many others in sociology.

Baudrillard, Jean (1929–) French social theorist who, in works such as *La Société de consommation* (1970) and *Simulations* (1983), has been influential in POSTMODERNISM. Baudrillard draws particularly on SEMIOLOGY to argue that modern-day consumption in particular entails the 'active manipulation of SIGNS', so that in modern society the production of the sign and the commodity have come together to produce the *commodity-sign*. An endless reduplication of signs, images and SIMULATIONS, launched through the media and elsewhere, in the end effaces all distinction between image and reality. The overproduction of such signs, images and simulations has the effect of producing a 'loss of stable meaning', which is advanced as a characteristic of POSTMODERNITY. See also HYPERREALITY.

Bauman, Zygmunt (1925–) British-based, Polish-born sociologist whose recent prolific writings in social theory have attracted wide attention. His best known work has been on modernity and postmodernity (including *Modernity and the Holocaust*, 1989, and *Life in Fragments*, 1995) and on INTELLECTUALS *(Legislators and Interpreters*, 1987). Although aware of the cultures of control associated with modernity, Bauman sees an openness, and with this the possibility of renewed moralities, arising from the discursive culture of MODERNITY/POSTMODERNITY and POSTMODERNISM. See also GENOCIDE.

Bayes' theorem a theorem stating the probability of an event occurring if another event has occurred. Bayesian statistics is concerned with the revision of opinion in the light of new information, i.e. hypotheses are set up, tested, and revised in the light of the data collected. On each successive occasion there emerges a different probability of the hypothesis being correct – 'prior opinions are changed by data, through the operation of Bayes' theorem, to yield posterior opinions' (Phillips, 1973).

Beauvoir, Simone de (1908–86) French feminist writer, whose main contribution to social theory – in *The Second Sex* (1953) – was an account of PATRIARCHY in which the 'feminine' is seen, in Hegelian terms, as culturally constructed, as 'other than' male. This 'otherness' is explained as arising from the historical cultural fact of the SEXUAL DIVISION OF LABOUR, but is in part also determined by women's sexual reproductive capacity, which restricts women's freedom compared with that of men. The only answer she suggests is that women should refrain from marriage and from childbirth and the responsibilities of motherhood.

Beck, Ulrich (1944–) German sociologist, best known for his 'landmark' volume *Risk Society – Towards a New Modernity* (1992, originally 1986) in which he argued that contemporary societies, compared with previous societies, are characterized, not so much by 'high risk', but by new kinds of risk arising from REFLEXIVE MODERNIZATION (see U. Beck, A. Giddens and S. Lash, 1994). It is the universality and the inescapability of risk that characterizes the new RISK SOCIETY. Beck's distinctive ideas can be seen as pointing to a 'third way' between modernist and postmodernist theories of contemporary society.

Becker, Howard S. (1928–) US sociologist whose work within the SYMBOLIC INTERACTIONIST tradition has made an important contribution to the study of student culture, LABELLING THEORY and the SOCIOLOGY OF ART. His most influential works are *Boys in White: Student Culture in a Medical World* (with Blanche Geer, Everett

Hughes and Anselm Strauss, 1961), *Making the Grade* (with Blanche Geer and Everett Hughes, 1968), *Outsiders: Studies in the Sociology of Deviance* (1963) and *Sociological Work* (1970). While focusing on the behaviour of individuals in groups and organizations, Becker's treatment of these was uncompromisingly sociological. The responses of individuals, e.g. to medical treatment, are seen as depending far less 'on the individual psychology of patients than on the relations between the healers and the sick. The actions of deviants stem less from their personalities than from the interactions between them, other deviants, and agents of social control'. See also DEVIANCE, HIERARCHY OF CREDIBILITY, MAKING THE GRADE, DRUG TAKING FOR PLEASURE.

behaviour 1 the alteration, movement or response of any entity, person or system acting within a particular context.
2 (PSYCHOLOGY) the externally observable response of an animal or human organism to an environmental stimulus (see also BEHAVIOURISM).

An important distinction is often made in sociology between automatic forms of behaviour described in 2 (e.g. jumping up after sitting on a drawing pin) and intended ACTION, where social meanings and purposes are also involved.

behavioural approach see BEHAVIOURALISM.

behaviouralism *or* **behavioural approach** a theoretical and empirical approach within US POLITICAL SCIENCE which emphasizes the importance of sociological and psychological determinants of political actions and behaviour rather than confining attention, as is traditional in political science, to narrowly political processes, e.g. constitutional arrangements, legislative procedures. See POLITICAL BEHAVIOUR; compare BEHAVIOURISM.

behavioural science(s) (especially in the US) the science or sciences of human and animal BEHAVIOUR. While sometimes suggested as an appropriate label for the social sciences as a whole (including psychology and political science as well as sociology), the close association of the term with BEHAVIOURISM has meant that there has been no general acceptance of the term, and little, if any, acceptance of it within sociology.

behaviourism 1 the school of psychology whose central precept is that the subject matter of psychology is observable behaviour only.
2 the study, generally through animal experiments, of the principles of learning (also called CONDITIONING), and the application of these principles to understanding and manipulating human behaviour.
3 (PHILOSOPHY, e.g. Ryle's *The Concept of Mind*, 1949) the notion that 'mental concepts may be analysed in terms of overt acts and utterances' (Flew, 1979). For Ryle, sense 1 mistakenly assumes exclusivity of the mental and physical, a DUALISM OF MIND and BODY.

Behaviourism as a school of psychology was founded in the US by E. L. Thorndike (1911) who proposed the Law of Effect. This states that behaviour which is rewarded tends to be repeated, while behaviour which is not rewarded tends to decrease. At much the same time, in Russia, I. Pavlov (1846–1936) was investigating the conditioned reflex. His experiments led to the formulation of the theory of *classical conditioning* (Pavlov, 1911).

The most influential and prolific behaviourist, however, is B.F. Skinner (1904–90), whose name has become almost synonymous with behaviourism and who invented the Skinner Box. This instrument provides a controlled environment within which to study animal learning (*operant conditioning*).

The main tenet of behaviourism as a school of psychology is that only observable behaviour can be scientifically studied. However, this includes verbal behaviour, which may express thoughts. Primarily, though, behaviourists prefer to disregard mental functions, or the effect of the organism, which is interposed between the observable stimulus (S) and the observable response (R). Only the S and R can be controlled and measured, therefore only they can be studied.

In order to study the principles of learning rigorously, the behaviours need to be simple and the procedures ethically acceptable. This has meant a concentration on animal experiments, often in the controlled environment of a Skinner Box where, typically, rats or pigeons can be studied learning to associate S (such as a lever or disk) and R (such as pressing or pecking) under various schedules of reinforcement (using food pellets as reinforcement). Such investigations have led to the development of a fund of knowledge about the circumstances under which conditioning takes place, and about what variables affect its strength and application.

These ideas were particularly influential in the 1930s and 40s, dominating academic psychology and pervading general culture, and particularly affecting child-rearing practices. Subsequently, their general influence within psychology has receded, but within the mental-health field the principles are still widely used. See BEHAVIOUR MODIFICATION.

Skinner has also been influential in the field of language learning (*Verbal Behaviour*, 1957). He proposed that a child learns language through a process of conditioning – his/her verbal behaviour is shaped by reinforcement towards the sounds of his/her native language. This contrasts with CHOMSKY's theory (see LANGUAGE ACQUISITION DEVICE).

behaviour modification *or* **behaviour therapy** the intentional alteration of human BEHAVIOUR by various techniques based on learning theory (see BEHAVIOURISM), particularly as used in clinical psychology. It rests on the premise that some problem behaviours involve faulty learning therefore can best be dealt with by relearning, i.e. retraining the individual's responses. Particular examples of this are systematic desensitization, token economies and AVERSION THERAPY.

Systematic desensitization is most usually used in the treatment of phobias (irrational fears) and involves replacing the unwanted response (fear) with a desired response (relaxation). This is done gradually (and systematically) by introducing the feared object or situation in the least frightening form to start with, while the person remains relaxed, and gradually increasing the exposure while relaxation is maintained. The reinforcer maintaining the improved responses is a sense of achievement, self-control and the possibility of a less restricted lifestyle.

Token economies are often used to control the behaviour of patients in mental hospitals or other institutions. This technique involves rewarding individuals with tokens when they perform desired behaviours, such as washing, dressing, clearing-up, being sociable, talking sensibly. The tokens can then be exchanged for rewards such as days out or any other treat regarded as desirable by the patient or inmate.

behaviour therapy see BEHAVIOUR MODIFICATION.

Being see DASEIN, HEIDEGGER.

belief system the configuration of beliefs which exists in a particular society or culture. The term may be used to refer to the entirety of the knowledge and beliefs within a society, including scientific and technological knowledge. It has more often been used to describe the patterns of religious beliefs and VALUES, and the central principles underlying these, which give distinctiveness and coherence to the modes of thought within a society or culture. See also WORLD VIEW.

Bell, Daniel (1919–) US essayist and sociologist whose various descriptions of modern society have achieved a wide but contested currency. In The *End of Ideology* (1960), he was among the first to suggest a sharp decline in the relevance of previously dominant class ideologies (see END-OF-IDEOLOGY THESIS). Later, in *The Coming* *of Post Industrial Society* (1973), he advanced the view that modern societies had become not only POSTINDUSTRIAL SOCIETIES but also knowledge-based, INFORMATION SOCIETIES, in which science and technology and professional and technical employment were now central. At this stage Bell's main message was one of an optimistic future and a society of declining social conflict. In *The Cultural Contradictions of Capitalism* (1976), however, the tone changes. Now Bell notes the new and unresolved tensions between the three competing 'axial principles' of modern society: techno-economic efficiency; universal CITIZENSHIP, political equality and entitlements to social welfare; and individual self-expression and hedonistic fulfilment (see also CULTURAL CONTRADICTIONS OF CAPITALISM, FISCAL CRISIS IN THE CAPITALIST STATE, LEGITIMATION CRISIS, SECTORAL CLEAVAGES). Thus Bell's sociological analysis of modern society can be said to have captured the changing fortunes and moods of modern society. See also FUTUROLOGY.

Bendix, Reinhardt (1916–91), German-born US sociologist, best known for his work on the interpretation of Max Weber's sociology (especially *Max Weber: an Intellectual Portrait,* 1960), and for his extensive work in historical and comparative sociology, including *Work and Authority in Industry* (1956), *Social Mobility in Industrial Society* (1959), and *Nation Building and Citizenship* (1964). See SOCIAL MOBILITY.

Benedict, Ruth (1887–1948) US cultural anthropologist who followed in the tradition of Franz BOAS in adopting a culturally relativist orientation to comparative anthropology. Her research contributions primarily involved a psychologically oriented exploration of the relationship of culture to personality, and she has been influential in the study of race. In her best-known book, *Patterns of Culture* (1935), she sought to demonstrate how conceptions of psychological normality are culturally produced and highly variable, and that personality traits highly valued by one society may be negatively viewed in another. Margaret MEAD was perhaps her most famous pupil. See also CULTURE AND PERSONALITY SCHOOL.

benefice 1 (in contemporary usage) a living from a church office or the property attached to a church.

2 (historically, and in sociology) the institution in Western European feudalism whereby a vassal was given land or a position by an overlord from which the vassal could gain an income. Especially where land was involved, more commonly this was known as a fief. See FEUDALISM AND FEUDAL SOCIETY.

Benjamin, Walter (1892–1940) German cultural theorist associated with the FRANKFURT SCHOOL OF CRITICAL THEORY. Benjamin's materialist dialectics were rooted in both Jewish mysticism and historical materialism. History as progress had to be blown apart, and cultural commodities could be rescued or transformed into 'dialectical images' which illuminated the revolutionary possibilities of the present (see *Illuminations*, 1955, and *One Way Street*, 1974). His work is regarded as particularly important today for its contribution to neo-Marxist theories of AESTHETICS and 'mass culture'. Part of his work constituted a theoretical analysis of the writing of the socialist playwright Berthold Brecht. Brecht's influence changed the direction of Benjamin's thoughts from critical negation to revolutionary affirmation of a collective revolutionary subject (see *Understanding Brecht,* 1973). At odds with ADORNO, who was pessimistic about the critical potential of 'mass art', Benjamin remained hopeful that a progressive potential would be found. Whereas Adorno retained, and even extended, an attachment to the classical 'modernist' (and bourgeois) distinction between high culture and other mass cultural forms, Benjamin questioned this distinction. In doing so he embraced many orientations which later became characteristic of POSTMODERNISM.

Bentham, Jeremy (1748–1832) English legal, political and social theorist and social reformer, and one of the founders of modern philosophical UTILITARIANISM. As a legal theorist, Bentham challenged the adequacy of the COMMON LAW tradition; he was even more critical of conceptions of natural law (see NATURAL RIGHTS AND NATURAL LAW), which he described as 'nonsense on stilts'. In place of these, Bentham advocated legislation and the general codification of laws, and LEGAL POSITIVISM. His interest in prison reform also led him to suggest designs for the modern prison – see PANOPTICAN.

Berger, Peter (1929–) Viennese-born US social theorist and sociologist of religion. In *The Social Construction of Reality* (with Thomas Luckmann, 1966), he provides an account of the role of COMMON-SENSE KNOWLEDGE in the social construction of everyday life and institutions, which he develops from the phenomenological perspective of Alfred SCHUTZ. In his studies of religion, including the *The Social Reality of Religion* (1969), he has suggested, controversially, that sociologists should adopt a 'methodologically atheist' stance and not seek to discuss whether religion is anything more than a social creation. He has also written a highly readable introduction to sociology, *An Invitation to Sociology* (1966), which is a hymn to the pleasures of sociology, 'a royal game among academic disciplines', according to Berger. See also STRUCTURE AND AGENCY, PHENOMENOLOGICAL SOCIOLOGY.

Bergson, Henri (1859–1941) French philosopher whose work on TIME has influenced sociological thinking. In *Time and Free Will* (1889) he contrasted time as experienced in everyday life ('continuous duration') with time as represented in scientific thinking.

Bernstein, Basil (1924–) social theorist and specialist in the SOCIOLOGY OF EDUCATION, who is best known for his pioneering work on SOCIOLINGUISTICS and his examination of the relationship between social class and children's acquisition and use of language in the context of the family and the school. His earliest papers, in the 1960s, established the existence of working-class 'restricted' codes and middle-class 'elaborated' codes of formal and public language (see ELABORATED CODES AND RESTRICTED CODES). These language theories, and his empirical research, were widely disseminated in Britain and the rest of the world.

Concentration on the sociolinguistic aspects of Bernstein's work has distracted attention from his wider interest in the distribution of power and the principles of social control (Bernstein, *Class, Codes and Control* vols. 1-3 (1971–7)). His approach is essentially a structuralist one, and he draws heavily on the work of DURKHEIM. These aspects are most clearly seen in his work on the organization, transmission and evaluation of educational knowledge. Education is essentially a form of knowledge code; how it is organized, transmitted and evaluated reflects the modes of social control. The curriculum is constructed as separate or combined units of knowledge which are classified in some way, where CLASSIFICATION refers to the boundary relationships between domains of knowledge. The term is paralleled by the concept of 'framing' which refers to the manner in which educational knowledge is transmitted. Bernstein suggests that, empirically, the message systems of 'classification' and 'framing' are realized in collection and integrated codes which underpin the curriculum of schools and have consequences for order and control. A collection code has strongly classified and bounded domains. Students can select only clearly separated contents in the form of specifically defined subjects, e.g. history, geography, chemistry, physics. An integrated code consists of contents which have an open relationship with each other, e.g. social studies, science. Thus the organization of knowledge is mirrored in the educational philosophy embedded in each code and its relationship to the principles of power and control. The collection code implies didactic teaching where 'facts' are inculcated. The integrated code implies a theory of teaching and learning predicated on the self-regulation of individuals or groups of pupils.

Bernstein, Eduard (1850–1932) German Social Democratic theorist who is mostly associated with REVISIONISM within Marxism. In his major work, *Die Voraussetzungen des Socialismus* (1899), he argued that an extension of political rights within capitalist societies would gradually transform these societies and avert economic crises without the necessity for violent revolution or DICTATORSHIP OF THE PROLETARIAT.

Beveridge Report a report setting out the principles which informed the creation of the British WELFARE STATE immediately after World War II. The formal title of the report is *Social Insurance and Allied Services* (published in 1942), but it is more commonly known after its author, William Beveridge (1879–1963).

Influenced by a KEYNESIAN ECONOMIC model which promoted full employment, and following the interwar economic depressions, Beveridge wanted to create a social policy which would eradicate what he considered to be the five great problems of idleness, ignorance, disease, squalor and want. The report advocated the introduction of social insurance to provide a universal system of social security (including family allowances) and a universal, comprehensive and free NATIONAL HEALTH SERVICE. Although the Beveridge Report gained wide support, it has been criticized for establishing a meagre system of benefits and for reinforcing a wife's economic dependence on her husband since, according to the scheme, in the case of a married couple, only the man could claim. See also POVERTY.

bias 1 any situation in which the accuracy, RELIABILITY, VALIDITY, etc. of sociological data or findings are held to be distorted by the limitations of a research method employed, or by a researcher's or a theorist's presuppositions (e.g. political or moral beliefs). See also OBJECTIVITY, VALUE FREEDOM AND VALUE NEUTRALITY.
2 in a more narrowly technical sense, in statistical analysis, a difference between a hypothetical 'true value' of a variable in a population and that obtained in a particular sample of respondents. See also BIASED SAMPLE.

biased sample a population SAMPLE which is not a true reflection of the parent population (see BIAS 2), i.e. not a REPRESENTATIVE SAMPLE.

When the incidence of a certain occurrence or piece of behaviour in a population is to be investigated, e.g. voting intention, it is often impossible to examine the total population, so a sample of this population is taken. For this sample to produce acceptable data, it must be a true representation of the parent population, so it is essential that it is selected in a way that ensures this. If this is not managed, bias will result and the information collected will not truly reflect the population being studied. Thus, to select a sample by questioning people in the street will bias it against people who do not walk, do not go shopping, are at work or school all day. Postal QUESTIONNAIRES attempt to overcome this type of bias, but are likely to be biased against those who do not bother to fill in questionnaires and return them, and against the illiterate. To keep bias to a minimum, if random sampling is not possible, it is necessary to select the sample carefully by matching all relevant parameters of the population, e.g. age, class, residence, etc., and to ensure as high a response rate as possible, probably by personal INTERVIEWS.

bilateral descent (ANTHROPOLOGY) a term describing a kinship system in which links are recognized through both sexes.

bilineal descent (ANTHROPOLOGY),
1 a synonym for DOUBLE DESCENT.
2 (less frequently) a term for NONUNILINEAL DESCENT systems.

bimodal distribution see MEASURES OF CENTRAL TENDENCY.

binary conceptual system see DECONSTRUCTION. LÉVI-STRAUSS.

binary system of higher education the system of HIGHER EDUCATION which operated in the UK between 1965 and 1991, in which education was provided by UNIVERSITIES and POLYTECHNICS. Universities awarded their own degrees; those of polytechnics were awarded by the Council for National Academic Awards (CNAA). Although formally of the same status, differences between the two types of institution reflected their different historical development. While an overlap existed between the two types of institution, polytechnics provided a wider range of vocational and part-time courses. Differences also existed in the occupational destinations of graduates, with graduates of polytechnics sometimes experiencing greater difficulty in gaining graduate level employment (see also GRADUATE LABOUR MARKET). The creation of the NEW UNIVERSITIES in 1991 marked the formal ending of the binary system. However, many of the differences between the previous universities and polytechnics (not least in levels of research) remain as differences between older and new universities. See also MASS HIGHER EDUCATION.

biographical method the use of personal documents (such as letters or diaries) to construct sociological accounts. See LIFE HISTORY, ZNANIECKI.

biomechanical (or **biomedical**) **model of illness** a model of illness based on a conception of the body as a physical system which may break down, and need treatment to restore it to good working order. Although there is a good deal of informal health care undertaken outside of medical settings, this model suggests that people normally go to see a doctor when they have a painful or life-threatening condition which cannot be cured by self-medication. It is a model of illness made up of the following elements:
(a) that normally people are either free of symptoms of ill health or are unaware that they are ill;
(b) that illness consists of deviation from a set of biological norms;
(c) that emotional or physical changes which are biological in origin make people aware that something is wrong;
(d) that the initial response to something being wrong is the use of lay remedies such as rest or perhaps a proprietary medicine;
(e) that if the symptoms persist or get worse people will visit the doctor;
(f) that at this point the person is either diagnosed as sick and treated by the doctor, or assured that there is nothing wrong;
(g) that the person who has been diagnosed as sick follows a course of treatment prescribed to make them well, at which point they are pronounced cured.

Sociologists have challenged this model and distinguished between disease as a biological category and illness as a social category. Disease refers to biological states such as a fractured limb or a tubercular lung; illness refers to both the subjective feeling of being unwell and the social status of sick person. See also SYMPTOM ICEBERG. TRIVIAL CONSULTATION.

biopolitics (FOUCAULT' s term) the form of political reason/intervention in which the power to take life is replaced by the power to foster life or disallow it – leading to a disciplining of the human BODY and 'soul', and a regulation of the population. See also PANOPTICAN, CONFESSIONAL TECHNOLOGIES.

birth certificate a certificate issued on the registration of the birth of a child. First instituted in 1837 in England and Wales, it shows the full name of the child, his or her sex, the names of the parents (including the former surname of the mother) and the father's occupation. Birth certificates provide the historical sociologist with a source of data with which to study life histories, fertility patterns and illegitimacy. See also DEATH CERTIFICATE, MARRIAGE CERTIFICATE. PARISH REGISTER.

birth cohort study the LONGITUDINAL STUDY of a sample born at a particular time in a particular year. British examples are the

Medical Research Council National Survey of Health and Development, 1946 and the National Child Development Survey, 1958.

birth rate the number of live births per 1000 people of all ages in one year. In post-World War II UK the birth rate rose until the mid-1960s and has since declined. Since 1951 the highest birth rate was in 1964 with 18.8 live births per 1000 people, and the lowest was in 1977 with 11.7 live births per 1000 people.

The overall birth rate is sometimes referred to as the *crude birth rate*. Various other '*age specific*' measures of the rate can be calculated to provide more reliable projections of POPULATION trends. There is some suggestion that birth rate changes may be related to economic cycles, but this is not a simple relationship. Variables affecting birth rate, including length of marriage, the age structure of the population and contraceptive methods used, interact in a complex manner with economic factors. See also DEATH RATE, FERTILITY, DEMOGRAPHY, FECUNDITY. DEMOGRAPHIC TRANSITION, POPULATION.

black a term used to refer to a variety of non-white ethnic groups. Black is a preferred form, especially among ethnic groups of African origins, reflecting a pride and identity in being black. The use of the term is associated with the rise of black political activism in the US in the 1960s, and is reflected in the slogan 'Black is Beautiful'. Other terms to describe black people, such as coloured, Negro or Negress, are now generally considered offensive.

In the UK (and elsewhere), however, there is controversy about the use of the term to describe 'non-white' persons of Asian origin. Many Asians object to the use of the word 'black' to describe them and argue that this usage confuses the identity of a large number of very different ethnic groups such as Pakistanis, Bangladeshis, Indians, West Indians, Africans and so on. The counter argument is that 'non-white' persons in the UK can be subject to DISCRIMINATION and institutionalized RACISM whatever their ethnic or national origins. In this sense, groups of both African and Asian origin share, to a significant extent, a common experience. See also BLACK POWER MOVEMENT, NEGRITUDE.

black-coated worker (more especially of male workers) a routine clerical or office worker. The more generally used sociological term for this category of workers is WHITE-COLLAR WORKER.

The term 'black-coated worker' was first given sociological currency by LOCKWOOD (1958) in an historical account of a group of such workers and a critique of simple PROLETARIANIZATION arguments. Lockwood distinguished between 'market', 'work' and 'status' situations (see MULTIDIMENSIONAL ANALYSIS OF SOCIAL STRATIFICATION). Historically there existed a clear separation in status, salary and conditions between office workers and most sections of the working class. More recently, the MARKET SITUATION of manual and routine non-manual workers to some extent converged. In WORK SITUATIONS and STATUS SITUATIONS, however, there remained pronounced differences. Among other things, manual and non-manual workers were physically separated at work and black-coated workers retained a higher level of prestige than manual workers. This explained differences in CLASS CONSCIOUSNESS, and political attitudes, with black-coated workers being more likely to see themselves as MIDDLE CLASS and to vote for the Conservative Party. In a postscript to the study, in a new edition of *The Black-coated Worker*, Lockwood rejects any suggestion that office workers have experienced either proletarianization or radical DESKILLING. See also SUBJECTIVE AND OBJECTIVE CLASS, RELATIVE DEPRIVATION.

black economy see INFORMAL ECONOMY.

black Muslims a number of BLACK American-Islamic religious, social and cultural movements and their adherents. During the 20th century a number of SECTS and SOCIAL MOVEMENTS grew up within the American black community based loosely on Islamic principles and drawing on the Koran. The most influential of these sects was the Nation of Islam, led, from the early 1950s through to 1975, by Elijah Muhammad.

The Nation of Islam held the belief that 'white' society was the cause of evil and that American blacks should strive to create a separate and self-sufficient state exclusively for blacks. Black Muslims believed that no accommodation could be reached with the white power structure. The Nation of Islam encouraged the creation of separate shops, schools, hospitals, industries and financial institutions in an attempt to free blacks from the economic and cultural power of white society in the US.

Many black Muslims were at the centre of the American BLACK POWER MOVEMENT in the 1960s and early 1970s. The widespread influence of the Nation of Islam was enhanced by the adherence of well-known figures such as Malcolm X, the black radical, and Muhammad Ali, the boxing champion first known as Cassius Clay. After Elijah Muhammad's death in 1975, the Nation of Islam, and indeed the black Muslim movements in general, became more fragmented and less influential.

black power movement a militant SOCIAL MOVEMENT, originating in the US in the mid-1960s, which emphasized the role of the white-dominated power structure in subordinating black people. It argued that power had to be taken by blacks, from whites, in order to materially improve the situation of black people. The movement was one of a number of radical responses amongst black activists to the perceived failure of the CIVIL RIGHTS MOVEMENT to achieve real improvements in the conditions of black people, and its concentration on the segregated, rural, Southern states at the expense of urban ghettoes. The black power movement has been particularly associated with the takeover of the Student Nonviolent Coordinating Committee (SNCC) by a group of more radical members, the most prominent being Stokely Carmichael. Two contemporary quotes serve to underline the developments. SNCC (pronounced 'Snick'), since its inception in 1960, had been at the forefront of more confrontational and high-profile CIVIL RIGHTS activities, including college sit-ins, Freedom Rides (integrated buses), voter-registration drives, etc. In a book written just before the emergence of the black power movement. Paul Jacobs and Saul Lindau (1966) wrote: 'The weary veterans of harassment, arrest, beatings, and the psychological torture of living in the South have begun to re-examine their objectives at the very time they confront the full and often subtle power of the American economic and political system.' In the same year, writing about the emergence of black power, Carmichael wrote: 'We had to work for power because this country does not function by morality, love and nonviolence, but by power ... integration is a subterfuge to maintain white supremacy' (reprinted in Floyd Barbour (ed.), 1969). This shift, drawing on a number of black separatist and black pride themes, castigated 'the system' as racist and unreformable, and emphasized black autonomy and self reliance.

Black Report the report of the Working Group on Inequalities in Health chaired by Sir Douglas Black, Chief Scientist at the Department of Health and President of the Royal College of Physicians which was published in 1980. A more accessible version was published as *Inequalities in Health* by Peter Townsend and Nick Davidson. The Black Report reviewed UK health statistics (MORBIDITY RATE and MORTALITY RATE and access to health care services) and compared them with figures for other EC and Scandinavian countries. It found:

(a) at all ages male mortality rates are greater than female mortality rates;

(b) the gap between the mortality rates of employed men in classes I and IV had increased between 1949 and 1972;

(c) the mortality rates for men in classes III, IV and V deteriorated or stayed the same in this period, but relative to the combined mortality rates of classes I and II they had increased;

(d) the picture of female mortality was similar, a deterioration for married and single women in the most numerous category, class IV;
(e) a reduction in deaths per 1000 live births for all groups, but a relative excess in classes IV and V combined, over classes I and II combined, between 1959 and 1972;
(f) a decline in maternal mortality for all groups, but a persistent class differential;
(g) no significant improvements in the life expectancy and life chances of children up to the age of 14 from all classes.

The Report found that there was a class gradient in illness and mortality, and that this gradient was replicated in a stratified access to, and use of, health-care facilities. The conclusion was that the significant factors affecting health were income, occupational characteristics, education, housing and lifestyle, all of which lie beyond the power of the NHS to change.

The committee made a number of far-reaching policy recommendations which concentrated on three areas:
(a) improved facilities and resources for the health of mothers and children;
(b) priority for disabled people in order to improve the quality of their lives in general, allow them to be cared for in their own homes, and to reduce the risk of them needing institutional care;
(c) priority for preventative and educational action to encourage good health and discourage unhealthy habits like smoking.

The overall conclusion, however, was that without a government strategy to reduce poverty, none of these recommendations would be entirely effective.

Blau, Peter (1918–2002) US sociologist who first made his reputation as an organization theorist with works such as *The Dynamics of Bureaucracy* (1955) and (with W. Scott) *Formal Organizations: A Comparative Approach* (1962). Subsequently, with O. Duncan, he also contributed an important empirical study on occupational structure, *The American Occupational Structure* (1967). In *Exchange and Power* (1964) he formulated a version of EXCHANGE THEORY in which his goal was to 'derive complex from simpler processes without the reductionist fallacy of ignoring emergent properties'. For Blau, 'social exchange' is the 'central principle of social life, and even relationships such as love and friendship can be analysed as relations of exchange'. The institutions of gift exchange in simple societies reveal underlying principles that apply to social exchange in general, for example, 'that reciprocated benefactions create social bonds among peers, whereas unreciprocated ones produce differentiation of status'. Anxious to avoid a merely tautological use of the notion of social exchange, Blau limits its reference to actions contingent on rewarding reactions from others, which would cease where these reactions were not forthcoming.

Bloch, Marc (1886–1944) French medieval historian who taught in Strasbourg and, from 1936, at the Sorbonne in Paris. His influence in sociology is mainly through his important book *Feudal Society*, published in English in 1961, in which he stressed the workings of feudal society as a whole, rather than emphasizing either the political or economic aspects which other theorists favoured. He was cofounder (1931) of the *Annales d'histoire économique et sociale* (see ANNALES SCHOOL). He was murdered by the Gestapo in 1944 for his role in the French Resistance. See also FEUDALISM AND FEUDAL SOCIETY.

blue-collar worker American synonym for a manual worker. The contradistinction involved is with WHITE-COLLAR WORKER.

Blumer, Herbert (1900–87) US sociologist who was a student and a teacher at the University of Chicago. He is best known as a teacher and writer in the symbolic interactionist tradition deriving from G. H. MEAD (see Blumer, *Symbolic Interactionism*, 1969). He coined the term SYMBOLIC INTERACTIONISM. See also VARIABLE.

Boas, Franz (1858–1942) German-born anthropologist who played a pioneering role in the foundation of modern CULTURAL ANTHROPOLOGY. Opposed to evolutionary theory, Boas was especially influential in establishing the ethnographic techniques which dominate modern anthropology. He emphasised the relativity of cultures and the importance of understanding these in their own terms.

body the physical form of the individual human being, which, however, is equally a social product, given that human biological capacities are in many areas underdetermined by biology and profoundly shaped by cultural definitions and social influences.

Although not always fully explicit, numerous topic areas in sociology (e.g. the SOCIOLOGY OF HEALTH AND MEDICINE, or the positionings of the body in face-to-face interaction as studied by GOFFMAN) raise central questions about the body, and the basic characteristics of the body (e.g. its vulnerability and finitude, and constraints on its mobility in time and space) possess crucial social implications. Examples of the latter are that every human society must preserve the basic material conditions for the health and welfare and reproduction of human bodies. The vulnerability of the body also means that the threat of VIOLENCE is a decisive factor in both the maintenance and the limitation of political POWER.

Recently the sociological study of the body (see also SOCIOLOGY OF THE BODY) has become a more central point of focus in the discipline, as seen from the attention given to the work of FOUCAULT or ELIAS on historical changes in the regulation of the body, and the study of the body as a medium of communication (see also BODY LANGUAGE) through gestures, posture, cosmetics and clothing. Feminist theory in particular has drawn attention to the stereotypical use of female bodies, and parts of bodies, in ADVERTISING and pornography, and also to the differences between the masculine and feminine body ideals in Western culture (see also FOOD. ANOREXIA NERVOSA).

In classical PHILOSOPHY, a central issue has been the mind-body relation (see DESCARTES, DUALISM), which finds echoes in many modern sociological debates (e.g. conceptions of FREE WILL). However, as MERLEAU-PONTY, among others, points out, any action always involves 'bodily being', so an outright dualism of mind and body is not appropriate. Finally (whatever plausibility may exist for modern conceptions of a DECENTRED SELF), as the physical site of the 'person', the boundaries and continuity of the individual body are significant in any identification, identity and continuities of the social SELF, although far from being their only basis.

In recent decades, attention to the constitution of the body has been particularly intense, influenced by FEMINISM as well as FOUCAULT (see Featherstone and Turner, 1996, in the founding issue of the journal *Body & Society*). See also POST-FEMINISM, BUTLER.

body language communication by gesture, posture and other *nonverbal* signs. Argyle (1967 and 1969) and Morris (1978) have both documented detailed observations of human nonverbal communication. Body language may include unintended SIGNS as well as intended communication.

In sociology, the appropriate positionings of the BODY in social ENCOUNTERS have been studied by social theorists, notably GOFFMAN. See also FACE-WORK.

Bogardus scale see SOCIAL DISTANCE.

bolshevik (from the Russian *bol'shinstovo*, majority) a member of the Leninist majority of the Russian Social Democratic Party in 1903, the forerunner of the Communist Party of the Soviet Union. Thus, by extension, the term *bolshevism* has also come to refer to any revolutionary communist party which adopts a similar 'vanguard conception' of the role of the party in leading the working class (see also POLITICAL PARTY).

bolshevism see BOLSHEVIK.

Bonapartism (MARXISM) a form of government in capitalist society in which the executive is controlled by a dictator, who in turn controls other institutions of the state and society. For MARX, in his *The Eighteenth Brumaire of Louis Bonaparte*, this form represented a stalemate in class relations with the capitalist class unable to rule through parliamentary means and the working class unable to achieve dominance. The example Marx analysed was of Louis Bonaparte in France, who became Napoleon III in 1851 after a coup d'état. Marx argued that the regime still sought the development of capitalism.

Subsequent writers have seen this as an example of the RELATIVE AUTONOMY (OF THE STATE). Various examples have been claimed in the 20th century, especially in THIRD WORLD societies where the relatively weak social class formations may underlie the frequency of military dictatorships stepping in to resolve political conflicts where no one social class is strong enough to dominate over others. Such examples may be distinguished from FASCISM, since mass parties are not used either to come to power or to sustain the dictatorship in power, and there may be no articulated fascist ideology. However, the concept may be too broad to account adequately for all the various circumstances in which dictatorships emerge and hence there is debate about its precise applicability.

Booth, Charles James (1840–1916) a businessman, shipowner and social reformer who recognized the need for systematic and reliable data to support the case for social reform. He was the first person to develop and use the SURVEY METHOD to collect data on POVERTY and income. His statistical findings were published in *Life and Labour of the People* (1889–91) and *Life and Labour of the People in London* (1891–1903). He was particularly concerned about the aged poor and was influential in the creation of the Old Age Pensions Act, 1908. See also SOCIAL SURVEY, SOCIAL ADMINISTRATION, ROWNTREE.

boundary maintenance see SOCIAL SYSTEM.

bounded rationality a model of human action in which choices are seen as limited and imperfect in terms of knowledge of the situation and expected outcomes; action is therefore never completely rational. The concept originated in the work of March and Simon (1958) and Simon (1957a & b) on DECISION MAKING in organizations. Their work was critical of the model or IDEAL TYPE of perfect rationality presented in economic theories of the firm; in contrast to the assumption of profit maximization in economic theory, March and Simon argued that actual behaviour in organizations was SATISFICING rather than 'optimizing' in terms of the achievement of goals. This approach to 'subjective rationality' has been influential in the sociology of organizations (see ORGANIZATION THEORY) because it demonstrated the way in which organizational structure (DIVISION OF LABOUR, SOCIALIZATION, AUTHORITY) and channels of communication limit the range of solutions considered.

Bourdieu, Pierre (1930–2003) French professor of sociology at the College de France, Paris, who has made significant contributions to general SOCIOLOGICAL THEORY in attempting to find a middle way between action and structure, and is well known for his work in the sociology of CULTURE and for the application of those ideas to the SOCIOLOGY OF EDUCATION (see CULTURAL CAPITAL). He has drawn on the work of a diverse range of theorists, such as MARX, DURKHEIM and WEBER, to develop a distinctive theory of the maintenance of social order. His major works include *Outline of a Theory of Practice* (1977), *The School as a Conservative Force* (1966) and *Reproduction in Education, Society and Culture* (1977). Other influential works by him include *Distinction* (1984) and *Homo Academicus* (1988). See also HABITUS, STRUCTURE AND AGENCY.

bourgeoisie (MARXISM) in capitalist societies, the social class comprising owners of capital. Thus, CAPITALIST is primarily an economic category, and bourgeoisie a social one. Non-Marxist sociological approaches to SOCIAL STRATIFICATION tend not to use the term, not least because the debates around the MANAGERIAL REVOLUTION in twentieth century capitalism raise the question as to whether a social class based on the ownership of capital any longer exists. In more general usage, the term *bourgeois* is often used to describe the lifestyles of the MIDDLE-CLASS(ES). Williams (1976) has a useful discussion of changing and differing usages of the word. See also, ÉLITE, UPPER CLASS, RULING CLASS.

bourgeoisification see EMBOURGEOISEMENT, EMBOURGEOISEMENT THESIS.

Bowlby, John (1907–90) the founder of infant-mother ATTACHMENT theory (Bowlby, 1958; *Attachment and Loss*, 1969). Bowlby trained as a child analyst under the supervision of Melanie KLEIN and worked as a psychiatrist at the London Child Guidance Clinic. The original spur for Bowlby's investigation of the nature of the tie between a mother and her child came from the World Health Organization, concerned that many children were suffering from the adverse effects of care in institutions, particularly as a result of the disruptions of the 1939–45 war. He published his first findings in 1951, concentrating on the role maternal care played in shaping the child's subsequent state of mental health. In developing a theory of attachment, Bowlby drew on his experience in the field of psychoanalysis, but his approach was unique since it combined the retrospective psychoanalytical approach to childhood experiences with ethological data from scientific studies of the development of other species. Some of Bowlby's original ideas (e.g. MATERNAL DEPRIVATION) have been questioned in the light of more recent evidence, but his theory has provided the framework for all subsequent investigations into the child's attachment to the mother figure. Bowlby's attachment theory has strongly influenced the disciplines of psychology, psychiatry and social work, and his popular writings have shaped the way many perceive the psychological development and welfare of the child.

Brahman, see CASTE.

Braudel, Fernand (1902–85) influential historian, associated with the ANNALES SCHOOL. His best-known work, translated as *The Mediterranean and the Mediterranean World of the Age of Philip II* (2 vols., 1972–73, originally 1949, expanded in 1966), exemplifies the approach characteristic of members of the school, which is to move beyond conventional political histories by focusing in detail on the material basis of political events, while also tracing their global interconnections. In his analysis of the change in the direction of Spain's foreign policy under Philip II (towards the Atlantic and away from the Mediterranean), demographic and cultural as well as economic data are combined with more conventional political analysis. Braudel was interested in the different pace of social change in different eras and in different areas of social reality. Beneath the short-term 'events' uppermost in conventional histories, there are longer-term changes which take centuries or millennia. In these terms, in *Civilization and Capitalism* (trans. 1973–82), Braudel presents an account of the development of the world economy from the Middle Ages to the Industrial Revolution. Critics of Braudel complain that, in de-emphasizing the independent significance of political 'events', his work may have gone too far in redressing the balance between social and political history. For others, Braudel's work has been inspirational, leading modern comparative sociological historians such as WALLERSTEIN to use it as a model for their own.

Braverman thesis see PROLETARIANIZATION, LABOUR PROCESS, DESKILLING.

bricolage the process of transforming the meaning of objects or symbols through novel uses or unconventional arrangements of unrelated things. The term is used in CULTURAL STUDIES; see FASHION.

Bricolage is a French term and was introduced, in a somewhat different context, by Claude LÉVI-STRAUSS in *The Savage Mind*, and subsequently used by his translators who could find no suitable English equivalent. He used it to refer to the (*bricoleur's*) practice of creating things out of whatever materials come to hand – the structure and the outcome being more important than the constituent parts which themselves are changed through the act of creation.

brideprice and bridewealth (ANTHROPOLOGY) a payment from the groom's kin to the bride's kin at marriage. The term 'brideprice' is rarely used now because of the implication that the woman is being purchased. It is considered to be an inappropriate Western metaphor for a practice that occurs in many cultures, usually those with PATRILINEAL DESCENT systems.

Buddhism a Far Eastern ethical religion deriving from the teachings of Buddha, 'the enlightened one', a Hindu nobleman in 6th-century BC Nepal. Subsequently, Buddhism has spread widely and has taken several forms. The road to salvation, according to Buddha, is self-denial, self-discipline and meditation, with the goal of escape from the endless cycle of reincarnation which would otherwise occur. *Nirvana*, or complete spiritual fulfilment, is the ultimate objective. As such, the orientation of Buddhism has often been, in Weber's terminology, 'other-worldly'. At times, however, Buddhism has also been a highly political religion, as in Lamaism or as part of protest movements within Third World societies.

built environment see SOCIOLOGY OF THE BUILT ENVIRONMENT.

Bukharin, Nikolai (1888–1938) a leading member of the Bolshevik Party before and after the 1917 Russian Revolution. He wrote on IMPERIALISM and, while he had disagreements with Lenin, was regarded as one of the most brilliant young members of the leadership. He took a major role in the economic debates of the 1920s, eventually favouring the gradual road to socialism represented by the New Economic Policy introduced in 1921. He edited the daily party paper from 1917 to 1929, but when he opposed STALIN's forced industrialization programme he was removed from the editorship. He continued to be a leading member of the party, but was eventually expelled from it in 1937 and then executed during the period of the Moscow trials.

bulimia see ANOREXIA NERVOSA.

bureaucracy

1 a type of organization in which administration is based upon impersonal, written rules and a hierarchy of offices; there is a clear distinction between 'the office' and its incumbent, and official positions are filled on the basis of formal qualifications. The concept was first systematically defined by WEBER (see IDEAL TYPE), who provided the frame of reference for much of the sociological research into modern large-scale organizations.
2 (literally) rule by officials, and hence bureaucrats or 'the bureaucracy', denoting the people who implement the rules or actually 'govern'. This was the original use of the term by the French physiocrats in the 18th century, which was taken up in political theory rather than sociology (Albrow, 1970).
3 (pejorative) denoting organizations which are inefficient due to cumbersome rules, 'red tape' and time-wasting procedures. The idea that bureaucracy is synonymous with inefficiency is frequently alluded to in everyday language, and also in subsequent criticism of Weber's ideal type of 'rational bureaucracy'.

Weber locates the analysis of bureaucracy within a theory of power, DOMINATION and legitimacy (see LEGITIMATE AUTHORITY) in which

modern rational bureaucracy is most closely approximated in 'legal-rational forms of domination' (Weber, 1922) dependent upon the development of a money economy, the free market, legal codification and the expansion of administration (particularly in the STATE). Weber's ideal type of bureaucracy involves:
(a) domination based upon written rules in a hierarchy of specialized offices;
(b) recruitment based upon qualifications;
(c) offices that are impersonal and clearly distinguished from incumbents; they are also segregated from private life and private property.

Consequently, office holding is a 'vocation' based upon expert training, offering a salary with pension and tenure, and a career ladder in which promotion depends upon seniority and/or ability.

In its pure form, rational bureaucracy is seen as technically superior to all previous forms of administration (such as patriarchal, patrimonialism) by virtue of its speed, predictability, precision and dispassionate treatment of 'cases' without regard to personal considerations. Thus Weber distinguished between rational bureaucracy and earlier forms of bureaucracy in ancient societies which were based upon personal allegiance to the ruler and payment in kind. Modern bureaucracy pervades state administration and all the major institutions in capitalist society, including the military, the church, education and private enterprise.

The spread of bureaucracy exemplified the process of RATIONALIZATION in the modern world, with paradoxical consequences. On the one hand, bureaucracy is 'formally rational' and 'efficient' like a machine, but it also carries with it a threat to democracy and human freedom which is dehumanizing, and the denial of fundamental values and of what Weber called *substantive rationality* (see RATIONALITY). In this sense, the ultimate foundation of bureaucracy is irrational.

Weber's pessimism about the advance of bureaucratic power under capitalism is reflected in his view of bureaucracy as inevitable, even under socialism. The only question becomes 'who runs the bureaucratic machine?' (compare IRON LAW OF OLIGARCHY). The conflict between bureaucracy and democracy was a theme running through the works of élite theorists such as MOSCA (1884), as well as the idea of a 'managerial revolution' (Burnham, 1943). See also FASCISM, CORPORATISM, ELITE THEORY, MANAGERIAL REVOLUTION.

MARX, in contrast to Weber, limited his brief discussion of bureaucracy to an aspect of a theory of the state. Bureaucracy is parasitic, serving the interests of the ruling class as an instrument of class domination; it has no autonomous basis of power but is dependent upon the power of private capital. In a future socialist society, bureaucracy, like the state, would 'wither away' (see STATE, SOCIALISM, BOLSHEVIK, RULING CLASS). The differences between Marx and Weber over the nature of power and class have provided the basis for much of the subsequent debate about the power structure of Soviet and East-European societies, in which bureaucracy was deeply entrenched (see LENIN, TROTSKY, STATE CAPITALISM AND STATE MONOPOLY CAPITALISM). The problem of the relation between bureaucracy and socialism was clearly portrayed by Djilas (1957) who saw the party bureaucracy in Eastern Europe as a NEW CLASS based upon control of the state rather than private property (see also ORIENTAL DESPOTISM for a similar debate over the significance of bureaucratic power in relation to Marx's analysis of Asiatic societies).

Thus Weber's influence is evident in the analysis of the contradictions of socialism. Conversely, one of the most important strands of criticism of Weber's bureaucracy has come from the Marxist perspective. For example, MARCUSE (1968) argued that Weber's discussion of formal rationality paid scant attention to the uses of bureaucracy as a form of capitalist domination because it assumed that the techniques of bureaucratic control were neutral and inevitable. This raises the question of whether it is possible to talk about the 'formal rationality' of administration without reference to the purposes or goals to which the bureaucratic administration is put. In a similar vein, the Marxist critique of Weber stresses the class basis of bureaucratic domination and therefore its temporary nature as opposed to Weber's pessimism. Weber's emphasis on the indestructibility of bureaucracy was also criticized from a different point of view in a famous essay by GOULDNER (1955a) which criticized the 'metaphysical pathos' inherent in Weber's fatalistic formulations which present bureaucracy as negating all possibility of human choice, ignoring the possibility of alternative forms of bureaucracy more consistent with democracy. For example, in another study, Gouldner contrasts 'representative' with 'punishment-centred' bureaucracy (GOULDNER, 1954).

Post-Weber, the study of bureaucracy has included a large number of empirical studies and criticisms of the ideal type which form the basis for modern ORGANIZATION THEORY (see also ORGANIZATION). The results of this type of research indicate that actual bureaucracies do not operate in accordance with Weber's ideal type, due to the existence of informal structures and the conflicting interests of subgroups within bureaucracies, and the inflexibility of formal rules which lead to inefficiency.
For example, the studies undertaken by MERTON and by Selznick (1966) have become minor classics on the way in which bureaucratic rules may be dysfunctional and give rise to unintended consequences. The rules become ends in themselves rather than means to ends (see GOAL DISPLACEMENT, FUNCTIONALISM). Blau's study of a federal law-enforcement agency (1955) demonstrates that informal practices are more efficient than strict adherence to in flexible formal rules. In addition, formal rules may be used by organizational members to further their own interests in opposition to official goals (Crozier, 1964).

Post-Weber research has generated an interesting literature in its own right, but its significance as a critique of Weber is still a controversial issue (Albrow, 1970; Mouzelis, 1975). There is no doubt that much of the criticism involved misunderstandings about Weber's approach, and reduced Weber's study of the wider social consequences of bureaucracy to a narrow concern with organizational efficiency. Confusion also enters into the evaluation of the ideal type – how it is to be assessed and whether it conceals hypotheses. However, even if the ideal type is vindicated, problems remain with Weber's formulations, namely the absence of any 'meaningful understanding' (a method advocated by Weber) of the actions of subordinates in bureaucracies, and whether alternative ideal types of bureaucracy prove more useful.

Recent research has seen a reintroduction of Weberian themes in terms of the critique of LABOUR PROCESS theory and managerial control. The analysis of internal LABOUR MARKETS and bureaucratic control has been used to modify the focus of labour process on the logic of DESKILLING based upon scientific management. The earlier, postwar, narrow analysis of organizational efficiency has given way to concerns about the development of capitalism and structures of domination which were central to Marx and Weber. See also MCDONALDIZATION.

business cycle see TRADE CYCLE OR BUSINESS CYCLE.

busing the transportation by bus of children of a particular ethnic group from one residential area into another residential area of different ethnic mix, with the aim of achieving an ethnic or 'racial' balance in schools. The term has its origin in the US, and the practice has been largely confined to that country.

Busing began after the 1954 Supreme Court ruling (*Brown v. Board of Education*) that segregated education was illegal in the US and that separate facilities for BLACK and white children could not provide equal opportunities. As a means of creating equal educational opportunity busing has been the subject of fierce controversy in the US. Busing was introduced on a very small scale within a few Local Education Authorities in the UK in the 1970s, but was soon abandoned. It is now being used in South Africa.

Butler, Judith (1956–) U.S. feminist scholar, whose best known work, *Gender Trouble* (1990) and *Bodies That Matter* (1993), argues that feminism mistakenly followed the same route as the patriarchal meta-narratives it tried to overturn by treating women and men in fixed sex/gender categories. She maintained that this approach reinforced the existing binary view of gender relations, contributing to the repetition of old essentialist identity constructs. Butler explains that gender is performative – a role that is acted out by socially constituted subjects who merely repeat a culturally naturalized discourse of 'compulsory heterosexuality' which aligns anatomical sex with sexual desire. This process, she states, contributes to the devaluation of other sexualities and restricts possibilities for sex/gender exploration by maintaining that we have an 'authentic' inner essence that dictates our identity formation. Influenced by the deconstructive and psychoanalytic work of theorists such as Michel FOUCAULT, Julia KRISTEVA and Jacques LACAN, she argues that the answer to this problem lies in removing sex/gender as a restrictive code. Butler promotes parody as a way to subvert established conventions. Here, individuals can perform flexible identities that resist dominant practices. Her theories have been widely adopted within the growing rhetoric of QUEER THEORY, which finds her use of parody a potent political strategy for destabilizing existing heterosexual norms.

C

cacique see CAUDILLISMO.

cadre 1 the permanent establishment forming the framework or nucleus of a regiment.
2 by extension, an established political unit, or a member of such a political unit. The term is applied especially to élite groupings within communist parties.

capital 1 the accumulated wealth embodied in the MEANS OF PRODUCTION or available, or potentially available, for the creation or purchase of the means of production. For MARX, capital is privately owned wealth or VALUE used to generate SURPLUS VALUE (see CAPITALISM AND CAPITALIST MODE OF PRODUCTION).
2 in a more general sense, any 'asset', financial or otherwise, immediately usable, or potentially usable, as a source of income (see also HUMAN CAPITAL, CULTURAL CAPITAL).
While capital in sense 2 exists in all societies, in the more restricted sense 1, as used by Marx, it involves a society-wide dominance of private capital which is specific to capitalism.
Marx insists that capital must not be seen as a 'thing' (see REIFICATION, COMMODITY FETISHISM) but as a socioeconomic relation which only appears thing-like (see APPEARANCE AND REALITY).

capital accumulation see ACCUMULATION OF CAPITAL.

capitalism and **capitalist mode of production**

That form of economy in which:
(a) the MEANS OF PRODUCTION (CAPITAL) are privately owned and privately controlled;
(b) LABOUR POWER is purchased by the payment of money wages by the owners of capital (capitalists);
(c) the goal of production is the making of profit by the sale of COMMODITIES in a competitive free market;
(d) profit is appropriated by the owners of capital (see SURPLUS VALUE);
(e) the system is inherently dynamic, given its basis in the competitive accumulation of capital (see ACCUMULATION OF CAPITAL).

Capitalism can also be described as 'generalized commodity production' (Mandel, 1962), in the important sense that 'domestic consumption', as well as 'production', issues in commodities, since human labour is also a commodity.

For MARX and for WEBER, whose work has exerted a profound influence on the conceptualization and understanding of capitalism, *capitalism* and the *capitalist mode of production* (the latter term is the one most used by Marx) are IDEAL-TYPE concepts. Thus, in practice, no society or economy will be found which corresponds exactly to the pure type. Actual economies will usually be found to combine elements from several different theoretical forms of MODES OF PRODUCTION. For example, Western societies, though predominantly capitalist, are in actuality MIXED ECONOMIES, combining elements of socialist and capitalist economic arrangements, although they may still be seen as predominantly CAPITALIST SOCIETIES. Thus, capitalism takes varying forms which can often be expressed as involving systematic departures from the pure-type of competitive capitalism, e.g. MONOPOLY CAPITALISM and ADVANCED CAPITALISM.

While they agreed on many aspects of the definition of capitalism, Marx and Weber differed considerably in the details of their characterization of capitalism. For Marx, whilst the surface appearances of capitalist market relations suggest that this form of economy is 'fair', the underlying reality is that the central economic and social relations between capitalists and labour involve EXPLOITATION (see also CAPITALIST LABOUR CONTRACT, ALIENATION). For Weber, notwithstanding that capitalism has irrational features, the central feature of Western capitalism is its 'rational' character in contrast with earlier forms of economy (see RATIONALIZATION, TYPES OF SOCIAL ACTION).

As well as a concern to characterize capitalism as an economic and social system, interest in sociology has also focused on the origins of capitalism, its relations with other types of economic system, (see DEPENDENCY THEORY) and the forces tending to bring about its transformation or replacement.

Origins of capitalism. Whereas Marx emphasized the existence of inherent features within the economic relations of FEUDALISM as leading to the emergence of capitalism, many other sociologists, including Weber, have stressed the independent influence of ideas (see PROTESTANT ETHIC). A further, but disputed, theoretical approach explains the initial appearance of capitalism in Western rather than Asian societies in terms of the existence of decisive environmental and cultural differences between East and West (see ASIATIC MODE OF PRODUCTION AND ASIATIC SOCIETY, HYDRAULIC SOCIETY, ORIENTAL DESPOTISM). Significant debates also exist within Marxist theory and historiography between those who emphasize inherent features of feudalism in the TRANSITION FROM FEUDALISM TO CAPITALISM (e.g. Dobb, 1946) and those for whom more 'incidental' features are decisive (e.g. the influx of gold from the new world or demographic changes, including epidemics which change the balance of power within feudalism). Much hinges on such a division of view within Marxism. For whilst the former position makes it possible to sustain a model of inherent forces in social change in which capitalism can everywhere be expected to replace precapitalist social formations, a focus on more accidental features of change throws into doubt any such assumption.

Transformation of capitalism and transition to socialism. Extensive controversy also surrounds the factors which may lead to the transformation of capitalism. Within classical versions of Marxism, ADVANCED CAPITALISM was regarded as containing inherent contradictions (e.g. increasing cut-throat competition between capitalists, increasing tendency to crisis, increasing class divisions) expected to lead to proletarian revolution and the replacement of capitalism by socialism. Where actual replacement of capitalism has occurred, however, this has usually been politically engineered and taken place in more peripheral economies, without Marx's conditions for such transitions being wholly present. For Weber, and for many modern sociologists, no inherent tendency to final crisis in capitalism can be assumed (compare ORGANIC COMPOSITION OF CAPITAL, TENDENCY TO DECLINING RATE OF PROFIT). On the contrary, capitalism's capacity for self-adjustment is emphasized by many theorists, with recurrent economic crises seen as playing a role in this adjustment rather than sounding the death knell of capitalism (see also CRISES OF CAPITALISM).

Capitalism and 'postcapitalism'. Claims that a separation of ownership and control has occurred in modern Western societies have led to the suggestion by some theorists that these societies might be better referred to as 'managerialist' or even 'postcapitalist' rather than capitalist societies (see MANAGERIAL REVOLUTION). For most theorists, however, the essential features of capitalist societies (e.g. private ownership of the means of production, production for profit, a managerial class which still functions as a capitalist class, the ecological unfriendliness of capitalism) remain, although changes in the form of capitalism, resulting from its inherently dynamic and unstable nature, are acknowledged (see also CULTURAL CONTRADICTIONS OF CAPITALISM, FISCAL CRISIS IN THE CAPITALIST STATE, LEGITIMATION CRISIS). Alternatives to capitalism, however, are seen as similarly problematic (see SOCIALISM, COMMUNISM).

At the turn of the millennium, the ascendancy of capitalism has never been so great. Although its problems and contradictions remain – see FOURTH WORLD, GLOBALIZATION – the dynamism and effectiveness of capitalism, plus its global power, make its continuation (albeit with continued adjustment) the most likely option for the foreseeable future (e.g. see W. Hutton and A. GIDDENS, eds, *On the Edge – Living with Global Capitalism*, 2000).

capitalist an owner of CAPITAL, who may or may not be directly involved in production. See CAPITALISM AND CAPITALIST MODE OF PRODUCTION.

capitalist labour contract the exchange of *wage-labour* (in strict terms, labour-time or LABOUR-POWER) for wages between workers and capitalists. According to MARX, while 'formally free' and apparently fair, when fully analysed this relationship is seen to be 'exploitive'. The reason for this is that the capitalist expropriates the SURPLUS VALUE generated by labour which remains once the wages required for the reproduction of labour have been paid. The capacity of capitalists to do this arises from:
(a) their ownership of the MEANS OF PRODUCTION;
(b) the existence of a RESERVE ARMY OF LABOUR, which together with the competition between capitalists, tends to depress wages towards the subsistence level;
(c) the greater capacity of capitalists than workers to withstand strikes and lockouts;
(d) the greater capacity of capitalists to enlist the support of the state.

It is clear that Marx's analysis underestimated the power of trades unions and governments, as well as the competitive power of skilled labour, which historically in Western capitalist societies has raised wages well above subsistence levels. On the other hand, inequalities and a fundamental lack of symmetry in the market position and bargaining power in the relationship between capitalist and labour remain. Accordingly, many non-Marxist sociologists (e.g. GIDDENS, 1981), as well as Marxist sociologists, have continued to regard the asymmetry in the capitalist labour contract as a distinctive feature of the class structure of capitalist societies.

capitalist society *or* **capitalism** any society based on a capitalist economy or where capitalist ownership of the means of production plays a principal role. See CAPITALISM AND CAPITALIST MODE OF PRODUCTION.

capitalist state (MARXISM) the form of STATE in capitalist society which, according to some versions of Marxism, operates predominantly in the interests of CAPITALISM, contributing directly to its reproduction. For Miliband (1966), for example, any apparent PLURALISM in the state institutions and political representation within capitalist societies can be discounted, since the fundamental fact remains that state institutions reproduce capitalism (see also RULING CLASS). Against this, however, it is evident that the form of the state in capitalist societies varies widely, differing according to the specific institutional forms of the connections between the economy, CIVIL SOCIETY, and the state, and that these different kinds of state – liberal-democratic, totalitarian-fascist, etc. – have major social and economic significance. See also LIBERAL DEMOCRACY, TOTALITARIANISM.

carceral organization any organization, such as the prison system or mental hospitals, in which individuals are held confined for punishment or correction and prevented from 'normal' social relations in the wider society. The existence of such specialized institutions of incarceration is held by some to be a particular feature of modern societies (e.g. FOUCAULT, 1975). See also TOTAL INSTITUTION OR TOTAL ORGANIZATION, SURVEILLANCE.

care 1 the work involved in supporting people who, because of physical frailty, chronic illness or other forms of incapacity and disability, are incapable of leading an autonomous existence.
2 other kinds of carework, e.g. in child-rearing (see CHILD CARE) and DOMESTIC LABOUR. This should be distinguished from care in sense 1.

Care in sense 1 operates over a wide range of social relations. A clear dividing line can be drawn between formal and informal care (see Abrams, 1978) as it exists in contemporary industrial societies. *Formal care* refers to services provided by agents of organization (statutory, voluntary and/or private) to people within clearly defined categories of need. *Informal care* is personally directed towards certain people who have a social relationship with their *carer* – usually a family member, and most often a spouse (Parker, 1993), or female relative.

Feminist sociologists (see also FEMINISM) have had a major impact on the understanding of care and caring relationships. They have argued that caring is 'a gendered concept' and that women constitute the majority of carers both informally, in the private sphere, and as low-paid care workers ('care assistants') in the formal sector (Finch and Groves, 1982; Ungerson, 1987; Lewis and Meredith, 1988). Studies of caring have examined the complex reasons why women care and the particular problems and difficulties they face. Social policies involving decarceration and COMMUNITY CARE, the decline of neighbour-hood and COMMUNITY associated with increasing SOCIAL (and geographical) MOBILITY, have placed an increasing burden on individual women carers. There is some evidence that women are reluctant to enter caring relationships with female relatives but lack viable alternatives (Cotterill, 1994). Recent research using data from the 1980 British General Household Survey has also pointed to the significant contribution made by male carers, particularly men who care for their wives (Arber and Gilbert, 1989).

carer see CARE.

career 1 the sequence(s) of professional or occupational positions in the life course of an individual.

2 (by analogy with 1) any individual pattern or progression in a nonoccupational life course, e.g., the 'deviant career' of the drug user (BECKER, 1953) or the MORAL CAREER of the mental patient (GOFFMAN, 1964).

Occupational careers may either consist of a sequenced progression in terms of a hierarchy of status and income (as typical of many middle-class careers, see PROFESSIONS), or lack any clear structure or progression, as is more usual for manual workers. Gender differences affecting access to careers has been a recent topic of importance in the sociology of labour markets (e.g. Dex, 1985). See LABOUR MARKET, DUAL LABOUR MARKET.

cargo cult a form of MILLENARIAN OR MILLENNIAL MOVEMENT widespread in Melanesia in the modern colonial era, in which followers of the CULT seek to achieve the delivery of cargoes of Western consumer goods by means of MAGIC and RITUAL, e.g. the building of 'airstrips' and models of planes. Such cults involve the combination of Western and native beliefs in a context of ANOMIE and disruption of the local culture, sometimes by successive waves of colonialism. Based on assumptions in the native religion about the supernatural origins of material resources as well as on an inadequate knowledge of the Western culture, when more adequate knowledge became available, these movements have tended to transform into politico-religious movements (see Worsley, *The Trumpet Shall Sound*, 1968).

carnival historical and continuing forms of social ritual which allow temporary reversals of the social order in which social rules (e.g. sexual mores) are transgressed and mockery made of the rich and powerful. See also LIMINALITY, BAKHTIN, ROLE REVERSAL.

case study the study of a single instance of a phenomenon either for its own sake (e.g. a particular person or a strike), or as an exemplar or PARADIGM case of a general phenomenon, perhaps as a test of a general proposition (e.g. de TOCQUEVILLE's study of America, 1835–40).

casework a method of investigation, care and advice used in SOCIAL WORK and some counselling situations. It involves looking at current personal problems within the context of the client's personal history. Crucial to this is the keeping of a record of the interactions between the social worker and the client by the social worker, in order to illuminate the complex of causes and effects involved in the client's current problems.

cash crop any agricultural crop grown for the market rather than for subsistence.

Historically, the increasing importance of production for markets – including such phenomena as PLANTATION agriculture, AGRIBUSINESS, MONOCULTURE – is a central feature of social and economic development with very wide implications, including changes in LAND TENURE and forms of labour. As well as whatever new opportunities production for market brings, it also introduces into previously largely subsistence PEASANT economies new uncertainties and disruptions associated with market forces, where 'natural' disasters such as FAMINE from pestilence, flood or drought had formerly posed the main problems.

In the THIRD WORLD, a process of substitution of cash crops for others has been associated with processes of MODERNIZATION or DEPENDENCY and is often under the influence of foreign markets and foreign corporations. However, in Third World countries, with the growth of URBANIZATION, internal markets are often just as important. Whilst in some cases it is possible to see the substitution of some crops for others, e.g. carnations and coffee for maize and beans in Colombia, at other times the same crop may be both a subsistence and a cash crop, e.g. rice in many Asian countries. In this case, the process of movement to cash cropping may involve fewer varieties of crops being grown, having a similar effect of forcing the producer into the market to buy food previously grown for subsistence. See also SUBSISTENCE ECONOMY OR SOCIETY.

cash nexus a concept that states the centrality of money relationships underpinning social relations especially in capitalist societies. The idea is associated with MARX.

caste

A form of SOCIAL STRATIFICATION which involves a system of hierarchically ranked, closed, endogamous strata, the membership of which is ascribed, and between which contact is restricted and mobility theoretically impossible. Although it reflects economic inequalities, by virtue of the occupations typically followed by, or permitted to, members, caste stratification is ultimately rooted in noneconomic criteria. In its purest form, in Hindu India, the caste principle is religious: castes are ranked in accordance with the degree of 'ritual purity' ascribed to members and to their activities. Some commentators, however, extend the term to cover situations in which divisions are underpinned by racial antipathies, supported perhaps by legal sanctions, as in the cases of South Africa (see APARTHEID) and, until recently, the segregated southern United States (e.g. see Dollard's *Caste and Class in a Southern Town*, 1937). The etymology of the term caste is also disputed. 'Caste' derives from the Portuguese *casta*, but whether this was originally simply a general term for class or category, or more specifically associated with conceptions of cleanliness and purity, remains unclear.

Historically, the most developed form, and some would argue the only true form, of caste stratification has occurred in India in association with HINDUISM. More than 3000 years old, the origins of this system are obscure. They probably lie in the twin bases of ethnicity and occupational specialization. India's vast subcontinental area was settled by a variety of ethnic groups, and relations between them were often shaped by conquest and by the fact that they carried specialized occupational skills. The caste system, therefore, appears to have developed out of patterns of military, political and social subordination, occupational specialization and ethnic antipathies involving ritual and taboo barriers to contact. From these, the development of the system was guaranteed by two facts: firstly, the groupings provided suitable units for collectivizing the rulers' arrangements for gathering taxes and tributes; secondly, there existed a powerful priesthood (the *Brahmans*) which was capable of elaborating the taboos into a consistent body of ritual regulations which could be enforced in alliance with the secular rulers.

The system which the *Brahmans* perfected was founded on five main divisions, four caste groups (*Varna*) and an outcaste group, the *untouchables.* These were, and are, ranked in a hierarchy of ritual purity derived from the lifestyle and occupations permitted to, and monopolized by, their members; the highest castes are those of the *Brahmans* and the *Khasatriyas,* the latter being the secular and military ruler and landlord caste. Beneath these come the castes of the entrepreneurial middle classes (the *Vaishyas*) and the workers, servants and slaves (the *Shudras*). Finally, and in strict terms, outside the hierarchy stand the outcastes or untouchables (*Harijans*) who, performing only the most degrading occupational tasks, are considered to be ritually impure. The varna, however, constitute only the broadest divisions within the system. More significant in determining everyday social practices is the subdivision of the varna into several thousand, usually regionally-based, individual castes and subcastes, the *Jati* (strictly translated, separate 'breeds' and 'species'). Each of these jati has its own social rank and body of caste regulations, designed, firstly, to maintain the ritual exclusiveness of the group by restricting or prohibiting marriage, COMMENSALITY, and social and physical contact across caste boundaries. Secondly, they ritually regulate the occupations, and the techniques associated with them, which members are allowed to follow. These regulations are supported by temporal as well as spiritual sanctions derived from the punitive powers of the caste authorities, public opinion and Hindu theodicy.

Hindu theodicy is associated with a belief in reincarnation. Individuals' caste positions are held to be either a reward or a punishment for their fidelity, or lack of it, in observing the rules of the castes of their previous incarnations. Since caste rank was congenital and fixed during any one incarnation, the only hope of upward mobility lay in individuals securing a higher rebirth through the faithful discharge of caste obligations. This provided a powerful incentive for adherence to caste rules, especially since violations were punished in the present incarnation and brought the certainty of a degraded rebirth in the next. In Hindu thinking, two general sets of doctrines underpin this framework of spiritual and social control: *dharma,* the overall order of all things natural and social, including social behaviour and social relations proper to a member of a particular caste, and *karma,* the general doctrine of reincarnation.

WEBER traced the overwhelming traditionalism of the Hindu peoples to these sources. He also argued that the caste system hindered the development of CAPITALISM in India for at least three reasons: firstly, because the divisions of the caste system prevented the urban 'middle classes' from combining to establish the rights of freedom of persons and property on which capitalism is based; secondly, because the multiplicity of special caste laws, framed in the religious interest, prevented the emergence of a uniform and 'universalistic' legal system suitable to capitalist development; thirdly, because the ritual stereotyping of occupations and techniques associated with caste hindered the mobility of labour and the application of new technologies.

The reality of caste, however, is different from its theoretical injunctions. One difference of importance is the existence of the process known as *sanskritization,* in which particular jati may succeed in raising their location in the status hierarchy by gradually assuming the behaviour and beliefs appropriate to members of a higher caste. In practice, somewhat at odds with Weber's view, the industrial development that has taken place in India since the 1900s has meant that patterns of work behaviour have sometimes adjusted to new economic requirements rather than remaining constrained by caste. As a consequence, the relationship between the caste system and economic development must be regarded as more flexible than sometimes assumed. Officially, since independence in 1947, caste divisions no longer receive state backing. In practice, their social significance remains considerable. Among the standard general works on caste are: V. Bougle, *Essays on the Caste System* (1970) and L. Dumont, *Homo Hierarchicus, the Caste System and its Implications* (1970). See also CLASS, SOCIAL CLOSURE; compare ESTATES, SLAVERY.

Castells, Manuel (1942–) Spanish-born sociologist, who first rose to prominence in the 1970s as a Marxian urban sociologist, especially researching and theorizing the role of URBAN SOCIAL MOVEMENTS. Increasingly operating, both in his teaching and his research, on a global stage, subsequently Castells has written more in a post-Marxist mode, focusing on the transformation of the global. *The Informational City* (1989) marked a transition in his work, in that he argued that developments in INFORMATION TECHNOLOGY were transforming patterns of regional development. His *magnum opus*, the three volumes of *The Information Age: Economy Society and Culture* (1996–8) have been widely hailed as a *tour de force*. The work surveys the information-driven, post cold war global economy (see also NETWORK SOCIETY), analysing both its dynamism (especially of new cultural regions such as the Asian Pacific) and its new patterns of inequality.

cataclysm a major physical and/or social upheaval that disrupts a previous ecological and/or social order to such an extent as to lead to the extinction of species and/or the elimination of a society. For example, it has been suggested that rather than merely endogenous social factors, forces such as climatic change (e.g. from volcanic eruption, meteorites) and/or epidemic diseases may have been responsible for periodic cataclysmic changes in social life. Such events as these, it has been suggested, may be behind the collapse of some South American societies and the replacement of feudal by capitalist society.

categorical discrimination see DISCRIMINATION.

categorical imperative see KANT, HYPOTHETICAL IMPERATIVE.

category 1 a conceptual class or set.
2 (PHILOSOPHY) a fundamental class or kind (e.g. ARISTOTLE's 10 classes of all modes of being).
3 *pl.* KANT's a priori modes of understanding (e.g. 'causality', 'substance') which he believed shaped all our perceptions of the world.

catharsis release of emotional energy, producing relief from tension. The term is most specifically used in PSYCHOANALYSIS where it describes the process in which repressed memories and emotions are brought into consciousness, sometimes involving transference to the analyst. In thus making them explicit, and the patient reexperiencing them consciously, they are depowered and the personality becomes freer.

caudillismo a system of rule by one man using violence or the threat of violence for political ends (a Spanish word used in the 19th-century to refer to regional or national military rulers who emerged in Latin America after independence from Spain). The term is now more generally used to refer to localized, powerful individuals who may call upon followers, either within or outside a state system, to use violence or the threat of violence to coerce others. In Mexico *cacique* means the same, or is the preferred term, when applied to local, rather than regional or national, power brokers.

causal adequacy see POSTULATE OF ADEQUACY.

causal explanation see EXPLANATION.

causality and causal relationship the relationship between two events, such that one brings about the other. Usually a causal relationship is claimed where:
(a) a spatial and temporal contiguity exists between two events;
(b) one event (the cause) precedes the other;
(c) the second event appears unlikely to have happened without the first event having occurred.

Where it also appears that a particular type of event always or usually occurs in a particular way, i.e. a 'lawlike' relationship, this is usually regarded as further reinforcing a claim that a causal relationship exists. It should be noted, however, that a lawlike association may exist between two events *without* this implying a causal relationship. A distinction can also be drawn between an 'immediate cause' (e.g. striking a match to light a fire) and more underlying 'explanatory' causation (e.g. the presence of oxygen in the atmosphere).

Philosophers, especially recently, have not been happy with the concepts of cause and causality. The concepts are difficult to reconcile with conceptions of logical implications in classical LOGIC. For example, if we refer to an increase in prices caused by increased taxation, the increase in taxation is neither a 'necessary' nor a 'sufficient' condition for an increase in prices. Furthermore, epistemologically, the provisional nature of scientific knowledge always means that claimed 'causal relationships' can never be stated conclusively.

Further issues concerning sociology specifically are:

(a) whether the sense in which 'cause' and 'causation' arise in connection with purposive actions is compatible with conceptions of causality in physical science (e.g. see WINCH); and
(b) whether FUNCTIONAL EXPLANATION is a form of causal analysis. See also EXPLANATION.

causal modelling a family of techniques of statistical modelling aimed at providing specification and testing of the causal relations underlying correlations between a number of variables. Based on the work of Herbert Simon (1957a), and pioneered in sociology especially by Hubert Blalock (1961), the approach requires the researcher to formulate and test successive theoretical models of the causal relations between variables, seeking a model which best fits the data. Included under the general category of causal modelling are PATH ANALYSIS and LOG LINEAR ANALYSIS. Causal modelling has been criticized as dependent on initial assumptions which cannot be regarded as fully tested by the data. Technical sophistication may disguise this. Nonetheless, causal modelling is important in making possible a more satisfactory exploration of causal relations than is achieved in simpler forms of correlation analysis.

causal relationship see CAUSALITY AND CAUSAL RELATIONSHIP.

cause any immediate, or more indirect, factor precipitating an outcome. See also CAUSALITY AND CAUSAL RELATIONSHIP.

census a government-sponsored, universal and obligatory survey of all individuals in a geographical area. The British Census is a major source of SECONDARY DATA because:
(a) it offers data on a comprehensive range of topics, many of which are not included in other surveys;
(b) its large size permits the analysis of some topics in greater detail;
(c) its size and scope permit the analysis of numerous interrelationships.

With the introduction of punched-card processing in 1911, and the use of computers in 1961, the amount of information that can be collected and processed has been dramatically increased.

The Census Act, 1920, requires that a census be taken in Britain at intervals of not less than five years. With the exception of the 1966 Census (so far the only quinquennial census), censuses have been taken in Britain since 1801 (except in 1941 when there was no census).

The earliest censuses (1801–31) took the form of simple head counts. Self-completion forms were introduced in 1841. Since 1961 the census has involved most households completing a simple questionnaire and every tenth household completing a more detailed questionnaire.

The census has a number of important applications for the sociologist, including:
(a) studies of SOCIAL STRATIFICATION;
(b) analysis of changing trends reflected in housing, education, work, etc.;
(c) studies of particular groups. Following demand from local authorities, academic researchers, market-research organizations, central government, and other organizations, Small Area Statistics have been introduced, based on the enumeration districts which comprise 500 people on average, which may also be aggregated to gain a picture of a particular area such as a parliamentary constituency, a school catchment area or a health authority district.

The census has also become a fruitful area for historical research and there is a growing interest in time-series research, or *cliometrics* in which modern statistical techniques are applied to historical data. See also SOCIAL SURVEY, FAMILY EXPENDITURE SURVEY, GENERAL HOUSEHOLD SURVEY, OFFICIAL STATISTICS, STATISTICS AND STATISTICAL ANALYSIS.

central tendency see MEASURES OF CENTRAL TENDENCY.

centre and periphery a depiction of the division of the world into dominant, mainly industrial, capitalist countries, and others, mainly in the THIRD WORLD, which are weaker politically and economically. Whilst the terms now have wide usage in sociology and a varied history, they are most commonly associated with WALLERSTEIN and the WORLD SYSTEMS approach. Wallerstein (1974) argued that from the 16th century onwards a capitalist world system began to emerge, with England, France and the Netherlands as the core countries having strong centralized political systems and mercantile economies. As a part of the process, other countries became subordinated to the core and provided cheap labour, most commonly unfree labour in the form of SLAVERY OR DEBT PEONAGE. These became the periphery countries supplying raw materials, foodstuffs and luxury goods to merchants from the core who dominated world trade.

Later the concept of *semiperiphery* was introduced by Wallerstein and others to describe those countries which, in the 20th century, have achieved some level of industrialization, are less dominated by the economies of the core, and which have achieved some levels of political centralization and civic political organization. Most of the southern European countries, some Latin American countries, e.g. Argentina, Brazil, Chile, and some Asian countries, such as South Korea, have been described as semiperipheral.

Whilst the world systems approach has been criticized for its over-reliance on the market as its main analytical focus (Brenner, 1977), the usage is now so widespread that adherence to Wallerstein's approach should not be assumed when writers use these terms.

Centre for Contemporary Cultural Studies (CCCS) see CULTURAL STUDIES.

Chalcolithic period the copper and stone age, regarded as occurring in the period 5000 BC to 3500 BC.

chance 1 the PROBABILITY of an event, such as the occurrence of heads or tails on the toss of a coin.

2 social or physical outcomes which are unforseen and perhaps inherently unpredictable.

Chance arises from the existence of physical or social processes which involve random events, a multiplicity of interacting variables in 'open systems' (including the changeability of actors' choices), and because actors' intentions often have UNANTICIPATED CONSEQUENCES. While an inherent CONTINGENCY in social events is seen by some theorists as ruling out general theories, this neglects the availability of generalized 'probabilistic' accounts and the fact that it is the goal of general theories to abstract from particular events (and provide EXPLANATION or analytical frameworks), not necessarily to predict or control events.

Coping with chance in social life is a source of MAGIC and RELIGION and the basis of important leisure forms, including games of chance and GAMBLING. See also RISK SOCIETY.

change see SOCIAL CHANGE.

chaotic phenomena see COMPLEXITY AND CHAOS THEORY.

charisma and **charismatic authority** special personal qualities or powers claimed by and for an individual (e.g. a religious or a political leader), making him or her capable of influencing large numbers of people who may become the followers of this person. This form of authority, based on an affectual or emotional commitment to a leader, as well as a belief in the extraordinary personal qualities of the leader, is one of three main types of LEGITIMATE AUTHORITY (OR POLITICAL LEGITIMACY) identified by Max WEBER. The term was originally a purely religious one, meaning the 'gift of grace'. In a religious context, it still refers to individuals or, in some cases, groups of believers, who claim to possess special powers, e.g. speaking in tongues, healing, etc.

chattel slavery see SLAVERY.

Chicago school the pioneering grouping of urban sociologists and social theorists located at the University of Chicago in the interwar years.

The eminence of Chicago among American universities, and the city's distinctive Midwestern voice in American affairs, has meant that Chicago has been the centre of numerous major movements in modern social thought, including philosophical PRAGMATISM and SYMBOLIC INTERACTIONISM, as well as the Chicago school of urban sociology. Founded in 1892, Chicago's Department of Sociology was the first to be established in an American university. Its founder, Albion SMALL, and his successor, Robert PARK, developed an approach to urban social analysis distinguished by careful empirical research and a particular model of urban ecology. Drawing on Darwinian ideas, a model of urban ecological processes was developed which presented urban competition over land and housing as resulting in the spatial organization of cities as a series of concentric rings, each with its own shifting functional focus and also subdivided into distinctive neighbourhoods and subcultures (see also URBAN ECOLOGY, URBAN SOCIOLOGY). Chicago has been described as an ideal laboratory for urban social research, and members of the Chicago school were responsible for a stream of classic works in urban sociology, amongst them Thomas and Znaniecki's *The Polish Peasant in Europe and America* (1917), Park and Burgess's *The City* (1925), Wirth's *The Ghetto* (1928) and Zorbaugh's *The Goldcoast and the Slum* (1929).

Chicano a person of Mexican origin or descent living in the US. Once a pejorative term, Chicano was adopted in the 1960s to give the (then) 8–10 million Mexican Americans an identity and political focus. 'Chicanismo' became a description of the movement to restore Mexican dignity, culture and power.

chiefdom a form of centralized social organization relying primarily on allegiance and not on formal coercive institutions. US evolutionary anthropologists regard it as existing prior to the STATE and as a development from the TRIBE. Chiefdoms are characterized by the emergence of patterns of social stratification and an economic system based on the redistribution of goods, but the distinction between states and tribes is often tenuous. See also SEGMENTARY STATES.

child abuse the inflicting of injury or psychological damage on a minor through assault, sexual exploitation or emotional harm. The awareness of child abuse internationally has developed very unevenly. Even in societies where concern is widespread, services for the investigation and amelioration of abuse are often under-resourced.

Research has been undertaken principally by psychologists and those associated with the SOCIAL WORK services to children and their families. Attempts at explanation have focused upon indices of deprivation, the faulty SOCIALIZATION of carers, and, more recently, and especially in relation to sexual abuse, male power.

child care 1 (generically) any matter associated with the upbringing and welfare of children, both familial and in relation to welfare services. Sociologists have concerned themselves with aspects of both. Studies of child care have included a focus on SOCIALIZATION historically and comparatively across class and cultural groups. Similarly, issues such as nursery provision, the educational system, primary health care and poverty in relation to children's welfare have all attracted much sociological attention. See also CHILD DEVELOPMENT, CHILDHOOD.

2 (more narrowly) the role of the child-care officer (see the Seebohm Report), a SOCIAL WORKER who has a duty to investigate any situation in which a child's welfare is thought to be at risk as a result of abuse, neglect or desertion or because a child is offending or is deemed to be beyond control. See also CHILD ABUSE.

child development the changes in physical, psychological and social behaviour that occur systematically with increasing age throughout childhood. The study of child development is concerned with both structural or maturational and environmental (learning and experience) influences, with much emphasis placed on the relationship between events in early childhood and later behavioural effects. See also NATURE-NURTURE DEBATE.

childhood a stage in the LIFE COURSE characterized by dependent status, usually, though not necessarily, due to biological immaturity. There are historical and cultural variations in the ways in which people understand age, and the division of the human age span into stages and meaningful categories is referred to as the *social construction of age.* According to Philippe Aries (*Centuries of Childhood,* 1962), the concept of childhood as a critical stage in the development of the person leads to particular ways of understanding and organizing the lives of young people which are highly variable, both historically and between societies. See also CHILD DEVELOPMENT, SOCIALIZATION, ANNALES SCHOOL.

chiliasm a belief that Jesus Christ will reign on earth for one thousand years. See MILLENARIANISM AND MILLENNIAL MOVEMENTS.

chi square (c2) a statistical test for use with nominal data (see CRITERIA AND LEVELS OF MEASUREMENT). The EXPERIMENTAL HYPOTHESIS predicts how many subjects in each group being tested will fall into certain categories if there are no differences between the groups, and the chi-square test compares the observed frequencies with the expected frequencies. The larger the difference between the observed and expected frequency, the more likely that there is a statistically significant difference between the categories.

Chodorow, Nancy (1944–) US sociologist whose influential work *The Reproduction of Mothering* (1978) explored the question: how does mothering reproduce GENDER identity? Her account, utilizing object relations theory, suggests that, unlike boys, girls do not have to give up their relationships with their mothers. Thus, for Chodorow, it is masculinity rather than femininity that can be seen as the detour in the development of identity. See also OEDIPUS COMPLEX.

Chomsky, Avron Noam (1928–) US theorist in LINGUISTICS whose major innovations in theories of LANGUAGE helped to move linguistics to a central place within the social sciences. Influenced by SAUSSURE and especially by JAKOBSON, and rejecting the BEHAVIOURISM of Bloomfield and Skinner, Chomsky's greatest achievement – in *Syntactic Structures* (1957) – was the development of a *transformational grammar.* In this, a set of 'phrase structure rules' provides 'deep structural' information about the sentences of a language, together with a set of transformational rules for generating 'surface structures'. There are also phonological and semantic components to Chomsky's theory. A main assumption of Chomsky's is that human linguistic COMPETENCE is innate and that the universals of grammatical DEEP STRUCTURE reflect this. Apart from the effectiveness of his own 'generative' models of grammar, further evidence for the innateness of fundamental grammatical structures is provided by the rapidity and accuracy with which children master the structures of language, suggesting that language is not simply learned and the rules of language picked-up 'inductively' as suggested by behaviourists (see also LANGUAGE ACQUISITION DEVICE). Thus, the capacity for language is similar to the acquisition and use of number; though a developmental account is appropriate, learning is triggered, rather than entirely formed, by 'experience'. There exist individual differences in the use of language, and languages vary, but the generalities of language structure and acquisition are seen as universal. Philosophically, the suggestion of innate ideas or categories locates Chomsky within 'rationalist' and 'idealist' schools of thought (see IDEALISM). This contrasts with EMPIRICISM – in which the MIND is regarded as *tabula rasa* – as Chomsky makes explicit in his 'debate' with Skinnerian theories of language acquisition.

Chomsky has also written extensively and in a highly engaged way on contemporary affairs, particularly in opposition to the Vietnam War. He sometimes denies that there exists any connection between such writing and his work in linguistics, though others have suggested that there is a connection between his egalitarian and syndicalist political viewpoint and his emphasis on universal linguistic capacity.

It is Chomsky's linguistic theories that have been of major importance, even if there remain many who question the extent of his emphasis on the universals of grammar, or that an emphasis primarily on syntax is sufficient to exhibit how diversity and process in human societies are also related to language. In recent years, in linguistics and in social science generally, a far greater emphasis has been placed on the systematic study of SEMANTICS and PRAGMATICS.

Christianity a monotheistic salvation religion originating in 1st-century Palestine, from where it spread to become the dominant religion in Europe and in European overseas settlements. The evolution of the Christian community was marked by divisions concerning church order and doctrine.

As a result, contemporary Christianity is split into three broad tendencies:

(a) the Western Catholic Church, which rests on the primacy of Rome;

(b) 14 autocephalous Eastern Orthodox Churches, dating from the 11th century;

(c) a multiplicity of Protestant bodies, dating from the 16th century and thereafter.

Accordingly, Christian organizational patterns are complex and differentiated between CHURCH, SECT and DENOMINATION (Troeltsch, 1912). Forms (a) and (b) are of the church type, while PROTESTANTISM furnishes examples of all three patterns.

Christianity rests on a belief in a personal God who is held to have created the universe and to be omnipotent, omniscient and just. Humanity, by contrast, has fallen from grace; it has sinned and is worthy of divine punishment. Thanks to the intervention of a saviour, Jesus Christ, however, salvation from this punishment becomes possible; Christians believe that Christ was the Son of God, and that his death constituted an atonement to God for their sins.

The question as to how individual believers can achieve 'salvation' has proved divisive within Christianity, and has major sociological significance. Notably, WEBER held that one answer to the question, the doctrine of predestination, was the driving force behind Protestant ASCETICISM (see the PROTESTANT ETHIC). Weber also held that Christianity's insistence on the ritual equality of all believers had sociological significance, preventing the emergence of CASTE-like divisions which might have destroyed the unity of the Western bourgeoisie and weakened its transformative revolutionary potential. Others have reinforced this line of argument by suggesting that the antiauthoritarian tendencies of 17th-century Protestant sects did much to foster democratic values (see Walzer, 1966).

While Christianity has had an important impact on historical development (not least the tension between church and state which has been a feature of European compared with Asian societies), today it is widely held to have a declining influence in Western societies. Nevertheless, its role in the recent transformation of Eastern Europe has been considerable and there remains sociological interest in sectarianism (see Wilson, 1967 and 1970) and in the overall nature and extent of religious belief and practices in modern societies (see, for example, Lenski, 1961), as well as in the causes, consequences and extent of SECULARIZATION (Martin, 1969).

church **1** any body of people, social institutions and associated beliefs and practices, constituting a distinctive religious grouping, e.g. the Methodist Church.

2 the Christian church as a whole.

In a more technical sociological sense (as initiated by Troeltsch and by Weber), distinctions are also drawn between the church as any well-established religious body, and DENOMINATIONS, SECTS and CULTS, which, together with 'churches', can be seen as making up a continuum of types of religious organization (see CHURCH-SECT TYPOLOGY).

church-sect typology a conceptualization of *types of religious organization* initially suggested by Weber and Troeltsch, and extended by Howard Becker (1950) and others, which suggests a continuum, and to some extent also a developmental sequence, of types of religious organizations running from CHURCH through DENOMINATION to SECT and CULT, making up a four-point typology of religious organizations. Sometimes a fifth category is also added, as in Fig. 3, in which the term *Ecclesia* refers to a supranational, formally organized, religious organization such as the Roman Catholic Church.

The developmental sequence involved in this typology shows that new cults and sects always tend to appear. Sects in particular can be seen as the dynamic element in religious organization, demanding high commitment

Ecclesia	*Church*	*Denomination*	*Sect*	*Cult*
Well-established	Well-established	A 'cooled-down' sect	Relatively dynamic	Fluid; often transient
Adjustment to the social order	Adjustment to the social order	Adjustment to the social order	Divergence from or challenge to religion in its established form, perhaps accompanied by withdrawal from or challenge to society-social exclusiveness	Rejection of or retreat from aspects of the outside world; also associated with social deviance
Formally organized; bureaucratic; hierarchical	Formally organized bureaucratic; hierarchical	Formally organized	Relatively informal organization; but sometimes authoritarian	Informal organization
Supranational membership; membership ascribed at birth	Wide membership; membership ascribed at birth	Substantial, relatively stable membership	Relatively exclusive membership; high level of commitment; new members make positive choice to join	Limited, often localized participation; participation from personal choice; often associated with social marginality

Fig. 3 **Church-sect typology.**

from their members and capable of leading to rapid religious, and also in some cases, political and economic change (see PROTESTANT ETHIC). Of course, many sects and cults simply fail to develop and often wither and disappear. When they survive and grow, however, the tendency in the long run is for them to become more formally organized, more bureaucratic and more hierarchical, and, ultimately, more conservative. In doing so they then pose less of a challenge to, and even become part of, the mainstream of society – the prize, but also the penalty, of success.

While the conceptions involved in the church-sect typology work well enough as ideal types in the discussion of most Western forms of religion, reflecting as they do mainly Christian patterns of religious organization, they are less useful in relation to non-Western religions. See also NEW RELIGIOUS MOVEMENTS.

Cicourel, Aaron (1928–) US ethnomethodologist whose influential *Method and Measurement in Sociology* evaluated the place of statistical and mathematical work in social science, in the light of the situated, judgmental and negotiated character of all social categorization. Often taken to be a devastating critique of orthodox sociologies (see MEASUREMENT BY FIAT, OFFICIAL STATISTICS), it in fact left open a wide range of possibilities. In his later work Cicourel has continued to seek a *rapprochement* between ETHNOMETHODOLOGY and other kinds of sociology, as well as continuing to contribute to a wide range of studies of familiar sociological topics, e.g. DEVIANCE and education, in which a rethinking of the place and nature of categorical work in social life is central.

circuits of capital (MARXISM) the circular movement in which, in capitalist production, CAPITAL produces SURPLUS VALUE. In this process, money capital is used first for the purchase of LABOUR POWER and raw materials and plant, then transformed into commodities (see COMMODITIES AND COMMODITY PRODUCTION), and finally, by the sale of these commodities, turned back again into money capital. In a profitable enterprise the full process leads to the return of the original money capital and the addition of surplus value, the difference between the VALUE of the goods created and the value of the labour power (and labour power embodied in the original capital) expended. With the *realization* of both a return of the original money capital and the accumulation of additional capital, the entire process begins again. See also CAPITALISM AND CAPITALIST MODE OF PRODUCTION, CRISES OF CAPITALISM, ACCUMULATION (OR EXPANDED OR EXTENDED REPRODUCTION) OF CAPITAL.

circulation (MARXISM) the sphere of the exchange of goods and services, as opposed to the sphere of PRODUCTION.

circulation of élites PARETO's term for the endless cycle of renewal and replacement of ÉLITES, in which political élites of one type are replaced by another. The tendency Pareto described was for élites with one psychological orientation, *lions* (distinguished by their possession of conservative 'sentiments' conducive to 'the persistence of aggregates), to alternate with more innovative, but more untrustworthy, *foxes* (distinguished by their 'instinct for combinations'). See also RESIDUES AND DERIVATIONS, ÉLITE THEORY.

citizen any member of a political community or STATE who enjoys clear rights and duties associated with this membership, i.e. who is not merely a 'subject'. Until modern times, with only a few exceptions, *citizenship* was typically restricted to a relatively narrow group within a political community, or was entirely absent. In the modern NATION STATE, however, not only has citizenship become the usual pattern, but the number of people admitted to this status has expanded, with *universal suffrage* and full CITIZEN RIGHTS established as the normal pattern.

citizen rights the rights which CITIZENS are entitled to, or may lay claim to, especially in modern states.

Following T. H. MARSHALL (1950, 1963), three sets of rights can be identified as significant:
(a) *civil rights,* the right to freedom of expression and access to information, and the right to freedom of association and organization and equality before the law;
(b) *political rights,* the right to vote and to seek political office in free elections;
(c) *social and economic rights,* the right to welfare and social security, and perhaps full employment, but usually stopping well short of the right to share in the management of economic organizations, to break the prerogative of managers to manage and of capitalists to own and direct the use of their capital.

The granting of citizen rights in modern societies in part reflects the fact that, as the result of changed expectations, violence can be used only as a last resort by governments in these societies. Accordingly, populations must be mobilized and culturally and ideologically won over and brought to regard these regimes, at least to some degree, as politically legitimate (see also LEGITIMATE AUTHORITY (or POLITICAL LEGITIMACY), INCORPORATION, WELFARE STATE). At the same time, however, such rights had also to be won, by political activity and social and class conflict.

Whereas some theorists, such as Marshall, present the expansion of citizen rights as undermining, or at least 'domesticating' and institutionalizing, class conflict, other theorists prefer to emphasize a continuing role for class conflict in preserving such rights, and in seeking to extend these beyond the limits usually placed upon them in capitalist societies. See also CIVIL RIGHTS, CIVIL RIGHTS MOVEMENT, ENTITLEMENTS, SOCIAL CONTRACT THEORY, DAHRENDORF.

citizenship see CITIZEN.

citizens' juries a recently introduced technique of political consultation and social inquiry and decision making in which a representative group is assembled, presented with expert evidence from a variety of viewpoints and asked to make recommendations on political or social issues (see A. Coote and J. Leneghan, *Citizens' Juries,* IPPR, 1997) Compare FOCUS GROUP.

city an inhabited central place differentiated from a town or village by its greater size and by the range of activities practised within its boundaries, usually religious, military-political, economic, educational and cultural. Collectively, these activities involve the exercise of POWER over the surrounding countryside. The first cities in human history appeared in areas of fertile land where the production of an agricultural surplus liberated part of the population from land work and encouraged other specialized activities and trades. The city depends upon a flow of goods from the country and therefore its development is structured by the availability of communication and transport technology. See also CITY STATE, URBAN SOCIOLOGY, URBANIZATION.

city state a form of the preindustrial STATE based on a single city, e.g. the Greek *polis.* In their earliest forms (e.g. the numerous city states of the Near East and the Mediterranean region) these states were small. Nevertheless they represented a significant advance in the concentration of political and economic POWER compared with previous nonurban societies. This is indicated by their capacity to extend their hegemony over surrounding areas, sometimes becoming the basis of major empires, e.g. Athens and Rome. It has been characteristic of some city states that they have been based on a 'democratic association' of citizens (e.g. in Athens, all those who bear arms). They have also been a major source of significant 'modern' political ideas and ideologies, not least because a sharp division between citizens and non-citizens (including the appearance of an urban PROLETARIAT) led to new class division. See also ANCIENT SOCIETY.

civic culture see POLITICAL CULTURE.

civic entrepreneur a person employing business-like approaches to public sector or voluntary activities. Civic entrepreneurship can be regarded as part of a broader emphasis on value for money (VFM), consumerism, and disillusionment with old-style state activity. It is part of a 'new approach' which theorists such as Anthony GIDDENS termed the THIRD WAY.

civil disobedience any overt act(s) of deliberate lawbreaking with the aim of bringing to public attention the alleged illegitimacy of certain laws, or their lack of moral justification. The term was originally introduced by Henry David Thoreau (1817–62) in his essay on the duty of civil disobedience (1849), which supported the nonpayment of tax as protest against the government support of slavery. Perhaps its most famous exponent was Mahatma Gandhi in India in the 1920s. His broad strategy of peaceful civil disobedience was adopted by the Indian National Congress to protest against the British imperial government. The strategy has been adopted by several modern CIVIL RIGHTS MOVEMENTS such as those in the US and Northern Ireland. *See* also CIVIL RIGHTS.

civil inattention the ways in which an individual shows that he or she is aware that others are present without making those others the object of particular attention (GOFFMAN, *Behaviour in Public Places,* 1963). For example, the eyes of one person may glance at the other but not directly engage, or quickly disengage should a more direct engaging seem likely to occur. Civil inattention illustrates the existence of an 'interaction order' and 'interaction ritual' which Goffman sees as governing the general processes of social interactions (see INTERACTION, INTERACTION RITUAL AND INTERACTION ORDER).

civilization 1 the advanced cultural forms (e.g. central government, development of the arts and learning, articulated concern with morals and manners) associated with cities and the wider societies in which these are located. The term derives from the Latin *civis,* citizen.

2 a particular society or culture area possessing the above characteristics (e.g. 'Chinese civilization' or 'Western civilization').

Historically, use of the term was often strongly, and somewhat crudely, evaluative, e.g. the contrast with pre-existing stages such as SAVAGERY or BARBARISM. See also CIVILIZING PROCESS.

civilizing process the historical process in which, according to ELIAS (1939), people acquired a greater capacity for controlling their emotions. Elias indicates how in Western societies the pattern of living – 'structures of affects' – that came to be regarded as 'civilized', involved profound redefinitions of previously 'normal' and 'proper' behaviour. In a detailed 'sociogenetic' study of manners, social stratification and state formation, Elias shows how new standards of decorum and repugnance came into existence. See also FIGURATION, COURT SOCIETY.

civil liberties see CIVIL RIGHTS.

civil religion a set of beliefs, rites and symbols which indicate and celebrate the citizen's relation to CIVIL SOCIETY, NATION and STATE and their historical provenance and destiny. The term originated with Rousseau's distinction between the 'religion of man', which is a private matter between the individual and God, and the 'religion of the citizen', which is a public matter of the individual's relation to society and government. Civil religions seek to bind all members to society, tell them their duties, even move them to fight and die for their country if necessary. Rousseau's formulations influenced DURKHEIM, but the term only obtained its contemporary currency with Robert Bellah's (1967) work on the United States. Bellah describes America's self-understanding of a covenant with God which obliges her to carry out God's will on earth. He refers to statements from the founding fathers, the Declaration of Independence, presidential inaugural addresses from Washington's to Kennedy's, the Gettysburg Address and other pronouncements; symbols and monuments (i.e. sacred places) such as the motto of the US ('In God we trust'), the Lincoln Memorial and the Arlington National Cemetery; and celebrations and rituals such as Thanksgiving Day, Memorial Day, Veterans Day, saluting the flag and ceremonies in schools. Bellah acknowledges that American civil religion can degenerate into national self-idolatry and has subsequently written about the American broken covenant.

The myths, stories, images, icons, sites, figures, celebrations and rites of civil religions are religious in the Durkheimian sense; they are set apart from the mundanities of everyday life and are the object of awe, reverence or special respect. The collective representations in a civil religion are also genuinely civil, i.e. representative of society, rooted in 'we the people'; politicians who control the apparatus of the state may exploit them, but they also ignore them at their peril. By contrast, the collective representations of a 'political religion' are superimposed on society by those who control the state with a view to putting the political order beyond question. The best known example is that of the Soviet Union. Christel Lane (1981) examines the sacralization of the October Revolution, the Great Patriotic War and the heroic achievement of labour; the accompanying symbols and rites, such as October parades, visits to the Lenin Mausoleum, and the placing of photographs of Lenin in every public office; and the numerous calendric rites and rites of passage. Anyone doubting that this was a political, and not a civil, religion has only to note how little of it survives in Russia today.

An explicitly functionalist account of 'civil religion' in the UK was provided by Young and Shils (1953) at the time of the coronation and a famous English cricket victory.

civil rights the rights which are due to a CITIZEN by virtue of citizenship alone, and which are protected by the law. Thus civil rights can be distinguished from *human rights,* which may or may not be protected by the law, and which belong to all people whether or not they are enshrined in the law. In the US the Bill of Rights makes all human rights civil rights. In the UK, in the absence of a written bill of rights, it is more normal to refer to civil rights as *civil liberties.* See also CIVIL RIGHTS MOVEMENT(S), CIVIL DISOBEDIENCE.

civil rights movement(s) any political organization seeking to gain CIVIL RIGHTS for a particular group in a society. The best-known civil rights movement came into existence in the US with the aim of enforcing those civil rights guaranteed to blacks by the constitution but traditionally denied to them. It was influential in the passing of the Civil Rights Act 1964, which contained strong antidiscrimination legislation. Since the mid-1960s the movement has concentrated its efforts on ensuring that the legislation has been enforced. Several other organizations have consciously modelled themselves on the American Civil Rights Movement. Most notably, the Northern Ireland Civil Rights Association was founded in 1968 to force the issue of civil rights for Roman Catholics into the political arena. See also CIVIL DISOBEDIENCE.

civil society (as used by HEGEL and MARX) market and economic relations (in contrast with the activity of the STATE); a realm intermediate between the family and the state. More generally, the realm of wider social relations and public participation, as against the narrower operations of the state or of the economy.

The earliest usages of the term in political and social philosophy were to contrast both 'civil society' and 'civil government' with 'natural society' or the 'state of nature'. In the Scottish Enlightenment, Adam FERGUSON used the term in contrasting Western CIVILIZATION, and its associated forms of government and politics, with non-Western forms of society and their more 'despotic forms of government (see also ORIENTAL DESPOTISM). The economic and political freedoms associated with civil society are regarded by Marxists as sometimes apparent rather than real (e.g. protecting the interests of private property and capital and enshrining significant freedoms, but instilling selfish individualism and masking underlying economic exploitation, ALIENATION, the loss of earlier community, etc.). However, within Marxism, as well as in sociology generally, the historical significance of the differentiation of civil society from 'nature', the family, and the 'state' is acknowledged on all sides. Distinctions in any of the above senses between civil society and the state operate, even if, as emphasized by GRAMSCI, the state plays a role in the establishment of civil society, and the establishment of civil society also plays a part in protecting or in changing particular state forms (compare PUBLIC SPHERE). See also CIVIL RIGHTS, PUBLIC SPHERE.

civil war armed conflict, often protracted, in which politically organized groups within a STATE contest for political control of the state, or for or against the establishment of all or part of that state in a new form. Major civil wars, such as the American Civil War (1861–65) or the Spanish Civil War (1936–39), may represent highly significant watersheds in the life of a nation state or society. For example, the English Civil War (1642–48) sounded the death-knell of English ABSOLUTISM, and, as suggested by Barrington MOORE (1967), the American Civil War, with the victory of the industrial North over the slave-owning Southern states, can be seen as confirming the supremacy of capitalism throughout the entirety of the North American continent. Since civil wars may bring revolutionary change, and many revolutions involve armed struggle, it is sometimes difficult to decide when to speak of civil wars and when REBELLION or REVOLUTION. The Russian Revolution, for example, led to a protracted internal war before the success of the revolution was confirmed. See also MILITARY INTERVENTION.

Cixous, Hélène (1937–) Algerian-born French feminist theorist, who in works such as *The Newly Born Woman* (1986) applies poststructuralist and psychoanalytical theory in an analysis of the potential for women to subvert theoretical and social structures. For her, 'woman' is the product of linguistic DIFFERENCE (e.g. binary oppositions such as culture/nature, activity/passivity) but the 'feminine' is a source of energy and diversity. For example, 'feminine writing' (not always by women), which operates on difference and plurality, can display the diversity and transgression of 'libidinal femininity'. See also OTHERNESS.

clan (ANTHROPOLOGY) a kinship term which describes a body of people claiming common UNILINEAL DESCENT. This may be MATRILINEAL or PATRILINEAL, but not both. Often clans are distinguished from others by reference to an ancestor who may be non-human or mythical (see TOTEMISM). Compare SIB.

class

1 the hierarchical distinctions that exist between individuals or groups (e.g. occupational groups) within a society. In this general sense class is an alternative general term to SOCIAL STRATIFICATION. The term 'social class' is also widely used as a general synonym for 'class'.

2 any particular position within a social stratification system or class system, e.g. 'middle class', 'working class', etc.

3 (*social classes*) the descriptive classificatory categories used by the Registrar General in the collection and analysis of CENSUS data; in 1961, for example, the Registrar General's division of the population into five 'social classes'.

4 (*occupational class*) descriptive classification of the total population into broad 'occupational classes' or 'socioeconomic status groups', e.g. 'manual and non-manual' classes, as well as more elaborated classifications (see OCCUPATIONAL SCALES).
5 the particular form of 'open', rather than 'closed', stratification of class system found within modern industrial societies, in which individual and collective SOCIAL MOBILITY is relatively commonplace (compare CASTE, ESTATE).
6 (MARXISM) the economically determined and inherently conflictual divisions of society based on ownership and non-ownership of property, e.g. lord and serf in feudal society (see FEUDALISM AND FEUDAL SOCIETY), BOURGEOISIE and PROLETARIAT in capitalist societies, which characterize all large-scale societies and which are held ultimately to determine the destiny of each type of society. Marx also identifies a multiplicity of lesser classes and groupings which influence the outcome of political and social conflicts.
7 (WEBER, 1922) differences between categories or groups of persons in their 'typical probabilities' of 'procuring goods', 'gaining positions in life' and 'finding inner satisfaction' – LIFE CHANCES. Thus, for Weber, 'class' means 'all persons in the same class situation', what ever the basis of this and whatever its implications may be for the longer-term destiny of societies (see also CLASS, STATUS AND PARTY). Weber identified a number of overlapping possible bases of class situation, based on ownership and non-ownership of property and also including reference to different kinds of property and the different kinds of income that this yields. In particular, he identifies:
(a) property classes;
(b) commercial classes, somewhat misleadingly so-called, since these include individuals able to safeguard their position through political or organization activity, e.g. professionals or others monopolizing qualifications, as well as entrepreneurs possessing other bases of monopoly;
(c) social classes, the 'totality' of such class situations, defined in terms of situations within which 'individual and generational mobility is easy and typically occurs'. The main 'social classes' identified by Weber in this sense are: (i) the working class, (ii) the petty bourgeoisie, (iii) the 'propertyless' intelligentsia and specialists, (iv) classes privileged by property and education.

Class situations, and the social classes these give rise to, may be 'positively privileged' or 'negatively privileged', with various 'middle classes' in between. Since mobility among, and the instability of, class positions is considerable, for Weber 'social class' is highly variable, and only sometimes are these the bases of class consciousness or collective action.

In the UK, the first dictionary use of 'class' occurred in the 17th century, in T. Blount's *Glossographia*. Apart from military and school usage, he noted that the term described a 'distribution of people according to their several Degrees'. The term came into general use in a similar way; as one which described differences of birth, occupation, wealth, ability, property, etc.

An overall, but no absolute, distinction can be drawn between those conceptions of 'class' which set out to be mainly 'descriptive' (e.g. senses **3** and **4**) and those which are more 'analytical' (e.g. senses **6** and **7**).

Descriptive classificatory approaches: for more on the main descriptive approaches see SOCIAL STRATIFICATION, OCCUPATIONAL SCALES.

Analytical conceptions of class: Marx. Of the analytical approaches to class, the most influential uses in sociology undoubtedly stem from MARX, although he acknowledged that the term had originated earlier, in particular in the work of Enlightenment social theorists and French socialists.

In Marx's own work the term has a number of different applications, but the essential aspects of Marx's general model of social class are clear:
(a) Every society has to produce a surplus to feed, house and clothe dependent children, the sick and the elderly. Class differences begin when one group of people claim resources that are not consumed for immediate survival as their private property;
(b) Classes therefore are defined in terms of ownership (or non-ownership) of productive property which makes the taking of the surplus possible. At different times in human history different forms of property (e.g. slaves, water, land, capital) have been crucial in shaping social relationships, but all class systems are characterized by two major classes. The most important class relationship as far as Marx was concerned was that found in CAPITALISM, between the bourgeoisie and the proletariat;
(c) The historical importance of classes, for Marx, is that they are intrinsically exploitative: one class, because it takes the surplus produced by another class, exploits and oppresses that class, and therefore conflict is an inevitable product of class relationships. The conflicts associated with class antagonisms are the most important factor in social change: ultimately it is class conflicts, associated with underlying social and economic CONTRADICTIONS, which transform societies;
(d) Marx distinguishes between the 'objective' aspects of class, as set out in (b) above, and the 'subjective' aspects, i.e. the fact of membership of a class is not necessarily accompanied by an awareness of membership or a feeling of political identity with the interests of a class. It is only when members of a class realize their common interests and act together to gain them that one can fully talk about a social class.

It should be noted that the above is a theoretical model and, as such, should not be taken as simply descriptive of any historical situation but as indicating the most important structure and processes for understanding social relations and for directing empirical work. In his own empirical work Marx introduced a number of factors into his understanding of social class. In *The 18th Brumaire of Louis Bonaparte* (1852), for example, he discusses the French peasantry of the mid-19th century and he comes close to a formal definition of class which includes variables such as a shared culture and a national political organization.

Major problems arising out of Marx's work have inspired most of the subsequent sociological work on class:
(a) the fact that Marx's account of classes and the role of class in pre-capitalist societies was relatively limited leads to questions as to whether class has the centrality of importance in the generation of change in these societies, e.g. see CLASS-DIVIDED SOCIETY;
(b) the existence and growth of important groups other than the proletariat and the bourgeoisie;
(c) divisions within classes which have often proved as significant. politically, as divisions between classes (e.g. see CONTRADICTORY CLASS LOCATIONS);
(d) the important effect of factors other than social class on people's lives, GENDER and race in particular;
(e) the fact that CLASS CONSCIOUSNESS, in practice, has never shown evidence of a simple correspondence with Marx's view of objective class situation and, historically, for subordinate classes, has normally been much at variance with 'objective' conditions as defined by Marx.

Analytical conceptions of class: Weber. The most influential alternative theory of class is found in Max WEBER's work. Unlike Marx, Weber emphasized other factors which promoted inequality. In particular he considered status or honour and prestige as a distinct variable. He also emphasized the link between class and opportunity, arguing that a class is a category or group of people who share similar 'life chances'. With Marx, he saw ownership and non-ownership as a basic criterion, but Weber stressed divisions within classes (partly based on social STATUS) and empirical changes in class boundaries to a much greater extent than Marx. Examples are Weber's distinction between ownership and commercial classes, and also the way that different skill levels divided the working class in terms of life chances. Here Weber is emphasizing the importance of 'markets' rather than simply ownership or non-ownership of property as the basis of inequality, i.e. level of skill and demand for skills determining differences in rewards. Weber also differs from Marx in seeing BUREAUCRACY, as well as class, as a fundamental nexus of power in modern societies.

Weber's stress on a variety of factors influencing opportunities and rewards (see also CLASS, STATUS AND PARTY) has made his approach to the analysis of class and social stratification very influential in sociological theory. In British sociology, for example, LOCKWOOD (1958), and later GOLDTHORPE and Lockwood et al. (1968 and 1969), emphasized the importance of taking account of 'status' as well as 'market situation' and 'work situation' (see also MULTIDIMENSIONAL ANALYSIS OF SOCIAL STRATIFICATION, BLACK-COATED WORKER, AFFLUENT WORKER). GIDDENS

(1981) has taken the emphasis on the market situation of individuals as important in qualifying Marx's view of class and power. Earlier critics of Marx's work also emphasized Weberian themes, notably theorists of MANAGERIAL REVOLUTION, STABLE DEMOCRACY, END-OF-IDEOLOGY THESIS (see also DAHRENDORF).

Analytical conceptions of class: modern approaches: Most recent approaches have tended to take either Marx or Weber as a starting point. There have been numerous attempts to adapt or refute elements of the classical approaches. Efforts to repair deficiencies in Marx's work, for example, as seen in studies by Poulantzas (1973), Carchedi (1977) and Wright (1978 and 1985), have been widely discussed. A common preoccupation of all these theorists is the problem of CLASS BOUNDARIES, of accounting for the position of the 'middle classes' (see INTERMEDIATE CLASSES AND INTERMEDIATE STRATA) within the Marxist theory of class. They all accept the deficiencies of the orthodox Marxist view of such groups as professionals, managers and white-collar workers, but they differ in their attempted solutions to the problem posed by the continued existence and role of this group, which the classical Marxian theory assumed in the long run would simply be assimilated into one or other of the two main classes in capitalism, or disappear.

Poulantzas follows ALTHUSSER's conception of the MODE OF PRODUCTION to argue that there are three relatively autonomous aspects of class relations: economic (PRODUCTIVE versus UNPRODUCTIVE LABOUR), political (supervision versus nonsupervision) and ideological (mental versus manual labour); and, hence, the definition of social classes cannot be purely economic. The direct production of commodities (the economic role) is still seen as the main criterion which defines the proletariat, but the situation is complicated by further relations of power. Any worker, productive or not, who occupies a subordinate position in any of the three spheres should be seen as a member of a distinct class: the 'new petty bourgeoisie'. Carchedi proposes a variation on this approach. He distinguishes between ownership and functional aspects of the capitalist labour relation. He argues that, as capitalism developed, production became more and more a collective process and, similarly, the function of the capitalist in controlling and organizing the labour force became separated from ownership with the growth of managerial hierarchies. The NEW MIDDLE CLASS exercises the function of capital (control and surveillance) without being part of the class which owns capital. Similarly, Wright (1978) distinguishes between ownership and control, arguing that people who do not own the means of production but have important powers as managers or semiautonomous professionals were in CONTRADICTORY CLASS LOCATIONS. In a later critique (1985), Wright re-emphasized ideas of property and exploitation as central to an understanding of class relations. Each of these approaches attempts to overcome the problems which the 'new middle classes' pose for Marxian accounts of class by treating power and control of the LABOUR PROCESS as in some way independently definitive of class relations. These 'new' approaches, therefore, despite their location within the Marxian tradition and different conceptual frameworks, bear, at some points, a striking resemblance to aspects of Weber's approach, the difference being, however, that they see their new approach as rehabilitating the Marxian view. The ultimate basis of class, and the fundamental dynamics of society, remain 'objective' economic class interests.

Many other writers have preferred to look more directly to Weber rather than to Marx to develop a more satisfactory theory of class. Among the most influential of these, along with Lockwood and Goldthorpe, has been Parkin (1971; 1974; 1979). Parkin draws on Weber's discussion of SOCIAL CLOSURE, the idea that groups try to monopolize resources and opportunities for their own benefit, and to deny resources and opportunities to others. The key point here is the idea of exclusion of nonmembers. In different societies, criteria of eligibility for membership of dominant classes differ: religion, ethnicity, gender, for example, are bases for exclusion in different societies. Birth into a particular group is a common criterion, so kinship and descent are crucial, and, in this type of rigid system, privileged groups can maximize closure to their own benefit very successfully. Closure in modern societies is not based upon descent, but distinct strategies of exclusion are nevertheless employed.

It should be noted that much empirical work on 'class' and social mobility operates with 'occupational definitions rather than with ones based on 'property' (see SOCIAL STRATIFICATION). Sociological approaches to class have also been much criticized recently for their 'gender blindness', that is, for being models of inequality relating to males only, and treating women's class positions as dependent on those of their male partners (see GENDER STRATIFICATION, MEDIATED CLASS LOCATIONS).

In Britain recently some theorists have seemed to propose an end to class and to the saliency of class analysis (e.g. Pahl, 1989). However, stripped of rhetoric, such claims represent less a call for a revaluation of the centrality of class (e.g. compare LIFESTYLE analysis) than a preference for particular versions of class analysis.

class awareness see CLASS CONSCIOUSNESS.

class boundaries the more or less clearly defined dividing lines held to exist between CLASSES within a society or particular types of society. Debates have existed particularly about the boundaries between classes in CAPITALIST SOCIETIES. Such debates have been especially important within Marxism, but also have a more general significance, both theoretically (e.g. in relation to assessments of CLASS INTERESTS and likely class action, see EMBOURGEOISEMENT, AFFLUENT WORKERS, CLASS IMAGERY, MULTIDIMENSIONAL ANALYSIS OF SOCIAL STRATIFICATION) or, more mundanely, in the construction of classificatory schemas in connection with analysis and accounts of SOCIAL STRATIFICATION and SOCIOECONOMIC STATUS.

Within Marxism and neo-Marxism, debates have centred not only on the location and the implications of the locations of class boundaries, but also on whether the assumption can be maintained that all individual or collective class positions can be 'located uniquely within particular classes', or whether there exist many class locations which in terms of main classes must be seen as CONTRADICTORY CLASS LOCATIONS. Theoretically and politically, a good deal hinges on decisions on the existence and location of class boundaries, e.g. the size, political role, and the centre of gravity and 'leadership' of the working class, or the role of INTERMEDIATE CLASSES OR INTERMEDIATE STRATA or the NEW MIDDLE CLASS. Theorists such as Eric Ohlin Wright (1985), for example, argued that groups such as the 'middle class within capitalist societies' are 'constituted by locations which are simultaneously in the capitalist class and the working class'. The implications of this, however, may or may not be seen as indicating a loss of saliency for Marx's basic notions of class (see COLLECTIVE LABOUR, GLOBAL CAPITALIST).

class capacity the organizational and cultural resources which are at the disposal of a CLASS. For example, a relative decline in WORKING-CLASS capacity over the last two decades can be explained not only in terms of declining numbers, but also in terms of an undermining of its organizational bases and communications networks with the decline of heavy industry and large factories and with the breakup of traditional working-class communities, etc. See also CLASS FORMATION.

class cleavage the class-based conflict in Western democracies between competing left- and right-wing political parties. As expressed by Lipset (*Political Parties*, 1960), in 'every modern democracy conflict among different groups is expressed through political parties which basically represent a "democratic expression of the class struggle"'. For Lipset, such forms of 'legitimate' and 'domesticated' class conflict, which replace earlier more socially disruptive forms, are a necessary requirement for a 'stable liberal democracy'. Modern stable democracies involve cleavage within CONSENSUS, the existence of a basic agreement on the political 'rules of the game', and arise from the gradual entry of the lower classes into the political system. See also END-OF-IDEOLOGY THESIS.

Lipset's characterization of class cleavage has come under attack from two directions: (a) from those who do not accept that the elimination of more 'traditional' forms of class conflict is an inevitable secular tendency in modern Western societies; (b) those who argue that a more fundamental CLASS DEALIGNMENT is occurring, leading to the replacement of class as the main basis of political cleavage (see WORKING-CLASS CONSERVATISM) by individualistic bases of identification (e.g. individual choice of LIFESTYLE).

class conflict 1 any political struggle between social classes on the basis of different CLASS INTERESTS.

2 an underlying conflict of interests between classes, whether or not this involves active political conflict.

Theories which use this concept operate within an adversarial view of classes, i.e. they typically consider that conflicts between classes are inevitable. Conflict exists over the distribution of power and wealth, and over issues like equality of opportunity, housing, education, working conditions and other sociopolitical matters. It is usually recognized, however, that such collective conflicts mostly occur without challenging the basis of the class system itself. For example, trade union conflicts over pay and conditions seek a better deal for a group within the existing framework. Social conflicts do not usually involve the mobilization of entire classes. Thus it is useful to distinguish between conflict *within* a system and conflict *about* it.

One of the founders of the conflict approach, MARX, foresaw an inevitable sharpening and radicalization of conflict, culminating in a revolutionary crisis. In practice, levels of conflict have very rarely been so threatening, and, in recent times, where a fundamental crisis has developed it has not been on the basis of one class in opposition to another, but has involved alliances and coalitions of different class groupings (e.g. students and workers in France in 1968, and similarly located groups in Eastern Europe in 1989 and 1990), and on varying bases (e.g. 'authority relations', 'exclusion' or 'inclusion'), as well as ownership and non-ownership of capital.

class consciousness the awareness, amongst members of a social CLASS, of common interests which are based on their own class situation and are in opposition to the interests of other classes. The term is particularly associated with MARXISM, where the concern is often either with the processes which foster the development of class consciousness in the PROLETARIAT, or involves discussions as to why such a consciousness has not developed. A basic distinction here is between a *class-in-itself* – the objective basis of class interests – and a *class-for-itself* – the consciousness of these interests. The basic idea is that a set of values and beliefs and a political organization will, or should, emerge in order to represent and realize the objective interests of a class. In the case of the WORKING CLASS, certain aspects of their work and life situations (exploitation, ALIENATION, periodic mass unemployment and poverty, etc.) are seen as facilitating a growing awareness of a common situation and encouraging a collective response. Most Marxists agree, however, that only a limited awareness and set of objectives are arrived at spontaneously. LENIN, for example, in a very influential pamphlet (1902), argued that, left to itself, the working class would develop only an 'economistic' consciousness, limited to demands for better pay and conditions within the capitalist system. Lenin, like many Marxists, was interested in the overthrow of CAPITALISM, not in its reform. Thus, he argued that a revolutionary ('vanguard') party was necessary to transform TRADE UNION CONSCIOUSNESS into political, 'revolutionary consciousness' and action. This has been a recurrent theme in Marxist writings on the proletariat – the issue of why a 'revolutionary class consciousness' has never developed among the working classes of the most developed capitalist states. In the 1920s and 30s, for example, LUKACS and GRAMSCI developed different critiques of 'crude' Marxism, emphasizing theoretical and cultural factors which impeded the development of 'true' consciousness or promoted the development of 'FALSE CONSCIOUSNESS'.

A substantial literature also exists on CLASS IMAGERY, the actual images of class possessed by social ACTORS, and, at the same time, sociologists have taken up the issue of the limits and possibilities of the notion of 'class consciousness' in the Marxian sense. This is a theme which also underlies debate on the NEW WORKING CLASS. MANN (1973) argued that one may find *awareness* of class membership and also group solidarity, but it is 'rather unlikely' that the working class can produce, independently, an alternative vision of a new society. This type of sociological approach seeks to do more than echo Lenin's 70-year-old conclusion. Instead, it attempts to operationalize the concept of working-class consciousness by identifying it as involving four elements:

(a) 'class identity' – the definition of oneself as working-class;
(b) 'class opposition' – the definition of an opposed (capitalist) class;
(c) 'class totality' – (a) and (b) taken as together defining the 'whole society';
(d) an alternative vision of society.

Mann concluded that British workers are usually limited to (a), only occasionally incorporating (b). See also HEGEMONY.

class dealignment the thesis, especially in connection with VOTING BEHAVIOUR in Britain, that a previous pattern of alignment between POLITICAL ATTITUDES and CLASS is breaking down and is being replaced by more fluid affiliations and more volatile patterns of voting (e.g. see Crewe et al., 1977; see also WORKING-CLASS CONSERVATISM, AFFLUENT WORKER, CLASS IMAGERY). The thesis finds some justification in the fact that working-class support for the Labour Party has declined in recent years, while middle-class support for the Labour Party and for parties other than the Conservative Party has increased. Alford (1967) has suggested that the extent of class voting within an electorate can be measured using an *index of class voting* computed as: the percentage of manual workers voting for 'Left' parties, minus the percentage of nonmanual workers voting for 'Left' parties. Crewe's thesis of 'class dealignment' would appear to rest on a similar conception of 'class voting' and 'non-class voting'. It can be argued, however, that this provides only one baseline for measures of class voting, and not necessarily the most cogent or significant one. Several possibilities can be noted:

(a) taking another baseline (e.g. Marxian conceptions of CLASS or sectoral interests, see SECTORAL CLEAVAGES), increasing middle-class support for parties other than the Conservative Party might be seen as reflecting a new recognition of 'class interests' among particular sections of nonmanual workers (see also NEW MIDDLE CLASS, MIDDLE-CLASS RADICALISM);

(b) there is the problem of how to take into account what Wright (1985, 1989) has referred to as MEDIATED CLASS LOCATIONS, especially the influence of a spouse's or partner's employment on the assessment of a voter's class location. In many studies of voting behaviour, including those of Butler and Stokes, and Crewe, this influence has not been taken into account. Studies have mainly used the occupation of the, usually male, 'HEAD OF HOUSEHOLD' as their main indicator of 'class'. For this second reason no less than the first, it is obvious that estimates of 'class' or 'class-deviant' voting will vary widely with different definitions of 'class'.

See also PARTY IDENTIFICATION, CLASS POLARIZATION.

class-divided society 1 any society in which there exist fundamental class divisions. 2 (GIDDENS, 1984) any agrarian State in which there is class division, but where this division 'is not the main basis of the principle of organization of the society'. As such, these forms of society are contrasted directly with modern forms, including CAPITALIST SOCIETY, in which class divisions are a main basis of the social organization and the central dynamic of society. In making this distinction, Giddens wished to undermine orthodox Marxist accounts of the dynamic role of class in all societies, i.e. 'the history of all societies as class struggle'. See also CLASS, STRATIFICATION, MARX, ASIATIC SOCIETY.

class domination the power exercised by one group over another by virtue of their respective CLASS positions. Class relations are generally agreed by sociologists to involve relationships of domination and subordination. These relationships are institutionalized and legitimated in different, more or less formal, ways in different societies. For example, customary rights and obligations may have great force in preindustrial societies, and it is usual to find that religious sanctions exist to regulate and normalize class relations. These forms of domination and legitimation are, like all others, ultimately backed up by the threat of political, juridical or military force. In more highly developed class societies, as relations become more impersonal and contractual, formal and legal regulations become much more important than tradition or religion, and the growth of centralized state power becomes a key mediating factor.

class formation the organized collectivities within a class structure and the processes by which these emerge.

The distinction between 'class structure' and 'class formation' can be seen as a basic, if often implicit, distinction in class analysis (Wright, 1985). If class structure can be seen as composed of those factors which establish the broad pattern of CLASS INTERESTS, class opportunities, life chances, etc. within a society, 'class formation' refers to the actual collectivities, class action, etc. which are generated on the basis of this structure. In classical Marxism, the relationship between class structure and class formation has sometimes been treated as relatively unproblematic. Neo-Marxist and Weberian approaches, on the other hand, have usually regarded the relationship as one requiring empirical exploration, although it is usually agreed the general conditions likely to be conducive to class formations can be identified, e.g. the conditions for the existence of CLASS CONSCIOUSNESS (see also CLASS CONFLICT, CLASS STRUGGLE).

class fraction (especially MARXISM) a division of any larger CLASS grouping, where differences in economic interests and ideologies lead to differences in lifestyle, political orientation, etc.

classical conditioning see CONDITIONING.

classical economists the major economic theorists, including Adam SMITH, Thomas MALTHUS, David Ricardo, John Stuart MILL, who, in the late 18th and early 19th centuries were responsible for the foundation of modern ECONOMICS. The classical economists analysed the working of the capitalist economy as the outcome of the economic interaction of landowners, capitalists and labour. Thus, the early economists were involved in a form of CLASS analysis which remains central to modern sociology, especially as the result of the work of MARX (see also MARXIAN ECONOMICS). Subsequently, with the 'marginalist revolution' in economics from the 1870s onwards (see NEOCLASSICAL ECONOMICS), development of the paths of sociology and mainstream economics tended to diverge, and economics became associated with the conduct of economic analysis in terms of the behaviour of abstract individuals (see also POLITICAL ECONOMY, ECONOMIC SOCIOLOGY, INSTITUTIONAL ECONOMICS).

class identity (usually) a SOCIAL ACTOR's subjective conception of class location (see SUBJECTIVE AND OBJECTIVE CLASS).

classification 1 any attempt to identify regularly occurring types of social structure, e.g. types of society, types of organization, types of social relationship.

In biology, the classification of animals and plants, which has sometimes been used as a model for sociological classification, has operated according to two main principles: (a) Linnaean classification (synchronic) of mutually exclusive possibilities; (b) the arrangement of types as an evolutionary (diachronic) sequence, representing evolutionary relationships.

While purists may claim that all particular phenomena are different and never absolutely identical, the aim of any classification is to place together all instances of a phenomenon whose similarities, and differences from other types of phenomena, are such as to justify the classification for particular theoretical purposes. See also TAXONOMY.

2 (SOCIOLOGY OF EDUCATION) the identification of the boundaries between different forms of human knowledge. In the formal educational process this relates to the organization of knowledge into curricula, or the various domains of educational activity. The term is a key concept in BERNSTEIN's theory of knowledge codes.

class-in-itself and class-for-itself see CLASS CONSCIOUSNESS.

class interest 1 (MARXISM) the 'objective' economic interests of a CLASS arising from its location within a MODE OF PRODUCTION.
2 (in a more general sense) any INTEREST that may be pursued or held to exist by, or on behalf of, members of a class.

Since it is clear that 2 may be at odds with 1, numerous questions arise as to the 'true' basis of class interests, or whether multiple bases of class interests must be acknowledged (see CLASS CONSCIOUSNESS, CLASS IMAGERY, IDEOLOGY). However, for analytical purposes both uses of the term persist.

class imagery

The ideas and images of class and class structure, and the distribution of power, held by SOCIAL ACTORS.

There have been many empirical studies of class attitudes and imagery, the great majority of which have been concerned with the manual working class. In the 1950s and 60s especially, many social commentators, not only sociologists, were interested in exploring the implications of changing lifestyles, particularly changes in patterns of family and work relationships within 'traditional' working-class communities (see also AFFLUENT SOCIETY, EMBOURGEOISEMENT THESIS, WORKING-CLASS CONSERVATISM). Influential North American and European studies also contributed to the discussion, e.g. those of Chinoy (1955), Popitz et al. (1957). In British sociology, significant studies were carried out by Abrams (1960) and Zweig (1961), but the classic paper was by LOCKWOOD, 'The sources of variation in working-class images of society' (1966, reprinted together with a number of papers on the theme in Bulmer, 1975).

Lockwood's article drew on a major study of conjugal relationships (Bott, 1957), which included a discussion of 'social imagery'. Bott had concluded that her respondents had two different 'models' of society: a 'power' model (also a 'them' and 'us' model), in which society was seen as divided into two fairly static, opposing classes ('working' and 'middle' classes), and a 'prestige' model, in which the class structure was seen as composed of a much larger number of groups arranged in a hierarchy of prestige. Bott also suggested that a preference for one or other of these two models could be explained as the outcome of the work and community experiences of people – their 'primary social experiences'. Lockwood drew on these ideas, identifying *three* types of 'social consciousness' within the working class linked to definite types of work and community structures (see Fig. 4):

(a) the traditional 'proletarian' worker, e.g. coal miners, dockworkers, and shipbuilders, having a 'power model' of society, i.e. where workers have a strong commitment both to their work and to fellow workers, and live in close, homogeneous communities;

(b) the traditional 'deferential' worker, who recognizes the leadership rights of a traditional elite and adopts a 'prestige hierarchy' model of class; these are typically workers in small 'family' firms or in agriculture, in paternalistic employment relations, and in a fixed-status hierarchy in the wider community of the town or village;

(c) the 'privatized' worker, who sees class differences in terms of a 'money model' of society; this group is seen as more 'home-centred' than communally orientated, and more 'instrumental' in its attitudes to work and politics.

Subsequently Lockwood's initial work was extended in a number of empirical studies, especially in the well-known studies of the AFFLUENT WORKER (GOLDTHORPE, LOCKWOOD, et al., 1968a & b, 1969).

Although mostly accepting the value of Lockwood's discussion, subsequent studies have, in general, revealed a more complex and contradictory picture of working-class class imagery. Notably, the lack of consideration of issues of gender or race by Lockwood has received criticism. Pollart (1981), for example, showed that the class images of women factory workers are frequently 'ambivalent', and constantly overlain by gender roles and the power relations associated with gender divisions. Others have also argued that most conventional studies of class imagery have paid insufficient attention to general structural and theoretical issues relating to class formation and development. Howard Newby, in his study of agricultural workers (1979), has argued, for example, that it is mistaken to see 'deference' as a simple or a single orientation, rather it is highly variable in form and often a relation of 'power' in which 'class imagery' is not paramount (see also DEFERENCE). For all this, the strength of research on class imagery, in contrast to much of the literature on CLASS CONSCIOUSNESS, is that it attempts to map empirically existing modes of consciousness among the working class.

Ideal type	*Social context*	*Class concepts*	*Likely party identification*
Traditional (proletarian)	Occupational and residential community	Two main classes, them and us; in terms of power and authority	Traditional Labour
Deferential	Small firm; agricultural; older workers; job involvement; status hierarchy	Three (or more) classes; in terms of lifestyle and social background – prestige model	Working-class Conservative
Privatized/ instrumental	Absence of occupational or residential community	Large central and residual classes; in terms of wealth and consumption	Labour support – conditional, but collective instrumentalism and potential militancy

Fig. 4 **Class Imagery.** Goldthorpe and Lockwood categories.

class location any 'objective' position within the class structure. See CONTRADICTORY CLASS LOCATIONS.

class polarization (MARXISM) the tendency for the inherently conflicting interests of the two main classes within CAPITALISM to result in an increasing consciousness of these differences, with the two classes eventually becoming opposing camps. According to Marx, this process comes about as the result of the tendency for the proletariat to experience 'immiseration' under capitalism, while at the same time also being thrown together in situations which will encourage collective action, e.g. in large factories and towns (see CLASS CONSCIOUSNESS). As part of this polarization, classes which stand in various INTERMEDIATE CLASS locations within capitalism also tend to be drawn into one camp or the other, mostly into the ranks of the proletariat, as tendencies to crisis within capitalism intensify.

It is obvious that Marx's hypothesis has not been borne out, at least in any straightforward way, partly because immiseration has not occurred on the scale Marx expected and also because class interests, and the foundations of class consciousness, are far more complex than he anticipated (see CLASS IMAGERY). On the other hand, a broadly class-based form of politics has become the norm within most Western liberal democracies (see POLITICAL CLEAVAGE, STABLE DEMOCRACY), despite some suggestions that CLASS DEALIGNMENT had removed this, and although the issue is much complicated by the continued existence of 'intermediate classes' (see also VOTING BEHAVIOUR).

Polarization, on a world scale, between rich and poor nations, is a further element of class polarization which can either be handled in terms of Marxian conceptions, or seen as involving a fundamental departure from his schemas (see DEPENDENCY THEORY, WALLERSTEIN).

classroom interaction a description of the activities of different participants in classroom activity. Interest in the nature of classroom relationships developed with increased research into the way in which educational institutions themselves shape educational outcomes. Using ethnographic techniques (see ETHNOGRAPHY) and concepts derived from SYMBOLIC INTERACTIONISM, researchers analyse the social interactions and values that comprise the social system of the classroom.

class situation see MULTIDIMENSIONAL ANALYSIS OF SOCIAL STRATIFICATION.

class society see CLASS-DIVIDED SOCIETY.

class, status and party three ideal-typical (see IDEAL TYPE), partly competing, partly interrelated, key ways in which, according to WEBER (1922), societies can be seen as hierarchically and politically divided.

We may speak of 'class', says Weber and his interpreters, when:

(a) a number of people have in common 'a specific causal component of their LIFE CHANCES';

(b) this component is determined by economic interests in the possession of goods and opportunities for income within commodity or labour markets.

Thus class may also be referred to as *market situation*. Classes in this sense need not be communities or collectivities; they merely represent 'possible', albeit 'frequent', bases of collective action. In contrast, for Weber, 'status' is normally a matter of actual *groupings* of individuals. As opposed to purely economically determined 'class situation', *status situation* is any typical component' of the life fate of people that is determined by a 'specific, positive or negative, social estimation of honour'. While 'status' can be linked with 'class', it need not be, and may also on occasions counteract it.

'Party' refers to POLITICAL PARTIES. In the circumstances in which these arise – especially, but not only, in modern societies – they may be based on 'status' or 'class', or both, or neither of these. Thus, for Weber, the analysis of class and social stratification could not be reduced to the simple terms sometimes involved in 'vulgar' versions of

Marxism and historical materialism. In Weber's analysis, though class interests may often be the basis of collective political and social action, there is no general tendency for class interests to lead to simple CLASS POLARIZATION or to REVOLUTIONARY CHANGE. Weber's ideas on 'class, status and party' have been widely influential, e.g. see MULTIDIMENSIONAL ANALYSIS OF SOCIAL STRATIFICATION. See also CLASS, SOCIAL STRATIFICATION.

class structure the general pattern of CLASS differences and relations within a society. See also CLASS FORMATION.

class struggle (MARXISM) any political and economic action (e.g. strikes, political movements) based on CLASS INTERESTS and necessary for the development of CLASS CONSCIOUSNESS and essential for a transition to socialism to occur. See also HEGEMONY, CAPITALISM AND CAPITALIST MODE OF PRODUCTION.

Clausewitz, Karl von (1780–1831) Prussian military theorist whose posthumously published masterpiece *On War* (1832–34) has influenced modern strategic theory and theories of WARFARE. Clausewitz's central ideas were premised on the assumption that STATES are sovereign, recognizing no authority above themselves. Since states promote their own interests, if necessary at the expense of other states, they are always potentially in conflict. Warfare, therefore, must be seen as a 'normal' occurrence in the relations between states, in a situation where there is no higher authority than states. In a famous phrase of Clausewitz, 'war is politics by other means'. See also TOTAL WAR, NEO-CLAUSEWITZIANS.

cleavage see POLITICAL CLEAVAGE, CLASS CLEAVAGE.

client and clientalism see PATRON-CLIENT RELATIONSHIP.

clinical sociology a practically-oriented approach to sociology, prevalent in North America, in which the aim is professional intervention in social life, especially in making evaluations of, and in seeking solutions to, social problems. Whether the 'clinical' model is an appropriate one for sociologists to adopt, however, is debatable; the term has gained little currency outside North America.

cliometrics see CENSUS.

clock-time the measurement of the passage of time in standard intervals and ultimately with reference to a fixed benchmark, e.g. Greenwich Mean Time. Although now taken for granted, the measurement of time in such standardized ways – and the 'tyranny of the clock' – is a relatively recent phenomenon in human societies, and is usually seen as associated with the rise of INSTRUMENTAL RATIONALITY and in particular Western capitalism. The term 'clock' derives from the bell towers which in pre-industrial societies were used to provide signals for the coordination of human activities. The first mechanical clocks are said to have been invented by monks as early as the 13th century and came into wide use in the 17th century. The coming of railways and other modern forms of transportation was a final stimulus necessitating the standardization of time. The regularized working hours of the modern FACTORY SYSTEM represented a significant break with earlier more informal patterns of DOMESTIC PRODUCTION (see Thompson, 1967), and it is significant that Marx's conception of SURPLUS VALUE is stated in terms of hours of labour-time.

cluster analysis a technique used to identify groups of objects or people that can be shown to be relatively distinct within a data set. The characteristics of those people within each cluster can then be explored. In market research, for example, cluster analysis has been used to identify groups of people for whom different marketing approaches would be appropriate.

There is a rich variety of clustering methods available. A common method is hierarchical clustering which can work either from 'bottom up' or from 'top down'. In 'agglomerative hierarchical clustering' (i.e. bottom up), the process begins with as many 'clusters' as cases. Using a mathematical criterion such as the standardized Euclidean distance, objects or people are successively joined together into clusters. In 'divisive hierarchical clustering' (i.e. top down), the process starts with one single cluster containing all cases, which is then broken down into smaller clusters.

There are many practical problems involved in the use of cluster analysis. The selection of variables to be included in the analysis, the choice of distance measure and the criteria for combining cases into clusters are all crucial. Because the selected clustering method can itself impose a certain amount of structure on the data, it is possible for spurious clusters to be obtained. In general, several different methods should be used. (See Anderberg, 1973, and Everitt, 1974, for full discussions of methods.)

cluster sample a method of SAMPLING which selects from groups (*clusters*) existing in the parent population, rather than assembling a RANDOM SAMPLE. This tends to be quicker and cheaper, but may lead to a BIASED SAMPLE if the clusters are not representative of the parent population. For example, polls taken of attitudes to government policy may be carried out in selected areas of the country thought to be representative, but, because of local political dynamics, this may not be the case.

cobweb theorem see CYCLE OR CYCLICAL PHENOMENA.

code the differential usage of a system or collection of SIGNS, marking differential social memberships. Codes may be conscious or unconscious. An influential example is BERNSTEIN's notion of differential usages of English, by which fundamental status and class differences are communicated and reproduced (see ELABORATED AND RESTRICTED CODES). Other examples include dress and fashion codes, with identities claimed or refused by items selected, and by the selection of terms, actions or items used as identification by formal and informal special interest groups, secret societies, sexual minorities or drug users.

coding the assignment of (generally) numerical codes to specific data in such a way as to allow analysis to be undertaken by means of computer or by hand. The need to code data in a meaningful way is common to much sociological research, whether it is describing a phenomenon or testing a sociological theory.

It is possible to differentiate between two basic types of coding – structured and unstructured – depending upon the type of data which is to be analysed, although the difference between them is blurred. STRUCTURED CODING can generally be used on primary data, i.e. that which the researcher collects directly. Unstructured coding is generally used with data which has been collected by the researcher from secondary sources. The main example of the use of structured coding is in QUESTIONNAIRE analysis, and that of unstructured coding in CONTENT ANALYSIS. See also UNSTRUCTURED DATA.

coefficient of association see CORRELATION.

coercion the use of physical or nonphysical force, or the threat of force, to achieve a social or political purpose. See also VIOLENCE, POWER.

cognatic (ANTHROPOLOGY) **1** a kinship term describing consanguinial relations (see CONSANGUINITY), i.e. those based on a blood/biological tie.

2 (in descent theory), a term describing NON-UNILINEAL DESCENT, i.e. descent traced through male and female links.

cognition the thinking process. Mental life can be considered as comprising both thinking and feeling elements: the cognitive and the emotional aspects of experience. Cognition is concerned with perception, memory, language, and problem solving. See also COGNITIVE SOCIOLOGY and COGNITIVE ANTHROPOLOGY.

cognitive anthropology the study that seeks to use the formal methods of LOGIC and LINGUISTICS in characterizing fields of culture, and the minds formed in those cultures. In the 1960s, the study of cultures moved away from tracking generalized belief systems (e.g. religion) towards the everyday or mundane classifications (or taxonomies) of things, persons and actions within particular cultures. Anthropology began to attend in detail to the way in which people's cognitions, their thoughts, reasonings and judgements, are necessarily bound up in their social activities. This was in line with developments generally in the social sciences, with increasing interest in what people 'know and think' as central to social organization. The ETHNOSCIENCES, in looking at categorizations of nature in non-Western thought, have had as deep an influence on the development of cognitive anthropology, as has linguistics. The central proposal has been that anthropology can use formal methods, rather than either those modelled on an empiricist reading of natural science, or on the uncontrolled interpretation associated with the humanities. The outcome is formal or quasi-formal statements of the rules and systemic alternatives, normally with reference to small fields of a culture. See also COMPONENTIAL ANALYSIS, SAPIR-WHORF HYPOTHESIS.

cognitive dissonance the experience of competing, opposing or contradictory thoughts, attitudes or actions leading to a feeling of tension and the need to achieve consonance. The term was introduced by Festinger (1957). In his definition dissonant cognitions exist when Belief A implies the negation of Belief B. For example, 'Smoking causes lung cancer' is dissonant with 'I smoke'. The dissonance can be reduced in a variety of ways, either by adjusting Belief A or Belief B. Belief A could be adjusted by disregarding medical reports that confirm the belief and by paying particular attention to sceptical reports. Belief B can be adjusted by smoking less, or smoking tobacco of a low carcinogenic type.

cognitive relativism see RELATIVISM.

cognitive science see PSYCHOLOGY.

cognitive sociology a term used by A. Cicourel, *Cognitive Sociology*, (1973) as an umbrella term to group together ETHNOMETHODOLOGY and other areas of non-positivistic cognitive science, including COGNITIVE ANTHROPOLOGY and SOCIOLINGUISTICS.

cohabitation see MARRIAGE.

cohesion see SOCIAL COHESION.

cohort a group of persons possessing a common characteristic, such as being born in the same year, or entering school on the same date. The term is usually used in making generalizations derived from quantitative data (see QUANTITATIVE RESEARCH TECHNIQUES).

cohort study see LONGITUDINAL STUDY, BIRTH COHORT STUDY.

cold war the state of hostility and political competition which existed between the two superpowers, the US and USSR, in the post-World War II period, which involved strategies of political subversion, spying, the promotion of regional wars between smaller powers, etc., but which stopped short of all-out war. Some commentators regard the period of the cold war as covering only the years of greatest mutual suspicion and hostility – 1945–55. For others, the era of cold war only ended with the advent of GLASNOST and PERESTROIKA, and the break-up of the Eastern military and economic bloc in 1989 and 1990. See also NUCLEAR DETERRENCE, BALANCE OF POWER.

collective action organized action by a group to promote its interests. See also FREE RIDER.

collective bargaining the negotiations about terms and conditions of employment which take place between an employer, or an employers association, and one or more TRADE UNIONS. Sociological interest in collective bargaining has involved, for example, consideration of the implications it has for the structure, aims and accomplishments of trade unions, the relations between managers and employees, and the dynamics of capitalist society; an underlying theme being the extent to which it is associated with the institutionalization of conflict and, relatedly, the separation of economic and political issues (see POSTCAPITALISM, INDUSTRIAL RELATIONS).

collective behaviour the action or behaviour of people in groups and crowds – *crowd behaviour* – where, as the result of physical proximity, and the protection and contagion of the group, the action of individuals is out-of-the-ordinary, tends to depart from routine standards of social demeanour, and may be more than usually explosive and unpredictable. In early sociological and social psychological theories of collective behaviour (notably in the work of Gustav LeBon, *The Crowd*, 1895), as well as in more recent theories (e.g. Smelser, 1962), it is seen as a potential threat to normal social order. As such, the various forms of collective behaviour, including such phenomena as rallies, riots and rebellions, sometimes play a significant part in SOCIAL MOVEMENTS and SOCIAL CHANGE.

collective conscience the shared beliefs and associated moral attitudes which operate as a unifying force within a society. As used especially by DURKHEIM, the term particularly refers to simpler societies based on mechanical solidarity, in which the DIVISION OF LABOUR is not advanced. In more complex societies, according to Durkheim, a shared collective conscience becomes less important, and social solidarity is based at least in part on reciprocity rather than likeness (see MECHANICAL AND ORGANIC SOLIDARITY). See also COLLECTIVE REPRESENTATION.

collective consumption any consumption of goods and services whose provision and management, to a degree, 'cannot be other than collective', and which the private sector finds it unprofitable to provide (Castells, 1977). Among such goods and services identified by Castells were public transport, housing, and leisure provision. The term was introduced by Castells in an attempt to achieve a focus on the distinctive features of URBAN SOCIAL MOVEMENTS, which he viewed as above all seeking to influence and control the spatially-bounded *collective consumption units* provided in the urban context.

Subsequently, the term has been taken up by other political sociologists and political scientists (e.g. Dunleavy, 1980) and used in a more general way as the basis of an overall analysis of SECTORAL DIVISIONS which cut across more conventional divisions of class: above all, the distinction between those who, as consumers or workers, are main beneficiaries of collective consumption, and those who are not. Both in Castells' work and in later inquiries, the focus on collective consumption emphasizes the tension between the necessity for collective provision of some goods and services, and the burden on capital which this provision represents (see also STATE EXPENDITURES, FISCAL CRISIS IN THE CAPITALIST STATE). It is this conflict that is seen as both generating urban social movements and as making sectoral divisions an important dimension of political cleavage in modern capitalist societies.

collective goods see PUBLIC GOODS.

collective labour (MARXISM) the combination of inputs of labour increasingly required for the production of a commodity, or commodities, within advanced forms of capitalism, in circumstances where the DIVISION OF LABOUR is well developed and individual workers no longer produce a commodity in its entirety.

collective representation the shared – hence social rather than individual – conceptions within a society. The term is DURKHEIM's, who argued that these conceptions must be the fundamental subject matter of sociology. For Durkheim, collective representations must be studied as 'social facts', external to any one individual. See SOCIAL FACTS AS THINGS.

collective unconscious see JUNG.

collectivism 1 any politicoeconomic doctrine which advocates communal or state ownership, and communal or state control of the means of production and distribution, e.g. COMMUNISM OR SOCIALISM.

2 any political system in which communal or state ownership and control of the means of production and distribution is the dominant mode of economic organization.

Actual forms of organization under

collectivism vary widely. Thus, in some contexts, collectivism may involve a large measure of collective self-management.

collectivity any grouping of individuals that 'cuts across the actor (see SOCIAL ACTOR) as a composite unit' (PARSONS, 1951).

collectivization the process of amalgamation of peasant holdings and private estates under state direction, e.g. the collectivization of agriculture by Stalin in the Soviet Union in the 1930s, and subsequently in other countries within the Soviet bloc. The term may also be applied to any organization of previously privately-owned property under state direction.

Collingwood, Robin (1889–1943) English archaeologist and philosopher, best known for his ideas on metaphysics and for what he had to say about historical explanation and understanding. Collingwood rejected positivist claims about the unity of knowledge, as well as a naive EMPIRICISM that knowledge of the external world could be obtained in an unfiltered manner from observation. In *An Essay on Metaphysics* (1940), he argued that the intellectual content of any given discipline, at a particular stage of its development, rested on 'absolute presuppositions' which were a priori, but specific to each discipline as well as each epoch. Thus, in ways that anticipate aspects of Thomas KUHN's conception of SCIENTIFIC PARADIGMS and scientific revolutions (see NORMAL SCIENCE AND REVOLUTIONARY SCIENCE), he sometimes wrote as if there were no common yardsticks of truth and falsity to which reference could be made in order to judge between different constellations of absolute presuppositions. More often, however, Collingwood simply wrote that different constellations underlie different modes of knowing. In the work which has exerted the greatest influence on sociology, *The Idea of History* (1946), he distinguished between 'scientific thinking', concerned with claims to laws established by observation and experiment, and distinctively 'historical thinking', in which the aim was to question the evidence in order to reveal the specific thought underlying human action. Hence his claim that 'all history is the history of thought'. Collingwood's ideas, which have some affinities with WITTGENSTEIN's emphasis on distinctive FORMS OF LIFE, have influenced thinking in sociology, particularly as the result of their influence on Peter WINCH.

colonialism the political rule, either directly or indirectly, of one society, country or nation over another.

Colonialism, however, involves more than just political rule. In the 20th century it has been particularly associated with one ETHNIC GROUP dominating another within the dominated group's territory. Thus, in this century, colonialism has been associated with European, white, Christian, wealthy rulers who have attempted to impose cultural values over the ruled by either devaluing or attempting to eradicate the colonized groups' religions, languages, customary laws and economic activities. Colonialism has therefore been seen by many sociologists as closely associated with the development of RACISM. Also in this century, colonization has been associated with the dominance of the colony's economy by the colonizer, and it is this that is one of the key differences which Marxist writers see as distinguishing 20th-century colonization from earlier forms. See IMPERIALISM, NEO-COLONIALISM.

Various forms of colonial rule have existed in history, but one important distinction is between *direct* and *indirect rule.* In this century, the British in Africa often relied on indirect rule, nominating indigenous people or institutions as representatives of the British crown, whilst the French imposed direct rule from Paris through French officials. See also ORIENTALISM, POST-COLONIAL THEORY.

colonization of the life-world see INTERNAL COLONIZATION OF THE LIFE-WORLD.

colour bar the systematic or institutionalized restriction on access to resources or social opportunities in which the basis of DISCRIMINATION is determined by socially established criteria of racial origin, especially criteria established by 'whites' and applied to 'blacks'.

coming out a social, psychological and political process which involves both public and private identification with the designation 'lesbian' or 'gay'. Crucially, the process involves internalization of the label 'homosexual' and acceptance of a lesbian or gay lifestyle. The term arose out of the re-emergence of radical sexual politics in the context of the wider radicalization of political culture in the 1960s. It was, and continues to be, a key concept within gay and lesbian politics because of the challenge it presents to the negative imagery surrounding HOMOSEXUALITY and the sociopolitical processes which render it invisible. Coming out involves a change in self-image for the individual which arises from an affirmation of his or her homosexuality. As a political strategy, the process challenges the normative frameworks surrounding institutionalized HETEROSEXUALITY.

command economy a 'planned economy', such as those prevailing in Eastern Europe until 1989–90, in which the economy is directed by the central state, and in which the market allocation of goods and services plays only a marginal role.

commensality the act of eating together (literally 'sharing the same table'); the social sharing of FOOD providing symbolic and social, as well as biological, sustenance. Both domestic and status relations are usually reflected in patterns of commensality, e.g. see CASTE. In more general terms, in a sense suggested by LÉVI-STRAUSS, 'food is both good to eat and think'.

commercial ethnography use of ethnographic techniques to inform design and marketing. As well as the mutual influence of commercial market-research and academic social-survey work, there has been an increasing adoption by commercial firms of 'qualitative' methods of investigating human activity. The most striking is the development of PARTICIPANT OBSERVATION, and a use of the methods of SOCIAL ANTHROPOLOGY as a means of discovering life styles in precise detail in order to tailor the design of products with precision. Investigators, with a cover story, seek to live a 'normal life', as close to the target community as possible. Pioneered by Japanese car firms in the US, and strikingly successful as a technique, it is ironic that what are usually regarded as 'soft' or 'unscientific' social-science methods have, in fact, remarkably powerful commercial applications.

commodification the process by which goods and services are increasingly produced for the market. Compare SUBSISTENCE ECONOMY.

commodities and commodity production economic goods produced for, and bought and sold in, a market.

commodity fetishism (MARXISM) the conferment of a 'naturalness' on material objects produced by human labour in capitalism when their character is really the result of social processes. Since commodities are the main form in which social relationships appear in capitalist society, this tendency to fetishism, according to Marx, is not surprising. However, it means that the real social processes in terms of LABOUR POWER and the EXPLOITATION of labour are hidden from view. Marx's analysis appears in the final section of chapter one of *Das Kapital*, Vol 1 (1976). Commodity fetishism is indicative of the more general perception, and hence misunderstanding, of economic and social relations that comes from regarding these as part of a 'natural' order. Marx regarded much POLITICAL ECONOMY as guilty of fetishizing the economy, thereby concealing underlying relationships. See also LABOUR THEORY OF VALUE, REIFICATION, CAPITAL.

commodity-sign see BAUDRILLARD.

common law a system of law, of which English law is the prime example, based on legal precedents created by judges. Thus, this system directly contrasts with more formally codified systems of 'civil law', such as those based on ROMAN LAW (e.g. Scottish law). In common-law systems, however, increasing legislative activity by the STATE has meant that 'statute law' also plays an important role within such systems.

common-sense knowledge the knowledge that guides and enables ordinary conduct in everyday life. According to SCHUTZ, common-sense knowledge consists of a huge bundle of understandings acquired through SOCIALIZATION, which resemble recipes for carrying out ordinary actions, such as responding to a greeting or using a telephone. ETHNOMETHODOLOGY studies PRACTICAL REASONING **2**, which is how this knowledge is *used* in SOCIAL ACTION. See also MUTUAL KNOWLEDGE.

commune 1 a group of families or individuals living and perhaps working together, and sharing some or all possessions as well as family and communal duties. Sometimes, but not always, the establishment of communes has been motivated by political ideologies, such as SOCIALISM, COMMUNISM or UTOPIANISM. They were briefly fashionable in California and elsewhere in the 1960s, a period of experimentation with 'alternative' ways of living (see COUNTER CULTURE OR ALTERNATIVE CULTURE). As 'exceptional' ways of living within the societies in which they occur, communes must be distinguished from communal forms of living which occur in many preindustrial societies. Because they are exceptional social forms and often at odds with the ideologies of mainstream society, and also because they must often work out basic problems of social organization from the start, communes have often been short-lived. One paradox in communes, for example, is that though often motivated by collectivist ideologies, they also embody concerns for individual self-development. Compare KIBBUTZ, SECT, CULT.

2 the revolutionary government established in Paris 1870–71 in the aftermath of the Franco-Prussian War of 1870. This has been regarded as a landmark in the history of REVOLUTIONS, as a classic case of the people seizing power, albeit only for a relatively brief period, March-May 1871, before it was crushed.

3 the agricultural and other collectives established in China under COMMUNISM in the period of the Great Leap Forward under MAO TSE-TUNG. More than 26,000 of these were created in an endeavour to produce a distinctively Chinese route to SOCIALISM.

communication(s) 1 the imparting or exchange of INFORMATION. Communication may be verbal or nonverbal, intended or unintended (see also SIGN, SEMIOTICS, BODY LANGUAGE).

2 the message(s) or unit(s) of information communicated.

3 (*pl.*) the 'means of communication', e.g. MASS MEDIA OF COMMUNICATION.

The human capacity for communication, especially through LANGUAGE, is far more extensive than that of any other animal. The capacity to communicate across time and space has expanded enormously in modern times (see TIME-SPACE DISTANCIATION) with the invention of WRITING, PRINTING, electronic communications – telegraph, telephone, radio – and media of mass communications, as well as the mechanization of transportation. A reduction of what geographers refer to as the 'friction of distance' has been particularly evident in the 20th century in the capacity to send messages over long distances at great speed. This has many implications, not least the increased capacity for social control this makes possible for the modern STATE.

communicative competence the means, including the rules, by which persons sustain communicative exchanges and interactions with others within a community. The term was coined by Hymes (1966) to focus attention on the skills and knowledge involved in human communication. It reflects the limitations in LINGUISTICS of concentration mainly on syntactic competence (compare CHOMSKY). Hymes indicates in the formulation of his S.P.E.A.K.I.N.G. acronym some of the elements of social situations which would have to be included: setting and scene, participants' ends, act sequence, 'key', instrumentalities, norms and genres. To imagine dealing with these in an integrated set of rules might seem to indicate an impossible ambition, and many critics would question whether a 'rule' formulation is appropriate. However, Hymes' conception points to a vital area of interest, and attempts to model 'communicative competence' will continue to command attention. Without resort to either 'psychologism' or 'sociologism', HABERMAS, for example, suggests communicative competence implies an 'ideal speech situation' from which discursive conceptions of truth and justice may be derived.

communism

1 a political ideology, deriving from SOCIALISM, and particularly from MARX and subsequent Marxists, which aims at the creation of societies in which private productive property, social CLASSES, and the state are absent.
2 a form of society which approximates to the socialist ideal.
3 any society in the 20th century ruled by a communist party.

The term emerged in the 19th century, and was adopted by Marx to designate the ideal society which socialists should attempt to create. With the revolutionary overthrow of capitalism, Marx envisaged the emergence of 'socialist societies' in which the state would still play a role; only with the transformation of all property relations and the withering away of the state would communism emerge. For most of the 19th-century, even political parties which adhered in some way to this programme still called themselves socialist. In 1918 the Russian Social-Democratic Labour Party changed its name to the Communist Party of the Soviet Union (BOLSHEVIK Party). From then on the term came to be primarily associated with parties and societies which at some stage were influenced by the USSR, even though, as with Trotskyist (see TROTSKY) and Maoist (see MAOISM) parties, there may have been splits from the USSR. LENIN had a decisive influence on 20th-century communism, primarily through his development of a theory of the party in which the basis of organization was *democratic centralism*, with a professional revolutionary leadership assuming the role of developing the theory and practice of revolutionary communism. Lenin's view was that without the revolutionary party the working class would rebel and revolt against the capitalist ruling class, with primarily economic rather than revolutionary political aims. Thus communism in the 20th-century is often equated with *Marxist-Leninist* thought.

Since the late 1920s, the concept has been decisively influenced by STALINISM. The international communist movement has been split over whether this represented a continuation or decisive break from Marxist-Leninist development. Thus supporters of Stalin continued to call the USSR communist, and, from 1948 until 1989, the Eastern European countries were linked to the USSR also. Others, in particular the various postwar European Trotskyist groups, saw these societies as either transitional (moving towards communism), as *state capitalist* or *degenerate workers' states*, or as new forms of society, neither capitalist nor socialist (see also STATE SOCIALIST SOCIETIES). Up until the 1970s, most of the European Communist Parties continued to support the USSR, but from that time on the development of EUROCOMMUNISM saw the emergence of tendencies within the European parties leading them to distance themselves from the Soviet Union and develop policies for political influence regarded as more appropriate to their own countries and the changed circumstances of the late 20th century. By the 1980s, the communist movement in Western Europe was varied, but exhibited declining membership and electoral support.

Outside of Europe, since the 1940s, various communist movements have appeared in the THIRD WORLD. Many of these rose to prominence alongside the nationalist movements for independence (see COLONIALISM and NEOCOLONIALISM). Communist parties came to power most noticeably in China, Vietnam, Angola, Mozambique and Cuba. Most were influenced by the model of party organization, state central planning and one-party policy inspired by Stalinism, even though Maoism in China, with its theoretical view of the primary role of the peasantry, might seem to have offered a theory of revolution more appropriate to the Third World.

For non-Marxist observers, the whole experience of 20th-century communist societies has supported the argument that communism means a lack of democracy, centralized state control over most aspects of society, rigid economies unable to sustain economic growth, and often tyrannical one-man dictatorships, as exemplified by Stalin in the USSR, Mao in China and Castro in Cuba. For some, this led to the development of the concept of TOTALITARIANISM, in which both fascist (see FASCISM) and communist states are contrasted with democratic market-based societies (see also DEMOCRACY, STABLE DEMOCRACY).

communitarianism a viewpoint on welfare issues that stresses common interests and common values arising from communal bonds. As such, communitarianism is opposed to purely individualistic conceptions of welfare. Communitarian conceptions have enjoyed resurgence recently as a reaction against the political ascendancy of conceptions of welfare based on crude market values. Communitarianism, however, is also sometimes associated with a romanticized cultural conservatism or with otherwise controversial ideas. For example, in his influential account of communitarianism, *The Spirit of Community* (1993), A. Etzioni suggests that the manufacture of new rights should be banned on the grounds that an 'inflation of rights' devalues more grounded moral claims.

community action the organization of groups to achieve change within the community. The term is most often associated with minority or disadvantaged groups. In particular, community action can be seen as an attempt by a disadvantaged or powerless group to organize and mobilize from a local or neighbourhood base. Community is seen to facilitate local participation in the political process, possibly in opposition to dominant beliefs and practices. See also COMMUNITY WORK, COMMUNITY DEVELOPMENT PROJECTS, URBAN SOCIAL MOVEMENT.

community and association see GEMEINSCHAFT AND GESELLSCHAFT, COMMUNITY, TÖNNIES.

community

Any set of social relationships operating within certain boundaries, locations or territories. The term (as used by both sociologists and geographers) has descriptive and prescriptive connotations in both popular and academic usage. It may refer to social relationships which take place within geographically defined areas or neighbourhoods, or to relationships which are not locally operative but exist at a more abstract, ideological level. For example, the term 'lesbian community' may refer to an actual settlement of women (e.g. 'lesbian ghetto', see E. Ettore, 1978), or it may refer to a collective of women sharing ideas and life styles, but not necessarily residing together in the same spatial area.

It has been suggested that the concept is one of the most difficult and controversial in modern society. Lowe (1986) suggests that it 'ranks only with the notion of class in this respect'. It is certainly a term which has attracted many different interpretations and has been subjected to wide use and abuse.

In popular usage, the term has often been associated with positive connotations, as in the phrases 'a sense of community' or 'community spirit'. It is clear that the term is not only descriptive, but also normative and ideological. Sociological discourse has often reinforced prescriptive usages of the term. Influenced by a tradition of 19th-century romanticism, some sociologists have regarded community as necessarily beneficial to human needs and social interaction. This tradition was particularly strong in the 19th century, but is by no means absent in 20th-century sociological thought.

In the 19th century, the German sociologist TÖNNIES drew a distinction between what he called GEMEINSCHAFT and GESELLSCHAFT. The former denoted community relationships which were characterized by their intimacy and durability: status was ascribed rather than achieved; and kin relationships took place within a shared territory and were made meaningful by a shared culture. Conversely, *Gesellschaft* gave rise to relationships which were impersonal, fleeting and contractual. Such relationships were both rational and calculative rather than affective: status was based on merit and was therefore achieved; and *gesellschaftlich* relationships were competitive and often characterized by anonymity and alienation. Tönnies believed that the processes of industrialization and urbanization would give rise to the destruction of *gemeinschaftlich* relationships and that *gesellschaftlich* relationships would consequently flourish. He was concerned by what he took to be the breakdown of traditional society, authority and the loss of community. In Tönnies' work we can see the high value he implicitly placed on the old social order and his ambivalence towards industrialization and urbanization (compare SIMMEL). It is this romanticized view of 'traditional society' that has given rise to the association of the concept of 'community' with ideas of social support, intimacy and security. Thus traditional communities have often been portrayed as close-knit and as facilitating cooperation and mutual aid between members. In contrast, the URBANIZATION process has been identified as destructive of both 'community' and communities. Research by Young and Willmott (1960) and Gans (1962) has, however, raised serious doubts about any such simple association between urbanization and 'loss of community'.

Sociologists have usually been less concerned with categorizing and identifying the physical and geographical characteristics of communities than with examining the nature and quality of the social relationships sustained by them. Recent sociology has also been concerned with the analysis of community action and collective resistance to social problems (Castells, 1976).

Whatever the definitional difficulties, all communities, both real and symbolic, exist and operate within boundaries or territories. Boundaries serve to demarcate social membership from nonmembership. Communities may be seen to be inclusive of some people and social groups, but exclusive of others. In some cases, community boundaries are rigidly maintained (e.g. some religious communities), in others the boundaries are more fluid and open.

Worsley (1987) has suggested that, despite the difficulties involved in theorizing about 'community' and communities', three broad meanings can be identified within sociological literature. The first he describes as 'community as locality'. Here the interpretation of the term comes closest to its geographical meaning of a 'human settlement within a fixed and bounded local territory'. Secondly, he suggests that 'community' has been used to denote a 'network of interrelationships' (Stacey, 1969). In this usage, community relationships can be characterized by conflict as well as by mutuality and reciprocity. In the third usage, community can be seen to refer to a particular type of social relationship; one that possesses certain qualities. It infers the existence of a 'community spirit' or 'community feeling'. This usage comes closest to a common-sense usage and does not necessarily imply the existence of a local geographical area or neighbourhood.

Community remains an important, if controversial, concept in sociology. See CHICAGO SCHOOL, COMMUNITY STUDIES, COMMUNITY CARE, COMMUNITARIANISM.

community care the care of individuals within the community as an alternative to institutional or long-stay residential care. It has its origins in relation to mental illness and the critique of institutionalization in the 1950s which led, in 1963, to the publication of *Health and Welfare: the Development of Community Care*. Since then, the term has been applied to provision for other groups, such as children and older people. In the 1980s, ideas about community care were developed by governments as a means of providing support for a growing number of needy people. This trend was initiated in 1982 with the publication of *Social Workers: Their Roles and Tasks, The Barclay Report*. Of more significance was the Green Paper by Sir Roy Griffiths entitled *Community Care: Agenda for Action,* which led to a White Paper in 1989 called *Caring for People: Community Care in the Next Decade and Beyond.* In this White Paper, community care is defined as the means of providing: 'the services and support which people who are affected by problems of ageing, mental illness, mental handicap or physical or sensory disability need to be able to live as independently as possible in their own homes, or in "homely" settings in the community'. The White Paper also recognized the need to give support to carers.

A further important dimension to the Griffiths Report and the White Paper was the philosophy that community care should be provided within the context of *welfare pluralism;* that is, that the WELFARE STATE and local authorities should not be the principle providers of care, rather, community care should be provided by a mixture of local authority, private and voluntary organizations. Although community care has been celebrated as a means of providing an alternative to institutional care (which is seen to lead to dependency), it has been criticized in a number of ways:

(a) its definition is unclear and commentators point to the difficulty in deciding whether community care is dichotomous with institutional care or whether they lie on a continuum of welfare provision;

(b) its lack of definition may mean that community care is little more than caring undertaken by relatives, friends and neighbours for little or no remuneration;

(c) feminist sociologists, in particular, have argued that community care is euphemistic for the work that women do in the family and in the community, and to promote community care is to reinforce the ideology of women performing the caring role in society;

(d) the sources of funding of community care are often unclear, and some critics have suggested that community care is a strategy for reducing the costs of welfare provision.

A number of empirical studies have demonstrated that most caring is undertaken by women, usually daughters and daughters-in-law. However, the number of male carers increased during the 1980s and some authors have speculated that the proportion of male carers might increase further as more women are encouraged to 'return to the labour market' to fill the shortage of labour predicted for the 21st century. On the other hand, historical analyses of women's work demonstrate that women have often been expected to undertake paid work whilst also caring for others in the family.

A cynical observation about community care, therefore, is that it is a means of providing for the welfare of others at a minimum of government expense. However, community-care programmes in other countries, such as Sweden, have demonstrated that community care can be a very good means of enabling needy people to live with some independence in the community, although the evidence from these schemes shows that effective community care can be more expensive than institutional care.

community development projects local schemes devised with the intention of promoting COMMUNITY ACTION and community development (see COMMUNITY WORK). With the realization that postwar urban settlements were both actual and potential sites of social conflict, a number of radical community projects were developed in the 1950s. This concern with the INNER CITY continued in the 1960s, and in 1969 the Home Office supported 12 action-research projects in areas of high social deprivation. They were locally based, and had the aim of finding new ways of satisfying need through improvements in service coordination and through community participation and self-help. Most of the community development projects were critical of liberal and consensual views of community work, and developed a Marxist critique of the home and the neighbourhood as the means by which capitalist social relations are reproduced, and attempted to engage people through group mobilization, social surveys and legal redress. Although their analyses of the city are extremely valuable to sociologists, they have been criticized for ignoring the role of women in the community and in society.

community politics the political concerns generated by residence in a particular locality or place, and the relationship of residents with the central STATE.

Community politics often arise from local concerns with urban spaces, as workplaces, residences and living areas, and the politics of URBANIZATION. In this sense, the early sociological explanations of community politics can be found in the writings of TÖNNIES (1887) and SIMMEL (1903), both of whom offered a critique of the social and political effects of the transformation of Europe, both seeing the movement from rural to urban living as marked by increasing disengagement from both social and political life. Their ideas were developed by WIRTH (1938), who argued that certain social and political actions were characteristic of the city. Wirth was a central figure in the CHICAGO SCHOOL, which developed a zonal model of the city. The overall approach became known as URBAN ECOLOGY. Its main assumption was that urban communities are organisms functioning according to laws which are different to those of the wider society. The approach argues that urbanism and the politics of the community must be seen as a distinct way of life (see URBANISM AS A WAY OF LIFE).

Throughout the 1960s and 70s, there was a dramatic increase in community groups and COMMUNITY ACTION in the 'inner cities' of the UK and other industrial societies including the US and France. This was reflected in a growing interest in the POLITICAL ECONOMY of urbanization and community politics by several writers who sought to combine Marxism with a theory of the 'social production' and organization of space. Castells (1977, 1978), for example, was concerned with the 'urban problematic': a series of everyday situations, housing, transport, redevelopment, the distribution of ethnic groups, the provision of shopping and recreation facilities. All of these areas Castells calls a *structured social process.* To understand this process, he suggested, it must be related to the political economy of STATE CAPITALISM AND STATE MONOPOLY CAPITALISM. For Castells, urban politics will develop new directions as contradictions widen between society's productive capacity and its social capacity to use its productive capacity. Because of this, social protest groups involved in community action (which he terms URBAN SOCIAL MOVEMENTS) will increasingly challenge the established order through the 'urban problematic'. Harvey (1973), however, has pointed out that problems commonly regarded as urban are not peculiar to the city but common to society and only made more manifest in urban settings. Within this approach to community politics, local issues, no matter how intensely felt or contested by local community groups, cannot be regarded as either local or urban. See also SECTORAL CLEAVAGES.

community power the distribution. The works of Floyd Hunter *Community Power Structure* (1963) and Robert Dahl *Who Governs?* (1961) are important examples of studies designed to test propositions about local political power. Controversy raged between the exponents of 'reputational' studies of power (asking respondents who they believed held power), and those based on a direct analysis of actual 'decisions' made within local communities. The different approaches have led to markedly different conclusions about community power. While the 'reputational' method tended to discover 'élites', the 'decisional' approach has more often led to the conclusion that no élite of community power-holders exists. This suggests that the method of research employed has played a major part in determining the outcome of the research. Another possibility is that the choice of method of study is also related to the political predispositions of the researchers.

A further difficulty in studies of community power is the issue of how to include *nondecisions,* i.e. situations in which a *mobilization of bias* exists (Bachrach and Baratz, 1962), so that key issues never reach the political agenda. For example, in a steel town like Gary, Indiana, studied by Crenson (1971), potential issues such as pollution simply did not arise as actual issues. See also S. Lukes (1974).

community study the empirical (usually ethnographic) study of the social relations and social structure within a clearly defined locality. Significant American examples of such studies include Lloyd Warner's *Yankee City* studies; while British examples include Dennis et al., *Coal is Our Life* (1956), a study of a Yorkshire mining community, and Margaret Stacey's *Tradition and Change: a study of Banbury* (1960), in which the focus was on a changing community, seen by the researchers as the meeting point of two cultures: the traditional local culture and that introduced by newcomers. In POLITICAL SCIENCE in America, these studies have been used to provide a unit of manageable size within which to test propositions about the distribution of POWER (see also COMMUNITY POWER).

community work a distinct movement aimed at stimulating local schemes for development, particularly of education, which started in colonial societies in the aftermath of World War II. It was originally known as *community development* and defined as 'a movement designed to create better living for the whole community, with the active participation and on the initiative of the local community' (HMSO *Community Development, A Handbook,* 1958). Used as a strategy by the British in Africa and by North Americans in South East Asia, its aims were contradictory in attempting both to maintain social control and facilitate independence.

In the UK in the 1950s, community work was seen as an appropriate response, within the context of a WELFARE STATE, to combat growing social tensions in British towns and cities. Some authors suggest that community work has a philosophical aim in attempting to recreate some form of GEMEINSCHAFT within fragmented urban settlements. Although the political values which led to its development may be considered pluralist or consensual, in the 1960s a more radical style developed with the COMMUNITY DEVELOPMENT PROJECTS whose practices were informed by a structuralist critique (see STRUCTURALISM) of capitalist society. More recently, community work has been criticized for its reliance on the work of women whilst ignoring the nature and work of women within the community. See also COMMUNITY ACTION, COMMUNITARIANISM.

comparative history the use of comparisons, and the examination of similarities and differences, between historical societies, with the aim of achieving greater understanding of the causal influences at work in particular or general cases (e.g. in the origins of capitalism, or in the origins and general nature of feudalism). Comparative history is often closely akin to HISTORICAL SOCIOLOGY. See also COMPARATIVE METHOD, ANNALES SCHOOL.

comparative method **1** any method that involves the examination of similarities and differences between phenomena or classes of phenomena with the aim of:

(a) establishing classifications and typologies of social phenomena; and

(b) the testing of hypotheses about casual relations by examining the empirical association and temporal ordering of factors.

2 specifically *cross-cultural* or *cross-societal* (including historical) comparison of similarities and differences between social phenomena with the above aims (see CROSS-CULTURAL COMPARISON, HUMAN RELATIONS AREA FILES).

Since the comparative method is used in the absence of strict experimentation in sociology, it is also sometimes referred to as the *quasi-experimental method.* See also EXPERIMENTAL METHOD.

An early systematization of the comparative method was provided by J. S. MILL. The three most used of these methods within sociology are outlined in Fig. 5. Explicit use of Mill's methods is seen in classical sociological studies such as DURKHEIM's *Suicide* (1897) and WEBER's *Protestant Ethic and the Spirit of Capitalism* (1904–05). The method of concomitant variation receives further elaboration and systematization in modern statistical analysis (especially see STATISTICS AND STATISTICAL ANALYSIS, CORRELATION).

Compared with the experimental method proper, the problems which occur when the comparative method is used arise from an in ability to manipulate truly 'independent' variables. The main problem is the possible influence of unknown variables which, in the natural settings observed, may affect in unknown ways the variables for which a direct causal or concomitant relation is suggested.

The early use of the comparative method in cross-cultural analysis was in the work of evolutionary sociologists who have often been accused of suspect judgements of similarity and difference, and of studying units out of context.

Generally, the use of the comparative method is not invalidated by such problems, but they do underline the difficulties which can attend the use of the method, especially in its cross-cultural forms.

	Antecedents	*Outcomes*
(a) Method of agreement		
empirical case 1	A,b,c	X
empirical case 2	A,d,e	X
empirical case n	A,f,g	X
	A is the only similarly occurring antecedent when X is the outcome	
	∴ A may be the cause of X	
(b) Method of difference		
empirical case 1	A,b,c	X
empirical case 2	b,c	not X
	A is the one difference found between the two otherwise identical cases when X occurs	
	∴ A may be the cause of X	
(c) Method of concomitant variations over a number of cases	the magnitude of A varies	the magnitude of X varies with the magnitude of A
	∴ A may be the cause of X	

Fig. 5 **Comparative method.** Mill's methods.

A more root-and-branch objection to the use of the comparative method in sociology arises from theorists who emphasize the importance of MEANINGFUL UNDERSTANDING AND EXPLANATION, or VERSTEHEN. In extreme cases (e.g. WINCH, 1958), no place is seen within sociology for the testing of general hypotheses of the conventional scientific kind. However, most sociologists reject the RELATIVISM involved in this view and continue to examine general hypotheses.

With implications for both experimental and quasi-experimental methods, modern philosophical analysis has rejected Mill's view that INDUCTION AND INDUCTIVE LOGIC and the comparative method can provide the conclusive proof possible in deductive LOGIC (see EMPIRICISM, FALSIFICATIONISM). However, this does not undermine the usefulness of the comparative method any more than it undermines the experimental; it merely points to there being no recipe for establishing causality.

comparative sociology any form of sociology that involves cross-societal or cross-cultural analysis. See also COMPARATIVE METHOD.

compensatory education a system of education designed to compensate pupils for the disadvantages they experience as a consequence of deficiencies in their social backgrounds and environments. Research undertaken by sociologists, mainly in the 1950s and early 1960s, suggested that children of lower-class parents, with disadvantaged cultural or ethnic backgrounds, regularly failed to achieve either academically or socially in school. Programmes of compensatory education were introduced in the US (Operation Headstart) and in the UK (Educational Priority Areas) during the 1960s and 70s. It is generally held that the approach has been unsuccessful, with poor levels of achievement by the socially disadvantaged continuing. The main reason for this is likely to be that piecemeal educational reforms of this sort, undertaken without any other kind of significant structural change, cannot compensate for the deficiencies of society, especially when schools themselves are part of society's value structures, and when pupils remain in the social setting which caused the initial problem. Also see ACCESS.

competence (especially ETHNOMETHODOLOGY, and by analogy with linguistic competence – see COMPETENCE AND PERFORMANCE) the fundamental capacities (TACIT KNOWLEDGE, etc.) displayed by social actors as 'skilled' participants ('members') in social contexts. See also SACKS.

competence and performance (LINGUISTICS) the distinction between the ability to use language (*competence*) and the actual verbalizations made (*performance*). This distinction is made in PSYCHOLINGUISTICS in particular where 'competence' more specifically describes the linguistic knowledge and grammar which is necessary to understand and speak one's own language, and 'performance' describes the particular utterances that speakers and listeners actually produce and understand. See also COMMUNICATIVE COMPETENCE, CHOMSKY, TRANSFORMATIONAL GRAMMAR, LANGUAGE ACQUISITION DEVICE.

competition any action in which one person or group vies with one or more other persons or groups to achieve an end, especially where the outcomes sought are scarce and not all can be successful in achieving these. Competition may be direct or indirect; it may or may not be normatively or socially regulated.

In ECONOMICS, the 'ideal' of competition between sellers in a market economy – the hidden hand regulating economic life – has been held to lead to low prices, equality of profits, and the promotion of economic efficiency. In the 19th century, the social benefits of competition were widely stressed by many schools of social theorists, e.g. UTILITARIANISM, SOCIAL DARWINISM, and the sociology of SPENCER. Influenced by economic and biological theories, members of the CHICAGO SCHOOL also made competition central to their accounts of

URBAN ECOLOGY. Thus, competition has often been assumed to be a universal, and a productive, element of the human condition.

By contrast, Marxism has viewed competition more as a specific requirement of CAPITALISM, in which the surface appearance of fairness and effectiveness is seen as belied by actual asymmetries of power and by the underlying contradictions and conflicts which competition generates. There also exist many other theories which stress the deleterious social and individual effects of competition in some of its forms, unless regulated or offset by other values (see COOPERATION, ALTRUISM).

The implication of such contrasting views would seem to be that competition is not best seen as a universal drive. Nor is it a phenomenon that should be viewed as wholly positive or wholly negative in its implications. Rather, it should be regarded (as by Weber) as a frequent aspect of social relations, with implications which require individual analysis in each case.

The concept of 'competition' overlaps with CONFLICT. Although the latter concept is more likely to be used to refer to situations which lack institutionalization or normative regulation, or lead to disruptive social tensions, no hard-and-fast distinction exists, as illustrated by the existence of such concepts as 'institutionalized conflict'.

competitive capitalism the early form and ideal type of Western capitalism in which competitive market relations predominate; hence this may also be termed *market capitalism* or *free market capitalism*. See also CAPITALISM AND CAPITALIST MODE OF PRODUCTION. Compare MONOPOLY, ADVANCED CAPITALISM.

complexity and chaos theory (chaotic phenemena) the origins of thinking on complexity and chaos can be found in 19th-century social theory (Herbert SPENCER on the evolution of societies from simple to complex structure through the processes of specialization and compounding), in 20th-century computer modelling and *fractal geometry* and in attempts to extend conceptualization of cause-effect relationships to include complex phenomena such as wave and cloud formation and the patterns of movement of people in crowds. Complexity tells us that what may appear disorganized at one level of view can be revealed to have order when the perspective is extended. Examples of this would be the straight line which can be made as a result of 'best fit' between points on a graph, the mapping of a coastline, or the patterns that emerge when a simple mathematical equation, as in the case of the *Mandelbrot set*, is repeated many times. Complexity points to the different types of causality that are found in linear or simple systems and non-linear or dynamic systems. When linear systems are nudged off centre they stay off centre. Non-linear or dynamic systems are self-centring though such regulatory systems as feedback, the autonomic nervous system in the human body and *fuzzy logic* in the design of some machines. Simple linear systems can produce complex systems and complex systems can function under a wide range of conditions (look at the diversity of the human diet in history and in different cultures today). Important concepts for understanding complex systems are the impact of randomness and sensitivity to, or dependence on, initial conditions. So *complexity theory* challenges three important assumptions in conventional science: that simple systems behave in simple ways, that complex systems have complex causes and that different systems behave differently. Complexity instead makes three arguments: that simple systems can behave in complex ways, that complex systems can have simple causes and that different systems can be driven by the same principles and behave similarly. The epistemological significance of complexity theory for sociology lies in the questions it poses about how we model the real world through our mathematical and conceptual versions of it. First, if we make our models complex in order to be faithful to reality does this aid understanding? If we make them simple in order to make them easier to handle or to aid understanding how do we avoid unproductive reductionism? Finally, how do we conceive of the relationship between the model and our realities?

compliance see TYPES OF COMPLIANCE.

componential analysis a technique, based in phonological LINGUISTICS, for analysing complex elements into their components. In semantics, for example, the meaning of 'woman' could be seen as analysable into 'human' + 'female', which would be the components. Thus, research in a field of COGNITIVE ANTHROPOLOGY may involve assembling the apparently available kinship terms, and then seeking to identify the underlying components or dimensions which, taken together, would yield a particular term. Thus, 'aunt' might involve 'female' + 'one generation older' + 'one distance of indirect descent'. 'Great aunt' would involve two generations, and so on. The ideal would be to account for all variation in the terminology of a field. Similar systems of relation and contrast have also been sought for actions themselves.

comprador capitalist an entrepreneur in colonial or THIRD WORLD countries who accumulates capital through acting as intermediary between indigenous producers and foreign merchants. 'Comprador' is a Spanish word meaning 'buyer'. In FRANK's analysis, such capitalists would only promote Third World dependency, since their economic interests were in the very economic transactions which he saw as existing at the heart of the dependency relationship. See also DEPENDENCY THEORY, UNDERDEVELOPMENT.

comprehensive education a form of secondary education in the UK in which pupils are generally taught in mixed ability groups or classes and for which there is no selective entry requirement.

Moves to develop a comprehensive system in England and Wales began during the 1960s after educational research demonstrated that secondary-modern school pupils designated as 'non-academic' were often highly successful in public examinations such as the General Certificate of Education (Floud, Halsey and Martin, 1956; Crowther, 1959; Jackson and Marsden, 1962). In addition, the 1960s were characterized by a growing concern with issues of inequality. Theorists began to argue (Halsey, Floud and Anderson, 1961; Swift, 1967) that the continued separation of social classes in education engendered by the tripartite secondary system (see EDUCATION ACTS) produced continual inequalities in education provision.

The Labour government of 1964–70 saw the introduction of comprehensive schools as a means of reducing such social divisiveness and ending separatism in education, thus creating greater equality of opportunity. It also saw it as a response to overwhelming technological and popular demands, and the elimination of a waste of talent (Marsden, 1971).

The implementation of comprehensive education has been uneven and incomplete. It has been estimated that only about 20% of secondary pupils attend 'true' comprehensives. In some local education authorities selective grammar schools exist side by side with comprehensives or are being reintroduced. Many middle-class children continue to be educated in the private sector. Thus middle-class pupils with ability are 'creamed off'. In some comprehensives children are 'streamed' (see STREAMING). In most they are organized in sets or bands for particular subjects, although some schools teach pupils in mixed-ability groups during years 1–3.

Whilst supporters of comprehensive education argue that it provides the only means of reducing inequality of educational opportunity (see Hargreaves, 1982), there exist major difficulties in realizing this aim (e.g. in inner city schools) and this is one reason why there is relatively little resistance to a retreat from comprehensive education.

Comte, Auguste

French social thinker who coined the term 'sociology'. Whether Comte should be seen as the founder of sociology is debatable, and depends on how one regards precursors to Comte's own sociology (including MONTESQUIEU, SAINT-SIMON or 18th-century Scottish thinkers such as Adam FERGUSON), whose thought was certainly sociological, although they did not use the term.

Born in the revolutionary era in France, and living through the post-revolutionary turmoil, Comte also witnessed the beginnings of the industrial revolution in that country. Associated with the foundation of modern POSITIVISM and the founder of a social movement dedicated to positive social reform, Comte's goal can be summed up by his own motto: 'Order and Progress'. A sign of his widespread influence is that today this is still the motto on the Brazilian Flag. His objective was to establish a new social science which would be both the basis of understanding society and bring about its radical reform. Always eccentric, and in later life at times considered actually mad, Comte at one stage confidently expected the Pope to resign in his favour. For all this, his contribution to modern social thought has been highly significant.

Comte's approach to sociology drew upon the work of Saint-Simon, the no-less-eccentric social thinker who once employed Comte as his secretary. The idea that society evolved through set stages, with European society as the pinnacle of this development, was current in the period of the French Enlightenment (see AGE OF ENLIGHTENMENT) in which Saint-Simon lived, and to which Comte was heir (see also CONDORCET). Comte's version of this view was his LAW OF THE THREE STAGES of social and intellectual development, a law which he advanced as one 'as firmly based as any in the sciences'. In terms of this, Comte saw society as progressing through 'Theological' and 'Metaphysical' stages, before finally reaching the modern 'Positive' age, an age to be ushered in by Comte's own positivism and sociology. In the Positive stage, an era of 'reliable' knowledge, new rational government and a 'Religion of Humanity', Comte expected society to be ruled by industrialists and bankers who would be educated and guided by sociologists. He described the new era as 'positive' to contrast it with the 'negative', critical revolutionary and speculative, 'Metaphysical' era, the function of which was merely to bring to an end the earlier 'Theological' (and monarchical) one. Parliaments would have no relevance in this new era; and no one would have any rights to stand against the new scientific morality which would be established; freedom would come from acting in conformity with the requirements of the laws of nature, including those discovered by sociology.

In his general sociological theory Comte distinguished between 'statics' and 'dynamics'. His 'statics', which states the requirements for social order, is echoed in later Durkheimian and FUNCTIONALIST sociology. He regarded the family as the 'social cell' and women's natural place as in the home; religion is seen as performing essential social functions. His account of 'dynamics', which emphasized the increasing importance of the DIVISION OF LABOUR in modern societies, also strongly influenced DURKHEIM.

It is Comte's earlier work, *Cours de philosophie positive* (1830–42), that is today regarded as his most serious contribution to the subject. His later writings, including *Système de politique positive* (1875–77) are regarded as more eccentric. The most accessible form in which to read Comte's work today is in collections of extracts such as those by Thompson (1975) and Andreski (1974).

It is easy to poke fun at Comte's sociology, given some of his obvious excesses, but in his lifetime he was highly influential. John Stuart MILL, a notably sober scholar, admired and sponsored his work, and Herbert SPENCER followed in his footsteps in adopting the term 'sociology', despite a markedly different view of society. Nor should his modern legacy simply be dismissed. His emphasis on the importance of both careful observation and comparative and historical study in sociology remains relevant. His conception of a HIERARCHY OF THE SCIENCES, each with its own appropriate approaches to knowledge, shows that he was far from slavish in applying a general model of 'scientific' knowledge to social science. The general view would probably be that Comte nevertheless underestimated the differences between the social sciences and the natural sciences. Thus, there are no strictly Comtean sociologists in modern sociology, although some are prepared to sing his praises (e.g. ELIAS, 1970).

conation mental aspects of doing, as opposed to feeling (affection) and thinking (cognition). The term now has limited currency, but was used by PARSONS.

concentration camp a special unit for the detention of those defined by governments as political and social 'undesirables'. Although special centres of internment, in this sense, had been established by the British government in the Boer War, and perhaps even earlier elsewhere, the term has come to refer in particular to the centres set up by the Nazis in Germany and in occupied Europe prior to and during World War II. In this form, the role of these institutions was not merely to detain or to correct behaviour, as in some earlier cases, but to demoralize to the point of death, or exterminate those detained, especially Jews, but also other groups such as Gypsies (see also ANTI-SEMITISM). Usually, institutions of this general type, including the forced labour camps established in the Soviet Union, are regarded as an instrument of TOTALITARIANISM, but there are continuities, although obvious differences, between such institutions and the modern institutions of incarceration (see PRISONS) which are a routine instrument of social control in modern societies of all types (see also SURVEILLANCE). Psychoanalytical theorists (notably Bettleheim, 1960, himself an internee) have studied the extremes of depersonalization and dehumanization with which concentration camps are associated (see also TOTAL INSTITUTION OR TOTAL ORGANIZATION). Bettleheim's suggestion is that those who survived death by attrition in camps did so by being able to preserve some 'areas of independent action', despite an environment which appears overwhelmingly 'total'. Those with no internal resources, dependent, for example, on outside props of status for their sense of self, were more likely to succumb. See also HOLOCAUST.

concentration of ownership a tendency noticed by MARX, among others, for the proportion of the population owning the MEANS OF PRODUCTION to decline. Marx regarded this tendency as a characteristic of ADVANCED CAPITALISM. The contrary thesis is a dispersal of ownership, including a widening of share ownership and indirect ownership (e.g. through pension schemes) – and of PUBLIC OWNERSHIP. Against this, a further argument is that even if formal ownership becomes more widespread, control of the means of production remains concentrated: the so-called *separation of ownership and control.*

concentric zone hypothesis see URBAN ECOLOGY.

concept the idea or meaning conveyed by a term. The construction of descriptive or explanatory concepts has a central role within any discipline. Given the absence of tightly articulated explanatory theories in sociology, what is usually referred to as SOCIOLOGICAL THEORY is made up of looser articulations of descriptive and explanatory concepts. See also SENSITIZING CONCEPT.

concomitant variation an empirical relationship in which the magnitude of a first variable varies with the magnitude of a second variable (see COMPARATIVE METHOD). The concomitant variation or CORRELATION between variables may be used as the test of a CAUSAL RELATIONSHIP between variables. The main causal hypotheses in Durkheim's *Suicide* (1897) were tested using this method.

concrete and abstract labour see ABSTRACT LABOUR.

concrete operational stage see PIAGET.

conditioned reflex an automatic response which has been trained or learnt. A reflex response is a naturally occurring response to a stimulus, for example, salivation is the natural response to the stimulus of food, while the knee jerk is the natural response to a tap below the knee. However, Pavlov (1911) demonstrated that if a neutral stimulus is associated with the natural stimulus, this neutral stimulus becomes conditioned and will alone evoke the response. This response is then called a 'conditioned reflex' (see CONDITIONING). The paradigm is useful in explaining faulty learning, especially of fear responses, i.e. the development of phobias.

Reflexes are automatic, often involving emotional responses, not only of fear, but also of anger, pleasure or other emotions. Many human emotional responses can be seen to have developed as a result of conditioning through previous experiences. The term *conditioned response* is now used in preference.

conditioned response see CONDITIONED REFLEX.

conditioning a term used in LEARNING THEORY or BEHAVIOURISM meaning the process of training or changing behaviour by association and reinforcement. There are two basic types of conditioning – classical and operant.

Classical conditioning was defined by I. Pavlov (1911) in his research on the salivary reflex in dogs. He observed that if a neutral stimulus (NS) is paired with an unconditioned stimulus (UCS) so that they become 'associated', then the NS develops the same ability to evoke a response as the UCS. Thus the NS becomes a conditioned stimulus (CS) and the response becomes a conditioned response (CR). This type of conditioning occurs only in involuntary behaviours such as salivation, sweating, heart rate and other behaviours controlled by the autonomic nervous system, and such a conditioned response may therefore be known as a CONDITIONED REFLEX. Reinforcement is delivered regardless of response, as it precedes it and is typically also the UCS (food in the case of Pavlov's experiment).

Operant or *instrumental conditioning* was defined and extensively researched by B.F. Skinner (1953). It involves training voluntary responses as the reinforcement is only delivered after the response and is contingent upon the response. Learning or conditioning involves the development of an association or bond between a stimulus and a response by reinforcing responses when they occur. Because reinforcement follows response, respondent behaviour can be manipulated by varying when the reinforcement is given (*schedules of reinforcement*). Learning is more resistant to extinction if the schedule of reinforcement used in training is related to the responses and is unpredictable. An example of this is gambling on a fruit machine. *Extinction* is the fading and disappearance of behaviour through non-reinforcement, e.g. socially unacceptable behaviour should be disregarded and not reinforced. Behaviour can be shaped towards a desirable end by the reinforcement of successive approximations to this. In this way, animals can be taught to do 'tricks' which would not be found in their normal repertoire of behaviour. Shaping principles underlie much of the control we exert over each other behaviour, especially children's.

Condorcet, Antoine, Marquis de (1743–94) French aristocrat, philosopher and social theorist who, in arguing for the discovery of laws of historical development, prefigured the concern of many subsequent thinkers (including COMTE and SAINT-SIMON) in proposing a broadly EVOLUTIONARY THEORY. Condorcet's main work was the *Sketch of an Historical Picture of the Progress of the Human Spirit* (1795). This conceptualized the evolutionary development of human society in terms of ten stages. The final stage would be a revolutionary period which would realize the perfection of humanity. This general outlook places Condorcet primarily within the Enlightenment (*see* AGE OF ENLIGHTENMENT) and modernist traditions of belief in both progress and in the ability of the intellect to subject the world to rational understanding and control. Condorcet believed progress to be contingent on education for all, and argued strongly for EQUALITY OF OPPORTUNITY. Just as radical were his claims for the emancipation of women, for birth control, for divorce and for civil marriage. The influence of Condorcet's thought – evolutionary, optimistic and radical – was widespread, and affected many thinkers apart from Comte and Saint-Simon.

confessional technologies (FOUCAULT) practices that embed individuals within conceptions of self/identity which through assisted self-examination (with psychiatrists, social workers, etc.) enable them to develop as 'normal'/'moral' persons. Such distinctively modern technologies operate by the construction of 'types' and agencies that involve both the constitution and 'policing' of behaviour.

confidence interval the range of values round the mean of a SAMPLE within which one can state the PROBABILITY of the observation being correct for the parent population. This is usually expressed in terms of standard deviation units. See also MEASURES OF DISPERSION, CRITERIA AND LEVELS OF MEASUREMENT.

configuration see FIGURATION.

conflict the overt struggle between individuals or groups within a society, or between nation states. In any society conflict may occur between (for example) two or more people, social movements, interest groupings, classes, genders, organizations, political parties, and ethnic, racial or religious collectivities. Conflict often arises because of competition over access to, or control over, scarce resources or opportunities.

Conflict may be *institutionalized:* regulated by sets of rules to which all participants agree, such as procedures of industrial arbitration, or the electoral process of democratic societies; or *unregulated,* such as the violence deployed by and against terrorist organizations or revolutionary movements. *Institutionalized conflict* is often taken as evidence of a healthy democratic process. The PLURALIST view of power regards society as a complex of competing interests, to the extent that democratic rules and institutions allow the articulation and resolution of conflict and prevent any one 'interest' group from always prevailing on every issue. See also CONFLICT THEORY.

conflict theory 1 any theory or collection of theories which emphasizes the role of CONFLICT (especially between groups and classes) in human societies.

2 more specifically, the relatively diffuse collection of theories that, in the 1960s, were ranged against, and contested the dominance of, Parsonian STRUCTURAL-FUNCTIONALISM and its emphasis on societies as mainly governed by value consensus and the internalization of institutionalized shared values. The main feature of such conflict theories was that:

(a) they accused functionalist sociologies of disregarding conflicts of value and interest in human societies, or at best regarding these as a secondary phenomenon;

(b) as an alternative to functionalism, they offered an account of both the integration of society and of social change which emphasized the role of POWER and COERCION and the pursuit of economic and political interests in human affairs, as well as the more general role of conflict.

While some versions of conflict theory were Marxist or influenced by Marxism (e.g. GOULDNER), others were not, and were advanced on a more eclectic basis. One important approach, for example, was based on the work of SIMMEL (e.g. Lewis Coser, 1956) and emphasized the social functions as well as the disruptive effects of conflict. Still others (e.g. DAHRENDORF, REX) emphasized the significance of WEBER as well as of Marx in the study of conflict. In a highly influential article ('Social integration and system integration', 1964), David LOCKWOOD underlined the importance of an approach in which conflict was more central than in functionalism, when he drew attention once again to the existence of 'social conflicts' and 'system contradictions', as well as 'social integration' and 'system integration', as major elements in social life (see also SOCIAL INTEGRATION AND SYSTEM INTEGRATION). In the 1970s and subsequently with the reflourishing of a full range of conflict theories, simple distinctions between 'functionalism' and 'conflict theory' are no longer important, and with this the usage of 'conflict theory' in sense 2 has faded.

confluent love see INTIMACY.

conformity (PSYCHOLOGY) behaviour controlled by group pressure. Groups have NORMS which group members are expected to abide by in order to maintain the integrity of the group. An individual feels the pressure of the group's expectations and tends to conform to them. See also SOCIAL CONTROL.

Social psychologists (e.g. ALLPORT, 1924; Sherif, 1935; Asch, 1952; Crutchfield, 1955) have investigated the effect of group pressure when the groups are impermanent and the members unknown to each other, as in an experimental situation. The degree of conformity has been found to depend on certain variables, such as the perceived prestige of the group, the amount of ambiguity in the judgements to be made, and the size of the group. These investigators also distinguish two types of conformity:

(a) *internalization* – the group's opinions are believed and internalized;

(b) *compliance* – outward agreement but internal disagreement. See also SOCIAL CONTROL.

Confucianism an ethical religion, rather than a religion founded on belief in god(s), which arose in the 6th century BC in China and was based on the teachings of Confucius, who was a teacher rather than a PROPHET. The goal of Confucians is to achieve harmony with the world and nature, a gentlemanly ideal. For many centuries Confucianism was the religion of the Chinese bureaucratic class – the *mandarins* or *literati* – whose administrative posts were gained through competitive examinations in classical knowledge. Confucianism is often regarded as playing a decisive role in the legitimation of Chinese society and in providing a unified CULTURE over many centuries, overcoming even the conquest of China by 'barbarian' outsiders.

conjugal of the marriage relationship. It is also becoming common to use the term to describe a long-term relationship between individuals who are not married.

conjugal family the FAMILY form consisting of a heterosexual pair and dependent children. Compare EXTENDED FAMILY.

conjugal roles the usually gendered roles of the adult partners within the CONJUGAL FAMILY. See also JOINT CONJUGAL ROLE RELATIONSHIP.

conjuncture (MARXISM) the balance of forces, particular ideologies, patterns of class consciousness, class interests, articulation of MODES OF PRODUCTION, etc., that in combination make up a particular pattern of social and economic CONTRADICTIONS, the 'moment in history', which may or may not be favourable to social change.

connubium (ANTHROPOLOGY) the relation between prescribed marital groups. If a certain group of males has either the power or the obligation to marry within a certain group of females, then they have connubium.

consanguinity (ANTHROPOLOGY) a kinship term expressing the relationship of DESCENT from a common ancestor. The tie is therefore based on biological facts as opposed to cultural facts (i.e. parental or sibling ties, not spouses). In theory, this opposes it to affinal relationships based on marriage, but 'facts' can rarely be classified so clearly. Adoption and fictive kinship constructions complicate the distinction in many societies. COGNATIC is an alternative term for consanguine.

conscience a person's sense of right and wrong which constrains behaviour and causes feelings of guilt if its demands are not met.

These moral strictures are learnt through SOCIALIZATION and therefore vary from person to person and culture to culture. The most important influence is that of the parents, who set standards for their child's behaviour both by example and by establishing rules, and who enforce the required behaviour by a system of rewards and punishments (see CONDITIONING). Parental and societal standards thus become internalized as the conscience.

FREUD's theory is particularly specific about the formation of the conscience, which he labels the SUPEREGO. This develops through IDENTIFICATION with the same sex parent and is essentially the child's idealization of the parent's moral values.

This emphasis on the parental and societal role may be considered limited by those who regard moral judgements as absolute. This view would suggest an innate moral sense and is particularly expressed in religion and mysticism. Compare COLLECTIVE CONSCIENCE.

consciousness that part of the human mind that is aware of a person's self, environment and mental activity. The conscious mind contains memories, current experience and thoughts which are available to awareness. The conscious mind in FREUD's theory is only a small part of mental life, most of which is hidden in the UNCONSCIOUS. See also PRACTICAL CONSCIOUSNESS, STRATIFICATIONAL MODEL OF SOCIAL ACTION AND CONSCIOUSNESS.

conscription see MILITARY-CIVILIAN RATIO.

consensual union usually a heterosexual couple living together as husband and wife but not legally married. See also MARRIAGE.

consensus the existence within a society, community or group, of a fundamental agreement on basic values. While some sociologists, notably Talcott PARSONS, emphasize the existence of such shared values as the basis of any persisting social order, other sociologists do not, pointing to the frequency with which social systems may be held together by reciprocal interests or by force. See also LEGITIMATE AUTHORITY, NORMATIVE FUNCTIONALISM, SOCIAL INTEGRATION AND SYSTEM INTEGRATION, POLITICAL CONSENSUS, DOMINANT IDEOLOGY THESIS.

consensus theory of truth see TRUTH.

conservatism 1 any social and political doctrine which seeks to defend the institutions and social values of the existing order.
2 any relatively stable set of POLITICAL ATTITUDES in support of the *status quo*, i.e. policies which seek to sustain or renovate rather than reconstruct the social fabric. As such, conservatism is the opposite of radicalism.
3 support for the British Conservative Party.

Conservative political ideology, in its modern forms, first manifested itself as a reaction to the French Revolution. Edmund Burke, in his *Reflections on the French Revolution* (1790), produced a classic statement in defence of the old order. His central argument was that the established social and political institutions should be defended because they existed; they had grown 'organically'. Hence, they were a better guide to action than any theoretical construction, no matter how rational the latter may seem. Burke's ideas have provided a core theme. Conservatism has rarely been based on any *overtly* stated political philosophy, since the danger is that it could be regarded as 'abstract' and 'ideological'.

Another persistent theme of traditional conservatism has been that the social order must be maintained by a leadership composed of ÉLITES holding key positions of political responsibility. The STATE is seen as playing a central role in guaranteeing the social order, authority, and the maintenance of social hierarchy. Inequalities are seen as necessary elements of society. Conservatives also stress the importance of custom and tradition as prerequisites of a stable social order. MANNHEIM (1953), however, distinguishes between conservatism and 'static traditionalism'. Conservative politics has often involved changes which have been seen as necessary for the preservation of the social order: renovation rather than reconstruction of the social fabric. Such notions rest on another central theme in conservative thought, the belief that the mass of people, because of their inherent qualities, including ignorance and selfishness, are unlikely to create a satisfactory social order through their own efforts. See also WORKING-CLASS CONSERVATISM, DEFERENCE, NEW RIGHT, THATCHERISM, PROPERTY.

consilience (E. O. Wilson, *Consilience*, 1998) the principle of a 'unity of knowledge'. Although his account is coloured by his association with SOCIOBIOLOGY, Wilson argues that 'nothing fundamental separates the course of human history from the course of physical history' and that a fluency of discourses across the existing boundaries of the social sciences, biology, environmental policy and ethics will build a far clearer view of the world.

conspicuous consumption a term coined by VEBLEN to help define the characteristics of the LEISURE CLASS. Rather than consuming goods or services for their utility, Veblen suggests that some consumption is for show alone, i.e. the demonstration of one's social STATUS. This idea has been re-examined in the work of Fred Hirsch (1977) on POSITIONAL GOODS, and by BOURDIEU (1984a).

conspiracy theory an element within a belief system in which social consequences, identified as harmful or unwanted, are seen as arising from the activities of groups believed able to influence the operation of power, economic decision-making, etc., in surreptitious ways. Members of successful religious or ethnic minority groups, political extremists, freemasons, etc., may be identified in such theories, e.g. the 'witch hunt' of members of the Communist Party (and alleged fellow travellers) carried out by Joseph McCarthy in the United States in the early 1950s, or the so-called 'Doctors' Plot' in the USSR prior to Stalin's death in 1953, in which Jewish doctors were accused of plotting to poison Stalin. Whether or not there are elements of truth in the claims made in such conspiracy theories, it is the exaggerated nature of the claims, and the often slender evidence advanced, that leads conspiracy theories to be regarded as a phenomenon requiring explanation rather than being seen as 'true' theories. Thus, they might be explained as arising from the believers' powerlessness and structurally precarious situation, and the need for the believers themselves to find a 'reason' for this and some hope of resolution.

constant capital and variable capital (MARXISM) the distinction between capital embodied in raw materials and plant and machinery, termed *constant capital* because it can bring no more to the value of output than its own value, and capital expended to purchase labour power, termed *variable capital* which, since it alone involves new work, is seen by Marx as possessing the capacity to create VALUE. See LABOUR THEORY OF VALUE, SURPLUS VALUE, ORGANIC COMPOSITION OF CAPITAL and CAPITALISM AND CAPITALIST MODE OF PRODUCTION.

constraint any restraining social influence which leads an individual to conform to social NORMS or social expectations.

For DURKHEIM, the distinctive SOCIAL FACTS, or sociological phenomena, that sociologists study can be recognized, above all, as 'those ways of acting ... capable of exercising an external constraint over the individual'. Durkheim recognized that such socially constraining forces may also be internalized by individuals, but it was an essential feature of his conception of such constraints that they had an origin external to the individual. Thus Durkheim's use of the term is much wider than the notion of 'constraint' in which the individual who wishes to act one way is made to act in another. As Lukes (1973) points out, Durkheim's use of the term 'constraint' at times suffers from considerable ambiguity, failing to distinguish clearly between:
(a) the authority of legal rules, customs, etc. as manifested by the sanctions brought to bear on violators of these;
(b) the necessity of following rules to carry out certain activities successfully (e.g. the rules of language);
(c) the 'causal influence' of 'morphological factors' such as the influence of established channels of communication or transportation on commerce or migration;
(d) psychological compulsions in a crowd or social movement;
(e) cultural determination and the influence of SOCIALIZATION.

However, Durkheim's overall intention is clear: to draw attention to the fact that distinctively *social* reality constrains, and is 'external' to the individual, in each and any of the above senses. See also COLLECTIVE CONSCIENCE, FREE WILL, DETERMINISM.

construct any theoretical or heuristic sociological concept. The use of the term 'construct' makes apparent the 'invented', mentally constructed, heuristic or explanatory purpose of many concepts in sociology. See also IDEAL TYPE.

consumer culture 1 the orientation in modern capitalist societies to the marketing and consumption of goods and services.
2 the 'status differentiated' and 'market segmented' culture of modern societies, in which individual tastes not only reflect the social locations (age, gender, occupation, ethnicity, etc.), but also the social values and individual LIFESTYLES, of consumers.

Whereas previously sociology has tended to regard consumer culture as manipulative and stage-managed, it is today evident that neither a model of cultural manipulation nor a model of individual 'consumer sovereignty', as preferred by economists, alone adequately describes the processes involved. As indicated by Featherstone (1990), in modern capitalist consumer societies, consumption:
(a) is continuously encouraged in order for production to occur, and to provide inducement to work;
(b) has become a significant source of status differentiation for all social groups;
(c) is a major source of our pleasures, and our dreams.

All three of these aspects of consumer culture must be seen as involving complex, sometimes contradictory, relations. On the one hand, new manipulations of wants undoubtedly occur, e.g. as with elements of the fictitious 'nostalgia' and 'PASTICHE' generated in association with tourism and the new 'heritage' industry (see Rojek, 1993). On the other hand – as suggested, for example, by theories of POST-FORDISM – production is increasingly oriented to specialist needs, allowing greater cultural variety and greater individual choice and self-expression. Thus the new interest in consumer culture has brought 'cultural questions to the fore' and is seeking to move beyond the merely negative evaluation of consumer pleasures associated with previous theories of MASS CULTURE. See also ADVERTISING, BAUDRILLARD, POSTMODERNISM.

consumer goods *or* **consumption goods** goods that satisfy immediate personal needs rather than goods used in the production of other goods and of services.

consumerism 1 the prioritization and promotion of a culture of CONSUMPTION – see also CONSUMER CULTURE, ADVERTISING, TELEVISION.

2 social movements directed at protecting or advancing the rights of consumers. See also CONSUMER MOVEMENT.

consumer movement those organizations which have grown up with the aim of informing and protecting the consumer of goods and services. In the UK, the Consumers Association is the prime example.

consumer sovereignty (ECONOMICS) the concept that in a MARKET ECONOMY the consumer of goods and services ultimately determines the continued production; and changes in the production, of these. The objection raised against this notion is that, while as social actors individual consumers have 'choice', this is constrained by the power of large producers to control the range of goods and services available to the consumer, e.g. through advertising (see also AFFLUENT SOCIETY, GALBRAITH). It follows from this, that in seeking to understand consumer behaviour one must study the overall social context in which the production of goods and services occurs, and not confine attention only to the tastes of consumers. See also CONSUMPTION, CONSUMER CULTURE, COLLECTIVE CONSUMPTION.

consumption the process in which goods or services are used to satisfy economic needs.

In comparison with production, sociologists have paid less attention to consumption. Often it has been viewed as a 'mere reflection' of production (see UNDERCONSUMPTION AND OVERPRODUCTION). When attention has focused on consumption behaviour, the focus has generally been on 'pathologies' of consumption – such as undernutrition, or over-indulgence in drugs or alcohol. Only more rarely, as Warde (1990) puts it, have sociologists examined consumption 'for its own sake'. According to Warde, a developing interest in recent years in a more well-rounded sociology of consumption has a number of sources:

(a) an interest in the implications of the expansion of LEISURE;

(b) the onset of ever more 'specialist niche' consumer markets associated with a move to POST-FORDISM in manufacturing;

(c) the privatization and recommodification of public services.

As a result of this, the new sociology of consumption has shown a renewed interest in two areas: first, the formation of taste, the pursuit of status as an aspect of the experience of personal gratification (see CONSUMER CULTURE), and, second, the area of COLLECTIVE CONSUMPTION.

contemporary history the study of contemporary events (i.e. events within living memory) using historical methods, including traditional methods such as documentary analysis as well as newer approaches such as ORAL HISTORY (see also HISTORY). Although the idea of contemporary history may appear paradoxical, and it faces difficulties such as prohibitions in the availability of key documents, contemporary history is a valid and scarcely new approach, in that historians have always studied the recent past.

content analysis a research technique for the objective, quantitative and systematic study of communication content. It involves charting or counting the incidence, or co-incidence, of particular items belonging to a set of (usually) predetermined categories. It has been used, for example, to explore political balance and bias in communication by counting the number of references or time allocation given to political groups. Critics of content analysis challenge the assumption that meanings can be studied quantitatively, arguing that meanings are conveyed by absence as well as presence, and by context rather than frequency. However, in its more sophisticated forms, content analysis can take account of these critiques, and can make a powerful contribution to sociological analysis (see also GLASGOW MEDIA GROUP).

contest and sponsored mobility contrasting modes of SOCIAL MOBILITY via education, identified by R. H. Turner (1960), in which children are either chosen to enter a selective system of secondary education and supported, financially and in other ways, in their passage though this system and ultimately into élite positions: *sponsored mobility;* or must engage in continuous open competition for educational and social advantage: *contest mobility.* Thus, while grammar schools are an example of sponsored mobility, COMPREHENSIVE EDUCATION is intended to produce contest mobility and more continuous EQUALITY OF OPPORTUNITY. In practice, there are likely to be elements of 'sponsorship' within any predominantly contest system. See also STREAMING.

contextual fallacy see ECOLOGICAL FALLACY OR WRONG-LEVEL FALLACY.

contingency uncertainty of social outcome. Conceptions of an inherent contingency of social events underpin much opposition to apparently deterministic theories of SOCIAL CHANGE such as some versions of MARXISM or EVOLUTIONARY THEORY. See also CHANCE.

contingency table see CROSS-TABULATION.

contingency theory an empirical approach within ORGANIZATION THEORY which correlates features of organizational structure with contingent aspects of the environment, technology, etc., and their effect upon organizational behaviour and performance. Contingency theory thus rejects the 'classical' idea of best organizing principles, and explains variation in organizational form as determined by environmental and technical conditions.

contingent see ANALYTIC AND SYNTHETIC.

continuous variable see VARIABLE.

contract see SOCIAL CONTRACT THEORY.

contradiction 1 The proposition that something is both the case and not the case at the same time. All argument and theory in science is systematically scrutinized in order to eliminate the presence of contradiction, for any proposition which involves, or leads to, contradiction is a logically impossible account of the world, and may be dismissed a priori. It is important to see that 'contradiction' in this sense involves a purely logical relation between statements. Thus, since to claim that a camel can both pass, and not pass, through the eye of a needle involves a contradiction of logic, and we know that the situation described cannot 'be the case'. Experiment is redundant. However, to claim simply that a camel can pass through the eye of a needle involves no logical contradiction. It is simply a claim about the world which experimentation with camels has (so far) shown to be empirically impossible.
2 *economic and social contradictions*: a key term of Marxist discourse, indicating a tension, opposition or conflict between two aspects of social structure or processes within a social whole. 'Contradiction' is held to be responsible for the dynamic properties of society. The proposition that all phenomena are composed of 'opposites' is one of the three laws of DIALECTICAL MATERIALISM. Marx himself was specifically interested in the application of dialectical analysis to the study of history, hence the term HISTORICAL MATERIALISM. Here, the notion of contradiction plays a central role in the analysis of social change. Marx argued that in all MODES OF PRODUCTION (prior to

communism) a contradiction eventually develops between the FORCES OF PRODUCTION and the RELATIONS OF PRODUCTION. Substantively, this contradiction is expressed in, and eventually resolved by, class conflict. Successful revolutionary struggle by the class which represents new relations of production then initiates a new cycle of change. See also DIALECTIC and CULTURAL CONTRADICTIONS OF CAPITALISM.

contradictory class locations 'non-polarized class locations', i.e. 'class locations within capitalism that are neither exploiters nor exploited' (Wright, 1985. 1989). As such, these are broadly equivalent to the Marxian conception of INTERMEDIATE CLASSES OR INTERMEDIATE STRATA, but these are given greater systematization by Wright, who seeks to provide a theory of potential 'class alliances' on this basis. The chief addition in Wright's analysis, compared with earlier ones, is that he takes into account what he terms 'organizational assets' and 'skill assets' (e.g. educational credentials) as well as more conventional 'assets in the means of production'. Twelve main class locations are identified in this way (see Fig. 6). Wright examines empirical variations in political attitudes in terms of these schema, although some critics have argued that his approach is 'over-formalistic and classificatory'.

control see SOCIAL CONTROL.

control condition see CONTROL GROUP.

control group *or* **control condition** a group matched with the EXPERIMENTAL GROUP in all aspects except that it is not treated with the INDEPENDENT VARIABLE whose effect is to be studied. A control group is an essential part of EXPERIMENTAL METHOD design, since, unless a comparison is made between two groups, one having been subject to the variable and one not, it is difficult to conclude that any change is due to that variable. See also CONTROL, STATISTICAL.

	Owners of mean of production	*Non-owners [wage labourers]*			Organization assets
Owns sufficient capital to hire workers and not work	1 Bourgeoisie	4 Expert managers	7 Semi-credentialled managers	10 Uncredentialled managers	+
Owns sufficient capital to hire workers but must work	2 Small employers	5 Expert supervisors	8 Semi-credentialled supervisors	11 Uncredentialled supervisors	> 0
Owns sufficient capital to work for self but not to hire workers	3 Petty bourgeoisie	6 Expert non-managers	9 Semi-credentialled workers	12 Proletarians	–
		+	> 0	–	
			Skill/credential assets		

Fig. 6 **Contradictory Class Locations.** In this figure (from Wright 1985), the interaction of three categories of 'assets' possessed by individuals produces 12 class locations, of which only 1 and 2 do not have contradictory elements. Organizational assets refer to appropriation of surplus 'based on hierarchy': 'skilled credential assets' to those deriving from education and training.

control, statistical a statistical technique for examining the effect of a further VARIABLE on a data set which has not initially taken account of this variable. For example, data on gender and voting behaviour may have been collected but the addition of age as a variable may provide fuller explanation of the pattern of association.

conurbation a continuous urban area resulting from the fusion of previously independent towns. The term was introduced by Patrick Geddes in *Cities in Evolution* (1915). Related terms are urban agglomeration and METROPOLITAN AREA.

convention 1 any existing regularized social practice or accepted rule or usage. For the most part in sociology, the term is not used in a sense that departs greatly from everyday usage.

2 in politics specifically, an established precedent in, or expectation of, procedures in political office, e.g. that the prime minister can call an election. Such expectations or conventions are not promulgated as written laws or formally stated rules, and thus are sometimes a matter of interpretation or dispute.

3 in the US, the political assemblies 'convened' to select presidential candidates.

conventionalism 1 (PSYCHOLOGY) an excessive or obsessional adherence to social conventions, sometimes seen as one of the components of, or a manifestation of, an AUTHORITARIAN PERSONALITY.

2 (PHILOSOPHY) the view that scientific knowledge is a matter of convention, rather than something that can be given an entirely secure basis resting on the nature of things, or as arising from unchanging methodological rules or procedures. As an epistemological and an ontological view, conventionalism is at odds with EMPIRICISM or REALISM. See also PRAGMATISM, POSITIVISM.

convergence and **convergence thesis** a process in which the structures of industrial societies are assumed to increasingly resemble each other, making conflicts between capitalism and socialism ultimately irrelevant. The idea that the core features of a new type of society, INDUSTRIAL SOCIETY, are determined by the logic of a basis in industrial production is present in the work of the earliest modern sociologists, notably SAINT-SIMON. However, the idea was taken a stage further, and given an important ideological twist, by modern functionalist sociologists, notably Kerr et al., (1962) in the 1950s and '60s, with the suggestion that the structure of modern societies would ultimately be determined by their technological and scientific basis rather than by politics.

The convergence thesis is an example of a non-Marxist TECHNOLOGICAL DETERMINISM. The idea had its heyday in the 1950s and 60s, a period of economic optimism and expansion, combined with COLD-WAR relations between the Soviet bloc and NATO countries. As the new political regimes in central and eastern Europe evolve, questions about the logic of (but also the obstacles to) convergence will again be on the agenda. See also END-OF-IDEOLOGY THESIS.

conversation(al) analysis an approach within ETHNOMETHODOLOGY which analyses naturally occurring forms of talk. The objective is to uncover those general principles which govern the organization of talk, e.g. the rules governing *turn-taking* (i.e. how a conversation is managed by its participants, H. SACKS et al., 1974), and the implications of these in specific contexts (e.g. in clinical relationships, Atkinson, 1981).

Cooley, Charles (1864–1929) US sociologist best known for his concept of the LOOKING-GLASS SELF. This theory, about the formulation and maintenance of the personality as reflected in the judgements (both real and imagined) of others, was developed by G. H. MEAD and the symbolic interactionists. Cooley was also responsible for making the distinction between the primary and secondary group (see PRIMARY group). In general, his sociology (*Social Organisation*, 1909) shared the CHICAGO SCHOOL's concern with the relationship between the SELF and the social GROUP. See also SYMBOLIC INTERACTIONISM.

cooling-out process In higher education 'the provision of readily available alternative achievements' (e.g. transfer from an engineering course to a lower-level course as an 'engineering aide') (Clark, 1960b). In this process 'the student does not clearly fail', unless he or she wishes to define it so, but instead transfers to some form of more immediate terminal qualification. In alleviating the emotional consequences of 'failure' in this way, the 'general result of cooling-out processes is that society can continue to encourage maximum effort without major disturbances from unfulfilled promises and expectations'.

co-operation 1 shared action to achieve a desired goal.
2 voluntary organizations of producers or consumers characterized by collaborative rather than competitive capitalist relations between those involved.

In the general sense 1, it is something of a paradox that those engaged in mutual conflict, even warfare, must often co-operate, at least to some degree, in order to maintain the conflict. Thus, the widespread existence of co-operation within social organizations and societies does not necessarily answer the question of whether co-operation or competition is the decisive social cement of societies, e.g. underlying the DIVISION OF LABOUR.

In sense 2, the major reference is to the co-operative organizations, and the wider Co-operative Movement dating from the early 19th century in Europe. These derived from the ideas of socialists such as Robert Owen (1771–1858) and the democratic and participatory principles established by the Rochdale Pioneers, who established the first retail co-operative in 1844. As producer and marketing organizations, co-operatives have been especially effective in agriculture. In general, in the context of a wider capitalist system, co-operative organizations have tended to suffer from undercapitalization and poor organization.

co-operative organization and **co-operative movement** see CO-OPERATION.

core and periphery see CENTRE AND PERIPHERY.

corporate crime see WHITE-COLLAR CRIME.

corporatism 1 as in Spain under Franco and more generally in association with FASCISM, the state control of major 'corporations' (e.g. labour organizations), with the aim of removing or suppressing social conflict, fostering nationalism, etc.
2 relations between government and key interest groups (see PRESSURE GROUPS), especially big business and TRADE UNIONS, involving:
(a) *intermediation* – bodies standing between the state and the individual citizen negotiate agreements with the government on behalf of their members (e.g. agreements on wages and prices);
(b) *incorporation* – the possession of a special status by these organizations (e.g. in the UK the CBI or the TUC), so that, in some respects, they become virtual extensions of government, what Middlemas, *Politics in an Industrial Society,* (1979) calls 'governing institutions'. The UK is often regarded as having moved in a corporatist direction in this second sense in the period 1960 to 1979, a tendency which was reversed with the election of the Thatcher government in 1979. Modern Austria is some times advanced as a more fully developed example of corporatism in sense 2, characterized by features lacking in the UK, including wide social agreement on the value of social partnership, compulsory membership of trade unions and employers organizations, and effective cooperation between capital and labour.

In a more general sense, 'intermediate organizations', and thus 'corporatist' social structures, were advanced as a solution to modern social ills by DURKHEIM. Corporatism is often regarded as one of the ways in which governments intervene to manage ADVANCED CAPITALISM. However, in the UK and elsewhere corporatism has been undermined by crises of accumulation and a reversal of consensus politics.

See FISCAL CRISIS IN THE CAPITALIST STATE, HABERMAS; see also SECTORAL CLEAVAGES.

correlation the *association* between two VARIABLES such that when one changes in magnitude the other one does also, i.e. there is a CONCOMITANT VARIATION. Correlation may be positive or negative. Positive correlation describes the situation in which, if one variable increases, so also does the other. Negative correlation describes the situation in which the variables vary inversely, one increasing when the other decreases.

Correlation can be measured by a statistic, the CORRELATION COEFFICIENT or *coefficient of association*, of which there exist several forms. Most of these focus on a linear relationship (i.e. a relationship in which the variation in one variable is directly proportional to the variation in the other). When presented graphically, for a perfect relationship between variables a straight line can be drawn through all points on the graph. Correlation coefficients are constructed essentially as measures of departure from this straight line. *Curvilinear correlation* occurs when the variation of the variables is non-linear, the rate of change of one being faster than the other.

When no association is found between variables they are said to have *statistical independence*. The technique of correlation analysis is mainly used on interval level data (see CRITERIA AND LEVELS OF MEASUREMENT), but tests also exist for other levels of data (see SPEARMAN RANK CORRELATION COEFFICIENT).

Finding a correlation does not imply causation. Spurious relationships can be found between variables so there has to be other evidence to support the inference of one variable influencing the other. It also must be remembered that the apparent association may be caused by a third factor influencing both variables systematically. For situations in which three or more variables are involved, techniques of MULTIVARIATE ANALYSIS exist. See also REGRESSION, CAUSAL MODELLING, PATH ANALYSIS.

correlation coefficient a measure of the association between two variables. See CORRELATION, PEARSON PRODUCT MOMENT CORRELATION COEFFICIENT, SPEARMAN RANK CORRELATION COEFFICIENT.

corruption 'the abandonment of expected standards of behaviour by those in authority for the sake of unsanctioned personal advantage' (Pinto-Duschinsky, 1987). One problem with such a definition is that in many societies corrupt practices, as specified by legal or administrative rules, may often be customary and widely accepted as normal behaviour. Such behaviour, as in some Third World countries or command economies, may be essential for the achievement of socially necessary outcomes. Nor is corruption confined to less-developed or state-socialist economies, as scandals such as the Watergate Affair or, in the UK, the Poulson Affair, demonstrate.

corvée labour a form of labour required by a state, or state representative, often as a form of rent, taxation or other tribute. Various societies in history have exhibited forms of corvée labour. Wittfogel (1957) saw it as a particular feature of ORIENTAL DESPOTISM, distinguishing this form from SERFDOM, in which labour obligations are extracted by a landlord rather than by a state.

cost-benefit analysis a technique for appraising the total economic costs and benefits (and ideally the total social costs and benefits expressed as economic costs) arising from any economic and social activity, especially new projects. Hitherto, the technique has been mainly used to appraise new, large, public projects. But, in an increasingly ecologically conscious era, the proposal now is that many more existing economic and social activities should be subject to full cost-benefit analysis, with many more costs, e.g. environmental, also included to a fuller extent than previously. Cost-benefit analysis is far from being a straightforward technique, however, and much depends on the assumptions on which a costing is made. Careful attention has always to be given to the range of external costs and the range of benefits to be included in the calculations, as well as to the basis on which these can be costed. The results usually leave scope for controversy.

cost-push inflation see INFLATION.

counselling the process of guiding a person during a stage of life when reassessments or decisions have to be made about himself or herself and his or her LIFE COURSE. As a practice, it is allied to PSYCHOTHERAPY, although less clinical, and more generally associated with normal responses to normal life events which may, nevertheless, create STRESS for some people who, therefore, choose to look for help and support. If this cannot be sufficiently provided by family and friends, a counsellor may be the choice.

The client-centred or PERSON-CENTRED COUNSELLING approach initiated by Carl ROGERS has been very influential in recent decades. This emphasizes the counsellor's role in 'enabling' the person to reach greater self-understanding and experience personal growth, and de-emphasizes any directive role. Other approaches, such as rational emotive therapy or the cognitive-behavioural approach, are far more directive.

Counsellors exist in a wide range of areas of expertise – marriage or careers guidance, students' problems, debt management, post-operative counselling, etc. Counselling may be paid or voluntary work. In the past, training has generally been provided by the organization for whom the counsellor has chosen to work, and has therefore been specific (e.g. courses for careers advisors in the public sector; marriage guidance training in the voluntary sector). However, standardization and publicly-funded generic courses were introduced in the late 1980s and early 90s.

counter culture *or* **alternative culture** any of the subcultures and *oppositional cultures* in which lifestyles, beliefs and values are distinct from those of the main or dominant culture, and which may challenge its central beliefs, ideals and institutions. Such groups may develop through isolation, threat or around common interests. Since the 1960s there has been a flowering of counter-cultural movements, such as the GREEN MOVEMENT, in Western societies.

counter-expertise the reservoirs of 'lay' expertise increasingly available in modern societies to contest the legitimacy of expert (and sometimes self-interested) claims to knowledge. Since expert claims to knowledge are often internally contested, and since the divided line between science and 'lay' knowledge is no longer clear-cut (see SCIENCE), any assumption that decision-making in modern societies must be controlled by experts and ÉLITES is unwarranted. Thus, as BECK (1992) suggests, the opportunity exists for 'social standards of relevance' to become more decisive.

counterfactual *or* **counterfactual conditional** a conditional statement, of the form 'if *a*, then *b*', in which the assertion is that 'were *a* to have occurred, then *b* would have followed', as in 'had the Greeks lost the Battle of Marathon, then a different historical outcome from the uniquely Western route to modernity would have been the outcome'. Since the 'antecedent' (the first clause of the statement) in such counterfactual statements is unfulfilled, the empirical assessment of the claim involved in the 'consequent' (the second clause) presents some difficulties. The plausibility of such statements depends on the possibility of citing convincing supporting evidence which can justify the conditional statement.

counter-revolution concerted, violent actions by social groups to reverse REVOLUTION. Often such actions are taken by groups ousted from power and can lead to civil war. A major example in the 20th century was the Russian Civil War from 1917 to 1921 with the counter-revolutionary Whites fighting against the BOLSHEVIK revolution.

countervailing power the existence of plural centres of power within a society

(GALBRAITH, 1952), e.g. a balance of power between labour and capital, and between private enterprise and the state. Although the existence of a degree of countervailing powers is usually regarded as a characteristic of the MIXED ECONOMIES and PLURALIST polities of modern Western capitalist societies, there is usually no suggestion that the balance of power between capital and labour is equal.

coup (d'état) the sudden overthrow of state power by unconstitutional, usually violent, means. In contrast to a revolutionary change in power, in a coup there may be no intention to change the social and economic set-up radically. Instead, a change in the governing group may be all that is intended. In recent decades, many coups have been military (see MILITARY INTERVENTION IN POLITICS). See also REVOLUTION.

court society the elaboration of etiquette and standards of 'cultivated' manners that occurred in the courts of Western European monarchs in the post-feudal era (Norbert ELIAS, *Court Society*, 1969, trans. 1983). Elias's book details the life of the king and his courtiers during the reign of Louis XIV in France. Elias argues that the growth of court society, whereby a warrior nobility was eventually replaced by a courtly nobility, is one instance of a general CIVILIZING PROCESS within European society. Court society is therefore a significant social formation and a major step in the development of the modern world. See also FIGURATION (or CONFIGURATION), FIGURATIONAL SOCIOLOGY.

covering-law model and **deductive nomological explanation** a model of scientific EXPLANATION particularly associated with Carl Hempel and Karl POPPER. In this model the defining feature of a scientific explanation is represented as resting on the operation of general SCIENTIFIC LAWS and initial condition statements (together known as the EXPLANANS) which logically entail the phenomenon thus explained (the EXPLANADUM). The basic model is as follows:

(a)	Law(s).	the *explanans*
(b)	Statements of initial conditions, which point to the applicability of the chosen laws to the case in hand.	
(c)	The phenomenon explained (or predicted) as a deduction from the above.	the *explanandum*

The laws involved are *universal conditional statements:* ('For any *a*, if *a*, then *b*'), for example, 'All water heated at the pressure existing at sea level boils at 100° C'. Whilst the basic model thus identifies SCIENCE as involving deterministic laws, 'probabilistic laws' (asserting 'if *a*, then a certain probability of *b*') can also be accommodated. An important distinction also made on the basis of the model is between scientific and nonscientific prediction: rather than being unconditional, scientific PREDICTION is conditional on the occurrence of the relevant initial conditions. The model is proposed as providing a unified account of the role of explanation, prediction and test in science, including a suggested 'logical symmetry' of explanation and prediction (see also FALSIFICATIONISM).

Criticism of the covering-law model has concentrated on its claims to provide a defining model of scientific explanation. There is no general acceptance that subsumption under empirical covering laws is a sufficient or a necessary condition for scientific explanation. Successful covering laws can be formulated without these being the basis of satisfactory explanation. A suggestion also made is that scientific explanation involves the identification of underlying causal 'mechanisms' which may not depend on empirical covering laws or involve prediction (see EXPLANATORY MECHANISM, REALISM); for example, while

Darwinian theory provides an important explanatory account, this is presented in terms of general mechanisms and is not predictive. In sociology in particular it is also clear that important kinds of explanation occur which are dependent neither on covering law nor on general mechanisms (for example, MEANINGFUL UNDERSTANDING AND EXPLANATION). Thus, while the covering-law model may be seen as adequately portraying one form of scientific explanation, there is no widespread acceptance that it provides an adequate overall model of this, or of the range of explanation in general. See also HYPOTHETICO-DEDUCTIVE EXPLANATION AND METHOD, EXPLANATION.

covert observation any observational study undertaken without the permission or awareness of the persons or organizations studied. Ethical objections are sometimes made to this way of proceeding. See also UNOBTRUSIVE MEASURES.

craft apprenticeship the traditional method of learning a craft in Britain (and often elsewhere), in which the trainee was attached by a legally-binding agreement, the 'indenture', to a master for a specific number of years as an unpaid worker. The goal of an apprentice was to become a master craftsman. However, an intermediate stage existed, that of 'journeyman', and, in practice, this was often the limit of the achievement of many craft workers. Connected with the earlier medieval system of craft guilds, as well as being a method of passing on the technical skills and 'trade secrets' associated with a particular craft, the system of craft apprenticeship was also a way of controlling entry into a craft (see also LABOUR ARISTOCRACY; compare PROFESSION and TRADE UNIONS).

In modern times, with the spread of industrialism and factory production, craft apprenticeship continues to exist, although it is in part transformed. In recent years, however, the association of the system with restrictive practices, and its being regarded in some quarters as a barrier to technical change and the more flexible management of labour, has led to the virtual dismantling of apprenticeship as a general system for the training of skilled craft labour. Its replacement, in the UK at least, has been with a system of training based on colleges and ad hoc agencies, and not with a systematic pattern of skills training of the kind that exists in some other countries, e.g. Germany. See also DESKILLING, LABOUR PROCESS.

creativity (PSYCHOLOGY) that aspect of INTELLIGENCE characterized by originality in thinking and problem solving. Creative ability involves the use of divergent thinking, with thoughts diverging towards solutions in a number of directions. Tests of creativity typically require the generation of as many appropriate responses as possible to a simple situation (e.g. unusual uses, word association). Positive correlations exist between intelligence tests and creativity tests over the full range of intelligence. However, tests of creativity do not predict intelligence within a narrower range of high IQ (INTELLIGENCE QUOTIENT) scores, nor do they predict creative achievements in artistic, literary or scientific fields.

credentialism the allocation of persons to social positions, especially occupations, on the basis of specific paper qualifications. Though these qualifications are, in particular, educational ones, this does not necessarily lead to either education for socially relevant need, or improved performance in occupations. There is a high demand for jobs in modern economies, which leads to considerable competition among applicants. The requirement is for educational credentials (certificates, diplomas, degrees), which regulate the flow of manpower. The pursuit of such credentials becomes an end in itself, leading to what Dore (1976) called the *'diploma disease'* – see also Berg's *The Great Training Robbery* (1970). The form and content of education is of secondary importance. What is of primary significance is the level of qualification attainable. The process is criticized as failing to meet the real needs of industrial societies because it tends to serve mainly as a method of selection in the entry to occupations, rather than providing a preparation for them (see SCREENING). It is also criticized for frustrating many of those who embark on higher education hoping to advance occupationally, since the number of appropriate jobs does not expand to match the expansion in the numbers 'qualified' to fill such posts.

An identical process, although potentially more insidious in its implications (according to Dore), is the way in which, in THIRD WORLD countries, credentialism and the attempt to emulate Western systems of secondary and higher education leads to the expansion of educational systems in a form which is inappropriate to the needs of the economies of these societies. For both developed and less-developed economies, however, the counter-argument can be made that the thesis of 'credentialism' undervalues the intrinsic value of extra education, both in employment, in providing specialist as well as general transferable skills (see also HUMAN CAPITAL. POSTCAPITALIST SOCIETY), and as a consumption good pursued for its own sake, rather than merely for reasons of gaining employment (see SOCIAL DEMAND FOR EDUCATION). See also GRADUATE LABOUR MARKET, HIGHER EDUCATION.

crime an infraction of the criminal law. Scholars have discussed the nature and causes of crime as far back as written history shows. A related issue is that of morality, consequently, until comparatively recently, crime was seen as the proper sphere of theological and philosophical comment. In general, sociologists have tended to argue against absolutist conceptions of crime and have opposed psychological and biological explanations of why people commit crimes. Many sociologists have discussed the issue of crime in terms of morality, but, unlike the majority of earlier writers, they tended not to use an absolute or universal notion of morality, but view moral precepts in particular historical and cultural settings. DURKHEIM, for example, argued that laws changed with changes in social structure; he saw a historical shift from MECHANICAL to ORGANIC SOLIDARITY (from traditional, simple societies to complex, industrial ones) as involving a transformation in social relations which could be understood in moral terms and studied through changes in legal codes. He also argued that a certain level of crime was functional for society; this was indicated by the fact that no known society was free of crime. More significantly, crime served to strengthen morality by uniting the community against the criminal.

Whilst not being as absolutist as earlier philosophies, Durkheim's is still a highly generalized discussion of crime. Other sociological traditions have focused on the problem in more specific ways. Examples of this include discussions of the ways in which employment laws change, for example, either to criminalize or legalize strikes, depending on complex balances in the relative powers of employees and employers. There is clearly some merit in this approach of linking the development of criminal law to the interests of particular classes or vested interests, but the more general moral dimension is also clearly important. For example, laws relating to sexuality may have connections with property and inheritance, but they defy analysis in terms of particular class interests. HOMOSEXUALITY is a case in point. The expression of male homosexual desire was a criminal offence in the UK until 1969. The fact that private homosexual acts between consenting adults were decriminalized, following the recommendation of the Wolfenden Report (1967), indicates a change in the conception of the role of criminal law in regulating private conduct. In fact, it signalled that ideas about crime and criminals do not reflect absolute standards, but change over time and differ between cultures. The fact that these legal changes remain controversial, however, and that gay men and women are still marginalized and discriminated against, as the MORAL PANIC over AIDS has shown, indicates that the relation between criminal laws and culture is a complex one.

Generally, sociological approaches have tried to explain the relative nature of crime and its causes, as well as the effects of crime on communities and victims. See also CRIMINOLOGY, LABELLING THEORY, DEVIANCE, VICTIMOLOGY, CRIMINAL JUSTICE SYSTEM, FOUCAULT.

crime statistics the official statistics recording 'serious crime', which in England and Wales are compiled from the record of 'notifiable offences' which each police force is required to assemble. As with all OFFICIAL STATISTICS, debate exists as to the reliability of these statistics as indicators of the incidence of crime. Plainly such statistics can record only reported crime. Apart from this, numerous 'biases' and sources of inaccuracies exist in the collection of statistics. For example some categories of crime (e.g. WHITE-COLLAR CRIMES, crimes by women) appear to be systematically underrecorded, the result of police decisions not to prosecute, while other categories of crime (e.g. 'mugging', drug offences), which are the subject of public concern, may attract disproportionate police attention; there are also differences over time and between different police forces in the efficiency with which statistics are collected. An alternative source of data on the incidence of crime are *crime surveys* (e.g. Jones et al., 1986). In Britain, these indicate that official statistics of crime underestimate the actual incidence of some categories of crime by a factor of five (for vandalism, minor thefts, etc.), with smaller, but still substantial, underrecording occurring for other categories of crime.

criminal justice system the set of institutions developed as the STATE response to CRIME and criminals. In England and Wales, the main elements of the criminal justice system are the POLICE, the magistracy and crown courts, the Crown Prosecution Service and the prison system, although some aspects of social work and the Probation Service are intrinsic to the system. These institutions are organized and administered separately, though they are all answerable, at some level, to the Home Office. Aspects of the criminal justice systems of Scotland and Northern Ireland are significantly different from the English model: 'Diplock' courts in Northern Ireland, for example, try many 'terrorist' and some other offenders without using the jury system, while in Scotland the unique office of the procurator fiscal is central to the prosecution of criminal trials. There has been very little sociological work on the criminal justice system as a whole. Most studies concentrate on some particular aspect of the system or some specific issue relating to policing, the work of the courts, sentencing, etc. An exception to this is Fitzgerald and Muncie's (1987) overview.

criminology

A branch of study which has traditionally focused on a number of aspects of the nature and causes of CRIME and the criminal element in society. It is debatable whether this area of study may be called a discipline in its own right as it has tended rather to focus only on one problem andits ramifications from a variety of disciplinary and epistemological perspectives.

Interest in crime and the infraction of rules is found throughout written history. Morality tales about the effect of lawbreaking are found in ancient Greece and, before that, in pre-Hellenic Babylon in legal codes established around 2000 BC. In modern times, a systematic interest in crime grew with the massive social changes associated with the take-off of capitalism in the 18th century. The break-up of traditional societies, the dislocation of forms of social control effective in small-scale and rural societies, and the emergence of new property and class relations, reflected in the political revolutions of the time, all led to a growth of interest in the conditions of social order, and its obverse. Interest in crime was a corollary of this.

In the 18th-century, the 'classical' school in law assumed the existence of human rationality and free will, and therefore the rational calculation of the costs and benefits of any action. The implication for criminal policy was to make the cost of infraction greater than the potential benefits. (This model has much in common with more recent deterrent theories.)

Positivist criminology may be seen, in part, as a reaction to the 'classical' tradition, but also as part of the general growth of positivist explanation in the 19th century. Its best-known exponent was Cesare LOMBROSO, an Italian physician. Lombroso and his followers espoused a biological determinism opposed to the notion of free will. On the basis of measurements of prison inmates and the postmortem examination of some convicts, he argued that criminality was associated with 'atavism' – by which he meant the survival of traits characteristic of a more primitive stage of human evolution. These genetic 'throwbacks' were associated with 'the ferocious instincts of primitive humanity and the inferior animals'. By the early years of this century Lombroso's work was thoroughly discredited. However, genetic/biological explanations have recurred from time to time, for example, in psychologists' contributions to criminology.

There is a variety of sociological approaches to crime and criminality, most of which are opposed to individualistic and biologistic accounts.

One tendency, incorporating a number of theoretical traditions, is 'social pathology'. The basic theme here is that, rather than problems with individuals, it is social problems which cause criminal behaviour.

Classical Marxist accounts (e.g. by Engels and Bonger) relate crime to inherent features of CAPITALISM, including poverty and the degradation of the working class, and the effects of greed and exploitation in creating a 'criminogenic' culture. This emphasis re-emerged in sociology in the 1970s with the growing influence of Marxism on the discipline. In the US, there has been a long-standing interest in the sociological explanation of crime, much of it influenced by the CHICAGO SCHOOL. Early Chicago school authors developed the notion of 'cultural transmission'. Studying high-crime areas in Chicago between 1900 and 1925, they argued that in such areas delinquency was a tradition. Delinquent values were transmitted by PEER GROUPS and gangs. Individuals were effectively socialized into delinquency. There is also a well-established interest in the broader explanation of DEVIANCE, e.g. in ANOMIE theory and in LABELLING THEORY.

These arguments were expanded in DELINQUENT SUBCULTURE and in

DIFFERENTIAL ASSOCIATION theories. Attempts have also been made to synthesize these different theoretical tendencies by Cloward and Ohlin (1960) in particular, who brought together cultural transmission and anomie theories. They showed how 'structures of opportunity' for legitimate or illegitimate use of resources vary. Cloward and Ohlin identify one section of the 'lower class' as particularly likely to take up the chances available for delinquency: those 'seeking higher status within their own cultural milieu' and an alternative to a middle-class lifestyle, an illegal route to affluence within 'lower-class' culture (compare MERTON's use of ANOMIE).

Approaches such as these have been criticized on a number of grounds. For example, that they generally accept the legitimacy of 'legitimate' means and ends and assume that everyone else does likewise. Also the focus has been exclusively on lower-working-class males, with little examination of female criminality, WHITE-COLLAR CRIME, or 'crimes of the powerful'.

In the 1970s, in the UK and the USA, sociologists returned to a blend of labelling theory and Marxism, and issues of crime, social class and capitalism. In the UK, work in this style is exemplified by the 'critical criminology' of Taylor, Walton and Young (1973). Radical criminologists were united by a common ethos rather than an agreed theory. They were critical of positivist, functionalist, and labelling approaches, and offered instead a criminology which located the analysis of crime and law in the wider understanding of the CAPITALIST STATE and social class relations. Thus criminal law, policing and the prison system were portrayed as aspects of class domination. There is a clear legacy of labelling theory in this approach, but with an emphasis on the labelling of particular acts as 'deviant', as grounded in the logic and needs of capitalism. The radical perspective has been important in reviving sociological interest in the detailed analysis of aspects of the CRIMINAL JUSTICE SYSTEM – policing, courts and sentencing, and prisons.

Further development since the 1970s has been in the growth of feminist contributions to the study of crime and deviance. Apart from the resurgence of the Women's Movement, this interest has owed much to the development of radical criminology, but with an increasing recognition that gender issues cannot be simply incorporated within a class-based perspective. Work on criminal statistics, SUBCULTURES, violence against women, female criminality, sentencing, PRISONS and other issues all demonstrated the importance of gender as a specific issue and in informing general theoretical and empirical debates in criminology. A further development in recent years has been a shift in emphasis from a concern only with offenders, to a concern with the victims of crime (see VICTIMOLOGY).

Beyond the more conventional, predominantly empirical, grounded theoretic or critical Anglo-American approaches to the study of crime, the influence of the work of FOUCAULT has also had a major influence.

crises of capitalism (MARXISM) the periodic ECONOMIC CRISES which occur in capitalist economies in association with the TRADE CYCLE, which, according to some Marxists, tend to deepen as capitalism advances, although MARX himself did not take such a view consistently. A deepening of the crisis tendencies in capitalism is seen as associated with a contradiction between an increasing 'socialization' of production (e.g. increased interdependency between different parts of the capitalist system) and the lack of any general mechanism for its coordination. One way in which cyclical crisis tendencies in capitalist societies have been controlled, especially in the course of the 20th century, is by government intervention in the economy. Sometimes it has been suggested that such interventions have been counterproductive (see KEYNESIAN ECONOMICS, FISCAL CRISIS IN THE CAPITALIST STATE). However, alternative policies introduced to 'correct' such intervention-related tendencies to crisis, in their own way also involve interventions. Thus no entirely convincing economic arguments have been adduced that tendencies to periodic crisis within capitalism, and any long-run tendencies to deepening crisis, cannot be smoothed or overcome by government, or increasingly by inter-state, intervention. Periodic crises are the way capitalism as an overall system adapts to new conditions, with periods of crisis being soon followed by periods of rapid growth. Whether the requirement of capitalism for ceaseless economic accumulation will ultimately be undermined by crisis tendencies which are ecological in source is a different matter. See also IMPERIALISM, DEPENDENCY THEORY.

criteria and levels of measurement the rules which govern the assignment of an appropriate value, code or score to an observed phenomenon. The most widely used classification is that devised by Stevens (1946, 1951) who identified four levels of measurement – *nominal, ordinal, interval* and *ratio* – distinguished according to their ordering and distance properties.

In *nominal-level measurement* each value represents a distinct category, and the value is merely a label or name. Values are assigned to the variable without reference to the ordering or distances between categories, in much the same sense that people have forenames such as Thomas, Richard, Catherine and Martha. Thus, nominal level measures lack many of the properties which real numbers possess, and it is not possible to add, subtract, multiply and divide such variables.

In *ordinal-level measurement* values are arranged in a rank order, such that if *a* is greater than *b* and *b* is greater than *c*, then it follows that *a* is also greater than *c*, although ordinal-level measurements give no indication of the relative distances between categories. For example, political parties might be arranged on a scale ranking from left-wing to right-wing, and although it is possible to say (in the UK) that the Labour Party is more left-wing than the Liberal Democratic Party, which in turn is more left-wing than the Conservative Party, we do not know what the *relative* distances are between these parties.

Interval-level measurements are an extension of ordinal-level variables except that the distances between categories are now fixed and equal. The Celsius temperature scale is an example of such a variable in that a change in temperature from say 2° to 3° represents the same magnitude of change as an increase in temperature from 64° to 65 °C. However, interval-level scales are purely artificial constructions and the *zero point* is not inherently determined but, rather, is defined in terms of an arbitrarily agreed-upon definition. In consequence, the zero point, and even negative values on such scales, can represent real values. For example, it is possible to have a temperature of 0 °C and temperatures below this value. Because of their artificial and arbitrary nature, interval scales lack the property of proportionateness, and, in consequence, for example, 20 °C is not twice as hot as 10 °C.

Finally, *ratio-level measurements* make use of real numbers, and the distances between categories are fixed, equal and proportionate (Nachmias and Nachmias, 1976). The zero is now naturally defined and because of this *ratio comparisons* can now be made. For example, a two-metre-tall man has twice the height of a one-metre-tall boy.

The importance of Stevens' classification is that the statistical tests which it is permissible to use are determined by the variable type. Arranging Stevens' variables in order – nominal, ordinal, interval and ratio – it can be shown that a statistical test which can be applied to a lower-level variable can also be applied to a higher-level variable. Very few statistical tests can be undertaken on a nominal-level variable, whilst any statistical test can be applied to a ratio-interval measure. Most variables which are commonly employed in the social sciences are of a nominal or ordinal nature, and in consequence only a limited number of tests can be applied to them. In the case of ordinal variables, for example, no statistical tests which involve calculating the MEAN are permissable. However, given the more sophisticated tests which are available, many social scientists prefer to use statistical tests which involve the calculation of the mean and STANDARD DEVIATION, although they are only fully justified with higher-level measurements. Laboriz (1970) and Taylor (1983) have undertaken a series of statistical tests on the validity of this approach and have concluded that it is generally acceptable, provided that the ordinal variables used are not of a dichotomous (see below) or trichotomous nature.

Other social scientists have attempted to elaborate upon Stevens' schema. Fixed and ratio-interval data are often grouped together and called *continuous* data. Finally, *dichotomous* variables (which can take only one of two values, e.g. sex) are often treated as a separate level of measurement in their own right because they can be treated as nominal, ordinal, or fixed-interval measures, depending upon circumstances. See also MEASUREMENT BY FIAT.

criterion of demarcation (of science) see FALSIFICATIONISM.

critical cultural discourse unrestricted 'open' discussion of social issues, which offers the potential for the undermining of ideological justifications of society, the establishment of true accounts of social processes, and hence also the potentiality for 'human emancipation'. Contrary to theories of MASS SOCIETY, the increasing importance of educated mass 'publics' in modern industrial societies is regarded by some theorists (e.g. GOULDNER, HABERMAS) as promoting the conditions for such critical discourse, although no guarantees exist that these will be fully realized.

critical rationalism see FALSIFICATION, POPPER.

critical social psychology diverse approaches in psychology, which tend to take an engaged, anti-discriminatory and anti-essentialist standpoint, in order to understand and explain psychological phenomena as inseparable from the SOCIAL ORDER. In part, this is achieved by critiquing many of the bases upon which psychological 'truths' have been produced and reproduced. Critical social psychologists challenge psychology's individualistic focus (see also INDIVIDUALISM), its assumption of a rational, unitary, autonomous and (usually male) subject and its appropriation of a natural science paradigm within which human behaviour is decontextualized (see also POSITIVISM). Critical social psychological research tends to be informed by DECONSTRUCTION, social constructionism (see also SOCIAL CONSTRUCTION OF REALITY) and POSTMODERNISM as it attempts to understand psychological phenomena in their wider historical and cultural contexts. For this reason, critical social psychological work is multidisciplinary, drawing on CULTURAL STUDIES, LITERARY AND CULTURAL THEORY, SOCIOLOGY and WOMEN'S STUDIES, for instance, and usually employs

QUALITATIVE RESEARCH TECHNIQUES. Different forms of DISCOURSE ANALYSIS, some informed by FOUCAULT's theorizing, are commonly employed to offer INTERPRETATIONS or readings of talk and texts, which may be naturally occurring or part of research inquiry, such as qualitative interviews. The field of critical social psychology expanded in the 1990s, though its roots can be seen in forms of FEMINIST PSYCHOLOGY. Other forms of critical social psychology are *Historical Psychology*, an approach which explicates psychological research and theory in relation to the particular socio-historical contexts in which they are embedded, and *Narrative Psychology*, an approach which takes the telling of NARRATIVES to be the way through which we make sense of our lives and the lives of others. Critical social psychologists have drawn on psychoanalytic theory (see also PSYCHOANALYSIS).

critical theory see FRANKFURT SCHOOL OF CRITICAL THEORY.

cross-cultural comparison the comparison of a social phenomenon in different societies, and perhaps at different historical times, with the aim of establishing either: (a) the common 'causal' basis of shared features, including the existence of any orderly pattern to social evolution; or (b) the unique features of a particular culture or society. Sociologists have often held sharply contrasting views on the relative importance of these two goals of cross-cultural analysis. Most theorists have recognized the considerable difficulty of defining the units of analysis and of comparing like with like in cross-cultural comparisons. While theorists and researchers taking the first view have been prepared to risk advancing general propositions about the overall form and types of human societies, those taking the second view have used comparisons mainly to highlight differences, usually portraying their use of general concepts merely as aids to comparisons (i.e. as heuristic IDEAL TYPES), with their main goal the understanding of particular cultures. See also COMPARATIVE METHOD.

cross-cutting ties the conflicting, or potentially conflicting allegiances of individuals, e.g. conflict between ethnicity and class, or religion and class. It has been argued that the web of relationships associated with such cross-cutting ties is conducive to social stability because it inhibits or moderates conflict between groups. Individuals subject to cross-cutting ties tend to be pulled two-ways, and so are likely to act to prevent or to limit conflict, e.g. presenting both sides of the case. The existence of cross-cutting ties has sometimes been suggested as important in preserving STABLE DEMOCRACY, e.g. in counteracting extremes of class consciousness. See also COGNITIVE DISSONANCE.

cross-sectional study a method of examining a varied population at one point in time in order to gather data about people at different life stages, or in different circumstances. This method contrasts with LONGITUDINAL STUDIES which investigate groups over a time period, in order to observe the developmental process, the influence of changing circumstances. The advantage of cross-sectional study is that it is quicker, not dependent on changing resources or research teams, and reduces extraneous variables resulting from the passage of time. The disadvantage is that no account of change can be given.

cross-tabulation a *contingency table* method of displaying data by a 2 x 2 table in order to examine the relationship between two VARIABLES with a view to providing explanations; for example, the investigation of Heath et al. (1991) of the 1987 election showed that class is still an important variable in explaining voting behaviour. See Fig. 7.

If, as above, an association appears to exist, other variables may be introduced by further dividing the categories (e.g. by sex and age). The purpose of displaying data in this way is not only to examine what relationship there

	middle class	working class
Labour		
Conservative		

Fig. 7 **Cross-tabulation.**

may be between variables, but to explore this relationship by the further breakdowns that may be made, e.g. by eliminating 'spurious' relationships, explained by the prior influence of a third variable, or 'specifying' the interaction between three or more variables. See also LAZARSFELD, CORRELATION, MULTIVARIATE ANALYSIS.

crowd behaviour see COLLECTIVE BEHAVIOUR.

crude birth rate see BIRTH RATE.

crude death rate see DEATH RATE.

cult 1 in both developed and less developed societies, the most informal and often most transient type of religious organization or movement, usually distinguished from other forms of religious organization (see CHURCH-SECT TYPOLOGY) by its deviation from the dominant orthodoxies within the communities in which it operates. Sometimes involving a focus of allegiance to an inspirational or charismatic leader (see CHARISMA AND CHARISMATIC AUTHORITY), cults may combine elements from various religions (SYNCRETISM) or, like SECTS, from which cults are not always sharply distinguished, may result from separation from, or operate alongside, a single more established religion. In preindustrial or transitional societies, cults often coexist with more formally organized religions and perform specialized functions, including magical rites.

Within both underdeveloped and developed societies it is characteristic of cults that they recruit individuals who make a positive choice to become involved. In this, they are unlike more mainstream religious organizations, where recruitment is normally at birth and by family ties. Cults and cult membership are most common in locations of social disadvantage and/or rapid social change and great social fluidity (e.g. modern California). See also NEW RELIGIOUS MOVEMENTS.

2 within the Roman Catholic church, the beliefs and practices associated with a particular physical location, e.g. a shrine.

cult of personality the practice in totalitarian regimes in which the leader (e.g. Hitler, STALIN, MAO TSE-TUNG) is elevated to a position of total pre-eminence and presented as the source of all political wisdom, the architect of all worthwhile political and social outcomes, etc. In this process criticism of, and opposition to, the leader is suppressed, and popular political participation reduced to ritualistic celebrations of the life and achievements of the leader.

cultural anthropology (US) the ANTHROPOLOGY of human cultures. It is distinguished from UK SOCIAL ANTHROPOLOGY by virtue of its focus on the artefacts and practices of particular peoples rather than social structures, although the difference is easily overstated. In practice, this has meant a tendency to stress the material basis of culture, though ideational senses of culture are also important and are represented in cognitive and symbolic anthropology.

cultural assimilation see ASSIMILATION.

cultural capital wealth in the form of knowledge or ideas, which legitimate the maintenance of status and power.

As proposed by BOURDIEU in particular, the notion of cultural capital extends the Marxist idea of economic capital. It is suggested that possessors of this form of capital exert considerable power over other groups, using it to gain preferred occupational positions and to legitimate their claims to a greater share of economic capital. Thus a dominant class has the symbols (language, culture and artefacts) through which it can establish HEGEMONY. Bourdieu argues that the school, through the mechanism of awarding of certificates and diplomas, is a key institution by which the established order is maintained. The language, values, assumptions and models of success and failure adopted within schools are those of the dominant group. Thus, success in the educational system is largely dictated by the extent to which individuals have absorbed the dominant culture, and by how much cultural capital is shared by the dominant group, thus ideologically legitimating the existing social order.

It is, in part, as a result of the operation of cultural capital that the working class are often upstaged in the competition for educational and occupational honours. This is because not only does cultural capital bring inherent advantages in learning, etc., but it is also possibly a factor leading to an undervaluation of formal qualifications, credentialled skills, etc., and a preference for more loosely defined 'social characteristics' by some employers, e.g. a preference for middle-class graduates from élite institutions, even when they possess inferior formal qualifications.

The concept of cultural capital involves a view of the advantages of human capital that differs from the main alternative theory, the HUMAN CAPITAL theory (see also INTELLIGENCE). It is complementary to a further alternative to human capital theory, i.e. screening theory, which has some shared features and some differences of emphasis – see SCREENING. Compare also FUNCTIONALIST THEORY OF SOCIAL STRATIFICATION.

cultural contradictions of capitalism the thesis (BELL, 1976) that unresolved conflicts exist between three fundamental 'axial principles' in modern CAPITALIST SOCIETIES, i.e., economic (technoeconomic efficiency), political (political and social equality) and cultural (individual self-expression and hedonistic fulfilment), and that central problems in modern societies have these as their source. Compare FISCAL CRISIS IN THE CAPITALIST STATE. See also JUSTICE.

cultural deprivation the lack of appropriate cultural resources, e.g. language and knowledge. The concept has been used to account for the educational limitations of working-class and ethnic minority children. It was particularly influential in the late 1960s and early 1970s, both in the US and the UK. The Headstart Project in the former and the Educational Priority Area Project in the latter were designed to compensate working-class children for lack of parental interest, the failings of home and neighbourhood, and the inadequate provision of appropriate cultural experience. This *deficit theory* of educational failure has been heavily criticized because it suggests personal inadequacy. Some sociologists believe that the issue is one of cultural difference: the idea that the school incorporates social values and ideas of social knowledge which are distinct from those held by members of the working class.

cultural diffusion see DIFFUSION.

cultural evolution see EVOLUTIONARY THEORY and SOCIOCULTURAL EVOLUTION.

cultural hegemony see HEGEMONY.

cultural incorporation see INCORPORATION.

cultural integration see INTEGRATION.

cultural lag the hypothesis that social problems and conflicts are due to the failure of social institutions to keep pace with technological change. This hypothesis is based upon the assumption of TECHNOLOGICAL DETERMINISM and is associated with neoevolutionary theories of social change. The term was first used by Ogburn (1964). See also MODERNIZATION, TECHNOLOGY, FUNCTIONALISM, NEOEVOLUTIONISM.

cultural materialism (ANTHROPOLOGY) an approach (e.g. the work of Marvin Harris 1978) which suggests that the appropriate explanations of many aspects of human culture are material factors. In some aspects the approach is like that of MARX, but in Harris's work the determining features of importance are more usually of a demographic or environmental nature. Harris, for example, has proposed ecological/environmental explanations of social practices such as cannibalism, TABOOS and food prohibitions. See also HISTORICAL MATERIALISM, ENVIRONMENTAL DEPLETION, GEOGRAPHICAL DETERMINISM.

cultural pluralism 1 doctrines which emphasize the social advantages of cultural diversity and a fostering of cultural richness.

2 a social situation in which cultural diversity prevails. See also MULTICULTURALISM, PLURALISM, GLOBALIZATION OF CULTURE.

cultural relativism and **linguistic relativism** any doctrine that the concepts and values of one society or cultural area cannot be fully translated into, or fully understood in, other languages, i.e. that truly universal concepts and values are not available. See also RELATIVISM, FORMS OF LIFE, INCOMMENSURABILITY, TRANSLATION, SAPIR-WHORF HYPOTHESIS.

cultural reproduction the perpetuation of existing cultural forms, values and ideas. For BOURDIEU, it means the reproduction and perpetuation of the culture of the dominant classes to ensure their continued dominance. See also CULTURAL CAPITAL.

Cultural Revolution see MAO TSE-TUNG.

cultural studies the distinctive range of interdisciplinary approaches to the study of culture and society, which in sociology has been especially associated with the work of the UK Centre for Contemporary Cultural Studies (CCCS) at the University of Birmingham. Established in 1964 under the directorship of Richard Hoggart, the Centre took its principal inspiration from his influential book *The Uses of Literacy* (1958). The aim was to support and encourage research in the area of contemporary culture and society: cultural forms, institutions and practices, and their relation to wider patterns of social change. Following the departure of Hoggart to UNESCO in 1968, a sociologist, Stuart HALL, became director, until his move to the Open University in 1979.

The concerns of both the Centre and the main sociological strand of cultural studies in the UK have been:

(a) the social conditioning of cultural production and symbolic forms;

(b) the 'lived experience' of culture and its shaping by class, age, gender and ethnic relations;

(c) the relationships between economic and political institutions and processes and cultural forms. These include the work of the socialist literary critic, Raymond Williams (especially *Culture and Society*, 1958, and *The Long Revolution*, 1960 – see also the entry on 'Culture' in *Keywords*, 1976). Influenced by Williams and Hall, cultural studies derived many of its concepts from Marxism, but it always avoided 'reductionism', emphasizing instead the idea that culture is a product of power struggles between different social groups, based on age, gender and ethnicity, as well as economic divisions (class). For example, in the 1970s a series of *Working Papers in Cultural Studies*, produced by researchers at the CCCS (see Hall and Jefferson, 1976), which focused on youth SUBCULTURES, attracted wide attention (see RESISTANCE THROUGH RITUAL). Later, influenced by the ideas of GRAMSCI and ALTHUSSERIAN MARXISM, members of the Birmingham school explored the cultural implications of THATCHERISM. See also MASS CULTURE, LITERARY AND CULTURAL THEORY.

More recently, especially with an increasing centrality of the 'cultural industries' within the economy, numerous further areas of focus on 'cultural forms' can also be noticed in addition to those central in the work of the CCCS – see CONSUMER CULTURE, POSTMODERNITY AND POSTMODERNISM, SOCIOLOGY OF ART.

A further trend within cultural studies, notable in the last decade, has been an increasing emphasis on the importance of acknowledgement, study and celebration of cultural difference and diversity (e.g. influenced by the work of such key theorists as FOUCAULT and SAID). A so-called '*cultural turn*' in sociology – a shift not least within neo-Marxist theory – that emphasizes the 'relative autonomy' of culture and ideology from structural determination – see GRAMSCI, NEO-COLONIAL THEORY – has made 'cultural studies' often appear as a rival approach to 'sociology'. See also MEDIA STUDIES, SOCIOLOGY OF MASS COMMUNICATIONS.

cultural theory see LITERARY AND CULTURAL THEORY.

cultural turn see CULTURAL STUDIES.

culture

The human creation and use of symbols and artefacts. Culture may be taken as constituting the 'way of life' of an entire society, and this will include codes of manners, dress, language, rituals, norms of behaviour and systems of belief. Sociologists stress that human behaviour is primarily the result of nurture (social determinants) rather than nature (biological determinants) (see NATURE – NURTURE DEBATE). Indeed, human beings may be distinguished from other animals by their ability to collectively construct and transmit symbolic meanings (see LANGUAGE). Knowledge of a culture is acquired via a complex process which is fundamentally social in origin. Human beings are both acted on by culture and act back, and so generate new cultural forms and meanings. Thus, cultures are characterized by their historical nature, their relativity and their diversity (see CULTURAL RELATIVISM). They undergo change alongside changes in the economic, social and political organization of society. Furthermore, human beings initiate cultural transformation out of their unique capacity to be reflexive (see REFLEXIVITY).

It is possible to detect in many societies the belief that culture and nature are in conflict with one another; that culture must seek to conquer nature via the civilization process. Such a view can be found in the natural science traditions of Western societies. It is also a strong element in Freud's theory of culture, in which he sees culture arising out of the repression and sublimation of man's inbuilt drives (EROS and THANATOS). Many cultures, however, regard the relationship not as oppositional but as complementary. Recent feminist theories of culture have suggested that belief systems upholding an antagonistic relationship between nature and culture have proved ecologically dysfunctional. It can be suggested that human beings *are* nature, but that they possess a consciousness of nature (Griffin, 1982).

Human beings not only have the ability to construct cultural forms and are in turn sustained by those forms; they also possess the ability to theorize about culture itself. Implicit in many sociological approaches to the study of culture(s), have been prescriptive ideas on the relative merits of certain ways of life and cultural forms. For example, cultural theorists both within and outside of the discipline have drawn distinctions between 'high' and 'low' cultures, POPULAR CULTURE, folk culture and MASS CULTURE. The concept of mass culture has been used by both radical and conservative critics to express dissatisfaction about the state of contemporary arts, literature, language and culture generally. Although embracing very different political ideologies, both groups have suggested that 20th-century culture has been impoverished and diluted. In the place of an independent, well-informed and critical public, an unstructured and largely apathetic mass has arisen.

Radical theorists have argued that the threat to the quality of culture comes not from below but from above. Most specifically, it comes from what the FRANKFURT SCHOOL OF CRITICAL THEORY has identified as the 'capitalist *culture industry*'. In this view, the capitalist mass media have the ability to manipulate the tastes, wants and needs of the masses. In contrast, conservative and élitist theorists of culture, such as those put forward by Ortega y Gasset (1930) and T. S. Eliot (1948), identify the threat as coming from the masses themselves. The masses, through what the conservative theorists saw to be their increasing power, would jeopardize culturally creative élites.

In more general terms, sociologists would suggest that it is virtually impossible for any human behaviour to reside outside of cultural influences. What initially may appear to be natural features of our lives, for example, sexuality, ageing and death, are all made meaningful by culture and transformed by its influence. Even the consumption of FOOD, so apparently natural, is imbued with cultural meaning and custom. See also ANTHROPOLOGY, MASS SOCIETY, SUBCULTURE.

culture and personality school an approach (especially within CULTURAL ANTHROPOLOGY in the US in the 1930s and 1940s) which involved the application of psychological and psychoanalytical theory within ethnographic accounts. See also BATESON, BENEDICT, Margaret MEAD. A central assumption of the school was that personality types, including differences in *national character,* were formed by SOCIALIZATION (e.g. distinctive patterns of feeding and toilet training). A classic account in this vein is Ruth Benedict's *The Chrysanthemum and the Sword* (1946) which portrayed what were seen as the two sides of Japanese national character. Although controversial, the writings of the school reached a wide audience and influenced popular conceptions of socialization and cross-cultural differences, especially in the USA.

culture area (ANTHROPOLOGY) a geographical area in which the societies share common cultural features, including language type and social organizational forms: shared cultural features which are usually assumed to be related to fundamental features of the ecology of the area. However, any assumption of ecological determinism would be challenged by most theorists.

culture bearer (ANTHROPOLOGY) any individual, especially a migrant, who carries, and thus diffuses, cultural values and traits between societies. The role of culture bearers is particularly important within those cultures undergoing transition or experiencing threat from outside the culture.

culture industries see POPULAR CULTURE.

culture of poverty the way of life developed and reproduced by poor people; an explanation for the existence of POVERTY in terms of the cultural characteristics of the poor themselves. The term was first used by Oscar LEWIS (1961, 1968), who emphasized 'fatalism' as the particular aspect of UNDERCLASS subculture which ensured the inheritance of poverty. He argued that the CYCLE OF DEPRIVATION was self-perpetuating and that children were quickly socialized into the values and attitudes of being poor. Lewis argued that the 'culture of poverty' in underdeveloped societies, typified by a cash economy and high unemployment, inhibited the inculcation of the 'modern' values appropriate for social and economic development. The idea of a culture of poverty has been criticized, notably by Valentine (1968), for its concentration on the familial and local view of poverty which largely places responsibility for poverty on the individual and the family rather than examining the external influences which may preclude social and economic development.

As applied particularly to the Third World, the 'culture of poverty' argument can be seen as part of the general debate, which emerged from the work of Talcott PARSONS, about the importance of VALUES in helping or hindering the process of ECONOMIC AND SOCIAL DEVELOPMENT. In this way, 'backward' values, such as 'fatalism' and 'resignation', were contrasted with the modernizing values of 'enterprise' and 'achievement' visible in affluent capitalist societies (see also ACHIEVEMENT MOTIVATION).

More recent research suggests that people living in the poor shanty towns described by Lewis do not have a fatalistic attitude within a culture of poverty; rather families and neighbours work together to devise strategies in order to adapt and cope with their changing social and economic circumstances. The impoverished inhabitants of Third World barrios and bidonvilles are far from apathetic. Research has clearly shown (e.g. Roberts, 1978; Lomnitz, 1977) how far the qualities of enterprise and inventiveness are needed simply to ensure survival in such adverse circumstances. Typically, family and neighbours develop complicated survival strategies, often involving the articulation of many different forms of informal and formal economic activity. Thus, relatively little empirical support has been found for the 'culture of poverty' argument. Other explanations are therefore required for Third World poverty (see UNDERDEVELOPMENT).

culture shock the disruption of one's normal social perspectives (own society, subculture, membership groups) as the result of confrontation with an unfamiliar or alien culture. While culture shock can be psychologically unsettling and troublesome to individuals (as when violently removed from their own society or when this has been undermined by outside intervention), it can also be liberating, leading to a new depth of understanding of sociologically significant relationships. It is in this latter context that sociology and anthropology often pride themselves in providing an element of culture shock for new students of their disciplines. See also STRANGER.

curvilinear correlation see CORRELATION.

custom any established pattern(s) of behaviour within a community or society. As in everyday usage, the term refers to regularized social practices, or accepted rules of behaviour, which are informally regulated, and which mark off one cultural group from another. At another level, customary forms of action may be distinguished from 'rational' forms of action (see TYPES OF SOCIAL ACTION), e.g. as with TRADITIONAL ACTION, in which there is little consideration of alternative courses of action.

cyberculture the cultural sphere arising from the advent of high technology, quasi-instantaneous communication networks, and virtual reality. Against this background, the 1980s saw William Gibson emerge as the author of *cyberpunk* (promoting self-direction and opposition to central control). His key novel, *Neuromancer* (1984), became the first work of the science fiction genre to respond to the changing technological environment. Akin to other, later, cyberpunk writers such as Bruce Sterling, Gibson's work explored the possibilities for the evolution of humanity through the medium of *cyber-technology*. Following the cyberpunk genre and the earlier work of the Canadian media theorist Marshall McLuhan, this question of human evolution has also been taken further by various social and cultural commentators, most notably thinkers such as Arthur and Marilouise KROKER, whose *Ctheory* journal remains one of the premier cyber-sites dedicated to the analysis of technology and culture, Pierre Levy, whose texts *Collective Intelligence* (1997) and *Becoming Virtual* (1998) should be regarded as key books on humanity and emergence of cyber-consciousness, and Donna HARAWAY, whose work on the cyborg as the bio-technological body, *Simians, Cyborgs, and Women* (1991), addresses the issues raised by Gibson in his early cyber-fiction. For B. Kennedy (D. Bell and B. Kennedy, eds, *The Cybercultures Reader*, 2000) 'cyberculture marks the current state of ... twenty-first century experience ...a convergence of man, mind and technologies'. See also INTERNET.

cyberfeminism the use of images of the cyborg (also see HARAWAY) and CYBERCULTURE to rethink and retheorise gender and sexual identities.

cybernetic hierarchy the notion that social systems, like animal organisms or any complex systems, are governed by a hierarchical network of communications and regulating mechanisms, and that in social systems this means that cultural VALUES and the STATE and government play a decisive role in shaping and maintaining the system. It is in this context, for example, that Talcott PARSONS refers to the political subsystem of the social system as involving 'goal attainment'.

Parsons sees social life as organized in terms of two interrelated hierarchies (see Fig. 8):
(a) a four-fold hierarchy running from culture, social systems, personality systems, to the biological organism;
(b) a hierarchy within the social system, running from 'values' and 'norms' to 'collectivities' and 'roles'. See also CYBERNETICS, SOCIAL SYSTEM, STRUCTURAL-FUNCTIONALISM; compare CULTURAL MATERIALISM.

cybernetics 'the science of control and communication in the animal and the machine'. As coined by Nobert Weiner in the 1940s (see Weiner, 1949), and stimulated by the advent of modern computing, the term was intended to draw attention to common processes at work in systems of

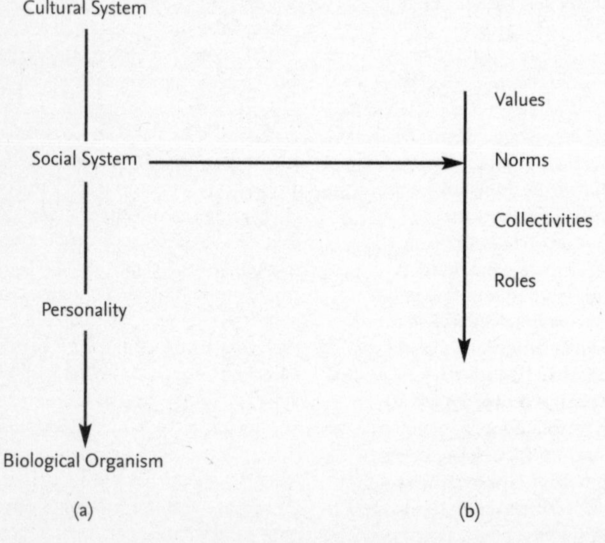

Fig. 8 **Cybernetic hierarchy.**

all types, whether these be mechanical servomechanisms (e.g. a thermostatically controlled central-heating system), biological organisms or SOCIAL SYSTEMS. The assumption is that all such systems regulate their relation to an external environment by the operation of a *feedback loop,* in which changes in the environment are communicated to the system in a manner which brings about a corresponding adjustment of the system to maintain a steady state, or other state appropriate to the effective functioning or survival of the system (see also CYBERNETIC HIERARCHY). Cybernetics and cybernetic analogies were in vogue in the 1950s and 60s, but subsequently they have suffered from a reaction against functionalist thinking and SCIENTISM in the social sciences. See also SYSTEMS THEORY, STRUCTURAL-FUNCTIONALISM.

cyberpunk see CYBERCULTURE.

cyberspace the communications 'space', including *virtual realities,* made available by the radically expanding world-wide network of electronic, especially computer-based, communications (e.g. the INTERNET). See also INFORMATION TECHNOLOGY.

cycle *or* **cyclical phenomena** any repetitive or recurring social processes in which a sequence of events is followed by a similar sequence on completion. Numerous social processes are accepted as manifesting a cyclical pattern (e.g. the life cycle); other suggested cyclical patterns (e.g. historical cycles, the CIRCULATION OF ÉLITES) are more controversial.

Bourdon and Bourricaud (1989) identify an important general category of cyclical phenomena, i.e. those that result when 'a process, in developing, causes a *negative feedback* to arise, which ends in a reversal of the process'. In ECONOMICS, the well-known *cobweb theorem* has this basis: producers tend to estimate future prices on the basis of current process, thus, they tend to produce an excess of products they think will be most profitable, and insufficient quantities of goods which they estimate will be less profitable, producing, when graphically expressed, a cyclical spider's web-like pattern of movements from one equilibrium position to another. A more straightforward example is provided by patterns of take-up of vaccination: high levels of vaccination lead to fewer illnesses due to a particular disease, leading to fewer vaccinations and a return of the disease, leading in turn to a renewal of take-up of vaccination. One attraction of conceptualizations of social reality as involving cyclical processes is that these can often be formulated mathematically, although such models rarely manifest themselves in a pure form in social life.

cycle of deprivation an account of the persistence of poverty which stresses the intergenerational transmission of social deprivation, principally through the mechanism of the FAMILY, although individual and community pathology are also implicated. The notion is linked with the CULTURE OF POVERTY thesis and was given political prominence by Keith Joseph, Minister for Social Services, in 1972.

The commitment of successive governments to urban aid programmes (EDUCATIONAL PRIORITY AREAS; COMMUNITY DEVELOPMENT PROJECTS sponsored by the Home Office and inner-city partnership schemes) reflects a concern with a supposed cycle of deprivation. Such an approach denies the importance of wider bases of structural inequality, and, as an exclusive basis to social policy, it has now been discredited.

Various other formulations or models have appeared which are variants of the cycles of deprivation theme. These alternative explanations acknowledge the significance of structural features such as changes in the occupational structure and unemployment. They also argue that the interrelationship between individuals, families and communities, on the one hand, and wider structural features on the other, are much more complex than Keith Joseph's simplistic version assumed.

d

Dahrendorf, Ralph (1928–) German-born sociologist, now a member of the British House of Lords, who has spent much of his working life in the UK, including some time as the Director of the London School of Economics. He is best known for his influential work *Class and Class Conflict in an Industrial Society* (1959), in which he proposed a reworking of traditional conceptions of class based on ownership (or non-ownership) of the means of production, replacing these with a definition of class in terms of patterns of authority. Dahrendorf retains the concept of class conflict, although he notes that in most developed capitalist societies this has undergone a process of INSTITUTIONALIZATION (see also DECOMPOSITION OF CAPITAL, DECOMPOSITION OF LABOUR). He has also written a number of comparative works examining CITIZENSHIP and democracy in modern society, including *Society and Democracy in Germany* (1967) and *The New Liberty* (1975). He has rejected as Utopian the idea that conflicts of interest based on differences in POWER can ever be removed, but has argued that the existence of CITIZEN RIGHTS and extension of EQUALITY OF OPPORTUNITY has the potential to reduce and control them.

dance see SOCIOLOGY OF MUSIC AND DANCE.

Darwin, Charles (1809–82) English naturalist whose theory of NATURAL SELECTION gave a revolutionary account of the origins of biological diversity. Darwin's ideas were presented in his *On the Origin of Species* (1859). The scientific approach which he defended, involving the gradual evolution of species over a massive time scale, has been as influential as its initial reception, especially by the church, was hostile. Darwin's theories were interpreted (quite wrongly, in fact) as a direct attack on the foundations of ecclesiastical life, God, the Bible and the Christian clergy.

Though Darwin is usually given the credit for the evolutionary hypothesis, similar ideas had been advanced by others, such as Erasmus Darwin (1731–1802) – Charles's grandfather – and Jean-Baptiste LAMARCK (1744–1829). With this historical foundation, and crucial theoretical contributions from Thomas MALTHUS (1766–1834) in demography, which suggested competition and conflict as crucial elements of population expansion, and from Sir Charles Lyell (1797–1875) in geology (the hypothesis that geological time, and hence the age of the earth, was infinitely greater than had previously been thought), Darwin's theory of evolution was, in reality, begging to be formulated. It is no surprise, then, that Darwin was not alone: Alfred Russel Wallace (1823–1913) independently and almost concurrently had come to exactly the same evolutionary conclusions.

Compared with earlier theories of biological change, the decisive contribution of Darwinian theory lay in its specification of the principal mechanism which governed development – natural selection. Darwin argued that in each generation of any species' offspring there would be some degree of random mutation, and natural variation. Any variation which enhanced the chances of survival would, over many generations, undergo a process of positive selection. Quite simply, those offspring lacking the feature would be less likely to survive, and less likely to reproduce.

Darwin could give no account of how reproduction ensured, on the one hand, identity, and on the other, variation. This had to await the development of a science of GENETICS. Nevertheless, his idea that variation, by allowing, for example, some members of a population to compete more successfully in a new or changed environment, could, over millennia, produce new species, was both simple and compelling. In sum, Darwin's ideas gave a coherent account of how a small number of simple forms could have given rise to a diversity of complex, differentiated and specialized species.

The importance of Darwin's ideas for sociology lie in two principal areas: firstly, the study of SOCIAL CHANGE, with particular reference to the EVOLUTIONARY THEORY of many 19th-century social philosophers, and their intellectual descendants, 20th-century NEOEVOLUTIONISM and theories of ECONOMIC AND SOCIAL DEVELOPMENT and MODERNIZATION; and, secondly, the social/racial engineering philosophy embraced by the school of SOCIAL DARWINISM.

Dasein (German) humankind's basic mode of participation in the world: 'Being-in-the-world' – a central concept in HEIDEGGER's philosophy. Three main aspects of *Dasein* were explored by Heidegger:
(a) 'facticity' – what is 'given', one's own origins;
(b) 'extentiality' – one's 'purposive being' and creative potential;
(c) the tendency to deny one's unique potential – a loss of '*authenticity*'.
'Unauthentic' action occurs in modes of being in which action is 'depersonalized', or regarded as 'objectivized'. See also EXISTENTIALISM.

data analysis the examination and processing of information gained from studies, such as surveys or experiments. Social data may be analysed by a variety of methods, including CROSS TABULATION, statistical tests (see STATISTICS AND STATISTICAL ANALYSIS) and computer programmes (e.g. see STATISTICAL PACKAGE FOR THE SOCIAL SCIENCES); punch cards were a common method used to collate information before more sophisticated computer analysis became possible. See also RESEARCH METHODS.

data archives *or* **data banks** repositories for the raw data collected in previous social surveys. Such data, today often made available to users in computer-readable form, may be used to reanalyse data, and used in SECONDARY ANALYSIS, which combines data from several surveys and over time. As well as containing the raw data on many classic studies, archives usually also have extensive holdings of data on changes over time in public opinion. In the UK, the main data archive is the ESRC Data Archive at the University of Essex. Data banks can be a source of inexpensive, highly relevant data. The disadvantages of using such data are that a researcher is likely to have less awareness of the limitations of the data than those who originally collected it, and, where data from several surveys are combined, problems of comparability are likely to arise (see also OFFICIAL STATISTICS). See also HUMAN RELATIONS AREA FILES.

data set a collection of information ('observations') made on a group of individuals and relating to certain VARIABLES in which the investigator is interested. This data may be gained from interviews, surveys, experiments, etc. See also DATA ANALYSIS, RESEARCH METHODS.

Dearing Report the report of the National Committee of Inquiry into Higher Education, chaired by Sir Ron Dearing in 1997 in response to MASS HIGHER EDUCATION, and a perceived 'funding crisis', in higher education in the UK. The Report proposed a variety of approaches to tuition fees and also argued for innovations in teaching and learning.

death and dying the cessation of life, which is today medically defined as 'brain death'. Sociologists have studied death and dying with an interest particularly in the sociocultural differences in the social provision for death and dying as socially managed processes involving the termination of membership of social groups, a form of 'status passage' (see also RITES OF PASSAGE). In the UK and some other Western societies, in contrast with previous eras, death has been treated as a taboo subject, with consequent difficulties for those in grief. Accordingly new provisions to cope with death and dying have been introduced, including *hospices* for the terminally ill, and *bereavement counselling*.

death certificate a certificate issued on the registration of a person's death. First instituted in 1837 in England and Wales, it shows the full name of the person, the date and cause of death, age at death, marital status, and the occupation of the deceased or his/her spouse. Death certificates provide the sociologist with a source of data with which to examine matters such as occupational illness and social-class differences in DEATH RATE. See also BIRTH CERTIFICATE, MARRIAGE CERTIFICATE, PARISH REGISTERS.

death rate *or* **mortality rate** the number of deaths per 1000 people in the population in a year – the *crude death rate*. Over the last 100 years the risk of death in the UK has been significantly reduced, particularly in the first few years of life. There is also a significant difference between the death rates of males and females according to age. In the UK, in 1961, the death rate for males under the age of one year was 24.8 compared with 19.3 for females. In 1986, the figures had fallen to 10.9 and 8.1 respectively. Similarly, the death rate for men over the age of 85 in 1961 was 258.6, and 215.9 for women. In 1986 these had fallen to 217.1 and 172.4 respectively. See also BIRTH RATE, STANDARDIZED MORTALITY RATIO, DEMOGRAPHY, LIFE EXPECTANCY.

de Beauvoir, Simone see BEAUVOIR.

debt peonage a coercive form of labour whereby the labourer is tied to an employer or landholder through indebtedness. It was a common method of ensuring a labour supply in AGRARIAN SOCIETIES until the 20th-century, although in some areas of the THIRD WORLD the practice persists illegally. Various forms of indebtedness were found: landowners sometimes paid taxes for the peasantry, requiring their labour services until payment had been made; sometimes labourers became indebted through transportation costs, such as was the case with Chinese immigrants to the US in the 19th century, when they worked without pay until their transport costs had been deemed to be covered. At its most extreme individuals were never able to work off the initial or subsequent debt which may even have been passed on to descendants. In such cases *debt slavery* may be the more appropriate term. See PEASANTS, PEASANT SOCIETY, LATIFUNDIUM.

debt slavery see DEBT PEONAGE.

decarceration see INCARCERATION (AND DECARCERATION).

decentred self *or* **decentred subject** a conception of the SELF, or the thinking and acting subject (see SUBJECT AND OBJECT), in which the self is no longer regarded as providing the kind of ultimate grounding for epistemological thinking that is often assumed in traditional forms of philosophy (e.g. EMPIRICISM). Particularly associated with STRUCTURALISM and POSTSTRUCTURALISM, the concept of a decentred self derives from three interconnected sources:
(a) from PSYCHOANALYSIS, the idea that the EGO is not 'master in its own home', and is influenced by the UNCONSCIOUS (see LACAN);
(b) from critical discourse with SAUSSURE'S linguistics, the conception that language consists of a system of SIGNS constituted by DIFFERENCE, so that the 'I' is 'only constituted as a sign' by virtue of its difference from 'you', 'we', 'they', etc., and as one element in that system, so that there can be no question of granting it philosophical privilege;

(c) from an emphasis on the 'autonomy' of culture, or the TEXT, in which the 'individual', or the 'author', exists nowhere.

In this view, rather than a single 'self', for any 'individual' person there always exist 'multiple selves' or 'quasi-selves', in which the 'self' exists only as a moment in a 'syntagmatic chain'. Whereas in structuralism the decentring of the self leads to the elevation of STRUCTURE as the pre-eminent basis of accounts of reality, in POST-STRUCTURALISM, neither the self nor structure are regarded as providing a secure basis. See also ALTHUSSER, ALTHUSSERIAN MARXISM, DECONSTRUCTION, DERRIDA, FOUCAULT.

decision making the processes by which individuals, or groups and organizations, decide actions or determine policies. Obviously, decision making covers a wide area, involving virtually the whole of human action. Sociologists, psychologists and political scientists, among others, have been interested in decision making in different ways, though there are overlapping interests. These perspectives include: formal analysis of the decision strategies of actors in competitive situations (as in THEORY OF GAMES, and in approaches derived from Economics, e.g. see EXCHANGE THEORY); analysis of decision-making behaviour in the dynamics of small groups (see GROUP DYNAMICS); studies of organizations (see ORGANIZATION THEORY); studies of access to political decision-making (see COMMUNITY POWER).

decisions and non-decisions see POWER, COMMUNITY POWER.

declining rate of profit see TENDENCY TO DECLINING RATE OF PROFIT.

decomposition of capital the process in which the ownership of CAPITAL, as the outcome of share ownership, becomes widely dispersed. The extent to which this process alters the effective control of major capitalists or the logic of CAPITALISM is much debated – see DAHRENDORF, MANAGERIAL REVOLUTION.

decomposition of labour the process in which the position of the WORKING CLASS becomes increasingly fragmented and in which this class can no longer be assumed to share consciousness or to act as a unitary force. See DAHRENDORF.

deconstruction a POSTSTRUCTURALIST intellectual movement particularly influential in France and the US since the late 1960s. The term is particularly associated with the work of the French philosopher Jacques DERRIDA who has developed powerful critiques, in particular of PHENOMENOLOGY, Saussurean linguistics, STRUCTURALISM and Lacanian psychoanalysis.

Derrida suggests that language is an unstable medium which cannot in any sense carry meaning or TRUTH directly. He has drawn attention to the ways in which Western philosophies have been dependent on METAPHOR and figurative rhetoric to construct 'origin', 'essence', or *binary conceptual systems* (e.g. nature/culture, masculine/feminine, rationalism/irrationalism) in which one term is constituted as the privileged norm setting up hierarchies of meaning which are then socially institutionalized. The project of deconstruction is to reveal the ambivalence of all TEXTS, which can only be understood in relation to other texts (*intertextuality*) and *not* in relation to any 'literal meaning' or normative truth.

By denying that we have any direct access to reality, unmediated by language, Derrida offers a critique of both POSITIVISM and phenomenology. He also traces the extent to which Western linguistics and philosophy have been permeated by *phonocentrism* – the privileged notion of speech as the voice or 'presence' of consciousness – and by *logocentrism* – the belief that the Word of the *transcendental signifier* (e.g. God, the World Spirit) may provide a foundation for a whole system of thought. Clearly, for Derrida, any such transcendental origin or essence of meaning is sheer fiction. Further, he argues that social ideologies elevate particular terms (e.g. Freedom, Justice, Authority) to the status of the source from which all other meanings are derived. But the problem here is how any such term pre-exists other meanings through which its meaning is in practice constituted. Thus, any thought system which is dependent upon a first principle is, for Derrida, 'metaphysical'.

In Derrida's view, then, LÉVI-STRAUSS consistently privileges a particular ethnocentric view of nature over culture; structuralism, generally, is dependent upon the project of constructing general laws based upon binary oppositions; LACAN (productively) sees the unconscious in terms of a language, but then falls into the trap of constituting the unconscious as the origin of 'truth'. Further, the relationship between deconstruction and MARXISM is a complex one. On the one hand Derrida has pointed to the extent to which Marxist theory has been dependent upon metaphor (e.g. base/superstructure) to erect a totalizing account of the world. On the other, he has, on occasion, declared himself to be a Marxist arguing that deconstruction is a political practice committed to uncovering false logics upon which social institutions maintain their power. While Derrida has continued to stress this progressive, radical critique, his work has been taken up by literary critics in the US in particular (the Yale School of Deconstructionists), stripped of its political force, and turned in a direction which focuses upon the 'undecidability' of meaning. Derrida himself has indicated the ways in which, ironically, such strategies of deconstruction can ultimately operate in the service of dominant political and economic institutions.

de-differentiation 1 any process in which previously more complex and variegated social arrangements are replaced by less complex patterns, e.g. the reduction of political pluralism under TOTALITARIANISM. 2 (a specifically postmodernist concept referring to) 'the collapse of the Modernist order of things'. Modernity is seen as dividing the social and natural world into pure, harmonized categories, defined and governed by reason. So private life was divided from public life, youth from old age, work from leisure, etc. Postmodernists believe that this Modernist order was always a myth and that this myth has now disintegrated. De-differentiation points to the unsustainability of rational order. It emphasizes the messiness, contrariness, ambiguity and incoherence of social life.

deductive explanation see HYPOTHETICO-DEDUCTIVE EXPLANATION AND METHOD; see also EXPLANATION, COVERING-LAW MODEL AND DEDUCTIVE NOMOLOGICAL EXPLANATION.

deductive nomological explanation see COVERING-LAW MODEL AND DEDUCTIVE NOMOLOGICAL EXPLANATION.

deep structure and surface structure the distinction, made by CHOMSKY (1965) in his theory of TRANSFORMATIONAL GRAMMAR, between the meaning of the communication (deep structure) and the surface form in which it is expressed (surface structure). Thus, for example, the deep structure of a sentence may be 'John gave the book to Jill', while this may be expressed in the surface structure as 'Jill received the book from John', or 'The book was given to Jill by John'. These grammatical changes are brought about by transformational grammar – the SYNTAX changes but the SEMANTICS does not.

defence mechanism (PSYCHOANALYSIS) the method by which the EGO transforms the energies of the ID to make them acceptable to reality. Defence mechanisms reduce biological tension and mental anxiety. The main defence mechanisms are:

(a) *denial,* where the instinctual urge is inhibited;

(b) *repression,* where it is made completely unconscious;

(c) *projection,* where the urge is inhibited in the self but attributed to another person;

(d) *reaction formation,* where the energies of the ID are redirected in the opposite direction;

(e) *intellectualization,* where unacceptable emotions are transformed by explanations making excuses for the undesirable behaviour;

(f) *sublimation*, where the energy of the ID is directed from the primary, but unacceptable, object to one that is socially acceptable. See also FREUD, LACAN.

deference 1 an attitude assumed to be based on the belief that there is a natural order of inferiority and superiority in which the inferior recognize the right of the superior to rule.

2 the outcome of a power relationship requiring a submissive response from a subordinated actor or group.

Most early work carried out within the framework of definition 1 was inspired by POLITICAL SCIENCE studies in the tradition of Bagehot (a 19th-century social commentator who, in *The English Constitution*, ascribed the relative stability of British society to its essentially deferential and, hence, élitist character). A number of voting and attitude studies used the notion of deference, in explanations of working-class VOTING BEHAVIOUR in the 1950s when manual workers' votes had clearly served to maintain Conservative governments in power. These studies were criticized on both operational and theoretical grounds. Operationally the studies employed crude indicators of 'deference' (e.g. McKenzie and Silver, 1968, labelled as 'deferential' all respondents who indicated a preference in general terms for a public-school-educated rather than a grammar-school-educated candidate for political office). Theoretically, the studies failed to explore with any precision the social structural and 'relational' dimensions of deference.

These dimensions are uppermost in sense 2 of deference, e.g. as formulated by H. Newby (1977). Drawing on a variety of earlier anthropological and historical studies, which indicated that deference did not always involve 'feelings of inferiority' but arose simply from a relationship of subordination and POWER, Newby was able to demonstrate the existence of deference in this sense in his study of agricultural workers. Thus for Newby deference is a 'form of social interaction which occurs in situations involving the exercise of traditional authority.' Deference, then, is better seen as conformity to a set of social expectations, to a ROLE, within a power structure, than merely as an attitude (see also G. Lenski, 1966). See also CLASS IMAGERY.

deferential worker and deferential voter see DEFERENCE, WORKING-CLASS CONSERVATISM.

deferred gratification the conscious postponement of immediate emotional satisfaction in order to achieve longer-term goals. Such an orientation to longer-term goals is, for example, sometimes seen as an important dimension of educational achievement (see Bernstein, 1971).

deficit theory see CULTURAL DEPRIVATION.

definition a statement or process by which the meaning of a term is conveyed. Ideally, a definition – *definiens* – will be logically equivalent to the word or term being defined – *the definiendum*. However, instead of such strict verbal definitions, *ostensive definitions* may be provided by pointing to examples or by providing general indications of use rather than strict definitions, e.g. in indicating the meaning of colour terms. Numerous further submeanings of the term 'definition' should also be noted, including:

(a) the distinction between 'descriptive' and 'stipulative' definitions, the former stating a meaning which already has currency, the latter a proposed or reformulated statement of meaning;

(b) the distinction between 'nominal' and 'real' definitions, where the intention of the latter is to move beyond a merely conventional statement of meaning to provide a definition of a phenomenon in terms of its underlying or 'real' structural determinants (see CONVENTIONALISM and REALISM). See also ANALYTIC AND SYNTHETIC, OPERATIONALISM.

definition of the situation a social situation as seen in the 'subjective' view of a particular social actor, group or subculture.

While not denying the importance of 'objective' factors in social life, the importance of taking account of the actor's definition of the situation in sociological analysis is summed up in the oft-quoted sociological aphorism: 'If one defines a situation as real, then it is real in its consequences' (W. I. Thomas, 1928).

deflation (ECONOMICS) a decrease over time in the general level of prices, coupled with an overall reduction in the level of economic activity, new investment, etc. (compare INFLATION). In modern capitalist economies, in which inflation tends to be endemic, deflation is usually relative rather than absolute, involving a reduction in rates of price increase rather than an absolute decrease in prices.

degradation ceremony the communicative work which transforms a person's entire status and identity to something lower (GARFINKEL, 1956). The guilty offender in a court trial, for example, is reduced to a degraded status as 'murderer' or 'thief. This has implications for the offender's total identity as a human being. According to Garfinkel, the existence of such ceremonies are in 'dialectical contrast' to, and also demonstrate, the 'ultimately valued, routine orders of personnel and action' within society. See also DEVIANCE AMPLIFICATION, ETHNOMETHODOLOGY.

degradation of work thesis see DESKILLING.

deindustrialization the process in which a previously industrialized or industrializing economy, or society, or region, reverts partly or wholly to a preindustrialized form. This process may occur as the outcome of international economic competition (see DEPENDENCY THEORY, also IMPERIALISM).

To some degree, the process may also occur within developed societies (e.g. the recent regional decline of manufacturing industries such as textiles or shipbuilding in parts of Western Europe). Nor is it simply a recent phenomenon. Rather, it can be seen as a 'normal' aspect of the workings of capitalism on an international stage at all phases of its development. According to WALLERSTEIN (1974), societies as different as Poland and India are examples of economies which underwent periods of deindustrialization in the course of the development of the world economy.

Deleuze, Gilles (1925–1995) French poststructuralist philosopher who most famously collaborated with Felix GUATTARI to critique Freud's theory of the Oedipus complex. Deleuze studied philosophy at the Sorbonne between 1944 and 1948 where he worked under Georges Canguilhem, Foucault's doctoral supervisor, and Jean Hyppolite, French translator of HEGEL's phenomenology. During the 1960s Deleuze produced his major individual study *Difference and Repetition* (1969). In this work Deleuze argued that a philosophy which could understand the endless play of difference and repetition should take over from structural knowledge which emphasised the relationship between the same and representation. Against the Hegelian quest for absolute knowledge, Deleuze discussed the need for a shift towards horizontal thought. Referring to the concept of the *rhizome*, he showed how difference could over-code previously fixed boundaries and move beyond the structuralist emphasis on the value of vertical knowledge.

In his 1962 work, *Nietzsche and Philosophy*, Deleuze argued that the idea of rhizomatic movement could be seen to follow the notion of the free play of forces which NIETZSCHE used to problematize the subject/object split. Following Nietzsche's theory, Deleuze argued that categories such as subject/object should be understood as values rather than truth. By overturning the singular and positing the multiple in such a way, Deleuze sought to emphasize the role of difference. His two-volume work with radical psychoanalyst Felix Guattari, *Anti-Oedipus: Capitalism and Schizophrenia: Volume I* (1972) and *A Thousand Plateaus: Capitalism and Schizophrenia: Volume II*

(1980), expanded upon this thesis by critiquing Freud's theory of the unitary ego, the desiring subject, and the Oedipus complex. For Deleuze and Guattari, Freud's conception of familial repression represented a reductivist categorisation and the imposition of vertical knowledge on a rhizomatic condition. In contrast to Freud, the two volumes of *Capitalism and Schizophrenia* argue that Oedipal repression is a psychoanalytic mythology which familizes a process of top-down capitalist oppression. See also: BATTAILLE, FREUD, ORDER/DIS-ORDER.

delinquency illegal or 'antisocial' acts, typically performed by young males. The emphasis on young males is not necessary in a strict sense, but has been a clear feature in sociological studies of the subject, which have commonly focused on WORKING CLASS youth PEER GROUPS, gangs or SUBCULTURES, or on aspirations and opportunities for young people.

The first sociologists to study the problem systematically were associated with the CHICAGO SCHOOL in the US. Starting with the influence of Robert PARK and W. E. Burgess in the 1920s, sociologists at the University of Chicago were encouraged to undertake empirical studies of neighbourhoods, gangs, etc., treating the city as a 'social laboratory'. Their lasting influence was in the development of area studies (the most criticized aspect of their work), and in arguments about 'social disorganization' and the importance of subcultures (or cultural transmission). Later US studies presented alternatives to the Chicago approach, or tried to develop themes which had been established by Chicago sociologists.

MERTON, for example, adapted DURKHEIM's notion of ANOMIE to suggest that a disparity between highly valued goals and legitimate opportunities to achieve goals could produce a number of deviant responses (see CRIMINOLOGY). Other researchers, notably A. K. Cohen (1955), developed the concept of subculture in relation to working-class male delinquency. He argued that delinquent subcultures provided an alternative source of status and respect for boys who did not take, or have access to, other 'solutions', like higher education or a stable adjustment to middle-class values. The values of the delinquent subculture were seen as a reaction to, and an inversion of, middle-class values. Some critics of Cohen pointed out that 'lower-class culture' had its own values which informed and shaped delinquent values. Those most commonly emphasized have been 'masculinist' values of 'toughness', autonomy and excitement. The work of Cloward and Ohlin (1960), emphasizing status and opportunities for legitimate and delinquent lifestyles, was an attempt to combine Merton's anomie theory with subculture theory. Critics of US subculture theory have tended to pick out the essentially FUNCTIONALIST assumptions about values, the positivistic, over-deterministic character of the work (see DELINQUENT DRIFT), the fact that females and middle-class youth are almost completely ignored, and, finally, the lack of empirical backing for many of the assumptions and arguments of 'classical' subculture theory.

In the UK, there has been a long-standing interest in juvenile crime and policy issues. Juveniles were very much the concern of the people who framed the Probation Act of 1907. Separate provision was made for juveniles in the Criminal Justice System (from 1933) and a number of Acts in the 1970s and 80s have been specifically directed at the problems of crime and treatment of young offenders. This interest has been stimulated by successive MORAL PANICS about YOUTH CULTURES – from teddy boys in the 1950s through a variety of 'youth subcultures' to FOOTBALL HOOLIGANS and 'lager louts' in recent years. Many sociologists have cast doubts on the argument that these phenomena are distinctively new (Pearson, 1983), and others have argued that the MASS MEDIA OF COMMUNICATION have played a significant role in defining working-class youth as a problem and in distorting and exaggerating the nature and significance of the issue (S. Cohen, 1973 and 1981). Even accepting the strength of these arguments, it is clear that juvenile crime and delinquency is a serious problem, requiring sociological research. CRIME STATISTICS in the 1980s suggest that, motoring offences apart, for both males and females, offending rates are highest amongst juveniles. This fact, together with the very high visibility of 'youth problems' which has been encouraged by the mass media, has stimulated a great deal of research by British sociologists. Early work questioned the value of the US gang studies for the British case (Downes, 1966). Rather different subculture models have been used, though, and are particularly associated with the Centre for Contemporary Cultural Studies (see CULTURAL STUDIES) at Birmingham University. Other studies have looked at the importance of 'anti-school' cultures (Willis, 1977) and at parental supervision and family life (Wilson and Herbert, 1978). Race has been a separate research area, in which much of the work has focused on the effects of deprivation, on RACISM, POLICING and political alienation (Beynon and Solomos, 1987; Institute of Race Relations, 1987). Equally important, the issue of gender has been raised in ways which do not simply accept the great discrepancy between male and female delinquency, but attempt to explain the reasons for the much lower involvement of females and for the quite different treatment which they receive in the Justice system (Carlen and Worrall, 1987). There is now a large British literature on different aspects of delinquency, characterized by a diversity of research interests and strategies. See also CRIMINOLOGY, DELINQUENT SUBCULTURE.

delinquent drift the idea that young offenders, who might otherwise respect law-abiding values and people, may *'drift'* into DELINQUENCY. The term is particularly associated with the US sociologists, David Matza and Gresham Sykes (Matza, 1964; Sykes and Matza, 1957). In arguing against the positivism and determinism of other theories of delinquency which were influential at the time, Matza suggested that the delinquent was a more active participant in the process of becoming deviant than those theories suggested. The drift into deviance is associated with a weakening of social controls, which the delinquent chooses to enhance by rationalizing or 'neutralizing' normative restraints. The important thing, for Sykes and Matza, is that these techniques of neutralization allow delinquents to value 'respectable' conduct and retain self-respect, while being deviant themselves. An emphasis on the deviants' own explanation of their actions is basic to the non-positivist stance of such theorists. Matza also elaborates on delinquents' feelings of injustice, which serve to weaken attachment to norms and excuse delinquency (1964). Sykes and Matza describe five techniques of neutralization:
(a) a denial of responsibility; instead accident, absent-mindedness, etc., are responsible;
(b) the act did not victimize anyone; no one was hurt, so there was 'no harm done';
(c) someone was victimized, but deserved what they got;
(d) condemning those who condemn you; police, judges and magistrates, newspaper editors, they all have some racket going;
(e) an appeal to higher loyalties; the delinquent act was done to help a relative or friend.

These techniques are important because 'neutralization enables drift'. Such rationalizations are commonplace in DELINQUENT SUBCULTURE.

delinquent subculture social GROUPS characterized by a commitment to values which are considered, within the dominant value system, to be criminal or antisocial.

The first sociological work in this area was carried out in the tradition of the CHICAGO SCHOOL. The earliest researchers (e.g. Shaw, 1930) used the interactionist approaches developed in the University of Chicago by G. H. MEAD and others, in studies of the high-crime, and mainly immigrant (Italian,

Polish, Irish, etc.), areas of the 'inner city'. In studying different areas of Chicago, Shaw and McKay (1929) found that there were much higher recorded rates of truancy and of juvenile delinquency in the relatively impoverished inner city areas, and that 80% of recorded delinquency was committed by groups of boys of a similar age. The research interest was thus directed onto the group, rather than on the individual, and the Chicago tradition emphasized SOCIALIZATION and the learning of delinquent values, i.e. the cultural transmission of deviant mores. They rejected individualistic explanations of criminality, arguing that the social conditions of the groups concerned encouraged the formation of subcultures, and that the problems of unemployment and lack of social acceptance (structural 'dislocations') engendered delinquent subcultures. The groups which took a delinquent path had a distinct set of values which determined status and 'acceptance' attitudes within the subculture. As Cohen (1955), in a classic study drawing on the interactionist approach, put it, 'the process whereby they "get that way" is no different from the process whereby others come to be conforming members of society'. This view, then, sees the subculture as a response and 'solution' to the poverty, low status, lack of opportunity, etc., of young people in the inner city. *Status frustration* at school and elsewhere is overcome by status and self-respect achieved within the value system of the delinquent subculture.

In the UK, the exploration of delinquent subcultures has continued in the work of researchers associated with the NATIONAL DEVIANCY CONFERENCE and the Centre for Contemporary Cultural Studies at Birmingham University (see CULTURAL STUDIES).

Delphi method a method of researching, with the aim of perhaps FORECASTING, future events. This involves marshalling the views, either by interviews or meetings, of a panel of 'experts' who are thought likely to be well placed to estimate future trends in the field in question. The method is named after the temple of Apollo at Delphi in Ancient Greece, famous for its oracle, whose priestesses were renowned for the highly cryptic character of their prophecies. How far 'experts' are always in the best position to provide useful forecasts of events is debatable. Experts, by definition having a particular view of the world, may be good at extrapolating trends or tendencies already well established, but they may be less good at spotting insidious change or the 'unexpected', which an outsider may be better placed to do. See also FUTUROLOGY.

demand elasticity see ELASTICITY OF SUPPLY AND DEMAND.

demand-pull inflation see INFLATION.

democracy

From the Greek, meaning 'rule by the people'. In modern times, those forms of government in which all full, adult members of a society or organization make up the policy-making body – *direct democracy* – or are represented by others who they elect to such a body – *representative democracy.* Until the 20th-century, democracy, in *either* of these forms, was a relatively rare phenomenon, confined to some city states, or to some organizations. Even in these cases, the number granted full citizenship or accorded full democratic rights was often limited – *limited democracy.* In both Greek city states and some modern Swiss cantons, only males are eligible to vote.

Direct democracy has only proved possible in a meaningful way in city states (e.g. the Greek *polis*) or similar settings, e.g. Swiss cantons. *Plebiscites* and *referenda*, in which people are asked to decide an issue are a form of direct democracy, but the timing and content of plebiscites and referenda usually rests with governments. PUBLIC OPINION POLLS have sometimes been presented as a new means of direct democracy. In practice, the polling of opinions can equally be regarded as a new tool helping governments and political parties, e.g. in managing election campaigns.

Representative democracy is usually seen as the only form of democratic government feasible for complex, large-scale modern societies. It is also argued that it is only in modern societies that economic and cultural resources exist to make representative democracy viable, e.g. the development of a participatory POLITICAL CULTURE, and the capacity to satisfy the demands for social welfare, etc., which representative democracies generate. See also CITIZEN RIGHTS.

As well as representative democracy, in the modern world most other forms of political system, including many single-party systems, usually attach to themselves the epithet 'democracy' – e.g. people's democracies – on the grounds that they involve rule in the interests of the people as a whole. Nor does this usage lack all sociological justification. State-dominated or 'totalitarian' expressions of democracy may be seen as one inherent tendency within modern political systems, an outcome which is only, and not always, avoided in most western societies by the preservation of plural élitist forms of democratic participation. See also ÉLITE THEORY, SOCIAL DEMOCRACY, STABLE DEMOCRACY, PLURAL ÉLITISM, IRON LAW OF OLIGARCHY, TOTALITARIANISM, TOCQUEVILLE, MOORE.

democratic centralism see COMMUNISM.

democratic élitism the theory that democratic participation in complex modern societies will inevitably be mainly restricted to participation in periodic elections for political leaders. As such, democratic élitism is another term for PLURAL ÉLITISM. The theory of democratic élitism has been challenged by those (for example, Bachrach, 1967) who emphasize the possibility of a 'developmental participation' that expands democratic capacities. See also DEMOCRACY, ÉLITE, ÉLITE THEORY.

demographic transition the changes in levels of fertility (see FERTILITY RATE) and mortality (see DEATH RATE) accompanying INDUSTRIALIZATION, which lead one pattern of population equilibrium, characteristic of preindustrial societies, to be replaced by a different equilibrium, characteristic of mature industrial societies.

This transition is held to involve three phases (see Fig. 9):

(a) a preindustrial phase, a situation in which high birth rates are balanced by high death rates, a position of rough equilibrium;
(b) an intermediate phase, in which death rates fall but birth rates remain high, a phase of rapid population growth;
(c) a concluding phase, in which birth rates fall, leading to a new equilibrium.

Explanations usually advanced for this pattern of population change are: improvements in public health in phase (b), followed by changes in economic and cultural orientations in phase (c), leading to a reduction in preferred family size.

If this pattern of demographic change can be taken as characterizing the classic historical process of industrialization, the question that today arises is whether the pattern is likely to be repeated in newly industrializing societies, or other contemporary societies undergoing MODERNIZATION. In many of these societies rates of population growth, and levels of social disruption, have been greater than in the middle phase in earlier European patterns of demographic transition. In some societies significant economic growth has been difficult to achieve, and population growth has not been associated with improvements in living standards. It remains to be seen whether a new equilibrium will be established under these very different circumstances.

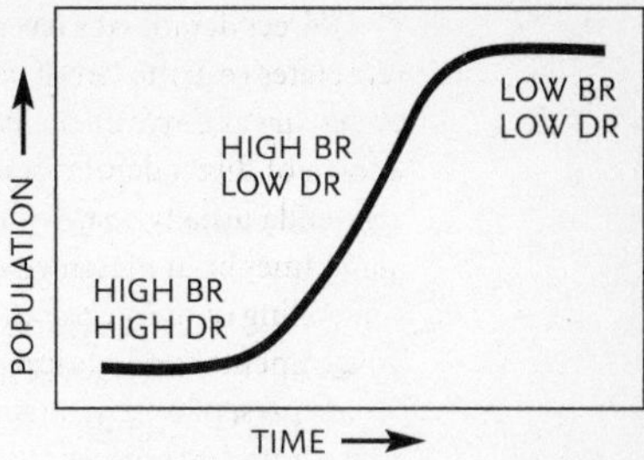

Fig. 9 **Demographic theory of transition.** Changes in rates of fertility and mortality accompanying industrialization in which, after a phase of rapid population increase, a previous pattern of population equilibrium involving high birth rates and high death rates is replaced by a different equilibrium involving low birth rates and low death rates.

demography

From the Greek *demos,* people. The statistical study of human populations with regard to their size and structure, i.e. their compositions by sex, age, marital status and ethnic origin, and to the changes to these populations, i.e. changes in their BIRTH RATES, DEATH RATES and MIGRATION. Philosophers and politicians have often been interested in the nature and size of populations. Plato, for example, recommended a static population for his ideal city. Politicians have been particularly concerned with over- and underpopulation. Laws were passed in Ancient Rome, for example, which sought to prevent population decline.

Most commentators agree that the systematic collection and study of population statistics originated with the publication of *Natural and Political Observations on the Bills of Mortality* by John Graunt in 1662. From 1629 onwards, the weekly 'Bills of Mortality' gave some indication of the causes of death within a population. Graunt used these bulletins to determine the biological and socioeconomic factors of mortality. He was one of the first people, therefore, to identify statistical regularities in human populations.

In the 17th and 18th centuries the collection of medical statistics developed in the study of health, disease and death. In 19th-century Europe, census taking improved and more reliable statistics became available for analysis. In the UK, the recording of death, then birth and marriage, rates was introduced after 1834 as the state came to recognize that population change was an actual phenomenon. These OFFICIAL

STATISTICS were known as *vital statistics.* The legal requirement to collect statistics made them more reliable, thus enabling demographers to apply more rigorous mathematical methods and facilitating their ability to forecast future population changes and developments. FORECASTING relies on assumptions made by the forecaster about populations; any forecast, therefore, is only as good as the assumptions that underlie it.

In the UK, population projections are made every two years in order to provide an estimate of the future population as an aid to planning. Based on the assumptions that mortality rates will continue to decline, that fertility rates will remain below replacement level, and that migration is negligible, it was expected that the population of the UK would total 57.5 million in 1991, rising to 60.0 million in the year 2025. The structure of the British population has changed; it is now getting older: 11% of the population were over the age of 65 in 1951, in 1986 that proportion had risen to 15%, and it is estimated to rise to nearly 19% by the year 2025.

There is a wide variety of reliable statistics available for demographic analysis in Britain; the ten-yearly CENSUS of Population (which is updated annually), the GENERAL HOUSEHOLD SURVEY, the FAMILY EXPENDITURE SURVEY, as well as the statistics compiled by government departments such as the Home Office and the Department of Social Security.

More recently, demographers have become interested in the study of populations in societies where there are few reliable statistics, and they have developed simple mathematical methods to analyse these. There has also been the development of HISTORICAL DEMOGRAPHY which similarly attempts to draw valid inferences from a limited range of available statistics such as local PARISH REGISTERS. These new developments contribute to the enduring discussion of the relationship between DEMOGRAPHIC TRANSITION and social change. See also BIRTH RATE, STANDARDIZED MORTALITY RATIO, FERTILITY, LIFE CHANCES, LIFE EXPECTANCY, EUGENICS.

denomination any subsection of the Christian Church (e.g. a former SECT, or a breakaway part of a former national church) which has become well established and has a substantial membership. Denominations are usually regarded as less dynamic than sects. As such, they are sometimes presented as the midpoint in a typology of forms of religious organization (see CHURCH-SECT TYPOLOGY).

dependency theory a theory of economic, social and political change which attempts to explain the continuing poverty, deprived social conditions and political instability of many poor countries in terms of their dominance by rich and powerful countries.

Dependency theory was first developed by economists in Latin America in the 1950s in opposition to the prevailing orthodoxy that THIRD WORLD countries could achieve MODERNIZATION and INDUSTRIALIZATION by following the examples of the already industrialized world. As it was developed by FRANK (1967b), the theory argues that Third World countries' problems were created by the colonial and trade dominance of Europe and the US. Their economies were shaped, firstly, by the needs of the advanced countries for agricultural and mineral goods, and, secondly, by the requirement to provide markets for the manufactured goods from the North. Any indigenous manufacturing in the Third World was suppressed by a combination of COMPETITION and political COERCION. Economic surpluses flowed out of the Third World through the repatriation of any profits, and terms of UNEQUAL EXCHANGE, whereby prices of Third World exports were comparatively lower than their manufactured imports, were employed. Thus, the Third World contributed to the economic growth and industrialization of Europe and the US, and that process created structures in the Third World which made industrialization there difficult or impossible. The Third World cannot repeat the experiences of the US or Europe because its starting point is different. In Frank's terms, it is underdeveloped, not undeveloped.

The theory was very influential in sociology in the 1970s. Whilst often termed neo-Marxist, it came under increasing criticism from Marxist writers. In particular, it has been criticized for concentrating on market rather than production relations. In one of the most rigorous critiques, Taylor (1979) has argued that the central concept of economic surplus is extremely weak. More general criticisms include its relative neglect of the contribution of internal social relations to problems which poor countries face, and the increasing diversity of their experiences. In the 1980s, many countries labelled Third World experienced significant processes of industrialization and rapid economic growth which most dependency analyses would seem to preclude. The main analysis within dependency theory which is most likely to endure is the work of Cardoso and Faletto (1979). This identifies different forms of dependency over time and space, and incorporates a detailed analysis of the class structure of Latin America. However, as Mouzelis (1988) argues, this too suffers from an over-general analysis which seems no longer adequate to embrace the diversity of experiences in Africa, Asia and Latin America. Roxborough (1984) adds that such overschematized analyses of history can now be improved as social scientific and historical studies become more adequate.

dependent industrialization the particular pattern of subordinate INDUSTRIALIZATION in the THIRD WORLD. The term implies that the 'classic' dependency of the Third World (see DEPENDENCY THEORY), involving the export of agricultural and mineral products and import of manufactured goods, has given way in some countries to a new era of manufacture of some goods, but with a reliance on the advanced countries for the import of capital goods and technical knowledge. Peter Evans (1979) is most associated with this argument in his work on Brazil and Mexico. He argues that dependent industrialization is characterized by a 'triple alliance' of foreign, state and national capital, with foreign capital directly investing in *high costs of entry manufacturing*, most commonly, consumer durables. The state is involved in the provision of high-cost infrastructural development, and local capital is involved in a variety of areas unprofitable to foreign capital. Since most of the production is geared to the internal market, this pattern assumes the prior development of middle classes in these countries, able to buy expensive consumer durables, and can be distinguished from EXPORT-ORIENTED INDUSTRIALIZATION characteristic of some other countries (e.g. Sri Lanka). In as much as foreign firms are involved in producing for these markets, Cardoso and Falletto (1979) have used the term 'internalization of imperialism' to denote the fact that foreign firms are located inside national boundaries (see also IMPERIALISM, NEOCOLONIALISM).

Many argue that this form of industrialization remains dependent because it is very difficult for the countries concerned to locate all aspects of the production process within their boundaries. Thus new 'bottlenecks' in development may occur, particularly in financing the purchase of capital goods and in the provision of extensive infrastructural developments. Support for this argument can be sought in the debt crisis that Brazil and Mexico met in 1982. During the 1970s both countries had borrowed heavily on the commercial banking market to finance industrialization projects, and their ability to borrow further, to pay the interest on existing debts, ended in the early 1980s. This corresponded with a decline in world markets precisely at a time when they needed to export to earn the resources to pay off the debts. Since 1982, with cutbacks in government spending, lack of new foreign investment and declining internal markets, because of austerity measures, the industrialization process has stagnated, and economic policies have been largely directed to paying off the foreign debt.

Whilst support for Evans' argument can be found using Latin American examples, Harris (1987) shows that the Asian countries of Hong Kong, Singapore, South Korea and Taiwan did not experience similar obstacles in the 1980s. Their export earnings were sufficient to pay their high levels of debt and, with the exception of Singapore, they had lower levels of foreign involvement and a wider range of industries, thus conforming more to a pattern of in dependent development. Not all NEWLY INDUSTRIALIZING COUNTRIES, therefore, are covered by the dependent industrialization label. See also MODERNIZATION.

dependent variable the measure of the effect of the INDEPENDENT VARIABLE. Thus, in an experiment, or in data analysis, the independent variable (for example, number of years in school) is manipulated, or otherwise controlled, and the effect of this manipulation is seen by the change in the dependent variable (for example, reading proficiency). See also EXPERIMENTAL METHOD.

depletion see ENVIRONMENTAL DEPLETION.

depression 1 (PSYCHOLOGY) a mood state characterized by despondency and pessimism, which may be short-lived but in its persistent forms may have its source in NEUROSIS or PSYCHOSIS. A further distinction is between reactive (to external stress) and endogenous forms.
2 (ECONOMICS), see TRADE CYCLE.

deprivation the lack of economic and emotional supports generally accepted as basic essentials of human experience. These include income and housing, and parental care (or an adequate substitute) for children. This recognizes that care, shelter and security are human needs (see also HUMANISTIC PSYCHOLOGY, MASLOW) the possession of which leads to a fuller, more comfortable life experience and allows a more complete development of the individual's potential. See also CYCLE OF DEPRIVATION, POVERTY, RELATIVE DEPRIVATION.

derivations see RESIDUES AND DERIVATIONS.

Derrida, Jacques (1930–2004) Algerian-born French philosopher whose ideas (e.g. *Writing and Difference*, 1978) have influenced sociological thinking in a number of areas, especially the implications for methodology of human LANGUAGE. Derrida is one of a number of philosophers in recent years to argue that philosophers have been simply mistaken in searching for underlying 'essences' or 'first principles'. Derrida's case, drawing critically on the ideas of HEIDEGGER and SAUSSURE, is that language, as a system of internal 'differences', cannot be the unambiguous carrier of TRUTH in the way assumed by many branches of traditional philosophy and by many social scientists, including LÉVI-STRAUSS (see also TEXT, DECONSTRUCTION). For Derrida the signifier has no stable relation to the signified. A sign (and *signification*) depends on a structure of difference, half of which is 'not that' (the relational *différence* – see DIFFERENCE) and the other half is 'not there' (*différance* – or 'deferral'), the fact that a meaning is never fully achieved, sliding under an endless chain of signifiers. Signifiers and signifieds are always becoming detached and forming new combinations. There is no end to the call for definition, and thus meaning is never transparent. As for Heidegger, for Derrida the sign, strictly speaking, must always stand 'under *erasure*', as necessary but inadequate. What this means is that, not only signs, but also human 'selves', must remain always in flux. The 'self is an uncertain effect, rather than the stable core and only origin of linguistic and thinking practices.

There are similarities in outcome, but also important differences of emphasis, between Derrida's POSTSTRUCTURALIST thinking and 'post-empiricist', 'antiepistemological' intellectual movements in the UK and US (compare KUHN, FEYERABEND). See also POSTMODERNISM.

Descartes, René (1596–1650) French philosopher and major exponent of modern RATIONALISM who, in his adult life, lived in Holland and Sweden. From an initial position of 'radical doubt', Descartes' rationalist philosophy was founded on his famous principle, *Cogito ergo sum* ('I think therefore I am'). A further feature of his philosophy was a DUALISM of MIND and body.

descent (ANTHROPOLOGY) the means by which individuals are allocated to specific ancestral groups. If a society has descent rules, they will specify the basis of the construction of LINEAGES, with all the rights and obligations which go with such membership. Descent may be based on PATRILINEAL, MATRILINEAL, BILATERAL or NON-UNILINEAL principles, and its discussion was central to postwar British SOCIAL ANTHROPOLOGY.

descent group a group in which all members have a common ancestor. See DESCENT, LINEAGE, PATRILINEAL DESCENT, MATRILINEAL DESCENT, BILATERAL DESCENT, NON-UNILINEAL DESCENT, COGNATIC, CONSANGUINITY.

deschooling arrangements to replace institutionalized forms of education in schools. Deschooling arguments were popular in both the US and the UK in the late 1960s and early 1970s, developing from the general cynicism and dissatisfaction expressed at that time with the nature of industrial society and the growing concentration of political and economic power. Schools came to be seen as agencies of a social system which legitimated the pursuit of qualifications at the expense of individual development. Writers such as ILLICH (1971), Reimer (1971) and Goodman (1956) suggested that schools converted liberal and humane purposes into repressive outcomes. They believed that, at the very least, schools play no more than a custodial role; at the very worst they are coercive. Pupils are socialized into dominant ideologies, understanding their own futures in competitive terms. Obedience to teachers and the lessons of the HIDDEN CURRICULUM prepare pupils for different places of work. Schools claim an educational monopoly and devalue all other forms of non-school knowledge. Such forms of schooling are detrimental to genuine forms of education and should therefore be replaced by alternatives. Suggested alternatives ranged from travelling teachers, on the old European 'friar' model, through information exchange networks, dependent on telephones and computers, in the US, to the establishment of schools outside the state and conventional private sector in the UK.

There was a very mixed reception for such ideas. In some cases they were enthusiastically accepted; in others they were reviled. The ideas can be criticized for their oversimplification of the relations of schools to society, although deschooling has value in its challenge to the idea that schooling is a 'good thing'. However, in denouncing all that is wrong in schools, it has ignored that which is successful. It remains arguable that those on whose behalf deschoolers speak would actually be gainers if conventional and traditional forms of schooling were abandoned.

description see THICK DESCRIPTION.

descriptive statistics see STATISTICS AND STATISTICAL ANALYSIS.

deskilling a process of job degradation in which work is progressively fragmented, and stripped of its complexity, discretionary content and knowledge base. The most important exposition of this concept (*degradation of work thesis*) is found in Braverman's theory of the LABOUR PROCESS based upon MARX. Deskilling is seen as a result of capitalist control of the labour process, in which management, using the principles of SCIENTIFIC MANAGEMENT, separates conception from execution and increasingly takes control of the labour process away from workers, leaving them with mundane, repetitive tasks. The argument that SKILL levels fall with the development of CAPITALISM and TECHNOLOGY is based upon 19th-century craft work as the model for skilled labour. In this theory, deskilling is a major cause of PROLETARIANIZATION in the class structure, reducing both skilled manual and clerical workers to a homogeneous working class.

In sharp contradiction to theories of the labour process, the thesis of POSTINDUSTRIAL SOCIETY posits a general upgrading of skills based upon INDUSTRIALIZATION. New technology is seen as creating the need for new skills, multi-skilling (*polyvalency*) and higher levels of qualification and technical expertise to replace the older craft skills of the 19th-century. Much of the debate about changing skill levels involves different definitions of skill and different types of evidence. For example, the evidence for skill upgrading has relied upon formal job classification and qualifications, whereas evidence for deskilling has analysed actual skills required in a job.

The deskilling argument has been criticized as deterministic and reliant upon a romanticized picture of the craft worker. Comparative research using CONTINGENCY THEORY has found evidence of both job upgrading and deskilling in different industrial sectors and societies, reflecting different managerial strategies, labour markets and other contingent factors. At the societal level, it is difficult to assess overall changes in skill levels, since economic restructuring may displace skills in old industries and create new skills in expanding sectors. In addition, whilst certain jobs may be deskilled, workers may not, since they may either be upwardly mobile (e.g. male clerical workers), or move into new jobs requiring higher levels of skill. Nevertheless, widespread empirical evidence for deskilling has been found in both the manufacturing and service sectors with mechanization and computerization. See also SKILL, NEW TECHNOLOGY, INTELLECTUAL LABOUR, FORDISM AND POST-FORDISM, CRAFT APPRENTICESHIP.

despotism see ORIENTAL DESPOTISM.

determinism **1** the assumption that a hypothetical omniscient observer would be in a position to predict outcomes at a time $t + 1, \ldots t + k$, etc., from knowledge at time t. Early classical sociology (e.g. COMTE's) can be seen as often adopting such a deterministic view of social structures, so that future social systems could be predicted, at least in principle, from present system states.

2 the less rigorous assumption that nothing occurs without it being caused (see also CAUSE, CAUSALITY AND CAUSAL RELATIONSHIP). However, since in social science, SOCIAL ACTORS may either have uncertain or unstable preferences which may alter social outcomes, a conception of universal causation which *includes* preferences (motives, reasons, etc.) as 'causes' cannot automatically assume predictability, even *in principle*.

Even within the physical sciences (e.g. so-called *indeterminism* in quantum mechanics) predictability cannot always be assumed. More straightforwardly, even such superficially simple phenomena as a leaf falling, although predictable in principle, cannot *in practice* be predicted, given the large number of variables involved.

Where social systems are highly structured, and the outcome of any one actor's individual behaviour can be shown to have little or no *independent* influence on the macro-structure of a system, relatively *deterministic* 'structural' accounts of social reality may be advanced, e.g. Marx's account of the working of competition in 'perfect markets'. On the other hand, where both actors' choices and social outcomes appear behaviourally and structurally 'undetermined', models which assume a degree of *actual* indeterminism are often proposed, i.e. explanatory accounts in sense **2** rather than in sense **1**. Accounts of this latter sort need not be regarded as 'unscientific' – rather they can be seen as providing EXPLANATIONS. See also FREE WILL, REFLEXIVITY, HISTORICISM, CHANCE, CONTINGENCY, UNANTICIPATED CONSEQUENCES OF SOCIAL ACTION, EVOLUTIONARY THEORY, FUNCTIONALISM. Compare OVERDETERMINACY.

deterrence see NUCLEAR DETERRENCE.

de Tocqueville, Alexis see TOCQUEVILLE.

deurbanization see URBANIZATION.

development see ECONOMIC AND SOCIAL DEVELOPMENT, CHILD DEVELOPMENT.

deviance any social behaviour which departs from that regarded as 'normal' or socially acceptable within a society or social context. Whilst deviance includes criminal behaviour, its sphere is far wider than this. Furthermore, not all criminal behaviour will always be labelled as deviance, e.g. minor traffic offences (see also CRIME, CRIMINOLOGY).

Although there are some recurring elements among the forms of social behaviour regarded as deviant within society, for the most part social deviance must be seen as a socially relative phenomenon, in that conceptions of normality and deviance are relative to social context and highly variable between different societies, different subcultures, etc.

As emphasized by Erving GOFFMAN, there is also an important sense in which all social actors are deviant in that no one conforms to all the canons of socially acceptable behaviour, none of us entirely fits any social ideal, and we are all sometimes in situations in which we are socially deviant.

A further crucial question is, 'What or who within society determines "deviance"?' As stressed by BECKER (1963), 'deviance is not a quality of the act ... but rather a consequence of the application by others of rules and sanctions'. Thus, the question of by whom, and how, deviance is 'labelled' becomes crucial to its explanation (see LABELLING THEORY).

Two main sociological approaches to the study of deviant behaviour can be identified. The first approach includes functionalist accounts of deviance. For example, in the work of DURKHEIM, two complementary usages of the term 'deviance' are found. In *The Rules of Sociological Method* (1895), he describes crime as 'normal', in that it is a universal phenomenon in societies, and is functional in that the concepts and ceremonies surrounding crime provide a 'social reaction' to crime and a ritual 'reaffirmation' of social values which strengthens the social order. In *Suicide* (1897), Durkheim focuses on deviance as a social problem arising from 'abnormal' or 'pathological' forms of social solidarity, particularly excessive individualism ('egoism') and ANOMIE.

Modern functionalist accounts of crime have largely followed Durkheim's. For example, for Parsons, deviance results from inadequate socialization, while Merton directly builds on Durkheim's concept of 'anomie'.

The second approach has developed, in particular, in opposition to the 'positivism' seen as underlying orthodox criminology and related approaches to the study of deviance. The starting point of such an alternative approach was the LABELLING THEORY of Becker and others. This was combined, especially in the work of the Radical Deviance Theorists (e.g. Taylor et al., 1973), with a revival of general critical debates about deviance and social control, including Marxian theories of crime. See also PRIMARY AND SECONDARY

DEVIANCE, DEVIANCE AMPLIFICATION. NATIONAL DEVIANCY CONFERENCE. Compare FOUCAULT.

deviance amplification a process in which the extent and seriousness of deviance is distorted and exaggerated, with the effect that social control agencies take a greater interest in the purported existence of the phenomenon and thus uncover, but actually 'construct', more examples of it, giving the impression that the initial distortion was actually a true representation.

The typical pattern of an 'amplification spiral' is as follows. For whatever reason, some issue is taken up by the MASS MEDIA OF COMMUNICATION – this may be glue sniffing, FOOTBALL HOOLIGANISM, the activities of 'lager louts', child abuse, or anything else which makes 'news'. The sensationalized representation of the event makes it appear that there is a new and dangerous problem which must be taken seriously. In practice, the problem, however dangerous or socially threatening, will not be new, but some dramatic example will have caught the attention of the media. Their distorted and sensationalized coverage creates a MORAL PANIC which also leads to increased police action and to more arrests of offenders. The higher arrest rate is seen as a confirmation of the growth of the problem. Judges and magistrates give exemplary sentences, to show 'society's' disapproval of this supposedly new problem. These sentences make news in themselves, and serve to keep the issue public. The police respond to this evidence of public concern with yet more arrests, and so on. In this process, a further dimension of amplification is that those persons newly labelled as deviant, become newly conscious of their 'difference', become part of new deviant networks, and may be driven to defensive action, all of which further ratchets the amplification.

Wilkins (1965) made the important point that minorities were the object of this exaggeration and distortion. Other major British studies of amplification have looked at MODS AND ROCKERS (Cohen, 1971, 1973), 'muggers' (Hall et al., 1978), drug users (J. Young, 1971) and similar groups. The concept has also been used to discuss issues like the criminalization of black communities, the presentation of gay men and women, and the AIDS panic.

More generally, it raises the issues of manipulation of public perceptions of minorities, and the powerlessness of minority groups to define their own images or control social reactions to them. See also HIERARCHY OF CREDIBILITY, BECKER, LABELLING THEORY.

deviance disavowal 'the refusal of those who are viewed as deviant to concur in the verdict' (F. Davis, 1964). The concept is intended to help understanding of ways in which, for example, 'socially deviant' persons, physically handicapped people, or criminals, may attempt to structure their interaction with 'normal', ablebodied, 'unblemished' people so as to minimize the effect of their deviancy on these relationships. See also STIGMA.

deviant career the process in which an individual comes to accept a deviant 'self-identity', and, often, to identify with a deviant SUBCULTURE. The concept is associated with LABELLING THEORY, indicating the fact that people are not born deviant, but only come to consider themselves as such through a process involving SOCIETAL REACTION. See also SECONDARY DEVIANCE, GOFFMANN.

deviant case (in research methodology) any social phenomenon presented as an exception to what is generally the case, and which therefore is of particular utility in *deviant case analysis* in allowing analysis of cause and effect of both the normal and the deviant case.

deviant case analysis see DEVIANT CASE.

Dewey, John (1859–1952) US pragmatist philosopher and writer on psychology and social affairs who also influenced American sociology, especially the work of G. H. MEAD. His contribution to PRAGMATISM (his own preferred term was 'instrumentalism') was to argue that knowledge is to be determined by its effectiveness, both in experiments and in practical accomplishments, and by its service to human interests and human needs. He rejected all forms of essentialism or idealist conceptions of knowledge which presented knowledge as timeless and as capable of being established by the solitary individual. He also rejected all forms of DUALISM (e.g. between mind and body or facts and values); for him, Man and nature were continuous, and knowledge always socially located.

dharma see CASTE.

diachronic see SYNCHRONIC AND DIACHRONIC.

dialectic 1 originally a term which simply meant LOGIC and/or METAPHYSICS (Williams, 1976).

2 (in German Idealist philosophy and in MARXISM) the process of contradiction and resolution – involving, or analogous to, the process of assertion, contradiction and agreement in an argument – in which conceptual and/or real world contradictions are resolved.

Formal logic licenses arguments, from given premises to conclusions according to strict rules, in which the conclusions are contained in the initial premises. However, ever since SOCRATES, thinkers have wanted to capture more of the reality of creative arguments, in which the conclusions reached involve genuine novelties. Socrates proceeded by a method of recurrent questioning of his interlocuters, multiplying their uncertainties, and enlarging their grasp by encouraging them to shift ground. In the 18th- and 19th-centuries, the attempt to establish inductive logic (see INDUCTION AND INDUCTIVE LOGIC) was another attempt to escape the formalism of conventional deductive logic. It was KANT and HEGEL, however, who first proposed the alternative of a fully-fledged *dialectical logic,* in which metaphysical and, for Hegel, the real world is 'Catholic' in its own self-understanding of what it wishes to reject, and its shape is in part fixed in that contradictions are surmounted in the course of 'world-history', realizing a more unified 'truth' – e.g. 'Protestant' preserves negation. Hegel's approach was taken up in MARXISM and in DIALECTICAL MATERIALISM. However, the interpretation of the dialectic as involving 'dialectical laws of nature' is usually regarded as a wrong interpretation: the opposite of a focus on the emergence of novelty. The notion of the dialectic in this latter sense lives on, however, in more open-ended conceptions of NEGATION AND NEGATIVITY, e.g. in the work of the FRANKFURT SCHOOL OF CRITICAL THEORY.

dialectical logic see DIALECTIC.

dialectical materialism the consolidation of MARX and ENGELS' main ideas as a 'scientific philosophy'. This scientistic rendering of MARXISM combined a Hegelian emphasis on MATERIALISM in asserting the DIALECTIC (contradiction and resolution) as the fundamental general law underlying all forms of development: in nature, in society, and in thought. Whereas Marx employed the dialectical method as the basis of HISTORICAL MATERIALISM, focusing exclusively on socioeconomic change, it is Engels (e.g. in *Dialectics of Nature*) who can be seen as taking the first step in formulating dialectical materialism, although he never used the term. It was the successors of Marx and Engels, including Plekanov (1856–1918) and LENIN, who formulated dialectical materialism in a fuller form. This became the 'official' version of Marxist doctrine under STALIN, and was a main source of the dogmatism, and economic determinism which characterized much Marxism in this period.

dialectic of control the two-way character of power as a form of control in which the less powerful are usually able to exert some control over the more powerful, e.g. the personal assistant who the manager must keep sweet if he or she is to perform his or her duties willingly. The assumption here is that purely 'alienative' forms of power are relatively rare (see TYPES OF COMPLIANCE).

diaspora (from the Greek *dia,* through, and *speiro,* scatter) the situation of any group of people dispersed, whether forcibly or voluntarily, throughout the world. Referring particularly to the Jewish experience, the term may be applied to any comparable migrant groups. In a world ever more subject to GLOBALIZATION, diasporic communities are increasingly a feature of the world and the social and political implications of these are much studied. See also POST-COLONIAL THEORY.

dictatorship of the proletariat (MARXISM) the form of government which Marx envisaged as emerging immediately after the revolutionary overthrow of capitalism and before the establishment of COMMUNISM. LENIN introduced the notion of dictatorship of the proletariat via the Communist Party, but because of the oppressive implications of the term, many Marxists no longer use it.

difference contrast, unlikeness. Three interrelated but distinct usages of the term are important:

1 (within SAUSSURE's linguistic theory) the presupposed (or 'absent') contrast(s) in any signification, necessary because meaning is never present in individual signifiers but gained (and never fully or finally) by contrast with other signifiers;

2 (for DERRIDA) an emphasis above all, on the open-endedness of *différence* and *djfférance,* as undermining 'several kingdoms', including the 'metaphysics of presence' and the 'logocentrism' of traditional philosophy (as well as some of Saussure's interpretations of his own linguistics). See also DECONSTRUCTION.

3 (more general use of the term) cultural differences of any kind.

Compare OTHERNESS.

differend 'a case of conflict, between (at least) two parties, that cannot be equitably resolved for lack of judgement applicable to both arguments' (J. LYOTARD, *The Differend – Phrases in Dispute,* 1983). Lyotard's concept is intended to indicate important aspects of the relationship between language and knowledge. As a POSTMODERN theorist, Lyotard is particularly concerned to show that science is now merely one amongst many ways of understanding the world (see also PERFORMATIVITY). If this levelling of knowledge claims is accepted, a choice presents itself: either one searches for some means of theorizing ways to arbitrate between claims (compare HABERMAS), or else the attempt to find stable and applicable criteria is abandoned. The concept of the differend and, indeed, Lyotard's work in general proceeds in the latter direction. Differends are thus associated with the divergences and disagreements that follow when two (or more) different DISCOURSE(S) or LANGUAGE GAME(S) meet, alhough differends are not, strictly speaking, these discourses themselves. Rather, a differend can be thought to have at least two sides, giving rise to two (or more) discourses. It follows that in each game there are *pertinent* (but not *necessary*) ways to proceed and, further, that new games (and thus new differends) will emerge. Such formulations should not be seen as suggesting that Lyotard propounds a framework or theory of language games *per se*. This would run the risk of producing a GRAND NARRATIVE, or, at least, would suggest that there is some external point beyond language. Both of these consequences would create serious tensions in relation to other major aspects of Lyotard's work. In exploring the highly contingent and incidental nature of language and phrases, Lyotard's concept of the differend reminds sociologists that conflict may be unavoidable and that states of equilibrium or stability may not endure. See also PAGANISM, INCOMMENSURABILITY.

differential association a theory of CRIME developed by Edwin H. Sutherland, in which criminal behaviour is viewed as learned behaviour resulting from contact with situations in which criminality is defined favourably. He argued that this theory could also account for the type of crime engaged in. Thus, in the appropriate contexts, favourable attitudes to tax evasion or 'fiddles' at work may be learned by people who are otherwise eminently law-abiding and respectable.

Working in the tradition of the CHICAGO SCHOOL, Sutherland was especially interested in street gangs and DELINQUENT SUBCULTURE. However, he intended his theory as a general theory of criminal behaviour, its significance lying in the argument that individuals learn to be criminal in precisely the same way that they learn to be law-abiding. He thus rejects those accounts of crime which explain it in terms of individual psychopathology. However, there is no acceptance in sociology that 'differential association' explains all aspects or all forms of crime. See also CRIMINOLOGY.

differential opportunity structure see OPPORTUNITY STRUCTURE.

differentiation see SOCIAL DIFFERENTIATION.

diffusion the spread of cultural traits (e.g. religious belief, technological ideas, language forms, etc.) or social practices from one society or group to another. The concept was first employed by the British anthropologist Edward TYLOR (in *Primitive Culture,* 1871) to explain the presence of non-indigenous cultural traits found within many societies. Such cultural diffusion has occurred on a wide scale throughout human history, so that, today, societies can even be said to exist as part of a single world society.

In social anthropology, and in sociology more generally, the existence of cultural diffusion is seen as presenting problems, especially for UNILINEAR theories of change which make the assumption that individual societies develop – mainly endogenously – through set stages (see also INTERSOCIETAL SYSTEMS). On the other hand, it should not be assumed that any cultural trait or social institution is compatible with any other, for this would be to assume that individual societies have no internal coherence.

The concept of diffusion has also been linked to the debate which emerged over theories of ECONOMIC AND SOCIAL DEVELOPMENT and MODERNIZATION. Theorists such as Talcott PARSONS (1964a) argued that the diffusion of social institutions (EVOLUTIONARY UNIVERSALS) and cultural values characteristic of Western capitalist democracies was essential if THIRD WORLD development was to occur. This position was trenchantly criticized by writers from the left, most notably Frank (1969), who pointed out that the diffusion of culture and institutions from Europe to the Third World was, in fact, centuries old, and rather than producing development, this colonial contact resulted in UNDERDEVELOPMENT.

In more mathematical usages of the term, similarities are seen as existing between patterns of social diffusion and those characteristic of EPIDEMIOLOGY, e.g. the logistical pattern of the spread of a contagious disease – proceeding slowly at first, with small numbers of persons involved, then more rapidly as more become involved and they also involve still others, but then slowing down as there are fewer new people to involve (see also DIFFUSION OF INNOVATIONS). However, although formal mathematical models of the type used in physical science can be illuminating, these are usually presented as 'heuristic devices', rather than models which will closely fit patterns of social diffusion which are likely to be seen as more complex and variable in form than those in the physical realm. One reason for this is that individual human beings and groups often resist change; and diffusion rarely occurs as the outcome of passive imitation (see also TWO-STEP FLOW OF COMMUNICATIONS; OPINION LEADERSHIP).

diffusion of innovations the adoption, and the social processes involved in the adoption, of technical innovations, new fashions, etc. One focus has been on the social and psychological characteristics of those who adopt innovations. Thus, Rogers (1983) proposed a three-stage model in which a relatively small number of people attuned to new developments in a field initially adopt the innovation, paving the way for the innovation to be adopted, in the medium-term, by a broad majority of the relevant population, but leaving a group of conservatives who either ignore or actively resist the innovation. A further focus is on 'innovative forms' (the extent of innovation involved in particular innovations, e.g. 'incremental', 'radical', 'technology systems', and 'technoeconomic paradigm' innovations in microprocessor technology) and on technical characteristics of the innovation which influence its range of application and take-up, e.g. while in the 1980s, 60% of all manufacturing establishments reported using microtechnology at some point in the production process, only 12.5% had incorporated such technology in their products (Northcott, 1988). Wider cultural and political factors, e.g. economic conditions, management strategies, traditions of industrial relations, also shape the detailed take-up of new technology.

Dilthey, Wilhelm (1833–1911) German idealist philosopher who argued for a methodological distinction to be made between the natural and the cultural sciences. Major works by him include *The Life of Schleiermachers* (1870) and *The Construction of the Historical World in the Cultural Sciences* (1910). A NEO-KANTIAN, he argued that whilst natural science should be practised in an essentially naturalistic manner, social science should be characterized by EMPATHIC UNDERSTANDING and a psychologistic understanding of cultural phenomena. The only proper way to understand the 'spirit of the age' (ZEITGEIST) is to interpret the WORLD VIEWS of its participants. He imported the term HERMENEUTICS from theology to describe this practice, but also used VERSTEHEN (understanding), a term which significantly influenced the thinking of Max WEBER. The two methods have since become distinct, though both are classed as interpretative. Dilthey's historical relativism, his conflation of the SUBJECT AND OBJECT (we are part of what we study) and his psychologistic approach on VERSTEHEN have all been criticized. His view of texts as objectifications of life, has been continued in the work of GADAMER. See also IDEALISM, GEISTESWISSENSCHAFTEN AND NATURWISSENSCHAFTEN, IDIOGRAPHIC AND NOMOTHETIC.

diploma disease see CREDENTIALISM.

direct and indirect rule see COLONIZATION.

disability **1** 'any restriction or lack (resulting from an impairment) of ability to perform an activity in the manner or within the range, considered normal for a human being' (World Health Organization).

2 'a form of social oppression resulting from a (socially constructed) environment unsuited to the needs of impaired people' (Peirson and Thomas, 1995). In emphasizing the socially constructed nature of, at least, part of the disadvantage and discrimination experienced by 'impaired' people, definition 2 emphasizes the political dimensions of disability and its remedy.

discourse and discourse formation the particular 'scientific' and specialist language(s), and associated ideas and social outcomes, which, according to FOUCAULT, must be seen as a major phenomenon of social POWER, and not simply a way of describing the world. For example, as the result of medical and scientific discourse(s), conceptions and the social handling of SEXUALITY or MADNESS have changed profoundly, in the 20th-century, from the previous 'non-scientific' view. It is an important aspect of Foucault's conception of discourse(s), that, in part at least, social phenomena are constructed from within a discourse; that there are no phenomena outside discourses. See also DISCOURSE ANALYSIS, EPISTEME; compare PARADIGM.

discourse analysis **1** forms of textual analysis (inspired by POSTSTRUCTURALISM) in which the aim is to exhibit the structure of DISCOURSE AND DISCOURSE FORMATIONS. The assumption is that a discourse has identifiable 'formation rules' which distinguish it from other discourses. Discourse analysis may focus on whole texts or the parts of texts. See also FOUCAULT, ARCHAEOLOGY 2, BARTHES.

2 (rather than an emphasis on the reader or viewer as just 'absorbing' TEXTS – as in 1) analysis of the role of the reader or viewer in *reading* and creating meaning. See also TELEVISION.

discourse ethics the conception that ethical agreements can be reached through 'communicative argumentation' aimed at a mutual, uncoerced understanding. See HABERMAS.

discourse theory see DISCOURSE ANALYSIS.

discrete variable see VARIABLE.

discriminant analysis see MULTIVARIATE ANALYSIS.

discrimination the process by which a member, or members, of a socially defined group is, or are, treated differently (especially unfairly) because of his/her/their membership of that group. To be selected for less favourable treatment, a social group may be constructed by reference to such features as race, ethnicity, gender or religion. A distinction can be drawn between 'categorical' and 'statistical' discrimination. *Categorical discrimination* is the unfavourable treatment of *all* persons socially assigned to a particular social category because the discriminator believes that this discrimination is required by his social group. *Statistical discrimination* refers to less favourable treatment of individuals based on the belief that there is a probability that their membership of a social group leads to them possessing less desirable characteristics.

In the UK, there are laws that deal with both sex and race discrimination: the *Sex Discrimination Act* (1975) and the *Race Relations Act* (1976). In both Acts, 'direct' discrimination is made illegal, in that a person may not be treated less favourably than another on the grounds of gender, colour, ethnicity or race. However, the *Race Relations Act* also attempts to tackle 'indirect' discrimination. This was defined as consisting of treatment which may be described as equal in a formal sense, as between different racial groups, but discriminatory in its effect upon a particular racial group. Indirect discrimination is the application of conditions or requirements which may mean that: '(1) the proportion of persons of a racial group who can comply with these is considerably smaller than the proportion of persons not of that racial group who can comply with them; (2) they are to the detriment of the persons who cannot comply with them; (3) they are not justifiable irrespective of the colour, race, nationality, or ethnic or national origins of the person to whom they are applied' (*A Guide to the Race Relations Act 1976* Home Office, 1977). See also POSITIVE DISCRIMINATION, RACE RELATIONS, SEGREGATION, GHETTO, PREJUDICE, SEX DISCRIMINATION.

discursive consciousness 'what actors are able to say, or to give verbal expression to, about social conditions, including especially the conditions of their own action' (GIDDENS, 1984). For Giddens, it is important to notice that such consciousness is not all that actors 'know', that alongside 'discursive knowledge' there also exists PRACTICAL KNOWLEDGE: what every actor knows, and needs to know, to get around in the social world, but cannot always express. See also STRATIFICATION MODEL OF SOCIAL ACTION AND CONSCIOUSNESS.

discursive formation see DISCOURSE AND DISCOURSE FORMATION, DISCOURSE ANALYSIS.

disease see ILLNESS.

disembedding and re-embedding mechanisms twin mechanisms operating especially in the modern world (GIDDENS, 1991):
(a) disembedding mechanisms are the 'abstract systems' (symbolic tokens – e.g. MONEY – and expert systems) that spread social relations across time and space and also produce insecurity and detachment from traditional social bonds;
(b) re-embedding mechanisms are the new forms of relationship and community (see INTIMACY) and new forms of politics (e.g. LIFE POLITICS) which appear as a response to the breakdown of traditional forms of social solidarity and an increasingly complex interplay between the local and the global.

See also RISK, TRUST, ONTOLOGICAL SECURITY AND INSECURITY, REFLEXIVE MODERNIZATION, GLOBALIZATION OF CULTURE.

disfunction see DYSFUNCTION.

disorganized capitalism the tendency of modern CAPITALISM, and its class structures, to become increasingly disorganized in the following respects (Offe, 1985; Lash and Urry, 1987):
(a) the growth of a 'world market', a decline in the regulation of national markets by dominant corporations, by tariffs, cartels, etc., and at the same time a declining capacity of individual nation states to control their own economic destinies. This includes a breakdown in 'neocorporatist' forms of state regulation and the provision of social welfare, which is associated with the appearance of contradictions between these state forms and the accumulation of capital (e.g. the appearance of 'fiscal crises');
(b) the expansion of the SERVICE CLASS(ES), existing between CAPITAL and LABOUR, and the appearance of 'new social movements' (e.g. ecological and women's movements), and a movement away from old 'class politics'; these developments are associated with the decline of labour-intensive traditional heavy industry in the West, as the result of the export of jobs to the Third World and with the introduction of new flexible, knowledge-based and labour-saving forms of work organization in new high tech and service areas of production;
(c) an increasing cultural fragmentation, pluralism, etc., including political pluralism, and the undermining of distinctive national identities, cultural values, etc.;
(d) a tendency for societies to be continuously transformed 'from above', and 'from below', so that ideas and cultures, industries and cities, as well as classes, are kept in a state of flux.

In contrast with earlier notions that ADVANCED CAPITALISM is *either* more organized than earlier forms of capitalism – by virtue of the introduction of state controls, monopoly, etc. – *or* will ultimately involve a final crisis, the concept of 'disorganized capitalism' in the above, modern, sense involves a doctrine neither of stability nor breakdown, but rather it sees continual adjustments within capitalism.

dispersion see MEASURES OF DISPERSION.

dissonance see COGNITIVE DISSONANCE.

distributed learning new forms of access to knowledge and distance learning available via the INTERNET. There are suggestions that these forms may lead to many new suppliers of education, competing with, and even replacing in some cases, traditional forms.

distribution of income and wealth the spread of material resources in a society. This is an indicator of social inequality for, by identifying the trends in the spread of resources, it is possible to ascertain whether a society is becoming more or less equal.

'Income' refers to the material resources obtained in the form of wages and salaries; through social benefits and pensions; through interest paid on investments; and from rents. There is no precise definition of WEALTH, but it generally refers to the accumulation of resources, both monetary and non-monetary. Although the number of 'self-made' rich people has increased, inherited wealth is still a vital element in any examination of who is wealthy. Being wealthy is a relative notion. For example, there are a number of people who might be considered 'super rich' who own over one billion pounds. A Gallup Poll undertaken in 1986 showed that over two thirds of the population believed someone to be wealthy if their level of wealth was over £200,000. Coincidentally, this corresponded to the level of wealth enjoyed by the richest 1% of the population.

Examining the distribution of income and wealth is very difficult for three reasons:
(a) the data are often inaccurate;
(b) the most appropriate unit of analysis is difficult to determine and might refer to individuals or families or households;
(c) it is difficult to evaluate non-monetary assets.

The Royal Commission on the Distribution of Income and Wealth (1974–79) used income tax returns to examine income distribution, supplementing its findings with data from the FAMILY EXPENDITURE SURVEY and the New Earnings Survey. Between 1976 and 1977 it found that the top 50% of the population received 75.9% of all in-come. Taxation slightly reduced this. Between 1979 and 1989, however, there was evidence of widening inequalities in income distribution. Between 1979 and 1987, for example, the top 20% of earners in the UK enjoyed a 22% increase in income, which is six times that of the bottom 20%. The Royal Commission found that wealth distribution, so far as it could be determined, was less equally distributed than income. That trend has continued. Between 1979 and 1988 inequalities in both disposable and final incomes widened. ('Final income' refers to 'disposable income' after the payment of indirect taxes, such as VAT and the council tax, and after the receipt of government benefits such as health and education services.)

All the evidence is that inequality has increased over the last two decades. This increase appears sharper in the US and UK, where the new economic policies associated with THATCHERISM have been especially pursued, and less in Europe where they have not. On a world-scale – and one aspect of GLOBALIZATION – the gap in incomes between the richest and poorest nations has also increased. See also POVERTY, CLASS, UNDERCLASS.

distributive justice see JUSTICE.

distributive power and collective power the distinction (drawn by PARSONS, *Structure and Process in Modern Societies*, 1960) between 'power by A over B' (*distributive power*) and the 'power of A and B combined' (*collective power*).

division of labour

1 the process whereby productive tasks become separated and more specialized. As used by the early classical economists such as Adam SMITH (1776), the term describes a specialization in workshops and the factory system, and explains the advantages accruing in terms of the increased efficiency and productivity of these new arrangements. In economic theory, the division of labour also gave rise to increased trade and exchange of goods and services based upon the 'law of comparative advantage' (see INTERNATIONAL TRADE). In sociology, specialization of productive tasks is seen as incorporating much more than economic efficiency in the narrow sense, and comprises a *technical division of labour* consisting of the subdivision of work tasks, hierarchies of skill and a structure of power and authority revealed in the relations between management and workers within the enterprise (see SCIENTIFIC MANAGEMENT, LABOUR PROCESS).

2 the process of occupational specialization in society as a whole, and the separation of social life into different activities and institutions such as the family, the state and the economy, denoted by the term *social division of labour*. In the writings of evolutionary sociologists such as DURKHEIM or PARSONS, the concept is indistinguishable from SOCIAL DIFFERENTIATION (see also EVOLUTIONARY THEORY). Sociological analysis of occupational specialization may refer to divisions within a society (see CLASS, LOCAL LABOUR MARKETS), sectoral patterns of employment (e.g. agriculture, manufacturing and services), and also to the concentration of particular occupations or productive tasks in Third World or advanced capitalist societies respectively (see INTERNATIONAL DIVISION OP LABOUR, UNEVEN DEVELOPMENT, WORLD SYSTEM).

The effects of both the social and technical divisions of labour figure centrally in theories of social stratification. In recent years, attention has focused not only upon class differences but also upon ethnic divisions, especially the gendered nature of jobs in the labour market, the separation of the PRIVATE AND PUBLIC SPHERES and the division of labour in the household (see SEXUAL DIVISION OF LABOUR, PATRIARCHY, DOMESTIC LABOUR, DUAL LABOUR MARKET). Thus, it is possible to talk of divisions of labour in the plural to include reproduction as well as production and the relation between commodity and non-commodity production.

DURKHEIM (1893) produced one of the most influential texts on the social division of labour. Developing an evolutionary theory of social change, he contrasts primitive and modern societies. The former are characterized by a low division of labour, a segmentary structure and a strong collective consciousness, or 'mechanical solidarity', as the basis of social order; modern societies exhibit a differentiated structure, greater individual consciousness and 'organic solidarity' (increased interdependence between the parts of society) (see MECHANICAL AND ORGANIC SOLIDARITY). It is the division of labour itself which functions to promote organic solidarity, based upon both the awareness of individuality fostered by specialization, and the corresponding dependence upon others. Thus Durkheim emphasized the social, and hence moral, functions of the division of labour, in opposition to Spencer and UTILITARIANISM which focused upon the individual pursuit of self-interest in a division of labour regulated only by contract. However, Durkheim was aware that organic solidarity was imperfectly realized in modern societies and he therefore postulated *abnormal forms of the division of labour:* the *anomic division of labour* and the *forced division of labour.* The former refers to situations in which the division of labour is not matched by appropriate forms of moral regulation (see ANOMIE), and the latter to coercive forms of the division of labour in which class conflict and inherited wealth prevent people from occupying positions appropriate to their natural abilities.

MARX's analysis of the division of labour contrasts markedly with that of Durkheim. Whereas Durkheim saw the solution to anomie as residing in the full development of an appropriately regulated division of labour, Marx linked the development of the division of labour to the emergence of private property, class divisions, exploitation and ALIENATION.

Under capitalism, the division of labour in machinofacture involves the progressive separation of mental from manual labour, and the subordination of labour to the requirements of commodity production. Marx traces the development of the division of labour through successive social epochs, involving the separation of towns from the countryside, the state from civil society, and industry from commerce, culminating in the extreme fragmentation of work in capitalist production. At the same time, the contradictory nature of capitalism is apparent in the capacity for increased wealth, and the need for economic cooperation in the division of labour which prefigures the eventual transcendence of capitalism by socialism. In *The German Ideology,* Marx envisages the abolition of the division of labour under socialism, along with the abolition of classes and private property. However, in his later works, reference is made to the continuation of a 'realm of necessity' in which a form of division of labour will continue to exist, but will be one without alienation or forced specialization.

Marx's critical analysis of the division of labour in the production process has been revived in recent years by interest in the labour process – particularly in the work of Braverman (1974). Labour process theory has focused upon the development of managerial control through the use of scientific management, mechanization and automation, in which labour is increasingly fragmented and deskilled (see DESKILLING).

divorce and marital separation the legal or socially sanctioned dissolution of a marriage – *divorce* – as distinguished from the severing, temporary or permanent, of a marital relationship – *separation* – which may or may not lead to divorce. Sociological studies of divorce have focused mostly upon two issues: firstly the variations in the divorce rate, both comparatively and within societies, and, secondly, the various social adjustments necessary to the process.

Variations in *divorce rates* may be accounted for by reference to both individual expectations and to the role of marriage within kin groups. Where expectations are predominantly those of the kin (as in arranged marriages), rates of marital breakdown are likely to be low. Where individual expectations are high, as in most Western societies, there is often an accompanying social acceptance of dissolution in order that those expectations might be fulfilled elsewhere. Within the UK, the virtual eradication of the 'marital offence' (*Divorce Reform Act,* 1969 and subsequently) within divorce proceedings could be viewed as part of this process.

Social and personal adjustment to divorce has been studied in great detail both by sociologists and those involved in family conciliation work. Divorce, or indeed separation, can have many dimensions, including emotional uncoupling, the negotiation of child-custody and child-care issues, the settling of property and maintenance issues, the realignment of social and community relationships, and the resultant personal adjustments.

divorce between ownership and control see MANAGERIAL REVOLUTION.

divorce rate the number of divorces per year divided by the total population, usually expressed as a rate per 1000. Other measures divide the number of divorces by the number of marriages. Although sometimes used as an indicator of social stability or social disorganization, the implications of changes in the divorce rate are open to wide differences of interpretation. See also DIVORCE AND MARITAL SEPARATION.

DNA (deoxyribonucleic acid) see GENETICS.

domestic cycle or developmental cycle of domestic group (particularly in ANTHROPOLOGY) the fact that any domestic group will experience different compositions over time as children are born and, when older, may leave the group, and as elderly members die. However, even in the same society, not all domestic groups will have the same developmental cycle.

domestic labour 1 the numerous, often repetitious tasks, including housework and child care, which serve to maintain the household. In most modern societies, domestic labour is unwaged, privatized and gendered. Women are primarily responsible for carrying out this servicing role and for ensuring that the physical and emotional needs of the family are met.

2 (MARXISM) the particular forms of work within the household or domestic setting which produce 'use values' rather than 'exchange values' (see USE VALUE AND EXCHANGE VALUE). To conceive of the household or the FAMILY as a MODE OF PRODUCTION, and to study its characteristics as a socioeconomic entity, involves a revision of the conventional way of viewing the home, which is to see it as an expressive institution, separated from the economics of the marketplace, in which men and women play out their expressive roles. The concept of domestic labour highlights the interconnections between the world of the home (the private domain) and the world of the factory and the office (the public sphere) (see also PRIVATE AND PUBLIC SPHERES).

In either sense, domestic labour services the economy in ways which are hidden by the ideology of the family and private life – it is the sphere of CULTURAL REPRODUCTION and SOCIAL REPRODUCTION in which people are raised and cared for as members of the family and enter into the economy as workers. In the domestic economy, women mainly service men through private personal services which are not classified or remunerated as 'real work'. Despite its importance in the national economy, domestic labour is not usually included in the GROSS NATIONAL PRODUCT, and this is one reason why 'Wages for Housework' was a demand made by some postwar women's groups who saw domestic labour as an essential aspect of women's oppression. Before the publication of A. Oakley's *The Sociology of Housework* (1974), the SOCIOLOGY OF WORK and the sociology of organizations had ignored this area of life.

A further aspect of domestic labour within the SEXUAL DIVISION OF LABOUR, is that women experience a double burden of work since they participate in both wage labour and unwaged domestic labour. Their primary responsibility in the domestic sphere is a key factor exacerbating their exploitation and subordination in the public sphere. This primacy was always apparent in history, but since the 19th century in Europe has been accentuated by the *separation of home from work* and the construction of the notion of *housewife:* a married woman whose primary role is to engage in domestic work, with paid work outside the home being secondary. Especially amongst the English Victorian upper and middle classes, this role became an ideal to which other classes aspired, but could not often achieve because of the economic necessity of having more than one wage or salary coming in to the household. When households were the focus of earned income or of self-provision, women often had important economic roles other than the domestic. Davidoff and Hall (1987), for example, show how male entrepreneurs in Birmingham in the early 19th-century depended heavily on the unpaid labour of their wives to establish their businesses. Only later, with expansion of the businesses, the development of new premises and the establishment of homes in the new suburbs, did wives cease participating and devote themselves to becoming housewives.

Since the 1970s, attempts to develop a political analysis of housework and child care in capitalist societies have focused on the *domestic labour debate.* This debate arose primarily from the work of S. James (1974) and M. Dalla Costa (1972), who utilized Italian social capital theory. In doing so they stressed the importance of analysing not only the position of the waged worker, but also that of the wageless. Both James and Dalla Costa argued that the wageless should demand wages and that housewives, in particular, should demand wages for housework. In doing so, the contradictions inherent in advanced capitalism would be intensified. James and Dalla Costa argued that the distinction between PRODUCTIVE AND UNPRODUCTIVE LABOUR was politically redundant, and that housework produced SURPLUS VALUE. Their work gave rise to two main Marxist responses, one of which sought to explore the implications of the 'demand for wages for housework campaign', whilst the other focused on the surplus-value question. The domestic labour debate is concerned with the extent to which Marxist categories can be used to explain the division of labour in the home, and whether the privatization of domestic labour is a necessary feature of capitalism. The debate has played a crucial role in highlighting the dual nature of women's work, and in demonstrating its usefulness to capitalism. A central theme of this debate has been the nature of the relationship of non-waged members of the working class to waged workers and to the 'family wage'. It fails, however, to explain why it is women, and not men, who have the responsibility for domestic labour. Miles (1986) argues that the debate fails to address a number of important issues. It does not deal with the question of gender domination nor does it explore the ways in which the interests of women and men of the same class may be divergent. By concentrating on what are assumed to be the common interests of working-class women and men, the debate avoids consideration of the part played by male violence in the subordination of women in the home. The debate fails to explore the lack of women's leisure time relative to men's, the position of children and the role played by men's control over women's sexuality and reproductive power. The domestic labour debate has also failed to address the contribution made by radical feminists in analysing the relationship between gender and class. Finally, attempts by feminists to examine the virtually universal oppression of women have been characterized as an ahistorical attempt to replace a class analysis of social relations by a gender analysis. It is, however, important to recognize that social class, gender and also race, are interactive features within advanced capitalism and indeed within most societies.

domestic production economic production located in the immediate producer's own home. This production may be for the producer's own use, for direct sale, or financed by and under the control of a capitalist. Domestic production in this last sense was one of the standard forms of capitalist production in the early stages of capitalism, before the introduction of the FACTORY SYSTEM. Although it has since become a marginal element of modern capitalist production, there are some suggestions that, partly as a consequence of the introduction of new forms of INFORMATION TECHNOLOGY which permit office work to be done from home, domestic production may again come to play a significant role in production.

domestic violence see WIFE BATTERING, CHILD ABUSE.

dominance (MARXISM) the 'dominant element' within a social formation – be this ideology, politics, or the economy – as determined by the particular requirements of the economic base at a point in time (ALTHUSSER, 1966). Althusser wished to draw attention to the internal complexity of social formations, even though these are determined by the economy 'in the final instance'. He contrasted this view with the 'Hegelian' conception of social 'totality'.

dominant class see RULING CLASS.

dominant culture the ruling cultural values and social practices within any society. As such the dominant culture may be contrasted with SUBCULTURE. See also POPULAR CULTURE.

dominant ideology thesis (MARXISM) the thesis that working-class subordination in capitalist societies is largely the outcome of the cultural dominance achieved by the capitalist ruling class. A strong criticism of the thesis has been mounted by Abercrombie et al., *The Dominant Ideology Thesis* (1980), who argue that proponents of the thesis tend to overestimate the importance of cultural integration in modern societies, and to underestimate the extent to which subordinate groups are capable of generating beliefs and values which run counter to prevailing ideologies. In this, the dominant ideology thesis can be seen as an analogue of structural-functionalist theories, which are widely regarded as overemphasizing the importance of shared values. See also RULING CLASS OR DOMINANT CLASS, HEGEMONY, GRAMSCI, IDEOLOGY, IDEOLOGICAL STATE APPARATUS AND REPRESSIVE STATE APPARATUS, INCORPORATION, CONSENSUS, SOCIAL INTEGRATION AND SYSTEM INTEGRATION.

domination 1 in a general sense, the POWER exerted by one person or group over another person or group.

2 in the more specific sense, used particularly by WEBER (1922) (a translation of the German word *Herrschaft*), the 'likelihood that a command within a given organization or society will be obeyed', which is distinguished from 'power' (*Macht*), the capacity of a social actor to impose his or her will on others despite resistance from them (see also LEGITIMATE AUTHORITY).

Weber also distinguishes between domination 'by virtue of authority' and economic forms of domination, in which the SOCIAL ACTOR, although formally free and motivated to pursue his or her own goals, is in fact highly constrained to act in one way.

double descent *or* **bilineal descent** a system of DESCENT in which there are 'Patriclans' and 'Matriclans' within the same group. They may each be used for different reasons, for example, inheritance of land may be through the male and inheritance of names through the female. A consequence of this is that an individual is a member of both a PATRILINEAL and a MATRILINEAL DESCENT group.

double hermeneutic (GIDDENS, 1984) the assumption that understanding in sociology and social science involves an understanding of social ACTION at two levels:
(a) the understanding of the 'meaningful social world as constituted by lay actors';
(b) the 'metalanguages invented by sociologists and social scientists to understand and explain social action'.
See also HERMENEUTICS, ETHNOMETHODOLOGY, VERSTEHEN.

Douglas, Mary (1921–) British social and cultural anthropologist who has made a particular study of RITUAL, symbolism and TABOO (e.g. *Purity and Danger,* 1966; *Natural Symbols,* 1970), much of this study possessing a special relevance for women's studies. She presents ritual prohibitions, including restrictions on women's activities, as occurring where social phenomena are held to 'threaten' existing classificatory systems.

downward mobility see SOCIAL MOBILITY.

dramaturgy an approach to social analysis, especially associated with Erving GOFFMAN, in which the theatre is the basis of an analogy with everyday life. In this analogy, social action is viewed as a 'performance' in which actors both play parts and stage-manage their actions, seeking to control the impressions they convey to others (*impression management*). The aim of actors is to present themselves in a generally favourable light and in ways appropriate to particular roles and social 'settings – the latter is Goffman's term for the physical trappings which signal particular roles or status. In a related way, SOCIAL ACTORS also cooperate as members of 'teams', seeking to preserve a 'front' while hiding from view the 'backstage' of social relations. Since actors will play different roles in different situations, they also on occasion find it necessary to practise *audience segregation,* withholding in a current situation any sign of those other roles they play which, if visible, would threaten the impression being given at the moment (e.g. the problems that would arise for a homosexual judge from any disclosure of his homosexuality). The model of interaction involved in dramaturgy turns on the inevitability of acting partly on inference. For Goffman, the social order is a precarious accomplishment, always liable to be disrupted by embarrassment and breaches of front.

Dreyfus Affair a *cause célèbre* in late-19th- and early-20th-century French politics, in terms of which most French intellectuals tended to take sides. Alfred Dreyfus (1859–1935) was a Jewish officer who was convicted by a military tribunal on the basis of forged documents but with a strong indication of ANTI-SEMITISM. Subsequently Dreyfus was rehabilitated. Generally the *Dreyfusards,* as the supporters of Dreyfus were called, were radicals, while those opposed to him were conservative or authoritarian.

drive see INSTINCT.

drug addiction *or* **drug dependency** a chronic physical and psychological compulsion or craving to take a drug, in which the person concerned must continue to take the drug in order to avoid unpleasant physical and psychological effects resulting from withdrawal from the drug. Compare DRUG TAKING FOR PLEASURE.

Many drugs can be associated with drug addiction and dependency, including sedatives (e.g. barbiturates), the opiates (e.g. heroin) and alcohol (see ALCOHOLISM). Drugs which do not lead to dependency include cannabis, the hallucinogens (e.g. lysergic acid – LSD), and stimulants such as cocaine and amphetamines. While so-called 'hard drugs' such as heroin attract the main attention of governments and researchers, addiction to alcohol is far more widespread. The indiscriminate medicinal use of barbiturates in the 1960s has also been responsible for much drug dependency. More recently, benzodiazepines (notably Valium) replaced barbiturates as a new source of medically induced drug dependency.

The control of addictive drugs has been a major concern of Western governments and the United Nations, but with mixed success. While government control of dangerous drugs reflects public concern, what needs explanation is why some non-addictive drugs, such as cannabis, are illegal, whilst other, more addictive drugs, such as tobacco and alcohol, are legal. Various explanations are offered for this phenomenon, including: the difficulty of controlling long-established drugs, and the occurrence of MORAL PANICS and mass media DEVIANCE AMPLIFICATION, and hence heightened controls and policing in relation to newly introduced drugs, particularly when these are associated with other forms of social DEVIANCE, and/or with lower status and ethnic minority groups.

drug taking for pleasure drug taking, where the aim is merely to gain or enhance gratification. Rather than ascribing some set of deviant impulses or motives which lead to drug 'abuse', some sociologists (e.g. BECKER, 'Becoming a Marijuana User', 1953) have been interested in exploring the social mechanisms which lead to drug taking for pleasure. Becker argues that the motivational chain involved in such cases is the reverse of that usually suggested by psychologists: the 'motivations' involved arise, like any other taste, as a socially acquired taste, in which the SOCIAL ACTOR is first introduced to the drug and then learns to enjoy it as a pleasurable sensation. As such, 'drug takers' do not differ 'psychologically' from other social actors; their drug taking can be explained primarily in sociological terms. See also LABELLING THEORY.

dual-career marriage the situation in which in contemporary industrial societies both partners in a relationship seek to maintain occupational CAREERS. Given the tensions between career and domestic commitments, especially on women (see DOMESTIC LABOUR), and also changes in the labour market (see FLEXIBLE LABOUR MARKETS), such arrangements are less common than is sometimes assumed.

dual economies *or* **dual societies** the coexistence of two different types of economies or societies within one nation state or colony. The term was originally coined by Boeke (1953) to describe the situation in colonial countries in which capitalist and noncapitalist sectors coexisted, but operated according to separate social and economic logics. Later, in MODERNIZATION theory, the meaning was taken up to refer to modern and traditional sectors within THIRD WORLD societies. More recently, the term has been applied to economies, such as Japan's, which are structured around a few very large corporations and a mass of small firms with very different labour relations, profitability, market control and security. The concept was criticized by FRANK (1967a) and other DEPENDENCY theorists. It implies that the two sectors are separate, whereas the counter-argument is that they are closely interlinked, with the modern, capitalist, large-scale sector dominating and shaping the other.

dualism any doctrine in which the fundamental forms of things, 'substances', reality, etc., are seen as of two contrasting types, without any possibility of one being reduced to the other, for example:
(a) (PHILOSOPHY) a distinction between 'material' things and 'mental' ideas;
(b) (SOCIOLOGY) distinctions between nature and nurture (see NATURE – NURTURE DEBATE), or between individual agency and the structural determination of social outcomes.

In philosophy, the alternative to dualism is *monism*, which asserts that 'things', substances, etc., are all of one basic kind, either 'material' in form (see MATERIALISM) or 'mental'. A further position, REALISM, argues that there is only one reality, even if this reality is 'stratified', i.e. contains fundamental differences of type, even if stopping short of dualism.

In current philosophy and sociology, rather than an outright 'dualism', a frequent position is to recognize the utility of thinking in terms of a *duality* of forms – mind and matter, or structure and agency – in which there exists a dialectical interaction between the two kinds of 'thing', but with no justification for sustaining a claim that there exist any ultimately irreducible kinds, e.g. see DUALITY OF STRUCTURE. See also DESCARTES, STRUCTURE AND AGENCY.

duality of structure (as formulated by Giddens, 1984) a conception of SOCIAL STRUCTURE as both 'the medium and the outcome' of social ACTION. See STRUCTURATION THEORY.

dual labour market the assumption that LABOUR MARKETS are systematically divided into two sectors: the *primary* and the *secondary*. The *primary* sector comprises relatively high-wage jobs with career prospects, while the jobs within the *secondary* sector lack these characteristics. The rationale for the division was that employers wished to offset the high cost of maintaining a stable, skilled core of workers by employing non-skilled workers to carry out the less central work activities on less favourable terms of employment and for less pay. Alternatively, companies may subcontract the work to small firms operating in a *secondary* labour market in the external environment. Typically, white adult males have enjoyed better access to *primary* sector jobs, while women and members of ethnic minorities have been over-represented within the *secondary* sector.

dual societies see DUAL ECONOMIES OR DUAL SOCIETIES.

Duhem-Quine thesis the view associated with the French philosopher of science, Pierre Duhem (1861–1916), and the American logician, Willard Quine (1908–) that SCIENCE consists of a complex network of assumptions, concepts, hypotheses and theories which are appraised 'as a whole', with no possibility of individual propositions being appraised in isolation from our entire system of beliefs. See also ANALYTIC AND SYNTHETIC, THEORY RELATIVITY.

durée the continuous flow of conduct and cognition in social life. In this view (see GIDDENS, 1984), social life is not seen as 'compounded of an aggregate or series of separate intentions, reasons and motives'. Nor is it regarded as the product of fixed structure. Rather, it is seen as a continuous process in which STRUCTURE AND AGENCY both play a part. Borrowing from the work of the social historian BRAUDEL, one may also talk of the *longue durée* of institutions as well as the repetitive *durée* of day-to-day social life.

Durkheim, Emile (1858–1917)

Along with MARX and WEBER, one of the triumvirate of major sociologists who did most to establish the shape of the modern subject. Of these three figures, Durkheim above all was quintessentially the sociologist, with his assertions that 'society *sui generis*' is the subject matter of sociology, and that 'social facts must always be explained by other social facts'. In a series of seminal works, Durkheim established many themes and contributed many concepts which continue to be important in modern sociology. Working within the tradition of POSITIVISM established by SAINT-SIMON and COMTE, but not wishing to refer to his own work as positivism, Durkheim's best-known dictum is to 'treat social facts as things'. By this he meant that social phenomena exist as an objective realm, are external to individuals, operate by their constraining or 'coercive' influence on individuals, and are general and collective. See also SOCIAL FACTS AS THINGS.

His first major work, *The Division of Labour in Society* (1893), rests on the important distinction he drew between MECHANICAL AND ORGANIC SOLIDARITY. His argument was that while in small-scale societies, with only a limited DIVISION OF LABOUR, people were bound together by similarity and a common COLLECTIVE CONSCIENCE, in more complex societies with an advanced division of labour, this division of labour itself acted as the basis of social integration. Two further vital concepts in Durkheim's sociology, which also make their first appearance in *The Division of Labour,* are his suggestion that in modern societies the division of labour is often marred by ANOMIE (i.e. is unregulated by society or social values), and that the division of labour is also often 'forced', which is to say that, as the result of unfairness and inefficiency in the operation of the educational system and in the processes of occupational selection, many people are made to occupy roles for which they are unsuited (see FORCED DIVISION OF LABOUR). Durkheim's objective in *The Division of Labour,* and subsequently, was to establish, both theoretically and practically, the conditions for social solidarity in modern societies which would combine individualism and collectivism. He rejected any suggestion (such as SPENCER's) that society could operate effectively on principles of self-interest, without collective norms. On the other hand, he was equally opposed to a strongly centralized state. He suggested, instead, that the organization of society into occupationally-based, intermediate groupings, standing between the state and the individual, might prove the best way to organize a modern society based on the division of labour. A network of such groups would perhaps be well placed to place moral restraints on egoism and to regulate the group conflicts which modern societies inevitably generate.

In *The Rules of Sociological Method* (1895), Durkheim laid out his overall approach to sociological explanation, including his doctrine of 'social facts as things'. But this work is perhaps equally important for its contribution to the formulation of modern FUNCTIONALISM. Central to Durkheim's functionalism was a distinction between healthy and 'pathological' forms of social organization. As Durkheim puts it, 'it is the function of the average organism that the physiologist studies; and the sociologist does the same'. 'It would be incomprehensible', Durkheim suggests, 'if the most widespread forms of organization were not the most advantageous'. Thus, the 'healthy', or the 'functional', social form is usually that which is present in the average at a given level of social development. For modern industrial societies, where the evolution of this type has not yet run its full course, Durkheim recognized that assessment of functionality was more difficult. Here, therefore, one must also seek to establish with some care that the generality of a phenomenon is actually bound up with the 'general conditions of collective life' for this social type. As well as establishing the function of a phenomenon, one must also always independently establish its cause.

In *Suicide* (1897), a work seen as a 'methodological classic' by some and as greatly flawed by others, Durkheim employed what would now be called the SECONDARY ANALYSIS of existing OFFICIAL STATISTICS, seeking to demonstrate how SUICIDE is a social, and thus a sociological, phenomenon rather than a purely individual one. After first 'eliminating' existing non-sociological explanations – including climatic factors and 'normal' and 'abnormal' psychological factors, such as 'racial' characteristics or insanity – three main types of suicide were identified by Durkheim as corresponding in each case to distinct types of social situation. Thus, *altruistic suicide,* he suggested, was caused by strong mechanical solidarity (e.g. the suicide of the old and infirm in simple societies, or suicides of honour in the army); *egoistic suicide,* he suggested, was caused by excessive individuation in modern societies (e.g. the higher incidence of suicide among Protestants compared with Jews or Catholics, and among the divorced compared with the married); and *anomic suicide* was said to result when disruptions of normal social expectations occurred (e.g. a sudden change in economic circumstances, and as a general tendency in modern societies in their unregulated forms). A fourth type of suicide – *fatalistic suicide* – also occurs where social regulation leaves no scope for autonomous action apart from death (e.g. the suicide of the slave). For those who admire it, *Suicide* is both a sophisticated work and a precursor of later forms of MULTIVARIATE ANALYSIS (see also CROSS-TABULATION). To its critics, however, it is a work in which Durkheim uses statistics in a manner that imposes MEASUREMENT BY FIAT, with little guarantee that actors' beliefs and values are as he assumed them to be.

In *Elementary Forms of Religious Life* (1912), Durkheim returned to an examination of the nature of the 'collective conscience' within simpler societies. This study of religious beliefs and practices in what he took to be their most elementary form (especially Australian aboriginal society) became the basis of much of the modern sociological study of religion (see RELIGION, FUNCTIONALIST THEORY OF RELIGION, SACRED AND PROFANE). The decisive idea in Durkheim's account of religion is that religion functions as a symbolic representation of society, in which the beliefs and practices relative to the 'sacred' continually reaffirm communal values. In view of this, one of the tasks of Durkheim's sociology was to discover what have since been called FUNCTIONAL ALTERNATIVES OR FUNCTIONAL EQUIVALENTS to religion in increasingly secular modern societies (see also CIVIL RELIGION; compare SECULARIZATION).

In addition to these four main works, Durkheim published much else, including numerous essays. Among the most important of these (written with Marcel Mauss) is *Primitive Classification* (1903), in which the basic categories of human thought, including time and space, and number, are seen as reflecting patterns of social organization. For example, classification is seen as reflecting the division of human societies into clans (see also SOCIOLOGY OF KNOWLEDGE). Also of importance are Durkheim's essays on TOTEMISM and on KINSHIP. Along with the ideas contained in *Elementary Forms,* these essays exerted a strong influence on the formation of modern STRUCTURALISM (see also MYTHOLOGIES).

As well as the works published in Durkheim's lifetime, many of his lectures, together with fragments of books left unfinished, were published after his death, including *Moral Education* (1925), *Socialism and Saint-Simon* (1928), and *Professional Ethic and Civic Morals* (1950). As one of the founding fathers of modern sociology, Durkheim was also associated with the journal which attracted around it many celebrated sociologists, anthropologists and historians, amongst them, Marcel Mauss, Maurice Halbwachs and Levy-Bruhl.

On socialism, Durkheim's position was sympathetic but non-Marxist. As pointed out by Gouldner (in the introduction to the English version of *Socialism and Saint-Simon*, 1959), contrary to suggestions that Durkheim was, above all, a conservative, an emphasis on social conflict and social change is an enduring element in his sociology, deriving from Saint-Simon. The possible role Durkheim saw for occupational intermediate groupings in modern societies places him closest to guild socialism. A 'moral conservative' Durkheim may sometimes have been, but he was not a political conservative. Nor was normative integration Durkheim's exclusive focus; relationships of reciprocal interdependence as well as normative integration are recognized as the basis of social order.

Debate surrounds Durkheim's work in general, as to how far it does, or does not, succeed in satisfactorily combining an emphasis on social structure with individual agency in sociological explanation (see also STRUCTURE AND AGENCY). For the most part, Durkheim's sociology has been seen as overstating general normative and social structural influences at the expense of individual agency, although it was always Durkheim's intention to leave scope for the latter within his sociology. Durkheim's two main goals were to establish sociology as an autonomous 'scientific' discipline, and to establish the practical requirements for social order in modern societies. In neither of these can Durkheim be regarded as having the last word. What is undeniable is that his influence on modern sociology has been immense, with many modern statements about the subject still being presented as positions either for or against Durkheim.

Two important biographical and critical studies on Durkheim's life and work are by Lukes (1973) and PARSONS (1937).

dyad and triad social interactions or relationships comprising two elements (*dyad*) or three elements (*triad*). As an aspect of his FORMAL SOCIOLOGY, SIMMEL suggested that certain properties of dyads and triads obtain whether the parties to the interaction or relationship are persons, organizations, or nation states, e.g. mediation or divide-and-rule is possible within the triad but not the dyad; the 'peculiar closeness' of the two compared with the three. The analysis of dyads and triads provides a particularly clear example of the character of FORMAL SOCIOLOGY, with its emphasis on recurring forms of social interaction.

dying see DEATH AND DYING.

dysfunction *or* **disfunction** any social activity seen as making a negative contribution to the maintenance or effective working of a functioning SOCIAL SYSTEM. See FUNCTIONALISM.

dystopia the reverse of UTOPIA, a possible or imaginary social place which is the worst of possible worlds.

e

ecclesia a term referring to a universal church, e.g. the Roman Catholic Church, in place of the more generic term CHURCH. See also CHURCH-SECT TYPOLOGY.

eclecticism any approach to analysis or research which mixes theoretically disparate perspectives.

ecodevelopment see SUSTAINABLE DEVELOPMENT.

ecological competition, ecological invasion and ecological succession see HUMAN ECOLOGY.

ecological fallacy *or* **wrong-level fallacy** the error of inferring that relationships established between two or more variables measured at an AGGREGATE level will also hold at the individual level. Care must be taken in research studies which use areas as the unit of analysis to avoid this error. For example, if an area is found to have a high percentage of unemployment and a high percentage of mental illness, any inference of a causal relationship at the individual level would be invalid. The problem is discussed in Robinson (1951) and Riley (1963).

ecology the study of the interactive relationship between living things and their ENVIRONMENT. The term became popularized in the 1980s due to a growing concern with the fragility of the Earth as a living system. A variety of indicators are acknowledged to be warnings that natural systems, evolved over millennia, are being threatened by the technological developments initiated by the Industrial Revolution and the resultant population explosion. Such indices include the extinction of many species of plants and animals, the depletion of the ozone layer, global warming and changes in weather patterns, pollution of large areas of land and water upsetting the natural balance of many smaller systems. See also GREEN MOVEMENT, HOMEOSTASIS, CHAOTIC PHENOMENA, COST–BENEFIT ANALYSIS. GAIA HYPOTHESIS. ENVIRONMENTAL DEPLETION, FAMINE, URBAN ECOLOGY, HUMAN ECOLOGY.

e-commerce sales of goods and services undertaken via the INTERNET and World-Wide Web.

econometrics quantitative economic analysis which combines economic theory with statistical analysis. Econometrics is employed in theoretical modelling, policy analysis and forecasting, as well as in historical analysis.

economic and social contradictions see CONTRADICTION 2.

economic and social development any change which results in increased economic productivity and prosperity, and new and more complex forms of SOCIAL STRUCTURE and organization. The study of such development was a central concern of classical sociological theory (see EVOLUTIONARY THEORY, SOCIAL CHANGE). In contemporary work, 'economic and social development' is usually used to refer to the specific *process* of industrialization in both its socialist and capitalist forms (compare ECONOMIC GROWTH). Although Barrington Moore's (1967) comparative and historical study continues to be influential, and new studies of changes in the developed capitalist world have attracted attention (SEE CONVERGENCE, POSTCAPITALIST SOCIETY, FORDISM AND POST-FORDISM, POSTINDUSTRIAL SOCIETY), much theoretical work is now devoted to current issues and problems of development in the THIRD WORLD. See also DEPENDENCY THEORY, DEPENDENT INDUSTRIALIZATION, NEOEVOLUTIONISM, UNDERDEVELOPMENT, UNEVEN DEVELOPMENT, MODERNIZATION.

Economic and Social Research Council (ESRC) the government-funded agency that provides grants for social research. Formerly the Social Science Research Council, the change of name was at the behest of a government minister, Sir Keith Joseph, who was unhappy with the appropriateness of the term 'science', and also anxious to focus on more economically relevant applied issues in social research.

economic crises periodic, or more irregularly occurring, phases in the working of the capitalist economy, in which economic accumulation is checked or halted, either as part of a regular cycle of alternating booms and depressions (see TRADE CYCLE), or as the outcome of exceptional circumstances, such as sudden restrictions on the supply of a vital commodity such as oil. In one view economic crises are functional for the capitalist system as a whole in that they promote a reshaping of production, restoring profitability and renewed accumulation. In MARXIAN ECONOMICS, there are suggestions that crises and depressions will tend to become more severe (see CRISES OF CAPITALISM), but no entirely convincing arguments have been given why this should be so. See also LONG-WAVE THEORY.

economic dependency see DEPENDENCY THEORY.

economic determinism see ECONOMIC INTERPRETATION OF HISTORY.

economic development see ECONOMIC AND SOCIAL DEVELOPMENT.

economic growth growth in the GROSS NATIONAL PRODUCT (GNP). A distinction can be drawn between theories of economic growth (in ECONOMICS) which emphasize primarily economic variables, such as levels of saving and investment (e.g. the Harrod-Domar model) and those which are more sociological and take account of wider social as well as more narrowly economic factors (e.g. SCHUMPETER or ROSTOW).

economic indicators see SOCIAL INDICATORS.

economic interpretation of history any approach to historical analysis which emphasizes the decisive importance of economic forces in history. Although especially associated with MARXISM (see also HISTORICAL MATERIALISM, ECONOMISM), such an emphasis is far from confined to this area. A significant non-Marxist example is the work of the US historian, Beard (1874–1948), whose *An Economic Interpretation of the Constitution* (1910) did much to alter the previous neglect of economic factors in American historiography.

economic man (ECONOMICS) the IDEAL-TYPE conception of the 'rational economic actor', in which the individual is assumed to seek to maximize his or her returns (satisfaction, UTILITY, profit) from economic activity. No assumption need be made that, in reality, the actor always does actually aim at, or, still less, succeed in such maximizing activity. Rather, the ideal type allows the construction of rational models of economic behaviour, so that departures from such a rational model can be studied. In sociology, many of Max WEBER's ideal types are posited as departures from rational types of behaviour, e.g. see TYPES OF SOCIAL ACTION.

economic reductionism see ECONOMIC INTERPRETATION OF HISTORY.

economic rent 1 payments (in money or in kind) made to the owner or controller of property for its use. Historically, in preindustrial societies, rent paid and received for LAND has been of major importance, e.g. under the FEUDAL MODE OF PRODUCTION. In MARXIAN ECONOMICS, with reference to situations where rent for land is levied in a context in which market relations exist, two main forms of rent are recognized: (a) *absolute rent,* the basic level of rent; and (b) *differential rent,* the extra rent obtained from land of higher than average productivity (not including any return on additional CAPITAL invested in improving the land).

Debate has existed (e.g. Hindess and Hirst, 1975) as to whether taxes on peasant production levied by the state constitute a fundamentally different MODE OF PRODUCTION (see also ASIATIC MODE OF PRODUCTION) from the forms of 'rent' that emerged in Western Europe, or whether the 'tax-rent' couple constitute a single mode of production. For some Marxists, the attraction of the latter view is that the idea of a single developmental sequence of modes of production can be preserved.

2 (ECONOMICS) *rent* or *quasi-rent,* any payment, or part payment, made for a FACTOR OF PRODUCTION, including human labour, which derives from an absolute shortage of supply (e.g. the fixed supply of land, inherent limitations in the supply of 'talent', outstanding musical or sporting abilities). Compare FUNCTIONALIST THEORY OF SOCIAL STRATIFICATION.

economics the specialist social science concerned with the study of economic behaviour. The term derives from the Greek for 'household management', and it has nowadays mainly replaced the earlier term for economic science, POLITICAL ECONOMY. The term can also be used to refer to the study of any behaviour in which there is a scarcity of means to achieve given ends (L. Robbins, *The Nature and Significance of Economic Science,* 1932).

A general distinction is drawn between *microeconomics,* which is concerned with the behaviour of individual units within an economy, such as individual consumers or firms, and *macroeconomics,* which is concerned with the study of aggregate economic activity, e.g. overall determinants of national income, levels of employment, etc.

Adam SMITH is usually regarded as the founding father of modern economics. The characteristic approach within the subject has been the method of simplification of IDEALIZATION (see also ECONOMIC MAN). This approach was developed by CLASSICAL ECONOMISTS, such as David Ricardo (1772–1823) and John Stuart MILL, and continued in NEOCLASSICAL ECONOMICS and in the work of modern economists.

Like sociology, although not to the same extent, economics has remained divided by competing perspectives. Important divisions within the modern subject exist between KEYNESIAN ECONOMICS and MONETARISM. Other distinctive approaches include MARXIAN ECONOMICS and INSTITUTIONAL ECONOMICS. See also RATIONAL CHOICE THEORY, EXCHANGE THEORY, THEORY OF GAMES, ECONOMIC SOCIOLOGY.

economic sociology the sociological study of the relations between the ECONOMY and other social institutions. Rather than being a specialist area of study within the discipline, the sociological analysis of economic life has been a central concern within many forms of general sociology. It is a central concern, for example, in the work of major classical sociologists such as MARX, WEBER and DURKHEIM. More specialist areas of sociological inquiry in which economic questions are uppermost include ORGANIZATION THEORY, INDUSTRIAL SOCIOLOGY, SOCIOLOGY OF WORK.

economic surplus the difference between what a country produces and what it consumes. This is a key concept in the work of the US Marxist economist, Paul Baran, and was developed by Baran and Paul Sweezy in their theory of MONOPOLY CAPITALISM (1966) and taken up by FRANK in UNDERDEVELOPMENT theory. Baran (1957) distinguished between three forms of economic surplus:

(a) actual economic surplus, which occurs in all societies, and is 'the difference between society's *actual* current output and *actual* current consumption'. Thus, the surplus is accumulated in savings and investments;
(b) potential economic surplus, being the difference between what *could* be produced in a given environment and 'what might be regarded as essential consumption'. This applies mainly to capitalist economies and is only realizable under reorganization of social arrangements. Economic surplus is lost because of excessive consumption, the existence of unproductive workers, poor organization of existing production processes and labour unemployment. In the THIRD WORLD, excessive consumption by élite groups eats up economic surplus, and in the monopoly capitalist countries, arms expenditure acts similarly;
(c) planned economic surplus, which applies to economic planning under socialism. (Baran's definition is, 'the difference between society's "optimum" output obtainable in a historically given natural and technological environment under conditions of planned "optimal" utilization of all available productive resources, and some chosen "optimal" volume of consumption'.) This assumes both a completely efficient use of resources, and control over consumption such that decisions can be made to produce whatever economic surplus is desired.

Many problems have been identified with this usage. Baran recognized that there were problems with measurement, but, despite his optimism, these have not been resolved, so that the OPERATIONALIZATION of the concept remains problematic. It is especially unclear how potential economic surplus can be measured. The notion has an intuitive appeal, but quantifying this is probably impossible. His concept of planned economic surplus seems utopian in the light of the experience of existing socialist societies, whose planning has been associated with excessive wastage and inefficient usage of resources. Further, whilst Baran claims to build on Marxian concepts, the relationship of this concept to those of SURPLUS VALUE and the LABOUR THEORY OF VALUE are tenuous.

economic take-off see ROSTOW.

economism (MARXISM) any theory or approach which emphasizes the economic determinants of social forms while failing to give adequate consideration to the RELATIVE AUTONOMY often possessed by IDEOLOGIES, the STATE, etc., and by human AGENCY.

economy 1 the organized management of human material resources, goods and services.

2 the social institutions concerned with the management, production and distribution of human resources.

It has been suggested that all major sociologies imply an economics. Both historians and sociologists have distinguished between different forms of society according to the tools that men and women use and the economic power they have at their disposal. In sociology, the most influential models of economic forms and their relation with types of society are those deriving from MARX and WEBER. A central issue running through much sociology is the extent of the determinancy of the economy, or institutional and cultural autonomy of other activities from the economy. See also MODE OF PRODUCTION, DIVISION OF LABOUR, ECONOMIC AND SOCIAL DEVELOPMENT, ECONOMIC INTERPRETATION OF HISTORY, ECONOMICS, POLITICAL ECONOMY, ECONOMIC SOCIOLOGY.

educability (SOCIOLOGY OF EDUCATION) the capacity to benefit from formal education, assumed to be affected by differences in patterns of child rearing and physical support.

education see SOCIOLOGY OF EDUCATION.

Education Acts legislation enacted in Parliament which has resulted in significant changes to the organization of the public education system, either as a whole or in certain sections of it. Such Acts have tended to follow, or sometimes herald, major changes in welfare or social policy. Thus, the 1870 Act provided school accommodation 'for all the children for whose elementary education efficient and suitable provision is not otherwise made', and followed other social reform legislation. The 1902 Act introduced a secular framework for the education system by placing it under the control of local education authorities, with some exceptions, which allowed for the existence of sectarian, Christian schools under specified conditions.

Probably the most important Act was passed in 1944, which laid the foundation of the contemporary education system. Its major contribution was to attempt to put into effect the notion of EQUALITY OF OPPORTUNITY through the provision of free secondary education for all, together with other support measures.

During the 1950s and 1960s, dissatisfaction with the tripartite secondary system grew significantly. The election of a Labour government in 1964 brought commitment to universal COMPREHENSIVE EDUCATION which was consolidated into the 1976 Act. This Act was repealed in 1979 on the election of the Conservative government.

Education Acts introduced during the 1980s continued to emphasize the extent to which they represented instruments of social policy and reflected contrasting political philosophies. These Acts quite specifically abandoned the principles of equality of opportunity and universal comprehensive education. Thus, the 1980 Education Act strengthened the provision of private schooling by introducing an Assisted Places Scheme which would reimburse fees for independent schools, but there is little evidence that poorer families benefit from it.

The 1980 Act extended the 'market economy' principle, the cornerstone of Thatcherite conservatism, in the system. The Act allows parents to send their children to schools of their choice. Critics argue that this will lead to the creation of a two-tier system of education in which the poorer classes will suffer. The 1988 Education Act, apart from introducing a National Curriculum, extended the 'market' philosophy by allowing schools to apply to become state, grant-aided schools by opting out of local authority control. See also SOCIOLOGY OF EDUCATION.

educational priority area a geographical location, usually in an inner-city area, designated for the receipt of special educational resources, based on the principle of POSITIVE DISCRIMINATION, in order to compensate for poor environmental conditions. Such areas were established after the publication of the Plowden Report in 1967. The report was based on extensive sociological research and argued for the importance of good primary education, especially for socially-deprived children. It argued that the major factor in a child's educational performance is the attitude of its parents to education. In locations of social, cultural and environmental deprivation, parental attitudes would be indifferent and children could be identified as suffering from educational handicaps. In such areas additional resources should be committed to improve the quality of educational experience and so compensate for the other disadvantages (see COMPENSATORY EDUCATION). The government accepted the report's advocacy of positive discrimination and made resources available, including rebuilding programmes, support for curriculum initiatives and special payments to teachers in EPA schools. Strategies were to be developed for forming close links with local communities through the development of community schools which would play a leading part in community regeneration.

The explicit acceptance of the principle of positive discrimination in favour of deprived groups represents a significant initiative in social policy and a recognition of the importance of social engineering in bringing about social change, although critics would argue that Educational Priority Areas have made little real difference to the alleviation of poverty and disadvantage.

effect size the size of effect which is found in a quantitative study. Different types of research design produce different effect sizes; for example, in correlational studies the size of *r* (the correlation coefficient) gives an impression of the strength of the association between two variables. Achieving statistical significance is dependent on the STATISTICAL POWER of the statistical test employed. Statistical power is largely dependent on two factors: the effect size and the sample size. Thus a small correlation could be found to be significant when a large sample has been employed, whereas a large correlation could be found not to be significant because a small sample was employed. Conversely, the effect size from a study is largely unaffected by the sample size. Accordingly, statistical significance is not a measure of the magnitude of a result and if researchers wish to compare studies then effect size should be employed. An additional role of effect size is in the synthesis of the results from a number of studies using META-ANALYSIS.

ego one of the three elements of the personality in FREUD's theory. The ego is that part of the personality which operates in direct contact with reality, attempting to control the demands of the ID according to the strictures of the SUPEREGO and with awareness of the real world. It therefore operates under the 'reality principle', in contrast to the id, which operates under the 'pleasure principle'. The id demands immediate gratification by direct means, so the ego's role is to assess whether these demands are realistically possible, and if not, to enforce delay of gratification until expression can be had in a socially appropriate form. See also DEFENCE MECHANISM.

egocentrism *or* **egocentricity** (PSYCHOLOGY) the state of being centred on the self. Though this term may be used to describe adult behaviour it is most theoretically useful in the context of CHILD DEVELOPMENT theory. According to PIAGET and later theorists, the child moves from a state of egocentrism during which experience is in terms of the self with little understanding of the point of view of 'others', to a state where the perspective of 'others' can be taken into account. This development process is thus seen as crucial to normal SOCIALIZATION, involving the emergence of the ability to predict other's behaviour, to take others into account and to act accordingly.

egoistic suicide the form of SUICIDE identified by DURKHEIM (1895) as being associated with 'excessive egoism', or individualism. As suggested by Durkheim, the incidence of egoistic suicide 'varies with the degree of integration of society'. For example, the reason that Protestants more frequently commit suicide than Catholics, Durkheim suggests, is that the collective beliefs and practices of the latter involve a stronger integration of the individual within the religious community, and far less sanction for individualism.

ego-psychology approaches within PSYCHOANALYSIS (see also NEO-FREUDIANS) that emphasize the EGO rather than the ID (see I. Craib, 1989). As Craib asserts: 'If object-relations theory is British psychoanalysis, then ego-psychology is American psychoanalysis' (see also OBJECT-RELATIONS SCHOOL). Ego-psychology exerted a strong influence on the theory of SOCIALIZATION developed by PARSONS. It is sometimes criticized as 'an ideological product of American capitalism', since its primary concern often appears to be a concern with individual adjustment to existing social conditions.

eidos the general features and characteristics of the ideas and, by extension, the main social institutions and activities, of a particular society. This relatively uncommon term was introduced by Gregory BATESON (1936), and also used by Charles Madge (1964).

Eisenstadt, Shmuel Noah (1923–) Israeli comparative sociologist and comparative historian known for his work on immigrant groups and on MODERNIZATION. The work which has attracted most attention is his *The Political System of Empires* (1967), a highly systematic attempt to compare historical, non-tribal, preindustrial political systems and to frame generalizations about the factors influencing the effectiveness, or otherwise, of this general type of political system. The volume contains nearly 100 pages of tabular comparisons of particular states, in which several metrics are employed to rank systems comparatively on a number of dimensions. The general hypothesis advanced is that to be effective, non-tribal, preindustrial political systems must be able to mobilize, and also generate, new, 'free-floating' material and cultural resources, prising these from traditional control, and must also mobilize the support of at least some leaders of local LINEAGES. Nevertheless, like most political systems (and in contrast with suggestions made about ORIENTAL DESPOTISM), such systems always contain contradictory elements and are inherently unstable.

Eisenstadt is known for his wide interest and academic productivity, ranging from the effects of immigration to the stabilizing effect of age stratification on society (see AGEING). In his pioneering study of *Israeli Society* (1967), and in *The Transformation of Israeli Society* (1985), he not only analysed an historically and sociologically unique case of nation building (the attempt to reconstruct a sovereign, national life that had ceased in AD 70), he also added a theoretically significant new dimension to the understanding of post-revolutionary societies.

elaborated codes and restricted codes specific forms of language and speech derived from particular social contexts, involving different orders of meaning. A *restricted code* is used in close communal circumstances, where there is legitimate expectation of shared presuppositions and understandings, and involves speech that is inexplicit, telescoped and indexical (see INDEXICAL EXPRESSION). An *elaborated code* makes no such presuppositions, is explicit in meaning, uses full forms of expression and 'objective' standards of reference. Bernstein argues that the English social classes manifest a differential familiarity with each mode of speech, with social and educational implications. However, the application of the concepts of elaborated and restricted codes to the speech patterns of middle- and working-class groups respectively, has not been universally accepted, and considerable scepticism has been expressed about their validity and usefulness since they were first introduced (see Labov, 1972).

elasticity of supply and demand (ECONOMICS) the degree of change in supply of a good or service in response to a change in the price offered by consumers (*elasticity/inelasticity of supply*); or degree of change in the quantity of goods and services demanded in response to a change in prices (*elasticity/inelasticity of demand* or *demand elasticity*). For example, the change in demand as a result of a price reduction may be small if the food is already in reasonable supply (inelasticity); and, where a fall in price reflects an overall increase in supply in a competitive market, this may also result in an overall reduction in the income of the suppliers.

electoral register (in the UK) a list of all electors entitled to vote in a local, parliamentary or European election. The electoral register is compiled in mid-October every year and shows the names and addresses of UK nationals aged 18 years and over, together with those who will attain that age during the lifetime of the register. Although some people fail to register, the electoral register is useful to the sociologist in that it provides an up-to-date list of inhabitants of a given area from which to draw random and non-random samples of the population for QUESTIONNAIRE and related studies.

electoral sociology the sociological study of elections and voting. This area of sociological study has been a shared enterprise between academic sociologists and behaviourally oriented political scientists (see also POLITICAL BEHAVIOUR). See VOTING BEHAVIOUR, PSEPHOLOGY.

electoral swing the movement between one major political party and another, between one election and the next. The movement is usually stated in percentage terms, as the percentage of the vote gained by one party, added to that gained by the second party, divided by two.

Electra complex see OEDIPUS COMPLEX.

Elias, Norbert (1897–1990) German-born sociologist who, after leaving Germany in the Hitler era, worked first in England and later in Ghana, Holland and Germany. He describes his approach to sociological analysis as FIGURATIONAL SOCIOLOGY, in which changing social 'configurations' – rather than societies – are analysed as the unintended outcome of the interactions of interdependent individuals (see also FIGURATION). His most important work, *The Civilizing Process* (1939), attracted little attention at the time of its publication in German. However, by the time the English edition appeared (2 vols. in 1978 and 1982), an 'Elias school', dedicated to promoting 'figurational sociology', had become well established in Holland and England (see P. Gleichman et al., 1977). The theme of *The Civilizing Process* is the relation between European state-formation and changes in individual patterns of behaviour and personality, including new forms of morality and individual self-control (see also CIVILIZING PROCESS). *The Court Society* (1969) deals with related themes. The theoretical underpinnings of figurational sociology are outlined in *What Is Sociology?* (1970). There are parallels between Elias's focus on 'figurations', rather than on individuals or societies as separate entities, and those approaches in modern sociology which emphasize the importance of modes of social analysis which acknowledge the interrelation between STRUCTURE AND AGENCY (see STRUCTURATION THEORY). Other works by Elias include *The Loneliness of the Dying* (1982) and *Involvement and Detachment* (1986).

élite literally 'the best or most talented members of society' (e.g. educational élite), however in sociology the term most usually refers to *political élites.* Here, the assumption of ÉLITE THEORY has been that a division between élites and MASSES is an inevitable feature of any complex modern society, and that the aspirations of radical democrats that the people as a whole could rule is mistaken.

élite theory the hypothesis that political élites are inevitable in complex modern societies. In its original form this theory was a sociological response to the relative failure of modern democratic movements, judged by their own highest objectives. Rather than power to the people, the advent of modern DEMOCRACY brought new bases of élite membership. Associated particularly with the pessimistic view of modern democracy taken by PARETO and, to a lesser extent MOSCA, élites were seen as an inevitable consequence of psychological differences between élites and MASSES and the organizational requirements of modern societies. See also IRON LAW OF OLIGARCHY, MICHELS. Compare RULING CLASS.

In its more recent form (see DEMOCRATIC ÉLITISM) élite theory has modified its pessimism about modern democracy. Building on arguments already implicit in the work of theorists such as Mosca and Michels that different bases of élite power have important social consequences, what some theorists (e.g. Dahl, 1961) now propose is that a democratic competition between rival representative élites constitutes the best practicable form of modern government. Compare POWER ÉLITE; see also STABLE DEMOCRACY.

The study of élites and the testing of élite theories has been a notably controversial area. While some researchers (e.g. Hunter, 1963) have pursued a 'reputational' approach asking respondents 'who holds power', others, including Dahl, have argued only the careful study of actual 'decisions' – the outcomes of the operation of power – can satisfactorily establish who in fact is powerful. Even this, however, is not decisive, for as Bachrach and Baratz (1962) have argued, the study of overt 'decisions' fails to explore the existence of 'non-decisions' (see COMMUNITY POWER), the many circumstances in which the balance of power may be such as to preclude political debate or political contest, so that no overt point of 'decision' is actually observable. See also POWER, MASS SOCIETY.

emancipation the collective freeing of a slave population in specific countries or colonial territories. The word is of Latin origin, meaning 'to transfer ownership'. The freeing of slave populations in the Western hemisphere has usually been by issue of a legal decree, i.e. an 'emancipation proclamation'. Britain abolished slavery in its empire in 1833, while in the US an emancipation proclamation was issued in 1862, but did not take effect until 1865, at the end of the Civil War.

emancipatory politics see LIFE POLITICS.

emancipatory theory see HABERMAS. See also LIFE POLITICS.

emburgeoisement *or* **bourgeoisification** the process of becoming bourgeois or, more generally, MIDDLE CLASS.

embourgeoisement thesis the argument that the working class in modern capitalism has adopted the lifestyle and political attitudes of the MIDDLE CLASSES. In the case of Britain, this thesis gained currency in the 1950s and 60s in a number of different spheres. Social commentators, political analysts and politicians contrasted the condition of the WORKING CLASS before the 1930s (in terms of income, housing, employment, health and leisure interests) with its improved situation after 1950. They argued, or assumed, that the establishment of the WELFARE STATE, relatively full employment, real improvements in living standards and the mass production of consumer goods, had removed material and cultural differences between the classes. They also attributed the success of the Conservative Party throughout the 1950s to these changes, arguing that material and social changes had had a major impact on working-class political consciousness, leading, again, to an identification with the middle classes (e.g. see Rose, 1960). These factors, welfare state, political conservativism, etc., led a number of sociologists to speculate about the end of ideology (see END-OF-IDEOLOGY THESIS) as a factor in voting and social behaviour.

A most interesting effect of the embourgeoisement thesis was its influence on the major political parties and in mass media coverage of politics during the period. Within sociology, some work (e.g. in studies of family relations) was thematically consistent with the embourgeoisement argument, but the most influential and most direct response to the thesis, the AFFLUENT WORKER studies, refuted it in terms of workers' attitudes, while earlier work on the extent and distribution of poverty had shown that there were still great numbers of people who did not enjoy a 'middle-class' standard of living. See also CLASS, CLASS CONSCIOUSNESS, CLASS IMAGERY, UNDERCLASS.

emergent evolution the distinctively social and cultural element in human evolution (see EVOLUTIONARY THEORY); those aspects of evolution that have carried human social evolution beyond merely physical and biological evolution, to social developments which are increasingly based primarily on CULTURE and cultural transformation. Compare SUPERORGANIC.

emergent properties any properties (of a social system or group) of which it can be asserted that they cannot be explained simply in terms of their origins or constituent parts – hence the notion that 'the whole is greater than the parts'. The term is especially identified with functionalist sociologies, such as Durkheim's, which emphasize the AUTONOMY OF SOCIOLOGY from other disciplines (i.e. that sociological accounts should not be subject to REDUCTIONISM). The notion of emergent properties has often been criticized. For example, it has been seen as leading to a reified account (see REIFICATION) of social reality, and to a loss of visibility and recognition of the influence of the individual actor. However, the conception of emergent properties need not be associated with the notion that there are *no* links with, or no influence of, underlying levels of reality, but merely that there may be aspects of social reality which cannot be satisfactorily explained reductively. In the physical sciences, too, emergent properties play an indispensable role (e.g. 'weather systems' in meteorology) where the complexity of reality and the unpredictability of the underlying variables defies a fully reductive account. In an important sense, the existence of separate disciplines in science is testimony to the existence of emergent properties; at the very least emergent properties prove analytically indispensable. The importance of these need not mean the existence of any absolute barriers to attempts at reductionistic analysis; simply that these attempts are unlikely ever to be *entirely* successful, and even if successful, will not overturn the utility of the conception of emergent properties. Compare HOLISM, METHODOLOGICAL INDIVIDUALISM.

emic and etic a distinction originating from LINGUISTICS (Pike, 1967), but now widely used in sociology and anthropology, between accounts made from a perspective indigenous or internal to a language or social situation (an *emic* account), and those made from a perspective external to the language or social context, including sociological observers' accounts (*etic* accounts). See also MEANINGFUL UNDERSTANDING, HERMENEUTICS, FORMS OF LIFE.

The original distinction stems from the linguistic terms *phonemic* and *phonetic.* Whereas a phonemic account rests on the speaker's own recognition of patterns of sound, phonetic accounts are based on the observer's model and measurement of these differences.

emigration see MIGRATION.

émigré a person living in enforced exile from his or her native country.

Emmanuel, Arghiri (1911–) Greek-born, French-based, Marxist economist of DEVELOPMENT who has sought to integrate aspects of the theory of INTERNATIONAL TRADE with Marx's general theory of VALUE (see UNEQUAL EXCHANGE).

emotional labour the face-to-face interaction and the sustained display of particular 'emotions' required by workers in particular occupations, such as air stewardesses or bar and casino staff. The term was introduced by A. Hochschild (*The Managed Heart: Commercialization of Human Feeling,* 1983). According to Hochschild, such work is guided by *'feeling rules'* (governing the appropriateness of particular emotions to particular social situations) and effectively means the COMMODIFICATION of emotions. As the service sector of most advanced economies expands (especially personal services) the number of people (often women) involved in emotional labour processes continues to rise.

empathic understanding a form of understanding and explanation achieved by imagining oneself in the role of the social actors whose actions one seeks to understand or explain. Since this form of explanation would appear to rest on a suspect introspective psychology, the method is often dismissed as 'unscientific' (Abel, 1977). Sometimes it is wrongly assumed, as by Abel, that all forms of MEANINGFUL UNDERSTANDING AND EXPLANATION are equally suspect, depending merely on introspection. However, the most widely used forms of interpretive explanation in sociology (e.g. in WEBER'S work) only impute meanings to actors where the likelihood of such meanings can be confirmed by prevailing social norms and values (see VERSTEHEN). See also EMPATHY.

empathy the feeling of being able to experience vicariously what another person is experiencing. The ability to empathize is crucial in many interpersonal relationships and social settings. If family members do not experience empathy with each other, discord is more likely than if a climate of EMPATHIC UNDERSTANDING exists. Close friends, by definition, have an empathic relationship.

Empathy is one of ROGERS' (1951) three conditions for a successful client-counsellor relationship, the other two being genuine warmth, and unconditional positive regard. Empathy is central to PERSON-CENTRED COUNSELLING, since this perspective holds the view that the client's problems can only be understood by the counsellor through experiencing the client's phenemonological field. For this empathy is required.

Empathy is also sometimes seen as central to techniques of MEANINGFUL UNDERSTANDING AND EXPLANATION widely used in sociology. See also EMPATHIC UNDERSTANDING, VERSTEHEN.

empirical 1 derived from systematic observation or experiment, as against speculative assertion or merely theoretical knowledge.
2 factually true but, as yet, theoretically unexplained. See also EMPIRICISM, ABSTRACTED EMPIRICISM, EMPIRICAL SOCIOLOGY.

empirical sociology any form of sociology which places emphasis on the collection and analysis of data. However, more specifically the term refers to forms of sociology using SOCIAL SURVEYS or carefully documented PARTICIPANT OBSERVATION.

Sociology of this latter type has represented a major strand within the discipline as a whole, especially within US sociology (e.g. empirical studies of SOCIAL STRATIFICATION, CLASS, VOTING BEHAVIOUR). This general approach to sociology has sometimes been criticized as failing to explore important questions of theory (see ABSTRACTED EMPIRICISM), or, in the case of questionnaire-based and statistical research, as involving MEASUREMENT BY FIAT (see ETHNOMETHODOLOGY, OFFICIAL STATISTICS). However, these charges can be countered as far too sweeping, by pointing to the existence of much empirical sociology in which significant theoretical hypotheses are explored (see EMPIRICISM, LAZARSFELD, THEORIES OF THE MIDDLE RANGE).

empiricism 1 the doctrine that all knowledge derives from experience as against a priori categories (the epistemological position of Hume, Locke, the Logical Positivists, etc.). Compare IDEALISM, EPISTEMOLOGY, POSITIVISM.
2 (pejorative) the use of empirical methods at the expense of a more adequate theoretical approach (see also ABSTRACTED EMPIRICISM).
3 (especially in MARXISM and the recent philosophy of science) the failure to recognize the theory-laden and the socially constructed, and reconstructable, character of concepts, and thus of 'facts' (see also THEORY RELATIVITY).

The 'problems of empiricism' in philosophy and the scientific method have long been recognized as the 'problem of induction': the provisional status of any universal generalization based only on a finite sequence of empirical observations (see INDUCTION AND INDUCTIVE LOGIC).

A further aspect of philosophical empiricism, given the lack of any clear solution to the problem of induction, is that it can lead to scepticism or RELATIVISM, for example, when formulated as a doctrine that we can only have a knowledge of our own sensations, with no necessary relation to a reality beyond this. In this form, empiricism becomes conjoined with IDEALISM, and both can end in scepticism or relativism.

Faced with such difficulties, many philosophers and sociologists have emphasized the importance of concepts, hypotheses and theories in science and sociology, and have asserted a realist, rather than an empiricist, methodology (see

REALISM). However, there are problems in the outright assertion of any overall philosophical or methodological position (see METHODOLOGY, SCIENCE).

While the importance of empirical methods and empirical knowledge finds wide acceptance within sociology, this does not imply 'empiricism' in the senses specified. See also EMPIRICAL SOCIOLOGY.

employment any activity engaged in for wages or salary.

In sociology, there has always been a healthy scepticism about the simple equating of paid employment with work, yet in the wider society the prevailing meaning of the word is just that – so, 'an active woman, running a house and bringing up children, is distinguished from a woman who works: that is to say, takes paid employment' (R. Williams, 1976).

Sociologists have long been aware that WAGE LABOUR, to give its technical name, is only a particular form of work, gaining its centrality and definition from the specific set of productive relations which occurs within capitalist, market-exchange economies. Work, in such societies, is identified with employment, which involves 'the sale and purchase of labour power as a commodity in a market, resulting in the direction of activity during "working hours" by persons who have acquired the right to do so by virtue of the labour contract' (Purcell, 1986). See also PRODUCTIVE AND UNPRODUCTIVE LABOUR, LABOUR THEORY OF VALUE, SOCIOLOGY OF WORK, PRIVATE AND PUBLIC SPHERES, DOMESTIC LABOUR.

encounter any meeting between two or more people in a face-to-face interaction. Everyday life is made up of a series of such interactions, some of them with persons we know well, but many others with people with whom we may have only a fleeting contact. Described by GOFFMAN (1961b, 1967, 1971) as situations of copresence, encounters involve SOCIAL ACTORS in 'positionings' of the body and knowledgeable attention to FACE WORK, creating and preserving the numerous, distinctive kinds of encounter that can be observed. See also FACE-TO-FACE INTERACTION, INTERACTION ORDER AND INTERACTION RITUAL.

encounter group see GROUP THERAPY.

enculturation (CULTURAL ANTHROPOLOGY) the informal and formal acquisition of cultural norms and practices. As such, the term is almost synonymous with SOCIALIZATION. Its use reflects the centrality of the concept of CULTURE within cultural anthropology. See also ACCULTURATION.

end-of-ideology thesis the viewpoint, especially prevalent in American political sociology in the late 1950s and early 1960s, that old-style, confrontational left-right ideologies were outmoded and were being replaced in Western democracies by a more consensual, competitive politics. The thesis, propounded for example by Daniel BELL (1960) and Seymour Martin LIPSET (1959), was based on the assumption that fundamental changes had occurred in the character of capitalism (e.g. the MANAGERIAL REVOLUTION), and that these changes, accompanied by full working-class participation in liberal democratic politics, had removed any basis for revolutionary political parties. According to Lipset, POLITICAL CLEAVAGE between political parties based on labour and those aligned with capital still played a crucial role in Western democracies, but class conflict had been 'domesticated' and was no longer a threat to the continuation of the political system or of capitalism (see also STABLE DEMOCRACY). With the upheavals of 1968, and for much of the 1970s and 80s, the return of a sharper confrontation between labour and capital, new urban and racial unrest, and a renewed polarization of political parties, 'the end of consensus politics' has sometimes seemed a more plausible hypothesis (see LEGITIMATION CRISIS). However, if conflicts remain, the continued absence of an effective socialist alternative to Western capitalist society – especially with the collapse of socialism in Eastern Europe in 1989 – has meant that an acceptance of social democratic politics is now widespread, even among parties of the left. In this sense, the ideological debate, although not 'ended', is more restricted than it once was. The most notable recent example of the end-of-ideology thesis is Francis Fukuyama's *The End of History and the Last Man* (1992), whose pseudo-Hegelian account of modernity is that history culminates in mature capitalism and democracy.

endogamy a rule prescribing marriage within a given social group. The group may belong to a LINEAGE, CASTE, CLASS, ethnic affiliation, or other type of social classification. The converse of endogamy is EXOGAMY. Since all marriage systems are both endogamous and exogamous, it is necessary to specify in detail the prescribed and the proscribed groups.

Engels, Friedrich (1820–95) German socialist. Born into a family engaged in the textile industry in Germany, as a student he was influenced by Hegelianism (see HEGEL) and became a socialist. He came to Manchester on family business and, in 1845, published *The Condition of the Working Class in England,* one of the most important contemporary analyses of the emergence of the working class with industrialization, in which he saw the working class as the revolutionary bearer of socialism. He began a long association with MARX in 1845 and, in collaboration with him, published *The Holy Family* in that year, *The German Ideology* in 1845–46, and *The Communist Manifesto* in 1848. These texts formed the basis of the development of Marx and Engels' political work in the formation of the First International, in which Engels played a key organizational role. In the next two decades, Engels provided financial support for Marx and his family while Marx worked on his major political economy of capitalism, and Engels was important both as a confidant of Marx and as a disseminator of his analyses. He further elaborated the concept of DIALECTICAL MATERIALISM, and first used the phrase 'materialist interpretation of history', and is often seen as promoting a deterministic reading of Marx. After Marx's death, Engels edited to publication the second and third volumes of *Das Kapital,* and was working on the fourth when he died. He was active in the setting up of the Second International.

In recent years, within sociology and anthropology, his most influential work has been *The Origin of The Family, Private Property and the State,* first published in 1884 (see MATRIARCHY). This is one of the few 19th-century analyses of history to incorporate the position of women and to attempt to understand the basis of gender inequality. It has informed many recent attempts to understand the role of women in history, and the bases of their subordination to men in so many known societies. This is despite the empirical weakness of his argument that there was an historical process from 'matriarchal societies', with women dominant within the family, to 'patriarchal societies' with the emergence of private property and men exerting control over the marriage and sexuality of women to ensure the transmission of property to their heirs. Recent work has further questioned his assumption of a biological-based sexual division of labour. The value of his work lies, however, in the questions he posed about the relationship between socioeconomic and gender relationships (see Sayers et al. (eds), 1987).

enlightenment see AGE OF ENLIGHTENMENT.

enterprise culture a set of values, symbols and practices which include a commitment to profitmaking, enterprise, innovation, initiative, self-reliance, creativity and competition. In the 1980s, the UK Government established an 'enterprise initiative' scheme which aims to develop graduates with skills and experience relevant to industry by funding initiatives in higher education which promote the skills and values associated with enterprise. Popular criticism of sociology often refers to its critical stance towards enterprise, profit and individualism. Sociological research on enterprise culture can be found in studies of ORGANIZATIONAL CULTURE and of the WELFARE STATE and SOCIAL POLICY. See also NEW RIGHT IDEOLOGY.

entitlements the rights to social welfare payments and provision which exist in most modern societies for all CITIZENS, but which are also the subject of dispute. For example, L. Mead (*Beyond Entitlements*, 1985) has argued that one-sided talk of entitlements has led to the neglect of 'obligations'. All Western capitalist states have experienced problems in sustaining both welfare provision and 'capitalist accumulation' (see FISCAL CRISIS IN THE CAPITALIST STATE, CULTURAL CONTRADICTIONS OF CAPITALISM, LEGITIMATION CRISIS, THATCHERISM). On the other hand, there are many who argue that a recognition of the rights of all citizens and workers to basic entitlements at a high minimum level (i.e. a new SOCIAL CONTRACT) is essential if the modern conception of CITIZENSHIP and CITIZEN RIGHTS is to be maintained and extended. See also UNDERCLASS.

entrepreneur any owner of capital who is engaged in the management of an enterprise for the sale of goods or services for profit. Classical economics focused on entrepreneurial activity as a factor of production in which risk taking was the key attribute of the entrepreneur. Classical microeconomic theory of the firm also assumed the existence of an individual entrepreneur as the basis for decision making in terms of profit maximization. In contrast, sociological study of entrepreneurs has been concerned in particular with their position within the class structure, their values and their relations to other class groupings (see also MIDDLE CLASS). Features of entrepreneurship variously include: values of independence, innovation, competition and a belief in enterprise and profit making (see also PROTESTANT ETHIC, ENTERPRISE CULTURE). Recent organizational research has identified the phenomenon of *intrapreneurship:* the development of entrepreneurial attitudes and behaviour of employees within the enterprise.

Empirical research into entrepreneurs has indicated that they do not comprise a homogeneous category, but include the self-employed, small employers, owner-controllers and owner-directors (Scase and Goffe, 1982). Sociological analysis of the self-employed – small proprietors, artisans and tradespeople – has occupied a problematic place in the study of the changing class structure of capitalist societies in terms of their position between large-scale capital and the working class (see PETTY BOURGEOISIE). Interest in the self-employed has been renewed recently with the proliferation of small businesses and research into the INFORMAL ECONOMY. The class position of owner-controllers and owner-directors has figured prominently in the analysis of the separation of ownership from control, and of the RULING CLASS in advanced capitalist societies. See also MANAGERIAL REVOLUTION, POSTCAPITALISM AND POSTCAPITALIST SOCIETY.

entropy see SYSTEMS THEORY.

environment the surroundings, or context, within which humans, animals or objects exist or act. The term's meaning is therefore wide, and is understood more precisely only within the context in which it is itself used.

Specifically, 'environment' is taken to mean, in association with 'learning' and 'experience', the sum of outside influences on the organism, and is to be distinguished from the inherited potential which is also influential in development and behaviour (see NATURE – NURTURE DEBATE).

A quite distinct usage is in relation to the natural world system, which is currently seen as fragile and threatened by the human technology developed since the Industrial Revolution, and the escalation of population which has resulted from it. This is a prime concern of the GREEN MOVEMENT and ECOLOGY generally.

These two usages by no means cover the many and various ways in which the term 'environment' can be used, but serve to illustrate the diversity of possible uses. See also SYSTEMS THEORY.

environmental depletion the process in which the stocks of available physical and economic resources tend to run down or become degraded as the result of processes such as the *intensification of agriculture*, mining, industrial pollution, physical overcrowding, etc. The idea that the world has reached a situation in which it must pay careful attention to the relative, or even absolute, degradation of the physical and social environment has only recently gained prominence (see GREEN MOVEMENT, SUSTAINABLE DEVELOPMENT, POSITIONAL GOODS AND POSITIONALITY). However, some theorists, e.g. Marvin Harris (1978), have even suggested that the process has been visible in human societies over a far longer period. According to Harris, Stone-Age peoples may have lived far happier and healthier lives than many of those who have come after them. From his viewpoint of CULTURAL MATERIALISM, Harris also suggests that many of the cultural, political and socioeconomic transformations undergone by societies in the modern historical era can be explained as the outcome of environmental pressures. These outcomes include the subordination of women, the need for settled agriculture and for state direction, and prohibitions on meat eating in some cultures. However, such claims are obviously far more controversial than the general claim that environmental depletion is not a recent problem, and has major implications.

epidemiology the study of the incidence and distribution of MORBIDITY and mortality in order to identify the role of nonbiological factors in sickness and health, for example, the relative significance of occupation, geographical location, class, gender, ethnicity, consumption patterns and lifestyle.

Originally the study of plagues and their relationship to population growth and economic development, the method was also called *medical mapping* when it was being developed in the 19th-century, at the same time as the sanitary reform movement. It provided evidence that the control of illness could be effected by public health measures. Although epidemiological research is informed by medical frames of reference, it is heavily used by sociologists interested in the social distribution of sickness (see BLACK REPORT).

epiphenomena and phenomena see APPEARANCE AND REALITY.

episode any 'historically located sequence of change' (e.g. the origins of PRISTINE STATES) with 'a specific opening, trend of events and outcome', but not a part of any necessary sequence of social development (GIDDENS, 1981). See also EPISODIC CHARACTERIZATION.

episodic characterization a theoretical approach in the study of social change in which change is represented as 'discontinuous' and 'historically CONTINGENT', rather than corresponding to an evolutionary or developmental pattern (see also EPISODE). This approach has been central in the work of a number of prominent historical sociologists, including Michael MANN (1986), Ernest GELLNER (1964) and Anthony GIDDENS. As expressed by Michael Mann, the thinking behind this view is that while general evolutionary theory may be applied up to, and including, the Neolithic Revolution, 'general social evolution ceased (with) the emergence of civilization', when distinctively historical change, not subject to laws, takes over. In Gellner's phrase, historical change does not fit any simple 'world growth story'.

Those sociologists who emphasize 'episodic characterizations' usually stand opposed to such doctrines as HISTORICAL MATERIALISM, as well as to EVOLUTIONARY THEORIES, in sociology. However, supporters of the latter positions claim that the identification of evolutionary sequences is not incompatible with a recognition that historical change has 'accidental', as well as general, features (see Jary, 1991).

episteme (Greek) any structure of knowledge, or, in terms used by FOUCAULT, *discourse formation,* which determines the way in which the world is experienced or 'seen'. As such, there are similarities between the notion of episteme and the concepts of PARADIGM or PROBLEMATIQUE (see also EPISTEMOLOGICAL BREAK).

epistemological anarchism the doctrine that there is no certain epistemological grounding, that there exists no single 'scientific method', that 'anything goes' (*methodological anarchism*) – see FEYERABEND, METHODOLOGICAL PLURALISM.

epistemological break (in science) the 'revolutionary' replacement of one theoretical framework – PARADIGM or PROBLEMATIQUE – by another. In the view of Thomas KUHN or Louis ALTHUSSER, the relations between rival or successive paradigms is always liable to be one of disjuncture and INCOMMENSURABILITY, in which the central concepts and procedures of one paradigm or problematique are unstatable in the language of the other: to quote Paul FEYERABEND, different paradigms involve different 'worlds' (see also FORMS OF LIFE). In the work of Althusser, the concept of the epistemological break is central to the sharp distinction he draws between the early 'humanistic' writings and the later 'scientific' writings of Marx.

epistemology (from the Greek *episteme,* knowledge) the branch of philosophy concerned with the theory (or theories) of knowledge, which seeks to inform us how we can know the world. Epistemology shares with ONTOLOGY, which is concerned to establish the kinds of things which exist, the claim to be the bedrock of all philosophical thinking and all knowledge.

An important division in epistemology is that between EMPIRICISM and RATIONALISM or IDEALISM. Whilst empiricists make our direct experience of the world the basis of all knowledge, rationalists and idealists argue that our knowledge of the world is governed by fixed and a *priori* concepts or CATEGORIES (e.g. conceptions of 'substance', 'causality') which structure our every thought and argument and therefore our experience or perception of reality (see also KANT).

In most forms of epistemology, the pure thought of the individual thinking 'ego', the philosopher, has been taken as providing the route to the ultimate understanding of knowledge and the bedrock on which the epistemological theory advanced is based (see DESCARTES). Recently, however, more sociological forms of epistemology have emerged which have sought to 'decentre' the role played by the traditional individual 'subject' in philosophy (see SUBJECT AND OBJECT, SUBJECT, STRUCTURALISM, DECONSTRUCTION), emphasizing instead the way in which knowledge is shaped by social structure, FORMS OF LIFE, etc. Thus the way is now open for much of the ground previously occupied by philosophy to be taken over by sociological accounts of knowledge and of science (see SOCIOLOGY OF KNOWLEDGE, SOCIOLOGY OF SCIENCE, KUHN, FEYERABEND).

Since any theory of knowledge must of necessity refer also to itself, it would be wrong to suggest that sociological theories of knowledge can any more avoid the element of circularity that must attend any theory of knowledge than could traditional philosophy. What such a sociological theory can however achieve is to dispense with the tendency to dogmatic closure in epistemological thinking of a kind which so often have been apparent in more traditional theories, with their claims to have reached bedrock. Once knowledge, including scientific knowledge, is seen clearly as a socially constructed phenomenon, the expectation of any final doctrines about the nature of knowledge can be seen as misplaced. See also SCIENCE.

epoché the placing in parentheses, or *bracketing,* of any aspect(s) of reality for methodological purposes. For example, the analysis of 'structure' while holding individual agency in parenthesis (see Giddens, 1984). The concept of *epoché* derives from HUSSERL'S PHENOMENOLOGY, where it was intended as a technique for allowing penetration to the underlying grounds of our knowledge by thinking away conventional, including scientific, assumptions. The device has been applied within sociology, particularly by SCHUTZ, and, influenced by him, also within ETHNOMETHODOLOGY, with the aim of uncovering the grounds of our everyday social knowledge and SOCIAL COMPETENCE.

equality a state of being equal in some respect. Although some religious doctrines hold that all people are in some sense equal at birth, most sociological discussions have focused on equality as an aspect of social context. The lack of equality – *inequality* – is a vital element in examinations of SOCIAL STRATIFICATION and CLASS.

Following the French Revolution and the growth of LIBERAL DEMOCRACIES, equality has usually been interpreted to mean equality between individuals or CITIZENS within a number of contexts. For example, LIBERAL DEMOCRACY assumes that all individuals are equal in law, have political equality. These equalities have often been translated into a series of constitutional rights: the right to a fair trial, the right to hold political office, and the right to fair selection procedures regardless of social background (see also CITIZEN RIGHTS). However, this liberal-democratic concern with individual equality does not assume equality of income and wealth, and critics have argued that the unequal DISTRIBUTION OF INCOME AND WEALTH undermines all the other attempts at equality since the holders of material resources have an advantage over other citizens. Sociologists have found this a fruitful issue for empirical research and have demonstrated how material resources affect people's life chances. For example, material resources have been seen to affect a child's progress in the education system (see EQUALITY OF OPPORTUNITY), and have also been seen to affect access to legal representation.

In the UK, the WELFARE STATE is often perceived as promoting equality, and there are a number of ways in which social policies have been considered to be egalitarian. Le Grande (1982) suggests five different models of equality in the context of social policy:
(a) *equality of public expenditure*, whereby everyone receives the same amount of support;
(b) *equality of final income*, where public resources are directed at those with greater need;
(c) *equality of use*, where everyone receives the same service although that service might be more expensive to provide in one part of the country compared with another;
(d) EQUALITY OF OPPORTUNITY;
(e) *equality of outcome*, where resources are provided so that every one is equal after a service has been given. This notion is one that has been particularly developed in socialist political ideologies.

Although the welfare state is perceived as egalitarian, empirical research has demonstrated that in the major areas of welfare policy in the UK – housing, health, education, income maintenance and *personal social services* – inequalities have persisted and, in some cases, actually increased.

In the 1970s and 80s, a number of Western liberal democracies, such as the UK and the US, elected governments holding the belief that the egalitarian objectives of welfare are wasteful and unfair. See also ROUSSEAU, JUSTICE.

equality of opportunity the idea that all persons, regardless of class, age, race or gender, should have equal rights to compete for and attain sought-after positions in society. In the 20th century, the concept has played an important part in the search to achieve a more just, more equal and fair, distribution of society's wealth and benefits. It has been especially central in debates surrounding education.

In the 1944 Education Act in England and Wales, 'equality of opportunity' meant the right to equal access to a system of secondary education which enabled children to develop their natural abilities and talents, irrespective of class position. The 11+ examination was designed as an 'objective', and therefore fair, device to assess these abilities in order that children would be placed in the education best suited to their needs and aptitudes. Research conducted, in the late 1950s and after, in the UK and the US, suggested that such an outcome was not being obtained. This led to a re-evaluation of the definition of equality of opportunity. Instead of an emphasis on 'equality of access' attention turned to the goal of achieving greater 'equality of outcome'. The new task was to alter the pattern of educational provision to compensate for the existence of social disadvantages. During the late 1960s and early 1970s various educational policy reforms such as the wider introduction of COMPREHENSIVE EDUCATION (replacing selective schools in many areas), COMPENSATORY EDUCATION schemes, and 'positive discrimination' were introduced.

Both the sociological literature and wider public debate have focused on two major issues concerning equality of opportunity, in either its narrower or its wider sense:
(a) the extent to which it is socially desirable, feasible, realistic; and
(b) the extent to which particular educational innovations aimed at achieving increased equality of educational opportunity have been successful or unsuccessful. On the first count, some critics have argued that attempts to engineer equality of outcome conflict with individual freedom. Critics have also argued that educational chances have failed because differences in social background are too pronounced to be removed by educational reforms alone.

equality of outcome see EQUALITY.

equilibrium see SOCIAL EQUILIBRIUM.

Eros the life instinct in FREUD's theory of personality. Eros involves all instincts leading towards survival, so is not synonymous with the sex drive, although this is central to it. Eros is creative, in contrast to its opposite, THANATOS, the death instinct, which is destructive.

eroticism sexual excitement or desire, and the changing social constructions of this. Theorists such as Michel FOUCAULT, *The History of Sexuality* (1979) have done much to document how SEXUALITY, the erotic realm and the discourses of eroticism (both scientific and literary) are transformed in every historical period and also have political dimensions (see also ROMANTIC LOVE). At a more empirical level, researchers such as Alfred Kinsey et al. (1948 and 1953) have sought to provide a comprehensive account of the range of erotic *sexual behaviour*. It is plain that eroticism and the objects of eroticism, which may or may not involve direct behaviour with other persons, take many forms, only a minority of these directly involving sexual reproduction. Most forms, and the greatest incidence of sexual behaviour, can be described as 'recreational', much of this as part of a continuing sexual relationship, although varying between different cultures and in different periods in the life cycle.

esprit de corps (French, literally 'corporate spirit') feelings of pride, etc., in belonging to a cohesive group, e.g. a military unit.

ESRC see ECONOMIC AND SOCIAL RESEARCH COUNCIL.

essentialism the view that philosophy or science is able to reach and represent absolute TRUTH(s), e.g. the necessary or essential properties, or 'essences', of objects. PLATO's theory of ideal forms is an example of essentialism.

Today the term is often a negative one, used by philosophers who oppose essentialism and emphasize the provisional or conventional nature of knowledge (see also CONVENTIONALISM, NOMINALISM, OPERATIONALISM OR OPERATIONISM, RELATIVISM, POST-EMPIRICISM, DECONSTRUCTION, REALISM).

essentially contested concept a category of general concepts in the social sciences, e.g.

POWER, the application of which, according to Gallie (1955) and Lukes (1974), is inherently a matter of dispute. The reason given for this is that competing versions of concepts such as 'power' inevitably involve relativity to VALUES. According to this view, hypotheses using concepts such as 'power' can be appraised empirically, but will remain relative to the evaluative framework within which the particular versions of the concept are couched. There are parallels between this notion and Weber's earlier view that social science propositions are VALUE-RELATIVE (see also VALUE FREEDOM AND VALUE NEUTRALITY). See also POWER.

Establishment, the the institutions, and the holders of élite positions within them, popularly regarded as constituting the culturally and politically dominant sector of society, especially members of traditionally dominant groups. Used particularly in the 1950s and 60s, it is now a term in general use, without any precise sociological meaning. Generally, it is seen as including the monarchy and the peerage, members of government and top civil servants, the Conservative Party as a whole, leading London-based members of top professions, old boys of leading public schools and Oxford and Cambridge, and so on. Sometimes leading Labour politicians, trade-union leaders, press barons, etc., are also included. Compare UPPER CLASS.

estate (in preindustrial society) a SOCIAL STRATUM within a system of SOCIAL STRATIFICATION, distinguished by a specific set of legally-defined rights and duties. The estate system is particularly associated with European, and especially French and German, feudal and postfeudal, so-called STÄNDESTAAT societies, although there were broadly similar systems in Russia, Japan and China. Estates might vary from locality to locality, but within their own area they had rigorously ordered boundaries and value systems, and the main divisions are conventionally defined as being between nobility, clergy and commoners. The rise of 'gentry', 'professional' and other groupings might complicate status divisions on a local basis, but the regulation of rights to offices, titles, property etc., and, less formally, of whom it was appropriate to 'know' and how it was appropriate to know them, was a defining feature of estates.

Estates formed 'communities' in the sense used by WEBER, whose conception of STATUS GROUP owes a great deal to his understanding of the historical conformation of estates. The elements of exclusiveness and 'acceptability', common life chances, and shared culture and experience, are found in different historical situations, but the aspects of legal regulation and relatively fixed boundaries define the estate system (compare CASTE). See also FEUDALISM.

esteem negative or positive evaluation of *individual* qualities or performance (compare STATUS). The term is sometimes used synonymously with STATUS, sense **2**, but the preferred usage is to preserve the distinct meanings in which 'esteem' has a reference only to individual qualities and performance, while 'status' usually relates to systems of SOCIAL STRATIFICATION or CLASS.

estimation see STATISTICS AND STATISTICAL ANALYSIS.

et cetera principle (ETHNOMETHODOLOGY) a 'members' method' for dealing with practical situations not fully covered by a general principle. The following of an instruction or the application of a social rule cannot cover every eventuality practically encountered. On such occasions persons interpret the instruction or rule as containing an implicit *et cetera,* principle which brings within the rule's remit those circumstances not explicitly covered by it. Following a rule is not a mechanical procedure, but involves PRACTICAL REASONING on the part of the person concerned. See also RULES.

ethical indifference the doctrine that sociology, in its main research and theorizing, should no more occupy itself centrally with ethical concerns than should the natural sciences. This view has been taken recently, for example, by the ETHNOMETHODOLOGISTS, who have wanted to establish a new focus on careful 'descriptions' of the everyday social competence and social practices of members of society, and to do this free of any distracting requirement to 'judge' these practices. While, in part, this celebration of 'ethical indifference' rests on the aim of advancing the 'empirical' understanding of social action, it also derives from a view that sociology possesses no special basis on which to make value judgements which are not already possessed by the lay member of society. The 'social competence' possessed by SOCIAL ACTORS is seen as establishing each actor as a 'moral agent'. Compare VALUE FREEDOM AND VALUE NEUTRALITY.

ethical neutrality see VALUE FREEDOM AND VALUE NEUTRALITY, sense 3.

ethics 1 the moral code of a person or society. 2 the branch of PHILOSOPHY concerned with how we ought to act in order to be moral. Two predominant schools of thought can be identified:
(a) those which emphasize that matters of right and wrong should be decided only by an analysis of the consequences of action (e.g. UTILITARIANISM); and
(b) those which assert that at least some duties are independent of consequences (e.g. not telling lies). Generally in the social sciences (a) has had more significance than (b). Other topics in ethics are similar to those that occur in sociology, e.g. issues surrounding the FACT-VALUE DISTINCTION and VALUE FREEDOM AND VALUE NEUTRALITY.
3 a moral code that guides the conduct of a professional group such as medical doctors or lawyers. For sociologists and social researchers in the UK two quasi-official ethical governing exist, one published by the British Sociological Association, the other by the Market Research Society.

ethnic group a group of people sharing an identity which arises from a collective sense of a distinctive history (see also ETHNICITY). Ethnic groups possess their own CULTURE CUSTOMS, NORMS, beliefs and traditions. There is usually a common LANGUAGE, and boundary maintenance is observed between members and non-members. As well as by birth, ethnic group membership may be acquired through marriage or other socially sanctioned routes.

Whilst socially perceived racial characteristics may be a feature of such groups, ethnic groups are not synonymous with racial groups (see RACE). According to C. Peach et al. (1981), British academic concern with the subject of ethnicity increased as a result of black immigration in the postwar period. Thus, despite the presence of immigrants, refugees and ethnic minorities prior to this period, it was the combination of racial and ethnic distinctiveness which gave rise to both popular and academic interest in the subject. One result of this has been the confusion of the term 'ethnic minority' with racial minority, in the UK culture.

The anthropologist, Narroll (1964), stressed the importance of shared cultural values and a group awareness of cultural distinctiveness as key elements in ethnic group membership. Barth (1970) places emphasis on group organization and the maintenance of ethnic boundaries via ETHNIC MARKERS. He suggests that the boundaries between ethnic groups are maintained not through isolation, as Narroll argues, but through social processes of exclusion and incorporation, i.e. ethnic group members identify themselves in terms of ethnic categories and are in turn recognized as members by outsiders. REX (1986), in turn, has criticized Barth for his failure to consider conflict between ethnic groups and for his imprecise use of the term 'group'. Rex also raises the question, immigrants aside, of the continued saliency of ethnic groupings in complex industrial societies and the utility of the concept as a precise basis of classification.

In societies in turmoil, however, ethnic groupings retain their importance and may be given added salience (or constructed) by political conflict, as in the former Yugoslavia, where the highly charged phrase 'ethnic cleansing' has appeared. An important distinction must therefore be drawn between those ethnic groups which consciously seek to assert their ethnicity, and those seen as ethnic minorities by more powerful groups (see also HOLOCAUST, GENOCIDE). In such cases, ethnic characteristics may be exaggerated or created to serve group interests and cohesion as well as to fuel conflict. The reverse side of the coin is when complex symbolic practices may be mobilized not to accentuate boundaries and divisions between groups, but to understate these in order to maximize INTEGRATION or ASSIMILATION. For example, in contemporary Britain, Pakistani Christian refugees may seek to minimize group differences. There are also cases in which ethnic group differences may be formulated in a climate of CULTURAL PLURALISM.

Where ethnicity is the basis for minority status, discriminatory practices against such groups may be legitimated by institutionalized means. As is widely apparent, ethnic minority status often seriously jeopardizes an individual's or group's life chances, particularly in relation to health, housing and employment.

It should also be noted that approaches to social stratification based on economic inequality find it difficult to treat the question of ethnicity adequately. See STATUS CONSISTENCY AND INCONSISTENCY. See also RACISM.

ethnicity a shared racial, linguistic or national identity of a social group. See also NATIONALISM.

Ethnicity is an imprecise term which has given rise to some degree of conceptual confusion (see also ETHNIC GROUP). It is often conflated with other terms such as *racial group*.

Ethnicity can incorporate several forms of collective identity, including cultural, religious, national and subcultural forms. A distinction may be drawn between *cultural ethnicity* and *political ethnicity*. The former refers to a belief in a shared language, religion or other such cultural values and practices. The latter refers to the political awareness or mobilization of a group on a (real or assumed) ethnic basis.

Although ethnicity is often used in relation to a group's assumed racial identity, strictly racial attributes (see RACE) are not necessarily, or even usually, the defining feature of ethnic groups.

ethnic marker the means whereby the social boundaries between ETHNIC GROUPS are maintained. Territoriality, history, LANGUAGE, and SYMBOLS may all serve as ethnic markers emphasizing distinctions between one ethnic group and another.

ethnocentrism 1 the attitude of prejudice or mistrust towards outsiders which may exist within a social group; a way of perceiving one's own cultural group (in-group) in relation to others (out-groups). The term was introduced by W. G. SUMNER (1906) and involves the belief that one's own group is the most important, or is culturally superior to other groups. Thus, one's own culture is considered to be racially, morally and culturally of greater value or significance than that of others, and one becomes distrustful of those defined as outsiders. It also involves an incapacity to acknowledge that cultural differentiation does not imply the inferiority of those groups who are ethnically distinct from one's own.

2 a characteristic of certain personality types. The ethnocentric personality is described by T. Adorno et al. (1950) in *The Authoritarian Personality* (see AUTHORITARIAN PERSONALITY). Initially this study was concerned with the social and psychological aspects of anti-Semitism, but developed into a study of its more general correlates. Adorno et al. were concerned with explaining attitudes towards other 'out-groups' in American society, such as homosexuals and ethnic minorities, and maintained that antagonism towards one 'out-group' (e.g. Jews) seldom existed in

isolation. They found that ethnocentrism tended to be associated with authoritarianism, dogmatism and rigidity, political and economic conservatism, and an implicit anti-democratic ideology. Thus, hostility towards one 'out-group' (see IN-GROUP AND OUT-GROUP) was often generalized and projected onto other 'out-groups'. See also PREJUDICE, DISCRIMINATION, RACISM OR RACIALISM, ATTITUDE, ATTITUDE SCALE.

ethnography the direct observation of an organization or small society, and the written description produced. Often the method of observation involves PARTICIPANT OBSERVATION. The ethnographic method (sometimes also referred to as FIELDWORK) is a basic method in SOCIAL ANTHROPOLOGY, It is also a method used in some areas of sociology, e.g. COMMUNITY STUDIES. Usually a researcher gathers data by living and working in the society or social setting being researched, seeking to immerse himself or herself as fully as possible in the activities under observation, but at the same time keeping careful records of these activities.

In anthropology, an emphasis on the importance of the ethnographic method was initially associated with the functionalist school, which encouraged an analysis of the internal structure and function of single societies rather than historical or comparative studies (see FUNCTIONALISM). However, there is no inherent reason why ethnographic and comparative approaches should not be seen as complementary, or why ethnography should simply be associated with one theoretical school.

ethnology the comparative historical study of peoples and cultures within their environments.

In the USA and parts of Europe 'ethnology' has sometimes served as an all-encompassing concept for human studies, including various mixes of archaeology, study of material culture, linguistics, sociology, together with social, cultural, and physical anthropology, which may also include sociology as a sub-part.

There has been resistance to such an overarching view. British social anthropology, for example, has usually distanced itself from the all-encompassing 'grand' historical view implied by the ethnological enterprise. RADCLIFFE-BROWN and others advocated ethnographic studies of the social organization of peoples in the 'here and now' as a methodological departure from ethnologies, and historicism, although retaining a concern for comparative study.

In contrast, American cultural anthropology, following the lead of BOAS and of Kroeber (*Anthropology: Race, Language, Culture, Psychology*, 1923) has championed the ambitious all-encompassing broad sweep of ethnological enquiry alongside ethnographic studies, as nothing less than the classification and taxonomization of the 'total' history of humankind in all its physical, material and cultural manifestations.

ethnoscience(s) (SOCIAL ANTHROPOLOGY) the study of the indigenous bodies of knowledge within a culture area. Thus, *ethnobotany* records local botanical knowledge and plant taxonomies, and *ethnoecology* records local knowledge of ecological factors; while *ethnohistory*, which possesses similarities with 'history from below' (see HISTORY WORKSHOP JOURNAL), seeks to provide an historical account from the point of view of the society under discussion, using the oral historical record within the community. In general, the prefix *ethno-* used in this context refers to an analysis from the point of view of the 'folk' culture(s) being studied.

The ethnosciences are now seen as having some value in achieving ecologically sensitive forms of development, and forms of development also in tune with local needs. The recovery of 'lost' knowledge that the ethnosciences represent also raises questions about the progressive nature of orthodox SCIENCE and about RATIONALITY. See also MULTICULTURALISM, COGNITIVE ANTHROPOLOGY. Compare ETHNOGRAPHY, ETHNOMETHODOLOGY.

ethnomethodology

The theoretical and specialist approach within sociology, initiated by Harold GARFINKEL, which sets out to uncover the methods (*members' methods*) and social competence that we, as members of social groups, employ in constructing our sense of social reality. Ethnomethodologists claim that mainstream sociologists have failed to study, or even to show any awareness of, members' possession of social competence, treating members merely as 'cultural dopes', rather than acknowledging that social reality is created by individuals.

For ethnomethodologists, social reality is always to be seen as the 'rational accomplishment' of individuals. Whereas conventional sociologists, e.g. DURKHEIM in *Suicide* or the symbolic interactionists, are seen as taking actors' capacity to construct 'meanings' merely as an unexamined 'resource', ethnomethodology makes the 'methods' and TACIT KNOWLEDGE that members possess into a 'topic' for analysis. What ethnomethodologists seek to do is to analyse the ACCOUNTS provided by members in particular contexts (hence the extensive use of transcripts of ordinary conversation). In this, there are some similarities and continuities with SYMBOLIC INTERACTIONISM. Beyond this, however, ethnomethodologists have sought to reveal the more universal recurring *members' methods* involved in 'doing' social life, e.g. organized 'turn-taking' in talk (see also CONVERSATION ANALYSIS, SACKS).

While ethnomethodology claims to have arrived at universal generalizations, the form of these generalizations (e.g. indicating a persistent indexicality (see INDEXICAL EXPRESSION) in members' accounts) suggests that the type of generalizations traditionally sought by sociology are unlikely to be achieved, or at least the claims for them are premature. By the same token, many of the research methods and assumptions about method and measurement in conventional sociology are criticized by ethnomethodologists as involving MEASUREMENT BY FIAT (see A. Cicourel, 1964).

Although ethnomethodology was at first presented as an alternative to conventional sociology, the insights drawn from it have in many instances been incorporated into more mainstream approaches, notably in the work of Anthony GIDDENS (1976a and subsequently) – see also STRATIFICATIONAL MODEL OF SOCIAL ACTION AND CONSCIOUSNESS, DOUBLE HERMENEUTIC. By far the best general overview of ethnomethodology is J. Heritage, *Garfinkel and Ethnomethodology* (1984). See also FIXED-CHOICE QUESTIONNAIRES, AGGREGATE DATA ANALYSIS. OFFICIAL STATISTICS. PRACTICAL REASONING.

ethology 1 a term used by J. S. MILL for the 'science of character', which he believed would become the basis of explanations within the moral sciences, using the inverse deductive method.

2 the science of animal behaviour, especially where the findings of this study are intended to be extrapolated to the study of human behaviour. Ethology in this sense can be highly controversial, being objected to especially by those sociologists who emphasize the distinctiveness of human consciousness. See also SOCIOBIOLOGY.

etic see EMIC AND ETIC.

etiology *or* **aetiology** the study of causation, especially of diseases, social pathologies, etc. (e.g. Durkheim's *Suicide*, 1897).

etymology inquiry into and accounts of sources and development of words. In modern linguistics, a distinction is drawn between the diachronic study of language (etymology), and its synchronic study (structural analysis) (see SYNCHRONIC AND DIACHRONIC). Etymology's concern is with the origins and changes in meaning of particular words, and also with the historical ancestry of groups or 'families' of languages, e.g. Indo-European, Amerindian, etc.

eufunctional (pertaining to a social activity) contributing to the maintenance or effective working of a functioning SOCIAL SYSTEM. See also DYSFUNCTION, FUNCTIONALISM.

eugenics the study of human heredity, founded by Francis Galton (*Hereditary Genius*, 1870), which led him and his followers to propose selective policies designed to improve the stock, e.g. fiscal and other policies to discourage child-rearing by those intellectually least well-endowed. Apart from wider ethical considerations, such policies assume a relationship between heredity and intellectual and cultural characteristics which has not been demonstrated.

eurocommunism a term denoting the political changes that occurred in the Communist parties of Western Europe (particularly the French, Italian, Spanish and British Communist parties) during the 1970s, involving the development of national, liberal and democratic strategies for the achievement of socialism (Machin, 1983). In his book *Eurocommunism and the State* (1977), Santiago Carrillo, the Spanish Communist leader, rejected the Russian model of revolutionary socialist development as being inappropriate for advanced capitalist societies. The only way forward for Communist parties was 'by the democratic, multi-party, parliamentary road'. Eurocommunists also asserted their independence from the Soviet government, which was criticized for its internal repression of dissidents and for the military occupation of Czechoslovakia in 1968. See also COMMUNISM, SOCIALISM. STATE SOCIALIST COUNTRIES.

evaluation a practice aimed at assessing worth or value, particularly of projects and services. The process can be viewed as objectively measuring value using quasi-scientific methods (see PERFORMANCE INDICATORS, AUDIT) or conversely, more subjectively-orientated reports and commentaries, especially drawing on QUALITATIVE RESEARCH TECHNIQUES. A further distinction can be drawn between evaluation which takes place during the lifetime of a programme, with the aim of improving the way in which it operates (see FORMATIVE EVALUATION) and evaluation that takes place at the end of a project or fixed period of time, and retrospectively states how well it has performed (see SUMMATIVE EVALUATION). The need for accountability – including evaluation – has increased as a result of THATCHERISM e.g. the introduction of the PURCHASER-PROVIDER SPLIT, especially in welfare services formerly provided by the public sector.

evangelism the emphasis of certain Protestant sects on personal conversion and faith in atonement through the death of Christ as a means of salvation. The political and social influence of mass evangelism is usually conservative in nature.

Evans-Pritchard, Sir Edward Evan (1902–73) British structural-functionalist social anthropologist. His major works include *Witchcraft, Magic and Oracles among the Azande* (1937), *The Nuer* (1940), *Kinship and Marriage among the Nuer* (1951) and *Nuer Religion* (1956). After being trained by MALINOWSKI, Evans-Pritchard undertook ETHNOGRAPHY in the southern Sudan. His writings illustrate both the rationality of apparently pre-logical thought (among the Azande) and the possibility of a peacefully anarchic stateless society (as exemplified by the Nuer). Though he is usually classed as a structural functionalist, his writings stress the affinity of anthropology to history, and not to science. In contrast to his predecessor at Oxford, RADCLIFFE-BROWN, he felt that to search for universal laws of social behaviour was pointless. His particular interest in religion is seen as being a result of his conversion to Catholicism in 1940. That his influence is still so great is probably a result of his focus on humanistic description. He characterized himself as 'first an ethnographer and second a social anthropologist'.

evidence based medicine see EVIDENCE SUPPORTED HEALTH CARE.

evidence supported health care a term has replaced evidence based medicine in the light of the focus on primary and community care in health policy and the UK government's intention to subject treatment and care management regimes to the same scrutiny as drug therapeutics to which evidence based medicine generally refers. See also PRIMARY CARE GROUPS, SYSTEMATIC REVIEW, NATIONAL INSTITUTE FOR CLINICAL EXCELLENCE.

evolution see DARWIN, EVOLUTIONARY THEORY.

evolutionary psychology a branch of PSYCHOLOGY that seeks to identify universal human psychological mechanisms/capacities by grounding exploration in a 'reverse engineering', in assumptions about those environments – specifically HUNTER-GATHERER society – in which human capacities will have evolved by Darwinian natural and sexual selection. It regards itself as far from neglecting CULTURE and learning, but as potentially providing a better grounding and understanding of these, not reductionistically, but in a manner which acknowledges 'emergence'. Topics treated in this way, include LANGUAGE capacity, EXCHANGE, COOPERATION (see Barkow, Cosmides and Tooby). Although criticized by theorists such as Gould (19), as involving '*just so stories*', lacking crucial tests, evolutionary psychology presents itself as a 'scientifically realist' theory.

evolved psychological mechanism universal human psychological capacities assumed to have evolved by natural selection (see EVOLUTIONARY PSYCHOLOGY).

evolutionary sociology

Any form of sociology which emphasizes continuities between biological evolution and sociocultural evolution. Notwithstanding the many excesses and oversimplifications of much previous EVOLUTIONARY THEORY in sociology, Runciman (1989), for example, suggests 'that there is no escape from the recognition that any substantive social theory is and cannot but be evolutionary.' What Runciman means by this is that:

(a) while in major part 'extra organic' (see also SUPERORGANIC, EMERGENT EVOLUTION), human social capacities are biologically based;

(b) though no simple pattern of UNILINEAR social development has occurred and prediction is out of the question (as is it also in relation to biological evolution), it remains possible to discuss social evolution in terms of a historical sequence of development (compare EVOLUTIONARY UNIVERSALS) in which later developments depend on those earlier; (c) in these circumstances, it makes sense to employ the concept of social 'selection' (while at the same time specifying what the 'advantage' is) to explain why certain social practices have become established.

Not all sociologists would agree with Runciman's assessment, although many would (see also NEOEVOLUTIONISM, SOCIOCULTURAL EVOLUTION). If few would quarrel with (a) and (b) of Runciman's three points, the main source of disagreement is whether terms such as 'selection' and 'adaptation', imported from biology can have any very precise content compared with their use in biology (see also FUNCTIONAL(IST) EXPLANATION). Some sociologists, notably GIDDENS and MANN recently, have also rejected any conception of 'serial history', proposing instead a purely EPISODIC CHARACTERIZATION of social change, presenting this as thus also a rejection of evolutionary (and functionalist) thinking. Yet, in practice, they too appear to find it difficult to escape evolutionary thinking in something like Runciman's broad terms (see Wright, 1983, Jary, 1991).

Issues often arise especially in the more particular claims for 'adaptation', functionally effective SOCIAL DIFFERENTIATION, etc., actually made by modern evolutionary sociologists (e.g. see MODERNIZATION). A further general issue is whether evaluative conceptions such as PROGRESS, have any place in modern evolutionary thinking. Evolutionary theorists are also divided on the issue of whether the general principle of 'evolution' has any implications for the choice between 'unplanned' and gradual evolution ('social mutations') or planned development (see HISTORICISM sense **2**, RATIONALIZATION). Evolutionary sociology in its modern forms has moved a long way from the crude notions of SOCIAL DARWINISM (misapplied biological ANALOGIES, racist theories, and sweeping applications of such notions as the 'survival of the fittest') advanced in the 19th century, but it remains controversial. See also SPENCER, PARSONS, HABERMAS.

evolutionary theory **1** the explanation of the origin, development and diversity of biological species proposed by Charles DARWIN and by Alfred Russel Wallace (1823–1913).

2 the explanation of SOCIAL CHANGE in terms of Darwinian principles.

Darwin's work influenced many 19th-century social theorists, including MORGAN, HOBHOUSE, TYLOR, WARD and SPENCER (although the latter also introduced evolutionary conceptions of his own prior to Darwin's theory – see SURVIVAL OF THE FITTEST). The international ascendancy of Britain's economy and polity during the Victorian age had created a social atmosphere and an intellectual climate that was particularly receptive to ideas of progress and advancement. Darwin's theory, which seemed to establish these trends as features of biological development, was, in this sense, waiting to be heard. The imperial strength of Britain and the dominance of Western culture could, rather crudely, be read as nothing more than the outcome of a natural law which always assured the ascendancy of 'the best'.

Evolutionary theory, then, in the social sphere, saw the newly industrialized countries of the 19th century as representing the most advanced stage of a long-term process of development which had begun with very much simpler kinds of society. Contemporary pre-industrial, or peasant, or simple hunting and gathering societies could be conceived as living examples of earlier stages of development which the industrial world had left far behind. Evolutionary theory, therefore, typically combined two propositions: first, that evolutionary advancement involved the development of complex forms of social organization from simple ones, via the increasing differentiation of social structure (see SOCIAL DIFFERENTIATION) and specialization of function; second, that these structural changes involved a parallel process of continuing moral, intellectual and aesthetic development. Darwin's theory, applied to social development, thus resulted in a distinction between CIVILIZATION and BARBARISM which was especially convenient in an age of IMPERIALISM.

The impact of Darwin's ideas on social theory in the 19th century was immense. The politics of social evolutionism could appeal as much to those interested in legitimating the status quo as to those (like MARX) interested in changing it. Yet the receptivity of social theorists to such ideas should have been tempered with caution. Darwin had developed his account of change primarily to explain diversity and adaptation among species in which consciousness, reflexivity and creativity (or CULTURE) could be ignored as a significant variable. But it was precisely these facts which made human society possible. Ironically, there *was* an evolutionary paradigm available which could take the cultural variable on board. It was not, however, the one elaborated by Darwin, but by his rival theorist, Jean Baptiste LAMARCK, who had argued for the inheritance of *acquired* characteristics in the evolutionary process. Darwin had rejected this, relying instead on the principles of *random* variation and NATURAL SELECTION. Yet it is precisely the capacity of individuals and societies to learn from each other – to acquire culture or copy crucial cultural developments (such as writing and measuring) – which is distinctive to human social life. Strangely, in pinning its flag to what was destined to be the most successful version of the evolutionary paradigm – Darwinism – social theory largely ignored the thesis which arguably had more to offer, that of Lamarck.

By the early decades of the 20th century, evolutionism was falling into disfavour among social scientists. A precipitating cause may have been the catastrophic slaughter and barbarism of the 1914–18 war, which was hardly an advertisement for a supposedly enlightened Europe which had undergone a civilizing process. More fundamentally, three main difficulties with 19th-century theories of social evolution had by then become increasingly apparent. First, the assumption of unilinearity (see UNILINEAR) – that there was one path of development through which all societies would pass; second, an inability to say much about the stages of development intermediate between simple and complex societies, and the processes which produced change; and third, the value-laden proposition that social development involved moral enlightenment, ethnocentrically conceived in European terms.

The second half of the 20th century saw a revival of interest in problems of development as Third World issues began to force themselves onto political agendas. This produced new versions of evolutionary theory (see NEOEVOLUTIONISM, SOCIOCULTURAL EVOLUTION, EVOLUTIONARY UNIVERSALS), and eventually a reopening of critical debate, especially by the UNDERDEVELOPMENT school. See also

SURVIVAL OF THE FITTEST, ECONOMIC AND SOCIAL DEVELOPMENT, EVOLUTIONARY SOCIOLOGY.

evolutionary universals as defined by PARSONS (1964a), those developmental steps in social change which 'increase the adaptive capacity' of human societies, and without which 'further major developmental steps would be blocked'. According to Parsons, evolutionary universals are 'organizational developments' that are 'hit upon more than once', comparable, say, with the development of vision in the organic world. By 'adaptation', Parsons means not only 'adjustment to an environment', but also the ability to cope with an increasingly wide range of environmental factors, including 'adaptive advantage' over other less developed societies. Once the symbol replaces the gene as the main agency of human development, four basic areas of social provision are important:
(a) RELIGION, performing Durkheimian functions;
(b) COMMUNICATION, especially language;
(c) KINSHIP, including INCEST TABOO and EXOGAMY/ENDOGAMY RULES;
(d) TECHNOLOGY, the primary adaptive relation with the environment.
As the result of these initial changes, bringing economic and organizational 'functional advantage', the next pair of advantages seen as important by Parsons in breaking out from the 'primitive stage', are:
(e) SOCIAL STRATIFICATION, social prestige and economic advantages attaching to some groups, lineages, etc.;
(f) a differentiated structure providing political and cultural legitimation.

As Parsons puts it, the differentiation of advantage for some groups tends to 'converge with the functional need for centralization of responsibility'. Stratification releases and centralizes resources for further development, breaking with traditionalism. LITERACY, at first the monopoly of only a minority, accentuates stratification and a tendency to primacy of cultural differentiation at this stage. In turn, stratification of all types is itself a source of 'strain' requiring new cultural legitimation.

Five further evolutionary universals, built on the previous ones, follow:
(g) BUREAUCRACY, i.e. the Weberian separation of administrative office from kinship and traditionalism;
(h) MONEY and markets, in which money, as 'the symbolic medium for resources', increases the mobility of resources, 'emancipating these for ascriptive bonds' (see also PATTERN VARIABLES);
(i) a universalistic legal system;
(j) the invention of the 'democratic association', especially its application to large-scale societies from the 18th-century onwards, though with its origins in Greece and Rome, and the early Christian church;
(k) SCIENCE.

Criticisms of Parsons' conception of evolutionary universals are in many ways the usual criticisms of EVOLUTIONARY THEORY in sociology: for example, the lack of any great precision in the use of terms such as 'adaptation', and the absence of direct parallels with evolutionary conceptions in biology. It is notable how often in describing his evolutionary universals, Parsons uses such phrases as 'probably decisive', 'by and large' and 'very difficult to pin down'. For all this, the general steps identified by Parsons as important in human development are not markedly different from those that were identified by WEBER or by MARX. In other words, what is most at issue is whether there is anything new in Parsons' formulation, and whether such developmental steps are best formulated within a specifically 'evolutionary' frame of reference. See also NEOEVOLUTIONISM, EVOLUTIONARY SOCIOLOGY, SOCIOCULTURAL EVOLUTION.

evolutionism see EVOLUTIONARY THEORY.

exchange 1 the transfer of economic goods or services, whether by trading or by other means.
2 any process in which people in their everyday social relations gain mutual benefit.

3 any social interaction that may have as one aspect an exchange of goods or services, but which also serves the purpose of social bonding (see GIFT EXCHANGE AND GIFT RELATIONSHIP). In simple societies there are generalized patterns of exchange of a variety of goods and services (including, for example, ceremonial goods or even marriage partners), in which the givers do not themselves immediately receive directly from those to whom they give. In their various manifestations, these forms of exchange can be seen as not only, or even primarily, economic; rather they reinforce established social relationships, e.g. enhancing the prestige of the giver. See also KULA RING.
4 any social interaction which can be interpreted as involving *reciprocal benefits* or 'exchanges', e.g. relationships between superordinates and subordinates (even master and slave), as well as relationships involving mutual affection and love. See also EXCHANGE THEORY.

exchange theory a theoretical perspective based on SIMMEL's insight that 'all contacts among men rest on the schema of giving and returning the equivalence (BLAU, 1964). The approach also draws upon economics and behavioural psychology, viewing individuals as always seeking to maximize rewards from their interactions with others (see also HOMANS). As a mode of analysis, exchange theory is associated with interesting hypotheses about social behaviour, e.g. Blau's suggestion that people tend to marry partners able to offer equivalent social assets. Critics of the approach, however, regard it as providing a model which is, at best, capable of presenting only a partial account of human social relations. Limitations of the approach suggested are: its tautological assumptions that social relations *always* involve exchange relations; its failure to deal adequately with such phenomena as traditional action or general values, and the great variety of human emotions. See also RATIONAL CHOICE THEORY.

exchange value see USE VALUE AND EXCHANGE VALUE.

existentialism a philosophical movement stressing personal responsibility and choice. Drawing on the works of KIERKEGAARD and NIETZSCHE, it was developed in the 20th century by HEIDEGGER, SARTRE and MERLEAU-PONTY. Heidegger elaborated his ideas against the phenomenological philosophy of HUSSERL., asserting human embedment in social life and our inability to theorize from outside it. The first section of *Being and Time* (1929) formulates the concept of DASEIN (being-in-the-world) and the primacy of language as a means of ordering experience. From this foundation, Heidegger then moves to establish the distinction between authentic and inauthentic action – the two being distinguished by the degree of self-awareness and commitment associated with particular choices. Sartre and Merleau-Ponty extended and elaborated on these foundations (to Heidegger's disgust) to make existentialism a dominant intellectual current in postwar Europe. Their journal, *Les Temps Modernes,* and Sartre's many literary and philosophical works, synthesized existential and Marxist themes in a search for a foundation for action that was not in 'bad faith'. Sartre's many plays and novels explored the nature of individual consciousness and freedom, and he came to be seen by some as the conscience of a generation. Existential thought has had an important influence on social scientific thinking, from LAING's radical psychiatry and phenomenological Marxism to a poststructuralist interest in the early Heidegger's stress on language. Though often dismissed as purely a moral philosophy, it also provides much in terms of exploring the nature of social life for the individual.

exogamy a rule prescribing marriage outside a given social group. The group may belong to a LINEAGE, CASTE, CLASS, ethnic affiliation or other social classification. Structural anthropologists have seen this practice as an exchange of women between groups which contributes to social stability. It may, therefore, be enforced by the use of

INCEST TABOOS. The converse of exogamy is ENDOGAMY.

expanded or extended reproduction of capital (MARXISM) that part of SURPLUS VALUE which is advanced as new capital to expand the activity of capitalist enterprise or economy. See also ACCUMULATION (OR EXPANDED OR EXTENDED REPRODUCTION) OF CAPITAL.

experimental condition see EXPERIMENTAL GROUP.

experimental group *or* **experimental condition** the group which receives the INDEPENDENT VARIABLE in an experiment. Typically, in the EXPERIMENTAL METHOD, the EXPERIMENTAL HYPOTHESIS is tested by treating the experimental group with the independent variable to be investigated, and comparing any resultant effect (measured by the DEPENDENT VARIABLE) with any change observed in the CONTROL GROUP. If a statistically significant difference is found between the dependent measures in experimental and control groups, then the experimental hypothesis is upheld. If there is no statistically significant difference, then the NULL HYPOTHESIS is upheld.

experimental hypothesis the statement that there will be a statistically significant difference between the EXPERIMENTAL GROUP and the CONTROL GROUP, and that this difference will have been caused by the INDEPENDENT VARIABLE under investigation.

When an experiment is set up, or observational data collected, this is done in order to test a hypothesis, or theory, which has been developed from previous work. This is the experimental hypothesis, which states what the expected difference is between the groups if the theory is correct. The converse hypothesis, or NULL HYPOTHESIS, is also conventionally stated – that the predictions from the theory are incorrect. See also DEPENDENT VARIABLE, EXPERIMENTAL METHOD.

experimental method the scientific method used to test an EXPERIMENTAL HYPOTHESIS by comparing an EXPERIMENTAL GROUP which has been subjected to an INDEPENDENT VARIABLE, with a CONTROL GROUP which has not. This is the method of choice in PSYCHOLOGY, but sociology has developed diverse methodologies to cope with less controllable data. See RESEARCH METHODS, QUANTITATIVE RESEARCH TECHNIQUES, COMPARATIVE METHOD, CAUSAL MODELLING.

explanandum the occurrence, phenomenon, etc., made plain in any explanation; the subject of an explanation. See EXPLANATION, COVERING-LAW MODEL AND DEDUCTIVE NOMOLOGICAL EXPLANATION, EXPLANANS.

explanans any explanatory account, particularly a formal deductive explanatory account, by which a particular occurrence or general phenomenon is explained (see EXPLANATION, COVERING-LAW MODEL AND DEDUCTIVE NOMOLOGICAL EXPLANATION, EXPLANANDUM).

explanation

Any account in which an occurrence or general phenomenon is made intelligible by identification of its CAUSE, nature, interrelations, etc. In more formal terms, the occurrence or phenomenon explained is the *explanandum*, the explanatory account, the *explanans*, which, in physical science, will usually involve SCIENTIFIC LAWS, EXPLANATORY THEORIES, etc., but in the social sciences may also involve actors' meanings, REASONS, and so on. Thus in sociology, explanation may take any one of a number

of forms (which are not necessarily always mutually exclusive):
(a) *causal explanation*, which may embrace various types of explanation, but in its most basic form involves the identification of an immediate precipitating cause or causes of a particular occurrence, e.g. the cause of a fire identified as the dropping of a cigarette. In their more limited forms, causal explanations usually involve numerous unstated background assumptions about physical laws, etc. (see also CAUSALITY AND CAUSAL RELATIONSHIP);
(b) *deductive explanation*, in which an explanandum is deduced, i.e. follows logically from established generalizations of general laws (see HYPOTHETIC-DEDUCTIVE EXPLANATION, VERSTEHEN, INTERPRETATIVE SOCIOLOGY, COVERING-LAW MODEL AND DEDUCTIVE NOMOLOGICAL EXPLANATION, FORMAL THEORY;
(c) *probablistic explanation*, in which a specifiable probability (a chance of less than 100% and more than 0%, i.e. in probability theory a chance less than 1 and greater than 0) is taken as explaining the occurrence of an event, e.g. the appearance of breast cancer in a woman whose mother and sisters have already had the disease. Strictly speaking, rather than explaining a single event, probability explanations relate to the likelihood of a particular distribution of occurrences in an infinite series of events. On their own they are usually seen as unsatisfactory as explanations, at least until further background factors explaining the probabilities are also identified, e.g. in the case of breast cancer, the discovery of genetic predispositions, etc.)
(d) *'meaningful' and 'purposive' explanations*, in which actors' meanings and/or desires, reasons, intentions, purposes, etc., explain an event or a social situation (see MEANINGFUL UNDERSTANDING AND MEANINGFUL EXPLANATION, PURPOSIVE EXPLANATION);
(e) *functional(ist) explanations*, in which the 'functional requirements' of systems explain outcomes (see FUNCTIONAL(IST) EXPLANATION);
(f) *evolutionary or ecological explanations*, which explain the persistence of natural species, types of social system, etc., in terms of their selection by and adaptation to an external environment (see EVOLUTIONARY THEORY);
(g) *teleological explanations* (see also TELEOLOGY), in which purposes, goals, or system end-states, rather than antecedent causes, are seen as decisive. Such explanations may be made with reference to human or animal purposes, to the needs and goals of human societies, or to the more arcane operation of processes such as 'world spirit' (as for HEGEL) or human destiny. Functional explanation in many of its sociological forms also involves teleological explanation, although, in this case, recourse to such explanation is not always regarded as incompatible in principle with a reduction to antecedent causes.

explanatory mechanism any scientific account of the causal factors (or 'causal powers') underlying a general phenomenon, e.g. 'natural selection' (in EVOLUTIONARY THEORY), or contradictory modes of production and class conflict (in MARXISM). The term has gained in currency recently as a result of the influence within sociology of the SCIENTIFIC REALISM of Rom Harré (1970 and, with E. Madden, 1975) and Roy Bhaskar (1975, 1979 and 1986), in which the formulation of 'explanatory mechanisms' is presented as the core of scientific EXPLANATION. This account of science and scientific explanation is preferred to those couched in terms of empirical regularities and general laws (e.g. the COVERING-LAW MODEL) for a number of reasons, above all that laws can be either empirical regularities or 'universal' and 'transfactual', but not both. The use of the term 'explanatory mechanism' both bypasses the problems associated with EMPIRICISM (see also POSITIVISM) and offers a way of recognizing the variety of forms taken by scientific explanatory accounts.

explanatory theory any theory which advances an EXPLANATION of a phenomenon or class of phenomena. Although explanatory theories can take many forms (see also HYPOTHETICO-DEDUCTIVE EXPLANATION AND METHOD, SOCIOLOGICAL THEORY, MEANINGFUL UNDERSTANDING AND EXPLANATION, FUNCTIONAL(IST) EXPLANATION), a general assumption is made that the 'facts' rarely speak for themselves in explaining phenomena.

exploitation (and **appropriation**) (MARXISM) the acquisition (*appropriation*) of the 'surplus product' by the individuals or class which owns and controls the MEANS OF PRODUCTION. More strictly, in terms of the LABOUR THEORY OF VALUE, exploitation involves the expropriation of SURPLUS VALUE.

Serious reservations are often expressed about the theoretical and empirical cogency of the labour theory of value (see also VALUE). However, conceptions of exploitation in capitalist, or other types, of society which do not depend on acceptance of the labour theory of value can still carry much force in accounts of CAPITALISM AND CAPITALIST MODE OF PRODUCTION. Thus, Hodgson (1982) has argued that we might, without such dependence, identify 'bargaining exploitation', resulting from the unequal bargaining strengths in the negotiation of a contract, as well as class exploitation, resulting from unequal distribution of the means of production (see also Roemer, 1982). Similarly, Wright (1985) has argued that if we pose the question, 'if one of the classes would disappear, would there be more consumption and/or less toil for the other class?', and the answer is 'yes', then there is exploitation, whether or not one accepts the labour theory of value. This leaves open the question, however, of whether these are satisfactory conceptions of exploitation. It is characteristic of all of these accounts that they arise from formal, a priori analysis, rather than from empirical analysis of the functions performed by classes, or any very adequate analysis of the practical implications or feasibility of the new social arrangements that would be required to eliminate exploitation.

The relations between exploitation and oppression and levels of political consciousness is a further topic of some importance. See CLASS, CONTRADICTORY CLASS LOCATIONS, JUSTICE.

exploratory data analysis a form of statistical analysis which begins by exploring data rather than testing clearly formulated prior hypotheses. Exploratory data analysis does as it says: it explores the pattern of the data set under analysis, considering its range, level, outliers, batching it before graphing and transforming it. The MINITAB computer package, for example, contains these techniques in its sub-programmes. In either qualitative or quantitative forms, the purpose of exploratory data analysis is to follow parallel procedures in the interrogation of statistics, i.e. generating hypotheses through exploring the data before turning to confirmatory statistics to test those hypotheses.

exponential growth change in a variable (e.g. population – see MALTHUS) where the increase is geometric, i.e. at an increasing ratio.

export-oriented industrialization reliance on external markets for manufactured goods as the main impetus towards a country's INDUSTRIALIZATION. It is a term usually applied to those THIRD WORLD countries which have attempted to find niches in the world market where advantages of low labour costs may make their goods cheaper than those produced in industrial countries. In Third World countries low incomes may mean a limited internal market, initially, for mass consumption goods which, nevertheless, can be produced relatively cheaply. The strategy has been successful for some countries, such as South Korea which exports a wide range of manufactured goods (from clothing to ships), and less successful for others which have been unable to increase the range of manufactured goods exported. The success of this strategy will depend on the opportunities in the world market at any particular time, the success of state investment and general economic policies, the nature of organized labour and whether it is successful in raising wage levels, and the degree of political and social stability within a country. See also DEPENDENT INDUSTRIALIZATION, NEW INTERNATIONAL DIVISION OF LABOUR, NEWLY INDUSTRIALIZING COUNTRIES.

extended family the unit formed both by family members who are in the nuclear family and those who are not, but are still considered to be close relatives. While the *nuclear family* is composed of a couple and their children, the family group is 'extended' when the grandparents, aunts and uncles, cousins, nieces and nephews, or any selection of these, are included.

Extended families living together as a unit in one location occur more often in preindustrial societies, rather than in industrial societies where the nuclear family is sometimes seen as more compatible with the needs of modern economies. Sec also FAMILY, SOCIOLOGY OF THE FAMILY.

extensive and intensive power a contrast drawn by MANN (1986) between 'the ability to organize large numbers of people over far-flung territories', albeit fairly minimally (*extensive power*) and 'the ability to organize tightly and command a high mobilization or commitment' within a territory (*intensive power*). The distinction is an important one in Mann's account of the differences between pre-industrial empires and modern nation-states.

extraversion (*or* **extroversion**) **and introversion** a personality trait (see TRAIT THEORY) characterized, in the case of extraversion, by orientation towards the outside world, sociability and impulsiveness, and, in the case of introversion, by orientation towards the inner world of the self, shyness and caution. The extraversion-introversion typology was first described by JUNG (1928). It is one of the three central dimensions of personality in the model of personality structure proposed by H. Eysenck (1953), and in this context may be measured using the Eysenck Personality Inventory (EPD. A biological basis for extraversion-introversion in terms of cortical inhibition-excitation has also been postulated (H. Eysenck, 1967).

f

Fabianism *see* FABIAN SOCIETY.

Fabian Society a society founded in Britain in 1884 to advance democratic SOCIALISM while pursuing a policy of 'gradualism' rather than REVOLUTION. The name derives from a Roman general, Fabius Cunctator, who gained victories by avoiding pitched battles. Well-known Fabians include Sydney and Beatrice WEBB, and the dramatist George Bernard Shaw. The society still survives, and as an approach to social research and social policy and SOCIAL REFORM, *Fabianism* remains an important orientation in British left-wing politics.

face-to-face interaction social interaction between individuals, which occurs in a situation of immediate co-presence and reciprocal influence. See also INTERACTION, ENCOUNTERS, GOFFMAN.

face-work the sequence of interaction in which a potential or actual 'loss of face' is dealt with by those involved in interaction. For GOFFMAN, such sequences are sufficiently standardized to be regarded as 'ritual', e.g. a 'transgression' is noted; the 'transgressor' acknowledges this (e.g. 'silly me'); this recognition is accepted by other parties to the interaction; the offender registers his gratitude for this. In Goffman's work and in related forms of sociology such as ETHNOMETHODOLOGY, the existence of such relatively standardized sequences are seen as a central element in the everyday social order.

factor analysis a MULTIVARIATE statistical technique in which the covariances (or CORRELATIONS) between a large set of observed VARIABLES are explained in terms of a small number of new variables called factors. The ideas originated in the work on correlation by Galton and Spearman, and were developed primarily in studies of intelligence. Most applications are found in psychology and sociology.

The technique is 'variable directed', with no distinction between INDEPENDENT and DEPENDENT VARIABLES in the data set. There are four steps to the analysis. The first is to derive a correlation matrix in which each variable in the data set is correlated with all the other variables. The next step is to extract the factors. The aim of this stage is to determine the minimum number of factors that can account adequately for the observed correlations between the original variables. If the number of factors identified is close to the number of original variables, there is little point to the factor analysis. Sometimes it is difficult to assign a meaningful name to the factors. The purpose of the third (optional) step, rotation, is to find simpler and more easily interpretable factors. If a satisfactory model has been derived, the fourth step is to compute scores for each factor for each case in the data set. The factor scores can then be used in subsequent analyses.

Factor analysis attracts a lot of criticism (Chatfield and Collins, 1980). The observed correlation matrix is generally assumed to have been constructed using product moment correlations. Hence, the usual assumptions of an interval measurement, normal distributions and homogeneity of variance are needed. Against this, it is argued the technique is fairly robust. Another problem is that the different methods of extraction and rotation tend to produce different solutions. Further, although factors may be clearly identified from the analysis, it may be difficult to give them a meaningful interpretation. Despite the need for so many judgmental decisions in its use, factor analysis remains a useful exploratory tool.

factors of production (ECONOMICS) the different resources that are combined in production: natural resources, labour and CAPITAL. In sociological analysis, and in Marxism, emphasis is placed on understanding the socioeconomic relations which production involves.

factory system the system of production introduced widely after the advent of the INDUSTRIAL REVOLUTION, in which workers were brought together in increasingly large units, making possible the application of new means of inanimate power (water power, steam), an extension of the DIVISION OF LABOUR, and a closer overall control of the LABOUR PROCESS. The relative importance of these three factors is debated, but some commentators suggest that the importance of the last of these has been underestimated. The factory system replaced earlier systems of artisan craft production and the *putting-out system,* in which workers were provided with materials and resources to finance the productive processes for work undertaken on their own premises.

fact-value distinction the distinction (often associated with HUME and the Logical Positivists) between factual assertions and moral assertions as two distinct classes of assertions, and the claim that moral assertions cannot be derived logically from factual assertions. While some sociologists have accepted the terms of this distinction (including, significantly, Max WEBER), other sociologists have refused to accept such a limitation on the significance of social science on the grounds that, for all practical purposes, facts and theories both inform and influence values, and that to deny this is to suggest an 'irrationalism' of values which is unwarranted. As GOULDNER (1973) remarks, 'one possible meaning of the term "objectivity" in social science is the contribution it might make to a human unity of mankind'. See also VALUE FREEDOM AND VALUE NEUTRALITY, VALUE RELEVANCE, BECKER, HIERARCHY OF CREDIBILITY.

false consciousness any form of CLASS CONSCIOUSNESS, IDEOLOGY or social imagery which is held to be inappropriate to the 'real' or 'objective' class situation or CLASS INTERESTS of the actor. The concept, although not used as such by MARX, is developed from his theory. In particular, it derives from the argument that ideologies and consciousness, generally, are products of social structure and represent real relationships of domination and oppression. It followed that, in time, the PROLETARIAT would come to realize its position as an oppressed and exploited class and put that realization to political use through revolutionary struggle.

A major problem facing Marxists has been that a widespread revolutionary consciousness has never emerged among the proletariat. Thus, after the extension of the vote to nearly all adult males, Engels wrote to Marx complaining about how the working class had 'disgraced itself' by giving political support to the Liberal Party at election time. In the period up to the 1950s the concept of 'false consciousness' was frequently referred to in accounting for the failure of a revolutionary working class to develop.

One persistent theme, established by LENIN, was that, unaided, the proletariat would develop only a 'reformist', 'economistic' or trade union consciousness. It required the organization of a revolutionary VANGUARD PARTY to transform the working class's limited awareness into a truly progressive 'political' consciousness based on the reality of the working-class situation. Other explanations included the idea that the formation of a revolutionary proletariat was impeded by factors such as NATIONALISM or IMPERIALISM, or even that sport and non-political diversions, in effect, sublimated the revolutionary impulse (see also LEISURE, INCORPORATION).

Theoretically, the concept has also been important in revising central perspectives within MARXISM. Georg LUKACS (1971), for example, writing in the 1920s, argued for the need for much more attention to be paid to the issue of consciousness than had been paid by the 'vulgar' Marxists who assumed an inevitable move to worldwide revolution. These themes have continued an interest in the study of MASS CULTURE, in the work of the FRANKFURT SCHOOL OF CRITICAL THEORY, and, more recently, in the work of the Birmingham Centre for Contemporary Cultural Studies (see CULTURAL STUDIES).

For sociologists generally, the idea of 'false consciousness' has posed a number of problems. It has been criticized for the 'élitist' implication that 'we know what the working class needs better than the working class does'. More pertinently, it may be seen to divert attention away from the need to research the actual ideas and consciousness of working-class groups and their social sources. It also requires that one accepts the Marxist theory of CLASS and embraces the idea that revolution is a logical necessity and inevitable consequence of social class relations. Although in recent times the notion of 'false consciousness' has tended to fall into disuse, in both Marxism and Marxist sociology the idea of HEGEMONY has replaced it as a popular conceptual tool in the discussion of working-class consciousness (for example in the work of the Birmingham Centre for Contemporary Cultural Studies). However, it can be argued that 'hegemony' has at least some of the same drawbacks of the earlier concept. See also IDEOLOGY.

falsification 1 the empirical disproof or refutation of a scientific hypothesis or proposed law. In this general sense, the falsification or the empirical confirmation or verification of propositions of all types is a routine feature of much sociology.
2 (more strictly) an alternative procedure to VERIFICATION. See FALSIFICATIONISM. See also VERIFICATION PRINCIPLE.

falsificationism the methodological position (particularly associated with Karl Popper, 1934) based on the notion that while an inductive universal generalization can never be finally verified, given the ever-present possibility of new and potentially refuting evidence, a single nonsupporting occurrence can refute a hypothesis (e.g. a single black swan refutes the general hypothesis that 'all swans are white'). According to this view (and in contrast with LOGICAL POSITIVISM, see also EMPIRICISM), science can be defined in terms of the 'falsifiability' rather than the 'verifiability' of its theories and hypotheses, and the essential provisionality of scientific knowledge acknowledged. For Popper, the 'falsifiability' of a discipline's propositions is the decisive *criterion of demarcation* between science and non-science.

A virtue of this 'realist', rather than empiricist, position, is that it recognizes the importance of hypotheses and theories within science, and of changes in scientific knowledge, thus also captures something of the 'critical spirit' of science. Hence, this position is sometimes also referred to as *critical rationalism.*

Although it has attracted some support among social scientists, critics of falsificationism challenge its cogency on a number of counts:
(a) that 'the facts' which are put forward as the basis of the 'independent' test of theories and hypotheses are themselves 'theory-laden' – experiments, for example, are both constituted *by* and interpreted *using* theories;
(b) in practice, in science, and contrary to the position that can be termed *naive falsificationism,* it turns out that a single refutation is rarely decisive, the rejection and replacement of theories being a matter of a more overall judgement of the cogency and effectiveness of theories;

(c) the attempt (see Lakatos and Musgrave, 1970) to replace naive falsificationism with a *sophisticated falsificationism,* in which an overall judgement is made between *progressive* and *degenerating scientific research programmes,* fails to overcome the problems of falsificationism, for if no single observation is decisive, falsification loses its distinctive position; it no longer provides a clear cut rule of thumb in the day-to day procedures of science, or any clear overall demarcation between science and non-science.

For many commentators (e.g. see FEYERABEND, 1975), the procedures suggested for science by falsificationists simply fail to fit the past and present activities of science, and if used strictly would be likely to cripple it. See also COVERING-LAW MODEL AND DEDUCTIVE NOMOLOGICAL EXPLANATION, HYPOTHETICO-DEDUCTIVE EXPLANATION AND METHOD, SOCIOLOGY OF SCIENCE, SCIENTIFIC PARADIGM.

family

A group of people, related by KINSHIP or similar close ties, in which the adults assume responsibility for the care and upbringing of their natural or adopted children.

Historically and comparatively, there have been wide variations in the family form. In order to analyse these differing family arrangements, sociologists have used the key notions of the EXTENDED FAMILY and the *nuclear family.* The extended family refers to a group of people, related by kinship, where more than two GENERATIONS of relatives live together (or in very close proximity), usually forming a single HOUSEHOLD. The nuclear family comprises merely parents (or parent) and their dependent child(ren). Sociologists have argued that the nuclear family form has developed as a concomitant of industrialization (although there have been suggestions recently that the prior existence of individualistic family structures may have contributed to the rise of industrialism). With the geographical and social mobility normally associated with industrial development, sociologists have argued that the nuclear family has become socially and geographically isolated from wider kin networks, leading to what is known as the *privatized nuclear family.*

There remain wide variations in the forms which extended and nuclear families take, depending on social and cultural NORMS. For example, extended families vary according to kin structures, including polygamous family forms. Similarly, the number of children to be found in nuclear families differs widely. For example, in the UK, the trend has been towards having fewer children; and in China couples are prohibited from having more than one child.

As well as differences between societies, each family goes through a life cycle, and most individuals undergo several changes in family role in the course of their own lifetimes (see FAMILY OF ORIGIN OR ORIENTATION and FAMILY OF PROCREATION).

Recent changes in patterns of family life in Britain and in many Western societies, include:
(a) the increasing importance placed on personal fulfilment, overriding previously more dominant economic considerations;
(b) the increasing percentage of stable reproductive and cohabiting relationships outside conventional marriage patterns;
(c) the increasing incidence of DIVORCE and remarriage;
(d) an increase in the number of single-parent families, especially fatherless families.

A further change in the nuclear family, which may occur as a consequence of an ageing population, is an increase in the number of nuclear families which are caring for dependent parents (see COMMUNITY CARE). See also SOCIOLOGY OF THE FAMILY, SOCIALIZATION, MARRIAGE, DIVORCE.

Family Expenditure Survey (FES) a UK government SOCIAL SURVEY which gathers information on spending patterns. It was initiated in January 1957 and is the longest-standing multipurpose survey in the UK. Responsibility for it is shared between the Department of Employment and the Office of Population Censuses and Surveys. Originally, its purpose was to provide information for the Retail Price Index, but its scope has widened and it is now a major source of data on the characteristics and circumstances of households. Apart from changes taking account of new services and commodities, the type of information collected has remained unaltered. For the first ten years it was based on a sample of 5000 addresses. From 1967 the sample has been approximately 11,000 addresses with about 7000 households cooperating. The scope is very comprehensive and respondents are asked to keep a record of all expenditure within a given period, including housing costs, telephone bills, insurance payments and certain types of credit. See also OFFICIAL STATISTICS, CENSUS, GENERAL HOUSEHOLD SURVEY.

family of origin or orientation the NUCLEAR, or EXTENDED FAMILY within which a person was raised. As a chief agent of SOCIALIZATION, the family of origin provides the social, cultural and linguistic background with which the person may continue to identify and be influenced by throughout life.

family of procreation the NUCLEAR FAMILY that a heterosexual couple found when they produce, or procreate, a child.

family therapy a treatment, usually for disturbed children, employing PSYCHOTHERAPEUTIC or COUNSELLING methods, based on the premise that a child's behaviour is the product of a complex of interacting family relationships. To understand why a child is unhappy or exhibiting behaviour problems it is essential that he or she is regarded as part of the family system, therefore the whole family is seen by the therapist. By being able to assess where the stresses are within the family, the therapist is able to suggest ways in which the balance may be restored. The 'problem' behaviour may be 'referred' from another part of the family system (e.g. when the parents are not happy in their marital relationship), and, similarly, it will be affecting the rest of the family system. Adjustment to one part of the system will have repercussions on other parts, therefore the whole family is involved in the treatment process (see SYSTEMS THEORY for the theoretical concepts involved).

famine widespread food shortages leading to starvation and a high death rate within a given population. During a famine people die not only of hunger but from a variety of diseases to which they become increasingly vulnerable. Sen (1981) has argued that starvation arises from the condition of people not *having* enough to eat, and not as a result of there not *being* enough food to eat. Famine generally occurs when there is a sudden collapse of the level of food consumption, rather than as the result of a long-term decline, and people die because of the lack of time available to counteract the factors that lead to low consumption. It rarely occurs that a population is without any food (the Netherlands under German occupation during World War II may be one example), rather, Sen argues that it is changes in people's entitlement to food which is altered. Thus famine is linked to the distribution as well as the production of food, and the vulnerability of some groups, rather than others, within a population. Historically, famine has been precipitated by events such as serious floods or pestilence, but in the 20th-century major famines have been closely associated with warfare, as with Ethiopia and Mozambique in the 1970s and 80s, or with profound political upheavals, as with the consolidation of Stalinism in the 1930s in the USSR, and Maoism in China in the late 1950s. In all of these cases, however, only some social groups lost their entitlement to food, whilst others retained theirs or acquired new ones.

Fanon, Frantz (1925-1961) Martinique-born psychiatrist and anti-colonial revolutionary writer whose critique of COLONIALISM and support for Algerian nationalism and revolutionary armed struggle was expressed in the influential works *Black Skin, White Masks* (1952) and *The Wretched of the Earth* (1961) profoundly influenced radical movements in the 1960s. Born into a middle-class family in the French colony, Fanon volunteered to fight with the Free French in World War II, and remained in France after the war to study medicine and psychiatry. Informed by his upbringing on a colonized island and his later experience as a black intellectual in France, *Black Skin, White Masks* exposes how the colonizer/colonized relationship both degrades the indigenous culture and imposes an alternative set of social and cultural values upon the colonized through education and language. Conceiving himself from within French culture, Fanon was able to see how the colonized subject is produced as lacking in relation to the dominant cultural group. This has the negative psychological effect of suppressing black consciousness as a way of promoting the dominant ideological position. In response to this condition Fanon saw resistance as revolutionary action. While actively involved in Algerian nationalist politics he developed his later work *Studies in a Dying Colonialism* (1959) and *Toward the African Revolution* (1964) where he formulated a revolutionary political manifesto aimed at overthrowing colonial rule. In his final work, *The Wretched of the Earth*, he argues for total revolution in order that the constraints of the past can be overturned and replaced by a new emancipated world. This, according to Fanon, can only be achieved by the peasantry or those under the most extreme oppression. His ideas have been widely adopted within POST-COLONIAL THEORY.

fanzines magazines dealing with a single aspect of popular culture, which are produced on photocopiers or small presses by fans for fans, and circulated mainly by other means than through mainstream commercial channels. Providing an alternative to the products of mass publishing and the mass entertainment industry, fanzines in the UK, such as *Sniffin' Glue* or *When Saturday Comes*, have proliferated over the last 15 years, dealing especially with rock and pop music and also with football. Fanzines can be seen as enabling a 'users' view' (and sometimes also a radical reinterpretation or defence) of popular cultural forms by people who would otherwise be excluded from any means of written expression about, or control over, mainstream institutions in the production of MASS CULTURE. As such, they can be seen as an example of the existence of a continued 'contestation' over cultural institutions of the kind suggested by sport and leisure theorists such as Gruneau (1982 and 1983) and Donnelly (1988) – see Jary et al. (1991).

fascism a political ideology forming the basis of political parties and movements which emerged in Europe between the two world wars, which was the basis of the extreme nationalist governments of Italy 1922–43 and Germany 1933–45, and has been continued through parties in many countries since the 1940s. Unlike other political ideologies of the 20th-century, fascism has no large body of systematic intellectual work elaborating its political philosophy, in part because anti-intellectualism is a constituent element of the ideology, so the tenets of fascism are not clearly delineated. One basis, however, is the preference for voluntarism over determinism or materialism, leading to the view that the human will, particularly as exercised by the strong leader, can overcome structural obstacles and make possible what others would see as impossible. This view has affinities with the philosophical writings of Friedrich NIETZSCHE, from whose work German fascists drew.

The following are some of the main constituents in fascist writings and actions: extreme racist nationalism linked with territorial expansion; virulent anti-communism combined with intolerance of most other political ideologies and independent working-class organizations; the open use and glorification of physical violence and terror against these groups; a reliance on a mass party organized around a powerful leadership, and once in power engaged in most areas of civil life and depending on continual mass mobilization to sustain support for the leadership; the glorification of militarism, the cult of the presumed masculine virtues, with women defined mainly as mothers and supporters of men; predominant support from the middle classes who are the main, though not exclusive, mass support.

The experience of fascism varies. The vicious ANTI-SEMITISM of the German Nazi party was not found originally in Mussolini's Italy. In postwar Europe, fascist parties have been less open on anti-Semitism, their racism more commonly being expressed against people of non-European origin. However, British fascists in their party writings claim that postwar immigration into Britain from the Commonwealth was promoted by Zionists to weaken the racial stock, and anti-Semitism has been a persistent feature of fascist organization and thought elsewhere.

Fascism is a specifically 20th-century phenomenon: unlike earlier 19th-century authoritarian and militaristic governments, it depends on the use of mass party organizations both to come to power and to sustain itself in power. The biological notions of race upon which it builds were only developed in the latter half of the 19th century and had widespread acceptance in Europe in the early part of the 20th century, for example in the EUGENICS movement. NATIONALISM, too, was developed as the basis of political organization and mobilization from the mid-19th century. Despite these continuities with other general intellectual and political thought, fascism is often thought of as unique in its association of racism, nationalism, mass mobilization and expansionism in such a violent form.

Explanations for the emergence of fascism continue to be the subject of extensive debate. The debates centre around the role of socioeconomic forces linked to the crisis of Western capitalism in the aftermath of World War I; the specific political characters of Germany and Italy with relatively late emergence of national unity and parliamentary democracy; the general problems of industrial modernization which give rise to social crises at particular points of transition, especially from small-scale competitive capitalism to large-scale and wider industrial capitalism; and the psychological motivation of fascist leaders and their supporters (see AUTHORITARIAN PERSONALITY). See Kitchen (1976) for a general discussion, and Kershaw (1989) for the debates on Germany. See also NATIONAL SOCIALISM, HOLOCAUST.

fashion modes of behaviour or dress 'in which the key feature is rapid and continual changing of styles' (E. Wilson, *Adorned in Dreams: Fashion and Modernity*, 1985). However, although centred on dress, fashion can be a feature of any area of life. Fashion is associated with three aspects of 'modernity':
(a) culture of consumerism and perpetual change created by ADVERTISING, and fuelled by the MASS MEDIA OF COMMUNICATION;
(b) conformity and differentiation – as Simmel (1905) suggests, fashion supports the differentiation of self but at the same time lightens the load of responsibility for actions as this is shared with others;
(c) the more accessible affordability of 'fashion goods' and 'style' as an option in choice of clothes, furniture, or similar goods which enables people to exercise an element of control over their immediate social environment and presentation of self and social identity (cf. LIFESTYLE).

D. Hebdige (*Subculture: The Meaning of Style*, 1979) argues that different subcultures make their own style through the creative juxtaposition – or BRICOLAGE – of different clothes or objects. Thus fashion is subject to the same assessment as other forms of popular culture. It contains elements of both creative expression and manipulation.

fatalistic suicide a form of SUICIDE identified by DURKHEIM (1897) which arises from 'oppressive regulation' and from 'physical or moral despotism', e.g. the suicide of slaves. Thus, Durkheim suggested that this form of suicide could be considered the opposite of ANOMIC SUICIDE.

fecundity the physiological capacity to reproduce. This physical aspect must be distinguished from the social, economic and psychological influences which affect actual reproduction. Compare FERTILITY. See also DEMOGRAPHY, POPULATION, BIRTH RATE.

feedback loop see CYBERNETICS.

feeling rules see EMOTIONAL LABOUR.

female gaze the proposed creation of a counterpoint to the predominance of a 'male GAZE' in narrative cinema and western popular culture (Laura Mulvey, 1975), in which women appear, for example, as sex objects. It was John Berger, the art historian, who said, 'men look, women appear'. The proposal of Mulvey and others is that an objectification of women will only be overcome if women gain more control of the production of visual popular culture.

femininity the characteristics associated with the female sex. The historical (often masculinist) study of femininity documents feminine identity linked to passivity, nurturing, co-operation, gentleness and relation to motherhood, with an emphasis upon the relegation of women to the private sphere, the sphere of domesticity. Feminists and sociologists have challenged the stereotypes relating to 'femininity', 'feminine identity' and the binary categories man/mind, woman/nature which dominate many conceptions of sexual difference, including the reduction of sociocultural processes to biological givens. For French feminist theorists (e.g. CIXOUS, KRISTEVA) 'feminine' is an arbitrary category given to woman's appearance or behaviour by patriarchy. For Sue Lees (*Sugar and Spice: Sexuality and Adolescent Girls*, 1993), changing the social constructions of masculinity and femininity will mean a fundamental shift in our conceptions of femininity and MASCULINITY within the context of dominant conceptions of rationality and morality.

feminism

1 a holistic theory concerned with the nature of women's global oppression and subordination to men.
2 a sociopolitical theory and practice which aims to free all women from male supremacy and exploitation.
3 a social movement encompassing strategic confrontations with the sex-class system.
4 an ideology which stands in dialectical opposition to all misogynous ideologies and practices. See also POST-FEMINISM.

Feminism has a long history and can, arguably, be traced back to the 15th century (Kelly, 1982), and women's resistance to subordination certainly predates the emergence of feminism as a fully articulated ideology and practice (Rowbotham, 1972). The roots of modern feminist thought are conventionally traced back to the late 18th century and to the works of Mary Wollstonecraft. Since the 19th century there have been numerous manifestations of feminist activity followed by periods of relative invisibility. The 'first wave' of feminism is frequently located between the mid-19th century and the early 20th century. The 'second wave' has been identified with the re-emergence of feminism in the late 1960s and has persisted as a social movement into the present. There have, however, been many 'waves' and Sarah (1982) has criticized the idea of 'first' and 'second waves' as ethnocentric.

Whereas feminism in the late 1960s was concerned with understanding and documenting an oppression believed to be commonly experienced by *all* women, much contemporary feminist writing emphasizes the diversity of women's relationship not only to the male social order but also to each other. It is more accurate, therefore, to talk of feminisms than feminism. Sebestyen (1978) charted over ten political tendencies within feminism, ranging from a liberal, equal rights position to a female supremacist strand. Palmer (1989) listed the following tendencies – academic feminism, cultural feminism, lesbian feminism, liberal feminism, psychoanalytic feminism, political lesbianism, radical feminism and socialist feminism. Furthermore, black feminism has been concerned with the implicit and explicit racism within feminist thought and has stressed the particular issues concerning the lives of black women (Lorde, 1979). The original four demands of the 'second wave' – equal pay now, equal education and opportunities, free contraception, abortion on demand and free 24-hour nurseries – have been identified as the primary concerns of white, Western women. Access to food, fuel and water are the primary needs of many THIRD WORLD women. Feminism has been identified with white women's culture, and many black women favour the term 'womanist' (Walker, 1983). *Ecofeminism* suggests that an end to the oppression of women is bound up with ecological values, and that women should be centrally concerned with ending the exploitation of the ecosystem (Collard, 1988). Ecofeminism has been particularly strong within radical feminism and within the GREEN MOVEMENT.

Case (1988) has followed the convention of distinguishing between two major theoretical divisions within feminism, namely, radical feminism and materialist (socialist) feminism. The former is characterized by the belief that PATRIARCHY is the major and universal cause of women's oppression, and that the power invested in men is the root problem. Radical feminism, the predominant form of feminism in the US, has fostered the notion of an exclusively women's culture, together with a belief in the need to organize separately from men. Materialist (socialist) feminism is critical of the essentialism implicit in radical feminism and the ahistorical approach to patriarchy. Materialist feminism has its roots in MARXISM and prioritizes SOCIAL CLASS as the factor determining the situation of women within CAPITALISM. This approach is therefore concerned with the interaction between the dialectic of class and GENDER. Not without theoretical problems, Hartmann (1979) has characterized the 'marriage' between Marxism and feminism as an unhappy one. The division between radical feminists, who wish to organize separately from men, and materialist feminists who seek solidarity with 'supportive' men, continues unresolved.

Academic feminism has made an impact on the teaching and research carried out in many academic institutions. WOMEN'S STUDIES courses have been concerned with revising and challenging a wide variety of academic disciplines including sociology, history and English literature. Academic feminism has been concerned to criticize the 'sex-blind' nature of academic knowledge. Within sociology there has been a growing literature on the position of women in society and the development of a specifically feminist research methodology (Stanley and Wise, 1983).

Whilst there is no single ideological position uniting all feminists, most would accept that the subordination of women to men is the result of socioeconomic factors and not the effect of biological determinism. Hence, there is a commonly held belief that major social change culminating in women's liberation is possible. At present, feminism remains a vital and visible social movement, particularly successful in the area of cultural creativity. Despite media references to the Post-Feminist Era, the continuing social inequality of women and its eradication remains at the core of feminism in all its forms. See also MATRIARCHY.

feminist epistemology (and feminist methodology) feminist theories of knowledge which suggest that traditional EPISTEMOLOGY has understated the importance of areas of knowledge that have been uppermost in feminine experience and in women's lives. According to Coward and Ellis (1977), traditional epistemological theory has been either too empiricist or too rationalist. In the view of Stanley and Wise (1983) and Hilary Rose (1986), feminist research methods (*feminist methodology*) and a truly feminist epistemology must reflect women's lived experience and place greater emphasis on affectual rationalities.

feminist psychology approaches to psychology which draw on FEMINIST THEORY to critique mainstream psychology for its tendency to focus on the experience of men as the 'norm'. Its aim, therefore, is to both incorporate an understanding of women's psychological experience and also detail the often sexist and heterosexist underpinnings of much mainstream psychological research. Many feminist psychologists in the UK take a critical approach, drawing on different combinations of social constructionism (see also SOCIAL CONSTRUCTION OF REALITY), POSTMODERNISM or psychoanalytic theory (see also PSYCHOANALYSIS) in order to question how GENDER is constructed and to challenge gender inequality and 'common-sense' understandings of gender difference. Feminist psychologists understand that 'women' do not constitute a homogeneous group, and seek to understand other divisions which impact on women's lives, such as social class, ethnicity and sexual orientation. There are recurrent debates within feminist psychology about the political expediency of taking relativistic (see also RELATIVISM) or psychoanalytic approaches (because of the latter's phallocentrism), as these challenge the standpoint from which a feminist researcher can make claims. See also CRITICAL SOCIAL PSYCHOLOGY.

feminist theory a theory (see also FEMINISM) which, with the political and social changes of the 1960s and 70s, has challenged traditional conceptions of femininity and GENDER. As Humm (1989) points out, feminist theory 'both challenges, and is shaped by the academy and society'. It has been, above all, characteristic of the explosion of recent theories, including the work of Hélène CIXOUS, Kate Millet (1970), Juliet Mitchell (1974), Sheila Rowbotham (1973) and many more, that these theories 'describe the historical, psychological, sexual, and racial experiences of women', not just academically, but as an indication of 'how feminism can be a source of power'. Because of this, tensions have existed between feminist theory and sociology, especially given that it has challenged the fact that much sociology has been a sociology of men, stating men's viewpoints. But feminist theory, in so far as it is not always in itself sociology, has contributed to an important reconstruction of sociological perspectives in many areas.

feminization (of occupation) the process, historically, in which certain occupations which women have entered (e.g. school teaching, nursing) have become regarded as women's work, with a consequent loss of income and status.

Ferguson, Adam (1723–1816) a philosopher who was a central figure in the SCOTTISH ENLIGHTENMENT and, in effect, a practitioner of sociology before Auguste COMTE had even coined the term. Ferguson, whose work influenced MARX among many others, was particularly interested in the process of historical change, which he understood within a broadly evolutionary framework (see EVOLUTIONARY THEORY). *An Essay on the History of Civil Society* (1767) discusses the emergence of civilized society from prior states characterized as 'savage and barbaric' – a theme which was to become familiar in the social theories of later thinkers.

For Ferguson, civil society was just that – refined, morally sensitive and politically sophisticated. Yet the achievement of this condition was not a guarantee of its stability or longevity. What distinguished SAVAGERY from BARBARISM was the institution of private property, and it was the kind of egoistic, individualistic and self-interested pursuit of wealth which this institution encouraged, progressively embedded as it was in the increasingly complex DIVISION OF LABOUR and network of commercial relations characteristic of CIVIL SOCIETY, that could dissolve the social bonds between the individual and society and lead to the degeneration of civil society into political despotism. Like Emile DURKHEIM after him, Ferguson was acutely aware of the problems of social order posed by economic individualism; like Marx, he under stood the alienating (see ALIENATION) effects of a capitalistic division of labour.

fertility (and **fertility rate**) 1 (*fertility*) the physical capacity of a woman or man to sexually reproduce.

2 (*fertility and infertility rate*) the extent of *actual* childbearing in a population, usually expressed as a combination of the crude BIRTH RATE, that is births per thousand of a population, and the *total fertility rate*, being the average number of children women bear, currently below 2.0 in most industrialized countries. Compare FECUNDITY.

Fertility in sense 2 is affected by social factors such as income and housing conditions, contraceptive methods, religious and social attitudes to contraception and family size, and age of marriage. Fertility characteristically declines with INDUSTRIALIZATION (see DEMOGRAPHIC TRANSITION) and can be controlled by government strictures. For example, the Chinese government aims to restrict population growth by limiting fertility through social measures, while Russia, France and the UK have adopted various policies in the recent past to encourage higher fertility among their populations. The economic depressions of the 1930s led to lower fertility, alarming the British government, which then introduced a policy of encouraging larger families. The postwar 'baby boom' can be regarded as the result of both government policy and the end of hostilities.

fetish 1 (in religious belief or magic) any object in which a spirit is seen as embodied; the worship of such an object being *fetishism* (see also ANIMISM).

2 (more generally, especially in psychology, PSYCHOANALYSIS) any object of obsessive devotion or interest, especially objects or parts of the body other than those usually regarded as erogenous, e.g. articles of clothing, feet. See also COMMODITY FETISHISM.

feud relations of continuing mutual hostility between groups where one group has been wronged by the other (e.g. one of its number has been murdered) and retribution is sought. Usually different LINEAGE groups or clans are involved. Feuding relationships occur in situations of kin solidarity, in which an individual can rely on support from relatives. They occur particularly in societies (e.g. SEGMENTARY SOCIETIES) which lack central political or legal authority, but where the fear of being involved in a feud acts as a major deterrent against wrongdoing. A retaliatory killing may end a feud, but other resolutions, such as the payment of compensation, may also bring it to an end.

feudalism and **feudal society** a type of agrarian society in which land is held conditional upon military or other service, and in which there is a hierarchy of political power based upon contractual rights and obligations, usually with a monarch at the head, and in which unfree PEASANTS work the land as SERFS. There are a number of significant debates surrounding the term and this definition would be disputed by many contributors to the controversies. The main areas of debate are:

(a) whether feudalism evolved only in Europe and Japan or has occurred more widely. Most writers would agree that much of Western Europe between *c.* AD 1000–1400 (the so-called Middle Ages) could be described as feudal, and for longer in Eastern Europe. The period in Japan known as the

Tokugawa (1603–1868) has such key similarities with Europe that the term has been widely applied there. Beyond that, there are strong disagreements which link to the second area of debate;
(b) whether feudalism is seen as a societal form, or whether the term applies to a set of institutions which may be found in a range of societies.

If feudalism is defined in the latter sense, then political or economic aspects are also usually defined. Politically, feudalism is generally seen as the dominance of a militarized land-possessing group linked in a hierarchy of *vassalage* in which subordinates owed allegiance and military service to a superior through a personal contract, and the superior (or lord) in return provided protection and advancement for the vassal. In Europe, this involved a chain of lord-vassal relationships from the monarch downwards. Economically, feudalism can be defined as centring around the holding of land conditional upon services (in Europe, the *fief*), with the peasants being unfree serfs who, through various forms of rent, gave up a surplus to the land holder. Typically, production would not be for the market, although markets did develop.

If the institutional approach is taken, then it may be possible to identify feudal land-holding in societies where feudal political relationships do not exist. This, for example, has been argued for the HACIENDA in colonial Spanish America. However, within contemporary sociology (e.g. MANN, 1986; ANDERSON, 1974a & b) there is a preference for defining feudalism as a type of society incorporating certain political, economic, social, and, more problematically, ideological or cultural elements, even though (e.g. by Anderson), it may be recognized that there can be variations, such as differences between Southern, Western and Eastern Europe. It is this societal approach which leads to few instances of feudalism being identified in the world. The arguments about a restrictive or general usage of the term cuts across other debates within sociology. Thus some Marxists, such as Anderson, keep to a restrictive use, whilst the influence of Maoist work leads others to identify feudalism in a variety of agrarian societies. See also FEUDAL MODE OF PRODUCTION.

feudal mode of production (MARXISM) the MODE OF PRODUCTION which Marx saw as historically preceding CAPITALISM in Western Europe, and in which the RELATIONS OF PRODUCTION were characterized by feudal landlords using political and legal power to extract an ECONOMIC SURPLUS from an unfree peasantry in the form of *feudal rent* (see SERFDOM). Marx saw this mode of production as emerging out of ANCIENT SOCIETY and the social forms introduced into Western Europe by the Germanic tribes who invaded the Roman Empire. Land was held on condition of providing rent or service to an overlord.

Marx also saw the feudal mode of production as associated with a considerable development of productive forces with the introduction of mills, heavy-wheeled ploughs and other innovations which increased agricultural productivity. For Marx, the growth of towns signified a new event in history since, for the first time, the relations of production in the towns differed from those on the land. Thus, unlike previous modes of production, the towns were not a continuation of the countryside, but the two were increasingly in opposition. This dynamic between the social relations of town and countryside, together with the development of trade and manufacturing in the towns, were important elements in Marx's analysis of the dynamic of the feudal mode of production and the TRANSITION FROM FEUDALISM TO CAPITALISM. See also FEUDALISM AND FEUDAL SOCIETY; NONCAPITALIST AND PRECAPITALIST MODES OF PRODUCTION; compare ASIATIC MODE OF PRODUCTION.

Feyerabend, Paul K. (1924–94) Austrian-born philosopher of science who worked in the UK and US as well as in Europe.

Influenced by Wittgenstein's later philosophy, his main work has involved a repudiation of the FALSIFICATIONISM of Karl POPPER. His best-known works are *Against Method* (1975) and *Science in a Free Society* (1978), in which he rejects the idea of a universal scientific method.

Like Thomas KUHN, between whose work and Feyerabend's there exist many affinities, the account of science which emerges is one which places great emphasis on science as a 'flesh and blood activity'. and a socially located one, that cannot be understood in formalistic or simple rationalistic terms. To those 'scientific rationalists' (such as Popper and Imre Lakatos) who claim to have located a universal scientific method, Feyerabend's answer is that the only universal rule in science is that 'anything goes'. One main reason why Feyerabend rejects falsificationism as a universal method is the INCOMMENSURABILITY of scientific terms and the THEORY-RELATIVITY, therefore, of the interpretation of any potentially refuting empirical data. Under these circumstances, Feyerabend's view is that 'pluralism' and a 'proliferation of theories' may often be the best policy, something that is not encouraged by falsificationism. A major part of Feyerabend's objective, especially in his later work, is to debunk the over-rationalist pretensions of modern science, its 'church-like' status in modern society, and the 'rule of experts' to which this often gives rise. His aim is to return scientific judgements to the public domain (an argument which he bases, in part, on J. S. MILL's On *Liberty*).

The frequent charge that Feyerabend's view of science involves 'irrationalism' is one that his polemical and iconoclastic postures have sometimes tended to encourage. However, Feyerabend is often deliberately deceptive on these matters, preparing traps for dogmatic rationalists to mislead them into more dogmatic expressions of their own position. His own general position, however, is clearly not intended to promote a philosophical relativism – since this is simply another form of philosophical dogmatism. Instead, like Kuhn, Feyerabend wishes to emphasize the way that science and knowledge generally depend on a variety of methods. In this context, while knowledge claims are sometimes relative to a particular scientific paradigm or particular FORMS OF LIFE (as in a simple society), on other occasions more general claims to 'realism' may also be mounted (in Feyerabend, 1981, he talks in these terms of 'two argumentative chains'). Feyerabend's point, however, is that there exist no final rules of method, no single identifiable basis of rationality. The rationalists are wrong to suggest otherwise, betraying their own claims to a 'critical' philosophy or to science. There is a similarity between Feyerabend's view and that of Richard Bernstein (1983) who has called for philosophical and sociological thinking on these matters to move 'beyond objectivism or relativism' (compare HABERMAS, with whom Feyerabend himself identifies continuities, but also differences).

fief see FEUDALISM.

field theory (PSYCHOLOGY) a theoretical and experimental approach to the study of behaviour associated with Kurt Lewin (*Field Theory*, 1951), which views mental events and behaviour as the outcome of a nexus of forces analogous to those seen as operating within field theory in the physical sciences. Deriving in part from GESTALT THEORY, the approach involved taking a holistic and a dynamic view of psychological events as 'systems of energy' – systems of psychological energy, which Lewin sought to represent mathematically. See also GROUP DYNAMICS.

fieldwork research that is carried out in the field, as opposed to the laboratory, library, etc. Fieldwork is the investigation of real-life situations through observation and informal or unstructured interviewing. Ingold (1989) has defined the specific character of anthropological fieldwork as 'the search for participant understanding through long-term immersion in an initially alien setting'. See also ETHNOGRAPHY, QUALITATIVE

RESEARCH, CASE STUDY, INTERPRETATIVE SOCIOLOGY.

figuration *or* **configuration** the 'nexus of interdependencies between people', the 'chains of functions' and 'axes of tensions' – both of cooperation and conflict – which can be identified in any social context (ELIAS, 1978). The concept is the central analytical concept of Norbert Elias's FIGURATIONAL SOCIOLOGY. Elias rejects any model of Man as *homo clausus* – the closed or discrete individual. Equally, however, he also rejects purely structural forms of explanation. It is the model of the 'dance' or the 'game' which Elias suggests best illustrates the focus he seeks to achieve in social analysis. The 'image of the mobile figurations of interdependent people on a dance floor (or playing a sport-game) which makes it easier to imagine states, cities, families and also entire social systems as figurations' (ELIAS, 1939). See also CIVILIZING PROCESS, COURT SOCIETY.

figurational sociology the sociological approach of Norbert ELIAS and those influenced by his writing. The concept of FIGURATION is de scribed by ELIAS (1939, 1970) and further reformulated in works by Goudsblom (1977), Dunning and Sheard (1979) and Mennell (1985). *Eliasian Sociology*, as it is sometimes called, has been more influential on the Continent, especially in Holland and Elias' native Germany, than in the UK and North America. In the UK, the chief applications have been in the fields of SOCIOLOGY OF SPORT, SOCIOLOGY OF LEISURE and CULTURAL STUDIES.

filiation an anthropological term for the recognition of relationships between parents and offspring. DESCENT is the addition of a significant number of filiations.

finance capital (MARXISM) the form of CAPITAL, which according to Hilferding (1910) (see AUSTRO-MARXISM), involves a tight integration of 'financial capital' (capital in the hands of bankers) and 'industrial capital', and occurs when CAPITALISM has reached an advanced stage of concentration and centralization, and MONOPOLY. Hilferding's ideas on the character and crisis tendencies associated with 'finance capitalism' (including the necessity for IMPERIALISM) influenced LENIN's thinking.

first World see THIRD WORLD.

fiscal crisis in the capitalist state a tendency to crisis in the contemporary CAPITALIST STATE seen as arising from a contradiction between the achievement of social harmony and legitimacy (e.g. by the provision of social welfare) and the need to maintain the conditions for profitability and the ACCUMULATION OF CAPITAL (O'Connor, 1973). The upshot of the CONTRADICTION stemming from these dual requirements is a tendency to increase the 'tax burden' on capital as a result of an 'overload' of demands within the capitalist state. Two outcomes may result from this: either a reduction of unprofitable 'state expenditures' must occur so that capital accumulation can continue, or a transition to socialism will take place in which the accumulation of capital is no longer a requirement. In recent years in Western capitalist states, it is the former option which has usually been taken, and this has generally occurred without the crisis in legitimacy expected by some commentators (see LEGITIMATION CRISIS). See also OVERLOAD ON THE STATE, BELL, THATCHERISM.

fixed capital in orthodox economic theory, assets such as buildings and machinery that are bought by a firm for long-term use rather than for resale. See, CAPITAL, CONSTANT AND VARIABLE CAPITAL.

fixed-choice questionnaire a QUESTIONNAIRE in which all (or most) of the questions are fixed choice, such that RESPONDENTS are provided with a range of optional (and often precoded) answers and are asked to indicate which applies to them. While this type of questionnaire is useful in collecting standardized data, the use of fixed-choice questions is sometimes criticized for wrongly imposing the researcher's meanings (see MEASUREMENT BY FIAT, CICOUREL). See also CODING.

flaneur a stroller, watcher, observer. The concept has poetic origins in the work of Charles Baudelaire (e.g. *Art in Paris*, 1845–62). He used it to encapsulate the new, metropolitan character type of the 1840s: the man in the urban crowd, the man whose outlook is shaped by the mobile gallery of metropolitan existence. The most notable sociological application of the concept is to be found in the work of Walter BENJAMIN (1983). In his *Arcades* project he presents the city as a labyrinth or a multi-layered social universe. Benjamin plays on the ambiguity of the concept to convey the sense of a stroller-watcher of urban forms as well as a detective or unscrambler of codes. The concept has been criticized by feminists for marginalizing women's distinctive urban experience. Wolff (1985) attempts to retrieve this experience with the concept of the *flaneuse*, or 'the woman in the crowd'. Recent work on postmodernism, urban sociology and the sociology of consumption has used the concept of *flanerie* to refer to looking, observing (social types, configurations and urban milieux), decoding the hieroglyphics of the city (spatial images, architecture, advertising and the general 'sign economy') and reading texts and images about the city.

flexible labour markets market conditions in which professional and occupational restrictions on the employment and payment of labour are dismantled, e.g. by competitive pressures in the world economy, and by government action undermining the powers of TRADE UNIONS. Moves to time-limited contracts, part-time work, the end of lifelong CAREERS and increasing insecurity of employment are all aspects of the process. Flexible labour markets are an aspect of the move to FLEXIBLE PRODUCTION and can be seen as a less humane face of this phenomenon.

flexible production the ability to switch rapidly from the manufacture of one product to another. Flexible production is a key element of post-Fordism and contrasts with the inflexible production of standardized products for mass consumption which was characteristic of Fordism (see FORDISM AND POST-FORDISM). Flexible production has been made possible by the development of new technologies which allow rapid product switches with a minimum of downtime, as well as by the adoption of more organic forms of business organization, by decentralization, by subcontracting, by developing skill-flexible core workforces, and by the GLOBALIZATION OF PRODUCTION. Systems of flexible production help to create the material possibilities for the individual selection/choice of life style and identity which is held to be a characteristic of the postmodernist age (see POSTMODERNITY AND POSTMODERNISM).

flexible specialization see NEW TECHNOLOGY, HUMAN-CENTRED TECHNOLOGY.

focus group a research method in which selected groups of people participate in focused discussion on a research issue. Groups may meet on more than one occasion. The method is seen as having some advantages over single-person interviews in allowing a more extended working out of individual and collective viewpoints. As well as a method used in sociology, it is also widely used by political parties and in MARKET RESEARCH.

folk devils any stereotypical, 'socially constructed' cultural types identified as socially threatening by other members of society; e.g. in the 1960s, high-profile and newsworthy youth subcultures such as MODS AND ROCKERS.

The 'folk devil' is a cultural type akin to the 'hero', the 'villain' or the 'fool'. The term was developed by Cohen (*Folk Devils and Moral Panics*, 1973), who explored the phenomenon of Mods and Rockers and sought to show how social typing, or labelling, of 'rule breakers' occurs. Such people are labelled as 'socially deviant' and threatening, and all subsequent interpretation of their actions is in terms of the status to which they have been assigned. The study of folk devils and MORAL PANICS belongs to the wider study of the relations between the MASS MEDIA OF COMMUNICATION and the social construction of social problems. See also LABELLING THEORY, DEVIANCE, DEVIANCE AMPLIFICATION.

folk society an ideal-typical conception of *primitive* or *simple* society. The term was applied by REDFIELD to denote small, isolated groups, characterized and controlled informally by sacred values. Kinship relations predominate, and culture is transmitted orally. The moral order is paramount, resulting in a relatively static society that develops indigenously. Redfield contrasted folk society with its polar opposite of urban society, and conceived of societies as lying on a continuum between the two. See also RURAL-URBAN CONTINUUM.

folk-urban continuum see RURAL-URBAN CONTINUUM.

folkways the everyday customs of a social group or community (W. SUMNER, 1906). Folkways are contrasted with MORES, being less strongly sanctioned and less abstractly organized.

food any natural or processed substance ingested by a living organism and metabolized into energy and body tissue. Food is fundamental to wellbeing as well as to existence.

Sociological interest in the production, preparation and consumption of foods is concerned with the ways in which social roles and relationships arise in relation to food. The allocation of food involves power and privilege, and social norms and roles often define who may prepare and eat different kinds of foods, and when and where they may be eaten. Given this, there can be no question of a *sociology of food* which is not dependent on central areas of sociology, e.g. different MODES OF PRODUCTION and patterns of trade, as well as more obvious areas such as the sociology of agriculture and food processing and food distribution (see AGRICULTURAL REVOLUTION, AGRIBUSINESS, TERMS OF TRADE, FAMINE, GREEN REVOLUTION).

Within a more focused study of the sociology of food, a main topic of interest has been that in offering and accepting food, people engage in forms of symbolic interaction using foodstuffs as a language and as a form of EXCHANGE to express and cement social relationships (see also COMMENSALITY). Sociologists and anthropologists (notably LÉVI-STRAUSS) have also been interested in the manner in which material objects become defined as fit for human consumption, and in the social values expressed by cooking, serving and eating different kinds of food. Women can be seen as having an ambivalent relationship to food because feeding the family well is both a social obligation and a source of personal satisfaction, while eating well may be associated with fears of gaining weight, or lack of self control, sometimes leading to eating disorders (see ANOREXIA NERVOSA; see also BODY, DOMESTIC LABOUR). The overall sociological study of systems of food processing and food distribution in modern societies can be integrated with more 'microscopic' studies. For example, new ways of food processing (e.g. pre-prepared and fast foods) which reduce the role of the FAMILY as a 'production unit', may be marketed by ADVERTISING which reinforces its importance as a 'consumption unit', demanding new standards in 'motherhood' or in feminine physical appearance. Finally, changes in food manufacturing and food distribution in Western countries (e.g. supermarkets, concentrations of ownership, and increases in the horizontal and vertical integration of the production process, the Common Agricultural Policy) have implications for agriculture, and may profoundly affect welfare, in primary-product producing countries.

football hooliganism the violent crowd disorder, and associated football-related disturbances away from football grounds, which first attracted major public and media attention in the 1960s. After initial attempts to explain football violence in terms of the

psychological characteristics of the 'hooligans' (Harrington, 1968), more recently a variety of sociological explanations have been suggested:
(a) opposition to the commercialization of football and the growing distance between players and the owners of clubs on the one hand, and ordinary working-class supporters on the other (Taylor, 1971);
(b) rather than 'true' violence, behaviour which appears disordered and threatening in fact often has its own 'rules of disorder': is ritualized (Marsh et al., 1978);
(c) deriving from LABELLING THEORY and DEVIANCE AMPLIFICATION (see Cohen, 1973), 'hooliganism' is seen as a media-amplified MORAL PANIC;
(d) since football violence has a long history, increased modern attention to it is a reflection of a 'civilizing' tendency in society, which has resulted in a lower societal tolerance of violence of the kind long associated with working-class conceptions of masculinity but now socially unacceptable (Dunning et al., 1988) (see also CIVILIZING PROCESS.

Arguably, each of these explanations has some justification.

forced division of labour see DIVISION OF LABOUR.

forced labour camp see CONCENTRATION CAMP.

forces of production (MARXISM) the material bases of production, including raw materials, tools and instruments, sometimes also including the technical division of labour. The term is often equivalent to the MEANS OF PRODUCTION, although this concept may be narrower, excluding the technical division of labour. See also MODE OF PRODUCTION, RELATIONS OF PRODUCTION.

Fordism (and **post-Fordism)** methods of organizing production in advanced industrial societies associated with Henry Ford. Although the fundamental reference point of both concepts is the production process, the terms are often used as a way of conveying associated social and political consequences. Thus, while Henry Ford's great initiative in manufacturing was the mass production of a standardized product at a price that would generate mass consumption, this also implied:
(a) capital-intensive, large-scale plant;
(b) an inflexible production process;
(c) rigid hierarchical and bureaucratic managerial structures;
(d) the use of semiskilled labour performing repetitive and routine tasks, often subject to the discipline of SCIENTIFIC MANAGEMENT;
(e) a tendency towards strong unionization and the vulnerability of production to industrial action;
(f) the protection of national markets.

Though Ford's innovations began, in the interwar period, with the production of cars, his methods were rapidly employed in other sectors of manufacturing, and were increasingly seen as the organizational basis on which the advanced economies could continue to develop and, especially after World War II, prosper. It should also be noted that Fordist ideas of scale, centrality of control, standardization and mass consumption not only influenced the agenda of capitalist production, but also underpinned the nature of Soviet industrialization and the creation and delivery of welfare services in the free-market democracies (e.g. in the UK welfare state).

Post-Fordism refers to the new economic possibilities opened up by the rise of microchip technology, computers and robotics in the production and exchange of information and commodities. In contrast to Fordism, the distinguishing feature of the post-Fordist era is usually held to be the foundation of smaller units of enterprise, catering for segmented markets by the FLEXIBLE PRODUCTION of specialized goods or services. Associated social and economic changes involved in the post-Fordist transition are:

(a) the decline of old manufacturing and 'smokestack' industries (together with the emergence of the so-called 'sunrise' computer-based enterprises);
(b) more flexible, decentralized forms of the labour process and of work organization;
(c) a reorganized labour market, into a skill-flexible core of employees and a time-flexible periphery of low-paid insecure workers performing contract labour;
(d) a consequent decline of the traditional, unionized blue-collar working class, and the pre-eminence within the occupational structure of white-collar, professional, technical, managerial and other service sector employees;
(e) the feminization of many labour processes affected by the new technology;
(f) the promotion of types of consumption around the concept of individually chosen lifestyles, with an emphasis, therefore, on taste, distinctiveness, packaging and appearance;
(g) the dominance and autonomy of multinational corporations in a global process of capitalist production;
(h) a NEW INTERNATIONAL DIVISION OF LABOUR, based on the new flexibility, within which global production can be organized.

The precise dating of the transition from Fordism to post-Fordism is impossible. Indeed, debate continues about the utility and content of both concepts. The least that can be said is that different sectors of national economies are differentially affected (for example, the fast-food business continues to expand on classic Fordist principles in the so-called post-Fordist era), and that, internationally, the implications of post-Fordism are rather obviously different for economies such as the UK's on the one hand and, for example, Bangladesh's on the other. As an analytical device, the term Fordism was used by Antonio GRAMSCI to emphasize Fordism's pivotal role as an 'hegemonic' form of industrial organization (see HEGEMONY), a form of control that mixed persuasion with compulsion, e.g. high wages, welfare provision. See also POSTINDUSTRIAL SOCIETY, NEW TECHNOLOGY, DISORGANIZED CAPITALISM.

forecasting the attempt to estimate future social occurrences. Compared with the more wide-ranging, often social science based, theorizing and speculation involved in FUTUROLOGY, forecasting can be distinguished as having a more specific focus (e.g. short-term economic forecasts, political-risk analysis). However, no sharp distinction exists between the two, and general observations which apply to futurology also apply to forecasting. See also DELPHI METHOD.

formal and informal structure the distinction between procedures and communications in an organization which are prescribed by written rules, and those which depend more upon ad hoc, personal interaction within work groups. The contrast between formal and informal structure (or organization) emerged from the debate about Weber's IDEAL TYPE OF BUREAUCRACY within ORGANIZATION THEORY (Compare ORGANIZATIONAL CULTURE). Critiques of Weber's ideal-type focused upon the neglect of informal organization and the ways in which adherence to formal rules can lead to inefficiency and detract from the official goals of an organization. See also GOAL DISPLACEMENT.

The Hawthorne Experiments were a famous example of the study of informal norms and expectations in work groups (see HAWTHORNE EFFECT, HUMAN RELATIONS SCHOOL). Studies in organizational sociology have demonstrated the ways in which informal practices bend or circumvent formal rules. From a functionalist perspective, such practices may be seen as conducive to organizational commitment (Katz, 1968), while other studies (e.g. Beynon, 1973), emphasize the role of informal work groups as forms of resistance and opposition to the aims of management.

The distinction between formal and informal structure has also been elaborated and operationalized as a key structural variable in organizations. The extent of formalization has been measured empirically in comparisons between organizational types (see CONTINGENCY THEORY). This approach differs markedly from the study of rule negotiation and informal organizational cultures (see ETHNOGRAPHY).

formal and substantive rationality the distinction between the *formal rationality* of, say, economic action, as the 'quantitative calculation or accounting which is technically possible and which is actually applied', and *substantive rationality,* which refers to rational social action which occurs 'under some criterion (past, present or potential) of ultimate value' (WEBER, 1922). Weber, although suspicious of the social implications of too narrow an application of the former (see RATIONALIZATION), nevertheless regarded the latter as so 'full of ambiguities' as to render any possibility of its systematization out of the question, since it involves 'an infinite number of possible value scales'. It is in this context that Weber is sometimes regarded as an 'irrationalist'. Other sociologists and philosophers (e.g. see FRANKFURT SCHOOL OF CRITICAL THEORY, HABERMAS) have taken a different view, and argued that contributions to improvements in 'substantive rationality' must be a central focus of sociological effort. See also RATIONALITY, HYPERRATIONALITY.

formally free labour see FREE WAGE LABOUR, CAPITALIST LABOUR CONTRACT.

formal operational stage see PIAGET.

formal organization see FORMAL AND INFORMAL STRUCTURE.

formal sociology a theoretical approach in sociology which focuses attention on the universal recurring social 'forms' which underlie the varying 'content' of social interaction (see FORM AND CONTENT, DYAD AND TRIAD). Georg SIMMEL, whose sociology is most identified with this approach, referred to accounts of these forms as amounting to a 'geometry of social life'. Following KANT, to indicate that these possess an a priori (or 'necessary') character as well as an empirical expression, Simmel presented his 'forms' as *synthetic a priori* concepts. Thus, these concepts are different from either conventional a priori concepts (which are purely 'analytic'), or conventional empirical concepts (which are purely 'synthetic'). Among the social forms and other general concepts discussed by Simmel are 'competition' and 'conflict', SOCIABILITY, and the STRANGER.

While Simmel did not found a 'school' in any strict sense, numerous influences of his formal sociology can be identified, in the work of Von Weise, the CHICAGO SCHOOL, and GOFFMAN. See also CONFLICT THEORY.

formal theory and formalization of theory the rendering of theoretical propositions relating to a particular phenomenon so that they form a set of logically and deductively interrelated propositions, and in which some of these propositions are seen as *axioms* or *premisses,* from which the remainder can be deduced as *theorems.* Zetterberg (1965), for example, sought a *formalization* of Durkheim's *Division of Labour* (1893) in these terms, presenting the following ten propositions:
(a) the greater the division of labour, the greater the consensus;
(b) the greater the solidarity, the greater the number of associates per member;
(c) the greater the number of associates per member, the greater the consensus;
(d) the greater the consensus, the smaller the number of rejections of deviants;
(e) the greater the division of labour, the smaller the number of rejections of deviants;
(f) the greater the number of associates per member, the smaller the number of rejections of deviants;
(g) the greater the division of labour, the greater the solidarity;
(h) the greater the solidarity, the greater the consensus;
(i) the greater the number of associates per member, the greater the division of labour;
(j) the greater the solidarity, the smaller the number of rejections of deviants.

Zetterberg selects propositions (g)–(j) as the axioms from which the remainder can be deduced. While formalizations of this sort can have their uses, particularly in revealing logical weaknesses in the previous non-formal statement of a theory, they are not usually regarded as essential, in science or in sociology.

formative (*or* decision-making) evaluation a policy- or decision-oriented process-based form of assessment or EVALUATION of organisations or activities. This can be carried out before, during or after a project takes place. The information generated is used to inform decisions about the manner and effectiveness in which a project operates. The aim is to improve the on-going operation of a programme or organization, for example by improving systems, sharing 'good practice' and collecting information to assist on-going decision-making. Compare SUMMATIVE EVALUATION.

form and content the distinction drawn, especially by SIMMEL, between the universal, recurring (abstract and A PRIORI) *forms* of social interaction (e.g. 'conflict' or 'competition') and the variable *content* given these forms in specific social situations. FORMAL SOCIOLOGY investigates the similarities of form evident in all areas of social life. See also DYAD AND TRIAD, SOCIABILITY.

forms of life the multiplicity of circumscribed language-embedded social practices which, according to WITTGENSTEIN (1953), characterize social life. The socially-located and conventional character of all languages is emphasized by Wittgenstein. In this interpretation of the nature and limits of language, all 'descriptions' and accounts, and hence all SOCIAL ACTION, are relative to language and to the social contexts in which a particular language is used. In a strict sense, there is nothing that can be said outside the language and context, hence translations are problematic.

One consequence of Wittgenstein's view has been to encourage those forms of philosophy and social science which tend towards a 'relativistic' conception of social studies. It also had a seminal influence on the construction of modern LINGUISTIC PHILOSOPHY, which has emphasized the need for analysis of the many particular uses of language (see also SPEECH ACTS).

In sociology, the concept lends support to the notion that the main task of the discipline should be the MEANINGFUL UNDERSTANDING AND EXPLANATION of the distinctive beliefs and practices of particular societies or social movements (see WINCH), and an 'empathic' understanding of historical societies (compare COLLINGWOOD).

Related to the above, the concept has also been important in arguments for a 'discontinuous' view of scientific change. Thus both KUHN's and FEYERABEND's conception of SCIENTIFIC PARADIGM, and associated conceptions such as INCOMMENSURABILITY, draw explicitly on Wittgenstein's notion of forms of life. One of the best ways of describing what a scientific paradigm involves is that it is a 'form of life'. See also TRUTH, RELATIVISM; compare GADAMER, HERMENEUTICS, FUSION OF HORIZONS.

Foucault, Michel (1926–84) a major figure in the great French philosophical debate on reason, language, knowledge and power, whose work was influenced by MARX, FREUD, NIETZSCHE and BATAILLE and has exerted a massive influence throughout sociology as well as in CULTURAL STUDIES. Although sometimes referred to as a 'structuralist' he usually rejected this label (see STRUCTURALISM, POSTSTRUCTURALISM). He is perhaps best seen as a 'poststructuralist' in the sense that he wished to discover the non-rational scaffolding of 'reason', but without any commitment to either an underlying order or a finally determinant power in the construction. Seeing himself as working in the 'wreckage of history', and enlarging on Nietzsche's linkage of knowledge with power (*power/knowledge*), he sought to locate (see *The Order of Things*, 1966) the 'discursive practices' (DISCOURSE AND DISCOURSE FORMATION; EPISTEME) which at different places and times exert 'power', not least over human bodies, but also increasingly over the 'soul'. Modern medicine, psychiatry and social work and such new professions are all potent examples of contemporary 'disciplinary power'. Although he would not have seen himself as a sociologist, Foucault's historical studies of MADNESS (*Madness and Civilization*, 1962), of medical knowledge, imprisonment (*Discipline and Punish*, 1975) and SEXUALITY (*History of Sexuality*, 1979) have been a major focus of interest for sociologists and have stimulated much debate and research. Foucault challenges directly the Enlightenment idea that knowledge leads straightforwardly to liberation. Instead, knowledge is seen as a subtle basis of new means of social and self/bodily control (see also SURVEILLANCE). Since people are always striving to gain some control over their lives, resistance movements do emerge (see TRANSGRESSION), but there is no guarantee that such movements will not simply spawn new bases of alienating social power. Critics of Foucault have argued that his attack on Reason undermines the 'self' as well as the grounds for any effective social critique. See also ARCHAEOLOGY 2, GENEALOGY, PANOPTICAN, CONFESSIONAL TECHNOLOGIES.

Fourth World those countries, mainly in contemporary Africa and Asia, which are the poorest in the world. The term is used to distinguish certain countries within the usual category of the THIRD WORLD, especially in the light of the economic stagnation of some countries during the 1970s and 1980s. It is a recent term not yet established in general usage.

fractal geometry the geometry of complex topologies/structures. There have suggestions, especially recently, that social reality is inherently 'fractal', its topologies 'bizarre' (see Law, 1999). With modern computers, the presentation of these structures visually has become more accessible.

frame (and frame analysis) the 'basic frameworks of understanding' or 'principles of organization of experience' for making sense of social events (GOFFMAN, 1974). *Frame analysis* refers to 'the examination of this organization of experience' in general and in particular terms (e.g. what makes a joke a joke, or a mistake a mistake), and to the 'vulnerabilities' to which any frame is subject.

frame of reference the basic assumptions delimiting the subject matter of any discipline or approach. For example, PARSONS and Shils (1951) state, 'The frame of reference of the theory of action involves actors, a situation of action, and the orientation of the actor to that situation.'

Frank, Andre Gunder (1929–2005) German-born economist who has held professorial posts in development studies and economics at numerous universities in Latin America, Europe and the US. Whilst by training an economist, deriving some of his key concepts on ECONOMIC SURPLUS from the Marxist political economist Paul Baran, he has been one of the most influential writers within the SOCIOLOGY OF DEVELOPMENT. Frank is best known for his theory of UNDERDEVELOPMENT which had an impact on sociology through his critique, in *Sociology of Development and the Underdevelopment of Sociology* (1967a), of the structural-functionalist theory of development influenced by PARSONS and Almond and Coleman (1960). His best-known substantive work is on Latin America, especially *Capitalism and Underdevelopment in Latin America* (1967b) and the collection of articles in *Latin America: Underdevelopment or Revolution* (1969). In the 1970s and 80s his work was taken up by the WORLD SYSTEM theorists, and Frank himself continued to write on global aspects of capitalism and its effects on THIRD WORLD countries. His later writings, such as *Crisis in the World Economy* (1980), have been less influential in sociology than his earlier works. See also CENTRE AND

PERIPHERY, METROPOLIS-SATELLITE, DEPENDENCY THEORY.

Frankfurt school of critical theory the grouping of left-wing thinkers and a style of radical social theory associated with members of the Frankfurt Institute for Social Research, which was founded in 1922 by Felix Weil, a wealthy political scientist with a strong commitment to Marxist radicalism. During the Nazi era the institute moved to New York, returning to Frankfurt in 1949. It was disbanded in 1969, but its influence continues, notably, recently, in the work of Jürgen HABERMAS. Many leading left-wing theorists were formally associated with the school, including Theodor ADORNO, Walter BENJAMIN, Erich FROMM, Max HORKHEIMER (Director of the Institute 1931–58), and Herbert MARCUSE.

The distinctive approach of the Frankfurt school of critical theory was a brand of neo-Marxist thinking which took issue with both Western POSITIVISM and Marxist SCIENTISM, and was at the same time critical of both Western capitalism and the forms of society created by bolshevik socialism. Among the important contributions made by Frankfurt school theorists have been:

(a) debate on an appropriate non-positivist epistemology for the social sciences;

(b) accounts of the dominant structural and cultural formations of capitalist and socialist societies;

(c) the combination of ideas drawn from MARX and FREUD, resulting in a radicalization of Freudian theory and the provision of Marxism with a fuller theory of personality.

Such features of the work of members of the school were based, above all, on a recovery of the philosophical thinking of the young Marx and a 'revision' of prevailing, 'official', Soviet interpretations of MARXISM which were seen by Frankfurt theorists as economistic and over-determinist.

Despite such shared themes, the work of members of the school does not result in a single unified view. Not only did individual theorists pursue their own distinctive lines of research, but, collectively, members of the school continually shifted the terms of their analysis of modern society in response to the massive political and economic changes that have occurred since the institute's formation, including the rise of fascism and the eclipse of revolutionary movements in the West. At first, institute members expected the transformation of competitive capitalism into monopoly capitalism and fascism to lead directly to socialism. Later, the mood of some members of the school, notably Adorno and Horkheimer, became increasingly pessimistic, portraying the working class as ever more manipulated by the new modes of MASS CULTURE, and as unlikely to develop revolutionary modes of consciousness in the future. Other theorists, especially Marcuse, remained more optimistic, identifying new sources of revolutionary consciousness outside the traditional proletariat, e.g. ethnic minorities and students. Whether pessimistic or optimistic about the prospects of revolution, however, all Frankfurt school theorists can be identified as continuing to explore a shared theme: the perversion of the ideals of Enlightenment rationality by a narrow and dehumanizing 'technical rationality' seen as embodied in both Western capitalist and Soviet Marxist forms of social organization, a technical rationality with which positivistic and scientistic forms of social science must be seen as colluding, and which critical theory must seek to combat. Accessible accounts of the work of the school are provided by M. Jay, *The Dialectical Imagination* (1973) and by D. Held, *Introduction to Critical Theory* (1980).

Frazer, Sir James (1854–1941) UK classicist and anthropologist whose major work is *The Golden Bough* (1890). The orientalist W. Robertson-Smith had suggested that TOTEMISM might be the original religion, on the basis that it was an example of a clan worshipping something other than itself. Frazer expanded this insight into a monumental volume that combined biblical references, classical myth, ETHNOGRAPHY and folklore to illustrate a theory of the development of mystical thought. Like COMTE, he postulated that the most primitive form of thought was MAGIC, followed by RELIGION, with SCIENCE at the apex. The implication that Christianity was descended from totemism had considerable impact on thought at the time. Although his influence on literature and theology has been notable (T. S. Eliot being the best-known example), amongst anthropologists he has come to be regarded with some suspicion for 'armchair theorizing' and for his evolutionary schema.

free market capitalism see COMPETITIVE CAPITALISM.

free rider a person who gains from a collectively provided benefit without bearing any of the costs of gaining this. In a seminal text, M. Olson, *The Logic of Collective Action* (1965) employs the prisoner's dilemma game (see THEORY OF GAMES) to indicate that, where the group is large and any benefits of COLLECTIVE ACTION cannot be withheld from non-participants in the action, it will be 'rational' for individuals to free ride.

free trade economic exchange between states without tariff or other restrictions. This first became a major issue in 18th-century Europe when states were still enforcing *mercantilist* policies through international monopolies of trading arrangements and protection of their economies from goods from outside. Increasingly, pressure came from some countries, and then from industrialists, to withdraw these barriers, thus opening up markets and increasing competition. In the UK, this culminated in the debates over the Corn Laws in the early 19th-century, resulting in the victory of the proponents of free trade.

Behind the movement towards free trade was the economic theory that there would be economic benefit if countries concentrated their economic activities in areas in which they had a *comparative advantage* and could produce more efficiently than others. The counter-argument to this is that free trade benefited, and continues to benefit, the most economically advanced countries. Thus, many countries which industrialized later than Europe and the US instituted import controls to protect their nascent manufacturing industries.

free wage labour the form of labour in which the labourer is politically and legally free, i.e. to sell his or her labour to the highest bidder, and free from constraints on his or her life outside work.

The concept is a central one in both MARX's and WEBER's account of CAPITALISM. In noncapitalist social formations, a labourer is induced, through political, legal, or violent means of social control exercised by the nonproducer, to give up part of what is produced. Under capitalism, in contrast, the economic surplus is extracted by purely economic means, and the labourer is *formally free* to change employers in a way that is often not so in pre-capitalist systems.

For both Marx and Weber, the appearance of free wage labour has many positive features, and is a progressive social force. Both Marx and Weber agree, however, that the freedom involved can sometimes be illusory, since in practice it is often the employer rather than labourer who benefits most from this freedom, in that by hiring and firing labour he obtains greater flexibility in the use of CAPITAL than he would if he had a continuous responsibility for the maintenance of a labour force, as under SLAVERY OF FEUDALISM. Proletarian labour, on the other hand, since it no longer has any rights of ownership over the MEANS OF PRODUCTION, can be in a weak bargaining position (see also CAPITALIST LABOUR CONTRACT).

Whilst all members of the PROLETARIAT are free wage labourers, the reverse is not so, since people may engage in free wage labour but still own their own means of production. This was the case in 17th- and 18th-century Britain where free wage labour emerged on the land, but people were not entirely dependent on wage for their livelihood. A similar situation exists in some THIRD WORLD societies today.

free will the proposition that human beings are able to act according to the dictates of their own will (compare DETERMINISM). Doctrines of free will take a variety of forms, e.g.:
(a) that human beings are morally responsible for their own actions – as in the Protestant world-view;
(b) that they have the capacity to carry out their own projects, and that to behave as if this were not so is to act in 'bad faith' (see EXISTENTIALISM);
(c) that they possess a capacity for REFLEXIVITY which is central to an understanding of both the nature of human action and the social construction of reality, e.g. modern forms of symbolic interactionist and interpretive sociology, which emphasize human AGENCY.

Some forms of structural sociology and behaviouristic psychology appear to leave no room for 'free will', being oriented towards discovering causal explanations of social actions and social structures. However, the identification of actors' reasons and purposes can provide explanations for the 'choices' and 'decisions' they make (as in buying goods, or voting). Thus reasons possess causality, even though wider sociological causation is also involved. 'Causality' in social events therefore need not preclude 'free will' as long as the conception of this is not mystical, i.e. does not imply that human action is exempt from ordinary conceptions of physical and social causality.

Equally, however, there is no necessity to use the term 'free will' in sociology. Most of what can be stated in terms of 'free will' can be perfectly well stated, and is arguably better stated, in terms of 'choice' or 'decision', without recourse to such a potentially misleading term as 'free will'. Examples might be: in drawing a distinction between situations in which we do not feel under compulsion to act in a certain way, and those where we feel that we have little or no choice; or in drawing attention to social outcomes which might have been different if actors who could have acted differently had done so, and those which appear to have been more structurally determined. See also CAUSALITY AND CAUSAL RELATIONSHIPS, STRUCTURE AND AGENCY, VOLUNTARISM, POWER, RATIONAL CHOICE THEORY, METHODOLOGICAL INDIVIDUALISM, UNANTICIPATED CONSEQUENCES OF SOCIAL ACTION.

Freire, Paulo (1921–1997) radical educationalist. His best known work *Pedagogy of the Oppressed* was translated into English in 1972. Freire used learning to facilitate the development of consciousness amongst oppressed and marginalised groups. Though he did not propose a singular set of pedagogical methods to achieve this, the goal of PRAXIS remained constant throughout his work. He believed that effective learning and the development of critical thinking led students to engage with the world around them and the various subjugatory structures that might confront them. Despite the fact that much of Freire's work took place in his native Brazil, and in developing countries, some contemporary Western educationalists have sought to apply his ideas in economically and politically peripheral areas, such as deprived inner city communities (see SOCIAL EXCLUSION). He has influenced adult educators in the non-formal sector in the UK, and his ideas have also informed some of the more radical notions of CITIZENSHIP. Though Freire's work is widely respected, it has been subjected to some criticism, particularly his understanding of oppression. For example, a person may be oppressed in one sphere (e.g. that of work), but may simultaneously be the oppressor in another (e.g. to his wife or family). See also SOCIOLOGY OF EDUCATION and PARTICIPATORY ACTION RESEARCH.

frequency distribution the number of times each value of a variable occurs in a set of observations.

Sex	*Number*	*Relative Frequency*	*Adjusted Frequency*
Male	2,300	56.1%	60.5%
Female	1,500	36.6%	37.5%
Unknown	300	7.3%	–
Total	4,100	100.0%	100.0%

Fig. 10 **Frequency distribution.**

A frequency-distribution table is a simple way of representing sociological observations. It consists of at least two columns: the left-hand one contains the values which a variable may take, and the right-hand one contains the number of times each value occurs. An additional right-hand column can also be included to show the percentage distribution. In Fig. 10 the number of male and female respondents to a questionnaire are shown. See also BAR CHART. HISTOGRAM. PIE CHART, which can also be used to represent distributions.

Freud, Sigmund (1856–1939) the founding father of PSYCHOANALYSIS and one of the most important figures in the development of PSYCHOLOGY as a discipline. His theory of the structure of the PERSONALITY, its development and its dynamics, evolved over the course of his life. He influenced many students and colleagues who often developed aspects of his theory according to their own ideas (see e.g. JUNG). This has meant the growth of several psychoanalytic 'schools' which have taken up rather different positions to his own (see NEOFREUDIANS, OBJECT-RELATIONS SCHOOL).

Freud was responsible for the development of a theory of the mind and for a method of treatment for mental illness. His theory of the mind involves the division of mental experience into the conscious and the UNCONSCIOUS, and the structure of the personality into the ID, EGO and SUPEREGO. He regarded the id as fundamental, containing the inherited biological disposition of the individual, with the ego and superego developing through the formative first five years of life. His theory, therefore, is 'developmental' and describes the process of personality development as part of a process of SOCIALIZATION in which sexuality and gender differentiation play a central role (e.g. see OEDIPUS COMPLEX). This process takes place in stages, and each stage must be worked through satisfactorily for a positive outcome to emerge. If there are problems experienced in the correct resolution of a stage, then personality problems occur and cause adult maladjustments. It is then that psychoanalysis may be necessary to uncover the causes withinthe unconscious, bringing them to consciousness, and so resolving the problem.

Especially in works such as *Civilization and its Discontents,* but dispersed throughout his work, Freud also offers a general psychosocial theory which has been variously taken up within sociology (e.g. MARCUSE's *Eros and Civilization,* 1955).

Elements of Freud's theory have become accepted psychological concepts – the 'unconscious' and the role of early experience in personality development are particularly important – and the widely used method of 'talking therapy' has developed from his original patient/analyst dialogue. Freud's concepts have also been widely influential, and much adapted, in sociology and philosophy; see for example MARCUSE, LACAN, FROMM, CIXOUS.

friendship a relationship between persons well known to each other which involves liking and affection, and may also involve mutual obligations such as loyalty. In contrast to kinship or other ASCRIBED STATUSES, friendship relationships are difficult to specify with precision since they are, above all, characterized by their fluid and voluntary nature and vary greatly in duration and intensity. As stated by Seymour-Smith (1986), 'The study of friendship is part of the study of social networks, of RECIPROCITY, and of relationships created by individuals in the social space which is left undetermined by the system of kin or other obligatory relationships.' From the limited amount of research on friendship in modern societies that has been done, it can be suggested that friendship is a significant factor in personal wellbeing, but that most adults regard themselves as having relatively few close friends (Suttles, 1970). However, there are marked gender differences, women commonly having more close friends than men, and regarding these relationships as more central in their lives. Among children, friendship and relations with peers play an important part in the process of SOCIALIZATION. See also PEER GROUP, INTIMACY, SOCIOMETRICS.

Fromm, Erich (1900–80) German-born radical social psychologist and psychoanalytical theorist, and onetime member of the FRANKFURT SCHOOL OF CRITICAL THEORY, who moved to America in 1934. In his best-known book, *Fear of Freedom* (1941), Fromm argued that human beings often lack the psychological resources to cope with individual freedom, suggesting that the rise of fascism could be, at least in part, explained by a longing for a return to the authoritarianism of pre-individualistic society. The solution proposed by Fromm was spontaneous love: the affirmation of others. In *The Sane Society* (1955), he argued that technological growth without altruism would be socially destructive. Fromm wrote many other works reiterating these, his main themes. See also NEO-FREUDIANS.

front region any social context or public locale in which a specific 'performance' is required of, or produced by, SOCIAL ACTORS, in order to create or preserve a particular impression, e.g. the doctor's surgery or the lecturer's podium. Compare BACK REGION. See also GOFFMAN, DRAMATURGY.

frustration-aggression hypothesis the theory that frustration increases the likelihood of aggressive behaviour, and aggressive behaviour results from frustration. This involves a circular argument, and, in fact, original proponents of the theory also accepted aggression as an innate drive (see FREUD). A modified version of the theory takes account of the observation that not all aggressive behaviour involves frustration and not all frustration results in aggression – behaviour is also affected by situational factors and by SOCIALIZATION. Nevertheless, the link between frustration and aggression is still accepted.

full employment 1 the policy of many governments in the late 1930s and in the immediate postwar period, which was to seek to maintain high levels of employment. In practice this has usually meant a level of employment below that in which all those seeking work are employed.

2 (KEYNESIAN ECONOMICS) the level of employment which a capitalist economy can sustain (e.g. without excessive inflation). KEYNES recognized that the level of unemployment would always be greater than zero, owing to the number of workers changing jobs, some seeking jobs who were unfit for work, etc., but he assumed that, by government management of demand, higher levels of employment could be sustained than in the past.

In fact, the levels of 'full employment' that Keynes believed possible have proved difficult for governments to obtain without leading to inflationary pressures on the economy (see also INFLATION, MONETARISM).

function the consequence for a social system of a social occurrence, where this occurrence is regarded as making an essential contribution to the working and maintenance of this system. See FUNCTIONALISM, STRUCTURAL-FUNCTIONALISM, PARSONS, MERTON, FUNCTIONAL(IST) EXPLANATION, FUNCTIONAL PREREQUISITES, POSTULATE OF FUNCTIONAL INDISPENSABILITY.

A distinction is also made between consequences of social action that are *intended* and recognized by the actors involved, and consequences that are *unintended* and unrecognized by the actors involved. See MANIFEST AND LATENT FUNCTIONS, MERTON, INTENDED AND UNINTENDED CONSEQUENCES OF SOCIAL ACTION.

functional alternative *or* **functional equivalent** any institutional arrangements seen as fulfilling the same FUNCTION, or broadly the same function, in answering the essential needs of a society or social system. Thus, secular CIVIL RELIGIONS (see also SOCIOLOGY OF RELIGION) may perform the same basic functions (e.g. in providing social integration) as conventional religions. The conditions for identification of functional equivalents are controversial, however, and may be difficult to specify (see FUNCTIONAL(IST) EXPLANATION). See also FUNCTIONALISM, FUNCTIONAL PREREQUISITES, POSTULATE OF FUNCTIONAL INDISPENSABILITY OR UNIVERSAL FUNCTIONALISM.

functional imperatives see FUNCTIONAL PREREQUISITES.

functional indispensability see POSTULATE OF FUNCTIONAL INDISPENSABILITY.

functionalism

Theories in sociology and social anthropology which explain social institutions primarily in terms of the FUNCTIONS they perform. To talk of the function of something is to account for a social activity or phenomenon by referring to its consequences for the operation of some other social activity, institution, or society as a whole. Modern functionalists treat societies as SYSTEMS of interacting, and self-regulating, parts.

In the 19th century, social thinkers theorized about society in terms of an *organic analogy.* As Herbert SPENCER wrote: 'All kinds of creatures are alike in so far as each exhibits cooperation among its components for the benefit of the whole; and this trait, common to them, is a trait common also to societies'. The idea of studying social life in terms of social functions was also central in early 20th-century British SOCIAL ANTHROPOLOGY. Both RADCLIFFE-BROWN and MALINOWSKI used the concept of function suggesting that society could be conceptualized as made up of *interdependent parts* that operate together to meet different social *needs.*

In the 1950s and early 1960s, 'structural-functionalism' was the dominant theoretical perspective in North American sociology. In the 1950s, the functionalist approach was associated especially with a form of SYSTEMS THEORY (see also STRUCTURAL-FUNCTIONALISM), articulated by Talcott PARSONS at Harvard University. Parsons' theories were widely influential, though there was critical dissent from other functionalists (see MERTON) and from non-functionalists (e.g. MILLS). In the 1970s and

1980s, functionalism's star waned, partly as a result of internal theoretical weaknesses, but also from changes in the political climate (see also GOULDNER).

One central area of debate has concerned the nature of FUNCTIONAL(IST) EXPLANATION. A further major area of debate has concerned its treatment of social order, social conflict and social change. One criticism is that the functionalist perspective neglects the independent 'agency' of individual social actors, in general tending to operate with an 'oversocialized conception' of the human subject (see OVER-SOCIALIZED CONCEPTION OF MAN), e.g. treating people as 'cultural dopes' (see ETHNOMETHODOLOGY). Social ROLES are seen as essentially prescribed by NORMS and static expectations of behaviour, rather than actively 'taken' and recreated through *interaction* with others (compare SYMBOLIC INTERACTIONISM). It has also often been suggested that a functionalist perspective has difficulty in accounting for social conflict and instability.

All of these criticisms of functionalism have some substance, but are also an overstatement. Parsons in particular sought to combine an 'action frame of reference' with an emphasis on system and social functions. And, while often concentrating on the conditions of 'social order' (including the functions of SOCIAL CONFLICT), both historically (e.g. as for Spencer) as well as in Parsons' later work, functionalism has usually also sought to combine the analysis of social order with an EVOLUTIONARY THEORY of social change: a model of increasing SOCIAL DIFFERENTIATION, of increasing functional adaption of society (see also EVOLUTIONARY SOCIOLOGY, EVOLUTIONARY UNIVERSALS). These models of social change have in turn been widely criticized (e.g. see MODERNIZATION, DEPENDENCY THEORY) but their existence shows that it is as a *particular* model of change, rather than a theory which neglects change, that functionalism must be discussed.

Despite the many criticisms, both the term 'function' and the functionalist perspective retain widespread significance in sociology, for they involve a concern with the crucial issue of the interrelationship of parts to wholes in human society and the relationship between SOCIAL STRUCTURE and human AGENCY, as well as issues of social order and social change.

functional(ist) explanation EXPLANATION of the persistence of any feature of a SOCIETY or SOCIAL SYSTEM (and at the same time an explanation for the persistence of the society or social system itself) in which this feature, usually along with others, is seen as making an essential contribution to the maintenance of the society or social system. Thus, perversely, according to some commentators, an aspect of the functionalist explanation is that the consequences of an activity are in part an explanation of its own existence.

Often functional(ist) explanation involves a recourse to *organic analogies,* in which societies or social systems are seen as akin to biological organisms in which specified organs can be identified which fulfil specific system 'needs'. For example, just as the function of the heart is to circulate the blood, the indispensable function of government may be suggested as establishing and implementing 'policies for society' (see also FUNCTIONAL PREREQUISITES, EVOLUTIONARY SOCIOLOGY). Alternatively, analogies with servo-mechanical systems may be proposed (see also SYSTEM, SYSTEMS THEORY, CYBERNETICS).

According to Hempel (1959), in so far as it proves an adequate basis for explanation, functional(ist) explanation can be a form of deductive nomological explanation (see COVERING-LAW MODEL AND DEDUCTIVE NOMOLOGICAL EXPLANATION), possessing the following characteristics (where 'i' stands for any item or trait, within a system 's' at a time 't', and where 'c' stands for the 'conditions' or 'setting' in which the system operates):

(a) at a time t, s functions adequately in a setting of kind c, characterized by specific internal and external conditions (statement of initial conditions);
(b) s functions adequately in a setting of kind c only if a certain necessary condition, n, is satisfied (law);
(c) if trait i were present in s then, as an effect, condition n would be satisfied (law);
(d) (hence) at a time t, trait i is present in s (the EXPLANANDUM).

Criticisms of proposed examples of functional explanation are made by Hempel and others on a number of grounds:

(a) that human societies and social systems are different from biological organisms in that they lack precise boundaries, change in form over time, do not exist as clearly demarcated species, are not born and do not die in the clear-cut way in which biological organisms do, and thus do not have clear-cut 'needs' or 'functional requirements' or clearly identified organs fulfilling these. Thus, a major problem exists in specifying the conditions for the 'survival', 'efficiency', 'adjustment', 'adaptation', etc., of social systems in general, or of types of social system;
(b) that no one has yet provided an adequate overall functionalist (and evolutionary) account of human societies which identifies the 'units selected' (compare NATURAL SELECTION, GENETICS) or confirms that institutions have in fact evolved on the basis of such units;
(c) that even if broad 'functional needs' can be identified, any number of different items or traits may fulfil the required functions, e.g. a system of social welfare in modern societies may be provided by the state, by private insurance, or by political parties or criminal organizations, or any mixture of these (see FUNCTIONAL ALTERNATIVES, MERTON. POSTULATE OF FUNCTIONAL INDISPENSABILITY);
(d) that even if it might explain the persistence of a system trait or institution (e.g. in terms of its present contribution), functional explanation is no substitute for a historical causal explanation of how an institutional arrangement came into existence, especially so where 'evolutionary accounts' are not seen as providing an adequate account;
(e) given the problems outlined in (a), (b) and (c) (and also that human social systems are 'open' systems), functional explanation adds nothing to causal or purposive explanations (see Fig. 11) (GIDDENS, 1976).

In particular, the argument can be made against functional explanation, that would-be functional explanations for the persistence of institutions in sociology fail to identify mechanisms which link the suggested functional need with the appearance of its claimed consequences (see also SOCIAL REPRODUCTION). Thus, taking this all into account, for GIDDENS, a so-called 'latent function', such as that of the Hopi rain dance in providing social integration and a 'unitary value system' for a small society, can be perfectly well restated without loss, as *simply* an 'unintended' outcome. We only mystify the phenomenon by suggesting that 'functional needs' account for this. In such circumstances the concept of function is redundant. We may use the term 'function' to refer to the intended purpose of a machine, etc., e.g. the function of the 'ballcock' is to regulate the quantity of water supplied to a water closet.

Functional(ist) explanation

social activities

functional consequence

functional needs

(a)

Purposive explanation

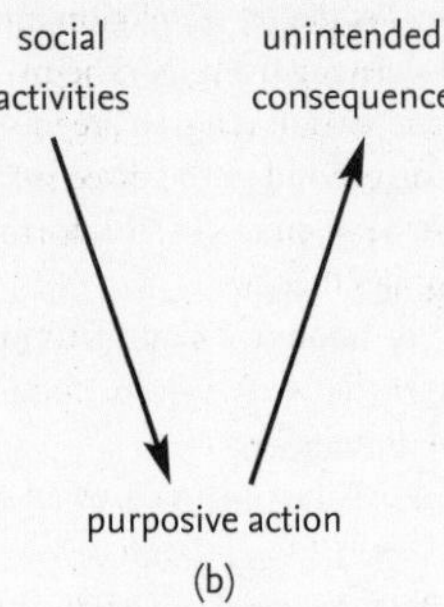

(b)

Fig. 11 **Functional(ist) explanation.** In contrast with other kinds of explanation, e.g. purposive explanation (b) functional explanation (a) explains the occurrence of a phenomenon in terms of the functional needs of a system. One argument against functional explanation is that where the 'mechanisms' of the system in question remain unclear, reference to 'system needs' adds nothing to purposive explanations and will mislead. Unintended consequences may still be acknowledged, but not system needs.

In the same way, the 'functions' of a political party, where intended functions are involved, may also be quite properly referred to. But reference to latent functions or to system needs in other terms than with reference to intentions, as in 'functional explanation' of the above type, remains obscure;

(f) that, in general, one may always 'define' a particular institution or trait as 'essential' to a particular system, but this risks becoming a 'tautology', and merely 'descriptive' rather than explanatory, unless some further independent reasons can be given for regarding the relations between the system and the institutions identified as functionally significant.

Notwithstanding such criticisms, and whatever the problems of functional explanation, functional analysis remains a common feature of sociological accounts. The notion that particular societies or social systems have particular *requirements* seems inescapable in sociological analysis (compare Davis, 1948), even if these cannot always be precisely specified. Whether or not these requirements should be called 'functional' requirements, risking misleading biological analogies, would seem to be the issue.

functional(ist) theory of religion

theoretical accounts of RELIGION which explain its origins, and also its continuation, in terms of the contribution it makes to society (see also FUNCTION, FUNCTIONAL(IST) EXPLANATION). The most influential of these theories by far is DURKHEIM's, and his ideas were further explored by RADCLIFFE-BROWN. MALINOWSKI's theory is also functionalist, and in many ways a broadly functionalist account of religion – albeit with marked variations, in emphasis – is behind many of the mainstream sociological accounts of religion on offer. If 'function' is used in a general sense, functional(ist) theories of religion extend from COMTE and the earlier evolutionary sociologists to modern functionalism, and even include Marxism. Though regarding it as eventually dispensable, MARX saw religion as 'the opiate of the proletariat', in that it performs social and individual functions.

In its modern form, the functional(ist) theory of religion has two strands: within modern structural-functionalism, and within structuralist theories. There also exist numerous theories and empirical accounts which are presented as counter-theories.

In modern structural-functionalism (especially in the work of PARSONS, the functionalist theory of religion most directly deriving from Durkheim) three main functions of religion are identified, which correspond to the three MODES OF MOTIVATIONAL ORIENTATION formulated in Parsonian theory:

(a) the provision of a central, ultimately unifying, belief system – the 'cognitive' function of religion;

(b) the provision of ceremony and RITUAL, seen as possessing a central role in fostering social solidarity – the 'affective' dimension of religion;

(c) the enunciation of ethical principles, and along with this the bolstering of ethical values by positive and negative sanctions – the 'evaluative' aspect of religion;

All of these contribute to the 'essential' role religion is seen as playing in the maintenance of social solidarity (compare Durkheim's similar emphasis – see CIVIL RELIGION). Durkheim's notion that religious beliefs are direct representations of society, however, is dropped.

Structuralist theories of religion have also built upon Durkheim's functionalism, but in a different way from structural-functionalism. In these, it is the 'sociology of knowledge' aspect of Durkheim's theory, played down by structural-functionalists, which remains more central, e.g. accounts of the part played by MYTHOLOGIES in the organization of social activities (see LÉVI-STRAUSS).

A counterbalance to either functionalist or structuralist theories, with their emphasis on general outcomes, exists in the many empirical studies of religion which explore the effects of religion in a more ad hoc way, i.e. are not tied to any one set of general assumptions.

As a relatively loose general framework involving accounts of the contribution made by religion to society, functionalism retains a wide currency, especially its general injunction to look for 'latent' function (see MANIFEST AND LATENT FUNCTIONS) and UNANTICIPATED CONSEQUENCES OF SOCIAL ACTION. The fact that religion divides as well as unites is *not* necessarily a problem, for this can be accommodated within functionalist theory, since it is the provision of social solidarity by religion that both unites and divides societies. Rather, the main problem is in achieving a *precise* meaning when claiming that religion fulfils 'functional needs'. Once one begins to talk of 'FUNCTIONAL ALTERNATIVES' for conventional religion (e.g. 'civil religion' or modern international sport), a functionalist account tends to lose out in arguments involving its most central claim, that religion provides for *universal* human needs which only religion can answer.

functional(ist) theory of social stratification an account of the origins and persistence of SOCIAL STRATIFICATION in terms of the contribution this makes to human societies. The theory is provided by modern US functionalist sociologists, especially Davis and Moore (1945). For Davis and Moore, social stratification comes into existence as an institutionalized form and persists as the 'device by which societies ensure that the most important positions' are 'filled by the most qualified persons'. The positions which carry the greatest rewards and the highest rank are those 'which have the greatest importance for society' and also require the 'greatest training or talent'. Together, these two factors interact to determine the precise form of any particular system of stratification. As societies evolve so do their specific requirements of a system of social stratification (e.g. from priests to specialists in high tech), but new requirements do not result in the elimination of social stratification.

Critics of the functional(ist) theory make a number of main points (especially see Tumin, 1953):

(a) it provides no adequate discussion of the way in which differences in rewards and status arise simply from the operation of POWER. Regarding the correlation between income and education, for example, there are three components which might explain this correlation: (i) superiority in skills, (ii) social background and/or social values, (iii) native abilities.

The first of these might conceivably also incorporate the other two, but only if labour markets are fully competitive. The argument against the functionalist theory is that usually labour markets are not fully competitive, with factors such as 'ascription' and CULTURAL CAPITAL often playing a role in the determination of incomes and status;
(b) the assessment of 'functional needs' is also suspect, tending to involve a circular argument that the best rewarded in society are also the most important/scarcest in supply, with. no clear independent demonstration of their social indispensability;
(c) no indication is given of why stratification *must* involve differential financial rewards or steep hierarchies of status, rather than more variegated differences in individual prestige, since Davis and Moore themselves suggest that 'humour and diversion' and 'self-respect and ego expansion' may alone serve to motivate social actors. Thus, the case against the possibility of a far more equal society has not been made by the functional(ist) theory (see also EQUALITY);
(d) no adequate account is taken of the way in which social stratification inhibits participation in education and the achievement of social ends. Davis and Moore do suggest the functional inappropriateness of too great an emphasis on ascription in modern societies. However, they fail to discuss how all systems of social stratification tend to generate such ascriptive elements.

Functionalists seek to reply to such criticisms by arguing, as did DURKHEIM, that anything that becomes established in society is likely to perform essential functions. However, as Durkheim agreed (especially in relation to particular types of society, when the evolution of that societal type is incomplete), an independent argument for functional importance is essential. The argument against the functionalist theory of social structure is that such an independent case has not been forthcoming.

The message is not so much that functional analysis of social stratification is, in principle, impossible, but that this needs to be handled with greater caution. See also FUNCTIONAL(IST) EXPLANATION.

functional prerequisites the provisions that all societies are required to make in order for any society to come into existence or to survive. The identification of functional prerequisites – also known as *functional imperatives* – is controversial.

As formulated by Aberle et al. (1950) – who first defined 'society' as 'a group of human beings sharing a self-sufficient system of action which is capable of existing longer than the life span of an individual, the group being recruited at least in part by sexual reproduction of the members' – nine functional prerequisites can be identified:
(a) 'provision for adequate relationship to the environment and for sexual recruitment';
(b) 'role differentiation and role assignment';
(c) 'communication';
(d) 'shared cognitive organization';
(e) 'a shared articulation of goals';
(f) 'the normative regulation of means';
(g) 'the regulation of affective expression';
(h) 'socialization';
(i) 'effective control of disruptive forms of behaviour'.

A rather different formulation of functional prerequisites is the four-fold set of functional 'problems' identified by PARSONS (1983) (see SUBSYSTEMS MODEL).

Apart from the functionalist bias towards 'normative integration' in all such proposals of functional prerequisites (see OVERSOCIALIZED CONCEPTION OF MAN), a general problem is in reaching agreement on the exact number and detailed specification of prerequisites. GIDDENS (1976b), for example, points out that Aberle et al.'s identification of 'functional prerequisites' involve either 'tautologies' and simply follow logically from these authors' initial definition of society, or else they involve assumptions about 'adaptive capacity' which are contentious and are arguably misplaced in sociology.

Compare also EVOLUTIONARY UNIVERSALS.

Further Education (FE) in England the sector of post-compulsory education now supported by the Further Education Funding Council (FEFC) but excluding HIGHER EDUCATION, sixth form colleges and INDEPENDENT SECTOR providers. Teaching is at a range of levels, including unaccredited courses, basic skills and level 1, 2 and 3 qualifications; and includes vocational, work-based, academic and leisure learning. The blurring of boundaries between FE and HE, particularly as result of the Further and Higher Education Act 1992, has resulted in some FE colleges providing HE courses. The latter reflects the move to MASS HIGHER EDUCATION.

fusion of horizons the merging of perspectives which in HERMENEUTICS is seen as an essential feature of the understanding of an unfamiliar TEXT or culture (GADAMER, 1960). For Gadamer, such 'understanding is not a matter of forgetting our own horizons of meanings and putting ourselves within that of the alien text or the alien society' (Outhwaite, 1985) and therefore not a matter of 'detachment'; instead, it involves a '*rapprochement* between our present world ... and the different world we seek to appraise'.

The concept stands opposed to two ideas: (a) that we can expect to understand and explain alien cultures and societies by imposing an external 'grid'; and (b) that we can never hope to understand (or translate) such ideas. Rather 'truth' can be the outcome of such a fusion.

The idea of INTERSUBJECTIVITY as the basis of scientific knowledge or political agreements has a similar basis (compare FEYERABEND, HABERMAS), although the fusion of horizons for Gadamer is far from being the basis for 'emancipatory knowledge' it is for Habermas. However, the similarity indicates that Gadamer's hermeneutics does not necessarily involve the degree of RELATIVISM sometimes suggested.

future shock (by analogy with the term CULTURE SHOCK) the shock provided by the 'perception' of future possibilities in a world that is changing at an ever-increasing rate and in a way that disrupts people's perspectives and tends to bring confusion. The term was coined by Alvin Toffler (1970).

futurology **1** the purported science of prognosis (Flechtheim, 1965).
2 any attempt to undertake long-term, large-scale social and economic FORECASTING. Rather than being defined as a separate science, efforts to illuminate the future are better seen as one aspect of the numerous individual social sciences, with sociology often playing a central role.

As indicated by Daniel BELL (1965, 1973), the varieties of social-science activity that can be involved in statements about the future must be carefully distinguished. They include:
(a) academically grounded general speculation;
(b) the simple extrapolation of existing trends or tendencies, or probability generalizations, based on the existing behaviour of known populations or natural phenomena;
(c) theoretical general models of the kind associated with Marxism, and developmental social-evolutionary theories of various kinds, including models of exponential growth;
(d) the 'prediction' of specific events.

As suggested by POPPER, the distinction must be drawn between 'prophecy' (e.g. claims to predict the future made by 'vulgar' versions of Marxism or evolutionary theory) and 'scientific prediction', which is always a matter of universal conditional statements and 'if, then' in form (see also HISTORICISM). Apart from our knowledge of what Bell refers to as 'structural certainties' (e.g. the date of the next US presidential election), exact prediction is rare in the social sciences, given the complexity of the variables involved, including human choice, the fact that most social systems are 'open systems'. The various attempts to chart future possibilities remain valuable, however, as long as the limitations and caveats which must attach to them are not ignored. See also SELF-FULFILLING AND SELF-DESTROYING PROPHECY.

g

Gadamer, Hans Georg (1900–) German social philosopher and major proponent of phenomenological HERMENEUTICS. His major work is *Truth and Method* (1960). Drawing on EXISTENTIALISM (HEIDEGGER in particular) and the work of DILTHEY he argues that any engagement with the unfamiliar involves a negotiation of our prejudices. These 'prejudgings' cannot simply be overcome with rhetoric about objectivity. Instead, he advocates that a search for scientific truth should be abandoned in favour of a sensitive investigation of our own responses to that which is strange to us. This involves a mediation of past and present, and inevitably reflects the way that the interpreter (re)constructs history. In order to achieve a FUSION OF HORIZONS with the 'other', we must enter the *hermeneutic circle* in which the text can only be understood as a manifestation of a world view, and a world view as the synthesis of a number of such texts. Gadamer has been criticized by many for his RELATIVISM, and by HABERMAS for his neglect of power in language, but he remains a key influence on sociological EPISTEMOLOGY.

Gaia hypothesis an hypothesis developed by the British scientist, James Lovelock, to suggest that the earth is one living system, such that the distinction between organic and inorganic matter is false. Gaia was an ancient Greek goddess of the earth and fertility. Contrary to established scientific notions, Lovelock argues that a conducive physical environment did not first exist within which living organisms could develop, but rather the living organisms create the necessary physical environment for their survival. This leads to the concept of the planet earth as a CYBERNETIC system. In the late 1980s, the Gaia movement emerged as one of the environmental groups increasingly influential in national and international politics.

Galbraith, John K. (1908–) Canadian-born US economist, social commentator, author of best-selling books and popular broadcaster, whose analysis of modern capitalist society is at once a critique of modern society and of orthodox academic economics. Galbraith's approach places him in the tradition of institutional economics, an approach which emphasizes the study of the real world and historical economic institutions, rather than the creation of abstract economic models, as the best route to an understanding of economic life. Not surprisingly, the significance of his work has not always been accepted by more orthodox economists.

Among his most influential works was *The Affluent Society* (1958). In this, he took the view that modern industrial societies such as America had moved beyond economic scarcity, but had failed to adjust their economic theory or their economic practice to allow adequate resources to be devoted to public expenditure. Alongside the existence of 'private affluence', Galbraith saw 'public squalor'.

Earlier, in *American Capitalism* (1952), Galbraith had advanced a conception of the modern American economy as governed by 'countervailing forces', meaning that America was neither a conventional market-driven capitalist economy nor a system directly subject to public control. This same general theme was carried forward in *The New Industrial State* (1967), in which Galbraith identified power in America as being in the hands of a new TECHNOSTRUCTURE.

Galbraith's ideas contributed to the climate in which public expenditure increased in the 1960s and 70s. It might appear that, in the 1980s, his work has become outmoded by the shift back to a market economy and new restrictions on public expenditure. Alternatively, his work can be seen as providing a continuing critique of restrictions on public expenditure.

Gallup, George (1901–84) US social researcher and pioneer in the development and application of modern SAMPLE survey techniques in the study of political attitudes and public opinion. So much is Gallup associated with the development of this mode of research, that this form of SOCIAL SURVEY is now often referred to as the *Gallup poll.* Gallup was among the first to show that an accurate gauging of voting intention and political 'opinions' was possible by the study of REPRESENTATIVE SAMPLES of the electorate. Gallup believed that the use of his technique made governments and political parties more democratically responsive. Equally, however, the many commercially-run polling agencies that now sample political attitudes in countries across the world also provide governments with a useful tool in the advantageous timing of elections.

Gallup poll see GALLUP.

gambling the staking of money on the outcome of games or events involving chance or skill. Although in most modern societies gambling is legal (and indeed often a major source of state revenue), religious and moral prohibitions still exert some degree of constraint. For a minority of people gambling can become a form of addictive behaviour; for most people, however, it involves a limited and controlled outlay, and may serve important social functions in addition to the chance for material gain (e.g. bingo). Even serious gamblers are usually disciplined rather than compulsive, planning expenditure, limiting losses and husbanding any winnings (D. Downes et al., *Gambling Work and Lesiure,* 1976).

In a wider sense, much conventional, 'speculative', economic activity also involves elements of gambling – e.g. on stocks and shares.

game theory see THEORY OF GAMES.

gangs relatively closed groups of (usually) working-class youth, with identifiable leadership roles, and often associated with particular territories and deviant activity. The first sociological work on gangs was influenced by the interactionist perspective developed by the CHICAGO SCHOOL. Subsequent classic studies (e.g. Cohen, 1955; Whyte, 1955) continued to employ this perspective, examining the way in which individuals were socialized into the SUBCULTURE of the group, the nature of the value system which this represented, and its function for individual members. More recently, sociological research has examined the MORAL PANICS created by gangs of MODS AND ROCKERS (Cohen, 1973) and by FOOTBALL HOOLIGANISM (Taylor, 1971; Marsh et al., 1978; Dunning et al., 1988). Most of the classic studies of gangs have been concerned with white working-class youth, indicating the need for further empirical work in the area of race, ethnicity and gender. See also CRIMINOLOGY, DELINQUENCY, DELINQUENT SUBCULTURE, LABELLING THEORY, FOLK DEVILS, DEVIANCE AMPLIFICATION, RESISTANCE THROUGH RITUAL.

Garfinkel, Harold (1917–) US sociologist and founder of the theoretical and specialist approach of ETHNOMETHODOLOGY.

Influenced especially by SCHUTZ, Garfinkel's contention in *Studies in Ethnomethodology* (1967) is that conventional sociology has neglected the study of the ethnomethods (*members' methods*) possessed by ordinary members of society and used by them in the ordinary conduct of their social lives. Garfinkel claimed to have revealed the existence of these methods by noting the outcome of informal experiments in which, for example, he encouraged his students to act as lodgers in their own homes. According to Garfinkel, what these and similar experiments demonstrate is the existence of the 'taken-for-granted assumptions' in social interaction and also the indexicality (see INDEXICAL EXPRESSION) of members' ACCOUNTS. Along with the member's creative capacity, this latter feature of members' accounts is seen as invalidating the scientific stance of much conventional sociology. See also DEGRADATION CEREMONY, ET CETERA PRINCIPLE.

garrison state Harold Lasswell's (1941) term for a form of state and society, regarded by him as incipient in the US, in which huge military expenditures and a military siege mentality become associated with restrictions on liberties. See also MILITARY-INDUSTRIAL COMPLEX, MILITARISM.

gatekeepers the individuals or groups in an organization who regulate either access to goods and services (in the case of social welfare provision), or the flow of information (in the case of politics or the news media). See also TWO-STEP FLOW OF MASS COMMUNICATIONS.

gatherings any situations, those 'strips' of time and space, in which SOCIAL ACTORS come together in face-to-face interaction (GOFFMAN, 1963). In moving into, or initiating, such contexts of copresence, social actors make themselves 'available', a process which involves the mutual monitoring of one another's actions. Gatherings may be either fleeting, including the polite discourse of routine greetings, or longer-lasting, in which the paraphernalia in which they are located may be planned and regularized, e.g. the fixed timing and formal arrangement of tables and chairs in a seminar. But all gatherings, however trivial they may seem, are implicated in larger social structures and, in turn, have implications for these social structures.

gaze the 'look', or viewpoint, inherent in particular cultural products. The concept originated in an article, 'Visual pleasure and narrative cinema' (Mulvey, 1975), which appeared in the critical film journal, *Screen*. Mulvey suggested that since most films are made by males, the 'gaze' of films is usually to objectify women – voyeuristically and stereotypically – from the point of view of the male spectator. Subsequently, the term has been used in related ways, for example, to refer more widely to the FEMALE GAZE.

Geisteswissenschaften* and *Naturwissenschaften (German) general terms to refer to the human and social sciences (the sciences of the spirit) and the natural or physical sciences. The. German usage, especially by DILTHEY, seems to have derived in part from a translation of John Stuart MILL's distinction between the 'moral' and the physical sciences. The distinction is now mainly associated with the view that the human and social sciences, since they deal with human meanings and purposes, must be constituted and must operate using different methods than those appropriate to the physical sciences (see MEANINGFUL UNDERSTANDING AND EXPLANATION, VERSTEHEN, HERMENEUTICS, RICKERT, WINDELBAND, WEBER).

Gellner, Ernest (1925–95), Czech-born, English social theorist, social philosopher and social anthropologist whose wide-ranging, often iconoclastic, writings included critical discussion of analytical philosophy (*Words and Things*, 1959), ethnographic studies (*The Saints of the Atlas*, 1969), studies of psychoanalysis (*The Psychoanalytic Movement*, 1985), of nationalism (*Nations and Nationalism*, 1983), of Soviet thought (*State and Society in Soviet Thought*, 1988), as well as general studies of social change and historical development (*Plough, Sword and Book*, 1988), and, in addition, numerous articles and books on methodological topics (e.g. *Relativism in the Social Sciences,* 1985). Running through all of these works is a persistent defence of rationalism, in which changes in knowledge are seen as decisive in social change. Gellner was especially impatient with approaches within the social sciences deriving from WITTGENSTEIN's second philosophy, which he presents as a 'new idealism' (Gellner, 1974). See also WINCH, EPISODIC CHARACTERIZATION, WORLD GROWTH STORY.

Gemeinschaft* and *Gesellschaft the German sociologist TÖNNIES' (1887) twin IDEAL-TYPE concepts referring to contrasting types of social relationship and, by extension, types of society. *Gemeinschaft* (usually translated as 'community') refers to relationships which are spontaneous and 'affective', tend to be related to a person's overall social status, are repeated or long-enduring (as in relationships with kin), and occur in a context involving cultural homogeneity. Characteristically, these are the relationships within families and within simpler, small-scale and premodern societies, including peasant societies. *Gesellschaft* (usually translated as 'association') refers to relationships which are individualistic, impersonal, competitive, calculative and contractual, often employing explicit conceptions of rationality and efficiency. Relationships of this type are characteristic of modern urban industrial societies in which the DIVISION OF LABOUR is advanced. For Tönnies, such relationships involved a loss of the naturalness and mutuality of earlier *Gemeinschaft* relationships. See also COMMUNITY.

Tönnies derived aspects of his concept from Henry MAINE's distinction between status and contract. Compare also Max Weber's TYPES OF SOCIAL ACTION, Talcott Parsons' PATTERN VARIABLES and Emile Durkheim's MECHANICAL AND ORGANIC SOLIDARITY. See also Herbert Spencer (MILITANT AND INDUSTRIAL SOCIETY) and Robert Redfield (RURAL-URBAN CONTINUUM).

gender

1 (common usage) the distinction between males and females according to anatomical sex.

2 (sociological usage) a social division frequently based on, but not necessarily coincidental with, anatomical sex. Thus, sociological usage of the term gender can be at odds with everyday usage.

Sociologists and social psychologists argue that while sex refers to the biological characteristics by which human beings are categorized as 'male', 'female', or in rare instances 'hermaphrodite' (in which the biological characteristics of both sexes are actually or apparently combined), gender refers to the social and social-psychological attributes by which human beings are categorized as 'masculine', 'feminine' or 'androgynous' (in which the social-psychological characteristics of both genders are intentionally or unintentionally combined). Many sociologists stress that within sociological discourse gender should be used when referring to the socially-created division of society into those who are masculine and those who are feminine. Whereas 'male' and 'female' are terms reserved for biological differences between men and women and boys and girls, 'masculine' and 'feminine' are reserved for culturally-imposed behavioural and temperamental traits deemed socially appropriate to the sexes. These traits are learnt via a complex and continuing process of SOCIALIZATION.

Anthropologists (e.g. Margaret MEAD) and psychologists, as well as sociologists, have stressed that gender is not biologically determined but socially and culturally defined. Gender is seen as culturally and historically relative, i.e. the meaning, interpretation and expression of gender varies both within and between cultures, and is subject to historical modification. Social factors such as class, age, race and ethnicity also shape the specific meaning, expression and experience of gender, underlining the fact that gender cannot be equated in any simplistic way with sex or SEXUALITY. See FEMINIST THEORY.

gender differentiation the process in which biological differences between males and females are assigned social significance and are used as a means of social classification. In most known cultures, anatomical sex is used as a basis for GENDER differentiation. In some cultures, the biological differences between sexes may be exaggerated and in others minimized. Thus, the biological differences between the sexes cannot be regarded as having inherent or universal meaning.

gender identity the sense of self associated with cultural definitions of masculinity and femininity (see GENDER). Gender identity is not so much acted out as subjectively experienced. It is the psychological internalization of masculine or feminine traits. Gender identity arises out of a complex process of interaction between self and others. The existence of transvestite and transsexual identities indicates that gender is not dependent upon sex alone, and arises from the construction of gender identities.

gender ideology a system of ideas whereby GENDER differences and GENDER STRATIFICATION receive social justification, including justification in terms of 'natural' differences or supernatural beliefs. As Oakley (1974) has argued, sociologists have sometimes tended to reproduce the 'common-sense' ideologies surrounding gender differences in an uncritical way.

gender role the social expectations arising from conceptions surrounding GENDER and the behavioural expression of these, including forms of speech, mannerisms, demeanour, dress and gesture (see also GENDER IDENTITY). Masculine and feminine ideas are often deemed to be mutually exclusive, and in some societies the role behaviours may be polarized, e.g. the equation of passivity with the feminine role, and activity with the masculine role. Prescriptions concerning gender role behaviour are particularly apparent in the sexual division of labour in male and female work situations (see also DUAL LABOUR MARKET).

gender stratification any process by which gender becomes the basis of SOCIAL STRATIFICATION, in which the perceived differences between the genders become ranked and evaluated in a systematic way. Stratification by gender was often rendered invisible, or misrepresented, by earlier sociologists. Frequently, gender stratification has been subsumed under social class or ethnicity. The importance of gender as a system of stratification, particularly as a system in which feminized persons are ranked and rewarded below masculinized persons, has been mainly stressed by sociologists influenced by feminism (see FEMINISM, FEMINIST THEORY). Feminist sociologists, for example, have employed the concept of PATRIARCHY in conceptualizing and analysing the present and historical oppression of women.

genealogy 1 the tracing of DESCENT relationships. These accounts are important in societies with LINEAGE systems, where it is common for the older members of the society to be the genealogical experts. Anthropologists have demonstrated that it is not necessary for the version of ancestry to be biologically correct – it may include reference to mythical beings or animals. Attention has also been paid to the possibility of strategic manipulation of genealogy to reflect current political interests.

2 (FOUCAULT's account of his preferred method) the historical reconstruction of how we have become what we are which acts as an immanent critique of what we are and is directed against the practical achievement of human autonomy (D. Owen, *Maturity and Modernity,* 1994). This approach to the study and interpretation of history was first proposed by NIETZSCHE and a crucial aspect of the work of both Nietzsche and Foucault is a questioning of the view that historical processes are mono-causal, linear and necessarily progressive. In *On the Genealogy of Morals* (1887), Nietzsche criticizes (and rejects) the notion that history is underscored by gradual ethical advancements by claiming that ideas of morality are the products of contestation and struggle. These struggles tend not to be recorded by the victors, however, as this would reveal the finite nature of that particular value system. With regard to the dominant Christian values of the West Nietzche attempts to uncover the historical processes which surrounded their emergence in order to show that they are neither eternal nor transcendental and can thus be criticized and supplanted. Foucault's genealogical approach applies this form of critique to other beliefs and tries to show that although modern values are often informed by extensive bodies of knowledge they are not less historical, finite or fragile that those of traditional religion. Much of his work focuses on the status of scientific knowledge, particularly that of the human sciences. The 'truths' that the disciplines in these latter fields (e.g. anthropology, psychology) claim to have discovered are questioned by investigating their respective pasts and showing that they are underpinned by unscientific irrational and partial assumptions. See DISCOURSE, EPISTMOLOGY, POSTSTRUCTURALISM.

General Household Survey (GHS) a multipurpose UK government SOCIAL SURVEY designed to be used by all government departments, and which also provides an invaluable source of SECONDARY DATA for the social scientist. It was started in 1971 under the auspices of the Office of Population Censuses and Surveys. It is a continuous survey and is therefore useful for filling in the time gaps between other surveys, such as the CENSUS, and for identifying trends. Five main areas of investigation are included: family data, housing, education, employment and health. Although most of the information collected is factual, some attitudinal data are also collected, such as information on job satisfaction and attitudes to pay (which have been collected since 1974). See also OFFICIAL STATISTICS, STATISTICS AND STATISTICAL ANALYSIS, FAMILY EXPENDITURE SURVEY.

generalized other the general concept of 'other SOCIAL ACTORS' which individuals abstract from the common elements they find in the attitudes and actions of others. According to G. H. MEAD, whose term this is, it is by 'taking the role of the generalized other' that the individual internalizes shared values and thus is able to engage in complex cooperative processes.

General Register Office the national depository which records all births, marriages and deaths registered as occurring in England and Wales since 1837 (situated in St Catherine's House, London). Scotland has its own General Register Office at New Register House, Edinburgh. See also BIRTH CERTIFICATE, DEATH CERTIFICATE, MARRIAGE CERTIFICATE, DEMOGRAPHY.

general systems theory see SYSTEMS THEORY.

general will see ROUSSEAU.

generation 1 a body of people who were born in the same period, variously defined. 2 the period between the birth of such a group and the birth of their children, which, for demographic purposes, is usually accepted as 30 years.

MANNHEIM distinguished between generation as location (a *birth cohort*), and generation as actuality, where there is a sense of belonging to a group because of shared experience or feeling, e.g. the Sixties Generation, the Vietnam Generation. See also AGE SET, AGE GROUP, AGEING, LIFE COURSE.

generative anthropology a theory of human origins in which American philosopher/anthropologist Eric Gans elaborates on GIRARD's notions of mimetic desire and sacrifice. Generative anthropology is advanced by Gans' most important books *The Origin of Language* (1981), *The End of Culture* (1985), *Science and Faith* (1990), *Originary Thinking* (1993), and *Signs of Paradox* (1997). In these works Gans argues that the evolution of humanity was made possible by the figure of the sign. According to this thesis the original sign was produced by the stalemate which occurred when a group of mimetic animals gathered around an object of collective desire. Because the object lay at the centre of the circle, with the animals forming the periphery, Gans argues that no single animal could appropriate the object without sparking a mimetic war of 'all against all'. As each animal reached for the object the others followed, as the others followed so the model animal, the originator of the first action, drew back for fear of igniting a frenzied struggle. Following this theory of '*homo-mimeticus*' we can understand how Gans uses Girard's concept of MIMETIC DESIRE to explain the development of the sacred. Akin to LACAN's category of the symbolic, the object was elevated above the early human group. It was made sacred because it seemed to stand beyond appropriative action. This factor in turn elevated its worth, which further contributed to the prohibition against its possession and consumption. Elevated beyond the original scene of the aborted gesture of appropriation, what Lacan would call the real, this inflated idea of the object became the originary sign. Long after the original object had lost its worth and been divided up amongst the main protagonists, the symbol continued to influence the group. In relation to its elevated position the early humans began to represent lack, they were bound together, fixed by its centrality and omnipotence. For Gans the creation of the sign is the origin of language and the structure upon which the early social sphere was built. In religious terms the invention of the sign represents the birth of God.

Generative anthropology sees the periodic consumption of the scapegoat as the attempt to re-state the legitimacy of the sacred at times of disorder and undifferentiation. By re-staging the originary scene, the destruction of the body of the victim pays homage to the symbolic omnipotence afforded the transcendental sign. This is why Girard's scapegoat is a paradoxical figure – at once loathed, as the embodiment of otherness, and sacrilized as the cure for social disorder. See also ANTHROPOLOGY; GIRARD, ORIGINARY POSITION, REVENGE.

genetic engineering the process of artificially combining genetic material to produce new varieties of plants and animals or new medical treatments. The process is controversial, given that there may be unknown ecological implications. The uncertainty involved is characteristic of the new 'manufactured' risks seen as characterizing the RISK SOCIETY. See also HUMAN GENOME PROJECT.

genetics the study of inheritance through transmission of characteristics by genes. The founder of the science of genetics was Gregor Mendel (1822–84), an Austrian monk who observed the changes produced in successive generations of pea plants by cross-fertilizing plants with different characteristics (i.e. selective breeding).

The genes are formed from DNA (deoxyribonucleic acid), a large molecule in the form of a double helix, the nucleotide bases of which can be arranged in a variety of ways to code specific information about the characteristic the gene represents. Genes are carried by chromosomes, threadlike structures which are found in pairs in virtually all living cells. The genes carry the specification ('blueprint') for the potential development of the organism. Genetic codes are species specific (so that breeding cannot take place between species), but allow for individual variation among members of a species. The only cases in which two individual members of the same species have identical genetic information are monozygotic twins (individuals produced by a division of an already fertilized egg) or clones (asexual or genetically engineered reproduction).

genocide the deliberate and systematic destruction of a whole nation, or an ethnic, 'racial' or cultural group. Though earlier periods in history have witnessed institutionalized violence against particular groups (for example, religious dissidents, indigenous peoples, 'witches'), often conducted by or on behalf of the Church and state, there are persuasive arguments for the claim that it is only under the conditions associated with late MODERNITY that genocide becomes a reality (Horowitz, 1980). BAUMAN's study (1989) of the Nazi Holocaust is perhaps the best known example of this thesis. If modernity is understood to involve the emergence of the NATION STATE and the elaboration of a BUREAUCRACY capable of keeping under surveillance and regulating its population, with the enhancement of scientific and technological power and the development of INSTRUMENTAL RATIONALITY as the dominant mode of thought and action, then the capacity of 'modern times' to effect the systematic destruction of populations is clear.

The 20th century continued to furnish examples of genocide, including the 'killing fields' of Pol Pot's Cambodia, the inter-tribal massacres in Rwanda and the persecution of the East Timoreans by the Indonesian government, adding weight to the claim that genocide has become one of the unacceptable faces of modernity.

genome the overall genetic constitution of an organism/species as constituted by the chromosomal make-up of every member (the term arises from a combination of the terms 'gene' and 'chromosome'). See also GENETICS, HUMAN GENOME PROJECT.

genotype (and **phenotype**) the unique collection of genes an individual receives from both parents as a result of cell division (meiosis) and fusion of the ovum and sperm (fertilization). All these genes have the potential to determine, or help determine, characteristics of the individual, but not all will in fact exert an influence since they are received from both parents and the gene for a characteristic, e.g. eye colour, from one parent may be dominant over that from the other parent. The genotype therefore expresses genetic potential, and even though genes may not be expressed in the individual they will be passed on to the offspring.

While the genotype is the total genetic potential of the individual, the *phenotype* is the actual expression of the genes as the individual. The phenotype therefore describes the pattern of genes that have influenced the development of the individual, e.g. the gene for the individual's eye colour, but not for the eye colour not exhibited, though still carried in the genotype.

gentrification the renovation and upgrading of buildings, either by programmes of planned urban regeneration or as a result of purchasing decisions made by higher-earning, white-collar, professional and managerial individuals intent on modernizing cheap, dilapidated property in previously unfashionable urban areas. Whether gentrification is planned or unplanned, the poorer sections of the community are often displaced or their needs discounted. The process is also sometimes known as *urban recycling*.

gentry a group of non-aristocratic landowners in England, from the 15th-century to the early 20th-century, whose size of landholding and wealth varied, but was usually enough to sustain a particular way of life which included education and a degree of leisure (Mingay, *The Gentry: the Rise and Fall of a Ruling Class,* 1976). The English gentry are seen as important for the introduction of capitalist agriculture. The term has also been applied to other societies, especially by Eberhard (1965), to conceptualize the combination of landholding and scholarship in Imperial China.

geographical determinism any analytical viewpoint that suggests that different patterns of human culture and social organization are determined by geographical factors such as climate, terrain, etc. The view has a long ancestry, stretching back to the ancient Greeks. However, although many social theorists, e.g. MONTESQUIEU, have placed a strong emphasis on the importance of geography, most see it as one factor influencing social arrangements, not usually a predetermining one. Compare CULTURAL MATERIALISM, WITTFOGEL.

geography the discipline concerned with the description and explanation of the changing spatial relationships of terrestrial phenomena in interrelation with humanity. As such, geography is both a physical science and a social science, ranging from physical geography, on the one hand (including geomorphology and climatology), to human geography on the other. The coverage of the discipline means that it overlaps with sociology and social anthropology, and with other social sciences such as economics. In the past, geography has drawn on sociology more often than sociology has on geography. More recently, however, the exchange of ideas has been greater in both directions, with leading sociologists (e.g. GIDDENS) importing 'time–space' conceptions, central in geographical analysis, into a central place within sociological analysis (see also TIME-GEOGRAPHY, HAGERSTRAND, TIME-SPACE DISTANCIATION). Other recent exchanges of ideas between geography and sociology have occurred in URBAN SOCIOLOGY, where the work of prominent geographers such as Castells (1978) and Harvey (1989) has exerted a strong influence on developments in sociology (see also URBAN SOCIAL MOVEMENTS).

gerontology the study of AGEING and of elderly people. It focuses on the societal consequences of a rising proportion of older people in the population, the personal experience of ageing, particularly in societies where youthfulness is prized, and also the social status of older people. Issues of current sociological debate are the degree to which the problems associated with old age are socially produced through ageist ideologies which deny status and resources to older people and result in enforced dependency through retirement and inadequate social services; historically and culturally, comparative studies of the social status of older age groups; the systems of social classification which overlie chronological ageing. An emerging issue is the frequent invisibility of age as a theoretical issue for sociology in the same way that gender was until recently. See also OLD AGE.

Gesellschaft see GEMEINSCHAFT AND GESELLSCHAFT.

Gestalt theory a theory developed by the Frankfurt school of psychologists in the early 20th-century, which emphasized the organization and meaning imposed on sensory data during the process of perception. An often quoted summary of Gestalt theory (*Gestalt* = whole or pattern) is the phrase 'the whole is more than the sum of the parts'. General laws of perceptual organization were described (e.g. proximity, similarity, law of *Prägnanz* or 'good form'), and a now highly dubious account of corresponding brain action proposed, in which percepts were represented by stability in cortical field patterns. Gestalt psychologists (e.g. Kurt Koffka, Wolfgang Köhler and Max Wertheimer) also believed perceptual organization to be innate (see NATURE-NURTURE DEBATE). Today, only the descriptive level of Gestalt theory finds general acceptance.

ghetto a segregated area of a city characterized by common ethnic and cultural characteristics. The term originated in the Middle Ages in Europe as the name for areas of cities in which Jews were constrained to live. The term was adopted more generally in sociology by the CHICAGO SCHOOL, and particularly by Wirth (*The Ghetto,* 1928). Ghetto has now taken on a meaning which implies not only homogeneity of ethnic and cultural population, but also the concentration of socially-disadvantaged and minority groups in the most impoverished inner city areas. The term is often used in emotive, racist and imprecise ways.

Giddens, Anthony (1938–) British sociologist who, in a prolific career, has established himself, first, as a leading interpreter of classical sociological theory (notably *Capitalism and Modern Social Theory,* 1971), secondly, as a significant contributor to modern analysis of class and stratification (e.g. *The Class Structure of the Advanced Societies,* 1973), thirdly, especially in the 1980s with his formulation of STRUCTURATION THEORY, as an important general sociological theorist in his own right, fourthly as a leading theorist of GLOBALIZATION and RISK SOCIETY, and finally as a leading 'public intellectual' and major influence on NEW LABOUR and the politics of the THIRD WAY.

His firmest reputation is for structuration theory. Beginning with *New Rules of Sociological Method* (1976) and *Central Problems of Sociological Theory* (1979) and culminating in *The Constitution of Society* (1984), this work has been widely influential, not only in sociology. Structuration theory advances an account of the interrelation of STRUCTURE AND AGENCY (see also DUALITY OF STRUCTURE) in which primacy is granted to neither. In a continuing series of works, including *A Contemporary Critique of Historical Materialism* (1981), *The Nation State and Violence* (1985) and *The Consequences of Modernity* (1990), this conception was then deployed in mounting a critique of evolutionary and developmental theories in sociology, and in advancing an alternative account of social change, in which emphasises 'contingency'. In *The Consequences of Modernity* and *Modernity and Self-Identity* (1991) Giddens also takes issue with theories of POSTMODERNITY and POSTMODERNISM, arguing instead for a conception of RADICALIZED MODERNITY in which most of the changes presented as 'postmodernity' (e.g. post-empiricist epistemology, centrifugal tendencies in social transformation) are seen as already implicit in modernity. In these works and also in *The Transformation of Intimacy* (1992), he explores the wider implications of 'radicalized modernity', including shifting conceptions of 'self-identity' (see INTIMACY, NARCISSISM, ONTOLOGICAL SECURITY AND INSECURITY, LIFE POLITICS), and new possibilities of social transformation and democratization, leading Giddens into an interesting 'debate' with BECK (see Beck et al., 1994) about the implications of 'RISK SOCIETY' – see also REFLEXIVE MODERNIZATION.

In recent years Giddens' writing has been oriented especially to influencing political and social change. The key works of this latest phase are *Beyond Left and Right* (1994), *The Third Way – the Renewal of Social Democracy* (1998) and the *Third Way and Its Critics* (2000) – see also THIRD WAY. The themes of the earlier phases of his work are still apparent but the target audience is now the public sphere, rather than sociology narrowly. In 1999, Giddens delivered the prestigious BBC Reith Lectures, via multi-media, to a global audience, with the theme of a 'runaway world' – in some ways the medium was the message. The lectures were subsequently published as *Runaway World – How Globalisation is Reshaping Our Lives* (1999). There are critics of this new phase (see King, 1999) but Giddens' thesis is that we live in a world with a future that is 'without guarantees' but we can make a difference. His aim is to speak to this agency and makes no apology for the change of voice that this involves, although he does acknowledge that there may be a 'trade-off' between academic rigour and public communication.

Overall accounts and discussion of Giddens can be found in Bryant and Jary (1990 and 2000) and Craib (1992). See also LIFE-WORLD, STRATIFICATION MODEL OF SOCIAL ACTION AND CONSCIOUSNESS, POWER, EVOLUTIONARY SOCIOLOGY, TIME–SPACE DISTANCIATION, INTERSOCIETAL SYSTEMS, NATION STATE.

gift exchange *or* **gift relationship** a reciprocal relationship of exchanging goods and services. Marcel MAUSS wrote a seminal book, *The Gift* (1925), in which he argued that gift-giving and taking is one of the bonds that cohere societies. Systems like the KULA RING and POTLATCH provide a system of obligations that comprise a network of 'presentations' which fuse economic, spiritual and political values into a unified system. These insights were elaborated by the anthropologist LÉVI-STRAUSS into a structural theory of group alliance in which he argues that patterns of giving, receiving and repaying, as individuals and groups, reflect the deepest structures of societies. This was applied, in particular, to the movement of women in and out of a patrilineage (see PATRILINEAL DESCENT).

TITMUSS also used these ideas in his *The Gift Relationship* (1970), a study of blood donors in the UK, US and USSR. Titmuss argues that the giving of blood in the UK, without material reward, reflects a sense of community that the other two countries do not have. The analysis of ALTRUISM in Titmuss's examination of the British blood donor service and the idea of the unilateral, anonymous and voluntary gift has been important in discussions of SOCIAL POLICY.

Ideas of exchange have also been applied to other areas of formal gift-giving in industrialized societies (e.g. the exchange of birthday presents), but the presence of complex market mechanisms complicates simplistic formulations of exchange. Compare EXCHANGE THEORY.

Ginsberg, Morris (1889–1970) Lithuanian-born sociologist and social philosopher who continued in the footsteps of HOBHOUSE as professor of sociology at the London School of Economics. At LSE, and as one of only the small number of British professors of sociology in the interwar years, Ginsberg's teaching and work (including *Essays in Sociology and Social Philosophy*, 1956; *Sociology*, 1934) influenced generations of British sociologists. The relatively ungrounded moralizing tone of much his work now appears outmoded. His work can be seen as the end of a tradition associated with Hobhouse, rather than as pointing in any new directions.

Girard, Rene (1923–) French philosopher, social theorist, and literary critic whose most famous texts include *The Scapegoat* (1986), *Violence and the Sacred* (1977), and *Things Hidden Since the Foundation of the World* (1993). In these books Girard discusses an array of biblical texts and literary examples in order to argue that human culture is grounded in the violence of 'all against one'. Focusing on the fate of the victim, he calls this event the foundational murder. He explains how the selection of the sacrificial body unites the collective against a common victim. In *The Scapegoat* Girard argues we can understand the function of the foundational murder by reading the stories written about demagogic occurrences. He shows how the scapegoat myths that surround the violence of 'all against one' both idolize the sacrifice, for its ability to re-unite the social, and legitimate the violence of the collective sphere, to justify the indiscriminate choice of an otherwise innocent victim. He elaborates on this paradox in *Violence and the Sacred* by showing how the scapegoat's role as a site for the outpouring of collective violence leads to its retrospective elevation to the level of the sacred. Regarding the relation between self/other which creates the need for constant violence, Girard writes about the notion of mimetic desire. Akin to thinkers such as Hegel and Lacan, mimetic desire reveals Girard's affinity with the idea that the consciousness of the self is dependent on the presence of the other. In *Things Hidden Since the Foundation of the World*, which Girard wrote with Jean-Michel Oughourlian and Guy Lefort, this resemblance is clarified by the theory of inter-dividual psychology. According to the thesis outlined by inter-dividual psychology, the tension between differentiation and un-differentiation is worked out by the effects of mimetic desire. When conflictual-mimesis leads the rivalous self/other towards a state of un-differentiation violence ensues and one of the couple is expelled in order to re-state the notion of the differentiated self. Here we can see how the fate of the scapegoat hinges on the order/dis-order of the collective sphere. For Girard, un-differentiation at the level of the collective, what he sometimes calls the crisis of degree, leads to the attempt to re-order social relations. This is the key function of the scapegoat. The victim turns the violence of 'all against all' (un-differentiation) into the violence of 'all against one' (differentiation) by virtue of its role as a symbol for the re-statement of otherness.

From the perspective of biblical exegesis, Girard argues that the social system which requires the periodic death of victims is Satanic. Referring to the etymological root of the name Satan, 'he who prepares ambushes', Girard argues that the story of the crucifixion should act as a moral barrier to further acts of collective ambush. For Girard, Christ's role as the zero-degree sacrifice, the ultimate scapegoat whose death over-codes any attempts at justification in scapegoat mythology, reminds humanity of the violence which grounds the notions of the independent self and the differentiated collective. See also: GENERATIVE ANTHROPOLOGY, MIMETIC DESIRE, ORDER/DIS-ORDER, ORIGINARY POSITION, REVENGE.

Glasgow Media Group a group of Glasgow University-based researchers, formed in 1974, whose critical studies of television news broadcasting have attracted much attention. The main publications of the group are: *Bad News* (1976), *More Bad News* (1980), *Really Bad News* (1982) and *War and Peace News* (1985). Concerned about the 'agenda-setting role of media', the main focus of the work of the group has been on the way in which news is constructed, especially its alleged use of slanted STEREOTYPES and its tendency to 'affirmation of the status quo'. Analysing news reports by utilizing CONTENT ANALYSIS along with modes of analysis drawn from the work of the ethnomethodologist Harvey Sacks, the Glasgow Group suggest that there exists an implicit 'ideology' within news broadcasting. They also quote the semiologist Roland BARTHES, that 'reluctance to display its codes is a mark of a bourgeois society and the mass culture which has developed from it'. See also MASS MEDIA OF COMMUNICATION.

glasnost the Russian word for 'openness', referring, from 1985 to 1991 in the USSR, to increased freedom of expression and organization in political and public life. General Secretary GORBACHEV initially reduced censorship of the theatre, films and the press, allowed publication of previously banned books, generally encouraged discussion, freed certain political prisoners, allowed greater freedom of movement and more openness to Western culture. This was both a reaction against the political organizations of STALINISM and an effort to open up debate about policies, such as those contained in PERESTROIKA, which some sections of the Soviet leadership saw as necessary to lift the USSR out of economic stagnation. By 1991 when the USSR ceased to exist, Soviet people interpreted it in far wider ways than the leadership had originally envisaged. Even the role of the Communist Party of the Soviet Union was being criticized, and several republics were seeking forms of independence from Moscow. See also PERESTROIKA.

global capitalist the totality of the roles, institutions and locations performing the function of CAPITAL within a given capitalist society or internationally. The concept of 'global capitalist' is intended to convey the fact that although the ownership of capital is widely dispersed, and the control of SURPLUS VALUE appropriation diffused among many different kinds and grades of employees (see also CONTRADICTORY CLASS LOCATIONS), the ACCUMULATION OF CAPITAL is unimpeded. In short, the use of the term 'global capitalist' is intended to convey the view that changes in terms of ownership and control of capital do not mean the achievement of a 'postcapitalist' society. See also SEPARATION OF OWNERSHIP FROM CONTROL.

globalization

A mulifaceted process in which the world is becoming more and more interconnected and communication is becoming instanteneous. Aspects of this process include:

(a) the transformation of the spatial arrangement and organization of social relations involving 'action at a distance', a stretching of social relations and transactions (and power), including instantaneous communications across time-space;

(b) the increasing extensity, intensity, velocity and impact of global social relations and transactions (see Held et al. 1999);

(c) the creation of new networks and nodes – the 'network society' (CASTELLS) – associated with the new levels of dependence on knowledge/information and 'expert systems – the 'information' or 'knowledge society' – as well as the new risks associated with this – RISK SOCIETY;

(d) a dialect between the global and the local in which (consistent with a dialect of power and the duality of structure) the outcome is not a simple triumph of the centre over the periphery, mere 'Americanization', or suchlike (see also MCDONALDIZATION).

As Held et al. (1999) suggest, a 'vibrant' ongoing debate exists on the characterization of globalization between three groups of theorists:

(a) 'hyperglobalizers' (e.g. Ohmae 1990; 1995) for whom global marketization is the main driver;

(b) 'sceptics' (notably Hirst and Thompson 1996a and b), who play down the level and distinctiveness of the change;

(c) 'transformationalists', including GIDDENS, for whom globalization is a distinctive new phase such that societies and states across the globe are experiencing profound social as well as economic changes – a 'massive shake-out' of social relations, economies, governance and politics – as they seek to adapt to an increasingly interconnected but also unpredictable and uncertain world.

In contrast with WALLERSTEIN's more economistic account, Giddens sees globalization as a complex multi-dimensional process involving a dialectical relationship between the global and the local, including a sideways stretch, breaking down state boundaries and creating new international agencies (including NGOs) but also leading to new global inequalities and stratification.

globalization of culture the tendency for worldwide diffusion of cultural patterns. As suggested by GIDDENS (1994), 'globalization cannot today simply be understood as Westernization'. It is a process which can also increase CULTURAL PLURALISM, e.g. the diffusion and fusion of musical forms such as jazz or 'world music'.

globalization of production the integration of economic activities by units of private capital on a world scale. Globalization is a key element of post-Fordism (see FORDISM AND POST-FORDISM), and resides in the ability of the MULTINATIONAL COMPANY OR CORPORATION to harmonize, integrate and make its production flexible (see FLEXIBLE PRODUCTION). This ability has been enormously enhanced by the new technologies of communication and robotics. Final products can be assembled from many individual units, made in a large number of different countries, and can be flexibly produced to meet changing demand and to fill individualized market niches. Production thus becomes spatially structured, with multinationals organizing activity internationally in order to take advantage of different wage rates and different levels of unionization, to force employees to compete with each other, and to develop coherent global strategies of accumulation. Compare WORLD SYSTEM, PLURALIZATION OF CULTURE.

GNP see GROSS NATIONAL PRODUCT.

goal attainment see SUBSYSTEMS MODEL.

goal displacement the process by which means designed to achieve goals become ends in themselves. The concept was first used by MERTON (1949) to explain how the inflexibility of formal rules can lead to individuals using tactics of survival which displace the official goals of an organization. Merton's example revealed how government officials tended to act in ways which protected their interests rather than served the public. A similar, classic, case study of goal displacement was identified in Selznick's research on the Tennessee Valley Water Authority (1966) which revealed that democratic ideals of the Authority were subverted by officials in furtherance of their own departmental interests. Although MICHELS (1911) did not use the term, his IRON LAW OF OLIGARCHY was an early example of goal displacement, represented by the conflict between democratic principles and bureaucracy.

The concept of goal displacement belongs to the language of functionalism and implies the existence of both 'organizational goals' and 'dysfunctional' activities. See also MANIFEST AND LATENT FUNCTIONS, BOUNDED RATIONALITY, DYSFUNCTION.

Goffman, Erving (1922–82) Canadian-born US sociologist and prolific author who made a unique contribution to the study of face-to-face interaction in everyday life in a number of interrelated areas. In *The Presentation of Self in Everyday Life* (1959), the central perspective is DRAMATURGY, a focus carried forward in *Encounters* (1961) and *Behaviour in Public Places* (1963). In *Stigma* (1964) and *Asylums* (1961), the social construction of deviant identities, and the actor's management of these, is explored. In *Frame Analysis* (1974) and *Forms of Talk* (1981), his attention turns to an examination of the ways in which we define, or *frame*, the world as real, and how framing remains always a precarious accomplishment. Throughout all the stages of Goffman's work, he displayed an unceasing capacity to generate new concepts and conceptual schemas of great ingenuity. An abiding focus of his work was to exhibit social FORMS, those general recurring features of social life which lie beneath the specific content of social life (see also FORM AND CONTENT).

Although standing, broadly, in the symbolic interactionist tradition, and concentrating his attention on face-to-face phenomena, Goffman's interests lay in displaying how even our most minute and apparently insignificant activities are socially structured and surrounded by RITUAL. In his later work, with its focus on the 'syntax' of framing, Goffman moved closer to the analytical concerns of ETHNOMETHODOLOGY and CONVERSATION ANALYSIS.

His methods of research included PARTICIPANT OBSERVATION and close analysis of various kinds of naturally occurring social documents and happenings (e.g. advertising images, radio talk). The establishment of the validity of his conceptual schemes would appear to depend, mainly, on his ability to provide persuasive demonstration of their analytical power (a mixture of FORMAL SOCIOLOGY and ANALYTIC INDUCTION). A major element in Goffman's success was his flair as a social observer, which is not easily emulated.

Critics of Goffman's sociology have commented on its author's 'demonic detachment', that it is peopled by actors who 'lack individual qualities', and that it presents society as a 'big con'. Nevertheless, even if Goffman's approach may not present people in the round, his sociology possesses great strengths, not least in its steady production of many SENSITIZING CONCEPTS taken up, to good effect, by other sociologists.
See also CAREER, ROLE DISTANCE, STIGMA, ENCOUNTER, FRAME, INTERACTION, INTERACTION RITUAL AND INTERACTION ORDER, STRATEGIC INTERACTION, TOTAL INSTITUTION OR TOTAL ORGANIZATION.

Goldthorpe, John (1935–) British sociologist best known for his empirical work on SOCIAL STRATIFICATION, CLASS and SOCIAL MOBILITY, which include (with David LOCKWOOD and others) the influential AFFLUENT WORKER studies (Goldthorpe, Lockwood et al., 1968–69), and the Nuffield College, Oxford, SOCIAL MOBILITY Studies, directed by him, published as *Social Mobility and Class Structure in Modern Britain* (1980, revised 1987). The methodological implications, as much as the empirical conclusions, of both sets of studies have been important (see Goldthorpe and Hope, *The Social Grading of Occupations*, 1974) and subject to considerable debate (see Bulmer, 1975; see also MULTI DIMENSIONAL ANALYSIS OF SOCIAL STRATIFICATION, CLASS IMAGERY, OCCUPATIONAL SCALES). Goldthorpe has also made occasional trenchant interventions in debates on sociological theory, on the virtues and vices of ETHNOMETHODOLOGY, on INDUSTRIAL RELATIONS, on class and gender, and on INFLATION.

Goldthorpe-Llewellyn scale see OCCUPATIONAL SCALES.

goodness of fit the degree to which observations in a data set conform to an expected distribution predicted from a model. See also CHI SQUARE (χ^2).

Gorbachev, Mikhail (1931–) Russian statesman elected General Secretary of the Communist Party of the Soviet Union in March 1985 and President of the USSR in April 1990 until deposed from power with the break-up of the USSR. As General Secretary, he was responsible for introducing fundamental changes in the USSR around GLASNOST and PERESTROIKA, and for changing international relations with Western Europe and the US.

Gouldner, Alvin (1920–80) US sociologist whose contributions to sociological theory were wide ranging. Although strongly influenced by MARXISM, he was not a Marxist in any strict sense. His best-known work, *The Coming Crisis in Western Sociology* (1971), might be seen as a postmortem on modern STRUCTURAL-FUNCTIONALISM. He had earlier made his name with *Patterns of Industrial Bureaucracy* (1954), which has become a modern classic. In this, he provided an empirical examination of the way in which inefficient administration and industrial conflict may result from the attempt to introduce disciplinary rules which leave little scope for human autonomy. In a number of further works, including *The Two Marxisms* (1980) and *The Future of the Intellectuals and the Rise of the New Class* (1979) (see NEW CLASS, INTELLIGENTSIA), he sought to establish a new route for critical thinking in the social sciences between a seriously flawed FUNCTIONALISM and an unreformed Marxism. Throughout his life, he was always concerned to explore relations of involvement and detachment arising in the social sciences, being critical of those, like WEBER, who argued strongly for detachment (see *For Sociology*, 1973), or who denied the possibility of the goal of an objective grounding for values. In *The Dialectic of Ideology and Technology* (1976), he developed these themes, exploring the implications for public participation of both new thinking in epistemology and changes in communications technology. See also BUREAUCRACY, CRITICAL CULTURAL DISCOURSE, NEW CLASS, VALUE FREEDOM.

graduate labour market that sector of the LABOUR MARKET in which only, or mainly, graduates are employed. This market has recently expanded to include an increasingly wide range of employment, as the number of graduates seeking jobs expands and as more employers seek to, or are willing to, employ them. This involves a *downward substitution* of graduates for non-graduates, from the point of view of graduates, and an *upward substitution* from the point of view of employers.

Directly related to the expansion of HIGHER EDUCATION in modern societies in recent decades (see also MASS HIGHER EDUCATION, UNIVERSITY, POLYTECHNIC, NEW UNIVERSITY), the implications of this transformation of graduate employment have been a matter of considerable speculation, including discussion of the possible consequences of:

(a) shortages of graduates in some areas (e.g. some branches of engineering), alongside an apparent oversupply in others;

(b) the appearance, for the first time, of graduate unemployment, or longer periods of job search than previously;

(c) the possible 'underemployment' of some graduates as some move down-market, i.e. the apparent paradox of 'educational upgrading' coupled with 'underutilization of abilities' (Berg, 1970).

Such problems are sometimes made the basis of arguments for a check to the expansion in higher education overall, especially in areas of low employer demand, and a redirection of some resources to shortage areas (see also CREDENTIALISM). Another viewpoint, however, is that the problems are mainly ones of adjustment to the new conditions provided by an expanded supply of educated labour, and the value of a continued expansion of higher education should not be in doubt (see POSTINDUSTRIAL SOCIETY; see also SOCIAL DEMAND FOR EDUCATION).

grammar the systematic description of the structure of a language. Grammars seek to state the rules by which the elements making up a language are formed and combined. These elements, although they now seem obvious and natural, are theoretical terms within grammar, such as noun, verb and adjective. At its most familiar level *syntax*, grammar looks at the construction of sentences from combinations of elements, including those elements that make up words, and the phrases that words make up. The discipline of LINGUISTICS is grounded in grammar. The procedures now extend to other 'levels', e.g. those of meaning (SEMANTICS) and the context of action (PRAGMATICS). See also SAUSSURE, CHOMSKY, DEEP, STRUCTURE AND SURFACE STRUCTURE.

Gramsci, Antonio (1891–1937) Italian revolutionary Marxist and political theorist whose concept of HEGEMONY has been influential in modern sociology. Gramsci was born into a poor Sardinian family. In 1911 he won a scholarship to the University of Turin where he studied linguistics. Because of increasing political commitments he left the University to become a leading socialist journalist and theorist of the Turin factory councils movement of 1919–20. Gramsci saw direct democracy based on factory councils as destined to replace parliamentary democracy. This would enable the mass of the population to participate directly in the making of political decisions. In 1924, Gramsci became secretary of the Italian Communist Party. But with the growth of FASCISM he was arrested in 1926. At his trial the official prosecutor demanded that the judge 'stop this brain working for twenty years'. Prison did not silence him, but inspired him to write his major theoretical achievement, the *Prison Notebooks*. These cover a wide range of subjects, the common link being the application of MARXISM to the problems of Italian history and society. His strategy for change was based upon organizing the northern working class and the southern peasantry, and welding a revolutionary alliance between them. See also INTELLECTUALS, FORDISM AND POST-FORDISM, CULTURAL STUDIES.

grand narratives and **metanarratives** general conceptions (compare NARRATIVES) such as 'the emancipation of the subject', which for LYOTARD (1984) have been characteristic of the 'sciences' of 'modernity', and which have usually legitimized themselves with reference to such metadiscourses. It is a central part of Lyotard's critique of modernity that, in a 'postmodern' era, such grand narratives lose their legitimacy. The paradox exists, however: is not Lyotard's theory itself yet another grand narrative? See also POSTMODERNITY AND POSTMODERNISM.

grand theory see MILLS.

gratification the process of satisfying needs or goals, and the state of satisfaction which results from the fulfilment of such needs or goals.

green movement a social movement whose prime concern is with ecological issues (see ECOLOGY). While this is broad-based, encompassing concern over environmental pollution, preservation of wildlife and of the traditional countryside, and the control of building development, the movement has a strong political wing which has been a powerful lobby during the 1980s. The Green Party has been most in evidence in West Germany and Holland, only emerging significantly in the UK in the late 1980s, with the renaming of the Ecology Party. However, many supporters would not regard their allegiance as conventionally political, but as based on practical issues with which they can be directly involved, through their purchasing habits, their leisure pursuits, or by contributing to conservation bodies.

green revolution the introduction of new species of crops and new techniques leading to greater crop yields. This began in Mexico in the 1950s, and from the mid-1960s new high-yielding varieties of rice and wheat were introduced in many THIRD WORLD countries. The most noticeable applications were in the Indian subcontinent where new strains of rice enabled *double-cropping*, eliminating a fallow period in the agricultural cycle. For a while these innovations were seen by many as solving food-supply problems. However, new problems arose, one of the most significant being that the new strains require heavy inputs of fertilizer, pesticides and machinery. For Third World countries, these can be very expensive imports, and small farmers have been unable to gain access to the credit financing necessary for full advantage to be taken. Generally a process of *increasing* impoverishment of poor farmers has resulted, with increasing income inequalities, a concentration of landholding and variable increases in food supplies. As Griffin (1979) points out, this was an example of a *technological fix* approach based on assumptions that technical solutions can operate independently of the institutional environment. He sums up by saying 'the story of the green revolution is the story of a revolution that failed'. See also INTERMEDIATE TECHNOLOGY.

Gresham's Law (ECONOMICS) the hypothesis, associated with the Elizabethan merchant-financier, Sir Robert Gresham, that 'bad money tends to drive good money out of circulation', where 'bad money' is money which contains less bullion value for a stated face value than 'good money'. The 'law' is particularly of interest as an early, archetypal, example of many laws in economics which assume individuals act rationally (see FORMAL AND SUBSTANTIVE RATIONALITY). See also IDEAL TYPE.

gross national product (GNP) (ECONOMICS) the total money value of the final goods and services produced in an economy in any year, including income from overseas property.

grounded theory any form of sociological theory that is built up gradually from the careful naturalistic observation of a selected social phenomenon (see also ANALYTICAL INDUCTION). As outlined by Glaser and Strauss *The Discovery of Grounded Theory* (1968), sociological theorizing of this type contrasts with more abstract general theories of the 'hypothetico-deductive' type (see HYPOTHETICO-DEDUCTIVE EXPLANATION AND METHOD). Compare also THEORIES OF THE MIDDLE RANGE.

group dynamics the processes involved in interaction within social GROUPS. Interest in sociology has focused especially on shifting patterns of tension, conflict, adjustment and cohesion within groups, as well as on styles of leadership.

group

Any collectivity or plurality of individuals (people or things) bounded by informal or formal criteria of membership. A *social group* exists when members engage in social interactions involving reciprocal ROLES and integrative ties. The contrast can be drawn between a social group and a mere *social category*, the latter referring to any category of individuals sharing a socially relevant characteristic (e.g. age or sex), but not associated within any bounded pattern of interactions or integrative ties. In terms of membership, social groups may be either relatively *open* and fluid (e.g. friendship groups), or *closed* and fixed (e.g. Masonic Lodges).

Any social group, therefore, will have a specified basis of social interaction, though the nature and extent of this will vary greatly between groups. Social groups of various types can be seen as the building blocks from which other types and levels of social organization are built. Alternatively, the term 'social group', as for Albion SMALL (1905), is 'the most general and colourless term used in sociology to refer to combinations of persons'. See also PRIMARY GROUP, GROUP DYNAMICS, REFERENCE GROUP, SOCIAL INTEGRATION AND SYSTEM INTEGRATION, SOCIETY, DESCENT GROUP, PEER GROUP, PRESSURE GROUP, STATUS GROUP, IN-GROUP AND OUT-GROUP.

The best-known theoretical and experimental approach in the study of group dynamics, and the one with which the term is most associated, is the FIELD THEORY of Kurt Lewin (1951); however, an awareness of the importance of group dynamics in a more general sense is evident in the work of many sociologists and social psychologists, including SIMMEL, MAYO, MORENO, Robert Bales (1950) and PARSONS (see DYAD AND TRIAD, HAWTHORN EFFECT, SOCIOMETRY, OPINION LEADERS AND OPINION LEADERSHIP, CONFORMITY, GROUP THERAPY).

group therapy the practice of treating psychological disturbance through a face-to-face group process of sharing experiences and emotions and, through this, moving towards greater self-understanding and adjustment. This form of therapy was introduced in the 1930s by J. L. MORENO, who founded psychodrama and sociodrama, and coined the terms. Since the 1940s, Carl ROGERS has actively developed the method, particularly in *encounter groups* which aim to provide a developmental experience for people termed 'normals'. Therapy groups, generally, have a group leader or 'facilitator', as the composition and the programme of a group needs to be carefully planned and controlled for its purpose to be realized in all members. A variety of theoretical approaches may underpin this type of therapy, for example, psychodynamic, Rogerian, feminist.

guerrilla warfare armed uprisings by irregular forces, depending for success on support from non-combatants. Such warfare is often sustained over long periods, and under certain circumstances can be successful against regular forces. In the 20th century, it has been seen in Mexico, China, Vietnam, Cuba, Central America and Afghanistan. See also WARFARE.

guild an association of craft workers, especially in preindustrial societies, formed to provide mutual aid and to control craft standards and entry into the trade (a form of SOCIAL CLOSURE). Compare PROFESSION, TRADE UNION.

Guttman scale, scalogram analysis *or* **scalogram method** an ATTITUDE SCALE, named after its designer, Guttman, which firstly assesses whether the attitude to be studied, e.g. racial prejudice, involves a single dimension. If it does, then it will be possible to arrange, hierarchically and ordinally, a series of attitude questions of increasing intensity such that agreement with a given statement implies agreement with statements of lower intensity. That is, they assume that a cut-off point exists within any set of attitude statements such that failure to endorse a particular item means that no item of greater intensity will be endorsed. Respondents' attitudes can then be compared by a simple score, and any individual's response towards any item is known from this score. In practice, perfect Guttman scales probably do not exist, and a 10% margin of error is generally considered to be acceptable. Compare LIKERT SCALE.

h

Habermas, Jürgen (1929–) German social theorist and leading living exponent of a style of radical social theorizing originating with the FRANKFURT SCHOOL OF CRITICAL THEORY. The range of Habermas's theorizing is extraordinary. He deals with most of the broad themes developed by earlier critical theorists, including epistemological questions and debate about the fundamental dynamics of advanced capitalist societies. In addition, he has sought to achieve a thoroughgoing synthesis of developments in social science and philosophy – including analytical philosophy, the philosophy of science, linguistics, political science and systems theory – that are of relevance in exploring the basis for a rational reconstruction of society on socialist lines.

With the starting point of a critique of the 'scientization of politics', Habermas has endeavoured to re-establish social scientific and political debate as an arena of 'open discourse'. Whereas historically, reason and science had been directed against ignorance and oppression, in Habermas' view in modern societies science and technical rationality now often function as ideologies, preventing the raising of fundamental questions about human ends. In *Knowledge and Human Interests* (1972, German original 1968), Habermas seeks to identify the proper spheres of three forms of scientific knowledge:
(a) *'empirical-analytical'* enquiry, concerned with establishing causal relations and grounded, above all, in an interest in controlling nature;
(b) *'hermeneutic'* enquiry, based on MEANINGFUL UNDERSTANDING and arising from the human need for mutual communication;
(c) *'critical'* and *'emancipatory'* forms of knowledge, seen as transcending the limits of the other two.

The terms in which Habermas elucidates the character of the third form of knowledge, (c), involve the formulation of a *'universal pragmatics'*, i.e. an account of the normative presuppositions ideally underlying all forms of human communication (Habermas, 1970a & b). All genuine attempts at communication have implicit in them claims to validity (truth, appropriateness and sincerity) (see also COMMUNICATIVE COMPETENCE). True rationality can be seen to be achieved only when this emerges from conditions which correspond to an *ideal speech situation,* in which all parties have equal opportunities to engage in dialogue, without undue domination by one party, without restriction and without ideological distortion. This model states the conditions for a critical and truly 'emancipatory' social science. Even if there are difficulties in realizing the model, it establishes a bench mark in terms of which the ideological distortions involved in existing forms of social science can be gauged.

In *Legitimation Crisis* (1975, original German edition 1973), Habermas turned his attention to an examination of tendencies to crisis in advanced capitalist societies. He portrays these societies as characterized by continued economic and class contradictions, and by a new politicization of administrative decisions as a result of increasing state intervention made necessary by economic contradictions, as well as by the new contradictions which these political interventions introduce. A tendency to 'legitimation crisis' is seen as occurring under these circumstances, especially in a situation in which previous bases of legitimacy (e.g. DEFERENCE) are not being renewed and where new social orientations (e.g. new welfare professionalism) are beginning to act as 'foreign bodies' within capitalism, producing a more critical political culture, potentially challenging to capitalism. Habermas acknowledges that tendencies to crisis in capitalist societies might be successfully managed, and that there are no guarantees that capitalism will be replaced. Nonetheless, he insists that the presence of economic and class contradictions and distorted rationality within capitalist societies are apparent once the procedures of critical theory are brought into play.

An aspect of Habermas's thinking which has perhaps been subject to most criticism is his use of SYSTEMS THEORY and evolutionary models of social development. On the former, Habermas now distinguishes between 'system integration' and 'social integration', the one concerned with material reproduction, the other a matter of cultural integration and socialization. It is the latter for which a systems analysis remains most appropriate. With regard to Habermas's use of EVOLUTIONARY THEORY a distinction is sometimes drawn between theories which emphasize ADAPTATION and Darwinian selection and those based on the notion of an 'unfolding' development. According to Outhwaite (1994), Habermas's use is closer to the latter, but his theorizing is 'reconstructive' (of the underlying developmental logic of a sequence) rather than deterministic or predictive. Evolution is then the 'ordered sequence of structural possibilities'; the models involved are of 'societal learning'. Actual, real historical changes are CONTINGENT, involving economic and cultural strands that are not jointly determined. For all this, a 'reconstructed historical materialism' is still seen by Habermas as remaining the best model of development, even if there must now be far less emphasis on 'labour' in any narrow sense and much more emphasis on family structures, culture, law, processes of democratization, and on the 'abstract principles' underlying 'new levels of societal learning'. The 'bearers of evolution' are societies *and* active subjects. Both system evolution and cognitive development are central.

Critics have sometimes regarded Habermas's overall theory as over-abstract, containing too little detailed history, and giving too little indication of a realizable, real-world political programme. However, if these are weaknesses, rather than an old style PHILOSOPHY OF HISTORY, Habermas's theory remains, as Outhwaite states, one intended to be 'tested in the discussive mode'. Demonstrating this, Habermas has shown a remarkable capacity to embrace the theories of others, making his the most comprehensive theoretical synthesis in contemporary sociology.

Habermas's combination of critical exegesis of the work of others with an elaboration of his own systematic theory has been immensely influential. The volume and complexity of his writing means that it is impossible to indicate all its ramifications in a relatively brief compass. In addition to the works noted, other main works by Habermas (English translations) include: *Theory and Practice* (1974), *Towards a Rational Society* (1970), *Communication and the Evolution of Society* (1979), *The Theory of Communicative Competence* (2 vols., 1984 and 1988), *The Structural Transformation of the Public Sphere* (1989) and *On the Logic of the Social Services* (1990). Summary and evaluation of his work is provided by McCarthy (1978), R. Bernstein (1976), and W. Outhwaite (1994).

habitus 'the durably installed generative principles' which produce and reproduce the 'practices' of a class or class fraction (BOURDIEU, 1977, 1984). Centrally, the habitus consists of a set of 'classificatory schemes' and 'ultimate values'. These, according to Bourdieu, are more fundamental than consciousness or language, and are the means by which groups succeed, or do not succeed, in imposing ways of seeing favourable to their own interests. While each habitus is set by historical and socially situated conditions, it also allows new forms and actions, but is far from allowing the 'creation of unpredictable (or unconditioned) novelty'.

hacendado see HACIENDA.

hacienda a large landed estate in Latin America worked by various forms of unfree labour, generally with mixed farming production for subsistence, a local or regional market, and for the consumption of the owner, the *hacendado.* This was one of the main ways in which agricultural production was organized in colonial Latin America until the 19th century, and in some cases into the 20th. For example, from the early 17th century in New Spain, now Mexico, the hacienda was 'a permanently inhabited territorial area, with both fallow and cultivated lands, granaries in which the products of the harvest were kept, houses for the owners and their managers, shacks for the workers, small craft workshops, and toolsheds' (Florescano, 1987). There livestock was raised and crops grown for mines and provincial towns. A variety of means of ensuring a labour supply were used, one of the most common being DEBT PEONAGE. Important for the organization and economic decisions within the hacienda were the political and status aspirations and consumption requirements of the *hacendado.* Haciendas were distinguished from PLANTATIONS in as much as the latter produced one crop, generally for export and often with corporate, rather than personal, forms of ownership.

FRANK (1969) has argued that haciendas were capitalist because they produced for the market. However, the absence of free wage labour and the low levels of capital accumulation have led most observers to argue against this. Production for the market is not a sufficient criterion for being called capitalist. Some observers use the term 'semi-feudal' as a general description.

The hacienda began to change in the 19th-century, after independence, through political interventions to establish free labour and with growing capitalist developments in agriculture. Duncan and Rutledge (1977) provide one useful summary of the variety of changes which took place: some haciendas were broken up by land reform, others became capitalist estates or plantations, but in some areas the hacienda persisted up until the mid-20th century.

Hall, Stuart (1932–) Jamaican-born sociologist, who, as a result of his association with the *New Left Review* and subsequent work with the Birmingham CENTRE FOR CONTEMPORARY CULTURAL STUDIES, has had an important influence, especially on CULTURAL STUDIES. See also NEW LEFT, ALTHUSSERIAN MARXISM, THATCHERISM.

Halsey, A. H. (1923–) British sociologist and Professor of Social and Administrative Studies at Oxford University who has published extensively on SOCIAL STRATIFICATION, SOCIAL MOBILITY and the SOCIOLOGY OF EDUCATION. The general thrust of his work is best expressed in *Change in British Society* (1978), a summary of his Reith Lectures in the same year. In that book, he is concerned with the extent to which the fundamental values of liberty, fraternity and equality can be realized in any society, and especially an advanced industrial one. He contrasts Weberian-liberal and Marxist explanations of SOCIAL CHANGE and argues that not all inequality can be accounted for as a consequence of CLASS. Rather, as did WEBER, he sees notions of party and STATUS as essential to an understanding of the complexities of social change, especially the changing distribution of power and advantage through economic, social and political processes. He concludes that none of the fundamental values identified are realized in the UK, and that there are serious obstacles to them being so. He is nevertheless cautiously optimistic that in the UK the 'rich traditions' of DEMOCRACY and citizenship offer the sort of basis for fraternity which ultimately transcend the conflicts engendered by class and lead to a new form of social integration. It is a social philosophy which was incorporated into the politics of newly created 'centre' parties in Britain in the 1980s.

Halsey's contribution to the study of social mobility is *Origins and Destinations* (1980) (with Heath and Ridge). Earlier in the sociology of education his reader *Education, Economy and Society* (1961) and *Social Class and Educational Opportunity* (1956) (both with Floud and Anderson) were highly influential books which influenced the course of sociological investigation into education for almost two decades. The concerns with equality, inequality of access and educational achievement in the sociology of education owe their origins to Halsey's early, influential work. The social experiments with COMPREHENSIVE EDUCATION, COMPENSATORY EDUCATION and community education, which spearheaded the drive towards the eradication of inequalities within postwar Britain, were the direct result of work inspired by Halsey and his colleagues.

Haraway, Donna (1944–) U.S. feminist social theorist who began her career as a biologist. This background informed her subsequent work in the field of the philosophy of science. Assessing the political considerations of scientific discourse, Haraway argues that the phallocentric model of knowledge is based on domination and oppression. Following the technological horrors of late modernity (such as Aucshwitz and Hiroshima), she maintains that we need a 'successor science' that promotes ethical considerations above the pursuit of money and prestige. For Haraway, science is reductionist because it often overlooks difference. Against this exclusionary discourse her book *Simians, Cyborgs and Women: The Reinvention of Nature* (1991) promotes the figure of the cyborg as a metaphor for the negotiation of difference within the scientific model. Here, the biotechnological hybrid transgresses the boundaries of the integrated subject, promoting a fluid model of identity. Although Haraway critiques science, she still argues in favour of its logical methodology unlike other postmodern theorists such as Jean-Francois LYOTARD whose book *The Postmodern Condition* (1984) appears to relativize knowledge by showing how science is just one of many competing 'language games'. See also CYBERCULTURE.

hard core Lakatos' term for that part of a scientific programme (see FALSIFICATIONISM) which is protected at all costs.

harried leisure class the situation experienced by increasing numbers of modern consumers of leisure in which, as the output of material goods increases, the time available to use them does not, but becomes more scarce relative to the goods and services available (S. Linder, 1970). Thus individuals are under increasing pressure to economize on their use of time, a situation exacerbated by the increasing costs of 'buying time' through the purchase of services.

haute bourgeoisie the wealthiest and most powerful sections of the BOURGEOISIE.

Hawthorne effect a term derived from the Hawthorne investigations (see HUMAN RELATIONS SCHOOL), in which the conduct of experiments produced changes in the behaviour of subjects because, firstly, they knew they were being observed, and, secondly, investigators developed friendly relationships with them. In the first instance, the Hawthorne effect made sense of the otherwise puzzling experimental finding of an inverse relationship between illumination (environmental change) and employee output. In the second instance, the attempt to assess the impact of a range of variables on the performance of employees, who were removed from their normal work situation, was rendered problematic, partly because over time investigators adopted a friendly supervisory relationship with the subjects. The difficulty in disentangling the effects of poorly controlled changes on the observed improvement in employee output was controversially resolved in favour of stressing the significance of employee preference for friendly supervision of cohesive and informal work groups. Indeed, this finding became the main platform in the prescriptions which human relations theorists proposed for effective management.

In both of the cases described above, the Hawthorne effect was associated with the way in which subjects interpreted and responded to poorly controlled experimental changes. As the researchers became aware of the need to consider the ways in which employees interpreted their work situation, other techniques of investigation, such as interviews and observation of natural settings, were adopted. Nevertheless, all of the phases in the research programme have been subjected to criticism, as has the interpretation of the findings (M. Rose, 1988). See also UNANTICIPATED CONSEQUENCES OF SOCIAL ACTION.

Hawthorne experiment see HAWTHORNE EFFECT.

Hayek, Friedrich von (1899–1992) Austrian-born economist and social philosopher who, as professor of Economics at the LSE (1931–50) and later when he moved to the USA, was highly influential in his opposition to central planning and advocacy of free market economics. Hayek's best-known general works include *The Road to Serfdom* (1944), *Individualism and the Economic Order* (1948) and the *Counter Revolution of Science* (1941; 1952).

headman (ANTHROPOLOGY) a leader within a small community. The term has been used to refer both to the leader of a BAND or TRIBE, or to a local leader within a larger political system such as a CHIEFDOM.

head of household traditionally the senior male of the household (i.e. 'breadwinner' in 19th-century terms), a tradition which has influenced social research definitions. In government surveys, the head of household has been defined as the man who is the owner or tenant of the house, or the man who lives with the woman who is the owner or tenant of the house. Therefore 'female-headed households' are confined to women living alone, or women-headed single-parent households, or women who are the tenant or owner living with older people.

This definition of head of household has consequences for the analysis of household situation: should members of a household be ascribed a social position according to the economic and social status of the, usually male, head of household? The debate on this overlaps with the debate on how social CLASS should be defined. In social surveys social class is measured by such variables as occupation (current job, job grade, responsibility in job), and/or education (highest qualification level achieved) and/or housing status. Should these variables be measured for the head of household and his social class then be assigned to all other members of the household? Can social class as measured in this way be assigned to other members of the family, e.g. the woman he lives with, 'his' children, etc.? Alternatively, is social class an individual attribute measured for each adult's own occupational, educational and housing status? Or, should social class be measured for the household through considering these variables for both male and female adults in the household?

Such questions have important repercussions for policy. In the collection of poverty statistics in the UK, it is assumed that resources are shared equitably within the family. If the head of household earns sufficient then the entire household is above the poverty line. However, many researchers have challenged this assumption and argued that although in some families resources may be equitably distributed, in others they are not and women and children may be living below the poverty line in families that appear adequately resourced by government criteria. See also WOMEN-HEADED HOUSEHOLDS, CLASS DEALIGNMENT.

health and medicine see SOCIOLOGY OF HEALTH AND MEDICINE.

Hegel, Georg Wilhelm Friedrich (1770–1831) influential German idealist and post-Kantian philosopher. His major works include *Phenomenology of Mind* (1807), *Philosophy of History* (1817) and *Philosophy of Right* (1821). He believed that the social world was essentially composed of ideas, manifested in the idea of the 'world (or 'absolute') spirit' (*Geist*). These ideas were to be discovered by a contemplative process of the mind 'alienating' itself from itself. The spirit is illustrated in history by the dialectical movement of ideas through time – a thesis combines with an antithesis to produce a higher synthesis (see DIALECTIC). This historical pattern unfolds with individuals (Napoleon is often cited) as mere pawns in its development. Hegel assumed that it would end with an eternal historical final synthesis and he appears to have believed that the Prussian state constituted such an ending. Despite his frequent evaluation as a philosopher of the right wing, his critique of alienating commercialism crucially influenced the young MARX who claimed to have rescued Hegel's thought from IDEALISM by placing the dialectic on its feet in the material world. See also IDEALISM.

hegemony

1 the power exercised by one social group over another.
2 the ideological/cultural domination of one class by another, achieved by 'engineering consensus' through controlling the content of cultural forms and major institutions.

In sense **2**, the term is derived from the work of GRAMSCI (1971), an Italian Marxist jailed by the fascists in the 1920s. He used the term to criticize the narrowness of approaches which focused only on the repressive potential of the capitalist state. Gramsci argued that the domination of ideas in the major institutions of capitalist society, including the Roman Catholic Church, the legal system, the education system, the mass communications media, etc., promoted the acceptance of ideas and beliefs which benefited the RULING CLASS. Gramsci compared civil society to a powerful system of 'fortresses and earthworks' standing behind the state. As a result, the problem of cultural hegemony was crucial to understanding the survival of capitalism. Gramsci concluded that before winning power the working class would have to undermine the hegemony of the ruling class by developing its own alternative hegemony. As well as exercising leadership, this required a cultural and ideological struggle in order to create a new socialist 'common sense', and thus change the way people think and behave. It followed, therefore, that a subordinate and oppressed class, in addition to organizing to resist physical coercion and repression, had to develop a systematic refutation of ruling ideas. In this sense, of political and theoretical struggle, the idea of hegemony, and often the term itself, was already established and in common use, for example in the Russian Marxist movements (see Anderson, 1977).

Where Gramsci most influenced later work was in shifting the emphasis from 'counter-hegemony' as a political necessity for subordinated groups, to hegemony as a factor in stabilizing an existing power structure. In a general sense, there is nothing new in this for sociologists. Weber, for example, writing more than a decade before Gramsci, had emphasized that the crude exercise of force was too unstable a method of guaranteeing the continuance of a system. A stable power system also needed a socially accepted principle of legitimation (see LEGITIMATE AUTHORITY). What distinguished Gramsci's contribution, and has influenced sociology in the last two decades, is the encouragement to investigate the ways in which specific institutions operated in the social reproduction of power relations and to examine wider theoretical issues in understanding belief structures, IDEOLOGY, etc. In the UK, the work of the Birmingham University Centre for Contemporary Cultural Studies (CCCS) (see CULTURAL STUDIES) was one important influence in the analysis and use of the concept. In recent years, there have been many studies which have used it in relation to issues such as working-class youth subcultures, the production of television news, and the development of state education.

Heidegger, Martin (1889–1976) German philosopher and leading contributor to PHENOMENOLOGY and EXISTENTIALISM. His philosophy has influenced modern sociological theory in a number of ways, notably his conception of what is distinctive about human beings: DASEIN, the so-called 'analytic of Man's Being'; and, related to this, his conception of TIME. What is distinct about Man is a capacity to understand himself, and although not master of his own origin, Man has the capacity to undertake 'authentic' actions, i.e. actions which do not retreat into anonymity, depersonalized objectivized modes of being, denying Man's distinctive capacities. In *Being and Time* (1929), Heidegger states the 'authentic self' as potentiality for action, an orientation towards the future (becoming), which involves possibilities and requires choice. The basic distinction which Heidegger draws between the *ontic* (entities or apparently 'real' things) and *ontological*, authentic 'Being', also has important implications for LANGUAGE. For Heidegger the 'ultimate signified' to which all 'signifiers' refer is the 'transcendental signified': Being. If in his earlier work Heidegger believed that Being could be addressed, later he did not, seeing all signification as open-ended. This feature of language Heidegger indicates by use of the technique of *erasure,* thus: to indicate both a word's necessity and its uncertainty. For Heidegger, traditional formulations of Western philosophy, which assumed the 'presencing' and grounding of the transcendental ego or subject, had become untenable. Heidegger attracted controversy mainly because of his association with FASCISM. However, the association has not hindered his ideas being taken up in a variety of applications – notably by SARTRE,

LACAN and DERRIDA and more generally in POSTSTRUCTURALISM (see also DECONSTRUCTION and POSTMODERNITY AND POSTMODERNISM). Heidegger's work has also influenced the SOCIAL PHENOMENOLOGY of SCHUTZ and Anthony GIDDENS' treatment of 'time' within STRUCTURATION THEORY.

herding society any form of society whose main subsistence comes from tending flocks and herds of domesticated animals (see PASTORALISM, NOMADS AND NOMADISM). In practice, subsistence needs are often met by a combination of herding with hunting and gathering and other forms of agriculture. See also HUNTER-GATHERER.

hermeneutic circle see GADAMER.

hermeneutics a theory and method of interpreting human action and artefacts. It derives from the term for interpreting biblical texts, a practice which involved detailed attempts to understand the 'authentic' version of the work. DILTHEY used the term (and also VERSTEHEN) to refer to the method of the 'cultural sciences', i.e. the subjects that forge 'shared understandings' between creator and interpreter. MANNHEIM made similar claims and enlarged upon the idea that the text could be seen as a document of a particular world view. GADAMER has attempted to validate his 'phenomenological hermeneutics' by invoking the idea of the *hermeneutic circle,* i.e. we can recognize and generalize a particular view only because we interpret instances of it, but can only understand a particular act or artefact with reference to the 'world view' that produced it. Gadamer argues that this process of validation is always provisional and never complete – our 'truth' can only ever be partial and must be subject to continual revision. Most recently hermeneutics has been developed by Ricoeur (1981), who has focused on its literary critical insights. He argues that the TEXT is in a key position as a mediator of tradition and uniqueness, and thus stands in a position of potential critique of both the world and the SELF. Similar possibilities have been opened up by HABERMAS with his 'critical hermeneutics' – an attempt to illustrate that any interpretation must take sides in a communication which is distorted by capitalist power relations.

Often criticized for its apparent celebration of RELATIVISM and SUBJECTIVITY, hermeneutics remains an approach that stimulates central debates within sociology. As Habermas points out, two features of hermeneutics have been vital:
(a) it reminds the social sciences of problems which arise from symbolic prestructuring of their subject matter; and
(b) it undermines simplistic, 'objectivist' understandings of the natural sciences (compare KUHN, FEYERABEND). See also FUSION OF HORIZONS. DOUBLE HERMENEUTIC.

heterosexuality 1 (common usage) the desire for sexual relationships with persons of the 'other' or 'opposite' sex.
2 (sociological usage) the privileged and dominant expression of sexuality in most known societies, which is often regarded as the 'natural' form of human sexual desire. In Western culture, heterosexuality has been normalized and prioritized over all other forms of human sexuality via institutional practices, including the law and social policy. Traditionally, sociologists have tended to take its 'normality' for granted, although, recently, sociologists such as MacIntosh have argued that heterosexuality should be regarded as sociologically problematic. Thus sociological theory should be directed at accounting for both the specific forms heterosexuality assumes in different cultures and its prevalence as the norm.
3 (usage in feminist sociology) a primarily political institution which has served to further the subordination of women to men. Rich (1980) has used the term *compulsory heterosexuality* to denote the social practices and prescriptions which ensure the continuance of heterosexuality as the privileged form of sexual orientation. Such practices penalize those who fail to conform,

whilst ensuring the inferiorization of those women who abide by the norms. Dworkin (1976) has defined heterosexuality as one of the major means whereby the sexual and social dominance of men over women is legitimated and reinforced. This view of heterosexuality has given rise to the growth of separatism within the feminist movement, and is challenged by those feminists who identify themselves as heterosexual. From this latter perspective, heterosexuality is a sexual preference which does not necessarily reinforce the imbalance of power between women and men.

heuristic device any general concept which is framed merely as an aid to analysis. WEBER sometimes presents his IDEAL TYPES as heuristic devices, as general concepts which are useful in the analysis of concrete historical cases but not an end in themselves.

hidden curriculum a set of values, attitudes, knowledge frames, which are embodied in the organization and processes of schooling and which are implicitly conveyed to pupils.

Although all schools have a formal curriculum comprising areas of academic knowledge which pupils are expected to acquire, it is the form of schooling, the messages transmitted as a result of its organization and practices, which is more powerful than the content of subjects. It promotes social control and an acceptance of the school's, and hence society's, authority structure.

Sociologists argue that the basic function of schooling is to reproduce society's VALUES and NORMS. Both structural-functionalists and Marxists agree on this, but for quite different reasons. The former argue that it is necessary in order to maintain the stability of the social order in the interest of all (see, for example, Parsons, 1959), whereas Marxists see the basic function of education as the reproduction of the social relations of capitalist economic production, and thus the maintenance of a class order which subordinates the proletariat. It is this latter function which is achieved predominantly through the hidden curriculum (see Bowles and Gintis, 1976).

hierarchy of credibility the notion (proposed by BECKER, 'Whose side are we on?', 1953) that societies are so organized that those who occupy top positions and positions of authority tend more readily to have their versions of the truth accepted, while the views of those who are 'underdogs' or 'outsiders' often go unrepresented, or are not taken seriously, or are represented only by 'official' accounts. Becker's opinion is that sociologists must side with the 'underdogs' or 'outsiders' if a more adequate overall view of society is to be obtained. The self-conscious pursuit of 'objectivity' and the avoidance of BIAS, or simply undertaking commissioned research for those in authority who can afford to pay, will result in research which is one-sided.

In siding with the 'underdog', Becker has been criticized (e.g. GOULDNER, 1973) for making proposals which undermine the attainment of objectivity, and suggesting, like WEBER, that sociology is always 'relative to values' (see also VALUE RELEVANCE). But his position is better seen as indicating that 'objectivity' is not easily achieved in sociology, and that many current practices designed to obtain it may have the opposite effect. See also OBJECTIVITY, VALUE FREEDOM AND VALUE NEUTRALITY, TRUTH, FUSION OF HORIZONS, DEVIANCE, LABELLING THEORY, AMPLIFICATION OF DEVIANCE.

hierarchy of needs see MASLOW.

hierarchy of the sciences a view of the sciences, first propounded by COMTE, in which the different sciences are seen as emerging in a definite sequence, with each science in the hierarchy being dependent upon, while also different in character from, and not simply reducible to, those below it (see Fig. 12). Though Comte saw a basic unity between the sciences (see POSITIVISM), sociology, as the 'Queen of the sciences' heading this hierarchy, is a synthesizing science, more complex than those disciplines below it.

SOCIOLOGY AND THE MORAL SCIENCES	↑	*INCREASING SPECIFICITY, COMPLEXITY, SYNTHESIS*
PHYSIOLOGY (BIOLOGY)		
CHEMISTRY		
PHYSICS		*RELATIVE SIMPLICITY, GENERALITY, 'ANALYTICAL'*
CELESTIAL PHYSICS (ASTRONOMY)		
MATHEMATICS	↓	

Fig. 12 **Hierarchy of the sciences.** According to this view of the sciences, first proposed by Comte (1798-1857), the sciences can be arranged in ascending order of complexity, with sciences higher in the hierarchy dependent, but not only dependent, on those below. Thus, sociology makes assumptions about the physical and biological world, but at the same time also involves an 'emergent' level of analysis different from and not reducible to those below.

Comte's view of the hierarchical arrangement of the sciences is still accepted in general terms (e.g. see Rose, 1973). However, the precise way in which sociology is 'scientific', and the extent of its differentiation from natural science, is much disputed.

One reason why sociology can be seen as dependent upon, but not reducible to, other sciences, is the number and the complexity of the variables involved. Thus, higher-level concepts, and accounts which simplify and summarize the many variables and relationships involved, are unavoidable. In biology and in sociology, however, where organisms pursue ends, and human actors are motivated by 'meanings', entirely new levels of analysis are introduced in which any simple reduction is unlikely to succeed. However, the precise implications of such new 'levels' for sociology are controversial, and often different from Comte's. See also REDUCTION, REDUCTIONISM, SUPERORGANIC, MEANINGFUL UNDERSTANDING AND EXPLANATION, MIND, HERMENEUTICS, VERSTEHEN.

high costs of entry manufacturing see DEPENDENT INDUSTRIALIZATION.

higher education the highest level of post-school education (see BINARY SYSTEM, UNIVERSITY, POLYTECHNIC, NEW UNIVERSITY). Although great differences between systems of higher education exist internationally, there are also some important common tendencies.

The expansion of higher education has been a feature of most countries in recent decades and the movement from 'élite' to MASS HIGHER EDUCATION has become well-established in most developed and in many developing countries, in which an increasing proportion of the relevant age group participate in higher education. The main differences between higher educational systems exist in the extent to which these are 'unitary' or have become 'differentiated' into separate subsystems (see Teichler, 1988), and in the extent to which individual systems have expanded. In the US and Japan, for example, enrolments in higher education either approach or exceed 50% of the relevant age group. The extent to which the expansion of higher education is effective in improving the economic performance and general social wellbeing of modern societies (see HUMAN CAPITAL, POSTCAPITALIST SOCIETY, INFORMATION SOCIETY, SOCIAL DEMAND FOR EDUCATION), or has consequences which are less desirable (see CREDENTIALISM, SCREENING AND THE SCREENING HYPOTHESIS), remains disputed. A balanced view would be to accept that this expansion has both positive and negative outcomes which need to be carefully analysed. See also GRADUATE LABOUR MARKET, INTELLECTUAL LABOUR.

Hinduism the main religion of India and the oldest of the great world religions. Hinduism is based on the doctrine of reincarnation and associated with the concept of CASTE. It is a polytheistic religion, with many gods and many different CULTS and practices, while JUDAISM, CHRISTIANITY and ISLAM are the main monotheistic religions.

histogram a diagrammatic representation of a FREQUENCY DISTRIBUTION, consisting of contiguous rectangles displaying interval-level data (see CRITERIA AND LEVELS OF MEASUREMENT) grouped into categories. In a histogram the width of the rectangle is proportional to the class interval under consideration, and the height is the associated frequency. The area of each bar is then proportional to the frequencies for each class interval (see Fig. 13). A histogram differs from a BAR CHART in that it is the areas of the rectangles which represent the relative frequencies.

historical demography the study of past patterns of population structure, FERTILITY, etc., using historical source material, especially for those periods prior to the first Census in 1801. In the UK, the subject has flourished particularly since the 1950s using data gathered from PARISH REGISTERS, wills, tombstones, and the like. The findings of this research (e.g. Laslett, 1972; Wrigley, 1966) have lead to a reappraisal of previous assumptions about the 'preindustrial family' (e.g. its 'extended' form). In more general terms, historical demography has thrown new light on the overall relation between family size and structure, patterns of sexual behaviour, social mobility and population change where data had been previously lacking. See also DEMOGRAPHY.

historical generalization any generalization about the past, which may or may not be true, e.g. 'the Danes plundered before they settled'. Such generalizations may be tested against the evidence, and may apply universally to the past, or to an aspect of the past. This is an important sense in which historiography and sociology may claim to be 'scientific'. It should also be noted that, contrary to some suggestions (see EMPATHIC UNDERSTANDING), such testable generalizations may refer to 'meaningful' as well as non-meaningful relations.

Historical generalizations have sometimes been seen as very different from scientific generalizations in that they do not assert fully-fledged universal conditional statements (see COVERING-LAW MODEL) which are intended to apply within their respective frames of reference (e.g. 'that all mammals suckle their young') utterly universally, i.e. to have an application to present and future events as well as to past events. Thus, scientific generalizations have

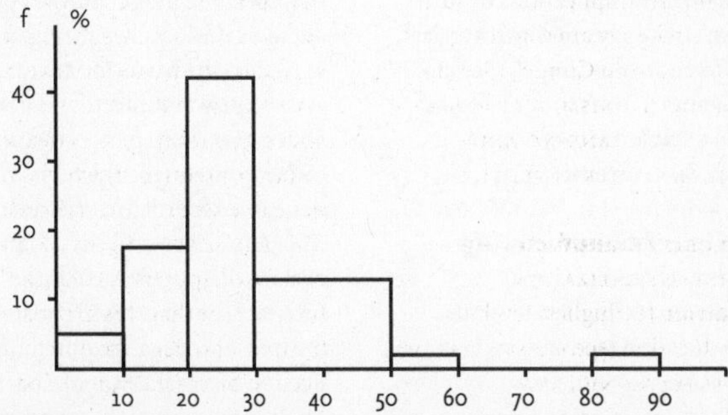

Fig. 13 **Histogram.** A diagrammatic representation (f=frequency) of a frequency distribution, consisting of contiguous rectangles, in which the width of each rectangle is proportional to the class interval under consideration and the area of each rectangle is proportional to the associated frequency.

been contrasted with merely '*accidental generalizations*' (e.g. a statement that all the stones in a particular box are black).

However many historical generalizations are not *merely* 'accidental generalizations' in the above sense, since they may refer to significant regularities in the past which have explanations and implications and may also have a universal basis (e.g. the general tendencies associated with PATRIMONIALISM or BUREAUCRACY). That events in history do sometimes have important 'accidental' causes (e.g. 'Cleopatra's nose') is not in dispute. Nor are historical generalizations usually easily reached, the reasons being:
(a) the complexity of the variables involved;
(b) the ability to manipulate the variables is limited to 'quasi-experimentation' (see COMPARATIVE METHOD);
(c) the limitations of available historical data, and uncertainties and disputes in their interpretation.

However, this need not imply that significant historical generalizations cannot be made or that generalizations with a more universal basis are confined only to the physical sciences. In one respect, historical generalizations may be more easily reached than universal generalizations in the sciences in that, by definition,, the past is completed and thus not subject further to the vagaries of human choice and future cases.

historical materialism a general term for MARX and ENGELS' conception of historical, social and economic change, and the method of analysis associated with this. The basic idea underlying Marx's MATERIALISM, as expressed in *A Contribution to Critique of Political Economy* (1859), is that 'in the social production of their life, men enter into definite relations that are indispensable and independent of their will, relations of production which correspond to a definite stage of the development of their productive forces'.

Unlike the more rigid, economic reductionism and scientism of the DIALECTICAL MATERIALISM propounded by later 'official Marxisms', historical materialism can be seen as allowing for a variety of interpretations. including 'humanistic' and 'voluntaristic' as well as deterministic' versions. Part of the warrant for the former is Marx's insistence that 'a distinction should always be made between the material transformation of the economic conditions of production which can be determined with the precision of natural science, and the legal, political, religious, aesthetic or philosophic, in short ideological, forms in which men become conscious of conflict and fight it out'. A further view of historical materialism is that it constitutes a 'method' (compare ECONOMIC INTERPRETATION OF HISTORY) in which the investigator is invited to focus on the role of economic factors in historical explanations, rather than a finished theory in which economic factors are claimed to have primacy. See also MARXISM, MARXIST SOCIOLOGY, BASE AND SUPERSTRUCTURE.

historical sociology 1 any sociology focused particularly on the study of past societies or using historical sources.
2 more particularly, those forms of comparative sociology which focus on historical societies, and on order and change within these societies (see also COMPARATIVE METHOD). Historical sociology in this second sense, after falling out of fashion (see HISTORICISM, EVOLUTIONARY THEORY, SOCIAL CHANGE), has come into vogue again in recent decades as the result of major works by such authors as MOORE and WALLERSTEIN in the US, and, in the UK, ANDERSON, MANN and ELIAS. There is also a sense in which all general theories of social change are historical sociologies. It is in this context that partisans of historical sociology, such as P. Abrams (1982), argue that it forms the central core of traditional sociology, and that its importance should be reasserted in modern sociology. An informative survey of the range of recent historical sociology is D. Smith *The Rise of Historical Sociology,* (1991). See also HISTORY.

historicism 1 any approach to the understanding of history which emphasizes the uniqueness of each historical epoch, suggesting that each historical situation or period can only be understood in its own terms. Usually historical understanding and/or explanation are seen as involving only those modes of explanation particularly appropriate to social studies or the human sciences (e.g. MEANINGFUL UNDERSTANDING AND EXPLANATION, HERMENEUTICS) and not those forms of explanation (see COVERING-LAW MODEL AND DEDUCTIVE NOMOLOGICAL EXPLANATION) widely regarded as uppermost in the physical sciences. See also COLLINGWOOD, DILTHEY, GADAMER, WINDELBAND, IDIOGRAPHIC AND NOMOTHETIC, GEISTESWISSENSCHAFTEN AND NATURWISSENSCHAFTEN.
2 Karl POPPER's extension of sense 1 to identify *two* distinct kinds of view which imply that explanation in historical and social studies is of a different order from our understanding of the physical world:
(a) *non-naturalistic historicism,* as in sense 1, and;
(b) *naturalistic historicism,* in which certain theorists in philosophy and sociology (notably HEGEL, COMTE and MARX) are seen as guilty of misunderstanding and misrepresenting the true nature of scientific prediction (POPPER, 1957) in claiming to be able to predict 'historical change'. Popper presents both forms of historicism as failing to appreciate the true character of scientific laws and theories, i.e. that scientific explanations and predictions are not 'unlimited', and are relative to specific 'initial conditions'. Popper refers to historical predictions, e.g. Marx's 'prediction' of the collapse of CAPITALISM) as unscientific 'prophecies'. In Popper's view, once the limited nature of scientific laws becomes appreciated arguments against the relevance of a proper use of scientific laws in historical explanations (non-naturalistic historicism) should also collapse, since reference to scientific laws need not be at odds with a recognition of the existence of elements of relative uniqueness in social situations (see also SITUATIONAL ANALYSIS AND SITUATIONAL LOGIC).

There exist some similarities (although some differences) between Popper's view and WEBER's opposition to HISTORICAL MATERIALISM and the latter's use of both meaningful explanation and IDEAL TYPES in historical sociological analysis. (Both Popper and Weber, for instance, take rational economic models as a benchmark.) Critics of Popper's view, however, accuse him of constructing a 'straw man' of the theorists he opposes, and point out that much of his argument relies on a prior acceptance of his disputed COVERING-LAW MODEL of science. This said, while differences in degree and perhaps kind between historical and social reality on the one hand, and physical reality on the other, are widely acknowledged in sociology and conceptions such as sense 1 above illuminate these, there is no general acceptance of the view implied in sense 1 that any simple distinction can be drawn between science and 'nonscience' (see also SCIENCE, SOCIOLOGY OF SCIENCE).

historicity 1 the distinctive historical quality or character of a social context. This aspect of social reality is emphasized by those sociologists who believe in the importance of an historical approach in bringing authenticity to social accounts. See also HISTORICISM, HERMENEUTICS.
2 the capacity of a society to reflect and to act upon itself. This term was first used by SARTRE, and is taken up by GIDDENS to characterize the capacities possessed especially by historical (as against 'prehistorical') societies.

historiography 1 the writing of HISTORY; written history.
2 the history of historical writing, together with discussion of the methodological questions raised by the construction of historical accounts. In many ways the discussions parallel methodological discussions in the social sciences in general, not least those in sociology.

history 1 the entirety of the past.
2 any written accounts of the past.
3 the recorded past (*recorded history*); the history of literate societies; societies in which there have survived written records of a recorded oral tradition (compare ARCHAEOLOGY).
4 the professional academic discipline concerned with the study of the past.

Historical writing takes many forms: popular, propagandist, as well as academic. Although in the latter form it is undertaken mainly by *historians,* academic historical writing is not confined to writers located within history as a discipline. Many sociological accounts have as their focus particular historical societies or selected general features of historical societies (see also HISTORICAL SOCIOLOGY). In addition each academic discipline also tends to produce accounts of its own history, e.g. the history of science, the history of art, etc.

The relationship between history and sociology as academic disciplines has been uneasy. Whereas for historians, the goal has usually been the understanding and explanation of specific historical situations, sociologists have more often viewed the findings about particular historical societies as a laboratory for testing more general propositions about society or particular types of society (see also COMPARATIVE METHOD). Such an overall distinction is, however, only partly justified, as is made clear by the presence of meaningful explanatory accounts within sociology (e.g. WEBER's *Protestant Ethic and the Spirit of Capitalism,* 1904–5) and by the frequent recourse to general propositions within academic history (see also MEANINGFUL UNDERSTANDING AND EXPLANATION, HERMENEUTICS). See too HISTORICAL GENERALIZATION, HISTORICISM, ANNALES SCHOOL, BRAUDEL, BLOCH, TILLY, MARX, MOORE, ANDERSON, MANN, HISTORICAL DEMOGRAPHY, HISTORY WORKSHOP JOURNAL, VERSTEHEN, IDEAL. TYPE, IDIOGRAPHIC AND NOMOTHETIC, GEISTESWISSENSCHAFTEN AND NATURWISSENSCHAFTEN.

history of ideas an interdisciplinary approach to the historical study of ideas which seeks to overcome the fragmentation of study in the modern history of thought (e.g. separate histories of sociology, science, philosophy, literature, etc.). The approach stresses the importance of study which focuses on the interrelationships between ideas in different disciplines (e.g. ideas like 'nature' or naturalism' which have importance across contexts).

history of mentalities an approach to historical study (as seen, for example, in the work of the French historians Fernand BRAUDEL, 1949, and Emanuel Le Roy Ladurie, 1978) in which the goal is the historical recovery and reconstruction of the ideas, emotions and mental structures of historical persons, especially the ideas of ordinary persons as well as the great and famous. In the work of Phillipe Aries (1962), the focus is on psychological investigation of the past, i.e. on PSYCHOHISTORY. In the work of Braudel, the *mentalities* are the mind sets, paradigms and points of view embedded in institutions which give coherence to, and make up the 'totality' of, a historical epoch. See also ANNALES SCHOOL.

History Workshop Journal a radical socialist and feminist journal and collective founded in the early 1970s. It has been especially associated with 'new ways' of doing and presenting historical research, e.g. *'history from below'* (an emphasis on social history and the history of everyday life and ordinary people, including ORAL HISTORY), an emphasis on interdisciplinarity, and on writing in ways accessible to a wide readership.

Hobbes, Thomas (1588–1679) English philosopher and political theorist responsible for the earliest self-conscious attempt to construct a 'science' of CIVIL SOCIETY from first principles derived from imagining what Man would be like in a state of nature, where all authority, political, moral and social, was lacking. His project was to follow the deductive reasoning of geometry, and his first principles were dictated by a philosophy that was both mechanistic and materialist. According to this view, society, like the human beings who are its simplest elements, is a machine. To understand how society works, one must take it apart in imagination, resolve it into its simplest elements, and then recompose it to a healthy functioning according to the laws of motion of these components. Hobbes distinguished between the artificial, made by Man, and the natural, found in the physical world. He then claimed that Man could only have certain knowledge of what men have created or made. Men could have certain knowledge of geometry because men themselves had created the theorems, propositions and figures of geometry. A like knowledge was possible of civil society, because men had also created this. The substance of Hobbes' political thinking is contained in *De Cive* (*Concerning the Citizen*) (1642) and *Leviathan* (1651). In these, he sought to demonstrate that Man's natural condition, in which all authority was lacking and in which he enjoyed a NATURAL RIGHT to everything that would assist his self-preservation, was one of unmitigated strife, in which there was no security for any human purpose. He then argued that since Man possessed reason, which was his capacity to know the causes of things, he was able to discover those principles of conduct which he ought, prudentially, to follow for his security and safety. These principles Hobbes called the 'convenient Articles of Peace', under which men agreed to lay down their natural right to everything and submit to absolute and undivided sovereign authority. Hobbes' conclusions here point in a monarchical direction, but he was always careful, when referring to this authority, to use the phrase 'one man, or assembly of men'. In the times in which he wrote – the English Civil War and its aftermath – it was not prudent to offend either royalist or parliamentary susceptibilities.

For commentators such as MacPherson (1962), Hobbes' thinking reflects a bourgeois individualism. For others, it came close to a Kantian view of 'moral obligation'. The question raised by Hobbes – the Hobbesian 'problem of order', as PARSONS puts it – remains a central question in sociology.

Hobhouse, Leonard Trelawny (1864–1929) British sociologist, and the leading figure in early British sociology, who is primarily remembered today for his contributions to COMPARATIVE SOCIOLOGY and, especially, to the SOCIOLOGY OF DEVELOPMENT. Hobhouse was a man of rich and varied interests, whose career exemplified a unity of theory and practice. Employment in journalism preceded his appointment to the new Martin White Professorship in Sociology at the London School of Economics. Politically, Hobhouse favoured the left, although he was well aware of the implications for personal liberty of a state bureaucratic form of socialism. For Hobhouse, a balance had to be struck between market and plan which enhanced individual freedom. His social philosophy is best expressed in his *Elements of Social Justice* (1922), a book which, in its conception of the relation between an economically regulating state and personal freedom, still remains relevant to socialist thought.

Apart from his major contributions to sociology, which included the comparative study, *Morals in Evolution* (1906) and the three-volume *Principles of Sociology* (1921-24), Hobhouse wrote on animal and social psychology, logic, epistemology, ethics and metaphysics as well as on social philosophy. However, the overarching theme of his work was the evolution of mind and society (see EVOLUTIONARY THEORY). For Hobhouse, the evolutionary process could be examined at three logically distinct levels: description, explanation and evaluation. Social development itself could be estimated in terms of four biologically orientated criteria:
(a) the increasing efficiency with which a Society is controlled and directed;
(b) a growing expansion in the scale and complexity of social organization;

(c) an extension of social cooperation in realizing human needs;
(d) the enhanced capacity for human fulfilment.

Hobhouse used historical and comparative evidence to suggest a general association between stages of social development and intellectual advance, manifested in the growth of science and technology, and ethical and religious reflection and art. A final concern was to examine development in terms of ethical standards. Here he employed his theory of *The Rational Good* (1921): development was ethically appropriate to the extent to which it promoted both social harmony and the realization of human capacities and potentialities. Progress was not inevitable, as the outbreak of World War I made clear. Yet, by the 1920s, he was cautiously optimistic that the regulation, efficiency and complexity of industrial societies had indeed been shown to be compatible with individual freedom and mutuality, that progress had been achieved, and that this could be advanced still further by the cooperative, self-conscious efforts of nation states. History will probably find his caution more justifiable than his optimism.

holism 1 any form of sociological theory which emphasizes the primacy of 'social structure', 'social system', etc., in determining social outcomes, and in sociological explanations. The opposite position is METHODOLOGICAL INDIVIDUALISM. As used by POPPER (1957), the term is mainly a pejorative one. See also SITUATIONAL LOGIC. 2 in a more neutral sense, the tendency of sociology, in contrast with other more specialized social sciences, to maintain an all-inclusive view of social phenomena.

Holocaust a general term for the atrocities committed by Hitler and the Nazi Party (see NATIONAL SOCIALISM) in Europe during World War II, and especially the systematic extermination of up to six million Jews in mass gas chambers and CONCENTRATION CAMPS. The term is derived from *holo* (whole) *kauston* (burnt) – 'burnt whole'. The Holocaust was meant to be part of the 'final solution' (*Die Endlosung*) to rid Europe of Jews and other 'undesirable' groups by the Nazis. See also BAUMAN. See also FASCISM, RACISM, GENOCIDE.

Homans, George (1910–89) US sociologist who, in 'Bringing Men Back In' (1964), his Presidential Address to the American Sociological Association, argued that social phenomena can only be explained by reference to the motivations of individual persons. In *The Human Group* (1950), he had earlier argued that, 'All grander sociologies must be true to the sociology of the group.' In *Social Behaviour: Its Elementary Forms* (1961), he stated that 'he had come to believe that the empirical propositions' in the former work could 'most easily be explained by two bodies of empirical general propositions already in existence: behavioral psychology and elementary economics'. Along with his fellow American, Peter BLAU, Homans is regarded as one of the main exponents of EXCHANGE THEORY.

homelessness the situation of having no home or permanent abode. Those in this situation include people living on the streets, in hostels, squats, or in temporary accommodation with no permanent right of tenure. Homelessness has become a major problem in Europe, North America, Australia and many other areas of the world in the past ten years, particularly among youth (S. Hutson and M. Liddiard, *Youth Homelessness. The Construction of a Social Issue*, 1994).

In Britain it is necessary to distinguish between different groups of homeless people according to their rights to social housing. The statutory homeless are those who have a right to social housing under the Homeless Persons Act, 1977 and Housing Act 1985, including homeless households with dependent children (both couple parent and single parent) and the homeless elderly over 60. Households do not just have to be in priority need, they should also be local and unintentionally homeless, but if they fulfil these conditions then the local authority must rehouse. The number of households accepted as homeless by local authorities per year has risen from just over 53,000 in 1978 to nearly 149,000 in 1991; four out of every five acceptances are households with children or where a woman is pregnant, and thus every year 400,000 persons are accepted as homeless including nearly 200,000 children.

However, local authorities reject at least 40 per cent of homeless applicants, and 'hidden homelessness' has grown. In the 1991 Census 198,000 households shared housekeeping at the same address and 95,000 households lived in non-permanent accommodation such as caravans and mobile homes. Both these figures have increased by 17 per cent compared with the census of 1981.

Households that are not accepted and young single people, who have never been included as a priority need group, have contributed to the extraordinary rise in the numbers of *non-statutory* homeless, people with no special rights to social housing. For London there are estimates of up to 120,000 homeless young single people, and nationally the estimate is 180,000 (J. Greve and E. Currie, *Homelessness,* 1990).

Some writers have seen the growth of homelessness as a result of the under-supply of social housing, others as a result of changing conditions of life for young people including high youth unemployment rates and changing patterns of family life. Both of these types of explanations have evidence to support them. Local authority housing completions in Britain have declined from 85,000 in 1979 to 2,000 in 1992. Housing Associations, which were to be the new providers of social housing, have not filled the gap. At the same time the employment rate for 16-year-old school leavers declined from 50 per cent in 1976 to 15 per cent in 1986. In 1994 the Government released a white paper, *Access to Local Authority and Housing Association Tenancies,* which proposed the repeal of all homeless persons legislation and a return to the provision of temporary accommodation only for the homeless. Nine thousand organizations wrote in to oppose the proposals, two to support.

homeostasis any process which regulates or maintains a system in a stable state in relation to a changing external environment in which this system operates. The term may be applied to mechanical systems or servomechanisms, to living beings, or to SOCIAL SYSTEMS. Although a central postulate of some sociological theories (especially see FUNCTIONALISM and STRUCTURAL-FUNCTIONALISM), the suggestion that social systems act in self-maintaining or self-equilibriating ways remains controversial. See also SYSTEMS THEORY.

homeworking a form of remunerated labour undertaken within the home. In the pre-factory era of manufacture, items would be delivered to households (the 'putting out' system) for further processing, and collected when this had been completed. In Europe, the practice continued after the introduction of factories, but probably declined until the late 20th-century when it was revived, especially with the introduction of more flexible patterns of production. In many contemporary Asian and Latin American countries, homeworking is very common, with parts of the production process contracted out. Its attraction for modern firms is that homeworkers (often women) represented a flexible and cheap labour force. Factory overhead costs are also reduced. Homeworking or 'outwork' should not be confused with DOMESTIC LABOUR. See also DOMESTIC PRODUCTION.

homo clausus see FIGURATION.

homo faber literally, 'man the worker'. The concept of work has undergone dramatic changes from ancient to contemporary societies. In Homeric society work was regarded as a natural part of the fabric of social life. The rich and the poor worked and did not despise manual labour. The unity between work and all aspects of culture was broken in the time of Classical Greece. A dual set of divisions were established between:

(a) work and the rest of life (contemplation, family life, politics, leisure); and (b) noble and ignoble work. These divisions were exploited and developed by successive social formations in the Middle Ages, the Renaissance, the Enlightenment, the 19th-century and the 20th-century. MARX regarded the labour exacted under the capitalist system of production as necessarily alienating. It did not satisfy the worker's innermost need for self-actualization and co-operation with the rest of society. At the same time Marx maintained that the *homo faber* model provided the most appropriate approach to understanding human affairs as through work men (and women) make themselves. Compare HOMO LUDENS.

homo ludens literally, 'man the player'. The fullest sociological treatment of the term is to be found in the work of Johan Huizinga (*Homo Ludens*, 1944). He argues that PLAY precedes culture in the development of human societies. Huizinga proposes an alternative model of social development in which the play-forms of *reverie*, irony and the capacity to imagine 'as if', are interpreted as being the spur to human innovation and growth. In addition to dominating SPORT and LEISURE, play forms are analysed as the basis of legal processes (the game of advocacy and defence), philosophy (the arts of rhetoric and sophistry) and war (mock battles and war-games). Huizinga's work was intended to rescue play from the marginal status which it has usually been assigned in the history of ideas. He was only partially successful. The conception of 'man the player' lacks the urgency or brutality of other metaphors of human development such as 'man the worker' and 'man the tyrant'. Nonetheless, *homo ludens* provides a challenging alternative view of history and society. Its full potential has yet to be realized. Compare HOMO FABER.

homophobia the fear of HOMOSEXUALITY. Although there has been some suggestion that homophobia may exist as a personality trait, it is more fruitful to examine the social conditions under which homosexual behaviour is proscribed (in England and Wales this happened in 1885, when male homosexuality was criminalized), and becomes an organizing principle for particular roles, identities and subcultures (Weeks, 1977).

Homo sapiens the biological term for human beings. The species term 'sapiens' means 'intelligent', as opposed to other species of the genus *Homo*, such as *Homo erectus*. Strictly, the term for the current variety of humans is *Homo sapiens sapiens*, as opposed to other subspecies of the species sapiens, such as *Homo sapiens neanderthalis*.

homosexuality the desire for sexual relationships with persons of the same biological sex. Usually, however, the term is used to describe social relationships between men, while LESBIANISM is used to denote such relationships between women.

A distinction needs to be made between homosexual behaviour, found in most known societies, and homosexuality as a particular role around which individuals construct identities, and communities or subcultures are formed. Weeks (1977) points out that the term 'homosexual' was first introduced into the English language in the 19th-century and that it was during this period that the social and historical factors involved in the development of homosexuality as a specific role occurred. The criminalization of male homosexuality in England and Wales in 1885 was an important part of this process. Moreover, the medical and psychiatric professions pathologized homosexuality, establishing it as a sickness open to their 'expert' intervention, and thus successfully medicalizing an area of social DEVIANCE. Homosexuality remained on the World Health Organization's list of pathologies until the 1970s.

According to Mort (1980), the legal reforms in England and Wales (1967) acted as an important catalyst for the emergence and radicalization of 'gay politics'. Alongside

FEMINISM, gay liberation movements challenged the essentialism of 19th-century sexology, and the medicalization of homosexuality, stressing the political and social dimensions of sexuality. Counter-ideologies were developed to challenge the stigmatization, discrimination and oppression encountered by lesbians and gay men. The term 'gay' was adopted, particularly by homosexual men, to challenge the negative labels attached to homosexuality by mainstream culture. Within the newly emergent and visible lesbian and gay subcultures, human sexuality has come to be seen as a combination of social forces, personal choice and sexual politics. The emphasis on choice was particularly evident in *political lesbianism,* which stressed woman identification as a political strategy against patriarchal relations. The implicit desexualization of lesbianism found in political lesbianism has highlighted divisions of an ideological nature within the lesbian community, and criticisms of sexist practices within gay male culture by lesbian feminists have given rise to the demand that the oppression of lesbians be theorized differently from that of gay men.

Kitzinger (1987) has challenged both the essentialist arguments and those which regard homosexuality as a matter of individual preference or political choice. In doing so, she has placed a renewed emphasis on social constructionism.

Whilst the 1960s and 70s may be regarded as a period of relative radicalism in Western societies for both lesbians and gay men, the socioeconomic conditions of the 1980s have engendered a moral backlash, exemplified by the growth of the New Right. and a series of MORAL PANICS over AIDS, lesbian motherhood and positive images of homosexuality. Sec also COMING OUT, PINK ECONOMY.

Hope-Goldthorpe scale see OCCUPATIONAL SCALES.

horizontal division of labour see SEXUAL DIVISION OF LABOUR.

Horkheimer, Max (1895–1973) German social theorist and leading member of the FRANKFURT SCHOOL OF CRITICAL THEORY. Beginning in the 1930s, he expounded his own and the Frankfurt school's conception of 'critical theory' in numerous essays and books. Taking as his point of departure the work of the young MARX and also HEGEL, his distinctive viewpoint was that a fundamental transformation of both theory and practice was required if modern civilization was ever to escape from its current alienative and exploitive form. Epistemologically, Horkheimer argued for a repudiation of all absolute doctrines, especially opposing any suggestion that it is ever satisfactory to take social phenomena at their face value. Thus both POSITIVISM and EMPIRICISM are rejected. Politically, Horkheimer argued against the assumption that a proletarian revolution would lead to human emancipation. What was required was the establishment of an open-ended conception of reason, capable of informing human values and breaking the link between 'knowledge' and human alienation. Works by Horkheimer include *Eclipse of Reason* (1947), *Critical Theory: Selected Essays* (1972), and (with Theodor ADORNO) *Dialectic of Enlightenment* (1972, original German edition, 1947). See also NEGATION AND NEGATIVITY.

horticulture a form of food cultivation which is effected by the use of hand tools, including digging-sticks or hoes. As such, horticulture is generally designated in anthropology as being less technologically developed than AGRICULTURE, in which ploughs and draft animals are employed (see Lenski and Lenski, 1970).

hospital an institution where the sick, wounded, infirm or incapacitated are nursed and given medical treatment. Originating in medieval places of refuge, such as hostels and hospices run by charitable and nursing orders of nuns, for the poor, the sick and social outcasts, the hospital emerged as a specialized institution during the period of

INDUSTRIALIZATION when the control and classification of social problems resulted in the differentiation of the hospital from the asylum and the workhouse.

Historians of medicine see the hospital as a key institution in the theoretical and social development of the PROFESSION. During the 19th century, medical practices were changing because of advancements in knowledge of anatomy and pathology. The status of medical doctors was being altered by changes in training and by medical registration which created a professional monopoly over healing. Teaching hospitals were the source of scientific training, research, specialization, practical techniques and a professional subculture. These hospitals admitted patients less on the basis of clinical need than on clinical interest, and they also created a new client group for the medical profession – their social equals and inferiors instead of the aristocrats who had hitherto employed doctors as part of their domestic retinue. The hospital was a vital institution also in the evolution of *nursing* as a profession, since it was in this setting that the Nightingale Reforms were put into practice: recruitment on the basis of 'vocation', training undertaken as part of the work process, the hygiene ideal, the practice of 'nursing the ward', and the social order of the hospital (which can be seen as paralleling the English bourgeois family of the time).

household 'a single person or a group of people who have the address as their only or main residence and who either share one meal a day or share living accommodation' (The Office of Population Censuses and Surveys). Nonrelated members are problematic in this definition, and sociologists have used two main types of household composition in discussing households:
(a) those based on the familial structure of the household, which identify the number, size and types of family in that household;
(b) those based on the age and sex structure, which identify the numbers of children, adults and, sometimes, people of pensionable age in the household.

The CENSUS uses both of these types. Different versions of the second type are used in the FAMILY EXPENDITURE SURVEY and the GENERAL HOUSEHOLD SURVEY. In the Census, the selection of the HEAD OF HOUSEHOLD is left to respondents to choose according to the criterion of 'chief economic supporter'.

These definitions closely relate household composition to family composition, and new types of social organization, such as flat sharing, sheltered accommodation for the elderly and student accommodation, call into question the adequacy of this type of definition. Critics have also queried the usefulness of the *head of household* definition since it is often assumed that a man is the head of the household regardless of the social position of any women living in the same household. See also HOMELESSNESS.

household allocative system the different ways in which household budgets are organized. The concept was developed by Jan Pahl (*Money and Marriage*, 1989). The households studied by Pahl were characterized by financial arrangements in which finances involved either 'husband or wife controlled pooling' of finances, or where the husband or the wife *alone* controlled money. These arrangements were found to be related to the socioeconomic characteristics of the household (e.g. total income, the relative contribution of husband and wife, educational background) as well as the degree of adherence to traditional patriarchal values (see PATRIARCHY), or more liberal ideals of sharing and equality.

housewife see DOMESTIC LABOUR.

housework the unwaged labour involved in maintaining the household and its members, such as cooking, cleaning, washing and ironing. In most modern societies, this work is privatized and feminized. Housework is concerned with the physical rather than the emotional tasks of caring for family members. Women, assumed to be 'natural'

CARE givers, typically undertake both roles. See DOMESTIC LABOUR.

housing see SOCIOLOGY OF HOUSING.

housing class see URBAN SOCIOLOGY.

human capital the productive investment of resources in human beings rather than in plant and machinery. In economics, such investment in human resources is appraised in comparison with levels of economic return from other kinds of investment. Clearly, investment in human capital begins in the family and continues in school and HIGHER EDUCATION, and is also affected by such inputs as provision for health care.

As a body of economic theory and associated empirical research, the *human-capital theory* of G. Becker, *Human Capital* (1975), explains income differentials as, in part at least, a return to human capital, e.g. the correlation between the number of years of formal education and earnings is so explained. The conclusion is often reached by human capital theorists that the returns to education are high. Similarly, POVERTY is sometimes explained as arising from a lack of human capital.

Challenges to the arguments of human-capital theory arise from a number of different sources, especially that the returns associated with education in fact arise from other sources, i.e. education may act merely as a filter or 'screen', and native ability or family background actually account for a significant proportion of the correlations between education and earnings (see SCREENING AND SCREENING HYPOTHESIS). Compare FUNCTIONALIST THEORY OF SOCIAL STRATIFICATION. See also CULTURAL CAPITAL.

human-centred technology an approach to technology design and work organization which aims to enhance the skills and abilities of users by according equal priority to human and organizational issues as well as technical design requirements. Also referred to in manufacturing as *anthropocentric production systems,* this approach is in direct contrast to the technical design philosophy which is based upon the engineering assumption that humans are a source of uncertainty and error in production, and are to be eventually replaced by computer-integrated systems in the 'unmanned factory of the future' (see also TECHNOLOGICAL DETERMINISM, NEW TECHNOLOGY). In its ideal-typical form, human-centred technology incorporates design criteria which allow a unity of conception and execution, skill enhancement (particularly the recognition of tacit skills), and a measure of worker control over work processes and technology through participative systems design.

Human-centred technology was at first associated with the work-humanization initiatives of the 1960s and 70s, such as the Volvo group technology experiments, job enrichment and job enlargement schemes, and the SOCIOTECHNICAL SYSTEMS APPROACH (see also QUALITY OF WORKING LIFE, HUMAN RELATIONS SCHOOL). More recently, human-centred technology is seen as a crucial feature of new production systems based upon *flexible specialization.* The theory of flexible specialization posits an emerging post-Fordist manufacturing strategy (see FORDISM AND POST-FORDISM) in which multiskilled and functionally flexible craft workers replace the Tayloristic work patterns of mass production. According to the theory of flexible specialization, human-centred technology is both more 'efficient' in management terms, and more humanitarian and democratic in terms of management – worker relations: a 'non-zero sum' worker-management relationship. Although an important corrective to the simplistic logic of DESKILLING implied by LABOUR PROCESS THEORY, critics of human-centred approaches to technology cast doubt upon the extent to which they are realized in practice and point to the negative consequences found in case studies, such as increased levels of stress and work intensification. Furthermore, critics of flexible specialization question the extent of genuine worker participation, and note the increase in peripheral workers on part-time or temporary contracts who support core workers enjoying greater job security and better conditions of work (see Wood, 1989).

human ecology the application of ecological principles to the understanding of the spatial distribution of social groups and the relationships among them. The approach was a product of the pioneering CHICAGO SCHOOL sociologists Robert PARK and Ernest Burgess, who employed it in their studies of urban society (see URBAN SOCIOLOGY). The term thus has often been used interchangeably with URBAN ECOLOGY. According to this view, cities develop in response to certain features of the physical environment (e.g. river banks) and act as 'a great sorting mechanism' in terms of the distribution of the populations which inhabit them. This process takes place according to the ecological principles of competition between social groups for scarce resources (*ecological competition*), for example, pressure on amenities and land drives up land values, by the invasion of urban space (*ecological invasion*) and by a succession of new populations (*ecological succession*). Eventually, this process creates a city with a series of concentric zones, in which inner city areas are characterized by commercial prosperity and decaying private houses, surrounded by older established neighbourhoods of workers, with the most affluent groups having retreated to the outlying suburbs. As groups continue to find central or near central zones unattractive, so further outward migration occurs, and new social groups (e.g. immigrant workers) move in.

The biologistic assumptions of human ecology meant that it eventually fell into disrepute, although Amos Hawley (*Human Ecology: A Theory of Community Structure*, 1950) attempted to revive the approach by focusing on the interdependence of occupationally differentiated areas, rather than on the competition between groups for scarce resources. Generally, however, it remains the case that the ecological approach of the Chicago school underplayed the importance of planning in terms of city development, and ignored the probable uniqueness of the USA experience compared with cities elsewhere.

Human Genome Project a multi-national project to map the human GENOME (i.e. of every gene on every human chromosome). Initiated in 1990, the project aims to complete its mapping early in the early decades of the present century. The traditional issues in nature and nurture – see NATURE-NURTURE DEBATE – arise in relation to the Project. There are those who expect that from the initial identification of genes links between specific genes and bodily functions, disease, etc will also be widely established and provide greatly enhanced understanding and a capacity to intervene. Others point to the limitations and dangers likely to be associated with such a reductionistic account. The likelihood is that while some matching of genes with functions will be tight (e.g. as already clear for some genetically inherited disease), many other areas will continue to require explanation beyond such reductionistic accounts.

humanism 1 a central focus on human needs and on human fulfilment without recourse to religious notions.

2 an emphasis on the creativity of humanity, and the autonomy and worth of the human SUBJECT.

3 the emphasis within the writings of the young MARX (including the concern with ALIENATION), seen by those who favour this period of Marx's work as less deterministic than his later work.

'Humanism' in philosophy and the social sciences has been a prime target of STRUCTURALISM and POSTSTRUCTURALISM, with their proclamation of the 'death of the subject', and the DECENTRED SELF. Humanistic Marxism is the object of criticism by Marxists who emphasize the later more 'scientific' Marx of *Capital*. (see ALTHUSSER). See also NIETZSCHE.

humanistic movement an influential movement within psychology which emphasizes the SELF and the power of individuals to realize their human potential (see SELF-ACTUALIZATION). In psychology, these ideas have been developed, in particular, by MASLOW and ROGERS who recognized that psychology was over-concerned with the abnormal (see PSYCHOANALYSIS) and the mechanistic (see BEHAVIOURISM). The humanistic school rectifies this imbalance in concerning itself primarily with human values, with understanding through EMPATHY and with the complexities of the person operating in a unique phenomenological field. See also PHENOMENOLOGY.

human nature the characteristics pertaining to human beings as a natural kind or species. Sociologists are generally agreed that, compared with other animals, the distinctive quality of human nature is its PLASTICITY. Rather than being born with specific INSTINCTS or predispositions, to be developed by maturation or automatically triggered by the environment, the BEHAVIOUR of human beings is influenced by CULTURE and SOCIALIZATION. Thus, suggestions that human beings are naturally acquisitive or aggressive can be countered by examples of societies in which acquisition or warfare are absent. Above all, human beings have developed the capacity for REFLEXIVITY, thus introducing the possibility of RATIONAL ACTION and rational social development. Against this, however, CIVILIZATION is sometimes seen as a veneer (e.g. Freud, *Civilization and its Discontents*), in which the instinctive aspect of human nature keeps breaking through, tending always to limit PROGRESS or rational development.

human needs see NEEDS, BASIC HUMAN NEEDS.

Human Relations Area files located at Yale University, this is an ambitious attempt to construct a coded, descriptive data base of comparative ETHNOGRAPHIC findings about the cultures of the world. The US anthropologist, G. P. Murdoch (1887–1985), was central to the enterprise, among the products of which was his *Ethnographic Atlas* (Murdoch, 1967).

human relations school an approach which seeks to understand and prescribe for workplace behaviour on the basis of the importance of work-group norms, communication and supervisory skills. This approach originates with the famous Hawthorne Studies (see HAWTHORNE EFFECT) which were undertaken at the Western Electric Company in the US during the depression of the 1920s and '30s (Roethlisberger and Dickson, 1939). In this research, the results were interpreted by the investigators as indicating the salience of group norms and styles of leadership for worker behaviour. Workers were seen as social beings operating in the social system of the workplace (Eldridge, 1971), and as having needs for social anchorage and belonging, which were not recognized by the rational, individualistic and materialistic assumptions of SCIENTIFIC MANAGEMENT.

Elton MAYO is sometimes regarded as the founding father who provided the theoretical underpinnings of this approach. Drawing on the Paretian notion of nonlogical action and sentiment (see PARETO), and the Durkheimian notion of ANOMIE, he thought that provision for social anchorage in the workplace could compensate for wider societal disorganization. Human relations techniques in industry could transform managers into brokers of social harmony. Some writers, however, mainly see Mayo as a popularizing publicity officer (M. Rose, 1988).

Subsequent developments within what has become a diverse approach involve, firstly, some inconclusive attempts to demonstrate the practical merit of human relations supervisory styles and participative approaches to organizational change (Coch and French, 1949). Secondly, others have drawn attention to the need to consider the tasks workers undertake and their implications for interaction. Attention has, for example, been given to the way in which technology influences tasks, work flow, interactions, group formation and supervisor-worker relationships. This shift to a more inclusive approach begins to question whether attitudes and supervisory styles can be altered independently of restructuring interactions, and therefore of certain features of formal organizations. These shifts in the level of analysis have begun to bridge the gap between the early anti-Taylorian, social-psychological emphasis on informal groups and the need to consider formal organizational arrangements. Similar arguments are to be found among later neo-human relations theorists who developed the model of 'self-actualizing man' (MASLOW, 1954; Herzberg, 1968), and sociotechnical-systems theorists (see SOCIOTECHNICAL SYSTEMS APPROACH).

Several related criticisms of this approach have been made, not least of which is the inadequate conceptualization of CONFLICT which tends to be located at the level of interpersonal relations, rather than in terms of structural inequalities in the distribution of POWER and resources, either within organizations themselves or the wider society. Relatedly, there has been a tendency to end analysis at the factory gates and offer in-plant solutions to problems on the basis of questionable social-psychological assumptions about the social needs of employees (Goldthorpe, 1968). Finally, the orientation of human relations research tends to reflect the values and interests of managers more than workers – a fact which, in the Hawthorne experiments, led to the selective interpretation of results from poorly designed experiments (Carey, 1967). However, it is important to note that these criticisms are not equally applicable to all the writers who are usually located within the human relations field, since they are not, in fact, easily classified as a 'school' or 'movement'. (M. Rose, 1988).

human resources management a term introduced in the latter part of the 20th century, which replaced the previous term *personnel management,* to refer to the branch of management that deals with the appointment, remuneration and training of employees. The import of the new term is double-edged in that while it was intended to encourage greater concern with 'staff development' and a culture of 'enhancement', it is also associated with a new flexibility, and arguably intensified exploitation, of labour. This dualism is evident, for example, in a UK government-backed initiative, 'Investors in People', which kite-marks organisations able to demonstrate 'exemplary' human resources and customer relations policies and practice.

human rights see CIVIL RIGHTS.

Hume, David (1711–76) SCOTTISH ENLIGHTENMENT philosopher generally regarded as a main influence on modern EMPIRICISM. Hume's examination of deductive and inductive logic led him to see limitations in both, and made him sceptical about the claims of RATIONALISM. His own philosophical position emphasized a knowledge confined to 'impressions' and 'ideas', in which there could be no certainty about the form of a world beyond these, e.g. no basis for claims for 'causality'. Although Hume also wrote at length on historical and social and economic topics, it is the methodological side of his thinking which has been important as an influence on social science (e.g. in discussions of the FACT-VALUE DISTINCTION), fostering an empirical emphasis in the study of society.

humour amusement, laughter, and the like created by the paradoxical, ironic outcomes of social situations, language, and the portrayal of these in literature, art and the theatre. Although humour is a universal feature of human societies and a diverse literature exists (not least the work of Freud), the treatment of humour, has been only fragmentary within sociology, despite its importance in social life. See M. Mulkay, *On Humour* (1988).

hunter-gatherer a member of a society which subsists by exploiting non-domestic/wild food resources. This strategy includes the hunting of large and small game animals, fishing, and the collection of various plant foods. A hunter-gatherer typically lives as part of a small camp or BAND made up of kin. The band is generally nomadic, with their movements following the availability of food, and there is a division of labour by age and sex: women collect plant foods and men hunt. Today, barely 30,000 of the world's population live by hunting and gathering, though it has supported life for 99% of humankind's existence.

Husserl, Edmund (1859–1938) German idealist philosopher and founder of modern PHENOMENOLOGY. His major works include *Ideas for a Pure Phenomenology and Phenomenological Philosophy* (1913) and *The Crisis of the Human Sciences and Transcendental Phenomenology* (1936). In an attempt to found certain knowledge, Husserl followed the method of Cartesian doubt (see DESCARTES) in reducing the objects of enquiry to those phenomena that we directly perceive, i.e. inner mental states. By 'bracketing off' the outside world and concentrating on consciousness it is possible to avoid unjustifiable ontological claims. Whilst his philosophy has been widely criticized for its subjectivity, it has been hugely influential. SCHUTZ's phenomenological sociology and HEIDEGGER'S EXISTENTIALISM are both based on the importance of phenomena as perceived. See also PHENOMENOLOGY. SOCIOLOGICAL PHENOMENOLOGY.

hybrid identity (U. Beck, 2000) a pattern of individual identity in post-traditional contemporary society in which individuals may move freely between multiple identities in a way partly of their own choosing, but which may sometimes lead to conflict and confusion. Beck also suggests that clearly defined roles may be in decline, social solidarity in retreat, social existence becoming 'conflictual coexistence', and that many of the previous traditional and industrial forms of society which nominally survive may in fact have become 'zombie categories', no longer reflecting actual patterns of existence. Thus, individuality in modern society 'can also be understood as radical non-identity'.

hydraulic society WITTFOGEL'S (1955) term for Asiatic society. He suggested that centralized and despotic state power could be explained as the outcome of the dependence of these Asiatic societies on extensive state-directed public works to provide and maintain irrigation and flood-control systems. However, Wittfogel's contention has not survived detailed empirical examination. Not only do many 'despotic' regimes possess no obvious hydraulic basis, many regimes with such a basis are not despotic (e.g. see Leach, 1959, Eberhard, 1965; compare Harris, 1978). At the very least, Wittfogel's explanation is vastly overextended.

Wittfogel's more general claim to have entirely undermined MARX's assumptions about the implications of materialism are similarly overstated. His argument that his work also demonstrated:

(a) that the TOTALITARIANISM of Russian as well as Chinese COMMUNISM could be explained as building on the despotic and hydraulic legacy; and

(b) the dependence of any future freedom on a resistance to all encroachments of state power are similarly challengable. Compare GEOGRAPHICAL DETERMINISM, CULTURAL MATERIALISM. See also ORIENTAL DESPOTISM, ASIATIC MODE OF PRODUCTION AND ASIATIC SOCIETY, ORIENTALISM.

hypergamy within CASTE, the process in which, on marriage, a woman may be allowed to move into a husband's caste (but a man may not move into that of his wife).

hyperinflation (ECONOMICS) an extreme type of INFLATION in which a very rapid exponential growth in prices occurs. The classic instance of hyperinflation was in

Germany in 1923. But there have been many instances since, e.g. Hungary in 1946, when a daily doubling of prices occurred, and Argentina in the period after the Falklands War.

hyperrationality 1 the one-sided application of systems-level rationality at the expense of the 'rationality' of the 'life-world' – INTERNAL COLONIZATION OF THE LIFE-WORLD.
2 the 'unprecedented', and 'far greater degree' of reliance, on 'rationality which Ritzer and Lemoyne (1991) see as decisive in the Japanese postwar economic 'miracle'. For these authors, Japanese success, and the creation of 'hyperrationality', has its origins in a fusion of Western and indigenous systems of 'formal rationality' with 'substantive, theoretical and practical rationality'. See also JAPANIZATION.

hyperreality 'the world of self-referential signs' – 'the new linguistic condition of society', according to BAUDRILLARD, in which the alleged 'real' is no more real than the thing which feigns it.

hypothesis any proposition which is advanced for testing or appraisal as a generalization about a phenomenon. See also EXPERIMENTAL HYPOTHESIS, NULL HYPOTHESIS, HYPOTHETICO-DEDUCTIVE EXPLANATION AND METHOD.

hypothetical imperative KANT's term for advice about action which has the form 'if you wish to achieve X, do Y'. Such advice, based on empirical evidence, is not binding, but optional. Thus it lacks the force of a *categorical imperative,* Kant's term for any moral injunction which can be held to possess a universal force. The basis of such categorical imperatives (e.g. 'thou shall not kill') is to 'act only on the maxim through which you can at the same time will that it should become a universal law'.

hypothetico-deductive explanation and method an alternative to INDUCTION based on the idea that HYPOTHESES are essential in science, as both the basis of proposed generalizations, and their test. In this approach or method, hypotheses and theories are advanced, and generalizations and predictions made, on the basis of deductions from these, with:
(a) successful prediction being taken as a test of the adequacy of the hypothesis and theory;
(b) explanation being seen as achieved once successful predictions have been made.

In its fullest (sometimes also logically formalized) form, hypothetico-deductive explanation and method results in a network of deductively interrelated propositions and theories. The emphasis on the importance of the advancing and the testing of hypotheses, or 'conjectures', has also meant that the hypothetico-deductive method is often allied with FALSIFICATION and FALSIFICATIONISM, although not always so. See also COVERING-LAW MODEL AND DEDUCTIVE NOMOLOGICAL EXPLANATION, and EXPLANATION. Objections to suggestions that the hypothetico-deductive method is *the* method of science should also be noted (see REALISM).

While a hypothetico-deductive approach to testing and theory, and the construction of formal theories, has been advocated in sociology (see FORMAL THEORY AND FORMALIZATION OF THEORY), it has also been sharply opposed (see GROUNDED THEORY, but compare ANALYTICAL INDUCTION).

i

iatrogenic disease any illness caused by doctors or pathogenic medicine which, according to ILLICH (1975), operates on three levels:
(a) *clinical* – the undesirable side effects of treatments administered to cure or exploit the patient or to protect the doctor from censure;
(b) *social* – where medical practice sponsors sickness by reinforcing a morbid society that encourages people to become consumers of curative, preventive, industrial and environmental medicine;
(c) *health-denying* – where the human potential to deal with vulnerability and weakness is eroded by reliance on medical solutions.

icon a person of major social celebrity – notably in film, popular and rock music or sport – who becomes an object of identification, hero worship and emulation. See C. Gledhill, *Stardom: Identity and Desire,* (1991) London: Routledge

id one of the three elements of PERSONALITY in FREUD's theory. It is the basis of personality, containing all the inherited resources, especially the INSTINCTS, and it is from the id that the other two elements, the EGO and the SUPEREGO, develop.

The id is in the UNCONSCIOUS part of the mind, and is closely linked to biological processes and operates under the *pleasure principle,* therefore seeking to gratify the instincts. Freud posits two main instincts – sex and aggression. Sex expresses the life instinct (EROS), and aggression the death instinct (THANATOS).

The desires of the id cannot be met realistically, so the ego develops to ensure the energies are released in a form acceptable to society. One means of transforming the instinctual energies into acceptable forms is through DEFENCE MECHANISMS.

idealism 1 (PHILOSOPHY) the doctrine that the world as encountered is in part or whole a construction of IDEAS.
2 (SOCIOLOGY) the doctrine that sociology must explain primarily by reference to the subjective and conscious intentions of persons (see also meaningful understanding and explanation).

In philosophy, sense 1 is one of the two basic possibilities that arise in considering the relations between, on one side, MIND or subject and, on the other, world or object (see SUBJECT AND OBJECT. EPISTEMOLOGY). For the world to be known by the subject, idealism suggests that there have to be guiding ideas or theories which unavoidably form the world as it is perceived or thought about. It regards its epistemological opposite, empiricism, as naive in supposing that the world as it really is can form, via the senses, a mind which is initially blank and passive.

Plato's idealism suggested that the objects of the world were in themselves imperfect versions of ideal objects which were their essences. Modern idealism derives from KANT and HEGEL. Kant suggests a two-way relation between mind and world, with the mind contributing universal forms by means of which the substantial and empirical world might be perceived and thought about. For Kant, this carries the implications that the world as it is in itself, unstructured by the mind, is unknowable; and that there is awareness, but not knowledge, of the mind as it is in itself – the 'noumenal' – and this is not structured by the forms which permit empirical knowledge, e.g. of space, time and causality. Hegel, rejecting Kant's unknowable 'world-in-itself', achieves a fully idealistic reconciliation by regarding mind and subject as essentially social and historical, and, simultaneously, the world as itself constructed or postulated in the successive categories of mind and subject. He attempted a revision of LOGIC (see DIALECTIC), with the world itself (not simply the 'mind') conceived as a succession of arguments.

The idea that mind constructs world rather than vice versa, is most evident within sense **2**, in the wide range of sociological theories that see the social world as the outcome of conscious human action, i.e. action that necessarily involves thought and 'ideas' on the part of persons. 'Persons' are 'subjects', essentially knowledgeable about the situations in which they are placed, who intend (see INTENTIONALITY) their actions. The explanation of action necessarily involves reference to those intentions, and normally 'interprets the meaning' of actions by reference to intention, motive and REASON. See also WINCH.

The most significant critique of sense **1** is that of Marx, who attempts a 'materialist' development of Hegel–Hegel put back on his feet – by which the shape of social history and development is not determined by successive postulations of 'ideas', i.e. the underlying movements of mind in the successions of the 'spirits' of particular 'ages', but by one range of social forces, particularly economic. For Marx, economic changes underlie all ideological changes. This emphasis on a socioeconomic substructure, he regards as a new form of MATERIALISM which nevertheless retains much of Hegel's 'dialectic' (see also DIALECTICAL MATERIALISM).

Recent discussion, in attempting to refurbish 'materialism', has extended Marx's critique to sense **2**, by emphasizing the 'material' aspects of subjectivity, in particular its construction in social location, as opposed to the idealist subject. In doing so, it represents both 'subject' and 'object', 'mind' and 'world', as constituted in essentially social and unconscious semiosis, and rooted in social practices.

idealization see IDEAL TYPE.

ideal speech situation see HABERMAS.

ideal type *or* pure type

Any conceptualization (*idealization*) of a general or particular phenomenon which, for analytical and explanatory purposes, represents this phenomenon only in its abstract or 'pure' (hence 'idealized') form(s). The foundations of ideal-type analysis in sociology derive from Max WEBER, who was influenced by the use of ideal types in economics. An element of idealization is a feature of any use of general concepts, whether in science, social science, or everyday life (see also TYPIFICATION). However there are variations in the extent to which concepts are idealized (compare TYPE, TYPOLOGY).

The most explicit use of abstract and idealized concepts occurs both in the physical sciences (e.g. the concept of the 'perfect vacuum') and the social sciences (e.g. in economics, the concept of 'perfect competition'). In the physical sciences, the use of idealizations allows a more simplified account of phenomena. This makes possible the formulation of high-level universal generalizations (SCIENTIFIC LAWS), in terms of which real world cases can be analysed and explained as more complex empirical departures.

Weber's use of ideal types occurred with a somewhat different aim. Most clearly apparent is what Weber did *not* mean by ideal types:
(a) they do not state an ethical ideal;
(b) they do not state an 'average' type;
(c) they do not 'exhaust reality', i.e. they do not correspond exactly to any empirical instances.

What Weber has to say more positively about ideal types is that:
(a) they are mental constructs which are ideal in the 'logical sense', i.e. they state a logical extreme;
(b) they 'distort' and abstract from reality;
(c) they can be used to formulate an abstract model of the general form and the interrelated causes and effects of a complex recurring phenomenon (e.g. BUREAUCRACY). A further requirement is that these concepts must be 'objectively possible', in that they must approximate to concrete realities and also be 'subjectively adequate', i.e. be understandable in terms of the subjective orientations of a hypothetical 'individual actor' (see also METHODOLOGICAL INDIVIDUALISM).

Weber's main use of ideal-type concepts was to provide clearly stated 'general' concepts (e.g. 'rational' or 'traditional' – see TYPES OF ACTION) which in turn can be used to allow the unambiguous statement of 'historical' concepts, formulated as departures from general ideal-types. Classification and comparison of phenomena and the appraisal of causal hypotheses are facilitated by this means. For example, while the specific ideal-type concept of the PROTESTANT ETHIC is formulated by Weber as approximating to 'rational action', and possessing causal significance in the rise of Western capitalism, Roman Catholicism and non-Western religions are formulated as historically specific types of traditional and nonrational action, which retard capitalism. Ideal types are used by Weber in *thought experiments* (e.g. Weber's estimation that rational capitalism would have originated in Asia as well as in Europe had there been any form of religion in Asia equivalent to Protestantism). Historical concepts formulated as specific departures from ideal types bring a precision which would otherwise be lacking in such comparative analysis.

It is clear from this that Weber's deployment of ideal-type concepts involves him in the use of explicit (or implicit) *type generalizations,* i.e. assumptions about the 'lawlike regularities' associated with the occurrence of empirical approximations of ideal-type concepts and models. In this way Weber refers to 'typical complexes of meaning' or 'established generalizations from experience', such as GRESHAM'S LAW (i.e. 'that bad money drives out good). Without assumptions of this kind there could be no appraisal of causal significance in ideal-type analysis.

In contrast with the position in the physical sciences, Weber does not in general envisage that an agreement on ideal-type concepts will emerge in sociology, or that such concepts will become the basis of a system of high-level general laws. At times, he refers to the role of ideal-type concepts as HEURISTIC, as merely aiding the clearer description and analysis of historical cases. Among the reasons for this limit on the 'scienticity' of sociology is the continued presence he sees for multiple perspectives within (see OBJECTIVITY AND NEUTRALITY, FACT AND VALUE). The difficulty that arises from Weber's position is that it renders ideal-type analysis in sociology essentially arbitrary.

Two main responses exist to this problem in Weber's approach. Critics, such as PARSONS (1937), argue that whatever differences of degree must be recognized between sociology and physical science, ideal-type analysis can only become coherent by seeking the cumulative development of general concepts and the development of a potentially unitary theory in sociology, avoiding Weber's 'type atomism'. Other critics (e.g. Winch, 1958) argue that ideal-type analysis should be dropped as utterly inappropriate to sociological analysis once this is seen as involving the 'meaningful understanding' of specific cases and not the development of general concepts and general theories.

identification the copying of another's behaviour closely with the desire to be as much like that person as possible.

The concept owes much to FREUD's notion of the resolution of the OEDIPUS COMPLEX through identification with the same-sex parent. This process leads to the internalization of the parent's moral values and the formation of the SUPEREGO.

The use is not always so strict. Identification is commonly used to describe a fleeting feeling of empathy with another person. See also IMITATION.

identity the sense, and continuity, of SELF that develops first as the child differentiates from parents and family and takes a place in society.

The NEO-FREUDIAN theorist. Erik Erikson, has proposed that there is a crisis of identity in adolescence. It is at this stage of development that a young person searches for an identity, trying out different friendship groups, different lifestyles, different career plans. Ideally, by the end of adolescence the identity has stabilized and the young person accepts him/herself, feeling at ease with this identity.

In Erikson's view, therefore, identity forms as a result of social interaction, and problems with identity occur if the adolescent feels alienated from society through, for example, ethnic differences or unemployment. See also IDENTIFICATION.

There are broad similarities but some differences in the emphasis on identity and the process of identity formation in sociology compared with psychology (see MEAD, COOLEY). See also SOCIAL IDENTITY.

In some versions of psychoanalytic theory, especially the poststructuralism of LACAN, identity is altogether more problematic. Lacan challenges the central presupposition involved in the question 'Who am I?', the assumption that there exists a Cartesian self. Instead 'identity' involves a dependence on a dialectic of self and others. While such a dialectic is, of course relatively commonplace in sociology, Lacan's formulation is distinguished by the far greater radicalism of its implications for identity. There is no PRESENCE, only language, and the lack of an identifiable core 'self', according to Lacan, can only be repaired by an 'imagined self, a 'phantasy' in which identity is only preserved by DEFENCE MECHANISMS such as 'denial'.

ideological state apparatus the institutions of the STATE which assist in reproducing the conditions of production of CAPITALISM. This is a term coined by the French Marxist philosopher Louis Althusser to describe the way institutions like schools, churches and the media function to support the state ideology. ALTHUSSER (1971) recognized that this reproduction was ensured not only by ideological state apparatuses, but also by the *repressive state apparatus* (army and police) which functioned principally by the use or threat of violence. How ever, no RULING CLASS could maintain state power over a long period if it lost HEGEMONY over the ideological apparatuses. Althusser has been criticized for giving too little importance to ideologies of resistance against the capitalist state in his formulation (see Elliott, 1987; Urry, 1981).

ideology

1 any system of ideas underlying and informing social and political action.
2 more particularly, any system of ideas which justifies or legitimates the subordination of one group by another.
3 an all-embracing encyclopaedic knowledge, capable of breaking down prejudice and of use in social reform. This sense would appear to be the original usage, when the term was coined by Antoine Destutt de Tracy in the period of social optimism in the French Enlightenment (see AGE OF ENLIGHTENMENT). Thus, between sense **3** and sense **2** there has occurred a full reversal of meaning. It is senses **1** and **2** which are now of prime interest.

In the work of MARX and ENGELS, which has had most influence in the development of the theory of ideology, the term had several connotations. In *The German Ideology*, Marx and Engels emphasized two points. The first was that ideologies presented a picture of the world from the point of view of a RULING CLASS. The second was that this picture was necessarily a distorted one because the interests of the ruling class are, by definition, partial and because they do not represent the interests of humanity in general. In later criticisms and developments, ideology is presented in terms of a social CLASS representing its particular sectional interests as 'natural' and universal (as the 'national interest', for example).

Many later writers have used the term in something like sense **2**, but in a more general way, to refer, for example, to GENDER IDEOLOGY, to race ideologies, and to generational ideologies. Such uses of the term involve the idea that all power relationships include doctrines of justification. For example, in the imperial era the subordination of black people was justified by ideas which emphasized the 'natural' superiority of white people and the enlightenment that imperialism could bring.

One significant challenge to Marx's view is provided by MANNHEIM'S SOCIOLOGY OF KNOWLEDGE. Mannheim argued that it was a mistake to see one class's viewpoint as wrong and another's as right. Sociologically, it was more valuable to see *all* belief systems as representing the interests of particular groups, including communist and socialist ideas, along with conservative ones. Mannheim followed Marx's usage in calling ideas which support the powerful 'ideologies', and ideas which opposed a given system or sought to justify a different one, UTOPIAS.

Modern Marxists have contributed to developments of Marx's theory of ideology, prompted especially by the failure of a revolutionary working class to emerge in Western capitalist societies, a fact which they have sought to explain, at least in part, as the outcome of ideology. Important examples of these approaches include:
(a) the FRANKFURT SCHOOL OF CRITICAL THEORY;
(b) GRAMSCI'S account of HEGEMONY, which in turn has also influenced work on the mass media and mass culture;
(c) ALTHUSSER'S conception of the IDEOLOGICAL STATE APPARATUS.

All these theories, however, have attracted criticism for exaggerating the significance of cultural ideas and VALUES in the maintenance of 'consensus' compared with economic and political POWER or everyday 'routines'. See DOMINANT IDEOLOGY THESIS. See also FALSE CONSCIOUSNESS, CLASS IMAGERY.

idiographic and **nomothetic** divergent orientations to social enquiry (and their associated methods): an idiographic focus is on cultural and historical particulars, using methods such as ETHNOGRAPHY and biography; while a nomothetic focus seeks to establish general laws following an explicitly natural-science model of knowledge.
The distinction was first conceptualized in these terms by the German neo-Kantian philosopher, WINDELBAND. In the late 19th century METHODENSTREIT, German theorists such as DILTHEY, RICKERT and Windelband debated which methods best suited particular social sciences, or whether the two methods could be combined (see Fig. 14). These concerns also influenced Max WEBER, who, like many sociologists subsequently, sought to combine both methods. See also GEISTESWISSENSCHAFTEN AND NATURWISSENSCHAFTEN, MEANINGFUL UNDERSTANDING AND EXPLANATION, IDEAL TYPE, VERSTEHEN, HERMENEUTICS. DOUBLE HERMENEUTIC.

idiographic method a method of investigation which is concerned with the individual or unique experience, rather than with generalities. Thus it is the opposite of a NOMOTHETIC approach. See IDEOGRAPHIC and Fig. 14. Compare ETHNOMETHODOLOGY, MEANINGFUL UNDERSTANDING AND EXPLANATION; see DILTHEY, RICKERT.

Illich, Ivan (1926–) Viennese-born libertarian philosopher, social critic, and one-time Roman Catholic priest, currently based in Mexico, whose provocative critique of economic development has attracted much attention. Illich regards so-called economic development as, in reality, leading to the destruction of the *vernacular skills* previously possessed by people in self-sufficient preindustrial economies.

Discipline	*Focus of Study/Method*
HISTORY *CULTURAL SCIENCES*	*IDIOGRAPHIC* Meaningful reality; empathic method [Dilthey] Unique determinations with respect to values [Rickert; Windelband]
SCIENCE, including *SOCIOLOGY* in its generalizing modes [Rickert] or excluding it [Dilthey]	*NOMOTHETIC* Causal law-like explanation

Fig. 14 **Idiographic and nomothetic.**

According to Illich, people have become increasingly dependent on professionals, experts and specialists for the satisfaction of many of their fundamental needs – e.g. the provision of health services and compulsory schooling. In Illich's terms, the provision of such services *have* often become *radical monopolies,* since, with the destruction of earlier traditions, there is often no longer any alternative but to have recourse to such expert provision, and in many ways the services offered by such experts are debilitating and dehumanizing. leading to 'passive consumption' and dependency. The solutions proposed by Illich are for more democratic, participatory structures that foster human autonomy, e.g. instead of compulsory education, access to a choice of 'educational frameworks'; instead of hierarchically controlled specialist services, the establishment of 'communication networks' for the mutual exchange of services. Another of Illich's suggestions is that 'high quanta of energy degrade social relations' as much as physical milieu, and that, accordingly, the bicycle is the mode of transport most compatible with egalitarian participatory principles. While Illich's thinking is utopian and polemical, his combination of a religious romantic conservatism with radical critique has stimulated sociological reflection. Main works by Illich are *Deschooling Society* (1972), *Tools for Conviviality* (1973), *Medical Nemesis: The Expropriation of Health* (1975) and *Shadow-work* (1981). See also DESCHOOLING, HIDDEN CURRICULUM, IATROGENIC DISEASE.

illness the state of feeling physically or emotionally unwell or sick, and, as such, different from having or suffering from a disease. The word 'ill' originally meant 'evil' or 'morally harmful'. Although they are not completely different categories, sociologists distinguish between illness as a social category, and *disease* as a medical category. The latter refers to clinical conditions and pathologies which are described, classified and published as a branch of medical expertise. Illness refers to the subjective experience of sickness, disease or bad health, and to socially and culturally generated and expressed concepts of physical, social and psychological abnormality. See also SICK ROLE, TRIVIAL CONSULTATION, SYMPTOM ICEBERG, SOCIOLOGY OF HEALTH AND ILLNESS.

illocutionary see SPEECH ACT.

imitation the copying of another's behaviour. Imitation as a means of learning has been investigated by social learning theorists (e.g. Bandura, 1977) who regard it as a significant means of learning, and an alternative to the CONDITIONING theories of behaviourists such as Skinner. The term *modelling* is also used in this context. Research suggests that strength of imitation depends on various environmental conditions, and especially the qualities of the model. Particularly significant are the nurturance and power of the model, and whether it is the same sex as the observer. See also IDENTIFICATION.

immigration see MIGRATION.

immiseration see RESERVE ARMY OF LABOUR.

imperative coordination the likelihood that a command within a given organization or society will be obeyed. The term is Timasheff's English translation (also adopted by PARSONS, 1964) of WEBER's concept *Herrschaft,* more usually translated as DOMINATION. As Parsons suggests, the term *Herrschaft* has no adequate translation in English. Parsons and Timasheff were attempting to bring out more clearly the distinction in Weber's work between POWER (*Macht*) – the capacity possessed by a SOCIAL ACTOR to carry out his or her own will 'despite resistance' from others – and *Herrschaft.* Where Weber is more particularly concerned with *legitime Herrschaft,* Parsons uses the term AUTHORITY. See also LEGITIMATE AUTHORITY OR POLITICAL LEGITIMACY.

imperfect competition see PERFECT COMPETITION.

imperialism

The political and economic domination of one country, or countries, by another, which leads either to alien rule imposed by force, or to economic domination and exploitation.

Within sociology, and the social sciences generally, there are two major perspectives. One emphasizes the political dimension of domination and traces imperialism back to ancient civilizations based on expansion, such as the Roman Empire. The other emphasizes the economic dimension and views imperialism as mainly a feature of the 20th century and of CAPITALISM. Although some writers would claim that direct colonial rule is a necessary part of the definition of imperialism, others would disagree. For example, they argue that the indirect political influence and economic dominance of the US constitutes imperialism, even though historically its colonial possessions have been few. With the decline of COLONIALISM since World War II, and the disappearance of the European empires, other writers, such as J. E. Goldthorpe (1975), have claimed that imperialism no longer exists. The emphasis on economic aspects is generally, though not exclusively, associated with MARXISM. This has been most influential in sociology in the UK in the last two decades. The approach is based on the work of LENIN. Whilst Lenin (1916) saw imperialism as an inherent feature of economic development in advanced capitalist countries, recent writers have concentrated more on the effects of imperialism upon the countries of Africa, Asia and Latin America. Deriving from the works of Marx as well as Lenin, imperialism is said to originate from the drive for profitability intrinsic to capitalism, and the continued need to find outlets for both capital and commodities. Accordingly, territorial expansion is a necessity for capitalist societies.

This involves using the THIRD WORLD as a focus of investment and as a source of profits, markets for goods and suppliers of raw materials.

The effect on Third World countries is primarily seen as that of holding back internal development by concentrating their economies on a limited range of activities, often owned by foreigners, and involving a transfer of resources to the advanced capitalist countries. However, even within the Marxist approach there are disagreements, since Warren's work (1980) argues that colonialism and imperialism have helped promote capitalist development in the Third World rather than held it back (compare DEPENDENCY THEORY). Warren claims that this is in fact closer to Marx's original view. See also NEOCOLONIALISM, LUXEMBURG.

implicit religion 'aspects of ordinary life which seem to contain an inherently religious element … whether or not they are expressed in ways that are traditionally described as "religious"' (*Implicit Religion* – the Journal of the Centre for the Study of Implicit Religion in Contemporary Society). The concept is a relatively novel, and perhaps a questionable, one, but is intended to extend the understanding of human behaviour by deploying insights from the academic study of religion to the wider study of society. See also CIVIL RELIGION.

import substitution the process whereby countries begin to produce certain goods for themselves instead of importing them. Given the heavy reliance of many THIRD WORLD countries on importing manufactured goods, one strategy they have tried to adopt is that of import-substitution industrialization. This has been successful where the goods can be produced with simple machinery and low capital costs. However, many countries have run into problems when such manufacturing involves high capital costs, complex machinery which they do not produce themselves, or labour and technical skills which they do not possess. In such cases, instead of diversifying their economies, and becoming less reliant on manufactured exports, they have often witnessed a new set of problems with dependency on foreign capital and technical knowledge. Further, since the 1970s, the experience of starting up industries and the provision of the necessary infrastructure has led to the creation of INTERNATIONAL DEBT. See also DEPENDENCY THEORY.

impression management see DRAMATURGY.

incarceration (and **decarceration**) the separation of people from the normal routines of everyday life within organizations such as prisons, asylums, long-stay hospitals, the armed forces, and boarding schools. Long-term incarceration can lead to the problem of INSTITUTIONALIZATION, and so to problems of adjusting to independent existence, e.g. for former prisoners or patients.

Decarceration normally implies a more general policy of releasing people from institutions like mental hospitals. The policy of 'care in the community', embraced by Conservative governments in Britain in the 1990s, and in Italy before this, is an example of this philosophy. See also TOTAL INSTITUTION OR TOTAL ORGANIZATION.

incest taboo the prohibition on sexual relations between certain categories of kin, generally those of close blood relationship. Some form of incest taboo is found in all known societies, although the relationships which the taboo covers vary. Most common are child-parent and sibling relationships. Some societies actively encourage sexual relationships between cousins, whereas in other societies such relationships would be seen as incestuous. Other societies may not prohibit sexual relationships between certain categories, but would prohibit marriage between the same people.

Various explanations have been put forward for the universality of some form of incest taboo. Some have argued that the now known genetic consequences explain this. But not all human groups would have made this link, and cousin marriage preference would probably have not existed if this was the case. LÉVI-STRAUSS argued that it existed to ensure that people marry out of their social group and thus form alliances with other social groups. (However, sexual prohibitions are not the same as marriage rules.) FREUD's explanation rests on the strong attraction of incestuous relations, particularly between son and mother, and the taboo exists to reduce conflict within the nuclear family. The internalization of the taboo is, for Freud, an important part of the psychological development of the individual (see OEDIPUS COMPLEX).

Given the variety of ways in which the taboo is expressed, emphasis on its universality, and hence on universal explanations, is probably misplaced. Greater emphasis on why particular societies designate particular relationships as incestuous and not others may be a more fruitful line of inquiry.

incommensurability 1 a relation between scientific theories in which the propositions and overall content of the theories cannot be directly compared.

2 a conception of scientific theories which holds that all observations are theory-relative (see THEORY-RELATIVITY), and that there may exist no theory-neutral data language of the kind assumed by inductive, logical positivist or falsificationist conceptions of science. The conception is most associated with Thomas KUHN and Paul FEYERABEND and it is often assumed to also imply a more general RELATIVISM. However, this is not Feyerabend's view: incommensurability is seen as a possible, not a necessary, relation between theories. If theories cannot always be strictly compared in terms of a theory-neutral data language (or using any unambiguous or unchanging decision rule), the proponents of competing theories can enter into a dialogue with the aim of appreciating each other's view and reaching a decision on this basis. See also TRUTH. POSITIVISM, FALSIFICATIONISM.

incorporation 1 the process in which the occupational and political organizations of the working class are accommodated within capitalist society.

2 the argument that working-class consciousness has been shaped by the values and interests of other, dominant, classes.

The concepts have a place in the arguments about working-CLASS CONSCIOUSNESS and CLASS IMAGERY. The first usage, for example, is resonant of the arguments about a separate status group within the working class, especially in the 19th century – the LABOUR ARISTOCRACY. The second might be compared to discussions of HEGEMONY. Often the distinction between sense 1 and sense 2 is analytical; in practice, organization and consciousness are treated in an integrated, coextensive way.

Incorporation is one of many concepts which have been proposed to explain the predominantly reformist attitudes of the working classes of capitalist societies. It has been particularly influential in UK studies. The extension of citizenship, and voting and welfare rights, for example, and the establishment of 'respectable', skilled, male trade unionism after 1850, have been seen both as the product of working-class struggle and as a means of institutionalizing, and thus containing the level of, industrial and political conflict. The Parliamentary Labour Party has also been a major element in the incorporation of the working class into existing structures. In the 1960s, proposed and actual trade-union legislation which attempted to give the state a continuous role in monitoring and regulating relations between employers and unions has been explained in terms of the incorporation of union militancy into stable and routine state structures (see also CORPORATISM). Between 1945 and 1979 the involvement of trade-union leaders in government committees, the acceptance of knighthoods, etc., by union leaders, and the willingness of unionists to cooperate in state-inspired initiatives like ACAS, have all been seen as examples of incorporation, i.e. as reducing militancy by channelling potential conflict, leadership and values into forms which can be accommodated by the *status quo*.

independence the achievement of political independence by a colonized country after a period of colonial rule (see COLONIALISM). In the 20th century, nationalist independence movements grew in nearly every colony and were of primary importance in ending colonial rule in most THIRD WORLD countries after World War II. It was through these movements that European notions of NATIONALISM were introduced to the Third World, along with mass participation in politics. Independence in Latin America was achieved in the early part of the 19th century in the context of the Napoleonic Wars in which Spain was embroiled, but Africa and many countries in Asia did not achieve independence until the second half of the 20th century.

independence, statistical see CORRELATION.

independent sector generic term for the private and voluntary sectors, distinguishing them from the public sector, especially in relation to PRIVATIZATION associated with THATCHERISM.

independent variable the VARIABLE which is experimentally manipulated, or otherwise controlled, in order to observe its effect. For example, the speed limit may be systematically varied on certain roads and the effect of this measured in terms of road accident statistics. The speed restrictions would be the independent variable, the road accident figures the DEPENDENT VARIABLE. However, in social research it is often not possible to set up experiments to test theories, and observations have to be made from retrospective occurrences. Thus a study may be made, for example, of the effect of age of marriage on family size. In this example, age of marriage would be the independent variable, and family size would be the dependent variable. See also EXPERIMENTAL METHOD.

indeterminism see DETERMINISM.

indexical expression any word or expression which draws its sense only from the immediate context of its use (e.g. personal pronouns). *Indexicality* can be seen as a frequent feature of social concepts (and also many sociological concepts), a feature which means that SOCIAL ACTORS (as well as sociologists) must often undertake careful interpretive work to determine the meanings prevailing within particular social settings (see also HERMENEUTICS).

For ethnomethodologists, the indexicality of social concepts and social accounts means that the kind of generalized sociological and scientific accounts sought by orthodox sociologists are unattainable. However, elements of indexicality can be seen as a feature of all concepts, including those in physical science (see also INCOMMENSURABILITY, SCIENTIFIC PARADIGM, RELATIVISM). While this certainly means that science can no longer reasonably be seen in simple positivist or empiricist terms as directly referring to phenomena, this does not prevent general theories being advanced. Likewise, elements of indexicality in sociological accounts need not preclude workable general accounts (compare ETHNOMETHODOLOGY).

indexicality see INDEXICAL EXPRESSION.

index number a measure which shows average changes over a period of time in the price, quantity or value of one, or a collection, of items. The RETAIL PRICE INDEX and the Index of Production are examples of indices that measure a collection (basket) of items.

Any series of figures can be put into index form. In a time series the chosen base year is set to 100 and all the changes are calculated relative to that base year. If there is only one variable in the index, this is done by obtaining the ratio of the current value to the base year value and multiplying by 100:

$$\text{index number} = \frac{\text{current value}}{\text{base value}} \times 100$$

If an index, for example the Index of Average Price of New Dwellings, contains only one variable, the calculation of the Index is straightforward. The construction of composite indices has to take into consideration the choice of items to be included, their availability and reliability, he need for weights, and the method of calculation. Most indices are weighted to reflect the relative importance of the various items. A Laspeyres index uses weights fixed in the base year. As time goes on this can make the weighting system unrepresentative. A Paasche index uses weights from the current year. This retains representation but makes comparison more difficult. One technique to overcome lack of representation is to relate the changes in the index to the previous year instead of the base year. This is known as 'chain basing'. Index numbers can also be re-based, i.e. a more recent year is used for the base year.

indicator see SOCIAL INDICATORS.

indigenous group any ethnic group originating and remaining in an area subject to colonization. North American Indians, Aboriginals and Maoris are all examples of ethnic groups who inhabited lands before colonial expansion (in North America, Australia and New Zealand respectively) and who have retained their distinctive identities. Such groups often appear to go through a sequence of defeat, despair and regeneration, if they have not been exterminated or their culture completely destroyed by the colonial power. The concept of 'indigenous group' is used by the United Nations to obtain lost rights for such groups. A similar term is 'native peoples'. See also MULTI-CULTURALISM.

indirect rule see COLONIALISM.

individual goods *or* **private goods** see PUBLIC GOODS.

individualism a ramifying collection of philosophical, political, economic, and religious doctrines, underlying which is a recognition of the autonomy of the individual human being in social action and affairs. Epistemological individualism has sought to locate the foundations of knowledge in individual perceptions or APPERCEPTIONS or experience (see also EMPIRICISM). Historically, individualism has been an important element in opposing the powers of the STATE (see also CITIZEN RIGHTS) and in justifications of private PROPERTY and the free play of markets. Religious individualism, the doctrine that Man stands next to God and requires no intermediaries, is characteristic of PROTESTANTISM. In the social sciences, METHODOLOGICAL INDIVIDUALISM is the view that social phenomena can ultimately only be explained in terms of facts about individuals.

Critics of doctrinaire forms of individualism argue that these ideas tend to rest on an asocial conception of the individual person, including in some cases even a denial that 'society' exists. The polar opposite of individualism, conceptions of 'structural determination' (see STRUCTURALISM), are seen as equally problematic by many critics. In seeking to resolve a DUALISM of individual and society many sociologists have adopted theories which emphasize an interaction between individual and society (see STRUCTURE AND AGENCY). This need not undermine conceptions of individual agency and 'moral responsibility', e.g. the potency of human purposes 'as causes' and the capacity of moral persuasion and social sanctions to influence these (see also FREE WILL). Competing valuations of individual and social interests remain. However, these no longer depend on conceptions of the absolute autonomy of the individual (compare DECENTRED SELF). See also AUTONOMOUS MAN AND PLASTIC MAN.

individual level data information collected from individuals by any form of research methodology, for example, INTERVIEWS, observational studies, QUESTIONNAIRES. Individual level data may subsequently be aggregated together into groups, e.g. households, school classes or social classes.

induction and **inductive logic** the process in which a general statement, suggesting a regular association between two or more variables, is derived from a series of empirical observations. In contrast with 'deductive' arguments, in which a conclusion follows logically from initial premises (*logical inference* – see LOGIC), no such strict logical necessity exists in connection with induction, even though, following MILL's formulation (see COMPARATIVE METHOD), this is some times referred to as *inductive logic.* The reason why no strict necessity exists in connection with inductive statements is that inductive argument depends upon generalization from a series of known cases: 'A_1 is b, A_2 is b, A_3 is b, etc.' to suggest that, therefore, any A *is likely to be* b. The views that scientific statements are only justifiable by further procedural rules such as FALSIFICATION or by 'realist' criteria, (see REALISM), arise in this context. See also EMPIRICISM, POPPER.

industrial conflict CONFLICTS, both overt and covert, which arise from the employment relationship and which are manifest in many different forms, from STRIKES and lockouts to time-wasting. The study of industrial conflict has involved:
(a) the classification of its different forms, e.g. visible and organized, such as strikes, or more hidden and informal, such as 'working to rule';
(b) study of the sources and consequences of these;
(c) consideration of the social processes by which activities actually become defined or labelled as 'conflict' (including media presentations of these – e.g. see GLASGOW MEDIA GROUP).

Sociology is one of several disciplines concerned with the sources, forms and consequences of both-conflict and cooperation in work organizations. As a discipline, it has in particular offered a perspective which locates the study of industrial conflict within a broad understanding of the nature of industrial societies. In this respect, the attempts of MARX, WEBER and DURKHEIM have been particularly influential and still inform discussion of industrial conflict. For example, by focusing on the way in which both formally FREE WAGE LABOUR and the espoused democratic values of capitalist societies are contradicted by the usually hierarchical nature of relations at work, sociologists have questioned those explanations of industrial conflict which either tend to offer crude psychological explanations or to regard it as simply 'irrational'. In all, four schools of thought can be identified in the study of industrial conflict (see also INDUSTRIAL RELATIONS):
(a) 'unitarians', who view conflict largely as an irrational aberration;
(b) 'pluralists', who regard organizations as inherently conflictual, but the conflicting interests within these as amenable to, and benefitting from, mutual accommodation;
(c) 'radical pluralists', who explain the persistence of conflicts as arising from fundamental inequalities of power and advantage;
(d) Marxists, who ground their analysis in assumptions deriving from Marxian conceptions of EXPLOITATION and conflict.
See also CONFLICT THEORY.

industrial democracy the participation of employees in the decision-making of a work organization. The participation may be total or shared with owner and managerial interests. Moreover, the decision-making may concern the organization as a whole, or only sub-groups within it. The main types are *workers' self-management* (e.g. the former Yugoslavia), *producer cooperatives* (e.g. Mondragon in the Basque province of Spain), and *codetermination* (e.g. Germany). At the shop-floor (i.e. sub-group) level, the creation of *autonomous work groups* and *quality of working life programmes* are examples of industrial democracy of a partial kind (Poole, 1986).

The general concept of industrial democracy has been much criticized by both pluralist and Marxist writers. The pluralist argument is that participation in management dilutes trade unions' ability to represent their members effectively in collective bargaining (Clegg, 1960). The pluralist critique amounts to an alternative definition of industrial democracy based upon opposition (through collective bargaining) rather than participation (see also COUNTERVAILING POWER, PLURALISM). The Marxist criticism is that it is not possible within a capitalist society to incrementally gain workers' control through employee participation in business enterprises (Hyman, 1984).

Historically, industrial democracy has its roots in French syndicalism which influenced early socialist thinking and trade unionism in the US and UK in the early decades of the 20th century. In the UK, the movement transmuted into guild socialism in the inter-war years (Pribicevic, 1959) and reappeared as a force in the 1960s largely as a consequence of the agitation of the Institute of Workers' Control (Coates and Topham, 1972). This group was active in supporting the establishment of cooperatives and worker directors on the boards of nationalized industries. In the UK, however, the biggest impetus towards implementing industrial democracy on a wide scale came in the 1970s, with the publication of the draft Fifth Directive of the EEC Commission in 1972. The British government's response was to set up the Bullock Committee of Inquiry on Industrial Democracy. This committee's principal recommendation was that workers should be represented, via trade union channels, on all companies employing over 2,000 workers. The proposals, however, were almost wholly ignored as none of the interested parties (government, employers, trade unions) found the recommendations palatable to them. In the 1980s there was (managerial) interest in participation on management's terms (i.e. quality circles) and in some extension of ownership through share schemes.

industrialization the general process by which economies and societies in which agriculture and the production of handicrafts predominate become transformed into economics and societies where manufacturing and related extractive industries are central. This process occurred first in the UK during the INDUSTRIAL REVOLUTION and was soon repeated in other Western European societies. Profound changes in the social organization of production and distribution are involved, especially a rapid increase in the DIVISION OF LABOUR, both between individuals and occupational groups and also between industrialized and nonindustrialized nations, changes which lead to a transformation of the techniques and the social organization of agriculture (see AGRICULTURAL REVOLUTION) as well as of extractive and manufacturing industry (see FACTORY SYSTEM, MASS PRODUCTION).

Criteria for delineating countries as industrialized or industrializing vary. The most commonly used indicators are: (a) the percentage of the labour force employed in the industrial and service sectors compared with primary production; (b) manufacturing output as a proportion of GROSS NATIONAL PRODUCT (GNP). However, other criteria such as levels of investment (see ECONOMIC TAKEOFF), the extent of URBANIZATION, levels of literacy, etc., may also be used as more general indicators of industrialization and of MODERNIZATION and development. Thus a country such as New Zealand which is mainly an exporter of primary products, but with a highly modernized agriculture, high literacy, etc., may be regarded as an industrialized country in the most general sense of the term.

The process of industrialization is closely

linked with the overall modernization of societies, especially the process of urbanization, the development of SCIENCE and TECHNOLOGY, and POLITICAL MODERNIZATION. Each of these changes can be viewed as either:
(a) a prerequisite of industrialization; or
(b) a direct consequence or requirement of it; or
(c) both of these.

While similarities exist in the overall pattern of industrialization in the first wave of European industrialized societies, important differences are also evident (e.g. in the role played by the state in initiating industrialization, limited in the UK but more extensive in Germany). Differences also exist between those countries which were part of the first wave of industrialization and those for which industrialization occurs later (e.g. whilst later entrants can gain advantage by learning from the mistakes of earlier entrants, they often find it difficult to compete with more established industrial economies, this sometimes restricting new entrants to a relationship of ECONOMIC DEPENDENCY) (see also IMPERIALISM, UNEQUAL EXCHANGE). As well as temporal differences of this sort, important regional differences also exist.

industrial relations the relations between employees and employers, and the study of these relations.

Sociology is but one of a variety of disciplines which have contributed to the study of this area.

Debate between competing theories led Fox (1965) to distinguish between unitarist and pluralist perspectives. In the unitarist perspective, cooperation is normal and organizational efficiency and rationality resides in managerial prerogative; conflict is seen as irrational and due to communications problems, agitators, etc. Pluralists, in contrast, regard conflicts between legitimate interest groups as normal, but resolvable through mutually advantageous collective bargaining procedures. This approach, exemplified in the Donovan Commission (1968), underpinned several reforms to British industrial relations in the I 970s, but has been subjected to several criticisms, e.g.:
(a) that in focusing on the failure of industrial relations institutions to regulate conflict, PLURALISM neglected the inequalities of power and advantage which generate conflict in the first place (Goldthorpe, 1974);
(b) that 'corporatist' or Marxist theories provide a better account of industrial relations (see CORPORATISM).

Thus theorists have focused on the attempts by successive postwar governments to deal with industrial relations problems through forms of state intervention which have involved tripartite arrangements (trade unions, employers and the state). Marxist scholars have remained unimpressed with the attempts to radicalize pluralism (Wood and Elliott, 1977). In the Marxist framework, the employment relationship is characterized by class exploitation and there can be no such thing as a fair wage. Conflict is endemic and employers constantly need to legitimate their control. Moreover, pluralist and corporatist views of the state are seen to be naive since capital is regarded as the main beneficiary of state intervention.

In stressing the need to consider employment relationships within the dynamics of capitalist society, a key feature of which is the way the conflict between capital and labour is expressed in class relationships and state activity, Marxists have both produced valuable insights and broadened the study of industrial relations. Nevertheless, this perspective also has its critics. Crouch (1982), for example, suggests that some Marxists underplay the constant choices about goals and means which employees have to make, whilst attempts to ascribe industrial conflict to class relations is unconvincing. The neoliberalist policies pursued by Conservative governments in the UK from the 1980s onwards, theoretically underpinned by the writings of Hayek and Friedman, are founded on a marked distrust of both corporatist institutions and trade unions, and express the unitarist view that many industrial relations problems derive from the excessive use of power by union officials (MacInnes, 1987).

In sum, as with most areas of sociological investigation, the study of industrial relations is marked by theoretical controversy. The above perspectives illustrate the point that perceptions of, and prescriptions for, solutions to industrial relations 'problems' are inextricably linked to particular theories.

Industrial Revolution the massive interrelated economic, technological and social changes, usually dated *c.* 1760–1850, in which the UK became a manufacturing economy based on a new machine technology and the FACTORY SYSTEM. As a result of these changes the UK also became the first INDUSTRIAL SOCIETY (see INDUSTRIALIZATION).

The decisive features of this industrial revolution were:

(a) increased CAPITALIST control over the LABOUR PROCESS and a greatly increased DIVISION OF LABOUR and consequent improvements in overall efficiency and productivity in factories and workshops;

(b) the invention of new machinery and the application first of improvements in water power and later steam power, in mining, manufacturing (especially textiles and iron and steel) and transport (roads, canals, railways and sea).

Once underway, the Industrial Revolution also brought rapid population growth (see DEMOGRAPHIC TRANSITION) and URBANIZATION with attendant social problems, such as urban squalor, ill-health and absence of effective urban administration.

Whether or not in its early stages the Industrial Revolution led to an absolute reduction in the STANDARD OF LIVING is a matter of some dispute (see Ashton, 1954). What is clear is that many categories of workers (e.g. handloom weavers) displaced by new machinery, and those subject to high levels of unemployment during periods of severe recession, suffered greatly, even if, as some commentators suggest, the overall effect of the new industrial society was generally to expand consumption and social welfare. Certainly the increased discipline – the tyranny of the new control over the labour process and of the clock (see E. P. THOMPSON, 1967) – was a new dimension unwelcome to and resisted by many workers.

The causes of the Industrial Revolution in the UK are complex and much disputed by economic historians. It is agreed, however, that once the revolution was underway it was the capacity of the new industries to provide new products, such as cheap cotton goods and household wares, both at home and overseas, which sustained the impetus to further economic growth and social change. See also ROSTOW, ECONOMIC AND SOCIAL DEVELOPMENT.

The onset of the Industrial Revolution in the UK was quickly followed by similar transformations in other European societies and in the US. Subsequently a number of these societies were able to outstrip Britain and to lead the way in a new period of economic and technological development (including electric power, the new chemicals industry, and radio and telecommunications) sometimes referred to as the *second industrial revolution.*

A further question of importance concerns the link between industrialization and CAPITALISM. Whilst it is clear that the first industrialization was the outcome of the prior appearance of capitalist social relations, it is equally apparent that industrialization was also initiated in SOCIALIST SOCIETIES (see also STATE CAPITALISM AND STATE MONOPOLY CAPITALISM).

industrial society 1 that form of society, or any particular society, in which INDUSTRIALIZATION and MODERNIZATION have occurred.

The general term originates from SAINT-SIMON who chose it to reflect the emerging central role of manufacturing industry in 18th-century Europe, in contrast with previous PREINDUSTRIAL SOCIETY and AGRARIAN SOCIETY.

As the basic form of modern society, the term 'industrial society' covers both CAPITALIST SOCIETIES, since both exhibit the following common features: factory-based production, a declining proportion of the population employed in agriculture, the separation of the household from production, increases in the level of production and improvements in productivity, urbanization, improvements in consumption and social welfare, the provision of mass education and the achievement of widespread literacy. Among other more disputed general features of industrial societies usually included are the tendency for extended family and kinship relationships to decline as the basis of social organization (see FAMILY, KINSHIP), and for religion to be undermined by SECULARIZATION.

2 a disputed model of modern society proposed as an alternative model to either 'capitalist society' or 'socialist society'. In this, more restricted sense of the term, a number of more specific propositions are advanced about modern society:

(a) that industrialization rather than capitalism or socialism is the decisive factor shaping modern society;

(b) that, rather than CLASS CONFLICTS of the dichotomous Marxian kind, CLASS and STATUS divisions occur which simply reflect divisions within the occupational structure of all industrial societies. Whilst these divisions result in a plurality of class and status conflicts (including SECTORAL CLEAVAGES), they occur in a manner which does not routinely undermine the basic effectiveness or continuity of these societies (see also CLASS STRATIFICATION, DAHRENDORF).

(c) that there are clear signs of an ultimate CONVERGENCE between capitalist and socialist societies (including domination by a TECHNOSTRUCTURE of managers and technical experts – see also MANAGERIAL REVOLUTION) so that these societies will in the end emerge as neither classically capitalist nor conventionally socialist in social and economic form. See also STATE SOCIALISM, STATE CAPITALISM AND STATE MONOPOLY CAPITALISM, POSTCAPITALIST SOCIETY, POSTINDUSTRIAL SOCIETY.

industrial sociology

The study of work as paid employment, and of industry. The chief concerns of this subdiscipline have been the division of labour, both social and technical (see also OCCUPATIONAL STRUCTURE); the experience of work; and the role and consequences of TECHNOLOGY within industry. In addition, the subject includes the study of industrial bureaucracies and INDUSTRIAL RELATIONS (see Burns, 1962). See also ORGANIZATION THEORY.

Industrial sociology has its roots in the analysis of INDUSTRIALIZATION provided by MARX, WEBER and DURKHEIM and has involved comparative studies between advanced industrial societies. However, much of industrial sociology has been concentrated on studies of the workplace, with cross-cultural issues dealt with implicitly by reference to North American texts (e.g. Blauner, 1964), leaving more explicit comparative analysis to ECONOMIC SOCIOLOGY or COMPARATIVE SOCIOLOGY. In consequence, the subdiscipline has been particularly concerned with the impact of industrialization in terms of the issues raised by worker attitudes and motivation, through a consideration of SCIENTIFIC MANAGEMENT, HUMAN RELATIONS and ALIENATION and POWER relations *within* industry.

This preoccupation with social relations and worker morale within the factory came under pressure with the development of the postindustrial thesis (see POSTINDUSTRIAL SOCIETY) in the 1960s and the emergence of the SERVICE SECTOR as a major employer of labour. More serious criticisms, in terms of their impact on the integrity of the subdiscipline, came in the 1970s. following, firstly, the rediscovery of the LABOUR PROCESS (P. Thompson, 1989) and, secondly, the development of FEMINIST THEORY. The common point of the criticisms was that industrial sociology was too limited in its major focus on factory work. The two critiques, however, differed markedly in their emphases. The labour process critique was more concerned with the POLITICAL ECONOMY and the relationship between, on the one hand, the organization and control of labour and on the other, the appropriation and realization of SURPLUS VALUE. The feminist critique was concerned with extending the domain and discourse to cover the following: the interrelationship between paid and unpaid work; gender issues; and the relation between work and society. In consequence of these criticisms, the focus of industrial sociology has changed recently from 'industry' to 'work' (see also SOCIOLOGY OF WORK).

inequality see EQUALITY.

infant mortality rate the number of infants who die within one year of their birth, per thousand live births. As in most industrial societies, in the UK the infant mortality rate has markedly declined. In 1901 it was over 150 per 1000 live births, in 1940 it was 61 per 1000 live births, in 1950 it was 31.2 per 1000 live births, and in 1988 it was 8.8 per 1000 live births. Infant mortality rates are an important indicator of the level of economic development, welfare provision, etc. within a society, and class-specific infant mortality rates are an important indicator of social inequalities.

infanticide 1 the killing of infants soon after they are born. Several reasons have been identified for the practice of infanticide, especially in nonindustrial societies:
(a) a means of population control, particularly in times of trouble such as FAMINE or war;
(b) a means of eliminating children with undesirable or unacceptable characteristics, such as disabled or sick children. Plato proposed infanticide as an ideal, and the infanticide of 'defective' children was practised in Sparta;
(c) a means of eliminating children whose birth is considered TABOO, such as breech births and twins;
(d) a means of reinforcing patriarchal values and behaviour; in many nonindustrial societies it was the practice to kill, or allow to die, many more girls than boys.
2 (in English law) the manslaughter of a child under the age of 12 months by the child's mother, according to the *Infanticide Act* of 1938.

inferential statistics see STATISTICS AND STATISTICAL ANALYSIS.

inflation (ECONOMICS) the increase over time in the general level of prices in an

economy. Inflation reduces the purchasing power of any unit of money. The rate of general inflation is usually measured using an index indicating the annual increase in consumer prices, such as the RETAIL PRICE INDEX. Two main types of inflation are identified by economists:
(a) *demand-pull inflation,* which occurs when there is excess demand at a time of full employment and little room exists for immediate increase in levels of output; and
(b) *cost-push inflation,* arising from an increase in the costs of inputs, including labour. An alternative explanation of demand-pull inflation proposed by MONETARIST economists is excessive creation of money.

Historically, periods of inflation were associated with the boom phase in the movement of the trade cycle. In Western capitalist economies in recent decades, inflation has been more continuous, a state of affairs which has been explained as the outcome of a prolonged post-World War II boom, increased effectiveness of trade union power, as well as increasing government intervention to protect full employment and the creation of money by governments and banks.

Attempts to control inflation by allowing increased levels of unemployment and by controlling money supply, though they have met with some success, may be effective in reducing inflation only by restricting growth and increasing social inequalities. Income policies involving voluntary agreements between government, employers and trade unions to control wages and prices have met with only limited success.

Although inflation has been studied mainly by economists, sociologists have been concerned to explore the wider social causes and effects of the phenomenon. As suggested by social theorists such as BELL and HABERMAS, a persistent tendency to inflation in modern Western societies would appear bound up with fundamental features of the social structure of these societies, e.g. the absence of consensus on a fair distribution of income; conflicts of interest inherent in the capitalist labour contract; and the ability of big business and organized labour to increase prices and wages while 'exporting crisis' – unemployment or a reduction in real incomes – to weaker economic sectors. One issue concerning the effects of inflation is whether inflation, or the problems generated by attempts to control inflation, presents the bigger problem. However, most governments try to control inflation, if only because persistent inflation can lead to a serious decline in export competitiveness. See also DEFLATION, STAGFLATION, CORPORATISM, LEGITIMATION CRISIS.

informal economy *or* **black economy** that assortment of paid work which takes place outside the formal structure of paid employment. It is not subject to the normal constraints of registration and taxation, and generally, therefore, is supported by cash-in-hand payments.

It is now realized that the study of formal employment does not exhaust the scope of the SOCIOLOGY OF WORK. Sociologist, Ray Pahl, and economist, Jonathan Gershuny published a provocative article (1980) in which they put forward the idea that there

Paid	*Unpaid*
wage-labour formal economy	domestic labour household economy
shadow wage-labour black economy	work outside employment communal economy

Fig. 15 **Informal economy.** Different types of work and economy.

were in fact three different economies – the formal, the informal and the household. In the formal economy, the one recognized by governments, people sell their ability to work for wages and salaries; in the informal economy people might do work 'off the books', i.e. receive cash but not declare it to the state (the real 'black economy'), or they might do a job for a neighbour or relative which would be repaid 'in kind'; in the household economy the role of women in performing routine cooking, cleaning and caring in the home is recognized, as well as 'do-it-yourself' jobs carried out by both men and women.

Since 1980, conferences have been held, research has flourished, and books and articles have been published on activities 'outside employment'. Fig. 15 summarizes different types of work and economy that have been identified by researchers.

A useful way of clarifying the differences (Pahl. 1984) is to imagine a woman ironing a garment at home. She could be ironing the garment before she delivers it to her employer for wages as an 'out-worker' (wage labour in the formal economy). She could be ironing the garment which she proposes to sell to get some extra cash with out declaring it to the state (wage labour or self-employment in the 'black economy'). She may be ironing the garment as a housewife for her husband upon whom she is financially dependent (domestic labour in the 'household economy'). Finally, she may be ironing the garment, with no expectation of payment, for a friend, neighbour or relative, or out of some obligation to the local church, club or other voluntary organization to which she belongs (work outside of employment in the 'communal economy').

Although some research suggests that the 'black economy' has grown during the economic crisis of the 1980s, it is important to keep its size and significance in perspective. In sum, work 'outside' formal employment needs to be studied in relation to that which goes on 'inside'. Researchers need to consider the *interconnections* between the two, and examine both how wage-labour relations penetrate unpaid work, and how socially generated ideologies shape patterns of waged work. There has been much discussion of the use of the term to account for economic activities in THIRD WORLD cities where many people do not have access to permanent employment. See also DOMESTIC LABOUR, DOMESTIC PRODUCTION, PRIVATE AND PUBLIC SPHERES.

informant see RESPONDENT OR INFORMANT.

information any unit of data or knowledge. The character and extent of the recorded information available to a society is a major differentiating feature between types of society. For example, in its possession of written records a literate culture possesses a decisive adaptive advantage compared with a nonliterate culture. This is seen, for example, in the rise to supremacy of the STATE, which was associated from the outset with the development of record-keeping and WRITING. The capacity possessed by modern societies to marshal and store information has grown massively in recent times as the result of major technological innovations such as printing, audio and video recorders, and especially computers. The centrality of knowledge and information in today's modern technological and highly administered societies has led some commentators to coin the term 'information society' to describe these societies (see POSTINDUSTRIAL SOCIETY). A further aspect of the increased capacity of modern societies to collect and store information is greatly increased power of the state in the monitoring and SURVEILLANCE of its citizens.

information explosion/information overload arising from the centrality of information in INFORMATION SOCIETIES, the suggestion is that there now exists an over-abundance of information that risks undermining communication, and drowns out some voices, especially in a world of media concentration and message manipulation. Against this there are those who argue that the information explosion and new media have, at least, the potential to democratize communications.

information society a currently fashionable description of contemporary societies in which information technology and knowledge occupations are seen as occupying a dominant position. A critical discussion of the general concept is provided by F. Webster, *Theories of the Information Society* (1995). His conclusion is that while there has undoubtedly been a transformation of means of communication and an information explosion, it is premature to talk of the 'information society' as wholly supplanting previously established patterns of social relations. See also INTERNET, CASTELLS, POSTINDUSTRIAL SOCIETY, KNOWLEDGE SOCIETY.

information technology (IT) a general term applied to all computer-based technologies of human communication. It can be viewed as a broad sub-type of NEW TECHNOLOGY. Office automation is the most widely implemented form of information technology and has had major implications for the organization and experience of clerical work. This development has stimulated much sociological research and commentary on the issues of DESKILLING and PROLETARIANIZATION as well as the feminization of clerical work (Crompton and Jones, 1984; Webster, 1996). Information technology underpins the flow of information (i.e. information systems) within and between organizations and societies giving rise to increasing dependency on global networks including the Internet (CASTELLS, 1996). The increasing reliance on computer-based information systems has also given rise to concerns over the electronic power of the state (Lyons, 1988) and the possibility that information technology turns work organizations into the new panopticans in which everyone is under continual surveillance and control, an interpretation that draws directly on the work of FOUCAULT.

Information technology can be said to have begun in 1943, with the building of the Colossus computing machine in the UK in order to break the German Enigma code. By the late 1950s computers had been introduced into the major British banks, and were being used within accounts departments a little later (Mumford and Banks, 1967). At this point, the technology was limited to routine activities, involving the computation of data rather than the communication of information. However, with the development of more powerful interactive (i.e. 'real time' computer systems), and of smaller computers (minis and micros) coupled with 'off the shelf' programs (generally known as 'software packages'), information technology has spread throughout industry, and has now extended into people's homes and leisure activity. The main development in information technology in recent years has been the digital integration of information and telecommunications technologies, such as fax machines and electronic mail and currently between cell phones and 'palm top' computers. The divide between information and communication technologies has now been virtually eroded; they are now common technologies of communication.

infrastructure the basic physical structure of a society or an organization, especially the stock of fixed capital equipment in a country, e.g. means of transport, schools and factories, etc.

in-group and **out-group** twin terms introduced by Graham SUMNER (1906) to refer to insiders in a particular 'we' relationship, in contrast with outsiders to the relationship.

inheritance the transmission of rights to PROPERTY. It is usually distinguished from SUCCESSION by focusing the latter on the transmission of rights to a particular office or status. See also KINSHIP.

inner city an area of urban settlement with high levels of social problems and poverty. The term is sometimes used as a codeword for 'immigrant area' by those who regard 'the problems of the inner city' as problems of minority cultures and not as a concentration of the social problems of capitalist societies. See also ZONE OF TRANSITION, URBAN SOCIOLOGY, URBANISM AS A WAY OF LIFE, URBANIZATION.

inner-directedness see OTHER-DIRECTEDNESS.

instinct 1 (ETHOLOGY) the innate, motivating drives leading to species-specific behaviour patterns. Instinctive behaviour in animals is usually observed to be released by a specific stimulus, stereotyped (a 'fixed action pattern'), not learnt or open to change, e.g. nest-building or courting rituals. Some human behaviour, e.g. maternal behaviour, is commonly regarded as instinctive. However, maternal behaviour is far more complex, even in animals, and is certainly affected by learning, though some psychologists would regard it as primarily learnt and not therefore instinctive in humans. Though some human behaviour may be based on inherited tendencies, the development of the human brain has meant that behaviour is far less reliant on 'built-in' mechanisms, and much more controlled by learning and choice. Animals lower down the PHYLOGENETIC SCALE have proportionately less brain area for learning, and more for instinctive processes, so their behaviour is less plastic and more predictable, i.e. controlled by instinct rather than learning. 2 (PSYCHOANALYSIS), in FREUD's theory of personality dynamics, an inherited, motivating force, or *drive* found in the UNCONSCIOUS. See EROS, THANATOS.

instinct for combinations see RESIDUES AND DERIVATIONS.

Institute for Economic Affairs a right-wing THINK TANK whose contribution to neo-liberal thinking especially influenced the Conservative Government of Margaret Thatcher.

Institute for Public Policy Research established in 1988, and modelled on the influential right-wing INSTITUTE FOR ECONOMIC AFFAIRS, this left-wing UK THINK TANK has had a notable influence on key elements in the evolution of the thinking of NEW LABOUR, including its policies on constitutional reform, political participation (see CITIZENS' JURIES), environmental and regional policy, its thinking on NEW PUBLIC MANAGEMENT, and its educational policies.

institution an established order comprising rule-bound and standardized behaviour patterns. The term is widely acknowledged to be used in a variety of ways, and hence often ambiguously. SOCIAL INSTITUTION refers to arrangements involving large numbers of people whose behaviour is guided by NORMS and ROLES. In functionalist theory (see FUNCTIONALISM), the concept of institution is linked to that of FUNCTIONAL PREREQUISITES OR FUNCTIONAL IMPERATIVES. MALINOWSKI lists seven social institutions which meet biological and social-psychological NEEDS. GOFFMAN uses the term TOTAL INSTITUTION to refer to bureaucratically organized establishments (see BUREAUCRACY) in which the inmates have little possibility of escape from the norms and roles of the administrative structure. INSTITUTIONALIZATION refers to the process whereby the norms and roles expected in various social settings are developed and learned. Although this often involves an OVERSOCIALIZED CONCEPTION OF MAN, researchers influenced by PHENOMENOLOGICAL SOCIOLOGY stress the creative and adaptive aspects of social life.

institutional economics approaches to economic analysis which emphasize the role of socioeconomic institutions and organizations in the causation of economic events. In a narrow sense, institutional economics was a movement opposed to the abstractions and excessive formalism of much orthodox economic analysis, and was especially associated with the work of Thorstein VEBLEN. More widely, the approach can be said to be consistent with much sociological analysis of economic life, which has been more interested in grounding theories of economic life in behavioural and institutional inquiry than has economics (see ECONOMIC SOCIOLOGY).

institutionalization 1 the process, as well as the outcome of the process, in which social activities become regularized and routinized as stable, social-structural features. See also INSTITUTION.

2 the process, and the resulting condition, in which SOCIAL ACTORS incarcerated for long periods in TOTAL INSTITUTIONS, such as prisons or mental hospitals, become incapable of, or disabled for, independent social life outside the institution.

institutional reflexivity 'the regularized use of knowledge about circumstances of social life as a constitutive element in its organization and transformation' (GIDDENS, 1991). See also REFLEXIVE MODERNIZATION.

instrumental conditioning see CONDITIONING.

instrumental rationality the subjection of activity to the criterion of effectiveness alone' (GELLNER, 1988). This form of rationality is often regarded as the essence of the process of RATIONALIZATION underlying the transformation of premodern, PREINDUSTRIAL SOCIETIES to modern INDUSTRIAL SOCIETIES. See also TYPES OF SOCIAL ACTION, RATIONALITY.

integration 1 the extent to which an individual experiences a sense of belonging to a social group or collectivity by virtue of sharing its norms, values, beliefs, etc. Integration is a key concept of Emile DURKHEIM's sociology, and is one of the two main variables which he used in his seminal explanation of variations in rates of SUICIDE.

2 the extent to which the activity or function of different institutions or subsystems within society complement rather than contradict each other. For example, the family is integrated within the economic systems of advanced industrial societies to the extent that it sustains and reproduces labour power (but no other commodity), while acting as a unit of consumption (rather than production).

3 the presence of specific institutions which promote the complementary and coordinated activity of other subsystems of society. The development of institutions of integration of this kind (such as written language, formal legal systems) is one of the FUNCTIONAL PREREQUISITES OR FUNCTIONAL IMPERATIVES of all social systems, and a key to social development in neoevolutionary theory (see NEOEVOLUTIONISM).

The use of the concept of integration in all three senses is a characteristic of FUNCTIONALISM, and especially of the work of Talcott PARSONS. *Malintegration* simply implies a lack, or absence of, integration or integrative mechanisms. For example, egoistic suicide is, for Durkheim, a result of the malintegration of the individual within the group; economic growth may suffer if the educational system fails to integrate its activity and goals with those of the economy; the important evolutionary advance (see EVOLUTIONARY THEORY) of the separation of power from office represented by the democratic association cannot survive without the supremacy of the integrative mechanism represented by the rule of law. See also SOCIAL SOLIDARITY, MECHANICAL AND ORGANIC SOLIDARITY, SOCIAL INTEGRATION AND SYSTEM INTEGRATION.

intellectual labour (especially MARXISM) all those forms of labour in which the work is by the brain rather than by the hand. The claim is made that in modern capitalist societies (and perhaps in all modern societies) the tendency is for these forms of nonmanual labour to grow in importance, and to do so as the result of a DESKILLING of manual labour as well as some forms of routine nonmanual labour. In this way, knowledge and skills that were previously possessed by workers as a whole (e.g. craft skills) become displaced, and are replaced by the new concentrations of skills that constitute intellectual labour. The growth of a number of distinct types of intellectual labour is said to occur in this process, especially supervisory workers and management, and new technical workers, the designers and repairers of advanced machines. Among Marxist sociologists (e.g. Sohn-Rethel, 1978), the suggestion is that much of the growth of such forms of labour serves the purpose of more effective EXPLOITATION of labour, and that noncapitalist planned economies will be able to dispense with some parts of such labour, reuniting intellectual and manual labour within the single worker. However, two points can be made against this view: that the growth of intellectual labour may be more a consequence of general advances in knowledge and the division of labour, which are only partly connected with CAPITALISM and which lead to general efficiency as well as to exploitation; and that deskilling may be occurring *generally* to a much lesser extent than suggested, and for different reasons in that it is restricted to some occupational groups. Thus, a general increase in the knowledge and skills of the workforce overall may be a consequence of the importance of intellectual labour in modern economies, exemplified by an overall increase in nonmanual labour (see also INFORMATION SOCIETY, Daniel BELL). However, the fact that intellectual labour expands in importance, for whatever reasons, does mean a loss of skills and power for some groups, and an increasing fragmentation of working-class interests may be one consequence of this (see CLASS CONSCIOUSNESS).

intellectuals persons, typically well-educated, who engage their intellect in work which they believe to be of cultural importance. In English, 'intellectual' as a noun first appeared in the early 19th century, and early usage was often pejorative. Sociological interest largely centres on intellectuals as a distinct social group (see INTELLIGENTSIA). In addition, three episodes in French social thought are worth noting. First, the social scientist Henri de SAINT-SIMON introduced the military concept of a vanguard, or *avant-garde*, to social thought in the early 19th century, although his reference was not to intellectuals as such, but rather to scientists, whose positive knowledge would enable them alone to direct the development of France and other industrial societies. Second, in 1896, the politician Georges Clemenceau labelled the defenders of Dreyfus as 'intellectuals' (see DREYFUS AFFAIR), so beginning modern usage. The label was promptly adopted as a badge of honour by DURKHEIM and others. Third, the philosopher Julien Benda condemned intellectuals for their readiness to serve particular social and political interests and to betray their true calling – the disinterested pursuit of universal truth and justice – in his *La Trahison des Clercs* (1927).

Intellectuals, interests and truth also figure in the writings of Antonio GRAMSCI between the wars. Gramsci notes the partiality of (communities of) intellectuals – producers and disseminators of knowledge – and their role in the generation of both hegemony and resistance. In particular, he distinguishes '*traditional intellectuals*' who, however self-deludingly, uphold the autonomy of intellectuals, from '*organic intellectuals*', including technical specialists, who acknowledge a functional relation, however nuanced, to dominant or oppositional classes and groups within a given socio-economic formation.

Finally, the term '*public intellectual*' is increasingly used in America, and now Britain, to refer to intellectuals in the PUBLIC SPHERE who set agendas, inform debate and influence opinion. Anthony GIDDENS' articulation of a 'THIRD WAY' politics beyond left and right provides an example. See also MANNHEIM.

intelligence a person's intellectual ability or potential for rational thought and behaviour. The nature and measurement of intelligence is one of the most controversial topics in the social sciences. The central debate concerns what we mean by the concept of intelligence. Early theories assumed a quite narrow range of cognitive abilities such as abstract reasoning, comprehension and memory, though they differed in the emphasis placed on the existence of a general factor of intelligence, common across all skills (e.g. Spearman), versus a number of distinct primary mental abilities (e.g. Thurstone). More recent views tend to broaden the concept to include such skills as practical problem-solving, social skills and creativity.

A second debate centres on the extent to which intelligence is inherited biologically, or acquired as a result of environmental experience and socialization (see NATURE – NURTURE DEBATE). Many methods have been devised to research this issue, including the study of identical twins and adopted children, but the *relative* contributions of heredity and environment remain unclear.

Models of the nature of intelligence have important implications for educational processes. One influential model finds expression in cognitive developmental theories which emphasize the importance of the interaction between inherited potential and environmental experience; This approach is exemplified in the work of PIAGET (1932) and Bruner (1968), both of whom identified qualitatively different stages of mental development and learning. These theorists have exerted considerable influence on the structure of educational provision in recent decades.

intelligence quotient (IQ) a unit used in the field of INTELLIGENCE measurement and testing as an index of an individual's intelligence relative to a comparable population with respect to age. A *ratio IQ* is the IQ expressed as a ratio of mental age (as measured by a test) to chronological age, and multiplied by 100 to avoid decimals:

$$IQ = \frac{\text{Mental Age (MA)}}{\text{Chronological Age (CA)}} \times 100$$

The average child at any one chronological age will therefore score 100 on the appropriate set of IQ test items. This was the original IQ measure first used in 1916 in the Stanford-Binet Test.

Modern tests make use of standard scores, which express the individual's distance from the mean in terms of the standard deviation, and assume a normal distribution. In a variant of this, the *deviation IQ*, the mean is 100 and a standard deviation of 15 or 16 is usual.

It is important to note the difference between these measures, since the deviation IQ is not a ratio of mental age to chronological age, and the measured IQs derived from it will depend on the standard deviation used in the test. See also INTELLIGENCE TEST.

intelligence test a set of items, usually arranged in ascending order of difficulty, which test an individual's level of INTELLIGENCE by generating an estimate of their IQ (INTELLIGENCE QUOTIENT). Among the best-known general tests are the Wechsler Adult Intelligence Scale, the British Ability Scales, and the Wechsler Intelligence Scale for Children. More specialized tests (e.g. Ravens Progressive Matrices), as well as subscales within many general tests, provide separate measures of more specific cognitive abilities such as spatial ability.

The development of testing procedures has been based on the assumption that the greater proportion of ability is inherited. Tests are therefore designed to measure innate ability, while controlling for environmental and cultural factors. Many critics, however, claim that it is not possible to achieve this aim, and that test results remain culturally biased towards the norms and values of dominant groups in society. According to this view intelligence tests therefore fail to reflect the true intelligence levels of subordinate class, race or gender groups.

The educational and political significance of intelligence testing can be seen in the fierce reaction to Jensen's reopening of the NATURE – NURTURE DEBATE in 1969 (see L. Kamin, *The Science and Politics of I.Q.*). Jensen's claim that 80% of intelligence was due to genetic factors was followed with even more controversial arguments attributing a significant proportion of the lower test performance of American blacks to this cause. Test results were therefore suggested as legitimizing the differential educational treatment received in schools by different social groups.

Within the field of education, educationists have often argued that concentration on intelligence testing and the automatic equation of a high IQ score with brightness and achievement have straitjacketed the education system for over half a century (e.g. the effects of 11+ in allocating children to different types of educational provision and experience). Others have consistently defended the predictive powers of IQ tests. Currently there tends to be more agreement that tests are neither wholly neutral nor wholly valid (see VALIDITY), but they remain a useful diagnostic tool in the assessment of cognitive and learning difficulties.

intelligentsia 1 a SOCIAL STRATUM of INTELLECTUALS with a self-appointed responsibility for guiding the future welfare and development of the nation. The term is of mid-19th-century Polish and Russian origin, and is like CASTE in that some sociologists consider it applicable only to a particular place and time, whilst others believe it to be more generally extendable. **2** any constellation of educated, but unpropertied, individuals with some consciousness of its distinctive role either in a national society or in a culture area transcending national boundaries. For example, there have been intelligentsias in this sense in some African societies before and after independence.

'Intelligentsia' and 'INTELLECTUALS' are not synonymous. Thus there have been and are intellectuals in Britain but not an intelligentsia in either sense **1** or **2**.

The first sense of intelligentsia arose in the 19th century when Poland was partitioned between Prussia (later Germany), Russia and Austria. Those few who possessed the secondary school leaving certificate, the *matura*, and who thus knew their Polish literature and history, considered themselves to be guardians of the national culture. As such they supplied the leadership for many oppositional movements. Very often they were the sons of pauperized nobility and GENTRY; they retained gentry values and disdained the bourgeois pursuits of trade and industry. Following the restoration of the Polish state in 1918, the intelligentsia played a leading part in government and administration but was then decimated in World War II.

After 1945, the Communist Party claimed for itself the leading role in the development of Poland and set out to eliminate all rivals. The 'classical' intelligentsia ceased to exist. According to the official Marxist formula, the new Poland had two 'nonantagonistic classes', the workers and the peasants, and the stratum of the intelligentsia. Reference to a separate stratum (not class) of the intelligentsia acknowledged that its relation to the means of production was similar to that of the working class, yet aspects of its culture and consciousness continued to set it apart. Entry to the intelligentsia was now defined in terms of completion of higher, rather than secondary, education, and the majority of graduates were now in science and engineering. This led to a distinction between the creative or cultural intelligentsia, and the vastly more numerous technical intelligentsia whose residual attachment to old intelligentsia values was much less evident.

In 19th-century Russia, a *declassé* fraction of the nobility sought to maintain elements of its traditional style of life in an urban setting (thereby guaranteeing its distinction from the BOURGEOISIE), whilst leading the nation to its destiny. The latter required abolition of tsarism, and the residues of feudalism, by whatever means, and a general commitment to progressive causes. Following the October Revolution in 1917, the creative intelligentsia at first flourished, but Stalin could not countenance its independence and put an end to it. The official Marxist formula of two classes and the stratum of the intelligentsia kept alive the term but that is all.

Sense 2 of the term intelligentsia is consistent with the German *Intelligenz.* Alfred Weber originated the notion of a socially unattached intelligentsia, but it is Mannheim's formulation which is best known: 'In every society there are social groups whose special task it is to provide an interpretation of the world for that society. We call these the intelligentsia' (MANNHEIM, 1936). He suggested that they tend either to affiliate voluntarily 'with one or other of the various antagonistic classes' (cf GRAMSCI on organic INTELLECTUALS), or try to fulfil 'their mission as the predestined advocate of the intellectual interests of the whole' (MANNHEIM, 1929).

More recent analyses of the class position of the intelligentsia include Konrad and Szelényi (1979) and Gouldner (1979). According to Konrad and Szelényi's account of 'intellectuals on the road to class power' in the industrially backward state socialist societies of Eastern Europe, the intelligentsia were 'organized into a government-bureaucratic ruling class', and took the lead in modernization, 'replacing a weak bourgeoisie incapable of breaking with feudalism'. Gouldner (1979) argues that in all parts of the emerging world socioeconomic order, humanist intellectuals and the technical intelligentsia constitute a new class which contests the control of economics hitherto exercised either by businessmen or by party leaders (cf BELL on INFORMATION SOCIETIES).

intended and unintended consequences of social action see UNANTICIPATED CONSEQUENCES (OF SOCIAL ACTION).

intensification of agriculture see ENVIRONMENTAL DEPLETION.

intensive power see EXTENSIVE AND INTENSIVE POWER.

intentionality 1 the purposiveness of human action. As SCHUTZ and the proponents of ETHNOMETHODOLOGY underline, intentionality does not, as sometimes suggested, consist only of a series of discrete purposes. It exists also in more 'tacit' forms of actor's 'knowledgeability' (i.e. in what GIDDENS (1984) terms PRACTICAL KNOWLEDGE OR PRACTICAL CONSCIOUSNESS), as well as in the DISCURSIVE CONSCIOUSNESS of the actor. See also STRATIFICATION MODEL OF SOCIAL ACTION AND CONSCIOUSNESS.
2 (PHILOSOPHY) for HUSSERL and SARTRE, the 'reaching out towards an object' involved in human consciousness.

interaction (STATISTICS) the compounded effect that two or more INDEPENDENT VARIABLES may have on the DEPENDENT VARIABLE when they act together. In examining the effect of the variables in an experiment, the individual effect of each may not explain the total variation. In such instances it is therefore appropriate to use a statistical test such as ANALYSIS OF VARIANCE which is designed to assess the effect of the interaction between the variables as well as the specific effect of each.

interaction, interaction ritual and **interaction order** the processes and manner in which social actors relate to each other, especially in face-to-face ENCOUNTERS.

While patterns of interaction have long been studied by social scientists (e.g. small groups by social psychologists, or BODY LANGUAGE by psychologists), the fundamental, trans-situational structure of interaction was often considered only incidentally. It is only with the work of Goffman that these structures have begun to be more fully explored. GOFFMAN (1963) defines a 'social order' as the 'consequences of any set of moral norms that regulates the way in which persons pursue their objectives'. Such moral norms are equivalent to the 'traffic rules' of social interaction. This 'public order', or *interaction order,* which governs the form and processes, though not the content, of social interaction, stands at the heart of Goffman's sociology (e.g. see CIVIL INATTENTION). What Goffman then means by *interaction ritual* is that a ritual cooperation exists, and 'ritual codes', in upholding the enactment of a shared reality, e.g. in allowing the actors with whom one interacts to preserve face (see FACE-WORK).

As early as 1951, Gregory Bateson suggested the possibility that interaction might be seen as a communication system, with perhaps a SYNTAX. Goffman's work appears to build on these early notions (see Kendon, 1988).

interest articulation see AGGREGATION.

interest group see PRESSURE GROUP.

interests the particular social outcomes held to benefit a particular individual or group. Such interests may be those recognized and pursued by the person or group, or they may be identified by others, including social scientists, as underlying or 'objective' interests, unrecognized by the persons concerned. MARXISM is an example of a theory in which the distinction between apparent interests and underlying, objective, interests plays an important role (see FALSE CONSCIOUSNESS).

intergenerational and intragenerational mobility see SOCIAL MOBILITY.

intermediate classes *or* **intermediate strata** (MARXISM) in CAPITALIST SOCIETY, those CLASSES standing intermediate between the capitalist (or bourgeois) class and the PROLETARIAT, and belonging to neither (see Fig. 16). As summarized by Hodges (1961), these class groupings can be seen as consisting of 'transitional' classes of four basic types:

(A) Basic dichotomous ideal type of classes under capitalism:

	BOURGEOIS/CAPITALIST CLASS:	*PROLETARIAT:*
(a)	ownership of capital	propertyless – wage earners
(b)	'unproductive' and exploitive – expropriating surplus value	'productive' and exploited – producing 'surplus value' which is expropriated by capitalists
(c)	political oppressors	politically oppressed

(B) Trichotomous class pattern: real world patterns of class

BOURGEOIS	INTERMEDIATE CLASSES	PROLETARIAT
	(all those who fall outside the dichotomous model of class)	
	i) *artisans* – standing 'outside' capitalism, as neither users of capital nor employed by capitalists	
	ii) *petty bourgeoisie* – limited use of capital or employment of labour	
	iii) *commercial and supervisory groups* – 'realisers' of capital on behalf of capitalists, rather than (usually) producers of surplus value	
	iv) *new middle class* – professional and technical workers	

Fig. 16 **Intermediate class** *or* **intermediate strata:** the several types of class groupings which under capitalism fall outside the simple Marxist dichotomous model of class and class conflict.

(a) 'artisans', who employ no-one and are not themselves employed, who because of this might be seen as lying 'outside the capitalist system', and hence also outside its system of classes;
(b) the PETTY BOURGEOISIE, i.e. those relatively small employers who are relatively limited users of capital, and are themselves often 'politically oppressed' under capitalism;
(c) commercial and supervisory intermediate class groups acting on behalf of capitalists, primarily as the 'realizers' rather than producers of SURPLUS VALUE who, while their income derives from the proceeds of the exploitation of the proletariat, are themselves often politically oppressed, and may sometimes be exploited given that they also sometimes produce surplus value;
(d) the 'NEW MIDDLE CLASS', i.e. professional, technical experts who, while partly productive in the sense that they produce surplus value, and may themselves be exploited, also receive salaries which in part are the fruits of exploitation. They can also be seen as being denied full power under capitalism, and thus potentially have interests in the replacement of capitalism, although benefiting from it in part.

In the classical Marxist view, these class locations are seen as likely to be transitional under capitalism, though in different ways. Thus (a) and (b) can be held to consist mainly of a survival from precapitalist patterns of class, and as tending to decline in importance, while (c) and (d) are hypothesized to crystallize into capitalist or proletarian positions, given the tendency for CLASS POLARIZATION to occur in capitalist societies. In the main, this process of crystallization was assumed likely to be in the direction of PROLETARIANIZATION, or at least include an increasing recognition by the members of these classes of interests opposed to capitalism. Subsequent empirical patterns of class locations, CLASS CONSCIOUSNESS and class action among intermediate groups, however, suggest a complexity of CLASS INTERESTS, which has lead to a great variety of neo-Marxist and non-Marxist accounts and theories of class within capitalist societies and the place of intermediate class groupings within these. See also CAPITALISM AND CAPITALIST MODE OF PRODUCTION, CLASS BOUNDARIES, MULTIDIMENSIONAL ANALYSIS OF SOCIAL STRATIFICATION, COLLECTIVE LABOUR, CONTRADICTORY CLASS LOCATIONS, DAHRENDORF, INTELLECTUAL LABOUR, NEW CLASS, PROFESSION, SERVICE CLASS, SOCIAL CLOSURE, STATUS CONSISTENCY AND INCONSISTENCY.

intermediate group *or* **secondary group** any group (e.g. VOLUNTARY ASSOCIATION) that can be seen as occupying an intermediate position between central state institutions and PRIMARY GROUPS such as the family or other face-to-face groupings. The number and variety of such intermediate and secondary groups is sometimes suggested as providing an important counterbalance to tendencies towards MASS SOCIETY in modern industrial societies.

intermediate societies societies of size and complexity intermediate between simple societies and modern industrial societies, and intermediate in 'developmental' sequence.

intermediate strata see INTERMEDIATE CLASSES OR INTERMEDIATE STRATA.

intermediate technology production techniques which avoid the NEW TECHNOLOGY and capital-intensive nature of Western production systems, but are an improvement on indigenous methods. The use of intermediate technology is increasingly proposed as APPROPRIATE TECHNOLOGY for some THIRD WORLD countries (see also UNDERDEVELOPMENT) which lack the infrastructure to adopt advanced technology satisfactorily and may not benefit economically or socially from export-oriented capitalist production (see also DEPENDENCY THEORY, DEPENDENT INDUSTRIALIZATION, NEOCOLONIALISM, UNEQUAL EXCHANGE. GREEN REVOLUTION).

Following E. F. Schumacher's (1973) prescription that 'small is beautiful', local schemes for irrigation, conservation, organic farming, etc., using indigenous skills and locally available resources, have been encouraged, enabling the population to exert more control over their lives. Such schemes are also proposed as 'ecologically friendly', avoiding the ENVIRONMENTAL DEPLETION that may result from inappropriate enterprise, and as providing a preferred basis for long-term development. (Such development is increasingly proposed as ecologically appropriate for more 'advanced' societies.) See also ETHNOSCIENCES, MULTICULTURALISM, SUSTAINABLE DEVELOPMENT.

internal colonialism the incorporation of culturally distinct groups by a dominant group into one national identity, centralized political rule and a national economy. In many analyses the process has similarities with external COLONIALISM, whereby one state subordinates another. In contemporary literature on this subject there are two main areas where the concept is at the centre of analysis. One is in Latin American scholarship, where the term has been used to analyse the relationship between Europeanized social groups and indigenous groups (often called Indians) with different languages, beliefs and ways of life. Stavenhagen (1975) argues that internal colonialism emerged in Latin American countries with independence from Spain and Portugal in the 19th century and with the development of capitalist economies. Indian communities lost their lands, were made to work for strangers, were integrated into a monetary economy and incorporated into national political structures. This led to a form of ethnic stratification which, in Stavenhagen's analysis, operates alongside changing social class relationships.

In Europe and the US, the concept has been used to discuss ethnic and race relations and the emergence of nationalist movements within established nation states. The term gained currency with the civil rights and black power movements in the US in the 1960s, when comparisons were drawn between the position of black people in the US and the situation in Africa, where European colonialism was giving way to independent states. Hechter (1975) produced one of the most influential academic formulations of the concept, and, by using it to analyse national development in the UK, widened the debate. Hechter used aspects of WORLD SYSTEMS analysis to argue that internal colonialism involves the subordination of peripheral cultural groups by core dominant groups partly as a result of the uneven industrialization of territories. Those groups in the most advanced regions achieve dominance over those groups in the less advanced. Later this may lead to the emergence of nationalist movements in those regions, as was the case in some European countries and Canada in the late 1960s. See also NATIONALISM, CENTRE AND PERIPHERY, IMPERIALISM.

internal colonization of the life-world the penetration of forms of economic and administrative rationality into areas of 'communicative practice' which specialize in cultural transmission (HABERMAS, *Theory of Communicative Action*, 1984–88). The outcome, according to Habermas, is a 'cultural impoverishment' of everyday life, and an associated 'loss of meaning' and 'loss of freedom'.

internalization the acceptance and incorporation of the standards or beliefs of other persons, or of society, by the individual. Internalization is a basic concept in FREUD's theory of personality development. The child's conscience (SUPEREGO) is formed by internalizing society's MORES, as represented by the parents' personal values and standards. As suggested by this psychodynamic usage, the total acceptance of beliefs and values is usually implied when the concept is employed in a more general way. However, some expressed attitudes or behaviours may be based on social pressures, such as CONFORMITY, and involve *compliance* rather than internalization. See also SOCIALIZATION, OVERSOCIALIZED CONCEPTION OF MAN.

internalization of imperialism see DEPENDENT INDUSTRIALIZATION.

internal labour market see LABOUR MARKET.

international debt 1 the 'amount of money' which the government of a country, or its private institutions, owes to other countries, external banks or international agencies. 2 the total amount of such debt in the world.

This has become a major problem since the late 1970s for many THIRD WORLD countries, and some others, such as Poland, which have borrowed heavily on the international markets for more than a decade. Many countries have found difficulty in paying the interest on the debt. This means that the total amount of debt is not decreasing. In the late 1980s, this was seen as a major problem for prospective world trade and for economic growth in the Third World. In 1988, one of the most indebted countries, Brazil, owed $120 billion to external institutions and this had not declined by the mid-1990s. During the 1980s and 1990s many countries in Latin America and Africa adopted policies of structural adjustment involving balanced internal budgets and an increased focus on exports: these were often required by the International Monetary Fund. See also DEPENDENCY THEORY, DEPENDENT INDUSTRIALIZATION, UNEQUAL EXCHANGE.

international division of labour see INTERNATIONAL TRADE, UNEQUAL EXCHANGE.

international relations both the relations between nations and the study of these relationships. As a policy-oriented academic study, international relations is a hybrid discipline, drawing upon historiography and political science as well as on sociology.

The most significant actors in international relations are usually considered to be sovereign NATION STATES. Given that states are sovereign powers, the formal relation between these is one in which there exists no higher authority than the nation states themselves. It is for this reason that WARFARE, or the threat of or the avoidance of warfare, has figured so prominently in both the practice of international relations and as the subject matter of the discipline (see also STRATEGIC THEORY, DETERRENCE THEORY, ARMS RACE). The economic and the political relations between states are also the subject of study, as is the operation of international organizations.

It is in terms of the specificity of its substantive focus, rather than in the range of methods employed, that the discipline of international relations is distinguished from sociology. Thus, most of the approaches, theories and topics of international relations also occur, actually or potentially, as subsections of sociology (see NATION-STATE SYSTEM, WORLD SYSTEM).

international trade the sale or exchange of goods and services between countries. According to the *law of comparative advantage,* proposed by the 19th-century political economist Ricardo, a country will ideally produce only those goods and services in the production of which it possesses such advantage that it can produce these more cheaply than other producers. In theory at least, therefore, the international division of labour that results should benefit all nations. However, the extent to which each country benefits depends on the favourableness or otherwise of the TERMS OF TRADE which operate for the commodities and services which it imports and exports. Thus, in recent years many developing nations have experienced adverse and often worsening terms of trade, especially as a result of declining relative prices for food and agricultural raw materials in situations where, in the short run at least, they are unable to shift their output to other areas of production. See DEPENDENCY THEORY, UNEQUAL EXCHANGE, IMPERIALISM.

Internet the global, distributed packet-switching network that interconnects computers. The Internet was initially developed by the US Defense Department in the 1970s as a safeguard against the failure of military communications systems during a nuclear attack. By the mid-1980s Internet technology was being appropriated by educational and research institutions as well as businesses and government organizations where it was widely viewed as an opportunity to document and access information. The

Internet is now present in millions of organizations and private households around the globe and is essentially available to anyone with access to a personal computer and a telephone line. Its wide variety of uses range from what are regarded as legitimate applications such as advertising, shopping, library catalogues, newspaper archives, and financial pages, to its use for recreational or illicit 'surfing': 'chat-rooms', gossip, and eroticism. Because of its use by individuals and groups wanting to broadcast and access illicit or illegal material, the Internet is often regarded as providing a democratic forum for underground subcultures and organizations to communicate their desires, beliefs, and political agendas. These democratizing implications also extend to the economy with consumers being able to access the best (cheapest) prices and products available. However, there is the issue that these possibilities remain limited to those with access to the technology and knowledge. The immense amount of information available on the Internet and the know-how required to make effective use of the technology restrict the applications for the average 'surfer' who may spend hours moving between trivial sites. Alongside possibilities for global networking runs the danger that information-rich countries will monopolize both the technology and know-how required to distribute information and exclude dispossessed nations from the advantages available to those with access to the World Wide Web. See also CYBERCULTURE, INFORMATION SOCIETY, NETWORK SOCIETY.

interpellation the process by which individuals become social subjects. According to ALTHUSSER (1971), people are actually the 'bearers of structures' rather than 'autonomous subjects'. Yet, if capitalist relations of production are to be reproduced, each person must be constituted as an independent individual. This is the function of IDEOLOGY. Individuals are constituted or interpellated as subjects by 'hailing' or addressing them as, for example, 'the people'. In this way, the capitalist state is able to address individuals in terms of a democratic discourse as autonomous subjects, while recruiting them into a political process whose real function is the preservation, co-ordination and reproduction of the conditions for successful capital accumulation.

interpolation see MEASURES OF CENTRAL TENDENCY.

interpretation (and **interpretive understanding**) a method that stresses the importance of understanding intentional human action. Semantically, any account is an interpretation. What distinguishes the interpretive paradigm from other movements is the recognition that any statement about the social world is necessarily relative to any other. It inevitably sets itself against the notion of the Durkheimian 'social fact' by asserting that 'facts' are always produced by specific people in certain circumstances for explicit reasons. There is little agreement on detail since interpretive sociologists cover a wide range of epistemological positions. The extreme subjectivist or relativist wing (HERMENEUTICS) takes the position that no single interpretation can predominate over another. SCHUTZ's phenomenological sociology occupies a fairly central position within the paradigm in attempting a systematic study of the intersubjective nature of social life. On the other hand, WEBER considered understanding (VERSTEHEN) to be a method of elucidating the motivations for action (not experience of action) which did not preclude the sociologist making generalizations from this data (see also IDEAL TYPES). ETHNOMETHODOLOGY is often classed as an INTERPRETIVE SOCIOLOGY, but this can only be partially valid since it gains much of its intellectual heritage from American EMPIRICISM. In sum, whilst there is a general commitment to EMPATHY and understanding the actor's point of view, the research that flows from interpretation is so varied as to be difficult to categorize as a school, possibly because the meaning of interpretation is itself subject to interpretation.

interpretative sociology

A variety of forms of sociology (including SYMBOLIC INTERACTIONISM, SOCIOLOGICAL PHENOMENOLOGY, and the approach of WEBER) united by an emphasis on the necessity for sociologists to grasp (i.e. to 'understand' or interpret) actors' 'meanings' (see also INTERPRETATION, MEANINGFUL UNDERSTANDING AND EXPLANATION, VERSTEHEN, HERMENEUTICS, DOUBLE HERMENEUTIC). In this argument all social reality is 'pre-interpreted' in that it only has form as (and is constituted by) the outcome of SOCIAL ACTORS' beliefs and interpretations. Thus it is, or ought to be, a truism that no form of sociology can proceed without at least a preliminary grasp of actors' meanings. DURKHEIM's suggestion, in *Rules,* that we can proceed to the objective study of 'social facts' without any reference to actors' purposes is wrong or misleading.

On a charitable reading, what Durkheim wanted to suggest was that sociology, if it genuinely wished to be a 'science', could not rest content merely with the social accounts contained in actors' meanings. Even here, however, most forms of sociology that refer to themselves as 'interpretative' part company with Durkheim, arguing that the pre-interpreted reality with which sociologists deal precludes a positivistic approach, especially given that the actions of social actors can change meanings and are not only the outcome of received meanings.

Among the various forms of sociology that adopt this stance, some (e.g. the proposals of WINCH) suggest that an understanding of actors' meanings can alone suffice in providing descriptions *and* explanations of social action. More usually, however, the argument is that the 'meaningful' character of social reality and sociological explanation restricts, but does not eliminate, the possibility of accounts of social reality which move beyond actors' meanings. For example, for Weber, IDEAL TYPES play an important role in the formulation and testing of historical hypotheses; in a not dissimilar way, within SYMBOLIC INTERACTIONISM, general SENSITIZING CONCEPTS play an important role in the analysis of particular cases; and in GOFFMAN's sociology the generation of general conceptual frameworks is central. In all such approaches (though there exist many disagreements), the aim is to achieve a 'non-positivistic' formulation of social science that does not violate the premises that actors' meanings must always be 'understood' and that actors' social competence and actors' choice precludes deterministic 'law-like accounts' of social reality. Whether wider 'structural', or even scientifically 'causal', forms of sociological analysis can also ultimately be constructed on an interpretative basis, raises a farther set of questions which have received a variety of answers (e.g. compare PARSONS' functionalism or the STRUCTURATION THEORY of GIDDENS) (see also STRUCTURE AND AGENCY).

intersocietal systems any social arrangements or social systems which 'cut across whatever dividing lines exist between SOCIETIES or societal totalities' (GIDDENS, 1984). The claim of Giddens is that sociologists have often failed to take into account the importance of intersocietal systems. According to MANN (1986), sociologists have often conceived of society as 'an unproblematic, unitary totality', and as the 'total unit of analysis', when, in fact, this concept, at best, applies only to modern NATION STATES. Usually, historically, 'societies' lacked such clear boundaries. Moreover, given the interdependence of modern nation states as part of a worldwide economic and NATION-STATE SYSTEM (see also WORLD SYSTEM), modern nation states cannot be properly understood as isolated social systems. See also TIME-SPACE DISTANCIATION.

intersubjectivity shared experiences between people; agreements on knowledge, etc. The existence of 'intersubjectivity', since it need make no claims to OBJECTIVISM, counteracts such doctrines as SOLIPSISM, RELATIVISM and INCOMMENSURABILITY, all of which suggest barriers to working agreements on 'knowledge'. See also LIFE-WORLD.

intertextuality see DECONSTRUCTION.

interval level measurement see CRITERIA AND LEVELS OF MEASUREMENT.

intervening variable a VARIABLE which mediates the effect of an INDEPENDENT VARIABLE on a DEPENDENT VARIABLE. This may be an internal mechanism whose existence is hypothesized from the effects it is observed to have (e.g. the effect of the organism which intervenes between the S [stimulus] and R [response] in behaviouristic psychology), or another external explanatory variable (e.g. social class has an observed effect on morbidity, but this is mediated by income, diet, housing, etc.).

interview a method of collecting social data at the INDIVIDUAL LEVEL. This face-to-face method ensures a higher RESPONSE RATE than POSTAL QUESTIONNAIRES, but can introduce INTERVIEWER BIAS by the effect different interviewers have on the quality, VALIDITY and RELIABILITY of the data so collected.

Interviews may be *structured,* with the interviewer asking set questions and the respondents' replies being immediately categorized. This format allows ease of analysis and less possibility of interviewer bias, but the data will not be as 'rich' as that elicited by an unstructured design (and may be subject to problems such as MEASUREMENT BY FIAT – see also CICOUREL). Unstructured interviews are desirable when the initial exploration of an area is being made, and hypotheses for further investigation being generated, or when the depth of the data required is more important than ease of analysis. See QUALITATIVE RESEARCH and QUANTITATIVE RESEARCH TECHNIQUES.

interviewer bias the BIAS which may be introduced into social-research findings when the social background (e.g. social class, ethnic background or gender) of an interviewer affects the response made at an interview. For example, as well as a mistrust or lack of rapport between an interviewer and an interviewee, there may exist *over-rapport,* in which an interviewer relates to the interviewee as if certain responses can be taken for granted, thus distorting outcomes.

intimacy sexual and personal relations characterized by closeness and personal disclosure. A recent analysis is provided by GIDDENS (*The Transformation of Intimacy,* 1992), who focuses on the changing character of the *'pair relationship'* in modern societies including homosexual as well as heterosexual relationships, and FRIENDSHIP relationships as well as sexual relationships. Three central concepts are employed in this analysis:

(a) the *pure relationship,* a relationship maintained for its own sake;

(b) *plastic sexuality,* sexuality freed from considerations of property relations;
(c) *confluent love,* the self-consciously conditional, revisable love relationship, a relationship that must be continuously worked at to ensure the mutual commitment and trust it requires of both partners.

The origins of the 'pure relationship', according to Giddens, are 'separation of sexuality from the reproductive function', made possible especially by modern contraception. In these circumstances the possibility of confluent love emerges. Child–parent relations also tend increasingly to approximate to the pattern of the pure relationship, and as Janet Finch (*Family Obligations and Social Change,* 1989) points out, kinship relations in general become increasingly dependent for their continuation on a 'working out' of relationships. For Giddens, intimacy involves above all an emotional communication with oneself and others, in a context of equality in which 'TRUST has to be won and actively sustained'.

intragenerational mobility see SOCIAL MOBILITY.

intrapreneurship see ENTREPRENEUR.

introversion see EXTRAVERSION and INTROVERSION.

invention the act or process of devising a new machine, technique, etc. As such, invention is sometimes presented in science, in historiography, and especially in popular thinking, as an individual matter and as a catalogue of discrete events associated with named persons, e.g. Watt's steam engine or Arkwright's spinning jenny – a phenomenon of individual genius, individual psychology and individual CREATIVITY, rather than something to be explained sociologically. In fact, however, inventions are often collective products, tending to occur as part of general waves of cultural and economic development (as in the INDUSTRIAL REVOLUTION in the UK), in association with particular SCIENTIFIC PARADIGMS, or craft traditions guided by 'scientific discoveries', rather than as isolated events. In much of modern industry, technological innovation, and also scientific discovery in general, is far more a matter of routine, bureaucratized 'research and development' than of individual creativity, though obviously this plays a part. See also DIFFUSION OF INNOVATIONS, STRUCTURALISM, STRUCTURE AND AGENCY.

invisible hand a term used by Adam Smith (1776) to indicate the way in which the pursuit of individual self-interest in a free market actually ensures the maximum overall benefit for everyone. Smith's arguments have typically been employed by the NEW RIGHT in promoting the deregulation of labour markets and the doctrine of minimalist government.

Irigaray, Luce (1932–) Belgian-born philosopher and psychoanalyst noted for her association with French psychoanalyst Jacques LACAN In contrast to Simone de BEAUVOIR, for whom women constitute the Other, Irigaray argues that because both Self and Other are understood from within a phallocentric (male-centred) signifying economy, in which women are the unrepresentable real, she has no language or identity of her own. To counteract this imbalance of power women must therefore create themselves in the symbolic in order to be valued by culture. Irigaray's aim in writing is to present herself as a subject at the centre of self-creativity without submitting to the masculine order. As such her work varies between poetic and instructive rather than the orthodox academic form which she would argue reinforces a phallocentric symbolic order. Her most notable work includes *Speculum of the Other Woman* (1985), *An Ethics of Sexual Difference* (1993) *and Je, Tu, Nous: Toward a Culture of Difference* (1993).

iron law of oligarchy the tendency for political organizations (POLITICAL PARTIES and TRADES UNIONS) to become oligarchic, however much they may seek internal democracy. 'He who says organization, says oligarchy', said MICHELS, who first formulated this law in his book *Political Parties* in 1911. Michels' suggestion was that once parties move beyond the fluid participatory structures which often accompany their formation, they inevitably become more bureaucratic and more centrally controlled, falling under the domination of a professional leadership. In this process the original goals of the organization may also be replaced by more narrowly instrumental goals including a concern for the maintenance of the organization (see also GOAL DISPLACEMENT). Three sets of factors were identified by Michels as central in this process:

(a) '*technical factors*', i.e. the need to maintain an effective fighting machine, but when this happens the machine develops its own vested interests, and is able to control agenda and communications, manage internal opposition; etc.

(b) '*psychological characteristics of leaders*', i.e. that they may be gifted orators, relish the psychic rewards of leadership, come to share the motivations and interests of a wider political elite, and thus tend to cling to power at all costs;

(c) '*psychological characteristics of the mass*', i.e. that the rank and file members of political organizations tend to be apathetic, are willing to be led, are readily swayed by mass oratory, and venerate the leadership.

Critics of Michels' 'iron law' point out that the tendency to oligarchy in political organizations is highly variable. For example, it may be a feature of trade unions more than of political parties. The extent of oligarchy is also affected by the characteristics of the membership and by the constitutional context in which the organizations in question operate (e.g. see LIPSET, 1960, and MacKenzie, 1963). Nevertheless, Michels' work has exerted a strong influence on the study of political parties and trade union democracy. See also ÉLITE THEORY.

irrationalism see RATIONALISM.

Islam the second largest of the monotheistic world religions, deriving from the teachings of the prophet Mohammed in the 7th-century. As the single all-powerful god, Allah is held to require from all believers absolute allegiance and worship five times a day. Other duties include pilgrimage to the holy city of Mecca, Mohammed's birthplace. Muslims, the believers in Islam, acknowledge Moses and Jesus as prophets, but Mohammed is Allah's final and supreme prophet.

An explanation of the origins of Islam proposed by Montgomery Watt (1961) is that Islam originated among previously nomadic tribesmen, who on moving on to an urban context acquired a more integrative and more universalistic belief system. Watt points out that Mohammed was a member of a relatively disadvantaged lineage within increasingly wealthy Meccan society. Ousted from Mecca and migrating to Medina (where he 'ruled', initially as an 'outside' arbiter – compare SEGMENTARY SOCIETY), one effect of his prophecy was to legitimize attacks (the first *jihads*, or holy wars) on Mecca's lucrative camel trains, at a time when political conditions were such as to force much formerly seaborne trade overland, making the rewards for attack larger than usual. On this basis, Islam came to espouse what MANN (1986) refers to as a 'quasi-egalitarian' doctrine.

In its Middle Eastern and North African homeland, Islam has been the basis of numerous theocratic political empires, beginning with the empire created by Mohammed, and continued to the present day in the Iranian Islamic revolution. Like Christianity, Islam has been riven by theological and political division, notably the division between *Sunni*, more libertarian, and *Shi'ite*, more authoritarian, forms.

j

Jakobson, Roman (1896–1982) Russian-born, post-Saussurean theorist in LINGUISTICS and formalistic literary studies who had a major influence on the development of modern theoretical linguistics and STRUCTURALISM. In the analysis of literature and poetry, his approach was innovative, employing a 'structural' analysis in which 'form' was separated from 'content'. A founder member of the 'Prague school' of linguistics, his main technical contribution to linguistics was in the study of *phonology* (i.e. the sound systems of LANGUAGE), in which sounds were analysed to reveal a comparatively simple set of binary oppositions underlying human speech. More generally, in the analysis of languages and human sign systems (see also SEMIOTICS), he suggested the existence of 'structural invariants' and that the apparent differences between cultures were merely 'surface' features. Driven from Europe by Nazism, it was as a European cultural theorist in the New World that he had his widest influence. Among those profoundly influenced by his thinking were LÉVI-STRAUSS and CHOMSKY, who were his associates in New York. His emphasis on linguistic universals presented a contrast with the more culturally relativist view of language propounded by American anthropologists such as Boas and Sapir (see SAPIR-WHORF HYPOTHESIS). In his linguistic theories, the use of psychology was also different from the prevailing American view in the 1940s and 50s. While pioneering American theorists of linguistics, such as Leonard Bloomfield, were wedded to a behaviouristic view, Jakobson's emphasis was philosophically 'rationalist', with its emphasis on innate cognitive structures which were universal, rather than on an acquisition of language seen as arising primarily from interactions with the social environment and from stimulus and response. Especially as the result of Chomsky's success, it is Jakobson's rationalistic formalism which has, on the whole, triumphed in linguistics. But this formalism, and its associated concentration on the universal structures of language, while it saw off behaviouristic accounts, also contained limitations, e.g. the lack of any very adequate treatment of SEMANTICS and the contextuality of language, or of linguistic and social 'creativity' and 'agency'. These overstatements and omissions were also to become 'weaknesses' of structuralism as this emerged as a modern movement, partly as a result of Jacobson's influence. See also STRUCTURE AND AGENCY, PRAGMATICS, POSTSTRUCTURALISM.

James, William (1842–1910) US psychologist and pragmatist philosopher – see PRAGMATISM.

Jameson, Fredric (1934–) US Marxist literary critic, cultural theorist and major interlocutor with POSTMODERNISM, whose influences include Frye and McLuhan. Jameson's argument is that what appears as postmodernity is part of 'the cultural logic of late capitalism' and it is this that brings about cultural fragmentation. Jameson has defended the Marxist project against postmodern writers such as LYOTARD and BAUDRILLARD whose work proclaims the end of the meta-narrative and the disintegration of macropolitical discourse. Whereas these thinkers' version of postmodernism threatens to collapse truth claims and introduce relativism, Jameson's theory of the postmodern as 'the cultural logic of late capitalism' attempts to save political knowledge by arguing that it is not enough to simply relate signs to other signs. In contrast to Baudrillard's theory of hyper-reality and Lyotard's idea of language games, Jameson suggests we must go beyond the idea of the independent matrix of signification and ground postmodernism in the politico-economic sphere. In *The Political Unconscious* (1981) Jameson elaborates on this theory by arguing that a close reading of postmodern textuality can excavate the sign's political motivation. His next major work, the *New Left Review* article 'Postmodernism, or, the Cultural Logic of Late-Capitalism' (1984), extended this thesis by suggesting that the project aimed at uncovering the bias of the sign could be related to the concept of 'cognitive mapping' as a method for situating the time/space relativism promoted by postmodern discourse. Later turned into a book-length study *Postmodernism, or, the Cultural Logic of Late-Capitalism* (1991) argued that cognitive mapping should be seen as a critical response to the curious depthless nature of postmodern culture.

Japanization the adoption of Japanese organizational practices by organizations in other societies. The key elements include JUST-IN-TIME supplier relations and stockless production; continuous improvement and zero-defects; TOTAL QUALITY MANAGEMENT and quality circles; employee involvement, training and lifetime employment; corporate welfare, seniority wage systems and enterprise unions. Two broad issues are raised in debates about Japanization. The first issue centres on the model of Japanese practices which are supposedly being transferred to other societies. In this respect differences can be observed between those theorists who use a broad and/or static model which contextualize it within Japanese society, and those who employ a more restricted model of Japanese practices which are seen to have emerged incrementally. Those using the former model find, perhaps not surprisingly, little evidence for Japanization in the UK whilst those using the latter are more open-minded (Wood, 1991; Ackroyd et al., 1988). The second issue concerns an evaluation of the benefits of Japanization. Those theorists who use a 'received' (some would say idealized) model point to the many advantages which flow from worker empowerment, transformed employee attitudes and industrial relations, FLEXIBLE PRODUCTION systems (see FORDISM AND POST-FORDISM), innovative capacity, and the efficient production of quality artefacts. Other theorists suggest that 'reality' is somewhat different. In particular, Japanese practices are perceived as Neo-Fordist systems which:

(a) reduce worker autonomy through systematic surveillance and lateral pressure in ways which involve work intensification;
(b) shift some of the costs and problems of production onto 'squeezed' smaller suppliers; and
(c) involve a dual economy in which employees in the supplying firms are unprotected and poorly paid due, in part, to the need of larger firms to offset the cost of using practices such as permanent employment and seniority pay systems.

jati see CASTE.

'Jim Crow' Laws the common slang name in the US for laws in the Southern states which enforced SEGREGATION of white and black persons in transport, education, marriage, leisure facilities and so on. These laws were common in the Southern US from 1883 to 1954 despite the emancipation of black slaves in 1865. All over the South, 'whites only' and 'blacks only' signs were a visible reminder of the inferior status of black Americans. The Supreme Court ruled in 1896 (*Plessey v. Ferguson*) that 'separate but equal' facilities for blacks and whites were legal. Until 1954, when the Supreme Court reversed its view (*Brown v. Board of Education*), separate, but very inferior and unequal, provision for blacks was the order of the day in the South. Originally, 'Jim Crow' was a common and pejorative slave name.

job enlargement see JOB REDESIGN.

job enrichment see JOB REDESIGN.

job redesign an approach to the design of work which seeks to offset the negative social and psychological implications of directly supervised, simple and routine tasks through the provision of wider tasks, increased autonomy and feedback on performance. See also QUALITY OF WORKING LIFE, SOCIOTECHNICAL SYSTEMS APPROACH.

There have been several approaches to job design which, operating at different levels, have sought to offset the negative aspects of SCIENTIFIC MANAGEMENT. The first level at which job redesign operates involves adjusting the horizontal division of labour. *Job rotation* seeks to increase the variety of work an employee does by providing for mobility between specialized jobs. *Job enlargement* combines two or more previously specialized activities within one job. Critics of job redesign at this level point out that employees are unlikely to be satisfied by jobs which deny them the opportunity to exercise judgement and discretion. Little is to be gained by piling one boring job on top of another. Hence, proponents of *job enrichment* suggest that there is a need to reconstitute the vertical division of labour so that some traditionally managerial tasks, such as deciding on work methods, are built into the jobs of workers. Sociotechnical systems theory, which stresses the need to consider more than individual responsibility and judgement, can be seen to be compatible with the extension of job enrichment to tasks which are more technologically interdependent (Child, 1985). For example, self-regulating, multi-skilled work groups reduce the need for direct supervision and enhance the judgement. discretion and skill requirements of employees.

job satisfaction a fit between what employees seek from work and their actual experience. Studies of job satisfaction have made a general distinction between intrinsic and extrinsic sources of satisfaction. There has been debate about whether job expectations derive from psychological needs or from socially generated and, therefore, variable expectations. Approaches differ in terms of whether or not orientations are single-stranded (e.g. economic) or more complex and multi-stranded, and whether or not factors inside or outside the workplace are more important for satisfaction. The stance which theories take affects both their explanation of, and remedies for, job dissatisfaction – see Brown (1991). See also ORIENTATIONS TO WORK.

joint conjugal role relationship a division of labour within a household that involves a sharing of household tasks between partners. The term was first used by Elizabeth Bott (1957) who suggested that such relationships were most often found in communities with high geographical and social mobility. The fragmentation of family and kin relationships consequent on such conditions is said to have disrupted the traditional pattern of the SEGREGATED CONJUGAL ROLE RELATIONSHIP and led to men becoming more involved in the home. An increase in working women, unemployed men and the existence of new social values are suggested as contributing to the increasing interchangeability of gender roles in the late 20th-century. Despite the suggestion that such families are more egalitarian, there is much evidence that the existence of gender segregation in household tasks is highly persistent. See also DOMESTIC LABOUR, SEXUAL DIVISION OF LABOUR.

joking relationship the anthropological term for ritualized insulting behaviour. RADCLIFFE-BROWN is credited with identifying widespread patterns of insult and stealing practised on the mother's brother by the sister's son. He interpreted this as a means of releasing the tensions inherent in certain social structural arrangements. 'Mother-in-law jokes' are often seen as an example of the same phenomenon in UK culture.

Judaism the oldest of the three most widespread monotheistic world religions. Initially the religion of a nomadic tribe, the ancient Hebrews, around 1000 BC Judaism emerged as a religion different from those of surrounding tribes, marked off by belief in a single omnipotent God. Weber's explanation for the rise of Judaism is that it came about as a response to the political weakness of the Hebrews compared with surrounding powers. The concept of the Jews as the 'chosen people' of such an all-powerful God, a God who also punished his people for their moral shortcomings, arose as an 'explanation' for that political weakness. Over the years, Judaism survived as an autonomous religion despite the fact that for most of the time there was no Jewish state.

Both CHRISTIANITY and ISLAM, the two other main monotheistic world religions, were to some degree offshoots of Judaism. See also SOCIOLOGY OF RELIGION.

Jung, Carl Gustav (1875–1961) psychologist. Born in Switzerland and medically trained, he became a psychiatrist and admirer of FREUD. However, in *The Psychology of the Unconscious* (1912), his personal development away from PSYCHOANALYSIS was evident and he distanced himself from Freud, his subsequent work being known as Analytic Psychology. He travelled widely, observing African cultures and the Indians of the Americas and of the East, and making various European visits.

Jung's extensive knowledge of the religions, mythology, philosophy and symbolism of many cultures became incorporated into his theory of the *collective unconscious.* To him, the deepest levels of the UNCONSCIOUS contain inherited universal *archetypes* – ideas or symbols common to all cultures, which are made manifest in dreams, myths and stories. Jungian psychology tends towards the mystical, which perhaps explains its popularity in recent years. His therapeutic method involved assisting patients to contact the healing powers within themselves, in the collective unconscious.

His more specific influence on psychology and analysis includes his introduction of the terms INTROVERSION and EXTRAVERSION to describe personality characteristics; the Word Association Test; and the notion of personality *complexes* which are comprised of associated emotions or ideas and are revealed through word association or dream interpretation.

jurisprudence legal and sociological theories which seek to situate the body of laws and legal institutions in an overall social context. Thus, jurisprudence to some extent overlaps with the SOCIOLOGY OF LAW.

Historically, it is possible to identify the following subdivisions of jurisprudence:
(a) *legal positivism,* e.g. Kelsen's conception of law as an objectively statable, hierarchical system of norms, or Hart's view of law as resting on 'basic norms'. This view of law has been seen as 'in tune' with traditional legal professionalism, and viewed by its practitioners as involving theories requiring little input from social science. Jeremy BENTHAM's application of utilitarianism to legal reform can also be seen as a form of legal positivism;
(b) *natural law theories* (see NATURAL RIGHTS AND NATURAL LAW), theories which were a main target of the legal positivists;
(c) *historical and evolutionary theories,* e.g. MAINE's theories, and Savigny's account of laws as reflecting the custom or *Volkgeist* of a nation or people;
(d) *conflict theories,* theories which emphasize the conflicts of interest underlying the formation and social control functions of legal systems, e.g. Roscoe Pound's 'pluralism';
(e) *legal realism,* US approaches influenced by PRAGMATISM, which emphasized the social basis, and fluid, 'living character' of law.

All of the above approaches have exerted an influence on the sociology of law, but a recent resurgence of sociolegal studies has owed much to a new vein of empirical sociological studies of legal systems and he operation of the law.

justice 1 the general principle that individuals should receive what they deserve. The definition, a common-sense one, has also received many philosophical formulations, including classical philosophers from ARISTOTLE to KANT. More recently, the ideas of the US philosopher John RAWLS (*A Theory of Justice*, 1971) have been highly influential.

2 *legal justice*, sometimes called 'corrective justice', the application of the law, and the administration of the legal institutions, which in modern societies are mainly operated by trained legal professionals. Here conceptions of formal or procedural fairness are uppermost, i.e. the operation of the law according to prescribed principles or 'due process' (e.g. 'the rule of law'). See also CRIMINAL JUSTICE SYSTEM.

3 *social justice*, general conceptions of 'social fairness', which may or may not be at odds with conceptions of 'individual justice', or with conceptions of justice in sense **2**. Competing conceptions of social justice also exist. For example, Utilitarian conceptions of justice, which emphasize an assessment of collective benefit as the overriding consideration, are at odds with conceptions which emphasize a balance of individual and collective rights.

While influenced by philosophical conceptions, sociologists have generally attempted to avoid the abstractions and definitional debates which have characterized philosophical works on justice. The major location of sociological work has been in discussions of political and CIVIL RIGHTS and particularly welfare and social policy. The central focus has been on *distributive justice*, i.e. the substantive allocation of benefits, rather than merely formal or procedural conceptions of justice.

It is as an example of a philosophical approach which combines formal and substantive concerns that Rawls' discussion has attracted particular attention. Defining justice as 'fairness', Rawls asks what people would be likely to regard as fair in a hypothetical 'original position' in which a 'veil of ignorance' prevents them having knowledge of their own possession of social characteristics. Rawls' suggestion is that inequalities are acceptable only if they leave all people better off. Thus Rawls also supports state interference. A contrary view (e.g. Robert Nozick's (1974) elegant defence of the '*minimalist state*') is that justice consists in the recognition and protection of individual rights, including PROPERTY rights.

Although the differences between conceptions of justice may appear sharp, and often overlain with ideology, empirical resolutions should not be ruled out. For example, theories as apparently divergent as those of Rawls, Nozick, or Hayek (1944) all involve arguments about aggregate economic benefits and their distribution which potentially at least are empirically resolvable, however difficult in practice this may be to achieve (compare ESSENTIALLY CONTESTED CONCEPT, HABERMAS). One route, for example, taken by Barrington MOORE (1972, 1978) is to focus on 'injustice', his assumption being that agreements on this will be more easily reached. See also BASIC HUMAN RIGHTS, EQUALITY, EQUALITY OF OPPORTUNITY, NATURAL RIGHTS AND NATURAL LAW, EXPLOITATION, DISCRIMINATION, SOCIAL CONTRACT THEORY.

just-in-time management a production system through which parts are delivered by suppliers to producers in the exact number and to a specified quality when and where they are needed at each stage of the production process. It is a flexible system, pioneered by Toyota, which seeks to curtail the costs of production by reducing inventories and is associated with long-term producer and supplier relations based on mutual help. See Wood (1991). See also JAPANIZATION, NEW TECHNOLOGY.

Kant, Immanuel (1724–1804) pre-eminent German philosopher, whose major works include *Critique of Pure Reason* (1781), *Critique of Practical Reason* (1788), and *Critique of Judgement* (1790). He argued that our minds structure our experience of the world; we can never know the 'things-in-themselves' (*Dinge-an-sich*), only the 'things-as-they-seem'; never 'noumena', only 'phenomena' (see also RATIONALISM). He went on to suggest that certain CATEGORIES (particularly substance and causality) may not be in the world-as-it-is, but conditions of our knowing it at all. These 'pure percepts of the understanding' were 'synthetic A PRIORI' truths, because without them it would be impossible to make any sense of the world. Kant's 'critical philosophy', described by him as a 'Copernican Revolution in philosophy', saved knowledge from scepticism, but only by jettisoning traditional claims to absolute knowledge.

As a social and moral philosopher Kant is best known for:
(a) his concept of the person in which determinism in the phenomenal realm is not seen as incompatible with freedom to act; and
(b) his concept of *categorical imperative* – a method to guide free human action – which can be paraphrased as 'act as if your actions should be taken as indicative of a general law of behaviour' or 'think what would happen if everyone did this'.

Kant's immense influence has a number of sources:
(a) it can be seen to result from his attempt to straddle both EMPIRICISM and IDEALISM;
(b) his distinction between phenomenal and noumenal realms, and his concept of the person, provides a basis for numerous distinctions between natural and social science (see NEO-KANTIAN, RICKERT, WINDELBAND, WEBER).

karma see CASTE.

Kennedy Report the UK report of the Widening Participation Committee (full title: *Learning Works, Widening Participation in Further Education*, 1997) chaired by Helena Kennedy QC. The Committee was established in December 1994 by the Further Education Funding Council to advise on the identification of under-represented groups in the sector and how funding arrangements should be developed to facilitate WIDENING PARTICIPATION. The Report is significant in placing FURTHER EDUCATION at the centre of a national strategy to widen participation and build a LEARNING SOCIETY (compare LIFELONG LEARNING). A broad recommendation was the rejection of business-orientated approaches to education promoted under THATCHERISM and the implementation of strategic partnerships, i.e. alliances of local 'stakeholders' to promote 'social inclusion'. See also SOCIAL EXCLUSION.

Keynes, John Maynard (1883–1946) English economist who, in the 1930s, transformed economic thinking and was influential in changing the way in which governments tackled high UNEMPLOYMENT at times of economic recession. Keynes' seminal work was *The General Theory of Employment, Interest and Money* (1936). Before Keynes, most economists had assumed that economies would tend to achieve FULL EMPLOYMENT unaided as the outcome of *Say's Law*, the natural tendency of supply and demand to match. At a time of prolonged worldwide recession and high levels of unemployment, Keynes showed that this was not so, that recessions are not always self-correcting, and that falling wages and falling rates of interest would not always be sufficient to bring unused capital and unemployed workers back into use. Accordingly, Keynes argued that government intervention in the economy to influence the level of aggregate demand was necessary if economies were to function effectively. See also KEYNESIAN ECONOMICS.

Keynesian economics (ECONOMICS) an account of the working of macroeconomic systems first propounded by John Maynard KEYNES, in which it is assumed that the economy is not self-managing and that governments must act to avoid prolonged recessions and secure FULL EMPLOYMENT. Directly at odds with much that had been previously assumed (see NEOCLASSICAL ECONOMICS), Keynes proposed government management of the economy – through monetary as well as fiscal policies – in which government expenditure would be increased at times of recession and reduced at times of FULL EMPLOYMENT and INFLATION, thus controlling aggregate demand within the economy. The adoption of Keynesian policies by governments seemed to be successful until the 1960s, when inflation and lack of economic growth began to emerge as a problem. Since then, while Keynesian economics still has many supporters, other macroeconomic theories, notably MONETARISM, have been in the ascendant.

kibbutz (*pl.* kibbutzim) small socialistic agricultural communities (of between 50 and 1000 or more members) established in modern Israel, with the aim, among other things, of producing an alternative to the conventional FAMILY. The objective has been to achieve social equality between men and women by making both child-rearing and work a collective responsibility (although links between children and their biological parents remain strong). Assessments of kibbutzim (see Bettleheim, 1969) suggest that they have been more successful in child-rearing than in achieving an overall equalization in the DIVISION OF LABOUR and relations between the sexes.

kinship

In ANTHROPOLOGY the social relationships and LINEAGE groups characterized by, and bound together through, a system of well-defined customs, rights and obligations. Kin relationships may derive either from descent or may be established through affinity. In so-called 'simple societies', the most important STATUSES are those defined predominantly in terms of kinship and, consequently, anthropologists have directed a great deal of attention to the structure and meaning attached both to kinship and to kinship nomenclature. Many early anthropologists (e.g. MORGAN, 1870) contended that a link could be established between types of kinship nomenclature systems and the stage of evolutionary development reached by a particular society. More recently, anthropological studies have cast doubt on this approach.

In sociology, kinship has been given less priority as, in the main, modern industrialized societies are not so influenced by kinship systems. Sociologists have tended to focus attention on the functions, role and structure of the FAMILY, rather than on wider kin networks. D. Gittens (1985) has questioned the existence of any one identifiable FAMILY form and has suggested that sociologists should be concerned with 'families' rather than 'the family'. Feminist sociologists have noted the important role played by women in maintaining and sustaining kin networks. Women are identified as 'kin keepers'.

Studies of kinship are concerned with the structure of relationships within the domestic domain and the way these relate to socioeconomic and political spheres. Kinship is considered by many theorists to constitute the primary bond between people, and the one most resistant to change. The anthropologist Meyer Fortes (1969) maintained that ties of kinship are particularly binding, creating (for the most part) inescapable claims and obligations. In general terms, students of kinship systems are concerned with three main areas:

(a) modes of DESCENT and INHERITANCE;
(b) forms of MARRIAGE and the associated rules of residence;
(c) the regulation of SEXUALITY through INCEST TABOOS.

Whilst kinship systems appear to be a universal feature of social organization, Goody (amongst others) has stressed that major differences exist between societies in terms of specific kinship characteristics. Goody notes that major differences exist between societies in terms of inheritance systems. In Eurasian societies, diverging inheritance is common. This is a form of bilateral inheritance where property goes to children of both sexes. Such a system is largely absent in Africa. Inheritance may occur *inter vivos* at marriage, as in the dowry system, or on the death of the property holder – *mortis causa.* Goody also notes that in many Eurasian societies women inherit male property, although there are various restrictions on the type of property and the amount. For instance, under Salic law women cannot inherit land, and under Muslim law they are restricted to half the property. In some Eurasian societies women do not inherit property on the death of the holder, but on marriage, in the form of a dowry. Dowry systems vary, being either direct or indirect, as in the case of BRIDEPRICE or bridewealth. In Africa, dowry systems tend to occur only in those societies, either Muslim or Christian, which have come under the influence of Mediterranean law and custom.

Where this influence is absent, property transferred at marriage takes the form of bridewealth. In this case, the property tends to be transferred between the male kin of the groom and that of the bride. Goody suggests that African societies are largely characterized by what he calls 'homogeneous inheritance'. In this case, a man's property is transferred exclusively to members of his own clan or lineage. The property passes down to members of the same sex irrespective of the system of descent.

Much of the work on kinship is concerned with the structure of descent systems and forms of marriage. The major types of descent are PATRILINEAL, MATRILINEAL, DOUBLE and BILATERAL DESCENT. Goody notes that the existence of different descent systems does not necessarily coincide with major economic differences between societies. G. P. Murdock (1949) regarded the institution of marriage as a universal feature of society. He contended that marriage exists 'when the economic and sexual functions are united into one relationship'. Murdock believed that marriage necessarily involved residential cohabitation and provided the basis for the NUCLEAR FAMILY. He has been challenged by numerous theorists, e.g. Goody (1971). Furthermore, marriage is not necessarily characterized by the union of heterosexual partners. The Nuer, Cheyenne and Azande all endorsed 'homosexual' marriage under certain circumstances. 'Ghost' marriages were practised amongst the Nuer and in traditional Chinese society.

In many societies the choice of marriage partner is prescribed or proscribed by law. *Endogamous marriage* prescribes that marriage shall take place within certain specified groups. *Exogamous marriage* only permits marriage outside specified groups.

In most societies social and/or legal norms prescribe the number of spouses allowed to any one woman or man. In general, marriage systems are either *polygamous* or *monogamous.* Group marriage is virtually unknown. Polygamous marriage takes two major forms: POLYGYNY, in which a man is permitted to have more than one wife, and POLYANDRY, in which a woman is permitted to have more than one husband. Polyandry is a relatively rare phenomenon. Monogamy, where the individual is allowed only one spouse, is the most common form of marriage. The work of LÉVI-STRAUSS (1949) suggests that a system of exchange forms the basis to the rules of marriage.

All human societies formulate rules to govern and restrict sexual relations between certain kinds of relative. An incestuous relationship is one which violates these taboos. Whilst INCEST TABOOS discouraging sexual relations among those defined as primary relatives are virtually universal, the precise nature of these taboos varies from culture to culture. One of the consequences of incest taboos is that CONJUGAL families cannot be independent or self-sufficient in the selection of sexual partners.

Marriage usually requires that one or both members of the couple must be relocated. Kinship rules of residence vary. In PATRILOCAL systems the bride is normally expected to move to, or near, the parental home of the groom. This is the most common form of residence. MATRILOCAL residence requires that the groom moves to, or near, the parental home of the bride. *Neolocal* residence requires that the couple establish a domicile separate from either parental home; *avunculocal* residence that the couple establish a home in or near the dwelling of the groom's maternal uncle. *Bilocal* residence allows the establishment of a home with either parent. See also EXTENDED FAMILY.

Klein, Melanie (1882–1950) an Austrian psychoanalyst who regarded the early experience of the child within the primary ATTACHMENT relationship as fundamental to personality development. Influenced by Karl Abraham's theory of 'object relations', she identified the mother as the primary object, at first experienced as merged with the baby, but gradually seen as separate. This changing relationship is regarded as the source of anxiety and depression by Klein, whose emphasis is on innate forces originating in the child. This contrasts with the position of the NEO-FREUDIANS. Melanie Klein developed a technique for psychoanalysing children as young as two years old through interpreting their play with special toys provided in the clinic setting. See also NARCISSISM, OBJECT RELATIONS SCHOOL, WINNICOTT.

knowledge society see INFORMATION SOCIETY, BELL.

Kondratieff cycles trade cycles of very long duration (about 55 years) named after the Russian economist N. Kondratieff. See LONG-WAVE THEORY, SCHUMPETER.

Kristeva, Julia (1941–) Bulgarian-born linguistic theorist and psychoanalyst who emigrated to France in 1966. Influenced by BAKHTIN, her most discussed work is perhaps her theory – expounded in The *Revolution in Poetic Language* (1974) – of the *'semiotic'*, 'pre-linguistic', pre-Oedipal dimensions of personality which become submerged by language and social conventions but are reflected in the work of the avant-garde. She promoted a shift away from the Saussurian concept of LANGUAGE towards a poststructuralist view that emphasized linguistic complexity. Kristeva has made significant contributions to feminist theory, although rejecting the idea of an ultimately distinctive feminine voice.

Kroker, Arthur (1945–) Canadian media theorist whose major influences include Marshall McLuhan, Harold Innis, Jean BAUDRILLARD, Gilles DELEUZE, and Friedrich NIETZSCHE. Kroker's key works consider the effects of technology on the socio-political/socio-cultural sphere. Books such as *The Post-Modern Scene: Excremental Culture and Hyper-Aesthetics* (1987), *Body Invaders: Panic Sex in America* (1988), and *The Possessed Individual: Technology and New French Theory* (1992) use postmodernism as both a critical tool and a stylistic guide. In Kroker's early work *The Postmodern Scene*, which he wrote with David Cook, the idea of postmodernism is seen as excremental. Unlike Fredric JAMESON, who is critical of the celebration of the postmodern as waste, Kroker's work refers to the Nietzschean/Bataillean theory of excess and obscenity. Against Jameson, Kroker argues we should see excremental culture as a means for transgressive action. Although postmodern depthlessness is potentially dangerous it is precisely this contingent feature which makes excremental culture a potentially useful revolutionary tool. In later texts such as *Body Invaders*, a collection of essays which he co-edited with his wife Marilouise, and *The Possessed Individual*, a critical assessment of French theory, Kroker clarified this position. In the former the authors show how panic sex can be used to illustrate America's technological determinism. Mirroring Bataille's reading of the sex act in *The Accursed Share* (1991), they argue that America's hysterical response to the body should be seen in terms of an attempt to discipline an increase of unreason and excess. Following this text, *The Possessed Individual* confirmed that Kroker's work has been heavily influenced by a critical engagement with French philosophy. Writers such as BATAILLE, FOUCAULT, LYOTARD, Deleuze, and Baudrillard are central to his thought. As well as his engagement with poststructuralism/postmodernism in these key texts, Kroker is also editor of the on-line journal *Ctheory*. See also POSTMODERNISM.

Kuhn, Thomas (1922–1996) US historian of science whose sociological accounts of science have done much to undermine conventional, 'abstract', general philosophical accounts such as EMPIRICISM and FALSIFICATIONISM. In Kuhn's view there simply is no universal scientific method in terms of which the achievements of science can be presented in an abstract general form (see also FEYERABEND).

Kuhn's central thesis is that science can only be properly understood as a historically and socially located product. In understanding a particular scientific approach, the historian of science must learn to apply its central concepts in the same way as a scientist working within a particular tradition applies those concepts. This being so, the study of science becomes no different from the study of any other group or community studied by the sociologist or anthropologist. Kuhn specifically notes the affinities between his own methods and HERMENEUTICS and MEANINGFUL UNDERSTANDING AND EXPLANATION, and between his own central concept of SCIENTIFIC PARADIGM and the Wittgensteinian notion of FORMS OF LIFE.

In his most influential work, *The Structure of Scientific Revolutions* (1962), Kuhn advances a general account of science in which he sees it as undergoing periods of 'revolutionary' change in which previously established notions are overturned. Central to this account is Kuhn's claim that the upheavals are such (e.g. the INCOMMENSURABILITY of the scientific concepts that reign supreme before and after) that conventional notions of cumulative 'scientific progress' cannot be sustained (see NORMAL AND REVOLUTIONARY SCIENCE).

Critics of Kuhn reject the tendency to philosophical RELATIVISM involved in such an account of science. However, a rejection of conventional philosophical accounts of scientific rationalism, and an advocacy of historical, sociological and psychological accounts of science, need not imply support for a doctrine of outright philosophical relativism (see also SCIENCE). It must be said, however, that Kuhn himself has been ambiguous on these issues.

Ku Klux Klan a secret racist organization founded in the Southern United States in 1865 to promote and uphold 'white' supremacy. It has been (and is) the most virulent white racist organization in the US, and has international links. The Ku Klux Klan (KKK or Klan) is devoted to maintaining the alleged superiority of the white Anglo-Saxon Protestant (WASP).

This highly secretive underground organization has been responsible for lynching, killing, bombing and intimidating blacks and other opponents throughout the last 125 years. The KKK manifesto states: 'Our main and fundamental objective is the maintenance of the supremacy of the white race … History and physiology teach us that we belong to a race which nature has endowed with an evident superiority over all other races …'

It is best known for its members' wearing of white robes and hoods as they publicly terrorize their victims. However, the KKK engages in less violent, if covert, political activity, and while it is impossible to be accurate about the extent of its membership, at times estimated to be over one million, the influence of the Klan is still considerable.

kula ring a system of reciprocal exchange found in the Melanesian Islands. It was described by MALINOWSKI in his *Argonauts of the Western Pacific* (1922). Within the Trobriand Islands, certain groups of tribes on specific islands continually exchange ritual objects. Necklaces circulate in one direction around the ring, and armshells in the other. He saw the long journeys and extensive ceremonials required in order to service the practice as functionally necessary to ensure the stability of this group of communities. Integrative patterns of status and prestige are produced which are often compared to those produced by the POTLATCH system of the Canadian Northwest. The emphasis on the importance of exchange is paralleled in the theories of M. Mauss and LÉVI-STRAUSS. See also EXCHANGE THEORY.

kurtosis see MEASURES OF DISPERSION.

L

labelling theory an analysis of the social processes involved in the social attribution ('labelling') of positive or (more commonly) negative characteristics to acts, individuals or groups. This approach has been particularly influential in the sociology of deviance. It developed within the interactionist perspective (see SYMBOLIC INTERACTIONISM) and is sometimes also referred to as SOCIETAL REACTION theory.

The classic statement of labelling theory is by H. S. BECKER (1963) in which he pursued insights developed by earlier theorists like Tannenbaum (1938) and Lemert (1951), and argued that acts are not 'naturally' good or bad: normality and deviance are socially defined (see also DRUG TAKING FOR PLEASURE). In Becker's famous formula, 'deviance is *not* a quality of the act a person commits but rather a consequence of the application by others of rules and sanctions to an *"offender"*'. This may seem no more than a sociological application of truisms like 'give a dog a bad name' or 'throw enough mud and it will stick'. What takes the labelling approach beyond common sense or cliché is the way in which the symbolic interactionist approach is drawn on to explore the effects of negative labels on individuals' self-conceptions, especially the development of 'deviant identity', DEVIANT CAREER, and deviant subcultures. Examples are the way in which 'societal reaction' – the condemnation and criminalization of specific types of social act by judges, media, police, etc. – can be shown to lead social actors to alter their individual identities, and to adopt the values of deviant subcultures which the labelling process itself helps to create (see also DEVIANCE AMPLIFICATION, MORAL PANICS, FOLK DEVILS).

The labelling approach gained great currency in the 1960s and 70s, and constitutes a movement away from 'Positivist' approaches in the study of deviance. The antipositivist aspect is found especially in the fact that unlike many previous approaches, normality and deviance were not seen as unproblematic but as 'issues' to be studied in their own right. An important outcome of the labelling approach has been its establishment of a distinctive interactionist approach to SOCIAL PROBLEMS. Issues which researchers have studied in these terms have included the 'social construction' and regulation of mental illness (e.g. see ANTIPSYCHIATRY), the effects of labelling in classrooms, or gender labels. Since interactionist approaches not only raised the question, 'Who gets labelled?', but also, 'Who labels?', and why ostensibly the same acts, when committed by people from different social backgrounds are responded to by labellers (e.g. the police or courts) in different ways, Marxists and conflict theorists have also developed an interest in labelling theory.

Labelling theory has been criticized on numerous grounds, e.g. for presenting an over-deterministic account of the effects of labelling, for ignoring the element of moral choice by actors, and for romanticizing deviance and ignoring victims. Also, the approach largely ignores pre-existing individual psychological predispositions which may, in part, explain individual deviance, offering accounts which are complementary to those provided by labelling theory. Finally, there exist many forms of criminal or deviant behaviour which cannot be explained by the reaction of social control agencies, e.g. CRIMES such as embezzlement, or gay social identity.

labour aristocracy a group (or groups) within the WORKING CLASS in Victorian Britain, seen as holding a privileged position, either economically or socially, or both.

Most of the writings on the labour aristocracy concentrate on whether such a category of workers actually existed, and if so, what were its essential features and its role in segmenting the working class in Victorian Britain.

Several writers (e.g. Crossick, 1978; Hobsbawm, 1968) have identified a fraction of the working class, roughly those identified with the apprenticed trades, who were separate in several ways from both other segments of the working class and the middle class. This distinctiveness included high stable earnings, a low rate of marriage into other class groups, distinctive non-work and leisure pastimes and social values, and a strong belief in trade unionism and in voluntary cooperative action.

One criticism of this, however, is that it does not consider fully the politics of the workplace or the process whereby the labour aristocracy was created. This question has been addressed by several further studies (Foster, 1974; Stedman Jones, 1975; Gray, 1975). One question concerns the political role of the labour aristocracy. Foster claims the labour aristocracy greatly weakened working-class opposition to capitalism, identifying them as a conduit for the transmission of 'bourgeois values'. Gray introduces a sophisticated notion of HEGEMONY, acknowledging a labour aristocracy with some level of autonomy, but recognizing that any ensuing struggles must remain locked within a framework of subordination.

The labour aristocracy can be usefully conceived as a temporary product of a particular phase of the development of British capitalism. From the mid-19th-century onwards, their experience had more in common with the rest of the working class than as an autonomous grouping.

labour market the economic relations between the buyers (employers) and sellers (workers) of labour power. In classical economics the assumption is that the supply of labour would be determined by its price (i.e. wage levels). Alternative economic models point to the existence of relatively autonomous, i.e. non-competing, *internal* labour markets within firms which could not be explained by the classical model; referred to as the *Balkanization* of labour markets by Clark Kerr (1954). These *internal* (firm specific) markets are connected to the *external* labour markets through recruitment mechanisms (i.e. criteria for selection), referred to as *ports of entry*, which explicitly emphasize educational qualifications, technical merit and experience, but also implicitly include criteria premised on tradition, geographic location and even prejudice.

Sociologists became particularly interested in labour market analysis in the early 1970s in their attempts to better explain the variations of employment experience between different social categories, in particular women, ethnic groups and the young (Fevre, 1992). This was initially attempted by reference to the *dual* labour market model which comprises two sectors: *primary* and *secondary*. This model was initially developed by economists, notably by Doeringer and Piore (1971), who postulated that employers paid high wages and offered good career prospects only insofar as is necessary to ensure that they retained a stable group of *primary* sector workers. It is this group of workers who possess the necessary skills and commitment to ensure the firm could remain competitive by adapting to any technological changes necessary. It is for this reason, it is argued, that primary sector jobs are to be found in the larger corporation, for it is they that invest most in maintaining their dominance of the market through the application of technological innovation. The policy of maintaining a core of *primary* sector workers (who are usually adult white males) is, however, expensive, and in order for it to be viable, other groups of workers have to accept lower wages and poor, or less good, conditions of employment. In this *secondary* sector (usually comprised of young adults, women, blacks and other ethnic groups), employers can tolerate much higher rates of labour turnover because the tasks performed are generally viewed as less skilled and less crucial to the production process. This *secondary* sector may be included within the company or located within smaller firms that subcontract to it.

While, in general terms, the *dual market* model can account for some of the variability in labour market conditions, it has been found to be limited in its explanatory power. This is, in part, because it is based on a technologically deterministic assumption that companies pursue labour market policies solely in order to maintain their economic dominance through the application of technology (Rubery, 1978). It is also the case that the model fails to explain why the social groups associated with the two parts of the dual labour market are as they are, e.g. why women tend to get *secondary* sector jobs. In adopting labour market forms of analysis, sociologists have attempted to overcome these limitations, notably by the development of the concept of *segmentation* (see SEGMENTED LABOUR MARKET), and the identification of *local* labour markets (see LOCAL LABOUR MARKET). Both developments emphasize the socio-historical patterns that underpin labour market behaviour and the integral interconnections between work and non-work institutions (e.g. the family). See also FLEXIBLE LABOUR MARKETS.

labour power 1 a general term for those employed within an organization.
2 (MARXISM) the capacity to work which is bought and employed by capitalists and from which the capitalist extracts SURPLUS VALUE (see also LABOUR THEORY OF VALUE). The distinction made by MARX between 'labour' and 'labour power' is an important one in Marx's economics and his theory of CAPITALISM AND CAPITALIST MODE OF PRODUCTION (see ALTHUSSER and Balibar, 1968; Hodgson, 1982). Unlike labour, labour power can be traded in a market and is an object of possession. Under capitalism, the hiring of labour power, involves an agreement by the worker to submit to the employer's authority for a set period of time. The employer then has freedom to use this labour power, and the surplus product created, as he wishes. It is this labour power which is the source of surplus value.

labour process

The process by which products are created by human labour for the satisfaction of human needs. Marx, from whom the term originally derived, outlined (1857) the basic components of the labour process as:

(a) purposeful activity (work);
(b) the object on which work is performed;
(c) the instruments of that work.

Together, these elements of the labour process comprise what Marx called the 'means of production', including both the means of appropriating nature and the corresponding social relations of domination, subordination and property ownership in successive epochs of human history (see also HISTORICAL MATERIALISM, MODE OF PRODUCTION, ALIENATION.) Marx concentrated on the development of the capitalist labour process in which labour is subordinate to the capitalist who owns both the means of production and the products of labour. Capitalist production involved a specific social DIVISION OF LABOUR and the extraction of SURPLUS VALUE. Marx distinguished between 'formal' and 'real' subordination of labour. The former occurred in the early stages of capitalism in which formal ownership of the means of production did not entail direct control of labour in the production process. With the development of the factory system and the decline of traditional handicraft, 'machinofacture' entailed real subordination, based upon direct capitalist control of the labour process with increased factory discipline, and the subservience of workers to machines (Littler, 1982).

Contemporary interest in the labour process was stimulated by the publication of Braverman's (1974) *Labour and Monopoly Capital.* Braverman's main argument was that Marx's 'real subordination of labour' was only fully realized in the 20th century with the stage of MONOPOLY CAPITALISM. Capitalist control of the labour process was extended by the growth of modern management, and especially Taylorism (see SCIENTIFIC MANAGEMENT). Using evidence from the US, Braverman argued that Taylorism, along with widespread mechanization and computerization of tasks, involved a logic of DESKILLING and work degradation affecting both manual and non-manual workers. Braverman's seminal work on the labour process has been highly influential in the reawakening of interest in labour process theory, and in initiating a shift of orientation in the SOCIOLOGY OF WORK (see also ORGANIZATION THEORY, PROLETARIANIZATION).

Braverman's analysis of the labour process has been criticized and modified on several counts. First, the significance of Taylorism in the labour process is questioned. Comparative research has demonstrated that the influence of Taylorism was uneven and never fully implemented (Littler, op. cit.). This line of criticism has revealed the existence of a variety of managerial strategies of control, some of which do not depend upon straightforward deskilling, but upon workers' consent and 'responsible autonomy'. The idea of a logic of deskilling also depends upon questionable historical assumptions about a previous 'golden age' of skilled craft work. In addition, empirical research has shown the extent of deskilling to be uneven and coexistent with evidence of job up-grading. This debate reflects the difficulties of defining SKILL. Secondly, Braverman's analysis is criticized for being deterministic, since it ignores workers' capacity to resist strategies of job degradation, class struggle on the shop floor and the negotiated nature of work organization under capitalism.

Current research on the labour process has therefore substantially modified Braverman's analysis, and investigated the variety of managerial strategies of control, the extent of deskilling and upgrading between different occupations, different sectors of industry, and has taken into account cross-national comparisons (see FORDISM AND POST-FORDISM).

labour relations see INDUSTRIAL RELATIONS.

labour theory of value the doctrine, in classical economics (and especially in MARXIST ECONOMICS), that labour alone is the source of VALUE and that the value and price of commodities is directly related to the labour-time embodied in their production. On this formulation CAPITAL represents past or 'dead' labour, and this, together with new labour and land, is combined in the process of production.

Apart from general arguments for and against Marxism, debates also exist within Marxism over the extent to which empirical prices, profits, etc. bear a systematic and calculable relation to value in its theoretical sense. Often it is accepted that they do not, but that nevertheless the general concept of labour values is useful in indicating levels of 'exploitation', tendencies to crisis, etc. within capitalism (e.g. see Wright, 1981, 1985, 1989). On the other hand, even within Marxism, there are arguments that the labour theory of value is unjustified (see Steedman et al, 1981). Both Pierre Sraffa (1960), in a so-called 'neo-Ricardian' analysis, and Roemer (1982), using a game-theory approach, have elaborated the technical reasons for this. Sraffa, for example, argues that the standard of absolute 'value' cannot be 'labour' in the way that both Ricardo and Marx suggested, but must instead be the 'standard commodity' (in which the proportions in which commodities enter net outputs is assumed equal to that in which they enter the aggregate means of production); this standard commodity includes labour, but not labour exclusively. It can be argued, as by Hodgson (1982), that: 'the extent to which the propositions of *Capital* depend on the labour theory of value has been over estimated by both supporters and opponents of Marxian analysis', and that this analysis remains a powerful tool for the analysis of capitalist societies and capitalist economic relations, especially in its focus on production, forms of PROPERTY, and on inequalities – see also CAPITALIST LABOUR CONTRACT, EXPLOITATION, CONTRADICTORY CLASS LOCATIONS. Against this, there exist very real problems for Marxism from any detachment from the labour theory of value, not least an undermining of the LAW OF VALUE and doctrines of an inherent tendency to final crisis in capitalism that have been central, at least to 'scientistic' forms of Marxism (see CRISES OF CAPITALISM, ORGANIC COMPOSITION OF CAPITAL, TENDENCY TO DECLINING RATE OF PROFIT). Accordingly, the account of capitalism provided by contemporary Marxism is far less determinate than that given previously.

Lacan, Jacques (1901–81) French psychoanalyst whose work is particularly associated with POSTSTRUCTURALISM and involved a reinterpretation of the work of FREUD using concepts derived from structural LINGUISTICS. Freud's view of the SELF as both an entity created in particular circumstances, and as inherently split in its creation, can be opposed to humanist claims for the unity, integrity and creative power of the subject. Departing from an early commitment to humanist PHENOMENOLOGY, Lacan was influenced by structural linguistics, with its revelation of unknown orders underlying the transparency of consciousness. A semiotic rereading of Freud provides a comparable set of structures, with the realms of cognition and consciousness (including DEFENCE MECHANISMS) as the product of an underlying transformation of 'desire'. The conscious subject is a semiotic product involved in DISCOURSES it does not control, and which cannot readily be brought to consciousness. The location of the self in social (including gender) positions, preserves and creates spaces for semiotic work and play that evade all fixity. Lacan's contribution has been strikingly influential, e.g. in feminist thinking on the creation of gender identity. Lacan's early writings are assembled in *Ecrits* (1977). Other books by Lacan include *The Language of the Self* (1953), *Four Fundamental Concepts of Psychoanalysis* (1977b). See also PSYCHOANALYSIS, DECENTRED SELF AND DECENTRED SUBJECT, IDENTITY, DECONSTRUCTION

Laing, Ronald David (1927–89) Scottish psychiatrist and critic of orthodox psychiatry. His 'radical' critique (see ANTIPSYCHIATRY) grew from varied experience and interests. His initial clinical experience was with psychotic (see PSYCHOSIS) long-stay patients in a large mental hospital, and he subsequently undertook psychoanalytic (see PSYCHOANALYSIS) work with neurotic (see NEUROSIS) patients and their families at the Tavistock Clinic in London. He became interested in EXISTENTIALISM and the phenomenological experience of the person (see PHENOMENOLOGICAL PSYCHOLOGY). He developed the view that mental illness must be understood as individual experience within a social context, and particularly the family context, as perceived by the individual. In his view, mental illness may be seen as a valid response to this phenomenological experience, and treatment can be effected by understanding this and assisting the mentally-ill person to grow through it. His own practical application of the theory can be seen in the therapeutic community, Kingsley Hall, which he set up and worked in.

Laing developed his ideas during the 1950s and 60s, publishing *The Divided Self* (1959), about the schizophrenic experience, *The Self and Others* (1961) and *Sanity, Madness and the Family*, with Esterson (1964), both concerned with family dynamics, and *The Politics of Experience and the Bird of Paradise* (1967). His radical views on mental illness and its treatment and his refusal to label people as 'sane' or 'insane', but as making different responses to different phenomenological experience, have had significant influence on the orthodox view, substantially 'humanizing' it. However, with the perspective of a quarter of a century, his ideas are not regarded as being of central theoretical importance in the treatment of schizophrenia, but only as offering a useful perspective in some cases. The importance of family dynamics in the etiology of mental illness generally, and its treatment, is recognized in the development of FAMILY THERAPY.

laissez faire the doctrine that economic affairs, especially the interests of capital, are best left unrestricted by government action. The term derives originally from the ideas of the French physiocrats, but was developed by Adam SMITH and by the CLASSICAL ECONOMISTS.

laissez-faire capitalism that form of capitalism in which, in theory at least, the state seeks not to interfere with, or seeks to preserve, the free working of the economy. See LAISSEZ FAIRE. See also COMPETITIVE CAPITALISM.

Lamarck, Jean (1744–1829) French biologist remembered for his now discredited theory that traits acquired by an organism during its lifetime are inheritable. This theory was contested principally by Charles DARWIN (1809–82), who suggested the now widely accepted theory of organic evolution by random variation and NATURAL SELECTION. Lamarck's connection with the 20th century and with political theory lies in the preference which the Soviet state under Joseph STALIN gave to Lamarckian rather than Darwinian principles. The project of creating a new socialist state and a new socialist person meant that any theory of development and change which suggested the inheritability (and thus, by implication, the perfectability) of acquired characteristics would find favour. Michusin (1855–1935), a Russian horticulturalist, was among the first to earn the praise of the Soviet government for attempting to prove Lamarckian principles. The infamous biologist and agronomist, LYSENKO, continued Michusin's project. With Stalin's support, Lysenko imposed theoretical uniformity on the scientific community as director of the Institute of Genetics of the Academy of Sciences of the USSR (1940–65), and as president of the All-Union Academy of Agricultural Sciences. Lysenko's baleful influence on Soviet science was not dislodged until the mid-1960s. See also EVOLUTIONARY THEORY.

land 1 territory valued for its natural resources or its potential for human use for cultivation, living space or natural beauty.
2 the territory with which a particular people identify: 'this land is our land'.

In ECONOMICS, land is generally viewed as a FACTOR OF PRODUCTION. Sociologists and anthropologists have been mainly interested in the social relations involved in LAND TENURE and land use. In STATELESS SOCIETIES and AGRARIAN SOCIETIES there are various forms of land ownership with communal or corporate group ownership in the former and various forms of state and private ownership in the latter. However, often in these societies issues of *land ownership* may be secondary, or even the concept itself absent. Of more importance may be the issue of who has rights of use of the land (*usufruct*) and rights to the products of the land.

Different forms of land tenure and land use are often considered important by social scientists in distinguishing between different forms of society: for example, the holding of land on condition of providing service to a superior is characteristic of FEUDALISM, as opposed to the notion of private ownership characteristic of CAPITALISM. In capitalist societies, however, land is often not just another factor of production equivalent to others. Thus zoning may prevent certain uses of land in certain regions, as with the designation of National Parks in the UK, and most societies have planning regulations governing the use of land. More recently, the rise of environmental pressure groups has led to calls for limitations on land use, e.g. to control deforestation or the use of nitrate fertilizers.

land tenure the rights involved in holding land whether this involves ownership, renting or communal forms. The most common forms in contemporary industrial societies are *freehold,* involving ownership, and *leasehold,* involving some form of renting.

language

1 a system of symbolic communication, i.e. of vocal (and written) SIGNS, which arguably distinguishes human beings from all other species. Language is rule-governed and primarily comprised of a plurality of arbitrary conventional signs. These signs will have a common significance for all members of a linguistic group.
2 the 'crucial signifying practice in and through which the human subject is constructed and becomes a social being' (W. Mulford, 1983).
3 the most important, but not the only sign system of human society (some of which may also be referred to as language(s) – compare BODY LANGUAGE).

Language is the means whereby subjectivity is stabilized and crystallized (including 'knowledge' and SCIENCE, and the stretching of societies across time and space; see TIME–SPACE DISTANCIATION). Language also exists as an 'objective' institution independent of any individual user. In common with all aspects of human culture, language can be seen to be historical and subject to change. Currently there are between three and five thousand active languages and a large number of nonactive languages.

Human beings acquire knowledge of and competence in a specific language via a complex process of SOCIALIZATION. Whilst specific linguistic knowledge and competence is not an innate feature of human beings, the likelihood is that human beings are genetically endowed with a LANGUAGE ACQUISITION DEVICE. Most notably, Noam CHOMSKY has argued that we possess an innate capacity to grasp the rules of grammatical structure (see also DEEP STRUCTURE, GRAMMAR, SYNTAX, SAUSSURE, JACOBSON).

Often sociologists and social psychologists have been less concerned with the syntactic structure and related formal properties of language than with the relationship between language, ideology, knowledge and the social nature of verbal interaction. Social psychologists have tended to concentrate on the latter, whereas sociologists have tended to explore the relationship between language and nonlinguistic structural arrangements such as class and gender. The work of Basil BERNSTEIN (1971–77) however, has shown that different forms of social relation generate different forms of linguistic code. Bernstein has suggested that, within the context of schooling, lower-working-class children may be disadvantaged due to their utilization of a restricted linguistic code (see ELABORATED AND RESTRICTED CODES).

A distinction has been made by Scott (1977) and Turiel (1983) between linguistic competence and social communicative competence. They have suggested that communicative skill is dependent upon an individual's ability to combine both of these aspects of competence. Linguistic competence refers to the individual's command of both vocabulary and grammatical rules. Social communicative competence refers to the degree to which the *encoder* (person sending the message) is responsive to the social and linguistic characteristics of the *decoder* (audience). Recently it has been suggested that social competence and linguistic competence must be seen as highly interlinked, e.g. that SEMANTICS can only be formulated in terms of PRAGMATICS, i.e. language usage is above all to be understood contextually.

Sociologists and social psychologists (as well as philosophers – see LINGUISTIC PHILOSOPHY, FORMS OF LIFE, LANGUAGE GAMES, SPEECH ACTS, WITTGENSTEIN) have become increasingly interested in examining the complex and socially determined rules which govern linguistic action. For example, verbal interaction is characterized by rules relating to the structuring of conversation and to *turn-taking* (see CONVERSATION ANALYSIS). Ethnomethodologists have been particularly concerned with the unstated rules governing communicative interaction (see H. GARFINKEL, 1967, H. Sacks et al., 1974).

Other general areas of interest concern linguistic relativity. The nature of the relationship between language and our perception and understanding of the world has been approached from many perspectives, one of the most influential being the work of the linguists Benjamin Lee Whorf and Edward Sapir. The SAPIR-WHORF HYPOTHESIS contends that the kind of language someone uses determines the nature of that person's thinking about the world. It has been suggested by other theorists that language does not have this determining function and that language itself is in fact largely determined by experience.

A further growing field of investigation is the relationship between gender and language. Writers such as D. Spender (1980) have argued that language is 'man-made', whilst M. Daly (1981) has shown the 'androcentric' or 'phallocentric' nature of language. In its stead she argues for the necessity of 'gynocentric' language. Underlying these different approaches is the assumption that the oppression of women is both revealed in and sustained by language and the process of language interaction. Whilst such approaches are not new (see for example Herschberger, 1948; Merriam, 1964), the 'second wave of feminism' has given impetus to the development of such critiques and forms of analysis.

Last but not least, language has been increasingly employed as a 'model' for social relations in general, especially resting on the 'structural' rule-governed character of both. In STRUCTURALISM and POSTSTRUCTURALISM (see also LÉVI-STRAUSS, LACAN) social relations are not simply *like* language, they are a language; thus a further implication of this is that individual actions (in the same way as particular utterances) can be viewed as 'structural' outcomes (see also SYNTAGMATIC AND PARADIGMATIC, DECENTRED SELF). To its critics, however, *structuralism* loses touch with the creative power of the subject, evident not least in relation to language use, which involves a 'creative' grasping of rules which are interpreted and also sometimes transformed. Since, in view of the increasing recognition of the dependence of syntax on context, structural linguistics is no longer widely seen as providing an adequate model *even* of language, it is not surprising that it should fail to provide one for society. See also LINGUISTICS, SOCIOLINGUISTICS, SEMIOTICS, COGNITIVE ANTHROPOLOGY.

Language Acquisition Device (LAD) a hypothesized structure suggested by CHOMSKY (1962) as being innate in human beings and enabling them to easily acquire language. He bases his hypothesis on the observation that language is acquired apparently without effort in the first few years of life and the child can compose novel sentences never previously heard. The proposal is that humans have an innate predisposition to understand grammatical relationships, extract the 'rules' from the language they hear, and then use these in forming their own verbalizations. Not all psycholinguists agree with Chomsky s proposal, the most famous antagonist being the behaviourist psychologist B.F. Skinner (*Verbal Behaviour*, 1957), for whom 'learning' is the only explanation for language acquisition.

language games the conception of LANGUAGE as akin to an assemblage of different 'games', like chess, football, children's play and so forth, each governed by a different set of 'rules' and located in a different FORM OF LIFE, and with only very general 'family resemblances' in common (WITTGENSTEIN, 1953). According to Wittgenstein, we cannot generalize usefully about language, but must simply notice that language use follows from the rules and practices which operate in particular kinds of use (e.g. jokes, greetings, story telling, as well as science and philosophy) and particular social contexts. As with many games, a further feature of languages viewed as rule-following activities, is that, while rules are followed, they are never followed slavishly but always interpreted. This is a further dimension of the apparently 'relativistic' and inherently non-universalizing character of language as portrayed in Wittgenstein's 'second' philosophy variously interpreted by later philosophers and sociologists. See also RULES AND RULE-FOLLOWING, INCOMMENSURABILITY, KUHN, FEYERABEND.

langue* and *parole (LINGUISTICS) the distinction between LANGUAGE as a communal resource, a socially established system of linguistic units and rules (*langue*), and as actually produced speech (*parole*). Introduced by SAUSSURE, the distinction is an important one not only in theoretical linguistics, but also for its influence in the formation of the more diffuse body of ideas in social science known as STRUCTURALISM.

In his own work Saussure regarded the understanding of *langue* as the paramount concern of theoretical linguistics. The significance of this is that it places an emphasis on the internal 'structural' relations of language, even though language is constantly changed as the result of *parole*, i.e. by language use. In structuralism more generally, it is the same emphasis on structural explanations, sometimes to the exclusion of the individual subject or AGENCY, which is uppermost and which defines the approach, but which is also much criticized for its onesidedness.

latent function see MANIFEST AND LATENT FUNCTIONS.

latifundium (*pl.* latifundia) a generic term for a large landed estate in noncapitalist societies. It is a Latin word, referring initially to the large slave estates found in the Roman Empire. These survived in various forms in southern Europe during feudalism, and with the Spanish and Portuguese conquest of Latin America the term, and to some extent the forms of the latifundia, became known as HACIENDA and PLANTATION. The latifundia complex in Latin America often existed with *minifundia*, small landholdings either on or near the large estates often involved in restrictive tenancy arrangements, but which ensured a labour supply for the large estate.

law see SOCIOLOGY OF LAW, SCIENTIFIC LAW.

law of comparative advantage see INTERNATIONAL TRADE.

Law of the Three Stages a proposed historical sociological law formulated by COMTE in which knowledge and the general form of society is seen as moving through three stages:

(a) knowledge permeated by 'Theological' conceptions and a society dominated by priests and by monarchy;

(b) 'Metaphysical' speculative knowledge, associated with a 'negative' era of social criticism and political upheaval and revolution; (c) the modern era of 'Positive' scientific knowledge (see POSITIVISM) in which Comte expected that social reorganization guided by scientific knowledge would occur, and including the application of a scientific sociology.

Sociologists do not disagree with Comte that a growth in the importance of scientific knowledge is an important general feature of modern societies. There is much disagreement, however, over how far it is appropriate to regard sociology as an 'applied science' on a par with the natural sciences. Whether or not they accept the goal of scientific laws in sociology, there is general agreement that Comte's formulation of the Law of Three Stages lacks the precision (or perhaps even the correct testable or falsifiable form – see HISTORICISM) to gain acceptance as a truly lawlike statement.

law of value (MARXISM) the doctrine that a fall in the amount of labour embodied in a commodity as the result of technical change in the production process will bring about a reduction in the price or VALUE of a commodity, or will strongly tend to. This is a consequence of the acceptance of the LABOUR THEORY OF VALUE by Marx, who adopted this position from Ricardo. See ORGANIC COMPOSITION OF CAPITAL, TENDENCY TO DECLINING RATE OF PROFIT.

Lazarsfeld, Paul (1901–76) Austrian-born, later US-based social researcher and sociologist, who made an outstanding contribution to the development of survey research and techniques of quantitative data analysis in sociology (see Lazarsfeld and Rosenberg, *The Language of Social Research*, 1955). After early research in Austria on class and unemployment, he emigrated to the USA in 1933, working first on research into the mass media, before moving to Columbia University, where he set up what was to become one of the leading centres for empirical sociological research, the Bureau of Applied Social Research. Among the most famous of the studies with which he was associated were those on voting behaviour, including *The People's Choice* (1944), with Berelson and Gaudet and *Voting* (1954), with Berelson and McPhee (see also VOTING BEHAVIOUR). Criticism of his work, for example from C. Wright MILLS, that it amounted only to ABSTRACTED EMPIRICISM, is unfair, as it was Lazarsfeld who can claim to have first established the systematic SOCIAL SURVEY as an analytical sociological tool rather than merely a means of collecting facts or opinions. His systematization of methods of HYPOTHESIS testing using CROSS-TABULATIONS remains central in sociology. He also contributed much to the development of research methods in other areas, including the construction of indicators, and his contributions to MATHEMATICAL SOCIOLOGY were instrumental in helping to establish this as a distinctive subsection of sociological endeavour. He himself claimed that his research goal was always to seek THEORIES OF THE MIDDLE RANGE. The continuing influence of a number of his theories in mass communications research (see OPINION LEADER and the TWO-STEP FLOW IN MASS COMMUNICATIONS) is testimony to this.

leadership the abilities, qualities and behaviour associated with the ROLE of group leader. This role may be conferred on individuals on the basis of personal characteristics and experience, or through tradition and/or position occupied. However, contingency approaches to leadership have led to awareness that effective leaders are not so simply by virtue of specific characteristics or behaviour, rather, different styles of leadership (e.g. task-oriented *v.* relationship-oriented) are required by different situations. See also GROUP, GROUP DYNAMICS, LEGITIMATE AUTHORITY (OR POLITICAL LEGITIMACY), OPINION LEADER.

league tables (associated with the AUDIT SOCIETY) numerical rankings of organizations based on arithmetical aggregations of publically available 'performance indicators'. Although often 'unofficial' (e.g. constructed by newspapers), such tables play an increasing part in influencing organizational behaviour.

learning society and **learning organization** the concept of a society or organization in which learning and a culture of improvement and 'enhancement' is seen as increasingly central. The popularity of the concept in management theory and in the new politics of education (see also LIFELONG LEARNING) reflects the increasing centrality of knowledge and knowledge workers within the modern global economy.

learning theory see BEHAVIOURISM.

left-right continuum the division between radical or 'left-wing' POLITICAL PARTIES and orientations on the one hand, and conservative or 'right-wing' political parties and orientations on the other, originally so-called because of the arrangement of seating in the two sides of the French National Assembly. Subsequently the concept has persisted as a general term referring to the spectrum of political orientations, despite the obvious oversimplifications involved in any assumption that political issues and political parties can be arranged on a single continuum. One reason why confining political analysis merely to a left-right division is an oversimplification is that other dimensions, such as the liberal-authoritarian dimension, cross cut the left-right dimension. See Fig. 17. See also AUTHORITARIANISM, POLITICAL ATTITUDES.

legal positivism a form of legal theory in which the law is seen as capable of being expressed in formal and objective terms as a hierarchical system of general principles (see JURISPRUDENCE).

legal-rational authority see LEGITIMATE AUTHORITY.

legitimacy see LEGITIMATE AUTHORITY.

legitimate authority *or* **political legitimacy** any form of political rule in which the rulers successfully uphold a claim that they govern by right in accord with law, tradition or similar basis.

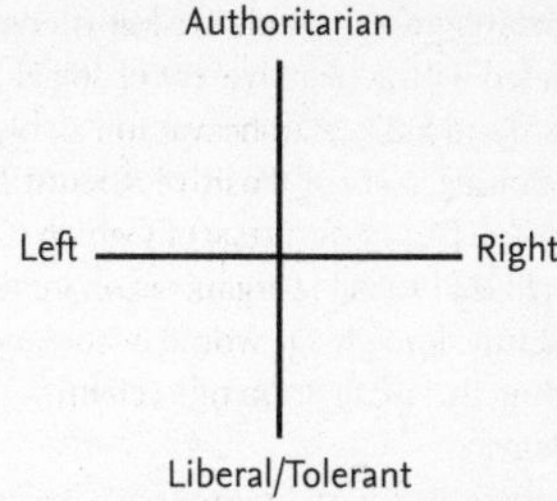

Fig. 17 **Left-Right Political Continuum.** The existence of a left-right continuum in politics is widely acknowledged, but this is also cross cut by a liberal-authoritarian dimension.

WEBER identified three 'pure types' of legitimate authority:

(a) *legal-rational authority*, resting on a belief in the legality of enacted rules and those achieving authority under these rules, e.g. elected representatives or civil servants;

(b) *traditional authority*, resting on an established belief in the sanctity of tradition and the acceptance of those chosen to rule in accordance with the customs and practices within this tradition, e.g. kings, queens or religious dignitaries;

(c) *charismatic authority*, resting on the devotion to an exceptional individual or leader and on the normative rules ordained by this individual, e.g. a prophet or warlord.

The last of these provides the dynamic or revolutionary element in Weber's overall account of political legitimacy. In the long run, how ever, e.g. after the death or departure of the exceptional teacher or leader, there occurs a *routinization of charisma*, and a reversion to traditional, or legal-rational, forms of authority. See also BUREAUCRACY, STATE, POWER, NATION STATE, SOVEREIGNTY, HOLMES, LEGITIMATION CRISIS.

legitimation the manner and the process in which a STATE OR POLITICAL SYSTEM receives justification. See LEGITIMATE AUTHORITY, LEGITIMATION CRISIS.

legitimation crisis the tendency of modern political systems, which depend on 'consent' for their maintenance of political AUTHORITY, to meet major problems amounting to 'crisis' in doing so. Such problems are seen as arising especially from contradictions and conflicts between the logic of capitalist accumulation and escalating demands for social welfare, as well as demands for increased participation and social equality.

From a neo-Marxist point of view, in *Legitimation Crisis* (1975) HABERMAS identified three main 'crisis tendencies' in capitalist societies:
(a) *economic crisis,* arising from fact that the state acting as the unconscious 'executive organ of the law or value' acts as the planning agent of 'united monopoly capital';
(b) *rationality crisis,* the 'destruction of administrative rationality' which occurs through: (i) the opposing interests of individual capitalists (e.g. between monopoly and non-monopoly forms of capitalism), and (ii) the production (necessary for continued existence of the system) of structures 'foreign to the system', such as welfare provision (including new types of welfare workers with new values);
(c) *legitimation and motivation crises* arising from the politicization of administrative interventions which results from the above, and from the erosion of previously important traditions (e.g. deference) and the 'overloading' of the existing political and economic system 'through universalistic value-systems ('new' needs)'.

Habermas's suggestion was that the state in future may prove unable to manage the tensions between competing values which such tendencies involve, especially in a context which encourages a new emphasis on rational critical discourse. In most Western states over the last decade, however, the tendencies to crisis (FISCAL CRISIS IN THE CAPITALIST STATE, as well as 'legitimation crisis') have been handled by rolling back the WELFARE STATE, a refashioning of justifications for the market economy, and by programmes of privatization, etc. See also THATCHERISM.

leisure 1 the time free from work and routine domestic responsibilities and available for use in recuperation, relaxation, hobbies, recreation, and cultural and artistic pursuits. 2 the activities occupying such 'free time'.

Theorists of leisure (see C. Rojek, *Capitalism and Leisure Theory* 1985) have generally either stressed the 'individual freedom' involved in leisure, compared with work or family responsibilities, or they have emphasized the illusion of this freedom, identifying the constraints on free choice arising from domestic responsibilities (especially on women's leisure) and the way in which leisure is shaped by the constraints arising from consumer culture and capitalist society.

Sociological interest in leisure grew in the 1980s. The sociology of leisure first developed out of INDUSTRIAL SOCIOLOGY in the 1950s during the era of 'affluence' which also spawned theories of POSTINDUSTRIAL SOCIETY. Dubin (1955) even argued that leisure was replacing work as a 'central life interest'. Subsequent research focused on exploration of the relationship between work and leisure (sec Parker, 1971; Roberts, 1970). This demonstrated the continued centrality of work and a complex pattern of work-leisure relations.

More recently an interest in leisure research has also emerged from two critical theoretical traditions: Marxist structuralism and radical cultural studies. Unlike earlier Marxist and 'critical' analysis of leisure, which tended to view leisure in modern society as largely 'constrained' by capitalism, these new approaches view leisure as a 'contested' sphere, characterized by increasing resistance to its commodification and standardization (see Home et al., 1987; Hall and Jefferson, 1976; Gruneau, 1983). Most recently leisure sociologists have embraced the many new issues raised by POSTMODERNITY AND POSTMODERNISM and by new interest in CONSUMER CULTURE. See also CULTURAL STUDIES, RESISTANCE THROUGH RITUAL.

Leisure, derived from the Latin *licere* 'to be allowed', shares a common root with 'licence'. It thus contains within itself the dualism of freedom and control, individual agency and constraint, with which modern sociological theorists have been concerned. See also SPORT, PLAY, SOCIABILITY.

leisure class a term coined by VEBLEN (*The Theory of the Leisure Class*, 1899) to refer to a particular stratum of the upper classes in the US in the latter half of the 19th-century. Veblen was critical of the *nouveaux riches*, who expressed disdain for all forms of manual and productive labour and sustained their own status position through acts of CONSPICUOUS CONSUMPTION and abstention from work.

leisure society the conception of a society in which work is losing its former centrality. Since the 19th-century, various commentators have used this phrase with little precision or consistency of meaning. In the second half of the 20th-century it has been used by writers in conjunction with other terms such as POSTINDUSTRIAL SOCIETY or POSTCAPITALIST SOCIETY, suggesting that fewer average hours of paid employment leads to a greater concern for leisure in such societies. Leisure, it is argued, comes to take on the centrality that paid employment had in the past. The notion of the leisure society is highly contested, however. The basic idea that fewer hours are spent working in modern industrial society than in the past is contestable on a number of counts, and both historical and comparative evidence suggests LEISURE was a central part of life in preindustrial societies.

Lenin, V. I. (1870–1924) (pseudonym of Vladimir Ilich Ulyanov) Russian statesman and Marxist theoretician. He is best known as the leader of the Bolshevik Party during the Russian Revolution of 1917 and, subsequently, until his death, the leading politician in the USSR and the Communist Party of the USSR. Lenin also contributed a large body of work to the theory and practice of MARXISM. A number of these works have had a significant impact within the social sciences, most notably: *The Development of Capitalism in Russia* (1899), which contributed to the analysis of changes and divisions amongst the peasantry (see PEASANTS) and to 20th-century theories of economic and political change; *Imperialism: the Highest Stage of Capitalism* (1916), which argued that the emergence of MONOPOLY CAPITAL was associated with the export of capital from the advanced capitalist world to the colonies and marked a new stage of capitalism from that analysed by MARX, and set in motion a debate in the social sciences which continues today (see IMPERIALISM); and *State and Revolution* (1917) which attempted to develop Marx's theory of the role of the state within capitalism and its role in future socialist and communist societies. Within Marxist political thought, Lenin's greatest influences have been, first, his theory of the revolutionary party, which he argued should comprise a 'vanguard leadership' based on 'democratic centralism' (see VANGUARD PARTY,. COMMUNISM), and vested with the task of leading the working class to revolutionary socialist ideas, and, secondly, his polemic against reformist, evolutionary paths to SOCIALISM and his argument that spontaneous action by the working class against the BOURGEOISIE will only raise economic demands and not lead to the revolutionary overthrow of the RULING CLASS. These ideas are contained in *What is to be Done?* (1902), ideas modified somewhat by Lenin's later political writings and political practice. There has been intense debate as to whether STALINISM resulted from, or was in complete contradiction to Lenin's thought and practice. See also REVOLUTION, STALIN.

Le Play, Fredéric (1806–82) French mining engineer and professor of metallurgy, and later an independent scholar and researcher, whose studies in sociology and involvement in industrial management and in public life (e.g. in organizing major international exhibitions) led to his making a wide-ranging contribution to the early development of empirical sociology. In particular, he used data gathered in pioneering interviews to provide accounts of working class family life and domestic economy (e.g. *Les Ouvriers Européens,* 1855). He regarded the family as the fundamental social unit, and its health and stability as an indicator of the overall state of society. He also proposed a more general classification of types of family, seeing the modern family as increasingly corresponding to an 'unstable' type, the outcome of unregulated urban and industrial change, poor housing and women's industrial work. A conservative politically, Le Play emphasized the importance of traditional values, including 'original sin'. This led him to emphasize the importance of establishing the social facts about the interrelation of society's interdependent parts, even if his own prejudgements often coloured his work.

lesbianism 1 a sexual categorization referring to female HOMOSEXUALITY. In this usage, sexual behaviour and sexual identification are taken as the primary factors denoted by the term.

2 (feminist usage) homoerotic desire between women, or, more widely, a specifically female experience involving the social, emotional and erotic bonding of women. In this usage lesbianism is seen as primarily a political category, placing less importance on the issue of genital sexuality and more on woman-identified experience.

Political lesbianism stresses that lesbianism is 'Far more than a sexual preference; it is a political stance' (Abbott and Love, 1972). Nestle (1981) challenges this approach for its misrepresentation of lesbian history and for its implicit desexualization of lesbian culture, Rich (1980) has suggested that lesbianism should, however, be regarded as one of the primary forms of resistance against 'compulsory heterosexuality' (see HETEROSEXUALITY). In this context, Rich (op. cit.) has distinguished between *lesbian existence* and the *lesbian continuum.* The former refers to conscious lesbian identification, the latter to a broad range of woman-identified experience or sisterhood. In both. Rich places less emphasis on sexual desire as the primary criterion for identification with lesbianism, and more on women's active, political resistance to heterosexual privilege.

Lesbianism is subjected to both social and legal control in many contemporary societies. In the UK, lesbianism is not subject to criminalization except in the armed forces. Lesbians, however, tend to be subject to control via the civil courts, particularly in custody cases involving the children of lesbian mothers. The history of lesbianism and its regulation via law and custom is different from that pertaining to male homosexuality, and has been the subject of both misrepresentation and invisibility.

less developed countries (LDCs) see THIRD WORLD.

levels of measurement see CRITERIA AND LEVELS OF MEASUREMENT.

Lévi-Strauss, Claude (1908–) Belgian-born, French social anthropologist, who is usually seen as an intellectual descendant of DURKHEIM and MAUSS, although also strongly influenced by MARX, FREUD and JACOBSON. A major figure in modern STRUCTURALISM, Lévi-Strauss claimed that Marx and Freud advanced the structuralist method of analysis by seeking to comprehend surface reality by reference to a deeper structural level. The central concerns in Lévi-Strauss's work are primitive classification and the study of KINSHIP and MYTHOLOGIES in TRIBAL SOCIETIES (see also TOTEMISM). His major translated works include *Structural Anthropology* (1963), *The Elementary Structures of Kinship* (1969), *The Savage Mind* (1969), *Totemism* (1963), and *Mythologies* (4 vols.) (1969–78). The distinctive feature of his work is the attempt to discover universal rules that underlie everyday activities and customs. Culture is held to embody principles which mirror essential features of the human mind

– 'binary classificatory systems'. The influence of LINGUISTICS, particularly phonology, led Lévi-Strauss to formulate the main task of anthropology as the discovery of semiotic, and hence cognitive, structures, deeply underlying the surfaces of social activity. It is in these terms that he locates neat systems of 'contrastive classes' underlying marriage systems and beneath myths. These structures are layered, and the same structures can underlie different surface patterns in different societies, so that one may illuminate another. It is the deepest layers which Lévi-Strauss sees as 'cognitive', and which permit the reconstruction of universals of the human mind. Although the layers of structure are systematic and ordered, they are not directly available to the consciousness that is constituted by them: they are unconscious structures, reconstructable in scientific logics. The existence of these logical systems has been challenged by recent thinkers, e.g. poststructuralists, who insist on the fragmentary, open, evasive and sliding character of semiotic underpinnings (see DECONSTRUCTION). But, in their critique of rational consciousness, and their 'decentring' of the subject, such critics continue a critique of the transparency of action, communication, institutions and history which sociology owes to Lévi-Strauss.

Lewis, Oscar (1914–71) US anthropologist who is best known for his concept of the CULTURE OF POVERTY which arose from his study of Mexican and Puerto Rican families. Lewis's books were highly popular, reaching an audience well beyond the usual academic boundaries.

Lewis's work was couched as a debate with the earlier work of Robert REDFIELD on Mexico. Whereas Redfield had described the peasants in his studies as a 'little community' and a 'folk society', Lewis, in contrast, found abject poverty and destitution among its inhabitants. Lewis's subsequent research included such notable LIFE HISTORY based studies as *Five Families,* 1959, *The Children of Sanchez,* 1961, *Pedro Martinez,* 1964, and *La Vida,* 1968. These studies firmly established the 'culture of poverty' concept, which implies that poverty is transmitted intergenerationally, encoded in the behavioural and cultural arrangements of family life. From this point of view, poverty's cultural dimension is deemed to be self-perpetuating. The culture of poverty' manifests itself in apparent social 'disorganization' and a personal sense of hopelessness and the perceived inability of the people involved to transform their lives.

In invoking 'culture' in an explanation of the behaviour of the poor in a manner which in part implied some criticism of them, it was inevitable that Lewis's claims would receive criticism. Integral to his work was the suggestion that life history research could stand on behalf of an entire culture. At the methodological level this turned out to be his Achilles heel and his work was subject to sweeping criticism by Valentine (1968) and Leacock (1971), who argued the inadequacy of life history at the family or individual level when what was required was wider ethnographic evidence based on field work at the community level.

liberal democracy the form of representative democracy in modern Western policies, distinguished by universal suffrage, electoral competition for power between POLITICAL PARTIES and the protection of CITIZEN RIGHTS. This form of government and politics became established in Europe only in the late 19th and early 20th century, and for most of the century has faced the challenge of alternative systems, especially those based on FASCISM and COMMUNISM. See also DEMOCRACY, STABLE DEMOCRACY, PLURALISM, PLURAL ÉLITISM, TOTALITARIANISM, CAPITALIST STATE.

liberalism a political doctrine developed in Europe from the 17th-century onwards, involving the rejection of authoritarian forms of government, the defence of freedoms of speech, association and religion, and the assertion of the right to private property. This theory of liberalism was primarily developed in the writings of the British philosophers John Stuart MILL, LOCKE, HUME and BENTHAM, and has been an enormously influential tradition in the development of Western democracies. Underpinning its precepts is the great ENLIGHTENMENT metanarrative of RATIONALITY, since a society founded upon liberal principles is the one, so it was argued, that self-interested, rational individuals would choose (see SOCIAL CONTRACT THEORY). The notions of choice, individual freedom and hostility to an overmighty or interfering state, which are embedded within liberalism, are also indissolubly linked to the LAISSEZ-FAIRE economics of Adam SMITH.

Liberalism has had many critics, especially from writers influenced by MARX who have regarded liberal democracy as 'the best political shell' for CAPITALISM, and also the basis of the legitimation of the continued oppression and EXPLOITATION of the working class. It has also had many advocates and apologists – most recently, with the collapse of COMMUNISM, Francis Fukuyama (1992), who celebrates the 'end of history' as the triumph of liberal democracy and capitalism over its ideological and historical rivals. Fukuyama should perhaps be less sanguine, especially if the principles of liberalism are being progressively eroded by a drift towards an anti- or a-rational postmodern world (see POSTMODERNISM AND POSTMODERNITY).

life chances the material advantages or disadvantages (e.g. material rewards, and social and cultural opportunities or lack of opportunities) that a typical member of a group or class can expect within a particular society. Originally a Weberian conception, and especially associated with WEBER's analysis of class and status, the concept has also been employed by DAHRENDORF (1979). Its focus is on inequality. Perhaps the most poignant of life chances is unequal distribution of health care, and associated inequality in life expectancy.

life course the process of personal change, from infancy through to old age and death, brought about as a result of the interaction between 'biographical events' and 'societal events'. The term is preferred by many to *life cycle* because, in recognizing that people do not experience their lives strictly in terms of chronology, it focuses on sociohistorical processes as both the result of human action and as a background to personal biography.

Life cycle may be regarded as the process of change and development of a person, an institution or an entity and is therefore similar in meaning to 'life course'. However, because it suggests a continuous and renewable process, as in 'the cycle of the seasons', it has connotations of inevitability, similarity and determinism which may be considered inappropriate to an understanding of how human lives are experienced at the level of individual personal relationships and in the context of the social and historical forces which influence lives. Both terms are often used interchangeably, but current preference is for 'life course' for the reasons given.

Sociological and psychological concern with the life course has grown in recent years. One of the first theorists to propose that development does not end when adulthood is reached, and who described eight successive stages of psychosocial development, was Erik Erikson (1963). Other classic authors include Charlotte Bühler (1953), whose work, like Erikson's, particularly illustrates the NATIVIST approach, emphasizing the common process underlying the human life course (this being closest to the definition *life cycle*). Other authors (e.g. Dohrenwend and Dohrenwend, 1974) have emphasized the effect of different experiences, i.e. the contrast between lives rather than their similarities (this being closest to the definition *life course*).

life crisis any disruptive life event, possibly entailing the loss of important relationships and social status, which requires personal adjustment and which may threaten the integrity of the SELF and its social relationships. An indicative list is bereavement, divorce, marriage, job loss or change, disability, retirement, migration, eviction. Because these may involve STRESS and anxiety, which are implicated in the causation of some diseases, life crises are an important area of study for the SOCIOLOGY OF HEALTH AND MEDICINE, as well as being a central factor for consideration in the fields of COUNSELLING and PSYCHOTHERAPY.

life cycle see LIFE COURSE.

life expectancy the number of years the average member of a social group can expect to live. This is largely determined by environmental factors, though improvements in these do not lead to an infinitely extendable life expectancy, since the maximum period of existence of a member of the human species remains at about 110 years and biological factors impose limits less than this for most humans. The average life expectancy at birth in the UK in the late 20th-century was for men 71, and for women 76, and this has changed little in the last half century. However, there is variation according to social class and region. Currently these demographic differences are widening, with life expectancy in the north of England and Scotland being significantly less than that in the south. See also BLACK REPORT, DEATH RATE AND MORTALITY RATE.

life history and life history method a sociological historical, or psychological account produced from face-to-face interviews (see also ORAL HISTORY) or from *personal documents,* such as diaries or letters.

lifelong learning part of the UK NEW LABOUR education agenda. This broad policy can be traced back to 'lifetime learning', originally proposed by the Conservative government (DFEE 1996). It stems from the conviction that a post-industrial society requires a more highly educated and skilled workforce, with greater flexibility; that a KNOWLEDGE SOCIETY requires higher levels of education (although this has been disputed – see CREDENTIALISM). A further assumption is workers must be prepared for more frequent CAREER changes as lifelong careers can no longer be expected. See also LEARNING SOCIETY.

A distinction can be drawn between 'mature students' entering education for the first time (an aspect of WIDENING PARTICIPATION – see also ACCESS) and those learners who are already well-qualified who are updating their knowledge, skills and qualifications (i.e. professional development).

life politics a possible new politics (according to GIDDENS, 1991) arising from the questions about 'self-actualization' and 'how we should live in a post-traditional order' and in a context of global interdependence. Such a politics is contrasted with the more conventional '*emancipatory politics*', concerned with combatting 'exploitation and oppression'.

lifestyle the manner in which an individual or group lives (see Polsky, 1969). Whilst the term has been used in a variety of contexts, it has recently been used especially in connection with the practice and discourses of ADVERTISING agencies and market research organizations. Conceptions of 'lifestyle' have become increasingly important in the marketing and advertising process since World War II, with the development of new forms of popular entertainment and new vehicles of mass communication, such as radio, cinema and television. The emergence of CONSUMER CULTURE and new consumer goods (e.g. cars, cigarettes, cosmetics) required new ways of selling. In the advertising process the success of a campaign increasingly relied upon the active identification of the consumer with the image of the product and advertisers have come to recognize the importance of understanding human motives and desires as an aid to effective communication and marketing. See also ADVERTISING, COMMERCIAL ETHNOGRAPHY.

life-world (*Lebenswelt*) the 'natural attitude' involved in everyday conceptions of reality, which includes 'not only the "nature" experienced.., but also the social world' (Schutz and Luckmann, *The Structures of the Life-World*, 1973).

Whereas HUSSERL'S PHENOMENOLOGY bracketed the 'life–world', for SCHUTZ it was the major task of SOCIAL PHENOMENOLOGY to uncover the basis of this 'natural habitat' of social life (of actors' social competence), with its central problem of human 'understanding'. For Schutz it is the 'taken-for-granted', 'routine' character of the life-world which is most striking (e.g. in contrast with SCIENCE). The 'stocks of knowledge' ('what everybody knows' – see also MUTUAL KNOWLEDGE) and the 'interpretive schemes' employed by social actors in bringing off everyday action, as made apparent by Schutz, become the subject matter of ETHNOMETHODOLOGY. Schutz's thinking has also influenced GIDDENS' formulation of STRUCTURATION THEORY. See also PRACTICAL CONSCIOUSNESS.

Likert scale a technique for measuring the strength of a person's ATTITUDE or predisposition towards a person, object, idea, phenomenon, etc. (Likert, 1932). Likert scales assume that attitudes lie on a simple, dichotomous continuum running from one extreme position through neutral to the other extreme, for example, capitalism/communism, religion/atheism.

Likert scales are subjective in nature, insofar as they are based on the replies given by individuals to a battery of questions. In constructing such scales a sample of respondents from the target population are presented with a large number of statements thought to have a bearing on the subject. For example, to construct a scale to measure the strength of religious belief respondents may be presented with statements such as: 'The laws relating to blasphemy are outdated and should be abolished'; 'We can be almost certain that human beings evolved from lower animals'; 'Every woman has the right to terminate an unwanted pregnancy if she so wishes', 'The miracles in the Bible happened just as they are described there'. Respondents are asked to indicate to what extent they agree or disagree with each statement, using a three-, five- or seven-point scale. A five-point scale is generally considered to be best. The replies given to each question are then coded (see CODING) so that a high score indicates a strong disposition towards the subject under consideration and a low score indicates its polar opposite. Finally, the Likert scale is constructed using those items whose scores correlate most closely with the overall scores, i.e. the scale has internal consistency and each item has predictability. This final form of the scale can then be administered to the population for whom it is intended.

The main problem with constructing Likert scales is that of ensuring that the individual items in the scale tap one dimension only. In measuring religious attitudes, as discussed above, for example, people's opinions about abortion are determined by many factors of which the individual's religious persuasion is only one. Various statistical techniques, such as FACTOR ANALYSIS have been devised which enable researchers to calculate the internal consistency of their scales. See also ATTITUDE SCALE AND MEASUREMENT, GUTTMAN SCALE.

liminality the situation of those in transit across the symbolic boundaries between statuses, especially in RITUALS (e.g. in RITE OF PASSAGE, CARNIVAL) – see A. van Gennep, *The Rites of Passage* (1909).

lineage and **lineage group** (ANTHROPOLOGY) a group of people who claim common DESCENT. The basis may be PATRILINEAL, MATRILINEAL, BILATERAL or NON-UNILINEAL. Lineage theory was at the centre of UK SOCIAL ANTHROPOLOGY from the 1940s to the 1960s, as discussed in the works of RADCLIFFE-BROWN, EVANS-PRITCHARD and M. Fortes. see also KINSHIP, SEGMENTARY SOCIETY.

lineage mode of production see NONCAPITALIST AND PRECAPITALIST MODES OF PRODUCTION.

linguistic analysis see ORDINARY LANGUAGE PHILOSOPHY, LINGUISTIC PHILOSOPHY.

linguistic philosophy 1 ANALYTICAL PHILOSOPHY in general.
2 ORDINARY LANGUAGE PHILOSOPHY in particular.
The latter is more common.

linguistics the academic study of LANGUAGE. Its centre is the possibility of GRAMMAR, i.e. describing language in terms of rules of abstract elements and their combinations. For example, sentences may be seen as made up of a subject and a predicate, with the predicate composed of a verb and an object. It includes descriptions of the sounds of a language, *phonology,* again attempted, with great success, in terms of the identification of simple elements and their combination.

Linguistics as so described has been a part of the classical education, with the systematic description of Latin and Greek grammars an important paradigm. In each intellectual era these possibilities are taken up in terms of broader interests: the 18th century investigated what appear to be relatively universal features of grammar, as aspects of a universal rationality; the 19th century investigated the history, transformation and 'evolution' of linguistic forms and patterns; and the 20th century sought a linguistic psychological and sociological science. Given that grammar and phonology do provide successful systematic descriptions, rare in the human disciplines, the scientized form of linguistics has been extremely influential in the social sciences. De SAUSSURE put forward a striking and plausible metatheory for a scientific linguistics, suggesting that it is the study of an autonomous subject matter, i.e. one conceptually separable from outside relationships. The linguistic system is composed of a system of contrasting elements existing on different levels of structure. Thus simple sound elements combine to make up minimal elements for the structural level above phonology, that of words and word parts (*morphology*). This kind of analysis was contrasted with the evolutionary views that preceded it, now regarded as a secondary study. The construction of an abstract system by linguists, attributed to people who 'use' language but cannot readily describe this use, has become a powerful model for social science (see also COMPETENCE AND PERFORMANCE). CHOMSKY gave it a psychological interpretation, arguing that a readiness for the system was a feature of human biological being, innate, and not learned. The underlying shape of the system would then be universal. Scientizing grammar led to the specification and investigation of further levels, e.g. SEMANTICS and PRAGMATICS.

In the French philosophical tradition, the Saussurean metatheory was extensively applied as a paradigm for the other social sciences, the doctrine of STRUCTURALISM. Society is seen as generally semiotic, i.e. sign-constituted. Controversy over this, in POSTSTRUCTURALISM and elsewhere, has been a substantial aspect of intellectual life in the human sciences in the late 20th-century. Can linguistics be extended to meaning and action? Is it a 'science', or some other kind of description? Is language describable in strict rules, or does it evade such formulation? Is human rationality the product of non-rational, unconscious systems? Do the uncertainties associated with reference and DIFFERENCE undermine the very conceptions of the individual and individual IDENTITY? These disputed questions are the legacy of the long tradition of linguistics for other social studies. Linguistics itself continues regardless of. their outcomes.

lions and foxes see CIRCULATION OF ÉLITES.

Lipset, Seymour M. (1922–) leading US political sociologist who, after his early work on radicalism, and on democracy and oligarchy in TRADE UNIONS (*Union Democracy,* 1956), has become best known for a number of influential general works on the social bases of liberal democracy and 'non-democracy', including *Political Man* (1960), *The First New Nation* (1963), and *Party Systems and Voter Alignments* (with S. Rokkan, 1967). See also POLITICAL CLEAVAGE,

CLASS CLEAVAGE, END-OF-IDEOLOGY THESIS, STABLE DEMOCRACY, IRON LAW OF OLIGARCHY, SOCIAL MOBILITY.

literacy 1 basic competence in reading and writing. In this basic sense the term was first used in the 19th-century, when *illiteracy* also first began to be seen as a social problem. Before this, with no mass provision for formal education, it was simply accepted that a majority of people would not be able to learn to read and write. In most preindustrial societies literacy was the preserve of a specialist and privileged group – scribes, bureaucrats, priests etc. – who often kept the written language complex (see CONFUCIANISM) or conducted written communications in non-indigenous languages. Thus, literacy was a vehicle for social exclusion. With the advent of PRINTING and the more ready availability of written works, the spread of literacy became a significant factor in the process of democratization of social life and increased public participation in decision-making.
2 by analogy with sense **1**, reference is sometimes also made to other forms of literacy, e.g. computer-literacy.

In modern societies a concern with literacy (and levels of literacy) has periodically been a major topic of political debate, e.g. the notion that 'we must educate our new masters' was an important part of the movement to increase public educational provision in the 19th century, although equally fears continued to be expressed that literacy was likely to be abused.

In functionalist and NEOEVOLUTIONARY forms of sociology, as well as more widely, near universal provision for basic literacy (and numeracy) is regarded as an essential requirement for the smooth functioning of a modern economy. See also NONLITERATE SOCIETY.

literary and cultural theory the analytical study of literature and related works of art (e.g. plays, films, televised drama).

Two approaches to the study of literature can be distinguished:
(a) the analytical study of literature considered part of élite culture, e.g. in Britain, the school of critics associated with F. R. Leavis, which emphasized the importance of teaching and upholding the canon of English literature;
(b) later, more radical approaches, which emphasize links with social theory, including sociology, and seek to break down the distinction between élite and MASS CULTURE, while critically appraising both.

An exceptionally clear student guide to the considerable complexity of this second strand of literary and cultural theory, which draws inspiration especially from POST-STRUCTURALISM, is provided by A. Easthope and K. McGowan (1992). Compare CULTURAL STUDIES; see also POPULAR CULTURE.

literati see CONFUCIANISM.

local labour market the market for jobs within a particular locale. At this level of analysis, specifics relating to the role of the family, social networks and employers within the local milieu all play their part in developing and sustaining the work expectations, attitudes and behaviour of individuals and groups. These can vary greatly between localities and influence the ways individuals, groups and employers respond to external LABOUR MARKET pressures, e.g. economic recession (Ashton et al., 1987). Studies of local labour markets add to our understanding of the dynamics of labour markets, in particular *segmentalism* (see SEGMENTED LABOUR MARKET) and emphasize the importance of local sociohistorical and cultural patterning of these relations.

Locke, John (1632–1704) English philosopher and political theorist, whose major political writing, the *Two Treatises of Government* (1690), was occasioned by his belief that the Stuart monarchs were seeking to restore ABSOLUTISM. In the *First Treatise*, he was concerned to demolish arguments about the patriarchal origins of political authority. Man's duty to God, under natural law, is to use his peculiarly human qualities – reason and free will. Political authority, properly so called, is limited to securing the conditions under which men can pursue these purposes (see NATURAL RIGHTS AND NATURAL LAW). This means that their property must be protected, and by 'property' Locke meant the 'lives, liberties, and estates' of men. Political authority is thus instituted by men in the *state of nature,* through contract, for their greater security; it is exercised according to trust, is sustained by an implicit contract, and consent can be withdrawn if that authority either proves incompetent or, as Locke thought likely, it oversteps the boundaries of the trust. Since civil government is entrusted to men who ultimately cannot be trusted, a right of popular resistance to political authority remains always in reserve as a deterrent to incipient absolutist and despotic pretensions. In putting forward a SOCIAL CONTRACT THEORY and limited constitutional government, Locke was to have a far greater influence on the American colonies and their post-independence constitutions, than he has ever had on the British political system. He was also an early proponent of the LABOUR THEORY OF VALUE, in that he argued that men legitimately appropriated land from the common stock by mixing their labour with it.

In EPISTEMOLOGY, Locke also laid the foundations of modern EMPIRICISM. He denied that men had innate knowledge, and rejected the rationalism of DESCARTES. In the *Essay on Human Understanding* (1690), he argued that all knowledge is derived from experience, either directly through the senses, or through reflection. Man could have intuitive knowledge of his own existence, and of mathematical truths, but his knowledge of the external world was conjectural and probabilistic. Locke's doctrine of the mind as a *tabula rasa* – a blank slate – indicates the extent of his empiricism. His interest in children's learning and the acquisition of ideas meant that aspects of his thinking also contributed to philosophical psychology. The SELF, for example, for Locke arises as a set of ideas and actions for which the individual takes responsibility. Like HOBBES, Locke's central doctrines are individualistic; more so than Hobbes', his proposals for CIVIL SOCIETY are for intellectual freedom and checks and balances.

Lockwood, David (1929–) British sociologist who has worked mainly at the LSE and the University of Essex, and whose main concern has been with the study of CLASS and SOCIAL STRATIFICATION, especially his studies of the BLACK-COATED WORKER (1958), and (with John GOLDTHORPE et al.) the AFFLUENT WORKER (Lockwood, 1966; Goldthorpe, Lockwood et al., 1988–89). See also MULTIDIMENSIONAL ANALYSIS OF SOCIAL STRATIFICATION, CLASS IMAGERY.

As well as his contributions to studies of class and stratification he has also made important interventions in central debates on SOCIOLOGICAL THEORY, notably his critiques of Talcott PARSONS and STRUCTURAL FUNCTIONALISM (see 'Some Remarks on the Social System', 1956, and 'Social Integration and System Integration', 1964) – see also SOCIAL INTEGRATION AND SYSTEM INTEGRATION His most recent book, *Solidarity and Schism* (1992), continues the discussion of these themes.

logic the branch of PHILOSOPHY concerned with analysis of the universal and context-free (A PRIORI) principles of sound reasoning and valid inference by which conclusions may be drawn from initial premises. These general principles are 'formal' in that they are abstract in character, and are usually also capable of being expressed in symbolic notation. An early formulation of logic, which held sway until modern times, was ARISTOTLE's systematization of the basis of the syllogism (also known as *propositional logic*). This was added to in the 19th-century by highly technical forms of logic, increasingly linked with mathematics. See also INDUCTION AND INDUCTIVE LOGIC, ANALYTIC AND SYNTHETIC, DIALECTIC, COVERING-LAW MODEL AND DEDUCTIVE NOMOLOGICAL EXPLANATION, POSITIVISM.

logical action and **non-logical action** see PARETO, RESIDUES AND DERIVATIONS.

logical positivism the philosophical doctrine of a group of philosophers – including R. Carnap (1891–1970) and O. Neurath (1882–1945) – known collectively as the *Vienna Circle*. See POSITIVISM.

logistic growth curve a pattern of growth characteristic of many social situations (see DEMOGRAPHIC TRANSITION, DIFFUSION OF INNOVATIONS) in which growth begins slowly, then increases rapidly, and finally stabilizes.

log linear analysis a technique of statistical analysis commonly used on CROSS-TABULATIONS of data. It transforms non-linear models into linear models by the use of logarithms. This is necessary because social data is often nominal or ordinal and therefore does not meet the assumptions needed by many statistical techniques (see CRITERIA AND LEVELS OF MEASUREMENT). It is a CAUSAL MODELLING device, involving setting up models to test against the data, successively adjusting the model till the best fit is found.

logocentrism and phonocentrism see DECONSTRUCTION.

Lombroso, Cesare (1836–1909) Italian criminologist who argued that certain individuals had criminal tendencies inbuilt at birth. Such people could be recognized by particular physical characteristics, such as the shape of the skull. Although Lombroso was prepared to accept that criminal behaviour could in some degree be learnt by 'normal' people, he clearly regarded most crime as the product of degenerate individuals, who were really biological 'throwbacks'. See also CRIMINOLOGY.

longitudinal study an investigation which involves making observations of the same group at sequential time intervals. Thus, a longitudinal study of a COHORT of children may be made to assess, for example, the effect of social class on school achievement (see BIRTH COHORT STUDY). Longitudinal studies are used by the National Children's Bureau to document various aspects of children's development in the UK. However, longitudinal studies are not only appropriate for studying human development or change, they may also be used to observe change over time within organizations.

The advantage of longitudinal studies compared with CROSS-SECTIONAL STUDIES is that the causal factor involved in a sequence of changes an be directly explored using data collected before and after changes (e.g. analysis of the effect of changes in the school curriculum). The main disadvantages are the greater expense of repeated study, the possible HAWTHORNE EFFECT of repeated studies and the influence of other changes which may be occurring concurrently (e.g. changes in the school curriculum may take place at the same time as changes in the resourcing of educational services). Compare PANEL STUDY.

longue durée see DURÉE.

long-wave theory the identification of long-term cycles of economic boom and slump in which the upturn in the cycle is caused by major technical innovations. The idea was first developed in the 1920s by the Soviet economist Kondratieff, who identified cycles of boom and recession totalling about fifty years which coincided with innovations such as cotton spinning in the 18th century and assembly-line mass production post-World War II. The theory has been taken up in the debate about innovations using microelectronics, seen as leading to movement out of the slump associated with the fourth KONDRATIEFF CYCLE in the 1980s (Freeman, 1982). See also SCHUMPETER.

looking-glass self the conception of the 'social self' as arising 'reflectively' as the outcome of the reaction to the opinion of others. This term was coined by Charles COOLEY, but the general idea is one that he shared with William James and SYMBOLIC INTERACTIONISM.

Lorenz, Konrad (1903–89) Austrian-born ethologist whose work was a cornerstone of the subject. Lorenz's main works include *On Aggression* (1966) and *Foundations of Ethology* (1978). See AGGRESSION.

Lukács, George (1885–1971) widely influential Hungarian Marxist, philosopher and literary theorist. The young Lukács attended the Universities of Budapest, Berlin and Heidelberg where he studied under George SIMMEL and Max WEBER. At the end of the First World War he joined the Communist Party and became Deputy Commissar for Education in the short-lived 1919 Hungarian Soviet Republic. His literary writings which attempted to develop a Marxist theory of AESTHETICS established him as a theorist of international distinction. The best-known book by Lukács, *History and Class Consciousness* (1923) covered several major themes, including the importance of HEGEL for the interpretation of Marx; Marx's theory of ALIENATION; and the relationship between ideology, class consciousness and revolution. In ways that later influenced members of the Western European NEW LEFT and members of the FRANKFURT SCHOOL OF CRITICAL THEORY, Lukács argued against scientistic interpretations of Marxism, emphasizing the importance of historical PRAXIS. In some tension with this view, however, he also gave strong support to Leninist conceptions of the supremacy of the Communist Party. In 1930 Lukács moved to the Soviet Union where he remained until 1945 when he was appointed Professor of Aesthetics and Philosophy at the University of Budapest. He was always a controversial figure, accused by his critics of condoning STALINISM. Nevertheless, during the Hungarian popular uprising of 1956 he was appointed Minister of Culture in Imre Nagy's government. Other major works by Lukács include *Theory of the Novel* (1920), *The Historical Novel* (1937), *The Young Hegel* (1948), *The Meaning of Contemporary Realism* (1963), On *Aesthetics* (1963), *Solzhenitsyn* (1969).

lumpenproletariat literally, the 'proletariat of rags', from the German *Lumpen* meaning 'rag'. MARX and ENGELS were two of the first 19th-century writers to recognize the existence of a class drawn from all classes, living on the margins of society, not in regular employment and gaining their subsistence mainly from crime. According to Marx, the composition of the Parisian lumpenproletariat in the mid-19th century included vagabonds, discharged soldiers and jailbirds, escaped galley slaves, swindlers, pickpockets, tricksters, gamblers, pimps, brothel-keepers, ragpickers and beggars. These groups were sharply differentiated from the industrial working class by both politics and by being outside the normal social relations of wage labour. Marx and Engels distrusted the lumpenproletariat because it did not make an obvious contribution in the struggle of the working class for socialism. They therefore considered the lumpenproletariat were 'the dangerous class', 'the social scum' whose parasitic ways of life prepared them for becoming bribed agents of reactionary elements in the ruling class. They threatened to lead workers into arbitrary violence and their highest forms of political activity were mob agitation and street fighting. These were primitive forms of political action, according to Marx and Engels, who maintained that where large scale capitalist production exists, modern revolution demands the mass seizure and control of the means of production by the working class.

Dissenting from the Marxist view, the African socialist, Fanon, in *The Wretched of the Earth* (1967), stressed that the lumpenproletariat or 'classless idlers' living in the shanty towns of Third World societies could play an important role in revolutionary struggles.

Luxemburg, Rosa (1870–1919) Polish Marxist revolutionary and theoretician who moved to Germany in 1898 and there played a major role in socialist revolutionary politics until her murder in Berlin. Her most important writings related to the question of reformist versus revolutionary politics, the national question, and the accumulation of capital. In the latter she contributed significantly to the Marxist analysis of IMPERIALISM by arguing that it was necessary for any capitalist economy to expand into non-capitalist economies because of its inability to absorb SURPLUS VALUE. The contradiction here was that when all the non-capitalist world had been absorbed, the capitalist system would be unable to accumulate and hence break down. More recently, with the rise of FEMINISM she has gained significance as one of the major Marxist figures of the early 20th-century who reflected on the relationship between her personal and public life.

Lyotard, Jean Francois (1924–98) French philosopher and a significant figure in POSTMODERNISM. Between 1949 and 1959 he taught philosophy at secondary schools before becoming professor of philosophy at the University of Paris VIII (St-Denis) until he retired in 1989. In the 1950s and 60s Lyotard was identified with Marxism. He was on the editorial committee of the socialist journal *Socialisme ou barbarie* and the left-wing newspaper *Pouvoir ouvrier.* He was also active in the events of May 1968. However, by the 1970s he seems largely to have renounced his Marxist past. His book (*The Postmodern Condition* 1984), prepared originally (1979) as a report on knowledge for the Quebec government, identified him in many circles as the father of postmodernism. The book refutes the idea of legitimacy in metanarratives (see GRAND NARRATIVE AND METANARRATIVE). It calls into question the French tradition of regarding society as a unity – a tradition which reached from COMTE and DURKHEIM through to SARTRE and Lefebvre. This tradition regarded the quest for knowledge to be legitimated either by the pure positivist dedication to impartiality and truth, or by the emancipation of a repressed subject (the proletariat). Lyotard argues that each of these bases for legitimacy is now contested so thoroughly that both are invalid. Moreover, there are no means of determining competing truth claims or the goals of knowledge. Borrowing from WITTGENSTEIN, Lyotard submits the science is best understood as a LANGUAGE GAME.

All of these arguments are consolidated in his later, more philosophical, work *The Differend* (1983). This is devoted to examining the neutralizing of players in language games. When a given field of DISCOURSE has become inflexible it tends to deny or eliminate different narratives and other voices. The Nazi death camps provide the most sickening twentieth-century example. *The Differend* calls for a more decentralized and diverse approach to questions of politics, history, culture and society. The emphasis is on enabling narratives and dialogues rather than repressing them.

Lyotard's sociology and philosophy have been heavily criticized. The main sociological criticisms are twofold: firstly, that his work is morally suspect because it fails to enable the reader to differentiate between the value of different positions; instead it reduces all propositions to a state of equivalence. Secondly, by announcing 'the end of politics' he encourages a political quiescence with the status quo. Nonetheless his attempt in *The Postmodern Condition* to pinpoint the features of postmodernity is rightly regarded as a benchmark work.

Lysenko, Trofim Denisovich (1898–1976) Russian plant breeder who claimed that plant behaviour and crop yields could be altered by treating seeds with changes of temperature, moisture levels etc. and, crucially, that these acquired characteristics could be inherited. He gained enormous influence over Soviet science under the patronage of STALIN, since the Soviet doctrine of the perfectability of the 'new Soviet man' favoured the evolutionary perspective of LAMARCK, which Lysenko followed. His views, however, were in direct opposition to the developing science of plant genetics in the West, and effectively destroyed Soviet developments in this area until his fall from favour along with Khrushchev in 1965. Lysenkoism is often cited as the classic example of the need to keep politics out of science, and was used during the COLD WAR as a convenient piece of anti-Soviet propaganda.

Machiavelli, Niccolo (1469–1527), Florentine diplomat and political theorist who is regarded as the first modern analyst of political POWER. His concern was twofold: the political instability of the Italian city states of his day, and the possibility of restoring to Italy the unity and greatness it had known under the Roman Republic. His main contribution to political thinking was in suggesting that in affairs of STATE a different morality had to prevail from that which governed private relations between men. A ruler who attempted to rule according to the dictates of Christian morality, for instance, would soon find himself ruined, for the simple reason that others would take advantage of him. In *The Prince* (1513), he argued that the overriding aim was the acquisition and consolidation of power. The prince, therefore, had to act according to circumstances, knowing how and when to break conventional moral codes. Ultimately, the prince had done all that could be expected of him if the political arrangements he bequeathed could be sustained by the engaged energies of an active citizenry. Though best known for *The Prince*, Machiavelli developed these ideas in other influential works, including The *Art of War* (1520) and *The Discourses on Titus Livius* (1532). See also NEO-MACHIAVELLIANS.

macrosociology the level of sociological analysis concerned with the analysis of whole societies, social structures at large, and social systems (compare MICROSOCIOLOGY). While the terms macro- and microsociology are used in sociology, the distinction is not as well-established or as central as the related distinction of micro- and macro- in ECONOMICS.

madness mental derangement ('insanity') which disrupts the 'normal' social functioning of an individual, leading to strange and unpredictable behaviour. In modern medical or psychiatric DISCOURSE, 'madness' is conceptualized and treated either as one of a number of physically grounded medical conditions (hence also treatable by drugs) or as a clinically identifiable personality disorder (see also PSYCHOSIS). In the sociological literature, it is more likely to be analysed as an example of the wider phenomenon of social LABELLING and SOCIAL CONTROL. For FOUCAULT, for instance, modern ways of handling 'madness' must be analysed as an aspect of the wider phenomena of social POWER and SURVEILLANCE, and social exclusion, in modern societies. Thus for sociological purposes there can be no question of any simple acceptance of the 'scientific' labels attached by 'experts'. In other societies and at other times, the kinds of behaviour now usually labelled 'insane' would be more variously labelled, e.g. as SHAMANISM, WITCHCRAFT, etc., and the social treatment of these would be similarly variable. In order to capture the social character of madness, there must be analysis of the social basis and social implications of madness. Medical and associated psychiatric conceptions will be part of this analysis, but can have no automatic priority in their own terms. See also LAING, SZASZ.

magic the attempt to activate supernatural or spiritual agencies in order to attain a specific outcome by ritualized means. Magic is not always readily distinguished from religious activity (see RELIGION), and in operation is often associated with it. However, an activity is usually identified as magic by its more instrumental, often more immediate, concern with the achievement of specific ends. In functionalist terms (see MALINOWSKI, 1948), magic is employed in situations where effective technologies to achieve the desired end are lacking. Thus the social function of magic is to allay anxieties and fulfil the need to do something, and it can also be cathartic (see also WITCHCRAFT AND SORCERY, SHAMAN).

In its broadest sense, magic is not only a feature of so-called 'primitive societies', but is also operative in modern societies, e.g. confidence in various pseudosciences, such as astrology, and in the survival of superstition. The interpenetration of 'true' technologies and ritualized magical activity can be seen as a pervasive feature of social activity, present even in modern medicine In all discussion of magic there is the difficulty that, since the distinction between empirical science and non-science is never a straightforward matter (see SCIENCE), the distinction between technology and magic is correspondingly blurred. It is the case that many of the users of magic do not operate with a sharp distinction between the natural and the supernatural. Thus magic is often an observer's concept rather than one shared by participants.

Maine, Henry James Sumner (1822–88) social philosopher and jurist best remembered for his *Ancient Law* (1861), which approaches the problem of social development in terms of the way in which legal systems evolved (see EVOLUTIONARY THEORY). The basic elements of Maine's understanding of SOCIAL CHANGE involve the development or evolution of societies based on kinship, family relationships, communal ownership, relations of status and political despotism to those based on territory, citizenship, private property, relations of contract and liberty. Maine's point was that legal terms could only be fully understood within a framework of social change.

The status/contract dichotomy was a variant of many attempts to conceptualize the evolutionary distinction between 'traditional and 'modern' society. Related formulations have come from SPENCER (MILITANT AND INDUSTRIAL SOCIETY), DURKHEIM (MECHANICAL AND ORGANIC SOLIDARITY), TÖNNIES (GEMEINSCHAFT AND GESELLSCHAFT), Robert M. MacIver (COMMUNITY AND ASSOCIATION) and Robert Redfield (RURAL-URBAN CONTINUUM).

making the grade process within modern HIGHER EDUCATION, and also schools, in which the 'faculty makes the rules' and students provide only the responses which faculties formally require, i.e. they direct their efforts largely at achieving good grades, neglecting the wider purposes of education (Becker et al., 1968). See also BECKER.

Malinowski, Bronislaw (1884–1942) Polish functionalist anthropologist. Major works include *Argonauts of the Western Pacific* (1922), *Crime and Custom in Savage Society* (1926), *Sex and Repression in Savage Society* (1927), *The Sexual Life of Savages* (1929) and *Magic, Science and Religion* (1948). He is best known for stressing the importance of ETHNOGRAPHY, or detailed participant observation, in ANTHROPOLOGY. His use of a detailed ethnographic diary is notable in this regard. Working in New Guinea and the Trobriand Islands (see KULA RING) he was able to provide detailed monographs on all aspects of the culture of these peoples. Together with RADCLIFFE-BROWN he shaped UK structural-functionalist (see STRUCTURAL-FUNCTIONALISM) anthropology whilst Professor at the London School of Economics from 1927 to 1938. His focus on the functional needs of sociocultural systems is indicated in *A Scientific Theory of Culture and Other Essays* (1944).

malintegation see INTEGRATION.

Malthus, Thomas (1766–1834) British clergyman, economist and demographer, particularly remembered for his thesis (in *Essay on the Principles of Population*, 1798) that there is a tendency for populations to increase at a geometric rate whilst food supply can only increase at an arithmetic rate. The implication is that a population, left unchecked, will reach a point where it cannot feed itself. He argued that a balance between a population and food supply is maintained either through 'positive checks' such as famine, disease and violence, or by 'preventative checks' such as late marriage, moral restraint and chastity. The political implication of this philosophy is that systems of poverty relief are ineffective, and Malthus believed that the poor should be responsible for themselves. Although Malthus only claimed that there is a tendency towards overpopulation, his ideas were used to justify the 1834 Poor Law Amendment Act in Britain, which required all poor relief claimants to enter the brutal regime of the workhouse. See also POPULATION, DEMOGRAPHY, DEMOGRAPHIC TRANSITION.

management science and administrative theory a set of universal principles and concepts concerned with the formal theory of organization (see ORGANIZATION THEORY). Sometimes referred to as the 'classical school of management', this approach developed in the early 20th-century, Henri Fayol (1841–1925) being the principle exponent of the movement. The ideas of the early management scientists contained a general set of principles concerned with efficient management practice and formal organization design: these included the principle of 'unity of command' (each person reports to only one boss) and 'hierarchy of authority' (authority runs down the organization from top to bottom). These principles were translated into an organizational blueprint or formal organizational chart which advocated 'tall' hierarchies of authority with 'small' spans of control. In other words, each position in a chain of command is responsible for a small number of subordinates. This form of organization was thought to increase efficiency and limit conflict.

Formal theories of organization complemented Taylor's principles of SCIENTIFIC MANAGEMENT by extending his study of the foreman and job design to management and the whole organization. Formal theories of administration have been influential in business and public administration; in the sociology of organizations they have been criticized as prescriptive and lacking in terms of empirical evidence or theoretical analysis of organization structure and behaviour. See also CONTINGENCY THEORY, FORMAL AND INFORMAL STRUCTURE, INTELLECTUAL LABOUR.

manager a person exercising responsibility for the coordination and control of work organizations. Managers are commonly divided into three strata: senior, middle and front-line, indicating a wide social and economic disparity within the category. The top echelons of managers include highly paid executives of multinational corporations, whilst the lowest include foremen who may earn little more than the manual workers they work beside and supervise. In recent debates, the main issue has concerned the class location of managers (Abercombie and Urry, 1983) which can be viewed as a continuation and extension of the older MANAGERIAL REVOLUTION debate. See also INTELLECTUAL LABOUR, CONTRADICTORY CLASS LOCATIONS.

mandarins see CONFUCIANISM.

manic depression see PSYCHOSIS.

manifest functions and **latent functions** the distinction between those functions of a social system which are intended and/or overtly recognized by the participants in that social system – *manifest functions* – and those functions which are hidden and remained unacknowledged by participants – *latent functions.* Merton's influential discussion of the distinction involves the raindances of the Hopi indians. These dances are intended to bring rain, but function to increase social integration. See also FUNCTIONALISM, UNANTICIPATED CONSEQUENCES AND UNINTENDED CONSEQUENCES (OF SOCIAL ACTION).

Mann, Michael (1942–) British historical sociologist and analyst of SOCIAL STRATIFICATION, whose book *The Sources of Social Power* (1986, volume 1 of a planned three-volume work) attracted critical acclaim from historians as well as sociologists. Having previously written incisively on contemporary political culture and class (e.g. *Consciousness and Action in the Western Working Class*, 1973), Mann turned his attention to historical analysis with the aim of bringing about a total reorientation in the treatment of POWER and SOCIAL CHANGE in sociology. The distinctive focus of Mann's approach to POWER is his insistence that it has four principal sources: economic, ideological, military and political, with none of these being alone decisive, and with no simple evolutionary or developmental pattern of social change (see also EPISODIC CHARACTERIZATION). The range and acuity of his account of the development and operation of power from neolithic times, through the civilization of the Near East, the classical age, and medieval Europe, to 1760 (the concluding point of volume 1) is remarkable. Volume 2 of Mann's planned trilogy, subtitled *The Rise of Classes and Nation-states 1760–1914*, appeared in 1993.

Mannheim Karl (1887–1947) Hungarian-born sociologist who was an enforced emigrant to England in 1933, and whose most important contributions to sociology were in the SOCIOLOGY OF KNOWLEDGE and in his writings on political issues of the day, including education and planning. In his main work *Ideology and Utopia* (1929) he systematizes distinctions between IDEOLOGY and UTOPIA as different kinds of belief system, the first performing the function of justification and preservation of a system, the second oriented to its change. More generally, in his SOCIOLOGY OF KNOWLEDGE, he argued that the main forms of knowledge are conditioned in various ways by the needs of social groups, although, contrary to MARX, not simply by class interests. He suggested that one way in which knowledge might escape RELATIVISM was if INTELLECTUALS adopted a 'free-floating' or non-aligned position. See also INTELLIGENTSIA.

managerial revolution

the growth in the number and professionalization of managers who do not own the companies they control. The idea of the separation of management from the ownership of business organizations, sometimes expressed as the *divorce between ownership and control*, is seen to rest largely on the progressive diffusion of shareholding at the same time as organizations both increase in size and become more technically complex. It is suggested that, as shareholding becomes both fragmented and 'absentee', and as the premium placed on professional, technical and administrative expertise increases, the professionalization of management fosters the emergence of a relatively homogeneous stratum of managers who both acquire effective control of organizations and have an orientation to both employees and wider society which is different to that of traditional capitalists. However, even when this thesis is accepted, there is debate about whether managers act either in their own distinct interest (Burnham, 1942) or with a broader social conscience, guided by professional values (Berle and Means, 1933). In any event the implications for developments in both stratification and CAPITALISM are profound. One theorist, for example, suggests that new authority relationships replace the traditional conflict of interests between employers and employees (DAHRENDORF, 1959). See also POSTCAPITALISM, POSTINDUSTRIALISM.

The thesis has not, however, remained unquestioned. Subsequent attempts to evaluate it involve more sophisticated analyses of patterns of shareholding (Zeitlin, 1974; Barratt-Brown, 1968), the stability and means of recruitment to board positions (Stanworth and Giddens, 1974), the values and ideologies of managers (Nichols, 1969), 'decision-making in process' (Pahl and Winkler, 1974), and corporate networks (Scott, 1979). Whilst these studies have their limitations, collectively they suggest that the managerial revolution thesis was premature. Some researchers have pointed to the similarity between owners and managers in their values, objectives and social origin, and have drawn attention to the way these similarities are upheld through connections and social activities (Nichols, 1969, Stanworth and Giddens, 1975; Whitley, 1974). It has also been suggested that those theorists who have based their arguments on analyses of shareholding concentration have done so on the basis of questionable methodology. In the approach adopted by Berle and Means, for example, both made dubious assumptions about the level of shareholding diffusion required for managerial control and encouraged the analysis of companies considered in isolation from others (Barratt-Brown, 1968; Zeitlin, 1974). Attempts to avoid such pitfalls have revealed a more complex and variable relationship between shareholding concentration and ownership control. Hence the particular constellation of investment patterns within and between companies will influence whether or not board members, who may collectively muster but a small percentage of total shares, can and do in fact control. Some theorists suggest, therefore, that whilst many shareholders are separated from company control, ownership is not. This is reinforced by findings that reveal the persistence, in some instances, and in particular sectors, of personal and family ownership and control of large corporations. Whilst the growth of both institutional investment in, and financial loans to, companies complicates the ownership-control relationship, it does not eliminate it. Indeed, given the tendency for these to go hand in hand with interlocking directorships, questions are raised about the progressive fragmentation of shareholding, the extent and implications of ties between institutional worlds, and the independence of managers (Hill, 1981).

Attempts to answer these questions are also significant for the broader analysis of the UPPER CLASS. In this respect, whilst the distinctions made between entrepreneurial, industrial and finance capitalists reveal subtle changes, e.g. in the intergenerational bases of CLASS composition, they do not preclude the persistence of a cohesive upper class which, aided by a network of interlocking directorships, has not relinquished significant control of capital to a 'managerial TECHNOSTRUCTURE' (Galbraith, 1979; Scott, 1979).

Among the more specific criticisms of the managerial revolution thesis are:

(a) a failure to distinguish between the allocative control exercised by top management (e.g. about future investment decisions) and the operational control of day-to-day corporate activities by lower managers (Pahl and Winkler, 1974);

(b) lack of recognition of the constraints exercised by the business environment, especially the way in which competition constrains and unifies management objectives in the direction of a balanced orientation to growth (investment) and dividends (shareholder earnings);

(c) the ignoring of historical and other contextual factors that may influence the kinds of management representation at boardroom level. In Britain, for example, personnel managers are regarded as less important in this respect than accountants and lawyers.

The managerial revolution thesis is clearly an important topic which is central to debates arising from attempts to theorize about contemporary society through concepts such as CAPITALISM, POSTCAPITALISM and POSTINDUSTRIALISM.

manual and non-manual labour the distinction between physical (manual or BLUE-COLLAR WORKERS) and mental (non-manual or WHITE-COLLAR WORKERS). OCCUPATIONAL SCALES typically employ the distinction as a basic measure of SOCIAL CLASS, It is important, however, to bear in mind that while these widely used scales broadly reflect the view that manual labour is 'working class' and mental labour 'middle class', this does not hold true for Marxist analyses, where class position is considered in terms of relations of power and the functions of different occupations vis-à-vis the process of CAPITAL ACCUMULATION (see CLASS, CLASS BOUNDARIES). Neither should it be assumed that the manual or non-manual content of occupations is fixed. Indeed, prior to the emergence of factory-based production systems, both elements were fused in the work of craftsmen and women. As craft labour was fragmented into discrete operations undertaken by factory workers, the mental or 'planning' element involved in the LABOUR PROCESS was removed and relocated at a supervisory level. This was the explicit aim of SCIENTIFIC MANAGEMENT. Today, technological change (see NEW TECHNOLOGY) continues to alter the nature of work, converting many former manual tasks (e.g. in the print industry) to white-collar work which involves the processing of information rather than the manipulation of things. In this sense, the shifting divide between manual and non-manual work is connected to the POSTINDUSTRIAL SOCIETY thesis, and to the emergence of *post-Fordism* (see FORDISM AND POST-FORDISM). In so far as some of these developments may involve JAPANIZATION, the 're-empowerment' of manual workers may actually involve the restoration of 'mental' elements to their work. See INTELLECTUAL LABOUR, MIDDLE CLASS(ES), WHITE-COLLAR WORKER, WORKING CLASS, PROLETARIANIZATION.

manumission see SLAVERY.

Maoism see MAO TSE-TUNG.

Mao Tse-tung (Mao Zedong) (1893–1976) one of the founding members of the Chinese Communist Party in 1921, who, in leading a prolonged rural movement from 1927 to 1949, developed a theory of socialist REVOLUTION based on the leading role of the peasantry. Mao argued that, in situations such as China, the CLASS STRUGGLE had reached stalemate with a small PROLETARIAT and a weak and dependent comprador bourgeoisie in towns (see COMPRADOR CAPITALIST), and a strong landed ARISTOCRACY in the countryside. From the Chinese Revolution of 1949 to his death Mao was effectively leader of the Republic of China, and under him various policies were at different times adopted with the aim of promoting socialist development.

Whilst it can be argued that during his leadership, in comparison with other THIRD WORLD countries, China saw increased prosperity of the rural population, in particular through the provision of health and welfare programmes, there were also times of major hardship. In 1959–62, the failure of one of his programmes, the Great Leap Forward, combined with climatic disasters, resulted in widespread famine (and as many as 50 million deaths according to some commentators). The *Cultural Revolution* from 1965 to 1970, which involved a dislodging of entrenched officials and old ways, was also in part an attempt by Mao to strengthen his position against growing opposition (see also CULT OF PERSONALITY). This resulted in widespread social disruption, with the internal exile or death of many deemed to be against the thought and practice of Mao embodied in the *Little Red Book* (which comprised quotations from his speeches and writings). During this period harsh censorship was enforced in particular against anything which reflected the influence of the 'paper tiger', Western IMPERIALISM.

Mao's relationship with the MARXISM of the Soviet Union was complex and contradictory. On the one hand, during the 1920s and 30s he publicly proclaimed loyalty to STALIN and in the 1950s adopted a five-year plan based on Stalin's centralized COMMAND ECONOMY. On the other hand, whilst leading the revolutionary movement in the countryside, his reliance on the peasantry was in conflict with prevailing Soviet theory. When the Japanese were defeated in 1945, Stalin recognized Mao's opponent, Chiang Kai-shek, and his party the Goumindang (the Nationalist Party), as the government of China, only recognizing Mao after he had come to power without Soviet help. Whether Mao had any allegiance to STALINISM is debatable, but the Sino-Soviet split in 1959 was justified by Mao on the grounds that after the death of Stalin in 1953, the Soviet Union was turning down a 'capitalist road'. In power the Chinese Communist Party adopted a highly centralized party organization along Stalinist lines, but it was probably the case that especially in rural areas there was far less detailed party and state control than in the Soviet Union. There was also what some commentators (see White, 1983) call a 'radical Maoism', since at times Mao was willing to encourage mass political participation to maintain the revolutionary process, and during the time of the Cultural Revolution there were limited attempts to achieve more democratic forms of organization and participation in factories and COMMUNES, the major local administrative bodies.

One interpretation of these different aspects of Mao's politics is that above all he was a supremely adaptable, and sometimes unscrupulous, politician. This can be seen in his reconciliation with the West in the early 1970s, seemingly contradicting his fifty-year opposition to all aspects of Western capitalism. This was on the one hand to develop an alliance against the Soviet Union and North Vietnam, and on the other to open the way to the trade and technology which China needed. Other interpretations generally tend to focus on one period of his life, conveniently ignoring contradictions in others. Thus, the political legacy of *Maoism*, comprising political groups who take their inspiration from Mao's life and work is fragmented, and often virulently so. One manifestation of Maoism is the *Khmer Rouge*, with its theory of social transformation based on mass terror. In Peru, since 1980, the *Sendero Luminoso* (Shining Path), have been fighting a guerrilla war in the countryside based on an uncompromising interpretation of Mao's thought and practice in the 1930s. See also COMMUNISM.

Marcuse, Herbert (1898–1979) widely influential German philosopher and social theorist. Marcuse studied philosophy at the Universities of Berlin and Freiburg (at the latter with the leading German philosophers HUSSERL and HEIDEGGER). He became a member of the Institute of Social Research (later referred to as the FRANKFURT SCHOOL OF CRITICAL THEORY) in 1933 and emigrated, with other members, to the US following the Nazi rise to power. Marcuse continued his association with the institute which had moved to Columbia University. Between 1942 and 1950 he worked as a researcher for the US government. Subsequently he held posts at leading US Universities before becoming an honorary professor at the Free University of Berlin.

Marcuse's wide-ranging interests covered all the current debates of his time: art and revolution, PHENOMENOLOGY, EXISTENTIALISM and the legacy of classical German philosophy, the nature of technological change, transformation in the capitalist mode of production, the rise of psychoanalysis, the nature of the individual and the problems of socialism, Marxism and the critical theory of society. Pippin et al. (eds.) (1988) have suggested that what gave unity to all these concerns was Marcuse's commitment to the task of developing critical theory in the light of the deficiencies of classical Marxism.

In his *Soviet Marxism* (1958) he argued that Marxism in the Soviet Union had lost its function as the ideology of revolution and instead had become the ideological prop of the *status quo*. In his diagnosis of capitalist societies, Marcuse thought that the pressures of consumerism had led to the total incorporation of the working class into the existing system. As a result, rather than looking to the workers as the revolutionary vanguard, Marcuse, in *One-Dimensional Man* (1964), put his faith in an alliance between radical intellectuals and 'the outcasts and outsiders, the exploited and persecuted of other races and other colors, the unemployed and the unemployables'. In May 1968 his vision of a 'non-repressive civilization' and total human emancipation inspired student radicals of the international NEW LEFT movement. Other major works by Marcuse include *Reason and Revolution: Hegel and the Rise of Social Theory* (1941); *Eros and Civilization: a Philosophical Inquiry into Freud* (1955), *An Essay on Liberation* (1969); *Counterrevolution and Revolt* (1972).

marginal analysis see NEOCLASSICAL ECONOMICS.

marginality the state of being part insider and part outsider to a social group. The term was perhaps first used by PARK (1928) to refer to the 'cultural hybrid' who shares 'the life and traditions of two distinct groups'. Park focused particularly on migrants, stressing the disorienting effects of marginality. However, the concept can obviously be used to refer to many types of *social marginality*, e.g. the marginality of the parvenu, the stigmatized, etc. See also STRANGER.

market capitalism or free market capitalism see COMPETITIVE CAPITALISM.

market economy an economic system in which production and allocation are determined mainly by decisions in competitive markets, rather than controlled by the STATE.

market research the use of sample surveys to establish consumer wants, e.g. the likely demand for a new product. Compare COMMERCIAL ETHNOGRAPHY. See also LIFESTYLE.

marital separation see DIVORCE.

market situation those aspects of the position of an individual or group within SOCIAL STRATIFICATION which are determined by market forces. It is one of three general dimensions of stratification seen as important by LOCKWOOD (1958 and 1966) and GOLDTHORPE and Lockwood (1968-69). For Marx, ownership or nonownership of the means of production were ultimately decisive in determining a person's overall class position. In Lockwood and Goldthorpe's analysis, strongly influenced by WEBER (see CLASS; CLASS, STATUS AND PARTY), three interrelated dimensions of social stratification must always be taken into account: WORK SITUATION, STATUS SITUATION and 'market situation'. See also MULTIDIMENSIONAL ANALYSIS OF SOCIAL STRATIFICATION.

marriage a socially acknowledged and sometimes legally ratified union between an adult male and an adult female. Some preindustrial societies recognize POLYGAMY, either POLYGYNY in which a man may be married to more than one woman, or, much more rarely, POLYANDRY, in which a woman may be married to more than one man. MONOGAMY, however, is by far the most common form of marriage, even in societies where polygamy is permitted. See also KINSHIP, FAMILY, SOCIOLOGY OF THE FAMILY.

In preindustrial societies marriage has been regulated by kin relationships and has for the most part reflected kin interests. Expectations would be either to marry within the group (ENDOGAMY), or in other societies the contrary, EXOGAMY. Within industrial societies personal choice is more prominent, with the idea of ROMANTIC LOVE, or 'affective individualism', having great influence. Choice of marital partner, however, would appear to operate generally within a narrow social range.

Another marital form increasingly found in industrial societies is *cohabitation,* where a male and female live together in a sexual relationship without marrying, although often as a prelude to marriage. On a much smaller scale there are also 'gay' (both LESBIAN and HOMOSEXUAL) marriages and communal arrangements.

The sociological study of marriage in industrial societies has a number of preoccupations currently, including:

(a) marriage rates – the number of adults that are married as a proportion of the adult population. This is a figure that seems to be influenced by a range of factors, including age at marriage, changes in FERTILITY, longevity, MIGRATION, wars and broad economic circumstances including the changing patterns in the employment of married women;

(b) the distribution of power within the marital relationship. The evidence is that this may be changing slowly. Across all social classes, however, the evidence is that economic and locational decisions are still made by men. The SYMMETRICAL FAMILY remains exceptional;

(c) the 'discovery' of violence within marriage. This has led to a substantial body of research revealing the widespread abuse of women within marriage in many societies and in all social classes (see WIFE BATTERING). Such studies have provided part of the feminist critique of the institutions of both marriage and the family;

(d) the factors affecting remarriage. Within industrial societies, remarriage is increasing among the divorced and the widowed. This phenomenon has led to the recognition of a new familial form, namely the *reconstituted family* (or stepfamily) involving the coming together of partners who bring with them the offspring of earlier relationships. Despite the growth in the divorce rate, remarriage in most industrial societies is increasingly popular, giving rise to the notion of *serial monogamy.*

marriage certificate a certificate issued on the registration of a couple's marriage. First issued in 1837 in England and Wales, it shows the full name of each marriage partner, their ages, occupations and addresses, and the names and occupations of their fathers. Marriage certificates not only provide the sociologist with a source of data with which to examine marriage patterns, but also enable matters such as occupational mobility to be examined. See also BIRTH CERTIFICATE, DEATH CERTIFICATE.

Marshall, Thomas H. (1893–1981) British sociologist who trained first as a historian, and whose discussion of citizenship and CITIZEN RIGHTS, *Citizenship and Class* (1950), remains the starting point of most modern discussions of the subject (see also CITIZEN). Marshall was interested in exploring the implications of an expansion of citizenship rights and welfare rights for class relations, and likewise, the implications of a continuation of class divisions and a capitalist economy for citizenship: a clash between democracy and egalitarianism in the civil and political realm and non-democracy and inequality in the economic realm. Commentators have sometimes regarded Marshall as over-sanguine in his judgement of the benefits flowing from the expansion of citizenship in modern Western societies. More recently, especially with the advent of THATCHERISM, his emphasis on the importance of citizen and welfare rights in establishing social fairness and in contributing to the maintenance of political legitimacy in these societies has increasingly been regarded as sound. His many essays on these topics and on the importance of an historical perspective in the understanding of modern society are collected together in *Sociology at the Crossroads* (1963).

Marx, Karl (1818–83)

German philosopher, economist and revolutionary. Of Jewish descent, he was born in Trier in the Rhineland and educated at the universities of Bonn and Berlin where he studied philosophy and law. At Berlin he came under the influence of HEGEL's philosophy and associated with a group of radical democrats who were trying to fashion the critical side of that philosophy to attack the Prussian state. This association cost Marx a post in the state-dominated university system. Thus began a career as an independent scholar, journalist and political activist which he pursued in the Rhineland, in travels throughout Europe from 1843, and thereafter in London, where he settled from 1849. In 1864 he participated in the establishment of the International Working Men's Association (the First International). The main works by Marx (sometimes written in association with ENGELS) include: *Poverty of Philosophy* (1847), *Communist Manifesto* (1848), *Grundrisse* (written 1857–58, first published only in 1939–41), *A Contribution to the Critique of Political Economy* (1859), *Capital* (volume 1, published in 1867, with volumes 2 and 3 published only after Marx's death).

Conventionally Marx's thought is held to derive from three main sources:
(a) French socialist thought, not least that of SAINT-SIMON, with whose work Marx was familiar before he went to university;
(b) Hegel's philosophy, the principles of which Marx modified but never entirely disavowed;
(c) English POLITICAL ECONOMY, on which Marx built but also went beyond. Experience of social conditions gained on his travels, and contact with radical and communist groups and individuals, notably Engels, with whom he formed a lifelong friendship and intellectual partnership from

1846, also played a part in Marx's transformation from a radical democrat to a communist revolutionary.

Marx's overall intellectual project encompassed several objectives. Briefly, he sought:
(a) to understand and explain the human condition as he found it in capitalist society;
(b) to lay bare the dynamic of that society and to lift the veil on its inner working and impact on human relations;
(c) to obtain a theoretical grasp of the mechanisms at work in the overall process of historical change in which capitalism was but a phase.

These projects were realized, albeit imperfectly, in Marx's philosophical, economic and political writings. These were not in any strict sense sociological, and Marx did not claim that they were. Nevertheless his thought has had a profound impact on the development of sociology; it has provided the point of departure for a wide-ranging tradition of scholarship and research, and has stimulated productive critical reactions from non-Marxist scholars.

Marx's efforts were informed by the belief that it was necessary not only to study society, but to change it. He had no hesitation, therefore, in making social science subserve the ends of the social liberation which he sought. Essentially he saw the human condition under capitalism (see CAPITALISM AND CAPITALIST MODE OF PRODUCTION) as being characterized by ALIENATION, a condition in which human beings were estranged from their world, and from their work, products, fellow creatures and themselves.

Alienation was an early preoccupation of Marx; it did not figure much in his later work which was concerned to provide an analysis of the inner workings of the capitalist economy framed against the background of a theory of history known as the 'materialist conception of history' (see HISTORICAL MATERIALISM). The theory is so called because it rests on the view that the economy is a primary influence on the formation and development of social structures, and on the ideas which people hold about themselves and their societies. Before people can philosophize, play politics, create art, etc., they must produce economic necessities. To do this they must enter into social relations of production (see RELATIONS OF PRODUCTION). According to Marx, economic relations constitute the base of society on which is erected the superstructure of non-economic institutions, the nature and scope of which are substantially determined by the base (see BASE AND SUPERSTRUCTURE). It is on account of this argument that critics have sometimes regarded Marx as simply an economic determinist. However, while occasionally ambiguous, Marx and Engels usually insisted that non-economic institutions, i.e. the state, religion, etc., were capable of playing a relatively autonomous role in social development. Nevertheless, in 'the last analysis', it is the productive relationships into which people enter that exercise the decisive influence. This is because the relations of production become CLASS relations, and because class relations are the constitutive bases of both social structure and social change.

Class was thus fundamental to Marx's analysis, though strangely he never provided a definitive definition of the concept. Clearly it is an economic category; classes are formed by groups of people who share a common interest by virtue of the fact that they stand together in a common relationship to the means of production. Classes can only form when the productive activity of a society yields a surplus above the subsistence needs of its members. A dominant group can then wrest ownership of, and control over, the means of production, and constitute itself into a RULING CLASS OR DOMINANT CLASS. This class appropriates to its own use the surplus produced by the rest of society, the members of which are rendered a subordinate class, forced to put its labour at the disposal of the possessing group. Marx referred to the process of surplus extraction as EXPLOITATION. Exploitation is basic to all forms of class society, though it takes different forms.

Marx's theory speaks of different types of MODES OF PRODUCTION. These were conceived of as a developmental sequence, since each one marked an advance in humanity's productive capacity and hence its mastery over nature. Marx thus postulated a *primitive communist* ('classless') society which was replaced by a series of class societies resting successively on SLAVERY, FEUDALISM and capitalism. The motor of change was held to be CLASS CONFLICT generated by the constant development of the forces of production. In each mode of production the relations of production were maintained by the dominant class because they were best fitted to the forces of production at their level of development within that mode. Within each mode, however, the forces of production were developed in novel ways that gave rise to new class formations, class conflict and REVOLUTION. Conflict arose because the relations of production maintained by the dominant class tended to strangle novel developments, provoking the rising class associated with new development to overthrow the old system and replace it with a new one. Thus, concretely, the feudal relations of production (the lord-serf relationship) acted as a brake on the capitalism that was developing within the womb of feudal society. Capitalists, therefore, had to overthrow the feudal relationships and replace them with a new set of relations between themselves, as the dominant class, and the propertyless PROLETARIAT, as the subordinate class.

In his economic writings Marx sought to expose the inner workings of the capitalist system. His analysis (see LABOUR THEORY OF VALUE, SURPLUS VALUE) convinced him that the system was riven with contradictions which were bound to bring it down; for technical economic reasons, he held that capitalists would suffer from a declining rate of profit, and that the system would be subject to periodic crises of *overproduction* (see CRISES OF CAPITALISM, ORGANIC COMPOSITION OF CAPITAL, TENDENCY TO DECLINING RATE OF PROFIT). Its ultimate downfall, however, seemed guaranteed by the antagonism that resulted from the conflict of interests between the working-class proletariat and the capitalist BOURGEOISIE.

Although Marx was aware of the existence of INTERMEDIATE CLASSES in capitalist society, his analysis convinced him that society was increasingly polarizing into two great hostile classes, the bourgeoisie and the proletariat. This antagonism resulted from an objective conflict of interest between the two groups; the bourgeoisie exploited the proletariat by paying less than the value of their labour, and through their private ownership of the means of production, frustrated the collective, social interest in the rational development of the productive forces at the disposal of society. Once the working class became conscious of these facts, Marx predicted that it would act to overthrow capitalist society and establish a new form of *classless society.*

The importance of 'human consciousness' needs to be emphasized within Marx's analysis. Revolutions did not happen automatically, and classes must become conscious of their interests before they could play their historic roles in the process of moving society forward. Marx held that consciousness developed as a reflection of the material conditions of existence to which classes were subject, though he recognized that ruling classes were capable of obstructing the development of consciousness in subordinate classes. The class which dominated economically also dominated in other spheres of life such as the state, politics, religion, etc. Thus it could also generate an IDEOLOGY, inducing a FALSE CONSCIOUSNESS which blinded the subordinate class to the true nature of the social relationships in which they were involved. Nevertheless Marx predicted the eventual victory of the proletariat in a revolution which would usher in a new era of human freedom.

That Marx's ideas should have been such a major factor in the Russian Revolution of 1917, in conditions he had not predicted, is a commentary on the power his ideas have exerted but is equally an indication of their weaknesses (see also COMMUNISM, SOCIALISM, LENIN, STALIN, STALINISM, STATE SOCIALISM).

Marx's social and economic analysis inspired generations of political activists, social critics and social scientists. Like Marx, they have emphasized that 'bourgeois' social science and social thought are often confined to 'appearances' and neither penetrate nor illuminate the true reality underpinning capitalist economic and social relationships. After Marx's death, especially in Soviet Marxism, aspects of Marx's ideas were taken to reveal the 'laws of motion of capitalist societies' (see DIALECTICAL MATERIALISM). Within Western Europe, the failure of the working class to combat FASCISM led politically committed Marxists (e.g. the FRANKFURT SCHOOL OF CRITICAL THEORY) to reappraise the working-class role in politics. More recently, Marxists have continued to differ fundamentally in their interpretations of Marx's thought. Some, such as ALTHUSSER, reject the philosophical, Hegel-influenced humanistic concerns of the early writings and insist that only the later writings with their scientific analyses of capitalist society are important. Others, for example E. P. THOMPSON (1978), dispute this, stressing both Marx's 'humanism' and the continuities in Marx's work.

Marx's output has also attracted much opposition and trenchant criticism. His economic writings and his evaluation of capitalist society have been widely challenged. His class analysis has been attacked on the grounds that it did not take sufficiently into account the rise of new 'middle class' groups, or affluence (see Parkin, 1979). This also suggests that his theory of social change and revolution is wrong. Marxists have responded by pointing out that Marx never set a time-scale for revolution, that the real worth of his analysis is in revealing the underlying mechanisms which sustain capitalism, but make its future uncertain. The resultant body of analysis shows that, notwithstanding criticism, the Marxist tradition remains an important and powerful influence within sociology, and within social science generally. See also MARXISM, MARXIST SOCIOLOGY, MARXIAN ECONOMICS.

Marxian economics the body of economic analysis deriving from the work of MARX, especially *Capital* (1867) (see also CLASSICAL ECONOMISTS). The distinctive approach of Marxian economists involves a general analysis of the long-run accumulation of capital, and developments and crises in the capitalist system (see CRISES OF CAPITALISM). While some Marxian economists apply Marx's own ideas rigidly, others, e.g. the work of Paul Baran and Paul Sweezy (1966), offer reinterpretations of these conceptions. For example, the LABOUR THEORY OF VALUE which is central in classical Marxist economics, is rejected by others, e.g. Pierre Sraffa (1960), Steedman et al. (1981), who nevertheless preserve many of Marx's essential insights compared with more orthodox economics (see also EXPLOITATION). Marxian economics has also been of particular importance in recent years in analysis of the world economy – see DEPENDENCY THEORY.

Marxism the total body of mainly theoretical work which aims to develop, amend or revise the original work of MARX by practitioners who identify themselves with the term. The term *Marxist* can be applied to such work or authors, but sometimes has a connotation of political commitment or activity which not all authors may share. Thus, for example, some academic sociologists may see themselves as working within the issues of Marxism, but reject the term Marxist because they do not share the political aims or commitments of Marxist organizations: *Marxian* may be the preferred description of their work. But there is variability in the use of these terms, in part reflecting the various nuances which have emerged within Marxism in the 20th-century, and the political problems which academics and intellectuals have had in various countries when identified with Marxism. 'I am interested in the problems of Marxism and find it philosophically and theoretically valid, but I am not a Marxist' might be how a Marxian sociologist would express the nuances.

It is only from the 1960s that Marxism has had a significant influence in Western Europe and the US within academic institutions (see MARXIST SOCIOLOGY). Before then, and outside of the Soviet bloc, Marxism's major developments came from intellectuals engaged in political organizations, and this influence continues alongside contributors in academia.

The main varieties of Marxism which have emerged in the 20th-century are:
(a) *Soviet Marxism,* which from the 1930s was dominated by STALINISM and developed a rigid 'scientific' and materialist view, seeing the natural sciences as the basic method of knowledge, but which became more varied after the death of Stalin;
(b) *Trotskyism* (see TROTSKY), which developed critical analyses of the nature of the USSR and of the changing nature of 20th-century capitalism, and which sees itself as the main heir of the *Marxist-Leninist* tradition, in terms of continuing to emphasize the importance of a revolutionary VANGUARD PARTY and the revolutionary potential of the working class;
(c) *Western Marxism,* which has been the main European intellectual current and most widely influential in academic spheres. Leading exponents were Antonio GRAMSCI, Karl Korsch (1886–1961), Georg LUKACS, Herbert MARCUSE and the FRANKFURT SCHOOL OF CRITICAL THEORY. All these were important for opening philosophical debates especially concerning the 'humanistic' or 'scientific' nature of Marxism, re-examining the Hegelian (see HEGEL) basis of Marxism, reacting to the crude materialism of Soviet Marxism, developing the analysis of culture, literature and psychology within Marxism, being more open to non-Marxist thought and attempting to incorporate it within Marxism. Examples of such work are Gramsci's analyses of the state and political processes, and Marcuse's use of Freudian analysis and SOCIAL PHENOMENOLOGY. From the 1960s, this current became more diverse within Europe, with the emergence of structuralist Marxism, especially from the work of Louis ALTHUSSER, who reacted against the perceived 'voluntarism' and 'humanism' of the earlier writers, and the rise of a renewed emphasis on Marxist political economy and the analysis of the dynamics of capitalism;
(d) *Third World Marxism,* concerned especially with exploring the differences between capitalism in the metropolitan and in the colonial and neocolonial countries, the relationship between national determination and the achievement of socialism, the role of the peasantry in the achievement of socialism, and the consequences of these questions for political action and organizations. These analyses showed that the predominant European varieties of Marxism did not provide adequate answers to these problems, and a large body of theoretical and political work has emerged on this from the 1920s. From Indian Marxists have come important analyses of the nature of colonial society and the peculiarities of capitalism within imperially dominated countries (see IMPERIALISM). From China emerged the theory and politics of MAOISM. From Latin America have come Marxist-inspired analyses of world capitalist development (see DEPENDENCY THEORY) and the political practice of *Castroism,* as a result of the experience of organizing revolutionary activity amongst the peasantry in prolonged guerrilla warfare; from Africa has come the theory of African Socialism (see SOCIALISM). Many countries contain major Marxist writers and thinkers who have contributed to a wide range of issues but who are mainly influential in their own society or region.

The above does not exhaust all the varieties

of Marxism. In Eastern Europe in the 1970s, important analyses developed countering the official Soviet communism (e.g. see NEW CLASS). Everywhere the growth of academic work has led to intense debate such that in academia there now exist many varieties of Marxism. Political beliefs, philosophical criteria, as well as questions of sociological relevance influence how these are viewed, but undoubtedly Marxism is now an important dimension of social scientific and sociological thinking, raising many questions not raised in other approaches.

Marxist-Leninism see COMMUNISM.

Marxist sociology approaches within academic sociology which utilize MARXISM. These grew in importance particularly in the 1960s in Europe and the US as a reaction to the perceived dominance of STRUCTURAL-FUNCTIONALISM and the political conservatism of established sociology. In the 20th century, the intellectual development of Marxism had taken place mainly outside academic institutions and was of limited direct influence in the social sciences. In the 1960s, there was wider questioning of the consensus models of society and of the presumed evolutionary nature of social change. Marxist sociology developed not just around conflict models of society and revolutionary models of social change (see CONFLICT THEORY), but also around methodological challenges. The assumed VALUE NEUTRALITY of orthodox social science was seen to be undermined by its privileged position within society and its practitioners' roles as advisors to large organizations and governments: 'The professional eyes of the sociologists are on the down people, and the professional palm of the sociologist is stretched towards the up people' (Nicolaus, 1972).

For some critics, the logic of this argument meant that Marxist sociology was a contradiction in terms: the academic pursuit of abstract knowledge divorced from the class struggle could only hinder socialist political ends. Others argued that Marxist academics had a political role through counteracting 'bourgeois ideology' within academic institutions and influencing future generations of students. The predominant approach, however, has been to utilize Marxist theory to develop a more adequate social science and to make that knowledge available to political groups.

During the 1970s and 80s, Marxist work had a wide influence within, first, sociology and historical studies, and then the other social sciences and literary studies. Often the debates were taken up in an eclectic fashion, so that the widespread use of Marxian concepts and ideas no longer necessarily reflected a political commitment to socialism or any identification of the user as a Marxist. See also AUSTRO-MARXISM, ANDERSON.

masculinity

the characteristics associated with the male sex. The historical study of masculinity documents 'manliness' as a code of conduct, heroism, strength, emphasis upon the public nature of man as natural, and monolithic dimensions of masculinity relating to objectivity, reason and CIVILIZING PROCESSES. Since the late 1970s masculinity has been studied in relation to continuity and change in its perceived forms and in relation to gender relations and sexual politics (Roper and Tosh, 1991; Brittan, 1989). The growing men's movement is giving voice to some of the differences and similarities between men in reflecting upon and defining interrelationships between men, masculinities, the women's movement and society (Seidler, 1991).

Of great importance to these debates is the interface with FEMINISM and the women's movement and the focus upon PATRIARCHY, power, male violence and oppression (Samuels, 1993). Samuels points out that since the early 1980s there has been an explosion of books on men's issues. In his examination of the men's movement he notes four overlapping dimensions: the experiential, the sociopolitical, the mythopoetic and the gay men's movements. The experiential is therapeutic in style, offering a chance to feel, cry, hug and confess. The sociopolitical is founded upon the notion that men should learn from feminism and work towards cooperative and non-hierarchical ways of achieving equality. There has been an increasing emphasis upon gender relations, power and sexual politics, most notably in the work of Robert Connell (1987). The mythopoetic movement is led by Robert Bly whose book *Iron John* (1990) uses a Grimm's fairy tale to develop the thesis that men need to regain contact with their spiritual, primal, Dionysian, 'hairy' selves. Men can be tough, decisive and gentle. In relation to the gay men's movement, Samuels points out that HOMOSEXUALITY is a recent category, that a thriving gay community undermines a social system that deploys HETEROSEXUALITY to maintain the control of women and that there are links to be made between the gay community and the sociopolitical dimensions to the men's movement(s). Hearn (1990; 1992), located within the sociopolitical movement and a leading theorist on masculinities and their relation to feminism and male violence, states that the category of men through 'absence, avoidance, ambivalence and alterity' becomes a taken-for-granted presence and central to the reproduction of dominant malestream ideologies and social practices. Men are the 'one' to women's 'other'(de BEAUVOIR, 1953). For Hearn, more careful work needs to be done on the interrelation of men's agency, subjectivity and practice and its relationship to men's structural power in reproducing that power and in potentially abolishing it.

Maslow, Abraham (1908–1970) American psychologist and member of the HUMANISTIC MOVEMENT in psychology, who developed a theory of motivation which was based on a *hierarchy of needs* (*Motivation and Personality*, 1954). He proposed that human needs can be categorized as: physiological, safety, love and belonging, esteem, and SELF-ACTUALIZATION. Higher needs cannot become important to the individual until lower needs have been satisfied. In *Towards a Psychology of Being* (1962) Maslow discussed how the uniqueness of the individual can be developed towards fulfilment, or *self-actualization*. This involves the achieving of potential, the fulfilling of *being needs* (which are distinguished from the *deficiency needs* of the lower levels of his hierarchy). To define his concept of self-actualization Maslow looked at the lives and personalities of people he considered to be self-actualized. He suggested that such people have greater acceptance of self and others, greater identification with humanity generally, higher levels of creativity and heightened perception, particularly of the natural world. Heightened awareness leads to *peak experiences* during which the individual feels 'at one' with the world.

Maslow's ideas have been taken up by a number of social philosophers and sociologists.

mass see MASS SOCIETY, ÉLITE THEORY.

mass communication see MASS MEDIA OF COMMUNICATION.

mass culture relatively standardized and homogeneous cultural products, and the associated cultural experiences, designed to appeal to large audiences.

One important conception of mass culture is the idea that goods mass-produced for consumption (including even gramophone records, reprints of great art, etc.) provide inherently inferior experiences. This has a long history, and is seen in the perspectives of literary critics such as F. R. Leavis, or neo-Marxists such as ADORNO, HORKHEIMER and BENJAMIN (see also MASS SOCIETY). In general, sociologists have dissented from such extreme views, usually regarding mass culture as a far more complex phenomenon. See POPULAR CULTURE, CULTURAL STUDIES.

mass customization mass means of production able to meet the highly *specific* individual needs of customers (compare MASS PRODUCTION). Mass customization has become possible as the result of NEW TECHNOLOGY – see also FLEXIBLE PRODUCTION, JUST-IN-TIME MANAGEMENT. The ability to differentiate products and markets is widely seen as one defining feature of a POSTMODERN social formation. Developments in E-COMMERCE may ultimately lead to a digitalized production and distribution system which collapses the distinction between manufacturing and services. Mass customization is part of what is meant by POSTINDUSTRIAL SOCIETY and a culture of POSTMODERNITY.

mass higher education any national system of HIGHER EDUCATION which has moved from 'élite' provision catering for only a small minority of the relevant age group, to one which allows for an ever-expanding mass entry, ultimately including the majority of the population. In the UK in the 1950s, when no more than 5% of the age group entered higher education, opponents of expansion argued that, as Kingsley Amis put it, 'more will mean worse'. However, in the UK and elsewhere élitist conceptions of higher education have generally lost ground to the proponents of mass higher education.

In the US and Japan participation in higher education already exceeds 50% of the relevant age group, and is expanding rapidly elsewhere. By the early 1990s, the proportion of school leavers entering higher education in the UK had increased to around 30%. The consequences of mass higher education, according to Martin Trow (1962), are that, at around 15% participation, 'élite' standards and patterns of provision can no longer be sustained across the entirety of a national system. The outcome has usually been a more 'differentiated' system of higher education. In the US an example of an extended hierarchy of many different types and levels of higher education exists, including the highest ranked research universities, and Ivy League colleges and universities, on the one hand, to the lowest ranked, community and two-year colleges on the other. The implications of such a transformation and differentiation of higher education for EQUALITY OF OPPORTUNITY in higher education and in subsequent employment are complex (see BINARY SYSTEM, CREDENTIALISM, SCREENING, GRADUATE LABOUR MARKET) as are many other features of the transformation of higher education. See POSTCAPITALISM and POSTCAPITALIST SOCIETY, INFORMATION SOCIETY.

massification see MASS SOCIETY.

mass media of communication the techniques and institutions through which centralized providers broadcast or distribute information and other forms of symbolic communication to large, heterogeneous and geographically dispersed *audiences*. The first medium of mass communication arrived with the invention of moveable type in the mid-15th century, but costs, government restrictions and low levels of literacy kept readerships both small and relatively specialized until the second half of the

19th-century, when the technologies and organizational forms devised to produce and sell goods were applied to the marketing and distribution of information and entertainment. First, the production of books and newspapers was transformed, and then in the 20th century, came the invention of the gramophone, radio, the cinema, and TELEVISION and video.

Today, the mass media are highly important economic, political and social institutions, in developed as well as developing societies. They are often large-scale organizations whose ownership is concentrated in the hands of the state or in the hands of a relatively small number of proprietors and shareholders, often with financial interests in several media. They make a significant contribution to the Gross National Product and exert a central influence on cultural forms. The occupational culture of media workers stresses the role they play in providing entertainment, information, and upholding the principles of free speech and the right to know, all of which are depicted as cornerstones of democratic societies. Critics, however, argue that the media do not operate simply as neutral channels of communication, but are actors in the cultural and political process and structurally allied to the powerful on whose behalf they can sometimes be seen as engineering consent. In reality, the influence of the mass media is complex and many-sided. See also SOCIOLOGY OF MASS COMMUNICATIONS, ADVERTISING, SEMIOTICS, CULTURAL STUDIES, GLASGOW MEDIA GROUP, CONSUMER CULTURE, POPULAR CULTURE, MASS SOCIETY, LEISURE, MORAL PANIC, HEGEMONY.

Mass Observation a research organization established in 1936–37 by Charles Madge and Tom Harrison, which continued during World War II and has recently been revived. It conducted social surveys by asking volunteer observers to write reports on their own and others' experiences, to keep diaries, and to answer QUESTIONNAIRES. In general, the approach was qualitative and unsystematic, which raised doubts about the representativeness of its findings.

mass production the production of long runs of standardized products for a mass market. This so-called 'Fordist' form of production was associated with a well-developed division of labour and a tendency to routinization of the LABOUR PROCESS. Subsequently, under post-Fordism, with the introduction of computer technology and more flexible production systems, mass production is disappearing (see FORDISM AND POST-FORDISM, FLEXIBLE PRODUCTION).

mass society a model of society which pessimistically depicts the social transformation brought about by modernization (e.g. urbanization, the democratization of politics and the growth of mass communications and popular education) as involving a process in which individuals become:

(a) increasingly detached from previous social groupings, i.e. a process of social fragmentation and atomization;

(b) increasingly open to commercial and political manipulation by centralized ÉLITES.

This process in which people are increasingly treated *en masse* is also referred to as the *massification* of society.

Diversity in the intellectual and political orientations of writers using the concept has resulted in a variety of theoretical meanings. However, general themes are a decline in social VALUES and COMMUNITY, a lack of moral core, and growing levels of social alienation. Because relationships between people are weakened the suggestion is that they become vulnerable to manipulative forces, to proposed simple solutions to problems, and to lowest common denominator forms of MASS CULTURE (forms of culture produced, sold and consumed in the same way as any other commodities for the masses). Theorists on the right (e.g. T. S. Eliot, 1948) have generally emphasized the threat to élite forms of 'high culture' presented by mass culture, and a loss of the social continuities associated with rule by traditional élites.

While also echoing some of these themes, theorists on the left (e.g. members of the FRANKFURT SCHOOL OF CRITICAL THEORY) have focused instead on the new opportunities for political manipulation of the masses by right-wing forces (e.g. FASCISM) and the general seductiveness of commercial forms of mass culture in incorporating the working class within CAPITALISM. More generally, in a now classical modern discussion, C. Wright MILLS contrasts modern forms of 'mass society' with a situation in which multiple 'publics' once existed. Mills argued that in a mass society':

(a) 'far fewer people express opinions than receive them';

(b) channels of opinion are relatively few and centrally controlled;

(c) the autonomy social actors once possessed in the formation of opinion is increasingly lost.

The heyday of the concept of mass society was in the period immediately before and after World War II. Subsequent research and theorizing has tended to suggest that the concept was too sweeping. Thus although, for example, it was influential in the early years of mass communications research (see MASS MEDIA OF COMMUNICATION), this research has resulted in studies which have demonstrated that the audience for the mass media is not an undifferentiated 'mass', that the manipulative power of the media is relatively limited and that the growth of POPULAR CULTURE did not occur at the expense of art or community (see also TWO-STEP FLOW OF MASS COMMUNICATIONS, LAZARSFELD). Similarly, research into forms of political behaviour and political participation in modern Western democratic societies has revealed no overall tendency to 'mass society' (see also PLURALISM).

material culture 1 'those aspects of CULTURE which govern the production and use of artefacts' (DOUGLAS, 1964).
2 the material products or artefacts actually produced by societies.

Debate about the reference of the term has focused on whether the objects or the ideas and social arrangements associated with the objects should be central. However, the study of material culture is bound to be concerned with the artefacts produced by a society, especially including its implements for the collection and hunting of food and the cultivation of plants, its modes of transportation, its means of housing and clothing, its techniques of food preparation and cooking, its art, and its magical and religious paraphernalia. An important part of sociology and social anthropology, the study of material culture is even more central in ARCHAEOLOGY, given that it has little to study but artefacts. See also CULTURAL MATERIALISM.

materialism (PHILOSOPHY) 1 the doctrine that nothing exists that is not 'matter'.
2 the doctrine that 'matter' is primary and thought or consciousness is secondary.

For either of these definitions the major contrast is IDEALISM. However, problems exist in saying exactly of what 'matter' consists, especially given the considerable uncertainty surrounding many of the entities, forces, etc. which populate modern scientific thinking. It has been suggested that the best way to identify the issues that lead to a materialist position (in sense 1 or 2) is to say what materialism opposes. One central position is an opposition to DUALISM, especially a dualism of MIND and BODY (see also DESCARTES). A main argument for opposition is the obscurity of notions such as Descartes' notion of the 'mind'. as an 'immaterial', non-extended, 'thinking substance'. The position of 'identity theorists', for example, is that any 'mind state' assumes a corresponding neurophysiological state (even if it is recognized that a particular mind state can never in practice be reduced analytically). Thus the goal of materialism is to head off any claims for a wholly separate, wholly immaterial realm. At the same time, the mind may be conceived (as for Bhaskar, 1979, 'emergent powers materialism') as a substance which is neither material or

immaterial; not a substance, but a complex of non-reducible powers. Compare also REALISM. See also HISTORICAL MATERIALISM and CULTURAL MATERIALISM, which usually involve MATERIALISM in senses 1 and 2, but are more concerned to make a statement about the fundamental nature of the causation of social phenomena:
(a) for *historical materialism*, the MODE OF PRODUCTION (the FORCES and the RELATIONS OF PRODUCTION) is the primary determinant of the constitutive role of human consciousness in producing and reproducing social life;
(b) for *cultural materialism*, ecological and environmental forces are decisive. See also DIALECTICAL MATERIALISM.

materialist interpretation of history see HISTORICAL MATERIALISM, ECONOMIC INTERPRETATION OF HISTORY.

maternal deprivation lack of contact between mother figure and child. The term was coined by BOWLBY (1958) who maintained that maternal deprivation in early life would lead to behavioural problems and delinquency in later childhood and adolescence. This link has subsequently been questioned, particularly by Rutter (*Maternal Deprivation Reassessed,* 1981), who argued that privation, rather than maternal deprivation, was the more likely cause of the problems shown by the children Bowlby studied.

mathematical sociology the use of mathematical procedures and mathematical models in sociology. The rationale for most mathematical sociology, as stated by James Coleman in *Introduction to Mathematical Sociology* (1964), is that: 'Mathematics provides a battery of languages, which when carefully fitted to a set of ideas, can lend these ideas great power'. Usually mathematical sociologists do not operate with the expectation that high-level, mathematically expressed general laws will be established in sociology. Rather they have made more limited claims that mathematics can be employed to good effect in illuminating areas of social life.

Examples of mathematical approaches which have enjoyed some influence in sociology are:
(a) the THEORY OF GAMES, deriving from the work of Herbert Simon and others;
(b) probabilistic *stochastic process models,* e.g. Markov chains, used in the modelling of population processes and social mobility (see Coleman, 1964);
(c) CAUSAL MODELLING, arising especially from the work of Blalock (1961);
(d) applications of 'finite' ('non-quantitative') mathematical models, as in Harrison White's analysis of the formal properties of kinship structures (*Anatomy of Kinship* 1953);
(e) applications of mathematical *graph theory* in the analysis of social networks (see P. Doreian, *Mathematics in the Study of Social Relations,* 1970).

The boundaries between mathematical sociology and STATISTICS AND STATISTICAL ANALYSIS are not easily drawn, but one distinction is that, while statistical analysis uses relatively standardized procedures, making standardized assumptions about the character of data, mathematical sociology uses a wider array of mathematical procedures and is more likely to involve the construction of theoretical models intended to achieve a more direct, more purpose-built, modelling of the area of social reality under analysis.

matriarchy any social organization based on female POWER. The literal meaning refers to the rule of the mother as head of the family, and can therefore be contrasted with the term PATRIARCHY, referring to the rule of the father.

The term is subject to much dispute both within the discipline of sociology and within feminist theory. Historically, the term was adopted by a number of 19th-century anthropologists and social theorists concerned with the origins of social organization and the family. Bachofen (1861) argued that the original family structure was matriarchal. In 1865 McLennan published *Primitive Marriage* in which he claimed that the origins of social organization were characterized by a matriarchal structure. ENGELS, influenced by the work of Lewis Henry MORGAN, wrote *The Origin of the Family, Private Property and the State* (1884) in which he argued that the primitive matriarchal clan predated patriarchy. Engels believed that the overthrow of 'mother right' led to the defeat of the female sex and culminated in the institution of the patriarchal family. Both women and children were thereby subordinated to the power and control of adult men. Thence arose the monogamous family unit based on the supremacy of the man. The main purpose of this unit was to produce heirs of undisputed paternity. Such accounts of the origins of social organization were disputed by writers such as Henry MAINE (*Ancient Law*, 1861) who argued that the original form of social organization was a corporate family group ruled over by a despotic patriarch. Such debates have assumed fresh impetus with the rise of feminist anthropology and feminist sociology. Much interest has been directed at the work of Engels as providing a possible explanation of the roots of female oppression, although recognized as flawed.

Debates continue as to whether matriarchal societies ever existed. Radical FEMINISM has focused more attention on this issue than other strands of feminist thought. Radical feminists argue that such societies did exist but patriarchal history has erased knowledge of them. The Greek island of Lesbos, 600 BC, is taken as an indication of the existence of a matriarchal era.

Within contemporary feminist thought, wider meanings of the term denote female supremacy, female-focused or female-orientated societies, and women-centred culture.

matrilateral *or* **uterine** (ANTHROPOLOGY) a KINSHIP term referring to relation on the mother's side. The opposite is PATRILATERAL. A system which recognizes both lines in DESCENT is termed BILATERAL DESCENT.

matrilineal descent *or* **uterine descent** (ANTHROPOLOGY) a UNILINEAL system of tracing DESCENT through females. This form of descent does not necessarily mean that women hold political or economic power; such a system would be called a MATRIARCHY. Early Victorian anthropologists suggested that this was the original form of descent, but it now appears that there is no evidence for this. The opposite is PATRILINEAL DESCENT.

matrilocal *or* **uxorilocal** the residence of a married couple with the wife's kin. Often this specifically means with the wife's mother, but not always, so the synonym 'uxorilocal' is often used to distance it from MATRILINEAL DESCENT.

Mauss, Marcel (1872–1950) French social anthropologist who collaborated with Emile DURKHEIM in the editorship of the ANNÉE SOCIOLOGIQUE and influenced LÉVI-STRAUSS. Among his most important studies are *Primitive Classification* (with Durkheim, 1902) and *The Gift* (1925). See GIFT EXCHANGE.

Mayo, Elton (1880–1949) a prominent figure within the HUMAN RELATIONS SCHOOL, who was associated with and wrote about the HAWTHORNE EFFECT. The interpretations he made of the Hawthorne experiments made him an influential figure within the human relations tradition. Echoing DURKHEIM, he felt that scientific and technical developments had outstripped the social skills and social arrangements of man, one consequence of which was widespread ANOMIE. This was evident, for example, in the spontaneous organization of informal groupings within industry, as revealed by the Hawthorne research. Mayo consequently advocated the development of social skills for managers who would provide for, communicate with and sensitively lead small work groups in industry, since these would provide social anchorage and meaning for otherwise anomic workers. In this way hope was held out for the ability of industry to provide for a satisfying and cooperative venture in an otherwise debilitating and individualistic society.

His ideas have, to varying and debated degrees, influenced both managerial practice and ideology and subsequent social and psychological research in industry (Mayo, 1949; Bendix, 1974; Rose, 1988).

McDonaldization (of society) 'the process by which the principles of the fast-food restaurant are coming to dominate more and more sectors of American society as well as the rest of the world' (G. Ritzer, *The McDonaldization of Society,* 1993). The forces behind this tendency, as described by Ritzer, are 'efficiency', 'calculability' and 'predictability', manifest in 'increased control and the replacement of human by nonhuman technology'. There are contradictions in this process, not least a loss of 'quality', which has to be counteracted by defining the new products favourably in extensive advertising. But the 'advantages' of McDonaldization are such that its principles have spread to many areas, including higher education. For a critique see B. Smart, *Resisting McDonaldization,*Sage, 1999.

Mead, George Herbert (1863–1931), US Pragmatist philosopher, sociologist and social psychologist, based at the University of Chicago, whose approach to sociology is today most identified with SYMBOLIC INTERACTIONISM. Mead termed his approach to sociology and social psychology 'social behaviourism' to distinguish it from the more orthodox psychological BEHAVIOURISM of Watson. Influenced especially by his fellow Pragmatist philosopher DEWEY and by Charles COOLEY, Mead's sociology and psychology emphasized the conscious mind and the self-awareness and self-regulation of SOCIAL ACTORS. In Mead's view, the SELF emerges from social interaction in which human beings, in 'taking the role of the other', internalize the attitudes of real and imagined others (see SIGNIFICANT OTHER). Drawing on Cooley's concept of the LOOKING-GLASS SELF, he postulated that the 'I' (myself as I am) is involved in a continual interaction with the 'Me' (myself as others see me). The 'Me' represents the attitudes of the social group, the GENERALIZED OTHER, and through role-taking in play and 'imaginative rehearsal' of interaction we internalize the group's values as our own. By continually reflecting on ourselves as others see us we become competent in the production and display of social symbols. Human nature is seen by Mead as part of evolution and nature, but the importance of language and symbolic communication as an aspect of this evolution is such as to free human action from natural determinism. Mead can be seen to represent the epitome of CHICAGO SCHOOL sociology in his attempt to articulate the relationship between the self and society. Herbert BLUMER took over Mead's lectures on his death, refined his social theory and coined the term SYMBOLIC INTERACTIONISM. Mead's main works, collected essays and lectures, all published after his death, are Mind, Self and Society (1932), The Philosophy of the Act (1938), and The Philosophy of the Present (1959). See also PRAGMATISM.

Mead, Margaret (1901–78) US CULTURAL ANTHROPOLOGIST. Major works include *Coming of Age in Samoa* (1928), *Growing Up in New Guinea* (1930), *Sex and Temperament in Three Primitive Societies* (1935). Her early work was concerned to illustrate that gendered patterns of behaviour were culturally, not biologically, determined. Her research into patterns of child-rearing was particularly influential in the NATURE-NURTURE DEBATE and instrumental in co-founding the US CULTURE AND PERSONALITY school. Her later work was concerned with applying the insights gained from her anthropology to US society, and though the accuracy of her ethnographies has been much criticized, her activities as an early feminist and reformer are still significant.

mean see MEASURES OF CENTRAL TENDENCY.

meaningful interpretation see MEANINGFUL UNDERSTANDING AND EXPLANATION.

meaningful social action *or* **meaningful action** see ACT OF ACTION, INTERPRETATION, VERSTEHEN, HERMENEUTICS, INTERPRETATIVE SOCIOLOGY.

meaningful sociology any form of sociology premised on the assumption:
(a) that social actors above all inhabit a universe of social 'meanings';
(b) that SOCIAL ACTION is *meaningful action*; and
(c) that social occurrences must be explained primarily as the outcome of actors' 'meanings', i.e. the beliefs, motives, purposes, reasons, etc. that lead to ACTIONS. The term is commonly applied to WEBER'S ACTION THEORY, but can equally apply to related approaches such as SYMBOLIC INTERACTIONISM. See also MEANINGFUL UNDERSTANDING AND EXPLANATION, INTERPRETATIVE SOCIOLOGY, VERSTEHEN.

meaningful understanding and explanation the comprehension of SOCIAL ACTORS' meanings (i.e. their beliefs, motives, purposes, reasons, etc. in any social context) which at one and the same time automatically constitute an explanation of their ACTIONS and of the social occurrences to which these give rise. See also VERSTEHEN, MEANINGFUL SOCIOLOGY, WEBER, WINCH, PURPOSIVE EXPLANATION, EMPATHY, INTERPRETATION, INTERPRETATIVE SOCIOLOGY.

means of production (MARXISM) the tools and machinery, plant, etc. used in production. In MARX's characterization of capitalism, the ownership and non-ownership of the means of production is central to his distinction between capitalists and proletarians. However, there exists a major ambiguity in Marxism as to whether the means of production (and the FORCES OF PRODUCTION, including the form and level of the technical development of the means of production) or the RELATIONS OF PRODUCTION have primacy in generating social transformations of the kind that are central in Marxism. Mostly, though with some exceptions (e.g. Cohen, 1978, who accords primacy to forces of production), theorists have emphasized the importance of an interaction between forces and relations of production.

measurement see CRITERIA AND LEVELS OF MEASUREMENT.

measurement by fiat 'measurement' (e.g. indirect indicators of a phenomenon) where 'we have only a prescientific or common-sense concept that on a priori grounds seems to be important but which we do not know how to measure directly' and, with some degree of arbitrariness, we impose a measure (W. Torgerson, *Theory and Method of Scaling*, 1958). CICOUREL (1964) has criticized such imposing of 'equivalence classes' without theoretical or empirical justification – a viewpoint influential in the establishment of ETHNOMETHODOLOGY.

measures of central tendency the different ways of conceptualizing the central or middle position of a group of observations, numbers, etc. There are three measures of central tendency: the *mode*, the *median* and the *mean*. The *mode* is the value which occurs most *often*. The *median* is the value which occupies the central position, having as many values below as above it. The *mean* (more commonly called the *average*) is found by adding together each individual value and dividing by the number of cases, or observations.

Sometimes a set of observations will yield a *bimodal distribution* (where two different values occur most often). Also, if there is an even number of observations there is no central value to represent the median. In this case the median may be taken to lie midway between the two centrally placed values.

Where there are many values in the distribution the approximate value of the median can be calculated by *interpolation*. The data is first grouped into a set number of bands and the median is taken as lying within the middle group, its value being calculated mathematically by estimating its position from the percentage of cases lying in the lower and higher bands.

The choice of which measure of central tendency to employ is determined by two factors: the level of measurement (see CRITERIA AND LEVELS OF MEASUREMENT) being employed and the amount of dispersion in the set of observations. Where a nominal-level measure is being employed, only the mode should be calculated. For example, if numerical values have been assigned to different types of accommodation, then the mode will show which is the most popular type of accommodation, but both the mean and the median would be meaningless. The median is best used with ordinal-level measures where the relative distances between categories is unknown (although it should be said that many social scientists do use the mean when dealing with ordinal-level variables because of the large number of statistical tests which can then be undertaken). Finally, the mean is generally the best statistic to use with interval level measures, except in those instances in which there are a number of extreme values which *skew* the distribution. For example, the mean incomes of a group of respondents may be skewed because of the inclusion in the sample of a few high-income earners. In such instances the median is often a better statistic to employ. Another instance where the median might be calculated is where data has been grouped and the 'highest' category is open-ended. For example, income might have been grouped in such a way that all earning over £100,000 per annum are grouped together and there is no upper limit to the amount which people in the category earn. In such a case the mean cannot be calculated, but the value of the median can be estimated by the process of *interpolation* mentioned above. See also MEASURES OF DISPERSION.

measures of dispersion the different ways of calculating the extent to which a set of observations, numbers, etc., are clustered together round a central point. Measures of dispersion are closely related to MEASURES OF CENTRAL TENDENCY. There are six measures: the *range, variance, standard deviation, standard error, skew,* and *kurtosis.*

The *range* is the simplest measure of dispersion; it relates to the actual spread of values and is equal to the maximum less the minimum value.

The *variance* is a measure of the dispersion of a set of values from the mean, and should only be used with interval-level measures. It measures the extent to which individual values are clustered around the mean. It is calculated by averaging the squared deviations from the mean, and in so doing it takes into account both negative values and the existence of unduly low and unduly high values. A low variance suggests that there is a high degree of homogeneity in the value and high variance is an indication of a low degree of homogeneity.

The *standard deviation* is simply the square root of the variance. It is used in preference to the variance because it is easier to interpret, having a value in the range of the values from which it is derived.

The *standard error* is an estimation of the extent to which the mean of a given set of scores drawn from a sample differs from the true mean score of the whole population. It should only be used with interval-level measures.

The *skew* attempts to estimate the extent to which a set of measures deviates from the symmetry of a normal distribution curve, whether to the left or the right. Where measures tend to be located to the right of the curve its value is negative.

The *kurtosis* shows the extent to which the 'curve' of a set of observations is flatter or more peaked than the normal distribution, whose kurtosis is zero. A peaked (narrower) distribution has a positive value and a flatter curve has a negative value.

mechanical and organic solidarity the distinction drawn by Emile DURKHEIM (1893) between two types of SOCIAL SOLIDARITY: *mechanical solidarity,* based on the similarity between individuals, the form of solidarity predominant in simple and less advanced societies, and *organic solidarity,* based on the DIVISION OF LABOUR, and complementarities between individuals, the form of solidarity ideally occurring in modern advanced societies. Durkheim

	Mechanical solidarity based on resemblances (predominant in less advanced societies)	*Organic solidarity based on division of labour (predominant in more advanced societies)*
(1) Morphological (structural) basis	Segmental type (first clan-based, later territorial) Little interdependence (social bonds relatively weak) Relatively low volume of population Relatively low material and normal density	Organized type (fusion of markets and growth of cities) Much interdependence (social bonds relatively strong) Relatively high volume of population Relatively high material and moral density
(2) Type of norms (typified by law)	Rules with repressive sanctions Prevalence of penal law	Rules with restitutive sanctions Prevalence of cooperative law (civil, commercial, procedural, administrative and constitutional law)
(3) (a) Formal features of *conscience collective*	High volume High intensity High determinateness Collective authority absolute	Low volume Low intensity Low determinateness More room for individual initiative and reflexion
(3) (b) Content of *conscience collective*	Highly religious Transcendental (superior to human interests and beyond discussion) Attaching supreme value to society and interests of society as a whole Concrete and specific	Increasingly secular Human-orientated (concerned with human interests and open to discussion) Attaching supreme value to individual dignity, equality of opportunity, work ethic and social justice Abstract and general

Fig. 18 **Mechanical and organic solidarity.** A summary of Durkheim's ideal types (from Lukes, 1973)

formulated the distinction between the two types of solidarity by identifying the demographic and morphological features basic to each type, the typical forms of law, and formal features and content of the *conscience collective*, which ought to be associated with each type (see Fig. 18).

The reality, Durkheim argued, was that in modern societies organic solidarity was as yet imperfectly realized. See also INTEGRATION.

media see MASS MEDIA OF COMMUNICATION.

median see MEASURES OF CENTRAL TENDENCY.

media studies see SOCIOLOGY OF MASS COMMUNICATIONS.

mediated class locations dimensions of individual locations within the class structure which arise from people's kinship networks and family structures, rather than from a direct relation to the process of production (i.e. personal occupations or personal ownership of productive assets). The term is proposed by Wright (1989), but the importance of such locations in influencing class orientation and political behaviour has long been evident (e.g. GOLDTHORPE and LOCKWOOD, 1969a).

medicalization 1 (in a medical context) the extension of medical authority into areas where lay and common-sense understandings and procedures once predominated, e.g. childbirth, where a medical frame of reference devalues the woman's perspective by stressing active management by professionals in order to minimize risk to mother and child at the same time as evaluating the success of the outcome by, mainly, technical criteria.
2 (more generally) the tendency to view undesirable conduct as illness requiring medical intervention, thus extending the realm of medical judgements into political, moral and social domains.

The concept has been criticized for presenting medicine as a unitary institution, for presenting lay and medical frames of reference as mutually exclusive, and for stressing the social control dimension of medicine without acknowledging the social value of medical work. It is regarded as a valuable concept because it focuses on issues of professional power and ideological domination. See also SOCIOLOGY OF HEALTH AND MEDICINE.

medical sociology see SOCIOLOGY OF HEALTH AND MEDICINE.

members' methods see ETHNOMETHODOLOGY.

Memmi, Albert (1920–)Tunisian born Jew whose most famous contribution to post-colonial theory is *The Colonizer and the Colonized* (1957). He described this book as a 'portrait of the protagonists of the colonial drama and the relationship that binds them' (1957: 145). According to Memmi, the project of the colonizer affects the colonized population at every level of social and psychological organisation. Apart from exposing the racism that informs the structure of the colonial institution, Memmi also focused on the ideology of the colonizer's culture. That is, the systems of thought which advance the view of the colonized's sub-humanity and legitimate oppressive legislation. Following FANON's reading of French colonial rule, Memmi used HEGEL's theory of the master/slave dialectic in order to explore the psychological relationship between colonizer and colonized. Through the concept of the '*Nero Complex*' he argued that the colonizer's mastery is dependent on the domination of the colonized consciousness. In suggesting an escape from this parasitic relationship Memmi discussed the potential for revolutionary action. He argued that the revolt of the colonized population should be seen as the built-in conclusion to the colonial process. By fighting against the colonizer's rule the colonized must reject the knowledge and language of the dominant culture. They must assert their own identity in order to escape colonial alienation and overthrow the dominance of the colonizer's ideology. Memmi continues to contribute to POST-COLONIAL THEORY. His most recent text *Racism* (1999) expanded upon his previous work in order to discuss the mechanics of wider racist discourse.

Mendel, Gregor see GENETICS.

mental illness disease of the mind. Mental illness varies from transitory episodes of anxiety or depression (see NEUROSES) which interfere with normal daily living through the mood changes involved, to the PSYCHOSES which may require in-patient psychiatric treatment to control the severe changes in mood and behaviour associated with them.

A sociology of mental illness has developed as a response to epidemiological studies which have pointed to social causes of mental illness (e.g. depression and bad housing), and from the impetus of the theories of the anti-psychiatrists, such as LAING (1960) and Szasz (1961). See also ANTI-PSYCHIATRY, MADNESS.

mental labour see INTELLECTUAL LABOUR, MANUAL AND NON-MANUAL LABOUR.

mercantilism the economic doctrine of state power and the merchant class in the 16th and 17th centuries, in which foreign trade that gave rise to a trade surplus in bullion was regarded as the main indicator of national wealth. Under this doctrine, trade was controlled by state power. In the 19th century, the doctrine was overturned by the arguments of CLASSICAL ECONOMISTS, and replaced by the doctrine of free trade and LAISSEZ-FAIRE, although 'protectionism' and state intervention in the economy have often re-emerged as rival doctrines.

meritocracy a form of society in which educational and social success is the outcome of ability (measured by IQ) and individual effort. The notion, given prominence by Michael Young (*The Rise of the Meritocracy*, 1958), figured prominently in the work of Fabian socialists who did much to promote it as a guiding principle to legitimate the changes sought in the 1944 Education Act and the subsequent drive to secondary reorganization along comprehensive lines. Meritocracy emphasizes equality of competition rather than equality of outcome, assuming that positions in an occupational hierarchy will be obtained as a result of achievement on merit against universal, objective criteria, rather than on ascribed criteria of age, gender, race, or inherited wealth. No person of quality, competence or appropriate character should be denied the opportunity to achieve a commensurate social status. Essential to the concept of meritocracy is the belief that only a limited pool of talent exists and that it is an important function of the education system to see that such talent is not wasted but is developed and fostered. (See also FUNCTIONALIST THEORY OF SOCIAL STRATIFICATION).

The principle of meritocracy is by no means universally accepted. Young himself was ambivalent about some of its consequences, e.g. a denuding of working-class culture and working-class leadership. Major criticisms have also come from those who argue that genuine EQUALITY can only be achieved by the adoption of strategies which are designed to produce greater equality as an end product of the system rather than at its starting point. In any event, those advocating the meritocratic view have to resolve the recurring difficulty of devising objective measures of ability. See also INTELLIGENCE.

Merleau-Ponty, Maurice (1908–61) French existentialist and phenomenological philosopher and social theorist, influenced by HUSSERL, who also worked with de BEAUVOIR and SARTRE. Influenced also by MARXISM he was critical *both* of conceptions of DETERMINISM and conceptions of the ultimate AUTONOMY of the SUBJECT. In the *Phenomenology of Perception* (trans. 1962, originally 1945) he affirmed the existence of a world independent of consciousness but a world on which the conscious agent acts, endowing it with meaning and with form. See also BODY.

Merton, Robert (1910–2003) leading US sociologist, who was a student of PARSONS, and became an influential voice of functionalist sociology in his own right. He was a colleague of LAZARSFELD's, as associate director of the Bureau of Applied Research at Columbia, and in his work Merton has tried to bridge the divide between the abstract theory of Parsons and the empirical survey work that typified much of modern American sociology. Merton's alternative to these he referred to as THEORIES OF THE MIDDLE RANGE, theories that connected with and organized empirical data, and empirical research which tested theory. His most influential general work is the collection of essays *Social Theory and Social Structure* (1949, subsequently enlarged and revised). This contains a number of seminal essays, including 'Manifest and latent functions' (see also MANIFEST AND LATENT FUNCTION, UNANTICIPATED CONSEQUENCES (OF SOCIAL ACTION), POSTULATE OF FUNCTIONAL INDISPENSABILITY) and 'Social structure and anomie' (see ANOMIE, CRIME, DEVIANCE). In these essays, and in a succession of further essays and books, he lived up to his claims for middle-range theory by both providing critiques and codifications of theoretical approaches (most notably FUNCTIONALISM), and applications of these approaches in empirical analysis. Of his own empirical work, the most significant are perhaps his contributions to the study of BUREAUCRACY, the SOCIOLOGY OF SCIENCE, and SOCIOLOGY OF MASS COMMUNICATIONS, as well as to ROLE THEORY and the analysis of RELATIVE DEPRIVATION and REFERENCE GROUPS. The following joint-authored and edited books are among his more important: *Mass Persuasion* (1946), *Continuities in Social Research* (1950), *A Reader in Bureaucracy* (1952), *The Student Physician* (1957). Although all of these have been influential, his doctoral dissertation on science, *Science, Technology and Society in Seventeenth Century England*, was particularly so. First published in 1938, it built upon WEBER's thesis on the relationships between Protestantism and capitalism, and was the work which made his reputation. Merton's hypothesis was that the growth of scientific activity in the 17th-century was closely related to social forces, including Puritan religion; a perspective which led to a sea-change in both the historical and the sociological analysis of science. Subsequently, Merton also wrote important essays on science as a social institution and on modes of organization and competition in scientific work (see *The Sociology of Science*, 1979). Although in recent years Merton's commitment to functionalism and a 'natural science' model of sociological theories has been extensively criticized (e.g. GIDDENS, 1977), the importance of his wide-ranging contribution to sociology is undoubted.

messianic movement see MILLENARIANISM.

meta-analysis a method by which the results of a number of quantitative studies can be analysed together to produce an overall impression from a field of research. This method lays emphasis on EFFECT SIZE as well as providing a SIGNIFICANCE TEST for the results. It has advantages over a conventional review in that it forces the analyst to evaluate the method and the results of a study more critically and that it provides an objective method for synthesizing the results from such studies. There are two basic approaches to meta-analysis. The first and most common approach involves combining the results from the studies in order to produce a single effect size, inferential statistic and probability. The second approach involves comparing studies which differ over some aspect of their method to see if the results of studies which utilized one design or measure differ from the results of studies employing a different design or method. By combining the results of a number of studies, meta-analysis can circumvent the problems of low STATISTICAL POWER which may characterize the individual studies. (See Cooper; 1998; Cooper and Hedges, 1994; Rosenthal, 1991)

metanarrative see GRAND NARRATIVE AND METANARRATIVE.

metalanguage any 'second order' language used to discuss a language; any set or system of propositions about propositions.

metaphor the application of a descriptive phrase or term to a phenomenon to which it does not literally apply (see also ANALOGY). In organizational theory, for example, metaphor can be a significant vehicle for highlighting different forms of organization (e.g. Morgan, 1995).

The role of metaphor in sociology and the sciences generally is considerable (e.g. the notion of light waves as 'particles') and is arguably indispensable. The value of metaphor is in suggesting new relationships or new explanatory mechanisms. However, its use can be problematic if metaphors are taken literally and their applicability is not confirmed by independent evidence.

In the STRUCTURALISM of LACAN and the SEMIOLOGY of BARTHES, metaphor and METONYMY in which one signifier takes the place of another, are seen as playing a central role in the overall process of signification. See also MODEL.

Linguistic analysis focuses on the use of metaphor by noting the differentiation between the *Speaker Utterance Meaning* (SUM) and *Literal Sentence Meaning* (LSM). (Searle, 1979), the difference between the intended meaning of the metaphor when uttered and the received meaning. It is difficult to distinguish between such a metaphor as 'my dentist is a butcher' and utterances as part of everyday dialogue. In the final analysis, all words are metaphors; a means of representing and conveying thought processes. Precise and literal reception of transmitted words cannot be guaranteed. There is always likely to be a difference between LSM and SUM because of a basic incompatibility of sensory description.

metaphysics 1 the branch of philosophy that deals with first principles, e.g. questions of 'existence', 'being' (see ONTOLOGY) and 'knowing' (see EPISTEMOLOGY).
2 (pejoratively – in POSITIVISM) merely speculative, empirical (i.e. nonscientific) doctrines or theories.

metatheory all or any second-order accounts of theories or second-order theories of theories.

methodenstreit methodological dispute between NEO-KANTIANS and naturalists in late 19th-century Germany. The former asserted that the natural and cultural sciences were different in kind and therefore needed different methodologies, the latter that the same methodology would do for both. The methods of HERMENEUTICS and VERSTEHEN became theoretically articulated during this period (see also IDIOGRAPHIC AND NOMOTHETIC). Running to some extent in parallel with these disputes, there were also disputes between the historical and the neoclassical school in economics, and debates about the role of VALUE JUDGEMENTS and issues of value freedom (see VALUE FREEDOM AND VALUE NEUTRALITY; see also WEBER). The term *methodenstreit* has also latterly been applied to the dispute between POPPER and ADORNO (amongst others) in Germany in the 1960s. Popper presented a falsificationist model (see FALSIFICATIONISM) of politically neutral social science which was hotly contested by critical theorists (see FRANKFURT SCHOOL OF CRITICAL THEORY).

methodological anarchism see EPISTEMOLOGICAL ANARCHISM.

methodological bracketing see EPOCHÉ.

methodological individualism theoretical positions holding that adequate sociological accounts necessarily involve reference to persons, their interpretations of their circumstances, and the reasons and motives for the actions they take. WEBER and POPPER both propose specifications by which all social categories, like 'capitalism' or 'the state', can be explicated by reference to real or abstract ('idealized') individuals or persons. In its more strident forms, methodological individualism proposes that all sociological explanations *must* begin and end with reference to individuals. To this, the standard objection is that individuals usually owe many of their defining features, e.g. of psychological disposition, to their cultures and their structural contexts, so the proposed termination is sociologically banal.

For a discussion of the issues see Lukes (1977). See also SITUATIONAL LOGIC AND SITUATIONAL ANALYSIS, HOLISM, STRATEGIC INTERACTION. Compare STRUCTURALISM, STRUCTURE AND AGENCY.

methodological pluralism the doctrine that, rather than slavish attachment to a limited number of scientific or research methods, a proliferation of methodologies and theories often pays off – see FEYERABEND.

methodology 1 the philosophical evaluation of investigative techniques within a discipline; a concern with the conceptual, theoretical and research aspects of knowledge.

2 the techniques and strategies employed within a discipline to manipulate data and acquire knowledge. Used in this narrow sense, methodology simply refers to the RESEARCH METHODS used by an investigator and does not question the validity or appropriateness of undertaking research.

Used in sense 1, methodology is an aspect of the EPISTEMOLOGICAL concern with the scientific status of sociology. Methodology was a central concern of Durkheim, Marx and Weber, who, respectively, attempted to demonstrate that they had developed a distinctive approach to the study of society and therefore to knowledge. By demonstrating the validity of new investigative techniques, they contributed to the development of sociology as a distinctive discipline.

In sociology, a central aspect of methodology 1 has been a comparison between sociology and the natural sciences. Natural science is often associated with the EXPERIMENTAL METHOD whereby one variable (the INDEPENDENT VARIABLE) is manipulated in a carefully controlled way. If consistent results are obtained, the scientist may draw conclusions about the cause and effects involved, or conclude that a previously made HYPOTHESIS is confirmed or denied. Since the experimental method is usually inapplicable in the social sciences, sociologists, therefore, have developed new techniques to achieve a degree of VALIDITY which corresponds to that of the natural sciences. DURKHEIM, for example, advocated the use of the COMPARATIVE METHOD, although this entails attempting to control a large number of variables. Alternatively, they have sought to develop methods which do not seek to emulate the natural science goal of scientific laws, but are more appropriate to the nature of social reality.

metonymy the substitution of a word referring to an attribute of a thing for the thing itself, e. the 'crown' to refer to the monarch. The role of metonymy in social life is a topic especially in SEMIOLOGY. See also METAPHOR, SYMBOL.

metropolis-satellite relationship a structure, both spatial and socioeconomic, in which a central region ('metropolis') dominates a peripheral region ('satellite') mainly through economic means. It is a concept developed by FRANK to describe the process whereby economic surpluses flow out of the THIRD WORLD into the industrial capitalist countries. The structure and process begins in the Third World where surpluses flow from rural and provincial regions into urban and commercial centres via the control of trade by indigenous and foreign merchants. Goods which are then exported to the advanced countries contribute to the flow of surpluses, the profits from trade accumulating in the advanced countries. Thus the world can be conceptualized as a series of metropolis-satellite relationships, with surpluses being syphoned off at each intermediate metropolis, which itself becomes the satellite of another. This relationship is central to Frank's explanation of the UNDERDEVELOPMENT of the satellites, which do not retain economic growth, and the development of the metropoles, which benefit from the absorption of economic surpluses.

The concept has been criticized for conflating spatial and socioeconomic processes; for imprecision in the concept of ECONOMIC SURPLUS; for inadequately explaining the mechanisms whereby surpluses flow in a certain direction; and for over-simplifying the relationship between the Third World and the industrial capitalist countries. See also CENTRE AND PERIPHERY, WORLD SYSTEM, CITY.

metropolitanization see URBANIZATION.

Michels, Robert (1876–1936) German sociologist and political scientist, best remembered for his book *Political Parties* (1911), in which he formulated the tendency for an IRON LAW OF OLIGARCHY to operate in formal democratic political organizations. It was a work which arose from Michels' disillusionment with the leadership of the German Social Democratic Party (SPD) (see also POLITICAL PARTY). A tension existed between Michels' critical indictment of the 'class betrayal' and reformism of the leadership of the German SPD and his suggestion that such a betrayal was perhaps inevitable, given the operation of the 'iron law of oligarchy'. In his later work, Michels' position achieved greater coherence, and he was one of a number of theorists (including his friend, Max WEBER) to advance a theory of the social benefits of limited representative democracy. This theory can be seen as the forerunner of the modern theory of STABLE DEMOCRACY. See also ÉLITE THEORY.

microsociology the level of sociological analysis in which the focus is on face-to-face interactions in everyday life, on behaviour in groups, etc. (see SYMBOLIC INTERACTIONISM, ETHNOMETHODOLOGY). While often concerned with understanding individual meanings (see MEANINGFUL UNDERSTANDING AND EXPLANATION), microsociology does not confine itself to particular forms of explanatory accounts. Compare MACROSOCIOLOGY.

middle class(es) the non-manual occupational groups(s) which are located between the UPPER and the WORKING CLASSES.

The term 'middle' itself reflects a widely perceived common-sense conception of a status hierarchy in which non-manual work is accorded greater prestige than manual work, but is recognized as socially inferior to groups with major property or political interests. The presence of a large middle class in capitalist societies has been a subject of interest for a number of reasons. Important changes in occupational structure, involving a large increase in non-manual occupations, have forced a re-examination of the concept of social CLASS, particularly with reference to the social and political role of the 'middle class(es)'.

Until the 19th century, there existed few relatively specialized occupational roles of the kind that now exist, e.g. accountancy, teaching, nursing. This is not to say that 'middle class' roles in banking and government, and in the traditional PROFESSIONS did not exist. However, in both industry and government, especially over the last 100 years, there has occurred an enormous expansion of non-manual occupations, while the number of manual workers has shrunk (see Fig. 19).

The growth of non-manual occupations, and also the persistence of small businesses and the professions, poses theoretical problems for some traditional approaches to CLASS and SOCIAL STRATIFICATION. Until recently, Marxist theory especially had no well-developed analysis of the nature and significance of the 'middle classes'. The problems are compounded by the great diversity of non-manual work which ranges

		1911	1921	1931	1951	1971
1	Professional					
	A higher	1.00	1.01	1.14	1.93	3.29
	B lower	3.05	3.52	4.46	4.70	7.78
2	Employers and managers					
	A employers	6.71	6.82	6.70	4.97	4.22
	B managers	3.43	3.64	3.66	5.53	8.21
3	Clerical workers	4.84	6.72	6.97	10.68	13.90
4	Foremen	1.29	1.44	1.54	2.62	3.87
5–7	Manual workers	79.67	76.85	76.53	69.58	58.23

Fig. 19 **Middle class.** The figure indicates the increasing middle-class proportion of the gainfully employed population of the UK in the period 1911–71 (percentages). (Adapted from Routh, 1980.)

from routine clerical work to relatively powerful managerial and professional roles, with the owners of independent small businesses in between. This has led to radically different ideas of where to locate the middle classes within the class structure. It has been argued, for instance, that a process of PROLETARIANIZATION has reduced the status, pay and working conditions of clerical workers to those of the manual working class. Others (e.g. Ehrenreich and Ehrenreich, 1979) have argued that the 'professional-managerial class' is a new and distinct class in its own right, while still others (e.g. Poulantzas, 1975) see the development of a NEW PETTY BOURGEOISIE (see also INTELLECTUAL LABOUR, CONTRADICTORY CLASS LOCATIONS).

Such differences in theoretical perspective reflect the diverse and ambiguous character of the middle class(es). It has often been argued, for instance, that non-manual occupations are distinguished by relatively higher pay, better working conditions, more opportunities for promotion, etc., than manual occupations. This argument cannot be sustained for women working in routine clerical jobs or behind shop counters; their WORK and MARKET SITUATION is quite different from that of higher middle-class occupations. On the other hand, routine white-collar workers do, on average, often work fewer hours per week than manual workers, and commonly enjoy great security of income, better sick pay and pension arrangements and greater job security. The further one moves up the status hierarchy the greater become the advantages of higher pay, career prospects and various 'perks' (e.g. company cars, low-interest loans or health insurance). The marked differences that exist within the middle class(es) mean that debates about their class situation and the implication of this for CLASS CONSCIOUSNESS, will continue to be held in sociology.
See also MULTIDIMENSIONAL ANALYSIS OF SOCIAL STRATIFICATION, CLASS IMAGERY, SOCIAL MOBILITY.

middle-class radicalism forms of political radicalism, including left-wing voting, by people from non-manual backgrounds. Parkin (1968) employed the term to refer to members of the Campaign for Nuclear Disarmament (CND). Middle-class radicalism is of interest in much the same way as WORKING-CLASS CONSERVATISM as a form of *class-deviant political action*, i.e. activity contrary to prevailing or expected class norms. Two distinct locations of types of 'middle class' class-deviant political activity can be identified:
(a) the *'lower middle class left'*, left-wing voting and action by those marginal to the middle class, e.g. routine manual workers; and
(b) the *'upper middle class left'*, forms of left-wing political activity particularly associated with membership of the caring professions and public sector employment (Jary, 1978).
See also VOTING BEHAVIOUR.

middle range theory see THEORIES OF THE MIDDLE RANGE.

midlife crisis doubt and anxiety experienced by many people in their fifth decade, 40 years being the entry point to the category middle age. This marks the end of their youthful period and of the opportunities and goals that life seemed to offer when they were young. People may reflect upon their lives, revalue their relationships and contemplate the prospect of the biological deterioration associated with AGEING. In occupational terms it involves acknowledging the limits to personal success and achievement, and in domestic terms it involves transition away from active parenting as children leave home to establish their own adult relationships.
See also LIFE COURSE, LIFE CRISIS.

migration the movement of people from one country to another, involving an intention to reside in the country of destination. *Emigration* refers to the movement out of a country, *immigration* refers to the movement of people into a country. There is an internationally agreed definition of an immigrant as someone who, having lived outside the country for at least one year, declares an intention to live in the country for at least one year. An emigrant is defined in the opposite way. Since World War II more people have emigrated from the UK than immigrated into it. In recent British history there have been three periods of marked immigration: Irish people 1800–61; Jewish people 1870–1911; and people from the New Commonwealth 1950–71. There have been a number of MORAL PANICS about immigration since 1945, focusing on the immigration of black people, and it is therefore important to distinguish between immigrants and black people; it is wrong to assume that an immigrant is black, and it is equally wrong to assume that a black person is an immigrant. See also LABOUR MIGRATION, ETHNIC GROUP, RACISM OR RACIALISM.

militant and industrial societies Herbert SPENCER's evolutionary distinction between two types of society: the earlier form of society based on 'compulsory cooperation', *militant society,* and the newer type of society into which militant societies evolve, *industrial society,* based on 'voluntary cooperation' (see Fig. 20). Spencer's conception of modern industrial society reflected his view that contemporary English society represented the highest stage of evolution. His typology formulates an idealized distinction. Spencer recognized that many societies had not reached his second stage. He was also acutely aware that modern societies displayed many signs of reverting to the militant form. However, he retained his belief that the industrial type was the most evolved form, and one which individuals and governments ought to seek to achieve.

militarism 1 the pursuit of war as an intrinsic value and the glorification of military ideals (e.g. in training the young, as in ancient Sparta).

2 the preponderance of military values and military practices within a society.

3 a proclivity in some societies for a section of the higher echelons to look for military solutions to political conflicts, and the readiness of the lower ranks to accept such solutions (GIDDENS, 1986).

In modern times, militaristic practices and militaristic ideologies have played a crucial part in the creation of national identities (see NATIONALISM, NATION STATE) and in the incorporation of the working class. Contrary to the expectations of certain of the classical sociologists (notably SPENCER), warfare and militarism have not declined in importance in the modern world (see also TOTAL WAR), although according to some theorists constraints on the exercise of warfare have emerged from the existence of nuclear weapons (see DETERRENCE, NUCLEAR DETERRENCE, MUTUAL ASSURED DESTRUCTION). See also WARFARE, MILITANT AND INDUSTRIAL SOCIETIES, ARMS RACE, CLAUSEWITZ, NEO-CLAUSEWITZIAN, MILITARY-INDUSTRIAL COMPLEX, GARRISON STATE, MILITARY INTERVENTION IN POLITICS.

military the armed forces of a STATE; pertaining to the armed forces or to WARFARE.

The Austrian sociologist Ludwig Gumplowitz (1838–1909) argued that military conquest was the origin both of the state and SOCIAL STRATIFICATION. Whether or not this view is accepted (and usually it is regarded as far too simple), it is clear the military play a crucial role in the maintenance of state power once this is established. Despite this, until recently sociological study of the military and of warfare has occupied only a relatively marginalized place within mainstream sociology. This neglect has been challenged recently by a number of theorists (e.g. MANN, 1983 and 1988). The argument is that in a world threatened with extinction by the military might of the two superpowers, and with MILITARISM today a more pervasive feature than in earlier societies, the study of warfare and the military ought to be more central. See also WARFARE, STRATEGIC THEORY.

military-civilian ratio the ratio of the military (and those in military-related occupations) to the total adult population (Andreski, *Military Organization and Society,*

Characteristic	Militant society	Industrial society
Dominant function or activity	Corporate defensive & offensive activity for preservation and aggrandizement	Peaceful, mutual rendering of individual services services
Principle of social coordination	Compulsory cooperation; regimentation by enforcement of orders; both positive and negative regulation of activity	Voluntary cooperation; regulation by contract and principles of justice; only negative regulation of activity
Relations between state and individual	Individuals exist for benefit of state; restraints on liberty, property, and mobility	State exists for benefit of individuals; freedom; few restraints on property and mobility
Relations between state and other organizations	All organizations public; private organizations excluded	Private organizations encouraged
Structure of state	Centralized	Decentralized
Structure of social stratification	Fixity of rank, occupation, and locality; inheritance of positions	Plasticity and openness of rank, occupation, and locality; movement between positions
Type of economic activity	Economic autonomy and self-sufficiency; little external trade; protectionism	Loss of economic autonomy; interdependence via peaceful trade; free trade
Valued social and personal characteristics	Patriotism; courage; reverence; loyalty; obedience; faith in authority; discipline	Independence; respect for others; resistance to coercion; individual initiative; truthfulness; kindness

Fig. 20 **Militant and industrial societies.** Spencer's contrasts between militant and industrial societies. This table (from Smelser, 1968) is derived from Herbert Spencer, *The Principles of Sociology*, 1897.

1954). While in preindustrial societies based on an armed citizenry this ratio was high (e.g. the city states of ancient Greece), it is considered more meaningful in modern states, where standing armies and a clear distinction between the civilian population and the military are a feature of the apparatus of the modern NATION STATE. This picture is complicated, however, by the existence in many of these states of the temporary compulsory enlistment, i.e. *conscription*, of a proportion of the civilian population, in times of peace as well as war. See also TOTAL WAR.

military-industrial complex a term introduced to the general public in a famous 1950s speech by President Eisenhower, in which he warned that the social structure of American society was becoming increasingly dominated by military and economic imperatives arising from the ARMS RACE. The suggestion that the capitalist economy has been dependent on a continuation of arms expenditure is controversial (compare TENDENCY TO DECLINING RATE OF PROFIT, OVERPRODUCTION AND UNDERCONSUMPTION). However, that the continuation of the COLD

WAR (e.g. Thompson, 1982) significantly distorted the economies and political systems of the major powers, limiting the possibility of reform, is borne out by changes in the subsequent era of greater detente, (see PERESTROIKA, GLASNOST), and the collapse of Soviet power.

military intervention (in politics) any military intervention in politics that extends beyond those minimal levels of influence which normally exist in constitutional democracies. Finer (*Man on Horseback*, 1962) identifies four levels of intervention by the military:
(a) influence;
(b) blackmail;
(c) displacement of civilian rulers;
(d) the supplanting of a civilian regime by a military one.

According to Finer, a formal separation of the military from politics, of the kind characteristic of modern constitutional states, is most readily maintained within Western industrialized democracies, where a strong POLITICAL CULTURE sustains the legitimacy of civilian political rule, and also defines military intervention as illegitimate. In Western industrialized societies, military intervention in politics tends to be limited to 'influence'. In contemporary societies, full military intervention, leading to the supplanting of civilian regimes by military regimes, is mainly a phenomenon of developing nations. However, it also occurs in more developed societies (e.g. Argentina) which lack a strong political culture legitimizing civilian rule.

Apart from the obvious factor, the possession of modern weaponry, further factors which enable or encourage military intervention are:
(a) where the military exist as an internally coherent group, possessing good communications and able to operate as a unit, in a context in which these attributes are lacking in other groups;
(b) where the military are able to claim to represent the nation as a whole, in situations in which civilian governments represent sectional interests;
(c) where members of the military may hope to benefit personally from intervention (e.g. expect to gain better equipment, improved salaries or improve promotion prospects).

It should not be assumed that military intervention automatically leads to right-wing regimes; there exist numerous examples to the contrary. The effectiveness of military regimes compared with civilian regimes in introducing social reforms is also an open question. It is usual, however, for periods of military rule to be of relatively short duration.

military society any form of society in which the military exerts a dominant or pervasive role. See also MILITARISM, MILITARY-INDUSTRIAL COMPLEX, GARRISON STATE, MILITARY INTERVENTION, MILITARY-CIVILIAN RATIO.

Mill, John Stuart (1806–73) English philosopher and leading 19th-century exponent of liberalism, who also took a keen interest in developments in social science and sociology, e.g. he sponsored COMTE's work. Apart from his own wide-ranging philosophical and more general work (including *Utilitarianism*, 1861a, *Representative Government*, 1861b, and *Principles of Political Economy*, 1848), Mill's own contribution to social science was made especially in his *A System of Logic* (1843). In this he provided a formal analysis of the main methods of INDUCTION AND INDUCTIVE LOGIC, which he advanced as the basis of empirical research and the scientific method in social science as well as natural science (see COMPARATIVE METHOD). Making the assumption of a 'uniformity of nature', Mill sought to combat traditional philosophical scepticism; however, he cannot be seen to have solved this problem (see FALSIFICATION).

Influenced by de TOCQUEVILLE, in *On Liberty* (1859) Mill argued against all forms of censorship and for a toleration of different viewpoints, one reason for this being that the development of knowledge required such openness – a viewpoint that can be interpreted as an argument against any fixed method (see FEYERABEND, TRUTH). Another reason was the importance of living life as one chooses, of allowing 'experiments in living' which do not threaten others. In *The Subjection of Women* (1869) he made out a case against gender inequality.

His contribution to UTILITARIANISM, the extension of the work of his father James Mill (1773–1836) and his godfather Jeremy BENTHAM, is also of sociological interest. Mill followed their views in making judgements of right and wrong a matter of the 'pleasure principle', the degree to which particular actions or social arrangements increase. or do not increase, overall 'happiness'. However, he differed from them in insisting that a distinction should be drawn between higher and lower forms of pleasure.

Millar, John (1735–1801) SCOTTISH ENLIGHTENMENT thinker and protosociologist, especially remembered for his *The Origin of the Distinction of Ranks* (1771). It was a distinctive feature of Millar's approach that he emphasized the importance of understanding the DIVISION OF LABOUR, and forms of subsistence and forms of property, in understanding social relations in general. For all this, most commentators regard his work as remaining in the tradition of 'moral philosophy' rather than ushering in a fully fledged sociological perspective.

millenarianism and millennial movement a type of religious, often also politico-religious, movement based on a belief in the imminence of a radical sociopolitical transformation by supernatural intervention – e.g., that the Messiah will return bringing a new millennium of one thousand years (hence the general term). In medieval and early modern Europe, millennial movements were movements mainly of the disadvantaged and the dispossessed (see Cohn, 1957). This pattern is repeated elsewhere, in for example the North American Indian Ghost Dancers or in the related phenomenon of CARGO CULTS. All such movements can be seen as pre-political responses to cultural disruption, which in time may give rise to non-millenarian forms of political movement. Equally however, many modern forms of political movement have been interpreted as involving elements of millenarianism in that they promise root-and-branch social and economic transformations for which there exists no immediate feasible means.

millennial movement see MILLENARIANISM.

Mills, C. Wright (1916–62) US sociologist and prominent critic of the two orthodoxies of American sociology in the 1950s: Parsonian functionalism and social survey research. The former he castigated as vacuous *'grand theory'* and the latter as 'ABSTRACTED EMPIRICISM'. In Mills' eyes these forms of sociology had ceased to raise truly significant questions about society. In his own sociology he sought to relate 'private ills' to 'public issues'. He was critical above all of the 'intellectual default' which he believed existed in modern sociology and modern society, i.e. the failure to intervene effectively in history.

As the editor and translator (with Hans Gerth) of selections from Max Weber (*From Max Weber: Essays in Sociology*, 1946) Mills argued for a sociological method grounded in historical understanding. Influenced also by SYMBOLIC INTERACTIONISM, in *Character and Social Structure* (1953) he also advocated a sociology which would interrelate 'character structure' with 'social structure'. *The Sociological Imagination* (1959) provides the most general summary statement of Mills' overall approach and attitudes.

Of his more substantive studies, two in particular attracted wide attention: *White Collar* (1951) and *The Power Élite* (1956). In the first of these Mills charted the declining importance and loss of public role of the 'old' independent 'middle class', whom he saw as being increasingly replaced by a 'new middle class', made up of bureaucratized office workers, salesmen, and the like. These were 'cheerful robots' according to Mills, with little control over their own lives. In *Power Élite*, Mills' more general thesis was that power in modern America was becoming more concentrated. Characteristically, three interrelated and overlapping groups of pivotal powerholders were identified by Mills: 'corporation chieftains', 'military warlords', and 'political bosses', all of whom Mills suggested could be comfortably accommodated in a medium-sized suburban cinema (see also ÉLITE THEORY). Although by their occupation of the commanding heights of American society, the members of this power élite have the potential to given a moral direction to society, in practice, according to Mills, their actions were often such as to constitute a 'higher immorality', e.g. a drift to World War III.

Critics of Mills' work have concentrated on two aspects: first, its relatively speculative empirical base and its populist tone, and secondly, its failure to relate systematically to other general theories of modern society, including PLURAL ÉLITISM and modern Marxism. However, Mills was an important and provocative voice in postwar American sociology, contributing to the development of a more critical stance.

mimetic desire concept which refers to the inter-dividual nature of desire. The idea of mimetic desire was introduced by the French thinker Rene GIRARD. It has since been appropriated by the American philosopher/anthropologist Eric Gans whose GENERATIVE ANTHROPOLOGY speculates about the role of mimetic desire in the evolution of humanity. Against Freud's theory of the independent nature of desire, Girard's theory follows Hegel and Lacan by arguing that the subjectivity of the self is based on the presence of the other. The concept of mimetic desire is also comparable with the ideas expressed by DELEUZE and GUATTARI. In *Anti-Oedipus* (1972) they argued that the role of desire in FREUD's OEDIPUS COMPLEX should be regarded as overly reductionist because it fails to take into account the way external sources of desire influence ego formation. For Girard the notion of mimetic desire refers to the self's reliance on the OTHER: the desire of the self is always mediated by the influence of the other that serves as its model. See also LACAN, JACQUES; ORDER/DIS-ORDER.

mind the mental faculties, mental experience of the human individual, involving self-consciousness, 'free will', thinking processes and unconscious processes. It is a hypothetical, and sometimes metaphysical, construct, which expresses a holistic capacity based on the neurophysiological processes of the brain, yet additively becoming more than these, i.e. an emergent property. Philosophically, there are disagreements about the way to express these properties. Major disputes have existed on the mind-body relation, on whether or not mind and body are to be conceptualized as separate 'immaterial' and 'material' realms (see DUALISM. MATERIALISM). Related debates (in PSYCHOLOGY) surround the doctrine of BEHAVIOURISM, that scientific psychology can proceed only by analysis of overt behaviour, not mental events. It should be noted, however, that doctrines such as philosophical materialism, which reject a dualism of mind and body, are not necessarily committed to a denial of 'emergent properties' of mind for many explanatory purposes. See also STRATIFICATIONAL MODEL OF SOCIAL ACTION AND CONSCIOUSNESS.

minifundia see LATIFUNDIUM.

Minitab (STATISTICS) a much-used software package for performing statistical analysis. Developed initially to help in the teaching of statistics, Minitab is fully interactive and based on the simple idea of entering numerical information in a worksheet of rows and columns, rather like a spreadsheet. Frequently updated, Minitab now has programs that enable it to handle many complex MULTIVARIATE ANALYSES and time-series analyses. Unlike many standard packages, Minitab is particularly strong in techniques associated with *exploratory data analysis* (*EDA*). For the analysis of survey data the package contains a wide range of statistical techniques and graphs; its one drawback is that labelling facilities are limited. Available in both mainframe and microcomputer versions, Minitab is regarded as one of the most 'user-friendly' statistical programs.

mixed economy an economic system which combines two or more contrasting forms of economic decision-making, especially the combination of market principles and state intervention. See also CAPITALISM AND CAPITALIST MODE OF PRODUCTION.

mobility see SOCIAL MOBILITY, OCCUPATIONAL MOBILITY.

mobilization see POLITICAL MOBILIZATION.

mobilization of bias see COMMUNITY POWER.

mode see MEASURES OF CENTRAL TENDENCY.

model 1 any representation of one phenomenon by another, e.g., ANALOGY OR METAPHOR.

2 any formal (i.e. mathematical or logically formal) representation of a set of relationships.

3 a physical or a pictorial or diagrammatic representation (including maps) of a set of relationships.

4 computer models, which can allow the simulation of real world processes.

In a final, looser sense, any abstract general concept (e.g. IDEAL TYPE) OF THEORY may sometimes be referred to as a 'model'.

Models vary in the degree to which they are regarded as approximating reality (their degree of *isomorphism* with the reality). Their functions also vary, and may be heuristic as well as explanatory, including: (a) the proposal of new hypotheses for exploration by suggesting comparisons between unfamiliar phenomena and those better known or better explained (e.g. between cultural and biological evolution); (b) the simplification of complex reality for analytical purposes by the provision of an unambiguous general concept (Weber's ideal type of BUREAUCRACY) or to highlight fundamental explanatory causal mechanisms in isolation from complicating factors (e.g. Marx's model of CAPITALISM AND CAPITALIST MODE OF PRODUCTION); (c) comparisons between the 'ideal' model and the real world (as in both Marx's and Weber's models, or the THEORY OF GAMES), intended to increase awareness of real world processes. Ultimately no clear-cut distinction exists between the terms 'model' and 'theory', since both of these terms imply some simplification of reality, necessary in order to achieve generality.

modelling see IMITATION.

mode of production (MARXISM) a particular combination of a specific set of RELATIONS OF PRODUCTION and FORCES OF PRODUCTION to form an historically specific way of organizing economic production. In recent years this has been an important concept for structuralist Marxists influenced by ALTHUSSER. See FEUDAL MODE OF PRODUCTION, ASIATIC MODE OF PRODUCTION, PRIMITIVE COMMUNISM, CAPITALISM, MARX.

modernism any cultural preference for 'the modern', for contemporary thought, style, etc., especially in architecture, music and art. In architecture, the modernism of Gropius and Le Corbusier was associated with the celebration of functionality and a belief in Man's ultimate ability to control his surroundings. In the arts more generally, however, modernism has often been associated with a rejection of 'realist' paradigms (e.g. surrealism). Featherstone (1988) summarizes the basic features of modernism in this sense as: 'an aesthetic self-consciousness and reflexiveness; a rejection of narrative structure in favour of simultaneity and montage; an exploration of the paradoxical, ambiguous and uncertain open-ended nature of reality; and a rejection of the notion of an integrated personality in favour of an emphasis upon the destructured, dehumanized subject.' According to Frederic JAMESON (1984), modernism in this general sense involves a break with the paradigm of 'representation' in theoretical discourse and in art, and a break with the 'realist' configuration associated with liberal capitalism. See also MODERNITY, POSTMODERNITY AND POSTMODERNISM, DECONSTRUCTION.

modernity the modern age, or the ideas and styles associated with this. In general historical terms, 'modernity' refers to the period since the Middle Ages and the RENAISSANCE and is associated with the replacement of TRADITIONAL SOCIETY by modern social forms (see MODERNIZATION). More specifically, it refers simply to the recent, to contemporary ways of doing things. If in one of its senses 'modernity' is seen as identified with a belief in rationality and the triumph of truth and science (see the ENLIGHTENMENT) it is now under attack from theorists who see the onset of a 'postmodern' era (see POSTMODERNITY AND POSTMODERNISM). Against this, for other theorists (as in Marx's phrase 'all that's solid melts into air'), the flux and uncertainty described as 'postmodern' can be seen as inherent in modernity itself.

modernization

1 the overall societal process, including INDUSTRIALIZATION, by which previously agrarian, historical and contemporary societies become developed. The overall contrast usually drawn is between premodern and modernized societies. The term includes a wider range of social processes than industrialization (see also POLITICAL MODERNIZATION). In classical sociological theory, modernization was conceptualized by DURKHEIM as involving a process of SOCIAL DIFFERENTIATION, by WEBER as a process of RATIONALIZATION, and by MARX as a process of COMMODIFICATION.
2 the more particular model of societal development, suggested especially by US functionalist sociologists in the 1950s and 60s, in which the decisive factor in modernization is the overcoming and replacement of traditional values and patterns of motivation hostile to social change and economic growth. In more general terms, structural-functionalist theories also emphasize the process of SOCIAL DIFFERENTIATION involved in modernization, including political PLURALISM (see also TRADITIONAL SOCIETIES, ACHIEVEMENT MOTIVATION).

While modernization **1** is an open-ended concept, modernization **2** has been widely criticized as a Western-centred approach. This criticism has been directed at the use of the concept (in the 1950s and 60s) by the STRUCTURAL-FUNCTIONALIST theorists, influenced by the work of PARSONS, to examine the prospects of development in THIRD WORLD societies.

Whilst there are important differences between authors, the main tenets of the structural-functionalist theory are:
(a) modern society is contrasted with TRADITIONAL SOCIETY which is seen as hindering economic development;
(b) change occurs through evolutionary stages which are broadly similar for all societies;
(c) Third World countries need agents to help them break out of tradition;
(d) such agents for change may either come from within the society, such as modernizing élites, or may come from outside, for example with the injection of capital or education models;

(e) DUAL ECONOMIES AND DUAL SOCIETIES may exist in contemporary Third World countries. Some regions persist in traditional forms, whilst others, especially urban areas, experience modernization;
(f) both the preferred and likely outcome are societies similar to those in Western Europe and the US. In this last respect authors share similar assumptions to CONVERGENCE theorists.

The criticisms came primarily from DEPENDENCY THEORY and UNDERDEVELOPMENT theorists in the late 1960s and subsequently. The main critical points were:
(a) modernization theory concentrated on internal social processes, thus ignoring the effects of COLONIALISM and NEOCOLONIALISM on the structure of Third World societies;
(b) the contrast between modern and traditional was both oversimplified and erroneous. FRANK argued that existing Third World societies were not in any sense traditional because they had been changed by centuries of contact with Northern countries. The obstacles to change were a creation of this contact;
(c) these were not dual societies because often the so-called traditional sectors were an integral part of the national economy;
(d) the evolutionary approach imposed a Western model of development and denied the possibility of novel forms of society emerging in the Third World;
(e) behind modernization theory were both political and ideological concerns. Many of the main theorists were from the US, involved in governmental advisory roles and explicitly committed to the curtailment of socialism or communism in the Third World. This was particularly seen in the 1960s when the US's 'Alliance for Progress' programme in Latin America was instituted in response to the Cuban Revolution of 1959 and which adopted many of the suggested policies and aims deriving from modernization theory. See also EVOLUTIONARY THEORY, NEOEVOLUTIONISM, SOCIOLOGY OF DEVELOPMENT, SOCIAL CHANGE, IMPERIALISM, CONVERGENCE.

modes of motivational orientation three forms or modes of *motivational orientation*, identified by Parsons and Shils (1951):
(a) *cognitive* (i.e. the perception of objects in terms of their characteristics and potential consequences);
(b) *cathartic* (i.e. the perception of objects in terms of the emotional needs of the actor);
(c) *evaluative* (in which the actor allocates energy among ends and attempts to optimize outcomes).

All three modes of orientation can be involved in any instance of social action, but equally particular instances or types of social action can be characterized by primarily involving one rather than the others. See also PATTERN VARIABLES, PARSONS. Compare TYPES OF SOCIAL ACTION.

mods and rockers significant examples of stylistic youth SUBCULTURES which emerged in the 1960s. *Mods* were a stylistic grouping based on motor scooters and smart dress, and *Rockers* a grouping riding powerful motorcycles and wearing heavy leathers. According to Hall et al. (1976) and Clarke et al. (1979), while Mods could be interpreted as the 'symbolic representation' of new working-class affluence through CONSPICUOUS CONSUMPTION and display, Rockers represented a reaffirmation of 'traditional' working-class values, including working-class community, male chauvinism, etc.

Such youth subcultural phenomena have been subject to considerable sociological scrutiny in Britain, particularly since the research carried out by S. Cohen (*Folk Devils and Moral Panics*, 1973). Incidents involving groups of Mods and Rockers at English seaside resorts between 1964 and 1966 were widely condemned in the press and broadcast news. Cohen uses them as a case study in the examination of the treatment of DEVIANCE by the MASS MEDIA. He argues that through the use of STEREOTYPES, symbols and imagery the media actively help construct FOLK DEVILS and generate large scale MORAL PANICS.

In the work of the Birmingham Centre for Contemporary Cultural Studies represented by Hall et al. (see also CULTURAL STUDIES), groupings such as Mods and Rockers are of interest in a different way, because they 'subvert the supposed (passive) role of the consumer and transform ... cultural meanings', constituting new forms of cultural identity and autonomy.

moiety (ANTHROPOLOGY) half a social group produced by the application of a social rule. The most common division is into two PATRILINEAL OF MATRILINEAL moieties on the basis of DESCENT, but other rules are also applied, such as residence or marriage.

monetarism a school of thought in economics and in politics that sees control of the money supply as the key to the management of the economy. Monetarists emphasize the need to match the supply of money (including credit) to the capacity of the economy to produce goods and services, if INFLATION is to be controlled and stop-go economic growth avoided. As well as having been a fashionable but controversial theory in academic ECONOMICS (compare KEYNESIAN ECONOMICS), monetarism has also been widely employed in the 1980s by Western governments. It provides a rationale for control of the economy through control of the money supply, including the control of rates of interest, and has also been used as justification for control of state expenditures, and thus the state borrowing which creates credit. The adoption of monetarism was an outcome of the seeming failure of Keynesian economics to prevent high inflation and high unemployment, a loss of international competitiveness and a squeeze on profits. All of these were suggested to be the result of an OVERLOAD ON THE STATE and the escalation of state expenditures.

The issues to which monetarism relates are not only a matter of monetary relations and fiscal policy, or the interests of nation states. Rather, as suggested long ago by MARX, such issues also involve the complex competing interests of multiple groups and classes, internationally as well as within nations. See also HABERMAS, THATCHERISM.

money any commodity or token generally acceptable as a medium of exchange, and in terms of which other goods and services may be priced. Originally the physical material used as money usually had an inherent usefulness as well as being a symbolic medium (e.g. gold). In modern societies money takes many forms, including paper and also machine-held records.

Absent in BARTER ECONOMIES, in which goods are exchanged directly, money can be seen as an important human invention (see also EVOLUTIONARY UNIVERSAL). As a 'symbolic medium for resources' (Parsons, 1963), money underlines the 'generalized instrumentality' of resources as against their more particular uses. Money, together with the development of MARKETS for resources, is immensely significant historically, for the following reasons:

(a) as a store of purchasing power or VALUE;

(b) as a unit of account or record; as a measurement of the relative value of goods and services whether or not these are actually to be sold;
(c) as *money capital*, the money used to finance production;
(d) as a source of credit.

For MARX in particular, and for the CLASSICAL ECONOMISTS generally, money played an indispensable role in the rise of CAPITALISM AND CAPITALIST MODE OF PRODUCTION. However, a number of its characteristics were also recognized as bringing problems. These arise from the storage and hoarding of money, and from situations in which goods cannot be sold for money, or credit obtained; one reason for ECONOMIC CRISES. For Marx, such crises have less to do with the characteristics of money as such, than with the character of CAPITALISM (see CRISES OF CAPITALISM; see also INFLATION, MONETARISM).

In a classic work, *The Philosophy of Money*, SIMMEL points to the fact that the transition to a money economy has far-reaching consequences beyond its role in the development of the economy. Not least, there is the general impetus it gave to rational calculation and a rationalistic world outlook, including scientific measurement. A further consequence was an increase in impersonal social relationships.

In the work of Parsons, analogies between the concept of money and the concept of POWER are also suggested. Thus political power can be seen as a generalized resource which can be used in many ways.

monoculture in agricultural practice, the concentration of one crop in a given area. This is generally associated with the growth of commercial agriculture and of CASH CROPPING, and can be contrasted with mixed farming more characteristic of agriculturalists growing for their own consumption. Whilst monoculture may have benefits for some crops, there may also be disadvantages: certain forms of mixed cropping may control pests and preserve the fertility of the soil, whereas monoculture is generally associated with increased use of pesticides and artificial fertilizers. For this reason monoculture is generally associated with large-scale organizations, such as PLANTATIONS, which can mobilize the resources for the necessary inputs and manage the marketing of the crop. Even then, problems for THIRD WORLD countries resulting from monoculture arise from dependence on a few crops for export earnings which are vulnerable to changes in world prices and demand, over which Third World countries may have little control. See also AGRIBUSINESS.

monogamy a MARRIAGE rule permitting only one partner to either sex. It may include prohibitions on remarriage, but where it does not the terms 'serial monogamy' or 'serial POLYGAMY' are sometimes used.

monopoly a commodity market for a particular product dominated by a single producer, who is thus able to control prices. Where a small number of producers dominate a market the term *oligopoly* is used. Compare PERFECT COMPETITION.

monopoly capitalism (MARXISM) that form or state of capitalism (see also ADVANCED CAPITALISM) in which concentrations of capital have brought about the development of cartels and monopolies which are able to manipulate and restrict the workings of a free competitive market.

monotheism the belief in the doctrine that there is only one God; religious belief systems based on this doctrine. Of the major world religions, only JUDAISM, CHRISTIANITY and ISLAM, are monotheistic, and they share a common root. According to Lenski and Lenski (1970), although rare in hunter-gatherer and horticultural societies, conceptions of a 'supreme being' become widespread in agrarian societies. Monotheism and a belief in a personal ethical God, however, appear only in the Near East. PARSONS regards the appearance of monotheism as a decisive developmental step encouraging the development of 'ethical universalism'. WEBER's account of the Jewish conception of the jealous God, Yahweh – 'Thou shall have no other gods but me' – and the notion of the 'chosen people', is that these conceptions were a response to the vulnerability of the tribes of Israel to foreign domination, problems 'explained' by the PROPHETS as a supreme God punishing his people for worshipping false gods.

Montesquieu, Baron Charles de (1689–1755) French aristocrat and early sociological thinker, chiefly remembered for the account of his massive social investigations contained in *The Spirit of the Laws* (1748). Educated in natural history, physiology and law, Montesquieu first came to the attention of Paris's social élite with the publication of his *Persian Letters* (1721), which examined familiar French customs from the point of view of the cultural outsider.

The Spirit of the Laws, however, is a more massive and seriously sociological study. It consists of 31 books, written over a period of 20 years, examining different forms of government, ecological influences on social structure, culture, trade, population, religion and law.

Montesquieu's conception of the precondition of political liberty, which he valued, was a form of PLURALISM, i.e. that freedom depended on a balance of power distributed among various groups or institutions. He was among the first to examine the legal apparatus of society in its social context, and is thus regarded as a founding figure in the SOCIOLOGY OF LAW. Montesquieu is also remembered for his advocacy of EMPIRICISM, and his early delineation of Asiatic despotism (see ASIATIC MODE OF PRODUCTION AND ASIATIC SOCIETY).

Moore, Barrington (1913–) US sociologist and social historian, whose most influential work *Social Origins of Dictatorship and Democracy* (1966) did much to rejuvenate comparative historical sociology, after an era dominated by overgeneralized functionalist and evolutionary accounts of social change. In his earlier works *Soviet Politics – The Dilemma of Power: The Role of Ideas in Social Change* (1950) and *Terror and Progress USSR* (1954), Moore had himself utilized functionalist modes of analysis in suggesting that the functional requirements associated with the necessity to industrialize had placed a limit on attempts to realize a socialist society. In *Social Origins of Dictatorship and Democracy*, however, rather than working with the idea of a single set of functional requirements for modernization, Moore's argument is that *three* distinctive historical routes to the modern world can be identified:

(a) a democratic, and capitalist, route – 'revolution from below' – based on commercialized agriculture and the powerful emergence of bourgeois interests (England, France, United States);

(b) a route leading ultimately to fascism – 'revolution from above' – where the bourgeois impetus was far weaker and modernization involved recourse to labour-repressive modes of work organization in agriculture by a traditional ruling group backed by strong political controls (Germany, Japan);

(c) a route leading to communist revolution, where neither the commercialization of agriculture nor a recourse to labour-repressive techniques by traditional ruling groups proved effective in the face of peasant solidarity (Russia, China).

Not all Moore's conclusions about these three routes have found universal acceptance (see Smith, 1983). Rather, it is the subtlety of his sifting of historical data while addressing general questions, which has impressed many sociologists and which has done much to stimulate the post-functionalist flowering of historical sociology evident in recent years. Barrington Moore's own subsequent work has failed to reach the heights achieved in *Social Origins*. It is of interest, however, that in *The Causes of Human Misery* (1978), an exercise in seeking conclusions on moral questions, he makes the suggestion that while social science is in a position to identify 'social evils', it is far less able to identify the basis of the good society. See also JUSTICE.

moral career the identifiable sequences in a labelling process in which a person's identity (particularly deviant identity) and moral status is progressively changed. For example, the moral career of the mental patient (GOFFMAN, *Stigma*, 1963) in which the patient is first 'sane', then a patient, and finally an expatient. In this process the entire biography of a person may be reinterpreted in the light of the 'moral' evaluations progressively imposed.

Compare DEGRADATION CEREMONY.

moral crusade a SOCIAL MOVEMENT, e.g. Mary Whitehouse's National Viewers' and Listeners' Association, in which members seek to mobilize support for the reassertion and enforcement of legal and social sanctions in defence of what are seen as fundamental moral values. Often, but not exclusively, these movements attract members with strong religious affiliations. In some sociological accounts, the suggestion is that they tend to attract members with particular personality needs, e.g. AUTHORITARIAN PERSONALITY, but there is no indication that this applies generally to membership. See also MORAL ENTREPRENEURS, PRESSURE GROUP.

moral entrepreneurs those members of society with the power to create or enforce rules (BECKER, *Outsiders: Studies in the Sociology of Deviance*, 1963). For Becker, for whom DEVIANCE represents 'publicly labelled wrongdoing', someone must call the public's attention to such wrongdoings. Deviance is the product of enterprise in the sense that there are:

(a) those who act to get rules made; and

(b) those who apply the rules once a rule has come into existence, so that offenders created by the abstract rules may be identified, apprehended and convicted.

Becker's interest is in reversing the emphasis of most social scientific research which concerns itself with the people who break rules. Instead, he suggests 'we must see deviance ... as a consequence of a process of interaction between people, some of whom, in the service of their own interests, make and enforce rules which catch others who, in the service of their own interests, have committed acts which are labelled deviant'. See also LABELLING THEORY, MORAL CRUSADE.

moral panic an exaggerated, media-amplified, social reaction to initially relatively minor acts of social DEVIANCE, e.g. social disturbances associated with MODS AND ROCKERS (S. Cohen, *Folk Devils and Moral Panics*, 1972). Such an overreaction by media, police, courts, governments and members of the public in 'labelling' and drawing attention, far from leading to an elimination of this behaviour, tends to amplify it. It does so by constructing role models for others to follow or by publicizing unruly or unsocial behaviour which might otherwise attract little attention. Some theorists also suggest that moral panics are encouraged by governments as useful in mobilizing political support by creating a common 'threat' (see Hall et al., *Policing the Crisis*, 1978). See also DEVIANCE AMPLIFICATION, LABELLING THEORY.

moral relativism see RELATIVISM.

moral statistics social data collected, e.g. in France in the 19th-century (preceding the development of sociology as a discipline), and seen to be indicative of social pathology, such as suicide, crime, illegitimacy and divorce. The concern for the collection of social data influenced social reformers in Britain, notably Edwin Chadwick (1800–90). See also SOCIAL ADMINISTRATION, SOCIAL REFORM, OFFICIAL STATISTICS.

morbidity rate the incidence of a certain disease or disorder in a population. This is generally calculated as the rate per 100,000 population in one year.

This is not as straightforward a measure to calculate as the DEATH RATE, since it is reliant on reporting of ILLNESS. Routine statistics are collected from the NHS, and are therefore dependent on the use of hospitals and GPs, and incomplete since they are not aware of illness and disability which does not involve them. Data may also be collected directly from the population, either by self-report (as in the GENERAL HOUSEHOLD SURVEY), or by screening a particular population or sample of a population.

Morbidity rates are of interest to the sociologist in that they vary according to social conditions and social classes. For example, the incidence of chest infections is higher in areas of POVERTY and poor housing, and the incidence of heart disease is related to diet, poverty and membership of the lower social classes. See also DEMOGRAPHY, EPIDEMIOLOGY, BLACK REPORT. SOCIOLOGY OF HEALTH AND MEDICINE.

Moreno, Jacob (1890–1974) Austrian-born, US psychologist who developed early forms of PSYCHOTHERAPY – *psychodrama* and *sociodrama* – which involve role-playing to act out troublesome emotions and relationships. Psychodrama may take place only between the person and therapist, or in groups when several or all members of the group may role-play. The more usual term for group role-playing is sociodrama (see also GROUP THERAPY). Moreno also developed the technique of SOCIOMETRY.

mores the accepted and strongly prescribed forms of behaviour within any society or community (W. G. Sumner, 1906). Mores are contrasted by SUMNER with FOLKWAYS in that the latter, though socially sanctioned, are less fundamental, less abstract in organization, and whose transgressions are less severely punished than those of mores.

Morgan, Lewis Henry (1818–81) American ethnologist and anthropologist, whose principal influence on sociology, and on Marxism, can be traced to his materialistic theory of social evolution (see EVOLUTIONARY THEORY) presented in *Ancient Society* (1877).

Morgan's first venture into ETHNOGRAPHY was a detailed study of the Iroquois Indians, the results of which were not published until 1891, after his death. Struck by the distinctive mode of relative classification, Morgan hypothesized that a search for similar systems abroad might establish the geographical origins of the American Indian. This led to a massive research effort. The result, which Morgan held to prove the 'Asiatic origin' of the tribes, appeared in 1871 (*Systems of Consanguinity and Affinity of the Human Family*).

Morgan's analysis of KINSHIP terminology suggested an evolutionary process, with family relationships developing through early promiscuity to 'civilized' monogamy. Later, Morgan was to give the hypothesis of a general process of social evolution more systematic attention. This resulted in his most famous work, *Ancient Society* (1877). Two approaches to SOCIAL CHANGE were explored: IDEALISM and MATERIALISM. According to the former, social INSTITUTIONS developed as a reflection of changing and accumulating human ideas; according to the latter, human CULTURE evolved to the extent that people were able to exert increasing control over nature. In this way human society moved through three basic stages: SAVAGERY, BARBARISM, and CIVILIZATION.

Morgan drew on a wide range of ethnographic data in pursuing these ideas, ranging from material on Australian aborigines to the societies of Ancient Greece and Rome. His idea of the evolutionary role of increasing control over the material reproduction of life resonated strongly with the materialist conception of history being evolved by Marx and Engels. For Morgan the history of property and the evolution of culture were inextricably linked. Moreover, the property-centredness of modern societies stood in the way of advance to a social order of greater justice. It is small wonder that *Ancient Society* became a classic text in the foundation of Marxist thought. Marx himself planned a text on Morgan, though this was never written. Engels, in *The Origin of the Family, Private Property and the State* (1884), explicitly recognized Morgan's independent formulation of historical materialism.

Morgan remains one of the founding figures in anthropology, and together with E. B. TYLOR and Herbert SPENCER, stands out as one of the great systematic evolutionary theorists of the 19th-century.

mortality rate see DEATH RATE.

Mosca, Gaetano (1858–1941) Italian political scientist and politician who, along with PARETO and Michels, is usually identified as one of the originators of ÉLITE THEORY. In Mosca's view, society always consisted of two 'classes' of individuals: the rulers and the ruled. Like Pareto, with whom he continuously contested the priority in formulating élite theory, Mosca regarded many of the justifications (*political formulae*) which surround rule as merely a veneer of rationalizations underpinning and preserving political power. He acknowledged that a distinction existed between political systems which were guided by 'liberal' principles (i.e. having an elected leadership) and those that were simply 'autocratic'. What he denied was that such an arrangement, including provision for recruitment of new entrants to the political élite, meant 'government by the people' or 'majority rule'. By the same token, although classes could be represented in government, there could be no question of rule by an entire class – least of all a 'classless society' – in the way suggested by Marx. Mosca's best-known work *Elementi di scienza politica* (1896), variously revised in successive editions was translated as *The Ruling Class* in 1939. It is a mistake to regard Mosca as an advocate of autocracy, rather his own preference was for particular forms of representative democracy. His theory can be seen as the forerunner of the influential modern theory of DEMOCRATIC ÉLITISM – with its celebration of representative élites, and its scaling down of what it regards as the unrealistic expectations associated with conceptions of participatory democracy and Marxism.

motivation (PSYCHOLOGY) the energizer of behaviour. This may be a physiological need, such as hunger, or it may be emotional, such as love, or it may involve the cognitive appraisal of a situation. Motivation may be *intrinsic*, the fulfilment of the need leading to personal satisfaction, or *extrinsic*, where the rewards are external to the individual rather than personally significant. See also MASLOW, NEEDS(S), VOCABULARY OF MOTIVES.

multiculturalism the acknowledgement and promotion of cultural pluralism. In opposition to the tendency in modern societies to cultural unification and universalization, multiculturalism both celebrates and seeks to protect cultural variety (e.g. minority languages), while at the same time focusing on the often unequal relationship of minority to mainstream cultures. After decades of persecution, the prospects of indigenous or immigrant cultures are now helped somewhat by the support they receive from international public opinion and the international community (e.g. the United Nations). See also PLURAL SOCIETY.

multidimensional analysis of social stratification any approach to the analysis of SOCIAL STRATIFICATION and CLASS which emphasizes the importance of a plurality of factors in the determination of the overall SOCIOECONOMIC STATUS or CLASS LOCATION of a person or particular category of persons. Often such a view is seen as stemming from WEBER's as against MARX's approach to the analysis of social stratification and class (see CLASS, STATUS AND PARTY). Among the most influential formulation in these terms is David LOCKWOOD's analysis of the class location of BLACK-COATED WORKERS, where he proposes three separate dimensions: MARKET SITUATION, WORK SITUATION and STATUS SITUATION. The importance of multiple dimensions to stratification, and the significance of these influencing CLASS CONSCIOUSNESS, was also central in the AFFLUENT WORKER studies, in which Lockwood and John GOLDTHORPE were the main researchers. More recently, the idea of sectoral interests which cross cut more conventional class locations has been advanced. (see SECTORAL CLEAVAGES).

While multiple dimensions of social stratification may be seen as undermining more unitary conceptions of 'class', especially Marxist conceptions, the argument is not decisive. Examples of Marxian forms of analysis which involve multidimensional analysis, include those emphasizing CONTRADICTORY CLASS LOCATIONS (see also INTERMEDIATE CLASSES OR INTERMEDIATE STRATA). The crucial difference between Marxian and non-Marxian theories lies more in what the implications of a multidimensional analysis are ultimately seen to be, e.g. whether or not analysis is conducted in terms of an assumption that 'objective' economic interests determine class relations and class conflict in the long-run. See also STATUS CONSISTENCY AND INCONSISTENCY.

multidimensional scaling see SCALING.

multinational company *or* **multinational corporation** a company which operates from a home base in one country with subsidiaries in others. The term *transnational company* has increasingly been preferred to describe large international corporations since they may not have an easily identifiable home base. World economy and trade is increasingly dominated by such companies which many authors see as outside the control of national governments. This raises issues of the control which such governments have over their own economies. Whilst the role of multinational companies has been decisive for the fate of THIRD WORLD economies and is central to the concept of IMPERIALISM and NEOIMPERIALISM, the largest companies have the majority of their investments in industrial countries. Investment in the Third World may not be the most important area for multinational companies, but they derive high profits from such investments and the effect on small Third World countries can be very significant. See also DEPENDENT INDUSTRIALIZATION, DEPENDENCY THEORY, UNEQUAL EXCHANGE.

multivariate analysis the analysis of data collected on several different VARIABLES. For example, in a study of housing provision, data may be collected on age, income, family size (the 'variables') of the population being studied. In analysing the data the effect of each of these variables can be examined, and also the interaction between them.

There is a wide range of multivariate techniques available but most aim to simplify the data in some way in order to clarify relationships between variables. The choice of method depends on the nature of the data, the type of problem and the objectives of the analysis. FACTOR ANALYSIS and principle component analysis are exploratory, and used to find new underlying variables. CLUSTER ANALYSIS seeks to find natural groupings of objects or individuals. *Discriminant analysis* is a technique designed to clarify the differentiation between groups influenced by the independent variable(s). Other techniques, e.g. multiple REGRESSION ANALYSIS, aim to explain the variation in one variable by means of the variation in two or more independent variables. MANOVA (multivariate analysis of variance), an extension of the univariate ANALYSIS OF VARIANCE, is used when there are multiple independent variables, as in the example above. An example of multivariate techniques for analysing categorical data is LOG-LINEAR ANALYSIS.

multiversity Clark KERR's (1982) conception of a multicentred and multifunctional HIGHER EDUCATION institution, containing within it a variety of levels and kinds of provision, e.g. élite and mass, nonvocational and vocational, etc. Kerr envisaged such institutions replacing the more unified traditional UNIVERSITY.

music see SOCIOLOGY OF MUSIC AND DANCE.

mutual knowledge 'the necessary respect' which the social analyst must have for the 'authenticity' of the social actor's knowledge (Giddens, 1984) Mutual knowledge is not corrigible in the light of any social science findings; it is the condition of coming up with any findings.

mutual(ly) assured destruction (MAD) (STRATEGIC THEORY) a situation where the nuclear arsenals of opposed nation states or alliances are approximately equivalent in capacity and invulnerability so that:
(a) neither could inflict sufficient damage on the other to immobilize it and prevent a retaliatory attack; and
(b) unacceptably high levels of destruction would inevitably result for both parties to the conflict if one were to launch an attack given that mechanisms for automatic retaliation are built-in to defence systems. Thus, assuming rational behaviour, the outcome of MAD was theorized to be that no attack will occur. Apart from the ever-present risk of nuclear war happening by accident, a further weakness of strategic thinking based on MAD is that it encouraged a continuous escalation of the ARMS RACE, including attempts to design defensive systems (e.g. the so-called 'Star Wars' programme) which would allow the possibility of victory in a nuclear war (see also SECOND STRIKE CAPABILITY). A further strategic option which earlier had also led to escalation of the arms race was the doctrine of 'flexible response': that in situations of limited attack, the ability to deliver an exactly appropriate level of response is required. This also led to the proliferation of new categories of nuclear weapons. See also NUCLEAR DETERRENCE.

myths and mythologies religious or sacred folktales, whose content concerns the origins or creation of the world, gods, a particular people or society, etc. Sometimes these stories, which have a particular importance in preliterate societies as part of an 'oral tradition' are acted out in RITUALS. See also NARRATIVES.

Mythologies have been of interest to anthropologists:
(a) as a source of quasi-historical data about societies which have no written record;
(b) as a coded indication of the central values of a society;
(c) as a heavily symbolic metaphorical expression of perennial psychic and social tensions e.g. the Oedipus myth (see also OEDIPUS COMPLEX, JUNG);
(d) as revealing, via the logics of myths, the universal structures of the human mind (e.g. the work of LÉVI-STRAUSS). It is the last of these that has recently attracted most interest and has generated much debate.

In LÉVI-STRAUSS's structuralist approach recurring universal *'binary oppositions'* are identified in myths, e.g. opposition between nature and culture, male and female, friendship and hostility. Lévi-Strauss quotes Mauss: 'Men communicate by symbols ... but they can only have those symbols and communicate by them because they have the same instincts.' Lévi-Strauss regards the function of myths as providing 'justifications' for the particular combination of all possible binary oppositions which have been actually adopted in a particular society. However, Lévi-Strauss is more interested in the complex transformations of mythologies across time and across cultures, as in the analysis of particular societies, in the way in which myths structure reality, and in what this reveals about 'primitive universal logic'. The main objection to Lévi-Strauss's structuralist analysis of mythologies, however, is that it is not clear how one can move beyond 'possible' interpretations of the universal logics of myths when many of these interpretations seem arbitrary and leave open other possible interpretations (see Leach, 1970). See also BARTHES.

naive falsificationism see FALSIFICATIONISM.

narcissism a stage of psychosexual development and a pathological psychological state, taken by some social theorists to describe late twentieth-century Western culture. Based on the Greek mythological character Narcissus (or *Narkissos*), who fell in love with his own image as reflected in a spring and whose fate was to fall in and drown, the term has been widely used by psychological theorists and practitioners and social theorists.

In psychoanalytical terms, narcissism refers to a phase of self-love in which the sexual object of desire is the self, representing a regression. The work of post-Freudians, particularly Melanie KLEIN, helped explain the precise process by which this is converted to a continuing disorder. Klein's research with children showed that, in early stages, a child makes no distinction between his/her ego and the surrounding environment. Failure to qualify this in later stages locks the individual into a kind of fusion of self with object images. The inability to differentiate between fantasy arid reality may lead the individual to internalize images of beauty, youth, wealth and omnipotence, a 'grandiose' conception of the self, which acts as a defence against all that seems bad in the environment.

Sociologically, the term is most recently associated with Christopher Lasch's *The Culture of Narcissism* (1991). Lasch employs the concept to characterize a profound cultural change in which a particular 'therapeutic outlook and sensibility' has come to exert an all-pervading effect on modern society. This outlook reinforces 'a pattern created by other cultural influences, in which the individual endlessly examines himself for signs of ageing and ill health, for telltale symptoms of psychic stress, for blemishes and flaws that might diminish his attractiveness'. There are obvious connections, but also important differences of emphasis, between Lasch's thesis and GIDDENS' (1991) proposal of identity crises in late modern society, where an intensified focus on the body and its presentation is a way of creating, sustaining and stabilizing the 'self' (see Shilling, 1993). Thus, for Giddens, unlike Lasch, contemporary *'regimes of the body'* are often positive.

Narodnik see POPULISM.

narratives the popular stories, myths, legends, and the like which bestow LEGITIMACY on social institutions, or accomplish other socially integrative work, by providing positive or negative models of behaviour. See also GRAND NARRATIVE AND METANARRATIVE.

nation a community of sentiment (Max WEBER, 1920) or an imagined community (B. Anderson, *Imagined Communities*, 1983) based on one or more of the following: race, ethnicity, language, religion, customs, political memory, and shared experience of the Other. A nation exists where a people succeeds in its claim to be one by securing recognition of it from others. Ethnicity has proved neither a necessary nor a sufficient condition of nationhood. According to Weber, modern nations usually need a state to protect their integrity and interests, and states usually need a nation if they are to command the allegiance of the individual. There are, however, many stateless nations, such as Scotland, and there have been many nationless (or multinational) states such as Prussia and the Soviet Union. Differences between ethnic nations (communities of descent) and civic nations (associations within a territory) have major implications for pluralism and the accommodation of difference, the character of civil society and the definition of citizenship.

national character see CULTURE AND PERSONALITY SCHOOL.

National Deviancy Conference a group of British sociologists, prominent in the late 1960s and 70s, interested in reconstituting 'traditional' *criminology* and the sociology of DEVIANCE. One of the founder members of the NDC (Cohen, 1981) summarized its interests as including four main themes:
(a) to emphasize the sociological dimension of criminology and integrate it into 'mainstream' sociological interests;
(b) to extend the insights of LABELLING THEORY and SOCIETAL REACTION theory in a more structurally and politically aware way;
(c) to emphasize the importance of the deviants' own understandings and meanings;
(d) to recognize the political character both of defining and of studying crime and deviance.

As Cohen argues, the 'ineptly named' NDC was important as a vehicle for developing new approaches to deviancy (sometimes known as *radical deviancy theory*), and laying the basis, for instance, for 'critical criminology' and later VICTIMOLOGY studies and for radical approaches in Social Work theory and practice (see RADICAL SOCIAL WORK). The emphasis on critical and political issues was very much of its time, and, as external political realities changed and internal theoretical divergences were developed, the NDC fragmented, although its influence is evident in the development and greatly increased status of criminological and deviancy issues within sociology.

National Health Service (NHS) the system of health care provided for all citizens by the UK government.

In 1948, after more than a century of public health reform, and in the centenary year of the first Public Health Act, the National Health Service was established. It occupies a unique position in British society because:
(a) it has the largest client group for social welfare since it provides care for people at all stages of the LIFE COURSE; and
(b) more than any other welfare institution established as a result of the BEVERIDGE REPORT of 1942, the NHS embodies the welfare principle – care as a social service rather than a market commodity. It is the subject of political debate because of New Right theories about the state and the responsibilities of individuals, and it is the subject of academic discussions concerning the power of the medical profession and the nature of illness and health in the UK.

The NHS was set up to provide a fully comprehensive service of curative and preventative medicine for physical and mental illness. The service was to be free at the point of treatment in accordance with the patient's medically defined needs. The means-test principle of eligibility was abolished and the service was funded centrally from insurance and taxation. Its architects believed that the NHS would mop up the pool of ill health and that full employment would combine with the other agencies of the welfare state to lead to higher standards of health and a long-term fall in demand for health services. This has not happened. Rising costs, changes in health expectations, changes in the pattern of disease, demographic change and the persistence of class-related illness (see BLACK REPORT) have resulted in high levels of demand. The balance of supply favours the acute, hospital, interventionist sector at the expense of the community, disability and geriatric sector. Garner (1979) refers to this as the 'no hope, no power' paradigm. These 'Cinderella' patients have no power themselves and no powerful medical interests ranged on their behalf. Their conditions require care rather than cure. In a profession where success is associated with high-technology medicine, conditions which hold out little hope of scientific advance or breakthrough are unattractive to ambitious doctors.

The development of the medical profession in the UK is inseparable from the history of the NHS since it guaranteed the medical monopoly and secured a number of professional rights, i.e.:
(a) the right to contract out of the NHS for private medicine;
(b) independence from some aspects of the NHS management structure for teaching hospitals;
(c) the right of the individual practitioner to prescribe whatever treatment he or she considered appropriate (clinical autonomy);
(d) systems of payment and administration which confirmed the status differentials between hospital doctors and general practitioners, consultants and the rest of the medical profession.

In the 1990s, the NHS has undergone reform. An internal market has been created with the intention of increasing the efficiency of service delivery and enhancing patient choice. The main change has been the institutionalization of a split between purchaser (Health Authority) and provider (hospitals, general practitioner and other services) with providers competing for service contracts. Hospitals and general practitioners have been encouraged to become 'trusts' or 'fundholders, i.e. units which function independently of Health Authority control. Other changes have involved the provision of a 'patient's charter', attempts to introduce performance-related pay for clinical staff, and decisions to abolish regional (but not District) Health Authorities. Critics of these changes are essentially anxious that the resort to market criteria is undermining the founding principle of the NHS (provision of care on the basis of need) with one that looks instead to costs and purchasing power.

National Institute for Clinical Excellence (NICE) an institute established in the UK in 1999 to carry out appraisals of existing and new health interventions. It was established by the Government in response to criticisms that some of the factors influencing health inequalities arise from variations in the treatments offered to patients due to clinical autonomy, the over-prescribing or use of expensive but not necessarily cost-effective drugs and restricted access to treatments because of local decisions on budget management (the 'post-code lottery in health care' as portrayed by the media). The Institute has the authority to issue clinical guidelines giving best practice advice for whole conditions or patient groups. The Institute is an important element in the drive towards EVIDENCE SUPPORTED HEALTH CARE, in that by providing information on the clinical and cost effectiveness of new and existing treatments it will support standards of best practice in health care and play a role in the licensing of new treatments. The first treatments examined were the anti-flu drug Ralenza, hip-replacement prostheses and the value of routine extraction of (non-symptomatic) wisdom teeth. See also SYSTEMATIC REVIEW.

nationalism 1 the belief in, and feeling of belonging to, a people united by common historical, linguistic and perhaps 'racial' or religious ties, where this people is identified with a particular territory and either constitutes a NATION STATE or has aspirations to do so.

2 Any related ideology which promotes the nation state as the most appropriate form for modern government.

Overwhelmingly, premodern states were not political communities in the sense of presenting themselves as based on a single people. Outside Europe and in Europe before the 16th-century, most states have not been nation states, but rather empires or relatively loosely consolidated territories.

Nationalism started life as a European phenomenon, an accompaniment especially of the reorganization and consolidation of modern Western European nation states in the 17th and 18th centuries. The nascent nation states of Western Europe invented nationalism, as a way of securing their political coherence and political autonomy in new political and economic conditions. In time, however, nationalism also came to represent the aspirations of peoples for self-determination.

It is undeniable that nationalism has bolstered existing nation states and created others by undermining earlier empires, but the expectation in sociology and social science generally has been that nationalism would prove a temporary phenomenon, to be replaced in the long run by internationalism (see MILITANT AND INDUSTRIAL SOCIETY) or by class interests (see MARXISM).

Two World Wars and the aftermath of these in which many more new nations have been created, have confirmed nationalism as a compelling force within the modern world. Once again – in Africa especially – new nation states were created as much by an invented nationalism as by any pre-existing 'nation'. The outcome is a worldwide state system, in which the modern nation state is now the dominant political form and in which nationalism remains a potent force, strongly influencing the relations between states, while sometimes threatening their internal coherence as new demands for recognition of nationhood emerge.

Sociological explanations for such a powerful role for nationalism have concentrated on three areas:
(a) the felt need for collective social identity in large impersonal societies;
(b) the fact that, far from undermining the expression of economic interests, it may reflect these interests;
(c) what Nairn (1977) has called, the 'janus-face' of modern nationalism, i.e. its usefulness as a vehicle for liberalism and radical ideas as well as a justification for violence and intolerant values.

nationalization see PUBLIC OWNERSHIP.

National Socialism *or* **Nazism** the doctrines and political movements associated with the National Socialist German Workers' Party. National Socialism began as a protest movement which especially embraced doctrines of German ('Aryan') racial superiority. It was as the leader of this party that the German World War II fascist leader, Adolf Hitler, rose to power. See also FASCISM.

nation state the modern form of STATE, possessing clearly defined borders, in which the boundaries of state and society tend to be coextensive, i.e. the territorial claims of the state typically correspond with cultural, linguistic and ethnic divisions (see also NATIONALISM). As such, these modern forms of state contrast with the most successful earlier state forms (e.g. preindustrial empires) which usually lacked the administrative or other resources to impose, such cultural integration.

As GIDDENS (1985) puts it, a decisive feature of modern nation states is that they are 'bordered power containers' enclosing far greater administrative intensity than traditional states. Furthermore, these modern states have also existed as part of a NATION-STATE SYSTEM of similarly constituted states, in which:
(a) WARFARE and the preparation for war played a fundamental consitutive role; and
(b) in providing a model, paved the way for all subsequent modern nation states, e.g. in Asia and Africa. In recent years, sociologists have tended to place a new emphasis on the role of the state in transforming the traditional world, often granting political institutions greater autonomy from, and sometimes even primacy over, economic institutions. See also ABSOLUTISM, SOVEREIGNTY, STANDING ARMY, ARMS RACE, CITIZEN, SURVEILLANCE, DEMOCRACY.

nation-state system the territorial division of the modern world into a network of 'national political communities' or NATION STATES, replacing the previous pattern of simple societies and imperial systems. This worldwide contemporary system of nation states (which originally derives from the Western European state-system which grew up in connection with ABSOLUTISM) has a number of decisive implications, above all, the crucial role of WARFARE, or its threat, in shaping the modern world. See also INTERNATIONAL RELATIONS, SOVEREIGNTY, NATIONALISM, STANDING ARMY, IMPERIALISM, CLAUSEWITZ, STRATEGIC THEORY, ARMS RACE, COLD WAR, INTERSOCIETAL SYSTEMS.

nativism 1 (PSYCHOLOGY) the theoretical stance which emphasizes the importance of heredity, the biological underpinnings of human behaviour, rather than the effect of the environment.

2 the negative orientation of any indigenous population to immigrants. See also NATURE – NURTURE DEBATE.

natural economy an economy in which money is either absent or very scarce, in which people produce for themselves with little or no trade within the economy or with other economies. A term which is now little used because of the problems with the word 'natural' and the question as to whether any such societies exist.

naturalistic research methods approaches to social research which emphasize the importance of the study of social life in naturally occurring settings. See also SYMBOLIC INTERACTIONISM.

natural law see NATURAL RIGHTS AND NATURAL LAW.

natural rights and natural law 1 (moral and political philosophy) originally, the doctrine that the principles of right conduct could be discovered by a process of rational enquiry into the nature of Man as God made him. For a political theorist such as John LOCKE, the laws of nature were the commands of God. From natural law, people derive rights to the means which they need in order to perform these duties.

2 the entitlements advanced as attaching to all human beings simply by virtue of their common humanity. While, in this second sense, *natural rights* may still be advanced as the foundation of normative theory, they are nowadays usually detached from their original religious basis, although conceptions that these rights are, or should be, 'self-evident', and that they provide a standard for all evaluations of political and legal rights, remain a powerful force in political discourse.

The connection between natural law, as the commands of God, and natural rights, was a strong element in the United States Declaration of Independence. Thereafter the language of rights becomes steadily divorced from its natural law setting, and, from the French Revolution onwards, takes off into the realm of the 'rights of man'. The 20th-century has added an array of economic and social rights to the original ones (see CIVIL RIGHTS. CITIZEN RIGHTS), but it is now relatively uncommon to meet the terms 'natural rights' and 'natural law' in their original usage, and these have virtually disappeared from everyday political discourse.

natural selection the process by which evolution takes place, involving the SURVIVAL OF THE FITTEST. The theory of evolution was proposed by Charles DARWIN and Alfred Russel Wallace in 1858 and was based on the observation that any characteristic found within a population exhibits variability. This means that some individuals will, as a result, have a survival advantage: they are more 'fit' for survival (and therefore more likely to reproduce and pass on their genes to the next generation) in the current environment. Thus, if skin pigmentation varies within a population living in equatorial regions, individuals with dark skin genes (which confer protection) are more likely to live to reproduce than those with lighter skin genes; and obversely in northern latitudes, where lighter skin maximizes the benefits of lower levels of sunshine. See also EVOLUTIONARY THEORY.

nature-nurture debate the debate surrounding the question of to what extent behaviour is the result of hereditary or innate influences (nature), or is determined by environment and learning (nurture). Assessing the relative contributions of each is extremely difficult, since both interact continually throughout development. Historically each side of the debate has had its support, *nativists* believing in hereditary determination and *empiricists* in the dominance of the environment. See also CHILD DEVELOPMENT, INTELLIGENCE.

Naturwissenschaften see GEISTESWISSENSCHAFTEN AND NATURWISSENSCHAFTEN.

Nazism see NATIONAL SOCIALISM.

need for achievement see ACHIEVEMENT MOTIVATION.

need(s) 1 the basic requirements necessary to sustain human life. MASLOW (1954) suggested a *hierarchy of needs* from the basic physiological needs for food, safety and shelter, to psychological needs of belonging, approval, love, and finally the need for SELF-ACTUALIZATION. Only the physiological needs are essential for sustaining life and, according to Maslow, must be fulfilled before higher needs can be met. Some sociologists have argued that the existence of human needs indicates that universal FUNCTIONAL PREREQUISITES for the survival of any society can be identified.

2 any socially acquired individual 'drive' (*personality need*), e.g. ACHIEVEMENT MOTIVATION.

3 a distinction may also be drawn between *basic needs* and *felt needs*. In ECONOMICS, the term *wants* is used to refer both to psychological and social 'felt needs' and also to the goods which stimulate these.

While many sociologists have registered their dissatisfaction with NEEDS 1, arguing that human needs are not universal but socially formed, conceptions of human needs have not been confined to psychologists or functionalist sociologists. Frankfurt School neo-Marxist sociologists (e.g. MARCUSE) refer to the 'false needs' created by capitalist societies, thus implying human 'needs'. Conceptions of 'absolute' and 'relative' POVERTY also depend on conceptions of physiological and social needs. See also BASIC HUMAN NEEDS.

negantropy see SYSTEMS THEORY.

negation 1 (LOGIC) a proposition that is the denial of another and is true only if the other is false.

2 (MARXISM) a phase or 'moment' in a dialectical process (see DIALECTIC) which negates a previous one, leading ultimately to a resolution ('negation of the negation'). In the work of members of the FRANKFURT SCHOOL OF CRITICAL THEORY (especially ADORNO's *Negative Dialectics*, 1973) *negativity* was expressed as an opposition to all fixed categories and to the 'administered world' to which both orthodox Marxism and POSITIVISM were seen to lead.

negative feedback see SYSTEMS THEORY.

negotiated order an influential idea in studies of organizations which sees social order as the emergent product of processes of negotiation (e.g. conferring, bargaining, making arrangements, compromising, reaching agreements) between persons and groups. Social order is not fixed and immutable but is open to revision and reorganization through these processes. See also ORGANIZATION THEORY.

negritude a cultural and political movement started in the 1930s to encourage the development of pride and dignity in the heritage of black peoples by rediscovering ancient African values and modes of thought. The movement was originally concerned with an artistic and cultural critique of Western societies, but was broadened into a more political programm[illegible] under the influence of Leopold Sengho[illegible] (poet and president of Senegal). Ne[illegible] was an attempt to raise the consc[illegible] of blacks throughout the worl[illegible] BLACK POWER MOVEMENT, [illegible] MOVEMENT, BLACK MUS[illegible]

neoclassical economics the approach to economic analysis, arising especially from the work of Alfred Marshall (1842–1924) and Leon Walras (1834–1910). This dominated ECONOMICS between 1870 and 1930. It replaced the explicitly sociopolitical analysis, in terms of land, capital and labour, which characterized the work of CLASSICAL ECONOMISTS, including MARX (see also POLITICAL ECONOMY), with a more formal analysis of the conditions for the optimal allocation of scarce resources. The approach can be described as 'subjectivist', since its central concept, *utility*, defined as the 'individual' satisfaction obtained from the consumption of a good or service, cannot be measured directly but can only be inferred from market behaviour. The approach is also known as *marginal analysis*, since its central assumption is that economic returns will be maximized whenever equilibria are reached in competitive markets, the point at which 'marginal utilities' or 'marginal revenues' cease (i.e. where no more of a good or service will be purchased, or where one more unit of production would yield a negative return). While earlier theories of VALUE based on the 'costs of production' found room for notions such as EXPLOITATION, no place exists for these in neoclassical theory. Thus it has been suggested that neoclassical economics be seen as involving special pleading on behalf of CAPITALISM AND CAPITALIST MODE OF PRODUCTION. Others, however, argue that the 'marginal revolution' in economics can be accounted for by the inherent superiority of this mode of analysis.

neo-Clausewitzians modern strategic theorists (e.g. Raymond ARON and Herman Kahn), whose thinking on warfare, including nuclear warfare, has been influenced by the 19th-century military theorist, Karl von CLAUSEWITZ. According to Rapoport (1968), the arguments of neo-Clausewitzians roceed along three lines:

) against the idea that war can be lawed;

(b) the identification of anticommunism and US ideology, especially during the COLD WAR period, with the defence of Western Civilization and the interests of humanity;

(c) an insistence that the extent and intensity of war can be controlled, but only by DETERRENCE.

neocolonialism 1 the attempt by former colonial powers to retain political and economic dominance over former colonies which have achieved formal political independence.

2 (more generally) the process whereby advanced industrial countries dominate THIRD WORLD countries regardless of whether colonial relationships previously existed. The term *neoimperialism* has a similar meaning although it is usually associated with a Marxist perspective. See also COLONIALISM, IMPERIALISM.

neoevolutionism a school of theory emerging in the middle of the 20th-century which attempted to revivify the explanation of SOCIAL CHANGE according to evolutionary principles (see DARWIN, EVOLUTIONARY THEORY).

Neoevolutionism probably received its most theoretically complex expression in the work of PARSONS (1964, 1966, 1971). The key texts here represent a systematic attempt to show that FUNCTIONALISM could produce an adequate account of social change, and that neoevolutionary theory could overcome the deficiencies of its forerunners. Nineteenth-century evolutionism has been compromised by three principle problems: its unidirectional assumptions (see UNILINEAR), an inability to specify adequately the intermediate stages of development between simple and complex societies, and a moralistic and ethnocentric view of progress.

The problem of unilinearity is dealt with, in the neoevolutionary approach, by drawing a distinction between the *general* evolutionary process, conceived in terms of crucial cultural, institutional or structural breakthroughs (such as language, writing, legal systems, money, markets, bureaucracy, stratification, etc.) achieved in different societies at different times, and the concrete evolution of any *specific* society. The development of these breakthroughs (or EVOLUTIONARY UNIVERSALS, as Parsons calls them) plays a critical part in his approach, for 'universals' enhance SOCIAL DIFFERENTIATION (see also FUNCTIONAL PREREQUISITES AND FUNCTIONAL IMPERATIVES) and so the 'general adaptive capacity of society'. Given that evolutionary universals may be 'borrowed' by, or diffused from, one society to another, the specific evolutionary path of any concrete society will not necessarily follow the general evolutionary pattern.

These concepts also allow Parsons to confront the issue of how to characterize intermediate stages of social development. Simply, this is achieved by using the degree of structural differentiation achieved, and kinds of integrative (see INTEGRATION AND MALINTEGRATION) solutions adopted. In effect, this is equivalent to the number and kinds of evolutionary universals which have been incorporated. Parsons identifies five distinct stages in the general evolutionary process, each of which is exemplified by historical or existing societies. The final stage, that of advanced industrialism, is the 'terminus' of the evolutionary process, and the future therefore of all currently existing societies which have not yet achieved industrialization.

The solution to the final problem – that of obtaining a value-free definition of evolutionary advance – should now be apparent. In Parsons' scheme, notions of 'progress' are reduced to the empirically specifiable concept of 'general adaptive capacity'. Other neoevolutionary theorists, for example the anthropologists Sahlins and Service (1960), share the Parsonian tactic of using empirically identifiable criteria. Rather than relying on a concept such as 'evolutionary universal', however, they suggest that evolutionary advance may be measured in terms of the efficiency with which societies are able to exploit energy resources, which is in turn related to enhanced autonomy from environmental factors, and the ability to displace and replace less advanced societies.

Parsons (1964) is specific that neoevolutionary theory has substantive implications for development policy in the Third World. It is on this issue that most of the deficiencies of the approach have come to light. A. C. FRANK's (1969) famous polemic points out that what neoevolutionary theory such as that of Parsons, or an economic version such as that proposed by W. W. ROSTOW (1960), lacks is the perception of an historical connection between development and UNDERDEVELOPMENT, i.e. that the development of the First World led to, and continues to sustain, the underdevelopment of the Third World. The Third World has continued to face problems of development, despite the centuries-long exposure to the diffusion of 'Western' evolutionary universals, and the values of 'achievement' and 'universalism' which underpin the patterns of role relationships in successful industrialized societies.

It is doubtful, too, whether Parsons actually succeeded (or even really meant to succeed) in producing a value-free theory of social change. Development is still conceived in Western terms. This is apparent in terms of the implications which neoevolutionary theory was meant to have for Third World governments interested in development, and even more so in terms of its implications for the developed communist world. One of the crucial evolutionary universals for Parsons is the 'democratic association' (held to separate POWER from bureaucratic office). Industrial societies lacking this political complex, like the USSR, are then held to be deviant or pathological examples of developmen[illegible] In this way, Parsonian theory can easi[illegible] supply theoretical justification for d[illegible] powers to intervene in Third W[illegible] where communist movemen[illegible] take control of the state.

Further important critical contributions may be found in GELLNER (1964), POPPER (1957) and BENDIX (1970). See also EVOLUTIONARY SOCIOLOGY.

neo-Freudians followers of FREUD who have modified his theory, often elaborating and clarifying its concepts and developing it further according to their own experience as analysts.

These theorists emphasize social and cultural influences on the PERSONALITY and de-emphasize the role of biological factors. They regard some parts of his theory, e.g. the emphasis on the role of the instincts and particularly of sex as central, as outdated, and they generally find no evidence for the OEDIPUS COMPLEX or the implied inferiority of women except as manifestations of cultural forces. Neurosis is seen as the outcome of problematic interpersonal relationships, and a healthy personality also as a social product.

Among the most influential neo-Freudians are: Erich FROMM, Erik Erikson, Carl JUNG, Karen Horney, Harry Stack Sullivan, Alfred Adler, David Rapaport. Though they can all be regarded as humanistic, their theories are personally distinctive and the above generalities are found in very different forms in their personal reworkings of Freudian theory. See also EGO-PSYCHOLOGY, OBJECT RELATIONS SCHOOL.

neoimperialism see NEOCOLONIALISM.

neo-Kantian applied to German social philosophical movements of the late 19th- and early 20th-century that attempted to 'return to KANT', acknowledging:

(a) an objective (or intersubjective) phenomenal realm (natural science); and

(b) the social realm, a realm of human ACTION and values. During the METHODENSTREIT of the 1890s, RICKERT and Windelband were particularly influential in reintroducing the idea that mind and mental CATEGORIES shape our perceptions of the world, and in stressing a distinction between the 'historical' and cultural sciences, concerned with unique configurations, and the 'natural' sciences, and insisted that the former required a method that recognized the specificity and value-related nature of their subject matter. They suggested that any attempt to analyse and describe the social world is thus bound to simplify either by imposing general categories or in interpreting reality in relation to its relevance for values. This way of thinking influenced both SIMMEL and WEBER. See also IDIOGRAPHIC AND NOMOTHETIC.

neo-liberalism see NEW RIGHT.

Neolithic Age the stage of human biological and cultural evolution characterized by the development of agriculture, domestication of animals and new kinds of stone tools. Literally it means 'new stone age' and is regarded as being the first great cultural revolution in human development following the PALAEOLITHIC AGE.

neo-Machiavellians a term sometimes applied to the group of political sociologists and political theorists, especially PARETO, MOSCA, and MICHELS, who in an analogous way to MACHIAVELLI, prided themselves on their 'realistic' analysis of political power, e.g. emphasis on the role of élites. See also ÉLITE, ÉLITE THEORY.

neo-Marxist denoting any recent theorists and theories which draw on Marx's thinking, or on the Marxist tradition, while at the same time revising and reorienting this, e.g. SARTRE's existentialist Marxism or HABERMAS's critical theory. See also MARXIST SOCIOLOGY, MARXISM.

neo-natal mortality rate a rate calculated by taking the number of infant deaths which occur in the first four weeks of life in any one year, divided by the total number of live births in the same year multiplied by one thousand. In most advanced societies, this rate can be seen to vary significantly by social class, with LIFE CHANCES increasing for children born in higher social classes.

neo-tribes a term used by M. Maffesoli (*Les temps des tribus*, 1991, tr. 1996) to refer to temporary social groups which cohere intensely around immediate consumption activity and then disperse into the general state of fragmented, nomadic anonymity which is said to characterize ordinary social life. Somewhat eccentrically, Maffesoli uses the case of the orgy as an example of this phenomenon. More commonplace examples are perhaps festival crowds, sports crowds, political gatherings and CARNIVAL groups. While the neo-tribe is only constituted sporadically as a physical entity, it subsists in continuous social life through magazines, television audiences, internet groupings, and the like.

network society (CASTELLS, 1996) the new global order formed by the emergence of new information and communication technologies, a 'space of flows' in which new patterns – 'networks' – of transnational economic and social relations are determined by the new technology.

network theory the doctrine, in the philosophy of science, associated with Duhem (1861–1916) and Mary Hesse (1980), that scientific statements cannot be appraised in isolation from the overall framework of concepts and theories in which they are stated. See also THEORY RELATIVITY, INCOMMENSURABILITY.

neurosis a disorder of the emotions with no underlying physical cause for the feelings of ill health it engenders. Neurosis is a term covering a variety of AFFECTIVE DISORDERS, such as anxiety, *depression* and obsessive states. Though there is no disease, there is considerable unhappiness. Mental health may be restored through various therapies, PSYCHOANALYSIS primarily being designed to help neurotics, but client-centred therapy (see Carl ROGERS) within the counselling movement, and cognitive BEHAVIOUR THERAPY are also appropriate. Neurosis should be distinguished from PSYCHOSIS which describes much more severe mental illness, such as schizophrenia.

neutralization of deviance the rationalizations of their own actions by which deviants (see DEVIANCE) minimize or justify their deviant acts. See DELINQUENT DRIFT.

new class the concept, first formulated by the Yugoslavian dissident writer Milovan Djilas in 1957, that eastern European societies had not succeeded in overthrowing class rule and were in fact dominated by a new dominant class of party bureaucrats.

More recently GOULDNER (1979) has generalized the notion, suggesting that, despite Marx's assumptions, the underclass in any revolution *never* come to power, nor do they seem likely to do so in future. Gouldner identifies five theories of the forms in which the 'new class' appears within modern societies:

(a) a new class of 'benign democrats' and managers, e.g. the theories of GALBRAITH, BELL, and of Berle and Means (1932);

(b) the new class as a 'master class', which is simply a further 'moment in a long-continuing circulation of historical élites', and still exploitative (e.g. Bakunin's view);

(c) the new class as 'old class ally', in which the new class are seen as 'dedicated professionals' who uplift the old moneyed class to a new 'collectivity-oriented' view (e.g. PARSONS);

(d) the new class as the 'servants of power', in which the moneyed or capitalist class retains power much as it always did (e.g. CHOMSKY, 1969, and Zeitlin, 1977);

(e) the new class as a 'flawed universal class' (Gouldner's own view); that the new class remains 'self-seeking' and out to control its own work situation, but is 'the best card that history has presently given us to play'.

Gouldner suggests that the new class in this fifth sense is growing, and is more powerful and independent than suggested by Chomsky but less powerful than suggested by Galbraith.

new deviancy theory a 'radical' approach to the study of DEVIANCE which has presented itself as an alternative to 'positivist' approaches which suggested that one could 'scientifically' establish biological, physiological, psychological or social determinants of deviance, and that a scientific approach necessitates an 'objective' and non-political stance. Against such deterministic perspectives, new deviancy theory emphasized an interactionist approach which took the understanding of the *meanings* of deviant actors, and the 'social construction' of deviance, as central. The common starting point for practitioners of new deviancy theory was LABELLING, emphasizing SOCIETAL REACTION rather than 'human nature' as a determinant of deviancy. Emerging in the late 1960s and early 70s, new deviancy theory argued that it was crucial to understand the political implications of deviance, and that the political stance of the researcher should be made explicit. The predominant politics of new deviancy theory were libertarian and hence anti-authority. Typically theorists 'took the side' of the deviant against various 'forces of reaction': the family, the police, courts, prisons and the state. This political stance had several consequences. One was an emphasis on the damaging effects of social control – an interest in prisons, for example, which emphasized the brutalizing effects of incarceration and the fact that imprisonment did not deter offenders. Other typical areas of interest were the users of 'soft' drugs (Young, 1971), and studies debunking popular myths about 'young hooligans' (Cohen, 1971). As Young later acknowledged, they tended to take 'easy' topics and frequently ignored the devastating effects of crime, e.g. on women, black people and the working class. For all this, new deviancy theory has been highly influential in developing later criminological approaches. These developments are summarized in Young (1988), and for a selection of papers showing a different line of development see Cohen (1988). See also NATIONAL DEVIANCY CONFERENCE.

new international division of labour (NIDL) the change in the world economy whereby some manufacturing processes are located in the THIRD WORLD. Frobel et al. (1980) offer the most systematic analysis of this process, arguing that changes in communication and transport in the 1970s, combined with slow-downs of growth and profitability in the most advanced capitalist industrial countries, have made the location of manufacturing in the Third World profitable. Most commonly, assembly processes in textiles and electrical goods were moved by TRANSNATIONAL COMPANIES to countries which had cheap and politically repressed labour forces. Typically the factories were located in Free Trade Zones without tariff or other barriers on imports or exports. Nearly all the production was exported, giving rise to the term *World Market Factories* and to EXPORT-ORIENTED INDUSTRIALIZATION. Changes in production processes, telecommunications and transport meant that large firms could use skilled and technical labour for some processes in advanced countries, and untrained, low-paid labour for routine processes in the South. Any one product could be assembled from components produced in several different countries.

Whilst the term has come into more general usage to account for the emergence of manufacturing processes in the South, the analysis provided by Frobel et al. is only partial. As Jenkins (1984 and 1986) has cogently argued, the industrialization process in the Third World is more complex and varied. Thus, little of the Latin American manufacturing capacity is located in World Market Factories or Free Trade Zones and much of the Southeast Asian industrialization is locally owned and covers a wider range of processes than routine assembly. But it remains true that some of the poorer and smaller Third World countries may only have this type of manufacturing. Recent changes may be leading to the reversal of this process. For example, computerization of textile production favours relocation back to Northern countries. See also NEWLY INDUSTRIALIZING COUNTRIES, DEPENDENT INDUSTRIALIZATION, DIVISION OF LABOUR.

New Labour a label applied to the British Labour Party after 1994/5. The term was deliberately coined to distance the Labour Party, under the leadership of Tony Blair, from the Party's postwar past and demonstrate that the Party had broken with Keynesian social democracy (see also KEYNESIAN ECONOMICS), abandoned collectivism and accepted the overall supremacy of the market economy. The deletion from Clause Four of the Party's constitution of the commitment to public ownership was a key stage in Labour's ideological transformation. Whilst Clause Four had exerted little effective influence over Party policy for generations, its revision in 1995 symbolized Labour's ideological shift.

The political values emphasised by New Labour include personal responsibility and partnership as well as the importance of community values and the SOCIAL INVESTMENT STATE. Although New Labour must be seen as a revisionist response to the British, and indeed the global, political landscape of the 1990s, the values New Labour identifies with are often depicted as a return to the ethical socialism held by the Party's founders. There are parallels especially with Clinton's Democratic Party in the US (in some respects employed as a direct model), and in recent years an 'ideological' gloss on new labour or new democratic has been provided by the concept of the THIRD WAY. During the 1990s changes to the Party's organisational structure strengthened the authority of the leadership and limited the capacity of constituency activists and affiliated trade unions to challenge the New Labour project.

New Left a loose grouping of intellectual movements in the UK and the US from the 1950s onwards, drawing on MARXISM, and concerned with promoting socialism. The New Left tended to be critical of the Soviet Union, and distanced itself from rigid forms of Marxist analysis. The Russian suppression of the Hungarian Revolution in 1956 was an important watershed, in which many of those subsequently active in the New Left left the Communist Party. The translation and greater availability of Marx's more 'humanistic' works and also the *Grundrisse* was also significant. In the UK, many leading intellectuals have been associated with the movement, including the historians Edward THOMPSON and Perry ANDERSON, the cultural theorist Raymond Williams and the sociologist Stuart HALL. The movement's leading theoretical journal is the *New Left Review.*

In a wider sense, the New Left also embraces other radical social and political movements, including the Campaign for Nuclear Disarmament, and the Feminist Movement. In the US, the CIVIL RIGHTS MOVEMENT and movements opposed to the Vietnam War can also be regarded as part of the New Left. Although links sometimes exist, the New Left is usually distinguished from Trotskyist or Maoist political organizations (more often seen as branches of the 'old Left') and from urban terrorist movements such as the Baader-Meinhof group or the Red Army Faction.

It is notable how over the years many of the initially radical ideas of the New Left, existing at first outside or only marginally within academia, have become incorporated as part of the broad academic mainstream of social science discourse (e.g. see CULTURAL STUDIES, HISTORY WORKSHOP JOURNAL). In the 1980s, in both the UK and the US, the New Left was counterbalanced by the appearance of a NEW RIGHT, finding expression in such research organizations as the Adam Smith Institute and the Centre for Policy Studies, and journals such as the *Salisbury Review.* However, the output of the New Right has yet to gain the kind of bridgehead in sociology gained by the New Left. See also RADICAL SOCIAL WORK.

newly industrializing countries a number of countries in southern Europe, Asia and Latin America which have developed industrial manufacturing capacity since the 1960s. The countries most commonly cited as belonging to this category are, in Europe, Spain, Portugal and Greece; in Asia, Hong

Kong, Singapore, Taiwan and South Korea; and in Latin America, Argentina, Brazil and Mexico. However, these do not have common experiences. The Asian countries have had the most independent industrialization with the emergence of indigenous corporations and strong state support leading to high levels of exports of manufactured goods. While they incurred INTERNATIONAL DEBT in this process, their export earnings are high enough to enable them to pay this, and in the 1980s their industrialization continued. The Latin American countries had higher levels of foreign investment, less successful state support and lower levels of exports of manufactured goods. The rise of international debt led to problems of payment and their industrialization declined in the 1980s as they reverted to exports of non-manufactured goods in attempts to earn foreign currency. Thus the Latin American countries have been described as having a pattern of DEPENDENT INDUSTRIALIZATION. Harris (1987) provides a good overview. See also IMPORT SUBSTITUTION.

new middle class see CONTRADICTORY CLASS LOCATIONS

new petty bourgeoisie categories of supervisory and mental workers (e.g. many office workers) who, according to neo-Marxist theorists such as Poulantazas (1975), should be placed outside the working class (even though they sometimes produce SURPLUS VALUE) but also should not be seen as part of the traditional BOURGEOISIE (since they do not own or control the means of production). In Poulantazas' view such workers are usually hostile to the working class and, like, the traditional petty bourgeoisie, remain caught between labour and capital. See also INTERMEDIATE CLASSES, CONTRADICTORY CLASS LOCATIONS.

New Public Management (NPM) forms of management that import techniques from business and private industry into the public sector. This form of management emphasises 'value for money' (VFM) as well as techniques such as TOTAL QUALITY MANAGEMENT (TQM). Sometimes these methods lead to full PRIVATIZATION. See also AUDIT.

new religious movements (NRM) sectarian or communitarian groups of worshippers, not necessarily Christian, who have usually undergone an intense conversion experience, and are often regarded with suspicion or even hostility by the public and press. Barker (1989) estimates that there are at least five hundred different new religious movements in the UK. This apparent diversity – expressed in the differences of outlook and constituency, and in the methods of recruitment of the many various groups – has been usefully conceptualized by Wallis (1984), who divides them into *'world rejecting'* (e.g. the Moonies, Hare Krishna), *'world affirming'* (e.g. Transcendental Meditation, Scientology) and *'world accommodating'* movements (e.g. evangelical, charismatic, *'born again'* Christian renewal groups).

World rejection movements expect their converts to reject their past lives, and to separate themselves from family and friends. The outside world is regarded with suspicion and hostility. Personal identity is submerged into the collective identity of the community, which always takes priority over the individual, and which encourages the sharing of possessions and affection. World affirming movements see the external world more benevolently. These movements tend to be more individualistic, with belief systems less clearly codified and articulated and acts of worship less organized. World affirming movements tend to regard everyone as having hidden potential and capacities which can be unlocked by believers and practitioners. Happiness and contentment are seen as something within everyone's grasp, provided that new ways of relating to the world (rather than rejecting or transforming it) are adopted. World accommodating movements tend to emphasize the importance of individual religious experience. Evangelical church groups are typical, where collective celebrations of faith are the vehicle for feelings of intense personal involvement with the spiritual and sacred realms addressed in acts of worship.

Though diverse and numerous, NRM tend individually to have only a small number of members. Public hostility is thus not justified by their numerical strength. Rather, this hostility should be seen as a product of the particular orientation which different groups adopt towards the world: in so far as world rejecting movements demand the total involvement of their members, and the breaking of family ties, anger and resentment are going to be almost inevitable consequences. NRM seem to have grown as a result of people's dissatisfaction with the kind of religious experience offered by the traditional Christian churches. Arguably, too, they can be seen as a response to the 'crisis of identity' in late modernity discussed by GIDDENS (1991). Given, however, the relatively small number of people actually involved in NRM, and the fact that they seem to appeal mostly to the young middle class, and then only for a few years, their recent growth cannot be seen as something which seriously offsets the trend towards SECULARIZATION. See also SECT, CULT, SOCIOLOGY OF RELIGION.

New Right the term applied to a range of ideologies and groups which aim to promote free-market, anti-welfarist, libertarian, and paradoxically sometimes socially authoritarian policies.

Several writers have questioned whether there is such a thing as a New Right, or if it is merely the old right reasserting its dominance. That this is the case in the UK may be indicated by the name of the leading research body, the Adam Smith Institute, as well as by the fact that some 'New Rightists' have called for a return to 'Victorian values'.

However, in another important sense the New Right is new. Its emergence has marked a radical break from the postwar consensus regarding economics and social welfare. The basic argument of this *radical right* is that the search for egalitarianism, and the equal distribution of resources, has deflected society's efforts away from the goals of individual freedom and economic growth and profit maximization (see also FISCAL CRISIS IN THE CAPITALIST STATE).

It is possible to identify several key values in such radical rightism:

(a) a stress on 'free-market' theory and the 'rolling back of the boundaries of the state, especially the WELFARE STATE;

(b) the efficiency of market-distributed rewards and incentives, compared with any system of bureaucratic planning. According to one of their major ideological sources, the works of Hayek (1944), any level of state economic planning represents the first step on the 'road to serfdom'. It is the state which impedes individual initiative, the major source of social prosperity;

(c) public spending is seen as parasitic on the private economy which generates wealth. High levels of taxation to fund public programmes lessen incentives to work and mean that the production of goods and services is less than it could be, thereby reducing economic growth. Any social welfare provision must not damage the system of rewards. Indeed, the New Right express a belief in structured inequality as necessary to reward 'success' and to provide the incentives necessary for the creation of wealth.

Alongside the *radical right* described above, a further strand of New Right ideology is the *authoritarian right*. Such thinkers largely agree with the virtues of free enterprise but argue for a strong state which provides a lead on matters of morals. They argue that the state should concern itself with issues of morals even at the expense of limiting individual freedom. Roger Scruton (1986), for example, has argued that the promotion of a 'normal' heterosexual family should underpin state intervention in social policy. The influence of the authoritarian right can also be seen in claims that previous state intervention has caused a wide range of social problems, such as promiscuity, divorce and single parenthood. See also MORAL CRUSADE; compare AUTHORITARIAN PERSONALITY, LEFT-RIGHT CONTINUUM.

Several writers have identified what they believe are the key characteristics of the New Right. Gamble (1985) has argued that the New Right is best identified by the emphasis it places on the role of a strong state in sustaining order, discipline and hierarchy. In the UK, it is this which explains the paradox of recent governments committed to a reduced role for the state but which have been more rather than less interventionist. Hall (1983) has identified as a main feature of the new right its 'authoritarian populism'. He argues that this differs from traditional CONSERVATISM, because rather than seeming to limit the political involvement of the masses, it makes a direct appeal to the masses, playing on prejudice. This creates a general climate of opinion which benefits conservative forces at the expense of the left.

Golding (1983) has argued that the most important impact of the New Right has been ideological. It has succeeded in converting LAISSEZ-FAIRE ideology into 'common sense' ideas which manifest as public concern surrounding the 'welfare burden'. See also THATCHERISM.

new social movements see SOCIAL MOVEMENTS, SUB-POLITICS.

new technology any form of technology which is more advanced or automated relative to that which preceded it in a given social context. The term is normally used to refer to information and communications technologies based upon microelectronics. 'New technology' entered the sociological vocabulary in the early 1970s. The term is used loosely, often left undefined, or assumed to include the various applications of microelectronics. Other 'new' technologies, such as biotechnology or the technologies of light, have, so far, received little attention from sociologists.

Developments in information technology have been heralded by some writers as a major qualitative advance in technology, compared to mechanization, such that they warrant the label 'information society' or 'second industrial revolution' (BELL, 1980). Studies of technology in the 1960s generally divided technical change into three broad stages: craft production, mechanization and automation (see TECHNOLOGY), but recent research has adopted more complex classifications to more accurately describe the changes involved with information technology. In manufacturing, three broad stages of AUTOMATION have been identified (Coombs, 1985), namely:
(a) primary mechanization, i.e. the transformation of raw materials into products;
(b) secondary mechanization, i.e. the mechanization of transfer of materials between machines (for example, the continuous-flow assembly line);
(c) tertiary mechanization, i.e. the use of information technology to control and program the operations of transformation and transfer in the overall production process.

Information technology therefore involves a considerable advance in process technology (the way things are done) which is more significant than developments in product technology (what is produced). The implications of process technology for work and employment have been examined in studies of economic growth and innovation (see LONG-WAVE THEORY, DIFFUSION OF INNOVATIONS) and, in sociology, in research into unemployment and the INFORMAL ECONOMY (Pahl and Gershuny, 1979). In the service sector the introduction of information technology has involved similar developments in process technology where the range of new computer and communications applications have automated the collection, processing and retrieval of information.

Sociological research into new technology has included its relationship to changes in occupational structure and unemployment and, in the workplace, changes in the nature of work and work organization. Research on the consequences of the introduction of new technology for overall employment levels is inconclusive. Automation eliminates many routine jobs in both manufacturing and services. At the same time, jobs requiring new skills are created, such as computer programming and highly skilled maintenance and technician jobs.

The consequences for employment and the future of work are difficult to estimate on balance, because the assumed 'effect' of new technology cannot be separated from managerial employment strategies and other causes of changes in employment such as the international division of labour, economic recession and the market for goods and services. Sociologists have also been concerned with changes in the pattern of employment and the labour market – e.g., the possible polarization of the workforce into a minority of 'technology winners' who are highly skilled and enjoy secure employment, and those who are 'technology losers' in the sense that their jobs are either deskilled or displaced altogether. These changes in the occupational structure also reveal inequalities based upon class, gender and race. See also DUAL LABOUR MARKET, SEGMENTED LABOUR MARKET.

These optimistic and pessimistic scenarios for new technology and work are also found in the research on changes in the quality of work. One line of argument develops the earlier work of Woodward (1970), Blauner (1964) and BELL (1980) (see TECHNOLOGY), to argue that new technology allows an increase in skill levels and more participative work organization. In contrast, LABOUR PROCESS THEORY has analysed the use of new technology for managerial control of the labour force and DESKILLING. Recent research (Piore and Sabel, 1984) into new technology in manufacturing has suggested that new forms of automation allow the possibility of *flexible specialization* – multi-skilled, 'high-trust' work – in contrast to Fordism and Taylorism as predominant features of earlier production systems geared to mass production. However, the evidence for these emerging new work forms is limited and confined to sectors such as metal-machining (see also FORDISM AND POST-FORDISM, SCIENTIFIC MANAGEMENT).

Applied sociological research on new technology has generally been critical of TECHNOLOGICAL DETERMINISM and supportive of programmes for human-centred technology.

new towns new urban centres, constructed under the New Towns Act 1946 and subsequent legislation, and built either entirely on a new site or by expanding an existing smaller town. The idea of new towns can be traced to Ebenezer Howard's earlier creation of 'garden cities'. Although new towns, mainly required to accommodate an increasing population, were intended to have a balanced social structure and a full range of social services and amenities, they have been criticized for failing to achieve these objectives.

new universities the universities created in England and Wales by the redesignation of the POLYTECHNICS in 1991, and in Scotland by the redesignation of non-university 'central institutions'. See also BINARY SYSTEM (OF HIGHER EDUCATION).

new working class a stratum within the WORKING CLASS that is seen as distinguished from the 'traditional' working class, firstly, by the fact that its members work as technicians in new forms of technologically based industry, and, secondly, by a greater trade union militancy, directed at issues of power and control rather than purely 'economistic' issues.

This use of the term was originated by a French writer, Serge Mallet, in 1963, and was adopted, in different ways, by other French authors, notably Alain Touraine and André Gorz (see Mallet, 1975; Gorz, 1967; Touraine, 1971). The argument in some ways recalls that of Blauner (1964). Both saw recent developments in the application of technology to work as having important consequences, but their conclusions are radically different. Blauner saw modern process industry as producing worker satisfaction and harmonious workplace relations. Mallet argued that, compared with the old working class, the work situation of workers in the new automated industries would inevitably produce demands for workers' control which, spreading throughout industry, would lead to a revolution in capitalist production relations. The nature of automated work, together with the need to maximize efficiency and productivity would produce a group of workers who were relatively highly trained, autonomous and highly integrated into the enterprise. These factors of community, knowledge and power (all encouraged by management in the interests of the enterprise) would facilitate the growth of confidence and demands 'to acquire control of the enterprise by and for the workers – and thus to a new political awareness ...' (Mallet, 1975, p. 105).

Mallet's original argument has been criticized and undermined by subsequent empirical studies. Studies of British automated companies by Nichols and Armstrong (1976) and Nichols and Beynon (1977), for example, showed that 'donkey work' was still common and that the 'new working class' remained a minority even in highly automated plants. These studies also suggested that work organization and management strategies were still successful in dividing workers and preventing the development of political organization. Similarly, in the best known 'test' of the 'new working class' thesis, Gallie (1978) studied three oil refineries, one in Britain and two in France, finding that technology did not have the effect claimed either by Blauner or by Mallet. Instead, distinct national differences between the work-forces existed, indicating that wider cultural factors were more important than technology, and no significant amount of support for workers' control was found, either in Britain or France. See also AFFLUENT WORKER, ALIENATION, EMBOURGEOISEMENT.

NGOs (non-government organizations) political and other types of organisation (e.g. Oxfam, Greenpeace) that operate on governments and play an increasingly significant role in the wider governance in the contemporary world, especially internationally.

Nietzsche, Friedrich (1844–1900) German thinker of the late 19th century who expressed the sharpest and most alarming doubts about the rationalism, humanism and scientism which he proposed had become the 'common sense' of the West, about the 'plausibility of the world'. This common sense, he suggested, meant a world of circumscribed possibilities and outcomes, framed by a single objective truth, prescribing essentially limited forms of human practice and endeavour. He regarded such assumptions as removing responsibility for actions, and as leading to a MASS SOCIETY of mediocrity, hypocrisy and failure. What is truth but 'a mobile army of metaphors, METONYMIES, anthropomorphisms?', asks Nietzsche. Truths are illusions when one has forgotten that they are illusions. He challenges objectivity by revealing the desire for power behind claims to knowledge, and by showing the impossibility, as well as the poverty, of a rationalist ethic. To both he opposes the open horizons of art, and of a striving for an excellence and superiority beyond the possible, with a necessary competition and élitism. The supposed political implications of this, including spurious links claimed by NATIONAL SOCIALISM, made him a favourite target, often unread, for liberals of all persuasions. Nevertheless, his ideas have influenced many sociological writers, notably WEBER and SIMMEL, and are echoed in the writings of leading theorists of POST-STRUCTURALISM and POSTMODERNISM, especially FOUCAULT and DERRIDA, whose views often draw directly on Nietzsche's work.

nomads and nomadism any people or society, e.g. the desert Bedouin of North Africa, distinguished by impermanence of place of residence, and who move from place to place in search of food or pasture. *Nomadism* may refer to the way of life of HUNTER-GATHERER societies as well as to PASTORALISM.

nomenklatura (in the USSR and state socialist Eastern European countries).
1 lists of names held by committees of the Communist Party from which were selected candidates for vacancies in state, party or social organizations, such as trade unions.
2 people holding positions as in **1** or on the nomination lists, and in particular those involved in the highest organizations in the countries, and who were identified by many observers as the rulers of these countries (Voslensky, 1984). Until the late 1980s in the USSR, the existence of such practices was not publicly acknowledged, but under the impetus of GLASNOST and PERESTROIKA, not only were they openly discussed, they were strongly criticized. Following the dramatic political changes which began in 1989 and which brought about the collapse of Communism, the system has broken down, but many *nomenklatura* individuals retain power and influence in other guises. See also STATE SOCIALIST SOCIETIES.

nominalism (PHILOSOPHY) the doctrine that 'universal' concepts which define general classes of things (e.g. redness, roundness) cannot be conceived of as having 'real existence' in the way that individual things exist (compare ESSENTIALISM).

nominal level measurement see CRITERIA AND LEVELS OF MEASUREMENT.

nomothetic see IDIOGRAPHIC AND NOMOTHETIC.

noncapitalist and precapitalist modes of production (MARXISM) the forms of economy and society which historically preceded the emergence of CAPITALISM and which in some societies may continue to exist together with the capitalist mode of production. Marx, especially in the *Grundrisse,* identified four main noncapitalist modes: 'primitive communism', the 'ancient', the 'Asiatic' and the 'feudal'. Despite variations between them, one distinguishing feature from the capitalist mode which the last three shared was that political power was used to extract ECONOMIC SURPLUS from labourers, who existed in various forms of unfreedom, whereas Marx argued that capitalism was based on FREE WAGE LABOUR, whose EXPLOITATION occurred through economic means alone.

Since the 1970s there have been various attempts, mainly by structuralist Marxists influenced by ALTHUSSER, to refine Marx's work, especially in the light of contemporary anthropological studies. In particular, the concept of primitive communism has been modified by French anthropologists (Rey, 1975; Terray, 1972) who developed the concept of *lineage mode of production* within which there are both hunting and gathering and horticultural societies (see HUNTER-GATHERER and HORTICULTURE). In this form elders (usually men) are seen to exert control over women, children and younger men through LINEAGE ties.

nondecisions see POWER, COMMUNITY POWER.

non-government organizations see NGOS.

nonliterate society a society in which the population do not have access to a system of writing. Whilst it is often regarded as being an evolutionary stage prior to civilization, this view takes no account of the possible complexity of oral traditions. Lengthy myths and systems of genealogy can be preserved by word of mouth, but the possibility of information being disseminated by texts and not individuals undoubtedly contributes to substantial cultural change. It is also important to note that there have been situations in which the minority do have access to writing but the majority do not, thus creating a privileged class of scribes with the power to define versions of the status quo for the nonliterate. See also LITERACY.

nonparametric statistics statistical methods used for the analysis of ordinal and categorical level sample data which do not require assumptions about the shape of the population distribution from which the samples have been drawn. Such statistics are often referred to as 'distribution-free statistics'. In contrast to PARAMETRIC STATISTICS, assumptions underlying the use of the methods are lenient and the formulae involved are simple and easy to use. Examples are the runs tests, the signs test and Cramer's V. Although such measures are popular in sociology, they have the disadvantages that they waste information if interval data is 'degraded' into categorical data, and that the tests are not as powerful as parametric tests (see also SIGNIFICANCE TEST). Against this, they are often more robust, i.e. they give the same results in spite of assumptions being violated. Hence, if the assumptions of a parametric test are not met, the use of an equivalent nonparametric test will still be valid.

nonresponse a problem in the social sciences caused by people not completing QUESTIONNAIRES, refusing to be interviewed, etc. Nonresponse is a common problem in sociological research, especially in those instances where a postal questionnaire is being used, where a RESPONSE RATE of above 50% is generally considered to be good.

In order to discuss ways of increasing the response rate it is necessary to consider briefly why people do not return questionnaires. Some people have died or moved before the questionnaires are sent out, whilst others simply refuse to complete questionnaires. Apart from people who have moved house, died, etc., probably the main reason why questionnaires are not returned is due to forgetfulness and inertia. This problem can be minimized in a number of ways. In constructing the questionnaire care should be taken in writing and ordering the questions to make it as simple and easy to complete as possible. The covering letter should be written so that the purposes of the study are explained and assurances should be given concerning the confidentiality of the data. A few days after sending the questionnaires a reminder card should be distributed, and second and even third copies of the questionnaire may be sent to nonrespondents, depending on finances. A shortened version of the questionnaire, asking key questions only, may be sent, or this may be administered by telephone.

A number of techniques exist which attempt to calculate the extent to which nonrespondents might differ from respondents. Depending on the data source, that data which is known about nonrespondents can be coded (see CODING) for analysis and comparison with respondents. For example, a study of young people using addresses obtained from careers offices may be able to build up a picture of nonrespondents which includes data on gender, age, examination results, employment status, etc. Also, replies can be weighted on the basis that respondents who reply to the final reminder have more in common with those from whom no response has been obtained than with those who replied earlier. It may also be possible to estimate some characteristics of the total population by using alternative data sources (e.g. other questionnaire studies, CENSUS material, etc.) and then the data can be weighted accordingly.

nonstructural social mobility see SOCIAL MOBILITY.

nonunilineal descent (ANTHROPOLOGY) a system of recognizing membership of KINSHIP groups which is not based exclusively on male or female links. Synonyms are COGNATIC or (less frequently) BILINEAL DESCENT.

nonverbal communication see BODY LANGUAGE, COMMUNICATION.

norm a standard or rule, regulating behaviour in a social setting. The idea that social life, as an ordered and continuous process, is dependent upon shared expectations and obligations, is commonly found in sociological approaches, although some place more emphasis on it than others. For DURKHEIM, society was theorized as a moral order. This perspective was influential in the development of modern FUNCTIONALISM, particularly in the work of PARSONS, where the concept of NORMATIVE ORDER is the central element of the SOCIAL SYSTEM. Here the idea of norms is related to SOCIALIZATION and ROLES. These prescriptions operate at every level of society, from individuals' actions in daily life, e.g. in table manners or classroom behaviour, to the formulation of legal systems in advanced societies. The concept of norms also implies that of SOCIAL CONTROL, i.e. positive or negative means of ensuring conformity and applying sanctions to deviant behaviour (see DEVIANCE).

Other sociological approaches deal with the issue of social order in rather different ways. In some, RULES are emphasized, rather than norms, whilst in others there is a greater emphasis on POWER and coercion.

normal distribution a continuous distribution of a random VARIABLE with its mean, median and mode equal (see MEASURES OF CENTRAL TENDENCY). Thus the normal curve is symmetrical, and bell-shaped as in Fig. 21 below. See also PROBABILITY, PARAMETRIC STATISTICS assume the parent population to have a normal distribution. In reality, a normal distribution is only approximated, and this is regarded as acceptable to fulfil this requirement of a parametric test.

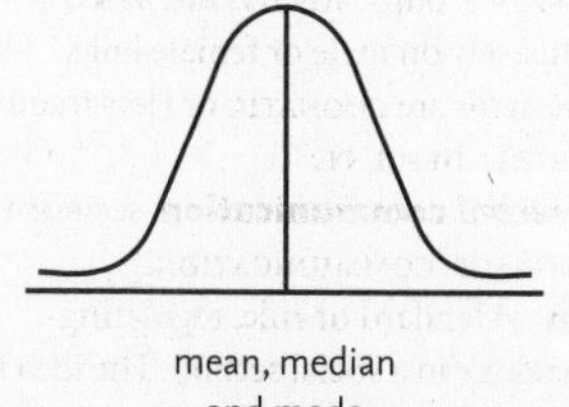

Fig. 21 **Normal Distribution.**

normal science and **revolutionary science** the important distinction, drawn by KUHN (1962), between periods of stability of concepts and assumptions in science, and periods of upheaval and rapid change. Contrary to the view that all science is characterized by bold attempts to falsify theories (see FALSIFICATIONISM), Kuhn sees *normal science* as usually involved in 'puzzle-solving' which accepts and works entirely within the assumptions of a particular SCIENTIFIC PARADIGM. Only when an established paradigm fails to generate new puzzles or is beset by major 'anomalies' do exceptional scientists turn to *revolutionary science* in which new paradigms are created. Examples of such revolutionary shifts cited by Kuhn are the Copernican and Newtonian revolutions, Dalton's new system in chemistry, and the work of Einstein. In periods of normal science, scientific work is characterized by psychological and social conformity and group solidarity. Scientific revolutions 'are like political revolutions', and must struggle to overcome such conformity, and when these occur 'there is no standard higher than the standard of the relevant community' (Kuhn, 1977).

normative relating to, or based on, NORMS.

normative functionalism those forms of FUNCTIONALISM which emphasize the importance of the part played by VALUES and value CONSENSUS in the overall INTEGRATION of societies. The charge is often made that these forms of functionalism give disproportionate weight to the importance of values and *normative integration* (including the internalization of values) in producing social integration. The STRUCTURAL-FUNCTIONALISM of Talcott PARSONS is often held to be a prime example. See also SOCIAL INTEGRATION AND SYSTEM INTEGRATION, OVERSOCIALIZED CONCEPTION OF MAN; compare DOMINANT IDEOLOGY THESIS.

normative integration see NORMATIVE FUNCTIONALISM.

normative order a system of rules and standards appropriate to a given social situation. In the work of PARSONS, a normative order is said to comprise two elements: VALUES and NORMS. Norms are rules which are specific to a given social situation, e.g. an assembly, a Christmas party. Thus they are seen as regulating action and relations within a group or system. Values are also moral and regulatory, but they have a wider significance in as much as they go beyond a specific situation and are seen as informing norms in different contexts and thus as serving to connect different systems. In Parsonian terms, therefore, the value aspect of the normative order is crucial in ensuring pattern maintenance (see SUBSYSTEMS MODEL).

normative theory any theory which seeks to establish the VALUES or norms which best fit the overall needs or requirements of society, either societies in general or particular societies, and which would be morally justified. For those who see the aim of modern social science as descriptive and explanatory and not 'prescriptive', such a goal for social science or sociology is not acceptable. Hence in these circumstances, the term 'normative theory' can be a pejorative term. For others, however, the aim of appraising and establishing values is an important goal, perhaps the most important goal, of the social sciences. See also FACT-VALUE DISTINCTION, VALUE JUDGEMENT, VALUE RELEVANCE, VALUE FREEDOM AND VALUE NEUTRALITY, FRANKFURT SCHOOL OF CRITICAL THEORY, POLITICAL SCIENCE, BEHAVIOURALISM.

norm of reciprocity the expectation that exists in many simple societies and also among kin and among friends in modern societies, that gifts or services must ultimately be reciprocated. Such exchanges are not strictly utilitarian and serve wider social functions and must be distinguished from more purely economically oriented exchange. See also GIFT EXCHANGE; compare EXCHANGE THEORY.

noumena and phenomena see KANT, RATIONALISM.

nuclear deterrence the capacity of a NATION STATE or alliance to protect itself from an attack using nuclear weapons by threatening retaliation which would result in wholesale destruction of the adversary's population and resources. Nuclear deterrence is above all a psychological concept, since a nation state or alliance must believe that an adversary has the capacity to retaliate if attacked and can credibly be expected to use it. The logic of nuclear deterrence is based upon twin assumptions:

(a) the RATIONALITY of decision-makers; and

(b) that both sides would be losers in the event of a nuclear conflict (see also MUTUAL ASSURED DESTRUCTION). Nuclear deterrence is often held to have prevented all-out wars between major powers in the post-World War II era. On the other hand, it does not prevent more limited conventional wars, and the invention of nuclear warfare has brought the ever-present threat of nuclear annihilation on a world scale. See also ARMS RACE, STRATEGIC THEORY, NATION-STATE SYSTEM.

nuclear family see FAMILY.

null hypothesis a working hypothesis which states that there will be no statistically significant difference between the EXPERIMENTAL GROUP and CONTROL GROUP.

When an experiment is set up, or observational data collected, this is designed to test a HYPOTHESIS, or theory, which has been developed from previous work. This is the EXPERIMENTAL HYPOTHESIS, and it states what the expected difference is between the groups if the theory is correct. The converse hypothesis is also conventionally stated: this is the null hypothesis, that predictions from the theory are incorrect, and there is no difference between the groups in the VARIABLE investigated. See also INDEPENDENT VARIABLE, DEPENDENT VARIABLE.

nursing see HOSPITAL.

O

object see SUBJECT AND OBJECT.

objective 1 (PHILOSOPHY) existing or held to exist independently of our percep-tions, e.g. being a material object.
2 free from distorting subjective (personal or emotional) bias. See also OBJECTIVITY, OBJECTIVISM, VALUE FREEDOM AND VALUE NEUTRALITY.

objective class see SUBJECTIVE AND OBJECTIVE CLASS.

objective test any test in which the responses are scored by reference to a set of correct answers so that, in this sense at least, no subjective assessment enters the scoring. See also FIXED-CHOICE QUESTIONNAIRE, QUESTIONNAIRE.

objectivism the view that it is possible to provide 'objective' representations and accounts of the external physical and social world, i.e. representations that capture these worlds accurately and reliably, without the importation of 'bias', or the view being coloured by one's own preferences and prejudices. It is now generally acknowledged that any simple doctrine that we are able directly to represent the world oversimplifies the degree to which we are able to achieve OBJECTIVITY. A rejection of objectivism, however, need not mean the outright endorsement of its opposite, RELATIVISM. A third argument, which today finds much support in modern sociology and philosophy (see Bernstein, 1983), is that we should seek in our epistemological thinking to move, 'beyond objectivism and relativism', since neither of these can be sustained as a general argument. See also EPISTEMOLOGY, FEYERABEND, KUHN. VALUE FREEDOM AND VALUE NEUTRALITY.

objectivity 1 accounts of the external world held to represent the world as it exists independently of our conceptions.
2 knowledge claimed to meet criteria of VALIDITY and RELIABILITY, and held to be free from BIAS. Most disciplines establish working criteria of objectivity in sense 2. However, they usually fall we short of providing more than conventional, 'working' answers to the question 'what constitutes objectivity?' in sense 1.

Problems arise as to whether objectivity is an attainable goal even for the physical sciences. Currently the philosophers' answer is that, in any strict sense, it is not, since our view of reality is mediated by our finite cognitive abilities and by the ever-changing theories and concepts which always structure our view of reality (see SCIENTIFIC PARADIGM, THEORY RELATIVITY, INCOMMENSURABILITY). Thus claims to knowledge are today more likely to be presented in terms of INTERSUBJECTIVITY and provisional agreements (compare REALISM).

For the social sciences there exist additional difficulties in conception 1, in that social reality does *not* exist independently of our collective conceptions of it. However, it can be seen as existing independently of any individual conceptions of it and to this degree as existing 'objectively'. Thus there seems no reason why social science should not aspire to 'objectivity', at least in sense 1, always accepting that this must *include* 'objective' accounts of what social actors hold 'subjectively' in constituting and reproducing their social worlds. That objective accounts may be difficult to achieve, must be recognized. What is *not* acceptable is any dogmatic assertion of 'objective' forms of 'measurement' (e.g. fixed-choice questionnaires insensitive to nuances of meaning) on the assumption that such methods constitute the only way in which social science can be rendered truly 'scientific' (see MEASUREMENT BY FIAT, CICOUREL, OFFICIAL STATISTICS; compare SOCIAL FACTS AS THINGS). See also EPISTEMOLOGY, TRUTH, ONTOLOGY, IDEALISM, POSITIVISM, EMPIRICISM, RELATIVISM, DECONSTRUCTION, POSTMODERNITY AND POSTMODERNISM.

objectivity and neutrality see VALUE FREEDOM AND VALUE NEUTRALITY.

Object Relations School the group of psychoanalysts, including Karl Abraham, Melanie KLEIN and Donald WINNICOTT, who developed FREUD's acknowledgement that the individual needs 'others' (people and things) with whom to interact to achieve fulfilment of instinctual needs. The significance of the object (which includes other people) is in the emotional meaning it, or its mental representation, has for the person. The emphasis of the Object Relations School in Europe can be contrasted with EGO PSYCHOLOGY in the USA, as displaying more ambivalence, and as having more depth, in its discussions of PERSONALITY and SOCIALIZATION.

occupational class see CLASS and OCCUPATIONAL SCALES.

occupational communities the traditional working-class communities formed where industries are able to provide stable employment to workforces. Some such industries (e.g. coalmining, shipbuilding) are concentrated in particular neighbourhoods, others (e.g. printing newspapers) involve unsocial hours. LOCKWOOD characterized the kind of worker found in occupational communities as 'traditional proletarian'. See CLASS IMAGERY.

occupational mobility the movement of individuals through different levels in a hierarchy of occupational positions (see OCCUPATIONAL SCALES). The case with which individuals may achieve this is usually an indication of the open or closed nature of the CLASS system of a particular society (GIDDENS, 1973). Occupational mobility may be upward or downward, and may be either individual or collective. The latter is often achieved through strategies of occupational closure, such as PROFESSIONALIZATION. The medical profession in the 19th-century is a good example of how successful this strategy can be in raising the income, STATUS and prestige of an occupation.

The degree of occupational mobility may be measured either inter-or intra-generationally. In these cases the extent of movement achieved is used as a measure of SOCIAL MOBILITY. This is a complex are a of research (Heath, 1981), since the comparison of rates of or chances for social mobility is complicated by variations in the grading of occupations on different scales, historical changes in the status of different kinds of work, the appearance of new kinds of jobs (e.g. those concerned with NEW TECHNOLOGY) and the decline of old ones (e.g. those in traditional 'smoke stack' industries), as well as genuine improvements in chances for upward mobility through better educational provision.

occupational prestige the subjective evaluation of the 'social honour' or 'standing' attached to an occupation. Conceptions of occupational prestige play an important part in the construction of OCCUPATIONAL SCALES which are used to measure SOCIAL CLASS and SOCIAL MOBILITY. See also STATUS.

occupational scales

Measures of the prestige, status, social standing and/or social class position of different occupations. Mainly used in the study of SOCIAL STRATIFICATION and SOCIAL MOBILITY, occupational scales are constructed in one of four ways – the intuitive, relational, constructed and reputational – all of which are based upon the premise that it is possible to arrange occupations hierarchically through similarities of market and status situation. In intuitive approaches, the researcher simply ranks occupations on the basis of his or her subjective assessment of their social standing in the community. In relational approaches, occupations are ranked on the assumption that people mix with others of broadly similar social standing to themselves. In constructed approaches, a number of different factors (such as income and levels of education) are used to rank occupations. In the reputational approach a group of people, chosen at random, are asked to rank occupations according to their perceived standing in the community and the social ranking of each occupation is then calculated on the basis of the replies.

Probably the occupational scale most widely used in the UK is the *Registrar General's Classification*, devised, using the intuitive approach, for use in the 1911 CENSUS and extensively modified for use in subsequent censuses. To use this schema details are needed of each individual's precise job title, employment status (self-employed/ employer/employee), industry of employment and educational qualifications. In its original form this had five SOCIAL CLASSES:

Class I (senior professionals) comprised doctors, lawyers, accountants, etc.;

Class II (intermediate occupations) comprised teachers, nurses and managers;

Class III comprised all people in skilled occupations, both white-collar and blue-collar;

Class IV comprised semi-skilled workers such as agricultural workers and machine moulders;

Class V consisted of labourers and others in unskilled occupations.

In 1961, Class III was subdivided into Class IIIN (white-collar workers such as clerks and shop assistants), and Class IIIM (manual workers such as underground workers in mines, welders and carpenters).

The main advantage of using the Registrar General's classification is that a detailed list of occupational titles is regularly produced, giving each occupation a number determined by its social class position, industry and employment status. These codes can then be combined to form the six social classes. In 1961 the Registrar General introduced a new form of coding in which occupations are assigned to 17 socioeconomic groups which can be further combined to form an alternative schema:

Class 1, professionals;
Class 2, employers and managers;
Class 3, intermediate and junior non-manual;
Class 4, skilled manual, foremen and own account;
Class 5, semiskilled and personal service;
Class 6, unskilled manual.

Further changes were introduced into the Registrar General's schema in 1981 in which occupations are coded in such a way as to make the schema comparable with the International Standard Classification of Occupations.

Historical data, such as that obtained from the 19th-century census enumeration books, cannot be coded using the Registrar General's classification because of the amount of detail necessary. However, Armstrong (1972) demonstrates how the 1951 classification can be adopted for use by historical sociologists.

One of the problems with the Registrar General's Occupational Scale is that, since it was constructed using the intuitive approach, it cannot easily be used to test sociological theories. For example, it cannot be used to identify the bourgeoisie and petty bourgeoisie. One attempt to overcome this problem has been made by GOLDTHORPE and Llewellyn (1977) who devised their own social class schema based upon the work of Hope and GOLDTHORPE (1974). The *Hope-Goldthorpe Scale* was constructed using the reputational approach, with occupations precoded according to the Registrar General's 1971 Classification, and then combined into 36 distinct, hierarchically arranged groups with similar levels of 'social desirability', and with separate categories for employers, managers, professionals, the self-employed, technical, white-collar, agricultural, supervisory and manual workers. These categories are recombined by Goldthorpe and Llewellyn into seven social classes. Class I, high-grade professionals, managers, administrators and large proprietors; Class II, lower grade professionals and managers, and higher grade technicians; Class III, routine non-manual workers; Class IV, small proprietors and the self-employed; Class V, lower grade technicians and supervisors of manual workers; Class VI, skilled manual workers; Class VII, semi-skilled and unskilled manual workers. The Hope-Goldthorpe schema was devised to study the occupations and social class positions of men so its use in studies of women's employment has been questioned.

occupational structure the DIVISION OF LABOUR within the economy, and by extension also society, largely in sectoral and status terms. Sectorally, the division of occupations has been classified into primary, secondary and tertiary sectors, a schema commonly used by sociologists studying INDUSTRIALIZATION and POSTINDUSTRIAL SOCIETY. In status terms the concept centrally informs the study of socioeconomic categories (CLASSES) for, in Parkin's (1971) classic statement, 'The backbone of the class structure ... of modern Western society, is the occupational order'.

Probably the best-known and most-used schema (within the UK) has been developed by GOLDTHORPE et al. (1980), derived from the earlier Hope-Goldthorpe Scales (see OCCUPATIONAL SCALES) for the analysis of SOCIAL MOBILITY. The concept has, historically, been blind to the involvement of women in the workforce, tending to focus on the occupations of adult males only (Walby, 1986).

occupational transition see SOCIAL MOBILITY.

Oedipus Complex the unconscious wish of little boys to kill the father and marry the mother (from the Greek legend of King Oedipus). This is regarded as integral to the Phallic Stage in FREUD's psychodynamic theory of development.

Freud suggested that between three and five years old a boy develops sexual jealousy of his father, and since his wishes cannot be realized in fact, he resolves the situation by realizing them vicariously through identifying with his father. This IDENTIFICATION involves internalizing the perceived moral standards of the father, thus forming the SUPEREGO. The obverse of the Oedipus Complex, for the little girl, is the *Electra Complex,* involving the unconscious wish to kill the mother and marry the father, though the term Oedipus Complex is generally used for both sexes.

Though the theory still has credibility among some psychoanalysts, feminist psychodynamic theorists have proposed other explanations for the development of the superego. Freud's theory was not a satisfactory explanation of female personality development. CHODOROW (1978) suggests that when gender awareness develops (between three and five years) a boy needs to differentiate from his mother with whom he has had a close physical and emotional identity. He therefore develops ways of coping with feelings of insecurity and a veneer of independence. A little girl does not have this need to differentiate, therefore she continues modelling on her mother and is thereby assisted in developing a mature personality. See also KRISTEVA, NARCISSISM.

official statistics any data collected and published by government departments. Such data have varied reliability and utility. Although many of these data can be highly valuable to the sociologist, e.g. those presented in the CENSUS, GENERAL HOUSEHOLD SURVEY and EXPENDITURE SURVEY, major debates exist concerning the limitations of official statistics (e.g. CRIME STATISTICS). The way in which statistics are collected, e.g. as a by-product of the work of administrative agencies, sometimes by a large number of untrained recorders, can lead to major inconsistencies, unreliability, and uncertainties about the meaning and worth of data. Also, statistics may possess positive or negative implications for the agencies and individuals that collect them, which can affect what is recorded. Finally, statistics are always collected for some purpose, which will usually be different from that of the sociological researcher; above all, they are the result of a process of categorization and the attachment of numbers which involves inherent difficulties of the kind identified particularly by ethnomethodologists (see CICOUREL, 1964). A classic example of the issues that can arise is the debate concerning DURKHEIM's use of Suicide statistics (see Douglas, 1967). See also MEASUREMENT BY FIAT.

old age the last part of the individual LIFE COURSE, associated with declining faculties, low social worth and detachment from previous social commitments. It is a social construct rather than a biological stage, since its onset and significance vary historically and culturally. See also AGEING, GERONTOLOGY.

oligarchy see IRON LAW OF OLIGARCHY.

oligopoly see MONOPOLY.

one-party system, one-party state *or* **one-party rule** a political system and state in which a single POLITICAL PARTY rules and where opposition political parties are not permitted or are precluded from rule. As well as being a feature, until recently, of eastern

European socialist and communist states and of other systems based on Marxism (see also VANGUARD PARTY), one-party systems have also been introduced by rulers in developing societies in which the existence of ethnic and tribal divisions (rather than modern class divisions) are claimed to provide an unsuitable basis for two-party or multi-party democracies (compare STABLE DEMOCRACY).

ontic see HEIDEGGER.

ontogenetic fallacy the conceptualization of 'the development and change of culture and society according to a model which applies, strictly speaking, only to the development of the individual (*ontogenesis*)' (P. Strydom, 1992). According to Strydom, HABERMAS commits this fallacy in his use of developmental logical models.

ontological security and insecurity the feelings of emotional and intellectual security or insecurity said to arise from the effectiveness or ineffectiveness of an individual's upbringing, especially early family relationships. According to psychoanalytic theorists, security depends on consistent and routine caring and an emotional exchange between parent and child in which the adult takes on the anxieties of the child so that these can be reinternalized by the child as bearable feelings.

ontology the branch of philosophy (and *metaphysics*) concerned to establish the nature of the fundamental kinds of thing which exist in the world (e.g. do MINDS exist?). Examples of philosophical ontological theory are PLATO's theory of 'forms', or recently, SCIENTIFIC REALISM, which asks what kinds of thing are presupposed by scientific theories.

Ontological arguments are also an explicit (or implicit) feature of sociological theory itself, e.g. DURKHEIM's conception of 'social facts', WEBER's (or the SYMBOLIC INTERACTIONIST's) emphasis on individual actors, or MARX's materialism and emphasis on modes and relations in production.

One argument (HUME's view) is that ontological inquiries are bound to be inconclusive, or are even pointless. Against this, the clarification of underlying assumptions is often important. Undoubtedly debate in sociology since COMTE, much of it broadly ontological in nature, has done much to clarify the nature, while also underlining the very great complexity, of social reality (social action, social structures, etc.). However, it has done so not as a separate realm of inquiry, but as an inherent part of sociological inquiry properly conducted. Philosophy can inform these discussions, but it is no longer regarded as the kind of *final* arbiter it was once assumed to be. The expectation must be that ontologies will change as knowledge and individual sciences and modes of study change (compare EPISTEMOLOGY, KUHN, FEYERABEND).

open-class societies see SOCIAL MOBILITY.

open-door college Burton Clark's (1960) term for those forms of HIGHER EDUCATION institution in which access is open to anyone possessing basic qualifications or sometimes with no formal qualifications. This being so, 'open-door colleges' are the polar opposite of 'élite' institutions. As discussed by Clark, open-door institutions will tend to adopt a 'service' orientation towards their clients, providing what is demanded rather than what they would ideally wish to provide. There are gains and losses in this arrangement in which student culture and extra-academic criteria generally tend to call the tune. According to Clark, it is likely that modern higher educational systems preserve a separate élite, academic provision as part of a diversified system of higher education (see MASS HIGHER EDUCATION).

open-ended question a type of question in a QUESTIONNAIRE in which the respondent's choice of answer is not prestructured but left entirely free. Analysis of open-ended questions is obviously less straightforward than for FIXED-CHOICE QUESTIONS, which can be pre-coded. However, open-ended questions have the advantage, of *not* imposing a frame of reference on respondents (see MEASUREMENT BY FIAT).

For this reason they may be preferred to fixed choice questions in some contexts and by some researchers (e.g. as an adjunct to PARTICIPANT OBSERVATION or in the early exploratory stages of research), and can be used alongside fixed-choice questions as appropriate. See also SOCIAL SURVEY.

open society Karl POPPER's conception of a 'free society' in which all forms of knowledge and all social policies can be openly criticized. He regards it as the only form of society compatible with his falsificationist and critical rationalist epistemology (see also FALSIFICATIONISM, HISTORICISM sense **2**). However, Popper's conception has been criticized (e.g. by FEYERABEND) as open only in an 'élitist' way and involving a 'guided exchange' between competing views where all the parties to an open debate are required to accept falsificationism. In this, Feyerabend finds Popper's concept less open, and less acceptable, than the conception of a liberal society found in J. S. MILL's *On Liberty* (1859).

operant conditioning see CONDITIONING.

operationalism or operationism the philosophical doctrine that defines scientific concepts entirely in terms of the working (i.e. 'operational') procedures with which they are associated. In the form proposed by the physicist P. W. Bridgman (1927), the doctrine, though intended to be 'empiricist' (e.g. to exclude all reference in science to 'unobservables'), in fact issues in a radical form of CONVENTIONALISM. In social science, an example of operationalism is the statement that 'intelligence is what intelligence tests measure'. Seen thus, the limitations of operationalism are obvious: science in all its forms would be condemned to possessing no rational way of judging between concepts in terms of 'realism', e.g. between different 'measures' of intelligence. Operationalism should be distinguished from OPERATIONALIZATION, which need not depend on operationalism.

operationalization the process of defining a concept empirically so that it can be measured, and so that repeated observations can be made which are RELIABLE and VALID. Thus intelligence can be defined as what INTELLIGENCE TESTS measure (though this is not recommended), and SOCIAL CLASS can be defined in terms of occupation, income and life style. The danger, as with any attempt at QUANTIFICATION, is that much information implicit in the original concept is lost by a categorization which tends to over-simplify. Where this occurs the operationalization may not be valid. Selection of relevant measures to be included in the quantification also introduces possibility of BIAS. See also OPERATIONALISM.

operationism see OPERATIONALISM.

opinion leaders the minority of individuals in any area of social life who influence the ideas of others. LAZARSFELD et al. (1944) introduced this term in connection with their account of VOTING BEHAVIOUR and a TWO-STEP FLOW OF MASS COMMUNICATIONS.

opinion poll see PUBLIC OPINION, GALLUP.

opportunity cost the opportunities foregone in undertaking one activity measured in terms of the other possibilities that might have been pursued using the same expenditure of resources. While opportunity cost is mainly a concept in economics, it also applies more generally to human existence. For example, given the finitude of time in the human life-span and the impossibility of doing many activities more than one at a time or other than in one-to-one interactions, opportunity costs are involved in many human activities, not only those in which economic resources are involved.

opportunity structure the social patterning of opportunities that are available to different individuals. Although originally conceived within deviancy theory (Cloward and Ohlin, 1960) as a way of developing Robert MERTON's work on ANOMIE by identifying variations in opportunities to engage in different kinds of illegitimate activity, the concept is now often employed in a general way to draw attention to the fact that social opportunities are rarely evenly or equally distributed. For example, the paucity of women in ÉLITE positions in society generally, as well as in particular organizations, is due to the fact that they confront a different opportunity structure compared with men; working-class underachievement in education is a product of the different opportunity structure which the home and school present to manual workers' children compared with those from professional backgrounds, etc. See also EQUALITY OF OPPORTUNITY.

oppositional culture see COUNTER CULTURE OR ALTERNATIVE CULTURE.

oral history a method of historical research, especially SOCIAL HISTORY, in which the recollections of living persons are collected (e.g. Thompson, 1981). The assumption is that the data collected in this way, particularly from ordinary people, will provide a valuable data archive for future as well as present historians. As for any historical sources, oral historical data require careful appraisal for reliability and representativeness. See also HISTORY, HISTORY WORKSHOP JOURNAL.

oral tradition the aspects of a society's CULTURE that are passed on by word of mouth. Some societies (see NONLITERATE SOCIETY) may rely solely on this method of documenting their history and GENEALOGY through song, poetry and narrative. In literate societies the oral tradition usually plays an increasingly marginal role in cultural transmission and may often stand in opposition to the dominant forms of representation. Whilst anthropologists have long been interested in folklore and story-telling, sociologists and social historians are now also using this method to document the histories of groups (e.g. women, ethnic minorities and the working class) who have not previously been focused upon in the written tradition. See also ORAL HISTORY.

order/dis-order the play of order and dis-order can be seen as an important motif in the work of many philosophers, social commentators, and cultural theorists. Thinkers such as NIETZSCHE, FREUD, KOJEVE, BATAILLE, LACAN, DELEUZE, DERRIDA, GIRARD, BAUDRILLARD, and LYOTARD have all addressed the relation between structure and the disintegration of organization. For the poststructuralist writers like Bataille, Lacan, Deleuze, and Derrida, Nietzshe's philosophy emphasised the idea that the absence of order should be seen as a space for the formation of non-repressive/ oppositional identities and cultures. Similarly, the postmodern writers, Lyotard and Baudrillard, have developed their ideas surrounding the end of modernity, the collapse of metanarratives, and the crisis of scientific legitimation out of the Nietzsche/Kojeve reading of Hegel's phenomenology. Like Freud's theory of the unconscious and Girard's analysis of the scapegoat mechanism, these thinkers showed how dis-order lurks at the heart of order.

ordinal level measurement see CRITERIA AND LEVELS OF MEASUREMENT.

ordinary language philosophy a detailed analysis of language in use. Also referred to as *linguistic philosophy* (or *analysis*), and *Oxford philosophy*, the term applies to a group of Oxford philosophers (including Austin and Ryle) influenced by the philosophy of WITTGENSTEIN. The aim of this ordinary language philosophy is to analyse natural language as a flexibly rule-governed practice. This approach contrasts with that of the logical positivists (see LOGICAL POSITIVISM), who wished to rid language of metaphysics by reducing it to an 'object language' capable of rigorous logical investigation. Ordinary language philosophers prefer to dissolve rather than solve problems, demonstrating that puzzlement often occurs only when metaphysics is used. Their own image of it is as a form of philosophy dispelling linguistic confusions, a view reflected in the title of Austin's *How to Do Things with Words* (1962).

Approaches in sociology which emphasize the importance of everyday language and talk (e.g. ETHNOMETHODOLOGY and CONVERSATIONAL ANALYSIS), have been influenced by ordinary language philosophy (see also SPEECH ACTS).

organic analogy see FUNCTION; see also ANALOGY.

organic composition of capital (MARXISM) the ratio between the mass of the means of production relative to labour employed in the production process, measured in value terms. It is therefore the ratio between CONSTANT AND VARIABLE CAPITAL. A closely related term in MARX's analysis is the *technical composition of capital* (the ratio of machines and plant to labour), which is not measured in value terms, and which seems to be a more straightforward concept but which in fact cannot be measured.

Central to Marx's analysis of the dynamic of capitalism is that there is a tendency for the organic composition of capital to increase. Increased competition between capitalists leads to individual capitalists attempting to increase the productivity of labour power and decrease the value of commodities via increased investment in machinery, constant capital. The value of constant capital increases more than the value of variable capital which is expended on labour power. The full implication of this process, as seen by Marx, is that it lies behind the TENDENCY TO DECLINING RATE OF PROFIT, since with less capital expended for labour power, which produces SURPLUS VALUE, and from which profit is derived, the rate of profit will fall (surplus value divided by constant and variable capital, S/C + V) as more capital is employed but less labour power. This will tend to occur even though the rate of SURPLUS VALUE (surplus value divided by variable capital, S/V) and the overall volume of profit will usually increase from the use of machinery.

The problems associated with this concept have led even sympathetic observers to argue that Marx does not achieve what he set out to do in *Das Kapital:* to show scientifically why capitalism 'digs its own grave'. Within Marxian analyses there have been various attempts either to show that Marx's original analysis does achieve its purpose, or that it is possible to complete the analysis satisfactorily.

organic intellectual see GRAMSCI, INTELLECTUALS.

organic solidarity see MECHANICAL AND ORGANIC SOLIDARITY.

organization

1 a type of collectivity established for the pursuit of specific aims or goals, characterized by a formal structure of rules, authority relations, a division of labour and limited membership or admission. The term is used mainly to refer to large-scale or 'complex organizations' which pervade all aspects of social life in modern society, e.g. business enterprises, schools, hospitals, churches, prisons, the military, political parties, trade unions, etc. Such organizations involve patterns of social relationships which differ from other social groups such as the family, peer groups, and neighbourhoods which are largely spontaneous, unplanned or informal (compare PRIMARY GROUP). Forms of association in organizations tend to occupy only a segment of a person's life (with the notable exception of TOTAL ORGANIZATIONS).

2 any purposeful arrangement of social activity or set of activities (compare SOCIAL STRUCTURE). Organization in this sense implies active control over human relations for specific ends. For example, the organization of work involves specifying the allocation and coordination of tasks, patterns of authority, forms of recruitment and employment relationships.

Although organization and BUREAUCRACY are frequently treated as synonymous, this is inappropriate, since while all modern bureaucracies are organizations, not all organizations are bureaucracies. WEBER, for example, was careful to distinguish organization (*Verband*) from bureaucracy since the former could include patterns of domination other than the 'legal-rational' type characteristic of modern bureaucracy. See also AUTHORITY.

The fundamental problem in defining organization in sense 1 concerns the specification of 'organizational goals'. To state that organizations have goals either reifies the collective concept 'organization' or assumes that the goals of an organization are identical to those defined by the power holders at the apex of the organization (see FUNCTIONALISM). Clearly, organizations, as such, have no goals. Rather, groups and individuals within organizations may hold a variety of different and competing goals. Organizational controllers may attempt to establish over-arching goals for the organization through selection, training, rewards and punishments, and the perpetuation of an 'organization culture', but the nature and extent of compliance by subordinates and the degree of cooperation and conflict within an organization can only be established by empirical research. This issue is reflected in the distinction between *formal and informal organization.* The former refers to the 'official' hierarchy and lines of authority, with their spans of control, as first described by formal theorists of organization and scientific management; the latter refers to the ways in which official rules are negotiated or subverted through the informal practices of subordinates as in the early Hawthorne experiments. See HUMAN RELATIONS SCHOOL

There is, in fact, no generally accepted definition of organization; its meaning varies in terms of the different theoretical approaches to organization in the literature (see ORGANIZATION THEORY).

organizational crime law-breaking by organizations such as businesses or state bureaucracies. Typical examples would be the flouting of health, hygiene or safety regulations, or the failure to observe pollution controls (S. Box, *Power, Crime and Mystification*, 1983). Precise figures are difficult to obtain, but organizational crime is certainly not insignificant. More working days each year are lost, for example, because of industrial injury and accident than through strikes, and many of these – perhaps 40% (J. Hagan, *Structural Criminology*, 1988) – are due to employer negligence.

Organizational crime (or 'crimes of the powerful') should be distinguished from WHITE-COLLAR CRIME, which usually implies criminal activity (such as embezzlement) exercised *against* organizations *by* their employees, and from *organized crime*, which refers to criminal organizations or networks involved in the *systematic* provision of illegal goods and services, such as those engaged in international drug trafficking.

organizational culture the particular configuration of norms, values, beliefs and ways of behaving that characterise the manner in which groups and individuals collaborate within organisations.

Controlling organizational culture became a prominent concern within British and American management schools in the 1980s as a result of three main factors:
(a) the challenge of Japanese competition;
(b) concern over the economic recovery of industry;
(c) the failure of previous methods of organizational design to overcome corporations inefficiencies, e.g. matrix structures. See also ORGANIZATION.

This concern with organizational culture was principally a prescriptive one, exemplified in the works of the American authors Deal and Kennedy (1982) and in the UK by Handy's four-part cultural schema (1984). Deal and Kennedy's (1982) analysis is prescriptive in intent and sets out to identify the particular rites and rituals of corporate life that constitute corporate cultures and they argue that business success relies on what they refer to as 'strong culture'. Successful corporations have 'values and beliefs to pass along – not just products' (ibid.). The authors describe organizational culture as possessing five elements: (i) business environment, (ii) values, (iii) heroes, (iv) rituals and (v) cultural network (i.e. informal communications). This model does have the merit of specifying what the dimensions of organizational culture are believed to be. Its main limitation is its assumption that organizational cultures need to be of a particular kind if the organization is to be successful. This conclusion results from a preparedness to over-generalize from research on a sample of powerful corporations. Such conclusions may be less applicable for organizations operating in different markets, with different technologies and employing lower numbers of highly qualified staff (see CONTINGENCY THEORY).

Handy (1985) offers a more complex model that is able to distinguish between different cultural forms and organizational types. This model is based on an earlier one designed to distinguish between organizational ideologies. Handy's view of organizational culture is, in general terms, similar to that of Deal and Kennedy (1982) in that organizational culture is '... founded and built over the years by the dominant groups in an organization' (ibid.). He, however, differs from them in arguing that there are four main types of culture, not just 'strong' and 'weak' cultures. The Handy schema lists *power, role, task* and *person* cultures as viable alternatives, each of which can be an effective culture within the appropriate context (1985).

One has to look elsewhere for sociologically informed and critical analyses. Casey's (1995) study of the US company she calls 'Hephaestus' (1995) and Watson's study of ZTC Ryland in the UK (1994) are such examples as is Parker's (2000) study of three organizations drawn from the public, service and manufacturing sectors of the UK economy. Within the managerialist literature generally it is difficult, however, to escape the sense that concern with culture shares some affinity with Orwellian brainwashing, a view argued strongly by Willmott (1993). Managerial discourse is not the only form. Sociologists have been actively interested in the phenomena for far longer whether as 'ideology' (MARX) or 'discourse' (FOUCAULT). There is, for example, a strong research tradition in the study of organizational cultures within the work of SYMBOLIC INTERACTIONISTS, for example Strauss et al's (1963) study of a hospital as a negotiated order.

organizational reach (MANN, *The Social Sources of Power*, 1986) the capacity and spread of organizations (e.g. of a STATE or economic system) to exert POWER at a

distance. Mann suggests a four-fold typology involving two dimensions:
(a) range of control, however loose, and tightness of control (see EXTENSIVE AND INTENSIVE POWER); and
(b) 'authoritative' (centrally directed) or diffused (more spontaneous) power. Thus, while modern state power is extensive and authoritative, the market exchange economy is extensive and diffused.

organizational sociology see ORGANIZATION THEORY.

organization man a standard character type held by some theorists (especially William Whyte, 1956) to be increasingly found within modern industrial, commercial and some scientific and government organizations, in which executives and managers in an important sense 'belong' to the organization, and are dominated by a 'social ethic' rather than an 'individual ethic', which leads to conformism and to mediocrity. Essentially the idea applies to Max WEBER's conception of, and fears about, modern BUREAUCRACY.

organization theory

1 the sociological and multidisciplinary analysis of organizational structure and the dynamics of social relationships in organizations. Topics studied comprise: formal and informal structures of control, task allocation, decision-making, management and professionals in organizations, innovation, technology and organizational change. Major contributing disciplines, apart from sociology, include psychology, economics, management science and administrative theory. The psychological emphasis upon individual behaviour is concerned with the study of motivation and reward, leadership and decision-making. This is frequently referred to under the title *Organization Theory and Behaviour*. Inputs from management science and administrative theory have tended to stress the relationship between organization design and behaviour and the 'efficiency' and 'effectiveness' of organization arrangements. Organization theory is a subject normally found on the curriculum of most business and management courses.

2 an alternative term for the specialist area, *Sociology of Organizations* or *Organizational Sociology*, its subject content is often indistinguishable from the applied field of organization theory. Nevertheless, the subdiscipline can be identified by the use of perspectives and discussion of issues closer to mainstream academic sociology and derived particularly from Weber's ideal type of bureaucracy. There is also a focus upon all types of organization including nonprofit-seeking ones such as schools, hospitals, prisons and mental institutions in an attempt to arrive at a general theory of organizations (e.g. PARSONS, 1956), develop typologies of organizations and explain similarities and differences in organizational structure. In practice, the boundaries between the multidisciplinary study of organization theory and the sociology of organizations are difficult to discern, since writers in these fields often publish in the same journals (e.g. *Administrative Science Quarterly*), and many organizational issues (such as

managerial strategy, decision-making and innovation) draw upon a multidisciplinary framework. Since the 1970s much sociological writing on organizations has adopted a more critical stance towards managerially defined applied issues and 'problems' in organizations, such as worker motivation and 'efficiency', in an attempt to re-establish the study of organizations in historical context and in relation to their wider society (for example, studies of the way in which class and gender inequalities are reproduced in organizational contexts e.g. Clegg and Dunkerley, 1970).

Weber's ideal type of bureaucracy provided the point of departure for the postwar development of a sociology of organizations. GOULDNER's (1955a) distinction between 'punishment-centred' and 'representative' bureaucracy and Burns and Stalker's (1961) comparison of 'mechanistic' and 'organic' forms of organization have been particularly influential for later research. Gouldner demonstrated how bureaucratic rules can be resisted and suggested that bureaucratization can take different forms with varying levels of participation by its members. The contrast between mechanistic and organic organization was used by Burns and Stalker to suggest that different organizational structures are appropriate depending on the degree of stability or uncertainty in the environment. Mechanistic structures are bureaucratic, hierarchical and rigid in contrast to organic structures which are flexible, decentralized and more able to cope with innovation and rapidly changing environments. Comparison between organizations was further elaborated in the attempt to develop general organization typologies based on, for example, the criterion of 'who benefits?' (BLAU, 1955) and on TYPES OF COMPLIANCE (Etzioni, 1961).

The subsequent development of organization theory reflects both the various theoretical approaches in sociology as a whole and the influence of managerial perspectives, particularly SCIENTIFIC MANAGEMENT and the HUMAN RELATIONS SCHOOL. FUNCTIONALISM has exerted a powerful influence on organizational theory either explicitly, as in the concept of the organization as a system (see SYSTEMS THEORY), or implicitly via assumptions about organizational 'survival' and 'adaptation' to the environment. Organizations have been conceptualized as 'open systems' with an emphasis on 'input-output' exchanges between the organization and its environment. In similar vein, the Tavistock Institute (Trist et al., 1963) has used the concept of 'sociotechnical system' (see SOCIOTECHNICAL SYSTEMS APPROACH) to describe the interaction between technical production requirements and social system needs and to demonstrate that a variety of forms of work organization are compatible with given types of technology allowing a degree of organizational choice.

CONTINGENCY THEORY (Pugh et al., 1968; Laurence and Lorsch, 1967), which drew on the work of Burns and Stalker, and Woodward's (1970) discussion of the connection between organizational structure and technological complexity in the production process, has synthesized many of these findings, and undermined the claim of Scientific Management that there is 'one best (organizational) way'. Instead, contingency theory argues for the empirical study of the variety of relations which exist between 'contextual variables' (e.g. size, technology, environment), types of organizational structure and performance. Interestingly, however, it has itself come under attack from theorists who, impressed by the success of Japanese managerial methods (Ouchi, 1981), have been anxious to reassert the need for universal principles, such as the importance of strong organizational culture (Peters and Wateman, 1982). In sociology, contingency theory has been heavily criticized for different reasons, namely its deterministic assumptions, empiricism, and the weakness of the correlations established. The neglect of power relations by contingency theorists has been stressed by Child (1985), who proposes a *strategic contingency* approach to organizations which concentrates upon the role of managerial choice in actively shaping organizational structures in response to contingencies. Contingent factors, such as the environment, are, in turn, not treated as 'independent variables' but partly chosen or controlled by powerful organizations (multinationals, for example). The study of power relations and decision-making in organizations has been influenced by Simon's (1957a & b) concept of BOUNDED RATIONALITY and includes the analysis of organizational 'micro-politics' (Perrow, 1979).

Interactionist contributions to organization theory have emphasized the socially constructed nature of organizational arrangements as 'negotiated orders' and the precariousness of organizational rules (Silverman, 1970) as a corrective to the 'top-down' systems view of organizational life. Perspectives derived from SYMBOLIC INTERACTIONISM have informed an expanding area of current research into organizational cultures using ETHNOGRAPHIC methods.

In recent years the realm of organization theory has been transformed by the entry of poststructuralist and 'culturalist' approaches – see ORGANIZATIONAL CULTURE.

organized crime see ORGANIZATIONAL CRIME.

organized labour see TRADE(S) UNIONS.

oriental despotism Karl Wittfogel's (1955) now largely discredited term for 'Asiatic society' (see ASIATIC MODE OF PRODUCTION AND ASIATIC SOCIETY) and types of social system which he felt were related to this. 'Asiatic society' was a form of society which, following Adam SMITH, MARX and J. S. MILL and much 19th-century European thought, Wittfogel saw as characterized by 'despotic' state power. This resulted from a necessity for public works to provide irrigation and flood control, hence his alternative term – HYDRAULIC SOCIETY. Oriental despotism was contrasted with Western European forms of constitutional, ultimately liberal constitutional, government. The absence of 'private property' (and CIVIL SOCIETY) was seen as a further decisive factor in accounting for this difference. While there remains much support for the contention that Western European development (including constitutional state forms) constitutes a distinctive route (e.g. see WEBER, ANDERSON), the idea that this can be explained simply, or even primarily, in terms of an 'hydraulic' social basis has not been accepted. See also ORIENTALISM.

orientalism 1 the academic study of the Orient, which has been variously defined as the Middle East, the Far East or most of Asia. 2 a more general perspective, intellectual, artistic or political, which sees the distinction between East and West as one of the fundamental divisions of the world. 3 'a Western style for dominating, restructuring and having authority over the Orient', (SAID, 1978; definitions 1 and 2 are derived from the same source).

Definition 3 is the subject of Said's analysis, wherein he argues that since the late 18th-century Western writers have constructed an image of the Orient centred around such concerns as the distinctiveness of the 'Oriental mind' as opposed to the 'Occidental mind'. Said argues that this corresponds to no empirical reality and reduces to insignificance the varieties of language, culture, social forms and political structures in the so-called Orient. This imagery has been a significant part of intellectual thought in the West since the AGE OF ENLIGHTENMENT. See also ORIENTAL DESPOTISM, ASIATIC MODE OF PRODUCTION AND ASIATIC SOCIETY, HYDRAULIC SOCIETY.

orientations to work the attitudes and motivation, and the overall subjective experience of work, associated with particular occupations or groups. A significant strand of sociological work in this area has been concerned with elaborating and developing the work of MARX on the ALIENATION of the worker produced within and by the capitalist LABOUR PROCESS. SCIENTIFIC MANAGEMENT (see also BRAVERMAN THESIS) was one early managerial strategy which, while aiming to maximize worker's efficiency, tended to increase levels of alienation. Robert Blauner (1964) subsequently argued that technological developments would tend eventually to enhance rather than erode the degree of control which workers could experience over their work, and so reduce the degree of alienation which they experienced (see ALIENATION). Later sociological research has questioned this hypothesis (see NEW WORKING CLASS).

In contrast to the tradition of scientific management, the HUMAN RELATIONS SCHOOL recognized the need of employees for social anchorage and recognition, and sought to increase satisfaction with work by recognizing the importance of work-group norms and the effect of styles of leadership. Elton MAYO's famous research, which initiated the human relations approach, has given rise to a continuing body of work concerned with the conditions and techniques which help to promote worker satisfaction (see MASLOW, Herzberg 1968, SOCIOTECHNICAL SYSTEMS APPROACH). The most recent initiatives in this area involve the new types of working arrangements associated with post-Fordism (see FORDISM AND POST-FORDISM) and JAPANIZATION.

The AFFLUENT WORKER studies of GOLDTHORPE, LOCKWOOD et al. (see also CLASS IMAGERY) have also pointed to the importance of the kinds of orientation which workers bring with them to the workplace, showing that workers sometimes express satisfaction with routine and repetitive manual tasks simply because work was well paid.

Much of the 'classical' sociological research in this area has focused on manual workers in jobs where control over the work process is often lacking. Professional, managerial, technical and scientific kinds of work, which have higher STATUS, greater responsibility and autonomy (see WORK SITUATION), as well as commanding higher financial rewards (see MARKET SITUATION), typically allow for greater intrinsic satisfaction. This view may be modified by the reorganization of the labour market, which has occurred in the 1980s and 1990s, where many professional kinds of work have undergone increasing levels of regulation and surveillance (e.g. teachers and doctors), where employment contracts are short-term and work is less secure, and where the labour process itself has been intensified at all occupational levels.

originary position the originary scene, the birth of the first sign (according to E. Gans, *Originary Thinking,* 1993), whose theory of GENERATIVE ANTHROPOLOGY speculates about the nature of human evolution, that is, the projection of the original abortive gesture of appropriation towards the level of symbolic representation. Also see: GIRARD, MIMETIC DESIRE.

ostensive definition see DEFINITION.

other-directedness an attitudinal orientation or personality type in which a person's sense of social identity is dependent upon the approval of others. In the two-fold schema proposed by RIESMAN (1950), other-directedness is contrasted with *inner-directedness,* in which a person's behaviour and sense of social identity is mainly governed by internalized standards and conscience. Riesman's suggestion was that modern societies like the US, dominated by mass consumption, were increasingly moving towards other-direction and an anxiety-riven conformity; a fear of not fitting in (other-direction), rather than a deeper sense of 'guilt' or 'shame' (inner-direction).

otherness the opposite or opposed element in a binary opposition such as self/other (ego/alter), East/West, or masculine/feminine.

The concept is important in FREUD and LACAN, and is variously employed elsewhere, e.g. SAID's account of ORIENTALISM, CIXOUS's conception of the 'feminine'.

out-group see IN-GROUP AND OUT-GROUP.

outwork see HOMEWORKING.

overdetermination 1 for FREUD the process in which a 'condensation' of a number of complex thoughts gives rise to a single image (as in recurring dreams).

2 by analogy with the above, the combined outcome of the multiple contradictions existing in the different areas of a 'social formation' at any given time, in which, according to Louis ALTHUSSER (1969), each contradiction is 'inseparable from the total structure of the social body' and is both determined by and in turn also determines this total structure. The existence of such overdetermination is seen as accounting for such phenomena as UNEVEN DEVELOPMENT, since complex 'overdeterminations' mean that no social formation develops simply.

overload on the state a situation in which the state in some modern Western capitalist and social-democratic societies is seen as suffering an overload on its resources as more demands are made upon it, e.g. provision of social welfare, education, and political legitimacy, at the same time as preserving the conditions for capitalist accumulation. See also FISCAL CRISIS IN THE CAPITALIST STATE, LEGITIMATION CRISIS, BELL, THATCHERISM.

overproduction see UNDERCONSUMPTION AND OVERPRODUCTION.

oversocialized conception of Man the charge (e.g. by Dennis Wrong, 1960) that functionalist theory, including the work of DURKHEIM and PARSONS, in answering 'the Hobbesian question' of what 'makes possible an enduring society' has tended to overstate the 'internalization of values'. Likewise, Marxian sociology is also seen as often taking an 'overintegrated view of society' in answering the question how 'complex societies manage and regulate and restrain ... conflicts between groups'. See also SOCIAL INTEGRATION AND SYSTEM INTEGRATION.

ownership and control see MANAGERIAL REVOLUTION.

Oxford philosophy see ORDINARY LANGUAGE PHILOSOPHY.

p

paganism 1 forms of religious practices regarded as heathen by Christianity.
2 (by analogy with 1) the practice, advocated by Jean Francois LYOTARD, of judging in the absence of criteria (*Just Gaming*, 1985). This is anathematical to traditional accounts of knowledge, ethics and art which have striven to delimit stable and coherent criteria. As a theorist of POSTMODERNISM, Lyotard rejects this project which he sees as impossible, primarily due to an increasing lack of faith in science and GRAND NARRATIVES. Though he does not shy from the not inconsiderable problems that arise here (e.g. how to judge between the claims of patriarchy and feminism, or between fascist and socialist) he maintains that paganism, with its emphasis on feelings, offers a viable way to engage with the current myriad of changes (see DIFFEREND and PERFORMATIVITY).

Palaeolithic Age the earliest stage of human biological and cultural development, characterized by a pre-agricultural lifestyle and the use of found tools. The term literally means 'old stone age' and is followed by the NEOLITHIC AGE. See HUNTER-GATHERERS.

palaeontology the study and dating of fossilized remains. The work of palaeontologists, sometimes working in close association with archaeologists and physical anthropologists, is of interest to sociologists for the light that it throws on human origins and on evolutionary processes in general. Evidence from palaeontology and from geology played a major role in the initial establishment of an evolutionary view of biological and human development during the 19th-century. See also EVOLUTIONARY THEORY.

panel study a technique for investigating change over time in the attitudes or opinions of a SAMPLE of people. This is a form of LONGITUDINAL STUDY, but is usually distinguished as being of shorter duration or more focused. It involves questioning the same sample at (regular) intervals to observe trends of opinion, e.g. voting intention and party preference before, during and after an election. As with any longitudinal study, this method may possess advantage compared with CROSS-SECTIONAL STUDIES, since the sample members remain constant, and change can be monitored using data gathered before and after it. Against this, some respondents may be lost through death, removal or lack of interest, and those that remain may become atypical through the experience of being panel members (compare HAWTHORNE EFFECT).

panoptican a design for PRISONS which was intended to allow warders to oversee every aspect of the inmates' lives. As such, the panoptican has often been regarded as symptomatic of a new emphasis on SURVEILLANCE and SOCIAL CONTROL in modern societies (see also FOUCAULT).

Invented by the English UTILITARIAN philosopher, Jeremy BENTHAM, in the early 19th-century, the panoptican was intended as a new, rational prison design, geared to personal reform as well as confinement and punishment. The idea did not only relate to the structure of the building, it involved a complete philosophy of imprisonment, incorporating ideological and organizational features as well as architectural ones. These included a strictly organized day, based around the reformatory influences of hard work and prayer, based on a single-cell system so as to avoid the moral contagion of association with other criminals. The physical design was intended to make perpetual observation and control possible. In many respects this idea broke sharply with previous conceptions of imprisonment and may be seen as part of a rationalization and rethinking of the role of imprisonment. It was linked to new ideas about the value of work: indeed, many writers have argued that there was an integral connection between the developing factory system and the regulation of the poor through the Poor Law and the reorganized prison system, although the early expressions of this theory are sometimes considered overstated. What is clear is that the panoptican may be seen in a context of major revision in the ideology of punishment and 'correction'. It influenced a number of prison projects in Britain, the US and elsewhere. See also CRIMINOLOGY.

paradigm 1 any example or representative instance of a concept or a theoretical approach, e.g. MERTON's (1949) summary exemplifying discussion of the strengths and pitfalls of functional analysis in sociology. In some branches of philosophy a 'paradigm case' is seen as providing an 'ostensive definition' of a concept.

2 see SCIENTIFIC PARADIGM.

paradigmatic see SYNTAGMATIC AND PARADIGMATIC.

parallel descent (ANTHROPOLOGY) a system in which males reckon ancestry through male links and females through female links. The system is to be distinguished from DOUBLE DESCENT in which both males and females are members of PATRILINEAL and MATRILINEAL DESCENT groups.

parametric statistics inferential statistics that assume that the population from which the SAMPLE has been drawn has a particular form, i.e. they involve hypotheses about population parameters. These assumptions are generally that the populations involved have a NORMAL DISTRIBUTION, that they have equal variances (see MEASURES OF DISPERSION) and that the data are at interval level (see CRITERIA AND LEVELS OF MEASUREMENT). Examples are the PEARSON PRODUCT MOMENT CORRELATION COEFFICIENT, multiple regression, and analysis of variance. Such procedures use all available information and tests are more powerful than nonparametric tests. In sociology, the problem of data that are not normally distributed in the population frequently arises. A transformation of scale, a reliance on the robustness of the technique, or a move to a nonparametric equivalent are the available solutions. Compare NONPARAMETRIC STATISTICS.

parasuicide see ATTEMPTED SUICIDE AND PARASUICIDE.

Pareto, Vilfredo (1848–1923) French-born, Italian engineer and social scientist who turned to sociology only in later life. In social science, he sought to apply the principles of mechanical systems in equilibrium to social systems, an approach which influenced Talcott PARSONS. He is best known in sociology for his work on political ÉLITES.

His first recognition in social science was as an economist, in which subject he is still remembered for his ideas on the distribution of income (see PARETO OPTIMALITY). Disillusioned with liberal politics and believing that political economy could not ignore psychological and sociological factors, the major focus of his sociological analysis was on social differentiation as an enduring feature of social and political life, including a distinction between élites and masses.

Critical of SPENCER's evolutionism as well as MARX's socialism, Pareto made the 'unequal distribution of capacities' the bedrock of sociological theory. He accepted neither liberal or Marxian conceptions of social progress. Rather he saw history as involving the endless CIRCULATION OF ÉLITES. According to Pareto: 'a political system in which the "people" expresses its will (supposing it had one, which is arguable) without cliques, intrigues, lobbies and factions, exists only as a pious wish of theorists. It is not observable in the past or present either in the West or anywhere else.'

As Pareto conceived of it, much of social life was governed by the operation of underlying nonrational psychological forces (see RESIDUES AND DERIVATIONS). These he believed had been ignored by most previous theorists, and had been given a proper scientific analysis only by him. Above all he distinguished between 'non-logical' and 'logical' forms of action (see LOGICAL AND NONLOGICAL ACTION). Previous theorists had simply underestimated the extent of the former, while overestimating the movement from non-rationality to rationality in human societies. Equilibrium in societies is seen by Pareto as something that can only be understood as the outcome of the complex interplay of sentiments and interests.

Pareto's major sociological work – *Trattoto di sociologia generale* – first published in Italy in 1916 (and translated as *The Mind and Society*, 1936) is a rambling treatise of very great length, in which, despite great pretensions to a new scientific rigour, his ideas are illustrated rather than systematically tested. While his contribution to ÉLITE THEORY and his conception of 'social system' influenced many (including Mussolini), no one now accepts the detail of his sociological thinking.

Pareto optimality a theoretical condition of the economy in which the distribution of economic welfare cannot be improved for any one individual without reducing the welfare of one or more other individuals. Thus a 'Pareto improvement' occurs when a reallocation of resources renders one or more persons better off. In any situation where more than one optimum is possible, Pareto optimality cannot be established.

pariah 1 in India, a member of a low CASTE (see HINDUISM) or 'untouchable' group, thus subject to ritual and social exclusion. 2 by analogy, any social outcast, or stigmatized individual or group.

parish register a list of the baptisms, marriages and burials performed in a church or chapel. Through the use of Anglican parish registers it is possible to examine a number of questions of interest to the historical sociologist and demographer. These include family structure, fertility rates, illegitimacy, infant mortality, birth and death rates, and, to a limited extent, occupational and geographical mobility.

Unfortunately not all parish registers have survived. In the 16th-century some churches failed to compile registers, gaps frequently exist in the records of some churches, especially during the Civil War period and many registers have been lost or damaged by fire or flood. From 1561, however, copies of the registers, The *Bishops' Transcripts* (BTs), were drawn up annually. Most of the surviving parish registers (together with the BTs) have now been deposited in *County Record Offices.*

Park, Robert (1864–1944) influential US sociologist and Professor of Sociology at the University of Chicago. As well as writing, with Ernest Burgess, a major general textbook on sociology (*Introduction to the Science of Society*), he is best remembered for his contributions to URBAN SOCIOLOGY and to the study of race relations. Park studied under William James and also under WINDELBAND and SIMMEL. His general sociology was eclectic, combining insights drawn from a variety of American and European sources. Along with other members of the CHICAGO SCHOOL, his influence on research methods was to attach a new importance to empirical studies in sociology, especially studies based on PARTICIPANT OBSERVATION.

parole see LANGUE AND PAROLE.

Parsons, Talcott (1902–79) American sociologist, who was arguably the most influential American sociologist of the 20th century, and the leading modern exponent of FUNCTIONALISM. Because his concerns ranged so widely, it is difficult to summarize even Parsons' main ideas briefly.

Amongst his earliest work was a translation of Max WEBER's *The Protestant Ethic and the Spirit of Capitalism,* which did much to introduce Weber's work to US sociologists. His first major volume in his own right, *The Structure of Social Action* (1937), involved an assessment of the theoretical legacy of PARETO, DURKHEIM and Weber – as usual in Parsons' work, Marx was a conspicuous omission. All three of these thinkers were presented as attempting to provide a solution to what Parsons called 'the problem of social order': why is it that society is not characterized by a 'Hobbesian' war of all against all?

In this first stage of his thinking, Parsons saw himself as working within an *'action frame of reference',* viewing social action as 'voluntaristic'. All three of his chosen theorists were presented as contributing to the repudiation of a merely 'positivistic theory of social action'. Based on their work, he saw himself as working towards the achievement of a single, coherent, 'analytical' sociological theory of voluntaristic social action. This involved a repudiation of all theories which represented social action merely as an automatic response to external stimuli, or sought to account for social order simply in terms of 'coercion' or 'self interest'.

For Parsons, in *The Structure of Social Action* and subsequently, the answer to the 'Hobbesian question' was that social action is engendered, although not simply determined, by shared NORMS and VALUES. These ideas were developed in the direction of functionalism and SYSTEMS THEORY, especially in *The Social System* (1951), and *Towards a General Theory of Action* (1951) (the latter written with Edward Shils). Three main aspects of Parsons' thinking in this period can be identified:

(a) the notion of FUNCTIONAL PREREQUISITES of society;
(b) a conception of social order which presents societies as internally interrelated and 'self-sustaining' SOCIAL SYSTEMS, operating in an 'external environment';
(c) the general theory of 'action systems', developed from the work of Robert Bales (e.g. *Working Papers in the Theory of Action,* Parsons, Bales and Shils, 1953) – see SUBSYSTEMS MODEL.

In a final phase of his work, Parsons also added to these a neoevolutionary model of social development (*Societies; Evolutionary and Comparative Perspectives,* 1966) (see EVOLUTIONARY UNIVERSALS, NEOEVOLUTIONARY THEORY). All these elements of Parsons' work were enormously influential at the time. Parsons' books became virtual bibles for a generation of functionalist sociologists. However, an increasing emphasis on the primacy of norms and values in his work, allied with his systems perspective (see CYBERNETIC HIERARCHY), also led to much criticism. For example, as well as the many general criticisms increasingly directed at functionalism and evolutionary theory (see FUNCTIONALIST EXPLANATION), the suspicion grew that Parsons' thinking (e.g. Parsons, 1964b; Parsons and Bales, 1955) involved an oversocialized conception of social action and fostered conservatism. The result of this was that in the 1970s and 80s, when the general dominance of functionalism within US sociology also declined, interest in Parsons' work waned although it has enjoyed a minor revival of late.

As well as his contributions to general theory, some of Parsons' briefer, more empirical, applications of his theory have also been significant and can be said to have stood the test of time rather better than his overall functionalist framework, e.g. essays on the SICK ROLE, on POWER, on education and on racial integration. In these Parsons displays a sharp analytical flair in the application of general conceptions to particular cases. Research inspired by the Parsonian conceptual legacy has also been extensive, especially research based on his conception of PATTERN VARIABLES. At its peak, Parsons' influence on American sociology was immense. In the UK, his role as a *bête noire* has tended to overshadow his considerable contribution to questions of how to theorize about society. See also SOCIAL INTEGRATION AND SYSTEM INTEGRATION, MILLS, MERTON, THEORIES OF THE MIDDLE RANGE, GOULDNER.

participant observation a method of social research in which the researcher becomes a participant in a naturally occurring social activity. Supporters of the method contrast it favourably with other research methods such as EXPERIMENTAL METHODS or FIXED-CHOICE QUESTIONNAIRES, which are seen as introducing artificiality into social observation and investigation.

In participant observation, data are collected informally in the course of a researcher's interactions in normal social life. However, the accurate recording of data and systematically focused intensive INTERVIEWS of key informants are normally an essential feature of the approach, and these are often also supplemented by documentary evidence.

While some participant observers have been content to write up their findings in the form of descriptive ETHNOGRAPHIES, claims to greater generalization may also be advanced (see ANALYTICAL INDUCTION). Participant observation is seen to good effect in the work of Erving GOFFMAN (1961a) on asylums or Howard BECKER (1953) on marijuana usage.

The generalizability of research findings need not be a problem for participant observation, but problems do arise in:
(a) the labour-intensive character, and the expense of the method given that lengthy periods of observation are usually required;
(b) the difficulty of minimizing and controlling the social researcher's influence on the social processes observed;
(c) ethical as well as methodological dilemmas in entering and leaving the field, including the decision to make the research overt or covert.

All three problems are equally applicable to *non-participant observation,* where the researcher refrains from active involvement in the behaviour under study. The HAWTHORNE EFFECT is a good example of the way in which subjects may alter behaviour when they are aware of being observed.

Whatever the problems of participant observation, it remains an invaluable method of sociological research, which is perhaps best seen as complementary to other approaches rather than as an outright alternative to them (see RESEARCH METHODS). Participant observation is an especially useful method where the social action being researched is deviant or covert. Participant observation can be described as a 'discovery-based approach' as well as a means of testing propositions.

participatory action research a form of ACTION RESEARCH. If the goals of traditional research have generally been restricted to trying to know, or understand aspects of society, participatory action research aims to change that which is studied. For this reason it is inherently political and involves researchers and researched working together to identify and resolve issues in a particular area. Thus, compared with more conventional research methods and approaches, participatory action research is more akin to PRAXIS in that assumes knowledge comes from interactive engagement with the world.

particularism the orientation of any culture or human grouping in which the values and criteria used in evaluating actions are internal to the group, without any reference to values or criteria which apply to human beings universally. Thus, many traditional cultures are seen as particularistic, while modern societies have increasingly tended to be dominated by universalistic criteria, by *universalism.* See also PATTERN VARIABLES.

parties of representation and parties of integration see POLITICAL PARTY.

partition the politically motivated division of an existing territory. Such divisions may involve changing existing state borders, and the enforced migration of residents. Partition can occur for several reasons: as a result of outside influence; following the departure of a colonialist power; or as a result of internal unrest. In Britain the term is primarily associated with the partition of Ireland in the 20th century.

party see POLITICAL PARTY.

party identification a voter's enduring link with a political party (Budge, 1976). In the UK Butler and Stokes (1969) sought to establish a respondent's party identification, asking the question: 'Generally speaking do you usually think of yourself as Conservative, Labour or Liberal?' Similar questions are widely elsewhere. Some early students of VOTING BEHAVIOUR assumed that voters might operate like individual consumers, with voting a matter of 'personal preference' and voters likely to be readily persuaded to change sides. Subsequent studies of 'party identification' have generally shown that this is not so, that in a majority of cases voters possess a 'party identification' to which they return even if in a particular election, or when polled in advance of an election, their 'voting intention' may sometimes differ from this. The increased volatility of voting behaviour in recent years (see also CLASS DEALIGNMENT) may have reduced the numbers of people who possess a persistent party identification (and also its strength), but it remains the case that individual voting behaviour possesses a continuity over elections. See also PARTY IMAGE, POLITICAL ATTITUDES, POLITICAL PARTICIPATION.

party system see POLITICAL PARTY.

passive resistance see SOCIAL MOVEMENTS.

pastiche the mixing of styles and *genres* which is characteristic of postmodern cultural forms (e.g. in architecture).

pastoralism and pastoral society a mode of subsistence economy and social organization, as among the Nuer of southern Sudan, in which the main livelihood is gained by tending flocks and herds of domesticated animals by moving on a regular basis or wandering with them in search of pasture. It has been suggested that pastoralism tends to be associated with egalitarianism and independence of mind (Spooner, 1973), but also with patriarchy. Whatever the truth of this, pastoralism and nomadic herding societies (see NOMADS AND NOMADISM) have historically been a frequent source of threat to more settled and more urban forms of society, and sometimes have been seen as a source of renewal within these – as for example, by the classical Arab social theorist Khaldun. See also AGRARIAN SOCIETY.

paternalism a system by which a government or organization deals with its subjects or employees by deploying an authoritarian family model of relationships, i.e. the directive but benevolent father dealing with a child. In such a relationship, the more powerful seeks to legitimate social, economic and political inequality by claiming that domination is in the best interests of the oppressed. The dominated are said to be child-like, i.e. immature and unable to look after their own affairs, therefore the government or organization must act *in loco parentis* (in the place of parents).

Paternalism is used widely as a legitimating ideology in pre-industrial societies, in colonial regimes and in personal relationships. Examples would include PATRON-CLIENT RELATIONSHIPS, the 'civilizing' mission of European powers in Africa, master-slave relationships in chattel slavery and some teacher-student relationships.

path analysis a statistical method using REGRESSION to quantify the relationships between VARIABLES. A causal model is generated, depicted by a *path diagram* which shows how the variables are assumed to effect or be affected by each other. The observed data is compared with this model and if it is compatible it can be concluded that the causal effects may be as depicted in the model; it is not proof that the paths of causation are correct. See also CAUSAL MODELLING.

patient role see SICK ROLE.

patriarch see PATRIARCHY.

patriarchy 1 a form of social organization in which a male (the *patriarch*) acts as head of the family/household, holding power over females and children (e.g. in Roman society). 2 any system whereby men achieve and maintain social, cultural and economic dominance over females and younger males. The term may refer to a pattern of organization within the family and households, etc., or within a whole society.

Although historically sociologists have mainly used the term descriptively, more recent usage by feminist sociologists has emphasized mainly its negative features. Analysis in sociology has been concerned with the origins and the implications of patriarchy. Although biological differences between men and women (e.g. physical strength in warfare) have sometimes been seen as the basis of patriarchy, the cultural and social sources of patriarchy, and its variations in form and importance, are equally striking.

Within FEMINIST THEORY, use of the term patriarchy has lead to the politicization of discussion of GENDER relations, enabling gender relations to be understood as predicated on inequalities of power.

patrilateral (ANTHROPOLOGY) a kinship term referring to relations on the father's side. The opposite is MATRILATERAL and the term for a system which recognizes both is BILATERAL.

patrilineal descent a UNILINEAL DESCENT system, tracing DESCENT through males. A synonym is AGNATIC. The opposite is MATRILINEAL DESCENT.

patrilocal residence of a married couple with husband's kin. Often this specifically means with the husband's father, but not always, so the synonym *virilocal* is often used to distance it from PATRILINEAL DESCENT.

patrimonialism any form of political domination or political authority based on 'personal' and bureaucratic power exerted by a royal household (WEBER, 1922). As such 'patrimonialism' is a relatively broad term, not referring to any particular type of political system. The crucial contrast between patrimonialism and other types of political power is that:
(a) this power is formally 'arbitrary'; and
(b) its administration is under the direct control of the ruler; (this means it involves the employment of retainers or slaves, mercenaries and conscripts, who themselves possess no independent basis of power, i.e. are *not* members of traditional landed aristocracy).

The limitation of patrimonialism, according to Weber, is that it was inherently unstable, tending to be subject to political upheavals, which arose from the emergence of rival centres of power. Since historically patrimonial systems were usually replaced by further patrimonial systems, their existence is seen as a barrier to any sustained economic and social transformation. Compare ORIENTAL DESPOTISM. See also EISENSTADT.

patron-client relationship any continuing relationship, often contractual, in which a powerful or influential person provides rewards and services to humbler and weaker persons in return for loyalty and support, and perhaps also including the reciprocal exchange of some services. Such relationships are found especially in simple or traditional societies; similar relationships may also exist between states.

The concept may cover personalized relationships and include instances where both coercion and consent are involved. It has been of particular importance in understanding relationships of the peasantry (see PEASANTS) with other groups in society, such as landlords or politicians. Usually the patron provides favours, services or protection in return for loyalty, political support, and maybe economic control. This relationship may extend outside the peasantry to a style of national politics in which electoral support is gained through fostering patron-client relationships, with a politician either giving or promising favours. Thus a system of *clientelism* may be one way of incorporating a wide population into national politics. Mouzelis (1986) discusses this and contrasts it with POPULISM as a form of political incorporation in parts of Latin America and the Balkans.

pattern maintenance see SUBSYSTEMS MODEL.

pattern variables the four (sometimes five) basic 'pattern-alternatives of value orientation' for individuals and cultures, according to PARSONS. On this formulation, cultures are seen as organizing action, and actors as faced with implicit 'choices' in relationships, in terms of four dichotomous alternative modes of orientation to social objects', including other actors:
(a) *affective involvement/affective neutrality* – orientation by the actor to immediate gratifications *or* the absence of such immediate gratification, e.g. eating a meal or watching a football match compared with work that does not engage one's emotions;
(b) *ascription/achievement* (also referred to as the *quality/performance* distinction) – judgements about 'social objects', including actors according to their membership or not of specified social categories *as against* judgements made in terms of more general criteria which apply to the actual performance of actors, e.g. in most societies gender is ascribed, while success at football or in a musical career involves achievement;
(c) *particularism/universalism* – the choice whether to treat a 'social object' in accordance with their standing in some particular relationship independently of general norms, *or* to treat it in accordance with 'a general norm covering all the objects in a category', e.g. a mother's relationship with her child may sometimes be particularistic but at other times involve universalistic criteria (appraising performance at school, for example);
(d) *diffuseness/specificity* – social relationships involving an across-the-board personal involvement, e.g. the mother-child relationship and family relationships in general, *or* relationships which have only a specified and limited purpose, e.g. a bus conductor issuing tickets.

A fifth variable, *collectivity-orientation/self-orientation,* originally proposed by Parsons, was subsequently dropped as being of a different order from the other four.

Parsons' conception of pattern variables was presented by him as deriving from previous characterizations of types of society such as TÖNNIES' distinction between GEMEINSCHAFT AND GESELLSCHAFT. He saw his pattern variables as providing an exhaustive general statement of the fundamental 'dilemmas' perennially facing all actors and involved in all social organization. Accordingly it was also possible to locate particular societies in terms of the schema (see Fig. 22).

	Achievement (what actors do)	Ascription (who actors are)
Universalism (general principles)	MODERN US	GERMANY IN THE LATE 19TH CENTURY
Particularism (particular values rather than general principles)	ANCIENT CHINA	COLONIAL SPANISH AMERICA

Fig. 22 **Pattern variables.** A location of examples of contrasting types of society in terms of their dominant cultural values, expressed in terms of Talcott Parsons' pattern variables.

While the vocabulary provided by the pattern variables has been widely used in both sociology theory and empirical research, Parsons' suggestion that these variables can be regarded as a formal derivation from his overall general theory of social systems is no longer convincing.

peace movements political movements, such as the Campaign for Nuclear Disarmament (CND), which have become increasingly influential in modern societies, especially since the end of World War II and with the build-up of nuclear armaments. These movements have tended to draw their support especially from public sector professionals (e.g. teachers and welfare workers; see also MIDDLE-CLASS RADICALISM). To some extent, however, association with such organizations cross-cuts the LEFT-RIGHT CONTINUUM of conventional party politics.

Pearson product moment correlation coefficient (*r*) a CORRELATION coefficient for use with continuous variables (interval or ratio scales) with a NORMAL DISTRIBUTION. A theoretical justification for the measure is that r^2 is the proportion of the variance in one of the variables that may be predicted from the other.

peasant differentiation see PEASANTS.

peasant politics the political activity and organization of PEASANTS. Until the 1960s the prevailing consensus within the social sciences was that peasants had little or no independent political organization and little impact on state politics. Since then this view has been fundamentally revised. It is now recognized that in the 20th-century the peasantry played decisive roles in the Russian Revolutions of 1905 and 1917, the Mexican revolution in the second decade and in a variety of anticolonial and national movements in the THIRD WORLD (see Wolf, 1971; Walton, 1984).

Several strands of analysis and questions can now be identified:

(a) Whether or not peasant politics can influence the state without the involvement of other social groups. Scott (1985) argues that peasants everywhere have probably used 'the ordinary weapons of relatively powerless groups: foot-dragging, dissimulation, false compliance, pilfering, feigned ignorance, slander, arson, sabotage, and so forth'. This resistance reflects rejection of dominant power groups but lacks coordination. At times this opposition may become more organized, but may be reflected in collective desertion rather than confrontation: MILLENARIANISM AND MILLENNIAL MOVEMENTS have been understood in this way. For confrontation with state and other political representatives, alliances with other groups may be necessary, since these introduce organizational forms and ideologies not generated by peasants. These may take various forms from urban-based political groups and organizations, depending on the historical context;

(b) Whether peasant political activity takes the form of organized opposition to or support for dominant political groupings and organizations, resistance, rebellion or revolution. Recently this has been a major area of investigation. One line of argument is that peasant demands everywhere tend to be limited and once these have been achieved peasants may lose interest in political activity. 'Land, peace and bread', or variations, have been common slogans, for peasants since the Russian Revolution. An example is the response of Zapata, one of the peasant leaders during the Mexican Revolution, on occupying the Presidential Palace in Mexico City: he chose to return to his native state since the demand for land rights had been achieved (Womack, 1969);

(c) Another line of enquiry has asked which groups within the peasantry are most likely to be involved in political activities. Alavi (1965) argued that middle peasants with land have enough economic leverage and resources to risk rebellion, whereas rich peasants are less likely to oppose the existing order and poor peasants without land have few resources to mobilize for action.

peasants 'small agricultural producers, who, with the help of simple equipment and the labour of their families, produce mostly for their own consumption, direct or indirect, and for the fulfilment of obligations to holders of political and economic power' (Shanin, 1988).

Until the 1960s, the peasantry were largely ignored in sociology as having no significant role to play in history. This was despite the now recognized point that peasants have existed for most of recorded history and in many parts of the world. From the 1960s the publication of key works, such as Wolf (1966) and Barrington MOORE (1967), began to change this perception, introducing to sociology perspectives developed in anthropology and political economy. The role of the peasantry in the Vietnam war, and the growth of peasant political activity in Latin America and Asia raised questions about the assumed passivity of the peasantry. Within Marxist work, partly under the influence of MAOISM (see MAO TSE-TUNG) and events in China around the 1949 Revolution and subsequently, there emerged the question of whether the peasantry in the Third World represented the revolutionary force of socialism. This was especially so in the light of analyses which saw the proletariat of the advanced capitalist world incorporated as a labour aristocracy into the dominant capitalist world. There is now a major area of interdisciplinary peasant studies. But, one of the most important debates is still over whether a distinctive category of peasantry can be identified both conceptually and empirically. Shanin presents one of the strongest and most influential defences of the concept. Drawing on all strands contributing to peasant studies this century, he argues that there are four main interrelated characteristics of the peasantry (Shanin, 1982; Shanin (ed.), 1988, Introduction):

(a) The family farm is the major economic unit around which production, labour and consumption are organized;

(b) Land husbandry is the main activity combined with minimal specialization and family training for tasks;

(c) There is a particular 'peasant way of life' based on the local village community which covers most areas of social life and culture and which distinguishes it from urban life and from those of other social groups;

(d) Peasants are politically, economically and socially subordinated to nonpeasant groups against whom they have devised various methods of resistance, rebellion or revolt;

There are two further subsidiary facets:

(e) A specific social dynamic involving a cyclical change over generations which irons out inequalities over time via land division and the rise and fall of the availability of family labour through the DOMESTIC CYCLE;

(f) Especially in the contemporary world, a common pattern of structural change, drawing peasants into market relationships, often through the influence of outside bodies such as AGRIBUSINESS, and incorporation into national politics. The precise outcome of these common changes is not predetermined.

According to circumstances, the peasantry may survive, they may migrate because of declining opportunities on the land, they may combine wage labour in urban or rural areas with some elements of land husbandry. becoming worker-peasants, they may become totally reliant on wage labour without land becoming a rural PROLETARIAT, or some combination of these.

Further, two general distinctions are usually made between peasants and other farmers. The first contrast is with TRIBAL peoples. Post (1972) distinguishes peasants as having:

(a) group or individual rather than communal land ownership;

(b) a social division of labour which is not exclusively based on kinship;

(c) an involvement in market relationships even though the extent of this will vary;

(d) political hierarchies which are not exclusively based on kinship and with a state structure to which they are subordinated; (e) a culture which is not as homogeneous as tribal people's. Peasant culture coexists with cultures of other groups in the same society.

The second contrast is with small CAPITALIST family-farmers who may rely predominantly on family labour, but who may also employ wage labour, who buy in seeds, fertilizer, livestock and so on, and sell most of the output rather than using it for the family's own consumption. Thus both inputs and outputs are COMMODITIES.

Peasants can be most clearly distinguished in AGRARIAN SOCIETIES. A key issue is what effect the emergence of CAPITALISM has on the peasantry. For some authors this raises the issue of *differentiation of the peasantry* which may increase with the development of capitalism. Following LENIN, one distinction is between rich peasants who have more land than they need for their own consumption and either rent it out or employ others to work it, middle peasants who conform to the definition of peasant used here, and poor peasants who do not have enough land to supply their own needs and who may have to sell their labour for an income. A graphic definition of a poor peasant is given by a Malaysian who said he 'had to shit on someone else's land' (Scott, 1985). An important debate has been whether, with the development of capitalism, rich peasants become capitalist farmers and poor peasants become PROLETARIANS, with middle peasants becoming one or the other.

Neglected in peasant studies until the last decade has been the question of GENDER. In the past, the structure of the peasant household was treated unproblematically but now it is increasingly recognized that PATRIARCHAL relationships are central. Thus women are frequently subordinated in many ways and carry a heavy burden of work. The division of labour between men and women varied in time and place but was rigid. Peasant women have limited public identity, and in extreme cases, such as China before the 20th century, scarcely counted as human beings.

There are several strong arguments that the concept of 'peasant' has no place in social-scientific analysis. Polly Hill (1986), drawing on her work in Africa and Asia, argues that there are such variations over time and place of the ways in which rural farmers make a living and organize their social life, that only a small proportion of people fit usual definitions of the peasantry: an individual over a lifetime may engage in trade, wage labour, small-plot farming, trucking, or employing others. Conceptually, others have argued that the term peasant has vague implications: one cannot read off from the definitions of 'peasant' implications for understanding the wider society, economy or politics in the same way that one can for other concepts. Finally there is debate whether the central importance attached to the peasant HOUSEHOLD in Shanin's and other formulations is appropriate. The focus on the household is derived from the work of the Soviet economist, Chayanov (see Thorner et al., 1966). However, given the extent of interhousehold activities, the importance of the village in many peasant communities, and the influence of nonpeasant groups on the peasants, it remains open to question as to whether the dynamics of peasant life are best approached with the household as the main unit of analysis. Some of these arguments are persuasive and still inform the current debates. See also PEASANT SOCIETY, PEASANT POLITICS, SERFDOM, TRANSITION FROM FEUDALISM TO CAPITALISM, SHARECROPPING.

peasant society small-scale social organization in which PEASANTS predominate with features distinctive from other social groupings. While sometimes the term is used to refer to a large SOCIETY in which peasants are the majority, most usages would limit the term to a narrower meaning approximating to COMMUNITY. Peasants live in various societies, mainly AGRARIAN SOCIETIES, within which there are other social groups, so that it is not possible to characterize the whole society by referring to one of those groups. However, within a village or region, peasant social relationships may dominate. Characteristically these may be centred around kin and family ties, the importance of access to land, a distrust of outsiders and a cyclical view of time. An area of debate is whether such commonalities can be easily distinguished given the wide range of locations it has been claimed that peasants have occupied for most of human history.

In any peasant community there will be people who are not analytically defined as peasants. These may be traders, truckers, moneylenders, labourers without land, craftspeople, who may command a similar income to peasants and who may have close social and economic links to peasants. People who are analytically defined as 'peasants' will often engage in some of these activities for part of their time. In the modern world in particular, there will also be people who may be more economically and socially distant from the peasantry. Most importantly these will be state functionaries, representatives of national or foreign corporations selling anything from tractors to pharmaceuticals, and there may be independent professionals: lawyers, physicians, etc. Some of these may be identified as *brokers* who mediate between the peasant village and the wider society. The larger the village, the more likely that these will be present, and even villages without them will have strong links with provincial towns where these nonpeasant groups are located. Thus, while definitions of the peasantry sometimes rest on the functioning of the household, it is essential to see how this is firmly integrated into a wider social, political and economic network. See also PEASANT POLITICS.

peculium see SLAVERY.

peer group a GROUP of individuals of equal status. The term is most generally applied to children and adolescents, who experience a very different influence on their SOCIALIZATION by interacting in groups of their own age, as compared to the hierarchical family experience. See also YOUTH CULTURE.

penology the systematic study of punishment, particularly imprisonment. The term was coined in the 19th-century along with the reorganization of the prison system and at a time of much debate about the purposes of imprisonment. In part, the introduction of the term reflected a 'positivistic' belief that a 'scientific' solution could be found to many human problems. See also FOUCAULT, PANOPTICAN.

peon an unfree PEASANT or rural labourer indebted to a landowner. See DEBT PEONAGE.

per capita income the income per head of the population of a country. This is a usual way of distinguishing between the relative WEALTH of countries, although there exist many problems in using it. Not least of the problems is the continued existence of 'subsistence' economic activity and a widespread INFORMAL ECONOMY in many societies. This means that much economic activity goes unrecorded. A further difficulty is that exchange rates (the basis of per capita calculations of differences in income) between different currencies often fail to reflect internal differences in the purchasing power of different currencies. Thus, while useful in establishing broad differences between nations, the notion of per capital income should be used with caution in making more detailed comparisons.

perception the reception and interpretation of stimuli. This involves sensory mechanisms and cognitive appraisal, and is influenced by prior learning experiences, emotional state, and current expectations. The significance of the term for sociologists is in acknowledgement of the individual interpretation of events which is socially and culturally influenced. Thus ATTITUDE, RACISM, PREJUDICE, STEREOTYPING have a perceptual aspect. See also GESTALT THEORY.

perestroika a Russian term meaning reconstruction. The term was adopted by GORBACHEV in the USSR from 1985 to 1989, to characterize the changes in the economy and society which he, and others, saw as necessary after two decades of slow economic growth. The precise policies were slow in being clarified, but in general involved reform of the state-planning system originated by STALIN, greater autonomy of individual enterprises, an increasing role for the market, increased freedom for family businesses and cooperatives and greater opening to foreign trade and foreign firms. Gorbachev also used the term alongside that of GLASNOST as a rallying call to the Soviet people to re-examine all aspects of their lives and to revitalize their motivation and their commitment to SOCIALISM. Even though Gorbachev at first thought that perestroika would be achieved rapidly, by 1990 the Soviet economy was still stagnating and Gorbachev was ousted from power in 1991.

perfect competition (ECONOMICS) the IDEAL-TYPE concept of a 'free market' in which:
(a) there exist many buyers and many sellers;
(b) units of the commodity are homogeneous;
(c) where any one buyer's purchases do not significantly alter the market price.
In addition, the assumption is also made that buyers and sellers possess full information, that there is freedom of entry to the market for new producers. who are able to sell on the same terms as existing producers.
The further implication is that no producer is in a position to make 'excess profits'.
Thus perfect competition is often equated with maximum economic efficiency.
Equally, however, it must not be ignored that the model is an ideal-type one. Thus, although real world conditions will sometimes be found which approximate to the ideal type, often they do not (see MONOPOLY).
And there can be no assumption that the achievement of 'free market' conditions will always produce optimum, efficient and 'fair' outcomes for all parties concerned (compare CAPITALIST LABOUR CONTRACT, UNEQUAL EXCHANGE).

performance see COMPETENCE AND PERFORMANCE.

performance indicators (and **performance targets**) a set of criteria used to measure, compare and assess the performance of an organization or project in order to establish its degree of success. Most performance indicator systems are based on one or more of four types of indicators:
(i) cost indicators – focusing on financial performance, such as profit and loss for a given period;
(ii) take-up and volume indicators, e.g. occupancy rates – these record the extent to which a service or programme, or aspects of provision are used, often being compared against maximum possible use or use in comparable contexts;
(iii) impact, or result indicators – measure the effect of a service by collecting information regarding the benefits produced; and
(iv) user reactions – gauge the degree of satisfaction experienced by recipients and consumers, through, for example, questionnaires, or by monitoring the number of complaints received.

The measurement of performance against explicit *performance targets* is a further feature of much contemporary use of performance indicators. (See also LEAGUE TABLES.)

Performance indicators and performance targets are a central feature of the forms of NEW PUBLIC MANAGEMENT introduced by governments. Although there is resistance – with claims that such systems can distort provision – these systems also have potential advantages in empowering clients and customers and can be attractive to managers of provision and services because they appear to offer clear and precise measurements thus simplifying complex situations. Criticisms remain, however. First, there is the issue of how best to identify appropriate targets and achievable goals. The aims and objectives of management may diverge from those of practitioners and users. Second, there is a danger that those who being assessed may be compelled to concentrate on targets, at the expense of other aspects of activity (which may be less amenable to measurement by indicators), thus leading to a general decline in standards. Finally, there is a lack of flexibility with regard to assessing a programme, for example, no account can be taken of unplanned outcomes; thus performance indicators are rarely a true reflection of work carried out. See also AUDIT, AUDIT SOCIETY, VALUATION, FORMATIVE EVALUATION, SUMMATIVE EVALUATION AND SOCIAL AUDIT.

performative see SPEECH ACT.

performativity a situation arising from the application of technology to science and scientific procedures explored by Jean Francois LYOTARD in his highly influential work *The Postmodern Condition: a report on knowledge* (1979). Lyotard notes that although technology initially aids scientists' EMPIRICAL inquiries, as MODERNITY matures this technology begins to dominate science. Science then becomes harnessed to the principle of 'optimal performance' – that is the maximising of outputs (information produced) for the minimum input of time and energy. Consequently, it is then possible to purchase proof in much the same way as a piece of equipment. Lyotard believes this relegates science to the status of a DISCOURSE OR LANGUAGE GAME, thus compromising its claim to a privileged view of reality. This, in turn, can be seen to create problems for traditional accounts of knowledge and EPISTEMOLOGY due to a subsequent lack of consensus regarding appropriate criteria with which to judge rival claims. Lyotard, however, does not view this situation as problematic holding that the reliance upon science was restrictive and tended to silence other voices and stifle other ways of knowing. See GRAND NARRATIVE, DIFFEREND, PAGANISM, LYOTARD.

periodization any division of prehistorical or historical time into definite eras or periods. Often, but not always, such periodizations have a technological basis, e.g. PALAEOLITHIC AND NEOLITHIC AGES.

periphery see CENTRE AND PERIPHERY.

perlocutionary act see SPEECH ACT.

permanent revolution (MARXISM) TROTSKY's conception of a REVOLUTION leading from a 'democratic revolution' to a 'socialist revolution' in a continuous process. The theory was developed by Trotsky in response to the 1905 revolution in Russia. He argued, against the orthodox Marxist interpretation, that the coming revolution in Russia would not first be a bourgeois revolution ushering in democracy and unfettered capitalism. The Russian bourgeoisie was too weak to confront successfully the landed aristocracy and Czar. Therefore the democratic revolution could only be defended by the proletariat leading the peasantry and petty bourgeoisie into a socialist revolution.

Later, in the 1930s, Trotsky widened the theory to apply to colonial or neocolonial societies where the indigenous bourgeoisie involved in political movements for national independence and democratization is seen as compromised by its links to imperialist powers. The theory was linked to Trotsky's conception of combined and UNEVEN DEVELOPMENT, which assumes that not all societies pass through the same stages to achieve either capitalism or socialism.

Peronism see POPULISM.

persistence of aggregates see RESIDUES AND DERIVATIONS.

personal construct theory a social psychological theory of PERSONALITY and social perception, part of the school of PHENOMENOLOGICAL PSYCHOLOGY, and based on the notion that each individual develops a unique personal construct system (their personality) made up of interrelated bipolar constructs (e.g. good–bad). This system is used to construe, i.e. anticipate and predict, future events, social and non-social, and therefore presents a model of the person which has been characterized through an analogy to scientific activity. Where prediction fails constructs should be modified or abandoned, though in reality this does not always occur, as in the case of those with stereotypical attitudes.

Personal construct theory has been formulated very precisely by its originator, George Kelly (Kelly, 1955), in terms of a fundamental postulate and eleven elaborative corollaries. Kelly also devised the *repertory grid technique* to elicit constructs. Individuals identify similarities and differences between triads of elements (e.g. people known to them), each identification being expressed as a construct, and all constructs then being applied to all elements, to generate the full grid. Applications of personal construct theory include psychotherapy and analyses of 'problem' behaviours such as stuttering and alcoholism.

personal documents see BIOGRAPHICAL METHOD, LIFE HISTORY.

personality the characteristic ways of behaving of any individual person. The 'personality' is therefore inferred from behaviour, and one's 'personality' is considered to be a cause of one's behaviour.

The study of personality forms a considerable area within PSYCHOLOGY. The various approaches to its study include the Type theories (e.g. introvert/extravert), the Trait theories (e.g. Cattell's 16 personality factors), Psychodynamic theories (e.g. FREUD's), and Social Learning theories (emphasizing the importance of experience). The Type and Trait theories aim to classify personalities but not to explain, while the Psychodynamic and Social Learning theories aim to explain why personality develops as it does. See also CULTURE AND PERSONALITY SCHOOL, PSYCHOANALYSIS.

person-centred counselling the approach to COUNSELLING pioneered by Carl ROGERS in the 1930s and 40s, and which regards the client/person as the essential focus of the therapeutic relationship. This may seem to go without saying, but Rogers' insight was that PSYCHOANALYSIS and other theoretical approaches *impose* a diagnosis and treatment on the client. He suggested that the client best understands his/her problem and ultimately it is from within that change/healing has to come. The counsellor, then, is seen as a facilitator, is nondirective, and responds to the client with genuineness, empathy and unconditional positive regard (Rogers' three core conditions). Only through understanding the client's phenomenological experience (see PHENOMENOLOGICAL PSYCHOLOGY) can the counsellor be effective in helping him/her to resolve his or her problems and take the right decisions for the future, and it is through experiencing this relationship with the counsellor that the client is enabled to take self-responsibility.

petite bourgeoisie see PETTY BOURGEOISIE.

petty bourgeoisie *or* ***petite bourgeoisie*** the class of small capitalist business owners. Some theorists also include self-employed artisans, middle and small peasantry and other smallholding farmers. The term has its origins in MARX's work. He distinguished between the social and economic situation of big and small businesses and argued that the logic of competition and successive economic crises in CAPITALISM is to encourage the growth of monopolistic big business (and CLASS POLARIZATION and PROLETARIANIZATION of the petty bourgeoisie). In practice, despite the insecurity and instability of small business ownership (only about 20% survive for more than five years, see Fidler, 1981), the rate of establishment of new small or independent concerns remains very high and may have been encouraged by high unemployment and recession. Empirical studies of the petty bourgeoisie suggest that their social and political attitudes can be characterized as individualistic and independent-minded, mistrustful of large organizations, generally conservative and antisocialist (Bechhofer et al., 1974). The support of members of the petty bourgeoisie is usually considered significant in the rise of European FASCISM in the 1920s and 30s in Germany (see Franz

Neumann, 1942). More generally, they are found disproportionately among the supporters of right-wing and extreme right-wing political movements. e.g. McCarthyism in the US (see BELL, 1964).

A recent theoretical redevelopment of the concept occurs in Poulantzas (1973). He has proposed that the non-manual MIDDLE CLASSES can be best conceptualized as a NEW PETTY BOURGEOISIE on the grounds that they are not members of the bourgeoisie, since they do not own the means of production, but nor can they (contrary to the PROLETARIANIZATION thesis) be members of the working class. Their role as assistants of capital and their ideological identification with capitalist interests makes it more appropriate to see them as identified with the 'old' petty bourgeoisie. In many ways, however, this theory is better seen in the context of the debate about the NEW MIDDLE CLASS than the traditional conception of the petty bourgeoisie (see CONTRADICTORY CLASS LOCATIONS).

petty commodity production (MARXISM) the production of goods for the market (commodities) by people who own the means of production but who may not usually hire waged labour. In non-Marxist terms these people are self-employed producers. The term *simple commodity production* usually means the same. The term is sometimes used for the economic activity of PEASANTS and has been much discussed as applicable to small-scale producers in contemporary THIRD WORLD cities. See COMMODITIES AND COMMODITY PRODUCTION.

phenomenalism the empiricist doctrine (e.g. advanced by J. S. MILL) that things 'are permanent possibilities of sensations'. Thus phenomenalism is not to be confused with PHENOMENOLOGY. DURKHEIM was influenced by phenomenalism.

phenomenological psychology a school of psychology that emphasizes the importance of the unique, subjective experience of the person. It regards the perception of events by the person as crucial to understanding why the person reacts as he or she does. The approach was influenced by HUSSERL and has been particularly influential within the HUMANISTIC MOVEMENT, where the SELF with its unique perspective is central and the realization of human potential, or SELF ACTUALIZATION, is the motivator of action. This perspective is seen in the PERSON-CENTRED COUNSELLING of Carl ROGERS.

phenomenological sociology sociological approaches deriving especially from the work of Alfred SCHUTZ (see also SOCIAL PHENOMENOLOGY, PHENOMENOLOGY).
The clearest contemporary expression of phenomenological sociology is BERGER and Luckmann's *The Social Construction of Reality* (1967). This influential text on the SOCIOLOGY OF KNOWLEDGE argues that all knowledge is socially constructed and oriented towards particular practical problems. 'Facts' can there fore never be neutral but are always reflective of why they are required. This stress on common-sense knowledge has influenced CONVERSATION ANALYSIS, ETHNOMETHODOLOGY, modern HERMENEUTICS and varieties of detailed ethnographic PARTICIPANT OBSERVATION, though the common strand is less a common method than an aversion to POSITIVISM, characterized by the use of QUANTITATIVE RESEARCH TECHNIQUES.

phenomenology 1 'the descriptive study of experiences' – a 'phenomenon' being any 'thing' perceived by our senses.
For example, the term was used by HEGEL in his *Phenomenology of Mind*, 1807; compare also KANT.
2 more recently, a philosophical approach particularly associated with Edmund HUSSERL in which philosophy is seen to rest fundamentally on the introspective examination of one's own intellectual processes in the experiencing of phenomena. A central doctrine of phenomenologists is that of the INTENTIONALITY of perception – we cannot simply be conscious, but must be conscious of something. In Husserl's *a priori*

rather than empirical method, all incidental aspects of the mental processes under inspection (all that which is not *directly* presented to the individual consciousness, e.g. extraneous conceptions) are *'bracketed'* (literally held in parentheses) to permit the systematic scrutiny of 'logical essences'. Thus, 'phenomenological reduction' is aimed at revealing the a priori essences of thought divested of the inconsistencies of perception.

Albeit with considerable variations in focus, phenomenology has exerted a major influence in sociology and in social analysis. Other philosophers and sociologists to adopt phenomenological methods include the EXISTENTIALIST philosopher Martin HEIDEGGER, existentialist Marxists (e.g. SARTRE and MERLEAU-PONTY), and Alfred SCHUTZ. The latter's SOCIAL PHENOMENOLOGY involves a critical appropriation of Husserl's approach, but an application of this to the study of the assumptions involved in, and the constitution of, everyday social knowledge – a focus on the LIFE-WORLD 'bracketed' in Husserl's original method. Applications of a phenomenological approach are also seen in the 'radical psychiatry' of LAING and Cooper. See also ETHNOMETHODOLOGY.

3 The term also continues in wider use to refer to any investigation of how things are experienced, e.g. the experience of works of art or architecture. Compare PHENOMENALISM.

phenotype see GENOTYPE (AND) PHENOTYPE.

philosophy the academic discipline concerned to define and understand a range of central and linked questions, especially questions about the general nature of knowledge, language and concepts, which recur, apparently, in all special fields of investigation and reflection.

'Philosophy' was once the generic term for human knowledge or world views, and it can be used in a sense wider than the academic, referring to a person's broad view of the world and his/her place in it, including an idea of what is valuable in life. As knowledge became specialized, philosophy was what remained, the questions which define it abstract, evasive and apparently deep. Philosophical questions also arise in connection with the bases, foundations or beginnings of the special disciplines. Thus, if in sociology one is interested in, say, the facts of female subjection, one might come to reflect on what the facts in a discipline like sociology actually amount to. This might provoke reflection on what 'facts' are, in general. The question 'what is a fact?' is a philosopher's question, not to be clinched by citing particular examples of 'facts' drawn from a science.

Some further examples of the very general questions that define philosophy are: 'How can we know anything?', 'What is there in the world?', 'How should we reason?', 'How should we act?' At this level of generality these define fields or branches of philosophy. Questions about what the world is made up of, its furniture, are the subject of ONTOLOGY. Questions about knowledge, what is certain, what probable and so on, are the subject of EPISTEMOLOGY. The philosophical study of reasoning is LOGIC, of oughts and obligations, ETHICS. If one asks 'What, in general, is science?', one is asking a question in the PHILOSOPHY OF SCIENCE, a major aspect of epistemology.

Philosophies attempt answers to these questions, usually seeking to answer them in an interlinked way. They are generally considered to be extremely difficult questions, often raising seemingly insoluble problems, perennial in their reappearance. For this reason, it is probably inappropriate to try to 'begin' with them, to try to make answers to them one's secure foundation, or to be seduced by their 'depth' from other preoccupations. Proposing and discussing answers to them can be an absorbing activity for persons of a particular cast of mind, and often attending to philosophical questions is a necessary activity when a discipline encounters a crisis. The radically different kinds of answers to all such questions has led to philosophy being divided into many different schools. A successful innovation in philosophy is likely to be a revelation of new possibilities that raise the old questions in new ways, rather than arriving at final solutions.

philosophy of history 1 critical and methodological reflection on the nature of HISTORY and HISTORIOGRAPHY.
2 large-scale speculative historical theories, claiming general laws or asserting general tendencies seen as operating throughout history. The philosophy of history in this second sense, influential especially in the 18th- and 19th-centuries (e.g. HEGEL), has on the whole gone out of fashion in the 20th-century. See also HISTORICISM, GRAND NARRATIVE AND METANARRATIVE.

philosophy of science the branch of PHILOSOPHY concerned with the nature and foundations of scientific knowledge. As such it is, in part, coexistent with ONTOLOGY and EPISTEMOLOGY, but in addition it also involves a more specific concern with the details of SCIENCE. Historically much of the concern of the philosophy of science has been prescriptive (see POSITIVISM, FALSIFICATIONISM), but as these approaches have run into problems (see KUHN, FEYERABEND) there has been a partial retreat from this emphasis, bringing the philosophy of science much closer to historical and SOCIAL STUDIES OF SCIENCE, and to the SOCIOLOGY OF SCIENCE and the SOCIOLOGY OF KNOWLEDGE.

phonocentrism see DECONSTRUCTION.

phratry (ANTHROPOLOGY) the grouping of two or more CLANS who claim a common ancestor, which may be mythical or nonhuman (see TOTEMISM).

phylogenetic scale the scale of animal life, ranging from the simplest organisms to the most complex. This incorporates the idea of evolution (see DARWIN, EVOLUTIONARY THEORY) from simple life forms with rudimentary reactions to environmental stimuli, to the complexity of the higher mammals with their specific and refined sensory systems, their capacity for learning from experience, and, in the case of humans, the ability to reflect on their own experience. The scale therefore not only represents increasing biological differentiation, but increasing brain capacity.

The concept is often used within the context of ETHOLOGY to indicate that the behaviour of animals lower down the scale is controlled by inherited behaviour patterns, often described as INSTINCTS, while animals higher up the scale are more 'open' to learning. The increased proportion of cortex in the human brain allows behaviour to be appreciably influenced by previous experience.

physical anthropology see ANTHROPOLOGY.

physiocrats a school of thought in economic thinking in 18th-century France, especially associated with Quesnay (1694–1774) and Turgot (1727–81). The physiocrats criticized the doctrine of the MERCANTILISTS, who argued that wealth arose from EXCHANGE. In their own theory they gave priority to agricultural production and LAND as the source of economic accumulation. Their ideas were taken further by the CLASSICAL ECONOMISTS, who made production in general the source of wealth. Both classical economists and physiocrats argued for LAISSEZ FAIRE and free trade.

Piaget, Jean (1896–1980) Genevan developmental psychologist, particularly significant for his stage theory of cognitive development.

Piaget's background was in zoology, and he retained a strong biological orientation, emphasizing the innate specification for development through a serial process of learning, each stage being the necessary foundation for the next (*e.g. The Origins of Intelligence in Children*, 1936, trans. 1952). This was not to deny the importance of the environment which he saw as an essential aspect of this process, though later theorists, such as Jerome Bruner, have tended to give environmental experience more weight than did Piaget. The four developmental stages were termed the *sensorimotor*, the *pre-*

operational, the *concrete operational* and the *formal operational*. Through the processes of ASSIMILATION AND ACCOMMODATION, the child gradually develops from sensing and responding at birth, to the capacity for abstract, hypothetico-deductive thought in the early teens. Piaget has been criticized for the rigidity of the stage theory and aspects of his methodology. His work was undoubtedly pioneering, stimulating much research which has supported the main tenets, but also indicated that the boundaries between stages should be regarded as 'fuzzy', and has also shown that the way in which children are assessed affects their responses, and therefore their stage categorization. See also EGOCENTRISM.

piecemeal social engineering the limited form of economic and social planning which Karl POPPER argued is all that is justified by social science knowledge. Popper's claim arises from his falsificationist epistemology (see FALSIFICATIONISM) and his view that knowledge – and hence social life – is inherently unpredictable (see HISTORICISM). He also argues that parallels can be drawn with biological evolution, that, as well as being unpredictable, social evolution best proceeds by small steps. See also EVOLUTIONARY SOCIOLOGY.

pie graph *or* **pie chart** a circular graph divided into sectors proportional to the magnitudes of the quantities represented (see Fig. 23).

pilgrimage a physical journey made to a sacred place which also represents a spiritual or emotional journey. The custom of pilgrimage is found in a wide range of cultures, and in most of the world's religions it is frequently associated with a shrine, the place where the body or relics of a saint or holy person are kept, and which may be the scene of miracles and offerings of money, flowers or symbolic objects.

In contemporary society the religious tradition continues. Alongside this is the growth in secular pilgrimage to places of cultural significance, such as Disneyland, or to the shrine of a dead hero, such as the grave of Elvis Presley, in Memphis, Tennessee (see C. King, 1993). Such journeys, whilst a feature of the modern tourist industry, demonstrate many of the features of traditional religious pilgrimage.

pillarization (translation of Dutch *verzuiling*) a stable vertical division of society in which patterns of political organization, including trade unions as well as political parties, are determined by religious or linguistic affiliations which substantially

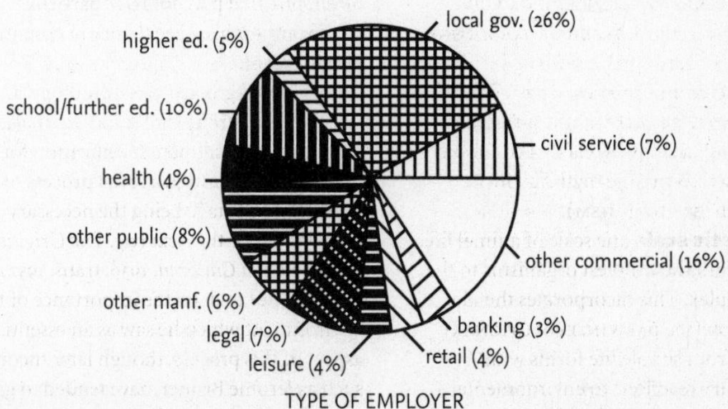

Fig. 23 **Pie graph** *or* **pie chart.** In the above example, sectors of the graph indicate the type of employment of Polytechnic and College social science graduates, three years after graduation.

override or cross-cut horizontal class divisions (compare SOCIAL STRATIFICATION). In Holland, where separate Calvinist, Roman Catholic, and secular organizations exist in many spheres of life, this pattern of social organization has become highly institutionalized, the basis of a 'segmented integration' and shared political power. Elsewhere, however, e.g. the Lebanon and Northern Ireland, pillarization has often been associated with instability and the failure of power-sharing. See also POLITICAL CLEAVAGE, STABLE DEMOCRACY.

pilot study a small-scale version of a planned experiment or observation, used to test the logistics and design of it. Thus, a questionnaire schedule may be 'piloted' on a small subsample of the proposed SAMPLE population to see if any of the questions give particular problems of interpretation, or lead to ambiguous responses that would be difficult to interpret as data. If the design works, without problems, then the main experiment can go ahead, but if problems have come to light these can be rectified first. It is also possible that a pilot study will suggest valuable extensions to the study, or restrictions of aspects that are unlikely to be helpful in the investigation.

pink economy a range of services, businesses, presses and clubs which serve the lesbian and gay communities, particularly in those Western cultures which have partly decriminalized HOMOSEXUALITY. Due to the greater economic power and social access afforded to men, the pink economy is predominantly owned and controlled by men. Lesbians tend to be marginalized within this economy.

planned economy see COMMAND ECONOMY.

planned obsolescence the deliberate introduction of regular changes in the design of consumer products with the aim of creating new demand by making earlier versions of a product appear outmoded. The fact that many products are no longer built to last, and often cannot be repaired, is sometimes seen as a further part of the same process. As well as being a way of improving the commercial returns of individual firms, the technique has been seen by some as a valuable way of keeping the overall capitalist economy buoyant. For others (e.g. Packard, 1957) such artificially built-in obsolescence is socially wasteful, and manipulates consumer need. Nowadays it is also seen as environmentally shortsighted, contributing to the depletion of resources and environmental pollution.

plantation a large agrarian estate, usually organized on a corporate basis, producing a single crop for a large-scale market. Often the owners will have interests outside of agriculture, in industry or commerce. Plantations may be either capitalist (employing wage-labour) or noncapitalist (using nonwage labour). Major examples of the use of nonwage labour were the slave plantations of North America, Brazil and the Caribbean, producing mainly sugar and cotton, from the 17th to the 19th-century. In colonial Africa and Asia, the establishment of tea and other plantations involved the colonial authorities using various forms of coercion in order to ensure a labour supply. In the 20th-century, plantations have increasingly been organized on capitalist lines with larger amounts of capital investment and relying on a small permanent labour force and salaried administrators supplemented with seasonal wage-labour mainly for harvesting. The seasonal labour may come from the locality, sometimes from PEASANTS who supplement their income with plantation work, but often involves longer-distance movements. Some people move from area to area following the various seasons of harvesting. This arrangement is common in parts of the THIRD WORLD with plantations now mainly producing for export and decisions about which crops are planted being influenced by the world market and consumption in the advanced capitalist countries.

plastic man see AUTONOMOUS MAN AND PLASTIC MAN.

Plato (428–348 BC) major Greek philosopher, pupil of SOCRATES, and teacher of ARISTOTLE. Living most of his life in Athens, Plato contributed to many areas of PHILOSOPHY, and his ideas exerted a many-sided influence on Western social thought, e.g. on political science, and on theories of education. The most fundamental feature of Plato's philosophical thinking is his theory of 'forms', in which observable reality, constantly in flux and in decay, is regarded as a departure from pure forms or 'ideas', e.g. the idea 'triangle' or the idea 'horse', which are 'necessary' and unchanging. Plato was impressed by the apparent certainties of mathematics, which led him to posit a realm of pure ideas – immaterial but nonmental, and known by intuition rather than empirical inquiry. Such IDEALISM permeates Plato's social and political writings as much as his more purely philosophical thought. It is exemplified in his best-known work *The Republic,* written, like much of his work, as a series of dialogues, in which a pure form of polity is outlined. In this ideal republic, philosophers, as the wisest and the best, would rule, employing censorship in education, and requiring the obedience of the majority. A connection between Plato's authoritarianism and Plato's idealism has been suggested by theorists such as POPPER.

play any activity which is voluntary, gives pleasure, and has no apparent goal other than enjoyment.

A classical conceptualization of the play form in social life is Simmel's concept of SOCIABILITY. However, although to achieve its purpose sociability ideally must be divorced from ulterior 'serious' purpose, the importance of the functions served by sociability and play are left in no doubt. See also HOMO LUDENS, LEISURE, SOCIOLOGY OF SPORT.

The functions of play within child socialization are equally an important issue. Play is widely seen as essential for physical development, for learning skills and social behaviour and for personality development (see Millar, 1968, for full discussion).

Play therapy is used as a technique for understanding young children's psychological problems and helping to resolve them (See KLEIN).

plural élitism the doctrine that power in modern liberal democratic states is shared between a multiplicity of competing ÉLITES (e.g. Dahl, 1967). Plural élite theorists acknowledge that in complex modern industrial societies élites will inevitably dominate. In this they are at one with classical ÉLITE THEORY. Modern plural élite theory differs from classical élite theory, however, in two key respects:

(a) in accepting that élite in modern liberal democratic societies are representative élites – thus while the people may not rule, the people's élite do;

(b) in asserting that in modern liberal democracies, power is either shared between multiple élites or these élites compete openly and continuously for political power without any one group achieving a lasting dominance over the others. It is in these terms that modern élite theory distinguishes between democracies and non-democracies. See also POLITICAL CLEAVAGE, STABLE DEMOCRACY.

Critics of plural élitist theory (e.g. *The Theory of Democratic Élitism,* Bachrach, 1967) object, first, to what they see as its tendency to understate systematic biases in the actual distribution of power in modern societies (see also NONDECISIONS, MOBILIZATION OF BIAS) and, secondly, to the restricted conception of political participation and individual development with which a 'democratic élitism' is associated. In responding to these criticisms, plural élite theorists point to the greater realism of their own view of DEMOCRACY compared with traditional models, further insisting that the distinctions between democracies and non-democracies captured by their models reflect key differences between actual political systems.

pluralism the situation within a state or social organization in which power is shared (or held to be shared) among a multiplicity of groups and organizations. The original use of the term was in association with opposition to the Hegelian conception of the unitary state. In a socialist conception of pluralism, *Guild Socialism,* the dispersal of economic and political power to occupational groups was proposed as an ideal. However, the most important use of the term in modern sociology and political science is the suggestion that modern Western liberal democracies are pluralistic polities, in which a plurality of groups and/or élites either share power or continuously compete for power (see also PLURAL ÉLITISM). Compare PLURAL SOCIETY.

plural society any society in which there exists a formal division into distinct racial, linguistic or religious groupings. Such distinctions may be horizontal (see also SOCIAL STRATIFICATION) or vertical (see PILLARIZATION). See also MULTICULTURALISM; compare PLURALISM.

police (and policing) the organized civil force and agency of SOCIAL CONTROL, which, in the service of the STATE, is charged with preserving law and order. It does this by protecting persons and property and bringing wrongdoers to JUSTICE, and acting as a deterrent to CRIME.

The first full-time and professional force (the Metropolitan Police) was established in Britain in 1829. Today it is funded and overseen by the Home Office. Other forces are funded in part by the central state and partly by local taxation and are responsible in theory to Police Authorities comprising local councillors, magistrates and the Chief Constable, as well as to the Home Office. (For the view that Police Authorities are more important in theory than in practice, see Simey, 1982.) In all forces the Chief Constable has an extremely powerful role in deciding on policing priorities and operational issues. This role has become even more important since the Police Act of 1964 and the reorganization of local government in the 1970s reduced the number of forces and greatly increased the size of individual policing areas.

As with other areas of the CRIMINAL JUSTICE SYSTEM in the UK, there has been a great expansion in sociological work on police and policing since the 1960s, and particularly in the 1980s. Much of the work has been in a radical or critical mode, in line with the reorientation of sociological approaches to crime and deviance from the late 1960s onwards. Some of these critical appraisals have had a clear effect on public opinion, and, to some extent on police practice. A notable example has been the feminist critique of police practices in regard to rape victims and victims of domestic violence and sexual abuse. Similarly, research criticizing police responsiveness to racial violence, while initially resented and dismissed by representatives of the Association of Chief Police Officers and of the Police Federation (the main organizations of senior and junior officers), was confirmed by a Home Office report (1981) and led to some changes in the system.

Other issues which have been prominent in sociological studies of policing have included the development of paramilitary styles of policing industrial disputes and political demonstrations; new technology and civil liberties issues; policing strategies – the debate on 'community policing' being a particular focus; police powers and accountability, and the politicization of the police. Amongst 'new deviancy theorists' (see NATIONAL DEVIANCY CONFERENCE) two divergent approaches have developed recently which might simplistically be described as:

(a) a more radical wing (e.g. Scraton, 1985);
(b) a more 'Fabian' and reformist wing, describing itself as 'new realism' (e.g. Kinsey, Lea and Young, 1986). These approaches, as is usual in the discipline, coexist with others.

The relationship between sociology, sociologists and the police has been and remains an uneasy one.

political activism see ACTIVISM.

political anthropology that part of social anthropology which focuses on the study of the POLITICAL PROCESSES and political institutions in SIMPLE SOCIETIES. As well as being a particular focus within social anthropology, the study of the politics of simpler societies is also an essential part of POLITICAL SOCIOLOGY.

A distinguishing feature of the political systems of simpler societies is that they do not always exist as a differentiated set of relatively specialized, explicitly political, institutions as they do in modern state societies (see SEGMENTARY SOCIETY, STATELESS SOCIETY).

political attitudes the relatively persistent psychological orientations and beliefs held to underpin political opinions and voting behaviour (see also ATTITUDE, ATTITUDE SCALE AND ATTITUDE MEASUREMENT).

Significant dimensions of political attitudes which researchers have sought to measure include:

(a) conceptions of 'political efficacy' (Budge, 1976), 'support for democracy' (e.g. Prothro and Grigg, 1960), levels of 'political tolerance' (Stouffer, 1955), 'authoritarianism' (see F-SCALE), 'protest potential' (Marsh, 1977), 'post-industrial attitudes' (Inglehart, 1977), etc.;

(b) the overall left-right organization of political beliefs (e.g. measures of 'Conservatism') (see also LEFT-RIGHT CONTINUUM).

There is little acceptance that such scales have been successful in establishing the existence of stable dimensions to political attitudes (see Robinson et al., 1968). As suggested by Form and Rytinna (1969) and Mann (1970), major problems can arise in the interpretation of 'attitudinal measures', and it is not clear that these possess major advantages over the more informal indicators of attitudes used in political sociology.

political behaviour any individual or collective participation or nonparticipation in the POLITICAL PROCESS. The term is most associated with the approach within American political science known as *behaviouralism* or *the behavioural approach*, which, rather than being concerned with formal political institutions, focuses especially on the empirical study of political behaviour, POLITICAL PARTICIPATION and nonparticipation, POLITICAL ATTITUDES and public opinion (see also POLITICAL SCIENCE, POLITICAL SYSTEMS). While it is credited with the introduction of a more empirical sociological approach within political science, its weakness has sometimes been a narrow empiricism and a focus on the 'measureable' at the expense of theoretical relevance.

political cleavage the division within a political system into competing POLITICAL PARTIES where this leads to a two-party political system, or similar division into competing party blocs (especially a broad left-right division in the pattern of political allegiance), where patterns of allegiance are based primarily on class divisions. For a theorist such as LIPSET (1959), the pattern of political cleavage within a political system is the key to understanding and explaining different types of political system. Thus, whereas STABLE DEMOCRACIES have tended to be characterized by a clearly defined cleavage between class parties, though tempered by the existence of a fundamental CONSENSUS On 'the rules of the political game', other kinds of political system have lacked one or both of these requirements. See also CLASS CLEAVAGE, LEFT-RIGHT CONTINUUM.

political consensus 1 the existence, within a POLITICAL SYSTEM, of broad agreement on the 'rules of the political game' (LIPSET, 1960), i.e. the absence of major political parties (e.g. revolutionary parties) opposed to the continuation of the system.

2 the agreement between parties on more particular issues of policy, e.g. the 'postwar consensus' in postwar Britain on the fundamental principles of the WELFARE STATE, or on a policy of FULL EMPLOYMENT, usually held to have ended with the election

of the Thatcher government in 1979. See also CONSENSUS, LEGITIMATION CRISIS.

political culture the norms, beliefs and values within a political system. It is usually assumed that a particular political culture is built up as the result of a long historical development and that its distinctive character exerts a profound influence on the form and effectiveness, or otherwise, of the political system with which it is associated. The term is most associated with the systems approach (see POLITICAL SYSTEM) within political analysis, which was in vogue in the 1950s and 60s in the US (e.g. G. Almond and S. Verba, *The Civic Culture*, 1965). The approach has been of most value in stimulating cross-cultural comparative research on political cultures, e.g. Almond's distinction between 'participatory', subject' and 'parochial' political orientations within political cultures. One central assumption of political-culture theorists is that the particular *civic culture* underlying liberal democracies such as the UK and the US, a mixture of participatory orientations tempered by political DEFERENCE, has been both a cause and effect of the greater political stability and effectiveness of these systems compared with other systems. From a different theoretical perspective, however, political culture can also be seen as involving cultural and ideological HEGEMONY. In this context, rather than being a sign of political effectiveness, political culture's role may be viewed as a conservative force preventing a social transition to more favourable social and political arrangements, (see also CULTURE, POLITICAL SOCIALIZATION).

political economy in the 19th century, the usual name for the academic discipline of ECONOMICS (see also CLASSICAL ECONOMISTS), the study of economic processes. The term 'political' economy reflected the fact that economics was then more directly concerned with the interrelation between economic theory and political action than has been true later. The superseding of the term political economy at the end of the 19th century corresponded with the idea that economics was now a pure 'science' and could be discussed apart from politics. Recently, however, the term has enjoyed something of a revival, especially among economists and sociologists wishing to reinstate a recognition that the subject matter of the discipline remains politically charged. The work of the classical political economists had been prompted by the growth of industrial capitalism and free trade, and was mainly directed at a justification of this new system and in furthering economic progress, or staving off disaster. MARX also wrote in part within this tradition, describing his own work on economics as a 'critique of political economy', and rejected any suggestions that the capitalist order could be seen as 'natural'. The revival of the term political economy has been made by economists and sociologists wishing to rejuvenate and reorient modern economic and socio-economic analysis in a way that returns it to the concerns uppermost in earlier political economy, including the work of Marx. S ee also MARXIAN ECONOMICS.

political formula(e) see MOSCA.

political image the positive or negative conceptions of its policies, programmes, and leaders which a POLITICAL PARTY has established within an electorate. The term was first used, early in the 20th-century, by the English political scientist Graham WALLAS. Influenced by sociological theorists of collective and mass behaviour, he suggested that the mind of the electorate is rather like a 'slow photographic plate', influenced by generalized past perceptions, and ATTITUDES and evaluations, built up over a long period, rather than guided by a rational appraisal of the policies of competing parties. Subsequently the term became widely used in studies of VOTING BEHAVIOUR. It has also been much employed by those consciously seeking to transform the political image of particular political parties, e.g. by political advertising.

political legitimacy see LEGITIMATE AUTHORITY.

political mobilization the aggregation and deployment of people and resources by the STATE (e.g. see EISENSTADT), or by a POLITICAL PARTY or SOCIAL MOVEMENT.

political modernization the process, usually seen as crucially affected by economic modernization, in which traditional or colonial forms of political organization and state-forms are replaced by Western state-forms, including modern POLITICAL PARTIES.

Identification of the socioeconomic requirements for 'political modernization' to succeed (education, the creation of appropriate POLITICAL CULTURE) was a central topic in the 1950s and 1960s in forms of POLITICAL SCIENCE and POLITICAL SOCIOLOGY influenced by SYSTEMS THEORY and STRUCTURAL-FUNCTIONALISM. Theories of political modernization of this type (e.g. D. Apter, *The Politics of Modernization,* 1965) usually adhered to a model of social development which saw Western European patterns of liberal democracy as the most rational and appropriate form of political development for non-European societies to pursue (see also STABLE DEMOCRACY). Understandably, such a Western-centred conception of political modernization was widely criticized. Thus the term is now used in a more open-ended way, to refer to the process of political modernization whatever its form.

political participation any individual or collective involvement in the political process. Research on political participation suggests a hierarchy of modes of participation. Thus while a majority of members of most societies participate in political discussions and in elections, relatively few are active in more formal political roles.

political party any association set up with the objective of gaining political power, usually but not always by electoral means. In contrast with PRESSURE GROUPS, which seek to influence political events by acting on governments and public opinion, parties can be distinguished as seeking to wield governmental power directly. The operation of political parties is central in the government and politics of modern industrial societies.

The early sociological study of political parties engaged with a series of questions raised by MICHELS, notably his argument that, what ever the differences in their political programmes and philosophy, political parties tend always to be dominated by ÉLITES. In reality, notwithstanding a general tendency for parties to be dominated by their leadership, with leaders drawn from socially advantaged backgrounds, empirical evidence suggests that parties vary greatly in the extent or permanence of such domination (see also IRON LAW OF OLIGARCHY). See ALSO POLITICAL PARTICIPATION, ÉLITE THEORY.

Apart from Michels, a useful contribution to the study of the internal organization of political parties is provided by Duverger (1964), who identifies four basic types of grass-roots organization:

(a) the *caucus,* e.g. a small group of political insiders acting either on their own behalf or on behalf of wider social groups they claim to represent;

(b) the *branch,* a local grouping established as part of a wider permanently organized democratic and bureaucratic structure;

(c) the *cell,* a carefully selected, highly and ideologically motivated group (e.g. within Communist parties), perhaps set up to operate covertly with the aim of fostering unrest or preparing for revolution;

(d) *militia* (as utilized by Fascist parties), political groupings organized on military lines and engaging in violence and political intimidation.

A further overall distinction of importance is that drawn by Sigmund Neumann (1956) between *parties of integration,* in which the lives of members are 'encased within ideologically linked activities', and *parties of representation*, which view their function as primarily one of securing votes in elections, without seeking to achieve ideological closure, seeing themselves as contestants in a 'give-and take' political game (Lipset, 1960). According to Lipset, parties of the latter type are an essential requirement for stable forms of liberal democracy, and the presence of major parties of the former type a significant barrier to this form of government (see STABLE DEMOCRACY).

A further important element in the sociological study of political parties is discussion of the origins and implications of different types of *party system*, e.g. differences between *one-party systems* (a feature mainly of communist and developing societies), *two-party systems* (associated mainly with first-past-the-post electoral systems as in the US or, for the most part, UK), *and multiparty systems*. This last form of party system occurs when elections are based on proportional representation and where political parties based on religious or ethnic divisions continue alongside parties based on class. In contrast, in two-party systems class is usually the predominant basis of political alignment, notwithstanding the fact that many voters vote across class lines (see also CLASS DEALIGNMENT).

political process the entirety of the social relations within a POLITICAL SYSTEM. While, traditionally, political science has focused on formal, constitutionally defined political processes, a sociological approach regards processes outside the political sphere as necessarily involved. See also POLITICAL SOCIOLOGY.

political rights see CITIZEN RIGHTS.

political science the science (or study) of POLITICS (sense 1) and government.

One of the oldest of systematic studies (see ARISTOTLE, PLATO, MACHIAVELLI, HOBBES, LOCKE), political studies has manifested great ambivalence on how, and whether, to present itself as a 'science'. Generally political scientists have divided into two (albeit often overlapping) schools of thought:

(a) those who describe (and compare) patterns of government and politics, drawing on the work of philosophers, historians, constitutional theorists, public administrators, etc., as well as collecting their own material, without any pretensions that political studies can ever be a 'science' in any natural science, or even social science, sense of the term;

(b) those who have wanted to bring political studies into far closer relation with the more avowedly 'scientific' social sciences, such as sociology, economics, and social psychology (e.g. see POLITICAL SYSTEM, POLITICAL BEHAVIOUR).

In this latter form especially, political science overlaps with POLITICAL SOCIOLOGY.

political socialization the process in any society in which the acquisition and internalization of political norms, values and beliefs occurs; the acquisition of POLITICAL CULTURE.

The study of political socialization, including child socialization, has been particularly important in those branches of political science and political sociology which have emphasized the role of political culture in the stability of POLITICAL SYSTEMS. Research into child political socialization faces significant problems. While a direct empirical study of the place of political ideas in child socialization has sometimes been possible, much research has of necessity had to rely on less reliable data based on adult recall of child socialization or on documentary evidence. See also AUTHORITARIAN PERSONALITY.

political system and political subsystem

1 the apparatus of government and the general arrangements for political decision-making within a society.

2 the subsystem of the SOCIAL SYSTEM which PARSONS identifies as concerned with 'goal attainment', i.e. establishing policies for society and setting the main collective goals for society and for other main subsystems of society (see Fig. 24), from which it also receives 'inputs'.

political sociology

the branch of sociology concerned with the study of politics or the political subsystems of society. Although a branch of sociology, political sociology also exists as a distinct approach within POLITICAL SCIENCE (see BEHAVIOURALISM, POLITICAL SYSTEM). In comparison with orthodox political science, both political sociology and the political sociological approach within political science insist that the investigation of political institutions must be treated as fully implicated in society not as a system that can be understood in isolation. The following main areas of study within political sociology can be identified:

(a) the general nature and functions of the STATE and the POLITICAL SYSTEM (or subsystem);

(b) the nature of POLITICAL PARTIES, PRESSURE GROUPS and political organizations and political movements of all kinds;

(c) empirical study of patterns of individual POLITICAL PARTICIPATION and POLITICAL BEHAVIOUR, including nonparticipation, e.g. empirical research on VOTING BEHAVIOUR;

(d) comparative research on the types of political system and the relative effectiveness and stability or instability of these;

(e) particular and general analysis of the relations between states, including WARFARE, and the location of states within the WORLD SYSTEM:

(f) running through all the above areas, perhaps something that political sociology has been most identified with, is the study of political ÉLITES and MASSES and the extent to which modern societies can be said to be dominated by a RULING CLASS (see MOSCA, PARETO, MARX). See also POWER, POLITICAL ANTHROPOLOGY.

The study of political phenomena has a long ancestry. Aristotle's *Politics* is often regarded as in many ways a work of political sociology. The same is true of the works of MACHIAVELLI, HOBBES and MONTESQUIEU, and many other political writers whose works anticipate aspects of the approach of modern political sociology.

In North American political science and sociology in the 1950s and 60s, a *systems approach* to political analysis was advanced by a number of theorists, notably Gabriel Almond, Robert Easton and Karl Deutsch (see also POLITICAL CULTURE). It was advanced as the new scientific way forward in political analysis and expected to replace traditional forms of political analysis. Although most of the more grandiose claims of the systems approach would now be rejected (see also SYSTEM, CYBERNETICS, SYSTEMS THEORY), the approach can be credited with achieving a degree of reorientation in traditional political science, bringing political science and political sociology closer together.

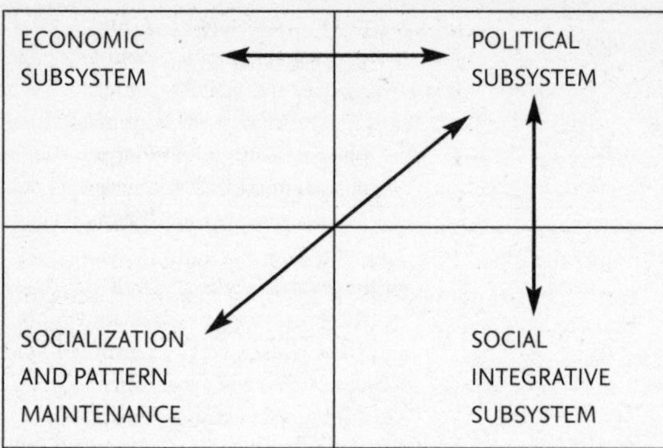

Fig. 24 **Political system** *or* **subsystem.** In political systems theory, the political system or subsystem is presented as setting goals and receiving 'inputs' from wider society. See also SUBSYSTEMS MODEL and Fig. 34.

politics 1 the processes within a STATE or organization (including groups of all kinds, e.g. families) concerned with influencing the content and implementation of the goals, policies, etc., it pursues, its *government* (compare POLITICAL SYSTEM).
2 the science or study of POLITICS 1 and government (see also POLITICAL SCIENCE).

polity 1 from the Greek *polis,* city state, now also used as a synonym for the modern state.
2 the subset of the social system concerned with politics.See also POLITICAL SYSTEM, POLITICS, POWER.

poll book a book showing the names of voters and details of how they voted in Parliamentary and other elections. Produced up to 1872, when the secret ballot was introduced in Britain, poll books are an invaluable source of information on voting behaviour in previous centuries. Poll books often contain information on the occupations of voters and have been used to show how different social groups voted in the past. Their value can be enhanced by using them in conjunction with other historical sources such as the 19th-century CENSUS enumeration books, TRADE DIRECTORIES and RATE BOOKS.

polyandry a form of plural marriage (POLYGAMY) where a woman has more than one husband. It is regarded as a functional strategy for ensuring reproductive stability when there is a shortage of women. Compare POLYGYNY.

polyarchy literally, 'the rule of the many'. In its widest usage in political science and sociology the term refers to any political system in which power is dispersed; thus its antonym is TOTALITARIANISM. As such polyarchy may take many forms, it is *not* synonymous only with LIBERAL DEMOCRACY, although it is sometimes used as if it were, e.g. by Dahl (1956; 1985). In sociology and in political science especially, a generic association is often seen between the existence of polyarchy and the rise of the modern NATIONSTATE. However, this is a relationship which has often been interrupted, and it ignores the existence of societies, prior to the emergence of nation states, in which power was relatively dispersed. See also CITIZENSHIP.

polygamy plural marriage involving more than one partner of the other sex; can be either POLYANDRY OR POLYGYNY. Compare MONOGAMY.

polygyny a form of plural marriage where a man has more than one wife. This is viewed as a strategy which allows powerful males to control reproductive resources and to tactically manipulate kin ties. Far more common than its opposite, POLYANDRY, it is a subclass of POLYGAMY.

polytechnic (in England and Wales between 1965 and 1991), the second tier of the HIGHER EDUCATION system (see BINARY SYSTEM). Elsewhere the use of the term is variable, and polytechnic institutions, as in France, may be of a higher status than universities. See also NEW UNIVERSITY.

polyvalency see DESKILLING.

Popper, Karl (1902–94) Austrian-born philosopher of science who worked from 1945 at the London School of Economics and is renowned for his advocacy over many years of FALSIFICATIONISM and 'critical rationalism'.

It was in his *Logic of Scientific Discovery* (1959, German 1934) that Popper first claimed to have 'solved the problem of empiricism' (see also EMPIRICISM, INDUCTION AND INDUCTIVE LOGIC), proposing a criterion of science based on the falsifiability rather than the verifiability of hypotheses (compare POSITIVISM, VERIFICATION PRINCIPLE). In taking this view Popper has also been a leading advocate of the COVERING-LAW MODEL of science, which is an integral part of his falsification view.

Although at first Popper's focus concerned mainly physical science, subsequently he extended the scope of his philosophy to include social science, notably in *The Poverty of Historicism* (1957) and *The Open Society and its Enemies* (1945). In the first of these Popper attacked those forms of historical social theory that claim a special status for the social sciences as historical sciences but in doing so either overstate the possibilities of scientific laws or see no possibility of these (see HISTORICISM). Both forms of theory were seen by Popper as failing to appreciate the true character of laws and theories in science and social science, i.e. that these involve limited, not unconditional, predictions.

In *The Open Society and its Enemies*, Popper continued his critique of 'historicism', focusing particularly on Hegel and Marx, whose historicism, he suggested, makes them 'enemies of the open society'. The OPEN SOCIETY is Popper's formulation of his preferred kind of society, a society in which individuals can aspire to change history and in which the future as a whole is recognized as inherently unpredictable. This form of society is the only one compatible with the kind of scientific laws that Popper believed possible in the social sciences, laws which are couched in terms of situational logic (see SITUATIONAL ANALYSIS AND SITUATIONAL LOGIC) and METHODOLOGICAL INDIVIDUALISM and make only limited predictions.

A similar reliance on this general epistemological view was also apparent in Popper's conception that PIECEMEAL SOCIAL ENGINEERING, rather than any utopian scheme, represents the only form of social planning which can be justified by social science.

In the exposition and elaboration of his views, Popper drew latterly on EVOLUTIONARY THEORY, arguing that, as in the biological world, knowledge and societies advance by gradual steps involving 'hopeful conjectures' which are sometimes successful, but which are unpredictable overall (see also EVOLUTIONARY SOCIOLOGY).

Although he presented it as 'anti-Positivist', Popper's philosophy remained broadly within the empiricist and positivist tradition with its claims for an absolute foundation for science and a unity of social and physical science.

In recent years Popper's position on science and social science has been subject to a number of damaging critiques, notably: (a) critiques of both the falsificationist and the covering-law model (see FEYERABEND, KUHN, SCIENTIFIC REALISM);

(b) critiques of methodological individualism;
(c) suggestions that part of the undoubted wide appeal of Popper's philosophy is ideological.

popular culture literally, the practices, likes and wants of the people. Popular culture operates in the context of high or élite culture with which it negotiates, struggles and reacts and which it simulates. In some readings, it is seen as the expression of the people. For example, Fiske (*Understanding Popular Culture,* 1989; *Reading the Popular,* 1989) stresses the capacity of popular culture to articulate the people's values. However, Fiske is reacting against a strong tradition which identifies popular culture with manipulation by market forces and the dominant class. The classic statement of this position is ADORNO and HORKHEIMER'S (1972) *'culture industry'* thesis. This thesis proposes that popular culture is managed by the producers of advertising, television, cinema, pop music and other branches of the mass communications industry. These agencies are alleged to produce conformity in the people. However, within the CULTURAL STUDIES tradition, popular culture has been theorized as a contradictory space. For example, Hall and Jefferson (1976) and Hall et al. (1978) recognize that popular culture is shaped by hegemonic forces. At the same time they read popular culture as territory in which the people genuinely resist hegemonic power. See also LEISURE, TELEVISION.

population 1 the totality of persons inhabiting a given location.
2 (STATISTICS) the aggregate of individuals or items from which a SAMPLE is drawn.

Quantitative aspects of the study of population are the subject matter of DEMOGRAPHY. Sociologists have been interested in moving beyond merely arithmetical analysis of population to achieve theories which can explain patterns of population change (e.g. variations in levels of FERTILITY, or 'push and pull' factors explaining MIGRATION). The study of tendencies in world population growth is a particularly important aspect, as is study of the social implications of particular national population profiles (e.g. an ageing population). See also MALTHUS, DEMOGRAPHIC TRANSITION, HISTORICAL DEMOGRAPHY.

population pyramid a two-dimensional graph used to display the age and gender structure of a population. See Fig. 25.

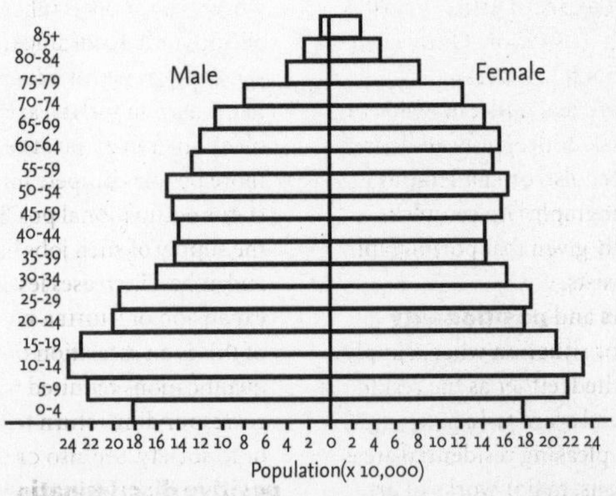

Fig. 25 **Population pyramid.** The above example represents the age structure of Scotland in 1976.

populism political movements or political parties which reflect a major disillusionment with conventional political parties and which have, or present themselves as having, the objective of returning political POWER to the mass of the people, e.g. the *Narodniks* in Russia in the late 19th-century, and the People's Party in the US in the same era. Populist movements have often been anti-urban, anti-industrial movements, and often also anti-big business. Sometimes they have been associated with CONSPIRACY THEORIES. In the 20th-century, the term has been applied to many political parties and to tendencies within political parties, which may be either left-wing or right-wing, e.g. the *Peronist* movement in Argentina, based on the urban working class, or FASCIST movements such as NATIONAL SOCIALISM in Germany.

Some political strategies employed by political parties may also be described as 'populist', even where the party as a whole would not usually be referred to as populist, e.g. in Britain, aspects of the strategy of the modern Conservative Party under THATCHERISM.

pornography erotic, sometimes violent or brutal, sexual representations (in e.g. literature or film) that meet social opposition on the grounds that they offend and degrade or exploit women or young people. A lack of literary or artistic merit is sometimes a further criterion. One view of pornography is that is provides opportunities for sexual outlet in which the male gaze, and male conceptions of desire, can still prevail (sec also QUEER THEORY). Attitudes to pornography are complex, however, especially given that pornography for women also exists.

positional goods and **positionality** any commodity or situation where supply is inherently limited, either as the result of physical or social scarcity (e.g. environmentally pleasing residential areas or holiday locations, major works of art, top jobs). The satisfactions obtained from such goods or situations derive in part from scarcity and social exclusiveness, as well as from the intrinsic satisfactions. The deficiencies in the supply of such goods cannot be overcome by normal economic growth.

In *Social Limits of Growth* (1977), Hirsch suggests that, as societies become richer, many of the extra goods, services and facilities sought by consumers cannot be acquired or used by all, without spoiling them for each other: 'what each of us can achieve, all cannot'. Thus as pointed out by Mishan (1967): 'The tourist in search of something different, inevitably erodes and destroys that difference by his enjoyment of it.' According to Hirsch, 'our existing concept of economic output is appropriate only for truly private goods, having no element of interdependence between consumption by different individuals'. Many of the environmental issues – problems of congestion, pollution, etc. – which increasingly arise in modern industrial societies, involve positionality in Hirsch's sense. The need for a distributional morality to support a limit to growth is emphasized by Hirsch. This view contrasts with the technocratic optimism usually associated with economist's theories of economic growth. See also PUBLIC GOODS.

positional jobs any sought-after jobs where the supply is inherently limited, e.g. all 'top jobs'. According to Hirsch (1977) the spiralling quest for educational achievement in modern industrial societies is a phenomenon of 'positionality'. More and more people compete for best-paid, high-status occupational positions. However, since the supply of such jobs is inherently limited, and at best increases less rapidly than the expansion of HIGHER EDUCATION, the result of this is an escalation of the formal qualifications required without any corresponding return to most individuals or to society. See also CREDENTIALISM.

positive discrimination social policies encouraging favourable treatment of socially disadvantaged 'minority' groups, especially in employment, education and housing. These policies aim to reverse historical trends of DISCRIMINATION and to create EQUALITY OF OPPORTUNITY. The term is roughly synonymous with *affirmative action* and *reverse discrimination*.

In the US, where affirmative action programmes have been in operation since the 1964 Civil Rights Act, these policies have created considerable controversy and litigation. In defending the concept of positive discrimination, President Lyndon Johnson said, 'You do not take a person who, for years, has been hobbled by chains and liberate him, bring him up to the starting line of a race and then say, "you are free to compete with all the others", and still justly believe that you have been completely fair'.

The arguments of those opposed to positive discrimination can be represented by the views of Glazer (1975), who argues that affirmative action 'has meant that we abandon the first principle of a liberal society, that the individual's interests and good and welfare are the test of a good society, for now we attach benefits and penalties to individuals simply on the basis of their race, color, and national origins.'

Despite calls for programmes of positive discrimination in the UK, it remains illegal under existing Sex Discrimination and Race Relations Acts.

positivism 1 the doctrine formulated by COMTE which asserts that the only true knowledge is scientific knowledge, i.e. knowledge which describes and explains the coexistence and succession of observable phenomena, including both physical and social phenomena. Comte's positivism had two dimensions:
(a) methodological (as above); and
(b) social and political, in that positive knowledge of social phenomena was expected to permit a new scientifically grounded intervention in politics and social affairs which would transform social life.
2 (*Logical Positivism*) the philosophical viewpoint of a group of philosophers in the 1920s and 30s known collectively as the Vienna Circle, whose ideas were in part based on Comte but presented as giving Comte's positivism a more secure logical basis. The central doctrine of the Vienna Circle, the *Verification Principle*, states that the only valid knowledge is knowledge which is verified by sensory experience. More strictly, the expectation was that scientific knowledge would ultimately find formulation in logically interrelated general propositions, grounded in statements about 'basic facts' stated in a strictly formulated 'sense datum' language. Some but not all members of the Vienna Circle also embraced Comte's project to extend the methods of the physical sciences to social science.
3 any sociological approach which operates on the general assumption that the methods of physical science (e.g. measurement, search for general laws, etc.) can be carried over into the social sciences.
4 (pejoratively) any sociological approach seen as falsely seeking to ape the methodology of the physical sciences.

In choosing the term 'positivism', Comte conveyed his intention to repudiate all reliance on earlier religious or speculative metaphysical bases of 'knowledge' (see LAW OF THREE STAGES). However, Comte regarded scientific knowledge as 'relative knowledge', not absolute. Absolute knowledge was, and always would be unavailable. Comte's social and political programme envisaged a new consensus on social issues and a reorganization of society on lines suggested by the new science of sociology. A role would exist for sociologists in government and in education, and in establishing a new 'Religion of Humanity'.

Since it was the work of a 'school' rather than an individual, the methodological position of Logical Positivism is more variegated than that of Comte, and in crucial respects at odds with his view. In the realm of ethics, for example, Logical Positivists were often associated with a doctrine that draws a sharp distinction between 'facts' (which are verifiable) and 'values' (which are not). While most philosophers associated with Logical Positivism maintained that science, including social science, could be expected to provide increasingly reliable knowledge, enabling the achievement of preferred goals, they did not usually accept that science can decide questions of value, 'ought' questions rather than 'is' statements (see also FACT-VALUE DISTINCTION).

Neither the details of Comte's methodological principles nor his social and political programme find strong support among modern sociologists. Nor has the attempt of the logical positivists to achieve a stricter logical formulation of positivism and 'science' proved durable.

Methodologically, a central problem of positivism arises from the so-called 'problem of empiricism': the lack of any conclusive basis for 'verification' in 'inductive logic' see INDUCTION AND INDUCTIVE LOGIC, EMPIRICISM). A further telling criticism – the so-called 'paradox of positivism' – is that the Verification Principle is itself unverifiable.

In recent years, new approaches in the philosophy and history of science (see SCIENCE, SCIENTIFIC PARADIGM) have shed doubt on the idea of a single philosophical basis to science. Positivism can be criticized for betraying its own conception of scientific knowledge as 'relative' knowledge and as dogmatizing about 'scientific method'. See also FALSIFICATIONISM.

If the above difficulties apply to Positivism in relation to physical science, further problems arise in relation to sociology specifically. The fact is that sociological positivism has not been successful in achieving either the expected unification of sociological knowledge, or a consensus on schemes for social and political reconstruction. For some sociologists, the failure of positivism points to the necessity to pursue sociology in other than conventionally 'scientific' terms – see MEANINGFUL SOCIOLOGY, VERSTEHEN.

C. Bryant, *Positivism in Social Theory and Research* (1985) is an accessible overview of the issues surrounding Positivism in sociology.

postal questionnaire see QUESTIONNAIRE. See also RESPONSE RATE and NONRESPONSE.

postcapitalism and postcapitalist society an envisaged new form of nonsocialist society in which capitalism is no longer the dominant basis of economic organization and in which the earlier confrontation between capital and labour is no longer the main basis of politics (e.g. DAHRENDORF, 1959). The idea of such a society is akin to the notion of a knowledge-based POSTINDUSTRIAL SOCIETY (see also INFORMATION SOCIETY) in which the dominant class is an educated professional class, rather than a traditional capitalist class.

post colonial theory a wide-ranging body of economic, social and cultural critique that investigates the conditions arising from and pertaining to the formation of empires, the impact of colonial rule and its aftermath. Generally indicating the time after World War II when imperial rule began to crumble in colonized nations, post colonialism raised issues of nationality, cultural identity and the use of language as a means of oppression. One of the most notable writers in this field was Frantz FANON whose contribution to the debate, *Black Skin, White Masks,* yielded further critique from writers such as Edward SAID and Albert MEMMI. Providing psychoanalytical, historical and cultural analysis of colonial rule, they argued that imperialism produced inferior subjects by devaluing the domestic language and culture, which in turn affected both their own sense of identity and outside perception of the culture. However, as post colonial theory emerged as a growing discourse, writers such as Homi Bhabha and Stuart HALL began to question the value of promoting an essentialist vision of society when identity has evolved beyond any set idea of singular subjectivity. Here notions of '*hybridity*' and '*syncretism*' have been developed in order to highlight the diasporic (see DIASPORA) and global nature of post-colonial culture, where the subject can make use of a myriad of identities in order to constitute a fluid self-image.

post empiricism the repudiation of the idea that science and knowledge can be grounded in entirely theory-neutral observations of the kind suggested by EMPIRICISM and POSITIVISM. Post empiricism involves an acceptance of accounts of science such as those proposed by KUHN and FEYERABEND. This need not imply that science or knowledge is an irrational or relativistic enterprise. However, it does mean that scientists and social scientists cannot escape the necessity to argue the reasons why one theory should be accepted and another rejected, that there exist no simple grounds for knowledge claims.

post feminism the viewpoint that earlier forms of FEMINISM have been replaced by a new phenomenon. The 1990s, in particular, were often characterised by the media as the post feminist decade; a rejection on the part of many women of the outdated feminism that had dominated the 70s and 80s, and a move beyond the 'hard-line' to the more amenable and photogenic 'girl power'.

According to Barrett (2000) post feminism:
(a) 'puts the feminine back into women's sense of identity and aspirations'; and
(b) sometimes incorporates ideas drawn from poststructuralist theory which cut away a good deal of the 'conceptual ground' on which earlier forms of feminism were based, including fixed notions of gender difference, ideas of gender equality, middle-class or western notions of feminism (Barrett, 2000). As Barrett notes, the prefix 'post' may refer to either or both that:
(a) we have moved 'beyond'; or
(b) 'come from' earlier feminism. Much of the manifest controversy that surrounds feminism/post-feminism hinges on whether (a) or (b) is emphasized. What is clear, however, is that post-feminism often incorporates a critique of previous assumptions about history, the SELF, the social, the political, the TEXT, knowledge and the West.

High profile women associated with post-feminism include Naomi Wolf, Katie Roiphe and Camille Paglia (see Gamble, 1999). All are critical of definitions of women as passive victims of patriarchy; thus they are reluctant to endorse feminist campaigns (such as those against pornography or date rape for example) and keen to generate more flexible discourses of power and subordination. However, this version of post-feminism has been challenged as impossibly utopian, an anti feminist betrayal of women's struggle which, in effect, delivers us back to pre-feminist times. Women are still expected to look slim, 'feminine' and eternally youthful while *also* bringing up the children *and* succeeding at their highflying career.

An alternative post feminist discourse emerged in the late 1990s. This view aims to extend rather than reject earlier theorizing and is associated with women like Rosi Braidotti, Ann Brooks, Judith BUTLER and Elspeth Probyn. Like the other 'posts' of recent years, particularly POSTSTRUCTURALISM, POSTMODERNISM and POST COLONIALISM, post feminism has been characterized as a break with a previous range of oppressive relations. However, Brooks (1997) argues that just as the 'post' of post colonialism should not imply colonial relations have been overturned, so *post* -feminism or *post*modernism should not be perceived as suggesting that patriarchal or modernist discourses have been superseded. In this view then, post feminism is feminism that has been dispersed into other areas of debate (eco-feminism, CYBERFEMINISM, POSTMODERNISM) as well as a set of debates that continue to engage with patriarchal discourses. In this way, post feminism challenges the hegemonic assumptions of earlier FEMINIST EPISTEMOLOGIES while remaining an important site of political mobilization.

post-Fordism see FORDISM AND POST-FORDISM.

postimperialism a concept in which the ending of COLONIALISM after World War II and the emergence of several major economic and political national groupings are associated with the end of exploitative relationships between nations characteristic of the period of IMPERIALISM from the end of the 19th-century until the mid-20th. This idea was particularly developed from the mid-1970s by political scientists in the US, notably Richard L. Sklar and David G. Becker (see Becker et al., 1987, for some key essays). They take the view that capitalism in the late 20th-century involves nonexploitative relations between nation states and a growing congruence between the interests of dominant classes internationally. Central to the analysis is not just the end of colonialism but the idea that MULTINATIONAL COMPANIES bring benefits to THIRD WORLD countries in the form of capital, secure markets and technologies. These companies no longer necessarily represent the national interests of their countries of origin, the industrial capitalist societies. Further, the bourgeoisie in the Third World involved in these enterprises are nationalistic, counter to FRANK's argument that they comprise a comprador bourgeoisie (see COMPRADOR CAPITALIST).

These arguments run counter to those of DEPENDENCY THEORY and many other contemporary approaches to the Third World. Whilst it is recognized that there are problems with nearly all such general approaches, postimperialism theory has had limited impact. This is because of disagreements over the beneficial role of multinational corporations for Third World countries and scepticism about the role of the national bourgeoisie in economic development. See also UNEQUAL EXCHANGE.

postindustrial society a conception of late-20th-century society which highlights the declining dependence of the societies on manufacturing industry, the rise of new service industries, and a new emphasis on the role of knowledge in production, consumption and leisure.

As formulated by Daniel Bell in *The Coming of Post-Industrial Society* (1974), modern societies, such as the US and many European societies, are seen as increasingly *information societies,* i.e. societies centred on knowledge and the production of new knowledge. An indication of this is the increased importance of HIGHER EDUCATION within these societies. According to Bell, knowledge is becoming the key source of innovation and the basis of social organization in these societies. This being so, new knowledge-based professional and occupational groups are also seen as increasingly achieving dominance within the class structures of these societies (see also TECHNOSTRUCTURE).

On this view, postindustrial societies may also be seen as a species of POSTCAPITALIST SOCIETY in which the owners of capital have conceded power to professional managers (compare MANAGERIAL REVOLUTION, SEPARATION OF OWNERSHIP AND CONTROL; see also CONVERGENCE). Although it finds some support, Bell's concept has also been widely criticized as failing to demonstrate that the undoubted increase in the importance of knowledge in modern societies actually does lead to a shift of economic power to a new class, especially to a new non-capitalist class.

In more general terms, there is relatively little acceptance that modern societies have moved beyond industrialism in any of the senses suggested. For example, if primary and manufacturing industry may seem to have declined in importance, this is deceptive, since much service production is production for manufacturing industry. Similarly, according to many commentators, the society of affluence and abundant LEISURE, often suggested as part of the idea of postindustrialism, remains a long way off (see also LEISURE SOCIETY).

postmodernity and **postmodernism**

Interrelated terms referring to:
(a) *postmodernity* – the cultural and ideological configuration taken to have replaced or be replacing MODERNITY;
(b) *postmodernism* – theories (including theories and new movements in architecture and the arts as well as social theories, e.g. POSTSTRUCTURALISM) implicated in or accounting for the change from modernity (and MODERNISM) to postmodernity. Variously defined, with different aspects of the general phenomenon emphasized by different theorists, 'postmodernity' is seen as involving such features as a world of 'flux, flow and fragmentation', without absolute values, an end of the dominance of an overarching belief in 'scientific' rationality and a unitary theory of PROGRESS, the replacement of empiricist theories of representation and TRUTH, and an increased emphasis on the importance of the unconscious, on free-floating signs and images, and a plurality of viewpoints. Theories of postmodernism offer an analysis of this condition while also contributing to it.

Associated also with the idea of a 'postindustrial age' (compare POSTINDUSTRIAL SOCIETY) theorists such as BAUDRILLARD (1983) and LYOTARD (1984) make central to postmodernity a shift from a 'productive' to a 'reproductive social order' in which SIMULATIONS and models – and more generally, SIGNS – increasingly constitute the world, so that any distinction between the appearance and the 'real' is lost. Lyotard, for example, speaks especially of the replacement of any GRAND NARRATIVE by more local 'accounts' of reality as distinctive of postmodernism and postmodernity. Baudrillard talks of the 'triumph of signifying culture'. Capturing the new orientation characteristic of postmodernism, compared with portrayals of modernity as an era or a definite period, the advent of postmodernity is often presented as a 'mood' or 'state of mind' (see Featherstone, 1988). If modernism as a movement in literature and the arts can also be distinguished by its rejection of an emphasis on representation, postmodernism carries this movement a stage further. A further feature of postmodernism seen by some theorists is that the boundaries between 'high' and 'low' culture tend to be broken down, e.g. cinema, jazz and rock music (see Lash, 1990). According to many theorists, post-modernist cultural movements, which often overlap with new political tendencies and social movements in contemporary society, are particularly associated with the increasing importance of new class fractions, e.g. 'expressive professions' within the SERVICE CLASS (see Lash and Urry, 1987).

Suggesting that a postmodern sociology – with its denial of 'truth' – is a contradiction in terms, BAUMAN, *Intimations of Postmodernity* (1992) has suggested that a sociology of postmodernism is the important task for sociology. Anthony GIDDENS (see also RADICALIZED MODERNITY) is another critic, who prefers the terms 'high modernity' or 'late modernity'. For him, 'the issues raised by postmodernity are more interesting than those suggested by postmodernism'.

Nonetheless, postmodernist sociologies and philosophies raise important issues – which are open to discursive evaluation – even if their denials of 'truth' may appear paradoxical or self-contradictory (see Sarup, 1993). It can be suggested that there perhaps exist two sides to post-modernism which should be disentangled: a 'hopeful' side, compatible with a 'continuation rationality' and progress (albeit in radically changed forms) and a 'less hopeful' side with no hope of avoiding licence and disorder. The hopeful side opposes dogmatic versions of rationality and can bring respect for different traditions while increasing the scope for individual self-fulfilment and creativity. The less hopeful side might seem to support the potential for relativism and a resurgence of intolerance. See also FORMS OF LIFE, DECENTRED SELF (OR SUBJECT), INCOMMENSURABILITY, STRUCTURALISM, DECONSTRUCTION. DISORGANIZED CAPITALISM.

post scarcity society the society of abundance in which scarcity has been eliminated, envisaged by some socialist thinkers. Counter-arguments suggest that there are always likely to be scarcities, including POSITIONAL GOODS, given that world resources are finite. A postindustrial, or postmodern, order might arise where the impetus to continuous accumulation associated with CAPITALISM was replaced by other goals, and it is in this sense that endemic scarcity might then cease.

poststructuralism a widely influential intellectual movement in France from the 1960s onwards, deriving from STRUCTURALISM but reinterpreting the latter's main assumptions about LANGUAGE and society as signifying systems. As such, poststructuralists utilized while also challenging the ascendancy of key structuralist theorists including SAUSSURE and LÉVI-STRAUSS. In the course of a root-and-branch questioning of traditional modes of philosophical and linguistic theorizing, they also challenged other major social theories, notably MARXISM.

The major theorists most usually associated with poststructuralism are DERRIDA and FOUCAULT (see also LACAN). Central aspects of previous linguistic theory 'deconstructured' by poststructuralism, especially by Derrida, include:
(a) a questioning of the implications of linguistic conceptions of DIFFERENCE, seen especially in Derrida's challenge to what he regards as SAUSSURE's still 'metaphysical' presuppositions about the SUBJECT and LANGUAGE, the priority given to speech' over 'writing' – see DECONSTRUCTION;
(b) a view that writing, too (see TEXTS), is also questionable as a source of any 'grounding' for objectivity or culture, the major reason for this being that, in addition to the 'arbitrary' connection between SIGNIFIER AND SIGNIFIED (as for Saussure), the relation between signifiers (via 'differences') is equally suspect, given that signifiers are always 'slipping under other signifiers', with no final definition possible.

postulate of adequacy **1** the doctrine (especially in SOCIAL PHENOMENOLOGY) that sociological accounts and explanations must be understandable to the social actor(s) involved in the social situations described or explained (see SCHUTZ, 1972).
2 the doctrine (particular to WEBER) that sociological explanations must be adequate

at the level of meaning (see also MEANINGFUL UNDERSTANDING AND EXPLANATION), but in addition they must also possess *causal adequacy*. This means that there must be indication that the events described are grounded empirically, including a grounding in empirical regularities, i.e. some probability that they would inevitably occur.

Not all sociologists accept Schutz's or even Weber's view, arguing instead that actors' understandings are frequently incoherent, and may be properly explained away or supplanted by sociological explanations, e.g. as merely surface meanings explicable in terms of underlying, perhaps UNCONSCIOUS meanings (see PSYCHOANALYSIS), or as FALSE CONSCIOUSNESS resulting from IDEOLOGY, or explicable without any reference to meanings (as in BEHAVIOURISM). In any of these cases, social outcomes may be seen as the UNANTICIPATED CONSEQUENCES OF SOCIAL ACTION.

GIDDENS' (1976a) response to this, in some ways a refinement of both Schutz's and Weber's views, is that, while sociological accounts should always start from actors' meanings, they must often move beyond these, although they must never ignore or discount the actors' concepts. The view also exists that even complex decodings and supplantings of actors' meanings by sociological accounts can be fed back to the actors involved for acceptance and for action (as intended, for example, in FREUD's psychoanalysis or in HABERMAS's proposals, based on Freud and Marx, for an 'emancipatory' social science). See also DOUBLE HERMENEUTIC.

postulate of functional indispensability *or* **universal functionalism** the doctrine, in some forms of FUNCTIONALISM (see also FUNCTION), that 'in every type of civilization, every custom, material object, idea and belief fulfils some vital function' (MALINOWSKI, 1926) and that 'no cultural forms survive unless they constitute responses which are adjustive or adaptive in some way' (Kluckholn, *Navaho Witchcraft*, 1944) – both of these quoted in Merton (1949). DURKHEIM (1897), though more cautious, nevertheless also made the assumption that the 'average form' in any type of society was likely to be functional for the type.

Robert MERTON in particular, in his famous 'codification of functional analysis' (Merton, 1949), challenged what he termed this 'postulate of universal functionalism', which he defined as holding 'that all standardized cultural forms have positive functions'. The alleged indispensability of religion', for example (see also FUNCTIONALIST THEORY OF RELIGION), is wrongly seen as based on the assumption 'that it is through "worship" and "supernatural prescriptions" *alone* that the necessary minimum "control over human conduct" and "integration in terms of sentiments and beliefs" can be achieved'. In challenging this view, Merton asserts that 'the same function may be diversely fulfilled by alternative items'. See FUNCTIONAL ALTERNATIVE, CIVIL RELIGION. See also FUNCTIONAL(IST) EXPLANATION.

potlatch a ritualized ceremony for the exchange of gifts and thereby the establishment of social standing and honour. It is found among various peoples of the northwest coast of North America. In its extreme form, potlatch could involve the symbolic public destruction of large amounts of goods, a practice which European colonizers banned. See also GIFT EXCHANGE AND GIFT RELATIONSHIP, KULA RING.

poverty the lack of sufficient material and cultural resources to sustain a healthy existence. Most discussions distinguish between *absolute* or *primary* poverty and *relative* or *secondary* poverty. 'Absolute poverty' refers to a lack of the basic requirements to sustain physical life; the subsistence poverty of not having sufficient food and adequate shelter. BOOTH and ROWNTREE were amongst the first researchers to demonstrate the widespread incidence of absolute poverty in the UK. 'Relative poverty' is used to demonstrate the inadequacy of definitions of absolute or primary poverty by referring to the cultural needs of individuals and families within the context of the rest of society. It is a relativistic definition which relates poverty not only to physical needs but also to the norms and expectations of society.

The study of poverty is central to any examination of social inequality, including an analysis of who is poor and the reasons for their poverty. In the UK, there is no set 'poverty line' although some commentators use eligibility for, and claiming of, social security benefits as a measure of the extent of poverty. Using this criterion, 17% of the British population, or about nine million people, were officially poor in 1986. However, this excludes all the people who were not eligible for social security support, those who did not claim support, those who were just above this arbitrary line, and those who fell into the POVERTY TRAP. Categories of poor people in industrialized societies usually include the unemployed, people in low-paid or part-time employment, the sick and disabled, older people, members of large families and single-parent families. Although the poor have often been blamed for their poverty, which is seen as the consequence of some form of personal inadequacy such as fecklessness or idleness, most studies explain the existence of poverty in terms of the social and economic structures of industrialized societies. Poverty studies have been criticized for not recognizing that poverty may result if the income of a man, although well above the poverty line, is not equitably shared between all members of the family; thus the burden of poverty falls particularly on women.

Just as poverty is seen to be an indicator of class and gender relations in an industrial society, so poverty has been seen as an indicator of unequal economic relations between different countries; the poverty of the Third World countries being directly related to the accumulation of wealth in developed countries (see UNDER-DEVELOPMENT).

poverty trap the situation where a slight increase in earnings leads to an individual or family being worse off overall as a consequence of losing entitlement to other benefits. People on low incomes may be eligible not only for social security support but may also make lower income tax and National Insurance (NI) contributions. A slight increase in their earnings may lead to the loss of their social security entitlement and put them in a position where they have to pay higher income tax and NI contributions; the slight increase in earnings may be considerably less than the extra amount they have to pay in NI and income tax contributions and their loss of social security support. The existence of a poverty trap is seen to be inevitable where there is a system of means-tested social security benefits.

A similar situation exists where single mothers may be considered to be in a poverty trap in so far as a woman in a reasonably well-paid job may have that income jeopardized by the need to pay for childcare. By taking a part-time job or giving up paid work altogether she may be able to look after her child or children, but is likely to lose any occupational benefits, including a pension, as well as her career prospects.

power élite the inner circle of powerholders in modern US society, according to C. Wright MILLS (1956). As portrayed by Mills, this élite group was composed of three loosely interlocking groups who had come to occupy the pivotal positions of power in modern American society: the heads of industry, military leaders, and leading politicians. Mills insisted that these three groups constituted a 'power élite' rather than a RULING CLASS (in the Marxian sense), in that the basis of their power is not simply economic. Instead, the relative unity possessed by the power élite is seen as arising from their shared cultural and psychological orientations, and often also their shared social origins. See also MILITARY-INDUSTRIAL COMPLEX.

The further main theory of modern political élites is PLURAL ÉLITISM, in which multiple élites are held to exist but not regarded as acting in a unified way.

power

1 the 'transformational capacity' possessed by human beings, i.e. 'the capacity to intervene in a given set of events so as in some way to alter them' (GIDDENS, 1985).
2 'the probability that one actor within a social relationship will be in a position to carry out his own will despite resistance' (WEBER, 1922).
3 the reproductive or the transformational capacity possessed by social structures, which may be seen as existing independently of the wills of individual actors, e.g. the power of market forces under capitalism.
4 (disciplinary, *knowledge/power* – *see* FOUCAULT, SURVEILLANCE, DISCOURSE AND DISCOURSE FORMATIONS).

Although power, especially in senses **2** to **4**, is often seen in negative terms, as involving coercion and conflicts of interest, all four senses of 'power' can also be seen in more positive terms, as 'enabling'. Power relationships may involve both interdependence and conflict. For PARSONS (1963), for example, power is the capacity to achieve social and societal objectives, and as such can be seen as analogous to MONEY, i.e. is the basis of a generalized capacity to attain goals.

As Giddens expresses it, power must be recognized as a primary concept in sociological analysis. It is potentially an aspect of all relationships, but one which he suggests has to be broken down into its various components before it can be used effectively in sociological analysis. A major distinction made by Giddens is between two types of resources involved in power (neither of which has primacy):
(a) control over material resources, i.e. economic or *allocative resources;*
(b) *authoritative resources,* including LEGITIMATE AUTHORITY but also numerous other expressions of *authoritative power,* e.g. 'surveillance'.

A further important distinction made by students of power (e.g. Bachrach and Baratz, 1962, and Lukes, 1974), is between the power visible in overt *decisions* and that involved in *nondecisions,* i.e. situations in which power is the outcome of a *mobilization of bias* within communities, the passive acceptance of established institutionalized power in which potential issues simply never reach the political arena.

Within structures or organizations we may also talk of the scope or intensity of the power or control which superordinates exert over subordinates. But control is never total. A DIALECTIC OF CONTROL can be said always to exist in that no agent (even a slave or child, or the inmates of a prison or an asylum) is ever totally powerless in a relationship, given that the active compliance of the subordinates is usually essential if a power relationship is not to become onerous for both parties to the relationship. Even when the balance of power between participants is unequal, there usually will be some reciprocities in power relationships (see also TOTAL INSTITUTION, VIOLENCE).

While power is an aspect of all areas of society and all institutions (e.g. in families, churches, groups and in organizations of all types), in modern societies the major concentrations are the power of:

(a) NATION STATES; and

(b) CAPITALISM. The first rests on the maintenance of LEGITIMATE AUTHORITY, but is ultimately grounded in physical violence. The second, in contrast to political power, is in its pure form quintessentially 'nonpolitical', and the major modern manifestation of 'allocative resources' in modern society. However, in modern Western societies, capitalism too plays a central role in the maintenance of 'political legitimacy', in view of its effectiveness and widespread acceptability compared with other economic systems, although some commentators regard this as involving ideological and CULTURAL INCORPORATION, contrary to long-term interests (compare LEGITIMATION CRISIS).

Studies of the distribution as well as the implications of power in modern society have occupied a central place in POLITICAL SOCIOLOGY, with its focus on ÉLITES and RULING CLASSES, on PARTIES and PRESSURE GROUPS, and on political and economic powerholders of all kinds. For Harold Laswell, for example, political sociology is about 'Who gets what, when and how'.

While some theorists such as C. Wright MILLS have suggested that modern societies are dominated by a narrow POWER ÉLITE, others including Robert Dahl or Seymour LIPSET strongly contest this view, seeing the situation as one involving PLURAL ÉLITES grounded in participant political cultures (see also STABLE DEMOCRACY). In an important study, followed by a seminal debate, Dahl sought to ground his viewpoint in empirical studies of community politics. However, his conclusions remain contested, being opposed particularly by those who point to his failure to take into account 'non-decisions' in reaching his conclusion that no one person or group is in a position to dominate (see also COMMUNITY POWER). A third main viewpoint is provided by Marxist theorists, who argue either that an overt capitalist ruling class exists or, more usually, a more diffused structural power, seen as arising from CAPITALISM's general allocative power, backed by control over what ALTHUSSER refers to as the IDEOLOGICAL STATE APPARATUS or else by a more diffuse HEGEMONY.

FEMINISM, in both its radical and materialist forms, has utilized the four definitions of power very effectively. The 'transformational capacity' of humans is regarded not as a neutral process, but one that is clearly gendered. Analyses of both social relationships and social structures have revealed persistent patterns of inequality based upon the subordination of women to men. Radical feminists have it that PATRIARCHY is a more fruitful paradigm for the analysis of power within social structures than class, status or purely political formations, whereas materialist feminists insist upon, minimally, the inclusion of the particular position of women within analyses of class in capitalist societies.

One thing evident from all such debates is that issues arise in the conceptualization and study of power which are not readily resolved. So much so that doubts have been raised (e.g. by Lukes, 1974) as to whether 'power' is not an ESSENTIALLY CONTESTED CONCEPT, by which Lukes means that the value issues surrounding it can never be resolved in empirical terms, or indeed ever satisfactorily resolved. There are similarities between Lukes' position and Max WEBER's (see VALUE RELEVANCE).

It can be argued, however, that both views are needlessly restrictive. The complexities and the contested character of the concept of 'power' can be acknowledged. But rather than singling out notoriously difficult concepts such as 'power' as having a special status, sociological inquiry might be better served simply by a recognition of the way in which many concepts in sociology tend to carry value loadings, leaving open the question of whether this makes them irresolvably contested. This would be closer to the viewpoint of Gallie (1955), the originator of the notion of 'contested concepts'.

Lukes is also cautious in the support he gives to any concept of structural power. This raises a final point about 'power' that must be mentioned: its overlap with both the concept of agency and the concept of structure, suggesting that Lukes' dismissal of 'structural power' is too sweeping. Although there are problems in the use of either of these concepts in isolation, recently their use as a paired-set has been held to offer greater prospect of a resolution of the problems that have attended the use of either alone (see STRUCTURE AND AGENCY).

power/knowledge (FOUCAULT) Although related to the dialectal identity of knowledge and power, this refers to the idea that 'forms of rationality open up fields of *possible* practices', and vice versa (D. Owen, *Maturity and Modernity*, 1994). The precise power/knowledge relationship can only be established by analysis of specific discursive and non-discursive practices.

practical knowledge *or* **practical consciousness** (especially in SOCIAL PHENOMENOLOGY and ETHNOMETHODOLOGY) 'what any social actor knows' in relation to his or her own action and social situation, but cannot necessarily express. Thus practical knowledge is often TACIT KNOWLEDGE, involving either a general or a specific social competence.

practical reasoning 1 thought directed to, and having outcomes in, social activity. This usage originates in PHILOSOPHY where it is contrasted with 'theoretical reason', considered as describing the world and its contents. Practical reason, by contrast, either emanates directly in action, or brings an immediate pressure to bear on it. It thus subsumes: considerations of the 'self' realizing and maximizing its goods, 'prudence', and considerations that restrict or encourage action or restraint from action in relation to others, i.e. 'morality'. The most dramatic claims to a special status for

practical reason derive from Aristotle's proposal of a *practical syllogism,* separate from theoretical syllogisms, in which an action itself (not a description or specification of an action) is held to follow logically from precedent premises, often summarized as a 'desire' and a 'belief. The effect is to render action itself 'logical', and this is held by some to be the source of the 'meanings' of action. Such logical connection is then held (e.g. Von Wright, 1971) to mark the fundamental difference between the explanation of human activity and the explanation of natural events (see also MEANINGFUL UNDERSTANDING AND EXPLANATION).
2 mundane or everyday thought in social situations. This ethnomethodological usage takes practical reasoning to be the central feature of routine social organization, and hence the subject matter of serious empirical sociology (see ETHNOMETHODOLOGY).

practical syllogism see PRACTICAL REASONING.

pragmatics the subdivision of LINGUISTICS concerned with the use of language in context. Pragmatics seeks to describe the systematic variation in the selection and production of linguistic items arising from the social environment. It is thus the most complex proposed 'level' of language study, and the one about which fundamental disagreements exist. It is not settled whether it can be a systematic study, perhaps focusing on permissible or favoured sequences of speech and action in systematically represented contexts, or whether it is a catch-all category for all those aspects of meaning, largely particular, which fall outside SEMANTICS. Influential approaches include SPEECH ACT theory, which, following Austin and Searle, seeks to specify the rules for 'bringing-off' actions in speech (e.g. promising) and ethnomethodological CONVERSATION ANALYSIS, which, with its detailed evidence of preferred sequences, can make a serious claim to being the first successful empirical pragmatics.

pragmatism a philosophical approach which embraces the work of a number of US philosophers, including C. S. Peirce (1839–1914), William JAMES and John DEWEY. Its central doctrine is that the meaning, and ultimately the TRUTH, of a concept or proposition relates merely to its practical effects. Thus for Peirce, scientific hypotheses should be judged by the testable deductions they permit, as well as by their simplicity, capacity to cope with new evidence, etc. For William James, ideas become true only in so far as they help us to interrelate our experiences. In at least some of their forms, CONVENTIONALISM and 'instrumentalism' are related doctrines to pragmatism; in all three, scientific laws and theories tend to be seen as principles which guide our actions, rather than as literal descriptions of the world. Similarities also exist with modern philosophical notions that all theories are 'underdetermined' by evidence, and that other criteria than 'empirical fit' are involved in our decisions about theories.

praxis (MARXISM) purposive action (including political action) to alter the material and social world, including Man himself. As a central general concept within Marxism, 'praxis' draws attention to the socially constructed nature of economic and social institutions and the possibility of changing these – humanity's capacity for freedom, which cannot be achieved entirely at the individual level. Praxis can be given more specific meanings, e.g. 'revolutionary praxis', but its main use is as a general concept capable of receiving a variety of emphases, for example, in some uses (within Marxism) a tension may exist between praxis and necessity.

preagrarian society see AGRARIAN SOCIETY.

precapitalist modes of production see NONCAPITALIST AND PRECAPITALIST MODES OF PRODUCTION.

prediction see SCIENTIFIC PREDICTION.

prejudice any opinion or ATTITUDE which is unjustified by the facts. The term tends to have a negative connotation both because a prejudiced person's opinions are unfounded and often not formed through first-hand experience, and also because the attitudes described are usually negative in relation to the object they are held about. However, one can hold a positive but prejudiced attitude.

Prejudice has been related to personality type (see AUTHORITARIAN PERSONALITY), and also to group membership. As with all attitudes, prejudices are the result of social learning within families and other social groups where opportunities for modelling and strong pressures towards conformity exist. See also STEREOTYPE, ETHNOCENTRISM.

preliterate society see NONLITERATE SOCIETY.

pre-operational stage see PIAGET.

presence (and **absence**) 1 the immediate social relations of copresence, compared with other actual or potential relations at a distance (*absence*) – see SOCIAL AND SYSTEM INTEGRATION.

2 (PHILOSOPHY, LINGUISTICS) the 'here and now', location of a 'knowing subject' assumed in traditional philosophy.

The method of DECONSTRUCTION employed by DERRIDA is an attack on what he terms the 'metaphysics of presence' in traditional philosophy (e.g. in HUSSERL) – the assumption that there is somewhere (e.g. a transcendental knowing subject) a site of immediate certainty. In Derrida's radicalized version of SAUSSURE's linguistics, signification and meaning, including the IDENTITY of the SELF, are always dependent on *absence* (see DIFFERENCE) and never complete.

presentations the totality of gift relationships which equalizes other relations (of kin, politics, economics, etc.). See GIFT EXCHANGE AND GIFT RELATIONSHIP.

pressure group (POLITICAL SCIENCE) any organized association of persons with the aim of influencing the policies and actions of governments or simply changing public opinion. In contrast with POLITICAL PARTIES, pressure groups do not seek to become the government, although in some cases organizations which begin as pressure groups may become political parties. The term *interest group* is mainly used interchangeably with pressure group.

A distinction can be drawn between: (a) groups which succeed, if only for a time, in establishing a continuing direct relationship with government (e.g. the National Farmers' Union and the Ministry of Agriculture, the British Medical Association and the Ministry of Health); (b) *attitudinal* or *promotional groups* (e.g. Shelter or CND), which mostly attempt to influence governments more indirectly by seeking to alter the general climate of public opinion.

Groups in the former category are usually based on a clearly defined economic interest. Their ability to establish a continuing direct relationship with government appears to depend on: (i) the claim to represent a significant proportion of potentially eligible membership, and (ii) advantages which arise for government as well as the interest group from a sustained cooperative relationship (see Eckstein (1960)).

The existence of a multiplicity of pressure groups of varying types is often regarded as an important indicator of the extent of political pluralism within a society. This may be so, but should not disguise the fact that major differences exist in the capacity of individuals to engage in effective pressure-group activity. See also PLURALISM. CORPORATISM, SOCIAL MOVEMENTS.

prestige see STATUS.

primal states see PRISTINE STATES.

primary care groups at the heart of the new NHS strategy in the UK, these groups came into being in 1999 and consist of groups of local healthcare and social care professionals (including social workers) who together with patient and Health Authority representatives take devolved responsibility for planning and implementing health policy in the context of local healthcare needs. Primary care groups are designed to replace the market principles in healthcare that the Conservative Government introduced with a new structure based around 'stakeholder' groups. Formally they have three main functions: to improve the health of, and address health inequalities in, their communities; to develop primary care and community services across the Primary Care Group and to advise on, or commission directly, a range of hospital services for patients within their area which appropriately meets patients needs. In the long run some PCGs will have Health Trust status and will be able to commission care, manage a devolved budget and have responsibility for primary care services within a locality. In policy terms they represent new forms of organizational partnerships between statutory and voluntary bodies in health and in social care.

primary deviance the initial act of rule breaking. Lemert (1961) used the term 'primary deviance' rather than DEVIANCE, but the latter is now in more common use. It has to be understood in relation to SECONDARY DEVIANCE.

primary education in Britain, the period of compulsory education usually received between the ages of 4 or 5 and 11 years. Considerable sociological research work has been undertaken on the primary school. It ranges from studies of STREAMING and other forms of school organization (Barker Lunn, 1970), to classroom labelling and interaction (Sharp and Green, 1975). The primary sector was the focus of the Plowden Report in 1967, the publication of which led to the establishment of EDUCATIONAL PRIORITY AREAS.

primary group a small group, such as the family, friends or colleagues at work. COOLEY (1909) classified groups into primary or *secondary groups.* The former have their own norms of conduct and involve much face-to-face interaction, whilst the latter are large and rarely involve direct interaction with all the members (e.g. a trade union or a political party).

primary poverty see POVERTY.

primary sector the sector of the economy (including AGRICULTURE and mining) concerned with the production and extraction of raw materials. See also SECONDARY SECTOR and SERVICE (OR TERTIARY) SECTOR.

primary sector of the labour market see DUAL LABOUR MARKET.

primary socialization see SOCIALIZATION 1.

primitive accumulation (MARXISM) the historical process whereby capital was originally amassed prior to CAPITALISM. In *Das Kapital* Marx asks how CAPITAL came into being before SURPLUS VALUE, which is only produced under capitalist social relationships. His answer was that the process of primitive accumulation involved, in England, the forcible expropriation of the peasantry from the land, making both land and labour available for agrarian capitalists who could then work the land for capitalist profit. This provided one of the main conditions for the emergence of capitalism: the separation of the producers from the means of production. A secondary factor in Marx's original formulation, but emphasized more strongly by some Marxists, was the role of colonialism in primitive accumulation. Marx in general sees that this had a role, through colonial plunder whereby wealth was extracted through noncapitalist means and transferred to Europe. However, to be transformed into capital there had also to be capitalist social relationships in Europe; hence its role can be seen as secondary. See also ACCUMULATION (OR EXPANDED OR EXTENDED REPRODUCTION) OF CAPITAL.

primitive communism see MARX.

primitive mentality see RATIONALITY, PRIMITIVE SOCIETY.

primitive society the least internally differentiated, and earliest, form(s) of human societies. As one of a number of terms (e.g. SIMPLE SOCIETY or SAVAGERY) also used to refer to such societies, the use of 'primitive society' suggests an elementary or basic level of technological and social organizational complexity. Theorists such as Levy-Bruhl (1923) have also proposed 'pre-logical' forms of *primitive mentality* associated with such levels of technological and social organization.

Notwithstanding the sympathetic and non-judgemental way that the term 'primitive society' has often been employed, the pejorative connotations of it have tended to lead to the use of alternative terms such as simple society, TRIBAL SOCIETY or NONLITERATE SOCIETY. However, none of these alternatives is able to entirely escape derogatory overtones. These arise from the basic cultural assumptions of modern societies in which modern society is seen as a superior form. The only solution is to continue to work towards accounts of premodern societies which do not automatically adopt such assumptions but explore the qualities of these forms of society in an open-ended way. See also EVOLUTIONARY THEORY.

primogeniture 1 the condition of being the first-born child.

2 the right of succession or inheritance of the first-born child. INHERITANCE systems vary between societies and are extremely important for the transmission and hence accumulation of property. Many Northern European societies practice primogeniture and this may be associated with greater accumulation of wealth and property than where these are dispersed amongst several members of a family. In particular, primogeniture prevents land-holdings being divided into ever smaller plots. In many societies, the first born usually means the first-born male.

printing the reproduction of text or pictures, especially in large numbers, by the machine technology arising from Caxton's inventions in the 15th-century. The development of printing is important as the first major step in the modern mechanization and extension of COMMUNICATIONS in human societies. Its implications include:

(a) an increased importance of the TEXT compared with the spoken word, including a heightened distinction between the influence of the text and its author's intentions;

(b) an enlargement of the PUBLIC SPHERE and scope for political discourse and POLITICAL PARTICIPATION in modern societies;

(c) its ushering in of the age of mass communications.

prisoners' dilemma a paradigm case in the THEORY OF GAMES, in which two prisoners, against whom there is some evidence of a crime but not enough to convict and who cannot communicate with each other, are each promised a light sentence if one of them confesses and the other, who would then be given a severe sentence, does not. If both confess they are promised a moderate sentence, but if neither confesses then both will receive a light sentence. The case this illustrates is the non-ZERO-SUM GAME, since there is no single 'rational' outcome. If neither confesses, both gain more than if both confess, but by not confessing they risk the most severe of the three possible penalties which will be imposed if only one confesses. Like all such hypothetical examples in game theory, the suggestion is that such models illuminate situations in the real world (even if they do not exactly match them). See also FREE RIDER.

prisons see PENOLOGY, FOUCAULT, PANOPTICAN.

pristine states *or* **primal states** the first STATES, believed to have arisen in the Middle East (and perhaps also in North India), from which all subsequent states – *secondary states* – are assumed to have developed, as both a defensive reaction to and modelled upon the first states. Fried (1967), Carneiro (1970) and Harris (1978) for example, make warfare a major factor in the origins of the first states. However, since warfare existed long before the existence of states, the decisive factors accounting for the rise of states were:

(a) the much closer proximity – or 'impactation' – of adjacent peoples in river valley societies (e.g. Mesopotamia before 3000 BC, Peru, 1st century AD, and Meso-

America, AD 300) which had undergone the AGRICULTURAL REVOLUTION but which were confined by natural barriers;
(b) the far greater competition for resources which occurred in these societies when, relative to population expansion, there may have been a DEPLETION of resources. Under conditions of food shortages and an escalation of conflicts between societies, a new coordination of populations is hypothesized as leading to an increasing incidence of warfare and the origin of states. The process involved the subordination of defeated groups within ever larger groupings, and also the incorporation of others who preferred to pay taxes and tribute rather than engage in warfare or flee beyond the reach of states.

Theories of the origins of the first states remain controversial. Compare SEGMENTARY STATE, EVOLUTIONARY UNIVERSALS, EISENSTADT. See also CULTURAL MATERIALISM.

private and public spheres

A dichotomous model of social relations which posits the separation between the domestic sphere of the family and that of socialized labour (wage work) and political activity. This model finds expression both commonsensically in phrases such as 'a woman's place is in the home' and within the social sciences (see Elshtain, 1981). It has been common practice for historians and social scientists to argue that industrialization and urbanization effected a separation between home and work, the personal and the political. This separation was gendered – the domestic sphere being associated with women and children, the public sphere with adult males. The domestic ideal of separate domains for men and women was particularly promoted in the 19th-century by the emergent middle classes and was given expression in 19th-century social policy and legislation. However, the splitting of the domestic from the economic and political spheres was, and continues to be, more ideological than empirical. It also serves as an example of the dualism found in much Western thought.

The work of Davidoff (1979) and Summers (1979) has questioned the historical existence of the dichotomy. Davidoff argues that the division between public and private spheres cannot be taken as given, even in the 19th-century. She argues that the existence of domestic service, the taking-in of lodgers, home work and the performance of a wide variety of subsidiary household tasks for payment indicates that the economy cannot be located solely outside the home. Summers documents the ways in which both middle- and upper-class women continually renegotiated the divisions between private and public in pursuit of their philanthropic work.

Siltanen and Stanworth (1984) also challenged the immutability of the boundaries between the spheres, criticizing both political and industrial sociology for taking the dichotomy for granted. Industrial sociology has operated according to the principle of the 'job model for men' and the 'gender model for women' (e.g. Blauner 1964). Men are defined in terms of their relationship to work and the economy, women in terms of their relationship to the family. Men's class position is therefore determined mainly by their place in the occupational structure, women's by their position in the family. Political sociology has often located both women and the private sphere outside politics. Political sociologists have characterized women as either apolitical or more conservative than men (e.g. see Dowse and Hughes, 1972). A 'male-stream' view of women's engagement with politics and economics has been fostered, rendering their involvement invisible or subject to misrepresentation.

The resurgence of feminism in the late 1960s was responsible for stressing the political nature of personal life, particularly in the areas of domestic labour, child care, sexuality, and male violence against women. Thus the definition of what constituted 'the political' was widened to incorporate the private sphere. Siltanen and Stanworth argue, however, that feminists have been less successful in challenging the dichotomy as a whole. For them the relationship *between* the spheres is a matter for political analysis, which must take account of the fluid nature of the spheres and reject a tendency to depict them as fixed. They argue that just as politics is not the prerogative of the public sphere, so the personal sphere enters into and influences the public sphere. Neither sphere is the exclusive domain of one gender. Men's involvement in the public sphere is influenced by their position in the domestic sphere, and, historically, women have occupied space in the public realm, and continue to do so. Furthermore, the state continues to engage with the private sphere, regulating and reconstructing it.

privatization **1** the sale or transfer of 'nationalized', publicly owned industries into private ownership and control. In the UK this process is particularly associated with the economic and social theories of THATCHERISM. The sale of shares in British Telecom, British Petroleum, British Gas, British Airways, and other companies is one aspect of this. In other areas the sale of council houses, and proposed changes in the WELFARE STATE, particularly in the funding of health and education, are comparable. See NEW RIGHT, NEW PUBLIC MANAGEMENT.
2 retreat of the individual from participation in political and PUBLIC activities.
3 a process in which traditional, working-class communal life styles are said to have been replaced by more family and home-centred ones, away from the older working-class housing and in relatively new housing estates. Sense **3** is particularly associated with the AFFLUENT WORKER study of GOLDTHORPE, LOCKWOOD et al. (1968–9). The focus of interest in this work is the hypothesis that significant changes in attitudes are associated with privatization. In particular, the breakdown of class loyalties, an 'instrumentalist' orientation to work, a new concern with living standards and status, a more pragmatic political orientation (rather than an 'automatic' support for the Labour Party), greater job mobility, and, generally, more individualistic attitudes. The Affluent Worker study is undoubtedly a 'classic' of British sociological research. Drawing on a number of themes which were popular in the 1950s and 60s, it has been a source for theoretical and

empirical work in the areas of working-class structure, CLASS CONSCIOUSNESS, and CLASS IMAGERY. Critics have indicated the oversimplification of Lockwood and Goldthorpe's categories, questioning their empirical usefulness in circumstances in which nontraditional class locations are associated with instrumentality and increased political militancy. Critics have also noted the lack of consideration given to factors other than social CLASS in the work: race, gender, religion, age, for example, may all affect attitudes (see Rose, 1988). As part of the reorientation of British sociology in the study of social class and class consciousness, though, this study of changing aspects of social class structure and consciousness remains of central importance.

privatized nuclear family see FAMILY.

probabilistic explanation see EXPLANATION.

probability (STATISTICS) a number ranging from 0 (impossible) to 1 (certain) that indicates how likely it is that a specific outcome will occur in the long run. *Probability theory* is concerned with setting up a list of rules for manipulating probabilities and calculating the probabilities of complex events. It predicts how random variables are likely to behave and provides a numerical estimate of that prediction. In sociology, it is particularly important for sampling procedures and statistical inference. See also EXPLANATION.

A *probability sample* is another name for a RANDOM SAMPLE, i.e. a sample selected in such a way that all units in the population have a known chance of selection. The advantage of using random (probability) samples in sociological research is that probability theory enables an estimate to be made of the amount of sampling error when sample results are generalized to the population. See SAMPLE AND SAMPLING.

Statistical inference deals with two related problems, the estimation of unknown population parameters and the testing of hypotheses from sample data. From sample data summary descriptive statistics are obtained, for example, the sample mean or the sample proportion. The Central Limit Theorem states that if random large samples of equal size are repeatedly drawn from any population, sample statistics such as the mean will have a normal (Gaussian) distribution. One property of this distribution is that there is a constant proportion of probabilities lying within a specified distance of the mean. It is this characteristic that allows statistical inferences from random sample statistics to populations. Calculating a sample mean does not allow a certain statement of what the population mean is, but with the knowledge of the sampling distribution an estimate of it can be made with a specific level of confidence, e.g. a probability of 0.95 (95%), or 0.99 (99%).

A SIGNIFICANCE TEST tests the probability of an observed result in sample data occurring by chance. Knowledge of the theoretical frequency distributions allows a probability value to be attached to the test statistic and if this is sufficiently low, e.g. $p=<0.05$ or $p=<0.01$, the NULL HYPOTHESIS is rejected (see SIGNIFICANCE TESTS). Both tests of significance and confidence levels are based on the laws of probability.

probability sample see PROBABILITY.

probability theory see PROBABILITY.

probation service a long-established form of specialized SOCIAL WORK (under the auspices of the Home Office) principally focused upon criminal offenders, but with a recent additional interest in the families of offenders and in matters associated with the welfare of children of divorcing couples. The core task for probation officers is the preparation of Pre-sentence Reports on proven offenders for the courts, to assist magistrates and judges in sentencing.
For those serving custodial sentences the probation officer has a generic welfare role both during incarceration and on the return of the offender to the community. The profession has shown a commitment to non-

custodial sentences, including the probation order, the community service order and forms of intermediate treatment. The training of probation officers includes substantial contributions from the field of sociology, including the sociology of crime and deviance.

problematique *or* **problematic** the system of questions and concepts which makes up any particular science (ALTHUSSER and Balibar, 1968). This concept plays a broadly equivalent role within the work of Louis Althusser to the concept of PARADIGM in the work of Thomas KUHN or the concept of EPISTEME in the work of FOUCAULT. As for Kuhn, in Althusser's view new scientific problematiques involve a revolutionary EPISTEMOLOGICAL BREAK with previous ways of thinking. Thus, Althusser argues that Marxism as a scientific problematique was born only after Marx's break with Hegelian ideas in 1845. Thereafter Marx operated within an implicit problematique, which later scientific Marxists developed.

problem of demarcation the problem(s) surrounding the identification of science, especially proposals for a single *criterion of demarcation of science*, such as the VERIFICATION PRINCIPLE or FALSIFICATIONISM (see also POSITIVISM).

problem of order see SOCIAL ORDER.

process sociology sometimes a preferred term for FIGURATIONAL SOCIOLOGY. Among figurational sociologists, the term is preferred because it better conveys the approach's emphasis on 'social process' rather than 'social structure'.

productive labour and **unproductive labour** (MARXISM) contrasting forms of labour within CAPITALISM AND CAPITALIST MODE OF PRODUCTION which arise as an implication of acceptance of the LABOUR THEORY OF VALUE. While *productive labour* refers to those forms of labour which create SURPLUS VALUE, *unproductive labour* refers to those forms of labour which do not do so. Only those forms of labour which in a fully socialized economy would be necessary are regarded as SOCIALLY NECESSARY LABOUR. All other forms of labour, which may be necessary within a capitalist economy for the 'realization' of surplus value rather than its creation (e.g. bank clerks) or for the ideological justification of capitalism (e.g. some forms of intellectual labour), are held not to constitute forms of 'productive labour'. If the labour theory of value is challenged, such Marxist conceptions of unproductive and unproductive labour lose much of their cogency. See also CONTRADICTORY CLASS LOCATIONS.

profane see SACRED AND PROFANE.

profession any MIDDLE-CLASS occupational group, characterized by claims to a high level of technical and intellectual expertise, autonomy in recruitment and discipline, and a commitment to public service. The 'traditional' professions are Law, Medicine, the Church and the Armed Forces, but both the term and its application are still debated. Among the reasons for this are the rise of new areas of technical knowledge and specialization and the everyday use of the term to refer to any and all occupations, or to distinguish between individuals who have exactly the same expertise by some nontechnical standard (e.g. money, social class). In the sociological literature, the debates have tended to concern problems of definition and the most significant features of professions.

Until the 1970s, there was a tendency in sociological work to discuss professions in their own terms and thus to reflect a functionalist ideology of expert public service as the main criterion for professional status. An early contribution (Flexner, 1915) exemplifies this. Flexner emphasized the intellectual, non-manual character of professions which necessitated long, specialist training in knowledge and techniques, their strong internal organization to deal with communication and discipline and their practical orientation, which was seen as altruistic – motivated by public service rather than personal profit.

Most sociological work until recently echoed these themes, emphasizing the high status which followed from these characteristics. Later functionalists continued to debate the nature of professions, emphasizing different elements but broadly agreeing on the essential points. Talcott PARSONS (1964a) took the argument further. He started with the familiar features of esoteric knowledge and altruism but added that by virtue of expertise and knowledge, the professional has authority over the lay person and that the characteristics of professionalism were a distinct and increasingly important feature of modern institutions. The implication that professionalization was occurring on an important scale has been a theme in much of the work on professions but has not always been developed in the same terms as Parsons or other functionalists. Whereas functionalists tended to emphasize the value to society, the high prestige and selflessness of professions, other approaches have emphasized power and self-interest. One might say that where the view from the professions emphasized the advantages of professionalism to the community, later critical approaches stressed the advantages to the professionals themselves. One of the earliest of these analyses was by Hughes (1952) who argued that professions did not simply operate to the benefit of clients, their organization and practices also protected and benefited the practitioners. In particular, the claim to authoritative knowledge means that only the professionals can judge whether work has been done properly and the professional organization can serve to defend the practitioner rather than the client. This critical view has been typical of more recent approaches. Johnson (1972), developed the argument on the relationship between client and practitioner. emphasizing the power which professionals have to define the needs and treatment of their clients and to resolve any disputes in their own favour. Parry and Parry (1976) studied the medical profession and argued that the 'producer–consumer' relationship is a less important consideration than the wish to establish a monopoly of practice – to get rid of rival medical approaches. The claim to unique competence, legally supported, is the basic strategy of professionalization. Self-regulation and control of recruitment are essential parts of the process. The advantages of professional (monopoly) status are to guarantee high material rewards, exclude outside judgement of performance and give guaranteed security of tenure to those allowed to practise.

This argument sees professionalization as a self-interested strategy and, in that sense, breaks down many of the distinctions which were formerly made between middle-class and working-class occupations. Skilled manual workers, for example, also have attempted to control recruitment by apprenticeships and to protect members' security by trade unionism and 'restrictive' job-definitions whereby permissibility to do particular jobs was strictly limited to a craft member. Manual workers, due to factors such as technological change and market situation in periods of high unemployment, have been less successful than professions in maintaining their monopoly privileges, but there are signs that the traditional professions are under pressure in their claims to monopoly and autonomy. The increasing popularity and success of alternative medicine, for example, and proposed changes in the legal profession, including the weakening of solicitors' effective monopoly on conveyancing and barristers' monopoly on higher court representation, are cases in point. These changes, though, have not diminished the popularity of professionalization as a strategy of SOCIAL MOBILITY, because material and prestige rewards are still apparent.

professionalization the process whereby an occupation succeeds in claiming the status, and therefore the rewards and privileges, of a PROFESSION.

profit see RATE OF PROFIT.

progress 1 a movement towards a desired objective; a development or advance, which is favourably regarded.
2 the result of social development, involving the enhancement of scientific and technological knowledge, economic productivity and the complexity of social organization.

Two main viewpoints in sociology on the idea of progress can be noticed:
(a) theories which embrace the concept in identifying the main historical route taken by progress, 20th-century theories such as Parsons' conception of EVOLUTIONARY UNIVERSALS, as well as 19th-century theories (see EVOLUTIONARY THEORY);
(b) theories, especially since the end of the 19th-century and the early 20th-century, which for a variety of reasons reject the idea of progress.

The concept of 'progress' lay at the core of early sociological thinking and is especially evident in the work of the discipline's founding trinity. For MARX, progress lay in the development of the forces of production and their eventual use, after revolutionary struggle, in the satisfaction of human need rather than private accumulation; for WEBER, somewhat more ambivalently, it lay in the RATIONALIZATION of economic, organizational, legal and scientific life; and for DURKHEIM in the enhanced possibilities for individual freedom in forms of organic solidarity (see MECHANICAL AND ORGANIC SOLIDARITY).

Much earlier 19th-century EVOLUTIONARY THEORY, however, had tended to see development as also involving a civilizing process, i.e. a transition from simple SAVAGERY and barbarism to the 'enlightenment' achieved by the European ruling, capitalist and Christian classes. Paleoevolutionism attempted to avoid this problem of value-laden definitions of progress by speaking of an increase in the 'general adaptive capacity of society' or the 'all round capability of culture' (M. Sahlins and E. Service, 1960).

A continuing characteristic of advanced and especially capitalist industrial societies is the rapidity of technological progress, with particular reference to the new technologies. The impact of these developments on economic and social life are a continuing source of debate, and are intimately connected with contemporary theories of SOCIAL CHANGE. See also MODERNIZATION, FORDISM AND POST-FORDISM, POSTINDUSTRIAL SOCIETY.

The alternative, more pessimistic, view of progress, however, includes:
(a) pessimism, especially associated with conservative thinking, e.g. from NEOMACHIAVELLIAN political theorists (e.g. PARETO, MICHELS) and NIETZSCHE, over the implications of 'mass democracy', MASS SOCIETY, etc.;
(b) pessimism associated with concrete political events, especially the end of the 'long peace' of the 19th century (which had led earlier theorists, e.g. SPENCER, to believe this would usher in a new 'pacific' age), including World War I, the rise of FASCISM in the interwar years culminating in World War II, and the threat of nuclear holocaust of the postwar era of COLD WAR. Added to this, there have arisen concerns about new threats to the environment, and questions have been raised about the sustainability of current patterns of economic growth.

The 20th-century retreat from POSITIVISM and EMPIRICISM, and the undermining of most forms of philosophical ESSENTIALISM, has been a further dimension questioning any simple assumptions about progress (see POSTMODERNITY AND POSTMODERNISM, DECONSTRUCTION).

progressive and degenerating scientific research programmes see FALSIFICATIONISM.

projective test an indirect test of personality in which individuals are assumed to reveal their personality traits by 'projecting' (see DEFENCE MECHANISM) them onto the deliberately ambiguous stimuli responded to. Examples include the

RORSCHACH INKBLOT TEST (Rorschach, 1921) and the Thematic Apperception Test (TAT) (Murray, 1943).

proletarianization 1 (MARXISM) the process whereby intermediate groups and classes (see INTERMEDIATE GROUPS) are reduced, by an inevitable logic of monopolization and capitalization, to the level of wage labourers. 2 in more recent sociology, the process in which the work situation of some middle-class workers becomes increasingly comparable to that of the manual working class, with consequent implications for trade union and political attitudes.

In the latter, more common sociological meaning, the focus has usually been on routine WHITE-COLLAR and office workers. One of the first extensive discussions of office work in this context was that of David LOCKWOOD (1958) (see BLACK-COATED WORKER), who concluded that tendencies to proletarianization were offset by differences in the STATUS and WORK SITUATION of these workers compared with manual workers. The argument was later taken up, notably in the work of Harry Braverman (1974), who suggested that the logic of capitalist development was to deskill and routinize work wherever possible, whether by the introduction of new technology or by the reorganization of work, broadly on the principle of SCIENTIFIC MANAGEMENT. The outcome of these changes in the labour process was to degrade work and make redundant previous status differentials. Braverman's thesis, however, has been the subject of an extensive debate. His work has been criticized, amongst other things, for over-simplifying the degree of deskilling, neglecting the development of new occupational groups with new and high-level skills, and ignoring the extent to which workers are able to resist management pressures. Also, continuing Lockwood's theme, while it is the case that the lower sectors of white-collar and MIDDLE-CLASS occupations are comparable to manual work in some terms, e.g. pay and autonomy, important differences remain in working conditions and, for some white-collar workers, job security, sick pay and promotion prospects. Routh (1980), for instance, showed that about 80% of male white-collar workers who started in routine office work were promoted during their working lives. This is not, though, the situation for women, who comprise about 70% of routine office workers and have far fewer opportunities for upward mobility (Crompton and Jones, 1984) (see also CONTRADICTORY CLASS LOCATIONS). The situation is also complicated by the ways in which gender expectations affect market and work situations. See also CLASS, SOCIAL STRATIFICATION, SOCIAL MOBILITY, MULTIDIMENSIONAL ANALYSIS OF SOCIAL STRATIFICATION, CLASS POLARIZATION, CLASS IMAGERY.

proletariat 1 (MARXISM) the class of propertyless labourers who live by selling their LABOUR POWER to capitalists in exchange for wages. The condition for employment is held to be 'exploitative', in that in creating VALUE workers increase the wealth and power of the bourgeoisie against their own interests (see SURPLUS VALUE, EXPLOITATION (AND APPROPRIATION)). Thus, in this perspective, the proletariat is conceptualized in an antagonistic relation to the bourgeoisie and is, inevitably, exploited and oppressed.
2 more generally, in sociology, the WORKING CLASS. See also PROLETARIANIZATION, CLASS.

property the rights of possession or ownership recognized within a society. Such possessions may be individually or collectively owned (including corporate as well as communal or state ownership), and include rights to LAND and housing, MEANS OF PRODUCTION or CAPITAL, and sometimes other human beings (see SLAVERY). Wide variations exist in the rights recognized within different societies, and these differences are often regarded as fundamental in determining overall differences between societies (see MODES OF

PRODUCTION). In their widest sense, rights of property include rights to alienate (to sell, will, etc.), but often may be limited to rights of control and rights to benefit from use. Historically – e.g. in many simple societies and preindustrial agrarian societies – 'absolute rights' of *private property* have been comparatively rare. Conceptions of 'absolute rights' of private property existed for a time in ANCIENT SOCIETY, but achieve a decisive importance only in CAPITALIST SOCIETIES – even then restrictions have usually remained.

Justifications of forms of property are an important part of the ideological legitimation which occurs in most societies, not least justifications of private property, notwithstanding that one of the justifications for private property has been the argument that it is a 'natural' form (see LOCKE, SMITH, CLASSICAL ECONOMISTS). Among important justifications for it have been the idea, especially influential in the period preceding modern capitalism, that individuals have a right to the fruits of their own labour (see also LABOUR THEORY OF VALUE). Arguments for unlimited rights to private property have been countered by an emphasis on the 'social' character of all production, the concept of social 'needs', and conceptions of social JUSTICE and ideals of EQUALITY (see also SOCIALISM, COMMUNISM). On the other hand the recognition of individual property rights has been emphasized as a significant source of limitations on STATE power, the development of CIVIL SOCIETY, and the appearance of modern CITIZEN RIGHTS (see also NEW RIGHT).

Sociological assessment of differences in, and consequences of differences between, societies in property rights is usually considered by sociologists to require more than regard merely to legal categories of property. An assessment of effective ownership and control, and the inequalities in wealth and income, life-chances, etc. related to these, is also essential. See also CONCENTRATION OF OWNERSHIP, PUBLIC OWNERSHIP.

prophet any 'individual bearer of charisma' (e.g. as demonstrated by ecstatic powers or MAGIC) who by virtue of his or her mission, 'proclaims a religious doctrine or divine commandment' (WEBER, 1922). For Weber, it is the 'personal call' and personal revelation of the prophet which distinguishes him or her from the *priest*, who has authority only as the 'servant of a sacred tradition'. Weber also notes that prophets have usually come from outside the priesthood.

A further significant distinction in Weber's discussion is that between *ethical prophecy*, in which the prophet proclaims God's will (e.g. Mohammed), and *exemplary prophecy*, where the prophet demonstrates by personal example the way to personal salvation (e.g. Buddha). According to Weber, the latter is characteristic of the Far East and the former appears initially in the Near East, and is associated with the appearance of conceptions of a personal, transcendental, ethical God only in this region. See also MONOTHEISM.

prostitution 1 (common usage) a practice involving sexual services for payment or other reward.

2 (legalistic usage) a sex-specific offence; although in England and Wales prostitution has technically been regarded as behaviour open to both women and men, in practice only women have been legally defined as common prostitutes and only women are prosecuted for the offences of loitering and soliciting related to prostitution. Legalistic definitions of prostitution, however, are culturally and historically relative. Prostitution is not always subject to criminalization and in some cultures the practice may be regarded as a sacred rite. In those societies where prostitution and related behaviours are criminalized it is typically the prostitute rather than the client whose behaviour is regulated, reflecting double standards of sexual morality.

3 (extralegal usage) an economic contract intrinsically equal to the practice of a man and woman contracting marriage primarily for economic reasons (see ENGELS, 1884).

Such attempts to go beyond the legal definitions of prostitution have been influential in feminist theory. Marx drew parallels between the economic prostitution of the worker and that of the prostitute. In doing so he neglected to consider the specific sexual exploitation and oppression experienced by women. Feminist theorists have also likened prostitution to marriage. Millet (1970) maintains that prostitution should be defined as the granting of sexual access on a relatively indiscriminate basis for payment. These approaches, however, fail to account for the particular stigmatization encountered by those women who work as prostitutes.

Traditionally, the sociological study of prostitution has taken place within the context of the sociology of crime and deviance (see CRIMINOLOGY and DEVIANCE). Thus sociologists have often uncritically accepted that prostitution should be regarded as primarily an example of rule-breaking behaviour or female deviancy. More recently, the impact of feminism has led to prostitution being examined within the context of wider gender relations and the socioeconomic position of women, particularly working-class and minority women. Sociologists have increasingly acknowledged accounts of prostitution given by prostitutes themselves, particularly those which present prostitution as part of the sex trade or sex industry. Arguably, it may, therefore, be as useful to examine prostitution in the context of the SOCIOLOGY OF WORK and occupations rather than in the context of deviant behaviour.

The rise of the prostitutes' rights movement since the late 1970s and the contradictory relationship with feminism and the women's movement has led to a shift in the contexts in which prostitution is studied and enters the public imagination (Scwambler and Scwambler, 1995). Aided by feminists, the discourse on prostitution has moved out of a legal/deviance framework and into a feminist framework which focused initially upon pornography and violence and latterly upon health issues in the AIDS era and prostitution as work (see V. Jennes, 1993). The prostitutes' rights movement emphasizes the profession of prostitute, and the rights, needs and civil liberties of adult women working in the sex industry, including the need for grassroots movements organized and managed by prostitutes and supported by 'experts' and 'professionals'.

Protestant ethic

A code of conduct derived from the redirection of Christian ASCETICISM by Puritan elements within Protestantism. Asceticism arose in CHRISTIANITY because zealous believers realized that methodical life-planning, self-control and self-denial were the best defences against the ethical inconsistency which offended God and so jeopardized the achievement of their ultimate end – salvation. In Catholicism, however, asceticism, was confined to the monasteries; it did not penetrate the lives of ordinary believers who remained trapped in the ethically inconsistent cycle of sin, repentance and renewed sin made possible by confession and indulgences. The Protestant ethic rested on a rejection of this dual morality and on an interpretation of monasticism as a selfish evasion of worldly responsibilities. Accordingly it demanded:

(a) that all believers maintain ethical consistency by means of ascetic regulation;

(b) that they do so, not in the monasteries, but in the faithful discharge of their worldly duties.

Principal among these duties were those associated with the believers' occupations (callings, vocations). It was this emphasis that provided WEBER with the grounds for the conclusion reached in *The Protestant Ethic and the Spirit of Capitalism* (1930): namely, that, insofar as it influenced human conduct, the Protestant ethic had a major impact on post-Reformation capitalism. According to Weber, capitalistic conduct was based on individualistic profit-seeking. More analysis, however, disclosed that individual capitalists were animated by a feeling of moral responsibility towards their resources, to increase them without limit by hard work, moderate consumption and saving for investment. All the elements of asceticism were present in the resultant conduct; it was methodically planned, self-controlled, self-denying – with reference to consumption and leisure – and single-mindedly directed towards the achievement of an ultimate end – economic acquisition and expansion.

Conduct like this seemed to Weber to be the result of a fundamental transformation in human character and values. Human beings were not *by nature* ascetic; they were easy-going and inconsistent, preferred leisure to disciplined work and regarded the single-minded devotion to economic acquisition as antisocial and immoral. Since the profit motive and capitalist institutions existed outside the post-Reformation West, without giving rise to ethically legitimated ascetic acquisitiveness, Weber did not think that economic interests provided sufficient incentive for human beings to break the mould of nature and impose ascetic regulation on themselves. So what did?

Weber thought that religion did, and he cited the example of Catholic monasticism to prove it. Once Puritanism redirected this asceticism the achievement of the zealous believers' ultimate end – the assurance of salvation – became linked to the discharge of their vocational obligations. God called Christians to serve Him by vocational activity. For this He gave them gifts of time, talent and resources and called them to work and save those resources so that His glory might be manifest in their use and increase. Idleness and thriftlessness, therefore, became the deadliest of sins, while the fruits of ascetically regulated diligence and thrift – growing profits and economic expansion – became valued as signs of God's blessing and thus provided believers with an assurance of salvation.

It was this need for assurance that forced people to undertake ascetic regulation. It arose because Puritan teachings about salvation caused anxiety. Puritans held that God granted salvation as a gift, either through predestination of a minority – as in Calvinism – or in an offer made directly to individuals – as in other traditions. Either way believers became anxious to assure themselves that they were amongst the saved. Since God dealt directly with individuals, proof could not be established through the mediation or sacramental ministry of the churches. It had to come through individual conviction developed by faith and a demonstration that God's grace had transformed an individual from the state of nature, indicated by ethical inconsistency, to the state of grace, proved through ascetic vocational conduct. Human character was thus changed; fear broke the mould of nature and forced people to become ruthless ascetics dedicated to work, saving and expansion.

Puritanism, therefore, provided capitalism with some signal services:
(a) it moulded a type of character ideally suited to expanding the system;
(b) it legitimated individualistic profit-seeking by making it a duty willed by God;
(c) it legitimated the division of labour by making specialist occupational activity a duty;
(d) it legitimated capitalist exploitation and work discipline by making conscientious labour a duty;
(e) it created a cultural climate in which poverty could be seen as a result of individual moral failings, i.e. idleness and thriftlessness, and so freed the successful, and the society, of responsibility of poverty. Capitalism, nevertheless, soon outgrew the religious origins of its spirit. In its developed form it rests on its own foundations; those who refuse to engage in capitalistically appropriate conduct will perish in the struggle for survival.

Weber's thesis generated a great unresolved conflict in which economic historians, church historians, theologians and other non-sociologists have taken part. Among other things, he has been accused of:
(a) failing to see that ethically uninhibited acquisitiveness and economic individualism were older than the Reformation (Robertson, 1933; Tawney, 1926);
(b) ignoring Protestant ethical reservations about acquisition (George and George, 1958; Hudson, 1949);
(c) ignoring Catholic and lay vocational teachings which were similar in purpose and content to those of the Puritans (Robertson, 1933; Samuelson, 1961). Much of this criticism is, however, based on misunderstandings. Weber was not trying to explain ethically uninhibited acquisitiveness or economic individualism, only the ascetic spirit which developed in capitalism after the Reformation. Nor did he ignore Puritan ethical reservations about acquisition; he admitted them but claimed that they were not directed against wealth as such, only its misuse in idleness and consumption. Weber was also aware of the non-Puritan teachings about vocational diligence. However he doubted their effectiveness because they were not supported by psychological sanctions of the sort which derived from the Puritan anxiety about salvation. For all this, Weber's thesis remains open to attack; some writers, for example, doubt that Puritanism generated psychological sanctions derived from anxiety

(Keating, 1985; McKinnon, 1988); Puritan writings on economic acquisition are ambiguous enough to sustain both pro- and anti-Weberian interpretations. When it is, finally, remembered that it is hard to establish unambiguously the direction of influence holding between religion and economic life – Marxists, for example, would argue for 'causation' in the opposite direction – it is easy to see why Weber's thesis retains an aura of plausibility, while at the same time attracting doubt. It is likely, therefore, to remain controversial so long as social scientists retain an interest in the problem to which it speaks.

Protestantism 1 those western Churches originating as distinct institutions at the time of the Reformation or by subsequent secession from Churches which originated at that time. 2 a system of Christian faith and practice based on the principles of the Reformation: that the Bible is the only source of revealed truth; the concept of justification by faith alone; and the universal priesthood of every believer. Protestantism also rests on negative views: it rejects the notion of the Church as an autonomous authority, beyond the voluntary association of its believers. The growth of Protestantism is often associated with distinctive features of Western European development. In particular WEBER claimed that the form capitalism took in Western Europe was dependent on what he called the PROTESTANT ETHIC. See also CHRISTIANITY, ROMAN CATHOLICISM. ASCETICISM.

psephology the study and analysis of voting and VOTING BEHAVIOUR (see ELECTORAL SOCIOLOGY). The term is derived from the Greek practice of voting by writing names on fragments of pottery or stones (Greek *psephos*, pebble). It is mainly in use in POLITICAL SCIENCE.

psychiatry the treatment of the mentally ill by medically trained practitioners. Psychiatry is a branch of general medicine, using drug treatment as a clinical resource, but also other physical methods such as surgery and ECT (electroconvulsive therapy). Thus, on the orthodox medical model, the patient is seen as having a specific dysfunction, and specific physical intervention is used to effect improvement. However, though physical intervention may be a first resort, the influence of PSYCHOANALYSIS, BEHAVIOUR THERAPY, and COUNSELLING and other nonphysical approaches to treating mental illness have considerably ameliorated this interventionist approach. Though the management of the PSYCHOSES is still very dependent on drug treatment, a variety of other techniques which emphasize the importance of the patient's perception and experience and the patient's role in their own treatment are used, and the appropriateness of behavioural techniques for changing behaviour is widely acknowledged in the profession. These methods are accepted as being of particular value for the neurotic patient (see NEUROSIS), and this, together with the evidence for severe problems of addiction arising from the prolonged use of tranquillizers, led to a swing from drug treatment to these 'softer' methods for the neurotic patient in the 1980s. See also PSYCHOTHERAPY, ANTIPSYCHIATRY, PHENOMENOLOGICAL PSYCHOLOGY.

psychoanalysis the theory and method of treating MENTAL ILLNESS by investigating the UNCONSCIOUS and understanding the dynamics of the PERSONALITY. It was originally developed by FREUD at the end of the 19th-century, working particularly with patients with emotional disorders, such as hysteria. Freud particularly used the techniques of free association and dream interpretation to explore the unconscious.

As well as Freud's own work and writings, a number of schools of thought within psychoanalysis (both as a therapy and as a wider theory) are also important – see NEO-FREUDIANS, OBJECT-RELATIONS SCHOOL.

As a therapy psychoanalysis is a lengthy process, taking perhaps several years, and a practitioner has to undergo a course of psychoanalysis himself or herself before being considered qualified to practise. The aim is to gain a full understanding of how one's current behaviour was developed as a result of past experiences, especially those of early childhood. These early experiences have to be brought to consciousness and confronted, leading to CATHARSIS, or a release of energy, with the result that the personality becomes freer, less restricted by having to control the energies of the ID, or operate under over-strict demands of the SUPEREGO.

In psychiatric practice, 100 years after its original development, the method is found to be most useful for neurotic disorders in patients who are highly motivated to recover and of good educational background as self-insight and an interest in the theoretical basis appear to be involved in a positive outcome. It has sometimes been criticized as having no better record for recovery than time alone (Eysenck, 1961), and is lengthy and expensive.

As a wider psychosocial theory, psychoanalysis has been influential (if controversial) in sociology and, more generally, in social theory (e.g. MARCUSE, structuralist theorists such as LACAN, PSYCHOHISTORY). Psychoanalytic theories have been especially influential recently in FEMINISM, FEMINIST THEORY and FEMINIST PSYCHOLOGY, although these theories constitute a major reworking of Freudian theory, especially in questioning the centrality of the symbolism of the phallus within Freud's writing and the problem that this presents for a genuinely feminist psychoanalytic theory (see CHODOROW, CIXOUS, KRISTEVA).

psychodrama see MORENO.

psychohistory the application of 'psychoanalytic forms of understanding to the study of history' (I. Craib, 1989). An exemplification of the approach is the work of E. Erikson (*Life History and the Historical Moment*, 1975).

psycholinguistics the study of linguistic behaviour, including language acquisition, grammar, and the relationship between language and thought. CHOMSKY is one of the crucial figures in this area, but see also SAPIR-WHORF HYPOTHESIS. See also LINGUISTICS, SOCIOLINGUISTICS.

psychologism the use of a psychological perspective to the exclusion of all others. Since PSYCHOLOGY's reference point is the individual, and SOCIOLOGY's is society, sociologists typically use psychologism as a term of abuse when explanation appears to be at an inappropriate individualistic level.

psychology the scientific study of behaviour. This includes human and animal behaviour (see also ETHOLOGY), but its particular concern is with mental events as revealed through behaviour, including introspection. As a separate discipline it has only existed since the late 19th-century, but in this time has encompassed several influential schools of thought, including PSYCHOANALYSIS, BEHAVIOURISM, the mental testing movement, and the HUMANISTIC MOVEMENT, their differences resting on ideological as well as theoretical and methodological predilections. For all this, mainstream psychology is a more homogeneous, more professionalized discipline than sociology, with a relatively high degree of agreement on the importance of experimental and statistical methods reflecting its different subject matter. Nevertheless, in a discipline which straddles physical and social science, and which has relations with many other disciplines, there is an acceptance of the appropriateness of different approaches and methods for different areas of the subject. Major topic areas within the discipline include comparative psychology (comparisons of human and animal behaviour), developmental psychology, cognitive psychology (including a central concern with perception, memory, language, and problem-solving; see also ARTIFICIAL INTELLIGENCE, EPISTEMOLOGY and LINGUISTICS), abnormal psychology, and SOCIAL PSYCHOLOGY. Numerous special applied psychologies exist (e.g. clinical psychology, educational psychology, occupational psychology and more recently, health psychology, counselling psychology and forensic psychology). Overlaps with sociology occur in a number of areas, especially in social psychology, which exists as a sub-field of both disciplines. Overlaps are greatest in those areas where the focus is on actors' 'meanings', 'naturally occurring situations' and a concern with contextualising psychological phenomena (see also CRITICAL SOCIAL PSYCHOLOGY, FEMINIST PSYCHOLOGY). See also PSYCHOTHERAPY, PSYCHIATRY.

psychosis severe mental illness in which the chief symptom is a distorted perception of reality. These distortions may include delusions and hallucinations, speech may be incoherent or inappropriate, there may be hyperactivity or complete social withdrawal. A wide variety of manifestations are evident but these are grouped generally under the terms *schizophrenia* and *manic-depression*. See also LAING, ANTI-PSYCHIATRY.

psychotherapy the clinical practice of healing the mind. Help for people with mental or psychological problems can come from many sources, from friends, family, voluntary workers, to counsellors, clinical psychologists, psychotherapists, psychiatrists. Psychotherapists are generally trained, often intensively and extensively trained, as Jungian or Freudian psychotherapists may be, but are not generally medically qualified. It is this that primarily distinguishes them from psychiatrists (see PSYCHIATRY). Psychotherapy aims to help the person in mental distress by a 'talking cure', examining past and present concerns and encouraging the person to understand themselves better. See also FREUD, JUNG, PSYCHOANALYSIS.

public goods *or* **collective goods** (ECONOMICS) commodities or services – e.g. defence, public parks, or urban clean air – which when supplied to one person are available to all. The contrast is with *individual or private goods,* which, in theory at least, are consumed privately.

According to Hirsch (1977), 'the central issue' involved in a consideration of the provision of private and public goods 'is an adding-up problem': what some individuals individually can obtain, all individuals and society cannot always get; and some things that societies might obtain cannot be obtained except by collective action. Thus society has to find some means of determining how such different sets of outcomes should be reconciled. If private decision-making provides no automatic best answer to such questions, nor necessarily do centrally controlled economies. Problems of overall coordination, and a lack of consideration for both true productivity and the external social costs of production, have beset both decentralized and centrally controlled economies. See also GALBRAITH, AFFLUENT SOCIETY, PARETO OPTIMALITY, SUBOPTIMALITY, POSITIONAL GOODS AND POSITIONALITY.

public opinion and **opinion polls** expressions of attitudes on political issues or current affairs by members of the general public. Since the advent of *opinion polls,* introduced by George GALLUP, the term has referred especially to statements of opinion collected in sample surveys. Compare MASS OBSERVATION. As pointed out by HABERMAS (1962), public opinion has a different meaning depending on whether it:
(a) is brought into play on the assumption that political and social power must be subject to public discourse; or
(b) is merely a construct to be manipulated in the service of government or powerful institutions. Habermas's concern is that in modern societies the critical content of 'public opinion' is often diluted. See also PUBLIC SPHERE.

public ownership the state ownership of some or all of the means of production. While the term can be used to apply to state ownership within COMMAND ECONOMIES, its main application has been to sectors of the economy within MIXED ECONOMIES which are state owned. An alternative term for the process in which industries are brought under state ownership is *nationalization.* In Britain the 1945 Labour government undertook an extensive programme of nationalization, including coal and gas, iron and steel, electricity, and civil aviation. Subsequently, the process has been reversed as the result of the radical programme of PRIVATIZATION under Conservative governments (see also THATCHERISM). Justifications for public ownership include the arguments that *public utilities,* especially 'natural monopolies', require public control, and the more general arguments that SOCIALISM and COMMUNISM are necessary to remove EXPLOITATION. Arguments against are that state ownership requires extensive bureaucratic controls, achieves less efficiency, and tends to reduce individual initiative and human freedoms. Between the pro- or anti- arguments, there also exist arguments for a balance between private and public ownership. While the command economies of Eastern Europe proved inefficient, it has not been established that public ownership and *state planning* are inherently inefficient. Empirical studies have discovered no simple pattern in differences between private and public corporations.

public sphere HABERMAS's (1962) term for the 'literate bourgeois public' (and later the 'public at large'), which can act as a critical counterbalance to the STATE. Habermas's historical portrayal of a 'critical forum' of independent voices free from state power is the basis of his later conception of politics and TRUTH, located in terms of an 'ideal speech situation'. Compare CIVIL SOCIETY; see also PUBLIC OPINION; PRIVATE AND PUBLIC SPHERE.

purchaser-provider split an aspect of the introduction in the UK of quasi-market mechanisms to the state and the public sector, initiated under the governments of Margaret Thatcher.

After World War II the State undertook the role of producer, supplier and coordinator of various services, including health and welfare. This began to change in the 1970s and with the advent of THATCHERISM in the 1980s these developments were taken further. A new minimal role for the state as buyer, rather than supplier, of services was created. These changes were ubiquitous, permeating local government too, where councils and authorities were compelled, by the Local Government Act of 1988 and the NHS and Community Care Act 1990, to allow INDEPENDENT SECTOR bodies to supply services. This has occurred through processes of Compulsory Competitive Tendering, and increased regulation. See also WELFARE STATE, PERFORMANCE INDICATORS, CIVIC ENTREPRENEURSHIP, AUDIT SOCIETY.

pure relationship see INTIMACY.

pure type see IDEAL TYPE.

purposive explanation an explanation of an occurrence as the outcome of an actor's own purposes and the purposive act(s) which follows from these purposes. Debate in philosophy and in sociology exists as to whether or not such explanations should be regarded as a species of 'causal explanation', explaining events that the actor 'makes happen'. For some theorists 'reasons are causes', and 'purposive explanations', 'causal explanations', but for others they are not. Either way, however, purposive explanations are not causal explanations in the Humean sense of 'universal' empirical regularities involving 'casual laws', in so far as they imply that actors could have acted differently. A crucial issue is whether purposive social action can be further explained, e.g. in 'structural terms' and/or in lawlike ways. See also ACTION, TELEOLOGY, FREE WILL, EXPLANATION.

putting-out system see FACTORY SYSTEM.

q

qualifying association any professional group that has succeeded in establishing a legally protected monopoly of training and access to an occupational area. See PROFESSION.

qualitative research techniques any research in which sociologists rely on their skills as empathic interviewer or observer to collect unique data about the problem they are investigating. Researchers may have a list of topics they will discuss with their informants in an unstructured way (a focused interview schedule or *aide-mémoire*) or may seek to uncover the informant's own 'narrative' or experience of the topic. Similarly, observation techniques may be more or less qualitative, the most qualitative being full PARTICIPANT OBSERVATION. These methods contrast with QUANTITATIVE RESEARCH TECHNIQUES where reliance is placed on the research instrument through which measurement is made, i.e. the structured questionnaire, the structured observation, or the experiment.

There is a strong emphasis on qualitative methods in ETHNOMETHODOLOGY and ETHNOGRAPHY. The data produced is considered to be 'rich' in detail and closer to the informant's perceived world while quantitative methods may lead to an impoverishment of data. Any classification of qualitative data can only be at the nominal level (see CRITERIA AND LEVELS OF MEASUREMENT). However, even among research teams fully committed to structured quantitative methods, qualitative methods are often used in the initial stages of an investigation when all aspects of survey design need to be assessed and information gained qualitatively is then used to produce the structured research instrument. See also RESEARCH METHODS.

quality and performance see PATTERN VARIABLES.

quality of working life (QWL) an approach to organizational and work design which advocates the merit of considering the well-being of employees, their participation in work-related decisions, and, relatedly, organizational effectiveness. The term originated in the US in the 1960s, but the underlying theoretical impetus derives from earlier European SOCIOTECHNICAL SYSTEMS writings and experiments, and QWL programmes have occurred in various countries. The QWL movement has been concerned with employee health, safety and job satisfaction, and has been associated with attempts to develop techniques and methods for improving the experience of work. These include JOB REDESIGN, autonomous work groups, and labour-management committees (Huse and Cummings, 1985). Critics of such programmes suggest that managers are the main beneficiaries. Autonomous work groups, it is argued, help to resolve management problems of control which typically arise from a Taylorian approach to work design (see SCIENTIFIC MANAGEMENT), and do so in ways which involve insignificant adjustment to managerial prerogative. Moreover, traditional work design is seen to be less suited to conditions of tight labour markets and turbulent environments. This kind of reasoning underpins some of the more critical assessments of QWL programmes, the popularity of which appears to have waned since the 1970s (Hill, 1981). Such views have to be placed alongside those of theorists and practitioners who suggest that employees also derive considerable benefits from participation in the redesign of work (Mumford, 1980).

quantification the transformation of observations into numerical data to assist analysis and comparison.

quantitative research techniques any research method that results in the data being expressed in numerical form.

There may be some dispute over the inclusion of *ordinal data,* since this describes the situation where categories of observations are assigned numbers because one category can be 'ordered'. Such data is generally considered to be quantitative even though the numbers have no real value or equal distance between them (see CRITERIA AND LEVELS OF MEASUREMENT). There is no dispute over the status of *interval* and *ratio data* within quantitative methods. See also RESEARCH METHODS for a discussion of the pros and cons of quantitative and qualitative research methods.

quasi-experimental method see COMPARATIVE METHOD.

Queer theory an approach to issues of sex and gender which has primarily arisen out of postmodernist thought. Queer theory rehabilitates the pejorative term 'queer' in order to denote nonconformist sexualities (not necessarily homosexualities) which serve to subvert and confront conventional categories of GENDER and SEXUALITY. These sexualities may include transgressive acts such as sadomasochism and the production of PORNOGRAPHY, TRANSVESTISM and gay camp.

In emphasizing the 'performative' aspects of gender and sexuality, Queer theory emphasizes their unnaturalness. From this perspective there are no fundamental identities underlying maleness or femaleness, HOMOSEXUALITY or HETEROSEXUALITY. Emanating from Queer Theory, queer politics seeks to destabilize and collapse existing categories of gender and sexuality. Both Queer theory and Queer politics may be regarded as coming into conflict with FEMINISM generally and lesbian feminism in particular. By emphasizing sexual pleasure as unproblematized they fail to address the role played by sexual politics in the subordination of women. (See S. Wilkinson and C. Kitzinger, 1994.)

questionnaire a form containing questions to be administered to a number of people mainly in order to obtain information and record opinions.

Social scientists use questionnaires to:
(a) examine the general characteristics of a population (e.g. age, sex, occupation, income, etc.);
(b) examine attitudes;
(c) establish the relationship between two variables (e.g. occupation and voting behaviour);
(d) test theories.

A number of problems exist in writing questions for questionnaires. Firstly, in wording the questions, care must be taken to try to ensure that the meaning which each respondent attaches to each question is the same. This means that when the questions are being written this should be done in relation to the target groups under study (see also PILOT STUDY). For example, in undertaking research with children the words used should be kept as simple as possible and long words avoided (e.g. 'job' rather than 'occupation', 'mum' rather than 'mother', etc.). A second problem is that of whether to use *unstructured* (open-ended) or *structured* (closed, or pre-coded) questions (see UNSTRUCTURED DATA and STRUCTURED CODING). The choice of which of these types of questions to use depends on the nature of the research topic and the means of administration. Where a relatively unexplored topic is being examined, open-ended questions might be preferred since the researcher may have little idea as to the range of possible replies. The same is often true where the questionnaire is being administered orally, since this enables the researcher to probe the replies given by respondents. Conversely, where postal or mail questionnaires are being used, precoded questions are generally preferred as this simplifies completion. A third problem concerns the sequence of the questions on the questionnaire. Generally, the questions should follow logically on from one another and they should be arranged in such a way that the order of the questions has as little effect as possible on how respondents answer subsequent questions. For example, when examining people's attitudes towards abortion a general question on whether abortion should be prohibited might be best placed before questions on possible reform of the abortion law. Finally, personal questions about age, sex, occupation and income, and possibly embarrassing questions should be placed at the end of the questionnaire.

Questionnaires can be administered in a number of ways:
(a) orally, by the researcher to the respondents in an interview situation;
(b) self-administered, where, for example, a teacher might give students questionnaires to be completed in the classroom;
(c) mail questionnaires, where they are sent to respondents through the post. The choice of how to administer a questionnaire depends on a number of factors, of which the nature of the research problems, the complexity of the questions, and cost are the most important. Where a relatively unexplored topic is being examined and many of the questions are open-ended, then interviews are preferred, and, conversely, where a large number of people are being researched and the questionnaire has many precoded questions, mail questionnaires are preferred. Finally, it should be mentioned that although postal questionnaires are relatively cheap to administer they suffer from the disadvantage of a high nonresponse rate (see NONRESPONSE).

Quetelet, Adolphe (1796–1874) Belgian scientist and pioneering social statistician and social reformer. Quetelet's approach was distinguished by the collection and analysis of large quantities of data, first to establish statistical regularities, and then to seek the underlying causes of social phenomena. His discovery of persistent regularities (e.g. associated with births and deaths, or crime) led him to expect that a social science could be established which would be on a par with the physical sciences. Thus he coined the term 'social physics' to describe his work. His major influence was on the development of social statistics.

quota sample a population SAMPLE selected by quotas from each defined portion of the population. The method of quota sampling does not fulfil the normal requirements of RANDOM SAMPLING. It involves breaking down the parent populations into strata (see STRATIFIED SAMPLING) according to relevant features (e.g. sex, age, social class, place of residence), and calculating how many individuals to include in each of these categories to reflect the parent population structure. At this stage randomness can be achieved, but once the size of each of these cells (i.e. the number of people of a certain sex, age and class living within a certain location) is decided, no attempt at randomness is made. Instead, the interviewers are instructed to achieve appropriate selections (quotas) to fulfil the requirements within each cell.

This lack of randomness in the selection of respondents means that though the interviewers achieve the correct proportion of the sexes, of age groups, of social class, etc., there is likely to be BIAS introduced on other VARIABLES since each member of the parent population has not had an equal chance of being chosen as a member of the sample (the criterion of randomness). MARKET RESEARCH and opinion polls commonly use this method for its cheapness and speed, but selecting a sample from individuals walking in town centres during daylight hours obviously risks biasing the sample on other variables than those specifically selected for.

r

race a scientifically discredited term previously used to describe biologically distinct groups of persons who were alleged to have characteristics of an unalterable nature. The concept has been used in the English language since the 16th-century. Its meaning has altered several times over the last 400 years in line with changing concepts about the nature of physical and cultural differences and, more importantly, the ideological uses of the concept to justify relationships of superiority and exploitation. Banton in *Racial Theories* (1987) provides a comprehensive account of the different uses of the concept of race.

Social scientists now recognize that 'race' is exclusively a socially constructed categorization which specifies rules for identification of a given group. Many writers will not use the term except in inverted commas to distance the use of the word from its historical and biological connotations. It is preferable to refer to ETHNICITY OR ETHNIC GROUPS. Despite the discredited nature of the concept of 'race', the idea still exerts a powerful influence in everyday language and ideology. See also RACE RELATIONS, RACISM, ETHNICITY, ETHNIC GROUP.

race relations 1 the social relations between ethnic or racial groups.

2 the academic study of these social relations.

In sociology, 'race relations' has focused upon the effects of DISCRIMINATION and RACISM on groups which have been singled out for such treatment, and also on the political struggle against racism. However, the use of the term 'race relations' is controversial on two main grounds. First, some sociologists argue that the term lends credence to the biological conception of race, which has no clear scientific foundation. Secondly, it can be argued that 'race relations' is not a distinctive area of social relations but can only be understood within the wider context of political and ideological processes and social relations in general.

racial discrimination see DISCRIMINATION, RACISM, RACE RELATIONS.

racism *or* **racialism** a set of beliefs, ideologies and social processes that discriminate against others on the basis of their supposed membership of a 'racial' group (see RACE, ETHNICITY). The term has been used in a variety of ways to describe both systems of thought and doctrines which justify the biological superiority of one social group over another, through to descriptions of practices and attitudes which produce racial DISCRIMINATION and disadvantage. The concept of racism is thoroughly reviewed by Robert Miles (*Racism*, 1989).

Writers such as Michael Banton (*The Idea of Race*, 1977) suggest that racism is a doctrine which asserts stable biological differences between groups standing in relationships of superiority and inferiority. Other writers such as John Rex (*Race and Ethnicity*, 1986), Martin Barker (*The New Racism*, 1981) and Robert Miles (op. cit.)

have variously argued that the essence of racism is the belief that there is a relationship between the membership of a socially created category and the possession of specific characteristics. The underlying explanation of these differences may be, for example, cultural, religious or historical, and need not be biological or pseudobiological.

In Europe, varieties of racist ideology have been used to justify colonial exploitation, aggression against nations and oppression of minority groups. Most of these ideologies, according to Banton, shared assumptions that:

(a) variations in the behaviour and constitution of individuals were to be explained as the expression of different underlying biological types of a permanent kind;
(b) differences between these types explained variations in the cultures of human populations;
(c) the distinctive nature of these types explained the superiority of Europeans in general and 'Aryans' in particular;
(d) the friction between nations and individuals of different type arise from these innate characteristics.

Racism played a key part in the rise and dominance of German FASCISM. The German nation as a 'pure RACE' was alleged to require the elimination of the biologically distinct and inferior Jews if it were to survive. This virulent and crude racism led to the death of some six million Jews (see HOLOCAUST).

Miles argues that 'the concept of racism should be used to refer to what can broadly be called an ideology ... racism works by attributing meanings to certain phenotypical and/or genetic characteristics of human beings in such a way as to create a system of categorization, and by attributing additional (negatively evaluated) characteristics to the people sorted into these categories. This process of signification is therefore the basis for the creation of a hierarchy of groups, and for establishing criteria by which to include and exclude groups of people in the process of allocating resources and services.'

Radcliffe-Brown, Alfred (1881–1955) UK structural functionalist anthropologist. His major work is *Structure and Function in Primitive Society,* (1952). With MALINOWSKI he shaped UK anthropology's preference for analysing social structure over culture. Much influenced by COMTE and DURKHEIM, he advocated a version of anthropology he called 'comparative sociology'. His fieldwork was carried out in the Andaman Islands and Australia, and his research made substantial contributions to the study of KINSHIP. Whilst his POSITIVISM and FUNCTIONALISM are now regarded as dated, his influence on a generation of UK anthropologists, teaching at numerous institutions, was immense.

radical deviancy theory see NATIONAL DEVIANCY CONFERENCE.

radicalized modernity a conception of MODERNITY which GIDDENS (1990; 1991) opposes to POSTMODERNITY and POSTMODERNISM by emphasizing thatL
(a) institutional developments rather than epistemological pluralism account for a sense of fragmentation in the late modern world;
(b) tendencies to integration and disintegration are *both* evident in the process of GLOBALIZATION OF CULTURE;
(c) the self is not dissolved or dismembered – rather possibilities for reflexive self-identity are enhanced;
(d) the pressing nature of global problems underpins truth claims;
(e) empowerment and appropriation are features of modern society, not merely powerlessness;
(f) post-modernity might be used to refer to movement beyond the institutions of modernity.

radical monopoly see ILLICH.

radical right see NEW RIGHT.

radical social work a term denoting attempts in the 1970s to achieve a fundamental reorientation of SOCIAL WORK practice ('radical' denotes a concerted attempt to change the *status quo*). The 1970s saw a loose movement known as radical social work, with its roots in an undifferentiated political left. Its main contention was that social problems, including those habitually addressed by social workers, had their roots in structural inequality, principally social CLASS, and not in personal inadequacy as earlier theory seemed to imply.

Key ingredients to radical social work as a method were *conscientizatian* (in Paolo Freire's sense), the *empowerment* of clients, the opening up of social work processes to public and indeed client participation, and attempts to make broad political alliances of 'progressive' forces (community groups, client groups, trade unions and political parties). In general, radical social workers perceived ambiguity in the state apparatus to the point that real gains were held to be achievable for the working classes.

Currently, a radical right (see NEW RIGHT) has emerged in social work, stressing individual, family, and to a lesser extent community responsibility for social problems. This has been associated with policy shifts in government, leading to the closing of large institutions for the mentally ill and handicapped, the growth of a private welfare sector, and the recent emphasis on COMMUNITY CARE in welfare provision. Faced with these changes the tendency has been for the radical left in social work to fragment, focusing on narrower, albeit significant, issues, such as RACISM, SEXISM and other aspects of EQUALITY.

random sample a SAMPLE from a parent population selected by ensuring that each member of that population has an equal chance of being selected. When this is observed the sample should have the same profile of features as the parent population, i.e. it should be a valid representation of it. Data collected by random sampling (assuming the sample is large enough) should reflect the parent population, but methods which are not random (e.g. QUOTA SAMPLING) cannot be relied on to do so. However, it is recognized that samples are not entirely accurate, thus account must be taken of SAMPLING ERROR.

The methods used to achieve random selection may be based on random number tables or, more usually in social surveys, on *systematic sampling*, i.e. selecting individuals, households, etc. according to their position on a list, such as the ELECTORAL REGISTER, when a sample of every name at a fixed interval, say the tenth on the list, is made. See also PROBABILITY.

range see MEASURES OF DISPERSION.

rank a position in a SOCIAL STATUS hierarchy. The familiar military usage reflects the wider use, which predates the language of social class.

ranking the ordering of items by preference, rather than according to an absolute scale. This results in ordinal data (see CRITERIA AND LEVELS OF MEASUREMENT). See also RATING, SCALING, GUTTMAN SCALE.

Rastafarian a BLACK movement, dating from the 1930s in Jamaica, but influential worldwide in the 1970s and 1980s, involving the 'deliverance' of black people to a new, free and sacred homeland in Africa. 'Rastafarian' is derived from Ras Tafari, the name of Haile Selassie I (Emperor of Ethiopia from 1930 to 1975) before he assumed his official title.

Rastafarian beliefs have their origins in the teaching and philosophy of Marcus Garvey (1887–1940) who organized the Universal Negro Improvement Association in the US at the beginning of the 20th century. He believed that integration with whites in the US was impossible and the foundation of a black homeland in Africa was necessary to restore the dignity and culture of black peoples.

Garvey's teachings were influential both in the US and the West Indies. His prophecies about a glorious kingdom and the return to Africa created interest in the crowning of Ras Tafari as the Emperor of Ethiopia. Followers of Garvey in Jamaica, though not Garvey himself, made connections between the prophecy of a black king (taken to be Haile Selassie) and the day of deliverance to a promised land (Ethiopia). They believed that Selassie was a Messiah who would organize the black exodus to Africa and end the domination of Western imperial powers. As such, the Rastafarian movement is often identified by sociologists as CULT-like, involving many of the features of millennial movements (see MILLENARIANISM AND MILLENNIAL MOVEMENTS).

By the middle of the 1970s Rastafarianism had become a potent cultural force in the West Indies and the beliefs became more internationalized, especially in parts of the US, UK and Australia.

Compare NEGRITUDE, BLACK MUSLIMS; see also BLACK POWER MOVEMENT.

rate book a book showing the names of householders, addresses, rateable values and rates payable on properties. Produced by local authorities in the 18th, 19th and 20th centuries, rate books are a valuable source of information on the wealth of individuals and the social structure of towns and cities in the period up to the early 20th century. Their value can be enhanced by using them in concert with the 19th-century CENSUS enumeration books.

rate of profit (MARXISM) the SURPLUS VALUE created in production, divided by the quantity of CONSTANT AND VARIABLE CAPITAL used in production (S/C + V). Since it can be calculated only indirectly in terms of theoretical labour values (see LABOUR THEORY OF VALUE), this means of determining profit differs from the empirical method used in orthodox economics and there are many problems in its interpretation. See also ORGANIC COMPOSITION OF CAPITAL, TENDENCY TO DECLINING RATE OF PROFIT.

rating the order of items by making judgements of absolute value, using a numerical scale. This results in interval data (see CRITERIA AND LEVELS OF MEASUREMENT). See also RANKING, SCALING, LIKERT SCALE.

ratio level measurement see CRITERIA AND LEVELS OF MEASUREMENT.

rational action see TYPES OF SOCIAL ACTION, RATIONALITY, LOGICAL AND NON-LOGICAL ACTION.

rational capitalism WEBER'S IDEAL TYPE of Western CAPITALISM, involving the systematic rational calculation of profit and loss (e.g. accountancy), in contrast with less rational, non-Western, preindustrial forms of capitalism. See also RATIONALITY, PROTESTANT ETHNIC.

rational choice theory a relatively formal approach to sociological and social science theorizing (e.g. drawing upon the THEORY OF GAMES notion of STRATEGIC INTERACTION and ECONOMICS), in which it is maintained that social life is principally capable of explanation as the outcome of the 'rational choices' of individual actors.

'When faced with several courses of action, people usually do what they believe is likely to have the best overall outcome. This deceptively simple sentence summarizes the theory of rational choice' (Elster, 1989). It is a form of theorizing characterized by the use of technically rigorous models of social behaviour, which seek to derive robust conclusions from a relatively small number of initial theoretical assumptions about 'rational behaviour'.

Rational choice theories have been in vogue over the last two decades, prompted by dissatisfaction with macroscopic and structural models in some circles but also by an increased centrality for the rhetoric of individual rational choice in many areas in economic and political life. Despite its often impressive formal architecture, and its undoubted value in illuminating some areas of social reality, two important limitations of rational choice theory can be noted (see Hollis, 1987):

(a) its relative lack of success in overcoming numerous technical difficulties (e.g. a regress in actors' expectations concerning the actions of others), which limit its formal rigour and undermine the direct applicability of its models;

(b) an association with positivist and pragmatist epistemologies, which has limited its attention to analysis of action located in norm-guided, rule-following and rule-changing social behaviour. See also EXCHANGE THEORY.

rationalism 1 a general confidence in the power of knowledge, both general principles and inductive or empirical knowledge, to describe and explain the world and to solve problems. Such a view was characteristic, for example, of the so-called 'age of reason' (see AGE OF ENLIGHTENMENT).

2 (PHILOSOPHY) any epistemological position which emphasizes the A PRIORI basis of knowledge and deductive theories (compare EMPIRICISM).

3 the doctrines associated with 17th- and 18th-century philosophers, including DESCARTES, Spinoza (1632–77), and Leibniz (1646–1716), that, using deductive methods, a unified knowledge can be attained by 'Reason' alone.

4 the epistemological position of KANT, which succeeded **3**, that, while assured knowledge of the real world, the world of 'things-in-themselves' or *noumena,* could not be achieved, it was possible to gain secure knowledge of the *phenomenal* world – the world as known to us. This was possible, according to Kant, given that the phenomenal world was conceptualized and perceived within a fixed frame provided by the human mind, e.g. the fixed *forms* of perception, i.e. 'space' and 'time'.

5 the Hegelian view (see HEGEL), that 'the cunning of reason' not only operates in individual thought, but is a general and a progressive process in history; a rational historical design which is fully revealed only as history unfolds but which is ultimately guaranteed. In what was intended to be a 'demystified form', this conception of 'reason' or 'rationalism' also influenced MARX.

In the 19th century, rationalism in any of these senses often gave way to *irrationalism,* e.g. in NIETZSCHE, a declining confidence in PROGRESS, endangered by world events as well as by sceptical movements in philosophy. However, rationalism in the sense of a belief in progress survives in a modified form in many areas of sociology and philosophy (e.g. see HABERMAS, EVOLUTIONARY THEORY). A further view is that it is a mistake to polarize rationalism and empiricism, since both of these play a role in human knowledge, which always involves both conception ('rationalism') and perception ('empiricism'), e.g. see FEYERABEND. See also RATIONALITY, RATIONALIZATION.

rationality 1 action which is effective in achieving the purposes which it is intended to achieve, i.e. the means are appropriate to the ends. In such a definition of *instrumental rationality,* no attempt need be made to appraise the rationality of the ends themselves. This conception of rationality, in which economic actors are assumed to seek to maximize their own economic returns, is often the basis of theorizing in ECONOMICS, much of this operating by the construction of idealized models (see IDEAL TYPES). For further conceptions of rational action, and questions about these, see FORMAL AND SUBSTANTIVE RATIONALITY, TYPES OF SOCIAL ACTION.

2 knowledge of beliefs which have been established scientifically, or on some other basis considered 'rational'. Such beliefs are implied in **1**, but the 'rationality' of knowledge and beliefs raises wider issues than the instrumental effectiveness of knowledge or beliefs, e.g. extensive philosophical debates (see EPISTEMOLOGY, ONTOLOGY, SCIENCE, RATIONALISM).

Other important debates concern the 'rationality' or otherwise of so-called *primitive mentality.* Lévy-Bruhl (1923) argued that, although MYTHOLOGIES and beliefs in preindustrial, prescientific societies may have a cognitive value, they reflect levels of mentality which are 'pre-logical'. An alternative view is that the myths and beliefs in such societies are 'rational' in the context in which they occur, see WINCH, MAGIC, RELATIVISM.

A rather different point is that many activities which at first sight appear 'irrational', on closer examination may be found to possess 'latent functions' (see LATENT AND MANIFEST FUNCTIONS), e.g. the 'conservatism' of many people in THIRD WORLD SOCIETIES, who may benefit economically, especially in old age, from having more children. In wider terms, 'nonrational beliefs', notably RELIGION, may perform general social functions, e.g. providing social integration (see also FUNCTIONALIST THEORY OF RELIGION). Such beliefs are sometimes regarded as encapsulating an accumulated institutional rationality, perhaps linked to survival. Conversely, actions which appear 'rational' from the narrow perspective of immediate instrumental rationality (e.g. cutting down the Brazilian rain forest) may be seen as 'nonrational', taking a wider view.

What all these considerations show is that the idea of 'rationality' is often difficult to define. While rationality in its simplest sense, 1, can sometimes be established without undue difficulty, only rarely can the means to an end be fully ordered (e.g. in terms of cost, availability, etc.), and actors often lack other salient information, even when this is potentially available (see THEORY OF GAMES, RATIONAL CHOICE THEORY, SATISFICING, BOUNDED RATIONALITY).

rationalization 1 the general tendency within modern capitalist societies for all institutions and most areas of life to be transformed by the application of RATIONALITY. As seen by WEBER, for example, such a process of rationalization is the master process which underlies the transformation of the economic, political and legal institutions of western societies (notably in the spread of BUREAUCRACY and of systematic forms of accountancy and law). Furthermore, the effects of this process are also evident in other sectors of society, e.g. the bureaucratization of science and learning, and developments in music and in religious organization.

Weber had major reservations about the implications of the operation of so seemingly inexorable a process, which he sometimes referred to as creating an 'iron cage' that would increasingly restrict individuality. He recognized that a narrow calculation of 'instrumental rationality' was likely to conflict with 'substantive rationality' i.e. the rationality of outcomes appraised in terms of wider human objectives. At the same time, however, in a world 'disenchanted' by rationality, he did not believe that a 'strictly scientific' basis existed for a generalized conception of human interests or human needs. Human beings possess freedom of action, and must therefore ultimately make their own choices (see also VALUE FREEDOM AND VALUE NEUTRALITY).

Other theorists have taken a more optimistic view of the outcome of the rationalization process. HABERMAS, for example, has suggested that 'human interests' will be identifiable in a context in which a truly democratic critical discourse exists (see also CRITICAL CULTURAL DISCOURSE). In general, however, sociologists have remained more agnostic on such issues (see also FORMAL AND SUBSTANTIVE RATIONALITY).

2 any after-the-act justification of an action which seeks to present this action in a favourable light, as having a coherent rationale, in circumstances where such a 'rational' reconstruction lacks plausibility (compare DEFENCE MECHANISMS).

PARETO regarded many social accounts, including most sociological and political theorizing, as involving rationalization in this general sense, as lacking a truly objective basis (see RESIDUES AND DERIVATIONS). Although emphasizing the importance of distinguishing rationality from nonrationality, Pareto had no illusions that rationality could ever become the guiding principle in social and political life; on the contrary, he is usually seen as a key figure in the pessimism about progress that typified much thinking in POLITICAL SOCIOLOGY at the turn of the 19th-century (see ÉLITE THEORY, NEOMACHIAVELLIANS).

Rawls, John (1921–2002) US social philosopher, whose major work *A Theory of Social Justice* (1971) propounds a 'contractarian' account of Human Rights, based on two principles:
(a) the *equality principle,* equal rights to basic liberties;
(b) the *difference principle,* in which inequalities are only justified if the worst-off fare better than they would in conditions of equal basic liberties. There are similarities with HABERMAS's emphasis on reason and universality.

Like Habermas's, Rawls' theory has generated enormous discussion, It has been suggested that he fails to resolve the problems of giving pre-eminence to civil and political rights over economic and social ones (e.g. see Doyal and Gough, *A Theory of Human Need,* 1991). As Doyal and Gough suggest, however, this critique of Rawls is not the same as assuming that a socialist society would readily resolve such issues. Nor is it to minimize the importance of the progress that has been made in meeting welfare needs in constitutionally governed societies. Seen in this context, Rawls' account is a powerful attempt to address central issues, and dilemmas, about JUSTICE. See also EQUALITY.

real income *or* **real wages** the value of the goods and services that can actually be bought with a given *money income* or given *money wages.* Thus while money wages may rise, real wages – measured in terms of the RETAIL PRICE INDEX – may fall, or vice versa, unless adjustments are constantly made to keep real incomes in line with inflation. The general tendency in Western economies has been on average for real wages to rise ahead of INFLATION, bringing numerous consequences, variously seen as benign or malign. However, the opposite tendency has also sometimes occurred, at least for some groups, with real wages failing to rise with inflation, leading to a real decline in living standards.

realism 1 (PHILOSOPHY) the ONTOLOGICAL assertion that the objects in the world have an existence independently of our conception or perception of them (see also SCIENTIFIC REALISM; compare MATERIALISM). In this form realism is opposed to philosophical NOMINALISM, SCEPTICISM (e.g. HUME), PHENOMENALISM, neutral monism (see MIND), OPERATIONISM, INSTRUMENTALISM, and also KANTIAN philosophy. Central to this notion (that can unite sense 1 and sense 3 below) is that a realistic science aims to describe the nature and especially the 'causal powers' of the things which exist independently of our descriptions of them (see Bhaskar, 1986).
2 (realist forms of idealist philosophy) the assertion of the existence outside time and space of abstract forms or universals which determine objects in the world. This includes the notion that the objects in the world are as we observe them (see IDEALISM).
3 (*sociological realism*) the assertion that social reality, social structures, social currents, etc., have an existence over and above the existence of individual actors (e.g. DURKHEIM's social reality *sui generis,* his conception of 'social facts as things'); compare METHODOLOGICAL INDIVIDUALISM.
4 (LITERARY AND CULTURAL THEORY) literary texts taken as providing a realistic account which, on analysis, can be shown as a 'realistic effect' in which the DISCOURSE 'positions the reader' (C. MacCabe, *Theoretical Essays,* 1985).

real wages see REAL INCOME.

reason the capacity of the human mind to make logical inferences, undertake rational arguments, understand the world, solve problems. What the nature, social determinants and limits of this capacity are, however, is much debated. See RATIONALISM, IDEALISM, EMPIRICISM, ONTOLOGY; see also PRACTICAL REASONING.

rebellion successful or unsuccessful mass uprisings against an existing set of rules, usually distinguished from REVOLUTION in that the system of power and authority is not fundamentally questioned, and also distinguished from COUPS D'ETAT in that the latter involve political 'insiders' rather than mass movements. Rebellions were a characteristic form of dynastic change in preindustrial empires. Glucksmann (1963) also sees these as endemic in traditional African states. Among typical groups involved in rebellions are slaves, peasants, and millenarian sects. The reason why rebellions rarely lead to revolutions is that forms of political organization based on CLASS and genuine structural alternatives in political and economic organization are both usually lacking before the advent of INDUSTRIAL SOCIETIES.

recession a period of lower than average economic growth.

reciprocity any relationship between two parties or things in which there is mutual action, giving and taking. See EXCHANGE, NORM OF RECIPROCITY, GIFT EXCHANGE AND GIFT RELATIONSHIP.

reconstituted family see MARRIAGE.

Redfield, Robert (1897–1958) US social anthropologist, whose studies of Mexican peasant communities led him to formulate influential conceptions of FOLK SOCIETY and the folk-urban continuum (see RURAL-URBAN CONTINUUM). Main works by Redfield are *The Folk Culture of Yucatan* (1941) and *Peasant Society and Culture* (1956).

redistribution the process of levelling of income and personal wealth through TAXATION and welfare benefits.

Debate has centred on the extent to which redistribution actually takes place, even where the expressed intention of government is a measure of levelling. Within the UK, for example, it would appear that the working class is more dependent on welfare benefits than the middle class. However, if all benefits are counted and contributions to National Insurance, income tax and various forms of local and indirect taxation are taken into account, they may contribute as much as, or more than, they receive. The debates are technical and much depends on the variables admitted to the discussion. There are, for example, clear class differences in the consumption of education, health and housing, all of which are in some sense subsidized by the state, and which may be taken into the reckoning.

redistributive chiefdom a type of economy and political system in a relatively complex form of TRIBAL SOCIETY in which the control of a central storehouse for a pool of communal goods is in the hands of a 'big man' or chief. According to some theories, such a form of political system can be seen as the forerunner of state formation proper (see Sahlins, 1972; Harris, 1978). Such redistributive systems allow the centre to accumulate goods and to utilize these for the enhancement of rank, and for the employment of specialist personnel such as priests, soldiers and craftsmen, and for the enhancement of the power and rank of the chief.

reductionism the doctrine that, either in practice or in principle, the propositions of one science can be explained in terms of the propositions of another, e.g. the reduction of chemistry to physics, or the reduction of sociology to psychology.

The contrasting doctrine is that particular sciences may be irreducible to other sciences. For Durkheim, for example, social reality is an 'emergent' reality, a reality *sui generis* irreducible to other sciences such as psychology. Similarly, those sociologists who emphasize human meanings as the basis of social explanations also see this level of analysis as irreducible. In practice, the relationships between the sciences are complex, with no pattern, or view of the pattern, of these relationships being in the ascendancy. Sometimes the subject matter of one science can be illuminated by analogies with, or reduction to, another; at other times attempted reductions of analogies will be misplaced or misleading. See also HIERARCHY OF THE SCIENCES.

reference group the actual (or notional) groups or social categories with which SOCIAL ACTORS identify and make comparisons in guiding their personal behaviour and social ATTITUDES, e.g. the identification of young people with rock stars, or sports people. The term was introduced by the social psychologist Muztafer Sherif in 1948. Reference groups may or may not be synonymous with a social actor's membership groups. Negative as well as positive reference groups may be involved. See also ANTICIPATORY SOCIALIZATION, RELATIVE DEPRIVATION.

reflexive modernization the conception (Beck et al., 1994) that: 'the more societies are modernized, the more agents (subjects) acquire the ability to reflect on the social conditions of their existence and to change them in that way'. Thus one *medium* of reflexive modernization is 'knowledge in its various forms – scientific knowledge, expert knowledge, everyday knowledge'. A further implication of reflexive modernization, however, is 'non-knowledge, inherent dynamism, the unseen and the unwilled' related to a latent disembedding and re-embedding of industrial society in which 'one type of scientization undermines the next'. 'There is growth – of obligations to justify things *and* of uncertainty. The latter conditions the former. The immanent pluralization of risks also calls the rationality of risk calculations into question'. Thus for theorists like Beck 'reflexive modernity' is a mixed blessing. While in some circumstances, burgeoning reflexivity may be 'emancipatory' (compare HABERMAS, GIDDENS) in others, the loss of 'certainty' brings an intensifying sense of rootlessness and increased risk (see also RISK SOCIETY; compare POSTMODERNISM), and a possible negation of industrial society.

reflexivity 1 the capacity possessed by an account or theory when it refers to itself, e.g. the sociology of knowledge, the sociology of sociology.

2 (particularly in ETHNOMETHODOLOGY and SYMBOLIC INTERACTIONISM) the idea that our everyday practical accounts are not only reflexive and self-referring but also socially constitutive of the situations to which they refer. On this view, reflexivity is a capacity possessed by social actors which is decisive in distinguishing human actors from animals.

It is a feature of reflexive social accounts and theories of all types that these accounts may also act to reproduce or to transform those social situations to which they refer.

reformism the label given to political and social policies whose object is to modify a political practice or aspect of social legislation without changing the fundamental political and social structure. For example, in the context of welfare states in capitalist societies, the term is used to refer to social policies which ameliorate social inequalities without challenging the capitalist economic system on which many of those inequalities are based. For example, postwar social security policies in Britain have been seen to ameliorate the hardship of primary POVERTY without fundamentally changing the unequal DISTRIBUTION OF INCOME AND WEALTH.

regionalization of action (GIDDENS, 1984) 'the temporal, spatial or time-space differentiation of regions' within or between different social *locales.* Regionalization is seen by theorists such as Balibar and ALTHUSSER, and Giddens as a counterbalance to the assumption that SOCIETIES always consist of unified social systems.

Registrar General's classification of occupations see OCCUPATIONAL SCALES.

regression *and* **regression analysis** a technique for analysing the relationship between two or more interval level VARIABLES (see CRITERIA AND LEVELS OF MEASUREMENT) in order to predict the value of one from the other, or others. For example, given a regression equation describing the relationship between income and years of education, income can be predicted once the years of education are known.

Multiple linear regression analysis is used when there are several independent interval level variables. For example, a linear equation could be derived which related income to years of education, age and years of job experience.

In many situations the researcher does not

know which, or how many, independent variables will provide a satisfactory model. There is a choice of methods for adding more independent variables to the model. See also CORRELATION, ANALYSIS OF VARIANCE, CAUSAL MODELLING, PATH ANALYSIS.

reification the interpretation of an abstract general concept (e.g. the STATE) as 'real', especially when this is considered to be done illegitimately or misleadingly. Thus METHODOLOGICAL INDIVIDUALISTS may take the view that others, e.g. functionalists, reify general concepts such as 'society' or 'structure.

Use of the term originated within MARXISM to refer to the tendency of many non-Marxists, as well as some Marxists, to attribute a rigid 'thinglike' status to what should more properly be seen as a complex and changing set of social relationships (see CAPITAL, COMMODITY FETISHISM). However, one sociologist's unacceptable reification may be perfectly acceptable to another. If all general concepts are considered abstract but with a potentially 'real' reference, any hard and fast distinction between legitimate and illegitimate reification collapses. Thus there is no standard line in sociology on what constitutes acceptable and unacceptable forms of reification.

relations of production (MARXISM) the economic and social relations established between producers and nonproducers in the course of economic production. These combine with particular MEANS OF PRODUCTION to form a MODE OF PRODUCTION. One of the key distinctions is between capitalist and noncapitalist modes of production (see CAPITALISM AND CAPITALIST MODE OF PRODUCTION, NONCAPITALIST AND PRECAPITALIST MODES OF PRODUCTION). In the former the producers are separated from the ownership of the means of production. In non-capitalist modes, producers such as PEASANTS are likely to own many of the means of production, but are confronted by nonproducers, such as landlords, who extract an ECONOMIC SURPLUS from the producers often via the use of political, military or ideological power.

relative autonomy (of the state) (MARXISM) the conception that STATE forms are not fully determined by the economic base (see RULING CLASS AND DOMINANT CLASS, BONAPARTISM).

relative deprivation the feelings felt and the judgements reached when an individual or members of a group compare themselves – and especially their social situation – adversely with some other individual within their group or with another group, e.g. the less well-off members of an occupational group with the more well-off. The notion is that it is not absolute standards which are important in making such judgements but the relative standards, or frame of reference, in terms of which people make judgements.

As indicated by Stouffer et al. (1949), relative deprivation, somewhat paradoxically, is more often felt when people compare their lot adversely with actual or imaginary others in situations with some similarity but not identical to their own, rather than those who occupy markedly different positions. Feelings of relative deprivation may be strongest in relation to others seen to be in a potentially competitive situation. As suggested by MERTON (1949), the bench mark group or groups with which comparisons are made constitute the REFERENCE GROUP(S) of the individuals or groups experiencing feelings and making judgements of relative deprivation. Thus, Runciman, in *Relative Deprivation and Social Justice* (1966), was able to demonstrate that political opinions and the meanings attached to class membership – (see SUBJECTIVE AND OBJECTIVE CLASS) were a function of reference groups and the associated feelings, possibly of relative deprivation. The pronounced attitudinal changes that can be brought about by change in the relative positions of social groups have been shown to be a potent source of political upheaval and revolutionary change (see Urry, 1973).

relative mobility see SOCIAL MOBILITY.

relative surplus value see SURPLUS VALUE.

relativism

An emphasis on the variety and differences of cultures, bodies of knowledge, conceptual schemes, theories, values, etc. The term covers a variety of sociological and philosophical positions, ranging from 'weak' to 'strong' forms.

At the weak end, the recognition of variety and difference appears to be little more than sociological common sense. However, strong versions of relativism, which can have powerful support, are the subject of much controversy.

For example, to claim 'strongly', that 'morals are relative' – *moral relativism* – is to claim that what is right is solely a local matter, to be judged so only within particular communities at particular times. This rules out attempts to judge between different moral schemes. Thus there would be no general basis for rejecting Nazi policies towards non-German racial groups.

Similarly, strong *cognitive relativism* suggests that SCIENCE and other ways of knowing, e.g. MAGIC, are simply different, involving truth claims from different standpoints, so that there are no overarching rules or procedures for deciding between such different belief systems. There may be no scientific grounds for saying 'X is a witch', but there can be entirely adequate grounds within witchcraft, or witchhunting, for saying that 'X is a witch', so that within such practices this is 'true without rational ground for privileging scientific truth'.

In contemporary sociology, some ETHNOMETHODOLOGISTS have argued that the meaning(s) of any categorization are essentially local achievements, unconstrained by any general definition, where any use does not bind future use.

To extreme critical relativists it is customary to reply: 'your theory that all theories are relative is self-defeating'. Enthusiastic relativists, however, embrace this response, suggesting that we must take responsibility for our decisions and choices, our own 'closures'. In this 'rationality' tends to fade into rhetoric, which relativists always assumed was so. See also TRUTH, OBJECTIVITY, PARADIGM, FORM(S) OF LIFE, SAPIR-WHORF HYPOTHESIS, WITTGENSTEIN, FEYERABEND, VALUE RELEVANCE.

reliability the dependability of data collected, or of the test or measurement used to collect it. A reliable measure is one which gives the same results if the same individuals are measured on more than one occasion.

Reliability describes consistency and this is commonly calculated by a CORRELATION COEFFICIENT. This may be done when social survey data is collected from two samples taken from the same population at the same time, or when the same test is completed by the same people on two different occasions (*test-retest reliability*), or when two different forms of a test are used (*alternate form reliability*), or when the similarity between the two halves of a test is calculated (*split-half reliability*).

Compare VALIDITY.

religion 1 the 'belief in spiritual beings' (Tylor, 1871) and the institutions and practices associated with these beliefs. **2** 'a unified system of beliefs and practices relative to sacred things', things set apart and held in awe, which unites the believers into a moral community or church (DURKHEIM, 1912) (see also SACRED AND PROFANE). On this definition, in terms of social FUNCTIONS, there is no ultimate distinction between religions which involve beliefs in spiritual beings or other supernatural phenomena and many other kinds of socially unifying ideas such as nationalism. The latter can be seen as FUNCTIONAL ALTERNATIVES OR FUNCTIONAL EQUIVALENTS of religion in the more conventional sense. Furthermore, even some beliefs and practices conventionally thought of as religions, such as CONFUCIANISM OR BUDDHISM, do not readily correspond to narrower standard dictionary definitions of religion which emphasize the worship of gods and spirits. Nor is a distinction between the supernatural and the empirical easy to draw uncontentiously. See also FUNCTIONALIST THEORY OF RELIGION. **3** any set of doctrines – 'theories in a hurry', according to GELLNER – providing overall answers to ultimate and existential questions for which there are no empirical answers. In comparison with definition **2**, this definition leaves open for empirical analysis the particular social effects or social functions of religion.

The virtue of either definition **2** or **3** above is that neither depends on contentious distinctions between the natural and the supernatural which may not be shared by religious believers. The problem with either of the definitions however is that they no longer provide any effective distinction between traditional forms of religious phenomena and other forms of belief systems or other forms of ritual behaviour, making it difficult, for example, to conceptualize phenomena such as SECULARIZATION. Under these circumstances, some sociologists have continued to operate with definitions which remain closer to definition **1**, despite the difficulties associated with it. See also SOCIOLOGY OF RELIGION, NEW RELIGIOUS MOVEMENTS, RITUAL.

Renaissance the revival of art, literature and learning in Western Europe in the 14th and 15th centuries which accompanied the rediscovery of the thought and work of the Ancients, e.g. the works of PLATO and ARISTOTLE. Typically, this has been seen not only as the rediscovery of the thought and work of the ancients, but as a rebirth of the human spirit, the birth of modern humanism.

rent see ECONOMIC RENT.

repertory grid technique see PERSONAL CONSTRUCT THEORY.

replication the collection of data under the same conditions as a previous study. This is often done to test the VALIDITY of the conclusions drawn, since faults in design or analysis may thereby be discovered.

representative sample a SAMPLE which is (or is assumed to be) a true reflection of the parent population, i.e. has the same profile of attributes, e.g. age structure, class structure, educational background. A representative sample is achieved by ensuring that its selection is entirely random (see RANDOM SAMPLE). It is essential that a sample is representative in order that the conclusions drawn from its study can be accepted as valid information about the parent population. See also SAMPLING ERROR, SAMPLING FRAME, PROBABILITY.

repressive state apparatus see IDEOLOGICAL STATE APPARATUS AND REPRESSIVE STATE APPARATUS.

reproduction see SOCIAL REPRODUCTION.

reproduction (of capital) see ACCUMULATION (OR EXPANDED OR EXTENDED REPRODUCTION) OF CAPITAL.

reproductive technologies various technologies applied to pregnancy and childbirth. These fall into three main categories: *managerial technology*, which includes the medical management of pre-pregnancy, pregnancy and birth; *contraceptive technology*, which ranges from the non-interventionist diaphragm or condom to hormone suppressants, intra-uterine devices, and sterilization; and *conceptive technologies,* which include artificial insemination, surrogacy, fertility drugs, embryo donation and storage, and *in vitro* fertilization. Feminists and medical sociologists have become increasingly interested in reproductive technologies on moral, medical and political grounds. At one extreme, Firestone (*The Dialectic of Sex*, 1971) has argued that the development of reproductive technologies are likely to liberate women from biological restrictions, whereas Mies and Shiva (*Ecofeminism*, 1993) condemn reproductive technology as sexist and racist exploitation. The latter argument views invasive technology as furthering a masculinist conception of science which shows little concern for 'nature' or for the choices of individuals, particularly women. Recent debates over ABORTION and the development of men's rights and foetal rights have, it is argued, further eroded the freedom of women to control their own bodies.

research methods

The investigative techniques employed within an academic discipline. In sociology, the range of methods is very wide, including many research methods also employed in other disciplines. For example, sociologists have used the critical techniques of the humanities in order to 'interrogate' TEXTS, paintings, buildings, etc., ethnographic techniques borrowed from ANTHROPOLOGY and applied to modern societies (see also ETHNOGRAPHY), and historical methods to understand the genesis of social forms.

Some of the most powerful techniques employed by sociologists are those the discipline shares with central and local government agencies, social survey methods based on SAMPLING, but the popular image of sociology as exclusively based on such methods is plainly erroneous. Among the array of further quantitative and qualitative research methods widely used in sociology are: PARTICIPANT OBSERVATION and other forms of 'direct observation', in-depth INTERVIEWS, ATTITUDE SCALING, CONTENT ANALYSIS, 'documentary analysis', SECONDARY DATA ANALYSIS (including reanalysis of OFFICIAL STATISTICS).

In a particular study, the methods chosen will depend upon a variety of considerations, including the following:

(a) the nature of the problem addressed (e.g. while a study of the incidence of ill-health among the elderly might be effective using questionnaires or medical records, study of deviant behaviour is likely to require participant observation);

(b) the theoretical stance and the preferred methods of the researcher or research team (e.g. symbolic interactionists are likely to prefer direct observation, less likely to operate with standardized variables);

(c) the time and money available (e.g. postal questionnaires are cheaper than face-to-face interviews; secondary data analysis cheaper than conducting new surveys);

(d) the type of research and evidence likely to carry conviction with the sponsors of the research and the audience for the research (e.g. the sponsors of research have often been regarded as preferring research which uses quantitative rather than qualitative data).

Of these, (b) is often most important, also influencing the kind of research problem which is chosen. Thus (a) and (b) are often closely interrelated. However, (c) and (d) operate as strong constraints on the choice of research methods.

Debates on the merits of quantitative and qualitative approaches can be fierce. Some researchers committed to quantitative survey methods refuse to acknowledge the strengths and validity of other methods, while others, whose preference is for direct observation, refuse to countenance quantitative techniques. However, a simple polarization of the two sets of techniques is unjustified. Denzin (1970) has suggested that, whenever possible, social research should seek to 'triangulate' different research methods (see TRIANGULATION OF APPROACHES). See also STATISTICS AND STATISTICAL ANALYSIS, METHODOLOGY, MATHEMATICAL SOCIOLOGY.

reserve army of labour unemployed workers, their number continuously renewed within capitalism, who by competing for jobs help to depress wages. In Marxism, the existence of this group is held to tend to force wages down to subsistence levels. Marxists, however, acknowledge that, in practice, a tendency to *immiseration* from this source is offset by a number of counteracting tendencies, including trade union action, which have increased the 'historical and moral' element in the value of labour power. Nevertheless, that unemployment remains a factor in the bargaining power possessed by labour, is seen in the correlation that exists between periods of full employment and wage increases and wage inflation.

residues and derivations a distinction drawn by PARETO, as part of his discussion of 'nonlogical' (or irrational) forms of action, in which *residues* are the uniform psychological bases underlying social action, and *derivations* the rationalizations or 'theories' which are advanced by social participants as justifications of their social actions. As Pareto saw it, many sociological theories are themselves derivations. He regarded his own theories, in replacing these, as establishing sociology on a new scientific footing (see Fig. 26).

Six main categories of residues were identified by Pareto, but only two of these: *the instinct for combinations* ('class I residues') and *the persistence of aggregates* ('class II residues'), are critical to an understanding of his approach. These play a central part in his theory of élites (see CIRCULATION OF ÉLITES).

resistance through ritual any ritualized styles of working-class youth culture and leisure behaviour – e.g. teddy boys – which can be interpreted as aimed at resistance to structural and cultural changes. The phrase gained currency after its use as the title of a collection of articles written by researchers at the CENTRE FOR CONTEMPORARY CULTURAL STUDIES in the mid-1970s. The title is indicative of the approach to the study of SUBCULTURES adopted by the CCCS and has been influential subsequently in studies of youth cultures, education, and deviance.

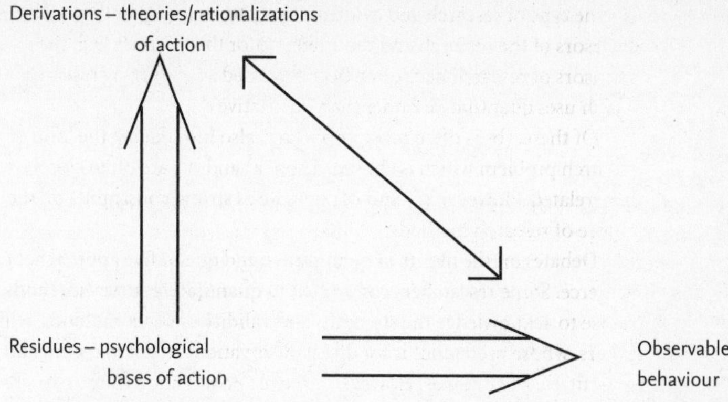

Fig. 26 **Residues and derivations.** As formulated by Pareto, the main causal origins of social action are located in the underlying psychological bases of this action. These bases explain both the action involved and the theories of this action advanced by social actors. Thus, these theories are seen by Pareto as 'derivations' from the underlying psychological bases. 'Residues' are the universal elements in social action left over once the more ephemeral derivations have been abstracted. For Pareto, they are the true basis of sociological explanations on which scientific sociological theory should be based. In comparison with the influence exerted by residues on derivations and on actions, the causal influence of derivations on action, or vice versa, is much more limited.

Youth subcultures such as MODS AND ROCKERS and punks, have been studied in this way (M. Brake, 1985). These youth subcultures arise at times of social upheaval – the collapse of community, whether associated with relative affluence or unemployment – and are thought to reflect 'negotiated responses' to these circumstances. In this process the products of mass culture are not simply accepted but richly interpreted, so as to express subcultural concerns.

respondent *or* **informant** any person replying to a social survey QUESTIONNAIRE or who answers questions in a social science INTERVIEW.

response cries those utterances, e.g. 'Oops', which are not obviously 'talk', in the sense of possessing a conscious communicative intent (GOFFMAN, 1981). Although apparently trivial and spontaneous in character, and often not deliberately aimed at communication, they nevertheless communicate a recognition by the SOCIAL ACTOR that he or she has transgressed the normal expectations of control over the body, that this lack of control was a mere accident, etc. As such, an analysis of response cries emphasizes the socially organized character of behaviour which at first sight may appear nonsocial.

response rate the proportion of individuals invited to participate in a study who actually do participate. In social surveys using SAMPLING the response rate is unlikely to be 100%; 90% or over would be considered very good, and over 70% is normally acceptable. The method of collecting data inevitably affects the response rate. Postal questionnaires generally have a low one, while personal INTERVIEWS achieve a higher rate. Reasons for NONRESPONSE include death, house removal, unwillingness to cooperate, not being available when the interviewer calls, etc. Because of this almost inevitable failure to achieve the selected sample, systematic error or BIAS is introduced and an assessment of the

VALIDITY of extrapolating from the sample to the parent population has to be made. There are various statistical techniques used to strengthen the level of confidence that is put on sample data.

restricted code see CODE and ELABORATED AND RESTRICTED CODES.

Retail Price Index (RPI) an index which measures the monthly change in the retail prices of a collection (basket) of typical goods and services bought by private households. It has been constructed since 1947. See also INDEX NUMBER, STANDARD OF LIVING.

revenge a retaliatory or retributive social act. For French thinker Rene GIRARD the concept of revenge is central to the problem of violence. Focusing on the idea of the blood feud, he shows how the mechanics of vengeance are contained within the effects of MIMETIC DESIRE. After one actor commits a violent act, mimetic desire ensures that the second actor's response reflects the severity of the original action. As such, violence becomes a self-sustaining effect; a vicious circle Girard calls the *skandalon* or Satan. Girard's analysis of biblical scripture illustrates this critique of revenge. He argues against the vengeful Old Testament deity, Yahweh, and the advice of 'an eye for an eye' and for the New Testament God of peace and forgiveness. For Girard, the importance of the New Testament God lay in the sacrificial offering of Christ. He argues that Christ represents the absolute scapegoat, the figure whose purity reminds the world of the evil nature of circular violence and revenge. See also ORDER/DIS-ORDER

reverse discrimination see positive DISCRIMINATION.

revisionism any attempts by socialist thinkers to reappraise and revise the revolutionary ideas of MARX in the light of changed economic and social conditions. The most famous of all revisionists was the German Social Democrat Eduard BERNSTEIN. In the late 1890s he argued that most of Marx's economic theory and predictions for the future had been disproved by new developments in the capitalist system. As a result: 'Peasants do not sink; the middle class does not disappear; crises do not grow even larger; misery and serfdom do not increase'. Bernstein concluded that 'the final aim' of the labour movement was unimportant. What was really crucial were the day-to-day battles to win improvements for workers living under capitalism. Socialism could only be achieved through a process of gradual and peaceful evolution entailing parliamentary reforms rather than violent working-class revolution. In the 1960s, there was an upsurge of revisionist ideas in many Western European Communist parties (see also EUROCOMMUNISM).

revolution 1 (political and social) 'the seizure of STATE power through violent means by the leaders of a mass movement where that power is subsequently used to initiate major processes of social reform' GIDDENS, 1989). This distinguishes revolutions from COUPS D'ÉTAT, which involve the use of force to seize power but without transforming the class structure and political system, and without mass support. The 20th century has seen revolutions occurring not in industrial societies but in rural peasant societies like Russia (1917), China (1949) and North Vietnam (1954). Various theories exist to try to explain revolutionary change, of which the most influential have been Marxist. An example of the application of MARXISM in an actual revolutionary situation is provided by LENIN in the context of Russia. He argues that a revolutionary situation is created when three elements come into play: when the masses can no longer live in the old way, the ruling classes can no longer rule in the old way, and when the suffering and poverty of the exploited and oppressed class has grown more acute than is usual. But the revolution will only be successful when the most crucial condition is fulfilled: the existence of a VANGUARD PARTY with the necessary Marxist programme, strategy, tactics and organizational discipline to guarantee victory. In her comparative study of revolutions Skocpol (1979) criticizes Marxist theories of revolution and argues for a state-centred approach. Specifically, she views international pressures such as wars or upper-class resistance to state reform as key factors leading to the breakdown of the administrative and military apparatus which in turn paves the way for revolution. See also MOORE, REVOLUTION FROM ABOVE.

2 (social) any major change in key aspects of a society which leads to a change in the nature of that society. This may refer to economic transformation, as in the INDUSTRIAL REVOLUTION, to changes in individual behaviour, as in the concept of a modern 'revolution in sexual behaviour', or to a revolution in knowledge, as in the 'scientific revolution' in 17th-century Europe, which laid the basis for all later developments in modern SCIENCE. Usage in this second sense tends to be highly variable, and may refer to comparatively long periods of time.

Originally, in the 17th century the concept of revolution referred to the process 'of passing through the stages of a cycle that ultimately lead back to a condition that is identical or similar to some antecedent one'. Today such CYCLES OR CYCLICAL PHENOMENA are not usually referred to as 'revolutions'.

One important issue in the study of revolutions (in sense **1** or **2**) is whether they form part of a more overarching 'evolutionary' or 'developmental' sequence in human affairs (see EVOLUTIONARY THEORY, EVOLUTIONARY SOCIOLOGY) or should receive only a more EPISODIC CHARACTERIZATION.

revolution from above a revolutionary transformation of society initiated and carried through by the existing rulers of society who maintain their dominant position in the post-revolutionary society. A debated example is that of Japan in 1868, when the Meiji Restoration was led by sections of the feudal ruling class who introduced radical changes in Japan's political and economic structure, leading to a process of capitalist industrialization and radical changes in state structure. The term is used by Barrington MOORE, to contrast such revolutions with the more classical conception of *revolution from below*, in which a previously dominant class is overthrown by a rising class or classes. See also REVOLUTION.

Rex, John (1925–) South-African born social theorist and social researcher (especially on race), who for an important part of his career was the Director of the Social Science Research Council (later ESRC) research unit on ethnic relations based first at Aston University and more latterly at the University of Warwick. His contributions to British sociology have been wide-ranging. In his first and influential book, *Key Problems of Sociological Theory* (1961), he offered a synthesis of classical approaches in sociology which emphasized the role of conflict alongside values and norms in human societies (see also CONFLICT THEORY). He continued to stress the importance of a broad approach to theory in sociology and became impatient when the revival of theory in British sociology which he had urged, and in which his own work had been greatly instrumental, led in his view to too great a willingness to jettison classical ideas and to follow current fashions, and also to a onesided emphasis on MARX. In the study of race his work has been consistently innovative, as well as radical, and has mixed theory with empirical research in a way that is comparatively rare in British sociology, introducing in particular the idea of HOUSING CLASSES. Examples of these studies are *Race, Community and Conflict* (1967), and *Colonial Immigrants in a British City* (1979) (with Sally Tomlinson). Other works by John Rex include *Sociology and the Demystification of the World* (1974), *Race, Colonialism and the City* (1970), and the influential collection of invited essays *Discovering Sociology* 1973).

rhizome a concept developed by Gilles DELEUZE and Félix GUATTARI in *Rhizome: an Introduction* (1976). At its simplest, the rhizome indicates a means of thinking other than in conventional, '*arborescent*' ways. Those latter forms are seen to have dominated Western thought, imposing on 'vertically inclined' structures which introduce hierarchies and specific, static 'placings'. In contrast, *rhizomic* approaches attempt to proceed in other directions, that is, outwards and horizontally avoiding regulation.

Rickert, Heinrich (1863–1936) German NEO-KANTIAN social philosopher, whose ideas influenced WEBER. His major works include *Science and History* (1899), and *The Limits of Natural Scientific Conceptualization* (1902). He argued that DILTHEY and WINDELBAND's separation of cultural and natural sciences made polar opposites out of a continuum. Like Windelband, Rickert argued that sociological and cultural studies could employ both IDIOGRAPHIC AND NOMOTHETIC methods. The complexity of social phenomena meant that all forms of knowledge involved simplification, i.e. relied on generalization or on accounts of phenomena in the light of their relevance for value. He accepted that at base all sociological knowledge was historical, but argued that it was possible to achieve greater objectivity than suggested by Dilthey. His proposal was a science of culture which sought to lay bare its essential components: 'constellations of meaning and value'. Rickert can be seen as the least subjectivist of the neo-Kantian school.

Riesman David (1909–2002) US sociologist and journalist whose work, especially *The Lonely Crowd* (written in 1950 with N. Glazer and R. Denney), was in vogue in the 1950s and early 60s. The hypothesis of the study was that the basic character type within US society was changing from an *inner-directed* to an *other-directed* type (see OTHER-DIRECTEDNESS), in which character is increasingly formed by the example of peers and contemporaries rather than as previously by 'internalized adult authority'. The work raised themes about modern society taken up subsequently by many theorists.

riot 1 (in English law) the use of unlawful violence on the part of at least twelve persons, in a way which would make 'a person of reasonable firmness' afraid for his or her safety.

2 (in sociology) large-scale public disorder involving violence to property and violent confrontation with the police.

Many sociological studies have been published in Britain in recent years, following urban unrest in St. Paul's, Bristol in 1980 and in many other towns and cities in the spring and summer of 1981 and autumn of 1985. No one cause has been accepted as the key to understanding why the unrest occurred, but a number of issues have been singled out as important. One of these is the term 'riot' itself. Many commentators have argued that the term is so loaded, morally and politically – involving only the viewpoint of the authorities – that it is specifically useless. Thus many have preferred to use more neutral phrases, like 'urban unrest', 'popular protest' and 'public disorder'.

The first type of explanation of riots tends to be of conspiracy, or the influence of outside agitators. So, in the Brixton and other disorders of 1981, political agitators were blamed; in the case of Handsworth in 1985, the police argued that the disorders were organized by drug dealers in order to protect their profits. These types of explanation have a history as long as the history of popular protest. Social historians have given accounts of magistrates and police responses to riots in the 18th and 19th centuries which bear an uncanny resemblance to official and media views of those in the 1980s. Sociologically, these explanations are interesting as ideological constructions. They are rarely proven, but usually serve to deflect attention from underlying social problems and tend to absolve the authorities from any responsibility for the occurrences.

Turning to sociological and related explanations of riots in Britain (except for policing strategies, Northern Ireland must be seen as a separate case), there have been a number of influences on theorizing of which perhaps the most important have been social historians' accounts of British riots in previous centuries and US sociologists' explanations of unrest in US cities in the 1960s. Most explanations have also involved some kind of dialogue with the Scarman Report (1981). Scarman's main arguments about the causes of the 1981 unrest concerned material conditions in the areas involved: unemployment, housing, work and other opportunities, together with heavy-handed and confrontational policing, exemplified in a 'stop and search' operation, 'Operation Swamp '81', which immediately preceded the unrest. His arguments are in line with sociological work on a number of counts, particularly in his rejection of conspiratorial ideas and emphasis on the reality of the problems faced by the 'rioters'. A number of strands have been variously emphasized by sociological researchers. These can be listed under four main headings:
(a) material conditions – all the major outbreaks of disorder occurred in localities with much higher rates of DEPRIVATION than average;
(b) POLICING – in virtually every case the first target of unrest was the police. Often disorders followed a specific police operation (e.g. in Bristol 1980, Brixton 1981, and Handsworth 1985) or were associated with high levels of policing. This situation was further complicated by;
(c) RACE – initially several police representatives and politicians gave racist accounts, making arguments about alien cultures, etc. Sociologists have tended to emphasize the importance of the ethnic dimension in different terms. It has long been argued that black people have been subjected to a process of *criminalization* (see Hall et al., 1978), and that institutionalized RACISM is a persistent and inflammatory problem (Policy Studies Institute, 1983). See also ETHNICITY;
(d) marginalization and ALIENATION – in some respects the existence of these is seen as particularly relevant to black British people, but their implication is wider (see Lea and Young, 1983; Hall, in Benyon and Solomos, 1987). The basic argument is that where people are effectively excluded from processes of political and cultural representation, where effective channels for expressing grievances are closed to them and they perceive a general indifference and even hostility to their situation, they may engage in violent unrest as the only means of expressing their anger and making their situation known, even when this may be likely to prove counter-productive. See also MARGINALITY.

All sociological explanations reject the view that unrest is simply 'irrational' or inspired by criminal or political conspirators. They also tend to play down arguments about the 'copycat effect', which would reduce explanations to the role of the MASS MEDIA in publicizing and amplifying riots (see AMPLIFICATION OF DEVIANCE). They emphasize that there are identifiable causes, found in the living conditions of the people involved, and understandable in rational terms as responses to those conditions. Compare COLLECTIVE BEHAVIOUR.

risk society a conception of the condition of modern society which asserts that we are today everywhere faced by 'manufactured uncertainty' (nuclear war, risk of science-induced ecological disaster) that has been created by the growth of human knowledge and its worldwide impact (BECK, 1992; Beck et al., 1994). See also REFLEXIVE MODERNIZATION, TRUST.

rite of passage *or* ***rite de passage*** the ceremony and RITUAL which may accompany the changes of STATUS that occur in the course of the life cycle, e.g. the MARRIAGE ceremony, or in present-day Britain, 18th-birthday parties. Such ceremonies are a way of drawing attention to changes in status and social identity; they are also a way of managing the tensions such changes may involve, e.g. the amalgamation of two families. An alternative term for such ritual is *status passage.* See also LIMINALITY, RITUAL.

ritual

1 any formal action which is set apart from profane action and which expresses sacred and religious meaning (see DURKHEIM; DOUGLAS). This usage of the term occurs in both anthropology and the sociology of religion.
2 'bodily action in relation to symbols' (Bocock, 1974).
3 any everyday practice which is characterized by its routine nature and by its significance to mundane social interaction. The term has been used by GOFFMAN (1972) to denote the routine practices of everyday life.

Ritual action may therefore be regarded as occurring in both the SACRED AND PROFANE domains of social life. In both cases it is the symbolic quality of the action which is its defining characteristic.

A distinction can be made between ritual or ritualistic behaviour and ritual action. *Ritual behaviour* is behaviour which is devoid of meaning, rigid and stereotypical. Ethologists may use the term to denote the routine and repetitive behaviours of animals during courtship and defence of territory. By contrast, *ritual action* is imbued with shared social meanings which are culturally transmitted through custom and tradition. *Ritual occasions* may be regarded as social situations which are separate and ceremonial. They are not necessarily characterized by rigidity and repetition, although these might be a feature of many rituals. Rituals may function as a conservative and cohesive force within a society, but they may also be the means for demonstrating social, political and cultural resistance (see Hall and Jefferson, 1976) – see RESISTANCE THROUGH RITUAL.

Whilst it has been common to study ritual action from perspectives within the SOCIOLOGY OF RELIGION, it is possible to suggest that ritual action is present in secular society. Bocock has argued that 'the category of ritual action is not well established within sociology', but he suggests that the term can be usefully employed to cover civic, aesthetic and political aspects of social life as well as rituals associated with the life-cycle. SECULARIZATION does not necessarily lead to a decline in ritual action. Such action may be present in the performing arts (e.g. mime and dance) and civic ceremonies (e.g. state funerals and graduation ceremonies) – see also CIVIC RELIGION.

Life-cycle rituals (see RITE OF PASSAGE) continue to have significance in both simple and complex societies. The growth and decay of the human body is a feature of all human societies and consequently necessitates social control and management. Life-cycle rituals are key areas enabling biological change to be made socially meaningful and significant. Life-

cycle rituals can be used both to integrate a newly born child into the group and to affirm the continued existence of a group in the event of the death of one of its members. Van Gennep (1909) suggested that rites of passage mark both biological changes and changes in social position. Rites of passage may be seen as characterized by a common structure involving:
(a) separation of the individual from the old order or previous social condition;
(b) a marginal or transitional phase which is highly sacred;
(c) a final stage which incorporates the individual into the new social order or status.

Ritual action may be seen to be present in all areas of social life and is one of the key means whereby both individuals and groups resolve problems encountered in both the sacred and profane aspects of social existence.

Rogers, Carl (1902–87) PHENOMENOLOGICAL psychologist within the HUMANISTIC MOVEMENT, best known for the development of client-centred or PERSON-CENTRED COUNSELLING (*Client-Centred Therapy*, 1951). His influence has been so extensive in the area of personal counselling that the methodology is often termed 'Rogerian'.

Central to Rogers' theory of personality, and to the humanistic movement generally, is the emphasis on a tendency towards 'personal growth'. He regards this as an 'innate organismic tendency', but problems in this developmental process may occur due to environmental constraints. Particularly, the person has a need for 'unconditional positive regard' from others if he or she is to develop positive self-regard. Parents particularly have a responsibility to provide unconditional positive regard and not to impose unrealistic 'conditions of worth'. If the person has undergone damaging experiences and lost, or not developed, a sense of self-worth then counselling/therapymay be necessary to generate it.

Phenomenological psychology sees the person as unique, with a unique personal perception of the world. Client-centred therapy therefore aims to facilitate the client in understanding their situation by allowing him/her to talk, and by reflecting back the content of this without further analysis or direction. This is done in a setting of empathy, genuine warmth and unconditional positive regard, the intention being to enhance positive self-regard and reduce the limiting conditions of worth. This technique has been developed in work with neurotics and it is within this group, particularly those who are verbal and highly motivated to get well, that it is most successful.

Rogers did not limit himself to individual psychotherapeutic counselling, but, as a humanistic psychologist, was concerned to assist everyone towards 'self-actualization'. He was active in developing group techniques (*Encounter Groups*, 1970) and also in applying his ideas within education (*Freedom to Learn*, 1969).

role 1 any relatively standardized social position, involving specific rights and obligations which an individual is expected or encouraged to perform, e.g. parental role. 2 'the dynamic aspect of STATUS', where 'status' refers to the position and 'role' to its performance (R. Linton, 1936); it is more usual, however, for the term 'role' to apply to both position and performance, with 'status' also being used as an alternative term for position. Roles may be *specific* or *diffuse*, *ascribed* or *achieved* – see PATTERN VARIABLES. In SYMBOLIC INTERACTIONISM the term 'role' is used differently. In this perspective social identities and social action are analysed as the outcome of 'taking the role of the other', rather than from adopting ready-made roles. *Role-playing*, a form of social training where people take part in group exercises in which they act out a range of social roles, has a similar basis. The expectation is that acting out social roles, including those with which one initially lacks sympathy, will bring greater social understanding.

In FUNCTIONALISM, the theory of role stresses the normative expectations attached to particular positions and the way in which roles are associated with INSTITUTIONS. The emphasis is on the acquisition and enacting of behaviour patterns determined by NORMS and rules. MERTON (1949) suggested the further notion of *role-set*, to refer to the range of role relationships associated with a given status. It is recognized that the individual is likely to encounter tensions (*role conflict*) in coping with the requirements of incompatible roles, e.g. the roles of worker and mother, or lecturer and researcher. The functional theory of role has been criticized, however, for sometimes implying a static, unchanging conception of social action.

The earlier, symbolic interactionist approach to 'role', associated with G. H. MEAD, contrasts with that of functionalism, in that for Mead 'role-taking' is mainly of interest as an essential process in the development of the SELF. Both adults and children establish conceptions of self by imagining themselves in others' positions (see also LOOKING-GLASS SELF), but there is no conception of fixed roles in the way central to functionalism, and the continually 'renegotiated' character of social action is emphasized.

The writings of GOFFMAN provided other examples of role analysis, e.g. the concept of ROLE DISTANCE, where the performer of a role adopts a subjective detachment from the role.

role conflict see ROLE.

role distance the subjective detachment displayed by a SOCIAL ACTOR while playing a ROLE, e.g. a waiter who may indicate to a customer that he is not *only* a waiter.

role-playing see ROLE.

role reversal any situation in which people exchange roles so that one plays the role of the other, e.g. master and servant, adult and child, male and female roles. In any societies institutionalized provision exists (e.g. Roman *saturnalia* – periods of feasting and social laxity) for such reversals to occur, seen as having the function of releasing the social tensions created by the constraints of ROLE. In present-day British society, office parties have been suggested as haying a similar function. See also CARNIVAL.

role-set see ROLE.

role theory any approaches in sociology that emphasize the importance of roles and 'role-taking' in shaping and maintaining social order and social organization. See ROLE.

Roman Catholicism the version of CHRISTIANITY held by the largest Christian denomination, the Roman Catholic Church. The RC Church claims universality and stresses the importance of unity with the Pope, the Bishop of Rome, as the successor of the apostle St. Peter. The RC Church broke with the Eastern (Orthodox) Church in the 11th-century, and there were further divisions in Western Christianity at the time of the Protestant Reformation (see PROTESTANTISM). The RC Church has always had a powerful political role and has exerted influence on both the formation of states and the shape of social and political institutions within them. It continues to play a major role internationally. It is difficult, however, to characterize the political nature of its current doctrine. Its stance on abortion and contraception, for example, has left it open to allegations that it is illiberal. On other issues, however, such as defence of human rights, for example in South Africa, Eastern Europe or Latin America, it is clearly progressive. Its internal structure remains authoritarian and hierarchical, but recent years have seen the laicization of its functions, revision of its central liturgies and more open relationships with other Churches. See also CHURCH, RELIGION, SOCIOLOGY OF RELIGION.

Roman law the code of LAW developed in ancient Rome, which today forms the basis of many modern European codes of law, e.g. in Scotland. It is characteristic of such codes of law that they have received systematic codification. In contrast, it is characteristic of English law, a *common law* system, that it is based far more on judge-made precedent and, in relative terms, lacks such systematic codification.

romantic love an intensity and idealization of a love relationship, in which the other is imbued with extraordinary virtue, beauty, etc., so that the relationship overrides all other considerations, including material ones. Conceptions of romantic love arose partly as a justification of extramarital sexual relations in contexts in which marital relationships were determined largely by economic considerations or by related expediencies. More generally, they are associated with the rise of more individualistic familial relationship, which, in Western Europe and elsewhere, replaced earlier patterns of values and relationships, such as arranged marriages. While rarely realized fully, the idea remains an element in the conceptions of companionate marriage, individualistic criteria in the choice of marriage and/or sexual partners, and the expectations attached to MARRIAGE in most modern societies, and can be a source of both heightened gratification and a sense of personal fulfilment or of disappointment and disruption in relationships. See also CONFLUENT LOVE, INTIMACY.

Rorschach Inkblot Test a device, designed by Rorschach (1921), to allow a person to *project* his/her personality so that problems may be uncovered and resolved. This is therefore a PROJECTIVE TEST, which is based on a holistic, phenomenological approach to understanding personality dynamics.

In practice, the client/patient is shown a series of ink-blot type patterns which are regarded as ambiguous stimuli. The ambiguity allows a variety of different interpretations to be put on them, and features selected from them. The client/patient is encouraged to talk about what he or she sees in the patterns, and the therapist uses these responses as clues to unconscious or difficult-to-voice concerns which can then be explored. A scoring system has been developed through observations made on various clinical and normal groups, but scoring is still necessarily subjective and interpretation of the responses is regarded as a skilled activity, requiring much experience.

Rostow, Walt (1916–) US economic historian who has made influential contributions to the study of ECONOMIC AND SOCIAL DEVELOPMENT and served in various advisory capacities with the Kennedy-Johnson administrations. His most famous work *Stages of Economic Growth* (1960) had the subtitle 'a non-communist manifesto'. Rostow identified five 'stages of economic growth': traditional society; preconditions for take-off; take-off; drive to maturity; and maturity. Levels of investment are regarded as decisive in launching societies on a growth trajectory. The study was intended to provide theoretical guidance on the solution of current problems of UNDERDEVELOPMENT applicable to all societies. The approach has been criticized by A.G. FRANK (1969), as being theoretically and empirically inadequate, and unlikely to provide an adequate recipe for development, because it ignores the history of imperialism and the dialectical interconnection of development with underdevelopment.

Rousseau, Jean-Jacques (1712–78) Swiss-born political and social theorist, who lived mainly in Paris, and was a leading, if ambiguous, figure in the French Enlightenment (see AGE OF ENLIGHTENMENT), and whose ideas were invoked in the French Revolution. His overriding concern was with human happiness, for which an essential condition was the freedom and autonomy of the will.

His critique of existing society identified the baleful effects of private PROPERTY which, in creating the unequal relationship of master and servant, enslaved all. Men could never recreate the 'natural' independence of premodern society, but by judicious education and democratic government they might ameliorate their condition. In *Emile* (1762), his major work on education, Rousseau indicates how the child might be brought to a state of physical and psychological self-sufficiency, through a system of personal tutoring geared to the child's own developing nature. It was Rousseau's argument that in seeking to perfect themselves, men had made the wrong choice about how they would live together. In the *Social Contract,* his major work of political philosophy, he was concerned to show men the choice they could have made. In the civil society of the *Social Contract,* each man is an equal member of a sovereign body – a classless, democratic assembly – which collectively determines the laws they will live under. All men surrender their rights and possessions to the body, which establishes both economic and political equality, and then each receives back from this body the same rights over others, that he allows others over himself. In such a condition of EQUALITY, men are able to make laws which genuinely apply to all, and since their only obedience is to laws they have themselves made, their wills remain free and autonomous, and they have the possibility of achieving happiness. In making laws, men give expression to the *general will,* which is the will of each person in so far as it refers to what they share as equal members of the sovereign body. Rousseau's view here has been seen as Utopian, but 'taking men as they are', he accepted that they each have a particular will, which is what differentiates them from every other, and that this will is always potentially in opposition to the general will. He advocated a number of devices to prevent the particular will from having its degenerative effects on the general will of the sovereign body. Men must be educated into citizenship, and their identity as citizens must be reinforced by, among other things, a CIVIL RELIGION. He did not believe that any human creation could last forever, and however perfect a society might be created, it would ultimately succumb to internal forces of destruction, centring on the individual particular will. Utopian or not, and however ambivalent was his own attitude to modernity, many of Rousseau's ideas, e.g. on inequality, on DEMOCRACY, on political legitimacy (see LEGITIMATE AUTHORITY), and on the moral community, have been widely influential, both within the social sciences and in political life. The major critique of his work is that it can be read as resolving issues, e.g. tensions between authority and liberty, which, if overlooked, can lead to TOTALITARIANISM. But equally, this work, and Rousseau's own ambivalence towards MODERNITY, illuminates such issues, and even finds some echoes in present-day movements such as POSTMODERNISM.

routinization 1 any social situation in which social action is repetitive and may be performed with a degree of motivational detachment and lack of involvement (see also ANOMIE).

2 (as employed by SCHUTZ, the ETHNOMETHODOLOGISTS and GIDDENS) the 'taken-for-granted' habitual character of most of the activities of 'everyday' social life: *routine.*

routinization of charisma see LEGITIMATE AUTHORITY.

Rowntree, Benjamin Seebohm (1871–1954) philanthropist and social reformer who had a significant influence on the development of the British WELFARE STATE as a result of his demonstration that the causes of poverty are located in structural features of society, such as the unequal DISTRIBUTION OF INCOME AND WEALTH, rather than being explained by the personal lifestyles of the poor. Born into the rich Quaker family famous for its chocolate factory in York, he emulated the poverty surveys of Charles BOOTH. In his three surveys of York, in 1898, 1936 and 1950, Rowntree sought to discover the causes of poverty as well as describing its incidence. In order to make valid claims for state intervention, he distinguished between primary and secondary POVERTY. Primary poverty, he argued, was the condition of an individual when he or she receives only subsistence to satisfy solely physiological needs; secondary poverty refers to the condition when the satisfaction of basic psychological and social needs, such as the ability to participate in the community and enjoy a social life, has been met. Rowntree also developed the notion of a CYCLE OF DEPRIVATION where one's chances of being poor may be influenced by one's position in the LIFE COURSE and one's family and social background. Rowntree's work was influential in the development of the first insurance-based social security policies and the BEVERIDGE REPORT. At the direction of Lloyd George, Rowntree was responsible for overseeing the welfare of munitions workers during World War I, and he helped to plan postwar housing policy. In subsequent years, Rowntree's notion of primary poverty has been criticized as being too restricted. However, he never intended that the provision of social security should be directed only at combating primary poverty.

rules and **rule-following** a general term for the normative codes, codes of signification, rules of games, and the like which play an utterly central role in the *constitution* (making a particular type of action what it is, e.g. a wedding or a funeral) and the *regulation* (e.g. criminal law or the rules of 'fair play' in sport) of particular forms of social life. Rules may be overt and on the surface or tacit and 'deep structural'.

It is a crucial characteristic of all 'rules' that they *do not* 'determine' action or behaviour in a 'lawlike' way, but require or leave room (potentially or actually) for 'choice'. However, an individual actor must follow the appropriate rules if he or she is to be taken as appropriately 'doing' particular types of action. *Rule-following,* then, is the *action* of an individual in 'conforming' to a rule and can be distinguished from 'predetermined' *behaviour,* such as drinking in response to thirst. The centrality of rule-following as the basis of human social structures is widely regarded as making human social systems different from most other kinds of system.

ruling class *or* **dominant class** 1 (MARXISM) within any society or social formation, that class which enjoys cultural, political as well as economic ascendancy (*class domination*) by virtue of its ownership and control over the MEANS OF PRODUCTION.
2 (non-Marxist POLITICAL SOCIOLOGY) *ruling* class – the minority which, in any society, always forms the political governing class – MOSCA *The Ruling* Class (1869) (see also ÉLITE AND ÉLITE THEORY).

In most Marxist usages but not all, the two terms 'ruling class' and 'dominant class' are virtually synonymous. In *The Communist Manifesto* Marx and Engels did write that in the modern representative state 'the bourgeoisie' will often hold 'exclusive political sway', that the state would be 'the executive committee of the bourgeoisie'. For most Marxists, however, even where such a 'ruling' or 'dominant class' does not govern directly (e.g. where, as in modern liberal democracies, government is in the hands of persons drawn from several different classes), this does not mean that the economically 'dominant class' is not the 'ruling class', since it may still 'rule' by virtue of its control over IDEOLOGIES, over dominant ideas, etc., stemming from its economic influence. As Marx and Engels wrote in *The German Ideology:* 'The ideas of the ruling class are, in every age, the ruling ideas; i.e. the class which is the *dominant* material force in society is at the same time its *dominant* intellectual force'. Thus, in this sense a 'ruling' or 'dominant' class may 'rule' even though it does not 'govern'. In some political circumstances, it is argued that it is to the clear advantage of an economically 'dominant class' that it does not rule or govern directly, for example when a sharing of central political power with other groups allows control to be exerted over diverse forces which are seen as 'condensed' at the political centre – see BONAPARTISM. In such circumstances, however, it can also be argued that the lack of class capacity preventing any one class from ruling directly can reflect a state of affairs in which there exists no economically and politically dominant class.

There are today many Marxists (e.g. see Poulantzas, 1973) who also emphasize that a tendency always exists for the state to possess a RELATIVE AUTONOMY – or even on occasions an absolute autonomy – from underlying economic forces. In this context, a distinction between the political 'ruling ÉLITE (S)' and the economically dominant class is one that usually needs to be made. A final problem for Marx ism is that *empirically* there often exist many difficulties in any actual identification of the ruling or the dominant class, especially in the study of historical forms of society, e.g. in ABSOLUTISM or ASIATIC MODE OF PRODUCTION OR ASIATIC SOCIETY.

For the users of the term 'ruling class' in sense **2**, the predominant concern has been different from that of most Marxists. Their goal has been to expose the pretensions of most modern claims to DEMOCRACY, including the claims of Marxists that true democracy might one day be achieved. According to Mosca the rulers will always be drawn from an 'organized minority'. Using abstract political justifications – which Mosca called *political formulae* – rulers everywhere seek to legitimize their political rule. In some cases the 'principles' which operate in the selection of political leaders and the social origins of such leaders may merit the 'empirical' use of such terms as 'representative democracy'. But even in these circumstances the 'ruling class' will always consist of, and be drawn from, a cultural and psychological minority of the population equipped to rule. See also PARETO, MILLS, POWER ÉLITE, GRAMSCI, HEGEMONY, DOMINANT IDEOLOGY THESIS.

Runciman, Walter (W. G.) (1934–) British sociologist and industrialist, who as an independent scholar and fellow of Trinity College Cambridge has produced a succession of commentaries, research monographs and theoretical works, especially in the areas of political sociology, class analysis, historical and comparative sociology, and sociological theory. A member of the House of Lords, he also chaired the Royal Commission on Criminal Justice. His first book, *Social Science and Political Theory* (1963), was a plea for Anglo-American political theory to give greater attention to European political sociology, especially the work of WEBER and SCHUMPETER. In *Relative Deprivation and Social Justice* (1966), he employed historical analysis and social survey data to show that actors' conceptions of social deprivation and class consciousness are relative rather than absolute, varying according to the social comparisons actually made by social actors (see RELATIVE DEPRIVATION, CLASS IMAGERY). Runciman argues that the conception of a 'just society' is a valid one, and should embrace notions such as equal provision for need, greater equality of educational opportunity, and increased opportunities for democratic political participation. However, he finds no indication that an automatic development of class consciousness and class action will occur which will lead to this outcome. Runciman's *magnum opus,* is a trilogy of volumes on sociological theory, of which two have been completed. The first of these *A Treatise on Social Theory,* Vol. 1, *The Methodology of the Social Sciences* (1983) identifies three main methods which have a legitimate place within sociology:

(a) theory-neutral 'reportage' of 'empirical facts' about the social order;

(b) theoretical explanation of overarching social structure;

(c) phenomenological 'description' of

the 'lived textures' of social lives, While the first and second of these are seen as broadly 'positivistic', the third is not, but is dependent on a 'coherence' rather than a 'correspondence' view of reality. The second volume of the Treatise, *Substantive Social Theory* (1989), consists of a wide-ranging comparative analysis and an evolutionary theory of social development in which the 'struggle' between different bases of social power, analogous to Darwinian 'natural selection', is central (see also EVOLUTIONARY SOCIOLOGY). The trilogy is to be concluded with a volume applying the concepts of volumes 1 and 2 to British social history. In all of this, Runciman regards the role of the sociologist as, ideally, that of the impartial benevolent observer. Runciman's 'evolutionism' has been subject to the standard criticisms directed at EVOLUTIONARY THEORY in modern sociology. The distinction he draws between his third and the first and second method has been criticized as over-polarized. But the breadth and the power of his sociological analysis, especially his historical comparative analysis, has been much admired.

rural sociology a branch of sociology concerned with the study of rural communities and agriculture. Rural sociology has existed as a clearly identified subdiscipline only in the US, where it was encouraged by state policies. Elsewhere the study of rural communities and agriculture has more often been subsumed within other areas of inquiry, including economic anthropology, peasant studies, and development studies. See also ECOLOGY, GREEN MOVEMENT.

rural-urban continuum the conception that, rather than a simple contrast between rural and urban communities, there exists a gradation of types of community, in terms of their size, density of population, extent of division of labour, isolation, sense of community solidarity, rates of social change, etc. The concept was introduced in the 1920s by SOROKIN and Zimmerman. Later REDFIELD relabelled the concept *folk-urban continuum*, but with the same basic notion. The notion is useful, since it is clear that the contrast between rural and urban communities varies greatly between societies and at different times. Historically, for example, the contrast was greater than in present-day Britain, where most rural communities exist in close relation with towns and are permeated by urban values. Compare GEMEINSCHAFT AND GESELLSCHAFT; see also FOLK SOCIETY.

S

Sacks, Harvey (1935–75) US sociologist prominent in ETHNOMETHODOLOGY and CONVERSATION ANALYSIS. Like his mentor Harold GARFINKEL, Sacks was influenced by the work of Talcott PARSONS. The theories and issues pursued by Sacks included the 'espousing a role', 'rules of conversational sequence','turn-taking', 'membership categorization devices', 'being chicken', 'suicide as a device for discovering if anybody cares'. Determinedly methodological in focus, what links these topics was a belief that conventional sociology neglected much of the underlying social COMPETENCE of social 'members' and what was really going on is social organization. Sacks sought empirical means to illuminate this. Much of Sacks published material was published from transcriptions, by Gail Jefferson, of lectures – see *Lectures on Conversation, Vol. 1 &2* (1992/5) (eds G. Jefferson and E. Schegloff.

sacred and profane a distinction particularly employed in sociology by DURKHEIM in which the *sacred*, which includes all phenomena which are set apart and revered, is distinguished from all other phenomena, the *profane*. For Durkheim, beliefs and practices in relation to the sacred are the defining feature of any RELIGION.

Said, Edward (1935–2003) Palestinian literary and social theorist and political activist in the cause of an independent Palestinian state, who from the late 1950s was based in the USA. The author of a number of works, his *Orientalism* (1978) captured the attention of sociologists with its vivid treatment of ORIENTALISM as a series of representations – categories, images, classifications – which have constructed 'the orient' as an object in Western cultural and social scientific understanding, and have at the same time helped to construct the West in opposition to this 'other'. Drawing on FOUCAULT's conception of DISCOURSE as a system of regulation, Said emphasizes the ideological force – POWER/KNOWLEDGE – of conceptions of orientalism.

Saint-Simon, Comte Henri de (1760–1825) French evolutionary and positivist social theorist who exercised a commanding influence on the development of sociology as a discipline (see EVOLUTIONARY THEORY, POSITIVISM). Saint-Simon's career was as iconoclastic as his sociology. An aristocrat of impeccable lineage, he fought in the American Revolution, and found himself imprisoned in the French Revolution. He subsequently amassed large profits from speculation in land, established a famous 'salon' which attracted France's intellectual élite, squandered his money, and from 1804 to the end of his life lived close to poverty. This period was his most productive in an intellectual sense and saw, towards its close, collaboration with Auguste COMTE.

The ideas of the Enlightenment, and especially those of MONTESQUIEU and CONDORCET, were influential in the formation of Saint-Simon's sociology. His own ideas were subsequently to inform those of Comte, and thus DURKHEIM, as well as

MARX. These theorists point to the main ingredients of Saint-Simon's work: his positivism and evolutionism on the one hand, and his SOCIALISM on the other.

Saint-Simon's evolutionary law argued that society passed through three stages, each characterized by different types of knowledge: the theological, the metaphysical and the positive (see LAW OF THREE STAGES). The positive stage coincided with the emergence of INDUSTRIAL SOCIETY, a term first coined by Saint-Simon himself. For Saint-Simon, industrial society was distinct from previous stages in three ways: the emergence of a single, albeit multilayered class (i.e. all those involved in industrial production); its technology, which completed society's struggle to dominate nature; and its potential for the transformation of the state from an instrument of domination to one of enlightened welfare and reform managed on behalf of the new industrial class by an intellectual élite informed by positive sociological knowledge.

Before this benevolent, élitist version of socialism could emerge, however, a transitional period of social dislocation and deregulation would inevitably occur, as the epistemological cement of social order characteristic of previous eras (religion), weakened under the impact of industrial society's secularism. Positive, scientific sociology or *social physics* as Saint-Simon put it, could, however, help hasten and smooth the transition to the new positive stage, and provide the basis of a new secular moral order.

Saint-Simon's ideas continue to reverberate through sociological work. Apart from his enormous influence on the contours of classical theory, Saint-Simon's concepts (of the centrality of knowledge to industrial society, and of the necessity for compatibility between its technologies and forms of social organization) have re-emerged in recent theory in terms of the ideas of CONVERGENCE and postindustrialism (see POSTINDUSTRIAL SOCIETY).

sample and **sampling** a selection of individuals made from a larger population (the parent population) and intended to reflect this population's characteristics in all significant respects. The purpose of taking a sample is to investigate features of the population in greater detail than could be done if the total population was used, and to draw inferences about this population. For these inferences to be valid (see VALIDITY) the sample must be truly representative, the only way to ensure this being to take a RANDOM SAMPLE. This involves using either *random numbers* or *systematic sampling.* Random numbers are used to ensure that every individual in the SAMPLING FRAME (e.g. an electoral register or mailing list) has an equal chance of being selected as a member of the sample. Systematic sampling involves randomly selecting the first individual from the list, then subsequently individuals at every fixed interval, e.g. every tenth person if a 10% sample is desired.

When the population to be studied is large and the sample relatively small, it may be efficient to use STRATIFIED SAMPLING. This technique involves dividing the population into strata, e.g. age groups, social classes, and drawing a random sample from each. This can improve the representativeness of the sample, since the size of the sample from each strata is made proportionate to the size of the strata in the total population. See also SAMPLING ERROR, CLUSTER SAMPLING, QUOTA SAMPLING, SNOWBALL SAMPLING, PROBABILITY.

sampling error the difference between the 'true' value of a characteristic within a population and the value estimated from a sample of that population. 'Error' occurs because no SAMPLE can be expected to exactly represent the parent population from which it was drawn. To minimize, and to be able to estimate, sampling error, it is necessary to ensure that the selection of the sample is RANDOM, and this is normally done by random numbers or systematic sampling. Sampling error is not the same as BIAS or systematic error, which may occur due to the process of data collection, but is nothing to do with the sample selection.

sampling frame the list of members of the total population of interest from which a SAMPLE for study can be drawn. For example, such a list may be the electoral register, if information about those with voting rights is being sought, or the family practitioner committee lists if a health survey is projected, or vehicle registration lists, if car ownership or road transport is under study.

sanction any means by which a moral code or social norm is enforced, either positively in the form of rewards or negatively by means of punishment. Sanctions may also be formal (e.g. legal penalties) or informal (e.g. ostracism). The operation of social sanctions is an all-pervasive factor in social relations.

sanskritization see CASTE.

Sapir-Whorf hypothesis the thesis that linguistic categories structure perceptual and cognitive ones. Two US anthropologists, Edward Sapir (1884–1934) and his student Benjamin Lee Whorf (1897–1941) are credited with this theory of *linguistic relativism.* Essentially the position states that our language structures our perception of the world. Whorf demonstrates this with his work on Hopi Indians, who appeared to have different concepts of space, time and matter from 'Standard Average European' language speakers. Another common example is the plurality of Inuit (Eskimo) words for 'snow', supposedly illustrating that they are attuned to elements of their environment that a non-Inuit would be unable to recognize. The strong version of the hypothesis is now rarely accepted, but debate still continues as to where language ends and material culture and social structure begin. See also RELATIVISM, FORM OF LIFE.

Sartre, Jean-Paul (1905–80) French existentialist philosopher and novelist, whose work blends EXISTENTIALISM with MARXISM. Sartre's method was influenced by HUSSERL'S PHENOMENOLOGY, but the central notion of his philosophy derives from HEIDEGGER. This is that although we cannot escape the 'givens' of our initial situation (its 'facticity') we are free to act to change it. Sartre draws a distinction between 'being-in-itself' (unconscious, 'thingness') and 'being-for-itself' (conscious, 'no-thingness' and action). Politicized by World War II and his association with the French Communist Party, his aim of overcoming the economic and social 'structures of choice' which restrict options, linked existentialism with Marxism. His *magnum opus* is *Being and Nothingness* (1956) and his main contribution to Marxism is *Critique of Dialectical Reason* (1960).

satellite see METROPOLIS-SATELLITE RELATIONSHIP.

satisficing the behaviour of an individual or firm in which, partly as the result of inadequate information, rather than seeking to maximize profits. etc. as in orthodox theories of economic rationality, a 'satisfactory' level of return is sought. Thus within the firm, organizational objectives such as increased size, prestige, or security, may have a greater priority than the maximization of profit. See also ORGANIZATIONAL CULTURE. ORGANIZATION THEORY.

Saussure, Ferdinand de (1857–1913) Swiss theorist who is generally regarded as the founder of modern structural linguistics. He was also a major influence on the wider intellectual movement known as STRUCTURALISM. His seminal work, *Cours de linguistique générale* (1916), was published posthumously, compiled from notes taken by his students. In this, SEMIOLOGY, the general study of all SIGN systems, is first distinguished from the more specific study of language. A number of interrelated distinctions are then introduced which have become central in theoretical linguistics and are often the taking-off points in structuralism:
(a) the distinction between LANGUE AND PAROLE, i.e. between the rules of language and actual instances of produced speech;
(b) the distinction between SYNCHRONY AND DIACHRONY, i.e. between the study of

language without reference to the past, only as an existing system of relationships, and the study of changes in language;
(c) the distinction between SYNTAGMATIC AND PARADIGMATIC (earlier called 'associative') relationships, i.e. between the combination of words in a particular chain of speech and the relationships of any particular term with related 'absent' terms within the language;
(d) the distinction between SIGNIFIER AND SIGNIFIED, i.e. between the term (its acoustical or written form) and the concept (the idea) signified by the term.

Other important notions in Saussure's linguistics are an emphasis on the arbitrary character of the relationship between the signifier and the signified, and the idea that the status or meaning or 'value' of each linguistic unit is established only in relation to all other units, i.e. is internal to the language, rather than in terms of an inherently determining phenomenon external to the language. Thus, in Saussure's well-known dictum, in languages 'there are only DIFFERENCES'.

The importance of Saussure's approach in launching theoretical linguistics on its modern course is undeniable, although the absence of any systematic treatment of SYNTAX OR PRAGMATICS in his work left gaps to be repaired by later theorists such as CHOMSKY. Because the emphasis in Saussure's work is on *langue* rather than *parole,* it is not surprising that this has been seen as leading to a onesided account of language. When employed analogically as in structuralism, this conception of language may also give rise to a onesided account of social structures. Finally, whilst an emphasis on internal relations within sign systems is consonant with an emphasis on the importance of understanding particular frames of reference (e.g. the study of particular scientific PARADIGMS, PROBLEMATIQUES, FORMS OF LIFE), it has been criticized for paving the way for conceptions of INCOMMENSURABILITY, and structuralist and poststructuralist conceptions of the 'death of the subject'. On the other hand, poststructuralist theorists such as DERRIDA who utilize Saussure's work see him as failing to realize fully the philosophical radicalism of his conceptions, given that it is not just a matter of the internality of the relation between signifier and signified that makes representation suspect, but that relations of difference are also always 'slippery'. See also POSTSTRUCTURALISM.

savagery one of the stages of development identified in early theories of SOCIAL EVOLUTION. MONTESQUIEU proposed that the three main stages of social development were:
(a) hunting or savagery;
(b) herding or BARBARISM; and
(c) CIVILIZATION.

The concept gained currency in the 19th-century through the distinction made between simple/primitive and complex/modern societies in EVOLUTIONARY THEORY. The term was inevitably pejorative, since evolutionary theory saw social development as also involving a 'civilizing' process. Thus 'savagery' was meant to convey a condition of brutal backwardness, the very opposite of the civilized manners, morals, intellect and taste of Europe's privileged classes.

Apart from its pejorative connotation, it was also inaccurate. Simple societies were not 'savage' in the way in which Europeans understood the term. The concept had its political uses in an age of expanding colonialism, but its adequacy as a description of non-European preindustrial societies could hardly survive events such as the 1914–18 war.

Say's Law see KEYNES.

scaling a method of measurement in the social sciences, which is applied particularly to the measurement of personality traits and of ATTITUDES. Central is the concept of a *continuum.* This means that personality types, for example, can be arranged or ordered in terms of dichotomous schemas (such as EXTRAVERSION AND INTROVERSION), and attitudes vary on a scale going from one extreme, through neutral, to the other extreme. When this is not possible and two or more dimensions are required for accurate description, *multidimensional scaling* is used (see Kruksall and Wish, *Multidimensional Scaling*, 1978.)

There are a number of ways of constructing such scales, but all rely on the assumption that personality traits or attitudes can be assessed from the responses given to statements or questions (see LIKERT SCALE). It is important that an equal number of positively and negatively loaded statements are used, and that only one dimension is tapped. Various statistical techniques are used to check the internal consistency of scales as they are developed.

QUESTIONNAIRES are the usual basis of scaling, but it can also be done from CONTENT ANALYSIS. See also ATTITUDE SCALE/MEASUREMENT, GUTTMAN SCALE, POLITICAL ATTITUDES.

scalogram analysis *or* **scalogram method** see GUTTMAN SCALE.

scapegoat a person or group made, unjustifiably, to bear the blame for the problems and misfortunes of others. The term originates from the Biblical Jewish custom of ritually transferring the sins of the people onto a goat and then sending the (scape) goat into the wilderness, taking with it the guilt of the people.

In the context of ethnic relations, people may shift responsibility for misfortune and frustration onto relatively powerless groups, often visibly identifiable minorities such as Jews, blacks or Asians. The concept of scapegoating is associated with theories of FRUSTRATION-AGGRESSION which suggest that when a person or a group is prevented from reaching a goal (frustration), this will raise their levels of aggression. If the cause of this frustration is too powerful, unknown or complex, aggression may be vented on a more accessible or vulnerable target.

Thus minority groups may be blamed for many social problems, unemployment, economic decline, crime, by a majority group, without the necessity to analyse the real causes of these problems. In recent times in Europe, Jews and blacks have been scapegoats for economic, political and social problems. In the most extreme form, Jews were targets for GENOCIDE by the Nazi regime in World War II.

scatter diagram or scattergram a diagram produced on a graph to illustrate the relationship between two variables by indicating the values of these for each case in the sample. It may be a first stage in data analysis, allowing 'eye-balling' of the data to observe any association or CORRELATION between the variables.

schedules of reinforcement see CONDITIONING.

schizophrenia see PSYCHOSIS.

Schumpeter, Joseph (1883–1950) Moravian-born, Austrian and US economist, politician and social theorist, whose distinctive approach combined economic and sociological analysis. In *The Theory of Economic Development* (1951, German 1912) and *Business Cycles* (1939) he advanced a general theory of fluctuations in economic growth (see LONG-WAVE THEORY). Three types of economic cycle were identified by Schumpeter, the most novel of which were KONDRATIEFF CYCLES (named after the Russian economist). These are periods of between 50 and 60 years initiated by a clustering of technical and commercial innovations – steam power (1787–1842), railways (1842–97) and subsequently electricity – creating new products and rapid advance, and brought to an end when the opportunities created by these innovations become exhausted.

Although, historically, economic growth and profit had been the outcome of entrepreneurial and technological innovation, Schumpeter also noticed an historical tendency for individual entrepreneurs to be replaced by a new class of industrial administrators. He also argued the need for long-term planning (not only Keynesian short-term planning, (see

KEYNESIAN ECONOMICS)) in modern societies to seek to control economic cycles. Although he rejected much of Marx's account of the onset of socialism, in *Capitalism, Socialism and Democracy* (1942), he suggested that the disappearance of the traditional entrepreneur and the need for economic planning meant that socialism was inevitable. He was not personally attracted by socialism, which he believed would undermine individualism and democracy.

Schutz, Alfred (1899–1959) Austrian-born sociologist and philosopher, a major architect of SOCIAL PHENOMENOLOGY, who, after his move to New York in 1935, worked as a banker.

Schutz's main work – e.g. *The Phenomenology of the Social World* (1967, German 1932) – involved the application of Edmund HUSSERL'S PHENOMENOLOGY to social phenomena, especially the phenomena of everyday life. This also involved Schutz in a critique of WEBER. According to Schutz, Weber 'does not ask how an actor's meaning is constituted or ... try to identify the unique and fundamental relations existing between the self and the other'.

The basic thesis of Schutz's social phenomenology is that sociology must work to uncover the concepts or TYPIFICATIONS by which actors, in intersubjective ways, organize their everyday actions and construct 'common-sense knowledge'. As he saw it, everyday knowledge, unlike scientific knowledge, cannot be studied by abstract methods. Rather, the careful inspection of everyday social life reveals that social actors operate with 'taken-for-granted assumptions' and 'stock knowledge' and achieve a 'reciprocity of perspective', a 'natural attitude' which must be seen as paramount' in social knowledge. Schutz's conception is that social order arises from the general presumption of a common world, but without this presumption being in any way a matter of normative consensus of the kind assumed by functionalism. (See also PRACTICAL KNOWLEDGE, LIFE-WORLD).

The paradox arising from Schutz's social phenomenology is that although a generalized account of the actor's constitution of social life is reached, this account suggests that there may be strict limits on the extent to which the macroscopic generalizations about social structures and social change which conventional sociologies have sought can ever by achieved. Schutz's ideas have been taken up by ETHNOMETHODOLOGY. The issue arising is whether scientific and everyday common-sense knowledge are as sharply differentiated as Schutz and the ethnomethodologists suggest, and whether general social structural accounts may still be possible, despite the undoubted elements of INDEXICALITY and REFLEXIVITY of everyday social accounts.

science 1 (most general sense) any systematic study of physical or social phenomena. 2 (more restricted sense) the study of physical and social phenomena where this involves observation, experiment, appropriate quantification and the search for universal general laws and explanations. 3 any specific branch of knowledge in either of the above senses (e.g. social science) (compare IDEOLOGY, MAGIC, RELIGION).

In sociology, and elsewhere, debate about science 2 centres on the extent to which it is necessary or possible to arrive at a strict definition of 'science', and at how far any definition which might be appropriate for the physical sciences is also appropriate for the social sciences, with their extra source of corrigibility for any generalizations proposed, namely human choice and the inherent fluidity of social action.

The general problems in the definition and identification of science 2 have increased recently as the result of a critical assault on conventional philosophies of knowledge and of science. Problems have arisen especially from the work of KUHN (1962) in which science is seen as the product of multiple perspectives and numerous groups and schools (see SCIENTIFIC PARADIGM) without any single identifiable set of procedures or identifying criteria making it possible to demarcate science as a whole. Neither POSITIVISM nor FALSIFICATIONISM, two previous main attempts to provide a 'criterion of demarcation' of science **2**, today find unreserved support (see also COVERING-LAW MODEL, SCIENTIFIC REALISM).

A widespread view is that, rather than being identifiable as a single pure form, science must now be seen as involving a complex process of social production, working upon and transforming previously existing knowledge, but with no single scientific method or straightforward distinction between science **2** and other forms of knowledge. As a socially located phenomenon, science must also be recognized as occurring in a context in which the cultural values and interests of scientists, and also the wider interests served by science, are always a potential influence on the knowledge produced (see also SOCIOLOGY OF SCIENCE, SOCIOLOGY OF KNOWLEDGE, OBJECTIVITY).

Some commentators have suggested that the only epistemological position now tenable is to recognize the inevitable relativity of scientific knowledge (see EPISTEMOLOGY, RELATIVISM). However, a return to broadly philosophical criteria for the identification of the 'truth' of hypotheses and theories remains possible. For example. HABERMAS (1970a & b) and FEYERABEND (1978) propose a 'consensus' or unrestricted discourse model of the conditions for knowledge. This sees the search for truth as requiring conditions which allow 'open discourse' on whatever evidence is offered in support of particular hypotheses, with the aim of arriving at a 'warranted consensus'. Current thinking on science, however, leaves the identification of 'science' as against 'nonscience' (e.g. compared with ideology) a much more open question than hitherto.

scientific law a statement of a uniform connection between empirical phenomena, to the effect that whenever and wherever conditions of a specified kind A occur, then so will certain conditions of another kind B. A law is a universal conditional statement of the form 'For any A, if A, then B'. Thus scientific laws are more than statements of fact, they make counterfactual claims, for example, that 'all water heated to 100 °C at sealevel and normal pressure will boil'.

As well as deterministic laws of this type there are also probabilistic laws of the form, 'For any A, if A, then a certain probability (less than 1 but more than 0) of B.

Laws may be empirical, theoretical, or idealized in form (compare IDEAL TYPE). The generalization achieved by scientific laws is often only possible by the formulation of laws in idealized form, e.g. involving such notions as 'frictionless surfaces' or 'perfect gases', with auxiliary assumptions being required for general laws to be applied to concrete cases.

On one view (see COVERING-LAW MODEL), the existence of laws is a central defining feature of science and scientific explanations. Competing conceptions of SCIENCE, however, give more central emphasis to explanatory mechanisms and EXPLANATORY THEORIES, which may involve scientific laws but need not do so (see also SCIENTIFIC REALISM).

scientific management

A set of principles governing the design of jobs which entail the separation of mental from manual labour, subdivision of tasks, deskilling, close managerial control of work effort and incentive wage payments.

The scientific management movement originated in the US in the 1890s, F. W. Taylor being its main proponent, hence the terms 'Taylorism' and 'scientific management' are often used interchangeably. Taylor was trained as an engineer and his principles of management were based on the philosophy that work design is capable of objective measurement by which work can be broken down into its constituent parts as various 'physical motions' which can be precisely timed (thus *time and motion study*) with a view to reorganizing jobs to achieve the most efficient use of effort to raise productivity. In this sense management would become 'scientific' rather than intuitive, discovering the laws governing work activity as a basis for a set of universal principles defining the 'best way' to organize work. Taylor's philosophy was also based on ideas from classical economics and a psychology which assumed that individuals were naturally lazy and instrumental in their attitude to work. Each individual would be paid in relation to their effort and motivated by economic reward. With scientific management trade unions would be obsolete and cooperation in the workplace would be ensured through the application of scientific principles and each worker pursuing their individual self-interest.

Scientific management advocated:

(a) the fragmentation of work into simple, routine operations;
(b) the standardization of each operation to eliminate idle times;
(c) the separation of conception from execution – the design and control of work being a management task.

Taylor's principles were primarily directed at the workplace but his methods also implied the functional division of management, including their separation from owners which was elaborated by the early proponents of MANAGEMENT SCIENCE into a formal blueprint for organizations, defining lines of authority and spans of control (see also ORGANIZATION THEORY).

Taylor's ideas were also an extension of earlier 19th-century approaches to factory organization and mechanization, notably the work of Andrew Ure and Charles Babbage. The 'Babbage Principle' (1832) asserted that skilled tasks should be fragmented into a skilled component and various deskilled associated tasks which allow each task to be paid at the lowest possible rate and workers perform only operations commensurate with their skill and training.

Sociological analysis of scientific management has focused upon two issues: first, its significance as a management ideology legitimating management control, and secondly, the extent to which scientific management was applied in practice in capitalist societies at various stages of their development. As an ideology, scientific management has enjoyed a pervasive influence over work organization and managerial thought up to the present day despite initial opposition from both trade unions and employers. As an ideology it contrasted strongly with earlier employers' attitudes of paternalism and welfarism and was the object of considerable criticism from later HUMAN RELATIONS approaches to management which rejected its individualistic, economistic assumptions about human motivation, and advocated instead task variety, group working and elf-fulfilment through work.

Recent debate in sociology has focused on the importance of Taylorism as a basis for managerial control under capitalism (see LABOUR PROCESS). It is clear that scientific management principles were never fully implemented in practice. Worker opposition and the need by employers to secure both work consent and flexibility in work organization meant the abandonment or modification of many of Taylor's original principles (see FORDISM AND POST-FORDISM). Nevertheless, elements of Taylorism, particularly deskilling, were and still are widespread both in manufacturing and office work (see TECHNOLOGY, SKILL). Scientific management was even influential in socialist societies via the works of Lenin and Gramsci but separated from the capitalist ideology which underpinned it.

scientific paradigm 'a universally recognized scientific achievement that for a time provides model problems and solutions to a community of practitioners' (KUHN, 1962). Kuhn has been criticized for using the term in a variety of senses (e.g. to refer to groups, FORMS OF LIFE, etc.). It is clear, however, that Kuhn's main reason for introducing the term was to draw attention to the fact that science is a 'flesh and blood' phenomenon and that the character and the achievements of science cannot be adequately understood as reducible to abstract theories (see also NORMAL AND REVOLUTIONARY SCIENCE). Once this is seen, the 'looseness' of the concept can be justified as reflecting a looseness in the subject matter.

While scientific paradigms are seen by Kuhn as a sign of the maturity of a scientific discipline and the social sciences viewed by him as 'preparadigmatic', it is also possible to talk of 'paradigms' in the social sciences, with the social sciences seen as 'multiparadigmatic' in a way that reflects the inherent difficulties and divergent interpretations of the subject matter.

Compare PROBLEMATIQUE, EPISTEME.

See also FEYERABEND, SCIENCE, SOCIOLOGY OF SCIENCE.

scientific realism (PHILOSOPHY OF SCIENCE) the assumption (Bhaskar, 1975, 1979), that a 'real world' exists independently of our senses, and that the objects of scientific thought are 'real structures, irreducible to the events they generate' (see also EXPLANATORY MECHANISM; compare REALISM). In presenting this as a new TRANSCENDENTAL ARGUMENT, Bhaskar has had considerable influence on methodological thinking in modern sociology, especially in providing support for 'structural explanations' and in combatting EMPIRICISM. What is not clear, however, is whether scientific realism carries quite the specific implications suggested by Bhaskar (e.g. support for MARX against WEBER or DURKHEIM).

scientific research programme see FALSIFICATIONISM.

scientific revolution see NORMAL AND REVOLUTIONARY SCIENCE, REVOLUTION (SENSE 2).

scientism any doctrine or approach held to involve oversimplified conceptions and unreal expectations of SCIENCE, and to misapply 'natural science' methods to the social sciences, including overconfidence in the capacity of science to solve social problems. Thus the term is mainly a pejorative one.

The notion that the success of the physical sciences could be readily repeated in the social sciences became well established in the 16th and 17th centuries and is seen later in COMTE'S POSITIVISM. Claims to a 'scientific basis' have been a feature of many other approaches in sociology, including MARXISM. Whether or not such approaches are held to be 'scientistic', however, is not a straightforward matter, since it depends on what one regards as proper or appropriate 'science' – both in general and in the context of social studies – and this, itself, is controversial. Thus at one extreme, accusations of 'scientism' have been associated with wholesale dismissals of natural science as a model for social science, whilst on other occasions they merely involve a repudiation of obvious excesses.

Scottish Enlightenment a general flowering of intellectual activity in Scotland at the end of the 18th century, including the work of some thinkers who are usually regarded as important precursors of modern sociological thought. Among the thinkers seen as falling into this category are Adam SMITH, Adam FERGUSON and John MILLAR. Among the wider group of intellectuals and scientists active in Scotland at this time was the philosopher David HUME. An important contribution to the Scottish Enlightenment was made by the Universities of Glasgow and Edinburgh, which unlike their English equivalents Oxford and Cambridge, were centres of innovation. Strong links also existed with the ENLIGHTENMENT in France. Orientations shared by most Scottish Enlightenment thinkers were:
(a) the importance attached to the necessity for empirical study of social institutions;
(b) a rejection of merely individualistic accounts of the nature and origins of social order;
(c) an assumption that society must be analysed as a natural and a moral order;
(d) an assumption that an underlying pattern of causation would eventually be uncovered (general principles or laws) explaining social reality. As was also true of the French Enlightenment, Scottish Enlightenment thinkers were optimistic that human societies would PROGRESS.

screening the use of academic qualifications as a means of selecting among candidates for employment, where it is the general level of academic qualification which is decisive rather than the particular content of the education. In this process, an employer may use educational qualifications, or sometimes also the type of institution attended, as a proxy for 'general intelligence', 'perseverance and motivation', or other 'social background', instead of being interested in the specific content of the education received. See also CULTURAL CAPITAL.

According to the *screening hypothesis*, it is the screening process rather than any direct economic return on education which explains part of the correlation between level of education and level of income. This hypothesis provides an account of the effects of education which is at odds with other hypotheses (compare HUMAN CAPITAL). See also CREDENTIALISM, CULTURAL CAPITAL.

secondary analysis any inquiry based on the reanalysis of previously analysed research data, e.g. publicly available data such as CENSUS data, or data available from data banks such as the ESRC Data Archive at Essex University. The advantages of using such data are their relative cheapness, since the data do not have to be collected, and the opportunity they can afford for longitudinal historical or cross-cultural analysis. The main disadvantage is that the researcher has far less control over the construction of variables and often has only limited knowledge of the manner and circumstances in which the data were collected. See also OFFICIAL STATISTICS.

secondary data analysis see SECONDARY ANALYSIS.

secondary deviance *or* **secondary deviation** the process whereby after an act of PRIMARY DEVIANCE an individual adopts a DEVIANT IDENTITY (Lemert, 1961). This involves a reconstruction of SELF in terms of attitudes, feelings and cultural or SUBCULTURAL affiliation. In common with the LABELLING perspective, Lemert sees this adaptation as identified with, and even produced by, SOCIETAL REACTION. See also DEVIANT CAREER.

secondary group see PRIMARY GROUP.

secondary poverty see POVERTY.

secondary sector the sector of the economy concerned with manufacture of goods, both CAPITAL goods (used in further production) and *consumer goods,* sold for immediate use. See also PRIMARY SECTOR, SERVICE SECTOR.

secondary sector (of the labour market) see DUAL LABOUR MARKET.

secondary socialization see SOCIALIZATION.

secondary states see PRISTINE STATES.

second order constructs theories about theories (see METATHEORY). Since all SOCIAL ACTORS themselves possess 'theories' about their own activities, *all* sociological theories can be seen as 'second order constructs', which must first of all grasp the social actor's 'first order constructs'. See also DOUBLE HERMENEUTIC.

second-strike capability (STRATEGIC THEORY) the ability of a defending STATE to absorb a nuclear 'first strike' and to have a capability to guarantee a counterattack of sufficient force to inflict massive destruction against an aggressor. During the 1960s the US and the USSR sought to maintain a second-strike capability by both increasing their nuclear arsenals and protecting nuclear weapons by siting them in underground silos, nuclear submarines, and constantly airborne aircraft. A consequence of the attempt to maintain a second-strike capability was an acceleration of the ARMS RACE. See also NUCLEAR DETERRENCE, MUTUAL ASSURED DESTRUCTION.

Second World see THIRD WORLD.

sect a religious, or sometimes a secular, social movement characterized by its opposition to and rejection of orthodox religious and/or secular institutions, doctrines and practices, e.g., the Shakers, Quakers, Amish Mennonites.

Sociologists have identified sectarianism with a relatively low level of institutionalization and with a tendency towards doctrinal heresy. Ernst Troeltsch (1912) distinguished between 'churches' and 'sects' (see also CHURCH-SECT TYPOLOGY). 'Churches' were characterized as conservative, orthodox, hierarchic, tradition – and ritual–bound, having a high degree of organization and institutionalization. By contrast, 'sects' were perfectionist, radical, egalitarian, manifesting a low degree of organization and institutionalization. 'Sectarians' valued spontaneous action above ritual practice. Troeltsch regarded sect and church as polar opposites. Troeltsch's work was concerned with sectarian movements within Christianity and is consequently difficult to apply outside of this context. This is particularly the case where many Third World sectarian movements are concerned.

More recently, Bryan Wilson (1973) has suggested that 'sects' may be regarded as 'self-distinguishing protest movements'. The protest may not necessarily be directed at orthodox churches but against state and other secular institutions within society. Wilson rejects Troeltsch's dichotomous model and suggests that it is useful to examine sectarian movements by reference to the relation between the following social factors: doctrine, degree of organization, form of association, social orientation and action. Wilson further suggests that 'sects' may be typified according to their 'responses to the world'. Many sectarian movements display some degree of conflict and tension with both the religious and secular social world. Consequently sectarians are often characterized by a desire to seek both deliverance and salvation from orthodox cultural forms, traditions and institutions. Wilson suggests that there are at least seven possible responses to the world and to the 'problem of evil' within it. He calls these the 'conversionist', 'revolutionist', 'introversionist', 'manipulationist', 'thaumaturgical', 'reformist' and 'utopian' responses.

By going beyond the concern with degree of organization and doctrinal heresy it is possible to examine sectarian movements which have arisen outside Christian culture. See also CULT, MILLENARIANISM AND MILLENNIAL MOVEMENT, CARGO CULTS, RELIGION, MAGIC, SOCIOLOGY OF RELIGION, NEW RELIGIOUS MOVEMENTS.

sectarianism the promotion of politically separatist policies on behalf of a SECT. Strictly speaking, a sectarian movement can only manifest itself when a grouping in society has broken away from the established religious body. This is usually due to differences in doctrinal belief or religious practice, although the beliefs of the breakaway group are not distinct enough to form the basis for a new religion. The term is often used, however, in a much more general way to distinguish any kind of separatist movement where a sect can have its basis in national or political identity as well as in religion. Hence, 'sectarianism' is often applied to the contemporary situation in Northern Ireland.

sectoral cleavages the bases of political interests and political action which, to some extent, cross-cut the basic left-right CLASS CLEAVAGE which has usually been regarded as central in politics (see Dunleavy, 1980). Significant sectoral cleavages include: (a) private and public-sector employment; (b) private and 'collective' consumption sectors (e.g. interests arising from the existence of public and private sectors in housing, transport, and the provision of welfare). See also URBAN SOCIAL MOVEMENTS, CORPORATISM.

secularization the process in modern societies in which religious ideas and organizations tend to lose influence when faced with science and other modern forms of knowledge. Included here are such phenomena as the decline in formal church membership (e.g. number of baptisms) or a reduced role for religion in formal education. However, the extent of secularization across Western societies is highly variable. Notably, for example, in the US religious membership has remained high, which is perhaps explained by the need for social location in a 'melting pot' society (Herberg, 1960). Nor has the formation and the membership of new CULTS and SECTS ceased in modern societies. Apart from this, a majority of members of most modern Western societies continue to profess religious beliefs, however truncated these may be and cut off from any fuller religious practice. That the secularization of society cannot be assumed to accompany modernization is also indicated by the resurgence of religion in some modernizing societies (e.g. recent Islamic revolutionary movements), or the importance of religion in more developed societies where it may exist in association with nationalist movements (e.g. in Poland), or may re-emerge in conditions of POSTMODERNITY.

segmental social structure DURKHEIM's characterization of 'mechanical solidarity' (see MECHANICAL AND ORGANIC SOLIDARITY) as a 'system of homogeneous segments that are similar to one another', e.g. a system of broadly identical clans or territorial districts, and individuals within these systems who are equally little differentiated from each other. Compare SEGMENTARY SOCIETIES.

segmentary societies forms of STATELESS SOCIETY, whose fundamental mode of social organization is a *lineage system* in which descent group membership is defined in terms of, sometimes notional, common ancestors (*apical* ancestor). Such systems, involve a hierarchical structure, which at each level defines expected bases of membership and opposition (see Fig. 27). A classical account of such a system is EVANS-PRITCHARD's (1940) account of the Nuer. However, this account, and the concept of segmentary society in general, has been criticized as presenting only an 'ideal' model of social relationships in such societies. See also SEGMENTARY STATES.

segmentary states forms of STATE society, with a central political authority and specialized political institutions including administrative staff, but having an underlying 'segmentary' structure (compare SEGMENTARY SOCIETIES), in which political allegiances are based on lineage groups, or on related forms of client-patron relations (see Southall, 1954). A segmentary structure,

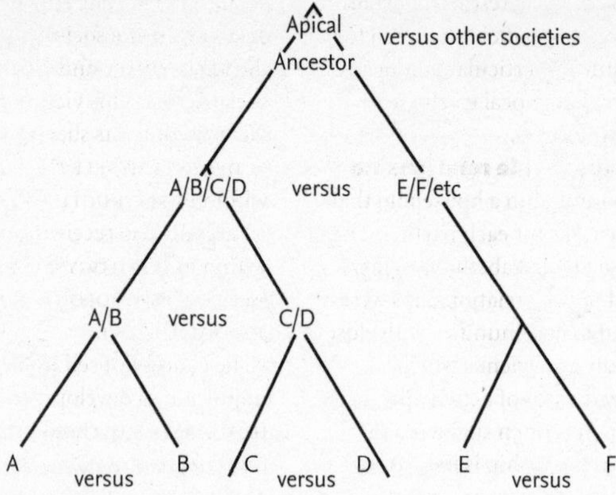

Fig. 27 **Segmentary societies.** At each level, membership of a descent group (A; A/B; A/B/C/D; etc.) defines the basis of allegiance and mutual support (e.g. in feuds).

in which primary loyalty is to the lineage group rather than the state, tends to produce somewhat fragile state forms. Segmentary states were a common form of state in precolonial Africa.

segmented labour market the structured variations in general levels of pay, career prospects, working conditions, formal skill content and status between jobs within and between primary and secondary labour market sectors (see DUAL LABOUR MARKET). The concept of *segmentalism* grew out of the realization among labour economists that companies exhibited an *internal labour market* structure that differentiated between various types of worker (see LABOUR MARKET). Sociological application of the model has led to the extension of the term *segmentalism* between companies and across industries as well as within companies (Freedman, 1976). Central to any consideration of *segmentalism* is the twin problematic of *skill* and *control*. SKILL is as much a socially structured phenomenon as it is a body of knowledge combined with physical dexterity. Moreover, the ability to sustain claims to skilled status is generally associated with relatively high levels of work autonomy and control. *Segmentalism*, therefore, permits the sociologist to differentiate between groups of workers in terms of their ability to sustain claims for skilled status and occupational autonomy and control. The social structuring of skill and occupational status also means that workers' expectations are constrained by socio-historical precedence in which white male workers have been viewed as being the only general category (as 'bread winners') for whom relatively high wages, skilled status and career prospects have been generally available. By contrast, women and ethnic groups of workers have had need of Equal Opportunity legislation to obtain the right even to be considered for such employment. However, the impact of international competition (GLOBALIZATION) on labour markets has led to a serious undermining of these labour market assumptions. No longer is it the case that large corporations and public sector organisations can be assumed to provide secure employment (Rubery, 1996: 27).

Segmentalism permits a finer delineation to be made in the analysis of labour markets than one simply premised upon a *dualistic* approach, for sociological research purposes it lacks the degree of specificity required for the empirical study of particular labour markets at regional and local levels (see LOCAL LABOUR MARKETS).

segregated conjugal-role relationship a division of labour within a household that involves separate tasks for each partner. The term was first used by Elizabeth Bott (1957), who suggested that such relationships were most often found in communities with close networks of family and friends which supported separate areas of activity for women and men. It is often suggested that this kind of role relationship is being replaced by the JOINT CONJUGAL-ROLE RELATIONSHIP, but there is much evidence to suggest that household tasks are still highly gender-segregated, ironing and car maintenance being the most often quoted examples. See also SYMMETRICAL FAMILY.

segregation the spatial separation of a RACE, CLASS OR ETHNIC GROUP by discriminatory means. Racial segregation can be enforced by law, as in the southern US until the 1950s, or in the system of APARTHEID in South Africa. Such segregation can take the form of separate facilities (schools, beaches, transport, etc.) or the establishment of racially homogeneous territories (as in the 'Bantustan' policy in South Africa pre-1991). In many countries, residential or educational segregation exists that does not have the force of law but results from economic and social DISCRIMINATION. See also GHETTO.

self a mental construction of the person, by the person, but inevitably formed from social experience. Thus the person sees him/herself reflected by others, in their reactions, and these are interpreted through the lattice of self-perception. MEAD (1934) is particularly associated with this idea of the self as being a social construction; self cannot exist without society – the self is where knowledge resides, but the knowledge is about society, which surrounds it. Theorists such as Mead and COOLEY (see SYMBOLIC INTERACTIONISM, LOOKING-GLASS SELF) and some sociologists also emphasize the REFLEXIVITY and creativity possessed by social actors. This view of the self and *self-identity* contrasts sharply with conceptions of DECENTRED SELF recently to the fore within POSTSTRUCTURALISM (e.g. LACAN).

The 'self' also receives varied formulation within PSYCHOLOGY and PSYCHOANALYSIS (see EGO-PSYCHOLOGY, OBJECT RELATIONS SCHOOL, LACAN).

The concept of self is particularly important to developmental and HUMANISTIC psychologists. Humanistic theorists (e.g. MASLOW, 1954) see the goal of the individual as SELF-ACTUALIZATION. (See also SOCIAL IDENTITY, PERSONALITY).

self-actualization the realization of personal potential. The term is associated with MASLOW's (1954) hierarchy of needs, where it is at the peak, only being achievable, according to his theory, if all other biological and social needs have been met. It is used more generally within the HUMANISTIC MOVEMENT to which the concepts of SELF and personal growth are central.

self-destroying prophecy see SELF-FULFILLING AND SELF-DESTROYING PROPHECY.

self-fulfilling and self-destroying prophecy two ever present possibilities that accompany any attempts at social or sociological generalization and prediction. These may either be:

(a) spuriously 'confirmed' merely as the outcome of their pronouncement, e.g. a stock exchange crash brought about by its expectation; or

(b) undermined, because on knowledge of these becoming available, people take action to prevent the outcome in question, e.g. uncongested roads at a predicted time of rush during a rail strike because people travel at other times to avoid the rush.

The occurrence of self-fulfilling and self-destroying predictions is an indication of VOLUNTARISM and choice in social behaviour (i.e. that it involves SOCIAL ACTION, which is purposive, in which events get monitored, is capable of reacting to feedback, etc.). Sometimes the fact that this happens is erected into a general principle (sic) that significant sociological generalizations, sociological laws, etc. are not possible in sociology or the social sciences. However, that social participants often have the capacity to change their actions does not mean that they always have this capacity, e.g. 'social structural' forces may intervene (see also STRUCTURE AND AGENCY). Thus all possibility of successful, non-spurious sociological generalizations is not ruled out by the existence of self-fulfilling and self-destroying hypotheses. See also HISTORICAL GENERALIZATIONS, FREE WILL.

self-help groups groups of people, often in some distress, set up for mutual support and assistance towards renewed psychological health. Self-help groups are part of the general group-therapy movement, and though having a group leader, or facilitator, is not regarded as obligatory it is usual to have one. The emphasis is on sharing a common experience and current emotions, and it is through this sharing and the deeper understanding of SELF and others it brings, that the healing process takes place. Such groups are commonly found in work with the bereaved, and with sufferers from eating disorders and alcoholism. See also SOCIOLOGY OF THE BODY.

self-identity the self-concept; the self as reflexively understood, as a continuing project – see also SELF.

semantic differential a device, designed by Osgood et al. (1957), to assess a person's phenomenological experience (see PHENOMENOLOGICAL PSYCHOLOGY). It is a way of standardizing and quantifying a person's assessments of objects/people/experiences according to several bipolar, seven-point scales. Thus, for example, the subject may be required to assess his or her mother according to the scale good – bad, choosing one of seven points on the continuum. This might be repeated for the scales warm – cold, happy – sad, or any other pairs of adjectives the investigator thinks is appropriate to gaining more understanding of the person's perception of the mother. At least 15 scales are normally required to provide an informative profile. Three main factors are involved, according to Osgood: Evaluative, Potency and Activity. The scores can be used to compare one subject's varying responses to different stimuli concepts, or responses from a group of individuals may be compared. Responses to a wide range of concepts and in varied settings, from therapeutic to consumer choice, can be assessed by this technique.

semantics the subdivision of LINGUISTICS concerned with meaning. Semantics attempts the systematic study of the assignment of meanings to minimal meaning-bearing elements and the combination of these in the production of more complex meaningful expressions. A variety of theories seek to account for semantic relations, ranging from behaviourist psychology, COMPONENTIAL ANALYSIS and theories based in modern logics, to sociological accounts taking meaning to be unavoidably a local achievement of interactive negotiation. Currently in logical semantics the search is on for an integrated SYNTAX and semantics. In this, syntax is framed as a structural vehicle for meanings, which moves from 'possible worlds' to 'truth values'. The project amounts to a technical reworking of the VERIFICATION PRINCIPLE that meaning is to be equated with a set of truth conditions. If the programme were to be successful it would possess important implications for sociology.

semiology *or* **semiotics** the general science of SIGNS, whether these signs appear in language, in literature or in the world of artefacts. As an aspect of STRUCTURALISM, semiology evolved from the linguistic studies of SAUSSURE. Its leading exponent was Roland BARTHES.

Although the idea of a general science of signs first appeared at the turn of the century in the work of Saussure, it was not until the

1960s, and in the fields of MASS MEDIA research and CULTURAL STUDIES that the idea was developed. In the realm of cultural studies semiology has involved the study of areas ignored by other disciplines (e.g. eating habits) and opened up the question of the relationships between cultural codes and power relationships. Its key concepts are the *signifier* (a thing, word or picture) and the *signified* (the mental picture or meaning indicated by the signifier), and the sign is the association or relationship established between them (see also SIGNIFIER AND SIGNIFIED). Some relationships may be fairly direct (*iconic*) and others may involve considerable mediation because of their arbitrariness. Semiology draws attention to the layers of meaning which may be embodied in a simple set of representations (e.g. the representations of 'Christmas' on greetings cards: Santa, Merrie England, Virgin and Child, fluffy animals, and so on). Barthes said that signs communicate latent as well as manifest meanings. They can signify moral values and they can generate feelings or attitudes in the viewer (e.g. a photograph of a Rottweiler = dog = power, a fighting dog = threat to children). Thus signs may be collected and organized into complex codes of communication. See also BRICOLAGE.

semiotic see KRISTEVA.

semi-periphery see CENTRE AND PERIPHERY.

sensitizing concept any sociological concept which, in contrast with fully operationalized or 'definitive concepts', 'merely suggests directions along which to look' (BLUMER, 1954). Whereas 'definitive concepts have specified empirical referents which can be readily operationalized, e.g. 'social class' operationalized in terms of income level or years of schooling, sensitizing concepts are less precise. They alert sociologists to certain aspects of social phenomena, e.g. GOFFMAN's concept of MORAL CAREER. However, no hard-and-fast distinction exists between the two kinds of concept.

sensorimotor stage see PIAGET.

separation of home from work see DOMESTIC LABOUR, PUBLIC AND PRIVATE SPHERES, FACTORY SYSTEM.

separation of ownership from control see MANAGERIAL REVOLUTION.

sequestration the forcible removal of goods and possessions, and, as used by FOUCAULT (1975), the enforced deprivation of personal liberty by the state in modern societies within specialized forms of CARCERAL ORGANIZATION.

sequestration of experience the separation in modern societies of day-to-day life from full contact with experiences such as madness, sickness and death which in historical societies forced people to confront and cope with disturbing existential questions. The effect of this sequestration, according to GIDDENS (1991), is a social and moral impoverishment that increases the incidence of ONTOLOGICAL INSECURITY.

serfdom an arrangement whereby unfree PEASANTS hold land on condition of payment of rent in labour, in kind or in cash. The practice is commonly associated with that of FEUDALISM in Europe, and for many analyses is one of the core features.

Unlike SLAVES, serfs normally possessed and owned some means of production such as agricultural equipment, but were usually tenants of the land. They had limited legal and judicial freedom, and were typically not free to buy and sell land, move, or even to marry without a landlord's consent. There were important regional variations, partly dependent on the power of the landlord to enforce restrictions. Serfs often had access to common land which gave them potential economic activities outside of the control of the landlord; the extent of this independence was often a source of conflict between the two groups. In some areas in Europe, although not in England after the Norman Conquest, not all land was claimed by a landlord, and this *allodial* land could be occupied by serfs who had escaped from a landlord's control. Serfdom changed over

time so that by the end of the feudal period in Western Europe, rent was more likely to be in cash, the extent of a landlord's control less, and in England during the 14th century, freehold rather than leasehold arrangements were more common. Hilton (1973) provides one of the most revealing analyses of the English experience. In Western Europe serfdom had largely disappeared by the end of the 15th century, but persisted in Eastern Europe for far longer; in Russia serfdom was not legally abolished until 1861. The reasons for its decline, and the differing experiences of East and West, are still subjects of intense debate and central to the analysis of the TRANSITION FROM FEUDALISM TO CAPITALISM. Amongst the possible explanations are:
(a) demographic changes whereby the decline of European population in the 14th century meant that landlords had to allow freedom to peasants in order to retain a labour force;
(b) class conflict between landlords and serfs within which serfs won their status of independent peasants through legal action and rebellion; the inherent political contradictions of feudalism meaning that in some countries, such as France, the crown supported peasant demands for freedom as a part of its conflict with powerful landlords;
(c) the emergence of overseas trade, especially with the discovery of the Americas, which fostered a money economy in Europe, enabling some peasants to buy out of feudal obligations. In Eastern Europe, it has been variously argued that either the less cohesive structure of peasant communities, or the greater cohesiveness of the feudal landlords, enabled the survival of feudal ties and serfdom for a longer period (see Holton, 1985, and Aston and Philipin (eds.), 1985).

serial monogamy see MARRIAGE.

service class administrative workers who act as the servants of CAPITAL (Renner, 1953) or in any way function, as employees, as part of the complex administrative and authoritative apparatuses which today run modern private and public organizations (DAHRENDORF, 1959). As used by GOLDTHORPE et al. (1980), the concept refers to the entirety of members of higher professional, higher technical, administrative and managerial occupations. See also OCCUPATIONAL SCALES.

service sector *or* **tertiary sector** the sector of the economy which provides personal or business services, e.g. tourism or insurance and banking. As such, the service sector is distinguished from the PRIMARY SECTOR and SECONDARY SECTORS of the economy. It is a usual correlate of economic development for the service sector to expand and the primary and secondary sectors to contract.

sex discrimination the practice whereby one sex is given preferential treatment over the other sex. In most societies this is observed as discrimination favouring men as against women.

In those societies characterized by patriarchal relations (see PATRIARCHY), women are systematically and routinely discriminated against in all areas of social life, that is, in both the PRIVATE AND PUBLIC SPHERES of social activity. Sexual discrimination is therefore institutionalized, and in this sense can be compared with racial discrimination. Sexist ideologies and discourses serve to reinforce such practices, thereby granting them legitimation and normalizing them. Importantly, sexual discrimination can be both implicit and explicit, overt and covert. Thus legislation designed to control discriminatory practices on the basis of sex differences, tends to be of limited effect, for example, the Sex Discrimination Act of 1975. Women in patriarchal societies are discriminated against in areas such as employment, political and religious office, housing and major areas of social policy, in relation to property and in both civil and criminal law. Women's position in the class structure, and other major social divisions such as age and race, may either reinforce or weaken the impact of sex discrimination. See also DUAL LABOUR MARKET, SEXUAL DIVISION OF LABOUR.

sexism 1 any attitudes and actions which overtly or covertly discriminate against women or men on the grounds of their SEX OR GENDER – see SEX DISCRIMINATION. 2 any devaluation or denigration of women or men, but particularly women, which is embodied in institutions and social relationships, e.g. the sexist use of language, such as the male personal pronoun, 'he', to refer to men and women. See also PATRIARCHY.

sexual behaviour see SEXUALITY, EROTICISM.

sexual division of labour a specific expression of the DIVISION OF LABOUR where workers are divided according to certain assumptions about 'men's work' and 'women's work'. The sexual division of labour is based upon gender divisions which, although socially constructed, are frequently believed to be the outcome of the 'natural' attributes and aptitudes of the sexes. Some form of sexual division of labour is apparent in most known societies but its particular manifestation and degree of differentiation is socially and historically relative. It is particularly marked in industrial societies, where it is accompanied by a distinction between unpaid DOMESTIC LABOUR and WAGE LABOUR, between the PRIVATE AND PUBLIC SPHERES. Whilst these spheres are gendered (the private sphere being associated with women, the public sphere with men) such divisions are more ideological than empirical. Preindustrial societies and, particularly, many stateless societies, are characterized by a less defined division between the public and the private spheres, and stateless societies generally have a less pronounced sexual division of labour.

In contemporary capitalist societies, women are concentrated in particular industries, services and caring professions. Women's experience of paid work is predominantly one of poorer working conditions, lower levels of pay and under-unionization relative to men. Despite the passing of the *Equal Pay Act 1970* and the *Sex Discrimination Act 1975* women in Britain continue to earn only approximately 75% of the average male hourly wage. Women are also more likely than men to engage in poorly paid 'homework', and part-time work and to experience insecure employment. Barrett (1988) has suggested that both a *vertical division of labour* and a *horizontal division of labour* characterize men and women's work. In the former men are advantaged with respect to pay and conditions of work. In the latter women are to be found concentrated in a limited number of occupations which both reflect and reinforce social expectations about femininity and domesticity. Coulson *et al.* (1975) have suggested that the difference between men's and women's work and the segregation of jobs according to gender amounts to 'industrial apartheid'.

It is important to recognize that such divisions must be understood by reference to a complex interaction between economic factors and the social order as a whole. Barron and Norris (1976) have argued that the labour market in capitalist societies is characterized by a division between the 'primary sector' (highly paid, secure, skills recognized) and the 'secondary sector' (low paid. insecure and deskilled). Men occupy most of the places in the primary sector whilst women are consigned to the secondary sector. Such an approach fails, however, to explain why it is women who occupy the secondary sector. (See also DUAL LABOUR MARKET.)

The concept of the RESERVE ARMY OF LABOUR has been used to explain the sexual division of labour in capitalist societies by reference to a Marxist theory of capital wage labour. It emphasizes the interests of the employer in ensuring a dispensable work force which can be returned to the domestic sphere during periods of economic recession. Married women's paid labour is seen as similar to migrant labour in that it too provides capital with an industrial reserve army. However, there is no perfect comparison between married women's work and that of migrant labour. The concentration of women in certain sectors makes it difficult for employers to find substitutes for them and their lower rates of pay may protect them from redundancy.

The failure of Marxist theory to explain why women occupy the positions they do in the labour market has prompted a concern with the issue of domestic labour in the family and women's responsibility for it (see DOMESTIC LABOUR DEBATE). The relationship between women's position in wage labour and their role in domestic work and child care has been stressed by many feminist sociologists. Barrett (1988) has argued that women's position as paid workers is strongly influenced by the structure of the family, women's role in reproduction and the 'ideology of domesticity'. Furthermore, the ideology of the 'family wage' in which men are regarded as the primary bread winners has functioned to keep women's wages lower than men's. Thus, the benefits derived by capital and by male workers must also be considered in any explanation. Cockburn (1983) has stressed the role played by organized male labour through its resistance to women's equality in paid work. Barrett (1988) has noted the labour movement's complicity with 'protective legislation' as a strategy for reducing competition from female workers. Precapitalist ideologies of gender render women vulnerable both to exploitation in the labour market and to oppression by men within the family. Women's domestic labour is deskilled by reference to the ideology of 'maternal instincts' and this deskilling carries over into paid work where women's involvement in caring and servicing work is seen as a natural outcome of gender attributes. Deem (1986) has shown that the impact of the sexual division of labour on women's leisure time has not been seriously considered within mainstream sociology. The study of women's work and women's leisure has been relatively neglected within the discipline until the late 1980s, when both Marxist and radical feminists started to address these issues.

sexuality 1 (common usage) a natural or essential property of the individual which finds expression through sexual activities and relationships.

2 an object of physiological, psychological and sociological investigation first established in the 19th-century by sexologists such as Havelock Ellis and Krafft-Ebing and the psychoanalyst FREUD, and continued by many others, e.g. Kinsey et al. (1948).

3 an area of social and cultural behaviour subject to state regulation and control, particularly in the context of prostitution and HOMOSEXUALITY.

4 (general sociological usage) personal and interpersonal expression of those socially constructed qualities, desires, roles and identities which have to do with sexual behaviour and activity.

5 a social process involving both institutional and experiential dimensions of sexual relationships.

6 a normative set of expectations concerning sexual practices.

7 preference for, or an orientation towards, specific forms of sexual expression and desire.

Sociological usages of the term frequently stress the social and cultural relativity of norms surrounding sexual behaviour and the sociohistorical construction of sexual identities and roles. In doing so, it contrasts with common usage which regards sexuality as a property largely intrinsic to the individual or as something which is determined by the early psychosexual experiences of the child (see FREUD). Writers such as FOUCAULT (1979) and Weeks (1985) have challenged naturalistic and essentialist arguments, referring to the way in which cultural definitions of sexuality and the control of the BODY are exercised 'among other ways' by the medium of systematic knowledge. Desire and the objects of desire are seen as being shaped by social forces (see also EROTICISM). Sexuality and its social constructions have featured in debates within feminist and gay politics, where androcentric and heterosexist definitions of sexuality are seen to be inimical to the interests of women and gays.

shaman a provider of religio-ethnomedical services in simple societies. Usually a part-time rather than a full-time practitioner, the shaman typically emerges as different from his clients by an ability to enter trance-like states or other abnormal states of consciousness. This is interpreted as involving a special capacity to make contact with and mobilize supernatural powers. The position of the shaman is based on these personal powers; this contrasts with the priest in more differentiated forms of religion, who is recruited to the organization. See also MAGIC, WITCHCRAFT AND SORCERY.

sharecropping an arrangement whereby a landholder receives a given amount of a harvest from those working the land. Various forms of land possession may be covered by this arrangement: the 'landholder' may or may not have absolute ownership of the land, and the share cropper may or may not have rights of possession of the land. The *Macmillan Dictionary of Anthropology* (Seymour-Smith, 1986) neatly summarizes sharecropping as an arrangement between a land-supplier and a labour-supplier. This is a common arrangement in AGRARIAN SOCIETIES and one of the various ways in which the PEASANTRY have access to land and its products. Examples have been found throughout history and in most areas of the world (Pearce, 1983). The most common arrangement historically has been for there to be a 50/50 split of the harvest between the labourer and the land-supplier. This arrangement seems to be most common when other means of labour control have broken down and the supervisory control of the land-supplier is weakened. Thus sharecropping became common in the postbellum southern United States after the abolition of slavery and persisted until the 1930s. Similarly, it has been argued that it rose in importance with the decline of SERFDOM in Europe. Sharecropping continues to exist in many parts of the contemporary THIRD WORLD, especially in Latin America and Asia. As with other noncapitalist rural labour arrangements, there is debate as to whether it is compatible with the spread of CAPITALISM. Thus it has been seen as transitional between tenant farming and wage labour.

shifting agriculture *or* **slash and burn** a type of nonintensive agriculture, practised in tropical forests where soil fertilities are low. It involves the clearing and burning of existing vegetation in order to cultivate crops. When the soil becomes depleted, or earlier, the society moves on to repeat the process elsewhere, often leaving the forest to regrow. Although perhaps ecologically sound, such forms of agriculture are threatened by economic development. Compare HUNTER-GATHERER.

shift work the organization of work into relays. Most common, within the UK, is the double day-shift, but three and four continuous 24-hour shift working is carried out in about a quarter of all work places (Millward and Stevens, 1986). The main reasons for shift working are to maximize the utilization of plant and equipment and thereby reduce costs, and to meet production targets and deadlines. It is also the case that certain industrial processes are, by their nature, continuous. This is particularly so with the continuous process technology associated with the petrochemical industry.

Workers' experience of shift work is that it is generally disruptive to their family and social life and deleterious to their health and physical wellbeing (Gallie, 1978).

Shift work is also commonly found among professional and technical workers associated with human services, notably in health care, but also covering commercial activities such as air transport. Here the pattern of recruitment and promotion (i.e. ANTICIPATORY SOCIALIZATION) may alter the workers' perceptions of the disruptions that shift work causes to their lives.

shudra (sudra) see CASTE.

sib a term used in US ANTHROPOLOGY to refer to a body of people claiming common UNILINEAL DESCENT. The more common term is CLAN.

sick role *or* **patient role** sickness viewed as a special status and as the basis of social identity, and distinguished from illness as a biomedical category.

The concept originated from PARSONS' (1951) discussion of the role of medicine in industrial societies and describes a form of socially sanctioned deviance possessing the following characteristics:

(a) the sick person is exempted from normal social responsibilities;
(b) the sick person cannot be expected to look after himself or herself;
(c) the sick person is expected to desire a return to normality;
(d) the sick person is expected to seek competent professional help.

According to Parsons, being sick interferes with normal social responsibilities and permits exemption from them. Consequently it may sometimes also be a status desired by those unwilling to meet their social obligations. Medicine therefore can be seen as having the function of social control in addition to a therapeutic one. It deters malingerers and promotes an awareness of social obligation among the sick.

Parsons' formulation has been subjected to much criticism on empirical and theoretical grounds. Nevertheless, the 'sick role' continues to be used as a sensitizing and organizing concept for empirical studies of interaction in clinical settings by the SOCIOLOGY OF HEALTH AND MEDICINE. See also SYMPTOM ICEBERG, TRIVIAL CONSULTATION.

sign **1** any direct indicator of an occurrence, e.g. the appearance of spots is a sign of measles (*natural signs*).

2 any SYMBOL, including the written marks for words, which stands for – or represents – both a meaning and an external thing which 'corresponds' to the meaning. Taking an 'empiricist' view, there is a sense in which signs 'picture' an external reality (see EMPIRICISM).

3 (modern LINGUISTICS and STRUCTURALISM) any *signifier* which *signifies* a concept or 'meaning', the *signified*. In this view, the relation between the SIGNIFIER and SIGNIFIED is internal to a particular language (see also LANGUE AND PAROLE, SAUSSURE).

As emphasized in SEMIOLOGY (OR SEMIOTICS), the general theory of signs, signs may take many forms, including *icons* (pictures), dress, conspicuous social display, etc. – thus 'referents' also signify – and all such signs are amenable to analysis in structural terms, i.e. as a system of 'DIFFERENCES'.

Compared with sense **1** (natural signs), senses **2** and **3** involve 'arbitrary' rather than natural signs. Sense **2** in particular, that our ability to refer depends on internal 'differences', also emphasizes that linguistic structures (at least the semantic structures) are 'social' not biological or individual in form (see also WITTGENSTEIN, FORMS OF LIFE, PARADIGM). Sense **3** is also central in modern POST-EMPIRICIST and POST-STRUCTURALIST thinking in philosophy, leading to celebrations or accusations of 'loss of reference' – see RELATIVISM, INCOMMENSURABILITY. But an emphasis on the 'internal relations' of sign systems need not imply lack of reference, merely that any system of reference cannot be guaranteed (see also FEYERABEND, KUHN). See also SEMANTICS, BODY LANGUAGE, METAPHOR.

significance test (STATISTICS) a test designed to assess whether an observed (numerical) result can have occurred by chance. The result of the test is expressed as a statistic (e.g. t-ratio, F-ratio) which can be assessed against different levels of probability. It is usual to accept a level of probability of 0.05, i.e. that there is only a 5% probability of the result having occurred by chance.

Examples of significance tests are the t-test (parametric) and the Wilcoxon (nonparametric) (see STATISTICS AND STATISTICAL ANALYSIS). These tests are designed to test for the significance of the observed difference between two groups of data. For example, in social survey work two samples may be taken, racial attitudes in cities with and without ethnic minority problems, perhaps. There may be an apparent difference (numerical) between these groups, but the groups were samples and therefore the data is subject to SAMPLING ERROR. The difference between them must therefore be tested to see if there is a statistically significant difference between them. Significance tests are designed to set up a NULL HYPOTHESIS, stating 'no difference', and the test result either confirms or disconfirms this.

significant other any SOCIAL ACTOR adopted as a role model by another social actor. The concept is particularly associated with G. H. MEAD.

signifier and signified (LINGUISTICS) with reference to any linguistic SIGN, the distinction between the term (its acoustical form) – the *signifier* – and the concept (or idea) signified by the term – the *signified.* The distinction was introduced by SAUSSURE. Further aspects of the sign emphasized by him were its essentially 'arbitrary' character, i.e. no inherent or necessary relationship between the signifier and the concept signified – thus, the term 'dog' in English is replaced by the different term 'chien' in French. Thus, the internal, essentially 'relational' character of language as a structure is emphasized. See also LANGUE AND PAROLE, SYNTAGMATIC AND PARADIGMATIC, DIFFERENCE, DECONSTRUCTION.

Simmel, Georg (1858–1918) German sociologist and philosopher whose extensive and stylish writings and brilliant lectures have ensured his place as one of the influential classical sociologists within the discipline, although not having the extent of influence of MARX, WEBER or DURKHEIM.

Simmel presented society as a 'web of interactions' (see SOCIATION). He is particularly remembered as the founder of FORMAL SOCIOLOGY, based on drawing a distinction between FORM AND CONTENT in social analysis, in which formal sociology deals with the universal recurring (abstract and *a priori*) 'forms' of social interaction examining the specifics of social interaction, i.e. its 'content', only in the light of these forms (see DYAD AND TRIAD, STRANGER, SOCIABILITY). For all this, there remain strong functionalist and evolutionary overtones in his work, e.g. he regarded social differentiation as bringing 'adaptation' (although also sometimes disorganization). For the most part, how ever, Simmel regarded claims for a fully unified sociological theory as, at the very least, premature.

Simmel's Jewish background meant that he never achieved the high academic positions his work undoubtedly merited. However, his work was highly influential. After his death, it was promoted in the US by the Chicago sociologists PARK and Burgess, where it influenced the tenor of the work of the CHICAGO SCHOOL Simmel's influence is also strongly in evidence in the work of GOFFMAN, with whom there are similarities of presentational style as well as method, and in the CONFLICT THEORY of L. Coser (Coser, 1956, 1965). Coser's work on the *'functions* of social conflict', also underlines an abiding feature of Simmel's sociology, an emphasis on the duality involved in many social forms.

Simmel wrote more than 30 books. As well as the several collections of his numerous essays and fragments from his work, especially *The Sociology of Georg Simmel* (Wolff, 1950) and *Conflict and the Web of Group Affiliations* (Simmel, 1955), the most important in recent discussions of his work have been his extended discussion of MONEY, *The Philosophy of Money* (1978) and his writings on leisure forms and urban life, which have been seen as anticipating many of the features of contemporary social life – e.g. flux and fragmentation – also emphasized in theories of POSTMODERNITY. A recent general discussion of Simmel's work is provided by Frisby, *Sociological Impressionism: a Reassessment of Georg Simmel's Social Theory* (1981).

simple commodity production see PETTY COMMODITY PRODUCTION.

simple reproduction of capital (MARXISM) the process whereby material and social elements of production are reproduced. Wages paid to workers enable them to live, and to present themselves for further work. The SURPLUS VALUE produced in the production process is used by the capitalist to replace raw materials and other capital consumed. However, in this form of reproduction there is no expansion, merely replacement. The main aspect of capitalism is its expansion, thus this form is analytic and likely to exist empirically in some sectors of the economy but not in normal times for the capitalist economy as a whole.

simple society the least internally differentiated, and earliest, form(s) of human societies. Along with PRIMITIVE SOCIETY, one of a number of terms used to refer to such societies, and less pejorative than alternatives, its use reflects an evolutionary view of human societies. The contrast drawn is with more internally differentiated, complex societies, and within such a perspective social development may be seen as progressing from simple to complex forms (e.g. Sahlins, 1971). In some respects, however, the term simple society is undoubtedly a misnomer, as can be seen for example in the frequently complex patterns of KINSHIP within these societies.

simulation the electronic copying or modelling of unique objects. The most famous sociological application of the term is by BAUDRILLARD (1983). He contends that contemporary society is so thoroughly saturated with electronic models and versions of unique objects that distinctions between reality and fiction are no longer valid. See also AURA, HYPERREALITY.

situational analysis and situational logic a methodological ideal, most closely associated with METHODOLOGICAL INDIVIDUALISM and the work of POPPER, in which it is proposed that social situations are analysed in terms of the motivations and goals of social actors and the logical implications of these, without recourse to either 'psychologism' or 'sociologism'.

skew see MEASURES OF DISPERSION.

skewed distribution a distribution of data obtained from a sample or population which does not show the NORMAL DISTRIBUTION of a bell-shaped curve. In a normal distribution the MEAN, MEDIAN and MODE fall in the same place – the curve is symmetrical. In a positively skewed distribution (Fig. 28a) the mode and median are less than the mean, while in a negatively skewed distribution (Fig. 28b) the mean is less than the median and mode. Some population characteristics have a normal distribution, e.g. height, others may be skewed, e.g. social class among students in higher education.

skill 1 (relating to a job or occupation) qualities required of a particular job in terms of the range and technical complexity of the

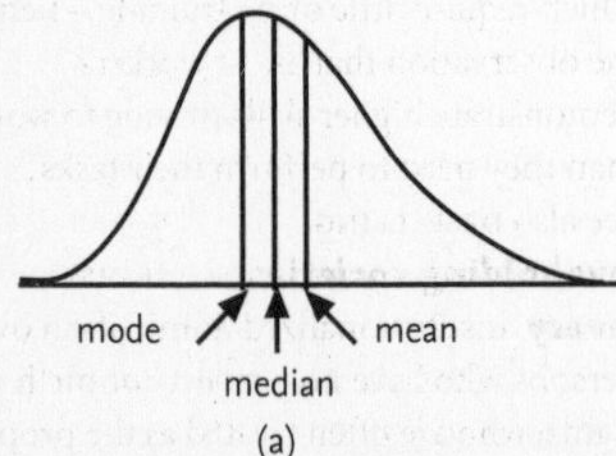

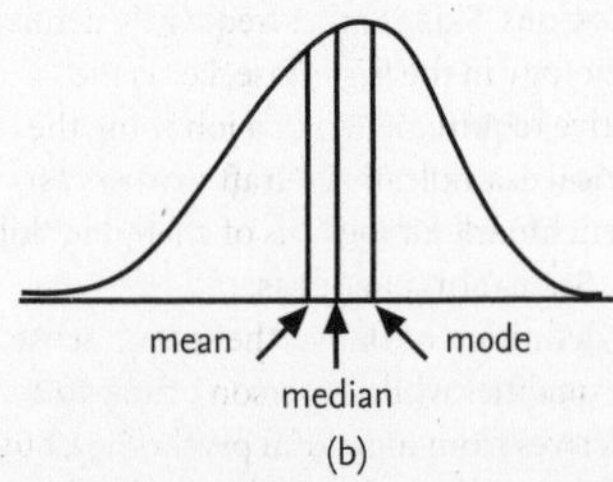

Fig. 28 **Skewed distribution.** (a) Positively skewed distribution. (b) Negatively skewed distribution.

tasks involved, level of discretion and control over how the work is performed, time needed to learn the job and the level of knowledge and training necessary.

2 (relating to a person) capabilities acquired by a person in his or her education and working life which may include one or more of the following: cognitive abilities (capacity for abstract thought, memory. concentration), manual dexterity, knowledge, and interpersonal abilities (ability to communicate, cooperate, empathize with others, leadership).

3 (social construct) a label attached to certain types of work or occupation as a result of custom and practice, union negotiation and job regulation which attracts differential rates of pay and status, and which are normally reflected in official classifications of occupations as 'skilled', 'semiskilled' or 'unskilled' in the division of labour.

4 (wider social sense) the most general capacities and COMPETENCE possessed by social actors, the sense in which participation in social life is always a 'skilled accomplishment'. The discussion that follows deals mainly with 'skill' in senses **1** and **3**.

Skill is an ambiguous concept in which its various meanings are often confused or inadequately defined. Different theoretical approaches to changes in skill levels and the empirical research supporting them depend critically on the way skill is defined. For example, theories of DESKILLING often use an 'objective' or technical definition of skill (**1** above) whereas arguments for upskilling define skill in terms of formal qualifications or official classifications of different occupations. Skill is most frequently defined in sociology in the first sense, i.e. as the objective requirements for a job using the historical example of the craft workers as the benchmark for analysis of changing skill levels. See LABOUR PROCESS.

The definition of skill in the second sense, as the qualities which a person brings to a job, derives from industrial psychology, but also informs discussion of the marketability and substitutability of skills in the labour market (see DUAL LABOUR MARKET). Skills acquired in this sense may depend partly on natural aptitudes although sociologists generally argue that most skills are learnt. Discussion of changes in the nature and level of skills has included analysis of the rise and decline of skills which are highly specialized and of transferable skills which are more indeterminate and less job specific and which may, therefore, command higher pay and status. The concept of skill as residing in the person is also important in the analysis of *tacit skills* which refer to the often unconscious and habitual skills which are learnt in the workplace through close familiarity with machines or work practices. Such tacit skills are frequently job specific and unrecognized in formal job status but are nevertheless critical to employers for the day to day operation of production or the provision of services.

The definition of skill as a social construct draws attention to the point that the definitions of skill above may not correspond in practice. Certain types of work may involve high levels of skill in the technical or objective sense but go unrewarded in the labour market, women's work being a notable example (see SEXUAL DIVISION OF LABOUR). Conversely, work may attract high pay and status via union negotiation or employers' strategies to 'divide and rule' their workforce such that job gradings bear little resemblance to actual differences in skill (see also INTERNAL LABOUR MARKET). Similarly, the profusion of 'semiskilled' job titles may refer to jobs which require little or no training – hence the observation that 'most workers demonstrate higher skills driving to work than they need to perform their tasks'. See also DESKILLING.

slaveholding societies see SLAVERY.

slavery institutionalized domination over persons who have no property or birth rights, who are often treated as the property of another, and who are subject to control in all aspects of their lives, with no enforceable limits. Such a system, in which the *slave* is dominated by a *slave master*, is often referred to as *chattel slavery*, which may be distinguished from other forms of unfreedom and unfree labour such as SERFDOM and debt bondage (see DEBT PEONAGE).

In the most comprehensive comparative study of slavery, O. Patterson (1982) argues that there are three universal features. First, a slave master has virtually unlimited rights of violence or threat of violence over a slave; secondly, a slave experiences 'natal alienation' being genealogically isolated and denied all rights of birth; thirdly, a slave has no honour.

Unlike other definitions of slavery, Patterson shows that in many societies masters had little interest in what slaves produced. For example, in kin-based societies in Africa, slaves were acquired as a means of increasing the number of dependants, and hence the prestige, of the master with little resulting economic difference between the master and slave. So the experience of Ancient Greece and Rome and the antebellum Southern states of North America from the 17th to the 19th century, where enslavement was primarily for labour purposes, cannot be incorporated in a general definition of slavery.

Patterson further questions the usual definition of slaves as being the property of the masters. He argues that, viewed comparatively, the concept of property in connection with slavery is socially variable with the legal recognition of absolute property common in Europe but not universal, emerging only with Roman law. This concept of absolute property may have emerged from the institution of slavery rather than the other way round. Patterson points out that other categories of dependants may be defined as the property of others, so that this in itself may not distinguish slaves: rather the distinctive feature is that slaves are denied rights of property (except for the *peculium* whereby the master invested partial and temporary rights of possession (see USUFRUCT) in the slave, but with ownership rights still vested in the master). Thus, in defining slavery, Patterson omits the concept of ownership and on the level of personal relations defines it as 'the permanent, violent domination of natally alienated and generally dishonoured persons'.

Near-universal correlates of slavery have been the sexual abuse of female slaves by their masters, the high frequency of concubinage and sometimes marriage between master and slave, and the rarity of enslavement of members of the master's own ETHNIC GROUP (with Russia in the 17th- and 18th-centuries being one of the few examples of such a practice).

Since slavery has existed in many known societies from the very beginning of human history, there have been many variations in the practice and institutions. Some societies such as Ancient Greece and Rome (see ANCIENT SOCIETY), the US, Brazil and many parts of the Caribbean from the late 17th century to the mid-19th, may be termed *slave-holding societies*, in as much as the ruling classes derived most of their wealth by extracting ECONOMIC SURPLUS from slaves, even though, as in Ancient Greece and Rome, this may not have been the most prevalent form of labour (de Ste. Croix, 1981). Other variations are in the means of enslavement, of which capture in warfare and kidnapping have historically been the most important, accounting for the majority of slaves in the Atlantic slave trade between the 17th and 19th centuries. Other means have included penal enslavement, the main source of slaves in Imperial China, and birth, with many variations between societies in how slave status was inherited, e.g. Roman practice was for slave status to derive from the mother, but under the Near Eastern and Islamic rule the higher status of the parents was decisive, meaning that children of mixed (slave and free) parentage usually became free. The means of acquiring slaves has also varied, internal or external trade being among the most common (Patterson even argues that slavery may have been involved with the origins of trade) and dowry and bride payments.

A final main variation concerns *manumission* practices, the freeing of slaves. The best-known slavery system in the modern world, that of the southern USA, is unusual in that manumission rates were amongst the lowest known. In many systems, slaves often became free on the death of their master, through marriage or concubinage with the master, especially in Islamic societies, by adoption, or through political manumission, e.g. by the state in recognition of acts of bravery in warfare. On freedom, however, the slave often remained in a dependent relationship with the ex-master, although, again, the US South was exceptional in granting such low status to freed slaves.

No known slave masters have succeeded in totally controlling all slaves or in having them accept totally their dishonoured status (compare DIALECTIC OF CONTROL). Thus slave rebellion has been a constant feature throughout history, although the lack of any ready basis for unity among slaves means that the only documented successful overthrow of a slavery system by rebellion was in San Domingo in the French Caribbean 1791–1803 (see James, 1980). As with all systems of domination, the sole use of violence as a means of control is self-destructive, so that various other incentives have figured, primarily the possibility of freedom, but also the right to acquire possessions which may be used to buy freedom. The extent to which slave systems subordinate psychologically, by the creation of a 'slave mentality' (e.g. 'Uncle Tomism'), has been challenged recently (see Weinstein and Gatell, 1979; Genovese, 1971).

Debate also exists as to whether slave systems are inherently inefficient compared with non-slave systems (e.g. involve more costs of social control, social subsistence and labour reproduction, and involve less flexibility in use of capital). Associated with this is the question of whether their elimination has been brought about primarily by economic or political considerations. The suggestion is that slave systems only become established where other forms of labour are in short supply and/or where a ready source of slave labour exists.

Small, Albion (1854–1926) US sociologist who at the University of Chicago in 1892 became the chairman of the first-ever graduate school in sociology, and in 1894 (with George Vincent) the author of the first textbook in sociology. In 1895 he also founded the *American Journal of Sociology*. In Small's view, sociology implemented a programme of analysis which began with Adam SMITH, and in his own work he sought to detach sociology from too close an identification with the approach of COMTE. Small wrote several books, including *General Sociology* (1905) and *The Origins of Sociology* (1924) but they are rarely read today.

Smith, Adam (1723–90) Scottish moral philosopher, best remembered for his *An Inquiry into the Nature and Causes of the Wealth of Nations* (1776) in which, after a seminal account of the DIVISION OF LABOUR, he proposed that the individual pursuit of self-interest and the unimpeded operation of the market acted as an 'invisible hand' resulting in the achievement of the 'common good'. A leading member of the SCOTTISH ENLIGHTENMENT, and a visitor to France where he met with leading French social and economic thinkers, Smith wrote on many topics apart from economic issues: on morality, on politics, on law, on language. In *The Theory of Moral Sentiments* (1779) he suggested that ethical judgements depend on persons imagining themselves in the position of others and can also be illuminated by considering how an ideal impartial observer might judge right and wrong. Although widely associated with advocacy of the doctrine of LAISSEZ FAIRE, Smith was not blind to the adverse implications of the division of labour, noting its potentially stultifying and dehumanizing effect on workers. He allowed that people might well wish to seek to limit such effects, but he believed that in reality governments were likely to be driven by narrow interests. See also CLASSICAL ECONOMISTS.

snowball sampling a method of selecting a SAMPLE by starting with a small selected group of respondents and asking these for further contacts. This is not therefore a RANDOM SAMPLE and no inferences about the characteristics of the parent population can be made from such a study. Its use is primarily in the collection of in-depth, qualitative data, perhaps on sensitive topics, where an obvious SAMPLING FRAME does not exist and the best method of selection is through personal contacts. Such a method might be used in an investigation of sexual habits or bereavement experiences.

sociability any social interaction which exists primarily 'for its own sake and for the fascination which in its own liberation from [social] ties, it diffuses' (Wolff, 1950). Simmel refers to this as the 'play-form of interaction' (see also FORM AND CONTENT). It need have 'no extrinsic results', and 'entirely depends upon the personalities among whom it occurs'. However, Simmel sees in sociability a capacity for transferring the 'seriousness and tragic to a symbolic and shadowy play-form' which can reveal reality obliquely. Thus, although much social interaction involves elements of sociability, the purer play-forms of sociability, e.g. parties or picnics, or mere talk, can be seen as possessing their own specific importance in social life. Although apparently and necessarily 'undirected' and 'unserious', they perform a definite role, first in providing relaxation, distraction, etc., but also in throwing a fresh light on 'serious' endeavours.

social 1 (of certain species of insects and some animal species, including humankind) living together in organized colonies or groups.
2 pertaining to human society and/or to human interaction in organizations, groups.

social action see ACTION, TYPES OF SOCIAL ACTION.

social actor any person who undertakes social ACTION. The term is used for the most part without any assumption that social actors always consciously 'stage-manage' their actions. However, as the use of concepts such as ROLE in sociology indicates, social action does often involve actors playing a 'part', although usually not without the possibility of actors interpreting and reshaping this. That much social action can profitably be understood by viewing it in *specifically* 'dramaturgical' terms is a view taken by some sociologists (see DRAMATURGY, GOFFMAN). Other sociologists (see ETHNOMETHODOLOGY) decline to use the term 'social actor' because of its dramaturgical connotations, preferring to use the term 'member' instead.

social administration 1 the academic field of study that developed out of a 19th-century concern with SOCIAL POLICY.
2 the practice of managing social agencies such as Social Service departments.

Pinker (1971) distinguishes between social administration sense 1 and sociology by arguing that although they share a common starting point, the development of industrial societies, sociology has been primarily concerned with the theoretical explanations of INDUSTRIALIZATION, whilst social administration has been concerned with the practical development of effective policies with which to tackle the problems that have accompanied industrialization, such as POVERTY, CRIME, ill-health, poor housing, etc. The origins of social administration, therefore, are usually located in a number of reforming individuals, such as BOOTH and ROWNTREE. This tradition is thought to have continued in the work of TITMUSS and can be seen to influence the work of a number of contemporary sociologists, such as Peter Townsend. It would be wrong, however, to suggest that the early sociologists were not interested in the policy implications of their work.

The academic development of social administration was institutionalized in social work training by the first university Social

Studies departments. Until recently, many sociologists have been critical of social administration for its lack of theory and for its REFORMIST political position. However, since the 1970s the sociology of social policy and social administration have been more closely integrated following a renewed sociological concern with WELFARE STATES, new theories of social policy and the development of comparative social policy. Some sociologists have suggested that these changes have led to the development of a 'new social administration'. See also APPLIED SOCIOLOGY, SOCIAL WORK, RADICAL SOCIAL WORK.

social and economic contradictions see CONTRADICTION.

social and economic development see ECONOMIC AND SOCIAL DEVELOPMENT.

social and economic rights see CITIZEN RIGHTS, BASIC HUMAN NEEDS.

social anthropology

The study (by Western investigators) of small-scale, 'simple', nonindustrial cultures and societies (see also ANTHROPOLOGY, CULTURAL ANTHROPOLOGY). As a discipline, it overlaps with sociology, sharing many of its theoretical orientations and its methodologies.

As a specialism, social anthropology developed in the 19th century as a scholastic offshoot of imperialist expansion, informed by and engaging in the scientific and pseudoscientific debates of the time. E. Leach (1982) distinguishes a number of tendencies amongst the 'founding fathers' in the period around 1840, united only in their preoccupation with 'exotic' cultures and at times their ETHNOCENTRICITY and arrogance.

The first major theoretical perspective to emerge was that of EVOLUTIONISM. In its time, the variety of evolutionism which became predominant was 'progressive' in the sense that it accepted that the people concerned were 'our fellow creatures', as a book of 1843 argued (quoted in Lienhardt, 1964). On the other hand, this evolutionary perspective was based on the racist assumption that the cultures of 'primitive' people belonged to an earlier and inferior stage of human history and that contemporary European observers could see in those cultures the 'savage' origins of their own societies. Sir Henry MAINE (1861) provides a good example: 'As societies do not advance concurrently, but at different rates of progress, there have been epochs at which men trained to habits of methodical observation have really been in a position to watch and describe the infancy of mankind'. These 'habits of methodical observation' and description were a prominent aspect of the development of the subject. In French, German and US studies, as well as British, intensive field-research into single societies became increasingly common and researchers qualified, criticized and, in many cases, dismissed earlier assumptions about the 'irrationality' and the 'barbarity' of 'primitive' cultures.

In the period after World War I, MALINOWSKI and RADCLIFFE-BROWN were instrumental in advancing the discussion of fieldwork and in establishing STRUCTURAL-FUNCTIONALISM as the dominant perspective in

British social anthropology. Influenced by the theoretical work of DURKHEIM, and emphasizing the importance of direct observation in the field, the anthropologists of this period published a great many studies of different cultures, tending to focus on the analysis of INSTITUTIONS. Thus patterns of KINSHIP, religious belief-systems, MAGIC, political systems, etc. were studied in great detail. As in other social sciences, different emphases and schools emerged and new theoretical debates and issues became important. STRUCTURALISM, particularly as developed in the work of LÉVI-STRAUSS, has been especially influential upon sociological theories.

In recent years, social anthropologists have also directed their attention to the study of their own and other urban, industrial societies, using the techniques and research practices developed in studying other cultures. This trend has made the discipline even harder to distinguish from sociology in many respects, other than by departmental boundaries or the self-definitions of practitioners. See also CULTURE, ETHNOGRAPHY.

social banditry a form of individual or group lawlessness and robbery in which those concerned are *not* regarded as simply criminals by public opinion.

A bandit, according to the *Shorter Oxford English Dictionary*, is 'one who is proscribed or outlawed; hence, a lawless desperate marauder'. But Hobsbawm (1969) has drawn a sharp distinction between criminal outlaws and social bandits. He claims that social banditry flourished in precapitalist agrarian societies. In these societies it was a primitive type of social protest by peasants against oppression and exploitation. The rural poor regarded social bandits as class heroes and as avengers of social injustice who robbed the rich to give to the poor. In return the bandits expected protection and support.

However, Hobsbawm's notion of the social bandit and the heroic claims made on its behalf have come in for criticism by Blok (1974). On the basis of his research in western Sicily, Blok argues that, far from being a simple form of peasant protest, banditry can just as easily be manipulated by ruling groups in order to extend their power. He rejects the concept of social banditry as being rooted in myth and legend.

social behaviourism see MEAD.

social capital (J. Coleman, *Public and Private High Schools: the Impact of Communities*, 1987) the resources, trust and networks that are constitutive of social capacity and empowerment. The provision of improved access to social capital for previously socially excluded groups has been a central aspect of recent emphasis on SOCIAL INCLUSION and the politics of the THIRD WAY. The strategy also seeks to replace 'deviant' – BLACK ECONOMY or criminal – coping strategies of the poor.

social category see GROUP.

social class see CLASS, SOCIAL STRATIFICATION.

social class scales see OCCUPATIONAL SCALES.

social closure the process by which groups seek to increase the advantages of their situation by monopolizing resources and restricting recruitment and access to their group. Examples of this are found in all privileged groups, e.g. marital 'eligibility' in European aristocracies; the system of apprenticeship for skilled manual trades; systems of accreditation and formal membership of professional associations for doctors and lawyers.

The term was first used by WEBER, and, in recent sociology, is particularly associated

social change

The difference between the current and antecedent condition of any selected aspect of social organization or structure.

The study of social change involves as a logical minimum the identification of the phenomenon to be studied, and the use of a historical perspective in order to identify the changes which it has undergone. In practice, this descriptive task is usually linked to the more difficult one of explanation, i.e. an attempt to specify the factor(s) which produced or caused the identified changes in the phenomenon studied. More simply, the objective is to show why change occurred in one way rather than another.

Social change is central to much sociological study and research, since neither societies nor their constituent parts are ever static. The whole range of theoretical perspectives and research methods available within sociology can be used in the study of social change. Clearly, a study of the SOCIALIZATION of, say, new recruits to the armed forces or police would require a different research strategy (participant or nonparticipant observation, for example) to one which examined changing patterns of social mobility within the class structures of contemporary industrial societies (sampling and questionnaire). A study of changing conditions of land tenure among 14th-century European peasants would, in turn, necessitate an approach based on the evidence of historical documents.

If it is true that sociology is always, in one way or another, examining social change, it is also true to say that sociology itself was a child of social change. It is no coincidence that sociology emerged as a discipline when theorists attempted to understand the nature of the dramatic social, economic and political upheavals associated with the industrial revolution of the 18th and 19th centuries in European societies. The seminal work of the three most important figures in early sociological thought – MARX, WEBER and DURKHEIM – can only really be understood in these terms.

Whilst these three theorists were interested in studying the nature and origins of industrial capitalist societies, they were by no means the only early sociological figures interested in social change. Indeed, a characteristic feature of late 18th- and 19th-century writing was its preoccupation with the topic. COMTE, drawing on the work of SAINT-SIMON, proposed a 'LAW OF THREE STAGES' in the intellectual and social development of societies. This law was, in effect, an EVOLUTIONARY THEORY of human society, and this grandiose concern to see history in terms of progress, direction and stages of development (see ECONOMIC AND SOCIAL DEVELOPMENT) was shared by many other theorists, e.g. CONDORCET, Herbert SPENCER, Lewis MORGAN, Sir Edward TYLOR, and Leonard T. HOBHOUSE.

Though these early models were problematic at a number of levels, interest in evolutionary approaches to social change has not been entirely abandoned by more recent thinkers. Talcott PARSONS (1966), the economist W. W. ROSTOW (1960) and the anthropologists M. D. Sahlins and R. E. Service (1960) have produced new work, more or less successful in remedying the deficiencies of earlier theorists.

Fundamental problems remain, however. Karl POPPER (1957), for example, has argued from a philosophical perspective that social development is inherently unpredictable (because it is affected by the growth of knowledge, which in itself is unpredictable) and, moreover, that development is a unique historical process, and though it may be possible to describe this in various ways, it cannot be explained in terms of any universal law (because a law explains the recurrence of identical events and cannot therefore be tested against, or explain, those which are unique (see also HISTORICISM)). E. GELLNER (1968) has also argued that the temporal ordering of stages of social development given by evolutionary theory is either redundant (if the mechanisms, sources or causes of change are identified) or insufficient (placing anything in a sequence does not, by itself, explain it).

Both Parsons and Rostow meant their work to have specific implications for development policy in the THIRD WORLD. Their insufficiency in this respect is highlighted by Popper's arguments. In particular, it is clear that the development of any society alters the context in which any other society can develop. No society can therefore repeat the developmental process of any other. This point has been trenchantly made by Gunder FRANK (1969), who argued that the development of the advanced industrial societies involved the underdevelopment of others.

At a less ambitious level, sociologists have also attempted to hypothesize about the general causes of social change within societies, rather than to bring their historical development under an evolutionary law. Here social change has been variously connected to:

(a) technological development;

(b) social CONFLICT (between races, religions, classes, for example);

(c) malintegration (see INTEGRATION) (of the parts of social structure or culture of a society, such as in Hinduism, caste and capitalism);

(d) the need for ADAPTATION within social systems (so that, for example, the development of efficient bureaucracies is an adaptive response of firms to a competitive economic environment);

(e) the impact of ideas (see IDEALISM) and belief systems on social action (most obviously, Weber's hypothesis of a connection between 'The Protestant Ethic and the Spirit of Capitalism');

(f) Marx's idea (see CLASS, HISTORICAL MATERIALISM) of class conflict generated by contradictions between the forces and relations of production in societies.

Such approaches are less ambitious than evolutionary theory. After all, they attempt (with the partial exception of Marx) to say what it is that produces social change, rather than to make predictions about the course of human history. At best, they provide more or less useful suggestions as to where the cause of change may lie when any particular social process is examined. Clearly, however, to argue that all social change in human groups, communities, institutions, organizations or societies in general is a result of conflict, or ideas, or adaptation, or whatever, is to overstate the case. Inevitably, the more ambitious the theoretical project, the more vulnerable it becomes. In one sense this hardly matters, for theories can remain heuristically useful, and a perfected general theory of social change is not a necessary preliminary to the normal business of sociological research. See also INDUSTRIALIZATION, MODERNIZATION, UNDERDEVELOPMENT, DEPENDENT INDUSTRIALIZATION, CONVERGENCE, POSTINDUSTRIAL SOCIETY, IMPERIALISM, WORLD SYSTEM, NEW INTERNATIONAL DIVISION OF LABOUR.

with the work of Frank Parkin (1979). Following Weber in the critique of Marxism, Parkin argues that property is only one basis for power, and only one form of social closure. The characteristics associated with different STATUS GROUPS, e.g. ethnicity, gender, skill level, religion, etc., can all be bases for closure strategies.

Parkin describes two types of closure strategy or process: *exclusion* and *usurpation*. Exclusion refers to practices which separate the group from 'outsiders'. The examples above, of aristocracy, professions and skilled artisans, are cases in point. Usurpation is a strategy adopted by low status or less privileged groups to gain advantages or resources which others are monopolizing; CIVIL RIGHTS MOVEMENTS illustrate this, or, in the Indian CASTE system, the process of *sanskritization*.

The two strategies should not always be regarded as alternatives, or as mutually exclusive. Protestant workers in Northern Ireland in the 1970s, for example, formed the Loyalist Association of Workers essentially to retain their privileges, i.e. they adopted an exclusion strategy with regard to Catholics. At the same time they continued normal processes of collective bargaining, involving occasional conflicts with employers, i.e. they attempted to increase their share of companies' profits (the usurpation of employers' and shareholders' privilege). Parkin calls this type of joint strategy a process of *dual closure*. It is particularly associated with intermediate groups in the class or status systems.

social cohesion the integration of group behaviour as a result of social bonds, attractions, or 'forces' that hold members of a group in interaction over a period of time. See also SOCIAL SOLIDARITY.

social construction of reality a formulation employed within some areas of sociology to emphasize the way in which social institutions and social life generally is socially produced rather than naturally given or determined.

At one level the claim is almost trivial, since our knowledge about ourselves, and about the social as well as the natural world, is mediated by CULTURE, and so is necessarily 'social' in origin. A specific emphasis on the social construction of reality is often made, however, to offset Durkheimian (see DURKHEIM) notions of society as a pregiven reality, consisting of constraining social facts (see SOCIAL FACTS AS THINGS) to which individuals are subject. The 'social constructionist' view, originating with THOMAS and members of the CHICAGO SCHOOL, was to emphasize instead the way in which the social world was continually reinvented (produced) by individuals, rather than as something which simply confronted them.

In reality, any simple DUALISM of individual selves (see SELF) and society is unsustainable. Society cannot exist without acting selves; in turn, the self is a product of society (see MEAD, COOLEY, STRUCTURE AND AGENCY, STRUCTURATION THEORY). Berger and Luckmann's *The Social Construction of Reality* (1697) – the text which first systematically introduced the concept of 'social construction' into sociology – is an early exploration of these themes. Since then the conception of 'social construction' has become much more widespread, e.g. in the study of DEVIANCE, especially LABELLING THEORY.

Some of the most wide-ranging debates and developments in terms of a social constructionist perspective have come when issues of ONTOLOGY are raised. This is especially the case where social reality might appear determined by the nature of physical realities such as bodies, diseases, or the natural world. Challenges to such assumptions have been forthcoming from theorists such as FOUCAULT for whom the BODY itself is seen as a product of particular discursive practices rather than biology (see SOCIOLOGY OF THE BODY); diseases can be reconceptualized as shifting modes of social response rather than an organic disruption (White, 1991; Bury, 1986; Nicolson and McLaughlin, 1987); and scientific knowledge can be analysed as the result of negotiations about the meaning of phenomena (see SOCIOLOGY OF SCIENCE) in which the rules about theoretical consistency, experimental adequacy and dissemination of information are flexibly interpreted according to a varying agenda of interests (see Mulkay, 1979).

social contract theory a theory of the origins and/or present basis of the STATE, which, in its simplest form, holds that the state arises from a 'contract' in which each member gives up his own 'natural rights' (see NATURAL RIGHTS AND NATURAL LAW) in return for new rights under the law (see also LOCKE, ROUSSEAU). Social contract theory does not apply to most historical cases of state formation, though it does apply to the foundation of new constitutions such as that of the US in 1787, which, in part at least, have been explicitly enacted under the guidance of social contract theory. Rather than as a straightforwardly explanatory or sociological theory, the historical role of contract theory is an ethical or logical theory, advanced to provide moral evaluation and reconstruction of existing constitutions, to justify revolutions, etc. See also JUSTICE, RAWLS.

social control practices developed by social groups of all kinds which enforce or encourage CONFORMITY and deal with behaviour which violates accepted norms.

Sociologists distinguish two basic processes of social control:

(a) INTERNALIZATION of norms and values. The process of SOCIALIZATION is much concerned with learning acceptable ways of acting as 'taken-for-granted', unquestioned imperatives or as social 'routines' (see also ETHNOMETHODOLOGY);

(b) the use of sanctions with regard to rule-breakers and non conforming acts. Sanctions may be positive, rewarding conforming conduct, or negative, punishing non-conformity to norms by means ranging from 'informal' sanctions like 'telling-off', ridiculing or ostracism, to 'formal' sanctions like a yellow card, a prison sentence, or execution. See also DEVIANCE. POLICE (AND POLICING).

Social Darwinism a term for social theories that apply Darwinian principles of NATURAL SELECTION to societies (see also DARWIN). The best-known proponents of this position were SPENCER (1820–1903) in the UK, and W. G. Sumner (1840–1910) in the US, both of whom argued forcefully that society should be viewed as if it were an adaptive organism (see SURVIVAL OF THE FITTEST). It is important to distinguish this from more generally evolutionist social perspectives which may not share the hard FUNCTIONALISM inherent in this approach, but simply a belief in some kind of directed social transformation (see EVOLUTIONARY SOCIOLOGY, SOCIOCULTURAL EVOLUTIONISM). The term is now almost always used pejoratively by social theorists who object to the importation of the biological analogy into the study of human social life. It is also regarded as politically problematic, since, if individuals and societies are subject to the survival of the fittest, then the status quo is always seen as justifiable. Social Darwinist ideas are now sometimes presented as SOCIOBIOLOGY.

social demand for education the demand for formal education not only for its benefits in employment, but also as a consumer good with intrinsic values in its own right. Viewing education in this way leads to a different emphasis from narrow, economic interpretations of the benefits.

Sociologists, such as Margaret Archer (1982), regard the 'expansionary search for opportunity' as the main force behind the expansion of education provision in developed societies, but may suggest that increased demand from successive cohorts tends to 'tip the opportunity curve out of the benefit zone'. In this context, Archer particularly notes that 'non-completion' of education now 'distributes liabilities'. She also suggests that members of the middle class are quicker than members of the working class to adapt their strategies to the new requirements of an expansionary pressure on entry to élite institutions and preferred occupational areas. (See also CREDENTIALISM, GRADUATE LABOUR MARKET).

social democracy political parties of the Left, whose programmes embrace SOCIALISM, but which pursue these objectives by electoral and parliamentary means, eschewing insurrection or violent revolution. Initially the term had a currency mainly within Marxism. In time, it has come to refer more widely to non-Marxist reformist parties of the Left, including the British Labour Party. Most recently it has been used to refer to political parties and policies which assert the value of plural social institutions and a MIXED ECONOMY, as against either a ONE-PARTY SYSTEM and a COMMAND ECONOMY, or the untrammelled working of a free MARKET ECONOMY.

social development see ECONOMIC AND SOCIAL DEVELOPMENT.

social deviance see DEVIANCE.

social differentiation the process whereby an institutional activity becomes divided and more specialized in two or more separate institutional activities. Differentiation is a term derived from biology to describe the specialization of functions in society in a process of social evolution. For example, the separation and specialization of the economic function of production from the institution of the family which retains the functions of reproduction and infant socialization. In PARSONS' (1977) model of the social system this process is described in more abstract terms such as the differentiation of the polity from the societal community. Social differentiation is also referred to as *structural differentiation* in functionalist theories of SOCIAL CHANGE (see FUNCTIONALISM).

Nineteenth-century evolutionary theories of social change (e.g. SPENCER) saw differentiation as a fundamental principle of social development in biology and sociology whereby societies increase in size and complexity in adapting to the environment (see EVOLUTIONARY THEORY). Differentiation was accompanied by the functional need for increased integration and interdependence in more complex societies. In the writings of DURKHEIM, social differentiation is identical to the social DIVISION OF LABOUR. Contemporary theories of social evolution retain the concept of differentiation as central to the general development of adaptive capacity in industrial societies (Sahlins and Service, 1960) and, in the case of Parsons' later work, to analyse the interdependence between the functional subsystems of modern society. See also MODERNIZATION.

social distance feelings or relations of 'aloofness and unapproachability', especially between members of different social strata. Conceptions of social distance are formally institutionalized in extreme systems of SOCIAL STRATIFICATION, such as APARTHEID and CASTE, but informally they exist in all societies. The term was introduced by PARK and Burgess (1924) and popularized by Bogardus (1933), who also formulated a *social-distance* (or *Bogardus*) *scale*, designed to portray the extent of tolerance or intolerance between social groups.

social equality see EQUALITY.

social equilibrium a state of persistence or balance between parts within a social system and/or in relation to its external environment. According to PARETO (1935), a social system is in equilibrium if when it is subjected to some modification a reaction takes place tending to restore it to its previous 'normal' state. Pareto's definition and his general approach to the study of social systems modelled on change in mechanical systems and on approaches in economics influenced a number of theorists, notably Henderson, HOMANS, PARSONS, and Dickson and Roeslisberger (1939). In the work of Parsons in particular, the assumption was made that, even if never fully equilibrated, social systems tend towards a state of equilibrium and can be analysed as functioning systems with self-equilibrating properties. See also FUNCTIONALISM, HOMEOSTASIS, CYBERNETICS, SYSTEMS THEORY; compare CHAOTIC PHENOMENA.

social evolution see EVOLUTIONARY THEORY, NEOEVOLUTIONISM.

social exclusion (and **social inclusion**) a form of social disadvantage encompassing economic and non-economic factors. The conception and existence of 'social exclusion' was debated in France in the 1980s and combating it has become part of the European agenda. Excluded individuals and groups are separated from institutions and wider society, and consequently from both rights and duties – e.g. the political, educational and civic (see also CITIZENSHIP). Social policy solutions aimed at achieving *social inclusion* focus on developing and enhancing SOCIAL CAPITAL and CULTURAL CAPITAL by making available improved education and training, healthcare and housing. For A. GIDDENS (*The Third Way*, 1998) social exclusion is a dual process operating at the top and bottom of society. While at the latter level it is usually involuntary, those higher up the socio-economic hierarchy may actively exclude themselves – for example by choosing private education, healthcare and so forth. This undermines the credibility – and eventually adequacy – of public sector provision, contributing further to social exclusion.

social facts as things 'a category of facts' with distinctive characteristics, 'consisting of ways of acting, thinking and feeling, external to the individual and endowed with a power of coercion by means of which they control him' (DURKHEIM, *The Rules of Sociological Method*, 1895). Durkheim formulated his sociology as resting 'wholly on the basic principle that social facts must be studied as things'. Durkheim recognized that 'there is no principle for which he had received more criticism' but argued that 'none is more fundamental' (DURKHEIM, 1897).

Sociologists remain divided between those who stress the externality and the independence of social facts from individuals, and those who emphasize that individuals participate fully in the construction of their own social lives (see also METHODOLOGICAL INDIVIDUALISM, STRUCTURE AND AGENCY). Durkheim's aim, however, was not so much to deny all possibility of individual construction of aspects of social reality as to maintain that social facts were in large measure external to particular individuals, and thus could be studied relatively objectively, e.g. as external 'social currents', such as patterns of law or variations between societies in rates of SUICIDE. Where Durkheim perhaps erred was in sometimes suggesting that this meant that sociologists could simply disregard the subjective ideas of individual actors. Instead it is dear that social phenomena such as suicide can only be studied effectively if the variable meanings individuals attach to social actions are fully investigated. As well as this, the artificial and constructed nature of many sociological data must also be noted (e.g. see MEASUREMENT BY FIAT). Thus, the proposal to treat 'social facts as things' (Durkheim's conception of a social reality *sui generis*), although undoubtedly of use in avoiding outright subjectivism and individualism in social analysis is usually regarded as providing a misleading rendering of the 'facticity' of social phenomena.

social formation (MARXISM) an actually existing society in which one or more MODES OF PRODUCTION may be dominant. The concept was developed by Althusserian Marxists (see ALTHUSSER) to distinguish a specifically Marxian concept equivalent to SOCIETY but without its perceived ideological connotations. Since any one social formation may have more than one mode of production, the concept potentially allows for greater refinement of the analysis of the variety of historical instances. (Although Marx used the terms 'social formation' and 'society' more or less interchangeably, he used the latter more often, (Bottomore et al., 1983)).

social group see GROUP.

social history historiography and historical analysis which concentrates attention on changes in the overall patterns of social life in societies, rather than merely on political events. See also HISTORY WORKSHOP JOURNAL.

social identity (SOCIAL PSYCHOLOGY) those aspects of the individual's self-concept which are derived from membership of and identification with social categories, e.g. race, gender, religion, occupation, and which are made salient in contexts where those social categories assume importance. Associated with each descriptive social identity is an evaluation which imparts positive or negative status. The social identity approach in modern social psychology originated in the work of Henri Tajfel, and his attempt to explain intergroup discrimination and conflict in 'minimal group' conditions, i.e. where group members are aware only of their group membership or category. Social categorization is followed by a social comparison process. In this in-group, members seek to maintain a positive social identity by comparing themselves with the out-group on dimensions which ensure a favourable self-concept is retained, creating positive distinctiveness. Where this is difficult, perceptions of the out-group may be distorted, resulting in PREJUDICE. Minority groups in society face a situation where their social identities are largely or wholly negative. Tajfel and Turner (1979) have described a number of different strategies minorities are likely to adopt as a means to attain more positive social identities. Social mobility strategies involve attempts to leave the minority group; social creativity strategies seek to change the dimension, value or focus of the comparison process; and social competition strategies challenge or instigate direct conflict with the majority.

Social identity theorists explicitly reject the notion of individualism and REDUCTIONISM in social psychology that has, for example, led to attempts to explain prejudice in TRAIT terms (e.g. AUTHORITARIAN PERSONALITY), or in terms of individual personality dynamics (e.g. SCAPEGOATING). While individuals do obviously act in terms of personal identities in many situations, the presence of salient out-group members is much more likely to foster behaviour consistent with social identity and in-group membership. Cognitive explanations of prejudice, such as STEREOTYPING, are also rejected on reductionist grounds, and because they fail to explain why comparisons between in- and out-group always occur on dimensions favourable to the in-group.

Studies in a number of contexts have confirmed the appropriateness of the social identity perspective as an explanation of intergroup behaviour; e.g. Brown (1978) on occupational groups seeking to maintain wage differentials; Giles and Johnson (1981) on the behaviour of ethnolinguistic groups. More recently the approach has also been used successfully to explain intragroup processes such as CONFORMITY, minority influence, and group polarization.

social inclusion see SOCIAL EXCLUSION (and SOCIAL INCLUSION).

social indicators any regularly collected social statistics which can be used to provide indication of changes in the general state of society, e.g. crime rates and health and mortality statistics. Parallels exist with well-established *economic indicators*, e.g. the RETAIL PRICE INDEX. However, there is far less agreement on the measurement and standardization of social indicators than for the most significant economic indicators. See also OFFICIAL STATISTICS.

social institution see INSTITUTION.

social interaction see INTERACTION, INTERACTION ORDER AND INTERACTION RITUAL.

social integration and **system integration** the distinction (LOCKWOOD, 1964) between INTEGRATION into society that arises from SOCIALIZATION and from agreement on values – *social integration* – and integration which occurs as the result of the operation of the social 'substratum', e.g. as unintended consequences of economic relations or structures of power – *system integration*. What Lockwood wished to stress was that the two forms of integration are not the same, and that any analysis of society must distinguish carefully between them, something he accused some forms of FUNCTIONALISM as failing to do.

As elaborated by GIDDENS (1984) (see Fig. 29), while social integration can be seen as

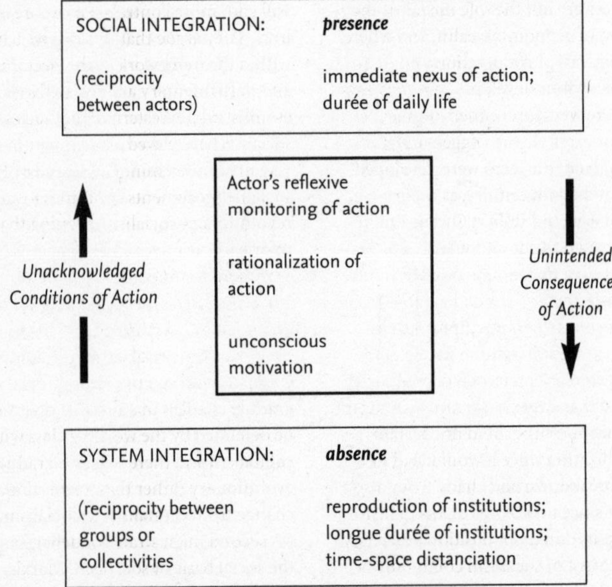

Fig. 29 **Social and system integration.**

arising particularly from the face-to-face interaction of individual social actors, system integration is far more a matter of interaction at a distance, and involves 'reproduced practices' which arise from the interrelation of groups and collectivities and the operation of institutions, processes which tend to occur behind the backs of the individuals involved.

social investment state a state that invests in its population and institutions with the aim of creating both SOCIAL CAPITAL and CULTURAL CAPITAL. This conception of the state is formulated to contrast with conventional notions of the WELFARE STATE, which is portrayed as creating 'dependency' and tax burden. See also THIRD WAY, NEW LABOUR, LIFELONG LEARNING.

socialism a political ideology with many variants which emerged in early 19th-century Britain and France, and which aims for societies in which poverty is eliminated, market forces are not the sole means of the distribution of economic wealth, and where the human ideals of cooperation and altruistic behaviour develop.

Whilst there were forerunners of this ideology, for example the Diggers in 17th-century England, the ideas were developed especially in the 19th century, as theory, e.g. by SAINT-SIMON and Robert Owen, and in practice through the development of cooperative societies and the nascent trade unions. MARX and ENGELS had a decisive influence through their attempts to show that socialism was a 'scientific necessity', rather than merely a preferred form of society. They argued that CAPITALISM AND CAPITALIST MODE OF PRODUCTION could not sustain human civilization since it would lead to economic breakdown and chaos. They also argued that since no RULING CLASS in history ever gave up its dominant position peacefully, the achievement of socialism could only be possible with the revolutionary overthrow of the BOURGEOISIE and thence capitalism.

From Marx and Engel's first socialist writings in the mid-19th century, differences between socialists have centred around one important issue:
(a) whether capitalism can be reformed and modified so that most of the ideas can be achieved within its framework (see also REVISIONISM, FABIAN SOCIETY AND FABIANISM); or
(b) whether it has first to be overthrown.

Today, those who advocate SOCIAL DEMOCRACY argue that capitalism is reformable (the position of most European Social Democratic Parties, including the British Labour Party). They argue that some combination of state supervision of the market and state ownership or regulation of selected sectors of the economy, combined with welfare measures and socialization into altruistic rather than selfish motivations, will achieve the aims of socialism. This form of society will be more democratic than forms of STATE SOCIALIST SOCIETY, in that political power will not be so centralized and people will gain more control in more areas of their lives. They argue that this can be achieved within the framework of the electoral politics and parliamentary and legislative procedures established in Western democracies, which socialists have played a major part in creating.

Against this, a minority strand of European socialist movements continues to support revolutionary socialism, arguing that reformist measures will be resisted by the dominant bourgeoisie, and that capitalism will not provide the framework for socialism and must be overthrown.

A recent variant of either of these positions exists in modern EUROCOMMUNISM, that gradual changes in a socialist direction can be defended by the working class within capitalism and there will be a gradual, evolutionary rather than revolutionary, change from capitalism to socialism.

A second main strand of debate concerns the social basis of socialism. Marxist and communist variants have tended to see the working class as the major social force capable of producing socialism, whereas social democrats have generally rejected a

Marxian analysis of social class and argued that the middle classes are as important, and that even sections of the capitalist class can be won over to socialist ideals (see also CLASS, CONTRADICTORY CLASS LOCATIONS).

Outside of Europe, socialist ideas have been adopted and modified and incorporated into non-European political ideologies. One important example is *African Socialism*, which developed in the 1950s independence movements around the idea that cooperative and communal forms of organization already existed in small-scale African societies, and that socialism could be built on the bases of these, especially as capitalism was weakly developed in Africa and therefore without entrenched indigenous capitalist interests. See also COMMUNISM, PUBLIC OWNERSHIP, PRIVATIZATION.

socialist societies see STATE SOCIALIST SOCIETIES, SOCIALISM.

socialization

1 (also called ENCULTURATION) the process in which the CULTURE of a society is transmitted to children; the modification from infancy of an individual's behaviour to conform with the demands of social life (see ACCULTURATION). In this sense, socialization is a FUNCTIONAL PREREQUISITE for any society, essential to any social life, as well as to the cultural and SOCIAL REPRODUCTION of both general and particular social forms. As emphasized by PARSONS and Bales (1955), socialization, undertaken in the FAMILY and elsewhere, involves both integration into society (ROLES, INSTITUTIONS, etc.) and the differentiation of one individual from another.

2 the replacement of private ownership of the means of production by PUBLIC OWNERSHIP.

3 (MARXISM) the tendency of capitalist production increasingly to depend on collective organization (e.g. the interrelation of many different processes). This is one important reason why MARX expected a transition to SOCIALISM (and common ownership of the means of production) ultimately to occur.

Of the three conceptions, **1** is the most important sociological and anthropological usage.

Because it is concerned with relationships between the individual and society, it is clear that socialization in this sense is a concept that bridges the disciplines of sociology and PSYCHOLOGY. Theories of socialization have concentrated on:

(a) cognitive development (e.g. PIAGET);

(b) acquisition of moral and personal identity through family relationships (e.g. FREUD);

(c) the acquisition of the SELF concept and social identity (e.g.G. H. MEAD);

(d) internalization of the moral categories and values of the group (e.g. DURKHEIM);

(e) the development of social skills which sustain interaction in all settings, chief of which is linguistic communication, through which the social and physical environment are appropriated and interpreted (e.g. BERNSTEIN).

A distinction is also sometimes drawn between two forms of socialization:

(a) the process involved in becoming an adult social being, with the focus largely on childhood – *primary socialization;* and

(b) the more general processes through which culture is transmitted (e.g. adult peers, media of communication, etc.) – *secondary socialization.*

According to D. Wrong (1961), it is useful to distinguish between these two forms of socialization **1**, but it is essential that the active, purposeful and reflexive dimensions of socialization, of relations between self and others, should be acknowledged for *both* forms of socialization (see OVERSOCIALIZED CONCEPTION OF MAN). See also NATURE – NURTURE DEBATE, DEVELOPMENT, LOOKING-GLASS SELF.

socially necessary labour (MARXISM) the labour time required to produce a commodity under average conditions at a certain level in the development of the means of production. For Marx, the socially necessary labour required to produce a commodity determines its VALUE, although value in this theoretical sense only indirectly determines actual exchange-values and prices. See also LABOUR THEORY OF VALUE, LABOUR POWER.

social marginality see MARGINALITY.

social mobility the movement of individuals (or sometimes groups) between different positions in the hierarchy(ies) of SOCIAL STRATIFICATION within any society. Within modern societies, CLASS positions within the OCCUPATIONAL STRUCTURE are usually of prime interest in studies of social mobility. Social mobility may involve movement up a class or status hierarchy – *upward mobility* – or down – *downward mobility.* It may take place from one generation to another – *intergenerational mobility* – where the focus of interest for sociology is on differences between the socioeconomic class or status of a person's FAMILY OF ORIGIN compared with his or her 'achieved' class or status position, or it may be more short-term, e.g. the ups and downs of an individual CAREER – *intragenerational mobility.* In sociology the main focus of study has been on differences in the volume and character of 'intergenerational mobility' within different societies. Interest has been greatest in levels of movement between manual and nonmanual socioeconomic status positions, and movement into and out of ÉLITE positions and the SERVICE CLASS. It is usually accepted that, in general, modern societies permit more mobility than earlier types of society, i.e. in comparative terms are *open-class societies.*

Systematic study of social mobility was pioneered by SOROKIN, who saw all societies as possessing 'selection agencies', which varied in form between different societies. As have sociologists in general, Sorokin conceived of social mobility, whatever its particular form, as performing vital social functions, e.g. promoting talent, acting as a 'safety valve'. Postwar study of social mobility in industrial societies began in earnest with the undertaking of large social surveys designed to establish overall levels of intergenerational social mobility (e.g. Glass, 1954; LIPSET and BENDIX, 1959). These studies seemed to suggest that levels of upward intergenerational social mobility – especially between manual and non-manual

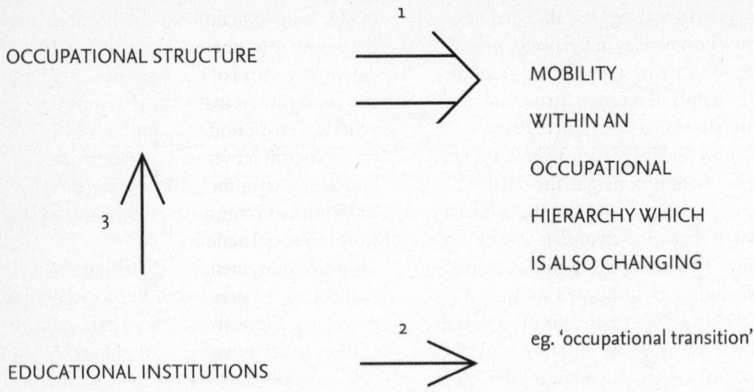

Fig. 30 **Social Mobility.** While changes in the occupational structure can be seen as the main determinant of the extent of opportunities for social mobility (1), and educational institutions act mainly as an avenue of social mobility which is particularly important in modern societies and can also influence who becomes mobile (2), educational institutions (3) also induce changes in the occupational structure.

occupations – were substantially the same in all industrial societies, despite differences in patterns of industrialization, educational structure, etc. Subsequent studies (see Miller, 1960) have refined this finding, pointing to considerable differences in the more detailed patterns of social mobility, e.g. Germany, Italy and Spain are less 'open' than Britain or the US, and socialist countries have generally had higher levels of social mobility than non-socialist countries (e.g. both eastern bloc countries and social democratic societies such as Sweden, see Heath, 1981).

A further important distinction in studies of social mobility is between *structural* and *nonstructural social mobility,* the former referring to movements made possible by fundamental changes in the form of the occupational structure (e.g. in the relative size of particular classes, status groups, etc.) within a particular society, the latter to any movements which do not involve such changes. As indicated in Fig. 30, one main assumption that can be stated in terms of this distinction is that occupational structures are often more fundamental in determining the form and volume of social mobility within a particular society or historical period – i.e. produce 'structural mobility' – than are differences in educational institutions, individual motivation, etc – i.e. nonstructural sources of mobility. However, although the capacity of the latter to affect levels of mobility may be limited, 'nonstructural' factors, such as education, do make a difference, not least where they act to induce changes in occupational structures, e.g. in encouraging 'occupational upgrading' or *occupational transition,* involving the 'substitution' of nongraduates by graduates, or the more general upgrading in the status and content of particular jobs (compare CREDENTIALISM).

While some researchers have concluded that rates of social mobility in the UK have remained relatively stable and have not increased during the postwar period, studies by GOLDTHORPE et al. (1980) have suggested that overall levels of upward mobility (including entry into the service class) may be higher than assumed. Goldthorpe's suggestion is that most of this increase can be accounted for as 'structural mobility'.

Where EQUALITY OF OPPORTUNITY between

social classes is the focus of attention, Glass (1954) argued that it is the extent of mobility *once* changes in the occupational distribution have been taken into account which is mainly of interest, 'structural mobility' should be discounted. Payne (1989), however, has argued against any such automatic assumption: that 'the relative chance of mobility ... *without* the artificial removal of structural change' is also of relevance. Thus, comparing studies across time (including Goldthorpe's study, conducted in 1972, with the 1984 Essex study, Marshall et al., 1988), we find that while the 'service class's success in retaining class positions does not diminish, the disadvantage experienced by those with working-class origins is ameliorated' (Payne, 1989).

Complex methodological problems attend all studies of social mobility, including problems of occupational classification (see also OCCUPATIONAL SCALES), reliance on respondents' memories, and the comparison of older generations with completed careers with younger generations whose careers are uncompleted. In the most advanced studies, highly sophisticated statistical and mathematical techniques may be employed, in which some have suggested 'techniques' and 'measurement' run ahead of sociological clarity or relevance. A final problem of major significance, is that most studies of social mobility have focused only on men. See also CONTEST AND SPONSORED MOBILITY, HIGHER EDUCATION.

social movement any broad social alliance of people who are associated in seeking to effect or to block an aspect of SOCIAL CHANGE within a society. Unlike POLITICAL PARTIES or some more highly organized interest or PRESSURE GROUPS, such movements may be only informally organized, although they may have links with political parties and more institutionalized groups, and in time they may lead to the formation of political parties.

Four distinct areas in which social movements operate in modern societies have been identified by GIDDENS (1985):

(a) democratic movements, concerned with establishing or maintaining political rights;
(b) labour movements, concerned with defensive control of the workplace and with contesting and transforming the more general distribution of economic power;
(c) ecological movements, concerned to limit the environmental and social damage resulting from transformation of the natural world by social action;
(d) peace movements, concerned with challenging the pervasive influence of military power and aggressive forms of nationalism.

Other social movements of importance in recent decades include women's movements and consumer movements. Although in part these types of social movement may act in complementary ways in modern societies, they may also be in conflict, e.g. a demand for work in conflict with ecological considerations. Such movements have also tended to generate contrary social movements concerned to oppose them, including conservative nationalist movements and movements aimed at blocking or reversing moral reforms.

Research on social movements, like research on political parties and interest groups generally, has focused on the social and psychological characteristics of those attracted to participate, the relations between leaders and led, and the social and political outcomes of such activity. One thing is clear: social movements are a fluid element within political and social systems, from which more formal political organizations arise and which may bring radical change. See also URBAN SOCIAL MOVEMENTS, COLLECTIVE BEHAVIOUR, ANOMIE, REVOLUTION, FASCISM, PEACE MOVEMENT.

social order the stable patterns of social expectations and social structure that exist in any society; the maintenance of these patterns. As such the term has a general rather than a specific reference. The problem of what makes societies cohere is sometimes referred to as the *problem of order* (see also PARSONS).

social organization any relatively stable pattern or structure within a society, and the process by which such a structure is created or maintained. The term is a highly general one overlapping with such terms as SOCIAL STRUCTURE, SOCIAL ORDER, etc. See also ORGANIZATION.

social pathology (by analogy with health and sickness in organisms) any condition of society regarded as unhealthy. With biological analogies currently being looked on with suspicion the term is now relatively little used, but was used by functionalist sociologists including DURKHEIM (1895). Durkheim drew a distinction between 'normal' and 'abnormal' states of society. He assumed that the 'average' condition in a particular type of society also represented the 'normal' and 'functional' condition for that type of society. On this basis pathological conditions could in principle also be identified. Thus while crime, for example, must be regarded as a normal feature of societies, an excessive incidence of crime could be seen as pathological. See also SOCIAL PROBLEMS, ABNORMAL.

social phenomenology a sociological approach, especially associated with the Austrian-American social philosopher and sociologist Alfred SCHUTZ, which investigates the taken-for-granted assumptions of and the processes involved in the constitution of social knowledge and social life (see also PHENOMENOLOGY). While a number of sociologists, notably BERGER and Luckmann (1967), have developed Schutz's ideas as a distinctive approach to the SOCIOLOGY OF KNOWLEDGE, these ideas have been especially influential in the development of ETHNOMETHODOLOGY, in which social phenomenology's concerns with the constitution of everyday life have received elaboration as a relatively self-contained theoretical approach or paradigm which is highly critical of 'orthodox sociology'. See also PHENOMENOLOGICAL SOCIOLOGY.

social philosophy any philosophical discussion which is presented as having implications either for:
(a) social life; or
(b) social science methodologies. The term is a general one, with no very specific reference.

social policy a field of study which entails the economic, political, sociolegal and sociological examination of the ways in which central and local governmental policies affect the lives of individuals and communities. Social policy is notoriously difficult to define and its use varies between authors. The term is often, though mistakenly, used in the context of SOCIAL ADMINISTRATION to refer to the institutionalized services provided by the WELFARE STATE, viz. housing, health, education, social security, personal social services and, in some cases, law. This approach to the study of social policy probably has its origins in the social policy courses introduced to train social workers. Authors who use this version of social policy do so to refer to the ways in which the state has assumed some social responsibility by intervening in a market economy to promote individual welfare. This type of discussion has led to enquiries about the distribution of goods and services and has, falsely, distinguished sharply between social policy and economic policy.

There are a number of criticisms of this use of the term:
(a) it lacks any theoretical analysis which precludes any sociological discussion of why policies are introduced and the unintended effects of their introduction;
(b) it leads to a conflation of social policy with the welfare state yet social policies occur outside the welfare state. As Titmuss argued, apartheid in South Africa is a social policy. Similarly, aspects of welfare lie outside the welfare state. Titmuss demonstrated, for example, that there are occupational welfare benefits such as pension schemes, help with housing and health costs, and so on, which some individuals receive from their employment;
(c) it often leads to a parochial concern with a 'history of legislations' in a particular

country and precludes the possibility of comparative analysis.

In the 1970s, a more critical approach to social policy developed which was informed by accompanying developments in sociological theory. In particular, Marxist and feminist sociologists developed new accounts of the relationship between social policies and the social structure.

Some authors have argued that the early sociologists had no interest in social policy. However, others have argued that a concern with social policy is implicit in the works of Durkheim, Marx and Weber.

Following the import of new and critical ideas about social policy its scope has been widened to include the comparative study of social policies in different societies. There has also been a renewed interest in the philosophical issues within the study of social policy such as the nature of JUSTICE, citizenship, NEEDS, etc. See also SOCIAL REFORM, SOCIAL PROBLEMS.

social problems aspects of social life seen to warrant concern and intervention, e.g. CRIME, domestic violence, child abuse, POVERTY, drug abuse. The identification of a 'social problem' is the outcome of social processes including a moral evaluation of people's behaviour. In analysing social problems it is important to identify the group of people for whom the behaviour is a 'problem'. For example, some authors have suggested that social policies dealing with poverty have been implemented to support the interests of landowners and owners of capital rather than to eliminate poverty out of humanitarian concern for the poor. The identification of a social problem suggests that there 'ought to be' some form of social intervention through SOCIAL POLICIES, new laws and new forms of social and COMMUNITY WORK, and some authors have suggested that there is a relationship between the 'social construction' of social problems, social policy and SOCIAL CONTROL. See also HIERARCHY OF CREDIBILITY.

social psychology a sub-field of both PSYCHOLOGY and sociology, which, according to ALLPORT, is concerned with the ways in which an individual's 'thought, feeling, and behaviour' are affected by the existence of others, e.g. by social interactions, by groups, relationships, etc. The focus on the individual within mainstream social psychology has been challenged especially by CRITICAL SOCIAL PSYCHOLOGY. Social psychology involves a variety of approaches, partly reflecting its multidisciplinary location. A further complication is that much work within sociology that might be labelled 'social psychology' (e.g. SYMBOLIC INTERACTIONISM) is not always labelled as such; rather it is often referred to as 'microsociology'. One of the first writers to use the term social psychology was W. McDougall who published *Introduction to Social Psychology* in 1908. Since the 1920s, social psychology has developed into a more 'fully fledged' field of study, also possessing wide-ranging applications, especially in the areas of education, social policy, work and mental health.

Despite its broad spectrum of approaches, social psychology can be seen as having a central interest in bridging between individual and social theories of human behaviour. Following Armistead (1974), two main traditions can be identified:
(a) *psychological social psychology,* characterized by its connections with general psychology, including an emphasis on experimentation; and
(b) *sociological social psychology,* influenced by the work of symbolic interactionists, laying stress on the social processes involved in the development of SELF-identity and on the role of LANGUAGE, and employing qualitative research methods, such as PARTICIPANT OBSERVATION.

An indication of the kinds of topics included as part of the subject matter of social psychology can be had by noting the main topics covered in Roger Brown's popular text *Social Psychology* (1965): SOCIALIZATION, including the acquisition of language; ROLES and STEREOTYPES; ACHIEVEMENT MOTIVATION; the AUTHORITARIAN PERSONALITY; ATTITUDES and attitude change; GROUP DYNAMICS; COLLECTIVE BEHAVIOUR. Remarkably the list of topics has changed relatively little since. Some commentators (e.g. Murphy, John and Brown, 1984), have suggested that social psychology faced a 'crisis' in the late 1960s and 70s, centred on the question of whether or not it should be a 'socially relevant' subject aimed at solving social problems. Influenced by the wider sociopolitical climate of the 1960s and 70s, radical social psychologists have argued for the necessity of uniting the 'personal' and the 'political' within the sub-field (again see CRITICAL SOCIAL PSYCHOLOGY). Writers such as Baker-Miller (1976) have also challenged what they see as the 'gender-blind' nature of much mainstream social psychology. However there continue to be many who argue that social psychology should have as its main aim the development of theory and knowledge about the individual in society. See also MORENO, SCALING, CONFORMITY, COGNITIVE DISSONANCE, PREJUDICE.

social reform political and social policies implemented with the aim of eliminating SOCIAL PROBLEMS. Social reform movements, and the bureaucratic administrative structures set up to implement such reforms, can be seen as a major feature differentiating modern industrial societies from earlier societies. A contrast is often made between 'social reform' which is incremental and gradualist, and social REVOLUTION. Fabians, such as Sidney and Beatrice WEBB (see also FABIAN SOCIETY AND FABIANISM), for example, viewed social reform as a method of 'social engineering' entailing the gradual improvement of provision of services and material goods, rejecting revolutionary change. Some critics have argued that many social reforms are essentially palliatives disguising fundamental social inequalities and problems rather than eliminating them. The reform of the National Health Service in 1974 was intended to improve the delivery of health services, but did little to address the causes of ill- health to be found in the social structure of society. Analysis of social reform also raises questions about the relationship between social science and value judgements.

social science

The entirety of those disciplines, or any particular discipline, concerned with the systematic study of social phenomena. No single conception of SCIENCE is implied by this usage, although there are sociologists who reject the notion that social studies should be seen as scientific in any sense based on the physical sciences.

A central issue that arises concerning the scientific status of social studies is how far the existence of meaningful purposive ACTION and choice in social life removes any possible basis for explanation involving general scientific laws. As well as questions about the effectiveness of explanation based on scientific laws, questions also arise as to the appropriate ethical posture to be adopted towards the human social actor.

For some sociologists, the essential features of social action mean that sociology can only explain satisfactorily using MEANINGFUL

UNDERSTANDING AND EXPLANATION and that scientific laws can play no part. However, whereas most sociologists recognize that important differences exist between the social and the physical sciences, they usually reject any suggestion that these differences mean that sociology must be seen as 'nonscience' because of this. The more usual position is to see the use of the term social science as justified by the existence in sociology of systematic RESEARCH METHODS, and both meaningful explanation and a variety of more general forms of sociological EXPLANATION. Thus, although there are important exceptions, sociologists will usually be found to regard sociology as scientific in one or more of the several senses in which the term science is used. Sociologists and philosophers who reject the term social science (e.g. Winch, 1958) usually do so on the basis of restrictive conceptions of science, when in reality conceptions of both physical and social science are both more open and more variegated than this. See also SCIENCE.

social reproduction 1 the process (including biological reproduction and SOCIALIZATION) by which societies reproduce their social institutions and social structure. It is usually assumed, especially of modern societies, that this process is accompanied by elements of social transformation as well as social reproduction.

2 (MARXISM) the maintenance of an existing MODE OF PRODUCTION and pattern of social relations within a particular society. Within capitalism, this is seen as the outcome of the continual reproduction and extended reproduction of capital (see ACCUMULATION (OR EXPANDED OR EXTENDED REPRODUCTION) OF CAPITAL AND CIRCUITS OF CAPITAL) and the associated maintenance of existing economic and social relations by recourse to IDEOLOGY. See also CULTURAL REPRODUCTION, ACCUMULATION OF CAPITAL.

social security a system of income maintenance provided by the state. Most systems have two components: a contributory system, which in the UK is labelled *National Insurance* (a system which underwrites benefits associated with unemployment, retirement and sickness), and a noncontributory 'safety net' which usually has some connection with conceptions of a poverty line. The former owes much to the thinking of Beveridge (see BEVERIDGE REPORT), the latter has its historical roots in Poor Law provision.

Sociologists of welfare have concerned themselves with a variety of related issues such as the relationship between ideology and social security systems taken as a whole, images of claimants, the notion of REDISTRIBUTION, and the relationship between social security and POVERTY. See also WELFARE STATE.

social services 1 any state-provided services which have a bearing on the quality of life of all citizens.

2 more narrowly, the organization and delivery of local authority SOCIAL WORK services in relation to children, the elderly, the disabled and the mentally ill (but excluding the PROBATION SERVICE except in Scotland). As well as state provision, Councils of Social Services are to be found within most localities. They are umbrella organizations to assist and coordinate voluntary social welfare provision. Both voluntary and statutory services are to be distinguished from the recent new burgeoning private sector.

Sociologists have interested themselves in the relationship between IDEOLOGY and the notions of social responsibility expressed in varying formulations of social policy. Thus the political right stress ideas of individual and familial responsibility, the political left the obligations of the state to individuals in guaranteeing some form of social minima. Marxists and others have recognized and studied the struggles within the state apparatus, both local and national, for the social wage. The recent emergence of the private sector has added another dimension to the voluntarism-statism debates.

The study of sociology has featured as a significant part of the education and training of professionals and quasiprofessionals who work within the social services. See also WELFARE STATE.

social settings the varying kinds of socially created 'locales' or 'regions' in time and space which provide the contexts of different types of social interaction, e.g. a courtroom or a school. Thus social setting refers to more than physical 'places', but rather to, what GIDDENS (1984), drawing upon GOFFMAN, refers to as a 'zoning' of social practices.

social solidarity the integration, and degree or type of integration, manifested by a society or group. The basis of social solidarity differs between simple societies and more complex societies. Thus in simple societies it is often based on relations of KINSHIP, and direct mutual relations and shared values. In relations between non-kin, and in more complex societies, social solidarity has various bases, e.g. see MECHANICAL AND ORGANIC SOLIDARITY. Whether in more complex societies social solidarity requires 'shared values', integrative RITUAL, etc., is debated (see CONSENSUS, DOMINANT IDEOLOGY THESIS, RELIGION, CIVIL RELIGION).

social statistics quantitative social data, such as crime statistics, details of marriage and family composition, housing, etc. The acquisition of such data is a fundamental concern in sociology. The term may also be used to refer to the methods used in this acquisition, including the SOCIAL SURVEY, INTERVIEWING, SAMPLING, etc. See also CENSUS, OFFICIAL STATISTICS, QUANTITATIVE RESEARCH TECHNIQUES, QUETELET.

social status see STATUS.

social stratification

The hierarchically organized structures of social inequality (ranks, status groups, etc.) which exist in any society (compare CLASS, especially **1** to **5**). As in geology, the term refers to a layered structuring or strata, but in sociology the layers consist of social groups, and the emphasis is on the ways in which inequalities between groups are structured and persist over time.

The term provides a focus in which distinctions can be made between the different forms of social ranking and inequality characterizing different societies or found within one society. In historical and comparative perspective, for example, one finds distinctions between SLAVE, CASTE, ESTATE and modern 'open class' societies. Also, one finds similar social characteristics structuring inequalities in different societies. Gender, ethnicity and age, for example, have in various ways been important in relations of domination and subordination in different historical periods and cultures. Access to or command over particular social resources have also been important in producing and sustaining inequalities. Examples here might include literacy (ancient China), religion (Mesopotamia or pre-conquest Inca and Aztec societies), military resources (in imperial territories throughout history). In addition, bureaucratic élites are extremely important in some societies – Eastern Europe and many Third World societies, for example. Gender divisions form a basis for social differentiation in all societies and, equally, relate to relations of domination and subordination. Similarly, ethnicity is a major factor in structuring inequalities in many societies.

Since there are very many bases on which human inequalities may be understood and upon which exploitation and oppression may be produced and reproduced, it is important to recognize that these variables are not mutually exclusive; for example, in the preindustrial world religious and military strata often coexisted along with those based on gender and ethnicity.

As well as the different bases of social stratification, the different shapes or structural profiles (e.g. steepness of hierarchy, number of steps in this hierarchy) of different systems can also be contrasted – see Fig. 31.

The usefulness of the term 'stratification' in allowing the discussion of different bases and forms of inequality has been largely instrumental in bringing the concept back into the mainstream of sociological debate in recent years. The term had become unfashionable with the revival of Marxian class analysis in the 1960s and 1970s. The feminist critique of conventional class analysis, for example, has demonstrated the independent significance of gender, cutting across class differences

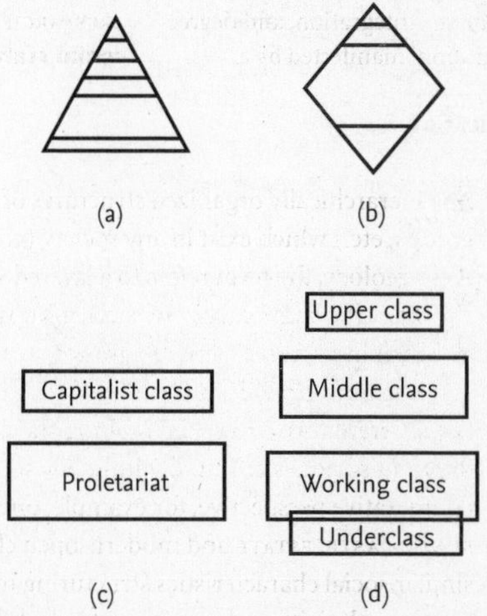

Fig. 31 **Social Stratification.** One way of representing alternative patterns of social stratification is diagrammatically. Thus, if some societies, including many traditional agrarian civilizations, exhibit (a) a steep pyramid structure, modern western societies can be represented as having a diamond shaped structure (b). In a similar way, in class analysis, the conflict potential of class structures can be represented diagrammatically. For example, (c) the two-class structure of ideal-type Marxian conceptions of capitalist society, or (d) the more complex three (or more) class structure which is sometimes seen as better representing the class structure of modern Western societies.

between women (see GENDER STRATIFICATION). In the same way, ethnic divisions cannot be simply reduced to conventional class divisions, and debates about ethnic inequalities have demonstrated the complexity of power and opportunity structures.

In addition to the emphases discussed above, FUNCTIONALISM has also stressed the historical and contemporary functional significance of systems of stratification. The best-known text in this tradition is Davis and Moore (1945). These authors argue that stratification is a FUNCTIONAL PREREQUISITE for *all* societies (see also FUNCTIONAL(IST) THEORY OF SOCIAL STRATIFICATION). Stratification is universally necessary due to the requirement of any society to motivate individuals to fill important social positions. Unequal rewards, including income and status, are seen as means whereby scarce talents are allocated to important positions. Davis and Moore describe social inequality as 'an unconsciously evolved device by which societies ensure that the most important positions are conscientiously filled by the most qualified persons'. They identify these positions historically as religious office, government, the economy and technical knowledge.

The functionalist approach has been criticized on numerous grounds, including its ideological implications. For example, the notion of 'functional importance' is challengeable – how can we demonstrate this without circularity of argument? Also, opportunities to develop skills are not equal in systems of stratification. Birth and inheritance of social position are important and recruitment into élite positions is routinely influenced by factors other than talent. Furthermore, the theory makes assumptions about individuals' motivations without evidence, and assumes that a period in higher education, for example, is a penalty for which future rewards have to be guaranteed. Finally, its views of society as an entity which has unequivocal requirements involves a questionable REIFICATION. On one view, particularly in its failure to consider the realities of power relations, the functionalist approach can be considered more as an ideological justification of inequalities than a satisfactory analysis of these. On the other hand, the view that stratification performs social functions which may be universal, cannot be ruled out in principle.

Sometimes the distinction is drawn between the relatively 'descriptive' approach of theorists who use the term 'social stratification', and the more analytical approach of those involved in 'class analysis' (see CLASS **6**, **7**). As shown from the above, this is an oversimplification. Rather than representing two diametrically opposed forms of analysis, a concern with 'stratification' and a concern with 'class' in reality involve two closely interrelated sets of terminology for the analysis of structured inequalities (see Westergaard and Resler, 1975, and SOCIAL MOBILITY).

social stratum 1 any identifiable 'layer' within a hierarchical system of SOCIAL STRATIFICATION, social STATUS positions, etc. (compare CLASS).
2 (formerly, in Eastern Europe) an identifiable grouping or category within a 'non-antagonistic' system of social stratification or social class. Such groupings or classes have been termed *social strata* and/or 'non-antagonistic' in acknowledgement of the claim that all such groups share in a common relation to the MEANS OF PRODUCTION. They remain identifiable since their different levels of education, culture, consciousness, etc. continue to set them apart. See also INTELLIGENTSIA.

social structure 1 any relatively enduring pattern or interrelationship of social elements, e.g. the CLASS structure.
2 the more or less enduring pattern of social arrangements within a particular society, group, or social organization, e.g. the 'social structure of Great Britain'.

No single agreed concept of social structure exists in sociology, despite its widespread usage. The definition employed depends upon the theoretical perspective within which the concept is used. For example, Herbert SPENCER was interested in showing how social structure, conceived as analogous with, if not identical to, a biological organism, became increasingly differentiated and more specialized as the result of 'social evolution'. MARX, on the other hand, stressed the overriding importance of the basis (or *infrastructure*) and the more or less dependent *superstructure,* as the two main components of social structure.

In general, disagreement exists as to whether the most decisive elements of social structure consist of the 'surface' rules, roles and social institutions (e.g. PARSONS, 1951, or Nadel, 1957), or whether these arise from mechanisms and processes which are hidden from view but which underpin social life, as for MARX or for LÉVI-STRAUSS (see also STRUCTURE, STRUCTURALISM).

Whilst a focus on the interrelation of social parts – and hence 'structural' thinking – can be seen as one of the defining features of sociology, numerous reservations exist about the uses to which the concept of social structure is put.

Disagreement and debate about the role of structural thinking in sociology derives from the differences of degree, if not of kind, which would seem to exist between the types of structures that exist in the physical and the biological world and social structures. Reservations exist particularly about the appropriateness of mechanical and biological analogies and the use of conceptions of HOMEOSTASIS, FUNCTION, SOCIAL SYSTEM as well as conceptions of TELEOLOGY in sociology (see FUNCTIONALISM).

The fact is that social structures do not possess the relatively clear-cut 'boundaries' in time and space of many physical and most biological structures, nor do they possess the precisely identifiable tendencies to homeostasis possessed by organic structures.

Reservations about structural thinking exist particularly in connection with functionalist thinking, but the identification of the 'essential' or central features of particular social structures, or types of social structure, is often controversial whether or not functional thinking is involved.

social studies of science the interdisciplinary study of the social context in the production of SCIENCE. As such the approach overlaps with both the SOCIOLOGY OF SCIENCE and the SOCIOLOGY OF KNOWLEDGE, as well as the history and the PHILOSOPHY OF SCIENCE, although those most associated with the approach have increasingly sought to distance themselves from the latter, above all wishing to instate the primacy of an 'empirical' approach in social studies of science. Adopting the doctrine of the so-called *'strong version of the sociology of science'* (i.e. that 'science' has to be explained by the same route as other forms of knowledge or belief, and can have no privileged status as 'truth' or be exempt from social explanation), has sometimes led those associated with the approach to be accused of 'relativism'. However, their intention is simply to place a study of science on the same basis as any other social phenomenon. Advocates of the approach are no more concerned to establish philosophical RELATIVISM than they have been to preserve traditional EPISTEMOLOGY.

social survey a comprehensive collection of data and information about people living in a specific area or administrative unit.

Social surveys aim to collect a great deal of data about individuals and their lifestyles by means of QUESTIONNAIRES and other QUANTITATIVE RESEARCH TECHNIQUES. They are undertaken for administrative as well as sociological purposes (see also MARKET RESEARCH).

In Britain, the first comprehensive social survey was probably the *Domesday Book*. The national CENSUSES held every ten years since 1801 can be regarded as national social surveys. The first major social surveys undertaken in the UK are generally considered to be those of Booth and Rowntree who looked at poverty in 19th-century London and York.

Today a number of social surveys are conducted on a regular basis by both private institutions and government departments. The *British Social Attitudes Survey* (BSAS) dates from 1983, and each year since 1971 the Home Office has undertaken a *General Household Survey* (GHS) (see Dale et al., 1988).

Although social surveys are often not explicitly sociological in orientation, they do provide the sociologist with a rich source of secondary data for the analysis of many sociological questions. For example, Booth's study of poverty in 19th-century London provides the historical sociologist with a considerable amount of data on life in that period, and the GHS provides the researcher with data on subjects as diverse as marriage and fertility patterns, employment and leisure.

social system 1 any, especially a relatively persistent, 'patterning of social relations across "time-space", understood as reproduced practices' (GIDDENS, 1984). Thus in this general sense, a SOCIETY, or any ORGANIZATION or GROUP constitutes a social system. For Giddens, however, social systems are highly variable in the degree to which they manifest a 'systematic pattern'. They 'rarely have the sort of internal unity' true of biological systems, or of the kind usually assumed by FUNCTIONALISM (see also SYSTEM, SYSTEMS THEORY). Compare also SOCIAL STRUCTURE, STRUCTURE.

2 (more specifically, as in FUNCTIONALISM) any persistent system of interaction between two or more social actors up to and including a unitary SOCIETY, especially where this is associated with a tendency of the system to *boundary maintenance*, i.e. to preserve its position *vis-a-vis* its external environment, whether this be other social systems or the physical world. In PARSONS' thinking (1951), and in most modern forms of functionalist and STRUCTURAL-FUNCTIONALIST sociology, such a conception of social system has been particularly associated with conceptions of FUNCTIONAL PREREQUISITES of societies and of societies as self-maintaining systems, etc. (see also SYSTEMS THEORY, SUBSYSTEMS MODEL).

social theory a term often used to refer to all or any general theoretical accounts of social relations, whatever their disciplinary base or origin. Thus a distinction can be drawn between SOCIOLOGICAL THEORY in a narrow sense, the theory produced by those fully identified with, and working within, paradigms clearly located within disciplinary sociology, and those theories produced outside it.

Given the open-ended and eclectic nature of sociology as a discipline (as discussed in the Introduction of this Dictionary), the distinction between sociological theory and social theory is not a hard-and-fast one, and many sociologists in fact prefer to work with whichever theories appear most relevant, whatever their disciplinary source (as indeed is often the case within this Dictionary). In doing this they may sometimes also prefer to present themselves as 'social theorists'.

social welfare the general state of health, wellbeing and happiness of individuals or a society. The extent to which provision for this should be the responsibility of the STATE or the individual is a central issue running through many debates in modern society. See also WELFARE STATE, JUSTICE.

social work the organized provision of personal welfare services to people in need, including the poor, the physically and mentally disabled, the aged, children in need, etc. Social work also includes work with delinquents and criminals, e.g. the probation service, which is as much an adjunct of policing as concerned simply with the provision of welfare. The twin goals of social welfare and social control can be seen as concerns present in most types of social work. Arising from the new urban conditions which accompanied rapid industrialization in the 19th-century, at first social work was provided by private individuals or voluntary bodies. In modern industrial societies, social work has become increasingly professionalized and is now mainly provided by statutory agencies. Training in social work has usually included a major emphasis on sociology. Psychoanalytic perspectives, and more recently a knowledge of law, have also figured strongly. Reflecting in part these disciplinary differences, orientations to social work have sometimes emphasized attitudinal or personality changes at the individual level as the key to effective intervention, while at other times, e.g. radical or Marxist orientations to social work, directing attention to the underlying socioeconomic causes of individual problems has been seen as part of the role of the social worker. See also RADICAL SOCIAL WORK.

sociation Kurt Wolff's rendering of SIMMEL's general term (*Vergesellschaftung*) referring to the conscious association of human beings (K. Wolff, 1950). A central concern of Simmel's sociology was to establish the general forms of sociation (see FORMAL SOCIOLOGY).

societal reaction the idea that the social response to an act which is seen as deviant can be crucial in its consequences, particularly in creating or encouraging a deviant lifestyle or identity, or DEVIANT CAREER. The term was first used in this special sense by Edwin Lemert (1951) who argued that the effects of actions of social control agencies (e.g. the POLICE, courts) were most significant in defining, changing or confirming deviance and the deviant actor. This is central to the distinction Lemert makes between PRIMARY DEVIANCE and SECONDARY DEVIANCE. The focus on the reactions of others has meant that the term is often associated with LABELLING THEORY, or with theories of SOCIAL CONTROL.

society

1 the totality of human relationships.

2 any self-perpetuating, human grouping occupying a relatively bounded territory, possessing its own more or less distinctive CULTURE and INSTITUTIONS, e.g. a particular people such as the Nuer or a long- or well-established NATION STATE, such as the UK or US.

Although one of the most basic concepts in sociology, a number of difficulties and disputes surround the use of the concept, especially in the second sense. If the concept of society in the second sense is usually fairly readily applied in the case of well-established nation states, which have their own familial, economic and political institutions and clear borders, the identification of the boundaries of a society is nothing like so easy in the case of, say, ancient empires, which usually consisted of relatively loose assemblies of different peoples, peasant communities, etc., with no conception of shared nationhood (see also NATIONALISM). As indicated by RUNCIMAN (1989), the range of actual 'societal membership' can be highly variable: a 'member of a local tribal group inhabiting an area on a boundary between zones of patrilineal and matrilineal inheritance; the member of a separate ethnic and religious community in a country ruled by a colonial power; the member of a separatist commune set up within a state'; and so on. The point at which historically a changing society should or should not be treated as the same society is a further issue which can present difficulties. Ultimately the capacity of members to interact with each other and the extent of this interaction, and, historically, the extent of cultural and institutional continuity, is the 'test' of whether the concept of a single society applies. This said, in even the apparently most clearly defined societies, such as nation states or a geographically and socially isolated 'simple society', there will be connections with other societies. Given the increasing globalization of modern social relations, some theorists (e.g. GIDDENS) have argued that the ever-present risk attached to an overemphasis on the concept of unitary societies in sociology is a failure to give sufficient attention to the major importance of inter-societal connections, multi-national organizations, etc.

For DURKHEIM and for some functionalists, 'society' also exists in a third sense. Durkheim promoted sociology as the 'science of society' and treated society as a distinct object, with a reality 'sui generis'. As an object of study it was distinct from and greater than the sum of its individual component parts. Its 'reality' was a 'moral power' external to and constraining human individuals (see SOCIAL FACTS AS THINGS). The issues raised by such further uses of the term have been some of the most contentious of all in sociology. In contrast with 'classical' sociological theory, it can be said that contemporary sociology has been increasingly reluctant to theorize society in this way (see HOLISM, METHODOLOGICAL, INDIVIDUALISM, STRUCTURE AND AGENCY). See also SOCIAL SYSTEM. FUNCTIONAL REQUISITES.

sociobiology theory and research within the field of evolutionary biology which seeks to provide biological explanations for the evolution of social behaviour and organization in animals and humans. Proponents of sociobiological theories (e.g. E. O. Wilson, 1975) regard the problem of the evolution of altruism as a major challenge, since altruism implies a sacrifice of individual fitness incompatible with classical evolutionary theory. Proponents of sociobiology have been criticized for arguing their case from selective evidence, for making claims for behavioural 'universals' speculatively and assuming their innate basis. See also ETHOLOGY, TERRITORIAL IMPERATIVE.

sociocultural evolution 'the process of change and development in human societies that results from cumulative change in their

stores of cultural information available' (Lenski and Lenski, 1970). For Lenski and Lenski, sociocultural evolution occurs on two levels:
(a) within individual societies;
(b) within the 'world-system of societies' in general as part of a process of *intersocietal selection.* Theorists such as Lenski and Lenski regard symbols as playing an analogous role (the transmission of information) within sociocultural systems and sociocultural evolution to that played by genes and NATURAL SELECTION in biological systems and biological evolution: in both processes continuity and change, variation and extinction, and innovation and selection, are evident – see also EVOLUTIONARY THEORY. Important differences between the two processes are recognized:
(a) while biological evolution is characterized by continuous differentiation and diversification (like the branching of a tree), it is characteristic of sociocultural evolution that societies merge or are eliminated, resulting in fewer rather than more societal types (differentiation, however, is an increasing feature within complex societies);
(b) in biological evolution simple species are not eliminated, but in sociocultural evolution they tend to be;
(c) in sociocultural evolution heritability involves transmission between generations which preserves useful learned behaviour, in biological evolution such *acquired characteristics* are not transmitted (see also LAMARCK); as a consequence, in comparison with biological evolution, sociocultural evolution is rapid and the potential exists for this to be brought under rational control.

The debate in sociology about evolutionary theory centres not so much on differences between social and biological evolution, since there is broad agreement on this. Rather debate centres on whether similarities or dissimilarities between biological and sociocultural change are regarded as uppermost. For sociocultural evolutionary theorists such as Lenski and Lenski, and some functionalist sociologists (e.g. see PARSONS, EVOLUTIONARY UNIVERSALS, NEOEVOLUTIONISM) similarities between the two mean that the term 'evolution' and evolutionary theory continue to have an important place in discussions of social change. For other sociologists, however, the differences between the two kinds of change are so great that continued talk of social evolution is not helpful and should be ended. See also EVOLUTIONARY SOCIOLOGY.

sociodrama see MORENO.

socioeconomic group see CLASS, SOCIAL STRATIFICATION.

socioeconomic status a person's overall standing within a social stratification system (LAZARSFELD et al., 1944; GOLDTHORPE AND HOPE, 1974). Imprecisions and uncertainties as to what such general notions refer to, compared with more analytically focused notions of CLASS and STATUS, have meant that the concept has attracted criticism (see MILLS, 1959). See also SOCIAL STRATIFICATION.

sociogram see SOCIOMETRY.

sociolegal studies see SOCIOLOGY OF LAW.

sociolinguistics a field of study, informed by both sociology and psychology, concerned with the social and cultural aspects and functions of LANGUAGE. Although sometimes narrowly identified with somewhat disparate, albeit important, topics such as language and social class (e.g. the work of Basil BERNSTEIN), language and ethnicity (e.g. Labov, 1967), language and gender, etc., potentially at least, sociolinguistics, has a much wider brief, including most aspects of language. One general area of major significance, for example, has been an emphasis on the importance of a sociological view of 'linguistic competence' and the inadequacy of a merely physiological and psychological view (e.g. Halliday's or HABERMAS's critique of CHOMSKY's theory of linguistic competence). Among further main areas of sociolinguistic concern are PRAGMATICS and SEMIOTICS. Accordingly, the argument can be advanced that sociolinguistics should be regarded as having an utterly central rather than a peripheral role within the general study of LINGUISTICS. See also COGNITIVE ANTHROPOLOGY.

sociological theory the range of abstract, general approaches and competing and complementary schools of thought which exist in sociology.

While sociological theory in this sense includes some theories which are 'formalized' or mathematical in form (see THEORY, MATHEMATICAL SOCIOLOGY), more usually 'theory' in sociology is looser in form, referring to the main 'approaches', intellectual paradigms, conceptual schemes, etc. which exist within the discipline.

The following are among the main general theoretical approaches usually identified within sociology:
(a) FUNCTIONALISM, sometimes but not always including EVOLUTIONARY SOCIOLOGY;
(b) SYMBOLIC INTERACTIONISM and INTERPRETATIVE SOCIOLOGY, including ACTION THEORY;
(c) MARXIST SOCIOLOGY and CONFLICT THEORY;
(d) FORMAL SOCIOLOGY;
(e) SOCIAL PHENOMENOLOGY and ETHNOMETHODOLOGY;
(f) STRUCTURALISM and POSTSTRUCTURALISM.

As well as these general approaches, the importance of which would usually be recognized by most sociologists, numerous theoretical approaches of lesser influence can also be identified (e.g. EXCHANGE THEORY or STRUCTURATION THEORY). In part all such general approaches can be seen as complementary, emphasizing different aspects of social reality (e.g. a complementarity between micro and macro approaches, or between theories of agency and theories of structure). Equally, however, they are also often presented as competing approaches.

Some sociologists, notably MERTON, calling for what he referred to as THEORIES OF THE MIDDLE RANGE, have sought to escape from the emphasis on competition between such general theoretical frameworks, placing a far greater emphasis on 'working' explanatory theories and SENSITIZING CONCEPTS that arise from research and interpret findings (see also GROUNDED THEORY, ANALYTICAL INDUCTION).

Other general distinctions between types of theoretical approach relate to:
(a) issues of EPISTEMOLOGY and ONTOLOGY, e.g. POSITIVISM versus CONVENTIONALISM or REALISM;
(b) distinctions between 'surface' and 'deep' STRUCTURE (see also SOCIAL STRUCTURE).

Compare SOCIAL THEORY.

sociology

A term coined by COMTE to describe the scientific and, more particularly, the positivistic, study of SOCIETY (see POSITIVISM). Since then, however, the term has gained a far wider currency to refer to the systematic study of the functioning, organization, development, and types of human societies, without this implying any particular model of 'science'. In some usage, the term can also encompass approaches which explicitly repudiate the relevance of a 'physical science' orientation to social study.

One problem immediately emerges about such a definition:
(a) it fails to distinguish sociology from SOCIAL SCIENCE in general;
(b) it fails to distinguish sociology from other, less generalist, social sciences.

Since no aspect of society is excluded from consideration by sociology, no simple distinction can be drawn between sociology and social science; in some usages the two terms are simply synonymous. More usually, however, whereas sociology necessarily overlaps with the subject matter of more specialist social sciences (e.g. ECONOMICS, POLITICAL SCIENCE), the discipline is conceived of by its practitioners as distinguished from these more focused social science disciplines by an avowedly 'holistic' perspective in social analysis, a commitment to analysis which studies the interrelation of social parts. This said, however, it has to be noted that sociology does not exist as a tightly integrated discipline; not only does the subject encompass many competing paradigms and approaches, it has also remained uniquely open to ideas imported from other disciplines, from PHILOSOPHY, from HISTORY, and so on, as well as from other social sciences, and from more general social and political discourse.

A further implication of such a view of sociology is that it does not begin with the work of Comte, but can also be regarded as embracing earlier systematic study of societies, including the plainly sociological thinking (although not so-called) of major classical philosophers such as PLATO OR ARISTOTLE, or, closer to modern times, SCOTTISH ENLIGHTENMENT thinkers, such as SMITH OR FERGUSON. There is a viewpoint in sociology, that sociology's concern as a discipline is with the distinctive problems of modern INDUSTRIAL SOCIETIES (GIDDENS, 1981). However, though this draws attention to an undoubted central emphasis within modern sociology, seen not least in the classical works of the giants of the discipline, such as MARX, WEBER, and DURKHEIM, it understates the range of the subject, which is a concern with all aspects and all types of society.

sociology of art an area of sociological analysis which includes with in its compass a concern with exploring the visual arts and sometimes also music, theatre, cinema, and literature. As such, the potential range of concepts and theories is diverse. Influential theoretical approaches have included Marxist and neo-Marxist – including STRUCTURALISM – as well as more conventionally sociological perspectives.

In the US, mainstream sociologists such as Coser (1978) and BECKER (1982) have focused on organizational and institutional analysis of the agencies involved in artistic and cultural production and their relations with audiences.

Whereas at one time Marxist approaches sought to analyse artistic products reductionistically, in terms of the metaphor of BASE AND SUPERSTRUCTURE, Marxists are today at the forefront of an emphasis on the importance of analysis of internal features of the artistic object or the text (see also HERMENEUTICS). Structuralist approaches, including SEMIOTIC analysis, exploring the complex codes involved in artistic products, have also been widely employed in recent years. Ultimately, however, it is a combination of an understanding of artistic production in its own terms and an account of its wider socioeconomic location and implications which continues to demarcate the sociology of art from more conventional non-sociological approaches to its analysis, such as literary criticism or art history. This said, it must also be recognized that much seminal work in the sociology of art has been interdisciplinary rather than narrowly sociological. See also AESTHETICS, SOCIOLOGY OF MASS COMMUNICATIONS, MODERNISM, LEISURE, CULTURAL STUDIES, BENJAMIN.

sociology of crime and deviance see CRIMINOLOGY, DEVIANCE.

sociology of development that branch of sociology concerned with the examination of social change from agrarian to industrial societies and particularly applied to study of the THIRD WORLD. More narrowly, the term is sometimes used to refer to those theories of social change associated with MODERNIZATION theory and neo-evolutionary approaches. This latter usage is now less common than in the 1970s when the sociology of development was contrasted with UNDERDEVELOPMENT or DEPENDENCY THEORY.

sociology of economic life see ECONOMIC SOCIOLOGY.

sociology of education the application of sociological theories, perspectives and research methods to an analysis of educational processes and practices. It is characteristic of industrial societies that, compared with previous societies, education is provided by specialized institutions. It is the performance of these institutions that is the central object of study in the sociology of education.

Although the emergence of the sociology of education as a distinct field of enquiry is of fairly recent origin, it has its roots in the early development of sociology, especially the FUNCTIONALISM of DURKHEIM. For Durkheim (1922), the process of education was to be understood in terms of its contribution to the promotion and maintenance of the social order. A related viewpoint (e.g. MANNHEIM) was to regard education as a means of solving problems and removing social antagonisms.

Until the 1950s, the sociology of education remained strongly influenced by such perspectives, although the development of the discipline owed much to the role of sociology in teacher training, especially in the US, as well as to the tradition of 'political arithmetic' in the UK. The latter tradition led to a range of surveys and statistical studies exploring the social influences on educational attainment, and educational and occupational selection and SOCIAL MOBILITY (e.g. Floud, HALSEY and Martin, 1957). Although these studies revealed the persistence of class and gender inequalities in educational opportunity, the assumption remained that education could become a means of social transformation in the long run. In the UK, the introduction of COMPREHENSIVE SCHOOLS, programmes of COMPENSATORY EDUCATION and the expansion of HIGHER EDUCATION in the 1950s and subsequently, were intended to achieve this end, creating not only a more equal society, but also eliminating unnecessary waste of the nation's human talent.

During the 1960s, a breakdown of the functionalist hegemony in sociology and an increasing pessimism about reformist policies in education, especially in the US, led to the emergence of a sociology of education markedly different in tenor. Sources of inequality lying outside the school were seen as intractable and fundamental questions were raised about both the traditional sociology of education and the assumed relationship between education and social reform. One aspect of this new phase in the sociology of education was to direct attention to features of schooling such as classroom interaction and curriculum organization, work which derived from the application of standard interactionist approaches. Other work was more radical (e.g. Young's work on the curriculum, and Bowles and Gintis's *Schooling in Capitalist America*, 1976), suggesting that schools function above all as agencies which necessarily reproduce the social relations of capitalist production. Part of the inspiration behind analysis of this type was Marxist (e.g. drawing on the conceptions of GRAMSCI and ALTHUSSER). Other sociologists, however, combined the thinking of Marx, Durkheim and Weber to achieve much the same outcome, e.g. BOURDIEU's arguments about the dependence of education on CULTURAL CAPITAL.

It would be wrong to imagine that later perspectives in the sociology of education have entirely replaced earlier ones. Nor should it be assumed that all attempts to expand educational opportunity have been to no avail. For example, in the UK the percentage of men and women entering higher education is now approaching parity, the overall proportion of schoolchildren entering higher education has substantially increased since the 1950s, and the number of entrants from working-class homes has also greatly increased. On the other hand, class differences in educational achievement remain striking and the role of educational systems in sustaining a class society equally apparent. See also BERNSTEIN, HIDDEN CURRICULUM, INTELLIGENCE, MERITOCRACY, CONTEXT AND SPONSORED MOBILITY.

sociology of health and medicine
the application of sociological approaches to the understanding of the experience, distribution and treatment of illness. This sub-area of the discipline has been a major growth area in terms of research and teaching, and in terms of membership it probably represents the largest section of both the British and American national sociological associations. The reasons for this expansion are perhaps twofold. The first has been the relatively greater access of workers in this area to research funds: both governments and medical sources have been anxious to promote research which could improve health policy and patient care. Secondly, it has become manifest that the profile of morbidity and mortality in the industrialized world is now dominated by so-called 'lifestyle diseases' (such as stroke, cancer and heart disease). As the name implies, the management of these problems often involves an adjustment to ways of living rather than subjection to a regime of drug therapy. Medicine has no 'magic bullets' to 'take out' these diseases (as antibiotics could with many infectious diseases), or immunization programmes to give prophylactic protection. Moreover, lifestyle diseases show a clear social class gradient, generally becoming less frequent as class position improves. There is also, then, a socially structured pattern of 'opportunity' for healthy living. Sociology has an obvious input to make in providing a fuller understanding of these 'chances for life'.

The expansion of health and medicine as an area of sociological concern can be dated from the seminal contribution made by PARSONS' analysis of the SICK ROLE. Parsons' interest, in fact, was part of a much larger theoretical project (1951) on the development of a complex functional model of society, but his contribution served to establish the area of medicine as an institution whose sociological study could enhance the theoretical development of the discipline itself. Herein lies a long-established (if, in the end, overdrawn) distinction between two sociologies of medicine: one a sociology *in* medicine, whose research agenda is set by governments, policy makers and clinicians, the other, a sociology *of* medicine, whose questions are determined much more *by* sociologists and *for* sociology.

Parsons' concept of the sick role was subjected to criticism and amendment (see, e.g., Morgan et al., 1985, for a recent overview of the major contributions here). Other topics of particular importance in the early expansion of the discipline were: medical education and socialization (MERTON et al.; 1957, BECKER et al., 1961); the social organization of death (Glasser and Strauss, 1965, 1968); mental illness (GOFFMAN, 1961a; Scheff, 1966); and the analysis of medicine as a profession (Freidson, 1970a, 1970b). FUNCTIONALISM and SYMBOLIC INTERACTIONISM were the major theoretical traditions which informed much of this early work.

As the sociology of health and medicine has grown both in terms of maturity and in the number and theoretical predilections of its practitioners, research has been extended into still further areas. There can now be hardly any substantive area in the field in which work still remains to be initiated. Among the topics which have been, and continue to be, of interest to contemporary researchers are: the relationship between medicine and capitalism; medicine as an instrument of social control (medicine and patriarchy and the medicalization of life have been two prominent themes here); gender and health, with particular reference to the role of women as paid and unpaid health workers; eating disorders (see ANOREXIA NERVOSA); inequalities in health and health provision, including those of race and gender as well as class; the social construction of medical knowledge; doctor-patient communication and interaction; patterns of help-seeking and compliance among patients; the holistic health movement and complementary therapies (see ALTERNATIVE MEDICINE); and, most recently, the study of sexual behaviour, with special reference to sexually transmitted diseases and AIDS.

sociology of housing an emerging specialist subject area in sociology, which seeks sociological explanations for a range of housing phenomena, ranging from patterns of housing tenure and provision, to patterns of inhabitation and household structures, to the meaning of 'house' and 'home' in different cultures. It is an area of study that overlaps with work in other disciplines, including human geography, planning, housing management, environmental psychology, urban sociology, policy studies and women's studies.

The sociology of housing in Britain has, in the past, been heavily influenced by prevailing modes of analysis in other sociological fields. Rex and Moore's (1967) analysis of housing provision in 'Sparkbrook' approached the subject from social stratification theory and developed the concept of HOUSING CLASS. In the 1980s Peter Saunders (*A Nation of Home Owners*, 1990) approached the sociology of housing from the perspective of CONSUMPTION. In the 1970s, however, in both France and Spain, two fundamental contributions were made in the work of Henri Lefebvre (1991) on the production of space and Manuel Castells (1977) on URBAN SOCIOLOGY, which made significant contributions to human geography and associated disciplines, especially in the United States. David Harvey (1989b) has synthesized and developed these perspectives and his work as a human geographer makes an important contribution to the debate on postmodernity (see POSTMODERNITY AND POSTMODERNISM).

At the microsociology level there has been a developing interest in the way people inhabit and transform their interiors and the meanings of their home. Some of this work is reminiscent of MASS OBSERVATION studies of the mantelpiece, but other work is concerned, as is the sociology of fashion, to explore the construction of SELF.

See also HOMELESSNESS.

sociology of industry see INDUSTRIAL SOCIOLOGY, SOCIOLOGY OF WORK.

sociology of knowledge the branch of sociology that studies the social processes involved in the production of knowledge. It is concerned with the understanding and explanation of knowledge in particular cases, and with the relations between the general form(s) of knowledge and social structure, including both the effects of knowledge and any social forces which condition either the form or the content of knowledge.

In a general sense, the sociology of knowledge (which may include among its subject matter all ideas and 'beliefs', as well as knowledge in a more exact sense, e.g. scientific knowledge or 'true' knowledge) is an integral part of many general theories in sociology, e.g. Comte's LAW OF THREE STAGES in the intellectual and social development of society. As such, the boundaries of the sociology of knowledge are not tight. It either includes or overlaps related branches of sociological study, such as the SOCIOLOGY

OF SCIENCE, the SOCIOLOGY OF RELIGION, the SOCIOLOGY OF ART and literature.

A further distinction often made is between the sociology of knowledge and EPISTEMOLOGY, the theory of theories of knowledge in philosophy. As illustrated by Comte's POSITIVISM, this boundary has not always been accepted in sociology. Durkheim's contribution was to suggest that a basic analogue exists between our fundamental modes of thought, e.g. our concepts of space and time, and our basic forms of social organization, especially our concepts of society. In recent years there has also been a strong movement within philosophy itself to approach epistemological questions in sociological ways, e.g. the work of KUHN on science.

Early approaches in the sociology of knowledge tended to be dominated by issues raised by Marxism. According to Marx and Engels, knowledge is often distorted by class interests. Thus the sociology of knowledge as initiated by Marxism focused mainly on the economic determination of leading ideas in a particular epoch or social formation (see also BASE AND SUPERSTRUCTURE, IDEOLOGY). This approach was both challenged and built upon by Karl MANNHEIM, who argued that group membership and social location of many kinds, not just class and economic interests, act in ways which condition the formation and outcome of knowledge. Marxism itself was also seen as no exception to this rule. One important distinction made by Mannheim was between 'realistic', 'ideological' and 'utopian' forms of knowledge. The social conditions conducive to each of these were also identified. Mannheim also wanted to overcome the tendency to RELATIVISM in the sociology of knowledge. His suggestion was that the knowledge accepted by socially unlocated, 'free-floating' intellectuals might provide the answer.

Mannheim was not alone in thinking that the sociology of knowledge must not confine itself to uncovering the social basis of 'false' claims to knowledge, but should try to contribute also to our identification of the social basis of 'true' knowledge. The work of Comte or Marx also stands four square with Mannheim in taking this no longer accepted view. The same objective is also uppermost in major attempts at synthesis in modern sociology, such as HABERMAS's model of three types of 'knowledge interests', or in modern sociological forms of scientific REALISM. If it cannot be said that sociology has solved such problems of knowledge in a once and for all way, neither is it the case that it has conceded the ground to outright relativism (see also POSTMODERNISM).

Today the sociology of knowledge is pursued at many levels, in particular in studies in the sociology of science, and in studies of the social construction of everyday knowledge (see SOCIAL PHENOMENOLOGY, ETHNOMETHODOLOGY).

sociology of law the sociological study of the social context, development and operation of *law:* the system of rules and sanctions, the specialist institutions and specialist personnel, and the several types of law (e.g. constitutional, civil, criminal) which constitute the legal system in complex societies.

In the development of this area of study the works of DURKHEIM and WEBER have been important as in other areas of sociology, but the development of the sociology of law is complicated by academic approaches overlapping with sociology, notably JURISPRUDENCE and, later, the development of *sociolegal studies.* The latter now exists as a strand of social science thinking and research (including psychology and economic analysis as well as inputs from sociology) and stands in critical relation with traditional orthodoxies in legal theory. CRIMINOLOGY and the wider study of DEVIANCE are further related areas of specialist study.

In the sociology of law and in sociolegal studies, utilitarian, individualistic and positivist views have been challenged by an interest in exploring the complexities of morality and mechanisms of social control. From Durkheim came the emphasis on the formal expression of what is pre-eminently social, viz, morality. This was explored in his discussion of the shift from MECHANICAL to ORGANIC SOLIDARITY, which included the distinction between 'repressive' and 'restitutive' law. From Weber's work has come an emphasis on the role of the development of rational and calculable law – legal rationalism – as a precondition for modern political developments and for capitalism. MARX's work, although less concerned with the detailed study of legal forms, has also influenced the study of law in a number of ways, ranging from studies of the role of class interests in the content of law, to debates about the overall form of 'bourgeois' legality – an interest inspired by the rediscovery of the work of Evgeny Pashukanis (1891–1937).

As well as such general theoretical bases, lower level empirical studies of the operation of legal institutions have been increasingly important, especially studies of the working of the CRIMINAL JUSTICE SYSTEM, including the operation of courts, police, etc., and PENOLOGY. See also NATURAL RIGHTS AND NATURAL LAW, COMMON LAW, ROMAN LAW.

sociology of leisure see LEISURE.

sociology of mass communications the subfield of sociology concerned with the study of the MASS MEDIA OF COMMUNICATIONS. In practice it has involved people from a variety of disciplines, bringing a multiplicity of theoretical perspectives. The central theoretical problem is the conceptualization of the relationship between the mass media and society and this has been undertaken through research into mass communication and power and influence, and the study of the mass media as institutions, the occupational cultures and practices of media workers, the audiences for mass communications, and the role of the mass media in the overall reproduction of culture. Three general perspectives have guided study: the first has been informed especially by SOCIAL PSYCHOLOGY, and has focused on the processes and effects of mass communications (e.g. see ADVERTISING); the second, has focused on mass communications institutions as ORGANIZATIONS and their broad social context; the third has been influenced by the structuralist perspective developed in the 1960s in which the focus is upon analysis of the messages, images and meanings conveyed by the mass media (see SEMIOLOGY).

sociology of music and dance the sociological study of music and dance as artistic and LEISURE forms possessing wide social significance.

As universal features of human societies, the functionalist view of both music and dance is that they perform social as well as individual expressive functions (e.g. religious dance). Early sociological study of music has focused most on the distinctions between élite and popular forms and the ideological implications of these (see ADORNO, BENJAMIN). More recently structuralist and semiological studies of music have been important, and the connections between musical and dance forms and particular subcultures (e.g. jazz and blues) and with YOUTH CULTURE has been an important topic in CULTURAL STUDIES (see also POPULAR CULTURE). An excellent survey of the main approaches to the sociological study of music is provided by R. Middleton, *Studying Popular Music* (1990).

sociology of organizations see ORGANIZATION THEORY.

sociology of religion the branch of sociology which deals with religious phenomena (see also RELIGION). Historically, the sociological analysis of religion was central in the analysis of most of the leading classical sociologists, notably WEBER and DURKHEIM. The ideas of these two theorists still constitute the core of the sociology of religion. Durkheim's work was concerned with the role of religion as a functional universal contributing to the integration of society. This remains the foundation of the FUNCTIONALIST THEORY OF RELIGION. Weber's concern was with the comparative analysis of the varying forms of religious belief and religious organizations, and the implications of these for the development of rationality and for social change (see PROTESTANT ETHIC, ASCETICISM, CONFUCIANISM, JUDAISM, CHURCH-SECT TYPOLOGY, THEODICY, PROPHECY). Prior to the work of Weber and Durkheim, the sociology of religion had viewed religion simply as 'error' (as for COMTE, or for MARX, e.g. the latter's conception of religion as the 'opiate of the masses'), or it had speculated about the origins of religion and the stages of its evolutionary development (see TYLOR, SPENCER).

More recently, the sociology of' religion has concentrated its attention on the process of SECULARIZATION occurring in Western societies. There have also been many studies of religious organizations (e.g. B. Wilson, 1967), especially 'fringe' religions and CULTS and SECTS (e.g. Scientology or the Moonies). In SOCIAL ANTHROPOLOGY, in HISTORICAL SOCIOLOGY, and in the study of contemporary non-European societies, comparative study of religion as a major social institution continues to occupy a central place in sociological analysis. See also CIVIL RELIGION, HINDUISM, ISLAM, BUDDHISM, CASTE.

sociology of science the branch of sociology concerned with study of the social processes involved in the production of scientific knowledge as well as the social implications of this knowledge, including TECHNOLOGY (see also SOCIOLOGY OF KNOWLEDGE, SCIENCE, SOCIAL STUDIES OF SCIENCE).

The pioneering work on the sociology of science was by Robert MERTON (1938) whose determinedly sociological work on 17th-century British science (especially the Royal Society) emphasized the mix of economic and military concerns, interests and religious beliefs (notably Protestantism) in the motives of early scientists. In his later work Merton also identified central social characteristics of science (e.g. the 'norm of universality', i.e. that, at least in principle, anyone ought to be able to check for themselves the validity of any scientific 'finding').

If Merton's later work identified 'ideal types' of scientific activity, subsequent work in the sociology of science has tended to break down any sharp distinction between science and other forms of knowledge. In recent years, sociologists have distinguished 'strong' and 'weak' versions of the sociology of science. If earlier 'weak approaches were based largely on the need to explain the social basis of 'false' claims to knowledge (scientific errors, 'parasciences' such as astrology, etc.), leaving the basis of 'true' knowledge a matter for the PHILOSOPHY OF SCIENCE, the more recent 'strong' approach has seen as its role the study and explanation of *all* forms of scientific knowledge (see also EPISTEMOLOGY).

One thing to emerge from this more even-handed treatment of 'true' and false' knowledge is that both of these forms share a common basis in everyday constructions of social reality, and problems in escaping INDEXICALITY and in establishing warrantabilty. Understanding of both kinds of knowledge is held to benefit from the study of the social impetus to new scientific ideas provided by economic and social interests, including the disciplinary and personal interests of the scientists.

Examples of recent detailed study in this expanded vein are:

(a) studies of the role of interests, fashions, etc. in particular disciplines or movements in science, e.g. the rise and fall of EUGENICS (Harwood, 1977), studies of IQ testing and even the history of mathematics;

(b) studies of the DIFFUSION of scientific ideas;

(c) studies of major 'scientific revolutions' (e.g. KUHN, 1962);

(d) ethnographic and related forms of close-up empirical analysis of the everyday social construction of scientific knowledge, e.g. in laboratories, the presentational arguments and graphic representations, etc. used by science, e.g. B. Latour and S. Woolgar, *Laboratory Life* (1979).

sociology of sport a subdiscipline of sociology which focuses upon the relationship between SPORT and society. The sociology of sport is concerned with the relationship between sport and other social institutions (the family, education, politics, and the economy), the social organization, social relations and group behaviour associated with different types of sport (e.g. élite or mass, amateur and professional, the class, gender or race relations that sport involves), and the social processes (such as ideological incorporation) that occur in conjunction with sport. Whilst once isolated from mainstream sociology, in recent years it has become more fully integrated. Most research has been conducted in North America, but a sociology of sport also exists in Eastern and Western Europe, in Australia and New Zealand and the UK, as well as in Japan. Leading exponents in the UK have included Norbert ELIAS and Eric Dunning (see Elias and Dunning, 1986), and John Hargreaves (1986). See also LEISURE, POPULAR CULTURE, FANZINES.

sociology of the body an important new area of specialism within sociology which has sought to repair a previous relative neglect of the BODY, and the implications of 'embodiment'.

In recent years there has been an increase in popular as well as academic interest in the body 'social'. Academic interest is related to the growing influence of FEMINISM, Foucauldian scholarship (see FOUCAULT) and postmodernism (see POSTMODERNITY AND POSTMODERNISM) – schools of thought which focus attention on the body as a social product as well as a physical entity. Popular interest in the body is indicated by the multimillion-dollar industries promoting exercise courses and weight reduction plans, the growth in popularity of self-help therapies and alternative medicine, and the emphasis on the body as an expression of individual identity. Further, the moral debates of the 1980s over contraception, ABORTION, PORNOGRAPHY, embryo experimentation and HOMOSEXUALITY, the emergence of AIDS, and more recent controversy over drug use in sport or genetic engineering, have raised issues of interest to the population as a whole as well as to sociologists. The emerging sociology of the body has contributed to an understanding of the social regulation of bodies, particularly by legal and medical institutions (Foucault, 1973; Turner, 1984, 1987, 1992) and particularly of those bodies perceived as 'other' or as 'out of control'. The sociology of the body has also been concerned with issues of CONSUMPTION (see Featherstone, 1991) and has addressed the important issues of SUBJECTIVITY, IDENTITY and the fashioning of the SELF (GIDDENS, 1991).

Recent developments in genetic manipulation, cloning techniques, the creation of transgenic organisms and artificial life forms (among others) have led to debate about the future of the body. Donna HARAWAY has argued that the human body is being encroached upon (by other organisms and by CYBORG technologies) at the same time as it extends into other areas like CYBERSPACE. Haraway argues that we are already cyborg, using machine technologies to transcend the limitations of the physical body; future generations are thus unlikely to be 'pure' human. In the 21st century then, our physical bodies as well as our cultural identities have become fully reflexive.

sociology of the built environment a recent emphasis in sociology which, according to some theorists, can be the umbrella to bring together a number of special studies previously handled separately, e.g. the SOCIOLOGY OF HOUSING, URBAN SOCIOLOGY, sociological analysis of movements in architecture and town planning. As both material artefacts and expressions of cultural values, the forms taken by individual buildings and by towns and cities are of interest at a number of levels, including:

(a) their relationship with both the commodification of space and resistances

to such commodification (see URBAN SOCIAL MOVEMENTS);
(b) the way the design and the planning of buildings and cities reflects cultural goals and cultural movements (e.g. the movement from the architectural 'modernism' of Corbusier or the Bauhaus school, with its principles of functionalism and fidelity to materials, to 'postmodernism', which has replaced the 'author' and consistent principles with pastiche);
(c) the way in which (a) and (b) are interrelated, e.g. the view that architectural 'postmodernism' comes in two forms: one a renewed subservience to commercial values, the other more 'oppositional' and seeking a revival of 'communal values' (Lash, 1989).

sociology of the family sociological inquiry directed at describing and explaining patterns of FAMILY life and variations in family structure. As such, the study of the family overlaps closely with the study of KINSHIP.

One continuing strand of inquiry, which can be traced to social anthropology, has been concerned with the comparative analysis of family and kinship structures. In association with this, evolutionary and developmental accounts of the transformation of family structures have also been important.

A second strand, which dominated much sociological discussion and research up until the 1960s, was the functionalist theory of the family, interested mainly in the 'universal' functions served by the family and the distinctive geographically mobile, *neolocal nuclear family* forms, which emerge to meet the particular functional requirements of industrial societies.

A more critical examination of family structures emerged in the 1960s, especially under the influence of new feminist sociologies and feminist critiques of social science (e.g. Morgan. 1975).

A final strand of sociological thinking, which has a long ancestry, is Marxist critiques of the family, in which an interest in the association between property relations and family structures has been central.

The functionalist theory of the family portrayed the elementary family unit (whether or not it is embedded in wider social relationships) as performing central social functions, such as:
(a) the regulation of sexual activity;
(b) the procreation of children, and the determination of FILIATION;
(c) the primary socialization of children;
(d) the provision of mutual emotional support for the couple.

These may be considered the core functions but the family usually also performs ancillary functions, although it may increasingly share these with other agencies ('an erosion of functions'). These include:
(e) the provision of housing and domestic services as well as general economic support for the family group;
(f) the provision of health care and welfare;
(g) support through the long period of education in modern societies.

Talcott PARSONS, a leading exponent of functionalist analysis also argued that within the family unit, while the male performed instrumental roles, the role of the woman was usually to perform 'expressive' roles.

Criticism of the functionalist view, and alternative sociological accounts of modern family structure, have made a number of central points and raised a number of general issues:
(a) the existence of a great variety of family forms in modern as well as traditional societies;
(b) the historical oversimplification of the extended/nuclear distinction as applied to preindustrial and industrial society, given that the nuclear family would appear to have preceded industrialism (see HISTORICAL DEMOGRAPHY), and the continued importance of extended kin in industrial society (as shown by Young and Wilmott, 1957);
(c) that the emotional and intimate ties of family conceal a high degree of conflict and in many cases actual violence, so that the study of the family can also be located within the study of social problems (see also WIFE BATTERING, RADICAL PSYCHIATRY);

(d) the importance of analysis of the family and of households in terms of power and authority relations, and also economic relations;
(e) that, at best, the functionalist's '"family" [especially functions (a) and (b)] is not the name of an entity which is universally found but a concept which has a universal application' (Harris, 1985);
(f) the difficulty of even identifying the family group in preindustrial simple societies. It is for this reason that the term 'family' has been relatively little used in social anthropology. See also MARRIAGE, DIVORCE AND SEPARATION.

sociology of work the sociological analysis of work and its organization, including unpaid as well as paid labour. The general subject matter is analysed within its wider social, comparative context, in particular its interrelations with social, economic and political institutions. GENDER, ETHNICITY and SOCIAL CLASS are central subjects (Grint, 1998). Work ideologies have also been a principle concern in relation to occupational specialization (e.g. professionalism). The central unifying theme is the DIVISION OF LABOUR.
The sub-discipline has also been the focus for debates concerning LABOUR PROCESS theory, NEW TECHNOLOGIES and LABOUR MARKET analysis within sociology.

The term 'sociology of work' became the generally accepted term for this sub-discipline partly as a consequence of the influence of the Open University course *People and Organizations* (cf. Esland and Salaman, 1975). This development was a reaction to the limitations sociologists found with INDUSTRIAL SOCIOLOGY, in particular, the preoccupation with manufacturing industry within industrial societies in consequence limiting industrial sociologists' ability to fully analyse many aspects of work. Examples of these, now studied in the 'sociology of work', include the dynamics of work relations and ideologies in relation to gender and race, the organization of domestic labour within society (see SEXUAL DIVISION OF LABOUR), and the effects of underemployment and unemployment.
See also EMPLOYMENT, ORGANIZATIONAL THEORY.

sociometry a widely used method of 'measurement' of social attractiveness within groups, invented by the Austrian-born US psychologist and psychiatrist Jacob MORENO. The technique involves the administration of a questionnaire in which respondents rank order the 'attractiveness' and 'unattractiveness' of fellow group members as coparticipants or colleagues, either generally or in particular activities. The results of these interpersonal choices are then plotted on a diagram, termed a *sociogram*, the configuration revealing sociometric 'stars' and 'rejectees'. and cliques of mutual positive appraisal and social 'isolates'.

sociotechnical systems approach a prescriptive approach to organizational design which, utilizing SYSTEMS THEORY, emphasizes the need to consider the interrelationship between social and technical systems.

The approach was developed by the Tavistock Institute of Human Relations largely as a critique both of classical approaches, which sought to establish universal principles of organizational design, and of the common practice of designing plant layout solely according to technical criteria (social and psychological considerations being an afterthought).
In contrast, the sociotechnical systems approach questioned the universalist assumption of 'one best way' and emphasized the possibility of organizational choice. Technology, for example, is seen as a limiting rather than a determining factor. This makes possible the consideration of alternative technical and social systems. Sociotechnical systems theory aims at systematizing the consideration of alternatives in order to facilitate the best choice. This would allow systems to meet their 'primary task' by optimizing the

relationship between technical efficiency and human satisfaction through diagnosing the 'best fit'. The classic illustration of this approach involved an analysis of technical change in postwar British coal mines (Trist et al., 1963).

Whilst some theorists and practitioners find much of value in the anti-universalist and humanistic stance of this approach, there are critics and sceptics. At a conceptual level the perspective can be seen to suffer from: (a) assumptions associated with systems theory (e.g. reification, system goals); (b) the possibility of a reductionist confusion of psychological and structural levels of understanding; (c) the charge of consultancy-based managerialist sociology (Brown, 1967; Silverman, 1970). Thus some theorists, having contrasted direct and indirect management control systems, point out that control and participation is limited to certain organizational issues and that consideration needs to be given, for example, to the distribution of the benefits of increased productivity. In addition, Mumford's case studies in participative sociotechnical systems design reveal some of the problems of resistance to designing bottom upwards, both from management and higher grade employees, and in the difficulties employees have in participating in design (Mumford, 1980).

Socrates (470–399 BC) Greek philosopher known mainly from his appearance in PLATO's Dialogues, who was executed in Athens for refusing to recant when accused of corrupting the young. Socrates appears to have been concerned mainly with ETHICS, which he concluded should not be a matter of custom or habit, but based on rational, deductive inquiry. Socrates' method of instruction – the *Socratic method* – was to initiate a series of questions and answers, designed to lead those involved to a re-examination of their fundamental beliefs.

soft systems methodology formulated by Peter Checkland in the 1970s as a method of coming to terms with 'soft' or ill-defined organizational problem contexts. The approach differs from traditonal management-oriented methods by virtue of its emphasis on learning, appreciative understanding and the recognition of different and competing 'world views'. Originally the method was promoted as a 7-stage iterative model that could be used to explore problem contexts encouraging iteration of polemical debate until a universal world view or 'accommodation of interests' could be achieved. SYSTEMS THEORY was used extensively in the original formulation; concentrating on emergent properties and holism rather than the reductionist techniques found in other approaches. In 1992 the methodology was reformulated in the face of its critics (Flood, Jackson & Keys 1990 et al) in order to focus more on learning and process, rather than formal systems theory.

soldier a serving member of an army. In its original sense the term meant a 'hired man', reflecting the fact that in premodern states, with some exceptions (e.g. Roman), rather than being conscripted to a citizen army, soldiers were recruited to the personal service of rulers or warlords on a more ad hoc basis. Compare STANDING ARMY.

solidarity see SOCIAL SOLIDARITY and MECHANICAL AND ORGANIC SOLIDARITY.

solipsism (PHILOSOPHY) the doctrine that the self – *my*self – is all that can be known to exist and that 'world' outside 'exists' only as the content of individual consciousness. The doctrine arises from a recognition that the 'objects' of our sense experience are 'mind-dependent'. However, solipsism is nowadays thought incoherent, e.g. WITTGENSTEIN argued that it is incompatible with the existence of the language in which the theory is expressed. The alternative view is REALISM, that the world outside can be 'known', although the limits of such knowledge of the world remains an issue.

Compare RELATIVISM.

sophisticated falsificationism see FALSIFICATIONISM.

sorcery see WITCHCRAFT AND SORCERY.

Sorel, Georges (1847–1922) French philosopher, social theorist and advocate of ANARCHO-SYNDICALISM, best known for his espousal of the roles of 'myth' and VIOLENCE in social affairs. His best-known work is *Reflections on Violence* (1908). Sorel believed in the overthrow of bourgeois society through class struggle, but came to the conclusion that orthodox Marxist accounts of the process were flawed by a tendency to interpret reality through the use of abstract concepts, predicated on the view that human beings were rational and so produced an ordered, regular society, open to scientific analysis and the discovery of laws from which predictions about future utopias could be derived. In Sorel's view, there were no social laws; reality was chaotic and disordered, and any order it exhibited was tenuous and derived from the imposition of human will, rooted, not in rationality, but in instinct. No revolution could be predicted. It could happen, but only as a result of spontaneous, willed action by the workers, which required solidarity. Two historical developments, however, militated against solidarity: the philosophies of trade and consumerism. Together these stimulated competition, mistrust, envy, bargaining and compromise which weakened both the bourgeoisie and the proletariat – the bourgeoisie was weakened by making concessions to the proletariat, which was, in turn, weakened by allowing itself to be bought off by the concessions. Revolutionary proletarians had, therefore, to eschew intellectualism, POLITICAL PARTIES and compromise. Instead they must develop their own ideas and seek to make the REVOLUTION at the point of production through direct action culminating in a general strike.

Sorel's thinking on myth and violence has been widely misunderstood. What he was mainly trying to do was to expose rationalist and bourgeois shallowness and hypocrisy. Myth consisted in ideas whose utility lay, not in their cognitive value, but in their power to evoke loyalty and to inspire action. All societies had myths which served these purposes. Likewise all societies employed violence, though usually for repressive and/or predatory purposes. The great myth of the workers was the *general strike;* it inspired them to revolutionary action, the violence of which promoted their solidarity by making them rely on each other as brothers and sisters in struggle. Likewise with violence. Provided it was neither repressive nor predatory, violence was liberating; its employment weeded out weaklings and compromisers, and so promoted a strong, committed workers' movement capable of overthrowing decadent bourgeois society. Sorel's ideas had some impact in France and Italy in the early 20th century. Subsequently, however, his thought had relatively little influence, and his ideas are significant today as one important expression of the non-rationalist turn taken by political sociological thought in the early 20th century (see also Neomachiavellans).

Sorokin, Pitirim (1889-1968) Russian-born US sociologist. Secretary to Prime Minister Kerensky in the provisional Russian government in 1917 and exiled from Russia in 1922, Sorokin settled in the US in 1924. His earliest sociological writing in English, *Sociology of Revolutions* (1925), drew upon his experience of the Russian Revolution. A pathbreaking study, *Social Mobility* (1927) emphasized the disruptive as well as the creative effects of social mobility. Sorokin's work subsequently was usually on the grand scale, as seen particularly in his studies of macro-historical change, e.g. *Social and Cultural Dynamics,* 4 vols. (1937–41) and his irreverent and provocative surveys of types of sociological theory, notably *Contemporary Sociological Theory* (1928) and *Sociological Theories of Today* (1966). Rather than accepting prevailing evolutionary or developmental models Sorokin regarded societies as best understood as subject to cyclical, though irregular, patterns of change. In the latter part of his career Sorokin's role in US sociology was increasingly on the margins as a somewhat eccentric critic of both American sociology and American society. Social disintegration and cultural crisis could only be overcome, he suggested, by a new altruism.

sovereignty the supreme, theoretically unrestricted, political POWER by which a STATE is identified. The concept acquired particular importance throughout Europe in the 16th and 17th centuries, in association with the formation of the modern NATION STATE (see also ABSOLUTISM, HOBBES).

Soviet Marxism see MARXISM.

Spearman rank correlation coefficient a NONPARAMETRIC STATISTICS test used for ordinal data (see CRITERIA AND LEVELS OF MEASUREMENT) when a CORRELATION between two VARIABLES is to be measured.

This test uses a ranking procedure to assess the degree of correlation. For example, if it is hypothesized that suicide rates in different countries vary with levels of church attendance, the suicide rates are put in rank order in one column, and the levels of church attendance are separately ranked in another. The correlation coefficient is calculated by a formula which uses the differences between the rankings.

specialization see DIVISION OF LABOUR.

specificity and diffuseness see PATTERN VARIABLES.

speech act or **illocutionary act** any social act which is accomplished by virtue of an utterance (e.g. promising, cursing). Associated especially with the philosophers J. Austin and J. Searle, the analysis of such illocutionary acts (and *perlocutionary acts* – the effects of an illocutionary act), is a central part of the subject matter of ORDINARY LANGUAGE PHILOSOPHY.

The analytical study of speech acts has affinities with a number of approaches in sociology, including the FORMAL SOCIOLOGY of SIMMEL, the work of GOFFMAN, and CONVERSATION ANALYSIS. The latter in particular is directly influenced by ordinary language philosophy (see also DEGRADATION CEREMONY). A further example of an approach influenced by the concept of speech act is the 'ethogenic' social psychology of Rom Harré (*Social Being*, 1979), which advances the idea of a possible 'grammar' of social encounters, one however, that would be far more complex than implied in philosophical conceptions of speech acts.

Spencer, Herbert (1820–1903) British social theorist, chiefly remembered for his contribution to the study of SOCIAL CHANGE from an EVOLUTIONARY perspective.

Born in Derby, after an unconventional schooling Spencer began a career as a railway engineer, but soon moved into journalism and later became an independent scholar.

His first major work, *Social Statics* (1850), revealed his firm commitment to economic individualism and the free market, a commitment that continued throughout his work and is one of the main reasons for the great popularity of his sociology in the US.

Spencer's early interest in geology had led him into the field of biology, and from there to the evolutionary theories of LAMARCK. These ideas became the informing principle of his social theory. As early as 1852, in a paper entitled 'A Theory of Population', Spencer had argued that the process of social DEVELOPMENT was decisively influenced by 'struggle (for existence) and 'fitness' (for survival). Thus he anticipated by some six years aspects of the theory of natural selection which Darwin and Wallace were to apply with such success to the organic world, but he did this while continuing to include Lamarckian assumptions. In *The Principles of Psychology* (1855), Spencer attempts to show how the evolutionary hypothesis could also illuminate mental development.

'Progress: its Law and Cause', an essay written in 1857, found Spencer arguing that the evolutionary principle was a law of universal applicability, defining development in the physical, organic and social spheres.

Evolutionary theory thus provided a basis for the unification of the sciences. Whatever trajectory of development was studied the movement was always towards increasing DIFFERENTIATION and INTEGRATION of structure. Systems, be they solar, biological or social, always manifested a tendency to move from a state where their constituent parts were homogeneous and loosely cohering, to one where they were increasingly heterogenous and integrated.

Spencer's later work, widely read and highly influential at the time, was concerned primarily with justifying this position, His *Synthetic Philosophy,* a multivolume project, covering sociology, psychology, biology and ethics, was one outcome. Thus, Spencer's sociology (e.g. his *Principles of Sociology,* 1876–96), should properly be seen as one subfield in which he sought the wider objective of securing consent to the universality of the evolutionary process.

Some of Spencer's concepts, such as those of 'differentiation' and 'integration', have retained their currency as sociological tools, especially within the SOCIAL SYSTEMS perspective and neoevolutionary work of Talcott Parsons. But Spencer's sociology is deeply compromised by his enthusiasm for unifying it with biology, and for his sometimes uncritical assumption that biological science could provide the appropriate concepts for studying society. If 'struggle' motivated organic evolution, so warfare was important in social development, promoting both internal social cohesion and the development of powerful, specialized industrial economies; if the development of sophisticated nervous systems in the animal world enhanced the survival capacity of certain species, the same was true of telecommunications systems in society, and so on. The connection between these views and Spencer's politics is obvious: if social conflict was an evolutionary positive, the market should be unregulated, and the state minimalist (*The Man Versus the State,* 1884).

Whatever the judgement made about these economic and political prescriptions for social wellbeing, the sociology from which Spencer derived them is not acceptable. Social systems are not biological systems. People create and transform the environment in which they live. They are moral beings, and 'the survival of the fittest' is also a moral judgement (see SOCIAL DARWINISM). Competition may often be productive but only in a context with a pre-existing framework of order and regulation rather than one of anarchy (compare DURKHEIM). The universality of the evolutionary process in the social sphere is also questionable; developmental patterns cannot be consistent, since the development of some societies alters the possibilities of change for others (see also DIFFUSION, MULTILINEAR EVOLUTION). The most compromising problem with Spencer's work, however, is the circularity of the logic he employs in its execution. It was small wonder that Spencer felt he had proved his evolutionary hypothesis in the social world since the evidence he used, the classification of different kinds of institutions and types of societies, was a classification derived from the very principles which the examples were supposed to prove. Spencer's legacy to sociology nevertheless remains an important one. He was a systems theorist, and was the first to make systematic use of STRUCTURAL-FUNCTIONAL analysis, still a mainstay of sociological explanation.

sponsored mobility see CONTEST AND SPONSORED MOBILITY.

sport individual or group recreational activities, usually physical, which involve interpersonal or intergroup competition, contests with nature (e.g. hunting), or the more general exercise of physical skills. While sports often take the form of 'games', not all games are sports (e.g. card games, various games of chance and strategy). Sport occurs in most societies. However, most modern forms of organized sport have their origins in the latter half of the 19th century, although some of these, such as horse racing, boxing, cricket and football have a much longer history. In modern societies the role of sport – including spectator and televised sport – is a significant one. See also SOCIOLOGY OF SPORT, PLAY, LEISURE.

SPSS see STATISTICAL PACKAGE FOR THE SOCIAL SCIENCES.

spurious correlation see MULTIVARIATE ANALYSIS.

stable democracy and **unstable democracy** a distinction drawn by LIPSET (1960) between *stable democracies,* defined as those polities which have enjoyed an 'uninterrupted continuation of political democracy since World War I and the absence of a major party opposed to the "rules of the game"', and *unstable democracies,* which fail to fulfil these conditions. For non-European/non-English-speaking nations, Lipset also distinguished between 'democracies' and 'unstable dictatorships' on the one hand and 'stable dictatorships'.

The factors sustaining 'stable democracy' according to Lipset are:

(a) POLITICAL CLEAVAGE between main competing POLITICAL PARTIES, institutionalizing broad class conflict between non-manual 'middle class' and manual 'working class';

(b) the historical replacement of previous main bases of political cleavage (e.g. religious, rural – urban, centre – periphery);

(c) broad 'consensus' on the fundamental legitimacy of prevailing political institutions, a 'secular' politics ('end of ideology'), and the absence of major PARTIES OF INTEGRATION opposing the rules of the political game;

(d) a socioeconomic system which is economically effective and delivers high levels of literacy, welfare, etc.;

(e) a fluid 'open' class structure and class mixing, which produces CROSS-CUTTING TIES and 'cross pressures' acting on the individual which help to moderate class conflict and competition between parties;

(f) a 'participatory political culture', including extensive participation in VOLUNTARY ASSOCIATIONS and a general strength of groups of all kinds which functions as a 'protective screen' against MASS SOCIETY (see also TWO-STEP FLOW OF MASS COMMUNICATIONS).

Reworking ideas drawn from classical POLITICAL SOCIOLOGY (especially TOCQUEVILLE and WEBER), Lipset also suggested that 'stable democracy' depends on an élite-mass structure in which representative élites (see PLURAL ÉLITISM) are central to the working of the system, and can also be seen as safeguarding 'central democratic values'. For Lipset, 'stable democracy' is not just another political system, it is 'the good society in action'. The theory of stable democracy in these general terms arose as a synthesis of behaviouralist and structural-functional and systems-theoretic approaches in US POLITICAL SCIENCE and political sociology. It has been influential (although also widely criticized) not only in discussions of western democracies but also in the discussion of POLITICAL MODERNIZATION and 'nation-building' in developing and THIRD WORLD nations (see also MILITARY INTERVENTION). Theories addressing the sources of stability and instability in democracies have gained a new lease of life in assessments of the newly emerging democracies of central and eastern Europe. See also ÉLITE, ÉLITE THEORY, MOSCA, MICHELS, SCHUMPETER, VOTING BEHAVIOUR, END-OF-IDEOLOGY THESIS; compare LEGITIMATION CRISIS.

stages of development specific economic, cultural, social or political forms which societies are thought to have to pass through to achieve a given destination. The concept is commonly used in evolutionary and neoevolutionary approaches to SOCIAL CHANGE. In understanding economic change ROSTOW's approach rests upon the delineation of stages. The whole concept has been much criticized because:

(a) stages are difficult to identify, and there are as many different classifications of stages as there are authors;

(b) it tends to be associated with mechanistic and deterministic approaches to social change;
(c) European history is generally used to construct various stages which are then seen as necessary for other societies to pass through (see MODERNIZATION);
(d) diffusion from one society to another will affect stages in differing societies;
(e) it is difficult to show that any one stage is a necessary prerequisite for the next (see UNEVEN DEVELOPMENT).

There is, however, some validity in the argument that there are very general stages which societies have to pass through, for example that an AGRARIAN SOCIETY has to exist before there can be an INDUSTRIAL SOCIETY, but there can be various forms contained within those categories. The history of the 20th-century in particular has shown that there are a variety of forms of agrarian society which experience transformations to industrial societies in a variety of ways. The fact that the variations seem to be finite does not necessarily justify the strong use of the concept of stages of development. See also INDUSTRIALIZATION. EVOLUTIONARY UNIVERSALS.

stagflation (ECONOMICS) a type of INFLATION in which wages and prices rise despite relatively low rates of economic growth and relatively high levels of unemployment. This phenomenon is explained in part by the existence of labour solidarity and effective trade-union action.

stakeholders the institutions, groups or individuals involved in, or affected by a project or programme, including beneficiaries or the target group, owners (or lead organisation), sponsor(s), other supporters and opponents. The use of the term has arisen especially as part of a movement in contemporary societies to empower 'users'. Stakeholders can be differentiated into primary and secondary or the active and the non-active, indicating those directly involved or affected, and those only indirectly affected. Sometimes donors are classified as secondary rather than primary stakeholders, and it follows that there are various sub-categories of stakeholders with differing interests; beneficiaries are unlikely to be a homogenous group, in the same way as departments within a government may have competing interests. The inclusion of stakeholders in programme planning and implementation is in keeping with notions of greater participation and thus democracy. Whether the term stakeholder should also include workers as well as shareholders and consumers as part of a *stakeholder society/ stakeholder capitalism* is also an issue. See also PARTICIPATORY ACTION RESEARCH.

Stalin, Joseph (1879–1953) leader of the Soviet Union from 1928 to 1953, who is held responsible for decisive features of STATE SOCIALIST SOCIETIES (see also STALINISM). A member of the BOLSHEVIK Party in Russia from 1904, Stalin was appointed General Secretary of the Party in 1922, and after the death of LENIN in 1924 he emerged from the ensuing power struggle as the dominant leader. At first he supported policies of gradual industrialization with controlled market mechanisms, as incorporated in the New Economic Policy initiated under Lenin, against those (including TROTSKY) who argued for the more rapid introduction of socialist industrialization. In 1924 and 1925, he introduced the policy of 'Socialism in One Country', which was opposed by those who saw this as contradicting the international nature of COMMUNISM. By 1929, partly in response to the failure of the New Economic Policy, Stalin adopted a policy of broad and rapid collectivization and industrialization combined with the consolidation of a party and state bureaucracy firmly under his dictatorial control. In the 1930s millions of peasants who opposed collectivization were murdered or starved to death, and thousands of political activists were murdered, some after the totally bogus Moscow Trials. Labour camps were also introduced, and the cult of Stalin as the father of the nation was established.

Defenders of Stalin argue that he made possible the industrial base from which the USSR was able to defeat Hitler's invasion from 1941, and that the defeat of the German Army, at a cost of 20,000,000 Soviet deaths, was decisive for the outcome of World War II. However, in 1939 Stalin had signed a nonaggression pact with Hitler and appeared surprised by the 1941 invasion. From 1945 onwards Stalin maintained his position in the USSR partly on the basis of his leadership during the war, and extended his influence into Eastern Europe, especially where the Red Army had liberated territories from German occupation. See also SOCIALISM, MARXISM, STALINISM.

Stalinism the economic and political policies and style of government and social and economic organization in the USSR (and in Eastern European socialist societies under the hegemony of the USSR) under the leadership of Joseph STALIN from the late 1920s until his death in 1953, and after. The term is a mainly pejorative one referring to many 'unattractive' features of these regimes such as:
(a) central control of most spheres of life, including the economy and intellectual life;
(b) bureaucratic controls using a 'mass party', itself centrally controlled;
(c) an official ideology;
(d) a CULT OF PERSONALITY around the leader of the party;
(e) the use of state-directed 'terror' and political purges.

While initially set up as People's Democracies with multiparty representation, from 1948 most Eastern European socialist states quickly became dominated by Communist Parties whose leadership owed their position to Stalin. In most countries, that leadership continued in power until the late 1980s, adopting the forms of dictatorial party organization and highly centralized state direction of the economy and society which Stalin had equated with communism. These regimes continued after the death of Stalin, despite the denunciation of the crimes of Stalin by Khrushchev in 1956. The extent to which de-Stalinization in the Soviet Union occurred before Gorbachev assumed the leadership in 1985 is debated. On the one hand, state central planning and control of the economy (see COMMAND ECONOMY) continued with only minor modifications. On the other hand, the arbitrary brutality of political control was considerably modified, although political prison camps remained, psychiatric wards rather than camps were used to control dissidents, and civil liberties and freedoms were few. Only with the emergence of GLASNOST and PERESTROIKA was the legacy of Stalin finally challenged fully.

The term Stalinism is also used to describe those political parties and organizations in the West which adopt highly centralized organization with rigid controls over members and who have often adopted an uncritical defence of the Soviet Union. See also TOTALITARIANISM, STATE SOCIALIST SOCIETIES.

standard deviation see MEASURES OF DISPERSION.

standard error see MEASURES OF DISPERSION.

standardized mortality ratio a way of calculating death rates in terms of the average for the group or population and then determining the degree to which local populations vary from that standard. For example, 100 is the number given to the average death rate for the UK and areas with SMRs of less than 100 have better life chances than areas where the SMR is above 100. See also OFFICIAL STATISTICS, DEATH RATE.

standard of living the level of material welfare, e.g. real purchasing power, of a person or household. As an average of all incomes, the standard of living of a nation may also be talked of as rising or falling. However, there are many difficulties with the concept. Obviously the same level of purchasing power will produce different standards of living in households with different numbers of dependents. In any case, the compilation of appropriate indices of purchasing power is far from straightforward, and comparisons between societies and across time are fraught with difficulties (e.g. the well-known debate on whether living standards rose or fell in the early decades of the industrial revolution). Issues also rise as to the relationship between the standard of living in such a relatively mechanical sense, and the 'quality of life', an even more subjective, but not less important, dimension. See also POVERTY.

stándestaat a postfeudal form of the STATE in some parts of Western Europe (e.g. France, Prussia) in which the broad ESTATES of the realm (e.g. nobility, burghers) possessed rights to be consulted by the ruler in affairs of state. The meetings of the *states-general* in France at the start of the 1789 Revolution were assemblies of representatives of estates. The existence of such groups, for which there exist no direct parallels outside Europe, has sometimes been seen as an important factor in the distinctive 'democratic', 'participatory' route taken by European politics.

standing army the establishment of an army as a body of enlisted, professional, regular soldiers under the direct control of the government. Although approached in form only exceptionally in premodern societies (e.g. the Roman legions), fully professionalized standing armies are a usual feature, and an important basis of the maintenance of the power, of modern NATION STATES. For GIDDENS (1985), the establishment and innovations in the control and tactics of standing armies – the 'Taylorism of this sphere' – are a greatly neglected aspect of the process of social development that leads to contemporary societies. See also MILITARY-CIVILIAN RATIO.

Stanford-Binet Test widely used INTELLIGENCE TEST for children. The original Binet Test was designed by Binet and Simon (published 1905) to select those French children who would not benefit from the normal schooling available, but needed special education. Its revisions in 1908 and 1911 were designed as a series of tests relevant to each yearly age group, the average child of that age being able to 'pass'. So in fact Binet defined what the average child of each age could do in terms of simple verbal and performance skills, i.e. standards or NORMS for each age were set (the concept of 'mental age' had appeared). The design was later adapted by Terman of Stanford University (US) to form the Stanford-Binet (1916), and it was Terman who introduced the concept of INTELLIGENCE QUOTIENT. This transformed the test scores into a quotient, making it possible to compare children in different age bands, or the same child as he or she grew older.

The Stanford-Binet tests are individual, in that they have to be administered on a one-to-one basis. They are therefore essentially diagnostic and require skilled administration. There have been two further revisions (1937, 1960). Revisions are necessary as the tests become obsolete, e.g. a picture of a buttoned boot would need to be replaced by a picture of a sandal, or, today, a training shoe. A test loses its VALIDITY if the items are no longer relevant to normal experience. The extensive and prolonged use of the Stanford-Binet Test has made it particularly valuable since each use provides further data, thus aiding diagnosis. However, new tests have appeared in recent years, the British Intelligence Scale (1977) having been designed to provide a replacement test for use in British schools.

state capitalism and state monopoly capitalism (MARXISM) an interpretation of Soviet society and similar planned or COMMAND ECONOMIES, in which the state élite is seen as acting as a surrogate capitalist class. This class is seen as continuing the 'historical role' of the capitalist class in the accumulation of capital in a situation where the bourgeois class has been overthrown but where the development of the means of production is insufficient as the basis for the full transition to socialism. Analogously, these terms may also be used (as for example, by LENIN, 1915) to refer to western forms of ADVANCED CAPITALISM, in which monopolistic concentrations of capital and overall state direction of the economy has occurred.

state

1 the apparatus of rule or government within a particular territory.
2 the overall territory and social system which is subject to a particular rule or domination. In this second sense the terms 'state' and 'SOCIETY' may sometimes be used interchangeably.

For WEBER, the crucial defining feature of any state is that it successfully upholds a claim 'to the monopoly of legitimate use of violence within its territory'. It should be stressed, however, that only in extreme circumstances do states depend mainly or entirely on the actual use of violence or physical coercion. These are normally used only in the last resort. The claims to political 'legitimacy' made by rulers usually provide a far more potent and effective basis for trouble-free political rule (see LEGITIMATE AUTHORIT Y). But the threat of force always remains in the background in the government of states, and, compared with those theories (e.g. NORMATIVE FUNCTIONALISM) which perhaps overemphasize the normative basis of state power, the importance of the threat of violence as an ever present factor in internal state power must not be neglected. Internationally, as a defensive and an offensive machine, sometimes resorting to WARFARE, the role of violence is again clearly evident.

The first states (see also PRISTINE STATES) appeared around 5,000 years ago, in the Middle East and elsewhere, probably as the outcome of the activity of REDISTRIBUTIVE CHIEFDOMS, or of warfare which led to conquest and class domination (see also ENGELS). Whatever their precise origins, however, there is agreement that the central appropriation of an economic surplus and SOCIAL STRATIFICATION are both an essential requirement and a consequence of the subsequent development of states.

Prior to the first states (see STATELESS SOCIETIES), the government of societies existed only as a set of functions diffused within the wider society among a number of institutions or organizations playing political roles, e.g. lineage groups, age groups, or general meetings. In contrast, modern states usually possess a set of clearly differentiated 'political' institutions, e.g. an executive, a legislature, a judiciary, armed forces, and police, etc. In comparison with modern NATION STATES, many earlier forms of the state (e.g. preindustrial empires), while possessing a differentiated state structure, can be characterized as having a far more fragmentary and contested domination over their territories. (See also CITY STATE, ORIENTAL DESPOTISM).

A further feature of modern states is that, whereas most forms of premodern state had only SUBJECTS, modern states have CITIZENS (i.e. full members of political communities increasingly enjoying the right to vote, the right to stand for office, freedom of expression, welfare rights; see

CIVIL RIGHTS, WELFARE STATE). A related distinction is that between state and CIVIL SOCIETY. This is an important distinction, especially in Marxism, where it provides a vocabulary to distinguish between state and society, or state and individual citizens or groups of citizens.

The sub-fields of sociology most concerned with study of the different kinds of state and POLITICAL SYSTEM and the implications of state power, are HISTORICAL SOCIOLOGY and POLITICAL SOCIOLOGY (see also POLITICAL SCIENCE, INTERNATIONAL RELATIONS). One central issue is whether state power can be explained autonomously or only in terms of underlying economic forces; see RELATIVE AUTONOMY (OF THE STATE), RULING CLASS. See also POWER, DEMOCRACY, LIBERAL DEMOCRACY, ONE-PARTY STATES, TOTALITARIANISM, STATE SOCIALIST SOCIETIES.

state expenditures the several different kinds of expenditure undertaken by the STATE. On the assumption that the state in capitalist society has two contradictory functions, accumulation and legitimization, O'Connor (1973) and Gough (1979) identify three main categories of expenditure:
(a) *social investment,* 'projects and services that increase the productivity of labour';
(b) *social consumption.* 'projects and services that lower the reproduction costs of labour';
(c) *social expenses,* projects and services which are required to maintain social harmony.

It is evident that the load on the state from state expenditures has increased historically, imposing, according to both O'Connor and Gough, 'new economic strains on the system', and 'simultaneously threatening both capitalist accumulation and political freedoms' (FISCAL CRISIS IN THE CAPITALIST STATE.) It is for this reason that the WELFARE STATE and state expenditures in general have been a site of central social and political conflict in recent decades (see also CULTURAL CONTRADICTIONS OF CAPITALISM. THATCHERISM, NEW RIGHT).

stateless societies various forms of society which lack a clearly identifiable STATE. Two main senses in which societies may be said to be 'stateless' can be noted:
(a) all forms of society which existed prior to the formation of the first central states (see PRISTINE STATES);
(b) those forms of society which as well as lacking the kind of clearly identified machinery of statehood (e.g. 'administrative' and military support for the leader) also seem to lack all formalized provision for stable leadership – so-called ACEPHALOUS (literally 'headless') societies. These forms of society are able to achieve coherence, sustain existence, even conduct warfare, without clearly differentiated state forms either because they are small enough to require no differentiated machinery or because they possess a complex 'segmentary structure'. See SEGMENTARY SOCIETIES. Compare SEGMENTARY STATES.

state monopoly capitalism see STATE CAPITALISM AND STATE MONOPOLY CAPITALISM.

state of nature see LOCKE.

state socialism see STATE SOCIALIST SOCIETIES.

state socialist societies the centrally directed socialist societies which emerged in the 20th century after revolutions or movements led by political parties adhering to communist or socialist political thought. The societies covered are diverse and include the USSR from 1918 to 1991; most Eastern European societies from 1948 until 1989; contemporary People's Republic of China, Cuba, Vietnam, Angola, Mozambique, Ethiopia, North Korea, Mongolia. Many of these societies are, however, currently

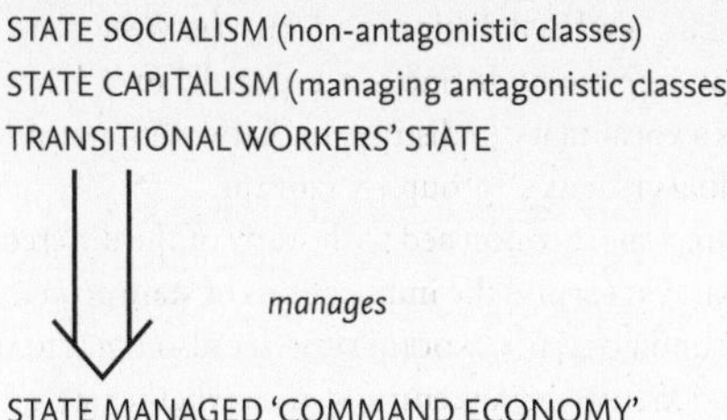

Fig. 32 **State socialist societies:** 'Official' and other Marxian conceptions of socialist societies, which regarded this form of society as either an evolving or as a degenerate form.

experiencing rapid change such that precise characterization and labelling is increasingly difficult.

There is much debate about the character of these societies which are more generally known as communist (see COMMUNISM). Some observers claim a more accurate characterization is TOTALITARIANISM, since these societies share features with nonsocialist societies without parliamentary democratic practices and institutions such as fascist states (see FASCISM). However, this tends to deny any distinguishing role for SOCIALISM in the formation and operation of these states.

Those commentators who saw the commitment to socialism – principally the abolition or severe curtailment of private productive property – as a differentiating feature of these states, found difficulty in reaching any clear agreement as to their precise nature. Some, following TROTSKY, argue that they fell well short of the ideals of a communist society, through their overcentralized and undemocratic political systems, their nationalistic rather than internationalistic policies, the privileges and often personal wealth of their political leaders, and the stagnation of their economies (see also STALINISM). This led to various terms, such as *state capitalism, degenerate workers' states*, and *bureaucratic socialism* (see Fig. 32) which denied their claim to being socialist. Others claim that they were forms of society *sui generis* which can be located neither within any Marxist scheme of classification (capitalist, socialist, communist, or transitional between these), nor within any existing non-Marxian typology of societies, such as democratic versus totalitarian. Nevertheless, their centralized state systems, their ideological commitment to some variant of communism or socialism, and the curtailments of private productive property, all pointed to some justification of the term 'state socialism' or state socialist societies' as a general term (see Post and Wright, 1989).

state terrorism 1 the form of TERRORISM used by some governments as part of their domestic and foreign policy. For example, in countries like the former Soviet Union, China and fascist Germany, state terror has taken the form of framed show trials, arbitrary arrests and detentions, bannings, massacres, torture and execution of members of political opposition groups.

2 the financial or 'moral' support given by some states to international TERRORIST ORGANIZATIONS.

statistical control see CONTROL, STATISTICAL.

statistical discrimination see DISCRIMINATION.

statistical independence see CORRELATION.

statistical inference see PROBABILITY, STATISTICS.

Statistical Package for the Social Sciences (SPSS) a package of statistical computer programs originally written over twenty years ago for the analysis of social science data. The statistical procedures range from simple frequencies to sophisticated multivariate techniques. It is particularly suitable for the analysis of survey data because it has extensive labelling, data modification and transformation facilities. The package is very flexible and includes procedures for producing 'tailor-made' tables and reports. It is also widely used for the analysis of experimental data, time series data, secondary analysis, and as a database management package. Versions are available which run on most computers and operating systems.

statistical power the probability of supporting a research hypothesis when it is true. Fisher's (1925) approach to inferential statistics was that a *Null hypothesis* should be tested. If the results were statistically significant then the Null hypothesis could be rejected. Neyman and Pearson (1928) pointed out that there is a second hypothesis involved in significance testing: the research hypothesis. If the results of a study achieve statistical significance then researchers may be committing a Type I error by rejecting the Null Hypothesis when it is in fact true. On the other hand, Neyman and Pearson noted that when a result fails to reach statistical significance a Type II error (which they called an error of the second type) may be committed: the failure to reject the Null hypothesis when the research hypothesis is true. Greater statistical power lessens the likelihood of committing a Type II error. Many writers (e.g. Cohen, 1988) argue that failure to consider statistical power renders statistical significance testing relatively meaningless.

statistics and statistical analysis the assembly and mathematical analysis of numerical data (e.g. CENSUS or SOCIAL SURVEY data). This involves description and inference. *Descriptive statistics* involve: (a) organizing the data using MEASURES OF CENTRAL TENDENCY and MEASURES OF DISPERSION, graphical representations (e.g. HISTOGRAMS and PIE-GRAPHS), and in its more sophisticated forms includes; (b) the use of measures of the 'association' between variables (e.g. CORRELATION and REGRESSION);
(c) *Inferential statistics* uses PROBABILITY theory and random sampling (see RANDOM SAMPLE) to permit inferences to be made from a sample to a larger population (see SIGNIFICANCE TESTS). The fundamental idea involved in statistical analysis of this type is that repeatable phenomena (e.g. tossing a coin) can be assumed to conform to an underlying probabilistic model. Thus an *estimation* is a 'best guess' about the features of a population derived from inferences made from a sample and to which is attached a level of probability that it is correct.

Modern statistical analysis has its roots in the work of 18th-century theorists such as Laplace, Poisson, and Gauss, and in the work of early 19th-century social statisticians such as QUETELET. However, the modern discipline stems especially from the work of Francis Galton (1822–1911) who formulated the concept of the NORMAL DISTRIBUTION and also popularized the 'correlation coefficient'. Karl Pearson (1859–1936), a student of Galton's, added notions of 'goodness of fit' (see CHI SQUARE) and W. S. Gossett (1876–1937) developed NONPARAMETRIC STATISTICS for situations where ratio or interval levels of measurement (see also CRITERIA AND LEVELS OF MEASUREMENT) cannot be assumed for small samples. Significance tests were added to the armoury of techniques by Ronald Fisher (1890–1962).

An important advance in recent decades has been the advent of high-speed and now widely available computer technology, which has removed much of the hard grind previously associated with the use of statistics (see STATISTICAL PACKAGE FOR THE SOCIAL SCIENCES (SPSS) and MINITAID. However, while there are many advantages of this development, one disadvantage is that it has sometimes encouraged the use of statistical techniques which are only half understood, thus leading to unwarranted inferences.

While statistical analysis is well established and has become an important adjunct to many disciplines, including most of the social sciences, it has been subjected to a number of criticisms, especially Selvin (1958) that the requirements for satisfactory use of significance tests are rarely met in the social sciences. There also exist notable divisions of view within the discipline of statistics, e.g. the division between orthodox and Bayesian statistics (see BAYES' THEOREM).

Compare MATHEMATICAL SOCIOLOGY.

status 1 any stable position within a social system associated with specific expectations, rights and duties. 'Status' in this sense is equivalent to ROLE, although it is the latter term which has the wider currency.
2 the positive or negative honour, prestige, power, etc., attaching to a position, or an individual person, within a system of SOCIAL STRATIFICATION (often referred to as *social status*).

Both conceptions derive from forms of society in which individual social locations were relatively fixed (see ASCRIBED STATUS, MAINE), for example by religion or by law (see CASTE, ESTATE). In modern societies status positions tend to be more fluid.
See also STATUS GROUP, CLASS, STATUS AND PARTY, SOCIOECONOMIC STATUS, STATUS CONSISTENCY AND INCONSISTENCY.

status and contract see MAINE.

status conflict the competition and vying for position and esteem which occurs within systems of SOCIAL STRATIFICATION based on STATUS 2 (see also STATUS GROUP). Status conflicts can be greatest between groups which stand in adjacent positions within a status hierarchy, and are thus direct competitors (see also RELATIVE DEPRIVATION, SOCIAL CLOSURE). This explains why a diminishing of distinctions of CLASS and rank, as in some modern societies, may be associated with a heightening of status tensions and status conflicts, since this leaves greater scope for competition around subtler distinctions of status (see also STATUS SYMBOL, RIESMAN, GOFFMAN). However competition and conflict between status groups also, exist in preindustrial and traditional societies (see CASTE, ESTATE). See also STATUS CONSISTENCY AND INCONSISTENCY.

status consistency and inconsistency the situation of either being ranked consistently across a range of status criteria (*status consistency* or *status congruence*), or being ranked inconsistently (*status inconsistency* or *status incongruence*), e.g. blacks or Hispanics in high status occupations. Sometimes the term *status crystallization* is also used.

Since modern societies usually involve the coexistence of parallel hierarchies of CLASS and STATUS (see also CLASS, STATUS AND PARTY; MULTIDIMENSIONAL ANALYSIS OF SOCIAL STRATIFICATION), Lenski (1966) has suggested that discrepancies in status, especially when acute, are associated with political radicalism. More generally, however, the empirical correlates of status inconsistency have themselves been inconsistent; as one sceptical comment expresses it, in the study of voting behaviour 'status inconsistency puts greater stress on theorists than voters' (Harrop and Miller, 1987).

status crystallization see STATUS CONSISTENCY AND STATUS INCONSISTENCY.

status group any group which can be identified in terms of a specific, 'positive or negative, social estimation of honour' (WEBER, 1922) within a system of SOCIAL

STRATIFICATION. The classical period of relatively clear-cut distinctions between status groups is the era of preindustrial empires. Clear STATUS hierarchies existed, for example, in India and China, as well as in preindustrial societies for Europe (see also CASTE, ESTATE). However, status groupings, and distinctions in status (even when loosely associated with status groups), continue as a significant dimension of social stratification in modern societies (see also CLASS, STATUS AND PARTY; MULTIDIMENSIONAL ANALYSIS OF SOCIAL STRATIFICATION).

status incongruence see STATUS CONSISTENCY AND INCONSISTENCY.

status inconsistency see STATUS CONSISTENCY AND INCONSISTENCY.

status passage see RITE OF PASSAGE.

status situation the prestige or 'social honour' associated with a particular occupation of position within a community – one of three main dimensions of social stratification identified by Lockwood (1958 and 1966) and Goldthorpe and Lockwood (1968a & b, 1969). Rather than market forces or ownership or non-ownership of the means of production alone being decisive in determining a person's overall position within the stratification system, three interrelated dimensions of social stratification are seen as significant: 'status situation', as well as WORK SITUATION and MARKET SITUATION. For example, an Anglican clergyman may enjoy relatively high status within a community, but his income (and market situation) may be low. See also MULTIDIMENSIONAL ANALYSIS OF SOCIAL STRATIFICATION, CLASS, STATUS AND PARTY, OCCUPATIONAL PRESTIGE, CLASS IMAGERY.

status symbol any commodity or service which is acquired as much or more for the favourable social evaluations it brings from others, and in terms of its enhancement of the acquirer's own self-perceptions. An early journalistic account of status symbols was provided by Packard (1959). A more sociologically sophisticated analysis, although he does not specifically use the term 'status symbol', is BOURDIEU'S *Distinction* (1979). For Bourdieu, matters of taste above all involve status claims. Thus the educated may go to the theatre rather than watch TV. One problem with the concept of status symbol, is that analysis of cultural products in terms of their status loadings tends to ignore other dimensions of preference. See also ADVERTISING, CONSUMER CULTURE, POSTMODERNITY AND POSTMODERNISM.

stereotype a set of inaccurate, simplistic generalizations about a group of individuals which enables others to categorize members of this group and treat them routinely according to these expectations. Thus stereotypes of RACIAL, SOCIAL CLASS, and GENDER groups are commonly held and lead to the perception and treatment of individuals according to unjustified preconceptions. See also PREJUDICE.

stigma any physical or social attribute or sign (e.g. physical deformity or a criminal record) which so devalues an actor's social identity as to 'disqualify from full social acceptance' (GOFFMAN, 1964). Different implications follow for the stigmatized person according to whether the stigma is visible (the individual is obviously 'discredited'), or hidden (the individual is potentially 'discreditable'). The latter allows a greater number of options to the stigmatized person to manage his or her stigma. But in both cases the actor's problem lies in finding a means of limiting, or even turning to some advantage, the damaging effects of the stigma. As well as of interest in its own right, the study of stigmatized identities also throws light on the social construction of 'normal' identities (see DEVIANCE).

stranger any person who is within a group or society but not entirely of that group of society. SIMMEL (Wolff. 1950) suggests three aspects of the social position of the stranger which define it in sociological terms:
(a) the position of the individual on the margin, part inside and part outside the group (see also MARGINALITY);

(b) a particular combination of remoteness and proximity (or SOCIAL DISTANCE) between the stranger and group members; (c) various further implications of the ROLE of the stranger and his or her interactions with the group which make this position of particular sociological interest.

A key feature of the role of the stranger identified by Simmel is the relative 'detachment' and 'objectivity' which he or she may bring, e.g. in settling disputes. This arises, according to Simmel, because the stranger 'imports qualities into the group which do not stem from the group'. This explains why the stranger also often meets with surprising openness and confidences. All of this applies, notwithstanding that strangers who arrive in large numbers, with their own cultures and groups, will often be mistrusted and may become persecuted members of the societies which they enter. However, even the individual stranger may become mistrusted, and be seen as a possible threat to group beliefs, e.g. in situations where his or her own 'vested interest' may be involved (see Schermer, 1988).

strategic contingency theory see ORGANIZATION THEORY.

strategic interaction interaction occurring in situations where one party's gain is the other party's loss, and thus the winning is defined by the losing and *vice versa.* Decision making in strategic situations may be quite complex, involving not only assessment of the other's knowledge state but also what the other party knows of the first party's knowledge state and likely strategy. GOFFMAN (1969) suggests that strategic interaction is a more commonplace feature of everyday life than is often acknowledged. The concept of social interaction may be effectively described in terms of strategies adopted by parties to the interaction, individual or collective. It avoids the view that interaction is the straightforward outcome of laws, or of rules, both of which tend to miss the openness of interaction. It also avoids the view that interaction is entirely a local accomplishment, and that any characterization of it in general terms is an arbitrary closure. If members can adopt and adapt goals and outline paths to those goals, without being bound to them, or if others can in turn recognize these, and similarly adopt and adapt existing strategies, then the sociologist can do simultaneous justice to choice, creativity and freedom, and, on the other hand, also to cultural patterning. Some of these patterns are obvious-but-unrecognized, but may be rendered strikingly explicit, as in the work of Goffman. They may also be formalized, as in the application of the THEORY OF GAMES.

strategic theory (INTERNATIONAL RELATIONS) theoretical analysis of the military and associated political strategies pursued by NATION STATES in advancing their own interests. Among the social science theories applied in this area have been 'decision theory' and the THEORY OF GAMES. See also ARMS RACE, BALANCE OF POWER, CLAUSEWITZ, COLD WAR, NUCLEAR DETERRENCE, MUTUAL ASSURED DESTRUCTION, NATION-STATE SYSTEM.

strategies of independence the ways which individuals find to maintain a measure of 'functional autonomy' within the organizations in which they work, creating social spaces for themselves (GOULDNER, 1959). Gouldner uses the example of 'strategies of independence', borrowed from E. C. Hughes, as part of his argument against making too strong assumptions about 'functional interdependence'.

stratification see SOCIAL STRATIFICATION.

stratificational model of social action and consciousness an interpretation of the human social actor (e.g. GIDDENS 1984), which emphasizes the existence of three layers of cognition and motivation: (a) DISCURSIVE CONSCIOUSNESS, i.e. what actors are able to say about social situations, including the conditions of their own action; (b) practical consciousness, what actors know or believe about social situations, including the conditions of their own

interaction, *but are unable to express* – i.e. tacit skills or PRACTICAL KNOWLEDGE (compare PRACTICAL REASONING);
(c) the UNCONSCIOUS.

The second of these areas of 'actors' knowledgeability' is seen by GIDDENS as neglected in sociological analysis, a neglect which, in Giddens' view, SCHUTZ's SOCIAL PHENOMENOLOGY and ETHNOMETHODOLOGY have drawn attention to and done much to remedy.

stratified sample a SAMPLE which is selected by first stratifying the parent population. The procedure involves dividing the population into strata relevant to the study to be undertaken, e.g. for a study of voting intention, social class and age may be relevant; for a study of attitudes to the benefit system, income level and employment status would be relevant. When the strata have been identified RANDOM SAMPLES are taken from each. As long as these samples are of sizes proportionate to the size of each stratum within the parent population (proportionate stratification), this method allows improved precision, particularly if a sample is being taken from a relatively large population, since it introduces some controlled restrictions on selection. However, disproportionate stratification may be used if a stratum is too small to yield a sufficiently large sample for analysis if the criterion for selection used in other strata is adopted.

stratum see SOCIAL STRATUM.

streaming a form of organization in schools where pupils are grouped according to their overall ability. This form of differentiation has been, and still remains, a common feature of UK schools, although there are numerous variations of it, such as 'banding' or 'setting'. There is also some evidence to suggest that, in primary schools at least, formal streaming is now much less common (Reid 1986). Its justification is to be found in the psychological tradition of education and derives from the evidence presented by Cyril Burt to the Hadow Committee in 1931. British use of streaming is almost unique. It is illegal in Norway, has been abolished in the Soviet Union, and is not used in the US or France.

Streaming rests on two basically simple beliefs: that since children vary in their ability (however this is defined) they learn best in classes of children with similar ability, and that such classes are better, or more easily, taught. By contrast, mixed ability classes are believed to hamper the learning of both bright and dull children and make teaching difficult. Literature in the SOCIOLOGY OF EDUCATION is replete with studies on the nature of streaming and its consequences for the educational achievement of children.

Children are allocated to different streams on the basis of standardized tests in English, Arithmetic and IQ tests (see INTELLIGENCE QUOTIENT), although some weight is also given to teachers' subjective assessments. Considerable research exists to suggest that streaming appears to favour children with particular ascribed characteristics, especially parental social class (Douglas, 1964). Other evidence suggests that streaming involves social as well as academic differentiation, where teachers, consciously or otherwise, discriminate between pupils according to perceptions of their social class origins (Barker Lunn, 1970). It leads to 'covert' streaming in both streamed and unstreamed classes.

Streaming practices have considerable effects on the life of a school and the performance of children. Several studies show that streaming is a self-fulfilling prophecy, others suggest that it reinforces social class differences, structures pupils' friendships and the development of informal cultures (Hargreaves, 1967; Lacey, 1970).

stress a state of tension produced by pressures or conflicting demands with which the person cannot adequately cope. This is therefore subjective in that different people experience the same event differently, and what is experienced as stress by one, may not be by another.

Stress, induced by life events, for example, is relevant in a consideration of psychological disorders (see NEUROSIS), sociological studies of social phenomena (e.g. SUICIDE), and in physical illness (e.g. heart disease). The holistic approach of PERSON-CENTRED COUNSELLING and much of ALTERNATIVE MEDICINE aims to treat the person within the context of the life experience and current problems. To use the mechanical analogy, the aim would be to strengthen the person in order to enable him/her to resist damage from life's pressures.

strikes temporary stoppages of work by a group of employees in order to express a grievance or enforce a demand (Hyman, 1984).

The strike is a basic sanction possessed by employees, the threat of which plays a large part in INDUSTRIAL RELATIONS. However it is typically an act of last resort, and only one of the means by which INDUSTRIAL CONFLICT is expressed. The popular view, particularly in the UK, that strikes are a major problem ignores a number of factors:
(a) consideration of strikes in isolation is liable to mislead as to the overall character of industrial relations;
(b) the number of working days lost as the result of strikes is small compared with those lost as the result of illness or accidents;
(c) strikes vary in character, from brief stoppages to drawn out trials of strength;
(d) discussion of strikes is plagued by definitional and measurement problems. Statistics of strikes record numbers per year, the extent of labour force involvement, working days lost, industrial location, and immediate cause. However international differences in criteria and the unreliability of British data reduce the value of comparisons;
(e) researchers have found it difficult to establish any simple links between the incidence of strikes and economic performance. For all these reasons accounting for the causes and assessing the implications of strikes would seem to involve a degree of complexity little captured by either public discussion or official statistics. There is little doubt that single-factor explanations of strikes (e.g. the presence of agitators, faulty communications, etc.) are inadequate. More satisfactory explanations have considered the range of local and national factors which affect employees' willingness and ability to undertake strikes, including the actions of employers and governments. See also TRADE(S) UNION, ARBITRATION AND CONCILIATION.

strong version of the sociology of science see SOCIAL STUDIES OF SCIENCE, SOCIOLOGY OF SCIENCE.

structural and frictional unemployment see UNEMPLOYMENT.

structural and nonstructural social mobility see SOCIAL MOBILITY.

structural anthropology the perspective that stresses the priority of cognitive structures in ordering experience. It is primarily associated with LÉVI-STRAUSS who took his lead from the linguist F. de SAUSSURE. Lévi-Strauss's studies of KINSHIP and SYMBOLISM were attempts to demonstrate that a simple set of logical principles underlay sociocultural systems. Myths, for example, could be understood as linguistic transformations of essentially binary oppositions, such as male – female, raw–cooked, and so on, which are constitutive of human thought. Structural anthropology treats cultural phenomena as if they were a language and then attempts to discover the grammar, or what the US linguist CHOMSKY has called the 'deep structure'. Whilst 'high structuralism' has been much criticized for its formalism, its methods have found general application in many areas of anthropology (E. Leach), sociology (ALTHUSSER, FOUCAULT) and literary criticism and SEMIOLOGY.

structural differentiation see SOCIAL DIFFERENTIATION.

structural-functionalism 1 theoretical approaches in which societies are conceptualized as SOCIAL SYSTEMS, and particular features of SOCIAL STRUCTURES are explained in terms of their contribution

to the maintenance of these systems, e.g. religious ritual explained in terms of the contribution it makes to social integration. As such, structural-functionalism can be seen as an alternative general term for FUNCTIONALISM. See also FUNCTION, FUNCTIONAL(IST) EXPLANATION.
2 (more specifically) the particular form of functional analysis associated with Talcott PARSONS, often distinguished from 'functionalism' in general, as 'structural-functionalism'. Sometimes the work of the modern functionalist school in SOCIAL ANTHROPOLOGY, including RADCLIFFE-BROWN and MALINOWSKI, is also referred to by this term.

structuralism

1 any sociological analysis in terms of SOCIAL STRUCTURE.
2 (more especially) any form of analysis in which 'structures' take priority (ontologically, methodologically, etc.) over human actors.
3 (in LINGUISTICS, e.g. SAUSSURE and CHOMSKY) an approach which concentrates analysis on the structural features of LANGUAGE(S); especially the study of the *synchronic* relations between linguistic elements rather than, as previously in linguistics, engaging in *diachronic*, historical or comparative study (see SYNCHRONIC AND DIACHRONIC).
4 those methodological and theoretical approaches to cultural and sociological analysis based on the assumption that societies can be analysed, analogously with language and linguistics (see sense **3**), as 'signifying systems'. In these approaches, the emphasis is on the analysis of 'unobservable' but detectable structural relations between 'conceptual elements' in social life (e.g. relations of opposition and contrast, or hierarchy). These conceptual elements are seen as the ultimate object of study in social science and the structural determinants of social reality. The view is that essentially the same methods of analysis apply, whether the phenomenon in question be, for example, a text, or a society. Structuralism in sociological analysis is seen in the work of the anthropologist Claude LÉVI-STRAUSS, the cultural semiologists Roland BARTHES and the psychoanalytic theorist Jacques LACAN. In the work of Lévi-Strauss, for example, social myths and, by extension, other social forms, are presented as arising from the tendency of the human mind to think in terms of binary opposites (e.g. 'the raw and the cooked', or in kinship relations, the marriageable and the unmarriageable).
5 any doctrine stating that social analysis should be concerned with exploring beneath 'surface appearances' in order to reach the deeper, ultimately more 'real', structures seen as determining social relations. Symptomatic of this general view is Marx's suggestion that 'if essence and appearance coincided there would be no need for science'. Although far from always being dependent on linguistic analogies, in recent years structuralism in this sense has gained a new impetus in borrowing some concepts from structuralism sense **4** (e.g. see ALTHUSSERIAN MARXISM).

For Lacan, structuralism succeeds by 'decentring' the previously central place of the individual in much social analysis. Likewise, for Foucault, individuals are no longer to be seen as the 'subjects' of history.

Critics of all types of structuralism in sociology argue that sociology must continue to take as central the human actor's involvement in the construction and reconstruction of meaning and the social world: structuralism is accused of an unjustified REIFICATION in its account of social reality. Among other objections to structuralism are a rejection of its ahistorical approach and the speculative and allegedly 'untestable' nature of much of its theorizing.

A halfway house between theories of structure and theories of individual agency has often been attempted. BERGER and Pullberg (1966), for example, propose a dialectical theory of the social construction of reality, in which 'social structure' does not stand on its own, 'apart from the human activity that produced it', but, that once created, 'is encountered by the individual (both) as an alien facticity (and) ... a coercive instrumentality'. More recently, GIDDENS has proposed a notion of DUALITY OF STRUCTURE involving both structure and individual agency. For Giddens, to enquire into the 'structuration' of social practices 'is to seek to explain how it comes about that structures are constituted through actions, and, reciprocally, how action is constituted structurally' (see also STRUCTURATION THEORY).

The debate over agency and structure in sociology can be seen as fundamental to the discipline and unlikely ever to be resolved. The debate revolves around the issue of whether or not there are underlying causes and UNANTICIPATED CONSEQUENCES (OF SOCIAL ACTION), and if so, how sociologists are able to investigate these. Whatever the reservations about structuralism, it is clear that conceptions of structuralism in all of the above senses must be acknowledged as a raising of central questions in sociological analysis that have been valuable in combating a one-sided individualism. Structuralism in senses **3**, **4** and **5** enjoyed a period as a vogue perspective in the 1960s and 70s, justifiably so, because it gave a new impetus to theoretical sociology in a number of areas (e.g. see SEMIOTICS). Equally, however, structuralism is often seen as itself unjustifiably one-sided, (see STRUCTURE AND AGENCY) even by some of its own previous leading proponents (see POSTSTRUCTURALISM).

structuration 'the structuring of social relations across time and space' (GIDDENS, 1984) as the result of the interaction of pre-existing STRUCTURE and individual agency. See DUALITY OF STRUCTURE, STRUCTURATION THEORY, STRUCTURE AND AGENCY.

structuration theory the approach to sociological theory adopted by Anthony GIDDENS, in which social relations are seen as structured in time and space as the outcome of the operation of a DUALITY OF STRUCTURE. In this approach (see Fig. 33) the intention is that neither agency or structure is accorded

	Structuralist or Voluntarist Theories	*Giddens' Structurationist Alternative*
Characterization of Structure	structure *or* agency	'duality of structure'; the interrelation of action and structure
Characterization of Actor	agents as supports of structure ('cultural dopes') *or* as purely voluntaristic	knowledgeability of actors/conscious intentionality – but in context of structure as medium and outcome of agency and interaction

Fig. 33 **Structuration theory.**

primacy in sociological explanations. Giddens presents structuration theory as an 'ontology' to aid analysis and as an orientation in social research, rather than a finished theory. However, opinion is divided as to how far Giddens has been successful in achieving his objective or whether his own work continues to exhibit a bias towards individual agency (see Bryant and Jary, 1990). See STRUCTURE AND AGENCY. Problems also exist with aspects of the conception of 'structure' used by Giddens (see also STRUCTURE, sense **2**) which refers to 'rules and resources' (including 'memory traces') and can be 'virtual' rather than possessing a particular time-space location (a conception that draws on STRUCTURALISM). In the view of some theorists (e.g. J. Thompson, 1989), this is to lose the substantive, institutional and constraining aspects uppermost in other senses of 'social structure'. However, a defence of Giddens would be that this sense of '*social* structure' is not lost in Giddens, even though the term 'structure' is reserved for 'rules and resources'.

structure **1** any arrangement of elements into a definite pattern. e.g. any institutionalized social arrangements (ROLES, ORGANIZATIONS etc.) e.g. the 'educational' or 'occupational structure' (see also SOCIAL STRUCTURE. STRUCTURAL-FUNCTIONALISM).

2 the rules (or 'deep structure') underlying and responsible for the production of a surface structure (especially structures analogous to GRAMMAR) (see also LINGUISTICS, LÉVI-STRAUSS). For GIDDENS (1984), for example, 'structure' in this latter sense refers to 'rules and resources', implicated in the reproduction of social systems (see also STRUCTURATION, STRUCTURATION THEORY). The distinction (sense **1** and **2**) drawn between 'surface' and 'deep structures' is also an important one in STRUCTURALISM (senses **3** and **5**).

Major criticisms are made by theorists from the SYMBOLIC INTERACTION, SOCIAL PHENOMENOLOGY and HERMENEUTIC traditions, who argue that sociology must make central human actors' involvement in the creation and recreation of the social world through symbolic meaning. People, not structures, can be seen as creating social order. Even if structures are treated as 'rules', then these also are created by people.

A compromise between theories of structure and theories of meaning has often been attempted by social theorists. In the 1960s P. L. Berger and associates proposed a 'dialectical' theory of the 'social construction of reality', in which 'social structure is not characterizable as a thing able to stand on its own, apart from the human activity that produced it', but, once created, 'is encountered by the individual (both) as an alien facticity (and) ... as a coercive instrumentality' (Berger and Pullberg, 1966). A humanly constructed reality only comes to take on the *appearance* of having been constructed by some external, non-human, force. GIDDENS' more recent proposal that 'structures' can always in principle be examined in terms of their structuration 'as a series of reproduced practices' (Giddens, 1976b), and that structures are 'both constraining and enabling', is another example of an approach offering a compromise between theories of action and theories of structure (see DUALITY OF STRUCTURE, STRUCTURATION, STRUCTURATION THEORY). See also STRUCTURE AND AGENCY.

structure and agency

The two main determinants of social outcomes which are recognized in sociology, but whose relative importance is much debated as a central issue in sociological theory. Three main general positions can be identified:
(a) doctrines (e.g. STRUCTURALISM, some forms of FUNCTIONALISM, ALTHUSSERIAN MARXISM) that social life is largely determined by social structure, and that individual agency can be explained mostly as the outcome of structure;
(b) doctrines (e.g. METHODOLOGICAL INDIVIDUALISM, SOCIAL PHENOMENOLOGY, ETHNOMETHODOLOGY) that reverse the emphasis, stressing instead the capacity of individuals – of 'individual agents' – to construct and reconstruct their worlds and the necessity of explanations in the actors' terms;
(c) approaches which, variously, emphasize the complementarity of the two processes, i.e. structural influences on human action and individual agency which is capable of changing social structure.

Despite many suggestions to the contrary (and notwithstanding that many difficulties and disagreements exist in defining STRUCTURE) most forms of sociological theory can be located in category (c), as recognizing the importance of both structural determinacy and individual agency. Crucial issues arise, however, in conceptualizing the relationship between the two, and it is here that a number of interesting formulations have emerged in recent years, especially those of BERGER and Luckmann (1967) and Berger and Pullberg (1966), Bhaskar (1979), and GIDDENS (1984) (see also BOURDIEU).

For Berger and Luckmann the relation between structure and agency is one in which society forms the individuals who create society in a continuous dialectic. For Bhaskar, a 'relational' and a 'transformational' view of the individual and society requires a stronger emphasis: 'society is both the ever present *condition* and the continually reproduced *outcome* of human agency'. Finally, Giddens, in perhaps the most sophisticated attempt to break free of the conception of a 'dualism' of structure and agency, argues for a conception of DUALITY of STRUCTURE in which:
(a) 'structure is both the medium and the outcome of the conduct it recursively organizes';
(b) 'structure' is defined as 'rules and resources', which do not exist outside of the actions but continuously impact on its production and reproduction; and
(c) analogies with physical structures, of the sort common in functionalism, are regarded as wholly illegitimate. In Giddens' formulation 'structure' must also be seen as both enabling and constraining.

Reformulations of relations between structure and agency have not ended debates about the appropriate conceptualization of relations between the two, or indeed about the prior, or interrelated, question of how 'agency' and 'structure' should be defined in the first place. Thus Layder (1981), for example, regards Giddens' conception of 'structure' as depriving this concept of any 'autonomous properties or pre-given facticity', and commentators have detected in Giddens' formulation a persistent 'bias' towards agency. Moreover, whatever sophistication general formulations of the structure-agency relations may achieve, disputes are likely to persist in particular application of such notions to 'concrete' historical cases. See also STRUCTURATION THEORY, AUTONOMOUS MAN AND PLASTIC MAN.

structured coding in QUESTIONNAIRE design, analysis is assisted by the questions being 'structured', so constraining response. Structured questions can be either *open-ended* or *closed.* Closed questions are those where respondents are presented with a list of options and are asked to indicate their answers by ticking a box or circling a number. Open-ended questions are those where respondents are asked to write down their replies which are then coded according to a pre-coded schema.

When using structured questions care must be taken that the questions asked refer to only one dimension. For example, religion has at least two distinct dimensions – the strength of each person's religious conviction and their nominal religion (into which they have been initiated). Care should also be taken to indicate that the answers are exclusive of one another.

Another problem is the purely practical one of including every possible reply in the coding schedule. The use of catch-all ('other) categories should be avoided as far as possible at the coding stage. since such a category may contain many different replies.

To assign numerical codes to the data the researcher should, where possible, make use of coding schemas which have been professionally designed by competent experts in the field of study. Not only does this procedure simplify the researcher's task but it also leads to the accumulation of data which is readily comparable. For example, in undertaking occupational research the researcher is generally advised to make use of the full Registrar General's classification devised for the analysis of CENSUS material.

Generally, however, the researcher is forced to develop his or her coding schema. This involves first taking account of the level of measurement (see CRITERIA AND LEVELS OF MEASUREMENT) which is being employed. Where interval variables are being employed the researcher is advised against precoding the data into a series of numerical bands since a precoded question might result in clustering within one band. Where a variable has ordinal properties it is generally best to code it as such as this will increase the number of statistical tests which are acceptable to use. When coding nominal data attention should be given to whether it is possible to group the data into a more convenient structure at a later stage of the research programme.

structure in dominance see DOMINANCE.

subculture any system of beliefs, values and norms which is shared and actively participated in by an appreciable minority of people within a particular culture. The relationship of the subculture to the so-called dominant culture has been identified as one of subordination and relative powerlessness. Power relations are therefore an important dimension of any sociological consideration of subculture.

Subcultures have been examined in terms of ETHNICITY, CLASS, DEVIANCE and YOUTH CULTURE. R. MERTON constructed a typology of possible responses to a dysjunction between means and goals. These responses might give rise to a number of different subcultures. S. Cohen (1971) has noted the emergence of a succession of youth subcultures in the postwar era, for example, in Britain, 'Teds', 'Mods', 'Rockers' and 'Punks'. It has been suggested that such subcultures serve as 'magical solutions' to the problems created for young working-class people in contemporary Western societies (Brake, 1980). They serve to provide a means of establishing both individual and group identity. They are discernible largely through stylistic expression, particularly language, demeanour, music, dress and dance.

Subcultures, like culture generally, are the result of collective creativity and are therefore subject to historical change and transformation. Feminist theorists such as McRobbie and Garber (1976), McRobbie (1991) have noted that gender is rarely considered in the study of subcultures. They have raised important questions concerning the relationship of young women to youth subcultures.
See also CULTURAL STUDIES, CULTURAL CAPITAL, CULTURAL DEPRIVATION, CULTURAL LAG, CULTURAL (AND LINGUISTIC) RELATIVISM.

subject and object (PHILOSOPHY) twin concepts, *subject* (person, mind, theorist, etc.) and *object* (external world), which have been central in much philosophical (and also sociological) discussion, especially EPISTEMOLOGY. The central issues have been: how the subject can come to 'know' the object, and how each is constituted (ONTOLOGY). Thus, an empiricist (see EMPIRICISM) may claim that the world is made up of 'things', and that the mind consists of 'ideas', and that the latter 'picture' or 'represent' the former. Alternatively in IDEALISM, ideas may be claimed to structure our perception of objects.

Recent movements in philosophy, (e.g. POSTSTRUCTURALISM, POST-EMPIRICISM) have sought to break with traditional conceptions of subject and object (see DECONSTRUCTION, DECENTRED SELF), and to move away from rigid conceptions of epistemology or ontology. In some forms, such a movement away from traditional conceptions of the foundations of knowledge has been associated with RELATIVISM (see also INCOMMENSURABILITY), but another view is that it can be presented as a move beyond objectivism *or* relativism (see FEYERABEND).

subjective and objective class a person's perception of his or her own class position, i.e. *subjective class* (or *class identity*), in contradistinction to that assessed in terms of either observable, or theoretically important, external elements of that person's CLASS position, i.e. *objective class*. No assumption need be made that in so far as the former differs from the latter, the subjective position is 'false', although this assumption may sometimes be made.

Discrepancies between subjective and objective class have often been regarded as significant in research into class and voting, e.g. proposed explanations of 'class-deviant' patterns of working-class voting behaviour in terms of subjective 'middle-class identity' (see also EMBOURGEOISEMENT, WORKING-CLASS CONSERVATISM). Butler and Stokes (1969) used the following question to elicit subjective social class: 'There's quite a bit of talk these days about different social classes. Most people say that they belong to either the middle class or the working class. Do you ever think of yourself as being in one of these classes?' However, fewer than 50% of respondents volunteer a 'subjective class' without further prompting. RUNCIMAN (1966) and GOLDTHORPE et al. (1989), among others, have exposed the equivocal 'meanings' associated with, for example, subjective 'middle-class identity', many of these incompatible with any simple hypothesis of EMBOURGEOISEMENT.

subjectivity the perspective of the person (subject); lack of objectivity. The range of attitudes towards this term indicates its essentially contentious nature. It is often used pejoratively within positivist sociology to derogate biased observation or methodology. At the other extreme it is celebrated by HERMENEUTICS as the only possible way to locate any attempts to theorize about the social. Any answer to the question as to whether subjectivity is inescapable or undesirable relies on ontological and epistemological assumptions about the nature of human beings' relationship to the concrete world. In practice the two terms are used as if they occupied ends of a continuum, greater or lesser degrees of subjectivity being claimed by various authors. Various attempts have been made to illustrate the way that subjectivities are objectively constructed and *vice versa* (see PARSONS, ALTHUSSER, GIDDENS, for example), but the dichotomy stubbornly refuses to disappear.

sublimation see DEFENCE MECHANISMS.

suboptimality (ECONOMICS and THEORY OF GAMES) any situation in which an 'optimal' – or best overall – outcome (e.g. income or benefit) from the point of view of a plurality of consumers and producers cannot be determined.

subpolitics this form of politics (including new trans-national forms), U. BECK suggests, may be replacing in importance traditional politics – e.g. consumer politics, the green movement. The old collective actors – trade unions, class parties, etc. – are 'being hollowed out' by the new political spaces and networks made possible by global society and new forms of reflexivity.

subsistence economy *or* **subsistence society** a society which is seen as producing enough for survival without any economic surplus. This is a commonly used term to describe simple societies such as TRIBES or HUNTER-GATHERERS, but problematic. Most societies produce beyond immediate needs, and in the past anthropologists tended to underestimate the extent to which contact between societies gave rise to trade. If these qualifications are held in mind it is a usable concept to refer to societies whose members may limit their surplus production, or for whom market transactions are of secondary consideration, and if it is recognized that there are problems in defining 'needs' and 'survival'. See also ECONOMIC SURPLUS, NATURAL ECONOMY.

substantive rationality see FORMAL AND SUBSTANTIVE RATIONALITY.

subsystems model (of action systems and social systems) the four-fold set of functional 'problems' identified by PARSONS (1953), and deriving from Bales (1950), in which any system of action and all social systems and societies are seen as required to cope with the following (see Fig. 34):
(a) the problem of adapting to the external environment of the system (*'adaptation'*, in Parson's schema, and in concrete terms 'the economy');
(b) the problem of achieving system goals (*'goal attainment'*, in concrete terms, the 'polity' or government);
(c) the problem of integrating the system (*'integration'*, in concrete terms, communities, associations and organizations);
(d) the problem of maintaining commitment to values (*'pattern maintenance'*, in concrete terms, the family, households and schools).

The working-out (often in intricate detail) of the relations between these analytical divisions formed a major part of the 'systems theoretic' phase in Parsons' FUNCTIONALISM. See also FUNCTIONAL PREREQUISITES, SYSTEM, SYSTEMS THEORY, STRUCTURAL-FUNCTIONALISM, SOCIAL SYSTEM.

suffrage the right to vote in elections.

suffragette a member of the militant female movement which, in the early part of the 20th-century, advocated the extension of the right to vote to women.

suicide 'all cases of death resulting directly or indirectly from a positive or negative act of the victim himself, which he knows will produce this result' (DURKHEIM, 1897). ATTEMPTED SUICIDE AND PARASUICIDE are different phenomena, requiring separate inquiry. Persons who have 'attempted suicide' or else feigned suicide, cannot

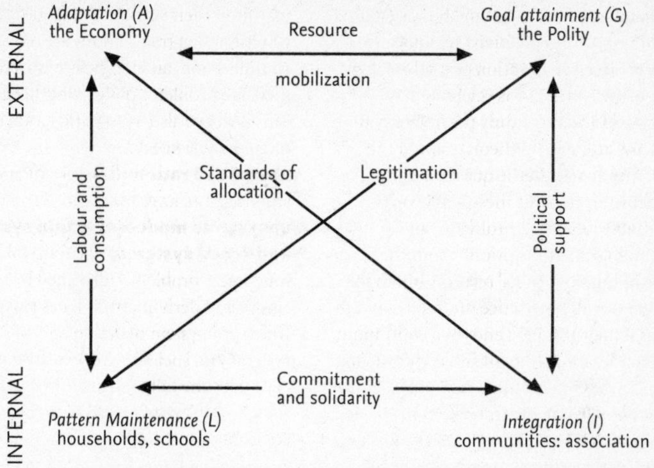

Fig. 34 **Subsystems model (of action systems and social systems).** As well as presenting the four subsystems, which according to Parsons all systems of action and social systems possess, this figure also indicates six main lines of interchange between subsystems as seen by him.

necessarily be studied as a guide to the behaviour of successful suicides.

DURKHEIM's analysis of suicide has been highly influential within sociology. His argument was that rates of suicide are related to the type and level of SOCIAL INTEGRATION within a society. Thus an explanation of these different rates required a distinctively sociological explanation. Using available published statistics, Durkheim first eliminated various environmental and psychological variables previously proposed as explaining suicide, before proposing that four distinctive types of suicide can be identified: EGOISTIC SUICIDE, ALTRUISTIC SUICIDE, ANOMIC SUICIDE, and FATALISTIC SUICIDE, each of these corresponding to a particular condition of society.

One central problem in Durkheim's account is that OFFICIAL STATISTICS undoubtedly distort and understate the overall incidence of suicide. It is also likely they do so more for some groups than others (e.g. Durkheim found Catholics less likely than Protestants to commit suicide, but Catholics may have greater reason to conceal suicide). Some sociologists (e.g. J. Douglas, *The Social Meaning of Suicide*, 1967) suggest that social research on suicide must first establish empirically how suicides are designated, e.g. by police, coroners, etc., before such social statistics can be used with any confidence, and that Durkheim failed to do this.

Despite reservations about Durkheim's work, aspects of his account have been confirmed by other theorists, e.g. Sainsbury (1955) who found that suicide rates in London boroughs were highest where levels of 'social disorganization' – e.g. levels of divorce, illegitimacy, etc. – were also highest. Sainsbury and Baraclough (1968) have also suggested that the rank order of suicide rates for immigrant groups to the US correlated closely with the rank order of suicide rates for their countries of origin, despite the fact that a different set of labellers were involved. Thus they suggest that, though official suicide statistics must be used with caution, they may be less unreliable than sometimes suggested. This view might be seen as gaining further support from regularities in the incidence of suicide which tend to recur across cultures, for example, higher rates among men than women, among the widowed and the divorced, among the unmarried and the childless, among the old compared with the young. Most of these findings are consistent with what Durkheim found.

summative (*or* objective-oriented) evaluation a retrospective review of how well an project or organization has performed (either after the programme has been completed or at set time intervals), enabling summary statements and judgements to be made. This approach often utilizes criteria against which achievements can be compared, e.g. an organization's performance can be measured against its aims and objectives, by measuring inputs and outputs, by using PERFORMANCE INDICATORS, comparing a similar organization or contrasting benefits accrued to beneficiaries with a control group. Summative or objective-oriented evaluation can be subdivided into 'process evaluation', which examines the use of inputs (such as time and money); and 'outcome evaluation', which considers the effectiveness of the outcome. See EVALUATION and FORMATIVE EVALUATION.

Sumner, William (1840–1910) early US sociologist, As an evolutionary theorist, influenced particularly by Herbert SPENCER, Sumner's work is today relatively little discussed. However, his best-known work, *Folkways* (1906), bequeathed a number of terms which have retained currency. See MORES, FOLKWAYS, ETHNOCENTRICISM, SOCIAL DARWINISM.

superego one of the three elements of the PERSONALITY in FREUD's theory. The superego is that part of the personality that operates as the conscience, aiming for perfection, controlling the function of the EGO by placing moral constraints on it.

Like the ego, the superego is said by Freud to develop from the ID in the first few years of life. He proposed that it was formed by the child internalizing the parent's perceived standards, and indirectly, therefore, society s standards. This came about through identification with the same-sex parent as resolution of the OEDIPUS COMPLEX. Freud's theory thus explained the development of a conscience in boys much better than in girls and he has been much criticized for the implied inferiority of women as a result. Feminist theorists such as Juliet Mitchell (1974) have explored this aspect of his theory.

superexploitation see UNEQUAL EXCHANGE.

superorganic (of human *social evolution*) superimposed upon, and surpassing, merely organic evolution. The term was introduced by Herbert SPENCER, and his choice of this term reflects his view that evolution must be viewed as a transformation that has taken place in three realms: the inorganic, organic, and superorganic. For Spencer, the superorganic is not a feature only of human evolution; it applies also to some social insects as well as many animals. But superorganic evolution is a central aspect particularly in human evolution.

Use of the term 'superorganic' (rather than the terms 'cultural' or CULTURE) reflects a commitment by Spencer that human social development can only be understood in evolutionary terms, in which, while different from biological evolution, human social evolution retains a basic continuity with biological evolution.

This leaves open the question of *how different* is social evolution. While for Spencer there were definite continuities between the three types of evolution – inorganic, organic, superorganic – other sociologists have not always agreed and have tended instead to emphasize a sharp break between human culture and all previous forms of evolution. See also EVOLUTIONARY SOCIOLOGY, SOCIOCULTURAL EVOLUTION.

superstructure see BASE AND SUPERSTRUCTURE.

surface structure (LINGUISTICS) see DEEP AND SURFACE STRUCTURE.

surplus labour (MARXISM) labour performed in all class societies, which is undertaken at the command of others or for payment, which enriches an exploiting class. In capitalism this labour produces SURPLUS VALUE. See also LABOUR POWER, LABOUR THEORY OF VALUE.

surplus value (MARXISM) the difference between the VALUE of capital at the start of the capitalist production process and the additional value of commodities which are produced. For Marx this added value only comes from the LABOUR POWER employed by the capitalist. The difference between value paid in wages and the value of the commodities produced is surplus value and is the rate of EXPLOITATION (AND APPROPRIATION). Profit for the capitalist comes out of surplus value, and is what remains when other costs such as constant capital (see CONSTANT AND VARIABLE CAPITAL) and of distribution have been met.

There are two forms of surplus value. *Absolute surplus value* is linked to the length of the working day: if a labourer produces in four hours the value, in commodities, of a day's wage, then the remaining hours worked are SURPLUS LABOUR within which absolute surplus value is produced. This may also be increased by lengthening the working day. However, since there are physical and often legal limits to the length of the working day, Marx argues that capitalists increase surplus value most generally by increasing *relative surplus value*, which is derived from increasing the productivity of labour such that, say, the value of a day's wages are produced in two rather than four hours. This process may involve both reorganization of the LABOUR PROCESS and the introduction of machinery. Hence this is linked in the Marxian analysis with the rising ORGANIC COMPOSITION OF CAPITAL.

The concept of surplus value is central to Marx's analysis of CAPITALISM since surplus value does not occur in noncapitalist modes of production. It is also central to some Marxian conceptualizations of social class, especially the distinction between PRODUCTIVE AND UNPRODUCTIVE LABOUR, since this refers to the production of surplus value. See also LABOUR THEORY OF VALUE.

surveillance the monitoring, and the associated direct or indirect forms of supervision and superintendence by the modern STATE, of the activities of its citizens. The capacity for surveillance possessed by modern NATION STATES has increased compared with those available to earlier forms of state, as the result of spectacular improvements in techniques for the collection and storage of INFORMATION and equally striking improvements in means of transport and communications.

For FOUCAULT, in *Discipline and Punish* (1975), the 'disciplinary power' of modern societies is an all-pervasive feature of these societies and a predominant feature of administrative power within them. Remedial and CARCERAL ORGANIZATIONS, which remove human liberty are not more than extreme forms of a generalized tendency to heightened surveillance within these societies.

Foucault's emphasis is disputed by many, however. Our heightened awareness of, and concern about, situations in which some individuals are subject to loss of liberty reflects the new importance of a concern for liberty within modern societies and the many areas of life in which liberties have increased. Nonetheless, few dispute that – for good and for ill – surveillance and control are an important characteristic of modern societies and the modern state. Compare ORIENTAL DESPOTISM, ABSOLUTISM. See also SEQUESTRATION, TOTALITARIANISM.

survey see SOCIAL SURVEY, SURVEY METHOD.

survey method a social science research technique using QUESTIONNAIRES and their analysis using various QUANTITATIVE and statistical techniques (see also SOCIAL SURVEY). In sociology the survey method is used for two main reasons:

(a) to describe a population and examine its principal characteristics, e.g. age, sex occupation, attitudes, etc.; and

(b) to test HYPOTHESES and examine the relationship between VARIABLES.

The main problems with the survey method include:

(a) the technique is non-experimental, i.e. the researcher cannot usually control

the conditions under which the research is conducted;
(b) researchers have to rely upon what RESPONDENTS tell them unless they are able to verify their findings with direct observations;
(c) the technique is atomistic, i.e. it examines individuals rather than whole communities.

Nevertheless, the survey method does have much to recommend it. It provides a cheap and relatively easy way to obtain a considerable amount of simply quantifiable data, which can be used to test and verify sociological hypotheses and identify further areas of research.

survival of the fittest an aphorism coined by Herbert SPENCER, and quoted by DARWIN in *On the Origin of Species* (1859). The theory argued:
(a) that reproduction in any species involved a certain degree of natural variation in the characteristics of offspring;
(b) that any variation which enhanced the survival capacity of certain members of a species over other members lacking that variation would be positively selected for in terms of reproduction chances; and
(c) that over millennia this process could account for: (i) the development of complex organisms from simple ones; and (ii) an enormous diversification of species from a small number of original organisms.

The concept of 'survival of the fittest' has had little explicit currency in sociology, except in terms of SOCIAL DARWINISM. See also EVOLUTIONARY THEORY, NEOEVOLUTIONISM, EVOLUTIONARY SOCIOLOGY.

sustainable development economic development which ensures that environmental depletion and degradation does not occur. The term *ecodevelopment* has a similar although narrower meaning. Used primarily in the 1970s to refer to problems of agricultural development in the THIRD WORLD where certain forms, such as exploitation of tropical rainforests, were seen as short-term measures with local and global consequences endangering that particular practice and other activities.

In the late 1980s the term came to have a wider application as concern with environmental issues grew. Criteria of sustainable development came to be applied to all forms of economic development which hitherto had ignored environmental effects which could undermine those very developments. So sustainable development would be seen as economic and social development which avoided pollution, conserved non-renewable energy forms, such as oil, and in general did not create future problems for which there were no easily available solutions.

Redclift (1987) provides a good discussion of the issues which sociologists have until recently tended to neglect. See also ECONOMIC DEVELOPMENT, ENVIRONMENTAL DEPLETION, GREEN REVOLUTION.

swing see ELECTORAL SWING.

symbol **1** a SIGN (see SIGN, sense **2**) in which the connection between the meaning and the sign is conventional rather than natural (SIGN, sense **1**).
2 an indirect representation of an underlying meaning, syndrome, etc. as, for example, in religious symbolism and RITUAL, or PSYCHOANALYSIS (see also METONYMY, LÉVI-STRAUSS).

Apart from the utterly central role of LANGUAGE in social life, symbolic communication occurs in a variety of further ways (see SEMIOLOGY, BODY LANGUAGE).

symbolic interactionism a theoretical approach in US sociology which seeks to explain action and interaction as the outcome of the meanings which actors attach to things and to social action, including themselves (see also REFLEXIVITY).

For symbolic interactionists, meanings 'do not reside in the object' but emerge from social processes. Emphasis is placed on the 'active', 'interpretive', and 'constructive' capacities or competence, possessed by human actors, as against the determining influence of social structures suggested by theoretical approaches such as FUNCTIONALISM.

The term was coined in 1937 by H. BLUMER, who summarizes the main principles of the

approach in terms of three propositions (Blumer, 1969):
(a) 'human beings act towards things on the basis of the meanings that things have for them';
(b) these meanings 'arise out of social interaction';
(c) social action results from a 'fitting together of individual lines of action'.

Theorists whose work stands predominantly within this tradition include George Herbert MEAD, Charles COOLEY, and Howard S. BECKER. An important sociologist whose work stands close to the symbolic interactionist tradition is Erving GOFFMAN.

Symbolic interactionism is sometimes seen as a sociologically oriented SOCIAL PSYCHOLOGY – indeed it has been described as the first properly 'social' social psychology of any kind. Thus, symbolic interactionism stands opposed to approaches in social psychology such as BEHAVIOURISM or ETHOLOGY. As Cooley put it, 'society is not a chicken yard'. Human action is seen as distinguished from animal behaviour above all by language and by the huge importance of symbolic communication of various kinds.

As well as being the main alternative theoretical approach to functionalism within modern American sociology, symbolic interactionism also provides the main alternative approach in social research to conventional SOCIAL SURVEY using fixed choice QUESTIONNAIRES and standardized VARIABLES. In place of these approaches, its preferred methods include PARTICIPANT OBSERVATION of actors in natural settings and intensive INTERVIEWS.

Although rejecting those approaches in psychology and sociology which seek deterministic universal laws or the discovery of overarching structural-functional regularities, symbolic interactionists do see a place for generalizations within sociology. Thus BECKER (1953) in his famous study of marijuana use for pleasure claims that his 'final generalization is a statement of those sequences of changes in attitude which occurred in every case ... and may be considered as an explanation of all cases'. Rather than a root-and-branch objection to generalization in sociology, symbolic interactionism calls for these to be appropriate to the particular subject matter of sociology (see ANALYTICAL INDUCTION, GROUNDED THEORY, DRUG-TAKING FOR PLEASURE).

A further feature of the approach is that it has often adopted a more socially radical posture than either functionalist or conventional social survey research, e.g. a 'reversal of the usual hierarchies of credibility' by exploring the perspective of 'the underdog' (BECKER, 1963).

The main criticism of symbolic interactionism is that in focusing exclusively on microsocial processes and subinstitutional phenomena, it understates the importance of macroscopic structures and historical factors, especially economic forces and institutionalized political power. Thus rather than exclusive perspectives, sociological foci on structure and action are seen as complementary perspectives by many theorists, e.g. GIDDENS (see also DUALITY OF STRUCTURE, STRUCTURATION THEORY).

A further critique, that symbolic interactionism fails to explore human creative competence in sufficient depth, is more internal to the interpretive and symbolic interactionist tradition (see SOCIAL PHENOMENOLOGY). A new sociological paradigm, ETHNOMETHODOLOGY, resulted from this critique.

symmetrical family (according to Young and Wilmott, 1973) the emerging form of FAMILY in industrial societies, distinguished by a sharing of domestic duties and a tendency for both husbands and wives to be in paid employment.

symptomatic reading (LITERARY AND CULTURAL THEORY) a reading of a TEXT that searches for underlying contradiction, absences, etc., which reveal 'what a text does not say' or cannot say.

symptom iceberg the submerged mountain of medically serious, personally troubling, painful or even life-threatening conditions which are never referred for professional help. It has been shown that people who possess severe symptoms and physical discomfort may nevertheless describe themselves as 'in good health', and when they describe themselves as 'in poor health' it does not follow that they act in the way assumed by the BIOMECHANICAL OR BIOMEDICAL MODEL OF ILLNESS and refer their symptoms for medical treatment. Definitions of illness and health are framed by the values of social groups as are the strategies deemed appropriate once a problem has been identified. The decision to go to a doctor for treatment depends, to a large degree, on the extent to which the troubling condition interferes with normal living patterns and social relationships. Illness behaviour and the acceptance of the SICK ROLE are part of a complex of self-referral patterns, systems of lay, folk and professional healing, and access to and distribution of health services. Even when a problem has been defined as suitable for medical referral, studies show that people may still not visit their doctor because they do not want to trouble the doctor, they are discouraged by the waiting room or appointments system or receptionist, they fear that the doctor will adopt a judgemental attitude, or they hope that the problem will go away.

synchronic see DIACHRONIC AND SYNCHRONIC.

synchrony and diachrony 1 (LINGUISTICS) the distinction between the study of language as an existing system of relationships and without reference to the past (*synchrony*) and the study of the changes in language over time (*diachrony*) – see also SAUSSURE.
2 (STRUCTURALISM) the distinction, deriving from the above, between an analysis and explanation of any feature of social life carried out with reference to existing 'structural' features of a society or social system, without reference to history (*synchrony*), and historical analysis which focuses on change (*diachrony*).
3 (similarly, but in sociology more generally) the distinction between accounts of social order and accounts of social change. For example, in his account of social evolutionary processes, Harré *Social Being* (1979) distinguishes between 'synchronic replicators' and 'diachronic selectors'.
In structuralism the distinction has often been associated with the downgrading of the significance of historical explanations, and an associated downgrading of the role of the SUBJECT and human agency, and the elevation of structural explanations to supreme status. However, there is no inherent reason why structural explanations and historical explanations should not be combined, or structural explanations combined with explanations in terms of the agency of individual human subjects (see STRUCTURE AND AGENCY, DUALITY OF STRUCTURE, STRUCTURATION THEORY). However, this is more easily said than done, with some sociologists, whether for convenience or for reasons of principle, preferring to concentrate on one or the other (see also EPOCHÉ).

syncretism the combination of elements from different religions or different cultural traditions. Syncretism in religious belief and practices has been especially associated with contexts, e.g. colonialism, in which a major religion is brought into contact with local religions, but it can also be seen as a general feature of the transformation of religions or cultures and of DIASPORAS. See also CULT, CARGO CULT, POSTCOLONIAL THEORY.

syndicalism see ANARCHO-SYNDICALISM.

syntagm (LINGUISTICS) any combination of words in a 'chain of speech'. See SYNTAGMATIC AND PARADIGMATIC.

syntagmatic and paradigmatic (LINGUISTICS) the distinction between the relationship of the combination of words in a chain of speech (a *syntagmatic* relationship) and the relationship of any particular term with 'associated', i.e. 'structurally interchangeable', absent terms (a *paradigmatic* relationship) (e. g. in the sentence 'she is sociologizing, 'she' might be replaced by 'he', 'is' by 'was', and 'sociologizing' by 'sleeping'). By analogy, any chain of social actions may sometimes also be referred to as 'syntagmatic' and the relationship of the 'units' in this action to other absent interchangeable possible units of action, 'paradigmatic'. See also SAUSSURE.

syntax see GRAMMAR.

synthetic see ANALYTIC AND SYNTHETIC.

systact a group or category of persons in specified ROLES, where these persons have, by virtue of these roles, 'a distinguishable and more than transiently similar location, and, on that account, a common interest' (RUNCIMAN, 1989). The term has been proposed by Runciman with the aim of making it 'easier to report and compare the institutions of different societies without having to be precommitted to a view on such vexed and theoretical questions' such as the difference between class and rank societies, 'ruling class' or 'governing élite'.

system 1 (in a loose general sense) any area of organized social provision (e.g. the 'educational system' or the 'transport system').
2 any set or group of interrelated elements or parts where a change in one part would affect some or all of the others parts (e.g. the solar system).
3 any set or group of elements or parts (e.g. an organism or a machine) organized for a definite purpose and in relation to an external environment. Such systems may be natural or man-made, and may be taken to include SOCIAL SYSTEMS. Hence a SOCIETY or a social ORGANIZATION may be deemed a system in this sense.

A system such as the solar system, which is little changed by its external environment, is referred to as a *closed system;* those, such as organisms or societies, which sustain themselves in response to changes in their environment are referred to as *open systems* (see also HOMEOSTASIS).

Although controversial, the concept in sense 3 has been important in social theory, which has often treated social relations, groups or societies as a set of interrelated parts which FUNCTION so as to maintain their boundaries with their wider environment. See also FUNCTIONALISM, PARSONS, FUNCTIONAL(IST) EXPLANATION, ORGANIC ANALOGY, TELEOLOGY, SYSTEMS THEORY, CYBERNETICS.

systematic desensitization see BEHAVIOUR MODIFICATION.

systematic review (of health care) a process of critical appraisal that evaluates the nature of the evidence in support of a treatment against the following test questions. Does it work (its efficacy)? How well does it work (effectiveness)? Is this the best of the available treatments in terms of cost-benefit? And also, can it be made available to those at risk, is it what people want and is it appropriate to their clinically-defined need? The research evidence in support of the treatment is evaluated against the following hierarchical order of strength of evidence: randomized clinical trials, robust experimental studies, robust observational studies, expert opinion and the endorsement of respected authorities. A number of factors underpin systematic review: the need to remove ineffective treatments, the need to establish scientifically agreed criteria for the introduction of new treatments, the need to demonstrate clinical effectiveness through the measurement of outcome and to provide a research-based system for resource allocation in treatment (see I. Crombie (1996) *The Pocket Guide to Critical Appraisal,* BMJ, London).

systematic sample see RANDOM SAMPLE.

system integration see SOCIAL INTEGRATION AND SYSTEM INTEGRATION.

systems approach see POLITICAL SYSTEM.

systems theory approaches to the study of SYSTEMS (especially SYSTEM, sense 3), which emphasize the general properties of goal-seeking systems – hence the term *general systems theory* is also used to refer to this approach (see also CYBERNETICS). These approaches were in vogue especially in the 1950s and 60s, and in sociology were particularly associated with the work of Talcott PARSONS, and with related theorists in POLITICAL SCIENCE (see also POLITICAL SYSTEM).

The view of general systems theorists is that the general concept of a 'system' can be applied to naturally occurring systems of many types, including SOCIAL SYSTEMS as well as biological and mechanical systems. The basic model is of mechanical systems (especially servomechanisms) and biological systems, which display such features as *negative feedback,* in which INFORMATION about the current state of the system feeds back to influence adjustment towards HOMEOSTASIS, correcting deviations from its basic goals.

The concept can be wider than this, however. It also incorporates ideas of knock-on effects spreading through a system, of *entropy* and *negantropy. Entropy* describes the natural state of a closed system in that it tends to use up its energy and run down (even if over a very long period). However, social systems are not closed, they can import energy, they have a transaction with the external environment and so can avoid entropy. Such open systems can survive to attain new steady states, adapting to changing conditions, achieving *negantropy*. Thus a crucial feature of general systems theory as applied to social systems is exchange with an environment, and ADAPTATION.

In sociology specifically, influenced by the systems thinking of Vilfredo PARETO, Parsons in particular worked with a number of theorists drawn from the physical as well as the social sciences, including L. Henderson. It is on this basis that Parsons produced a model of the 'social system' and of 'action systems' in general (see SUBSYSTEMS MODEL (OF ACTION SYSTEMS AND SOCIAL SYSTEMS)) which constituted the core of his STRUCTURAL-FUNCTIONALISM. The further objective was to integrate the study of different social sciences (ANTHROPOLOGY, PSYCHOLOGY, POLITICAL SCIENCE, ECONOMICS) under the umbrella of general systems theory.

Although hugely influential at the time, the attempt of Parsons and the many theorists associated with his work to found a new general theory of action systems and social systems is now adjudged a relative failure. The approach has been accused of making 'conservative' assumptions about the integration of social systems (see GOULDNER, LOCKWOOD), of too high levels of abstraction and propositions at times verging on tautology (see Black, 1961; MILLS, 1956), and a relative neglect of the independent influence of individual actors' agency, reflexivity, etc. (compare SYMBOLIC INTERACTIONISM, SOCIAL PHENOMENOLOGY, ETHNOMETHODOLOGY).

For all this, general systems theory, and systems thinking in related forms, remains an important influence in sociology and within the social sciences generally (e.g. see SOCIOTECHNICAL SYSTEMS APPROACH). Parsons' general approach has also been taken up recently by radical theorists such as C. Offe and Jurgen HABERMAS, for example, in the latter's analysis of the tendency to LEGITIMATION CRISIS in advanced capitalist societies, a model in which the four main tendencies examined correspond to the four subsystems in Parsons' earlier model.

Finally, general systems models remain of central importance in analysis of ecosystems, and relations between social systems and the physical environment.

Szasz, Thomas Stephen (1920–) American psychiatrist, best known for his influence on the ANTIPSYCHIATRY movement through *The Myth of Mental Illness* (1961). His name is often associated with that of LAING, since both criticized the diagnosis and treatment of schizophrenia (see PSYCHOSIS) in the 1950s and 60s. He was most critical of the role of psychiatrists in labelling as mad those people who do not conform to society's norms, and using their power to have them locked up. This meant that psychiatrists were primarily agents of social control, while patients were having their human freedoms denied.

t

taboo *or* **tabu** any ritual prohibition on certain activities. The term originally comes from Captain Cook's description of Polynesian custom. It may involve the avoidance of certain people, places, objects or actions, and the universal incest taboo is a much cited example of the latter. Much work on this area has been carried out from within anthropology in an attempt to explain why, for instance, different foods are avoided within various cultures. Functionalists prefer explanations of taboo and TOTEMISM in terms of group solidarity, whilst structuralists, such as M. DOUGLAS in *Purity and Danger* (1966), have focused on taboos as a problem in classifying ambiguity.

tabula rasa see LOCKE.

tacit knowledge any knowledge which the SOCIAL ACTOR possesses but may not be able to articulate, which enables him or her to perform competently within a general or specific social context.

tacit skills see SKILL.

take-off to maturity see ROSTOW.

Taoism the ancient Chinese philosophical and religious tradition (literally 'the school of the way') nominally based on the thinking of the legendary thinker Lao-tzu. Taoism is a theory which advocates an acceptance of the forces of nature and the importance of living in harmony with these. Whereas WEBER regarded CONFUCANISM as the philosophy of the ruling class, he regarded Taoist cults as popular religious forms in which the needs of the masses were accommodated.

Tarde, Gabriel (1843–1904) French social psychologist and criminologist whose studies of crime were couched in terms of an opposition to the biologistic reductionism of LOMBROSO. In sociology he is best remembered for *Les Lois de l'Imitation* (1890), a work singled out for criticism by DURKHEIM (*Le Suicide*, 1897) as underestimating the constraining external force of social currents.

Tawney, Richard (1880–1962) English economic historian and egalitarian social philosopher, influenced by his early association with the Workers' Educational Association (WEA) and by his lifelong Christianity. As an economic historian Tawney can be seen as a forerunner of modern approaches to economic and social history which emphasize working-class resistance to capitalist exploitation. As a social philosopher, in works such as *Equality* (1920) and *The Acquisitive Society* (1931), he raised fundamental questions about the morality of 20th-century social institutions. In sociology he is best remembered for his *Religion and the Rise of Capitalism* (1926). In this he agreed with WEBER's thesis that the individualism and worldliness associated with Calvinism and Puritanism were the moral engine of capitalist development, although he regarded Weber as failing to give sufficient emphasis to the two-way causal interaction between religion and economics.

taxation compulsory levies by central or local governments. Taxation takes many forms, e.g. on personal wealth and income, on corporate income or profits, on the purchases of goods and services, on imports and exports. A major general distinction between forms of taxation is between *progressive* forms (those proportional to income or wealth, e.g. income tax) and *regressive* forms (those levied at a flat rate, e.g. a poll tax). Historically, struggles by governments to increase state revenues, especially to fund WARFARE, were a major factor in state formation. As well as raising revenue, modern governments have also used changes in taxation ('fiscal policy') as an instrument of control over the economy, or to inhibit undesirable social activities (e.g. smoking). In modern times, taxation has been frequently used as a main means of *redistribution* of income and wealth. However, the extent to which redistribution actually occurs as the result of taxation is debated. In the UK, for example, it is clear that some elements of redistribution through taxation benefit the better-off more than they do poorer sections of the community (e.g. tax relief on mortgages, or educational grants). Overall, even with redistribution, the poor pay a greater proportion of their incomes in taxes than other social groups. See also FISCAL CRISIS IN THE CAPITALIST STATE, STATE EXPENDITURES.

taxonomy the theory and practice of CLASSIFICATION. As a scientific procedure taxonomy has been especially prominent in biology (e.g. hierarchical formal classificatory systems such as that of Linnaeus). Some proposed classifications of societies in sociology have used such classificatory systems as models (e.g. the work of Herbert SPENCER and W. G. RUNCIMAN). Although argument has raged in biology and elsewhere as to whether taxonomies should be seen as 'natural' or 'imposed', the only answer that can be given is that taxonomies are theory-relative, that when theories change taxonomies will also change, as in the move from pre- to post-Darwinian biology.

Taylorism see SCIENTIFIC MANAGEMENT.

technical composition of capital see ORGANIC COMPOSITION OF CAPITAL.

technological determinism the assumption that technology is both autonomous and has determinate effects on society. Technology is seen as political and as an INDEPENDENT VARIABLE in social change. This assumption is criticized for ignoring the social processes and choices which guide the use of technology and the variety of possible social arrangements which coexist with different types of technology. Marx s famous phrase – 'the handmill gives you society with the feudal lord; the steam-mill, society with the industrial capitalist' – is sometimes used (mistakenly) as an example of technological determinism. MARX, however, saw technology as intimately related to the social relations of production (compare HISTORICAL MATERIALISM). Technological determinism is associated with neoevolutionary theories which give technology primacy in the analysis of social change (see NEOEVOLUTIONISM, POSTINDUSTRIAL SOCIETY, CONVERGENCE), and empirical studies in the SOCIOLOGY OF WORK which describe the 'effects' of technology. See also CULTURAL LAG.

technology the practical application of knowledge and use of techniques in productive activities. This definition reflects a sociological concern with technology as a social product which incorporates both the 'hardware' of human artefacts such as tools and machines and the knowledge and ideas involved in different productive activities. Such knowledge need not depend upon science as its driving force: for example, the relatively simple forms of mechanization associated with the early industrial revolution. More recent developments in energy production and information technology may, however, depend upon innovations derived from organized science, (see also NEW TECHNOLOGY.) Sometimes technology is referred to in the narrow sense as machines, whereas wider definitions include productive systems as a whole and even work organization and the division of labour. The narrow definition tends to treat technology as autonomous and ignore the social processes involved in the design and choice of technology; more inclusive definitions make it difficult to distinguish between the technology and the social arrangements with which it is related. (See also SOCIOLOGY OF SCIENCE, TECHNOLOGICAL DETERMINISM.)

The role of technology in social change has been a longstanding issue in sociology, from Marx's analysis of the FORCES AND RELATIONS OF PRODUCTION to theories of INDUSTRIALIZATION, MODERNIZATION and POSTINDUSTRIAL/INFORMATION SOCIETY. These latter theories were developed in the 1960s and were based upon neoevolutionary assumptions. Technology was accorded a key determining role in shaping the social structure of advanced industrial societies. (See CONVERGENCE, CULTURAL LAG.)

In industrial sociology and the sociology of work, technology has also been identified as a key determining factor for work organization and ALIENATION. This has involved the classification of different types or levels of technology of which the most important have included:
(a) Blauner's (1964) classification of four types of technology – craft, machine-minding, assembly-line and process or automation. Blauner's inverted 'U' curve of alienation suggests that alienation is low in craft industries, reaches a peak in assembly-line technology, as in the car industry, and declines again with automation. His work has been criticized empirically and for its TECHNOLOGICAL DETERMINISM, especially by 'social action' theorists (Silverman, 1970; Goldthorpe, 1966);
(b) Woodward's (1970) classification of three types of production system based upon degree of technical complexity – small-batch and unit production, large-batch and mass production and finally process production. Each type was related to different organizational characteristics: for example, mass production led to the most bureaucratic form of authority structure. Different types of technology were seen to require appropriate organizational structures for optimum 'efficiency' (see also CONTINGENCY THEORY; compare SOCIOTECHNICAL SYSTEMS APPROACH).

Both Blauner and Woodward suggest an optimistic approach to technological change with the development of automation, reflected in new types of skilled work, less rigid work organization and increased job satisfaction. However, the debate about automation in the 1960s has now been subject to extensive theoretical and empirical reappraisal on the basis of research into information technologies. In contrast, LABOUR PROCESS theory, based upon a Marxist framework, has adopted a more critical perspective towards technology. Technical change is analysed as the product of capitalist control of the labour process rather than a politically neutral, autonomous development. Braverman's (1974) analysis of technology in the labour process was based upon Bright's (1958) classification of technology into 17 levels which progressively substitute machines for manual and then mental skills (see also DESKILLING). This critical analysis of technology is also evident in the work of the FRANKFURT SCHOOL and HABERMAS in particular, in which technology and 'technical rationality' is seen as a form of ideology.

technostructure the technical and bureaucratic class which GALBRAITH (1967) regards as replacing the previously dominant capitalist class (of private owners and entrepreneurs) within modern industrial societies. See also SEPARATION OF OWNERSHIP AND CONTROL, MANAGERIAL REVOLUTION, SERVICE CLASS.

teleology 1 (from the Greek *telos*, purpose) originally, the conception that all things have their own natural purposes (e.g. a stone thrown in the air which falls to the ground).
2 (later) the ultimate purpose of things, the doctrine of 'final causes', e.g. the doctrine that everything is God's design.
3 (more generally, including its use in sociology) any theory or account which suggests that the phenomena of nature or social phenomena can be explained not only by their prior causes but also by the end-states or purposes to which they are directed. As such, teleological accounts and explanations

include both PURPOSIVE EXPLANATIONS and FUNCTIONAL(IST) EXPLANATIONS. Also included are some forms of developmental and EVOLUTIONARY THEORY.

4 the process or processes by which teleological end-states are approached or achieved.

While teleological accounts in senses 1 or 2 fall largely outside social science, those in sense 3 remain widely used in everyday life and in both the physical and the social sciences. A central issue is whether in their acceptable forms, teleological explanations are reducible to more conventional causal accounts. Doctrines of 'historical inevitability', human destiny, etc. have been especially controversial. See also TELEOLOGICAL EXPLANATION.

teleological explanation EXPLANATIONS which have the form 'A occurs for the sake of B' (A. Woodfield, 1981). Three main forms of teleological explanation can be identified (see also TELEOLOGY):

(a) PURPOSIVE EXPLANATION, which is concerned with the goal-directed behaviour of animals, especially human beings, e.g. explanations in terms of purposes, motives, reasons, etc.;

(b) FUNCTIONAL(IST) EXPLANATIONS of biological or societal characteristics, explained: (i) as the result of a natural or social selection, and (ii) in terms of their continuing contribution (see FUNCTION) to the working and persistence of the plant, animal, society, etc. in question (see also SYSTEM, SYSTEMS THEORY, EVOLUTIONARY THEORY);

(c) accounts of the working of machines which relate to the design and purpose of the machine, including machines that 'behave' or 'function in an animal-like way (see also CYBERNETICS).

Everyone accepts that human beings act purposively. Furthermore, in explaining human social action it is clear that a knowledge of actors' beliefs and values will often do much to 'explain' their actions. The issue that arises is whether teleological explanations in this sense can suffice in sociology (as some sociologists and philosophers suggest, e.g. WINCH) or whether further, even wholly different, explanations are required for adequate sociological explanation, including the second type of teleological explanation(s) or causal explanations of other kinds (see SOCIAL FACTS AS THINGS, BEHAVIOURISM).

There is little disagreement that functional and evolutionary forms of teleological explanation are appropriately used in explanations of animal behaviour and of the biological realm generally. Usually it is argued that 'teleological' functional and evolutionary explanations are no more than one form of causal explanation. Proposed teleological explanations which involve the end-states or end-goals of societies have been far more controversial, for it is often argued that societies have neither aims nor needs apart from the aims and needs of individual human beings (see also METHODOLOGICAL INDIVIDUALISM). Against this, the view that functionalist and evolutionary accounts have a legitimate place in sociology continues strongly supported in many areas of sociology.

Other examples of general theories having a teleological element include Hegelian theory (see HEGEL) and MARXISM. In these cases the attempt is made to identify a general direction of history, in terms of which particular events can be understood. While much criticized (compare DIALECTICAL MATERIALISM, EPISODIC CHARACTERIZATION, POSTMODERNISM), the idea of a directionality in human history still figures in the work of many sociologists (see PROGRESS, EMANCIPATORY THEORY).

television (TV) (from a compression of the Greek *tele*, meaning far and distant, and *vision* (from Latin) the faculty of seeing) the apparatus for transmitting images and sounds, arguably the most culturally significant phenomenon of the late 20th century. The importance of television is so not simply because of its impact on LEISURE patterns, nor because of its purported effect on, among other things, violent behaviour, reading abilities and family relationships, nor even because of its ability to change conceptions of space and time and stimulate global awareness, but also because of its central role in the perpetuation of CONSUMERISM (see also ADVERTISING).

In 1949 less than 2% of homes in Britain and the USA had TV sets; now over 99% do. The time spent watching TV varies across age, class, gender and other factors. A popular soap opera in Britain will typically draw 13 million viewers, or about one quarter of the population. A global event, like the Super Bowl in the USA may attract 100 million viewers in the USA alone, and billions around the world. During such an event an advertiser will pay $900,000 for a 30-second commercial. This is crucial, for advertisers rather than viewers are the main customers television companies seek to accommodate. Commentators have suggested that TV networks rent out viewers to advertisers.

Apart from scaremongering critics who accuse TV of fostering all manner of unwanted behaviour, more thoughtful writers such as Neil Postman (*Amusing Ourselves to Death*, 1985) have bemoaned the passing of typography as the dominant cultural medium and likened TV to Huxley's 'soma' which induces an agreeable state of euphoria, but which drains critical powers. This view has much in common with earlier theorists from such diverse sources as the FRANKFURT SCHOOL OF CRITICAL THEORY and the Columbia School at New York: they agreed that TV, along with other MASS MEDIA OF COMMUNICATION, was politically soporific and geared to the maintenance of the status quo.

More recently, the rise of DISCOURSE ANALYSIS has led to a reorientation, with more emphasis laid on the role of the viewer in *reading*, rather than just absorbing TV's material. In the view of researchers like John Fiske (*Television Culture*, 1987), reading television involves viewers in creating *meaning:* they engage with the programme's text in an interpretative activity that shapes the discourse. While this has permitted a more active conception of the viewer, it has also diverted attention away from 'big' issues like the way in which TV influences our public behaviour, in particular our spending habits.

Tel Quel Group the group of French academics who edited the avant-garde literary journal *Tel Quel* which was influential in the development of STRUCTURALISM and SEMIOTICS in the 1960s (amongst them were Roland BARTHES and Julia KRISTEVA).

tendency to declining rate of profit (MARXISM) a long-term process identified by MARX as inherent in capitalism and linked to the appearance of recurrent, and deepening, economic crises. As more capital is invested in machinery, raw materials and other constant capital (see CONSTANT AND VARIABLE CAPITAL) in order to increase the competitiveness of individual capitalists, so others are forced to do the same. Thus the ORGANIC COMPOSITION OF CAPITAL in the capitalist economy as a whole increases with more value embodied in constant capital, and proportionately less in variable capital, labour power. According to the LABOUR THEORY OF VALUE, it is only labour power which creates new value in the production process and it is this from which surplus value is derived. Profit is derived from surplus value. Thus the argument is that with more capital as constant capital, which does not create new value, the rate of surplus value and hence of profit declines. As expanded accumulation (see ACCUMULATION (OR EXPANDED OR EXTENDED REPRODUCTION) OF CAPITAL) depends on the availability of surplus value for reinvestment, the declining rate of profit is associated with the emergence of crises and the conditions for the revolutionary overthrow of capitalism. It is important to emphasize that Marx is speaking of rates, and the absolute amount of profit may nevertheless rise, and in a capitalist economy as a whole, and not just isolated capitalist enterprises.

Here as elsewhere Marx sees a tendency, but there can be important factors counteracting it. These include increasing the rate of

EXPLOITATION by decreasing wages and decreasing the value of constant capital. Marx suggested that the organic composition of capital rises faster than these counteracting tendencies although he does not show how.

Several arguments have been made against Marx's analysis. It depends upon acceptance of the labour theory of value. Empirically it has proved difficult to test Marx's arguments, and the rate of profit has been maintained via a variety of mechanisms, many not envisaged by Marx. Short-term falls in the rate of profit have generally been overcome even if this has involved severe social dislocation. Further, even if rates of profit do show cyclical tendencies to rise and fall, it has by no means been established that this is for reasons outlined by Marx, and most current analyses start from different conceptual bases than the Marxian, for example KEYNESIAN ECONOMICS or MONETARISM.

terms of trade the changing overall ratio of the prices (or VALUES) a country must pay for the goods and services it imports and the prices (or values) it is able to obtain for the goods and services it exports. This is usually measured by a quotient obtained by dividing an index number of the prices of goods and services sold by an index number of those obtained. In recent decades, a deterioration in the terms of trade between developed and less developed countries has posed a persistent problem for the latter, brought about by, e.g.:
(a) the substitution of agricultural products by synthetic, industrially produced replacements; and
(b) the 'income elasticity' (see ELASTICITY OF SUPPLY AND DEMAND) for foodstuffs (i.e. people in developed societies can eat only so much food). Efforts to overcome the problem of adverse terms of trade for many of the goods produced by poorer countries include the diversification of their pattern of production for international markets, but this, if it can be achieved at all, is a long-term process in which some developing nations (e.g. those richer in natural resources, and achieving relative political stability) are more successful than others. See also INTERNATIONAL TRADE, UNEQUAL EXCHANGE.

territorial imperative the tendency of individuals or groups of individuals to protect their own territories (Ardrey, 1967). While the 'territorial behaviour' of some birds and animals is well established (see ETHOLOGY), the notion that some human behaviour is closely analogous, i.e. instinctive, is treated with much scepticism in sociology, along with other such suggestions made by SOCIOBIOLOGY.

territory the geographical area under the formal jurisdiction or control of a recognized political AUTHORITY. GIDDENS (1985) distinguished between the jurisdiction of modern NATION STATES, where the *borders* are strictly demarcated and highly administered, and the much more loosely defined and often contested and ill-defined *frontiers* of preindustrial empires. He sees this as an exemplification of the much greater control over time and space possessed by modern governments (see TIME-SPACE DISTANCIATION).

terrorism a form of politically motivated action combining psychological (fear inducing) and physical (violent action) components carried out by individuals or small groups with the aim of inducing communities or states to meet the terrorists' demands. The concept remains notoriously difficult to define with any precision. The major problem is summarized in the adage that 'one person's terrorist is another person's freedom fighter'. The issue is complicated further because some would argue that acts of terrorism do not belong exclusively to the politically motivated but may also be employed by criminals and psychopaths. However, *political terrorism* can be thought of as the use of violence by a group either acting on behalf of, or in opposition to, an established political authority.

In broad terms, it is possible to identify three major types of politically motivated terrorist behaviour:
(a) revolutionary terrorism;

(b) sub-revolutionary terrorism; and (c) terrorist action which is essentially repressive in nature (see also TERRORIST ORGANIZATIONS). Thus it is also necessary to differentiate between terrorism which is perpetrated by the state itself (see STATE TERRORISM) and actions which are undertaken by groups in pursuit of political change. Finally, it is possible to identify 'INTERNATIONAL TERRORISM', i.e. acts of terrorism which transcend the boundaries of one state. The tactics adopted by terrorists have been widespread. including kidnapping, bombs in public places, the 'hijacking' of aeroplanes, attacks on property, the extortion of ransom, raids on banks, and state oppression, arrests and torture.

Rubenstein (1987) suggests that terrorism usually springs from the political alienation of the INTELLIGENTSIA from both the ruling class and the masses. The former engages in repression and the latter is indifferent. This combination is particularly likely to appear in colonial situations although it may occur in any country where a social crisis generated by rapid and uneven economic development isolates intellectuals from the masses for whom they wish to act as political spokesman. The other precondition for terrorism occurs when a reform movement collapses or when it appears that such movement will not succeed in restructuring society. For advocates of terrorism, individual or small-group violence becomes the only means that can expose the fragility of the ruling class, raise the consciousness of the masses, and attract new members and supporters to the movement. Rubenstein shares the Marxist view that terrorists have rarely gained mass working-class support and have usually been ineffective in making social revolutions. As an instrument of political change, however, terrorism has often been effective, e.g. as an adjunct of nationalist movements.

terrorist organizations those organizations which exist specifically to engage in the pursuit of political goals by acts of TERRORISM. Such groups may either be organized by the state – STATE TERRORISM – or directly opposed to the state. Terrorist organizations have, however, a wide range of goals and aims. Their primary motivation may be nationalist (e.g. the Irish Republican Army), ideological (e.g. the Red Brigade), single issues (e.g. Animal Liberation Front) or religious (e.g. Islamic Jihad).

tertiary sector see SERVICE SECTOR.

text any written representation (e.g. books), or by extension other recorded symbolic representation (films, television programmes, art forms). Unlike 'speech', a text can have an independent existence beyond the writer and the context of its production. Rather than the authorial voice and the pre-given structures of LANGUAGE being decisive (as it sometimes seems for SAUSSURE), the text takes on a life of its own, so that meaning is gained from the relations between texts (intertexuality) – see also STRUCTURALISM, DECENTRED SELF. For DERRIDA (see also DECONSTRUCTION), any assumption that a text can have a definite meaning is misplaced, given that signifiers are always 'floating'. That texts do not simply 'assert their meanings' is a point of view made much of in modern research into MASS MEDIA OF COMMUNICATIONS such as TELEVISION. See also DECONSTRUCTION, POSTSTRUCTURALISM. Compare HERMENEUTICS.

Thanatos the death instinct in FREUD's theory of personality. Thanatos involves all instincts which are destructive, such as aggression. It is the opposite of EROS, the life instinct.

Thatcherism the economic and social policies associated with the British prime minister (1979–90) Margaret Thatcher, which replaced an era of KEYNESIAN ECONOMICS and 'consensualist' politics and CORPORATISM in the UK with an emphasis on MONETARISM and market mechanisms and a more confrontational style of politics, especially in the introduction of greater controls over trade unions.

Sociologists have debated the political character and implications of Thatcherism. While Stuart HALL et al. (eds) (*Policing the Crisis*, 1978, and *The Politics of Thatcherism*,

1983) have characterized the political style of Thatcherism as involving a marriage of free-market ideology, strong state, and 'authoritarian populism', Jessop et al., *Thatcherism*, (1989) present what they regard as a 'more rounded account of Thatcherism', analysable in terms of the interrelated implications of its 'social base', 'accumulation strategy', 'state strategy', and 'hegemonic project'. Thatcherism is seen as the Conservative Party's response to the continuing long-term relative decline in the British economy and in the capacity of the state to regulate economic and social relations (see also FISCAL CRISIS IN THE CAPITALIST STATE). In these circumstances, a new social base is sought in 'popular capitalism' (e.g. home ownership, a widening of share ownership based on PRIVATIZATION), while adopting an accumulation strategy which (in contrast with Germany or Japan) involves opening the economy to international capitalism. The main 'state strategy' associated with these moves is the fostering of 'neoliberal' state forms, including a rolling back of corporatist arrangements. Finally, a 'hegemonic project', involving acceptance of a degree of division into 'two nations' (e.g. the rejection of a 'social contract') and the building of a populist emphasis on law and order and *raison d'état*, has tended to replace the social inclusiveness associated with the 'postwar compromise'. The question remains whether this is too negative an assessment of Thatcherism, whether Thatcherism may succeed in building a long-term basis for its own continuation, including the achievement of lasting improvements in the performance of the British economy, genuine benefits for consumers and improvements in industrial relations recognized on all sides, or whether there are weaknesses in its economic and social strategies which will provoke a reaction.

theocracy government by a priesthood.

theodicy theological explanations for the existence of suffering and evil in the world despite divine presence. As used by WEBER, the concept refers to religious doctrines which legitimate social inequalities, or see purpose in evil, or promise compensation for suffering, e.g. the Hindu doctrine of kharma (see CASTE).

theories of the middle range 'theories that lie between the minor but necessary working hypotheses that evolve in abundance in day-to-day research and the all-inclusive systematic efforts to develop unified theory that will explain all the observed uniformities of social behaviour, organization and social change' (MERTON, 1949). As identified by Merton, compared with 'general theories' which may be remote from particular classes of social behaviour, such middle-range theories are 'close enough to observed data to be incorporated in propositions that permit empirical testing'. The construction of such theories was an important part of Merton's doctrine that in sociology pieces of empirical research were often too much divorced from one another. In the course of his own career in sociology Merton has been responsible for the development of important middle-range theories in many areas, including contributions to the theory of REFERENCE GROUPS, BUREAUCRACY, MASS COMMUNICATIONS, many of these represented in his *Social Theory and Social Structure* (1949 and subsequent editions). Compare MILLS, ABSTRACTED EMPIRICISM.

theory 1 (in physical science and in social science) any set of hypotheses or propositions, linked by logical or mathematical arguments, which is advanced to explain an area of empirical reality or type of phenomenon. See also FORMAL THEORY, MODEL.

2 in a looser sense, any abstract general account of an area of reality, usually including the use of formulation of general concepts. See also EXPLANATION, SOCIOLOGICAL THEORY.

Even in the physical sciences, the importance of theories in the strict logical or mathematical form is challenged by some philosophers and historians of science (see SCIENTIFIC PARADIGM, KUHN, FEYERABEND).

theory-laden (potentially, of any empirical assertion) relative to (i.e. presupposing) theoretical (e.g. ontological, epistemological, paradigmatic, etc.) assumptions. See also SCIENTIFIC PARADIGM, INCOMMENSURABILITY.

theory of games mathematical accounts of the hypothetical decision-making behaviour of two or more persons in situations where: (a) each has a finite choice between two or more courses of action ('strategies'); (b) the interests of each may be partly or wholly in conflict; (c) and for each person, numerical values can be attached to the 'utility' of every combination of outcomes. Developed especially by Von Neumann (see Von Neumann and Morgenstern (1944)), the theory of games builds on more conventional forms of rational modelling in ECONOMICS. Various real-world situations (e.g. the arms race, military alliances) possess at least some of the properties that allow them to be analysed in such terms. However, although it has had some influence on the way in which STRATEGIC INTERACTION is discussed in sociology (see also RATIONAL CHOICE THEORY, EXPLOITATION), the abstract mathematical theory of games makes assumptions, about the measurement of social utilities and the availability of information to actors, which in the social sciences are only infrequently justified. See also PRISONERS' DILEMMA, ZERO-SUM GAME, RATIONALITY, FREE RIDER.

theory of knowledge see EPISTEMOLOGY. See also SOCIOLOGY OF KNOWLEDGE, SCIENCE, SOCIOLOGY OF SCIENCE.

theory relativity the situation in which scientific terms and propositions are held to possess meaning only in the context of particular theories, SCIENTIFIC PARADIGMS, etc. See also INCOMMENSURABILITY, FORMS OF LIFE.

thick description (ANTHROPOLOGY) the provision of 'densely textured facts' about a social context, on the basis of which more general assertions about the role of culture in social life can be sustained (C. Geertz, *The Interpretation of Cultures*, 1973). Like the ETHNOMETHODOLOGISTS, Geertz's interpretive anthropology regards a minute attention to the fine details of everyday social life as the only feasible basis for more extended generalizations, but he makes no assumption that any 'thick description', however detailed, can ever be complete.

third sector a recent term for the voluntary sector of the economy, along side the state and capitalist private sector. In the UK the development of this sector has been encouraged by recent governments, both left and right, as a way of contracting, direct state provision.

Third Way the conception, as formulated by Anthony GIDDENS (*The Third Way- the Renewal of Social Democracy*, 1998, and the *Third Way and Its Critics*, 2000), advocating a 'renewal of social democracy' that moves beyond the parameters of the old Left-Right division of politics and meets the new demands of a global age (see also GLOBALIZATION). The proposals include: reform of the WELFARE STATE and the creation of a SOCIAL INVESTMENT STATE, some regulation of global financial markets, and the potential for a new global CITIZENSHIP. Third Way ideas have influenced both Clinton's Democratic Party in the US and Blair's NEW LABOUR in the UK. They are also being debated in the EU.

Third World countries mainly found in Asia, Africa and Latin America and the Caribbean, many having been colonies until the mid-20th-century, and today manifesting lower levels of INDUSTRIALIZATION and general living standards than the advanced industrial countries.

The term was first used in the early 1950s and taken up by Third World political leaders engaged in independence movements against European COLONIALISM. It signified the positive idea that politically and economically their countries would develop in ways different both from the *first world*, Western Europe and the US, and the *second world* of the USSR and the Soviet Bloc. Subsequently, the term has become associated with negative aspects of poor living standards, great social inequality, economic stagnation and political instability such that many people living in these countries now resent the use of the term. Alternatives preferred by some authors include underdeveloped, NEOCOLONIAL, *less developed countries* (LDCs), oppressed nations, peripheral or nonaligned countries. The recent emergence of NEWLY INDUSTRIALIZING COUNTRIES alongside countries that are stagnating or becoming poorer (sometimes referred to as the FOURTH WORLD), and the further division between socialist and non-socialist countries have highlighted the issue of whether such a blanket term is useful for referring to such a diverse range of countries. However, the term still has wide social scientific and general usage. Various attempts have been made to distinguish the Third World both qualitatively and quantitatively (see Thomas et al., 1994), and Worsley (1984) has defended its utility. See also SOCIOLOGY OF DEVELOPMENT, DEPENDENCY, UNDER-DEVELOPMENT, CENTRE AND PERIPHERY.

Thomas, William (1863–1947) pioneer American sociologist, founder member of the CHICAGO SCHOOL. His major work (with Znaniecki) is *The Polish Peasant in Europe and America* (1918–20). He is best known for his use of the LIFE HISTORY as a method of reflecting social history in the biographies of individuals. A theme running through his work is the link between culture and personality, explored through a method that places the individual at the centre of the analysis. He also formulated the idea of a SOCIAL ACTOR's definition of the situation', explained in his much quoted aphorism 'If men define situations as real, they are real in their consequences'.

Thompson, Edward P. (1924–93) British Marxist social historian, also associated with the NEW LEFT and as an activist leader of the Campaign for Nuclear Disarmament. His reputation as an outstanding historian rests especially on *The Making of the English Working Class* (1963), a seminal approach to historiography which helped to inspire a new generation of labour and social historians to focus on 'history from below'. This consists of an history not of the activities of political élites and dominant classes but a careful reconstruction of the consciousness and action of individuals and groups usually previously hidden from view in conventional history. It is a feature of Thompson's historical writing – which also includes *Whigs and Hunters* (1975) – that as well as reporting the past, it is also an engagement with the present, as in his influential article 'Time, Work-Discipline and Industrial Capitalism' (1967) where he speculates on the possibility of a synthesis of old and new time-senses in a future socialist society. Thompson belonged to the humanist wing of Marxism, emphasizing the role of human AGENCY, which in *The Poverty of Theory and Other Essays* (1978) led him to take issue with the structuralist Marxism of Louis ALTHUSSER. Thompson's writings on nuclear disarmament, e.g. *Protest and Survive* (1981) and *Beyond the Cold War* (1982), stressed the scope for breaking free from COLD WAR logic.

thought experiments see IDEAL TYPE.

Tilly, Charles (1926–) influential US historical sociologist, and head of the Center for Research on Social Organizations based at the University of Michigan. Tilly's work is remarkable, in that it has interested historians and sociologists alike. His methods, in works such as *From Mobilization to Revolution* (1978) and *Strikes in France, 1830–1968* (with Edward Shorter) (1974), has involved the assembly of large data sets and the testing of hypotheses over time. His historical inquiries have focused especially on the exploration of changes in the patterns of 'collective action' – including violent political action – which are associated with long-term structural transformations of society such as urbanization, industrialization, the expansion of the state, and the spread of capitalism. Rejecting those conceptions of 'collective action' that emphasize its basis mainly in social disorganization, Tilly's research findings have emphasized instead the increasingly 'strategic' character of such action. Other major works by Tilly include *The Vendée* (1964), regarded by many as his best book, *The Rebellious Century, 1830–1930* (with Louise and Richard Tilly) (1975), *As Sociology Meets History* (1981) and *European Revolution 1492–1992* (1993).

time the continuous passage of existence. Time may be measured with reference to any stable or periodic physical or social process. In the latter case, 'time' will often be stated with reference to clear physical periodicies that determine the units of social division, as for example, 'days' and 'years'. In many other respects, however, the divisions of 'time' (though still stated partly in terms of physical periodicies) depend on a patterning of social events which is relatively independent of such natural periodicies, as is so for 'weeks' or 'hours'. Various forms of generic 'social time' may also be identified, as for example, in the distinctions drawn by GIDDENS between:
(a) the repeated day-to-day *durée* – or 'reversible time' – of everyday social life;
(b) the *longue durée* involved in the persistence, as against the rise and fall, of social institutions and societies;
(c) the 'life span' of the individual – 'irreversible time'.

As well as this, in social life and in sociological and historical accounts an almost infinite number of more specific 'periodizations' can also be noticed, e.g. 'Victorian times', 'the Age of Reason'. See also CLOCK-TIME, TIME – SPACE DISTANCIATION.

Since time always exists as a fourth coordinate of *time-space* in specifying any event, it must obviously be an important component in any sociological account. A number of sociologists recently, however, have suggested that time has been relatively neglected in sociology, in that sociology has often been concerned with static structural models and has tended to neglect the great variety of ways in which social life is both temporally structured and, as the result of social processes occurring in time, socially transformed – see MANN (1986) and GIDDENS (1984). A resurgence of interest in time has been a feature of recent sociology and is also evident in other disciplines (e.g. see TIME-GEOGRAPHY), from which sociology has also drawn.

See also HISTORY, DUALITY OF STRUCTURE, TIME-SPACE EDGES, TIME-SPACE DISTANCIATION, HEIDEGGER.

time and motion study see SCIENTIFIC MANAGEMENT.

time budget studies a method of social inquiry, which requires respondents to keep accurate diaries of their daily activities, e.g. leisure activities over a set period (see Szalai, 1972). Usually respondents are asked to record accurately the activities they engage in at set intervals throughout a particular period, e.g. a day or a week. These data are then analysed to present time budgets of the activities of each individual, enabling an overall statement of the incidence of particular activities to be made, and comparisons to be made between individuals or groups.

time-geography an approach within GEOGRAPHY which focuses on the way in which social events are structured, '*through* time and *across* geographical space' (Hepple, 1985). Pioneered by geographers such as Hagerstrand (1975), the general ideas involved in this approach have been recently introduced into sociological thinking by GIDDENS (see also TIME–SPACE DISTANCIATION).

time series ideally, any set of data in which 'a well-defined quantity is recorded at successive equally-spaced time points over a specific period' (C. Marsh, 1988), e.g. the RETAIL PRICE INDEX. Where the data fail to fulfil all of these strict criteria, e.g. inadequately standardized variables, or gaps in the series, where the recording interval is not equally spaced, one may still speak of a time series if data over time are involved. However, the problems of interpretation of such a series will be much greater. An important source of time-series data is the CENSUS.

time–space distanciation the stretching of social relations and systems across time and space, resulting from advances in human techniques of transport and communications and hence social control (GIDDENS, 1985). See also DISEMBEDDING AND RE-EMBEDDING MECHANISMS.

time-space edges the 'connections, whether

conflictual or symbiotic', that 'exist between societies of different structural types', both *in* space and *across* time (GIDDENS, 1984). All societies are both social systems and at the same time in part constituted by their intersection with other social systems, both other SOCIETIES and INTERSOCIETAL SYSTEMS. The significance of the notion of time-space edges in Giddens' work is that not only the spatial location but also the temporal location in particular societies is seen as profoundly affecting the outcomes of action in these societies. See also WORLD-TIME, EPISODE, EPISODIC CHARACTERIZATION.

Titmuss, Richard (1907–73) British sociologist and influential postwar occupant of the chair of social administration at the LSE. As well as writing about social policy he played a direct role in the formulation of social policy as advisor to the Labour Party and several foreign governments. The central theme of his work is that the provision of social welfare should be more than about ensuring a safety net for the casualties of society. His main works include *Essays on the Welfare State* (1958), *Income Distribution and Social Change* (1962), and *The Gift Relationship* (1970). The last of these works, a study of blood donors, in which he sees the prevalence of 'donorship' as an 'indicator' of 'cultural values and the quality of human relationships' in a particular society, sums up much of what Titmuss stood for (see also GIFT RELATIONSHIP.) His view was that social policy should be aimed at fostering altruistic values and genuine community relations as well as overcoming inequalities and social disadvantage.

Tocqueville, Alexis de (1805–59) French political scientist and member of the Chamber of Deputies, widely considered to be one of the first comparative political and historical sociologists. His analysis of the political experience of America in the 1830s was undertaken in the belief that lessons could be learnt that would be applicable to Europe, especially France. In *Democracy in America* (1835–40) he argued that democracy – the condition of equality – was an irresistible tendency in modern societies, but that unchecked it held considerable dangers for 'liberty', by which he meant responsible self-government based on 'enlightened self-interest'. Democracy, because it tended to undermine all hierarchy and to abolish all intermediary bodies between the individual and society, was likely to be accompanied by two further tendencies: individualism and centralization, which together could lead to tyranny. In America, Tocqueville found these tendencies held in check, though not absent, by two factors. Firstly, the American colonies had been accustomed to self-government. Secondly, through the principle of federalism, the American constitution after the Revolution remained a fragmented one, providing multiple points of access for individuals to participate. Tocqueville's conclusion was that where democracy came without such prior establishment of 'liberty' it was likely to lead to tyranny. It was this scenario which, in *The Old Regime and the French Revolution* (1856), Tocqueville concluded had been enacted in France. Revolutionary France had lacked the conditions which made democracy compatible with liberty, including the lack of a strong middle class. In his comparative analysis of political arrangements Tocqueville especially emphasized what subsequently came to be called POLITICAL CULTURE. His analysis of the preconditions for, and character of, modern democracy strongly influenced later theorists. see DEMOCRACY, INTERMEDIATE GROUPS, PLURALISM, MASS SOCIETY.

token economy see BEHAVIOUR MODIFICATION.

Tönnies, Ferdinand (1855–1936) German sociologist and founder of the German Sociological Association, who is above all remembered for his coining of the terms GEMEINSCHAFT AND GESELLSCHAFT, which was based on a distinction between 'natural will' (*Wesenwille*), including habitual as well as instinctual action, and 'rational will' (*Kurwille*), including INSTRUMENTAL RATIONALITY. Both sets of distinctions were IDEAL TYPES, and were used by Tönnies to analyse historical changes in social organization, including the social problems created by the breakdown of traditional social structures. Tönnies' concepts, and aspects of his thesis of a loss of COMMUNITY in modern societies, are not dissimilar from those of WEBER or, to a lesser extent, MARX. They form one influence on the work of the CHICAGO SCHOOL. They were also one of the sources of PARSONS' formulation of PATTERN VARIABLES.

total institution *or* **total organization** any social organization (including prisons, monasteries, long-stay hospitals, boarding schools, and ships on long voyages) in which the members are required to live out their lives in isolation from wider society (see GOFFMAN, 1961). In contrast with 'normal' social life, in which people live in their own homes and usually work, sleep, eat and engage in leisure activities in a number of different locations, it is characteristic of total organizations that social action is confined to a single location. In these organizations there is no possibility of any complete escape from the administrative rules or values which prevail.

Research has concentrated on the sociological and social psychological consequences (e.g. INSTITUTIONALIZATION) that can arise from this form of life, and which exist for those in superordinate as well as subordinate positions. As suggested by Goffman, various 'mortifications of the self' (e.g. removal of personal possessions), may occur in total institutions (e.g. asylums or prisons), resulting in a reconstruction of the person to fit with the demands of the organization to an extent which could never be achieved in more open social contexts. This reconstruction, however, is never complete. There always remains scope for 'inmate culture' to exert some control over the formal organizational structure of a total organization.

totalitarianism a form of political rule, especially in modern times, in which power is centralized, and above all is able to penetrate into all corners and all aspects of social life.

Benjamin Barber's (1969) assertion that the term has been a 'conceptual harlot … belonging to no one but at the service of all', may be correct. Use of the term has often been heavily overladen with ideology, and often associated with sweeping evaluation rather than careful description and analysis. However, the main characteristics of totalitarian rule compared with previous forms of 'absolute' or despotic rule, and in comparison with most modern forms of democratic government, are clear. They are outlined by Friedrich (1954) as follows:
(a) an ideology of totalism;
(b) a single party committed to the ideology, usually led by one person, who rules as a DICTATOR;
(c) a fully developed secret police;
(d) state monopolistic control of: (i) mass communications, (ii) all organizations, including all economic organizations, and all weapons, the means of violence.

Such a system thus possesses means of SURVEILLANCE and terror on a scale simply unavailable to premodern regimes (compare ABSOLUTISM, ORIENTAL DESPOTISM), the use of which it justifies on grounds of national interest, and in terms of general ideologies, including RACISM, NATIONALISM AND COMMUNISM. (As Tolstoy prophetically observed, 'imagine Genghis Khan with a telephone'.) Because of these ideologies, and since totalitarianism is often based on SOCIAL MOVEMENTS which may enjoy wide support, it will rarely survive if based on force alone.

It is in the sharpness of the distinction often drawn between modern forms of totalitarianism and other modern forms of democratic government that the difficulties lie in use of the concept. One reason why too sharp a distinction is misplaced is that a totalizing tendency, including the use of general systems of surveillance, exists as a feature of all modern states. Furthermore, in totalitarian as well as non-totalitarian regimes, it is an ideology of democracy, in the sense of 'the rule of the many', that acts as a justification for the requirement for involvement and support that exists in both types of regime. In non-totalitarian regimes, of course, such a totalizing tendency is offset by the institutionalized acceptance of political opposition. However, even this distinction can be taken too far, if the assumption is made that no forms of opposition exist or can ever be effective in totalitarian systems. The presence of opposition in some form must be seen as an inherent feature of all systems. Compare LIBERAL DEMOCRACY.

total organization see TOTAL INSTITUTION.

total quality management (TQM) a managerial technique for the pursuit of continuous improvement through strategic, processual and cultural change in organizations. Studies of TQM in the UK suggests that it has a close relationship with Japanese industrial practice and the American 'school of excellence', and that there is considerable variability in the nature and impact of TQM in the UK.

Broadly, optimists regard TQM as having the potential to resolve some of the problems that managers experienced with 'quality circles' (see S Hill, 1991), whilst sceptics point to the disjuncture between the rhetoric and reality of TQM, although they recognize that, in association with the techniques of *human resource management* it may produce changes in behaviour in line with management objectives. Nevertheless, it is suggested that the rhetoric of 'devolution' and 'empowerment' is often undermined by the simultaneous use of forms of control which involve lateral, peer-group pressure and vertical information systems which buttress centralized control. Moreover, sceptics suggest that particular economic, political and cultural features make a full-blown system of TQM unlikely here (see Sewell and Wilkinson, 1992).

total war the form of modern warfare in which whole populations may be subject to mobilization either as soldiers or as labour, and in which whole populations are regarded as legitimate targets. Air warfare is a significant feature of modern warfare compared with the more limited conventional warfare of previous eras. However, the onset of mass CITIZENSHIP, and nationalist ideologies and citizen armies is equally significant.

totem see TOTEMISM.

totemism the practice of symbolically identifying humans with nonhuman objects (usually animals or plants). The classic case of totemism is when a clan claims an animal as a mythological ancestor: however, the term has also been used to cover a wide range of symbolic practices. Functional anthropologists, such as RADCLIFFE-BROWN, (under the influence of DURKHEIM) have explained totems in terms of their being symbols of group solidarity. FREUD, in *Totem and Taboo,* (1913) used the idea of a totem as a mediator between repressed culture and instinctive nature. Later, structural anthropologists, as exemplified by LÉVI-STRAUSS, focused on their capacity to express structures of difference between humans and animals. He argues that totemism, like TABOO, is yet another instance of nature being 'good to think with', that is to say, certain objects possess qualities that express vital features of human experience and are thus used to construct a mythology of the concrete.

trade cycle *or* **business cycle** fluctuating phases in the working of the capitalist economy. Periods of expansion of economic activity (*recovery* or *boom*) are followed by periods of slow-down or contraction (*recession* or *depression*) as economic demand and rates of profit fall. See also ECONOMIC CRISES, LONG-WAVE THEORY.

trade directories books containing the names, addresses and occupations of individuals, produced in the 18th, 19th- and early 20th-centuries for advertising purposes. Trade directories are a useful source of information on the social structure of towns and cities in previous eras. Their value can be enhanced by using them in concert with the 19th-century CENSUS enumeration books.

trade(s) union an employee organization primarily concerned with improving the conditions and rewards of the working lives of its members. Sociological analysis of trade unions has involved:

(a) distinguishing them from other forms of employee organizations;

(b) explaining their emergence, the forms they have taken, the objectives they have pursued, and the strategies they have adopted;
(c) examining trade-union government, levels of member involvement, and trade-union democracy;
(d) consideration of the impact of trade unions on work and wider society.

Internationally, differences in overall patterns of trade-union organization (e.g. number of unions, degree of centralization and involvement in government and level of membership) are striking; sociologists have also been interested in the implications of these differences.

Trade unions can be distinguished from PROFESSIONS, which are fully in control of the content of specific areas of work and often also able to control recruitment, and also from *staff associations*, which, as largely management-sponsored organizations, are often limited to a consultative role (see also UNIONATENESS).

Explanations for the emergence of, and variations in types and objectives of, trade unions have occasioned considerable debate. Fundamentally, however, trade unions can be regarded as attempts to offset the unequal relationship between employees and employers under capitalism (see also CAPITALIST LABOUR CONTRACT). Differences in the manner and degree to which different categories of workers were able to enhance their bargaining capacity accounted for historical differences between different kinds of trade-union organization, e.g. distinctions between 'craft', 'general' and 'industrial' unions. More recently, distinctions between different types of trade union have tended to break down, with the proliferation of new 'market-based unions' (i.e. accepting single union, single status, flexible working, no-strike agreements), and a debate within the trade union movement between 'traditionalists' and 'new realists'. The problems currently facing unions in Britain are those arising from the restructuring of the national and international economy, decline in membership (particularly in manufacturing), anti-trade-union legislation and reduced union political influence (see also CORPORATISM)

Analysis of the internal dynamics of trade unions has been largely concerned with testing MICHELS' thesis that as political organizations grow larger they become less democratic and more conservative (see also IRON LAW OR OLIGARCHY). Conclusive statements on this issue are difficult given the various measures of democracy that exist (e.g. responsive leadership, institutionalized opposition, active participation, effective representation of members' interests). It is clear, however, that variations in levels of 'democracy' are related to the characteristics of the membership of a union (e.g. social status) and the context in which the union operates (see also LIPSET).

A main strand of sociological debate about the social impact and effectiveness of trade unions has concerned their implications for CLASS CONSCIOUSNESS and whether they constitute any kind of threat to capitalism. Explanations for what are in fact usually seen as relatively limited trade-union objectives – at least in Britain – have focused on:
(a) the way in which they have segmented the labour movement by organizing around the stratification of occupations;
(b) the emergence of institutions through which conflict has become institutionalized and regulated; and
(c) union bureaucracy and member apathy.
See also INDUSTRIAL CONFLICT, INDUSTRIAL RELATIONS, STRIKES, INFLATION, TRADE-UNION CONSCIOUSNESS.

trade-union consciousness the limited, sectionalist, less than revolutionary, social-democratic consciousness which, according to Lenin, the working class spontaneously develops from the narrow 'conviction that it is necessary to combine in unions, fight employers and strive to compel governments to pass legislation' (LENIN, 1902). Since these ameliorative objectives serve to impede working-class unity and ensure subservience to bourgeois ideology, the theoretical and philosophical insights of intellectuals are necessary for the development of class consciousness. This thesis has influenced subsequent debates about TRADE UNIONS in capitalist societies. See also CLASS CONSCIOUSNESS.

traditional action see TYPES OF SOCIAL ACTION.

traditional authority see LEGITIMATE AUTHORITY.

traditional society a nonindustrial, predominantly rural society which is presumed to be static and contrasted with a modern, changing, INDUSTRIAL SOCIETY. The concept is widely used in the social sciences, but over the last few decades has come to be seen as very problematic and therefore avoided by many sociologists. The problems involved in its usages are:
(a) it is a term which has been used to describe a wide variety of societies which in fact differ markedly from each other (see AGRARIAN SOCIETY, TRIBAL SOCIETY, ANCIENT SOCIETY, FEUDAL SOCIETY);
(b) whilst the rates of SOCIAL CHANGE in such societies are slower than in industrial societies, it is erroneous to accept that no change occurs;
(c) the term gained usage within sociology when systematic knowledge of nonindustrial societies was weak, and increased knowledge no longer warrants the usage;
(d) it is associated with MODERNIZATION theory which has been criticized for delineating an oversimplified contrast between traditional and modern;
(e) the oversimplifications involved in the term lead either to a romanticized or a pejorative view of such societies.

An example of the problematic use of the term is when commentators argue that contemporary Japanese society differs from Western European society because of the stronger survival of traditional society within Japan. This ignores the facts that all societies carry features from the past in their present social arrangements, no societies have complete breaks between so-called traditional and modern, and that such features from the past may be more striking to Western observers because of their unfamiliarity, thus adding Eurocentricity to the list of problems. Further, in the case of Japan, in the 19th century the state actively decided to promote what were seen as aspects of traditional Japan for political purposes and for the establishment of Japanese national identity. Thus what is seen as 'traditional' is as likely to be an invention (see Hobsbawm and Ranger, 1983).

trait theory a form of personality theory which describes individual differences in terms of a number of relatively enduring independent *traits*. A trait is a bi-polar construct (e.g. clever – stupid; mean – generous), often represented by a scale on which individuals can be rated. Trait theories vary largely according to the number of independent traits believed to be necessary to provide a complete description of personality. Personality inventories provide a picture or profile of these trait scores, derived from responses to self-report questions. Examples include the Sixteen Personality Factor Questionnaire (16PF) (Cattell, 1963), and the California Psychological Inventory (CPI) (Gough, 1957). Indirect measurement of traits is also possible (see PROJECTIVE TESTS). A complementary view of personality is provided by *type theories* which characterize individuals by one of a much smaller number of dominant traits or types (see EXTRAVERSION).

transcendental argument (PHILOSOPHY) the assertion of 'what must be the case' (i.e. can be established A PRIORI) on the presupposition that we do have knowledge of the world. Thus KANT claimed to have established the concepts and principles that organize all our experience and are logically prior to this experience. Similarly Bhaskar (1989) argues for his version of scientific REALISM on the premise that it is possible to state what, ontologically speaking, the world 'must be like prior to any scientific investigation of it' for any science, including a social science, to be possible.

transcendental signifier see DECONSTRUCTION.

transsexual a person who experiences a profound and constant dislocation between his or her physiological sex and his or her ascribed GENDER. Sometimes there is a desire to change physiological sex so that this comes into line with subjective feelings of gender identity. The term 'transsexual' was introduced in 1953.

transsexualism the belief that dislocations between sex and gender can be remedied by a surgical restructuring of the sex organs. Radical feminists have been critical of this belief and the associated practices of the 'Transsexual Empire'. From this perspective transsexualism is primarily concerned with 'artifactual femaleness' and arises from an ideology fraught with normative assumptions (see J. Raymond, *The Transsexual Empire*, 1980).

transformational grammar see CHOMSKY.

transformational model of social activity a model of social activity advanced by Bhaskar (1979) based on the Aristotelian view that any productive activity presupposes both an *efficient* cause and a *material* cause. In this model, the social forms pre-existing social action constitute the material cause, and social action the means by which this pre-existing reality is either reproduced or transformed (see also STRUCTURE AND AGENCY). It is on the basis of this model of 'causal powers' that Bhaskar bases his 'realist' argument concerning both the possibility and ontological limits of sociological naturalism (see also SCIENTIFIC REALISM). See also TRANSCENDENTAL ARGUMENT.

transgression the practice of engaging with, and challenging, areas of knowledge and DISCOURSE by exploring their historically contingent conditions of emergence. For FOUCAULT transgression can be liberatory because it shows how taken-for-granted aspects of the self and subjectivity are neither universal nor necessary and are therefore open to change. It must be noted, however that the Foucauldean practice of transgression does not attempt to criticize or oppose by claiming that a true, deeper self lies beneath various historical layers of prejudices and assumptions. This would constitute a form of ESSENTIALISM, inferring that an unchanging set of qualities exists that can be discovered and to which one must then adhere. Here, one set of constraints is merely replaced with another. To avoid this, Foucault draws on Nietzsche's views of history.

transhumance the seasonal movement of human groups in search of pastures; for example, the movement from dry season to wet season pastures undertaken by the Nuer. See also PASTORALISM, NOMADS, HERDING SOCIETY.

transition from feudalism to capitalism the process in Western Europe between the 15th and 18th centuries by which feudal society was succeeded by capitalist society. The term is most often associated with Marxist approaches but a distinctive Weberian approach can also be identified.

Marxists disagree about the decisive factors involved in the process. MARX identified two main factors: the emergence of autonomous craft manufacturing in the feudal towns around which capital developed; and the growth of overseas trade, particularly with the emergence of trade with the Americas in the 16th century and the emergence of merchant capital. The development was limited while labourers were tied to the land either as SERFS or independent PEASANTS. In England the enclosures movement forced the peasantry off the land, thus providing a labour supply for the towns and wage-labour on the land. Other European countries were slower in developing this 'free' labour force. Marx also spoke of the feudal aristocracy being replaced by the new BOURGEOISIE, but more recent analyses have shown that this is an oversimplification, especially in England where sections of the aristocracy became capitalist landlords and later became involved in industrial capitalism. Subsequent Marxist debates have centred around whether the growth of trade, the transformation of the labour force, or class conflict within FEUDALISM were the most important aspects of this process. (See Hilton (ed.), 1976, and

Aston and Philipin (eds.), 1985, for two collections of key debates.)

The Weberian approach lays great emphasis upon the political changes in Western European feudalism, drawing on WEBER's observation that the key contradiction was between the attempts at centralization by the monarchy, and the local and regional powers invested in the feudal lords. Part of that contradiction was also expressed in the growth of towns as administrative and trading centres. Further, WEBER's thesis on the role of the PROTESTANT ETHIC introduces the role of beliefs in explaining social and economic change largely missing from the Marxist debate. However, Weber, in emphasizing such socioeconomic changes as the growth of trade, and transformations of labour force, should not be contrasted in any simplistic fashion with Marx.

This proviso is reflected in the appearance of recent works which examine the process drawing on both analytical traditions. Thus Perry ANDERSON (1974a & b) develops a Marxist approach which relies heavily on Weberian insights into the political contradictions and the role of the Christian Church, and Michael MANN (1986) provides an analysis drawing widely on both. See also CAPITALISM, SOCIAL CHANGE.

transition to socialism see CAPITALISM AND CAPITALIST MODE OF PRODUCTION.

translation the transformation of SIGNS and meanings, (especially languages), where these are initially unknown or alien, into a known and familiar set of signs and meanings. The question of the extent to which the ideas and language of one society or culture can have an adequate expression in the language of another society or culture has been an especially important one in SOCIAL ANTHROPOLOGY (e.g. see SAPIR-WHORF HYPOTHESIS). Issues also arise in sociology, especially where it is assumed that its subject matter is SEMIOTIC and meaningful, i.e. made up of SIGNS, so that an unknown society or set of social interactions is like an unknown language and the main task is one of translation. Quine (1960) has argued that any translation is in principle 'indeterminate', that any set of signs can equally well be translated by an indefinite list of alternative possibilities. Davidson (1984) suggests that this leaves no alternative other than a 'principle of charity', which assumes that others and their signs will resemble us and our own signs. However, the effect of questions raised about the indeterminacy of translation is to puncture any simple assumptions about ready translation or objectivity in social science. See also RELATIVISM, INCOMMENSURABILITY, FORMS OF LIFE, WITTGENSTEIN.

transnational company for many authors a preferred term for MULTINATIONAL COMPANY.

transvestism the practice of cross-dressing and associated ideologies supporting this practice.

transvestite a person who derives social, cultural and political affirmation and/or sexual pleasure from assuming the dress and demeanour of the opposite gender. Cross-dressing has a long history and is an important part of ritual performance in both sacred and profane social contexts. It has been an important feature of both western and eastern theatre and continues to be a key aspect of contemporary popular culture, e.g. in pantomime (Britain) and girls' opera (Japan). Periodically, popular music has been associated with cross-dressing and/or androgyny as a fashionable style. In the tradition of western medicine and psychotherapy, transvestites are deemed to be suffering from an underlying pathology or problem which should be treated and corrected. In contrast, the transvestite community regards transvestism as a sociopolitical identity and lifestyle. Although often conflated with gay and lesbian cultures, cross-dressing is neither restricted to these cultures nor a defining feature of them (M. Garber, *Vested Interests: Cross-Dressing and Cultural Anxiety*, 1992). Compare TRANSSEXUAL.

triad see DYAD AND TRIAD.

triangulation of approaches the employment of a number of different research techniques (see RESEARCH METHODS), in the belief that a variety of approaches offers the best chance of achieving VALIDITY.

tribe and tribal society 1 (usually) a pastoral or horticultural society whose members share cultural or linguistic characteristics and who are bound together by reciprocal social rights and obligations. Such a society has weak or nonexistent political centralization, but strong LINEAGE structures, important for social cohesion and interaction.

2 a concept developed by anthropologists from the 19th century onwards which attempted to categorize one type of stateless society, generally on an evolutionary scale (e.g. the sequence: BAND, tribe, CHIEFTAIN) but which is now often seen as, at the worst, a European imposed category which related inadequately to empirical reality, and, at best, a term over which no consensus exists.

Thus definition 1 is only an approximation to some of the concept's usage by some anthropologists, and definition 2 reflects the work of others, especially over the last two decades, who reject usage of the concept, prefer no narrow classification of such societies and would substitute the term ETHNIC GROUP. The debate is still current in anthropology. The concept has a general usage to refer to all stateless societies and is sometimes used as a synonym for PRIMITIVE OR SIMPLE SOCIETIES.

trivial consultation a form of inappropriate conduct where patients seek medical advice for problems that are neither medically relevant nor life-threatening. However salient the problems are for patients, they may be dismissed by doctors because they implicate factors beyond medical competence (domestic, financial, social or emotional) and because they cast the doctor in the role of general counsellor/advisor. They are a significant element in doctors' lack of job satisfaction because they are viewed as time-wasting.

Trotsky, Leon (Lyov Davidovich Bronstein) (1879–1940) a leading member of the Russian BOLSHEVIK Party which he joined during the 1917 Revolution. He was Commissar of War during the civil war which followed, but after the death of LENIN in 1924, he was increasingly in conflict with STALIN, resulting in his exile from the USSR in 1929. In exile he became a leading Marxist critic of the policies of the USSR, developing in *The Revolution Betrayed* the notion of a *degenerated workers' state,* dominated by a parasitic bureaucratic caste. In 1938 he formed the Fourth International as a means of continuing the commitment to revolutionary COMMUNISM centred around parties based on pre-Stalinist principles.

Trotsky is accepted as a major writer within the Marxist tradition. His *1905* and *History of the Russian Revolution* are seen, even by critics, as brilliant analyses. His major contributions to Marxist theory are the theories of PERMANENT REVOLUTION and *combined and uneven development,* in which he argued that not all societies have to go through a stage of mature CAPITALISM to achieve SOCIALISM.

In exile in Mexico, Trotsky was murdered by an agent of Stalin. Since his death his political legacy is evident in various, often relatively marginal, political organizations committed to Trotskyism. See MARXISM.

Trotskyism see MARXISM.

trust confidence in the reliability of a person or a system (GIDDENS, 1991). A degree of *basic trust* in others and institutions, acquired in childhood, is often viewed as essential to satisfactory long-term social relations (see ONTOLOGICAL SECURITY AND INSECURITY). With the detachment of individuals from traditional social bonds it is characteristic of modern societies that more abstract types of trust – e.g. MONEY or 'expert systems' – become central as relations are extended across distances of time-space (see TIME–SPACE DISTANCIATION, DISEMBEDDING AND RE-EMBEDDING MECHANISMS), though there are problems associated with these developments (see RISK SOCIETY, REFLEXIVE MODERNIZATION).

What Giddens (1994) terms *active trust* becomes increasingly significant in the degree to which *post-traditional social relations* require trust to be specifically cultivated in contexts ranging from intimate personal ties (see INTIMACY) through to global systems of interaction.

truth that which corresponds to the facts, e.g. in PHILOSOPHY, the *correspondence theory of truth.* Strictly interpreted, in which true propositions or ideas 'picture' or 'represent' the world, this is an 'empiricist' notion (see EMPIRICISM). However, this conception of truth has been challenged recently, e.g. by 'post-empiricist' conceptions of science (see KUHN, FEYERABEND, POST-EMPIRICISM, POSTSTRUCTURALISM, THEORY-RELATIVITY). Since both hypotheses and the 'facts' which 'test' these are 'theory-relative', 'truth' cannot be established simply by recourse to empiricist procedures such as VERIFICATION OF FALSIFICATION.

Alternative bases of truth-claims include the *consensus theory of truth,* in which 'truth' is a matter of social (including scientific) agreements on reality, reached in a context of 'open' discourse (see HABERMAS). Questions of correspondence with reality remain central, but cannot be settled in the way which empiricists suggest. See also DECONSTRUCTION, DERRIDA.

turn-taking see CONVERSATION ANALYSIS.

two-party system a political system (found in e.g. the UK or the USA) in which the electoral contest is dominated by two main parties. Generally one party is 'left wing', and the other 'right wing', but not always (e.g. the Republic of Ireland). An elective system based on single-member constituencies and first-past-the-post elections usually underlies this. The existence of such systems would also appear to depend on the elimination of social and political divisions (e.g. religious or ethnic) which might cross cut those based on class interest. See also CLASS CLEAVAGE, STABLE DEMOCRACY.

two-step flow in mass communications the idea, contrary to theories of MASS SOCIETY, that in a plural society the flow of mass communications is mediated by the action of OPINION-LEADERS, who function as GATE-KEEPERS in such a 'two-step flow' (LAZARSFELD, et al., 1944, Katz and Lazarsfeld, 1955). The idea has been a significant one in the development of theories of the MASS MEDIA OF COMMUNICATION. See also DIFFUSION OF INNOVATIONS.

Tylor, Edward (1832–1917) early anthropologist, whose *Researches into the Early History of Mankind and the Development of Civilization* (1865) did much to establish anthropology as a scientific discipline. He can also take credit for the introduction into English of the German, now standard anthropological and sociological usage of the term CULTURE. Drawing upon Darwinism and on discoveries in archaeology which suggested that cultures manifest a serial progression, the persistent theme of Tylor's approach was evolutionism. In *Primitive Culture* (1871) he applied this perspective to the development of RELIGION, which he suggested had developed through three stages: ANIMISM, polytheism, and MONOTHEISM. Tylor's works were works of synthesis based on comparative analysis in which he searched for evidence of cultural 'survivals' which could provide clues to sequences of social development. His emphasis on the possession of rich 'cultural' traditions by all peoples meant that his anthropology was relatively little marred by the overtones of racism often present in the work of other 19th-century evolutionary theorists. See also EVOLUTIONARY THEORY.

type any abstract or conceptual class or category which may or may not be seen as capable of straightforward empirical reference. Compare IDEAL TYPE. See also TYPOLOGY, TYPIFICATION.

type generalization see IDEAL TYPE.

types of compliance 'three means – physical, material, and symbolic – employed within organizations to make subjects comply', identified by Amitai Etzioni (*A Comparative Analysis of Complex Organizations,* 1961): (a) *coercive power,* resting 'on the application, or the threat of application of physical sanctions';

(b) *remunerative power,* based 'on control over material resources and rewards through allocation of salaries, wages', etc.;
(c) *normative power,* resting 'on the allocation and manipulation of symbolic rewards and deprivations'.

These three modes of compliance are associated with three kinds of involvement: *alienative, calculative,* and *moral.*

types of involvement see TYPES OF COMPLIANCE.

types of legitimate authority see LEGITIMATE AUTHORITY.

types of religious organization see CHURCH-SECT TYPOLOGY.

types of social action the four IDEAL TYPES of social action identified by Max WEBER:
(a) *zweckrational* or *instrumental action* (as in models of 'rational economic action' developed within economics), where the actor weights the relative efficiency of different available means to an end, and sometimes also the ends themselves, seeking to maximize benefits;
(b) *wertrational action* or *value rationality,* where the relative effectiveness of alternative means to an end may be assessed but the ends are accepted as given, perhaps as a moral imperative, as in the PROTESTANT WORK ETHIC;
(c) *affectual action,* where action is governed by emotion;
(d) *traditional action,* where action is governed by customary or habitual practice.

Related general typologies of social action include PARETO's distinction between 'logical' and 'non-logical' action (see also RESIDUES AND DERIVATIONS).

Weber's idealized typology, which states other forms of action as departures from the *zweckrational* type, is intended to provide a bench mark for the analysis of concrete actions and for comparing societies, and has been widely used in sociology. As well as the four pure types, Weber also allowed for 'mixed types' of action. Nonetheless, the criticism is made that in using his typology Weber failed to give adequate credence to systematization of 'substantive rationality' as against the 'formal' (i.e. 'formal calculable') form of rationality, despite his reservations about the narrow operation of the latter (see FORMAL and SUBSTANTIVE RATIONALITY). See also RATIONALITY, BUREAUCRACY.

typification the conceptual process by which both sociologists and social actors organize their knowledge of the social world, not in terms of the unique qualities of persons, things or events, but in terms of the typical features of these (see SCHUTZ, 1962-66).

Typification in sociology can be seen as no more than an extension of a process which already occurs in the social construction of everyday life by social actors. This fact has considerable significance in the eyes of those sociologists (see ETHNOMETHODOLOGY) who wish to deny that a sharp dividing line exists between the 'practical sociology' undertaken by everyday actors and 'conventional academic sociology'. The latter school of thought is seen as failing to recognize this approach as tending to underestimate the 'rational capacities' and 'cultural competence' of ordinary social actors, and thus failing to see that sociology must be built upon, and be compatible with, the 'rational accomplishments' of ordinary social actors.

Whether or not these criticisms of 'conventional academic sociology' are fully accepted, attention to the everyday social and cultural 'competence' and the typifications of social actors can be regarded as an essential element of modern sociological analysis (see GIDDENS, 1976a). But the implications of this for academic sociology remain controversial. There is no general acceptance of the view of ethnomethodologists that a total 'revolution' in sociology is necessary (see GOLDTHORPE, 1973).

typology any classificatory conceptual scheme (e.g. church, sect). It may or may not be logically exhaustive within its empirical frame of reference. The role and utility of any typology is relative to the theoretical perspective within which it is formulated. See also TYPE, IDEAL TYPE, TYPIFICATION.

U

unanticipated *or* **unintended consequences (of social action)** any consequences of social action which are unintended and unforeseen by social participants. That social actions have consequences which are unforeseen by SOCIAL ACTORS is a major part of the drive to undertake sociological analysis. The same impetus was often uppermost in many forms of social thought prior to modern sociology, for example, Adam SMITH's 'invisible hand' of market forces, an idea taken and transformed by MARX (see also APPEARANCE AND REALITY).

An important discussion of unanticipated consequences is Robert MERTON's discussion of MANIFEST AND LATENT FUNCTIONS, and SELF-FULFILLING AND SELF-DESTROYING PROPHECY. Within Marxism and modern STRUCTURALISM the analysis of underlying realities is central. It is also present as a main objective in many other forms of sociology, including Weberian sociology (e.g. Protestants did not intend to establish modern capitalism, but according to Weber, this is one outcome of their religious orientation – see PROTESTANT ETHIC).

Among the reasons why social participants do not always intend or comprehend the implications of their own actions are:
(a) layers of unconscious and subconscious mind beneath conscious intentions, including various modes of tacit knowledge and human social competence;
(b) long chains of interdependence in and between modern societies which no one is in a position to view, still less to anticipate, in their entirety;
(c) the operation of ideological distortions, cultural HEGEMONY, etc., which hide an accurate view of social relations from some or all social participants.

unconscious that part of the mental life that remains outside awareness.

The unconscious is a crucial concept in psychoanalytic theory (see PSYCHOANALYSIS), but since being used by FREUD it has entered our culture, is widely accepted and used in PSYCHOLOGY generally and by psychotherapists in particular.

Freud regarded the unconscious area of mental life as much larger than the conscious, and the analogy of the iceberg has often been made. According to him, this area contains the instincts and all memories and emotions that may once have been conscious but have been repressed. This unconscious material, of which the ID is part, is a dynamic force, providing the stimulus to all action. Freud developed the technique of psychoanalysis to explore the unconscious, as he believed that it was only by bringing troublesome elements of the unconscious to consciousness that mental distress could be alleviated, Interpretations of the role of the unconscious are also central in the many competing interpretations of Freud's theories within sociology and POSTSTRUCTURALISM, where a recourse to psychoanalytic theory has often been central – see LACAN, KRISTEVA, CIXOUS.

The term unconscious, and its obverse, *consciousness,* also have much wider usage than in psychoanalytic theory. Physiological consciousness describes the state of being aware of sensations, reacting to them, and experiencing thoughts and emotions, while the unconscious brain does not exhibit these features. Cognitive psychology makes a further distinction, between automatic and attentional behaviour. Conscious attention is not necessary for well-practised skills, e.g. driving. The conscious brain is seen as being able to engage at different levels of attention as appropriate to the task, thus distributing its capacities most efficiently. Automatic behaviour may be performed without conscious awareness, but is not unconscious in the physiological or the Freudian sense.

underclass social groups that are located at the bottom of the occupational class schema in some models (Runciman, 1990) or outside it in others (D. Smith, *Understanding the Underclass,* 1992). In some definitions the underclass consists of individuals who are unemployed, living on welfare, or existing off criminal activity; in other definitions the underclass consists of family units who live off welfare.

The second definition has become particularly important for writers of the NEW RIGHT who have identified some single-parent families as being a core element to the underclass (Charles Murray, *The Emerging British Underclass,* 1990; N. Dennis and G. Erdos, *The Family: Is it Just Another Lifestyle Choice,* 1992). Both George Gilder (*Wealth and Poverty,* 1992) and Charles Murray have created *structural* versions of the underclass thesis rather than cultural versions. In their arguments, it is economically rational for members of the underclass to exist on welfare because they can receive more in welfare benefits than in low wages; thus the demand that welfare benefits be cut. Their identification of welfare as a cause of the underclass distinguishes current New Right theories of the underclass from the 'culture of poverty' argument of Oscar LEWIS in the 1960s or the 'cycle of deprivation' argument of the British Conservative politician Keith Joseph in the 1970s.

Liberal sociologists have also written on the emerging underclass. In the United States, William Julius Wilson (*The Truly Disadvantaged: The Inner City, the Underclass and Public Policy,* 1987) linked three key groups who were likely to be dependent on income support and therefore also members of the underclass – the long-term unemployed, unskilled workers in erratic employment and young single mothers. His argument is that the 'marriageable pool' of traditional bread-winning males is shrinking because of rising unemployment and rising crime in the urban areas of the US, particularly in the black urban areas, and in these areas women are left to be single mothers. Wilson has thus produced a liberal explanation of the rise of crime and rise of single parents in the US through rising unemployment.

Wilson's thesis has been the subject of an extensive research programme in the USA (see C. Jenks and P. Peterson, *The Urban Underclass,* 1991). Many of the researchers are committed to a liberal view of welfare provision. Thus, Jenks' conclusion is that the concept of the underclass is unhelpful because the concept of classes is unhelpful; he argues that we should not over-correlate social problems. Charles Murray's response has been to argue that it is because of single mothers that the pool of marriageable men is shrinking – single mothers produce unemployed young men.

A recent study in the UK has sought to demonstrate the absence of a dependency culture among long-term claimants (H. Dean and P. Taylor-Gooby, 1992). However, this does not invalidate the entire underclass thesis, because of its wider structural basis. See also POVERTY, LUMPENPROLETARIAT, CYCLE OF DEPRIVATION, CULTURE OF POVERTY, GHETTO.

underconsumption and overproduction (MARXIAN ECONOMICS) the tendency of capitalist economies to generate insufficient demand, and hence insufficient consumption (*underconsumption*) to absorb all that is produced (*overproduction*). Taking the wider perspective of a possible future economy in which production is for 'use' or 'need', rather than profit, i.e. that which an economy might theoretically be capable of producing, 'underconsumption' will also involve *underproduction*. The problem in accepting a theory of 'underproduction', however, is that finding a means of avoiding underconsumption and overproduction has proved elusive in real world economies (see ECONOMIC SURPLUS). See also CRISES OF CAPITALISM.

underdevelopment 1 the general state of a society yet to undergo major social and economic development, particularly by INDUSTRIALIZATION and MODERNIZATION.
2 a process whereby a society, especially its economy, changes under the influence of another society which becomes dominant. Baran (1957), Furtado (1964) and FRANK (1967b) formulated the concept in opposition to prevailing economic theories of change in the THIRD WORLD, and in particular to the theory of MODERNIZATION in the SOCIOLOGY OF DEVELOPMENT. As argued by Frank and Baran, ECONOMIC SURPLUS is said to be transferred out of the dominated society, making economic growth there difficult or impossible. Commercial ports and élites in the Third World absorb some of the surplus, but most is absorbed in the dominant societies in a METROPOLIS-SATELLITE relationship. The underdeveloped economy has certain activities encouraged at the expense of others. The industrial countries were interested in developing mineral and agricultural products from the Third World as supplies to their own economies. The Third World countries were in turn seen as potential markets for manufactured goods. Thus, underdevelopment was a condition which already industrialized societies had not experienced. This led to the conclusion that the processes of industrialization experienced in Western Europe and the US were not repeatable in the Third World, not least since the starting points were radically different. This economic relationship had important consequences for social, political and cultural processes, so broadening out the concept of underdevelopment to embrace most aspects of society.

The concept has been criticized by Marxists for being overreliant on reference to market forces to explain economic problems in the Third World, for overstressing external rather than internal processes, for under-estimating the prospects of industrialization in the Third World, and for having a weak concept of economic surplus at its centre (Brenner, 1977). However, shorn of its more particular usages, the term is frequently used to refer to Third World societies because of the central notion that they confront problems of development different from those faced by the already industrialized countries. See also DEPENDENCY THEORY, WORLD SYSTEMS. Compare IMPERIALISM, ECONOMIC AND SOCIAL DEVELOPMENT, UNEVEN DEVELOPMENT.

understanding see MEANINGFUL UNDERSTANDING AND EXPLANATION, VERSTEHEN.

unemployment the state of not being employed in paid work, or self-employed, even though available for such activity. Unemployment is higher for men than for women and affects young people, especially those from ethnic minority groups, disproportionally more than other social groups.

Employment is important for self-esteem. Jahoda (1982) suggests that it fulfils a number of vital latent functions by providing the following:
(a) regular pattern of activities and time structure to the day;
(b) source of social contacts outside the household;
(c) participation in a wider collective purpose;

(d) social status and identity.

This list of characteristics, while suggestive, has provoked debate. Firstly, as Warr (1987) suggests, the categories can have negative as well as positive psychological effects depending on the degree of exposure. Secondly, because it fails to distinguish between the experiences of men and women (Gallie and Marsh, 1994: 17). Marsden's (1975) earlier qualitative study of a group of unemployed men clearly demonstrated that the impact of the loss of paid employment was devastating: anxiety about finding a new job and coping with financial worries undermined any attempt to enjoy the increased spare time they had. In the 1980s there was a major programme of research into this area. These studies showed that unemployment gave rise to higher levels of psychological distress among men. Warr (1987) reported research findings that unemployment was detrimental to the psychological wellbeing of men. Women's experience of unemployment is more complex (e.g. Marshall, 1984; Kelvin and Jarrett, 1985). In the past, women were more likely to be in less-skilled and less well-paid work with fewer career prospects. Similarly, women's traditional domestic role offered an alternative identity to their paid-work role. Whether this will remain unchanged for the future is questionable. Women have become increasingly active in the LABOUR MARKET (Grint, 1998: 209-14). More generally, the relationship between work and unemployment has been increasingly questioned as it has become clear that economic success at the national level does not necessarily translate into FULL EMPLOYMENT. New technologies and the service economy have far less need for labour than the older manufacturing ('smoke-stack') industries. Handy (1984) argued that we needed to look to having a portfolio of activities during our adult lives, including, possibly, child care, voluntary work and study as well as paid employment. Rifkin (1995), drawing largely on US evidence, has argued for a growth in the *social economy* or THIRD SECTOR, of non-profit organizations might provide a focus of activity for the otherwise 'underemployed' and improve the quality of life for the community and the individual too. His prognosis is an equivocal one, observing that mass unemployment can equally undermine the 'chances of a compassionate and caring society ...' (ibid: 247).

Rates of unemployment have fluctuated considerably over the course of the last century. In Western countries, unemployment reached a peak in the early 1930s, with some 20 per cent of the labour force being out of work in Britain. J.M. KEYNES strongly influenced public policy in Europe and USA at that time and more especially after 1945. State involvement in the economy became accepted in Western industrial societies as a means of underpinning a policy of FULL EMPLOYMENT and retaining a predominantly private sector market economy. By the mid-1970s the policy was losing its effectiveness. Rather than reducing unemployment levels increased state spending fuelled inflation rates instead. The three main factors are the following:

(a) rise in international competition – especially from Japan and other countries of the 'Pacific Rim';

(b) there have been several severe recessions in the global economy starting with the 'Oil crisis' of 1973;

(c) increasing use of new technologies has reduced the demand for labour.

Whereas, the UK unemployment rate was less than 2% in the 25 years after the end of World War II in 1945, by the 1980s it had risen to 12%. It dipped slightly during the decade but rose again to 10% in 1991. Economists refer to *structural* and *frictional* unemployment to distinguish between long-term or endemic (*structural*) unemployment inherent to the economic system and short term adjustments to the system that gives rise to *frictional* unemployment as the people in the labour market adjust to the new requirements in terms of training and skills etc. The distinction between *stock* and *flow* is also highly relevant particularly for sociological research. The official statistics record the *stock* of people claiming benefits. The monthly net change is relatively small but this disguises the *flow* of people into and out of unemployment i.e. there has been an underlying *stock* of *long-term* unemployed but there is also a *flow* of people who are out of work for 3 months or less. In Greater London in the mid-1980s only 20% of those registering unemployed for the first time would be out of work 3 months later (Marsh, 1988: 351). But for that 20% the chances of finding working in the next 3 months was far more dismal. In fact, 86% would not find employment.

unequal exchange trade between peripheral capitalist and centre capitalist countries which operates to the disadvantage of the former. The concept is particularly associated with the Marxist economist Arghiri Emmanuel (1972), who argued that low wages in peripheral countries lead to international exchanges which involve the flow of economic surplus to the core capitalist countries. In Marxist terms, in international exchange, centre capitalist countries exchange commodities in such a way as to acquire commodities embodying more labour time (i.e. greater VALUE) than the goods they exchange. This phenomenon is seen as not something that can be accounted for simply by differences in 'productivity' arising from training and capital inputs, etc. in more developed countries (see also LABOUR THEORY OF VALUE).

Emmanuel's suggestion is that the major cause of unequal exchange is the historically high wages in developed nations, resulting from the power of strong trade unions to maintain wages, compared with the low wages in poorer countries, resulting from a very great surplus of labour. The immobility of labour between countries prevents any tendency to the equalization of wages in these circumstances. The overall process of unequal exchange is also seen as accentuated by a high 'ethical wage' which becomes established in developed countries, and which also contributes to a cycle of growth, while in poor nations a vicious cycle of stagnation occurs, contributed to by both low wages and a poor return from overseas trade.

While Emmanuel argued that unequal exchange is the key to explaining how economic surplus is transferred, other Marxists have argued that the theory is not precise enough, and in particular that Emmanuel does not satisfactorily distinguish between labour values and prices. He also ignores that in addition to the exploitation that arises from unequal exchange there is exploitation by the processes of production within poorer nations. Amin (1980), for example, presents an account of the exploitation involved in unequal exchange which emphasizes the existence of NONCAPITALIST AND PRECAPITALIST MODES OF PRODUCTION alongside capitalist modes, which means that labour is available to capitalism in poorer nations without the necessity for any widespread provision of welfare programmes. This process, in which resources or values are thus transferred to the capitalist sector from the noncapitalist sector, is referred to as *superexploitation* by Amin. Since this capitalist sector may be indigenous (see COMPRADOR CAPITALISM) an analysis such as Amin's points to an appropriate role for analysis of internal CLASS CONFLICT within developing nations as well as an emphasis on divisions of interest between nations.

New competitive advantages enjoyed recently by some newly developing nations of the 'semi-periphery', and the consequent DEINDUSTRIALIZATION of some previous Western centres of industrial production – in which capital has moved to cheap labour – do not mean that the conditions for an unequal exchange have disappeared. For, although levels of employment may increase in the semi-periphery, this does not automatically mean high wages, and some profits from such relocated production will continue to be exported. However, the longer-term implications of such changes – which may or may not include lower levels of employment, lower wages and salaries in developed countries, and may or may not bring improvement in wages and a new diversity of production in developing societies – are not easily unravelled.

Many economists have suggested that changes now occurring in many developing nations indicate that these nations will increasingly be competing directly with established capitalist core economies, following in the steps of nations like Japan. There are also many economists and some sociologists who dispute whether richer nations can be said to exploit the poorer nations – have these nations been 'redeveloped' or UNDERDEVELOPED by colonialism and capitalism as Marxist and sociological DEPENDENCY THEORISTS suggest? Since theorists of different persuasions make judgements about 'fair' exchange in terms of different criteria (e.g. theoretical 'labour values' compared with simple prices and values are difficult to calculate), any simple resolution of the debates between the several sets of protagonists is unlikely.

Although the theories behind it may be in dispute, the concept of unequal exchange is still useful in that it indicates aspects of the nature of trade relationships existing between richer and poorer countries, between CENTRE AND PERIPHERY. See also INTERNATIONAL TRADE, TERMS OF TRADE, IMPERIALISM, UNEVEN DEVELOPMENT.

uneven development a term applied to countries, and areas within countries, to signify that capitalist economic development occurs at different rates and takes differing forms. Leading countries and areas may increase their lead, but more backward countries or areas may at a later stage leapfrog those which previously seemed to have an advantage. Further, a country may develop industrial capitalist centres but these may exist alongside noncapitalist sectors in the countryside or within urban areas. This may be the case with present THIRD WORLD countries, or as TROTSKY argued, with Russia before the 1917 revolution, when industrial capital is predominantly foreign-owned or influenced and in isolated pockets. The theory implies that at some time there may be advantages in this seeming backwardness. Trotsky and LENIN argued that it meant that Russia did not need to proceed through the same stages of capitalist development to achieve a socialist revolution. Some academic social scientists argue that through adopting the latest technology and organizational forms, the backward countries may be able to achieve a rapid breakthrough to catch up with the advanced industrial capitalist countries without having to go through the same long process they experienced (see Löwy, 1981).

unilineal descent DESCENT through one sex, therefore either PATRILINEAL or MATRILINEAL. Nonunilineal descent is sometimes called COGNATIC.

unilinear of any process of SOCIAL CHANGE or development which always proceeds in a single direction, through the same stages, and with the same results. The concept of unilinearity is actually a redundant one in sociology, for no process of social change is actually (or ever could be) unilinear. However, unilinear assumptions were a prominent feature of much 19th-century social theory. See also EVOLUTIONARY THEORY, DIFFUSION.

unintended consequences see UNANTICIPATED CONSEQUENCES OR UNINTENDED CONSEQUENCES (OF SOCIAL ACTION).

unionateness the extent to which employee organizations define themselves as TRADE UNIONS, maintain independence from employers, display a willingness to adopt COLLECTIVE BARGAINING and industrial action, and identify with the broader labour movement. Thus a contrast may be drawn between most manual trade unions, usually high on 'unionateness', and many 'white-collar' unions, often far less committed to the general ideals of trade unionism. See also INDUSTRIAL RELATIONS.

universal conditional statement see COVERING-LAW MODEL AND DEDUCTIVE NOMOLOGICAL EXPLANATION.

universalism see PARTICULARISM, PATTERN VARIABLES.

universal pragmatics see HABERMAS.

university the form of HIGHER EDUCATION institution which in most countries stands at the pinnacle of a hierarchy of types of institution providing post-school education. There are exceptions to such a generalization, however, e.g. in France the *grandes écoles,* which train personnel for top positions in the higher reaches of government and industry, stand above the universities in terms of prestige. The university being in origins a medieval institution, there are some European universities – including Oxford and Cambridge – that can claim continuity dating back to this era. Most modern institutions however are comparatively recent creations, a product in some instances of the latter half of the 19th century. Most are more recent still, a result of the rapid expansion of higher education in nearly all countries since World War II. This in turn reflects the fact that in almost all countries higher education now plays a dominant role in occupational selection, although the nature and value of the part played by higher education in this respect is disputed (see CREDENTIALISM, SCREENING, INTELLECTUAL LABOUR).

In addition to the differences already mentioned, other important differences also exist in the character of universities in different countries: e.g. Germany has a system dominated by the professoriat and with an emphasis on research and scholarship and a relatively restricted and closely controlled access, while the US system is much more under the control of administrators, but also 'open', allowing wide access to a high proportion of the population (see MASS HIGHER EDUCATION). See also NEW UNIVERSITIES.

As well as its teaching functions, research and social monitoring are also vital functions of the university. As Clark (1983) suggests, the capacity of the modern university is such as to 'appropriate functions'; thus for some commentators they are now utterly crucial to the essential character of modern knowledge-based societies. See INFORMATION SOCIETIES, POSTINDUSTRIAL SOCIETIES, BELL, LIFELONG LEARNING.

univocal reciprocity *or* **directional reciprocity** (ANTHROPOLOGY) a generalized pattern of social EXCHANGE (e.g. the exchange of women as brides) between families, groups, etc. in which the exchange is not direct, so that A may give to B, who in turn gives to C, who completes the circle by giving to A.

unobtrusive measures any methods of collecting data without the knowledge of the subject and without affecting the data. Examples are very varied, e.g. studies of garbage, wear on carpets, recording how much coffee is consumed in meetings. What these unobtrusive methods have in common is that they avoid the problem of 'subject reaction' to the study. Hence they are less likely to distort the observations than standard ways of collecting data such as the completion of a questionnaire or an attitude test. In the latter cases the subjects are bound to be aware that they are taking part in research and this can produce artificial results. Unobtrusive measures are often used within a QUALITATIVE RESEARCH design and can be especially useful in evaluation research to reduce any distorting reaction to the evaluation on the part of the people being evaluated.

unproductive labour see PRODUCTIVE AND UNPRODUCTIVE LABOUR.

unstable democracy see STABLE AND UNSTABLE DEMOCRACY.

unstructured data data which has been collected without reference to how it might eventually be coded. Some questions in survey questionnaires (and particularly in pilot questionnaires) yield data of this nature. Respondents are asked to give a direct verbal answer to a question for which there has been no precoding. Much data collected by qualitative researchers is unstructured, and content analysts studying newspapers, and historical sociologists studying old manuscript sources make use of unstructured data, because these sources were not compiled with their needs in mind. See also SCALING, QUALITATIVE RESEARCH, CONTENT ANALYSIS, HISTORICAL SOCIOLOGY. Compare STRUCTURED CODING.

untouchables see CASTE.

upper class the topmost class in any society. In modern British society this class can be said to consist of:
(a) a core of around 25,000 individuals who exercise strategic control over the economy (Scott, 1982);
(b) a wider group of individuals and families owning considerable, usually inherited, wealth, and distinguished by a distinctive lifestyle.

Since the numbers of individuals involved is relatively small, networks of relationships (e.g. public-school education, upper-class leisure pursuits) play an important part in sustaining the distinctive lifestyle and high social status, as well as the economic and political power, enjoyed by the upper-class. Persons whose family origins are upper-class are also prominent in élite professions, such as the administrative class of the civil service, the judiciary, and the upper echelons of the military, positions which may be seen as upper-class in their own right.

upward mobility see SOCIAL MOBILITY.

urban ecology the study of the city in terms of the social characteristics of areas or neighbourhoods, which originated in the University of Chicago in the 1920s. High rates of immigration into Chicago from Europe in the first two decades of the 20th century led to rapid urban growth and change, and stimulated research into the nature of urban living, the origins of social problems and the processes of urban growth and change through competition for space, changing land use and succession of functions. The early industrial city could be seen as being composed of three concentric zones or areas – the *concentric zone hypothesis.* These were the factory and business centre, the surrounding area of working-class residence, and then the areas occupied by the middle and professional classes. This is a reversal of the situation in the preindustrial city where the richer classes lived close to the central business district within the protective walls of the city, while the poorer people lived outside the city gates. However, as the industrial city grows into a metropolis, three developments occur:
(a) some productive enterprises move out of the centre into new industrial zones or trading estates where rents are lower and there are better networks of communication;
(b) the retailing and business zone grows and spreads into the neighbouring residential zone;
(c) the overall size of the city grows and creates suburbs and out-of-town shopping and amusement areas. See also URBANISM AS A WAY OF LIFE, URBAN SOCIOLOGY, ZONE OF TRANSITION, URBANIZATION, HUMAN ECOLOGY.

urbanism as a way of life the prevailing feature of modern society, (in the view of L. Wirth, 1938). Wirth regarded this feature as more salient than industrialism or capitalism, since the development of large cities and towns had created a break with 'society's natural situation'. The process of URBANIZATION had rendered ties of kinship less important and replaced them with relationships of an instrumental, transitory and superficial character. Urban settlements are characterized by size, density and heterogeneity, which in combination provide the basis for a complex division of labour and fundamental changes in the nature of social relationships. See also URBAN SOCIOLOGY.

urbanization

1 the statistical measure of the proportion of a country's population living in cities or settlements of a size defined variously by political, cultural or administrative criteria. The *rate of urbanization* describes changes in the proportion of urban to rural dwellers over time (the reverse process is described as the *rate of deurbanization*).

2 the social processes and relationships which are both the cause and consequence of the urban rather than rural way of life (see URBANISM AS A WAY OF LIFE).

G. Hurd et al. (1973) have suggested that historically the process of urbanization had three major stages. The first is identified as extending from the time when people first began to live in towns up until the 18th-century. During this stage few urban areas had more than 100,000 people. The second stage is the rapid growth in the size and number of cities contingent upon the process of INDUSTRIALIZATION. Tables drawn up by the United Nations Statistical Office show that between 73% and 85% of the populations in the industrial countries of the west live in cities. The third stage is *metropolitanization* which involves the centralization of people and wealth and of society's political, economic and cultural institutions (see P. Hall, *The World Cities,* 1977). Other writers would refer to a fourth stage of *deurbanization* via the growth of suburbs, migration to rural areas, alternative communities and planned 'new towns'.

In its earliest usage the term 'urbanize' meant 'to make urbane', to render something or someone polished or refined. The modern sense of 'to develop an urban character', or 'make into a city', emerged in the second half of the 19th-century when the city became a special object of study for social scientists and others who were concerned about the social consequences of the growth of industrial cities (see URBAN SOCIOLOGY). The relevance of the older usage is that it influenced the way in which thinkers conceptualized the rural and the urban and gave rise to two contrasting sets of images:

(a) the city as the locus of civilization, refinement, excitement, freedom and change, in contrast to what Marx described as 'rural idiocy';

(b) the country as the home of truth and of sharing in 'knowable communities' united by common values, in contrast to the alienation of the city. Raymond Williams examines these traditions in *The Country and the City* (1973), where he also says that in writings about the city from the 16th to the 19th century a number of themes emerge in sequence – money and law, wealth and luxury, the mob and the masses, and finally mobility and isolation. He says that in the past, as now, our real experience is of many different types of organization in the city and the country, yet our imagery is always of two opposed realities, the rural – urban dichotomy.

The dichotomy of two different sociocultural systems, one of which is broken down under the force of industrialization, was a prominent element in the study of preindustrial societies and of industrialization.

Although in Europe urbanization and industrialization did occur generally at the same time, it would be a mistake to see these two processes as necessarily contingent upon each other. For example, urbanization preceded industrialization in England in that a high and rising proportion of English people had lived in London from the time of its first phase of growth in the 16th century until the early 1700s when it was estimated to hold one-seventh of the population. London was a city created by agriculture and mercantile capital within an aristocratic political order which tried to arrest its growth by ordinances preventing the erection of buildings. The development of cities as centres of industrial activity came later, primarily in the Midlands and North of England, and parts of central Scotland. Today, in many parts of Africa, Asia and Latin America, there is rapid urban growth via migration and natural increase without any significant development in the direction of an industrial economy. See also URBAN ECOLOGY.

urban managers see URBAN SOCIOLOGY.

urban social movement a locally-based social and political movement arising in response to an increasing politicization of issues surrounding the provision of urban social services, including housing, transport and education. Restrictions on COLLECTIVE CONSUMPTION, associated, e.g. with the tendency to FISCAL CRISIS IN THE CAPITALIST STATE, are regarded as significant sources of these movements in recent decades. See also COMMUNITY POLITICS.

urban sociology

The study of social relationships and structures in the city. It is a subdiscipline of sociology whose development has been influenced by debate about the distinctiveness of its subject matter, by the willingness of researchers to adopt cross-disciplinary approaches, and by a social-problem orientation which has fostered research outside of the mainstream of intellectual change in sociology.

Early sociological writing about the city located the urban dimension within the broader compass of sociological theorizing. TÖNNIES, SIMMEL and WEBER in the 1890s addressed such issues as the characteristic forms of association and social life in urban environments, and the role of urban development in social change. With the establishment of the CHICAGO SCHOOL of sociologists in the 1920s, urban studies emerged as a distinct area of research. Focusing upon the issues of social order and organization, members of the Chicago school conducted empirical

research into the social characteristics of different areas within the city. For example, research on the ZONE OF TRANSITION (the area bordering the central business district characterized by high levels of migration, social heterogeneity and poor housing stock) explored the relationships between the incidence of social problems such as crime, mental illness, alcoholism and social cohesion. Urban sociology demonstrated that:
(a) socioeconomic factors were more significant than geographical or environmental factors in the genesis of social problems; and that
(b) meaning and social order exist in areas of apparent disorganization (see W. Whyte's study of Boston street-corner boys, *Street Corner Society*, 1955).

Although the Chicago school established a rich empirical tradition, its theoretical deficiencies led to a decline in urban sociology between the 1940s and 1960s with the exception of a number of community studies showing urban neighbourhoods to have forms of association commonly associated with rural communities (Gans, 1962, called them 'urban villages'). The theoretical poverty of the rural/urban typologies and the metropolitanization of society left urban sociology indistinguishable from the sociological analysis of advanced, industrial, capitalist societies. However, in the late 1960s urban sociology was revived under the influence of a new generation of (a) Weberian and (b) Marxist scholars:
(a) J. Rex and R. Moore published a study of housing and race relations in Sparkbrook, Birmingham (*Race, Community and Conflict*, 1967) which combined Burgess's insights into the dynamics of the zone of transition with Weber's ideas about the sociological significance of the meaningful actions of individuals. This work relocated urban sociology within the sociological mainstream and in turn stimulated discussion of Weberian stratification theory through the concept of the *housing class*. Because the housing market is structured around different forms of tenure it gives rise to new status groups or consumption classes whose interests do not necessarily coincide with economic class interests. Housing is a scarce resource whose distribution is influenced by a political group which Pahl termed *urban managers*. The degree of autonomy they possess vis-à-vis the central state, private capital and the local consumer of social goods is an empirical question, but according to Pahl their operations give rise to forms of social inequality and political struggle which are independent of the sphere of production;
(b) Marxist work on the city began with a critique of urban sociology as ideology. Lefebvre (1967) argued that urban sociology was an apology for capitalism because it failed to examine the ways in which space is actually produced and distributed in capitalist societies. Space is itself a commodity, a scarce and alienable resource, in this view. The contradictions between profit and need, exchange and use-value, the

individual versus the collective, are exemplified by the conflicting need of capital to exploit space for profit and the social requirements of the people. CASTELLS, although a Marxist, begins his analysis (*The Urban Question*, 1977) with the conventional interest in spatially significant social phenomena, but he does not regard space as such as a theoretically important issue. What is significant is the role of the urban system in the mode of production. Castells concentrates upon the reproduction of LABOUR POWER which he sees as being increasingly concentrated within particular spatial units where the provision of social goods and services is dependent upon the state. Centralization of services results in the collectivization of consumption. He sees the city as an important element in the struggle against capitalism because urban crises cut across class boundaries and give rise to social movements with a specifically urban base which can in turn create the conditions for new political alliances. These ideas stimulated discussion of COLLECTIVE CONSUMPTION, an underdeveloped concept in Marx's work, and the political economy of housing and rents. Marxist critics (Pickvance, 1976; Harvey 1973) have argued that these approaches must not replace class struggle with consumption and accumulation as the main factors in the analysis of capitalism.

use-value and exchange-value (MARXISM) the distinction between the usefulness of an object or service (COMMODITIES) produced within an economy, its *use-value*, and the ratio at which a commodity exchanges against others, its *exchange-value* (see also VALUE). While use-value is a precondition for any exchange value, the magnitude of the latter is not determined by use-value.

The distinction plays an important role in Marxist political economy, particularly in relation to the difference held to exist between, on the one hand, the exchange-value of the commodities that LABOUR POWER produces, and the exchange-value of labour power itself. The expropriation by capitalists of the SURPLUS VALUE created in this way is the source of the EXPLOITATION that Marx insists occurs as an inherent feature of capitalism. See also CAPITALISM AND CAPITALIST MODE OF PRODUCTION, LABOUR THEORY OF VALUE, RESERVE ARMY OF LABOUR.

usufruct the right of use of another's property without destroying or consuming that property. The concept derives from ROMAN LAW, and is in general use in the social sciences to designate property relations whereby either property ownership, particularly in land, is not established within a society, or where use rather than ownership may be the most important aspect of property relations.

uterine see MATRILINEAL DESCENT and MATRILATERAL.

utilitarianism a philosophical school of thought which holds that UTILITY entails the greatest happiness of the greatest number. It is usually associated with Jeremy BENTHAM (1748–1832) and John Stuart MILL (1806–73), although some would argue that the earlier philosophical works of HOBBES, HUME and LOCKE are also utilitarian. This philosophy holds that the realization of utility should be the proper goal in life, but may be hindered by selfish prejudice and ignorance. Behaviour which enhances happiness and reduces pain ought to be encouraged and behaviour which increases unhappiness ought to be proscribed. Utilitarianism, therefore, implies a model of social action in which individuals rationally pursue their own self-interests, with SOCIETY being no more than the aggregation of individuals brought together in the realization of their individual goals. Bentham applied these principles to ECONOMICS, SOCIAL POLICY and LAW. Utilitarianism influenced the creation of many of the 19th-century institutions, many of which still survive, such as the prison and the asylum (see PANOPTICAN). SPENCER was influenced by utilitarian ideas, although DURKHEIM was critical, arguing that SOCIAL ORDER is the outcome of cultural traditions that are not reducible to individual interests. See also JUSTICE.

utility (ECONOMICS) the satisfaction or pleasure that a person derives from the consumption of a good or service. In the work of CLASSICAL ECONOMISTS, it was assumed that utility might be measured on an absolute scale. In modern economics, the assumption is merely that individuals are at least able to rank the satisfactions they receive or expect to receive. It is on this basis that conceptions and forms of analysis central in modern economics, e.g. indifference curves, conceptions of marginal utility, are formulated (see NEOCLASSICAL ECONOMICS).

utopia (from the Greek, meaning 'nowhere') any imaginary society or place, intended to stand as an ethical or theoretical ideal or to provide an illuminating contrast with existing patterns of social organization. Utopia may be based on historically existing societies or located in the future. Well-known examples of utopias are PLATO's *Republic* and Sir Thomas More's *Utopia* (1516).

Assessments of the value of utopian thinking vary. By its advocates the use of utopian imagery is justified if it aids critical imagination and extends awareness of alternatives to existing forms of social organization. By its detractors it is seen as liable to mislead and to promote unreal expectations about social change. See also UTOPIANISM. Compare IDEAL TYPE.

utopian communities communities established with the aim of realizing, or moving towards, an ideal form of society, e.g. 19th-century socialist communities such as Robert Owen's New Harmony, or modern-day sectarian religious communities such as Jonestown (Guyana). Such communities have often been short-lived, but as 'social experiments' they have attracted considerable attention in sociology for the indication they may offer on the viability of alternative patterns of social organization. See UTOPIA, COMMUNES.

utopianism any form of social or political thinking or social theory which presents an ideal form of society as a realizable model of future society (see UTOPIA).

Such thinking has sometimes been criticized as fostering political objectives or political strategies which may have little empirical or theoretical basis (compare Marx's rejection of UTOPIAN SOCIALISM). For MANNHEIM (*Ideology and Utopia*, 1929), however, utopian ideas can be distinguished from most ideologies in always possessing a potentially 'transforming effect upon an existing historical social order'. In this sense utopianism may sometimes help to bring about at least some aspects of the ideal model of society which it advances (see also FRANKFURT SCHOOL OF CRITICAL THEORY). At the same time, Mannheim did not fail to notice that utopianism was often rooted in irrationalism. See also MILLENARIANISM, COLLECTIVE BEHAVIOUR.

utopian realism discussion of possible alternative social futures by the extrapolation of current trends (see GIDDENS, 1991).

utopian socialism early forms of modern socialist thinking (including the ideas of SAINT-SIMON, Fourier and Owen) criticized by MARX as 'utopian' (see UTOPIA, UTOPIAN COMMUNITIES) since they were seen by him as based on an inadequately scientific conception of the dynamics of capitalist society and the necessity of class struggle.

uxorilocal see MATRILOCAL.

V

validity the extent to which a measure, indicator or method of data collection possesses the quality of being sound or true as far as can be judged. For example, if a psychological measure, such as an intelligence test, is considered to be valid, this means that it is thought to measure what it sets out to measure. If social survey observations are said to have produced valid data, then they are considered to be true reflection of the phenomenon being studied in the population being studied (e.g. projections of voting behaviour), and the survey method could be said to have validity. Compare RELIABILITY.

In practice, in sociology and the social sciences generally, the relation between indicators and measures on the one hand and the underlying concepts they are taken to represent is often contested (see OFFICIAL STATISTICS, MEASUREMENT BY FIAT).

value (MARXISM) the quantity of LABOUR POWER, measured in units of labour time, which is on average necessary to produce a commodity. This for Marx is the basis of exchange-value. See LABOUR THEORY OF VALUE, USE-VALUE AND EXCHANGE-VALUE.

Marx accepted, indeed it was central to his way of working, that value in his sense did not always correspond closely to actual prices (empirical exchange-values). His argument was, however, that these concrete forms of value stood in a systematic relation to value in his theoretical sense and that this best revealed the social relations underlying the workings of a capitalist economy, e.g. its dependence on EXPLOITATION (see also APPEARANCE AND REALITY).

This conception of value is a highly controversial one even within Marxism. Regarded by some as the essential core of Marx's theory of capitalist society by which this theory stands or falls, by others it is seen to involve conceptual problems in application that render it impossible to use empirically or simply wrong. The main alternative, an empirical conception of value adopted by mainstream ECONOMICS, is that value is determined simply by economic scarcity, i.e. by supply and demand.

value consensus see CONSENSUS.

value freedom and **value neutrality**

1 the view that sociology can, and should, conduct research according to the dictates of 'science', excluding any influence of the researcher's own values (see VALUES sense 1).

2 the doctrine, particularly associated with Max WEBER (1949) – sometimes expressed as *value neutrality* – that sociologists, if they cannot ever hope to exclude all biases introduced into their work by their own values, can at least make clear what these values are and how they affect their work.

3 the doctrine of *value freedom* or *value neutrality* or (sometimes) *ethical neutrality*, that, while social science may establish the 'facts' about social reality, it cannot, in doing so, settle questions of ultimate VALUES 1, since a logical gap always exists between empirical evidence and moral actions, between facts and values (see FACT-VALUE DISTINCTION).

4 the doctrine, also particularly associated with Weber (and related to his acceptance of value freedom/value neutrality in senses 2 and 3) that the sociologist *qua* sociologist should *not* seek to pronounce on ultimate values, and especially should not seek to use his or her professional position as a teacher of students to seek to advance particular value positions.

The four senses of value freedom/value neutrality each raise problems. The problem with 1 is that it is difficult to exclude or even control all influence of the researcher's values on the choice and execution of social research, hence Weber's position, sense 2. Furthermore, it is not apparent that sociological research which starts from the researcher's values must inevitably lose in VALIDITY and OBJECTIVITY – if this were so then almost all the work of the major classical sociologists, including positivistically inclined sociologists such as DURKHEIM, would be fatally flawed. Moreover, the idea also seems out of gear with what we know about SCIENCE in general, i.e. it can never operate in a presuppositionless way (see also OBJECTIVITY, THEORY-RELATIVITY).

The alternative to sense 1 provided by Weber's conception of VALUE RELEVANCE, is that sociologists will inevitably be guided by a concern for values, but that so long as this is made clear it need not compromise the achievement of objectivity *within* the chosen frame of reference. However, the problem with this view, especially when made in conjunction with senses 3 and 4, is that it would appear to support a view of the arbitrariness and ultimate 'irrationalism' of values. For many sociologists, including Durkheim and MARX, such a view is simply unacceptable, and a more general scientific basis for values remains a goal (see also VALUE JUDGEMENT).

A more specific objection to Weber's doctrine of 'value freedom' in sense 3 is advanced by BECKER (1967; 1970) and GOULDNER (1956; 1973), and is that any acceptance of this doctrine enables sociologists, if they wish to, simply to undertake research for the rich and powerful who can afford to commission research or can readily set the agenda of 'social problems' seen as requiring attention (see HIERARCHY OF CREDIBILITY). See also ETHICAL INDIFFERENCE, RELATIVISM.

value judgement an ethical or moral evaluation, especially where this leads to a statement of what, on ethical or moral grounds, 'ought to be done'. In Logical Positivism (see POSITIVISM) the assumption is sometimes made that no 'value judgement' can ever be derived from a purely 'scientific' statement (see FACT-VALUE DISTINCTION). However, two other possibilities exist:
(a) that 'facts' and 'theories', although they can never dictate our 'values', can inform us about causal connections, etc., thus also indicating how we might go about achieving our ethical goals (this approximately was WEBER'S view; see also HYPOTHETICAL IMPERATIVE);
(b) that the notion of an insurmountable divorce between 'facts' and 'values' is false, and that whenever possible we should always seek to ground our ethical and moral positions and our value judgements on firm sociological foundations (the position, for example, of COMTE or DURKHEIM, or the FRANKFURT SCHOOL OF CRITICAL THEORY).

All three positions continue to be held by different sociologists in modern sociology. See also CATEGORICAL IMPERATIVE, KANT, BECKER, HIERARCHY OF CREDIBILITY.

value neutrality see VALUE FREEDOM AND VALUE NEUTRALITY.

value rationality see TYPES OF SOCIAL ACTION.

value relativity the proposition that all sociological knowledge is relative to particular values, and that these values, in turn, are also relative to social content. See RELATIVISM, VALUE RELEVANCE, OBJECTIVITY.

value relevance the doctrine that sociological research topics will inevitably, and rightly, often be chosen for their 'ethical interest', but that this need not prevent the researcher from seeking OBJECTIVITY within the particular frame-of-reference adopted.

The doctrine is especially associated with Max WEBER in association with his conception of VALUE FREEDOM AND VALUE NEUTRALITY (senses 2 and 4). This means that he identified three stages in the overall relation between values and sociological research:
(a) a researcher's values often influence the choice of topic;
(b) this need not prevent objective research, e.g. research establishing the empirical importance of particular values such as the PROTESTANT ETHIC; but
(c) the outcome of any research never amounts to the outright justification of particular values. See also FACT-VALUE DISTINCTION.

values 1 ethical ideals and beliefs. The term is often used to distinguish scientific knowledge from 'values', especially where such 'ethical' ideals, 'oughts', etc. are held not to be, or as inherently incapable of ever being, 'scientific'. See also FACT-VALUE DISTINCTION, POSITIVISM, VALUE FREEDOM AND VALUE NEUTRALITY.
2 the central beliefs and purposes of an individual or society. In Talcott PARSONS' structural-functionalism internalized 'shared values' are regarded as playing a decisive role in the social integration of any society (see also CONSENSUS). Criticism of this view is that it overstates the extent to which social integration depends on shared values and understates the importance of political or economic POWER (see also OVERSOCIALIZED CONCEPTION OF MAN; CONFLICT THEORY). Most sociologists recognize that societies can exist even though riven by value divisions, and that an adherence to prevailing beliefs and values is often expedient or pragmatic rather than deeply held (e.g. see DEFERENCE). Equally, however, most sociologists also acknowledge that naked economic or political force is rarely the sole basis of social integration (e.g. is an unstable basis of political power) and that values usually play an important role (see POLITICAL LEGITIMACY).
In a similar way to criticisms of functionalism, Marxist theories which posit a dominant role for IDEOLOGIES in the maintenance of social power are also criticized for overemphasizing the role of internalized beliefs and values (see DOMINANT IDEOLOGY THESIS).

vanguard party (MARXISM) a form of revolutionary POLITICAL PARTY aimed at providing leadership of the working class, and overthrow of the RULING CLASS. The conception was formulated by LENIN in his famous work *What is to be Done?* (1902), in which he dealt with the specific problems of party-building in Tsarist Russia, a political system which operated as a police state. In these circumstances, Lenin outlined the necessity for a strongly centralized and disciplined party organization, with full-time members, to provide the practical and theoretical training of revolutionaries, since he had no confidence that revolutionary consciousness would develop spontaneously. Without the creation of a vanguard, working-class consciousness would fail to advance beyond a limited TRADE-UNION CONSCIOUSNESS. Lenin has been criticized for setting aside questions of democratic accountability, and as paving the way for STALINISM. Harding (1977), however, stresses the importance of seeing Lenin's ideas in their historical context rather than as reflecting a principled opposition to democracy in all circumstances.

variable a characteristic which can be measured and which may vary along a continuum, *continuous variable* (e.g. height), be more *discrete* (e.g. family size) or be bipolar (e.g. sex). The term is commonly used in empirical social research to denote the representation of a social factor such as age, social class, employment status, years of education, which can be observed to affect other measures, such as income level (which may be influenced by all of those mentioned). Social and psychological research is particularly interested in defining what aspects of society or experience influence other social parameters or behaviours, with the intention of explaining social phenomena. On one view, for this to be managed scientifically, possible influences and possible effects have to be defined and quantified so that methods such as concomitant variation, survey research or experiment can be set up to test HYPOTHESES. It is these definitions and quantifications that result in the variables which are used in scientific data analysis. It should be noted that continuous variables are measured on an interval scale, while discrete variables often use nominal or ordinal measurement (see CRITERIA AND LEVELS OF MEASUREMENT).

In some traditions in sociology, however, the appropriateness of the concept of the variable in the above sense has been questioned. From the perspective of SYMBOLIC INTERACTIONISM, for example, Herbert BLUMER (1956) has suggested that the use of standardized variables in social analysis leads to a neglect of the close study required for the effective study of social situations and a distorted representation of social reality. Similar scepticism is voiced in approaches such as ETHNOMETHODOLOGY (see also MEASUREMENT BY FIAT, OFFICIAL STATISTICS).

variable capital see CONSTANT AND VARIABLE CAPITAL.

variance see MEASURES OF DISPERSION.

Varna see CASTE.

vassalage see FEUDALISM AND FEUDAL SOCIETY.

Veblen, Thornstein (1857–1929) US economist, sociologist and social critic, of Norwegian extraction, who founded the approach known as INSTITUTIONAL ECONOMICS. In the *Theory of the Leisure Class* (1899), Veblen presented an uncompromising critique of the lifestyle of emulation and CONSPICUOUS CONSUMPTION of the dominant social groupings in American society. In a further series of works, notably *The Theory of the Business Enterprise* (1904), *The Instinct for Workmanship* (1914), and *The Engineers and the Price System* (1921), he was responsible for an equally trenchant critical analysis of US capitalism, which he regarded as 'predatory' and 'parasitic'. Veblen's hope was that one day the LEISURE CLASS and modern corporate power would be replaced by the rule of engineers and that the human 'instinct for workmanship' would prevail. However, he was not surprised that capitalism should have led to world war, the origins of which he traced to Germany's late industrialization and its lack of a democratic political tradition. There is some similarity between Veblen's style of sociology (and the hostile response it often generated) and the later work of another major sociological critic of US society, C. Wright MILLS. However, the critical reception of Veblen's work reflects weakness in his methods as well as undoubted ideological resistance to his critique of US society.

verification any procedure regarded as establishing the TRUTH of a proposition or hypothesis.

verification principle the criterion of SCIENCE proposed by Logical Positivists (see POSITIVISM) that to be accepted as 'scientific' a proposition must be 'verifiable'. Problems with the concept of VERIFICATION (e.g. we can never establish with certainty universal propositions, such as 'all swans are white', since we can never know future cases) have led some theorists (notably POPPER) to suggest that this must be replaced as the criterion of scientific statements by the conception of 'falsifiability', since a single contrary instance (e.g. a single instance of a 'black swan') will falsify a universal proposition (see FALSIFICATION AND FALSIFICATIONISM). Because it is also proposed by Logical Positivists as a criterion of 'meaningfulness', a further criticism of the verification principle is that it leaves utterly unclear the status of the principle, which is itself unverifiable – the so-called 'paradox' of Positivism.

Verstehen the German word for 'understanding', which, when used in a sociological context in English-speaking sociology, usually refers to MEANINGFUL UNDERSTANDING, the procedure in which both social actors and sociologists 'interpret' and gain access to the meanings of others.

The German term is especially associated with the work of Max WEBER, who stated as 'the specific task of the sciences of action, ... the interpretation of action in terms of its subjective meaning' (Weber, 1922), distinguishing the social sciences from the natural sciences by the presence of such an orientation.

A confusion exists in the literature – illustrating the problems that can arise in any understanding of meanings! – as to whether in Weber's use *Verstehen* refers only to a doubtful psychologistic and 'introspective', 'empathic' understanding, in which the sociologist merely 'imagines' herself or himself in the place of a person or group, or whether – something capable of far more 'objective' evaluation – actors' 'subjective meanings' can be 'read off' from the existence of an explicit 'language' of social meanings which can be objectively demonstrated.

In fact, Weber's usage would appear to have involved elements of *both* of these possibilities, but in the former case he endeavoured to found any 'existential' psychological assumptions involved in 'empirical regularities of experience'. Nevertheless, there remain some critics who, wrongly, see Weber's, and *any*, use of *Verstehen* as *only* involving a doubtful introspective psychology (e.g. Abel, 1977). While others (e.g. WINCH, 1958, or Macintyre, 1962) argue that it would have been better if Weber had confined his use of *Verstehen* to meaningful understanding in the second sense, and not sought to merge meaningful understanding and 'causal explanation'.

What Weber meant by 'causal explanation' in the context of actors' meanings is another issue: either these could refer:
(a) to meanings *in themselves* functioning as 'causes' (a usage to which some philosophers object; compare WINCH); or
(b) *Verstehen* is a way of generating wider causal hypotheses based on 'universals' which, at least to some degree, must themselves in turn be 'verified' against experience. Again Weber does seem to have made reference to 'causes' in *both* of these senses. It is in this context that Weber's sociology may be seen as constituting a 'half-way house' between a purely positivistic sociology with no place for actors' meanings, and a purely 'interpretative sociology' with no place for causal analysis. In all of this Weber's view was that sociology should go as far as is appropriate in making sociology a science, and no further. Thus he insisted that actors' meanings and choices could never be reduced to merely physical or mechanical causation.

vertical division of labour see SEXUAL DIVISION OF LABOUR.

vertical mobility movement up or down a status hierarchy or other hierarchy in a system of SOCIAL STRATIFICATION. See also SOCIAL MOBILITY.

vicious cycle any situation in which an action (e.g. an attempt to resolve a social problem) tends to bring about a further reaction which offsets any gain brought about by the initial action, perhaps tending to bring a return to the state which led to the initial action or exacerbating the initial problem, e.g. an inflationary spiral in which incomes and prices chase each other, and where attempts to control inflation by increased taxation in themselves increase prices. In contrast, a *virtuous cycle* exists where an action to effect an outcome automatically leads to further outcomes which assist in the achieving of this outcome.

Vico, Giambattista (1688–1744) Italian social theorist, whose *New Science* (1725) is widely seen as the forerunner of the view that social science should not simply adopt the methods of the physical sciences. What men had made they could understand in different ways from their understanding of the natural world. Vico suggested that human civilization had developed through three stages – 'divine' and dominated by religion, 'heroic' and militaristic, and 'humanistic' and rational. However, he cautioned that cultural variations between different societies and different times were likely to preclude any simple developmental account of human societies. He also suggested that much historical change was 'cyclical'. Despite similarities between Vico's thinking and many ideas in modern sociology, there are few, if any, direct continuities with his work, which was for long largely forgotten.

victimless crime an act which is defined as an offence within a country's criminal law but which does not result in anyone's physical, financial or other harm. This issue came into sociological discussion in the late 1960s associated with LABELLING THEORY and the NATIONAL DEVIANCY CONFERENCE. Subsequent discussion has highlighted problems with the concept, particularly when the 'public at large' may be viewed as the 'victim' of such activities as soliciting by prostitutes or soft drug use.

victimology the study of the victims of crime.

This area has traditionally been marginal to the concerns of the vast majority of criminologists. The topic had been raised occasionally in arguments about the reliability of CRIMINAL STATISTICS, but was not treated systematically until the 1960s. The US President's Commission on Law Enforcement in 1965 sponsored the first major survey of crime victims, and found that the figure for unreported crime – the 'dark figure' – was much larger than had been assumed. It was also found that victimization and fear of crime were unequally distributed between different classes, different ethnic groups and between men and women. In addition, inner-city residents reported very high incidence of crime and great fear of crime which heavy police presence was not mitigating. The first official British victim survey (M. Hough and P. Mayhew, *The British Crime Survey*, 1983) replicated the US findings on the 'dark figure' of crime and the distribution of crime.

Theoretical approaches to victimology include a focus on the nature of the relation between victim and offender, e.g. the concept of 'victim precipitation'. At one extreme, e.g. the crime of rape, this psychologistic approach effectively 'blames' the victim for inviting the crime.

Other accounts, working from statistics, have focused on geographical, demographic or 'lifestyle' explanations.

In the UK, the major recent work in this field has taken a more sociological and structural line. It represents both a move away from the previous critical CRIMINOLOGY and an attempt to contribute to an understanding of the victim, especially in working-class areas, and to contribute to policy formation, particularly in relation to policing policy and victim support (e.g. Lea and Young, 1983; Jones, Maclean and Young, 1986).

Vienna circle see LOGICAL POSITIVISM.

violence the infliction of physical harm to the human body, or to human property, by physical force, using the body or weapons. The ability to marshal physical force is often a determining factor in social actions, e.g. in domestic relations between husbands and wives (see WIFE BATTERING), or parents and children. In politics, the sustaining of a claim to legitimate monopoly of control over the means of violence within a territory (including defence of the realm), is a defining feature of the STATE. Equally, however, the threat of a recourse to violence against rulers by the ruled acts as a major constraint on the powers of rulers. See also SOREL, REVOLUTION, WARFARE, MILITARY INTERVENTION (IN POLITICS).

Virilio, Paul (1932–) French philosopher, urbanist, and cultural theorist whose major influences include HEIDEGGER, DELEUZE, and FOUCAULT. Although Virilio started his career as an artist of stained glass, he soon turned to architecture and design. During the 1960s he worked with the architect Claude Parnet on several projects which explored the way design interacts with the wider socio-political environment, work published as *The Function of the Oblique* (1996). Expanding on this analysis of space, Virilio's first key text, *Bunker Archaeology* (1975), suggested that the governance of space could be related to the progress of the modern war-machine. In this book Virilio looked at the Atlantic Wall (during World War II Germany constructed 1,500 bunkers along the coast of France in order to prevent an allied invasion) to show how economics, politics, and technology impose a particular ideological position on design and architecture. Later in *Speed and Politics: An Essay on Dromology* (1977), Virilio expanded this theory by arguing that the increasing speed of the modern political-economy has led to the generalization of the war-machine, the disappearance of physical space, and the dominance of real time. Akin to Eric Alliez whose *Capital Time* (1996) explored the way capitalism re-codes our understanding of distance, Virilio's work shows how new technology has resulted in the collapse of physical distance and a renewed emphasis on the psychological category of time. In recent texts such as *The Vision Machine* (1994), *The Art of the Motor* (1995), and *Open Sky* (1997) Virilio argues that the end of space has led to an assault on time. Recalling the postmodern theories advanced by BAUDRILLARD's *Simulations* (1983), he suggests that the invention of quasi-instantanéous communication networks has led to the collapse of represented/representation dichotomy and the end of the real/image distinction. Where Virilio differs from Baudrillard's postmodernism is in his attempt to save the category of reality. His latest works, *Politics of the Very Worst* (1999) and *Information Bomb* (1999), explore the nature of the technological accident and its effects on the political economy. In such a way, Virilio refers to a level of reality that exists beyond the symbolic matrix addressed by Baudrillard's postmodernism. Also see JAMESON, KROKER, POSTMODERNISM.

virtuous cycle see VICIOUS CYCLE.

visual anthropology a recently established branch of social anthropology which investigates the visual dimensions of societies, and is based on the assumption that different cultures frequently involve a strongly visual component, i.e. they look different. The visual can be recorded in various ways, including sketches, photographs, film and videotape, and visual anthropology both employs and explores the implications of the use of such methods in sociology as well as anthropology (see Ball and Smith, 1991).

vital statistics see DEMOGRAPHY.

vocabularies of motive the verbalizations and terminologies employed by social actors, not only to describe their motives but to persuade others as to the acceptability of their actions. As used by MILLS (1940), such vocabularies of motivation do not refer to the universal psychic structure of the human organism, rather they are the typical terms in which, in particular societies, actors justify their actions. It is suggested by Gerth and Mills (1953) that these vocabularies become embedded in our individual and collective psychic structure, but in particular, rather than universal, ways.

voluntarism any theory predicated on the assumption that individual purposes, choice, decisions, etc. are a decisive element in social action. The polar opposite of voluntarism is DETERMINISM. However, often in sociology there is an acceptance that it is appropriate for theories to include both voluntaristic and deterministic elements, e.g. structural determinants which constrain but do not necessarily eliminate choice. Talcott PARSONS (1937), for example, refers to his theory of action as 'voluntaristic', in that it includes reference to 'subjective' elements and individual 'moral' choice. But this does not preclude him from advancing accounts of universal FUNCTIONAL PREREQUISITES. See also ACTION THEORY, STRUCTURE AND AGENCY, METHODOLOGICAL INDIVIDUALISM, FREE WILL.

voluntary association *or* **voluntary organization** any organization (political parties, recreational clubs, etc.) where membership is optional and not a standard requirement of membership of a particular society. As Pickvance (1986) states, there is 'general agreement that voluntary associations are not institutions in the sense of social structures devised to organize action in the main areas of social life, such as firms, schools, governments'. Pickvance also identifies four further usual criteria in both common-sense

and sociological definitions of voluntary associations:
(a) non-commercial orientation;
(b) they are public organizations in the sense that, formally at least, access is open to all;
(c) they are formally constituted organizations, often with an elected administration;
(d) they are nonstatutory, not established by law.

In the USA especially, voluntary associations have been widely identified as playing an indispensable role in the maintenance of STABLE DEMOCRACY, as fostering a participatory POLITICAL CULTURE and providing a training ground for political leaders. See also INTERMEDIATE (OR SECONDARY) GROUPS.

A renewed emphasis is being placed on voluntary and 'third sector' activity – including new partnerships with the state – in the less state-centred politics of the THIRD WAY. See also CIVIC ENTREPRENEUR.

voodoo *or* **voodooism** a syncretic religious CULT, probably of African origin, which is pervasive among the peasantry and urban poor in parts of the Caribbean and Central America, but most particularly in Haiti. Voodoo practices involve MAGIC and WITCHCRAFT, especially the use of charms and spells.

voting behaviour the decision-making processes and the social factors influencing patterns of voting.

Studies of voting behaviour have been of four main types: constituency studies, nationwide studies, cross-national studies, and those focused on particular categories of voters or the political implications of particular class locations. The seminal studies which influenced most later work were by LAZARSFELD et al. (1944) and Berelson et al. (1954) in the USA. These studies established the importance of socioeconomic variables such as socioeconomic status, religion, age, and gender as determinants of voting behaviour. They also made clear the part played by 'group pressures' and OPINION LEADERSHIP as influences on voting behaviour. The dominant paradigm which resulted was that most voting behaviour could be accounted for in terms of the PARTY IDENTIFICATION of voters, which for most individual voters was assumed to be relatively stable.

This model also informed the important study of the British electorate by Butler and Stokes (1969). These researchers painted a picture of voting behaviour in Britain in which, as well as being influenced by CLASS, voters tended to 'inherit' their party identification from their parents, where this had been 'strong', was shared by both parents, and was for main parties. With increased volatility of voting behaviour ('an erosion of partisanship', LIFESTYLE politics, etc.) this model of voting behaviour is now more limited in its scope (see also CLASS DEALIGNMENT). Since many focused studies of voting behaviour and political attitudes (e.g. McKenzie and Silver, 1968, on WORKING-CLASS CONSERVATISM, and GOLDTHORPE and LOCKWOOD, et al., 1968b, on AFFLUENT WORKERS) assumed the predominance of 'class-based voting', seeking to explain departures from this, an overall decline in 'class' voting also has implications for the interpretation of 'cross-class' patterns of voting, which are longer exceptional. See also PARTY IMAGE, POLITICAL ATTITUDES, STABLE DEMOCRACY, MIDDLE-CLASS LEFT.

Vygotsky, Lev Semyonovich (1896–1934) Russian psychologist, and leading figure in the Soviet School, whose view of the higher mental functions as retaining key features of the social interaction from which they derive is proving one of the most influential in modern psychology, especially in the USA. Of particular importance is his theory of the role of language in the development of thought (Vygotsky, *Thought and Language*, 1934, but translated only in 1986). The phenomenon of *private speech*, where children appear to use speech to regulate their own behaviour, results from the internalization of verbally-mediated exchanges with other individuals. In turn, private speech becomes internalized to form *inner speech*, such that mature verbal thought retains the social character of the exchanges from which it originated.

wage labour see CAPITALIST LABOUR CONTRACT.

wage-push inflation see INFLATION.

Wallas, Graham (1858–1932) English political scientist who is sometimes regarded as one of the founding fathers of the BEHAVIOURAL APPROACH in political analysis. His most influential book was *Human Nature in Politics* (1908), in which he argued for a greater emphasis on the role of the 'nonrational' factors in politics, including custom and human psychology. Perhaps his most potent contribution was to coin the term POLITICAL IMAGE.

Wallerstein, Immanuel (1930–) US sociologist and social historian, born in New York and educated at Columbia University. He researched primarily in Africa, between 1955 and 1970. The first volume of his *Modern World-System* appeared in 1974, and since 1976 he has been Distinguished Professor of Sociology at the State University of New York, Binghamton, and Director of the Fernand Braudel Center for the Study of Economies, Historical Systems, and Civilizations. His major contribution has been the development of WORLD SYSTEMS theory and the coordination of a large body of research which comprises interdisciplinary studies in sociology, economics, politics and history. The most general statements of his approach are contained in his *The Capitalist World-Economy* (1979), a collection of essays, and *Historical Capitalism* (1983). See also CENTRE AND PERIPHERY.

war see WARFARE.

Ward, Lester Frank (1841–1913) US sociologist and evolutionary theorist (see EVOLUTIONARY THEORY). He gained his degree in botany and law by part-time study, and went on to work and research in the fields of botany and geology before eventually accepting a professorship of sociology in 1906. Like other 19th-century social theorists, he made a distinction between the study of social process and change, and the description of social structure. His four-stage evolutionary theory was novel in its psychological approach, where an important role was found for purposive action, i.e. the human capacity to guide action in terms of knowledge about its likely consequences ('telesis').

Ward, following thinkers like COMTE, was a positivist (see POSITIVISM) in the sense that he was anxious to use sociological knowledge for political purposes. Indeed, he argued strongly that social reform should be based on, or at least be in accordance with, the laws identified by sociology. Using the evolutionary principle of 'telesis', Ward supported movements aimed at the emancipation of women, and of the industrial working class. He was a strong critic of social and economic inequality, and argued that the state could produce policies, such as universal education, which would help to promote egalitarianism. Among the more important of his works are *Pure Sociology* (1903), *Applied Sociology* (1906) and *The Psychic Factors of Civilization* (1906).

warfare 1 violent, usually armed, conflict between STATES or peoples.

2 comparable but not necessarily violent conflicts between classes, etc., but which stop short of war in sense **1**. The first of these uses is by far the most important and is dealt with here.

Warfare and preparation for warfare is often regarded as a near universal feature of human societies. This is sometimes explained by presence of innate human aggression as well as by the operation of a TERRITORIAL IMPERATIVE in human societies. Against this, however, it is also clear that the incidence of warfare is highly variable, and that in some societies there exists little recourse to warfare and no tradition of MILITARISM. Plainly, warfare is a culturally influenced phenomenon rather than simply biologically determined. Nor would there appear to be, in simple or in more developed societies, any straightforward pattern of ecological or territorial pressures which can provide an explanation of variations in the incidence of warfare. In modern societies in particular, warfare requires understanding in politicoeconomic terms.

As the historian TILLY remarks, 'the state made war, and war made the state'. In particular, as numerous commentators have insisted, the modern European NATION STATE can be seen as having been 'built for the battlefield' (ANDERSON, 1974b) – see ABSOLUTISM. Not only this, the entire modern NATION-STATE SYSTEM remains centred on sovereign nation states in which the threat of war is an everpresent possibility. and in which, at least until recently, the very survival of the world was threatened by the antagonism of 'superpowers' (see also STRATEGIC THEORY, ARMS RACE, COLD WAR). Under these circumstances, and given that the economic and the political side-effects of war have also been extensive (e.g. as a stimulus to reform or REVOLUTION or to political reaction), it is surprising that the study of warfare has not been more central in sociology. Now this is being remedied with a much greater attention being given to the subject by sociologists (e.g. the work of MANN and GIDDENS). A key general issue is how political and military changes and economic and social changes interact. Whereas classical Marxism and many other areas of social science have in the past tended to explain the former in terms of the latter (e.g. see IMPERIALISM), now the tendency is to give much greater credence to the reverse relationship.

See also MILITARY-CIVILIAN RATIO, MILITARY-INDUSTRIAL COMPLEX, STRATEGIC THEORY, CIVIL WAR.

Warner, William Lloyd (1898–1970) US sociologist best remembered for his much discussed COMMUNITY STUDIES of New England life.

wealth the value of the resources possessed by an individual or a society (compare CAPITAL).

An important issue in any society is the distribution of wealth *within it*. Usually, in all but the simplest of societies, the ownership of wealth is unequal, and the degree to which this is so is an important differentiating feature of types of society. In the modern world advanced industrial societies generally manifest less inequality of *income* than less developed societies, but inequalities in the distribution of wealth remain great, although these are often difficult to quantify, given the tendency of wealth to go often unreported – e.g. at the time of death – because it is subject to taxation.

The massive inequality in wealth which exists *between* societies – especially between FIRST and THIRD WORLD societies – is, of course, also a major feature distinguishing between nation states in the modern WORLD SYSTEM, and a major aspect of the potential economic and political instability of this system.

Webb, Sydney (1859–1947) and Beatrice, *née* Potter (1858–1943) English social researchers and social activists, who in partnership played a formative role in the development of labour history (e.g. *The History of Trade Unions*, 1894, and *Industrial Democracy*, 1897) founded the London School of Economics and Political Science, in 1895; wrote voluminously on local government (*History of English Local Government*, 9 vols, 1903–29); were responsible for the minority report of the Poor Law Commission (1905–7);

founded the *New Statesman* (1913); were influential in the Fabian Society and the British Labour Party; and were advocates in the cause of the USSR (*Soviet Communism: a New Civilization?*, 1935). Besides the twenty or so books written in collaboration, each wrote many more books and pamphlets separately. In *Our Partnership* (1948), describing their life and work, Beatrice Webb wrote that they regarded their concern with 'the study of social institutions' as 'sociology'. Not all modern sociologists would agree, for the Webbs' work often related only relatively obliquely to the most central concerns of sociology as a developing academic discipline. But that the Webbs contributed much to historical understanding, to empirical social investigation in the English tradition and to the promotion of social welfare is undeniable.

Weber, Max (1864–1920)

German economist, historian and major classical sociologist and, along with MARX and DURKHEIM, usually regarded as one of a 'trinity' of major classical sociologists. Weber was born in Erfurt, Thuringia, and educated at the Universities of Heidelberg, Berlin and Göttingen. After initial studies in philosophy and law, his interests gravitated towards economics, history and latterly sociology. As a result, Weber's scholarship cannot be confined within narrow disciplinary boundaries; he taught law in Berlin from 1892, before becoming professor of political economy at Freiburg in 1894, and professor of economics at Heidelberg in 1897, when a depressive illness interrupted his research and precluded further involvement in teaching until he accepted chairs in sociology at Vienna in 1918, and at Munich in the following year. Throughout his life Weber took an active interest in the social and political affairs of Germany; his politics were nationalist in tendency, yet critical, liberal and anti-authoritarian, especially in his defence of academic freedom against those who sought to make the universities subserve the interests of the state.

Weber's scholarly output is formidable in extent and controversial in its content and interpretation. In summary his aims were:
(a) to put the social sciences on a sound methodological footing;
(b) to establish their limits with respect to VALUE RELEVANCE and social policy issues;
(c) to provide a range of generalizations and concepts for application to the study of substantive problems;
(d) to contribute to the study of issues that interested him, especially those associated with the nature and origins of modern industrial society and of the process of rationalization that underpinned it.

In pursuit of these aims he wrote extensively on the methodology and philosophy of the social sciences (especially see Weber, *The Methodology f the Social Sciences* (ed. Finch), 1949), and contributed to the study of ancient society, economic history, the comparative religion and social structures of China, India and Europe, and, *inter alia,* to the sociologies of law, politics and music. For translations of these see *The Religions of China* (1951), *Ancient Judaism* (1952). *The Religion of India* (1958), *The City* (1958).

The most comprehensive systematization of his sociological thinking is *Wirtschaft und Gesellschaft* (1922). Bendix, *Max Weber: an Intellectual Portrait* (1960) remains a very useful overall guide to Weber's work; Gerth and Mills, *From Max Weber* (1946) is a 'classic' compilation.

For Weber, the aim of sociology was to achieve an *interpretative understanding* (see also MEANINGFUL UNDERSTANDING) of subjectively meaningful human action which exposed the actors' motives, at one level 'the causes' of ACTIONS, to view. Acting individuals constituted the only social reality, and so he was opposed to the use of collective concepts (like the STATE, SOCIETY etc.) unless these were firmly related to the actions of individuals. He also opposed the idea that the social sciences could discover laws, especially development laws, in the manner of the natural sciences, though he thought that social scientists could, and should, employ lawlike generalizations – statements of tendency – about the nature, course and consequences of human conduct. These were possible because human behaviour tended to follow more or less regular patterns. They were necessary in order to establish the causal adequacy of explanation (see POSTULATE OF ADEQUACY), and could be given statistical expression provided that the statistics were supported by a meaningful interpretation of the conduct to which they referred,

Weber's work abounds in generalizations, and in concepts ranging from a basic typology of social action (see TYPES OF SOCIAL ACTION to well-known constructs like BUREAUCRACY, CHARISMA, etc., all of which are designed to facilitate the analysis of action and to elucidate its causes, consequences and institutional expressions. Many of these concepts are IDEAL TYPES, i.e. logical simplifications of tendencies more or less present in a complex reality, constructed from a one-sidedly selective viewpoint by the sociologist. Weber insisted that scientific concepts cannot exhaust reality, which is infinite and too complex for the finite human mind to grasp completely. Concepts, therefore, could never stand as final, exhaustive, definitive accounts, but were rather HEURISTIC DEVICES against which reality could be compared and measured for the purposes of its further exploration and explanation.

The intimate connection between social sciences and values arose from this need for selectivity; social science was 'value relevant' in that the problems which scientists selected for study, and their conceptualization, were determined by the values of the scientists and/or those of their communities (see VALUE RELEVANCE). Yet social science also had to be value free insofar as values should not be allowed to intrude into the actual investigations and their results (see VALUE FREEDOM) and science could never finally validate value judgements, moral choices or political preferences. In this sense, the world of science and the world of moral and political choice were seen by Weber as logically disjunct. To assume otherwise would be to abdicate the human responsibility for making choices and standing by their consequences.

Weber held these views during the bitter debates about methodology and values which took place in early 20th-century German social science (see also METHODENSTREIT). At the same time he developed his own research interests which found a major focus in the process of rationalization underpinning modern industrial society. Weber applied the term RATIONALIZATION to the West in order to capture a process of disenchantment or demagification of the world, in which action was increasingly reduced to prosaic calculation and oriented to the routine administration of a world dominated by large-scale organizations and the specialized division of labour which found their ultimate expression in bureaucracy. Weber felt uneasy about this process which he saw as destructive of human vitality and freedom; the rule-bound bureaucratic *milieu* compelled people to become narrow specialists; orientation to its values made people into conforming moral cowards who preferred the security of the routine to the exercise of creative imagination and responsibility which were necessary for the preservation of human freedom – the highest ideal of the West.

Weber saw this process as uniquely European in origin. In a sweeping comparative analysis of European and Oriental religion and social structures – somewhat misleadingly subsumed under the rubric of the SOCIOLOGY OF RELIGION – he tries to show how human beings, orienting to different religious, social and political values, created ideas and structures that inhibited the process in the East and facilitated it in the West. In these studies he tried to indicate how Western religion alone broke the power of MAGIC and thus exercised a decisive influence, independently of economic interests, on the rationalization of economic and social life. Here also he sought to demonstrate how the decentralized Western political structure, together with the legacy of ROMAN LAW, created the conditions for the development of individual rights and rational administration which capitalism needed and further fostered as it grew. The much discussed, sometimes maligned and much misunderstood PROTESTANT ETHIC thesis (Weber, 1930) is, therefore, but a small fragment of a much larger analysis of Western capitalist society and its origins.

Weber's emphasis on the power of religious interests to influence human conduct makes it tempting to regard him as a thinker opposed to Marx. Yet this judgement may be too simple. Weber regarded MARX and NIETZSCHE as the two intellectual giants of his age. Thus, while he rejected the crude economic determinism of vulgar Marxists, it is by no means obvious that he imputed such determinism to Marx himself. Weber, in fact, accepted that economic interests were a prime, indeed often a decisive, mover in shaping human action. More, his concern about modern society's implications for human freedom and creativity have something in common with the concern that Marx expressed through his concept of ALIENATION. Nevertheless, Weber's analysis of the structure and dynamics of modern capitalist society differs from Marx's. He does not, for example, see it splitting up into two great hostile classes based on

property relations. Instead he saw the bases for conflict group formation as being wider, involving:
(a) a larger number of classes, determined by market relationships and thus by credentials and skills as well as property relations;
(b) potentially complicating considerations of status and party which provided possible foci for conflict independently of class (see also CLASS, STATUS AND PARTY, and MULTIDIMENSIONAL ANALYSIS OF SOCIAL STRATIFICATION).

Above all, however, Weber did not share Marx's optimism about the possibilities for liberation held to inhere in socialism. Insofar as socialism involved the centralization of economic and political power it would extend bureaucratization and thus intensify, rather than alleviate, the problems confronting freedom.

When it touches the future of Western society, therefore, Weber's work is shot through with pathos; it seems ironic to him that a people who established individual freedom should have created conditions that did so much to diminish it. His analysis of modern mass-democratic politics did little to reassure him. Based as they were on mass bureaucratic parties, led by individuals who compromised their ideals in the interests of preserving their organizations, and their jobs, these politics tended to be supportive of the *status quo* and provided little scope for critical input from the individual. Weber's longing for great charismatic leaders, for people who, by sheer force of their personalities, could rouse the masses and challenge the structure of bureaucratic domination, is perhaps understandable in the light of this analysis, even if it is a little distasteful in the light of a figure like Hitler. Weber, however, was not a proto-NAZI; he clearly believed in political conflict, in which the leaders and their parties competed for power through the mechanism of elections; he defended academic freedom and the rights of Jewish and Marxist intellectuals against a state that tended to discriminate against them. Nevertheless, his nationalism was undoubted, and this makes it difficult for some people to accept him as a liberal thinker (DAHRENDORF, 1967).

Weber's output has not escaped criticism. Some have suggested that he failed in his aim to provide an adequate foundation for a 'meaningful sociology' (SCHUTZ, 1967; WINCH, 1958), and, indeed, others have suggested that his empirical work is more concerned to elucidate the structural determinants of action than with meanings. His views on ethical neutrality have also come under attack (especially see GOULDNER, 1973), though they also attract considerable support in contemporary sociology. As Boudon and Bourricaud (1989) suggest, however, 'the Weberian heritage has furnished a series of continually relevant landmarks to those researchers who have not given up the association of both a wide-ranging historical-comparative perspective with careful institutional analysis and personal commitment with methodological detachment.'

welfare pluralism see COMMUNITY CARE.

welfare rights the legal entitlement to services provided for in SOCIAL POLICY. Welfare rights stand in contrast to those arrangements where GATEKEEPERS have the discretion to determine which people will receive a service and who will be denied. An examination of the British social-security system shows that, historically, both welfare rights and welfare discretion have been promoted at different times. Supporters of welfare rights argue that having legal *entitlements* is a means of ensuring that claimants are not at the mercy of the subjective value-judgements of the people who have control over welfare resources, such as social-security officers and housing managers. Critics of welfare rights have argued that claimants often do not know their rights and are placed in a demeaning situation by having to find advocates, such as the Citizens Advice Bureau. They also argue that the legal definition of entitlement cannot foresee all the circumstances when a need may arise and this may lead to some needy people being excluded from help when they could have been afforded support in a discretionary system.

welfare state the state provision of benefits and social services intended to improve the wellbeing of citizens. The term was introduced after the Second World War to refer to social legislation, particularly in the areas of health, education, income maintenance, housing and personal social services. The welfare state intervenes in people's lives at national and local levels. Since 1945, the welfare state has expanded its scope in the UK and it is now a major concern of government (in its cost and operation). Life in all modern Western societies is now affected by welfare concerns and the idea of a welfare society has a strong ideological appeal.

There are differing sociological explanations of the welfare state:

(a) the citizenship view, most developed in the work of T. H. MARSHALL, which suggests that the state needs to provide minimal welfare support to ensure that an individual can properly participate in a liberal-democratic society;

(b) the functionalist view expressed especially by PARSONS, that state intervention through social policy is necessary for resolving conflict in complex industrial societies;

(c) the Marxist view, which suggests that the welfare state has an ideological role in legitimating capitalist social relations, and that individuals give support to the state and to a capitalist economic system because they adhere to a belief in the welfare that a capitalist state provides.

Marxists have also argued that a welfare state supports the owners of the means of production by reducing the reproduction costs of labour; the welfare state's function is to provide a healthy, educated and well-housed labour force. Further, the conditions under which welfare support is given, that people receive minimal support and have to prove eligibility, are seen to act as a powerful means of social control. However, Marxists have also argued that there are aspects of the welfare state which are genuinely beneficial to the working classes, such as the National Health Service or rent subsidies. They have argued that these benefits are the result of political pressure coming from the labour movement. Marxists see the welfare state, therefore, as an arena of class conflict which is ambivalent in its operation, partially supporting the owners of the means of production and partially supporting the working classes. More recently, feminist sociologists have argued that explanations of the welfare state have ignored the relationship between women and the welfare state. They argue that many aspects of the welfare state were achieved by women working within the labour movement before 1945, such as the Women's Labour League and the Women's Cooperative Guild. They have also argued that the welfare state has been a powerful regulator of women's lives by sustaining ideas about the roles of women as carers. For example, the Beveridge Report of 1942 specifically excluded married women from being eligible for national insurance benefits; they were to be dependent on their husbands for any social security support. Feminists have also been critical of policies promoting COMMUNITY CARE, arguing that community care is euphemistic for the care that women provide for dependent relatives.

Following the introduction of monetarist policies and talk of FISCAL CRISIS in a number of Western societies since 1979, the idea of welfare being provided by the state has been questioned. Sober assessment of welfare policies, however, indicates that the welfare state is surviving these critiques, albeit in somewhat changed form. In the UK, levels of funding remain high. Government reforms throughout the 1980s and 1990s have been aimed more at changing the institutional arrangements of the welfare state by limiting the direct provision of welfare by state institutions, introducing quasi-markets and a separation of purchasers of services from providers, allowing schools and hospitals to manage themselves, and channelling state funding into an increasing number of private and voluntary organizations. The long-term implications of these changes, which certainly have as one aim 'value for money' (VFM) and a reduction of funding, remain to be assessed. See H. Glennerster and J. Midgley (eds), *The Radical Right and the Welfare States* (1991). See also SOCIAL POLICY, POVERTY, CITIZEN RIGHTS, NEW PUBLIC MANAGEMENT, AUDIT, PURCHASER-PROVIDER SPLIT.

Weltanschauung see WORLD VIEW.

***wertrational* action** see TYPES OF SOCIAL ACTION.

Western Marxism see MARXISM.

white-collar crime 'a crime committed by a person of respectability and high social status in the course of his occupation'. This is the definition which Edwin H. Sutherland gave in his book which started systematic sociological interest in this area: *White-collar Crime* (1949). Sutherland argues that criminal behaviour is not confined to working-class people. It is frequently, even routinely, found among people of high social status and respectability, but white-collar crimes are rarely treated as such.

Sutherland's focus was on crimes committed by managers and others in the course of their occupations, though the usage has often been broadened to include other areas of middle-class crime. In a study of 70 US corporations Sutherland found a large number of crimes including fraud, misrepresentation, infringe-ments of patents, and others. Much of his evidence did not come from criminal statistics but from the investigations of independent commissions, because very few of the offenders had been prosecuted. Even though the total amounts of money lost to companies, banks, etc., runs into many millions of pounds, it is still the case that white-collar crimes are very much under-represented in the CRIMINAL STATISTICS and are not stigmatized in the way that violent crimes or thefts from individuals are. The importance of Sutherland's work is in correcting common assumptions about the distribution of crime and in qualifying some arguments which have linked crime exclusively to deprivation.

white-collar worker a nonmanual employee. The term is mainly applied to those who occupy relatively routine posts in the lower sectors of nonmanual employment. A focus on differences in dress between nonmanual and manual workers reflects historical underlying differences in STATUS and WORK SITUATION, as well as MARKET SITUATION, between the two types of workers. See also MANUAL AND NONMANUAL LABOUR, MIDDLE CLASSES.

Whorf, Benjamin see SAPIR-WHORF HYPOTHESIS.

wife battering a colloquial term now also used in sociology to refer to the physical abuse of women by their husbands or partners. By feminist theorists, such physical abuse is held to be explicable, not only as the outcome of the greater physical strength of most males, but as an adjunct of a wider cultural climate that supports 'male domination'. The incidence of wife battering is difficult to determine, but, in the UK, an increased willingness of women to report such actions, and of police and other authorities to take action against it, has meant its greatly increased visibility.

will to power (NEIZSCHE) our individual capacity for cultural judgement and identity as autonomous agents.

Winch, Peter (1926–97) British philosopher, in the analytic tradition of WITTGENSTEIN, who has written primarily in moral philosophy, and, early in his career, on the philosophy of social science. His early contributions, notably *The Idea of a Social Science* (1958), have been enormously influential. Winch attacked the dominant form of sociology, which was a broadly positivist and functionalist one, arguing that fundamental investigations of social life must be philosophical (and ethical) rather than aping the natural sciences. For Winch social action is a matter of following (and breaking) the rules and conventions which underlie the meanings of actions, and which can be grasped or 'understood' by sociologists (see also RULES AND RULE FOLLOWING). Winch wanted specifically to exclude 'causation' (in the sense of 'constant conjunction' in David HUME's theory of causality). Social life, he suggested, is more like the unfolding of discourse than of chains of causation. He argued that the heart of philosophy – EPISTEMOLOGY – rests on rules and conventions (Wittgenstein's FORMS OF LIFE) and that philosophical and sociological investigations are therefore inseparable. His insistence on the variety of ways of living, each with a differently based epistemology, also seemed to result in the notion of 'truth' being 'relativized' leading Winch to be regarded as a social and cognitive relativist.

The refutation of Winch's arguments has been attempted by many. The most successful have challenged his Humean notion of science, arguing that a logical line cannot be drawn between 'causal' science and non-science, and that 'forms of life' cannot finally be circumscribed in the way that Winch suggests.

Windelband, Wilhelm (1848–1915) NEO-KANTIAN German philosopher, remembered largely for his distinction between two contrasting 'focuses of interest' in social studies: IDIOGRAPHIC AND NOMOTHETIC, the latter concerned with the discovery of scientific laws and the former the distinctive approach required when dealing with individual historical phenomena. Along with RICKERT, Windelband argued that whilst economics and sociology, in seeking to establish generalizations, could quite properly adopt a natural science methodology, it must also be recognized that historical and cultural studies often required the use of idiographic methods. One important emphasis in Windelband's work was the significance of values in the selection of problems for study in the cultural realm, a view which influenced WEBER (see VALUE RELEVANCE), although, unlike him, Windelband held open the possibility that universally valid ethical norms might be established.

winner-take-all society (coined by R. Frank, a society in which, in the name of merit, those who rise to the top obtain an ever-growing share of a societies resources, while those at the bottom receive less. This tendency is fuelled by an increasingly global market for highly skilled scarce labour (see also ECONOMIC RENT).

Winnicott, Donald (1896–1971) a British paediatrician, child psychiatrist and psychoanalyst who has been a major influence on psychoanalysis since the 1930s. A member of the OBJECT RELATIONS SCHOOL, he developed his theory of the child's gradual differentiation into a separate independent individual through his study of early infant – mother interaction and ATTACHMENT processes. Adult personality problems are traced to failures in this early relationship, and regression, in analysis, suggested as appropriate therapy to help resolve them. In contrast to KLEIN, Winnicott places great emphasis on the influence of the environment on development. Winnicott also defined the 'security' objects or toys that children often have as 'transitional objects', forming a support while the child moves towards independence.

Wirth, Louis (1897–1952) German-born, US sociologist and a member of the CHICAGO SCHOOL. His main contribution was to URBAN SOCIOLOGY – see URBANISM AS A WAY OF LIFE. His classic work is *The Ghetto* (1925).

witchcraft and sorcery the use of MAGIC in an attempt to achieve ends which are socially disapproved, e.g. harmful to the victim. Whilst the terms are often used interchangeably, distinctions are also drawn.

For Evans-Pritchard (1937), in *witchcraft* the powers claimed or alleged are typically seen as 'inherent' and portrayed as pervasive in the individual, whilst in *sorcery* these powers are regarded as learned and are usually more specific (see also SHAMAN).

Belief in witchcraft and sorcery occurs mainly in premodern societies. In tribal and preindustrial societies witchcraft functions as a mechanism for the expression of social strains and conflicts. According to Marwick (1970), accusations of witchcraft arise in contexts in which a misfortune occurs and an explanation is sought among those who may have some reason for practising witchcraft against the person experiencing the misfortune.

Wittfogel, Karl (1896–1988) German-born comparative sociologist best known for his work on Chinese society and for his controversial book *Oriental Despotism* (1957) (see ORIENTAL DESPOTISM). From 1925 until 1933 Wittfogel worked at the Institute for Social Research at Frankfurt (see FRANKFURT SCHOOL OF CRITICAL THEORY). Subsequently he moved to the United States.

Wittgenstein, Ludwig (1889–1951) Austrian-born philosopher whose influence on modern philosophy and on certain sectors of sociology has been immense. Wittgenstein is unusual among philosophers in making a major contribution to two divergent major movements within the subject:

(a) In the *Tractatus Logico-Philosophicus* (1923), language was presented as 'picturing' the world. According to this theory, the 'truth' or 'falsity of any proposition is ultimately a matter of its 'correspondence' or otherwise with the 'atomic facts', i.e. the 'ultimate simples' that make up the world. This view (connected with Russell's 'logical atomism') exerted a major influence on LOGICAL POSITIVISM;

(b) In *Philosophical Investigations* (1953), published posthumously, Wittgenstein – who had previously given up philosophy, believing his task completed with the *Tractatus* – repudiated his 'picture theory', advancing instead a theory in which language was seen as providing 'tools' which operate only within particular social contexts or in relation to particular tasks. This is the meaning of Wittgenstein's most influential concept at this stage: language as a FORM OF LIFE (see also LANGUAGE GAMES). Whereas in the *Tractatus* language was the basis of universal truths, a secure basis for science, now there were multiple languages, and any truth was relative to these. Arguably, Wittgenstein s later philosophy was implicit in his earlier view, for in quitting philosophy at this stage, he had reported himself as leaving unsaid, 'what cannot be said'. In his later philosophy, there is much that can be said, but nothing that can be said independently of particular languages.

It is in its 'second' form, that Wittgenstein's philosophy has exerted a ramifying influence on sociology, especially on SOCIAL PHENOMENOLOGY and ETHNOMETHODOLOGY, partly through its influence on LINGUISTIC PHILOSOPHY and partly more directly, and also through the work of Peter WINCH. It has also had a profound effect on historical and social studies of natural science, seen especially in the work of Thomas KUHN and Paul FEYERABEND. The influence of the later Wittgenstein has been seen as a baneful one by some sociological commentators, e.g. GELLNER (1974), who sees Wittgenstein's influence on Winch as ushering in a 'new idealism' and a 'new relativism'. For others (as for Winch), the MEANINGFUL UNDERSTANDING of social actors' beliefs and values in the particular social contexts in which these are located is of the essence in sociological analysis, and the subject's only goal. There is also a third view, however. For many, Wittgenstein's emphasis on first understanding social actors' beliefs and values before trying to explain them is what is most important and valuable. In such a viewpoint, there are direct parallels between what some sociologists have taken from Wittgenstein, and what can also be found in WEBER's conception of accounts of social reality: 'meaningful' and wider 'causal' explanations are combined.

women-headed households HOUSEHOLDS headed by women rather than men. The term has been used especially in connection with Third World and peasant economies where the norm is PATRIARCHY. Here the presence of such atypical households is liable to present special problems of poverty and disadvantage (e.g. Kumari, 1989). The sources of women-headed households include widowhood, desertion and divorce, and economic migration of the male partner.

women's liberation movement the multifaceted resurgence of Western FEMINISM from the 1960s. The experience of women activists in the CIVIL RIGHTS MOVEMENT in the US prompted them to focus on the necessity to struggle against the subordination of women. In contrast to earlier women's movements, the women's liberation movement stressed that the 'personal is political' and saw 'consciousness raising' as the basis for all theory and practice. The emphasis was therefore on a concrete personal politics which would enable women to analyse the nature of their oppression and struggle to overcome it.

The movement is diverse and nonhierarchical, loosely structured and without rigid principles. There are no leaders and a concern with the liberation of women finds expression in many different social contexts. The strands of the movement are, however, united around one major tenet, i.e. that all women share a common oppression and one that is not shared by men, who are identified as benefiting from it.

A major concern in the early years of the movement was with the importance of *sisterhood* – a sense of identifying with and belonging to a global community of women. Hooks (1981), amongst others, has stressed the inauthenticity of this concept in the face of continuing racism within the movement. In the 1980s the *divisions* between women began to be explored alongside the social factors which unite them.

Trivialization of the term women's liberation movement ('women's lib') by the Western mass media has led many feminists to use 'women's movement' in preference. In doing so there is a danger that awareness of the movement's commitment to feminist principles and to the goal of liberation may be eroded. Nevertheless 'women's movement' has the advantage of being the more inclusive term and allows connections to be made between women's struggles cross-culturally. See also FEMINIST THEORY.

women's studies a multidisciplinary approach to the analysis and understanding of the position and experience of women in patriarchal societies both past and present. Emerging alongside the growth of the WOMEN'S LIBERATION MOVEMENT in the late 1960s, women's studies programmes have been developed and expanded in higher education establishments in Europe and the US. Informed essentially by a commitment to feminist theories, methodologies and practice, women's studies programmes seek, via a woman-centred approach to learning, to challenge the misrepresentation of women found in traditional disciplines, including sociology. The content of women's studies courses has been shaped by feminists working within the humanities, natural sciences and social sciences. They have also been shaped by feminists working in the community, particularly in women's organizations. Thus women's studies programmes have emerged out of women's direct experience of and response to sexual exploitation and oppression. An essential aim of women's studies is to render visible women's engagement with society and culture whilst making explicit the masculine biases underpinning traditional knowledge. Women's studies programmes seek to challenge all major forms of discrimination and to question the rigid boundaries demarcating one academic subject from another. As such, they provide a radical critique of established academic knowledge and educational practice. The content of such programmes varies but most courses aim to combine a feminist analysis of women's oppression with the development of practical skills such as assertiveness training. Traditional methods of teaching and assessment are re-evaluated in the light of women's needs and links are drawn between theoretical concerns and the daily experience of women.

work see SOCIOLOGY OF WORK.

working class 1 manual workers, i.e. those who labour primarily with their hands, rather than with their brains (nonmanual workers). In this sense, in Britain the proportion of the population that is working class has declined steadily over the course of the 20th century. However, an issue exists as to whether, for some purposes, routine white-collar workers should also be included as part of the working class (see also PROLETARIANIZATION).

2 members of the PROLETARIAT, i.e. all those employed as wage labourers or salaried workers, who neither own nor control the MEANS OF PRODUCTION. In this second sense, the working class embraces by far the majority of the working population (but see also INTERMEDIATE CLASSES, CONTRADICTORY CLASS LOCATIONS).

In either sense 1 or 2, divisions, and variations in class consciousness, within the working class have also been a major interest – see WORKING-CLASS CONSERVATISM, LABOUR ARISTOCRACY, CLASS IMAGERY.

working-class conservatism (in the UK) manual working-class voting for the Conservative Party, and the attitudes associated with this. Since this behaviour deviates from the working-class norm, and is also sometimes seen as at odds with working-class interests, a number of explanations have been proposed:

(a) DEFERENCE, i.e. acceptance of the middle class and the Conservative party as the traditional ruling class, especially by older voters;

(b) a particular tendency to working-class Conservatism among women, explained in part by their different work locations and less frequent contact with traditional modes of working-class political organization such as trade unions;

(c) affluence and *embourgeoisement*, seen as occurring especially among voters moving from traditional working localities (see AFFLUENT WORKER, EMBOURGEOISEMENT THESIS);

(d) MEDIATED-CLASS LOCATIONS, e.g. '*middle-class connections*', such as a spouse or one or both parents with a nonmanual background, leading to 'cross-pressures' on manual working-class voters (see GOLDTHORPE et al., 1968a);

(e) a continuing tendency to generalized ideological incorporation of the working class existing in Western capitalist societies, resulting from an overall CULTURAL HEGEMONY achieved by right-wing values in these societies.

These explanations are sometimes complementary, each of them explaining only a part of the phenomenon, although not all of them are accepted by every theorist (e.g. see DOMINANT IDEOLOGY THESIS).

Whatever reasons, it is clear that the late 20th century has also witnessed a more general decline in working-class support for the Labour Party and perhaps an overall CLASS DEALIGNMENT (Crewe, 1977) in British politics, involving increased working-class support for the Conservative Party but also increased middle-class voting for the Labour Party (see also MIDDLE-CLASS RADICALISM). Some commentators have suggested that this points to a decline in the general salience of class in voting behaviour also shedding doubt on traditional conceptions of working-class interests and any interpretations of working-class conservatism as involving FALSE CONSCIOUSNESS. See also VOTING BEHAVIOUR, PARTY IDENTIFICATION.

work orientations see ORIENTATIONS TO WORK.

work situation the social relationships which workers enter into at their workplace. For LOCKWOOD (1958 and 1966) and GOLDTHORPE and Lockwood et al. (1968a), three interrelated dimensions of social stratification are significant in influencing a person's position within the stratification system: 'work situation', as well as MARKET SITUATION and STATUS SITUATION. For example, the fact that routine white-collar workers are more likely than manual workers to rub shoulders with management, is one reason for differences in their class consciousness and political attitudes compared with manual workers, even where their market situation is no better or may even be worse. See MULTIDIMENSIONAL ANALYSIS OF SOCIAL STRATIFICATION, CLASS, STATUS AND PARTY, AFFLUENT WORKER, CLASS IMAGERY.

world growth story the account of human affairs, criticized by GELLNER (1964), which presents the development of human societies as a history of 'all-embracing upward growth', dovetailing with biological evolutionism and with Darwinism. Those such as Gellner, GIDDENS OR MANN, who have argued strongly against this notion, prefer to see distinctively human history as involving the 'rise and fall of civilizations' and 'uneven development'; as 'episodic' rather than continuous (see also EPISODES, EPISODIC CHARACTERIZATION, EVOLUTIONARY THEORY).

world market factories (WMFs) see NEW INTERNATIONAL DIVISION OF LABOUR.

world system a conception of the modern social world which views it as comprising one interlinked entity with an international division of labour unregulated by any one political structure. The perspective was developed by WALLERSTEIN and has given

	Core nations	*Semi-Periphery*	*Periphery*
Capitalist ruling groups			
Broad middle strata – socially integrated			
Underclasses – malintegrated; disaffected, but lacking power			

Fig. 35 **World system.** Wallerstein's 'world-system' model in terms of a three-fold division of nation states each internally divided into a three-fold class system is at odds with either conventional theories of modernization or Marxian theories of social transformation and revolution. For Wallerstein, divisions between nations and between classes are interrelated aspects of the dynamics of the world system unlikely to change in the short term. There can be mobility by nations, or by individuals within classes, but the overall pattern of the system in terms of the above 3 x 3 model is likely to remain.

rise to a large body of work, especially in the US. The key concepts are that the capitalist world is divided into CENTRE AND PERIPHERY and semi-periphery, with Northern Europe since the 16th-century, and later the US, dominating world trade. The centre countries were those that developed strong nation states and a proletarianized free labour force. The peripheral countries, comprising most of the THIRD WORLD, had various forms of unfree labour, contemporarily low levels of proletarianization, with household organization of production and weak nation states. This provides a view of structure and change which challenges both conventional MARXIST and MODERNIZATION approaches and has affinities with DEPENDENCY THEORY. See Fig. 35. See also UNDERDEVELOPMENT, GLOBALIZATION.

world time a conception of time, introduced by Eberhard (1965), which emphasizes the way in which the conjuncture of types of society existing at a specific time or period in history profoundly affects the context and outcome of action and developments in particular societies. The importance of this notion is that it suggests that those theories which propose that all individual societies move through a single set sequence of evolutionary stages are wrong. See also TIME-SPACE EDGES, EPISODE, EPISODIC CHARACTERIZATION.

world view *or* ***Weltanshauung*** Max WEBER's term for the overarching belief system of a particular social group.

World Wide Web (www) the information organised on the INTERNET that utilises URL (Universal Resource Locator) characters to identify locations.

writing the encoding of the spoken word by inscribing symbols on a surface, usually paper, but also in other materials such as clay.

Writing, since it allows the storage of information on an altogether new scale, is a social innovation whose significance in social and economic development is profound. At first the preserve of an exclusive class, the ultimate spread of writing, and subsequently printing and other forms of mass communications dependent upon this, is a major source of both the modernization and democratization of societies. See also LITERACY.

wrong level fallacy see ECOLOGICAL FALLACY.

x, y

xenophobia an exaggerated hostility towards or fear of foreigners. See ETHNOCENTRISM.

youth culture the subcultural features which surround youth as a social category. These include:

(a) distinctive fashions and tastes, especially in music and clothes;

(b) social relationships centred on friendship and peer groups, rather than families;

(c) a relative centrality of leisure rather than work;

(d) a challenge to adult values, and individual experimentation with lifestyles;

(e) a degree of classlessness in leisure tastes and behaviour.

Although divisions between adult and youth are evident, youth culture is far from being completely uniform, but is divided by gender and ethnicity, as well as by class and education, and by a myriad competing cultural styles.

The rise of distinctive youth cultures in modern societies is associated with the central role of MASS MEDIA OF COMMUNICATIONS and with increasing affluence. These have created new markets in cultural products aimed primarily at young people. See also ADOLESCENCE, LIFE COURSE, RESISTANCE THROUGH RITUAL, LEISURE, POPULAR CULTURE.

youth unemployment a specific form of UNEMPLOYMENT associated with the period between leaving school and entry into employment. In the 1970s and 80s youth unemployment grew steadily in the UK and most of the Western world. Its persistence, and public policy measures designed to alleviate it, led to a number of research projects. An emphasis on labour supply factors (demographic change, high cost of labour, and lack of skills) led to arguments and policies for more vocationalism in education. Sociologists have tended to criticize 'supply side' arguments as 'blaming the victim' for being unemployed. Unemployment is seen by sociologists as a result of structural and institutional factors, rather than the characteristics of the particular social groups affected by it.

Yule's Q a measure of association (CORRELATION) invented by the mathematician G. V. Yule. Q can be used to calculate the association between two VARIABLES which can take only two possible values.

Z

Zeitgeist (German) the spirit of a particular age. This is a term particularly employed in the study of 19th-century romanticism, and denotes the essential beliefs and feelings of a particular epoch. See also DILTHEY.

zero-sum game any game or analogous social situation in which what one player or side loses the other gains (Von Neumann and Morgenstein, 1947). See also THEORY OF GAMES, PRISONERS' DILEMMA.

Zionism the political movement for the establishment and support of a natural homeland for the Jews in Palestine.

Znaniecki, Florian (1882–1958) Polish-born, US sociologist best known for his seminal work, *The Polish Peasant in Europe and America* (1918–20), which pioneered the employment of LIFE HISTORY AND LIFE HISTORY METHOD.

zone any area, especially within a town or city, possessing particular functions or characteristics. The occurrence of zones may be planned as well as unplanned (e.g. the zoning of school attendance, planning restrictions on industrial or commercial development). See also ZONE OF TRANSITION, URBAN ECOLOGY.

zone of transition an area of the city, according to the perspective of URBAN ECOLOGY, which borders the central business district. Although its socioeconomic make-up is constantly changing due to the processes of urban growth and relocation, it is characterized by high levels of migration (as poorer people and newcomers to the city move into the area and as well-off people move away to the 'better areas' of the suburbs), by social heterogeneity, multioccupation of dwellings and a high incidence of reported social problems such as crime, mental illness and alcoholism. The coincidence of social problems with the decline in housing stock and the spread of slums resulted in the recent past in programmes of slum clearance and the building of high-rise accommodation. Although the material fabric of the environment is regarded as important, urban ecology argues that the lack of social ties and sense of community found in these areas are the chief cause of social pathology.

More recently the term has been superseded by INNER CITY to denote the growth of settled communities of people of minority heritage backgrounds, people who emigrated to the UK for work during the phase of decolonization, and their descendants who experience discrimination, relative deprivation and low socioeconomic status and can be regarded as an UNDERCLASS in capitalist society. See also HUMAN ECOLOGY, URBAN SOCIOLOGY, URBANIZATION.

zweckrational action see TYPES OF SOCIAL ACTION.

Bibliography

This bibliography is not a comprehensive listing of all works cited in the text. It does not include many references where the title of the book or article has already been given in the text, either at the point where the reference occurs or listed under a 'person' headword. Thus, if not given immediately in the text, and if not listed in the bibliography, a reference such as Raymond ARON (1935) in the text leads to *German Sociology* (1935) within the entry **Aron, Raymond**.

Both in the text and the bibliography, the year given for each work is usually either the year of first publication, or, for some foreign language works, the year of a first English language edition. For works first published in the UK and the US in different but adjacent years, the year given is not always the earlier of the two. Details of place of publication and publishers given in the bibliography are sometimes for a more recent (more accessible) edition.

Abbot, S. and Love, B. 1972, *Sappho Was Right On Woman: a Liberated View of Lesbianism,* New York: Stein and Day.

Abel T. 1977, 'The operation called *Verstehen,*' in F. Dallmayr and T. McCarthy (eds.), *Understanding and Social Inquiry,* University of Notre Dame Press.

Abercrombie, N., Hill, S. and Turner, B. 1980, *The Dominant Ideology Thesis,* London: Allen and Unwin.

Abercrombie, N., Hill, S. and Turner, B. 1984, *Dictionary of Sociology,* Harmondsworth: Penguin.

Abercrombie, N. and Urry, J. 1983, *Capital, Labour and the Middle Classes,* London: Allen and Unwin.

Aberle, D. et al. 1950, 'The functional requisites of a society', *Ethics,* 60.

Abrams, M. 1960, 'The "Socialist Commentary Survey"' in M. Abrams and R. Rose (eds.) *Must Labour Lose?* Harmondsworth: Penguin.

Abrams, P. 1982, *Historical Sociology,* Shepton Mallet: Open Books.

Ackroyd, S. et al. 1988, 'The Japanization of British Industry', *Industrial Relations Journal,* 19.

Alavi, H. 1965, 'Peasants and revolution', *Socialist Register,* London: Merlin.

Albrow, M. 1970, *Bureaucracy,* London: Macmillan and Pall Mall Press.

Alford, R. 1967, 'Class and voting in the Anglo-American political systems', in *Party Systems and Voter Alignments,* S. Lipset and S. Rokkan (eds.), New York: Free Press.

Allport, G. 1935, 'Attitudes', in C. Murchison (ed.) *Handbook of Social Psychology,* Worcester, Mass.: Clark University Press.

Almond, G. 1958, 'Comparative study of interest groups and the political process', *American Political Science Review,* 52.

Almond, G. and Coleman, J. 1960, *The Politics of the Developing Areas,* Princeton: Princeton University Press.

Almond, G. and Verba, S. 1963, *The Civic Culture: Political Attitudes and Democracy in Five Nations,* Princeton: Princeton Univ. Press.

Amin, S. 1980, *Class and Nation Historically and in the Current Crisis,* London: Heinemann.

Anderberg M. 1973, *Cluster Analysis for Applications,* New York: Academic Press.

Anderson, P. 1977, 'The antinomies of Antonio Gramsci', *New Left Review,* 100 (November 1976–January 1977).

Andreski, S. 1954, *Military Organization and Society,* London: Routledge & Kegan Paul.

Andreski, S. (ed.) 1974, *The Essential Comte,* London: Croom Helm.

Arber, S. and Gilbert, J. 1989, 'Men: The Forgotten Carers', *Sociology,* 23.

Archer, M. 1979, *The Social Origins of Educational Systems,* Beverley Hills: Sage (abridged edn. 1984).

Archer, M. (ed.) 1982, *The Sociology of Educational Expansion,* Beverley Hills: Sage.

Ardrey, R. 1967, *The Territorial Imperative,* London: Collins.

Argyle, M. 1967, *The Psychology of Interpersonal Behaviour,* Harmondsworth: Penguin.

Argyle, M. 1969, *Social Interaction,* London: Methuen.

Ariès, P. 1962, *Centuries of Childhood,* Harmondsworth: Penguin.

Armistead, N. 1974, *Reconstructing Social Psychology,* Harmondsworth: Penguin.

Armstrong, W. 1972, 'The use of information about occupations', in E. Wrigley (ed.) 1972, *Nineteenth Century Society: Essays in the Use of Quantitative Methods for the Study of Social Data,* Cambridge: Cambridge University Press.

Asch, S. 1952, *Social Psychology,* Englewood Cliffs, NJ: Prentice-Hall.

Ashton, D., Maguire, M. and Spilsbury, M. 1987, 'Local labour markets and their impact on the life chances of youths', in R. Coles (ed.) *Young Careers,* Milton Keynes: Open University Press.

Ashton, T. 1954, 'The treatment of capitalism by historians', in F. Hayek, *Capitalism and the Historians,* London: Routledge & Kegan Paul.

Aston, T. and Philipin, C. (eds.) 1985, *The Brenner Debate: Agrarian Class Structure and Economic Development in Pre-Industrial Europe,* Cambridge: Cambridge University Press.

Atkinson, P. 1981, *The Clinical Experience: the Construction and Reconstruction of Medical Reality,* Farnborough: Gower.

Austin, J. 1962, *How to do Things with Words,* London: Oxford University Press.

Bachofen, J. 1861, 'Mother Right' in *Myth, Religion and Mother Right* (tr. R. Mannheim), Princeton: Princeton Univ. Press (1967).

Bachrach, P. 1967, *The Theory of Democratic Élitism: a Critique,* London: University of London Press.

Bachrach, P. and Baratz, M. 1962, 'The two faces of power', *American Political Science Review*, 56.

Baker-Miller, J. 1976, *Towards a New Psychology of Women*, Boston: Beacon Press.

Bales, R. 1950, *Interaction Process Analysis: a Method for the Study of Small Groups*. Cambridge, Mass.: Addison-Wesley.

Ball, M. and Smith G. 1991, *Analysing Visual Data*, California: Sage.

Bandura, A. 1977, *Social Learning Theory*, Englewood Cliffs, N.J.L: Prentice-Hall.

Banji, J. 1977, 'Modes of production in a materialist conception of history', *Capital and Class*, 3.

Baran, P. 1957, *The Political Economy of Growth*, New York: Monthly Review Press, and Harmondsworth: Penguin (1973).

Baran, P. and Sweezy, P. 1966, *Monopoly Capital*, Harmondsworth: Penguin.

Barber, B. 1969, 'Conceptual foundations of totalitarianism', in C. Friedrich, et al., *Totalitarianism in Perspective*, London: Pall Mall.

Barbour, F. (ed.) 1969, *The Black Power Revolt*, Boston: Collier MacMillan.

Barker, E. 1989, *New Religious Movements*, London: HMSO.

Barker Lunn, J. 1970, *Streaming in the Primary School*, National Foundation for Educational Research.

Barratt-Brown, M. 1968, 'The controllers of British industry', in K. Coates (ed.) *Can Workers Run Industry?* London: Sphere.

Barrett, M. 1988. *Women's Oppression Today*, London: Verso.

Barron, R. and Norris, S. 1976, 'Sexual divisions and the dual market', in D. Barker and S. Allen (eds.) *Dependence and Exploitation in Work and Marriage*, London: Longman.

Barth, F. 1970, *Ethnic Groups and Boundaries – The Social Organisation of Cultural Difference*, London: Allen and Unwin.

Bataille, G. 1992, *Theory of Religion*, New York: Zone Books.

Bateson, G. 1936, *Naven*, Cambridge: Cambridge University Press.

Bauman, Z. 1989, *Modernity and the Holocaust*, Cambridge: Polity Press.

Beard, C. 1910, *An Economic Interpretation of the Constitution*, New York: Macmillan.

Bechhofer, F. et al. 1974, 'The petite bourgeoisie in the class structure', in F. Parkin (ed.) *The Social Analysis of Class Structure*, London: Tavistock.

Beck, U., Giddens, A. and Lash, S. 1994, *Reflexive Modernization, Politics, Tradition and Aesthetics in the Modern Social Order*, Cambridge: Polity Press.

Becker, D., Frieden, J., Schtatz, S. and Sklar, R. 1987, *Postimperialism: International Capitalism and Development in the Late Twentieth Century*. Boulder and London: Lynne Rienner.

Becker, Howard, 1950, *Systematic Sociology*, New York: Wiley.

Becker, H.S. 1953, 'Becoming a marihuana user', The American Journal of Sociology, 59.

Becker, H.S. 1967, 'Whose side are we on?', *Social Problems*, 14.

Becker, H.S. 1982, *Art Worlds*, London: University of California Press.

Bell, D. (ed.) 1964, *The Radical Right* (rev. edn.), New York: Doubleday.

Bell, D. 1965, 'Twelve modes of prediction', in J. Gould (ed.) *Penguin Survey of the Social Sciences, 1965*, Harmondsworth: Penguin.

Bell, D. 1980, 'The social framework of the "information society"', in T. Forester, (ed.) *The Microelectronics Revolution*, Oxford: Basil Blackwell.

Bellah, B. 1967, 'Civil religion in America', *Daedalus*, vol.96.

Bellah, R. 1975, *The Broken Covenant*, New York, Seabury.

Bendix, R. 1960, *Max Weber: an Intellectual Portrait*, London: Heinemann.

Bendix, R. 1970, 'Tradition and modernity reconsidered', in *Embattled Reason*, New York: Oxford University Press.

Berelson, B., Lazarsfeld, P. and McPhee, W. 1954, *Voting*, Chicago: Chicago University Press.

Berg, I. 1970, *Education and Jobs: the Great Training Robbery*, Harmondsworth: Penguin (1973).

Berger, P. and Pullberg, S. 1966, 'Reification and the sociological critique of consciousness', *New Left Review*, 35.

Berger, P. and Luckmann T. 1967, *The Social Construction of Reality*, London: Allen Lane.

Berle, A. and Means, G. 1932, *The Modern Corporation and Private Property*, New York: Harcourt Brace.

Bernstein, B. 1971, 'On the classification and framing of educational knowledge', in M. Young (ed.) *Knowledge and Control*, London: Macmillan.

Bernstein, R. 1976, *The Restructuring of Social and Political Theory*, New York: Harcourt, Brace.

Bernstein, R. 1983, *Beyond Objectivism and Relativism*, Oxford: Blackwell.

Berthoud, R. 1976, *The Disadvantages of Inequality: A study of Social Deprivation*, MacDonald and Jane.

Bettleheim, B. 1960, *The Informed Heart: Autonomy in a Mass Age*, London: Thames and Hudson (1961).

Bettleheim, B. 1969, *The Children of the Dream*, London: Thames and Hudson.

Beynon, H. 1973, *Working for Ford*, Wakefield: E.P. Publishing.

Beynon, J. and Solomos, J. (eds.) 1987, *The Roots of Urban Unrest*, Oxford: Pergamon.

Bhaskar, R. 1975, *A Realist Theory of Science*, Leeds: Leeds Books.

Bhaskar, R. 1979, *The Possibility of Naturalism*, Brighton: Harvester.

Bhaskar, R. 1986, *Scientific Realism and Human Emancipation*, London: Verso.

Bhaskar, R. 1989, *Reclaiming Reality*, London: Verso.

Black, M. (ed.) 1961, *The Social Theories of Talcott Parsons*, Englewood Cliffs NJ: Prentice Hall.

Blalock, H. 1960, *Social Statistics*, New York: McGraw Hill.

Blalock, H. 1961, *Causal Inference in Non Experimental Research,* University of North Carolina Press.
Blau, P. and Scott, W. 1962, *Formal Organizations: A Comparative Approach,* San Francisco: Chandler.
Blauner, R. 1964, *Alienation and Freedom,* Chicago: Univ. of Chicago Press.
Blok, R. 1974, *The Mafia of a Sicilian Village* 1860–1960, Oxford: Oxford University Press.
Blumer, H. 1954. 'What's wrong with social theory?', *American Sociological Review,* 19.
Blumer, H. 1956, 'Sociological analysis and the variable', *American Sociological Review,* 21.
Bocock, R. 1974, *Ritual in Industrial Society,* London: Allen & Unwin.
Boeke, J. 1953, (rev. edn.) *Economics and Economic Policy of Dual Societies,* New York: Institute of Pacific Relations.
Bogardus, E. 1933, 'A social distance scale', *Sociology and Social Research,* 17.
Bott, E. 1957, Family and Social Network, London: Tavistock.
Bottomore, T. et al. (eds.) 1983, *A Dictionary of Marxist Thought,* Oxford: Blackwell.
Bourdieu, P. 1984b, quoted in J. Thompson, *Studies in the Theory of Ideology,* Cambridge: Polity Press.
Bourdon, R. and Bourricaud, F. 1989, *A Critical Dictionary of Sociology,* Routledge (original Fr. edn 1982).
Bowles, S. and Gintis, H. 1976, *Schooling in Capitalist America,* Routledge & Kegan Paul.
Brake, M. 1980, *The Sociology of Youth Culture and Youth Subcultures,* Routledge & Kegan Paul.
Brake, M. 1985, *Comparative Youth Culture: the Sociology of Youth Cultures in America, Britain and Canada,* London: Routledge.
Braverman, H. 1974, *Labour and Monopoly Capitalism: The Degradation of Work in the Twentieth Century,* New York: Monthly Review Press.
Brenner, R. 1977 'The origins of capitalist development: a critique of neo-Smithian Marxism', *New Left Review,* 104.
Bridgman, P. 1927, *Dimensional Analysis,* New Haven: Yale UP.
Bright J. 1958, *Automation and Management,* Cambridge, Mass.: Harvard Univ. Press.
Britten, A. 1989, *Masculinity and Power,* Oxford: Blackwell.
Brooks, A. *Postfeminisms: Feminism, Cultural Theory and Cultural Forms,* Routledge, London, 1997.
Brown, R. 1967, 'Research and consultancy in industrial enterprises', *Sociology,* 1.
Brown, R. 1978, 'Divided we fall: an analysis of relations between sections of a factory work-force', in H. Tajfel (ed.) *Differentiation Between Social Groups: Studies in the Social Psychology of Intergroup Relations.* London: Academic Press.
Brown, R. 1992, *Understanding Industrial Organizations in Industrial Sociology,* London: Routledge.
Bruner, J. 1968, *Towards a Theory of Instruction,* New York: Norton.
Bryant, C. 1985, *Positivism in Social Theory and Research,* London: Macmillan.
Bryant, C. and Jary, D. (eds.) 1991, *Giddens' Theory of Structuration: a Critical Appreciation,* London: Routledge.
Budge, I. 1976, *Agreement and Stability in Democracy,* Chicago: Markham.
Bühler, C. 1953, 'The curve of life as studied in biographies', *Journal of Applied Science,* 9.
Bulmer, M. (ed.) 1975, *Working Class Images of Society,* London: Routledge & Kegan Paul.
Burgess, R. (ed.) 1986, *Key Variables in Social Research,* London: Routledge & Kegan Paul.
Burke, E. 1790, *Reflections on the Revolution in France,* (ed. C. O'Brien) Harmondsworth: Penguin (1969).
Burnham, J. 1943, *The Managerial Revolution,* London: Putman.
Burns, T. 1961, 'Micro-politics: mechanisms of institutional change' *Admin. Sci. Quarterly, 6.*
Burns, T. 1962, 'The sociology of industry', in A. Welford (ed.), *Society: Problems and Methods of Study,* London: Routledge & Kegan Paul.
Burns, T. and Stalker G. 1961, *The Management of Innovation,* London: Tavistock.
Burrell, G. and Morgan G. 1979, *Sociological Paradigms and Organizational Analysis,* London: Heinemann.
Bury, M. 1986, 'Social Constructionism and the Development of Medical Sociology', *Sociology of Health and Illness,* 8.
Butler, D. and Stokes, D. 1969, *Political change in Britain,* London: Macmillan.
Butler, Judith 1990, *Gender Trouble: Feminism and the Subversion of Identity,* London: Routledge.
Butler, Judith 1993, *Bodies that Matter: On the Discursive Limits of Sex,* London: Routledge.
Byres, T. (ed.) 1983, *Sharecropping and Sharecroppers.* London: Frank Cass.
Carchedi, G. 1977, On *the Economic Identification of Social Classes,* London: Routledge & Kegan Paul.
Cardoso, F. and Faletto, E. 1979, *Dependency and Development in Latin America,* New York: University of California Press.
Carey, A. 1967, 'The Hawthorne studies', *American Sociological Review,* 32.
Carlen, P. and Worrall, A. (eds.) 1987, *Gender, Crime and Justice.* Milton Keynes: Open University.
Carneiro, R. 1970, 'A theory of the origin of the state', *Science,* 169.
Carrillo, S. 1977, *Eurocommunism and the State,* London: Lawrence and Wishart.
Case, S. 1988, *Feminism and the Theatre,* London: Macmillan.
Casey, C. 1995, *Work, Self and Society: After Industralism,* London: Routledge.
Cashmore, E. 1994a. *Dictionary of Race and Ethnic Relations* (3rd edn.), London: Routledge.
Cashmore, E. 1994b, ... *and there was television,* London: Routledge.

Castells, M. 1976, 'Theory and ideology in urban sociology', in C. Pickvance (ed.), *Urban Sociology,* London: Tavistock.

Castells, M. 1977, *The Urban Question: a Marxist Approach,* London: Edward Arnold.

Castells, M. 1978, *City, Class and Power,* London: Macmillan.

Castells, M. 1983, *The City and the Grassroots: a Cross-Cultural Theory of Urban Social Movements,* London: Edward Arnold.

Catell, R. 1963, *The Sixteen Personality Factor Questionnaire,* Illinois: Institute for Personality and Ability Testing.

Chatfield, C. and Collins, A. 1980, *Introduction to Multivariate Analysis,* London: Chapman and Hall.

Child, J. 1972, 'Organizational structure, environment and performance – the role of strategic choice', *Sociology,* 6.

Child, J. 1985, *Organizations: a Guide to Problems and Practice,* New York: Harper Row.

Chinoy, E. 1955, *Automobile Workers and the American Dream,* New York: Doubleday.

Chomsky, N. 1962, 'Explanatory models in linguistics', in E. Nagel, P. Suppes, and A. Tarski, (eds.) *Logic, Methodology and Philosophy of Science,* Stanford Univ. Press.

Chomsky, N. 1965, *Aspects of the Theory of Syntax,* Cambridge Mass.: MIT Press.

Chomsky, N. 1969, *American Power and the New Mandarins,* Harmondsworth: Penguin.

Cicourel, A. 1964, *Method and Measurement in Sociology,* New York: Free Press.

Clark, B. 1960a, *The Open Door College: a Case Study,* New York: McGraw Hill.

Clark, B. 1960b, 'The "cooling out" function in higher education'. *American Journal of Sociology,* 6.

Clark, B. 1983, *The Higher Education System: Academic Organization in Cross-National Perspective,* Berkeley: Univ of California Press.

Clarke, J., Critcher C. and Johnson R. 1979, *Working Class Culture,* London: Hutchinson.

Clegg, H. 1960, *A New Approach to Industrial Relations,* Oxford: Blackwell.

Clegg, S. and Dunkerley, D. 1980, *Organization, Class and Control,* London: Routledge & Kegan Paul.

Cloward, R. and Ohlin, L. 1960, *Delinquency and Opportunity.* New York: Collier-Macmillan.

Coates, K. and Topham, T. 1972, *The New Unionism,* London: Owen.

Coch, L. and French. J. 1949, 'Overcoming resistance to change', *Human Relations,* 1.

Cockburn, C. 1983, *Brothers,* London: Pluto.

Cohen, A. 1955, *Delinquent Boys,* Chicago: Free Press.

Cohen, G. 1978, *Karl Marx's Theory of History: a Defence,* Oxford: Clarendon Press.

Cohen, J. 1988, *Statistical Power Analysis for the Behavioural Sciences,* (2nd Edn) New Jersey, Lawrence Erlbaum.

Cohen, S. (ed.) 1971, *Images of Deviance,* Harmondsworth: Penguin.

Cohen, S. 1973, *Folk Devils and Moral Panics,* London: Paladin (rev. edn. 1980).

Cohen, S. 1981, 'Footprints in the sand', in M. Fitzgerald et al. (eds.) *Crime and Society,* Milton Keynes: Open University Press.

Cohen, S. 1988, *Visions of Social Control,* Cambridge: Polity Press.

Cohn, N. 1957, *The Pursuit of the Millennium,* London: Paladin.

Collard, A 1988, *Rape of the Wild,* London: The Women's Press.

Connell, R. 1987, *Gender and Power: Society, the Person and Sexual Politics,* Cambridge: Polity Press.

Coombs, R. 1978, 'Labour and Monopoly Capital', *New Left Review.*

Coombs, R. 1985, 'Automation, management strategies and labour process change', in D. Knights et al. (eds) *Job Redesign,* Aldershot: Gower.

Cooper, H. 1998, *Synthesizing Research: A Guide for Literature Reviews,* (3rd Edn.) London, Sage.

Cooper, H. and Hedges L. (eds.) 1994, *The Handbook of Research Synthesis,* New York, Russell Sage Foundation

Coser, L. 1956, *The Functions of Social Conflict,* New York: Free Press.

Coser, L. (ed.) 1965, *Georg Simmel,* Englewood Cliffs, NJ: Prentice Hall.

Coser, L. 1978, 'The Production of Culture', *Social Research,* 45.

Cotterill, P. 1994, *Friendly Relations? Mothers and their Daughters-in-Law,* London: Taylor and Francis.

Coulson, M., Magas, B. and Wainwright, H. 1975, 'The housewife and her labour under capitalism: a critique', in *New Left Review.*

Coward, R. and Ellis, J. 1977, *Language and Materialism,* London: Routledge & Kegan Paul.

Cowell, D. et al (eds.) 1982, *Policing the Riots,* Junction Books.

Craib, I. 1989, *Psychoanalysis and Social Theory,* Hemel Hempstead: Harvester.

Crensen, M. 1971, *The Un-Politics of Air Pollution,* London and Baltimore: Johns Hopkins Press.

Crewe, I., Alt, J. and Sarlvik, B. 1977, 'Partisan dealignment in Britain', *British Journal of Political Science,* 6.

Croix, de Ste. G. 1981, *The Class Struggle in the Ancient Greek World,* London: Duckworth.

Crompton, R and Jones, G. 1984, *White-Collar Proletariat: Deskilling and Gender in Clerical Work.* London: Macmillan.

Crossick, G. 1978, *An Artisan Élite in Victorian Society,* Beckenham: Croom Helm.

Crouch, C. 1982, *Trade Unions: The Logic of Collective Action,* London: Fontana.

Crow, B., Thomas, A. et al 1983, *Third World Atlas,* Milton Keynes: Open University Press.

Crow, B., Thorpe M. et al. 1988, *Survival and Change in the Third World,* Cambridge: Polity Press.

Crowther Report, The 1959, *Fifteen to Eighteen – Report of the Central Advisory Committee for Education,* London: HMSO.

Crozier, M. 1964, *The Bureaucratic Phenomenon,* London: Tavistock.
Crutchfield, R. 1955, 'Conformity and character', *American Psychologist,* 10.
Dahl, R. 1956, *A Preface to Democratic Theory,* Chicago University Press.
Dahl, R. 1961, *Who Governs?* New Haven and London: Yale University Press.
Dahl, R. 1985, *Polyarchy,* New Haven, Conn.: Yale University Press.
Dahrendorf, R. 1979, *Life Chances,* London: Weidenfeld & Nicolson.
Dale, A., Arber, S. and Procter, M. 1988, *Doing Secondary Analysis,* London: Unwin Hyman.
Dalla Costa, M. 1972, *The Power of Women and the Subversion of the Community,* Bristol: Falling Wall Press.
Daly, M. 1981, *Gyn-Ecology,* Boston: Beacon Press.
Davidoff, R. 1979, 'The separation of home from work' in S. Burnham, (ed.) *Fit work For Women,* London: Croom Helm.
Davidoff, L. and Hall, C. 1987, *Family Fortunes: Men and Women of the English Middle Class 1780–1850,* London: Hutchinson.
Davidson, D. 1984, *Enquiry into Truth and Interpretation,* Oxford: Oxford University Press.
Davis, F. 1964, 'Deviance disavowal: the management of strained interaction by the visibly handicapped', in H.S. Becker (ed.) 1967, *The Other Side,* New York: Free Press.
Davis, H. 1979, *Beyond Class Images,* London: Croom Helm.
Davis, K. 1948, *Human Society,* New York: Macmillan.
Davis, K. 1959, 'The myth of functional analysis as a special method in sociology and anthropology', *American Sociological Review,* 24.
Davis, K. and Moore, W. 1945, 'Some principles of social stratification', *American Sociological Review,* 10.
Dawe, A. 1971, 'The two sociologies', in K. Thompson and J. Tunstall (eds.) *Sociological Perspectives,* Harmondsworth: Penguin.
Dawkins, R. 1976, *The Selfish Gene,* London: Oxford University Press.
Deal, T. and Kennedy, A. 1988, *Corporate Culture,: The Rites and Rituals of Corporate Life,* Harmondsworth: Penguin (originally published US, 1982).
Dean, H. and Taylor-Gooby, P. 1992, *Dependency Culture: the Exploration of a Myth.* Hemel Hempstead: Harvester.
Deem, R. 1986, *All Work and No Play: The Sociology of Women and Leisure,* Milton Keynes: Open University Press.
Delphy, C. 1984, *Close to Home: a Materialist Analysis of Women's Oppression,* London: Hutchinson.
Demerath, H. and Peterson, R. (eds.), 1967, *System, Change and Conflict,* New York: Free Press.
Dennis, N., Henriques, F. and Slaughter, C. 1956, *Coal is Our Life,* London: Eyre and Spottiswoode.
Denzin, N. (ed.) 1970, *Sociological Methods: a Source Book,* Chicago: Aldine.
Dex, S. 1985, *The Sexual Division of Work: Conceptual Revolutions in the Social Sciences,* Brighton: Wheatsheaf.
Djilas, M. 1957, *The New Class,* London: Thames and Hudson.
Dobb, M. 1946, *Studies in the Development of Capitalism,* London: Routledge & Kegan Paul (1963).
Doeringer, P. and Piore, M. 1971, *Internal Labour Markets and Manpower Analysis,* Lexington, Mass.: D.C. Heath.
Dohrenwend, B. and Dohrenwend, B. (eds.) 1974, *Stressful Life Events: Their Nature and Effects.* New York: Wiley.
Donnelly, P. 1988 'Sport as a site for "popular" resistance', in Gruneau, R. (ed.) *Popular Cultures and Political Practices,* Canada: Garamond Press.
Dore R. 1976, *The Diploma Disease,* London: Allen and Unwin.
Douglas, Jack 1967, *The Social Meanings of Suicide,* Princeton: Princeton University Press.
Douglas, J.B. 1964, *The Home and the School,* London: MacGibbon & Kee.
Douglas, M. 1966, *Purity and Danger,* London: Routledge & Kegan Paul.
Downes, D. 1966, *The Delinquent Solution,* London: Routledge & Kegan Paul.
Dowse, R. and Hughes, J. 1972, *Political Sociology,* London: John Wiley.
Dubin, R. 1955, 'Industrial workers' worlds', *Social Problems, 3.*
Duncan, K. and Rutledge, I. (eds.) 1977, *Land and Labour in Latin America,* Cambridge: Cambridge University Press.
Dunleavy, P. 1980, 'The political implications of sectoral cleavages', *Political Studies,* 28.
Dunning, E., Murphy, P. and Williams, J. 1988, *The Roots of Football Hooliganism,* Routledge.
Dunning, E. and Sheard, K. 1979, *Barbarians, Gentlemen and Players: a Sociological Study,* London: Martin Robertson.
Duprese, M. 1981, *Family Structure in the Staffordshire Potteries,* Unpublished PhD thesis, University of Oxford.
Durkheim, E. 1922, *Education and Sociology,* Glencoe, Ill.: Free Press (1956).
Duverger, M. 1964, *Political Parties,* New York: Wiley.
Dworkin, A. 1976, *Our Blood: Prophecies and Discourses on Sexual Politics,* New York: Harper Row.
Easthope, A. and McGowan, K. 1992, *A Critical and Cultural Theory Reader,* Buckingham: Open University Press.
Eastlea, B. 1983, *Fathering the Unthinkable,* London: Pluto Press.
Eberhard, W. 1965, *Conquerers and Rulers,* Leiden: Brill.
Eckstein, H. 1960, *Pressure Group Politics,* London: Allen and Unwin.
Edwards, R. 1979, *Contested Terrain,* Heinemann: London.
Ehrenreich, R. and Ehrenreich, J. 1979, 'The professional and managerial class', in P. Walker (ed.)

Between Labour and Capital, New York: Monthly Review Press.

Eichenbaum, L. and Orbach, S. 1982, *Outside In, Inside Out,* Harmondsworth: Penguin.

Eisenstadt, S. 1956, *From Generation to Generation,* Chicago: Free Press.

Eldridge, J. 1971, *Sociology and Industrial Life,* London: Nelson.

Eldridge, J. 1980, *Recent British Sociology,* London: Macmillan.

Elias, N. and Dunning, E. 1986, *Quest for Excitement: Sport and Leisure in the Civilising Process,* Oxford: Blackwell.

Eliot, T.S. 1948, *Notes Towards the Definition of Culture,* London: Faber.

Elliott, G. 1987, *Althusser: The Detour of Theory,* London: Verso.

Elshtain, J. 1981, *Public Man, Private Woman,* Princeton: Princeton Univ. Press.

Elster, J. 1989, *Nuts and Bolts for the Social Sciences,* Cambridge University Press.

Erikson, E. 1950, *Childhood and Society,* Harmondsworth: Penguin (1963).

Esland, G. and Salaman, G. 1975, 'Towards a sociology of work' in G. Esland, J. Salaman and M. Speakman (eds.), *People and Work.,* Edinburgh: Holmes-McDougall/The Open University.

Ettore, E. 1978, 'Women, urban social movements and the lesbian ghetto', *International Journal of Urban and Regional Research,* 2.

Etzioni, A. 1961, *The Comparative Analysis of Complex Organizations,* New York: Free Press.

Evans, P. 1979. *Dependent Development: the Alliance of Multinationals, the State and Local Capital in Brazil,* Princeton: Princeton University Press.

Everitt, B. 1974, *Cluster Analysis,* London: Heinemann.

Eysenck, H. 1953, *The Structure of Human Personality,* London: Methuen.

Eysenck, H. 1961, *Handbook of Abnormal Psychology,* London: Pitman.

Eysenck, H. 1967, *The Biological Basis of Personality,* Springfield: Thomas.

Featherstone, M. 1988, 'In pursuit of the postmodern', in *Postmodernism,* special double issue of *Theory, Culture and Society,* 5.

Featherstone, M. 1990, 'Perspectives on consumer culture', *Sociology, 24.*

Featherstone, M. 1991, *Consumer Culture and Postmodernism.* London, Sage.

Feigenbaum, E. and McCordnuck, P. 1984, 'Land of the rising fifth generation', in *The Information Technology Revolution,* Oxford: Blackwell.

Ferguson, A. (1767) *An Essay on the History of Civil Society,* Philadelphia: Finley (8th. edn., 1819).

Fernandez, R. 1977, *The I, the Me and the You: an Introduction to Social Psychology,* New York: Praeger.

Festinger, L. 1957, *A Theory of Cognitive Dissonance,* Evanston, Ill.: Row, Peterson.

Fevre, R. 1992, *The Sociology of Labour Markets,* Hemel Hempstead: Harvester Wheatsheaf.

Feyerabend, P. 1981, *Problems of Empiricism.* (2 vols.), Cambridge: Cambridge Univ. Press.

Feyerabend, P. 1987, *Farewell to Reason,* London: Verso.

Fidler, J. 1981, *The British Business Élite,* Routledge & Kegan Paul.

Finch, J. & Groves, D. 1982, 'By Women, For Women: Caring for the Frail Elderly' *Women's Studies International Forum,* 5(5):427-38.

Fisher, R. 1925, *Statistical Methods for Research Workers,* New York, Hafner.

Fitzgerald, J. and Muncie J. 1987, *System of Justice,* Oxford: Blackwell.

Flechtheim, O. 1965, *History and Futurology,* Meisenheim am Glan.

Flew, A (ed.) 1979, *A Dictionary of Philosophy,* London: Pan Books.

Flexner, A. 1910, *Report on Medical Education in the United States and Canada,* New York: Carnegie.

Flexner, A. 1962, 'Is social work a profession?' in H. Becker, *Education for the Professions: the 61st Yearbook of the National Society for the Study of Education,* University of Chicago Press.

Florescano, E. 1987, 'The hacienda in New Spain', in L. Bethel (ed.), *Colonial Spanish America,* Cambridge: Cambridge University Press.

Floud, J., Halsey, A. and Martin, F. 1956, *Social Class and Educational Opportunity,* London: Heinemann.

Forester, T. 1987, *High-Tech Society,* Oxford: Basil Blackwell.

Form, W. and Rytinna, J. 1969, 'Ideological beliefs in the distribution of power in the US', *American Sociological Review,* 34.

Fortes, M. 1969, *Kinship and the Social Order: the Legacy of Lewis Henry Morgan,* London: Routledge & Kegan Paul.

Foster, J. 1974, *Class Struggle and the Industrial Revolution,* London: Methuen.

Foucault, M. 1972, *The Archaeology of Knowledge,* London: Tavistock.

Foucault, M. 1973, *The Birth of the Clinic,* London, Tavistock.

Fox, A. 1965, 'Industrial sociology and industrial relations' Research Paper No.3, *Royal Commission on Trade Unions and Employers' Associations.* London: HMSO.

Frank, A. 1967a, 'Sociology of development and underdevelopment of sociology', *Catalyst,* Summer 1967 (reprinted in Frank, 1969).

Frank, A. 1967b, *Capitalism and Underdevelopment in Latin America,* New York and London: Monthly Review Press.

Frank, A. 1969, *Latin America: Underdevelopment or Revolution,* Harmondsworth: Penguin.

Frank, A. 1980, *Crisis: in the World Economy,* London: Heinemann.

Freedman, M. 1976, *Labour Markets: Segments and Shelters.* New York: Allanhead, Osman/Universal Books.

Freeman, C. 1982, *Unemployment and Technical Innovation,* London: Frances Pinter.

Freidson, E. 1970a, *Professional Dominance,* Chicago: Aldine.

Freidson, E. 1970b, *Profession of Medicine,* New York: Dodd and Mead.

Fried, M. 1960, 'On the evolution of stratification and the state', in Diamond S. (ed.) *Culture in History,* New York: Columbia Univ Press.

Fried, M. 1967, *The Evolution of Political Society,* New York: Random House.

Friedman, A. 1977, *Industry and Labour: Class Struggle at Work and Monopoly Capitalism,* London: Macmillan.

Friedrich, C. 1954, *Totalitarianism,* Cambridge Mass.: Harvard University Press.

Frobel, F., Heinrichs, J. and Kreye, O. 1980, *The New International Division of Labour,* Cambridge: Cambridge University Press.

Fukuyama, F. 1992, *The End of History and the Last Man,* London: Hamish Hamilton.

Furtado, C. 1964, *Development and Underdevelopment,* Los Angeles: University of California Press.

Gadamer, H. 1960, *Truth and Method,* London: Sheed & Ward (Eng. trans. 1975).

Gallie, D. 1978, *In Search of the New Working Class,* Cambridge: Cambridge University Press.

Gallie, W. 1955, 'Essentially contested concepts', *Proceedings of the Aristotelian Society,* 56.

Galton, F. 1870, *Hereditary Genius,* New York: Appleton.

Gamble, A. 1985, *Britain in Decline* (2nd. revised edn.), London: Macmillan.

Gamble, A. 1988, *The Free Economy and the Strong State: The Politics of Thatcherism,* London: Macmillan.

Gamble, S. (ed.), *The Icon Critical Dictionary of Feminism and Postfeminism,* Icon Books, Cambridge, 1999.

Gans, E. 1993, *Originary Thinking,* Stanford: Stanford University Press.

Gans, E. 1997, *Signs of Paradox,* Stanford: Stanford University Press.

Gans, H. 1962, *The Urban Villagers: Groups and Class in the Life of Italian-Americans,* (2nd edn), New York: Free Press.

Garfinkel, H. 1956, 'The conditions of successful degradation ceremonies', *American Journal of Sociology,* 61.

Garner, L. 1979, *Your Money or Your Life,* Harmondsworth: Penguin.

Garrard, J. et al 1978, *The Middle Class in Politics,* Farnborough: Saxon House.

Geddes, P. 1915, *Cities in Evolution,* London: Williams & Norgate.

Geiger, T. 1949, *Die Stennung der Intelligenz in der Gesellschaft,* Stuttgart.

Gellner, E. 1974, 'The New Idealism – cause and meaning in the Social Sciences', reprinted in Giddens, A. (ed.), *Positivism and Sociology,* London: Heinemann.

Genovese, E. 1971, *In Red and Black,* London: Allen Lane.

Genovese, E. 1974, *Roll Jordan Roll: The World the Slaveholders Made,* New York: Knopf.

George, C. and George, K. 1961, *The Protestant Mind and the English Reformation,* London: Methuen.

Gerth, H. and Mills, C. 1953, *Character and Social Structure,* London: Routledge & Kegan Paul.

Gibson, W. 1984, *Neuromancer,* London: Voyager Books.

Giddens, A. 1976, 'Functionalism: Après la lutte' *Social Research,* 43.

Giddens, A. 1977, *Studies in Social and Political Theory,* London: Hutchinson.

Giddens, A 1982, *Profiles and Critiques in Social Theory,* London: Macmillan.

Giddens, A. 1987, 'Structuralism, post-structuralism', in A. Giddens and J. Turner (1987) *Social Theory Today,* Cambridge: Polity Press.

Giddens, A. 1989, *Sociology,* Cambridge; Polity Press.

Giddens, A. 1994, 'Living in a post-traditional society' in U. Beck, A. Giddens, and S. Lash, 1994.

Giles, H. & Johnson, P. 1981, 'The role of language in ethnic group relations', J.C. Turner and H. Giles (eds) *Intergroup Behaviour,* Oxford: Blackwell.

Gill, C. 1985, *Work, Unemployment and the New Technology,* Oxford: Blackwell.

Gittens, D. 1985, *The Family in Question,* London: Macmillan.

Glaser, B. 1968, *A Time for Dying,* Chicago: Aldine.

Glaser, B. and Strauss, A. 1965, *Awareness of Dying,* Chicago: Aldine.

Glaser, B. and Strauss, A. 1968, *The Discovery of Grounded Theory,* London: Weidenfeld & Nicholson.

Glass, D. (ed.) 1954, *Social Mobility in Britain,* London: Routledge & Kegan Paul.

Glazer, N. 1975, *Affirmative Discrimination,* New York: Basic Books.

Gleichman, P. et al. 1977, *Human Figurations,* Amsterdam: Sociologisch Tijdschift.

Gluckman, M. 1963, *Order and Rebellion in Tribal Africa,* London: Cohen and West.

Goffman, E. 1967, *Interaction Ritual: Essays on Face-To-Face Behaviour,* New York: Doubleday.

Goffman, E. 1969, *Strategic Interaction,* Philadelphia: Univ. of Pennsylvania Press.

Goffman, E. 1971, *Relations in Public: Microstudies of the Public Order,* London: Allen Lane.

Goffman, E. 1979, *Gender Advertisements,* London: Macmillan.

Golding, P. 1983, *'Rethinking common sense about social policy'* in D. Bull and P. Wilding (eds.), *Thatcherism and the Poor,* Child Poverty Action Group.

Goldthorpe, J.E. 1975, *The Sociology of the Third World: Disparity and Involvement,* Cambridge: Cambridge University Press (2nd. edn. 1984).

Goldthorpe, J.H. 1966, 'Attitudes and behaviour of car assembly workers – a deviant case and a theoretical critique', *British Journal of Sociology,* 27.

Goldthorpe, J.H. 1974, 'Industrial relations in Great Britain: a critique of reformism', reprinted in T. Clarke, and I. Clements, (eds.) *Trades Unions Under Capitalism,* London: Faber.

Goldthorpe, J.H. 1973, 'A revolution in sociology', *Sociology*, 7.

Goldthorpe, J.H. and Llewellyn, C. 1977, 'Class mobility in Britain: three theses examined', *Sociology*, 11.

Goldthorpe, J. H., Lockwood, D., Bechhofer, F. and Platt, J. 1968a, *The Affluent Worker: Industrial Attitudes and Behaviour*, Cambridge: Cambridge University Press.

Goldthorpe, J.H., Lockwood, D., Bechhofer, F. and Platt, J. 1968b, *The Affluent Worker: Political Attitudes and Behaviour*, Cambridge: Cambridge University Press.

Goldthorpe, J.H., Lockwood, D., Bechhofer, F. and Platt, J. 1969, *The Affluent Worker in the Class Structure*, Cambridge: Cambridge University Press.

Goode, W. and Hatt, P. 1952, *Methods in Social Research*, New York: McGraw-Hill.

Goodman, P. 1956, *Growing up Absurd*, New York: Vintage Books.

Goody, J. (ed.), 1971, *Kinship*, Harmondsworth: Penguin.

Gorz, A. 1967, *Strategy for Labour*, Boston: Beacon Press.

Goudsblom, J. 1977, *Sociology in the Balance*, Oxford: Blackwell.

Gough, H. 1957, *California Psychological Inventory*, Palo Alto: Consulting Psychologists Press.

Gough, I. 1979, *The Political Economy of the Welfare State*, London: Macmillan.

Gouldner, A. 1955a, *Wildcat Strike*, London: Routledge & Kegan Paul.

Gouldner, A. 1955b, 'Metaphysical pathos and the theory of bureaucracy', *American Political Science Review*, 49.

Gouldner, A. 1959, 'Reciprocity and autonomy in functional theory', in L. Gross (ed.) *Symposium on Sociological Theory*, New York: Harper Row.

Gray, R. 1976, *The Labour Aristocracy in Victorian Edinburgh*, Oxford: Clarendon Press.

Griffin, K. 1979, *The Political Economy of Agrarian Change: an Essay on the Green Revolution*, (2nd. edn.) London: Macmillan.

Griffin, S. 1982, *Made From This Earth*, London: Women's Press.

Grint, K. 1998, *The Sociology of Work*, (2nd edn.), Cambridge: Polity.

Gruneau, R. 1982, 'Sport and the debate on the state', *in* Cantelon, H. and Gruneau, R. (eds.) *Sport, Culture and the Modern State*, Univ.of Toronto Press.

Gruneau, R. 1983, *Class, Sports and Social Development*, Univ. of Massachusetts Press.

Guttman, L. 1950, 'The Basis for Scalogram Analysis', in L. Stouffer, L. Guttman, E. Suchman, P. Lazarsfeld, S. Srar and J. Clausen, *Measurement and Prediction*, Princeton: Princeton University Press.

Haber, R. and Fried, A. 1975, *An Introduction to Psychology*, New York:Holt, Rinehart and Winston.

Habermas, J. 1962, *The Structural Transformations of the Public Sphere*, Cambridge:Polity, (tr. 1986).

Hagerstrand, T. 1976 'Space, time and human conditions', in A. Karlqvist, *Dynamic Allocation of Urban Space*, Farnborough: Saxon House.

Hall, J. 1985, *Powers and Liberties*, Oxford: Blackwell.

Hall, S. 1983, in Hall and Jacques, 1983.

Hall, S. et al. 1978, *Policing the Crisis*, London: Macmillan.

Hall, S. and Jacques, M. (eds.) 1983, *The Politics of Thatcherism*, London: Lawrence and Wishart.

Hall, S. and Jefferson, T. 1976, *Resistance Through Rituals – Youth Cultures in Post War Britain*, London: Hutchinson.

Handy, C. 1984, *The Future of Work: A Guide to a Changing Society*, Oxford: Blackwell.

Handy, C. 1985, *Understanding Organizations*, Harmondsworth: Penguin Books, 3rd. edn.

Haraway, D. 1991, *Simians, Cyborgs, and Women*, London: Routledge.

Harding, N. 1977, *Lenin's Political Thought*, London: Macmillan.

Hargreaves, D. 1967, *Social Relations in a Secondary School*, London: Routledge & Kegan Paul.

Hargreaves, D. 1982, *The Challenge for the Comprehensive School*, London: Routledge & Kegan Paul.

Hargreaves, J. 1986, *Sport, Power and Culture*, Cambridge: Polity Press.

Harré, R. 1970, *The Principles of Scientific Thinking*, London: Macmillan.

Harré, R. 1979, *Social Being*, Oxford: Blackwell.

Harré, R. and Madden, E. 1975, *Causal Powers: a Theory of Natural Necessity*, Oxford: Blackwell.

Harrington, J. 1968, *Soccer Hooliganism*, Bristol: John Wright.

Harris, C. 1989, 'The Family', in A. Kuper and J. Kuper, (1985).

Harris, M. 1969, *The Rise of Anthropological Theory*, London: Routledge & Kegan Paul.

Harris, M. 1978, *Cannibals and Kings: the Origins of Cultures*, London: Fontana.

Harris, N. 1987, *The End of the Third World: Newly Industrializing Countries and the Decline of an Ideology*, Harmondsworth: Penguin.

Harris, O. 1981, 'Households as natural units', in K. Young, C. Wolkowitz and R. McCullah (eds.) *Of Marriage and the Market: Women's Subordination in International Perspective*, London: CSE Books.

Harrop, M. and Miller, W. 1987, *Elections and Voters: a Comparative Introduction*, London: Macmillan.

Hartmann, H. 1979, 'The unhappy marriage of Marxism and feminism', *Capital and Class*, Summer.

Harvey, D. 1973, *Social Justice and the City*, London: Edward Arnold.

Harvey, D. 1989a, *The Urban Experience*, Oxford: Blackwell.

Harvey, D. 1989b, *The Condition of Post Modernity*, Oxford: Blackwell.

Harwood, J. 1979, 'The race-intelligence controversy: a sociological approach', *Social Studies of Science*, 6 & 7.

Hayek, F. von 1944, *The Road to Serfdom*, London: Routledge & Kegan Paul.

Hearn, J. 1990, *Men, Masculinities and Social Theory,* London: Unwin Hyman.

Hearn, J. 1992, *Men in the Public Eye: The Construction and Deconstruction of Public Men and Public Patriarchies,* London: Routledge.

Heath, A. 1981, *Social Mobility,* London: Fontana.

Hebdige, D. 1979, *Subculture,* London: Methuen.

Hechter, M. 1975, *Internal Colonialism: the Celtic Fringe in British National Development, 1536–1966,* London: Routledge & Kegan Paul.

Held, D. 1980, *Introduction to Critical Theory,* London: Hutchinson.

Held, D. et al 1999, *Global Transformations,* Cambridge: Polity.

Hempel, C. 1959, 'The logic of functional analysis', in L. Gross (ed.) *Symposium on Sociological Theory,* New York: Harper Row.

Hepple, L. 1985, 'Time-space analysis', in A. Kuper and J. Kuper.

Herberg, W. 1960, *Protestant, Catholic, Jew,* New York: Doubleday.

Herzberg, F. 1968, *Work and the Nature of Man,* London: Staples Press.

Hesse, M. 1980, *Revolutions and Reconstructions in the Philosophy of Science,* Brighton: Harvester Press.

Hill, P. 1986, *Development Economics on Trial: The Anthropological Case for a Prosecution,* Cambridge: Cambridge University Press.

Hill, S. 1981, *Competition and Control at Work,* London: Heinemann.

Hill, S. 1991, 'Why quality circles failed but total quality management might succeed', *British Journal of Industrial Relations,* 29.

Hilton, R. 1973, *Bond Men Made Free: Medieval Peasant Movements and the English Rising of 1381,* London: Temple Smith.

Hilton, R. (ed.) 1976, *The Transition from Feudalism to Capitalism,* London: New Left Books.

Hindess, B. 1973, *The Use of Official Statistics,* London: Macmillan.

Hindess, B. and Hirst, P. 1975, *PreCapitalist Modes of Production,* London: Routledge & Kegan Paul.

Hirsch, F. 1977, *Social Limits to Growth,* London: Routledge & Kegan Paul.

Hirst, P. and Thompson, G. 1966, *Globalization in Question,* Cambridge: Polity.

Hobsbawm, E. 1964, 'The labour aristocracy', in E. Hobsbawm, *Labouring Men,* London: Weidenfeld & Nicolson.

Hobsbawm, E. 1969, *Bandits,* London: Weidenfeld and Nicolson.

Hobsbawm, E. and Ranger, T. (eds.) 1983, *The Invention of Tradition,* Cambridge: Cambridge University Press.

Hodges, D. 1961, 'The "intermediate classes" in Marxian theory', *Social Research,* 23.

Hodgson, G. 1982, *Capitalism, Value and Exploitation,* Oxford: Martin Robertson.

Hollis, M. 1977, *Models of Man,* Cambridge: Cambridge Univ. Press.

Hollis, M. 1987, *The Cunning of Reason,* Cambridge: Cambridge Univ. Press.

Holton, R. 1985, *The Transition from Feudalism to Capitalism,* Basingstoke and London: Macmillan.

Home, J., Jary, D. and Tomlinson, A. 1987 *Sport, Leisure and Social Relations,* London: Routledge/Sociological Review Monograph, 33.

Hooks, B. 1981, *Ain't I a Woman?* London: Pluto Press.

Hope, K. and Goldthorpe, J.H. 1974, *The Social Grading of Occupations:a New Approach and Scale,* Oxford: Clarendon Press.

Horowitz, I. 1980, *Taking Lives, Genocide and State Power,* Transaction Books.

Houlihan, B. 1994, *Sport and International Politics,* Hemel Hempstead: Harvester.

Hudson, W. 1949, 'Puritanism and the Spirit of Capitalism', *Church Times,* 18.

Hughes, E. 1952, *Men and Their Work,* Glencoe, Ill.: Free Press.

Humm, M. 1989, *A Dictionary of Feminist Theory,* London: Harvester/Wheatsheaf.

Hunter, F. 1963, *Community Power Structure,* New York: Anchor Books.

Hurd, G. et al. 1973, *Human Societies – an Introduction to Sociology,* London: Routledge & Kegan Paul.

Huse, E. and Cummings, T. 1985, *Organization, Development and Change,* (3rd ed.).

Hyman, R. 1984, *Strikes,* Glasgow: Fontana (3rd edn., originally, 1972).

Hymes, D. 1966, On *Communicative Competence,* Report of Research Planning Conference on Language Development among Disadvantaged Children, Yeshiva University.

Inglehart, R. 1977, *The Silent Revolution – Changing Values and Political Styles among Western Mass Publics,* Princeton: Princeton University Press.

Ingold, T. 1989, *BASAPP Newsletter,* 3.

Institute of Race Relations, 1987, *Policing Against Black People,* London: Institute of Race Relations.

Jackson, B. and Marsden, D. 1962, *Education and the Working Class,* London: Routledge & Kegan Paul.

Jacobs, P. and Lindau, S. 1966, *The New Radicals,* Harmondsworth: Penguin.

James, C. 1980 (first published 1938), *The Black Jacobins: Toussaint L'Ouverture and the San Domingo Revolution,* London: Allison and Busby.

James, S. 1974, 'Sex, race and working class power', *Race Today,* January.

Jameson, F. 1984, 'Post-modernism or the Cultural Logic of Late-Capitalism', *New Left Review,* 146.

Jameson, F. 1991, 'Post-modernism or the Cultural Logic of Late- Capitalism', London: Verso.

Jary, D. 1978, 'A new significance for the middle class left?' in Garrard et al, 1978.

Jary, D. 1991, 'Society as "time-traveller": Giddens on historical change, historical materialism and the nation-state in world society', in C. Bryant and D. Jary, 1991.

Jary, D., Horne, J. and Bucke, T. 1991, 'Football fanzines and football culture', in R. Frankenberg (ed.) *Cultural Aspects of Football, Sociological Review,* 39.

Jay, M. 1973, *The Dialectical Imagination,* London: Heinemann.
Jeffrey, P. 1979, *Frogs in a Well: Indian Women in Purdah,* London: Zed Press.
Jenkins, R. 1984, 'Divisions over the international division of labour', *Capital and Class,* 22.
Jenkins, R. 1986, *Transitional Corporations and the Latin American Motor Industry,* London: Macmillan.
Jennes V., 1993, *Making it Work: the Prostitutes' Rights Movement in Perspective,* New York: Aldinine Gryet.
Jensen, A. 1969, 'How much can we boost IQ and educational achievement?, *Harvard Educational Review,* 39.
Jessop, B. et al. 1984, 'Authoritarian populism, two nations and Thatcherism', *New Left Review,* 147.
Jessop, B., Bonnet, K., Bromley, S. and Ling, T. 1989, *Thatcherism,* Cambridge: Polity Press.
Johnson, T. 1972, *Professions and Power,* London: Macmillan.
Jones, T., Maclean, B. and Young, J. 1986, *The Islington Crime Survey: Crime, Victimization and Policing in Inner-City,* London: Gower.
Jung, C.G. 1928, *Collected Works,* London: Routledge & Kegan Paul.
Karabel, J. and Halsey, A. 1977, *Power and Ideology in Education,* New York: Oxford University Press.
Katz, D. and Kahn, R. 1966, *The Social Psychology of Organizations,* New York: Wiley.
Katz, E. and Lazarsfeld, P. 1955, *Personal Influence,* Glencoe, Ill: Free Press.
Katz, F. 1968, *Autonomy and Organization: the Limits of Social Control,* New York: Random House.
Keating, P. 1985, *Clerics and Capitalists: a Critique of the Weber Thesis,* Salford Papers in Sociology and Anthropology, 2.
Kelly, G. 1955, *The Psychology of Personal Constructs,* New York: Norton.
Kelly, J. 1982, 'Early feminist theory and the Querelle des Femmes, 1400-1789'. *Signs,* 8.
Kendon, A. 1988, 'Goffman's approach to face-to-face interaction', in P.Dolin, and A. Wootton, *Exploring the Interaction Order,* Cambridge: Polity Press.
Kerr, C. 1954, 'The Balkanization of labour markets', in E. Wight Bakke et al. (eds.) *Labour Mobility and Economic Opportunity,* Cambridge, Mass.: M.I.T. Press.
Kerr, C. 1982, *The Uses of the University,* Cambridge, Mass.: Harvard Univ Press (3rd ed.).
Kerr, C. 1983, *The Future of Industrial Societies: convergence or continuing diversity,* Harvard Univ. Press.
Kerr, C. et al. 1962, *Industrialism and Industrial Man,* London: Heineman
Kershaw, I. 1989, *The Nazi Dictatorship: Problems and Perspectives of Interpretation,* Edward Arnold: London (2nd edn.).
King, C. 1993, 'His truth goes marching on: Elvis Presley and the pilgrimage to Graceland', in I. Reader and T. Walter (eds) *Pilgrimages in Popular Culture,* London: Macmillan.
Kinsey, A. et al. 1948, *Sexual Behaviour in the Human Male,* Philadelphia: W. B. Saunders.
Kinsey, A. et al. 1953, *Sexual Behaviour in the Human Female,* Philadelphia: W.B. Saunders.
Kinsey, R., Lea, J. and Young, J. 1986, *Losing the Fight Against Crime,* Oxford: Blackwell.
Kitchen, M. 1976, *Fascism,* London: Macmillan.
Kitzinger, C. 1987, *The Social Construction of Lesbianism,* London: Sage.
Kluckhohn, C. 1944, *Navaho Witchcraft,* Boston: Beacon Press.
Konrád, G. and Szelényl, I. 1979, *The Intellectuals on the Road to Class Power,* Brighton: Harvester.
Kuhn, T. 1977, *The Essential Tension,* Chicago: Chicago University Press.
Kumari, R. 1989, *Women-headed Households in Rural India,* London: Sangam Books.
Kuper, A. and Kuper, J. 1985, *The Social Science Encyclopedia,* London: Routledge (1989).
Laboriz, S. 1970, 'The assignment of numbers to rank order categories', *American Sociological Review,* 33.
Labov, W. 1967, *The Social Stratification of English in New York City,* Washington, DC: Centre for Applied Linguistics.
Labov, W. 1972, 'The logic of non-standard English', in P. Giglioli (ed.) *Language and Social Context,* Penguin.
Lacey, C. 1970, *Hightown Grammar,* Manchester: Manchester University Press.
Lakatos, I 1976, *Proofs and Refutations: The Logic of Mathematical Discovery,* Cambridge: Cambridge University Press.
Lakatos, I. and Musgrave, A. (eds.) 1970, *Criticism and the Growth of Knowledge,* Cambridge: Cambridge Univ. Press.
Lane, L. 1981, *The Rites of Rulers: Ritual in Industrial Society – the Soviet Case,* Cambridge, CUP.
Lasch, C. 1991, *The Culture of Narcissism,* New York: Norton.
Lash, S. 1990, *The Sociology of Postmodernism,* London: Routledge.
Lash, S. and Urry, J. 1987, *The End of Organized Capitalism,* Cambridge: Polity Press.
Laslett, P. (ed.) 1972, *Household and Family in Past Time,* Cambridge: Cambridge Univ. Press.
Lasswell, H. 1941, 'The garrison state', *American Journal of Sociology,* 46.
Lawrence, P. and Lorsch, J. 1967, *Organization and Environment: Managing Differentiation and Integration,* Boston: Harvard Univ. Press.
Layder, D. 1981, *Structure, Interaction, and Social Theory,* London: Routledge & Kegan Paul.
Lea, J. and Young, J. 1983, *What is to be done about Law and Order?* Harmondsworth: Penguin.
Leach, E. 1954, *The Political Systems of Highland Burma,* Cambridge: Cambridge University Press.
Leach, E. 1959, 'Hydraulic Society in Ceylon', *Past and Present,* 15.
Leach, E. 1970, *Lévi-Strauss,* London: Fontana.
Leach, E. 1982, *Social Anthropology,* London: Fontana.

Leacock, E. (ed.) 1971 *The Culture of Poverty: A Critique*, New York: Simon and Schuster.

Le Bon, G. 1895, *The Crowd*, New York: Viking Press (1960).

Le Grande, J. 1982, *The Strategy of Equality: Redistribution and the Social Services*, London: Allen and Unwin.

Lefebvre, H. 1967, 'Neighbourhoods and neighbourhood life', in *Le quartier et la ville*, Cahiers de l'IAAURPA, 7.

Lefebvre, H. 1991 *The Production of Space*, Oxford: Blackwell.

Lemert, E. 1951, *Social Pathology: a Systematic Approach to Sociopathic Behaviour*, New Jersey: Prentice Hall.

Lemert, E. 1961, *Social Pathology*, New York: McGraw-Hill.

Lenin, V. 1902, 'What is to be done?' reprinted in T. Clarke and L. Clements, (eds.) *Trades Unions Under Capitalism*, (1977).

Lenin, V. 1916, *Imperialism, the Highest Stage of Capitalism*, New York:International Publishers (1939).

Lenk, K. 1982, 'Information and society' in G. Friedrichs and A. Schaff (eds.), *Microelectronics and Society: for Better or for Worse*, Oxford:Pergamon Press.

Lenski, G. 1961, *The Religious Factor*, New York: Doubleday.

Lenski, G. 1966, *Power and Privilege*, New York: McGraw-Hill.

Lenski, G. and Lenski, J. 1970, *Human Societies*, New York: McGraw Hill (5th edn., 1987).

Le Roy Ladurie, E. 1978, *Montaillou*, London: Scholar Press.

Lévi-Strauss, C. 1967, *The Scope of Anthropology*, London: Cape.

Lévy-Bruhl, L. 1923, *The Primitive Mentality*, Boston: Beacon Press.

Lewin, K. 1951, *Field Theory in Social Science*, New York: Harper.

Lewis, J. and Meredith, B. 1988, *Daughters Who Care: Daughters Caring for Mothers at Home*, London: Routledge.

Lienhardt, G. 1964, *Social Anthropology*, Oxford: Oxford University Press.

Likert, R. 1932, 'A Technique for the Measurement of Attitudes', *Archives of Psychology*, 40.

Linder, S. 1970, *The Harried Leisure Class*, New York, Columbia University Press.

Lindesmith, A.R. 1947, *Opiate Addiction*, Bloomington: Principia.

Linton, R. 1936, *The Study of Man*, New York: Appleton-Century.

Lipset, S. 1959, 'Political Sociology', in R. Merton et al. (eds.) *Sociology Today*, New York: Basic Books.

Lipset, S. and Bendix, R. 1959, *Social Mobility in Industrial Society*, Berkeley:University of California Press.

Littler, C. 1982, *The Development of the Labour Process in Capitalist Societies*, London: Heinemann.

Lockwood, D. 1956, 'Some remarks on the "Social System"', *British Journal of Sociology*, 7.

Lockwood, D. 1964, 'Social integration and system integration', in Z. Zollschan and W. Hirsch (eds.) *Explorations in Social Change*, London: Routledge & Kegan Paul.

Lockwood, D. 1966, 'Sources of variation in working class images of society', *Sociological Review*, 14.

Lomnitz, L. 1977, *Networks and Marginality: Life in a Mexican Shanty-town*, New York: Academic Press.

Lorder, A. 1979, 'Need', *Heresies*, 2.

Lowe, S. 1986, *Urban Social Movements: the City after Castells*, London: Macmillan.

Löwy, M. 1981, *The Politics of Combined and Uneven Development: the Theory of Permanent Revolution*, London: Verso.

Lukes, S. 1968, 'Methodological individualism reconsidered', *British Journal of Sociology* (reprinted in Lukes, 1977).

Lukes, S. 1973, *Emile Durkheim: His Life and Work*, London: Allen Lane.

Lukes, S. 1974, *Power: a Radical View*, London: Macmillan.

Lukes, S. 1977, *Essays in Social Theory*, London: Macmillan.

Lyon, D. 1988, *The Information Society: Issues and Illusions*, Cambridge: Polity Press.

Machin, H. (ed.) 1983, *National Communism in Western Europe: A Third Way to Socialism?* London: Methuen.

MacInnes, J. 1987, *Thatcherism at Work*, Oxford: Oxford University Press.

MacIntyre, A. 1962, 'A mistake about causality in social science', in P.Laslett and W. Runciman, *Philosophy, Politics and Society*, Second Series, Oxford: Blackwell.

MacPherson, C. 1962, *Possessive Individualism*, Oxford: Clarendon Press (1964).

Madge, C. 1964, *Society in the Mind*, London: Faber & Faber.

Mallet, S. 1975, *Essays on the New Working Class*, St. Louis: Telos Press.

Mandel, E. 1962, *Marxist Economic Theory*, London: Merlin.

Mann, M. 1970, 'The social cohesion of liberal democracy', *American Sociological Review*, 35.

Mann, M. 1983, *Student Encyclopedia of Sociology*, London: Macmillan.

Mann, M. 1988, *States, War and Capitalism: Studies in Political Sociology*, Oxford: Blackwell.

Mannheim, K. 1953, 'Conservative thought', in *Essays on Sociology and Social Psychology*, London: Routledge.

March, J. and Simon, H. 1958, *Organizations*, New York: Wiley.

Marcuse, H. 1968, *Negations: Essays in Critical Theory*, London: Allen Lane Press.

Marsden, D. 1971, *Politicians, Comprehensives and Equality*, Fabian Society Tract. London: Gollancz.

Marsden, D. 1982, *Workless*, (2nd edn.), London: Croom Helm.

Marsh, A. 1977, *Protest and Political Consciousness*, Beverley Hills: Sage.

Marsh, C. 1988, *Exploring Data: an Introduction to Data Analysis for the Social Sciences,* Cambridge: Polity Press.

Marsh, C. 1988, 'Unemployment in Britain'. In Gallie (ed.) *Employment in Britain,* Oxford: Blackwell.

Marsh, P., Rosser, E. and Harré, R. 1978, *The Rules of Disorder,* London: Routledge & Kegan Paul.

Marshall, 1984, 'On the significance of women's unemployment, its neglect and significance', *Sociological Review,* 32 (2): 234–59.

Marshall, G., Newby, H., Rose, D. and Vogler, C. 1988, *Social Class in Modern Britain,* London: Hutchinson.

Marshall, G. (ed.) 1994, *The Concise Oxford Dictionary of Sociology,* Oxford: Oxford University Press.

Martin, D. 1969, *The Religious and the Secular,* London: Routledge & Kegan Paul.

Marwick, M. (ed.) 1970, *Witchcraft and Sorcery,* Harmondsworth: Penguin (2nd. edn., 1982).

Matza, D. 1964, *Delinquency and Drift,* New York: Wiley.

Mayo, E. 1949, *The Social Problems of an Industrial Civilization,* London: Routledge & Kegan Paul.

McCarthy, T. 1978, *The Critical Theory of Jurgen Habermas,* London: Heinemann.

McClelland, D. 1961, *The Achieving Society,* Princeton: van Nostrand.

McKenzie, R. 1963, *British Political Parties,* London: Heinemann, (2nd edn.).

McKenzie, R. and Silver, A. 1968, *Angels in Marble,* London: Heinemann.

McKinnon, C. 1989, 'Calvinism and the infallible assurance of grace: the Weber thesis reconsidered', *British Journal of Sociology,* 39.

McLennan, J. 1865, *Primitive Marriage,* Edinburgh: Adam and Charles Black.

McRobbie, A. 1991, *Feminism and Youth Culture,* London: Macmillan.

McRobbie, A. and Gerber, J. 1976, 'Girls and ıb-cultures', in S. Hall and T. Jefferson, 1976.

ad, G.H. 1934, *Mind, Self and Society,* Chicago: hicago Univ. Press.

ad, L. 1985, *Beyond Entitlements, New York:* lacMillan.

mmi, A. 1957, *The Colonizer and the Colonized,* ondon: Earthscan Books.

nnell, S. 1985, *All Manner of Food: Eating and Taste in England and France,* Oxford: Blackwell.

Merton, R. 1949, *Social Theory and Social Structure,* Glencoe: Free Press. (3rd. edn. 1968).

Merton, R. 1957, 'Bureaucratic structure and personality' in R. Merton, *Social Theory and Social Structure,* revised edition.

Merton, R., Reader, G. and Kendall, P. 1957, *The Student Physician, Cambridge,* Mass: Harvard University Press.

Miles, A. 1986, Economism and feminism: a comment on the domestic labour debate', in R. Hamilton and M. Barrett (eds), *The Politics of Diversity,* London: Verso.

Miliband, R. 1966, *The State in Capitalist Society,* London: Weidenfeld and Nicolson.

Millar, S. 1968, The *Psychology of Play,* Harmondsworth: Penguin.

Miller, S. 1960, 'Comparative social mobility: trend report and a bibliography', *Current Sociology,* 9.

Millet, K. 1970, *Sexual Politics,* New York: Doubleday.

Mills, C. 1940, 'Situated actions and vocabularies of motive', *American Sociological Review,* 5.

Millward, N. and Stevens, M. 1986, *British Workplace Industrial Relations 1980–84: The DE/ESRC/PSI/ACAS Surveys,* Aldershot: Gower.

Mishan, E. 1967, *The Costs of Economic Growth,* London: Staple Press.

Mitchell, J. 1974, *Psychoanalysis and Feminism,* London: Allen Lane.

Moore, B. 1978, *Injustice: the Social Basis of Obedience and Revolt,* London: MacMillan.

Morgan, D. 1975, *Social Theory and the Family,* London: Routledge & Kegan Paul.

Morgan, G. 1986, *Images of Organization,* London: Sage.

Morgan, L. 1870, *Systems of Consanguinity and Affinity of the Human Family,* Washington, DC: Smithsonian Institute.

Morgan, M. 1985, *Sociological Approaches to Health and Medicine,* Beckenham: Croom Helm.

Morris, D. 1978, *Manwatching,* St. Albans: Triad/Panther.

Mort, F. 1980, 'Sexuality: regulation and contestation', in Gay Left Collective (ed.), *Homosexuality: Power and Politics,* London: Allison and Busby.

Mouzelis, N. 1975, *Organization and Bureaucracy,* London: Routledge & Kegan Paul.

Mouzelis, N. 1986, *Politics in the Semi-Periphery: Early Parliamentarism and Late Industrialisation in the Balkans and the Latin America,* London: Macmillan.

Mouzelis, N. 1988, 'Sociology of development: reflections on the present crisis', *Sociology,* 22.

Mulkay, M. 1979, *Science and the Sociology of Knowledge,* London: Allen and Unwin.

Mulvey, L. 1975, 'Visual pleasure and narrative cinema', *Screen,* 16.

Mumford, E. 1980, 'The participative design of clerical information systems: two case studies', in N. Bjorn-Anderson, *The Human Side of Information Processing,* Holland-Holland: IAG.

Mumford, E. and Banks, O. 1967, *The Computer and the Clerk,* London: Routledge & Kegan Paul.

Murdoch, G. 1967, *Ethnographic Atlas,* Pittsburg: University of Pittsburg Press.

Murdock, G. 1949, *Social Structure,* New York: Macmillan.

Murphy, J., John, M. and Brown, H. 1984, *Dialogues and Debates in Social Psychology,* Milton Keynes: Open University Press.

Myrdal, G. et al. 1944, *An American Dilemma,* New York: Harper Row.

Nachmias, D. and Nachmias, D. 1976, *Research Methods in Social Investigation,* London: Edward Arnold.

Nadel, S. 1957, *The Theory of Social Structure,* London: Cohen and West.

Nairn, T. 1977, *The Break Up of Britain,* London: New Left Books.

Narroll, R. 1964, 'Ethnic unit classification', *Current Anthropology,* 5.

Nestle, J. 1981, 'Butch-fem relationships: sexual courage in the 1950s', *Heresies,* 3.

Neumann, F. 1942, *Behemoth,* New York: Harper Torch. (trans. 1963).

Neumann, S. 1956, 'Towards a comparative study of political parties', in Neumann S. (ed.) *Modern Political Parties,* Chicago: University of Chicago Press.

Newby, H. 1977, *The Deferential Workers,* London: Allen Lane (Penguin, 1979).

Neyman J. and Pearson E. 1928, 'On the use and interpretation of certain test criteria for purposes of statistical inference. Parts I and II', *Biometrika,* 20, 174–240 and 263–294.

Nichols, T. 1969, *Ownership, Control and Ideology,* London: Allen and Unwin.

Nichols, T. and Armstrong, P. 1976, *Workers Divided,* London: Fontana.

Nichols, T. and Beynon, H. 1977, *Living with Capitalism,* Routledge & Kegan Paul.

Nicolaus, M. 1972, 'Sociology Liberation Movement', in Pateman T (ed.) *Counter Course: a Handbook of Course Criticism,* Harmondsworth: Penguin.

Nicolson, M. and McLaughlin, C. 1987, 'Social Constructionism and Medical Sociology: A Reply to M. Bury', *Sociology of Health and Illness,* 9.

Northcott, J. 1988, *The Impact of Micro Electronics in Industry,* London:PSI.

Nozick, R. 1974, *Anarchy, State and Utopia,* New York: Basic Books.

Oakley, A. 1974, *Housewife,* London: Allen Lane.

O'Connor, J. 1973, *The Fiscal Crisis of the State,* New York: St Martin's Press.

Offe, C. 1985, *Disorganized Capitalism,* Cambridge: Polity Press.

Ogburn, W. 1964, *On Culture and Social Change: Selected Papers,* Chicago University Press.

Okley, J. 1975, 'Gypsy women: models in conflict' in S. Ardener, (ed.) *Perceiving Women,* London: Dent.

O'Leary, B. *1989, The Asiatic mode of Production,* Oxford: Blackwell.

Omahe, K. 1990, *The Borderless State,* London: Collins.

Omahe, K. 1995, *The End of the Nation State,* New York: Free Press.

Ortega y Gasset, J. 1930, *The Revolt of the Masses,* London: Allen & Masses.

Osgood, C., Suci, G. and Tannenbaum, P. 1957, *The Measurement of Meaning,* Urbana: Univ. of Illinois Press.

Ouchi, N. 1981, *Theory Z: How American Business Can Meet the Japanese Challenge,* Reading, Mass.: Addison-Wesley.

Outhwaite, W. 1985, 'Gadamer', in Skinner, Q. (ed.) *The Return of Grand Theory,* Cambridge: Cambridge Univ. Press.

Outhwaite, W. 1994, *Habermas – a Critical Introduction,* Cambridge: Polity Press.

Outhwaite, W. and Bottomore T. 1993, *Blackwell Dictionary of Twentieth-Century Social Thought.* Oxford: Blackwell.

Packard, V. *1957, The Hidden Persuaders,* New York: McKay (Penguin, 1961).

Packard, V. 1959, *The Status Seekers,* New York: McKay (Penguin, 1961).

Pahl, R. 1984, *Divisions of Labour,* Oxford: Basil Blackwell.

Pahl, R. 1989, 'Is the emperor naked?, *International Journal of Urban and Regional Research,* 13.

Pahl, R. and Gershuny, J. 1979, 'Work outside employment – some preliminary speculations', *New University Quarterly,* 34.

Pahl, R. and Gershuny, J. 1980, 'Britain in the decade of the three economies', *New Society,* January 3rd.

Pahl, R. and Winkler, J. 1974, 'The coming corporatism', *New Society, 10.*

Palmer, P. 1989, *Contemporary Women's Fiction,* London: Harvester.

Park, R. 1928, 'Human migration and the marginal man', *American Journal of Sociology, 33.*

Parker, G. 1993, *With This Body: Caring and Disability in Marriage,* Milton Keynes: Open University Press.

Parker, M. 2000, *Organizational Culture and Identity,* London: Sage.

Parker, S. 1971, *The Future of Work and Leisure,* London: MacGibbon and Kee.

Parkin, F. 1968, *Middle Class Radicalism,* Manchester: Manchester University Press.

Parkin, F. 1971, *Class Inequality and Political Order,* London: MacGibbon and Kee.

Parkin, F. 1974, 'Strategies of social closure in class formation', in Parkin (ed.) *Social Analysis of the Class Structure,* London: Tavistock.

Parkin, F. 1979, *Marxism and Class Theory: A Bourgeois Critique,* London:Tavistock.

Parry, N. and Parry J. 1976, *The Rise of the Medical Profession,* London: Croom Helm.

Parsons, T. 1939, 'The professions and social structure', *Social Forces,* 17, reprinted in *Essays in Sociological Theory,* Free Press *(1954* and 1964, revised edn.).

Parsons, T. 1956, 'Suggestions for a sociological approach to the theory of organizations', *Administrative Science Quarterly, 1.*

Parsons, T. 1959, 'The school class as a social system' in A. Halsey. et al. (1961) *Education, Economy and Society, New* York: Free Press.

Parsons, T. 1963, 'On the concept of political power', *Proceedings of the American Philosophical Society, 107.*

Parsons, T. 1964a, 'Evolutionary universals in society', *American Sociological Review, 29.*

Parsons, T. 1964b, *Social Structure and Personality,* New York: Free Press.

Parsons, T. 1971, *The System of Modern Societies,* Englewood Cliffs, NJ: Prentice Hall.

Parsons, T. 1977, *The Evolution of Societies,* Englewood Cliffs, NJ: Prentice Hall.

Parsons, T. and Bales, R. 1955, *Family: Socialization and Interaction Process,* London: Routledge (1956).
Parsons, T., Bales, R. and Shils, E. 1963, *Working Papers on the Theory of Action,* Glencoe, Ill: Free Press.
Patterson, O. 1982, *Slavery and Social Death: a Comparative Study,* Cambridge, Mass. and London: Harvard Univ. Press.
Pavlov, I. 1911, *Conditioned Reflexes,* Oxford: Oxford University Press (1927).
Payne, G. 1989, 'Mobility and bias: a reply to Saunders', *Network,* 45.
Peach, P. 1981, *Ethnic Segregation in Cities,* London: Croom Helm.
Pearce, R. 'Sharecropping: Towards a Marxist View', in T. Byres (ed.) 1983.
Pearson, G. 1983, *Hooligan, a History of Respectable Fears.* London: Macmillan.
Perrow, C. 1979, *Complex Organizations: a Critical Essay,* Illinois: Scott Foreman.
Peters, T. and Waterman, R. 1982, *In Search of Excellence,* New York: Harper Row.
Pettigrew, A. 1973, *The Politics of Organizational Decision-Making,* London: Tavistock.
Phillips, L. 1973, *Bayesian Statistics for Social Scientists,* London: Nelson.
Piaget, J. 1932, *The Moral Judgement of the Child,* London: Routledge & Kegan Paul.
Pickvance, C. 1976, *Urban Sociology,* London: Tavistock.
Pickvance, C. 1984, 'Voluntary associations', in R. Burgess, 1986.
Pierson, J. and Thomas, M. 1995, *Collins Dictionary of Social Work,* HarperCollins.
Pike, K. 1967, *Language in Relation to a Unified Theory of the Structure of Human Behaviour,* Pt 1, Preliminary Edition, Glendale Summer Institute of Linguistics.
Pinker, R. 1971, *Social Theory and Social Policy,* London: Heinemann.
Pinto-Duschinsky, M. 1985, 'Corruption', in R. Kuper, and J. Kuper, 1985.
Piore, M. and Sabel, C. 1984, *The Second Industrial Divide,* New York:Basic Books.
Pippin, R., Feenberg, A., and Webel, C. (eds.), 1988, *Marcuse: Critical Theory and the Promise of Utopia,* London: Macmillan.
Policy Studies Institute, 1983, *Police and People in London,* (4 Vols.) London: Policy Studies Institute.
Pollart, A. 1981, *Girls, Wives, Factory Lives,* London: Macmillan.
Polsky, N. 1969, *Hustlers, Beats and Others,* Harmondsworth: Penguin.
Poole, M. 1966, *Workers' Participation in Industry,* London: Routledge.
Popitz, H. et al. 1957, 'The worker's image of society' in T. Burns (ed.) *Industrial Man,* Harmondsworth: Penguin.
Post, K. 1972, '"Peasantisation" and rural political movements in West Africa', *European Journal of Sociology,* 13.
Post, K. and Wright, P. 1989, *Socialism and Underdevelopment,* Routledge.
Poulantzas, N. 1973, *Political Power and Social Classes,* London: New Left Books.
Poulantzas, N. 1974, *Fascism and Dictatorship,* London: New Left Books.
Pribicevic, B. 1959, *The Shop Stewards' Movement and Workers' Control,* Oxford: Blackwell.
Price, R. and Bains, G. 1988, 'The labour force', in A. Halsey (ed.) *British Social Trends Since 1900: A Guide to the Changing Social Structure of Britain, (2nd. edn.),* London: Macmillan.
Prothro, G. and Grigg, C., 1960, 'Fundamental principles of democracy', *Journal of Politics,* 22.
Pugh, D. and Hickson, D. 1968, 'The comparative study of organizations' in D. Pym (ed.) *Industrial Society,* Harmondsworth: Penguin.
Purcell, K. 1986, 'Work, employment and unemployment', in R. Burgess, 1986.
Quine, W. 1960, *Word and Object,* Cambridge, Mass.: MIT Press.
Quine, W. *1987, Quiddities: an Intermittently Philosophical Dictionary,* Harmondsworth: Penguin Books.
Rapoport, A. (ed.) 1968, 'Introduction', to *Clausewitz,* Harmondsworth: Penguin.
Redclift, M. 1987, *Sustainable Development: Exploring the Contradictions,* London: Methuen.
Reid, I. 1986, *The Sociology of School and Education, Fontana.*
Reimer, E. 1971, *School is Dead: an Essay on Alternatives in Education,* Harmondsworth: Penguin.
Renner, K. 1953, 'The service class' in T. Bottomore and P. Goode (eds.), *Austro-Marxism,* 1978, Oxford: Oxford University Press.
Rex, J. and Moore, R. 1967, *Race, Community and Conflict,* Oxford: Oxford Univ. Press.
Rey, P-P. 1975, 'The lineage mode of production', *Critique of Anthropology,* 3.
Rich, A. 1980, 'Compulsory heterosexuality and lesbian existence', *Signs,* 5.
Richardson, L. 1960, *Statistics* of *Deadly Quarrels,* London: Stevens.
Ricoeur, P. 1981, *Hermeneutics and the Human Sciences,* Cambridge: Cambridge University Press.
Rifkin, J. 1995, *The Future of Work: The Decline of the Global Labor Force and the Dawn of the Post-Market Era,* New York: G.P. Putnam's Sons.
Riley, M. 1963, *Sociological Research: a Case Approach,* Vol.1. *New* York: Harcourt, Brace and World.
Ritzer, G. and LeMoyne, T. 1991, 'Hyperrationality': an Extension of Weberian and Non-Weberian Theory', in Ritzer G., *Metatheorizing in Sociology,* Lexington, Mass.: Lexington Books, pp. 93-115.
Roberts, B. 1978, *Cities of Peasants,* London: Arnold.
Robertson, H. 1933, *Aspects of the Rise of Economic Individualism,* Cambridge: Cambridge University Press.
Robinson, W. 1950, 'Ecological correlation and behaviour of individuals', *American Sociological Review,* 15.
Robinson, W. 1951, 'The logical structure of analytical induction', *American Sociological Review,* 16.

Robinson, W. et al. 1968, *Measures of Political Attitude,* University of Michigan.
Roemer, J. 1982, *A General Theory of Exploitation and Class,* Cambridge, Mass.: Harvard University Press.
Roethlisberger, F. and Dickson, W. 1939, *Management and the Worker,* Cambridge, Mass.: Harvard Univ. Press.
Rogers, C. 1986, *Freedom to Learn for the Eighties,* Colombus, Ohio: Charles Merrill.
Rogers, C.D. 1983, *The Family Tree Detective,* Manchester: Manchester University Press.
Rogers, E. 1983, *Diffusion of Innovations,* 3rd. edn., New York: Free Press.
Rojek, C. (1991) *Ways of Escape: Modern Transformations of Leisure and Travel,* London: Routledge.
Rokeach, M. 1960, *The Open and Closed Mind,* New York: Basic Books.
Roper, M. and Tosh, J. 1991, *Manful Assertions, Masculinities in Britain Since 1800,* London: Routledge.
Rorschach, H. 1921, *Psychodiagnostics: a Diagnostic Test based on Perception,* Berne: Huber (tr. 1942).
Rose, D. (ed.) 1988, *Social Stratification and Economic Change,* London: Hutchinson.
Rose, H. 1986, 'Women's work: women's knowledge', in J. Mitchell, and A. Oakley, (eds.) *What is Feminism?,* Oxford; Blackwell.
Rose, M. 1988, *Industrial Behaviour,* Harmondsworth: Penguin (2nd edn., 1st edn. 1975).
Rose, R. (ed.) 1960, *Must Labour Lose?* Harmondsworth: Penguin.
Rose, S. 1973, *The Conscious Brain,* London: Weidenfeld and Nicolson.
Rosenthal, R. 1991, *Meta-Analytic Procedures for Social Research,* (revised edition), London: Sage Publications.
Routh, G. 1980, *Occupation and Pay in Great Britain,* London: Macmillan.
Rowbotham, S. 1972, *Women, Resistance and Revolution,* New York: Penguin.
Rowbotham, S. 1973, *Women's Consciousness, Man's World,* Harmondsworth:Penguin.
Roxborough, I. 1984, 'Unity and diversity in Latin American history', *Journal of Latin American Studies,* 16.
Rubenstein, R. 1987, *Alchemists of Revolutions: Terrorism in the Modern World,* New York: Basic Books.
Rubery, J. 1996, 'The labour market outlook and the outlook for labour process analysis.' In R. Crompton, D. Gallie and K. Purcell (eds.), *Changing Forms of Employment: Organisations, Skills and Gender,* London: Routledge.
Rubery, J. 1978, 'Structured labour markets, worker organization and low pay.' *Cambridge Journal of Economics,* 2.
Runciman, W. I. 1990, 'How many classes are there in contemporary British society?', Sociology, 24.
Rushton, J. and Sorrentino, R. (eds.) 1981, *Altruism and Helping Behaviour:Social, Personality and Developmental Perspectives,* Hillsdale, NJ.
Sacks, H., Schegloff, E. and Jefferson, G. 1974, 'A simplest systematics for the organization of turn-taking for conversation', *Language,* 50.
Sahlins, M. 1971, *Culture and Practical Reason,* Chicago: Aldine.
Sahlins, M. 1972, *Stone Age Economics,* Chicago: Aldine.
Sahlins, M. and Service, E. 1960, *Evolution and Culture,* Ann Arbor: University of Michigan Press.
Said, Edward 1993, *Culture and Imperialism,* New York: Vintage Books.
Sainsbury, P. 1955, *Suicide in London: an Ecological Study,* London: Chapman.
Sainsbury, P. and Barraclough, B. 1968, 'Differences between suicide rates', *Nature,* 220.
Samuels, A. 1993. The *Political Psyche,* London: Routledge.
Samuelson, K. 1961, *Religion and Economic Action: a Critique of Max* Weber, New York: Harper.
Sarah, E. 1982, 'Towards a reassessment of feminist history', *Women's Studies International Forum,* 5.
Sarup, M. 1993, *An Introductory Guide to Post-Structuralism and Post-Modernism,* (2nd ed.) Hemel Hempstead; Harvester.
Sayers, J. et al. (eds.) 1987, *Engels Revisited: New Feminist Essays,* Tavistock:London.
Scarman, Lord 1981, *The Brixton Disorders,* London: HMSO.
Scase, R. and Goffee, R. 1982, *The Entrepreneurial Middle Class,* London: Croom Helm.
Scheff, T. 1966, *Being Mentally Ill,* Chicago: Aldine.
Schermer, H. 1988, *Towards a Sociological Model of the Stranger,* Staffordshire Polytechnic, Dept. of Sociology Occasional Paper, 9.
Schumacher, E. 1973, *Small is Beautiful,* Harmondsworth: Penguin.
Schutz, A. 1962–6, Collected *Papers,* Vol.1, The Hague: Nijhoff.
Schutz, A. and Luckmaun, T. 1973, *The Structures of the Life World,* London: Heinemann (1974).
Scott, J. 1979, *Corporations, Classes and Capitalism,* London: Hutchinson.
Scott, J. 1982, *The Upper Class,* London: Macmillan.
Scott, J.C. 1985, *Weapons of the Weak: Everyday Forms of Peasant Resistance,* New Haven and London: Yale University Press.
Scott, R.L. 1977, 'Communication as an International Social System', *Human Communication Research,* 3.
Scott, R. and Shore, A. 1979, *Why Sociology Does not Apply – A Study of the Uses of Sociology in Social Policy,* New York: Elsevier.
Scraton, P. 1982, 'Policing and institutionalized racism on Merseyside', in D. Cowell et al. 1982.
Scraton, P. 1985, *The State of the Police,* London: Pluto.
Scruton, R. 1986, *Sexual Desires: a Philosophical Investigation,* London: Weidenfeld.
Scwambler G. and Swambler A. (eds) 1995, *Rethinking Prostitution: Purchasing Sex in Britain in the 1990s,* London: Routledge.
Searle, J. 1969, *Expression and Meaning: Speech Act Theory and Pragmatics,* New York: World.
Searle, J. 1984, *Minds, Brains and Science,* London: Penguin Books.

Sebestyen, A. 1979, 'Tendencies in the Women's Liberation Movement', in *Feminist Practice: Notes from the Tenth Year,* London: Radical Feminist Collective.

Secord, P. and Backman, C. 1964, *Social Psychology,* New York: McGraw-Hill.

Seidler, V. 1991, *Recreating Sexual Politics: Men, Feminism and Politics,* London: Routledge.

Selznik, P., 1966, *TVA and the Grass Roots,* New York: Harper Torch Books.

Selvin, H. 1958, 'A critique of tests of significance in survey research', *American Sociological Review,* 23.

Sen, A. 1981, *Poverty and Famines: an Essay on Entitlement and Deprivation,* Oxford: Clarendon Press.

Sewell, G. and Wilkinson, B. 1992, 'Empowerment or emasculation? Shop floor surveillance in a total organization', in P. Blyton and P.Tunnball (eds) *Reassessing Human Resource Management,* London: Sage.

Seymour-Smith, C. 1986, *Macmillan Dictionary of Anthropology,* London: Macmillan.

Shanin, T. 1982, 'Defining peasants: conceptualisations and deconceptualisations', *Sociological Review,* 30.

Shanin, T. (ed.) 1988, *Peasants and Peasant Societies,* Harmondsworth: Penguin.

Sharp, R. and Green, A. 1975, *Education and Social Control,* Routledge & Kegan Paul.

Shaw, C. 1930, *The Jack Roller,* Chicago: University of Chicago Press.

Shaw, C. and McKay, H. 1929, *Juvenile Delinquency and Urban Areas,* Chicago: University of Chicago Press.

Shaw, M. (ed.) 1985, *Marxist Sociology Revisited: Critical Assessments,* London: Macmillan.

Sherif, M. 1935, 'A study of some social factors in perception', *Archives of Psychology,* 27.

Shilling, C. 1993. *The Body and Social Theory,* London: Sage.

Shils, E. and Young, M. 1953, 'The meaning of the Coronation' *Sociological Review,* 1.

Siltanen, J. and Stanworth, M. 1984, *Women and the Public Sphere,* London: Hutchinson.

Silverman, D. 1970, *The Theory of Organizations,* London: Heinemann.

Simey, M. 1982, 'Police authorities and accountability', in D. Cowell et al. 1982.

Simmel, G. 1903, 'Metropolis and mental life' in K. Woolf (ed.) 1950.

Simon, H. 1957a, Models of Man, New York: Wiley.

Simon, H. 1957b, *Administrative Behaviour,* New York: Macmillan.

Sinfield, A. 1981, *What Unemployment Means,* Oxford, Martin Robertson.

Skinner, B. 1953, *Science and Human Behaviour,* New York: Macmillan.

Skinner, B. 1957, Verbal *Behaviour,* New York: Appleton-Century Crofts.

Skocpol, T. 1979, *States and Social Revolutions: A comparative analysis of France, Russia and China,* Cambridge: Cambridge University Press.

Small, A. 1905, *General Sociology,* Chicago: University of Chicago Press.

Small, A. 1924, *The Origins of Sociology,* University of Chicago Press.

Smart, C. 1976, *Women, Crime and Criminology,* London: Routledge & Kegan Paul.

Smelser, N. 1962, *Collective Behaviour,* London: Routledge & Kegan Paul.

Smelser, N. 1968, *Essays in Sociological Explanation,* Englewood Cliffs, NJ.: Prentice Hall.

Smith, A. 1776, *An Inquiry into the Nature and Causes of the The Wealth of Nations,* London: Routledge.

Smith, D. 1983, *Barrington Moore Jr: Violence, Morality and Political Change,* London: Macmillan.

Sohn-Rethel, A. 1978, *Intellectual and Manual Labour,* London: Macmillan.

Southall, A. 1954, *Alur Society: a Study of Processes and Types of Domination,* Cambridge: Heffer.

Spencer, H. 1971, in K. Thompson and J. Tunstall, *Sociological Perspectives:Selected Readings,* Harmondsworth: Penguin.

Spender, D. 1980, *Man-Made Language,* London: Routledge & Kegan Paul.

Spooner, B. 1973, *The Cultural Ecology of Pastoral Nomads,* Reading, Mass.:Addison Wesley.

Sraffa, P. 1960, *The Production of Commodities by Means of Commodities,* London: Cambridge University Press.

Stacey, M. 1969, 'The myth of community studies', *British Journal of Sociology,* 20.

Stanley, L. and Wise, S. 1983, *Breaking Out: Feminist Consciousness and Feminist Research,* London: Routledge & Kegan Paul.

Stanworth, P. and Giddens, A. 1974, 'An economic élite: a demographic profile of company chairmen', in P. Stanworth and A. Giddens (eds.) *Élites and Power in British Society,* Cambridge: Cambridge University Press.

Stavenhagen, R. 1975, *Social Classes in Agrarian Societies,* New York: Anchor Press.

Stedman Jones, G. 1975, 'Class Struggle and the Industrial Revolution', reprinted in G. Steadman Jones, *Languages of Class,* 1983 Cambridge: Cambridge University Press.

Steedman, I. et al. 1981, *The Value Controversy,* London: Verso.

Stevens, S. 1944, 'On the theory of scales of measurement', *Science,* 103.

Stevens, S. 1951, 'Mathematics, measurements and psychophysics', in S. Stevens, (ed.) *Handbook of Experimental Psychology.* New York: Wiley.

Stouffer, S. 1955, *Communism, Conformity and Civil Liberties,* New York: Doubleday.

Stouffer, S. et al. 1949, *The American Soldier,* Princeton University Press.

Strauss, A., Schatzman, L., Ehrlich, D., Bucher, R. and Sabshin, M. 1963, 'The hospital and its negotiated order.' In E. Friedson (ed.) *The Hospital in Modern Society,* New York: Macmillan: 147–69.

Strydom, M. 1992, 'The ontogenetic fallacy: the immanent critique of Habermas's developmental logical theory of evolution', *Theory Culture and Society,* 9.

Summers, A. 1979, 'A home from home – Women's philanthropic work in the nineteenth century', in S. Burnham, (ed.) *Fit Work for Women*, London: Croom Helm.

Sumner, W. 1906, Folkways, New York: Doubleday (1959).

Suttles, G. 1970, 'Friendship as a social institution', in G. McCall et al., *Social Relationships*, Chicago.

Swift, D. 1967, 'Social class, mobility, ideology and 11 + success', *British Journal of Sociology*, 17.

Sykes, G. and Matza, D. 1957, 'Techniques of neutralisation', *American Sociological Review*, 22.

Szalai, A. 1972, *The Use of Time*, The Hague: Mouton.

Szasz, T. 1970, *The Manufacture of Madness*, London: Paladin.

Szasz, T. 1973, *Ideology and Insanity*, New York: Calder and Boyers.

Tajfel, H. and Turner, J. 1979, An integrative theory of intergroup conflict. In W.G. Austin and S. Worchel (eds) *The Social Psychology of Intergroup Relations.* Monterey: Brooks-Cole.

Tawney, 1926, *Religion and the Rise of Capitalism*, Harmondsworth: Penguin (1938).

Taylor, I. 1971, 'Football mad', in Dunning, E. (ed.) *The Sociology of Sport*, London: Frank Cass.

Taylor, J. 1979, *From Modernization to Modes of Production: A Critique of the Sociologies of Development and Underdevelopment*, London: Macmillan.

Taylor, I., Walton, P. and Young, J. 1973, *The New Criminology*, London: Routledge & Kegan Paul.

Taylor, L. 1981, *Justice for Victims of Crime*, London: Macmillan.

Taylor, M. 1983, 'Ordinal and interval scaling', *Journal of the Market Research Society*, 25.

Teichler, U. 1988, *Changing Patterns of the Higher Education System*, London: Jessica Kingsley Publishers.

Terray, E. 1972, *Marxism and 'Primitive' Societies*, New York: Monthly Review Press.

Thomas A. et al. 1994 *Third World Atlas*, Buckingham: Open University Press (2nd ed).

Thomas, W. (with Thomas, D.) 1928, *The Child in America*, New York: Knopf.

Thompson, E. 1967, 'Time, work-discipline and industrial capitalism', *Past and Present*, 38.

Thompson, E. 1978, 'The poverty of theory', in E. Thompson *The Poverty of Theory and Other Essays*, London: Merlin.

Thompson, E. 1982, *Zero Option*, London: Merlin.

Thompson, J. 1989, The theory of structuration', in Held, D. & Thompson, J. *Social Theory and Modern Societies, – Anthony Giddens and his Critics*, Cambridge University Press.

Thompson, K. 1976, *Auguste Comte: the Foundations of Sociology*, London:Nelson.

Thompson, P. 1989, *The Nature of Work*, (2nd. edn), London: Macmillan.

Thompson, T. 1981, *Edwardian Childhoods*, London: Routledge & Kegan Paul.

Thorndike, E. 1911, Animal *Intelligence*, New York: Macmillan.

Thorner, D., Ferblay, B. and Smith, R. 1966, *Chayanov on the Theory of Peasant Economy*, Homewood, Illinois: Richard D. Irwin.

Thurstone, L. and Chave, E. 1929, *The Measurement of Attitude.* Chicago:Univ. of Chicago Press.

Toffler, A. 1970, Future Shock, London: Bodley Head.

Tönnies, F. 1887, *Gemeinschaft und Gesellschaft* (tr. as Community and Society). London: Routledge (1955).

Touraine, A. 1971, The *Post-Industrial Society*, New York: Random House.

Trist, E., Higgins, G., Murray, H. and Pollock, A. 1963, *Organizational Choice*, London: Tavistock.

Troeltsch, E. 1912, *The Social Teachings of the Christian Churches*, London: Allen and Unwin (1956).

Trow, M. 1962, 'Reflections on the transition from élite to mass higher education', *Daedalus*, 90.

Tumin, M. 1953, 'Some principles of social stratification: a critical analysis', *American Sociological Review*, 18.

Turlel, E. 1983, *The Development of Social Knowledge*, Cambridge: Cambridge University Press.

Turner, B. 1984, *The Body and Society*, Oxford: Basil Blackwell.

Turner, B. 1987, *Medical Power and Social Knowledge*, London: Sage.

Turner, B. 1992, *Regulating Bodies: Essays in Medical Sociology*, London, Routledge.

Turner, R. 1960, 'Sponsored and contest mobility in the school system', *American Sociological Review*, 25.

Ungerson, C. 1987, *Policy is Personal: Sex, Gender and Informal Care*, London:Tavistock.

Urry, J. 1973, *Reference Groups and the Theory of Revolution*, London: Routledge & Kegan Paul.

Urry, J. 1981, *The Anatomy of Capitalist Societies*, London: Macmillan.

Valentine, C. 1968, *Culture and Poverty*, Chicago: University of Chicago Press.

Von Neumann, J. and Morgenstern, O. 1944, *Theory of Games and Economic Behaviour*, Princeton University Press.

Von Wright, G. 1971, *Explanation and Understanding*, London: Routledge & Kegan Paul.

Von Wright, G. 1983, *Philosophical Papers, Vol.1: Practical Reason*, Oxford: Basil Blackwell.

Voslensky, M. 1984, *Nomenklatura: Anatomy of the Soviet Ruling* Class, London: Bodley Head.

Walby, S. 1986, *Patriarchy at Work*, Cambridge: Polity Press.

Walker, A. 1980, 'Coming apart', in L. Lederer (ed.) *Take Back the Night: Women as Pornography*, New York: Morrow.

Walker, A. 1983, *In Search of Our Mother's Gardens*, New York: Harper Row.

Wallerstein, I. 1974, *The Modern World System: Capitalist Agriculture and the Origins of the European World-economy in the Sixteenth Century*, London: Academic Press.

Wallerstein, I. 1980, The Modern World System: *Mercantilism and the Consolidation of the European World-Economy, 1600–1750.* London: Academic Press.

Wallis, R. 1984, *The Elementary Forms of the New Religious Life*, London: Routledge and Kegan Paul.

Walton, J. 1984, *Reluctant Rebels: Comparative Studies of Revolution and Underdevelopment*, New York: Columbia University Press.

Walzer, M. 1966, The *Revolution of the Saints: A Study in the Origins of Radical Politics*, London: Weidenfeld & Nicolson.

Warde, A. 1990, 'Introduction to the sociology of consumption', *Sociology*, 24.

Warren, B. 1980, *Imperialism: Pioneer of Capitalism*, London: Verso.

Watson, T.J. 1994, *In Search of Management*, London: Routledge.

Watt, M. 1961, *Islam and the Integration of Society*, London: Routledge & Kegan Paul.

Weber, M. 1912, *The City*, Glencoe, Ill.: Free Press 1958.

Weber, M. 1922, *Wirtschaft und Gesellschaft*, translated as *Economy and Society: an Outline of Interpretive Sociology*, New York: Bedmmster Press (1968) (trans. G. Roth and G. Wittich).

Weber, M. 1930, *The Protestant Ethic and the Spirit of Capitalism*, London: Allen and Unwin, (original Ger. edn. 1904–5, rev. edn, 1920).

Weber, M. 1963, *The Sociology of Religion*, Boston, Mass.: Beacon, (original Ger. 1922).

Webster, J. 1996, *Shaping Women's Work: Gender, Employment and Information Technology*, London: Longman.

Weeks, J. 1977, *Coming Out: Homosexual Politics in Britain from the Nineteenth Century to the Present*, London: Quartet Books.

Weeks, J. 1985, *Sexuality and its Discontents*, London: Routledge & Kegan Paul.

Weiner, N. 1949, *Cybernetics: or Control and Communication in Man and Machine*, Cambridge, Mass.: MIT Press.

Weinstein, A. and Gatell, F., 1979, *American Negro Slavery*, Oxford: Oxford University Press (3rd edn.).

Weizenbaum, J. 1984, *Computer Power and Human Reason*, Harmondsworth: Penguin.

Westergaard, J. and Resler H. 1975, *Class in a Capitalist Society*, London: Heinemann.

White, G. 1983, 'Chinese development strategy after Mao', in G. White et al. (eds.), *Revolutionary Socialist Development in the Third World*, Brighton: Wheatsheaf Books.

White, K. 1991, 'The Sociology of Health and illness', *Current Sociology*, 39.

Whitford, Margare. 1991, *Luce Irigaray: Philosophy in the Feminine*, London: Routledge.

Whitley, R. 1974, 'The city and industry', in P. Stanworth and A. Giddens, (eds.) *Élites and Power in British Society*, Cambridge: Cambridge University Press.

Whyte, W. 1955, *Street Corner Society*, Chicago: Chicago University Press.

Whyte, W. 1956, *The Organization Man*, Harmondsworth: Penguin.

Wilkins, L. 1965, 'Some sociological factors in drug addiction control', in B. Rosenberg, I. Bernard and F. Howlen (eds.), *Mass Society in Crisis*, New York: Free Press.

Wilkins, L. 1975, *Social Deviance*, London: Tavistock.

Wilkinson, S. and Kitzinger, C. 1994, 'Dire Straights? – Contemporary Rehabilitation of Heterosexuality', in Griffin et al. (eds) 1994, *Stirring It: Challenges for Feminism*, London: Taylor and Francis.

Williams, R. 1973, *The Country and the City*, London: Chatto and Windus.

Williams, R. 1976, *Keywords*, London: Fontana (2nd edn. 1983).

Williamson, J. 1978, *Decoding Advertisements, Ideology and Meaning in Advertising*, London and New York: Marion Boyars.

Willis, P. 1977, *Learning to Labour*, Farnborough: Saxon House.

Willmott, H. 1993, 'Strength is Ignorance; Slavery is Freedom; Managing Culture in Modern Organisations', *Journal of Management Studies*, 30(4): 515-52.

Wilson, B. 1967, *Patterns of Sectarianism*, London: Heinemann.

Wilson, B. 1970, *Religious Sects*, London: Weidenfeld & Nicolson.

Wilson, B. 1973, *Magic and the Millennium*, London: Heinemann.

Wilson, E. 1975, *Sociobiology: the New Synthesis*, Cambridge Mass.: Harvard University Press.

Wilson, H. and Herbert, G. 1978, *Parents and Children in the Inner City*, London: Routledge & Kegan Paul.

Wirth, L. 1938, 'Urbanism as a way of life'. *American Journal of Sociology*, 44.

Wolf, E. 1966, *Peasants*, Engelwood Cliffs. NJ: Prentice Hall.

Wolf, E. 1971, *Peasant Wars of the Twentieth Century*. London: Faber & Faber.

Wolff, K. (ed.) 1950, *The Sociology of Georg Simmel*, New York, Free Press.

Wolpe, H. 1972, 'Capitalism and cheap labour power in South Africa: from segregation to apartheid', *Economy and Society*, 1.

Womack, jr. J. 1969, *Zapata and the Mexican Revolution*, London: Thames & Hudson.

Wood, S. 1989, *The Transformation of Work*, London: Hutchinson.

Wood, S. 1991, 'Japanization and/or Toyotaism', *Work, Employment and Society*, 5.

Wood, S. and Elliott, R. 1977, 'A critical evaluation of Fox's radicalisation of industrial relations theory' *Sociology*, 11.

Woodfield, A. 1981 'Teleology', in W. Brynum, E. Brown and R. Porter, *Dictionary of the History of Science*, London: Maanillan.

Woodward, J. 1965 (new edn. 1970), *Industrial Organization: Theory and Practice*, London: Oxford University Press.

Woolf, J. 1975, *Feminine Sentences*, Berkley: University of California Press.

Worsley, P. 1968, *The Trumpet Shall Sound*, (rev. edn), MacGibbon & Kee.

Worsley, P. 1984, *Three Worlds: Culture and World Development*, London: Weidenfeld and Nicolson.

Worsley, P. 1987, *New Introductory Sociology*, (3rd edn), London: Penguin.

Wright, E. 1978, *Class, Crises and the State*, London: New Left Books.

Wright, E. 1981, 'The value controversy and social research', in T. Steedman, 1981.

Wright, E. 1983, 'Giddens' critique of Marxism', *New Left Review*, 138.

Wright, E. 1985, *Classes*, London: Verso.

Wright, E. 1989, *The Debate on Classes*, London: Verso.

Wrigley, E. (ed.) 1966, *An Introduction to English Historical Demography*, London: Weidenfeld and Nicolson.

Wrong, D. 1961, 'The oversocialized conception of man in modern sociology', *American Sociological Review*, 26.

Young, J. 1971, *The Drugtakers: the Social Meaning of Drug Use*, London: McGibbon & Key.

Young, J. 1980, 'The Development of Criminology in Britain', *British Journal of Criminology*, 28.

Young, M. 1971, *Knowledge and Control*, London: Collier-Macmillan.

Young, M. and Wilmott, P. 1957, *Family and Kinship in East London*, Harmondsworth: Penguin (1960).

Young, M. and Wilmott, P. 1973 *The Symmetrical Family*, Harmondsworth: Penguin.

Zeitlin, M. 1974, 'Corporate ownership and control: the large corporation and the capitalist class', *American Journal of Sociology*, 80.

Zeitlin, M. 1977, *American Society Inc.: Studies of the Social Structure and Political Economy of the United States*, (2nd. edn) Chicago: Rand McNally.

Zetterberg, H. 1965, *On Theory and Verification in Sociology*, (3rd. edn), Totawa, NJ: Bedminster Press.

Zweig, F. 1961, *The Worker in an Affluent Society: Family Life and Industry*, London: Heinemann.

Finding sociology resources on the internet

The internet has a vast amount of information on sociology and related subjects available to academics, professional researchers, and laypeople alike. Finding reliable and free data should not be difficult although a few points need to be borne in mind. The material should be up to date. Small organizations and departments within academic institutions sometimes encounter funding difficulties and are unable to continue with their researches. Make sure to look at the 'Last updated' section of the main website page before using any data. Try clicking on the links to make sure that they have been maintained properly and do not result in error messages. Ideally information should be obtained from websites run by universities, research institutes, and other reputable organizations. Websites maintained by individuals may not be up to date and comprehensive. It is also possible that the prejudices of those maintaining the websites will be reflected in the content and list of links.

There is a very useful free 'tutorial' to finding and using sociological information on the internet, which can be found at:

www.vts.rdn.ac.uk/tutorial/sociologist

General sociology sites

There are a number of gateway sites that give access to many internet sites. These are the best places to start your internet researches, as the links they contain are carefully researched and maintained.

Social Science Information Gateway

www.sosig.ac.uk/sociology

This service aims to provide a trusted source of selected, high-quality internet information for researchers and students. Within the Sociology section of the site, there are specific categories for:

communication
community research
culture and popular culture
regional and country studies
schools and theories
social change
social movements
sociologists

and sections on the sociology of

adolescence, children, economics, education, gender, law and crime, medicine, politics, race and ethnicity, religion, sport, work, the elderly, the family.

Within the Social Science Information Gateway, there are also major sections on anthropology, social welfare, women's studies, and on research tools:

www.sosig.ac.uk/anthropology
www.sosig.ac.uk/social_welfare
www.sosig.ac.uk/women_studies
www.sosig.ac.uk/research_tools

SocioSite

http://www2.fmg.uva.nl/sociosite

The SocioSite is designed to give access to information and resources which are relevant for sociologists and other social scientists. It is based at the University of Amsterdam.

SocioWeb

www.socioweb.com

The SocioWeb is an independent guide to the sociological resources available on the internet.

The Virtual Library – Sociology
http://socserv2.mcmaster.ca/w3virtsoclib/
The Virtual Library is the oldest catalogue of the Web, started by Tim Berners-Lee, the creator of html and the Web itself, in 1991 at CERN in Geneva, Switzerland. It is run by a loose confederation of volunteers, who compile pages of key links for particular areas in which they are expert.

Sociological Tour Through Cyberspace
www.trinity.edu/~mkearl/index.html
This site features commentary, data analyses, occasional essays, as well as the requisite links. Additions and updates are made daily.

Sociology Central
www.sociology.org.uk
A site with links appropriate to those studying at senior school level.

Sociology Links
www.abacon.com/sociology/soclinks
A wide range of links provided by the US publisher Allyn and Baker.

BUBL Links Sociology
http://bubl.ac.uk/link/s/sociology.htm
Catalogue of internet resources for sociology, maintained by the University of Strathclyde.

Internet Resources for Sociologists
www.umsl.edu/~sociolog/resource.htm
A useful selection of internet resources, maintained by Robert Keel of the University of Missouri, St Louis.

Women's Studies Database
www.mith2.umd.edu/WomensStudies

Organizations

American Sociological Association
www.asanet.org

Association for the Teaching of Social Sciences
www.le.ac.uk/education/centres/ATSS/atss.html

The Australian Sociological Association
www.tasa.org.au

Australian Social Science Data Archive
http://assda.anu.edu.au/index.html

British Sociological Association
www.britsoc.co.uk

Canadian Council on Social Development
www.ccsd.ca

Canadian Sociology and Anthropology Association
www.csaa.ca

Economic and Social Research Council
www.esrc.ac.uk/ESRCInfoCentre/index.aspx

European Sociological Association
www.valt.helsinki.fi/esa

International Sociological Association
www.ucm.es/info/isa

International Social Science Council
www.unesco.org/ngo/issc

Society for Applied Sociology
www.appliedsoc.org

Society for the Study of Social Problems
www.sssp1.org

Sociological Association of Aotearoa New Zealand
http://saanz.science.org.nz

Social Research Association
www.the-sra.org.uk

Selected journals

American Journal of Sociology
www.journals.uchicago.edu/AJS

American Sociological Review
www.asanet.org/journals/asr

British Journal of Sociology Online
www.lse.ac.uk/serials/Bjs

Canadian Journal of Sociology Online
www.arts.ualberta.ca/cjscopy/events/news.html

Sociological Research Online
www.socresonline.org.uk

Social Research Update
www.soc.surrey.ac.uk/sru

Data

Internet Crossroads in Social Science Data
http://dpls.dacc.wisc.edu/newcrossroads/index.asp
Internet Crossroads, run by the Data and Program Library Services, University of Wisconsin, contains over 750 annotated links to data-related resources on the internet.

Australian Bureau of Statistics
www.abs.gov.au

Canadian Statistics (Statistics Canada)
www.statcan.ca

FedStats (the gateway to statistics from over 100 US Federal agencies)
www.fedstats.gov

Gender statistics (World Bank)
http://devdata.worldbank.org/genderstats/home.asp

New Zealand Statistics (Statistics New Zealand)
www.stats.govt.nz

Population Reference Bureau
www.prb.org

Social Science Data Archive
www2.fmg.uva.nl/sociosite/databases.html

UK Data Archive
www.data-archive.ac.uk

UK Statistics (Office for National Statistics)
www.statistics.gov.uk

US Census Bureau
www.census.gov

US Census Bureau International Database
www.census.gov/ipc/www/idbnew.html